A TREATISE

ON THE

GRAMMAR OF NEW TESTAMENT GREEK,

REGARDED AS

A SURE BASIS FOR NEW TESTAMENT EXEGESIS.

A TREATISE

ON THE

GRAMMAR

OF

NEW TESTAMENT GREEK,

REGARDED AS

A SURE BASIS FOR NEW TESTAMENT EXEGESIS.

BY DR. G. B. WINER.

Translated from the German, with Large Additions and Full Indices,

BY

REV. W. F. MOULTON, M.A., D.D.

Wipf and Stock Publishers
150 West Broadway • Eugene OR 97401
2001

A Treatise on the Grammar of New Testament Greek

By Winer, G.B.

ISBN: 1-57910-070-8

Reprinted by *Wipf and Stock Publishers*
150 West Broadway • Eugene OR 97401

Previously published by T & T Clark, 1882.

TO THE

RIGHT REVEREND C. J. ELLICOTT, D.D.,
LORD BISHOP OF GLOUCESTER AND BRISTOL,

THIS WORK IS DEDICATED

BY THE EDITOR,

IN EXPRESSION OF HIS REVERENT ESTEEM AND
LASTING GRATITUDE.

PREFACE TO THE SECOND EDITION.

I HAD hoped that I might be able to show my gratitude for the unexpected kindness of the welcome accorded to this work, by seeking to render it much more worthy of the acceptance of students; but the extreme pressure of other duties has compelled me to relinquish this hope for the present. It will be found that this edition is in the main a reprint of the first. The chief point of difference is the introduction into the text of all the new matter left by Winer for the seventh edition of the original work. A few paragraphs which I had previously abridged (see below, p. xiii.) are now given in full. Whilst, however, but few substantial changes have been made, both text and notes have been carefully revised. In the notes on Part II. (the Accidence) many slight alterations have been found necessary in order to bring the statements into accord with the best critical texts of the New Testament. Here, especially, I have to express my very great obligations to Professor Westcott and Dr. Hort for their kindness in allowing me the free use of their (in my judgment invaluable) edition of the text—soon, I trust, to be given to the world.

The very frequent references to Alexander Buttmann's *Grammar of the New Testament Greek* are in this edition adapted to the excellent translation by Professor Thayer,

PREFACE TO THE SECOND EDITION.

whose careful edition of Winer's Grammar has also been of much service.

As great care has been taken to avoid, as far as possible, any interference with the paging of the book, almost all references to the former edition will still be found correct.

WILLIAM F. MOULTON.

CAMBRIDGE, 21*st October* 1876.

PREFACE TO THE FIRST EDITION.

THE merits of Winer's *Grammatik des neutestamentlichen Sprachidioms* are so well known and so freely acknowledged, that it would be unbecoming in me to detain the reader by any lengthened remarks on the work, or on the subject of which it so fully treats. I shall therefore confine myself to a brief statement of the objects which have been kept in view in the present translation, and of the way in which I have sought to attain them.

When I was requested by Messrs. Clark to undertake this work, the translation published by them in 1859 was placed at my disposal. I have without hesitation availed myself of the liberty thus accorded, as the existence of common matter in the two editions will show; but the present is, in the most literal sense, a new translation, in the execution of which all accessible sources of help have been freely resorted to. Besides the edition just specified, the American translation by Messrs. Agnew and Ebbeke (Philadelphia, 1840) has sometimes been of service. Perhaps an apology is necessary for what will seem to some an excessive adherence to German structure and phraseology in certain paragraphs. If I have erred in this respect, it has been from a conviction that the nature of the book required unusual literalness of rendering, and that in some instances it was almost impossible to depart from the original form and at the same time preserve the meaning with technical exactness.

In deference to a strongly expressed opinion on the part of some whose judgment deserved respect, I have in a few instances ventured on a slight abridgment of the original, and have omitted a few references of little or no importance. At the foot of the page will be found a detailed statement of all the omissions I have made.[1]

---

[1] Winer's account of the New Testament Grammars of Pasor and Haab, and his relation of the disputes between the Purists and the Hebraists, I have condensed about one-half. I have not thought it necessary to retain all the references to certain authors who engaged in the Purist controversy, viz., Georgi (*Vindiciæ* and *Hierocriticus Sacer*), Schwarz (*Commentarii* and *ad Olearium*),

PREFACE TO THE FIRST EDITION.

All references to passages in the Old and New Testaments have been carefully verified. In each case, whether the passage is quoted at length, or merely indicated by chapter and verse, I have examined the reading. Variations which do not touch the question under consideration I have not thought it necessary to notice; but I trust that all instances in which a difference of reading affects the appositeness of the quotation are pointed out in my notes. Much labour would have been saved had it been possible to follow Winer's example, and abide (in the main) by the text of some particular edition of the Greek Testament. As this could not be done, the only alternative was to follow the reading which appeared to be most generally received by recent editors, referring expressly to conflicting opinions only in cases of special difficulty or importance. I have given most weight to Tischendorf, as Winer had done; and, wherever it was possible, have quoted from his eighth edition, now in course of publication. Before the completion of the Gospels in this edition, my references were made to his *Synopsis Evangelica* (ed. 2, 1864), which gave the only indication of his judgment as modified by the Codex Sinaiticus. If this MS. has in other parts of the New Testament confirmed the reading of his seventh edition (1859), I have sometimes ventured to quote this reading as Tischendorf's, without further qualification: otherwise, the edition is expressly stated. A considerable portion of this book was already in type when the fourth and fifth parts of his eighth edition and the fourth part of Tregelles' Greek Testament appeared. I need hardly say that Scrivener's collations of the texts of Lachmann and Tischendorf and of the Codex Sinaiticus have proved of essential service in this portion of my work.[1] In quotations from the Septuagint I have used Tischendorf's text (ed. 3, 1860) as the standard of comparison; when the readings of the leading MSS. differ in such a way as to affect the quotation, I have noted the variation. I may add, that in the numbering of the Psalms the Septuagint is followed throughout, unless the Hebrew text is under notice: Winer's practice was not uniform. In instances such as that just specified, and in many others where a correction was obviously needed, I have altered Winer's figures without calling attention to the change.

It has not been in my power to carry the work of verification as far as I could have wished. A marked characteristic of Winer's Grammar is the number of its references to com-

Palairet, Pfochen, Solanus, Fischer (*ad* Leusden. *Dial.*), or to Pasor's *Grammar*. In one place (p. 123, note 3) a note is abridged, and the titles of works quoted are slightly curtailed. With these exceptions, the whole of the original is reproduced.

[1] When the 'received text' which Winer quotes differs from the text of Stephens, I have referred to it as '*Elz.*;' otherwise, as '*Rec.*'

mentaries on classical writers. To many of the works cited I could not obtain access; and I confess that, judging from those quotations which I was able to verify, I cannot feel that I should have conferred much benefit on the student if I had succeeded in examining the whole: in most instances I have removed such references from the text into the notes, for the convenience of the reader. On the other hand, it has been my aim to secure all possible accuracy and completeness where standard grammatical authorities are cited. Every reference to the Greek Grammars of Buttmann (*Ausf. Sprachlehre*), Bernhardy, Matthiæ, and Madvig, Zumpt's *Latin Grammar*, Hermann's edition of Viger, Lobeck on Phrynichus, Lobeck's *Paralipomena*, and Klotz's *Commentary on Devarius*, has been carefully examined. The references to Rost's *Grammatik* and to K. W. Krüger's *Sprachlehre* have been altered so as to suit the most recent editions. In the case of Madvig, Matthiæ, and Zumpt, it seemed best to substitute sections for pages, that the reference might hold good both for the original works and for the English translations. In the sections on irregular and defective verbs, I have usually given references to Fishlake's translation of Buttmann, in the place of those which Winer gives to the original work : where the matter was not the same (i.e., where Lobeck's observations were important), I have given both.

In the additions I have made to the German work—which, independently of Indices, etc., constitute about one-sixth of this book—my main objects have been the following :—
(1.) To supplement the author's statements, and bring them into accordance with the present state of our knowledge.
(2.) To show under the different heads of the subject how much may be regarded as settled, and how much is still disputed border-land. (3.) By means of continuous references to English writers on Greek grammar and on New Testament Greek, to place the English reader in the position occupied by one who uses the original. (4.) To call further attention to the many striking coincidences between Modern Greek and the language in which the New Testament is written. No one can feel more keenly than myself that I have not fully succeeded in my endeavours; but I have spared no pains or effort to attain success, so far as it lay within my reach.

To assert that the original work is in many particulars below the standard of our present knowledge, is no more than to say that the last ten or twenty years, distinguished as they have been by so much zealous and accurate study of the Greek Testament, have not passed without yielding some fruit. The German scholars to whom we owe so heavy a debt of gratitude for their persistent and successful effort to obtain for New Testament Greek the scientific treatment which was its due, have left worthy successors both in their own country and in England. Of my deep obligations to some of our English scholars I shall subsequently speak in detail.

The edition of this Grammar which appeared in Germany in 1867, under the editorship of Dr. G. Lünemann of Göttingen, differs very slightly from the sixth edition, which is the basis of the present translation. The very scanty additions relate entirely to points of detail. As I was not at liberty to make use of these additions, I have carefully abstained from seeking any assistance from them: in many instances, however, they were already included in the matter I had myself supplied. I cannot part from this edition without expressing my surprise that a scholar of Dr. Lünemann's reputation should have left so many mistakes in the text, and should have contributed so little to the improvement of the great work with the care of which he had been entrusted.

By far the most important work on the grammar of New Testament Greek which has appeared during the last fourteen years is the *Grammatik des neutestamentlichen Sprachgebrauchs* by Alexander Buttmann (Berlin, 1859). The form which the author has chosen for his work is that of an appendix to his father's (Philip Buttmann's) *Griechische Grammatik*. The theoretical advantages of this plan cannot be doubted, as the grammarian is no longer required to concern himself with the usages of ordinary Greek, but is at liberty to confine his attention to what is peculiar in Hellenistic usage. On the other hand, the inconveniences which beset the practical use of the book, in the case of those who are unfamiliar with the particular Grammar chosen as the standard, are sufficiently great to detract seriously from the usefulness of a most valuable work. As this peculiarity of plan seemed to render it unlikely that A. Buttmann's Grammar would be translated, I have been the more anxious to place the most important of its contents within the reach of the English reader. There is a difference between the general tendencies shown by the writers of the two Grammars, which makes it especially useful to compare their treatment of the same subject. Winer, never perhaps entirely free from the influence of the period in which he began to write, when it was above all things necessary to convince the world that New Testament Greek had a right to claim scientific investigation, seems inclined at times to extenuate the difference between New Testament usage and that of classical writers. His successor, coming forward when, on the main question, the victory is already won, is able to concede much that once it seemed important to dispute; and indeed, unless I am mistaken, frequently goes to an extreme in this kind of generosity. For this and other reasons, I have sometimes exhibited in detail Buttmann's general treatment of an important point, believing that a comparison of the two writers would do more than anything else to illustrate the real character of the question. My notes will show that I have made great use of A. Buttmann's work; but I have frequently received suggestions where I have not had to acknowledge direct assistance. I am bound, however, in justice to myself, to say that, unless the writer's words are distinctly quoted, the statement made in my note rests on my own responsibility, Buttmann's observations having merely served as the basis of my own investigation.

I wish I could join in the commendation which has been bestowed on Schirlitz's *Grundzüge der neutest. Gräcität* (Giessen, 1861); but I would gladly save others the disappointment which the study of this work caused myself. To represent it as an independent work is really to do it the greatest injustice. For the most part, Schirlitz servilely follows Winer—in many instances copying the very order of his examples and remarks, and sometimes even reproducing obvious mistakes. There is very little evidence of independent judgment or research. The general arrangement of the book, however, is clear and useful: unfortunately, the advantage which is gained by presenting received results, disentangled from the arguments by which they have been sustained, is to a great extent sacrificed by the introduction of irrelevant matter (e.g., on the meanings of Hebrew proper names, etc.) belonging to the lexicon, and not to a treatise on grammar. I have further consulted Beelen's Latin version of the 5th edition of Winer's Grammar (Louvain, 1857), but not with much advantage. My obligations to K. H. A. Lipsius' *Grammat. Untersuchungen* (Leipsic, 1863) are acknowledged in the following pages.

Of German commentators, Meyer has justly received the largest share of my attention; partly on account of the general merits of his masterly Commentary, and partly because his successive editions take up and discuss every fresh contribution to the grammatical study of the language of the New Testament. I have, of course, made but few references to the writers already laid under contribution by Winer himself, as De Wette and others: where, however, new editions have been issued, I have often availed myself of their assistance. In cases where Winer quotes from a German work, or from a book which is not readily accessible, I have frequently sought to help the reader by supplying the pith of the quotation,

b

especially where Winer has chosen this mode of indicating his own opinion of a passage. My aim has been to make myself acquainted with everything of importance which has lately appeared in Germany in connexion with the subject of this book; and I trust the reader will not discover any omissions of a serious character.

To English works I have referred much more freely, as it has been a leading object with me to provide English readers with all the helps supplied by Winer to his countrymen. Whilst occasional references are made to a number of Grammars, Jelf's and Donaldson's are quoted systematically, as our leading English authorities. I may here observe that, with the exception of an occasional citation of Liddell and Scott or Rost and Palm in the place of Passow, these references to Jelf and Donaldson are the only additions of my own which are incorporated with the text. My regular practice has been to distinguish added matter by square brackets,—thus [ ]; but in the instances just specified the convenience of the reader seemed best served by a departure from strict uniformity. It is not necessary for me here to mention all the works of English scholars which are quoted in my notes. I have attached most importance to references to works of a distinctively grammatical character; but have striven to show my high sense of the value which belongs to many recent English editions of classical authors, by frequently directing the reader to their pages. I fear it will be held that I ought either to have done more, or not to have made the attempt; I could not, however, refrain from giving this kind of practical expression to the interest with which I have studied the notes of Shilleto, Paley, Jebb, Riddell, Sandys, and others.

Every page of this book will show how greatly I am indebted to our foremost English writers on New Testament Greek. The excellent treatises expressly devoted to the subject by Mr. Green and Mr. Webster I have used extensively; the latter, from the nature of its plan, is less frequently quoted than the former. I have very rarely neglected an opportunity of making use of the Commentaries of Professor Lightfoot and Dean Alford; and most gratefully do I acknowledge the assistance I have received from them throughout my work. My hearty thanks are due to the Rev. Dr. Dickson, Professor of Biblical Criticism in the University of Glasgow, and to the Rev. B. Hellier of Headingley, for the kind interest they have displayed in my undertaking, and for some useful suggestions. I have left until the last the name which is, and must remain, the first in my thoughts, whether they are resting on the present work or on my Greek Testament studies in general.

PREFACE TO THE FIRST EDITION.

The measure of my obligation to the Bishop of Gloucester and Bristol, who has generously permitted me to associate his name with this book, it is altogether out of my power to express. I feel sensitively that whatever I have done is unworthy of such an association; but if this book succeed in accomplishing anything for the accurate study of the Greek Testament, it will be through what I have learned from Bishop Ellicott's wise counsels, and from his noble Commentaries on St. Paul's Epistles.

I trust that the plan upon which I have made use of the various authorities now specified will commend itself to the judgment of my readers. I may perhaps anticipate an objection which may be raised, to the effect that the quotation of many opinions upon any subject tends to produce confusion, whereas the usefulness of a Grammar depends much on the directness and uniformity of its teaching. I am so far alive to the force of this objection, that I am inclined to think an amount of dogmatism and indifference to the views of others may for a time increase the teacher's power, and thus prove beneficial to the student. But, to say nothing of the effect which may be produced by the discovery that the teacher had spoken with equal confidence of the certain and of the questionable, the decisive tone of an independent work would have been strangely out of place if here assumed by me. My desire is to show where those scholars who best represent the present state of knowledge and opinion are in accord, and what points are still under discussion. I should be sorry to lie under the imputation of indefiniteness of opinion, when I have felt compelled to present conflicting views. I am convinced that clearly to state the amount of divergence which exists is to do something towards the removal of it. I have tried to bear in mind that this book may fall into the hands of different classes of readers, and have sometimes ventured to add an explanation which to many will seem superfluous, for the sake of inexperienced students. Where the author makes a statement which appears to me erroneous, in regard to matters of greater importance than details of language, I have usually appended a reference to some standard work containing an adequate answer or correction.

The only other subject requiring comment in connexion with the notes to this edition is the prominence which I have given to Modern Greek. I am persuaded that English scholars will not consider that I have gone too far in calling attention to its peculiarities in a work on New Testament Greek:[1] if I were commencing my task anew, I should attempt

[1] See an interesting article in the current number of the *Journal of Philology* (vol. ii. pp. 161--196).

to do much more in this way than I have done. The Grammars referred to are those of Mullach (*Grammatik der griechischen Vulgarsprache in historischer Entwicklung:* Berlin, 1856), J. Donaldson (Edinburgh, 1853), Sophocles (Boston, 1860), and occasionally Lüdemann's *Lehrbuch* (Leipsic, 1826).

Much labour has been spent upon the Indices. To the three contained in the German work (each of which is more than doubled in size) I have added a fourth, containing the principal passages from the Old Testament noticed in the book. The fulness of the Index of Subjects will, it is hoped, supply the want of more frequent references between the various parts of the work. . . . A Table of Authors cited, with dates, seemed especially desirable in a work like the present, which contains quotations from so wide a range of writers, flourishing at periods 2000 years apart. I have taken pains to secure accuracy in the dates. As a general rule, I have chosen for the 'floruit' of an author a point about mid-way between his entrance on manhood and the close of his life. I am here most largely indebted to Müller and Donaldson's *History of the Literature of Greece*, Dr. Smith's *Dictionary of Biography*, and Engelmann's *Bibliotheca Scriptorum Classicorum*. The notices contained in Liddell and Scott's Lexicon have been compared throughout: I must, however, confess myself unable to understand on what principle some of the dates are assigned.

Through various circumstances, I have been placed at a disadvantage in the correction of the proofs, and must beg the indulgence of the reader for the mistakes which will be found. Most of these, I trust, are noticed in the table of Errata; but it did not seem necessary to swell that list by including those errors (e.g., in the division of words) which are merely blemishes, and cannot lead any one astray.

I have extended these introductory remarks beyond the limit I had assigned myself. I will only add the expression of my earnest prayer, that He who can use for His glory the feeblest work of man may grant that mine may be instrumental in leading some to a fuller knowledge of His inspired Word.

WILLIAM F. MOULTON.

Richmond, *January* 7, 1870.

AUTHOR'S PREFACE.

When this Grammar first appeared, in 1822, the object proposed was, to check the unbounded arbitrariness with which the language of the New Testament had so long been handled in Commentaries and exegetical prelections, and, so far as the case admitted, to apply the results of the rational philology, as obtained and diffused by Hermann and his school, to the Greek of the New Testament. It was in truth needful that some voice should be raised which might call to account the deep-rooted empiricism of the expositors, and might strive to rescue the New Testament writers from the bondage of a perverted philology, which, while it styled itself sacred, showed not the slightest respect for the sacred authors and their well-considered phraseology.

The fundamental error—the $\pi\rho\hat{\omega}\tau o\nu\ \psi\epsilon\hat{v}\delta o\varsigma$—of this biblical philology, and consequently of the exegesis which was based upon it, really consisted in this, that neither the Hebrew language nor the Greek of the New Testament was regarded as a *living* idiom (Hermann, Eurip. *Med.* p. 401), designed for a medium of human intercourse. Had they been so regarded, —had scholars always asked themselves whether the deviations from the established laws of language, which were assumed to exist in the Bible to so enormous an extent, were compatible with the destination of a human language for the practical uses of life, they would not have so arbitrarily considered everything allowable, and taken pleasure in ascribing to the apostles in nearly every verse an *enallage*, or *use of the wrong form in the place of the right*. If we read certain Commentaries still current of the eighteenth and nineteenth centuries—for the older works of the period of the Reformation are almost entirely free from such perverseness—we must conclude that the peculiar characteristic of the New Testament language is an utter want of definiteness and regularity. For the expositors are continually pointing out instances of the use of a wrong tense, or a wrong case, or the comparative instead of the positive,—of ὁ for τις, *but* instead of *for*, *therefore* for *because*, *on the other side* for *on this side*, the relative for the sign of the apodosis (Isa. viii. 20¹). Amidst such erudition on the part of the interpreter, the reader becomes almost indignant at the unskilfulness of the sacred writers, who knew so little how to deal with words. One cannot conceive how such men could make themselves even generally intelligible in their oral discourses, in which this lawlessness of language must certainly have appeared in still stronger relief. Still more difficult is it to understand how they won over to Christianity a large number of educated men. Whilst, however, this play with *pro* and *idem quod* has a laughable, it has also a serious aspect. Does not Scripture—as a great philologer remarked long ago—thus become like a waxen nose, which a man may twist any way he pleases, in proportion to the scantiness of his knowledge of language? Would it have been impossible, or even difficult, for such a man as Storr, for example, had the task been assigned to him, to find in the words of the apostles any meaning which he pleased? And is such a view of the New Testament language compatible with the dignity of sacred writers?²

We should regard as simply devoid of understanding any man who, in the ordinary intercourse of life, could so pervert language as to say, 'I shall come to you to-day,' instead of 'I have come,' etc.; 'No prophet has arisen out of Galilee,' for 'No prophet shall arise out of Galilee' (John vii. 52); 'I call you no longer servants,' for 'I called you not merely servants' (John xv. 15); 'For Jesus himself testified that a prophet hath no honour in his own country,' for 'Although Jesus himself testified,' etc. (John iv. 44); 'I saw the forest with mag-

¹ [In this verse some regard אֲשֶׁר as introducing the apodosis, and therefore leave it untranslated (in English): thus Henderson (after Gesenius), 'There shall be no dawn to them.' Winer, with Ewald, renders the verse: Ad legem revertamur, ita profecto dicent, quibus non fulget aurora (*Simonis*, s.v.).]

² Hermann, *ad Vig.* p. 786: Diligenter caveant tirones, ne putent, viros spiritu sancto afflatos sprevisse sermonem mortalium, sed meminerint potius, illam interpretandi rationem, qua nonnulli theologorum utuntur, *nihil esse nisi blasphemiam.*

nificent foliage,' instead of 'I saw a forest,' etc. (John v. 1);[1] 'Send me the book, and I will read it,' for 'You will send me the book,' etc.; 'To whom it was revealed that . . .,' for 'To whom this was revealed, yet so that . . .' (1 Pet. i. 12);[2] 'Christ died, he has therefore risen again,' for 'but has risen again;' 'He is not more learned,' for 'He is not learned;' 'He rejoiced that he should see, . . . and he saw, and rejoiced,' for 'He would have rejoiced if he had seen, . . . even over that which he saw he rejoiced' (John viii. 56); 'He began to wash,' for 'He washed' (John xiii. 5); and the like. If all the examples of *quid pro quo* which during the past *decennia* a number of interpreters have put into the mouths of the apostles were collected together, the world would justly be astounded.

When I, at that time a young academic teacher, undertook to combat this unscientific procedure, I did not conceal from myself that there were men far better qualified for such a work; and indeed what I accomplished in the earlier editions of this Grammar was but imperfect. My attempt, however, met with friendly recognition from some men of eminence; first, from Vater and D. Schulz. Others pointed out, sometimes certainly with harshness, the imperfections of the book; and to these critics I owe much, not only in this work, but in all my exegetical labours. I enlarged the grammatical material by Excursuses, which followed the second edition in 1828. Extensive study of the writings of the Greek prose authors and of the Hellenistic Jews enabled me to make the third edition much more copious, and also more accurate. I have subsequently laboured incessantly in the improvement of the book; and I have been gladdened by the aid which philological and exegetical works have afforded in rich abundance for this purpose. Meanwhile the rational method of investigating the New Testament language has daily gained new friends; and the use made of this Grammar by commentators has become more and more apparent: even classical philologers have begun to notice the book. At the same time, I have always been far from thinking accurate grammatical explanation to be the only proper exposition of the New Testament;

---

[1] Kühnöl's reasoning, *Matt.* p. 120 sq., shows (*instar omnium*) how completely the commentators of the old school were destitute of critical perception.

[2] On this passage see my *Erlanger Pfingstprogr.* (1830).

and I have borne in silence the charge which some have brought against me, of being even an opponent of what is now called theological exposition.

The present edition, the sixth, will show on every page that I have striven to come nearer to the truth. I deeply lament, however, that in the very midst of my labours a nervous affection of the eyes brought me to the verge of total blindness. Hence I have been compelled to employ the eyes and hands of others in the completion of this edition; and I avail myself of this opportunity to express publicly my sincere thanks to all my young friends who have unremittingly assisted me: for it is only through their aid that I have been enabled to bring the work to a conclusion, which I had often despaired of being able to reach.

The change in the arrangement of the matter in Part III. will, I think, be approved of. In other respects, it has been my principal aim to treat every point with greater completeness and yet in smaller space than formerly: accordingly, the text of this Grammar now occupies about eight sheets fewer than in my last edition. With this view I have made use of abbreviations in the biblical and Greek quotations, as far as I possibly could.[1] I hope, however, that both these and the names of modern authors[2] will everywhere be intelligible. All the quotations have been verified anew; and, so far as I know, every scientific work that has appeared since 1844 has been turned to account, or at all events noticed.

In regard to the text of the New Testament, I have uniformly (except when dealing with a question of various readings) quoted from Dr. Tischendorf's second Leipsic edition [1849], which probably now has the widest circulation.

May the work with these improvements—certainly the last it will receive from my hands—accomplish what in its sphere it can accomplish for the knowledge of Biblical truth!

LEIPSIC, *October* 1855.

[1] The Greek writers are only quoted by the page when the division into chapters has not obtained currency: Plato, as edited by Stephanus; Strabo and Athenæus, by Casaubon; Demosthenes and Isocrates, by H. Wolf; Dionys. Hal. by Reiske; Dio Cassius by Reimarus; Dio Chrysost. by Morell.

[2] It may be observed that, instead of Kuinoel, the Latinised form of the name, Kühnöl (as the family name was written in German) is used throughout, except in Latin citations.

CONTENTS.

---o---

INTRODUCTION.

PAGE

ON THE OBJECT, TREATMENT, AND HISTORY OF N. T. GRAMMAR . . 1

PART I.

ON THE GENERAL CHARACTER OF THE N. T. DICTION, ESPECIALLY IN REGARD TO GRAMMAR.

Sect. i. Various Opinions respecting the Character of the N. T. Diction . 12
    ii. Basis of the N. T. Diction 20
    iii. Hebrew-Aramaic Colouring of the N. T. Diction 28
    iv. Grammatical Character of the N. T. Diction 37

PART II.

ACCIDENCE.

Sect. v. Orthography and Orthographical Principles 42
    vi. Accentuation 55
    vii. Punctuation 63
    viii. Unusual Forms in the First and Second Declensions . . 69
    ix. Unusual Forms in the Third Declension 73
    x. Declension of Foreign Words: Indeclinable Nouns . . 77
    xi. Declension and Comparison of Adjectives 80
    xii. Augment and Reduplication of Regular Verbs . . . 82
    xiii. Unusual Forms in Tenses and Persons of Regular Verbs . . 86
    xiv. Unusual Inflexions of Verbs in $\mu\iota$ and Irregular Verbs . . 93
    xv. Defective Verbs 98
    xvi. Formation of Derivative and Compound Words . . . 112

PART III.

SYNTAX.

A. SIGNIFICATION AND USE OF THE DIFFERENT PARTS OF SPEECH.

	PAGE
CHAP. I. The Article	129
Sect. xvii. The Article as a Pronoun	129
xviii. The Article before Nouns	131
xix. Omission of the Article before Nouns	147
xx. The Article with Attributives	163
CHAP. II. Pronouns	176
Sect. xxi. The Pronouns in general	176
xxii. Personal and Possessive Pronouns	178
xxiii. Demonstrative Pronouns	195
xxiv. Relative Pronouns	202
xxv. The Interrogative and Indefinite Pronoun τις	210
xxvi. Hebraistic modes of expressing certain Pronouns	214
CHAP. III. The Noun	217
Sect. xxvii. Number and Gender of Nouns	217
xxviii. The Cases in general	224
xxix. The Nominative and Vocative	226
xxx. The Genitive	230
xxxi. The Dative	260
xxxii. The Accusative	277
xxxiii. Verbs (neuter) connected by means of a Preposition with a Dependent Noun	291
xxxiv. Adjectives	293
xxxv. The Comparative Degree	300
xxxvi. The Superlative Degree	308
xxxvii. The Numerals	311
CHAP. IV. The Verb	314
Sect. xxxviii. The Active and Middle Voices	314
xxxix. The Passive Voice	326
xl. The Tenses	330
xli. The Indicative, Conjunctive, Optative Moods	351
xlii. The Conjunction ἄν with the Three Moods	378
xliii. The Imperative Mood	390
xliv. The Infinitive Mood	399
xlv. The Participle	427

CONTENTS.   xxvii

		PAGE
CHAP. V. The Particles		447
Sect. xlvi. The Particles in general		447
xlvii. The Prepositions in general, and those which govern the Genitive in particular		449
xlviii. Prepositions governing the Dative		480
xlix. Prepositions with the Accusative		494
l. Interchange, Accumulation, and Repetition of Prepositions		510
li. Use of Prepositions to form Periphrases		526
lii. Construction of Verbs compounded with Prepositions		529
liii. The Conjunctions		541
liv. The Adverbs		579
lv. The Negative Particles		593
lvi. Construction of the Negative Particles		627
lvii. The Interrogative Particles		638

B. THE STRUCTURE OF SENTENCES, AND THE COMBINATION OF SENTENCES INTO PERIODS.

Sect. lviii. The Sentence and its Elements in general	644
lix. Enlargement of the Simple Sentence in the Subject and Predicate : Attributives : Apposition	657
lx. Connexion of Sentences with one another : Periods	673
lxi. Position of Words and Clauses, especially when irregularly arranged (Hyperbaton)	684
lxii. Interrupted Structure of Sentences : Parenthesis	702
lxiii. Sentences in which the Construction is broken off or changed : Anacoluthon : Oratio variata	709
lxiv. Incomplete Structure : Ellipsis : Aposiopesis	726
lxv. Redundant Structure : Pleonasm (Redundance), Diffuseness	752
lxvi. Condensation and Resolution of Sentences (Breviloquence, Constructio prægnans, Attraction, etc.)	773
lxvii. Abnormal Relation of Particular Words in the Sentence (Hypallage)	786
lxviii. Regard to Sound in the Structure of Sentences : Paronomasia and Play upon Words (Annominatio) : Parallelism : Verse	793

INDEX.

I. Passages of the New Testament	801
II. Passages of the Old Testament and Apocrypha	818
III. Subjects	820
IV. Greek Words and Forms	830

LIST OF AUTHORS.

	B.C.	A.D.
Achilles Tatius		480 ?
Ælian		210
Ælian, the tactician		120
Æneas of Gaza		490
Æschines, the philosopher [1]	390	
Æschines, the orator		340
Æschylus	480	
Æsop [2]	600	
Agathias		560
Alciphron		200 ?
Alexander Numenius (p. 749)		150
Ammonius, the grammarian		390
Anacreon [3]	520	
Andocides	410	
Anna Comnena		1120
Anonymi *Chronologica* [4] (p. 698)		850
Antipater of Sidon (p. 733)	105	
Antiphon	435	
Antoninus Liberalis		160 ?
Antoninus, Marc. Aurelius		160
Aphthonius		300 ?
Apollodorus of Athens	140	
Apollonius Dyscolus		140
Apollonius Rhodius	200	
Appian		140
Aratus	270	
Aristænetus		470 ?
Aristarchus, the grammarian	170	
Aristeas [5]	270	
Aristides, the rhetorician		160
Aristophanes	410	
Aristotle	345	
Arrian		140
Artemidorus Daldianus		150
Athenæus		200

	B.C.	A.D.
Babrius	40 ?	
Barnabas, *Epistle* of, written about		100
Basilica, completed about		900
Callimachus	270	
Cananus, John		1430
Cantacuzenus, John V.		1355
Cebes	400	
Cedrenus, George		1060
Charax, John		?
Chariton		500 ?
Chrysostom, John		390
Cinnamus, John		1160
Clement of Alexandria		195
Clement of Rome, *Epistle* of, written about		95
Cleomedes		200 ?
Codinus, George		1440
Constantine Manasses		1160
Constantine Porphyrogenitus		940
Demetrius Ixion	20	
Demosthenes	345	
Dexippus, the historian		250
Dicæarchus	320	
Dinarchus	315	
Diodorus Siculus	30	
Diogenes Laërtius		210
Dion Cassius		200
Dion Chrysostom		95
Dionysius of Halicarnassus	20	
Dionysius Periegetes		300 ?
Dioscorides		100 ?
Ducas, Michael		1460

[1] The dialogues and letters ascribed to this philosopher, together with the other 'Epist. Socratis et Socraticorum,' are spurious.
[2] The collection of prose fables bearing Æsop's name is of very recent date. See Smith, *Dict. of Biogr.* i. 47 sq.
[3] Almost all that has come down to us under Anacreon's name is spurious. See Müller, *Lit. of Greece*, i. 245-249.
[4] Probably written by Georgius Hamartolus. See *Dict. of Biogr.* ii. 908.
[5] The letter which bears the name of Aristeas is spurious, but of early date,—not later than the first century B.C.

LIST OF AUTHORS.

	B.C.	A.D.
Ephraem the Syrian		350
Epictetus		90
Epimenides	. 600	
Epiphanius, Bishop of Cyprus		370
Epiphanius, the monk		1200?
Etymologicum Magnum		1000?
Eunapius		390
Euripides	. 435	
Eusebius of Cæsarea		315
Eustathius, the erotic writer		1100?
Eustathius, the grammarian		1160
Eustratius, the philosopher		1100
Galen		175
Geoponica compiled		940
George Acropolita		1260
George Chœroboscus		400?
George Pachymeres		1280
George Phranzes		1450
George the Pisidian		620
George the Syncellus		800
Glycas, Michael		1180?
Gorgias of Leontini	. 430	
Gregory of Corinth (Pardus)		1150
Gregory of Nazianzus		370
Gregory of Nyssa		375
Heliodorus		390
Hermas		140
Herodian, the grammarian		160
Herodian, the historian		215
Herodotus	. 440	
Hesiod	. 850?	
Hierocles (Neo-Platonist)		450
Himerius		355
Hippocrates	. 410	
Homer	. ?	
Hyperides	. 345	
Iamblichus		300
Ignatius, *Epistles* of, written about		107
Irenæus (Pacatus), the grammarian	. 10?	
Isæus	. 370	
Isocrates	. 380	
Josephus		75
Julian (Emperor)		355
Justin Martyr[1]		130
Leo Diaconus		980
Leo, the grammarian		940?
Leo VI. (the philosopher or tactician)		895
Libanius		360

	B.C.	A.D.
Longinus		250
Longus		400?
Lucian		170
Lycophron	. 280	
Lycurgus, the orator	. 355	
Lysias	. 400	
Macarius the Egyptian		350
Macho	. 280	
Malalas, John		600?
Malchus		500?
Manetho (author of 'Αποτιλεσματικά)		400?
Marinus, the philosopher		485
Maximus of Tyre		190
Meleager	. 60	
Menander	. 310	
Menander, the historian		590
Mœris		200?
Moschopuli, the (uncle and nephew)		1300?
Moschus	. 260	
Nicander	. 160	
Nicephorus Blemmidas		1260
Nicephorus Bryennius		1100
Nicephorus Gregoras		1335
Nicephorus of Constantinople (Patr.)		800
Nicephorus II. (Emperor): see p. 38		950
Nicetas Choniates		1190
Nicetas Eugenianus		1200?
Nilus		420
Œcumenius		950?
Œnomaus		150?
Olympiodorus (Neo-Platonist)		540
Origen		225
Orphic Poems (earliest)	. 500?	
Pæanius		400?
Palæphatus	. 300?	
Pausanias		160
Petrus Patricius		540
Phalaris, Epistles of		200?
Philo the Jew		30
Philostratus, Flavius[2]		220
Philostratus, Flavius,[3] of Lemnos		240
Photius		860
Phrynichus		170
Pindar	. 470	
Plato	. 380	
Plutarch		90
Pollux		170

[1] The date of his undisputed works is about 146 A.D.
[2] Author of *Vit. Apollonii, Vit. sophistarum, Imagines, Heroica*, etc.
[3] Author of another (smaller) work called *Imagines*.

LIST OF AUTHORS. xxxi

	B.C.	A.D.		B.C.	A.D.
Polyænus		150	Teles	300?	
Polybius	155		Themistius		360
Porphyry		280	Theocritus	275	
Priscus Panites		450	Theodoret		435
Proclus		455	Theodorus Gaza (p. 29)		1450
Procopius		540	Theodosius Diaconus		960
Psellus, Michael (the historian)		1070	Theodosius, the grammarian		350?
			Theognis	530	
Ptolemy		140	Theophanes continuatus[2]		940
			Theophanes Isaurus		800
Rosetta Inscription	196		Theophrastus	320	
			Theophylact (Abp. of Bulgaria)		1070
Scymnus of Chios[1]	80		Thomas Magister		1310
Sextus Empiricus		230	Thucydides	420	
Sibylline Oracles (earliest)	150		Tiberius (p. 749)		?
Simplicius		530			
Sophocles	440				
Stephanus of Byzantium		500?	Xenophon	390	
Stobæus		480?	Xenophon of Ephesus		?
Strabo	10				
Suidas		1050?	Zonaras		1115
Synesius		410	Zosimus		440

The Septuagint version may be ascribed to the period 280–160 B.C. Most of the Greek books which are usually included under the name 'Apocrypha' belong (in their Greek dress) to the next hundred years; the Prayer of Manasses and the third Book of Maccabees (and possibly other books) are later. The Psalms of Solomon may belong to the second century B.C., but the Greek translation was probably made at a much later date. The versions of Aquila, Symmachus, and Theodotion were executed in the second century A.D. To the same century are referred the Testaments of the Twelve Patriarchs (early), the Protevangel of James (150?), the Gospel of Nicodemus (first part—the 'Acts of Pilate'), the Acts of Paul and Thecla, the Acts of Thomas.

EDITIONS QUOTED.

Krüger, *Sprachlehre*: ed. 4, 1861–62.
Matthiæ, *Sprachlehre*: ed. 3, 1835.
Rost, *Grammatik*: ed. 7, 1856.
Buttmann, *Gr. Grammatik*: ed. 21, 1863.

Ewald, *Lehrbuch*: ed. 7, 1863.
Jelf, *Grammar*: ed. 3, 1861.
Veitch, *Greek Verbs*: ed. 3, 1871.
Green, *Gram. of the N. T.*: ed. 2, 1862.

In the case of works not specified here or in the Preface, the references are usually made to the last edition.

'Lob.' denotes Lobeck on Phrynichus; '*Irr. V.*,' Fishlake's translation of Buttmann's *Catalogue of Irregular Verbs* (ed. 3, 1866).

The notes appended by the former translator, Professor Masson, have the signature '*E. M.*'

---

[1] Author of a *Periegesis*, which is lost. The extant poem bearing the same name is of later date.
[2] See *Dict. of Biogr.* ii. 757.

CORRIGENDA.

Page 274, line 18, *after* ii. 15, *insert* [or rather, Jude 11.]

Page 336, line 2, *for* v. 4 *read* x. 4.

Page 588, line 10, *for* former *read* latter.

Page 592, line 23, *for* ὅπου *read* ποῦ.

N.B.—Where peculiarities in the form of words are in question (and therefore in a large number of the quotations contained in §§ v.–xvi. of this book), the references to the text of Westcott and Hort must be taken in connexion with pages 141–173 of their *Appendix*, where many *alternative readings* are given. When this *Appendix* was published (Sept. 1881), the greater part of the present volume was already in type.

INTRODUCTION.

ON THE OBJECT, TREATMENT, AND HISTORY OF N. T. GRAMMAR.

§ 1. THE peculiar language of the N. T., like every other language, presents two distinct aspects for scientific investigation. We may examine the several words in themselves as to their origin and significations—the *material* element; or we may consider these words as they are employed according to certain laws to form clauses and periods—the *formal* element. The former is the province of lexicography; the latter of grammar,[1] —which must be carefully distinguished from the laws of style (or rhetoric) of the N. T.

N. T. lexicography, of which the examination of synonyms is a very important part, though its importance has only of late been duly recognised, has hitherto been treated in a merely practical manner. A *theory* might however be constructed, for which the recently introduced term *lexicology* would be a convenient name. No such theory has as yet been fully developed for the N. T.; but this is the less surprising when we consider that the same want exists in connexion with the classical languages, and that our exegetical theology is still without a theory of Biblical criticism, higher and lower. Practical lexicography has however suffered materially from this deficiency, as might be easily shown by an examination of the lexicographical works on the N. T., even the most recent.[2]

A treatise on the laws of style or (to use the name adopted by Glass and by Bauer, the author of *Rhetorica Paulina*) the *Rhetoric* of the N. T. should investigate the peculiar features of the N. T. language as shown in free, original composition, conditioned merely by the character and aim of the writing,—first generally, and then with reference to the peculiarities of the *genera dicendi* and of the several

---

[1] On the separation of lexicography from grammar see an article by Pott, in the *Kieler allgem. Monatsschr.* July, 1851.
[2] For some remarks on the theory of lexicography see Schleiermacher, *Herneneutik*, pp. 49, 84. A contribution towards a comparative lexicography is furnished by Zeller, in his *Theol. Jahrb.* II. 443 sqq.

writers: compare Hand, *Lehrb. des lat. Styls*, p. 25 sq. Much yet remains to be done in this department, especially as regards the theory of the rhetorical figures, which have at all times been used most mischievously in N. T. interpretation. The preparatory labours of Bauer and D. Schulze [1] are of some use, and Wilke's compilation (*N. T. Rhetorik:* Dresden, 1843) is worthy of attention: Schleiermacher too gave excellent hints in his *Hermeneutik*. Biblical rhetoric would most appropriately include the treatment of the modes of reasoning employed in the discourses of Jesus and in the apostolic Epistles. By this arrangement, which agrees in principle with that adopted by the ancient rhetoricians, we should avoid the excessive subdivision of N. T. exegetics, and the separation of kindred subjects, which throw light on one another when studied in connexion.[2]

It may be incidentally remarked that our Encyclopædias still leave very much to be desired in their delineation of exegetical theology so called; and that in practice the hermeneutics are not properly distinguished from what we may call the *philology* [3] of the N. T.,—denoting by this name the whole of that province of exegetical theology which has just been sketched in outline.

§ 2. As the language in which the N. T. is written is a variety of Greek, the proper object of a N. T. grammar would be fully accomplished by a systematic grammatical comparison of the N. T. language with the written Greek of the same age and of the same description. As however this later Greek itself has not yet been fully examined as a whole, and as N. T. Greek displays in general the influence of a foreign tongue (the Hebrew-Aramæan), N. T. grammar must take a proportionately wider range, and investigate scientifically the laws according to which the Jewish writers of the N. T. wrote the Greek of their time.

Let us suppose, for instance, that a grammar of the Egyptian or Alexandrian dialect of Greek is required, that is, a grammar of the language used by the Greek-speaking inhabitants of Alexandria, gathered from all parts of the world. It will be necessary to collect together all the peculiarities which make this a distinct dialect: but a

---

[1] K. L. Bauer, *Rhetorica Paulina* (Hal. 1782), and *Philologia Thucydideo-Paulina* (Hal. 1773): under this head come also H. G. Tzschirner's *Observationes Pauli ap. epistolarum scriptoris ingenium concernentes* (Viteb. 1800).—J. D. Schulze, *Der schriftst. Werth und Character des Johannes* (Weissenf. 1803); and two similar treatises by the same author, on *Peter, Jude, and James* (Weissenf. 1802), and on *Mark* (in Keil and Tzschirner's *Analect.* Vol. II. and Vol. III.).

[2] Compare also Gersdorf, *Beiträge zur Sprachcharakterist. d. N. T.* p. 7; Keil, *Lehrb. der Hermeneutik*, p. 28; C. J. Kellmann, *Diss. de usu Rhetorices hermeneutico* (Gryph. 1766).

[3] I should prefer this old and intelligible appellation, "Philologia sacra N.T." (compare J. Ch. Beck, *Conspect. system. philol. sacræ:* Bas. 1760, 12 section.), to that which Schleiermacher proposes in accordance with ancient usage, "Grammar:" see Lücke on his *Hermeneutik*, p. 10.

mere accumulation of disjointed details will not be sufficient; we must search for the leading characteristics, and we must show, in every section of the grammar, how the general tendency of the dialect has affected the ordinary rules of Greek, by overlooking niceties, misusing analogies, etc. The grammar of the dialect will then be complete. Since the language of the N. T. is a variety of later Greek, a special N. T. grammar could only portray it as a species of a species, and would thus presuppose a grammar of the ordinary later Greek. But it is hardly possible even to form a conception of N. T. grammar so restricted, still less could such a conception be worked out with advantage. For in the first place, the grammar of later Greek, especially in its oral and popular form, has not as yet been scientifically investigated,[1] and hence the foundation which theory points out for a special N. T. grammar does not actually exist. Moreover, the N. T. language in itself is said also to exhibit the influence of a non-cognate tongue (the Hebrew-Aramæan) upon the Greek.

For these reasons the boundaries of N. T. grammar must be extended in two directions. It must first—since the reader brings with him the ordinary grammar of the written language—investigate the peculiarities of the later Greek in the N. T., according to the principles mentioned above; and secondly, it must point out the modifications which were introduced by the influence of the Hebrew-Aramæan on the Greek, the details being classified as before. It is not possible, however, to make a rigorous distinction between these two elements; for in the mind of the N. T. writers the mixture of the (later) Greek with the national (Jewish) had given rise to a *single* syntax, which must be recognised and exhibited in its unity.[2] This treatment of N. T. grammar will be changed in one respect only, when we are furnished with an independent grammar of later Greek. Then the N. T. grammarian will not, as now, be compelled to illustrate and prove by examples the peculiarities of the later language; a simple reference to these will suffice. On the other hand, the *polemic* element in grammars of the N. T., which combats

---

[1] Valuable material for this purpose, though rather of a lexical than of a grammatical character, will be found in Lobeck's notes on *Phrynichi Eclogæ* (Lips. 1820). Irmisch (*on Herodian*) and Fischer (*De vitiis Lexicor. N. T.*) had previously collected much that is serviceable. Abundant material for philological observations on "Græcitas fatiscens" has more recently been furnished by the corrected texts of the Byzantine writers and the Indices appended to most of them in the Bonn edition, though these Indices are very unequal in their merit; by Boissonade's notes in the *Anecdota Græca* (Paris, 1829, &c., 5 vols.), and in his editions of Marinus, Philostratus, Nicetas Eugenianus, Babrius, al.; and lastly by Mullach's edition of Hierocles (Berlin, 1853). Lobeck also constantly pays due attention to the later Greek element in his *Paralipomena Grammaticæ Gr.* (Lips. 1837, 2 parts); *Pathologiæ sermonis Gr. Proleg.* (Lips. 1843), and *Pathol. Græci serm. Elementa* (Königsb. 1853, I.); 'Ρηματικόν sive verbor. Gr. et nominum verball. Technologia (Königsb. 1846). [The 2nd volume of Lobeck's *Pathol. Elementa* appeared in 1862. In 1856 Mullach published a *Grammatik der griechischen Vulgarsprache* (Berlin).]

[2] Schleiermacher's remarks on the lexical treatment of Hebraisms (*Hermen.* p. 65) are worthy of attention.

inveterate and stubborn prejudices or errors revived anew, may gradually disappear: at present it is still necessary to vindicate the true character of the N. T. diction on this negative side also. For even very recently we have seen in the works of well-known commentators—as Kühnöl, Flatt, Klausen in his commentary on the Gospels—how deeply rooted was the old grammatical empiricism by which *ultra Fischerum* (or *ultra Storrium*) *sapere* was held in horror.

The notion of special grammars for the writings of different authors, as John or Paul, cannot be entertained. What is distinctive in the diction of particular writers, especially of those just named, has seldom any connexion with grammar. It consists almost entirely in a preference for certain words and phrases, or belongs to the rhetorical element, as indeed Blackwall's observations[1] show. The same may be said of most of the peculiarities in the arrangement of words. Hence Schulze and Schulz[2] have, on the whole, formed a more correct estimate of such specialities than Gersdorf, whose well-known work contributes even to verbal criticism no large store of *certain* results, and must have almost proved its own refutation, if it had been continued on its own principles.

§ 3. Although the study of the language of the N. T. is the fundamental condition of all true exegesis, Biblical philologers have until lately almost excluded N. T. grammar from the range of their scientific inquiries. The lexicography of the N. T. was the subject of repeated investigation; but the grammar was at most noticed only so far as it stood connected with the doctrine of the Hebraisms of the N. T.[3] Casp. Wyss (1650) and G. Pasor (1655) alone apprehended more completely the idea of N. T. grammar, but they were unable to obtain for it recognition as a distinct branch of exegetical study. After them, 160 years later, Haab was the first who handled the subject in a special treatise; but, apart from the fact that he confined his attention to the Hebraistic element, his somewhat uncritical

---

[1] *Sacred Classics*, I. p. 385 sqq. (London, 1727).

[2] His remarks on N. T. diction are contained in his dissertations on the Parable of the Steward (Bresl. 1821) and on the Lord's Supper (Leips. 1824, second improved ed. 1831), and in various reviews in Wachler's *Theol. Annalen*. Both dissertations are of an exegetical character, and hence the remarks (which are usually acute) are out of place, since they throw but little light on the exegesis. Textual criticism might turn his observations to good account, had but the distinguished writer been pleased to give them to us in a complete form. Compare also Schleiermacher, *Hermen.* p. 129.

[3] An honourable exception among the earlier commentators is the now nearly forgotten G. F. Heupel, who, in his copious and almost purely philological commentary on the Gospel of Mark (Strassburg, 1716), makes many good grammatical observations. The Greek scholarship of J. F. Hombergk in his *Parerga Sacra* (Amstel. 1719), and of H. Heisen in his *Novæ Hypotheses interpretandæ felicius Ep. Jacobi* (Brem. 1739), is more lexical than grammatical.

work was fitted rather to retard than to promote the progress of the science.

The first who in some degree collected and explained the grammatical peculiarities of the N. T. diction was the well-known Sal. Glass († 1656), the 3rd and 4th books of whose *Philologia Sacra* are entitled *Grammatica sacra* and *Gramm. sacræ Appendix.*[1] As however he makes Hebrew his point of departure throughout, and touches the N. T. language only so far as it agrees with Hebrew, his work—to say nothing of its incompleteness—can be mentioned in the history of N. T. grammar only as a feeble attempt. On the other hand, the historian must revive the memory of the two above-named writers, whose names are almost unknown, as indeed their works on this subject are forgotten. The first, Casp. Wyss, Professor of Greek in the Gymnasium of Zürich († 1659), published his *Dialectologia Sacra*[2] in 1650. In this work all the peculiarities of the N. T. diction, grammatically considered, are classified under the heads, *Dialectus Attica, Ionica, Dorica, Æolica, Bœotica, Poëtica,* Ἑβραΐζουσα, —certainly a most inconvenient arrangement, since kindred subjects are thus separated, and in many cases are noticed in four different parts of the work. The author too was not in advance of his age in acquaintance with the Greek dialects, as is proved by the very mention of a special *dialectus poëtica*, and as an examination of what he calls *Attic* will show still more clearly. As a collection of examples, however, in many sections absolutely complete, the work is meritorious; and the writer's moderation in regard to the grammatical Hebraisms of the N. T. deserved the imitation of his contemporaries.

George Pasor, Professor of Greek at Franeker († 1637), is well known as the author of a small N. T. Lexicon, which has been frequently republished, last of all by J. F. Fischer. He left amongst his papers a N. T. Grammar, which was published, with some additions and corrections of his own, by his son Matthias Pasor, Prof. of Theology at Gröningen († 1658), under the title, *G. Pasoris Grammatica Græca sacra N. T. in tres libros distributa* (Groning. 1655, pp. 787). This work is now a literary rarity,[3] though far better fitted than the lexicon to preserve the author's name in the memory of posterity. As the title indicates, the volume is divided into three books, of which the first contains the Accidence, the second (pp. 244–530) the Syntax, and the third seven appendices,—*de nominibus N. T., de verbis N. T., de verbis anomalis, de dialectis N. T., de accentibus, de*

---

[1] In Dathe's edition this *Grammatica sacra* constitutes the first book.

[2] *Dialectologia sacra, in qua quicquid per universum N. F. contextum in apostolica et voce et phrasi a communi Græcor. lingua eoque grammatica analogia discrepat, methodo congrua disponitur, accurate definitur et omnium sacri contextus exemplorum inductione illustratur.* Tigur. 1650, pp. 324 (without the Appendix).

[3] Even Foppen (*Bibliotheca belgica*, Tom. I. p. 342), who enumerates Pasor's other writings, does not mention this work. Its great rarity is attested by Salthen, *Cat. biblioth. libr. rar.* (Regiom. 1751), p. 470; and by D. Gerdesius, *Florileg. hist. crit. libr. var.* (Groning. 1763), p. 272.

praxi grammaticæ, de numeris s. arithmetica Græca. The most valuable parts of the work are the second book and the fourth appendix;[1] for in the first book and in most of the appendices the writer treats of well-known subjects belonging to general Greek grammar, and, for example, most needlessly gives full paradigms of Greek nouns and verbs. The Syntax is accurate and exhaustive. The author points out what is Hebraistic, but does not often adduce parallels from Greek authors. This useful book suffers from the want of a complete index.

In the interval between Pasor and Haab N. T. grammar received only incidental notice, in works on the style of the N. T., as in those of Leusden (*De dialectis N. T.*) and Olearius (*De stylo N. T.*, pp. 257–271). These writers, however, limited their attention almost entirely to Hebraisms; and by including amongst these much that is pure Greek they threw back into confusion the whole question of the grammatical structure of the N. T. Georgi was the first to show that many constructions usually regarded as Hebraisms belonged to genuine Greek usage, but he also sometimes falls into extremes. His writings passed into almost total neglect. Meanwhile Fischer gave currency anew to the works of Vorst and Leusden, and during many years Storr's well-known book[2] was able to exercise without restraint its pernicious influence on the exegesis of the N. T.

From the school of Storr now came forward Ph. H. Haab, Rector of Schweigern in the kingdom of Würtemberg († 1833), with his "Hebrew-Greek Grammar for the N. T., with a preface by F. G. von Süskind" (Tübing. 1815). Disregarding the genuine Greek element in the diction of the N. T., he confined his attention to the grammatical Hebraisms, and in the arrangement of his materials followed the works of Storr and Weckherlin.[3] If we are to believe a reviewer in Bengel's *Archiv* (vol. i. p. 406 sqq.), "the diligence, judgment, accuracy, nice and comprehensive philological knowledge, with which the author has accomplished his task, must secure for his work the approval of all friends of the thorough exegesis of the N. T." A different and almost directly opposite verdict is given by two scholars[4] who must in this field be regarded as thoroughly competent (and impartial) judges; and after long and manifold use of the book we are compelled to agree with these critics in all points. The great defect of the work consists in this,—that the author has not rightly understood the difference between the pure Greek and the Hebraistic

---

[1] This appendix had already been added by Pasor himself to the first edition of his *Syllabus Græco-Latinus omnium N. T. vocum* (Amstel. 1632), under the title, *Idea (syllabus brevis) Græcarum N. T. dialectorum*. At the close he promises the above complete *Grammatica N. T.*

[2] *Observatt. ad analog. et syntaxin Hebr.* (Stutt. 1779). Some acute grammatical observations, especially on *enallage temporum, particularum*, &c., are to be found in J. G. Straube, *Diss. de emphasi Gr. linguæ N. T.*, in Van den Honert's *Syntagma*, p. 70 sqq.

[3] Weckherlin, *Hebr. Grammat.* (2 parts).

[4] See the reviews in the *Neu. theol. Annal.* 1816, II. pp. 859-879, and (by de Wette?) the *A. L. Z.* 1816, N. 39-41, pp. 305-326.

elements in the language of the N. T. ; has accordingly adduced as Hebraistic very much which either is the common property of all cultivated languages, or, at all events, occurs in Greek as frequently as in Hebrew ; and, out of love to Storr's observations, has altogether misinterpreted a multitude of passages in the N. T. (for examples see below) by *forcing* Hebraisms upon them. Besides all this, everything is in confusion, the arrangement of materials is most arbitrary, and the book opens with a section on *Tropes !*—a subject which does not belong to grammar at all. Hence we cannot regard as too severe the words with which the second of the reviewers above mentioned concludes : " Seldom have we seen a book which has been so complete a failure, and against the use of which it has been necessary to give so emphatic a warning."

§ 4. The remarks scattered through commentaries on the N. T., books of observations, and exegetical monographs, though sometimes displaying very respectable learning, yet when all taken together presented no complete treatment of the grammar. But even their incompleteness does less to render these collections useless, than the uncritical empiricism which ruled Greek philology until the commencement of this century, and Hebrew much later still; as indeed this same empiricism has impressed on N. T. exegesis also the character of uncertainty and arbitrariness. The *rational* method of treatment, which seeks for the explanation of all the phenomena of languages, even of their anomalies, in the modes of thought which characterise nations and individual writers, has completely transformed the study of Greek. The same method must be applied to the language of the N. T. : then, and not till then, N. T. grammar receives a scientific character, and is elevated into a sure instrument for exegesis.

The main features of this empirical philology, so far as grammar is concerned, are the following :

(*a*) The grammatical structure of the language was apprehended only in rudest outline, and hence the mutual relation of allied forms, in which the genius of the Greek language is peculiarly shown,—as of the aorist and perfect, the conjunctive and optative, the two negatives οὐ and μή,—was left almost entirely undefined.

(*b*) Those forms whose true signification was generally recognised were confounded together by an unlimited *enallage*, in virtue of which one tense or case or particle might stand for another, even for one of a directly opposite meaning, e.g. preterite for future, ἀπό for πρός, etc.

(*c*) A host of ellipses were devised, and in the simplest sentences there was always something to be supplied.

The commentators applied these principles—which still appear in Fischer's copious *Animadv. ad Welleri Gramm. Gr.* (Lips. 1798 sqq.

3 spec.)—to the interpretation of the N. T. Nay they considered themselves justified in using still greater freedom than classical philologers, because (as they held) the Hebrew language, on the model of which the Greek of the N. T. was framed, had as its distinguishing characteristic the absence of all definiteness in forms and regularity of syntax, so that Hebrew syntax was treated, not as a connected whole, but only under *enallage* and solecism.[1] The ordinary commentaries on the N. T. exhibit in profusion the natural results of such principles, and Storr[2] earned the distinction of reducing this whole *farrago* of crude empirical canons of language into a kind of system. Apart from all other considerations, such canons of language necessarily gave unlimited scope for arbitrary interpretation, and it was easy to extract from the words of the sacred writers meanings directly contrary to each other.[3]

It was in Greek philology that the reformation commenced. A pupil of Reitz, Gottfr. Hermann, by his work *De emendanda ratione grammaticæ Græcæ* (1801), gave the first powerful impulse to the *rational*[4] investigation of this noble language. In the course of more than forty years this method has penetrated so deep, and has produced such solid results, that the face of Greek grammar is entirely changed. It has recently been combined with historical investigation,[5] and not without success. The principles of this method, which entitle it to the name of rational, are the following:

(*a*) The fundamental meaning of every grammatical form (case, tense, mood), or the idea which underlay this form in the mind of the

---

[1] The attempts made by better scholars to combat this empiricism were only partial and isolated. The Wittenberg Professors Balth. Stolberg (in his *Tractat. de solœcism. et barbarism. Gr. N. F. dictioni falso tributis*: Vit. 1681 and 1685) and Fr. Woken (in his *Pietas critica in hypallagas bibl.*: Viteb. 1718, and especially in his *Enallagæ e N. T. Gr. textus præcipuis et plurimis locis exterminatæ*: Viteb. 1730) exposed many blunders of the commentators, and on the whole very intelligently. J. C. Schwarz also shows creditable learning and acumen in his *Lib. de opinatis discipulor. Chr. solœcismis* (Cob. 1730). Such voices were however not listened to, or were drowned by a *contorte! artificiose!*

[2] How complete a contrast is presented by his acute countryman Alb. Bengel, in his *Gnomon!* Though he often falls into over-refined explanations, and attributes to the Apostles *his own* dialectic modes of thought, yet he left to posterity a model of careful and spirited exposition. He notices points of grammar,—compare *e.g.* A. iii. 19, xxvi. 2, 1 C. xii. 15, Mt. xviii. 17, H. vi. 4: in the lexical department he pays especial attention to the examination of synonyms.

[3] "Sunt," says Tittmann (*Synon. N. T.* I. p. 206), "qui grammaticarum legum observationem in N. T. interpretatione parum curent et, si scriptoris cujusdam verba grammatice i. e. ex legibus linguæ explicata sententiam . . . ab ipsorum opinione alienam prodant, nullam illarum legum rationem habeant, sed propria verborum vi neglecta scriptorem dixisse contendant, *quæ talibus verbis nemo sana mente præditus dicere unquam potuit.*" Hermann's sarcasm (*Vig.* 788) was quite just.

[4] I prefer "rational" to "philosophical," because the latter word may easily be misunderstood. All philological inquiry that is merely empirical is irrational: it deals with language as something merely external, and not as bearing the impress of thought. Compare Tittmann, *Syn.* p. 205 sq.

[5] G. Bernhardy, *Wissenschaftliche Syntax der gr. Sprache* (Berlin, 1829).

Greek nation, is exactly seized, and all the various uses of the form are deduced from this primary signification : by this means numberless ellipses have been demolished, and *enallage* has been confined within its natural (*i.e.*, narrow) limits.

(*b*) When the established laws of the language are violated, either in expressions of general currency, or in the usage of individual writers, the grammarian is at pains to show how the irregularity originated in the mind of the speaker or writer,—by anacoluthon, confusio duarum structurarum, attraction, constructio ad sensum, brachylogy, etc.

The language is thus presented as bearing the direct impress of Greek thought, and appears as a *living* idiom. The grammarian is not content with merely noticing the phenomena : he traces each form and turn of speech back into the thought of the speaker, and endeavours to lay hold of it as it comes into existence within the speaker's mind. Thus everything which is impossible in *thought* is rejected as impossible in *language;* as, for instance, that a writer could use the *future* tense when he wished to refer to the *past;* could say *to* for *from;* could call a man *wiser* when he wished to call him *wise;* could indicate a *cause* by *consequently;* could say, *I saw the man*, when he wished to express, *I saw a man*. For a long time, however, these elucidations of Greek grammar (and lexicography) remained altogether unnoticed by Biblical scholars. They adhered to the old Viger and to Storr, and thus separated themselves entirely from classical philologers, in the belief—which however no recent writer has distinctly expressed—that the N. T. Greek, as being Hebraistic, could not be subjected to such philosophical investigation. They would not see that Hebrew itself, like every other human language, both admits and requires rational treatment. Through Ewald's reiterated efforts this fact has now been made patent to all. All are convinced that, even in the Hebrew language, the ultimate explanation of phenomena must be sought in the national modes of thought, and that a nation characterised by simplicity could least of all be capable of transgressing the laws of all human language.[1] It is not now considered sufficient to assign to a preposition, for instance, the most different meanings, just as a superficially examined

---

[1] Rational investigation must be founded on historical. The whole field of the language must be historically surveyed, before we can discover the causes of the individual phenomena. The simpler the Hebrew language is, the easier is this process of discovery, for a simple language presupposes simple modes of thought. In the rational investigation of Hebrew the problem assigned us is, to reproduce the course of the Hebrew's thought; to conceive in our minds every transition from one meaning of a word to another, every construction and idiom of the language, as he conceived it; and thus discover how each of these grew up in his mind, for the spoken words are but the impress of the thought,—as indeed in this very language *thinking* is regarded as an *inward speaking* [*e.g.*, Gen. xvii. 17, Ps. x. 6]. To think of constructing *à priori* the laws of a language is absurd. It may be readily admitted that this rational system of investigation may be misused by individuals, as even the Greek philologers sometimes deal in subtleties ; but to persevere in insipid empiricism from the apprehension of such danger is disgraceful.

context may require : pains are taken to trace the transition from the fundamental signification of every particle to each of its secondary meanings, and the admission of meanings without such a process of derivation is regarded as an unscientific assumption. Nor is any one satisfied now with vaguely remarking that *non omnis* (by which no man of sense could mean anything but *not every one*) was used by the Hebrews as equivalent to *omnis non*, that is, *nullus;* he rather indicates in every instance the exact point on which the eye should be fixed.

Hence the object which grammar must in any case strive after is the *rational* treatment of the N. T. language: thus, and thus only, grammar obtains for itself a scientific basis, and in turn furnishes the same for exegesis. The materials offered by Greek philology must be carefully used ; but in using them we must by all means keep in mind that we cannot regard as established all the nice distinctions which scholars have laid down (so as, for instance, even to correct the text in accordance with them), and also that classical philology itself is progressive : indeed it has already been found necessary to modify many theories (e.g. the doctrine of εἰ with the conjunctive), and other points are still under discussion even amongst the best scholars —some of the constructions of ἄν, for example.

Since 1824, N. T. grammar has received very valuable contributions from Fritzsche, in particular, in his *Dissertt. in 2. Epist. ad Cor.* (Lips. 1824), his *Commentaries on Matthew and Mark,* his *Conjectan. in N. T.* (Lips. 1825, 2 spec.), and especially in his *Commentary on the Ep. to the Romans* (Hal. 1836). Here should also be mentioned the treatises by Gieseler and Bornemann in Rosenmüller's *Exeget. Repert.* (2nd vol.), Bornemann's *Scholia in Lucœ Evang.* (Lips. 1830), and in part his edition of the Acts of the Apostles.[1] Lastly, many grammatical problems have been discussed in the controversial correspondence between Fritzsche and Tholuck.[2] The philological investigation of the N. T. language has exerted more or less influence on all the numerous N. T. commentaries which have recently appeared,[3] whether emanating from the critical, the evangelical, or the philosophical school ; though only a few of the writers (as Van Hengel, Lücke, Bleek, Meyer) have given full attention to the grammatical element, or treated it with independent judgment.

---

[1] *Acta Apost. ad Cod. Cantabrig. fidem rec. et interpret. est* (Grossenhain, 1848, I.).

[2] Fritzsche, *Ueber die Verdienste D. Tholucks um die Schrifterklärung* (Halle, 1831). Tholuck, *Beiträge zur Spracherklärung des N. T.* (Halle, 1832). Fritzsche, *Präliminarien zur Abbitte und Ehrenerklärung, die ich gern dem D. Tholuck gewähren möchte* (Halle, 1832). Tholuck, *Noch ein ernstes Wort an D. Fritzsche* (Halle, 1832). In his *Commentary on the Ep. to the Hebrews* (Hamb. 1836, 1840, 1850), Tholuck laid more stress on philological investigation. The severe censure passed in an anonymous work, *Beiträge zur Erklärung des Br. an die Hebr.* (Leipz. 1840), has less reference to grammar than to Tholuck's treatment of the subject matter of the Epistle.

[3] Even on the commentaries of the excellent Baumgarten-Crusius, the weakest side of which is certainly the philological.

A sensible estimate of the better philological principles in their application to the N. T. has been given by A. G. Hölemann, in his *Comment. de interpretatione sacra cum profana feliciter conjungenda* (Lips. 1832).

N. T. grammar has recently made its way from Germany to England and North America, partly in a translation of the 4th edition of the present work[1] (London, 1840), partly in a distinct (independent?) treatise by W. Trollope (*Greek Grammar of the New Testament:* London, 1842). An earlier work on this subject by Moses Stuart (*Grammar of the New Testament Dialect:* Andover, 1841), I have not yet seen.[2]

The special grammatical characteristics of particular writers have begun to form a subject of inquiry (yet see above, p. 4): G. P. C. Kaiser, *Diss. de speciali Joa. Ap. grammatica culpa negligentiæ liberanda* (Erlang. 1824, II.), and *De speciali Petri Ap. gr. culpa. &c.* (Erlang. 1843).

---

[1] [Translated by Agnew and Ebbeke (Philadelphia, 1840). An earlier edition of Winer's Grammar had been translated in 1825 by M. Stuart and Robinson. In 1834 Prof. Stuart published a N. T. Grammar, part of which appeared in the *Biblical Cabinet*, vol. x.]

[2] [To this list the following works may be added: A. Buttmann, *Grammatik des neutest. Sprachgebrauchs: im Anschlusse an Ph. Buttmann's griech. Grammatik* (Berlin, 1859); Schirlitz, *Grundzüge der neutest. Gräcität* (Giessen, 1861); K. H. A. Lipsius, *Grammatische Untersuchungen über die biblische Gräcität; Ueber die Lesezeichen* (Leipzig, 1863); T. S. Green, *Treatise on the Grammar of the N. T.* (Bagster, 1842; 2d edition, considerably altered, 1862); W. Webster, *Syntax and Synonyms of the Greek Test.* (Rivingtons, 1864). In the later (the 3d and 4th) editions of Jelf's *Greek Grammar* considerable attention is given to the constructions of the Greek Testament. The Grammars of Winer and A. Buttmann have recently found a very able and careful translator in Professor Thayer, of Andover, Massachusetts. Another useful work, of a more elementary character, is Dr. S. G. Green's *Handbook to the Grammar of the N. T.* (1870, Rel. Tr. Society).]

PART I.

ON THE GENERAL CHARACTER OF N. T. DICTION, ESPECIALLY IN REGARD TO GRAMMAR.

Section I.

VARIOUS OPINIONS RESPECTING THE CHARACTER OF THE N. T. DICTION.

1. Though the character of the N. T. diction is in itself tolerably distinct, erroneous or at any rate incomplete and one-sided opinions respecting it were for a long time entertained by Biblical philologers. These opinions arose in part from want of acquaintance with the later Greek dialectology, but also from dogmatic considerations, through which, as is always the case, even clear intellects became incapable of discerning the line of exact exegesis. From the beginning of the 17th century the attempt had been repeatedly made by certain scholars (the Purists) to claim classic purity and elegance in every respect for the N. T. style; whilst by others (the Hebraists) the Hebrew colouring was not only recognised, but in some instances greatly exaggerated. The views of the Hebraists held the ascendancy about the close of the 17th century, though without having entirely superseded those of their rivals, some of whom were men of considerable learning. Half a century later the Purist party entirely died out, and the principles of the Hebraists, a little softened here and there, obtained general acceptance. It is only very lately that scholars have begun to see that these principles also are one-sided, and have rightly inclined towards the middle path, which had been generally indicated long before by Beza and H. Stephens.

The history of the various theories which were successively maintained, not without vehemence and considerable party bias, is given in brief by Morus, *Acroas. acad. sup. Hermeneut. N. T.* (ed. Eichstädt) vol. I. p. 216 sqq.; by Meyer, *Gesch. der Schrifterklär.* III. 342 sqq.

(comp. Eichstädt, *Pr. sententiar. de dictione scriptor. N. T. brevis censura:* Jen. 1845); and, with some important inaccuracies, by G. J. Planck, in his *Einleit. in d. theol. Wissenschaft*, II. 43 sqq. :[1] compare Stange, *Theol. Symmikta*, II. 295 sqq. On the literature connected with this subject see Walch, *Biblioth. Theol.* IV. 276 sqq.[2] The following outline of the controversy, in which the statements of the above-named writers are here and there corrected, will be sufficient for our purpose.

Erasmus had spoken of an "apostolorum sermo non solum impolitus et inconditus verum etiam imperfectus et perturbatus, aliquoties plane solœcissans." In reply to this, Beza, in a *Digressio de dono linguarum et apostol. sermone* (on Acts x. 46), pointed out the simplicity and force of N. T. diction, and in particular placed the Hebraisms (which, as is well known, he was far from denying) in a very favourable light, as "ejusmodi, ut nullo alio idiomate tam feliciter exprimi possint, imo interdum ne exprimi quidem,"—indeed as "gemmæ quibus (apostoli) scripta sua exornarint." After Beza, H. Stephens, in the Preface to his edition of the N. T. (1576), entered the lists against those "qui in his scriptis inculta omnia et horrida esse putant;" and took pains to show by examples the extent to which the niceties of Greek are observed in the N. T., and how the very Hebraisms give inimitable force and emphasis to its style. These niceties of style are, it is true, rather rhetorical than linguistic, and the Hebraisms are rated too high; but the views of these two excellent Greek scholars are evidently less extreme than is commonly supposed, and are on the whole nearer the truth than those of many later commentators.

Both Drusius and Glass acknowledged the existence of Hebraisms in the N. T., and gave illustrations of them without exciting opposition. The first advocate of extreme views was Seb. Pfochen. In his *Diatribe de linguæ Græcæ N. T. puritate* (Amst. 1629 : ed. 2, 1633), after having in the Preface defined the question under discussion to be, "an stylus N. T. sit vere Græcus nec ab aliorum Græcorum stylo alienior talisque, qui ab Homero, Demosthene aliisque Græcis intelligi potuisset," he endeavours to show by many examples (§ 81–129), "Græcos autores profanos eisdem phrasibus et verbis loquutos esse, quibus scriptores N. T." (§ 29). This juvenile production however —the principles of which were accepted by Erasmus Schmid, as his *Opus posthumum* (1658) shows—seems to have excited little attention at the time with its rigid Purism. The first who gave occasion (though indirectly) for controversy on the diction of the N. T. was the Hamburg Rector Joachim Junge (1637, 1639); though his real

---

[1] [This portion of Planck's work is translated in the *Biblical Cabinet*, vol. vii. pp. 67–71. The controversy is briefly sketched by Tregelles, in his edition of Horne's *Introduction*, vol. iv. p. 21 sq.]

[2] See also Baumgarten, *Polemik*, iii. 176 sqq. The opinions of the Fathers (especially the Apologists) on the style of the N. T. are given by J. Lami, *De erudit. Apostolor.* p. 138 sqq. They regard the subject more from a rhetorical than from a grammatical point of view. Theodoret (*Gr. affect. cur.*) triumphantly contrasts the σολοικισμοὶ ἁλιευτικοί with the ξυλλογισμοὶ ἀττικοί.

opinions as to the Hellenism (not barbarism) of the N. T. style [1] were admitted by his opponent, the Hamburg Pastor Jac. Grosse (1640), not indeed to be correct, but at all events to be free from insidious intent.[2] The latter writer, however, brought upon himself the censure of Dan. Wulfer (1640), who, in his *Innocentia Hellenistarum vindicata* (without date or place), complained of the want of clearness in Grosse's strictures.[3] Grosse had now to defend himself, not only against Wulfer, whom he proved to have misunderstood his meaning, but also (1641) against the Jena theologian Joh. Musæus (1641, 1642), who found fault with Grosse's inconsistencies and unsettled views, but wrote mainly in the interests of dogma (on verbal inspiration). Hence by degrees Grosse gave to the world five small treatises (1641, 1642), in defence, not of the classic elegance, but of the purity and dignity of the N. T. language.

Without entering into these disputes, which passed into hateful personalities, and which were almost entirely useless to science, Dan. Heinsius (1643) declared himself on the side of the Hellenism of the N. T. language; and Thomas Gataker (*De Novi Instrumenti stylo dissert.*, 1648) wrote expressly—with learning, but not without exaggeration—against the Purism of Pfochen. Joh. Vorst also now published (1658, 1665) the well-arranged collection of N. T. Hebraisms which for some time he had had in preparation: this work soon after fell under the censure of Hor. Vitringa, as being one-sided in a high degree.[4]

---

[1] In a German memorial to the department of ecclesiastical affairs (1637) Junge himself thus explains his true views: I have indeed said, and I still say, that there exists in the N. T. what is not really Greek. . . . The question *an N. T. scateat barbarismis* is so offensive a question, that no Christian man raised it before; . . . that barbarous formulas are to be found in the N. T. I have never been willing to allow, especially because the Greeks themselves recognise a barbarism as a *vitium*. [Lünemann refers to *J. Jungius " Ueber die Originalsprache des N. T." vom Jahre* 1637: *aufgefunden, zuerst herausgegeben und eingeleitet von* Joh. Geffcken (Hamb. 1863).]

[2] His two main theses are the following: "Quod quamvis evangelistæ et apostoli in N. T. non adeo ornato et nitido, tumido et affectato (!) dicendi genere usi sint . . . impium tamen, imo blasphemum sit, si quis inde S. literarum studiosus Græcum stylum . . . sugillare, vilipendere et juventuti suspectum facere ipsique vitia et notam solœcismorum et barbarismorum attricare contendat. . . . Quod nec patres, qui solœcismorum et barbarismorum meminerunt et apostolos idiotas fuisse scripserunt, nec illi autores, qui stylum N. T. Hellenisticum esse statuerunt, nec isti, qui in N. T. Ebraismos et Chaldaismos esse observarunt, stylum s. apostolorum contemserint, sugillarint eumque impuritatis alicujus accusarint cet."

[3] Grosse's work was strictly directed against a possible inference from the position that the Greek of the N. T. is not such as native Greek authors use, and in the main concerns adversaries that (at all events in Hamburg) had then no existence. Besides, he keeps throughout mainly on the negative side; as is shown, for example, by the résumé (p. 40 of Grosse's *Trias*): Etiamsi Græcus stylus apostolorum non sit tam ornatus et affectatus, ut fuit ille qui fuit florente Græcia, non Atticus ut Athenis, non Doricus ut Corinthi, non Ionicus ut Ephesi, non Æolicus ut Troade, fuit tamen vere Græcus ab omni solœcismorum et barbarismorum labe immunis.

[4] In the preface Vorst expresses his conviction, "sacros codices N. T. talibus et vocabulis et phrasibus, quæ Hebræam linguam sapiant, *scatere plane.*" Compare also his *Cogitata de stylo N. T.*, prefixed to Fischer's edition of his work on Hebraisms.

J. H. Böcler (1641) and J. Olearius (1668)[1] took a middle course, discriminating with greater care between the Hebrew and the Greek elements of the N. T. style; and with them J. Leusden agreed in the main, though he is inferior to Olearius in discretion.

By most, however, it was now regarded as a settled point that the Hebraisms must be allowed to be a very prominent element in the language of the N. T., and that they give to the style a colouring, not indeed barbarous, but widely removed from the standard of Greek purity.[2] This is the result arrived at by Mos. Solanus in a long-deferred but very judicious reply to Pfochen. Even J. Heinr. Michaelis (1707) and Ant. Blackwall (1727) did not venture to deny the Hebraisms: they endeavoured to prove that the diction of the N. T. writers, although not free from Hebraisms, still has all the qualities of an elegant style, and is in this respect not inferior to classic purity. The latter scholar commences his work (which abounds in good observations) with these words: "We are so far from denying that there are Hebraisms in the N. T., that *we esteem it a great advantage and beauty* to that sacred book that it abounds with them." Their writings, however, had as little effect on the now established opinion as those of the learned Ch. Siegm. Georgi, who in his *Vindiciæ N. T. ab Ebraismis* (1732) returned to the more rigid Purism, and defended his positions in his *Hierocriticus sacer* (1733). He was followed, with no greater success, by J. Conr. Schwarz, the chief aim of whose *Commentarii crit. et philol. linguæ Gr. N. T.* (Lips. 1736) was to prove that even those expressions which had been considered Hebraisms are pure Greek.[3] The last who joined these writers in combating the abuse of Hebraisms were El. Palairet (*Observatt. philol. crit. in N. T.:* Lugd. Bat. 1752)[4] and H. W. van Marle (*Florileg. observ. in epp. apostol.:* Lugd. Bat. 1758). Through the influence of the school of Ernesti a more correct estimate of the language of the N. T. became generally diffused over Germany:[5] compare Ernesti, *Instit. Interp.* I. 2, cap. 3. [*Bibl. Cab.* I. p. 103 sqq.]

[1] The *Stricturæ in Pfochen. diatrib.* by J. Coccejus were drawn up merely for private use, and were first published in Rhenferd's *Sammlung.*

[2] See also Werenfels, *Opusc.* I. p. 311 sqq.—Hemsterhuis on Lucian, *Dial. Mar.* 4. 3: "Eorum, qui orationem N. F. Græcam esse castigatissimam contendunt, opinio perquam mihi semper ridicula fuit visa." Blth. Stolberg also (*De solœcismis et barbarismis N. T.:* Viteb. 1681 and 1685) wished merely to vindicate the N. T. from blemishes unjustly ascribed to it; but in doing this he explained away many real Hebraisms.

[3] Conscious of certain victory Schwarz speaks thus in his preface (p. 8): "Olim Hebraismi, Syrismi, Chaldaismi, Rabinismi (sic!), Latinismi cet. celebrabantur nomina, ut vel scriptores sacri suam Græcæ dictionis ignorantiam prodere aut in Græco sermone tot linguarum notitiam ostentasse viderentur vel saltem interpretes illorum literatissimi et singularum locutionum perspicacissimi judicarentur. Sed *conata hæc ineptiarum et vanitatis ita sunt etiam a nobis convicta,* ut si qui cet." A satire on the Purists may be seen in *Somnium in quo præter cetera genius sec. vapulat* (Alteburg, 1761), p. 97 sqq.

[4] Supplements by Palairet himself are to be found in the *Biblioth. Brem. nova Cl.* 3, 4. In the main, however, Palairet quotes parallels almost exclusively for meanings and phrases which no man of judgment will regard as Hebraisms.

[5] Ernesti's judgment on the diction of the N. T. (*Diss. de difficult. interpret. grammat. N. T.* § 12) may here be recalled to mind: "Genus orationis in libris

Most of the (older) controversial works on this subject (those mentioned above and others besides) are collected in J. Rhenferd's *Dissertatt. philolog.-theolog. de stylo N. T. syntagma* (Leov. 1702), and in what may be considered a supplement to this work, Taco Hajo van den Honert, *Syntagma dissertatt. de stylo N. T. Græco* (Amst. 1703).[1]

We will endeavour briefly to describe the mode in which the Purists sought to establish their theory.[2]

Their efforts were mainly directed towards collecting from native Greek authors passages in which occur the identical words and phrases which in the N. T. are explained as Hebraisms. In general, no distinction was made between the rhetorical element and what properly belongs to language; but besides this the Purists overlooked the following facts:

(*a*) That many expressions and phrases (especially such as are figurative) are from their simplicity and naturalness the common property of all or of many languages, and therefore can no more be called Græcisms than Hebraisms.[3]

(*b*) That a distinction must be made between the diction of poetry and that of prose, and also between the figures which particular writers may now and then use to give elevation to their style (as *lumina orationis*) and those which have become an integral part of the language. If expressions used by Pindar, Æschylus, Euripides, &c., occur in the plain prose of the N. T.,[4] or if these expressions or rare Greek figures are here in regular and ordinary use, this furnishes no proof at all of the classical purity of N. T. Greek.

(*c*) That when the N. T. writers use a form of speech which is

N. T. esse e pure Græcis et Ebraicam maxime consuetudinem referentibus verbis formulisque dicendi mixtum et temperatum, id quidem adeo evidens est iis, qui satis Græce sciunt, *ut plane misericordia digni sint, qui omnia bene Græca esse contendant.*"

[1] The essays of Wulfer, Grosse, and Musæus, though of little importance in comparison with their size, should have been inserted in these collections; and the editors were wrong in admitting only one of Junge's treatises, the *Sententiæ doct. vir. de stylo N. T.* Compare further Blessig, *Præsidia interpret. N. T. ex auctoribus Græc.* (Argent. 1778), and Mittenzwey, *Locorum quorundam e Hutchinsoni ad Xenoph. Cyrop. notis, quibus purum et elegans N. T. dicendi genus defenditur, refutatio* (Coburg, 1763). A treatise by G. C. Draudius, *De stylo N. T.* in the *Primitt. Alsfeld.* Nürnb. 1736 (Neubauer, *Nachr. von jetzt lebenden Theol.* I. 253 sqq.), I have not seen.

[2] Some of the points are noticed by Mittenzwey in the essay mentioned in the last note.

[3] Hebrew, and therefore Hebraic Greek, possesses the qualities of simplicity and vividness in common with the language of Homer; but the particular expressions cannot be called Hebraisms in the one case or Græcisms in the other. Languages in general have many points of contact, especially as *popularly* spoken, for the popular language is always simple and graphic: in the scientific diction, framed by scholars, there is more divergence. Hence, for instance, most of the so-called Germanisms in Latin belong to the style of comedies, letters, etc.

[4] See on the other hand Krebs, *Observ. Præf.* p. 3. Leusden (*de Dialectis*, p. 37) says most absurdly, "Nos non fugit carmina istorum hominum (tragicor.) innumeris Hebraismis esse contaminata." Fischer accordingly finds Hebraisms in the poems of Homer (*ad Leusd.* p. 114).

SECT. I.] OPINIONS ON THE CHARACTER OF N. T. DICTION. 17

common to both languages, their education renders it, in general, more probable that the phrase was immediately derived from the Hebrew, and not borrowed from the refined written language of Greece.

(*d*) These uncritical collectors, moreover, raked together very many passages from Greek authors which contain (α) the same word, indeed, but in a different sense; or (β) phrases which are merely similar, not exactly parallel.

(*e*) They even used the Byzantine writers without scruple, though many constituents of the Hebraistic diction of the N. T. may have found their way into the language of these writers through the medium of the church,—a supposition which in particular instances may be shown to be even probable, comp. Niebuhr, *Index to Agathias*, s. v. ζημιοῦσθαι,—and though these writers at all events cannot be adduced as evidence for ancient Greek purity of expression.

(*f*) Lastly, they passed over many phrases altogether in silence, and were compelled to pass them over, because they are undeniably Hebraisms.[1]

Their evidence, therefore, was either incomplete or beside the mark. Most of the Purist writers, too, restricted themselves by preference to the lexical element; Georgi alone took up the grammatical, and treated it with a copiousness founded on extensive reading.

A few remarkable examples shall be given in proof of the above assertions.[2]

(*a*) On Mt. v. 6, πεινῶντες καὶ διψῶντες τὴν δικαιοσύνην, passages are adduced from Xenophon, Æschines, Lucian, Artemidorus, to prove that διψῆν in this (figurative) sense is pure Greek. But as the same figure is found (in Latin and) in almost all languages, it is no more a Græcism than a Hebraism. The same may be said of ἐσθίειν (κατεσθίειν) figur. *consume:* this cannot be proved from *Iliad* 23. 182 to be a Græcism, or from Dt. xxxii. 22, &c., to be a Hebraism, but is common to all languages. For the same reason we could well spare the parallels to γενεά *generation*, i.e. the men of a particular generation (Georgi, *Vind.* p. 39), to χείρ *power*, to ὁ κύριος τῆς οἰκίας, and the like. But it is really laughable to be referred on Mt. x. 27, κηρύξατε ἐπὶ τῶν δωμάτων, to Æsop 139. 1, ἔριφος ἐπί τινος δώματος ἑστώς. Such superfluous and indeed absurd observations abound in Pfochen's work.

(*b*) That κοιμᾶσθαι signifies *mori* is proved from *Iliad* 11. 241, κοιμήσατο χάλκεον ὕπνον (Georgi, *Vind.* p. 122 sqq.), and from Soph. *Electr.* 510; that σπέρμα is used by the Greeks also in the sense of *proles* is shown by passages mainly taken from the poets, as Eurip. *Iph. Aul.* 524, *Iph. Taur.* 987, *Hec.* 254, and Soph. *Electr.* 1508 (Georgi p. 87 sqq.); that ποιμαίνειν means *regere* is proved from Anacr. 57. 8; that ἰδεῖν or θεωρεῖν θάνατον is good Greek, from Soph.

---

[1] This applies also to J. E. Ostermann, whose *Positiones philologicæ Græcum N. T. contextum concernentes* are reprinted in Crenii *Exercitatt.* fasc. II. p. 485 sqq.

[2] Compare also Mori *Acroas. l. c.* p. 222 sqq.

2

Electr. 205 (Schwarz, *Comm.* p. 410), or from δέρκεσθαι κτύπον, σκότον, in the tragedians. For ποτήριον πίνειν in a figurative sense (Mt. xx. 22), Schwarz quotes Æschyl. *Agam.* 1397. The use of πίπτειν in the sense of *irritum esse*, which is one of the regular meanings of the corresponding Hebrew word, Schwarz defends by the figurative phrase in Plat. *Phileb.* 22 e, δοκεῖ ἡδονή σοι πεπτωκέναι καθαπερεὶ πληγεῖσα ὑπὸ τῶν νῦν δὴ λόγων.

(*c*) We may safely regard the phrase γινώσκειν ἄνδρα—though not unknown to the Greeks, see Jacobs *ad* Philostrat. *Imagg.* p. 583—as immediately derived by the N. T. writers from the very common אִישׁ יָדַע : in the N. T., therefore, it is a Hebraism. Similarly, σπλάγχνα *compassion*, ξηρά *land* as opposed to water (Fischer *ad* Leusd. *Dial.* 31), χεῖλος *shore*, στόμα as used of the sword, *edge*,[1] παχύνειν *to be stupid, foolish*, κύριος κυρίων, εἰσέρχεσθαι εἰς τὸν κόσμον, were probably formed in the first instance on the model of Hebrew words and phrases, and cannot be proved to be genuine Greek by parallels from Herodotus, Ælian, Xenophon, Diodorus Siculus, Philostratus, and others.

(*d*) (*a*) That ἐν is used by Greek writers to denote the instrument (which within certain limits is true), Pfochen proves from such passages as πλέων ἐν ταῖς ναυσί (Xen.), ἦλθε . . . ἐν νηῒ μελαίνῃ (Hesiod)! That good Greek authors use ῥῆμα for *res* is shown from Plat. *Legg.* 797 c, τούτου τοῦ τε ῥήματος καὶ τοῦ δόγματος οὐκ εἶναι ζημίαν μείζω, where ῥῆμα may be rendered *expression, assertion*. Χορτάζειν *fill, feed* (of men), is supported by Plat. *Rep.* 2. 372, where the word is used of *swine!* That ζητεῖν ψυχήν τινος is good Greek is shown from Eur. *Ion* 1112, Thuc. 6. 27, al., where ζητεῖν is used alone, in the sense of *insidiari*, or rather *search for* (in order to kill)! That ὀφείλημα signifies *sin* in pure Greek, Schwarz professes to prove from Plat. *Cratyl.* 400 c, where however ὀφειλόμενα means *debita*, as elsewhere. In the same way, most of the passages adduced by Georgi (*Hierocr.* p. 36 sq., 186 sq.), to prove that εἰς and ἐν are interchanged in the best Greek authors, as in the N. T., are altogether inappropriate. Compare also Krebs, *Obs.* p. 14 sq.

(β) To prove that εὑρίσκειν χάριν (ἔλεος) παρά τινι is not a Hebraism, Georgi (*Vind.* p. 116) quotes εὑρίσκεσθαι τὴν εἰρήνην, τὴν δωρεάν, from Demosthenes; as if the Hebraism did not rather consist in the whole phrase (for the use of *find* for *attain* is certainly no Hebraism), and as if the difference in the voice of the verb were of no consequence whatever. For ποτήριον *sors* Palairet quotes such phrases as κρατὴρ αἵματος (Aristoph. *Acharn.*); for πίπτειν *irritum esse* Schwarz brings forward Plat. *Euthyphr.* 14 d, οὐ χαμαὶ πεσεῖται ὅ, τι ἂν εἴποις· The familiar *merismus* ἀπὸ μικροῦ ἕως μεγάλου is claimed as pure Greek[2] on the authority of passages in which οὔτε μέγα οὔτε σμικρόν occurs. But it is not the *merismus* in itself that is Hebraistic, but

---

[1] Compare however Boissonade, *Nic.* p. 282.
[2] Georgi, *Vind.* p. 310 sqq., Schwarz, *Comment.* p. 917. Compare Schæfer, *Julian*, p. xxi.

only the precise phrase ἀπὸ μ. ἕως μεγ., which is not found earlier than Theophan. cont. p. 615 (Bekk.). Καρπὸς τῆς κοιλίας, ὀσφύος, is supported (Georgi, *Vind.* p. 304) by passages in which καρπός is used by itself of human offspring. That δύο δύο, *two and two*, is pure Greek, does not follow from πλέον πλέον, *more and more* (Aristoph. *Nub.*): instances must be produced in which the repeated cardinal stands for ἀνὰ δύο, ἀνὰ τρεῖς, κ.τ.λ. (§ 37. 3). That τιθέναι εἰς τὰ ὦτα is pure Greek, is not proved by ὅσσα δ' ἀκούσας εἰσεθέμην (Callim.): the latter phrase is of an entirely different character. These examples might be multiplied indefinitely. Georgi's defence (*Vind.* p. 25) of the use of ὁ ἀδελφός for *alter* from Arrian and Epictetus is especially ridiculous.

(*e*) Schwarz (p. 1245) quotes Nicetas, to prove that στηρίζειν τὸ πρόσωπον and ἐνωτίζεσθαι are pure Greek; and Palairet justifies the use of ἡ ξηρά for *continens* from Jo. Cinnam. *Hist.* 4. p. 183. Still more singular is Pfochen's reference to Lucian, *Mort. Peregr.* c. 13, as justifying the use of κοινός with the meaning *immundus*: Lucian is scoffingly using a Jewish (Christian) expression.

(*f*) Of the many words and phrases which these writers have entirely passed over in silence, we will only mention πρόσωπον λαμβάνειν, σὰρξ καὶ αἷμα, υἱὸς εἰρήνης, ἐξέρχεσθαι ἐξ ὀσφύος τινός, ποιεῖν ἔλεος (χάριν) μετά τινος, ἀποκρίνεσθαι when no proper question precedes, ἐξομολογεῖσθαι θεῷ *give thanks to God.* There are many others: see below § 3.

After Salmasius, whose work *De Lingua Hellenistica* had been entirely forgotten by later scholars, Sturz[1] first led the way to an accurate estimate of the N. T. language, especially in regard to its Greek basis. Hence Keil (*Lehrb. der Hermen.* p. 11 sq.), Bertholdt (*Einl. in d. Bib.* 1 Th. p. 155 sq.), Eichhorn (*Einl. ins N. T.* IV. p. 96 sqq.), and Schott (*Isagoge in N. T.* p. 497 sqq.), have treated this subject more satisfactorily than many earlier writers, though by no means exhaustively or with the necessary scientific precision. In both respects H. Planck has surpassed his predecessors, in his *De vera natura atque indole orationis Grœcæ N. T. Commentat.* (Gott. 1810):[2] avoiding a fundamental error into which Sturz had fallen, he was the first who clearly, and in the main accurately, unfolded the character of the N. T. diction.[3]

---

[1] F. W. Sturz, *De Dialecto Alexandrina* (Lips. 1784, Ger. 1788-1793; 2nd edition, enlarged, Lips. 1809). Valuable remarks on this work may be found in the *Heidelb. Jahrb.* 1810, Heft xviii. p. 266 sqq. [Sturz's treatise may also be found in Valpy's edition of Steph. *Thesaurus*, vol. I. p. cliii. sqq.]

[2] This treatise is included in Rosenmüller's *Commentationes Theologicæ*, I. i. p. 112 sqq. [It is translated in the *Biblical Cabinet*, vol. I. pp. 91-188.]

[3] Compare also his *Pr. Observatt. quœdam ad hist. verbi Gr. N. T.* (Gott. 1821, and in Rosenmüller's *Comm. Theol.* I. i. p. 193 sqq.) See further (De Wette in) the *A. Lit. Z.* 1816. No. xxix. p. 306.

Section II.

BASIS OF THE N. T. DICTION.

In the age of Alexander the Great and his successors the Greek language underwent an internal change of a twofold kind. On the one hand, a literary prose language was formed, having the Attic dialect as its basis, but distinguished from it by the admission of a *common* Greek element, and even by many provincialisms: this is known as ἡ κοινή or ἑλληνική διάλεκτος. On the other hand, there arose a language of common life, a popular spoken language, in which the peculiarities of the various dialects, which had hitherto been confined to particular sections of the Greek nation, were fused together, the Macedonian element being most prominent.[1] This spoken Greek—which again varied to some extent in the different provinces of Asia and Africa that were subject to the Macedonian rule—is the true basis of the language of the LXX and the Apocrypha, and also of the N. T. language. Its characteristics, amongst which must also be included a neglect of nice distinctions and a continued effort after perspicuity and convenience of expression, may fitly be divided into *Lexical* and *Grammatical*.

The older works on the Greek dialects are now nearly useless, especially as regards the κοινή διάλεκτος. The subject is best treated in brief by Matthiæ, *Ausf. Gramm.* §§ 1–8, and (still more thoroughly) by Buttmann, *Ausf. Sprachl.* I. 1–8 ; also, though not with perfect accuracy, by H. Planck, *l. c.* pp. 13–23 [*Bib. Cab.* I. 113 sqq.]. Compare also Tittmann, *Syn.* I. 262 sq., and Bernhardy p. 28 sqq. (Don. pp. 1–4.)[2]

The Jews of Egypt and Syria[3]—of these alone we are now speaking

---

[1] Sturz, p. 26 sqq. But the subject deserves a new and thorough investigation : it can scarcely be disposed of by such *dicta* as that quoted by Thiersch, *De Pent. Al.* p. 74.

[2] [The peculiarities of the Greek spoken in different countries and at different periods are carefully reviewed by Mullach, *Griech. Vulgarsprache*, pp. 1–107.]

[3] It is not possible to point out with exactness what belonged to the language of Alexandria, and what was or became peculiar to the Greek dialect of Syria (and Palestine) ; and the inquiry is not of great importance, even for the N. T. Eichhorn's attempt (*Einl. ins N. T.* IV. 124 sqq.) was a failure, and could not be otherwise, as it was conducted with little critical accuracy. Εὐχαριστεῖν, a word used by Demosthenes and by many writers from the time of Polybius, is said by Eichhorn to have been a *late addition* to the Alexandrian dialect ; and ξενίζειν, *hospitio excipere*, which is found in Xenophon and even in Homer, is pronounced Alexandrian ! To what extent Greek was spoken by the Jews of Syria (and Palestine), we need not here inquire. On this see Paulus, *De Judæis Palæst. Jesu et apost. tempore non Aram. dialecto sed Græca quoque locutis* (Jen. 1803) ; Hug, *Introd.* II. § 10 ; Winer, *RWB.* II. p. 502 ; Schleiermacher,

—learned Greek in the first instance by intercourse with those who spoke Greek, not from books;[1] hence we need not wonder that in writing they usually retained the peculiarities of the popular spoken language. To this class belonged the LXX, the N. T. writers, and the authors of the Palestinian apocryphal books. It is only in the writings of a few learned Jews who prized and studied Grecian literature, such as Philo and Josephus,[2] that we find a nearer approach to ordinary *written* Greek. We have but an imperfect knowledge of this spoken language,[3] but a comparison of Hellenistic Greek (apart from its Hebraic element) with the later written Greek enables us to infer that the spoken language had diverged still more widely than the written from ancient elegance, admitting new and provincial words and forms in greater number, neglecting more decidedly nice distinctions in construction and expression, misusing grammatical combinations through forgetfulness of their origin and principle, and extending farther many corruptions which were already appearing in the literary language. Its main characteristic, however, continued to be an intermixture of the previously distinct dialects (Lob. *Path.* I. 9), of such a kind that the Greek spoken in each province had as its basis the dialect formerly current there: thus Atticisms and Dorisms predominated in Alexandrian Greek. From the dialect spoken in Egypt, especially in Alexandria (*dialectus Alexandrina*),[4] Hellenistic Greek was immediately derived.

Herm. p. 61 sq. [See also Diodati, *De Christo Græce loquente* (Naples, 1767; reprinted 1843, with a preface by Dr. Dobbin); Davidson, *Introd. to N. T.* (1848) I. 37–44; Greswell, *Dissertations*, I. 136 sqq. (2nd ed.); Grinfield, *Apology for the LXX*, pp. 77, 184; Smith, *Dict. of Bible*, ii. 531; Roberts, *Discussions on the Gospels*, pp. 1–316. The subject is most fully examined by Dr. Roberts, whose conclusion is that Greek was "the common language of public intercourse" at this time. See further Schürer, *Lehrb. d. neut. Zeitgeschichte*, p. 376 sq.; and comp. Westcott, *St. John*, p. lviii.]

[1] That the reading of the LXX contributed to the formation of their Greek style makes no essential difference here, as we are now referring immediately to the national Greek element. It is now generally acknowledged that even the apostle Paul cannot be supposed to have received a learned Greek education (amongst others see Pfochen, p. 178). He certainly displays greater facility in writing Greek than the Palestinian apostles, but this he might easily acquire in Asia Minor and through his extensive intercourse with native Greeks, some of whom were persons of learning and distinction. Köster (*Stud. u. Krit.* 1854, 2), to prove that Paul formed his style on the model of Demosthenes, collects from this orator a number of parallel words and phrases; nearly all of these, however, Paul might acquire from the spoken language of educated Greeks, and others are not really parallel. In the case of men who moved so much among Greeks, copiousness and ease of style furnish no proof of acquaintance with Greek literature.

[2] A comparison of the earlier books of the *Antiquities* of Josephus with the corresponding portions of the LXX will clearly show that his style cannot be placed on the same level with that of the LXX, or even of the N. T., and will exhibit the difference between the Jewish and the Greek style of narration. Compare further Schleiermacher, *Herm.* p. 63.

[3] Hence it will never be possible to supply the want of which Schleiermacher complains (*Herm.* p. 59), and give a "complete view of the language of common life."

[4] On this subject (περὶ τῆς Ἀλεξανδρίων διαλέκτου) the grammarians Irenæus (Pacatus) and Demetrius Ixion wrote special treatises, which are now lost:

We proceed to trace in detail the later elements found in Hellenistic Greek, noticing first the lexical peculiarities, and then the grammatical, which are less conspicuous. This inquiry must be founded on the researches of Sturz, Planck, Lobeck, Boissonade, and others;[1] and to their works the reader is referred for citations—mainly from the writers of the κοινή, Polybius, Plutarch, Strabo, Ælian, Artemidorus, Appian, Heliodorus, Sextus Empiricus, Arrian, &c.[2]—in proof of the various particulars. We mark with an asterisk whatever appears to belong exclusively to the popular spoken language, and does not occur in any profane author.[3]

LEXICAL PECULIARITIES.

(a) The later dialect comprehended words and forms from all the dialects without distinction.[4]

(1) Attic: ὕαλος (ὕελος, Lob. p. 309), ὁ σκότος (τὸ σ.), ἀετός (αἰετός, Herm. *Præf. ad Soph. Aj.* p. 19), φιάλη (φιέλη), ἀλήθειν (Lob. p. 151),[5] πρύμνα (πρύμνη, Lob. p. 331), ἴλεως (ἴλαος).

(2) Doric: πιάζω (πιέζω) κλίβανος (κρίβανος, Lob. p. 179), ἡ λιμός (ὁ λ.), ποία *grass* (for ποίη or πόα); also probably βεμβράνας, quoted

---

see Sturz, p. 24, and comp. p. 19 sq. The well-known Rosetta inscription is a specimen of this dialect: other extant monuments will be found in A. Peyron's *Papyri Græci reg. Taurin. Musei Ægyptii ed. et illustrati* (Turin, 1827, 2 vols. 4to.), and his *Illustrazione di due papiri greco-egizi dell' imper. museo di Vienna* (in the *Memorie dell' academ. di Torino*, Tom. 33, p. 151 sqq., of the historical class); *Description of the Greek papyri in the British Museum* (London, 1839, Part i.); J. A. Letronne, *Recueil des inscriptions grecques et latines de l'Egypte &c.* (Paris, 1842, 1848, 2 tom.) [See also Mullach, *Vulgarsp.* p. 15 sqq.]

[1] But see also Olearius, *De Stylo N. T.* p. 279 sqq.

[2] The Fathers and the books of Roman law have hitherto been almost entirely neglected in the investigation of later Greek; to the latter frequent reference will be made in the course of this work. [See Mullach, p. 31 sqq., 51.] How far the N. T. diction through the medium of the Church affected the later Byzantine Greek, is reserved for special inquiry. The spurious apocryphal books of the O. T. (*Libri Pseudepigraphi*) and the apocryphal books of the N. T. are now accessible in a more complete form and with a better text (the latter books through the labours of Tischendorf), and may be used for points of detail: the style of these productions as a whole (though in this respect they differ among themselves) is so wretched, that the N. T. diction appears classic Greek in comparison. Compare Tisch. *De evangelior. apocryph. origine et usu,* in the *Verhandelingen uitgeven door het Haagsche Genootschap, &c.* (Pt. 12. 1851).

[3] The Greek grammarians, particularly Thomas Magister (latest edition, Ritschl's: Halle, 1832), specify as common Greek much that is found even in Attic writers: see *e.g.* θεμέλιος in Thom. M. p. 437, ἐρευνῶμαι *ib.* p. 363. Indeed they are not free from even gross mistakes; comp. Oudendorp *ad Thom. M.* p. 903. Much however that made its way into the written language *after* Alexander the Great may probably have existed in the spoken language at an earlier date: this was perhaps the case with στρηνᾶν, which we meet with first in the poets of the new comedy.—The N. T. writers sometimes use words and forms which are preferred by the Atticists, instead of those which they assign to common Greek: as χρηστότης, Th. M. p. 921,—ἡ (not ὁ) λαῖλαψ, *ib.* p. 564.

[4] [In this section, (*a*), I have added in each case *the other* form of the word: thus Lobeck speaks of ὕαλος as the Attic form, *not* ὕελος.]

[5] [Ἀλήθειν is rejected by the Atticists, and Lobeck *l.c.* agrees with them in the main: ἀλίω is the regular Attic form,—"the later writers used in the present ἀλήθω, which however was still an ancient form." *Irr. V. s. v.*]

by Zonaras from 2 Tim. iv. 13, where, however, all our MSS. have μεμβ., see Sturz, *Zonaræ glossæ sacræ* II. p. 16 (Grimmæ, 1820).

(3) Ionic : γογγύζω (Lob. p. 358), ῥήσσω (ῥήγνυμι), πρηνής (πρανής, —yet πρηνής is found in Aristotle, Lob. p. 431), βαθμός (βασμός, Lob. p. 324), σκορπίζειν (Lob. p. 218), ἄρσην, Buttm. I. 84 (Jelf 33), comp. Fritz. *Rom.* I. 78.[1] To Ionic and Doric Greek belong εἱλίσσειν (Rev. vi. 14 *v. l.*, comp. Matth. 12. 4), φύω in an intransitive sense, H. xii. 15, comp. Babr. 64.[2]

The grammarians note as Macedonian παρεμβολή *camp* (Lob. p. 377, comp. Schwarz, *Solœc. Ap.* 66), ῥύμη *street;* as of Cyrenæan origin, βουνός *hill* (Lob. p. 355) ;[3] as Syracusan, the imperative εἰπόν (Fritz. *Mark*, p. 515).

(*b*) Words which existed in the older language now received new meanings; as παρακαλεῖν and ἐρωτᾶν* *intreat*, παιδεύειν *chastise*,[4] εὐχαριστεῖν *thank* (Lob. p. 18), ἀνακλίνειν [ἀνακλίνεσθαι], ἀναπίπτειν, ἀνακεῖσθαι *recline at table* (Lob. p. 216), ἀποκριθῆναι *answer* (Lob. p. 108), ἀντιλέγειν *oppose*,[5] ἀποτάσσεσθαι *valere jubere, renuntiare* (Lob. p. 23), συγκρίνειν *compare* (Lob. p. 278), δαίμων, δαιμόνιον *evil spirit*,[6] ξύλον (*living*) *tree* (Lidd. and Scott s. v.), διαπονεῖσθαι *ægre ferre,** στέγειν *hold off, endure*,[7] σεβάζεσθαι *reverence* (=σέβεσθαι, Fritz. *Rom.* I. 74), συνίστημι *prove, establish* (Fritz. *Rom.* I. 159), χρηματίζειν *be called* (Fritz. *Rom.* II. 9), φθάνειν *come, arrive* (Fritz. *Rom.* II. 356), κεφαλίς *volume, roll* (Bleek on H. x. 7), εὐσχήμων *one of noble station* (Lob. p. 333), ψωμίζειν and χορτάζειν *feed, nourish*,*[8] ὀψώνιον *pay* (Sturz p. 187), ὀψάριον *fish*, ἐρεύγεσθαι *eloqui* (Lob. p. 63), ἐπιστέλλειν *write a letter* (ἐπιστολή), περισπᾶσθαι *negotiis distrahi* (Lob. p. 415), πτῶμα *corpse*[9] (Lob. p. 375), γεννήματα

---

[1] [Tischendorf now receives the Ionic εἶπεν in Mk. iv. 28, and in L. xiii. 34 the Doric ὄρνιξ : in Rev. iii. 16 ℵ has χλιερός.]

[2] [On the Æolic κτίννω (χύννω) see below, § 15 (Jelf 10. 6).]

[3] [On this word see Donaldson, *New Cr.* p. 701; Blakesley, *Herod.* i. 556 sqq.]

[4] [On this word and the next see Ellicott's notes on E. vi. 4, Col. i. 12.]

[5] [So Fritzsche (*Rom.* II. 428), " Valere serioribus Græcis ἀντιλέγειν non solum repugnare verbis sed etiam *reniti re et factis* frustra neges:" see also Alf. on H. xii. 3. Meyer (on Rom. x. 21) maintains that this verb always denotes opposition in *words.*]

[6] That is, as its inherent signification, for the word is used in reference to an evil demon as early as Homer (*Iliad* 8. 166) : of the same kind is also Dinarch. *adv. Demosth.* § 30. p. 155 (Bekker), a passage quoted by recent writers. Even the Byzantines, to speak with exactness, add κακός to δαίμων (Agath. 114. 4).

[7] [On this word see Alford on 1 C. ix. 12 ; on συνίστημι, Ellic. on G. ii. 18 ; on φθάνειν, Ellic. on Ph. iii. 16 ; on κεφαλίς, Alford on H. x. 7.]

[8] This extension of meaning might in itself be considered a Hebraism. It had become customary to use ψωμίζειν as entirely equivalent to הַאֲכִיל (comp. Grimm on Wis. xvi. 20), like χορτάζειν, which in Greek authors is not applied to persons. (Against Pfochen see Solanus in Rhenferd, p. 297.) It is uncertain whether δεκαδύο for δώδεκα belongs to the later spoken language, or whether it was coined by the LXX : the former supposition seems to me more probable, since δώδεκα is nearer than δεκαδύο to the Hebrew שְׁתֵּים עֶשְׂרֵה [See Lightfoot's note on G. i. 18, quoted below, § 37.]

[9] [Without any dependent genitive, as in Mt. xxiv. 28 ; see Lidd. and Scott s. v., and comp. Paley, Æsch. *Suppl.* 647 (662).]

fruges (Lob. p. 286), σχολή *school* (Lob. p. 401), θυρεός *large (door-shaped) shield* (Lob. p. 366), δῶμα *roof*, λοιβή *sacrifice* (Babr. 23. 5),[1] ῥύμη *street* (Lob. p. 404), παρρησία *assurance, confidence*, λαλιά *speech (dialect)*, λαμπάς *lamp*,[2] καταστολή *long robe*,[*][3] νυνί *now* (in Attic, *at this very moment*, see Fritz. *Rom.* I. 182), στάμνος not, as in classical Greek, a vessel for holding *liquids* merely (Babr. 108. 18). A special peculiarity is the use of neuter verbs in a transitive[4] or causative sense, as μαθητεύειν (Mt. xxviii. 19), θριαμβεύειν (2 C. ii. 14?—see however Meyer *in loc.*).[5] The LXX so use even ζῆν, βασιλεύειν, and many other verbs (comp. particularly Ps. xl. 3, cxviii. 50, cxxxvii. 7, al.), comp. § 32. 1: see Lydius, *de Re Mil.* 6. 3, and especially Lob. Soph. *Aj.* p. 382. Μέθυσος, used by earlier writers of women only, was now applied to both sexes (Lob. p. 151, Schæfer, *Ind. ad Æsop.* p. 144).

(*c*) Certain words and forms which in ancient Greek were rare, or were used only in poetry and in the higher style of composition, now came into ordinary use, and were indeed preferred, even in prose; as αὐθεντεῖν *to have authority over* (Lob. p. 120), μεσονύκτιον (Th. M. p. 609, Lob. p. 53), ἀλάλητος (?), θεοστυγής (Pollux I. 21), ἔσθησις (Th. M. p. 370), ἀλέκτωρ (ἀλεκτρυών, Lob. p. 229), βρέχειν *irrigare* (Lob. p. 291), ἔσθω (for ἐσθίω, *Irr. V.* s. v.). To this head Eichhorn (*Einl. ins N. T.* IV. 127) refers θέσθαι τι ἐν τῇ καρδίᾳ, on the ground that this phrase, which belongs to the stately language of the poets (especially the tragedians), is used by the N. T. writers in the plainest prose. But the Homeric ἐν φρεσὶ θέσθαι is only a similar, not an identical phrase. That which the same writer quotes as a stately formula, συντηρεῖν ἐν τῇ καρδίᾳ, never occurs without emphasis in the N. T. Κοράσιον, on the other hand, is an example of a word which passed from the language of ordinary life into the written language (compare the German *Mädel*), losing its accessory meaning (Lob. p. 74).[6]

(*d*) Many words which had long been in use received a new form or pronunciation, by which the older was in most cases superseded: as μετοικεσία (μετοικία), ἱκεσία (ἱκετεία, Lob. p. 504), ἀνάθεμα (ἀνάθημα),[7] ἀνάστεμα, γενέσια (γενέθλια, Lob. p. 104), γλωσ-

---

[1] [With the reading ἄρνα λοιβὴν παρασχεῖν; but Lachmann reads λοιπόν. The word does not occur in the Greek Bible.]

[2] [This meaning is given in Steph. *Thesaur.* (ed. Hase) and in Rost and Palm's *Lex.*, but Mt. xxv is the only example quoted. In the LXX λαμπάς is the regular equivalent of לַפִּיד *torch;* once, in Dan. v. 5 (Theodot.), it stands for נֶבְרַשְׁתָּא *candelabrum.* In Mt. xxv, Trench (*Syn.* s. v.), Olshausen, Jahn (*Arch. B.* § 40), and others suppose that a kind of torch is referred to: A. xx. 8 is similar.]

[3] [See Ellic. on 1 Tim. ii. 9.]

[4] Transitive verbs can be handled in construction more conveniently than intransitive. In later Greek we find even προςτάττειν τινά (*Acta Apocr.* p. 172), and in German "etwas widersprechen" is becoming more and more common. In mercantile language we hear "das Rüböl *ist gefragt.*"

[5] [Meyer renders this, "Who ever triumphs over us:" see Alf. *in loc.*]

[6] [It was formerly used only "in familiari sermone de puellis inferioris sortis, cum εὐτελισμῷ quodam:" Lob. *l. c.*]

[7] See Schæfer, *Plutarch* V. p. 11, [and Ellicott and Lightfoot on G. i. 8].

σόκομον (γλωσσοκομεῖον, Lob. p. 98), ἔκπαλαι (πάλαι, Lob. p. 45), ἐχθές (χθές), ἐξάπινα (ἐξαπίνης), αἴτημα (αἴτησις),[1] ψεῦσμα (ψεῦδος, Sallier ad Th. M. p. 927), ἀπάντησις (ἀπάντημα), ἥγησις (ἡγεμονία), λυχνία (λυχνίον, Lob. p. 314), νῖκος (νίκη, Lob. p. 647), οἰκοδομή (οἰκοδόμησις,[2] Lob. p. 490), ὀνειδισμός (Lob. p. 512, ὄνειδος, ὀνείδισμα Her. 2. 133), ὀπτασία (ὄψις), ἡ ὀρκωμοσία (τὰ ὀρκωμόσια), μισθαποδοσία (μισθοδοσία), συγκυρία (συγκύρησις), ἀποστασία (ἀπόστασις, Lob. p. 528), νουθεσία (νουθέτησις, Lob. p. 512), ἀπαρτισμός (ἀπάρτισις), μελίσσιος (μελίσσειος), ποταπός (ποδαπός, Lob. p. 56), βασίλισσα (βασίλεια),[3] μοιχαλίς (μοιχάς, Lob. p. 452), μονόφθαλμος (ἑτερόφθαλμος, Lob. p. 136), καμμύειν (καταμύειν, Sturz p. 173), ὄψιμος (ὄψιος, Lob. p. 52), ὁ πλησίον (ὁ πέλας), προσήλυτος (ἔπηλυς, Valck. ad Ammon. p. 32), φυσιοῦσθαι (φυσᾶν) *be puffed up* (used figur. Babr. 114), ἀτενίζειν since Polybius for ἀτενίζεσθαι (Rost and Palm s. v.), ἐκχύνειν (ἐκχέειν, Lob. p. 726), στήκω (from ἕστηκα *stand*, Buttm. II. 36), ἀργός as an adj. of *three* terminations (Lob. p. 105), πειθός, νοσσοί and νοσσιά (νεοσσοί, νεοσσιά, Th. M. p. 626, Lob. p. 206), πετάομαι (πέτομαι, Lob. p. 581), ἀπελπίζειν (ἀπογινώσκειν), ἐξυπνίζειν (ἀφυπνίζειν, Lob. p. 224), ῥαντίζειν (ῥαίνειν), δεκατοῦν (δεκατεύειν), ἀροτριᾶν (ἀροῦν, Lob. p. 254), βιβλαρίδιον* (βιβλίδιον, βιβλιδάριον), ψιχίον (ψίξ), ταμεῖον (ταμιεῖον, Lob. p. 493), καταποντίζειν (καταποντοῦν, Lob. p. 361), παραφρονία (παραφροσύνη),* πτύον (πτέον, Lob. p. 321), ψιθυριστής (ψίθυρος, Th. M. p. 927), ὠτάριον, and most of the diminutives in αριον, as παιδάριον, ὀνάριον (Fritz. *Mark*, p. 638). Ἀκρόβυστος and ἀκροβυστία are purely Alexandrian, having been first used by the LXX (Fritz. *Rom.* I. 136).

For verbs in μι we find forms in ω pure, as ὀμνύω for ὄμνυμι (Th. M. p. 648). Compare also ξυράω for ξυρέω (Th. M. p. 642, Phot. *Lex.* p. 313, Lob. p. 205, and *ad* Soph. *Aj.* p. 181), the present βαρέω for βαρύνω (Th. M. p. 141), σαροῦν for σαίρειν (Lob. p. 83), χολᾶν (χολοῦσθαι), ἐξὸν εἶναι for ἐξεῖναι (Foertsch, *De locis Lysiæ*, p. 60). Verbs used in the older written language as middle or deponent now receive active forms; as φρυάσσειν A. iv. 25 (from Ps. ii. 1), ἀγαλλιᾶν L. i. 47, εὐαγγελίζειν [Rev. x. 7, 1 Sam. xxxi. 9], Lob. p. 268. Compound verbs, where the meaning itself was not extended by the preposition, were preferred to the less graphic and less sonorous simple verbs;[4] and, as sometimes even compound

---

[1] [See Ellicott on Ph. iv. 6.]
[2] [And οἰκοδόμημα, Lob. *l. c.*; see Ellic. on E. ii. 21.]
[3] Similarly ἱέρισσα (*Papyr. Taur.* 9. 14) from ἱερεύς: compare further Sturz p. 173.
[4] That, conversely, simple verbs were sometimes used instead of compound by later writers, Tischendorf (*Stud. u. Krit.* 1842, p. 505) seeks to prove from the phrase βουλὴν τιθέναι, arguing that a classical author would have said β. προστιθέναι. But the two expressions probably have different meanings: see Raphel on A. xxvii. 12. More probable examples would be two verbs quoted below under (*e*), διυγματίζειν and θεατρίζειν—for which the written language has παραδειγματίζειν and ἐκθεατρίζειν,—and ταρταροῦν for καταταρταροῦν. Similarly the Prussian law style uses Führung for Aufführung. [See Tisch. *Proleg. N. T.* p. 59 (ed. 7), where several additional examples are given. The following are from the N. T.: ἐρωτᾶν Mk. viii. 5, κρύπτειν Mt. xi. 25, ἀρνήσασθαι L. ix. 23, ἀθροίζειν L. xxiv. 33, for which the more familiar ἐπερωτᾶν, ἀποκρύπτειν, ἀπαρνήσασθαι, συναθροίζειν, have been substituted in many MSS.]

verbs did not appear sufficiently expressive, many double compounds were formed.[1] For several nouns, mostly denoting parts of the human body, diminutive forms, losing their special meaning, came into common use in colloquial language; as ὠτίον (comp. Fischer, *Proluss.* p. 10, Lob. p. 211), φορτίον.[2] Lastly, many substantives received a change in gender, which was sometimes accompanied by a change of termination : see § 8. Rem. and § 9. Rem. 2.

(e) Entirely new words and expressions[3] were framed, especially by composition,—mainly in order to meet new wants: as ἀλλοτριοεπίσκοπος,* ἀνθρωπάρεσκος (Lob. p. 621), ὁλόκληρος, ἀγενεαλόγητος,* αἱματεκχυσία,* δικαιοκρισία, σιτομέτριον, νυχθήμερον (Sturz p. 186), πληροφορία (Theophan. p. 132), καλοποιεῖν (Lob. p. 199), αἰχμαλωτίζειν and αἰχμαλωτεύειν (for αἰχμάλωτον ποιεῖν, Th. M. p. 23, Lob. p. 442), μεσιτεύειν, γυμνητεύειν, ἀγαθοποιεῖν (ἀγαθοεργεῖν) for ἀγαθὸν ποιεῖν (Lob. p. 675), ἀγαλλίασις, ὁροθεσία, ἀντίλυτρον,* ἐκμυκτηρίζειν,* ἀλεκτοροφωνία (Lob. p. 229), ἀποκεφαλίζειν (Lob. p. 341), ἀνταποκρίνεσθαι (Æsop. 272, ed. De Fur.), ἐξουθενεῖν (Lob. p. 182, Schæf. *Ind. ad Æsop.* p. 135), ἐκκακεῖν,*[4] εὐδοκεῖν (Sturz p. 168, Fritz. *Rom.* II. 370), ὁμοιάζειν,* ἀγαθουργεῖν, ἀγαθωσύνη, διασκορπίζειν (Lob. p. 218), στρηνιᾶν (τρυφᾶν, Lob. p. 381), ἐγκρατεύομαι* (Lob. p. 442), οἰκοδεσπότης and οἰκοδεσποτεῖν (Lob. p. 373), λιθοβολεῖν, προσφάγιον (ὄψον, Sturz p. 191), λογία, κράββατος (σκίμπους, Lob. p. 63, Sturz p. 175), πεποίθησις (Lob. p. 295), σπίλος (κηλίς, Lob. p. 28), μάμμη (τήθη, Lob. p. 133), ῥαφίς (βελόνη, Lob. p. 90), ἀγριέλαιος (κότινος, Mœris p. 68), ἁγνότης,* ἁγιότης,* ἐπενδύτης, ἐκτενῶς and ἐκτένεια (Lob. p. 311), ἀπαράβατος (Lob. p. 313).

Under the last two heads, (d) and (e), certain classes of words deserve special mention. Later Greek was particularly rich in

(1) Substantives in μα, as κατάλυμα, ἀνταπόδομα, κατόρθωμα, ῥάπισμα, γέννημα, ἔκτρωμα (Lob. p. 209), βάπτισμα,* ἔνταλμα, ἱεροσύλημα :* see Pasor, *Gram.* pp. 571–574.

(2) Substantives compounded with συν, as συμμαθητής, συμπολίτης (Lob. p. 471).[5]

(3) Adjectives in ινος, as ὀρθρινός (Sturz p. 186), πρωϊνός, καθημερινός, ὀστράκινος, δερμάτινος (Lob. p. 51).

(4) Verbs in οω, ιζω, αζω, as ἀνακαινόω, δυναμόω, ἀφυπνόω, δολιόω, ἐξουδενόω,* σθενόω,* ὀρθρίζω,* δειγματίζω,* θεατρίζω, φυλακίζω,* ἱματίζω, ἀκουτίζω, πελεκίζω (Lob. p. 341), αἱρετίζω (Babr. 61, Boisson. *Anecd.* II. 318), σινιάζω.

---

[1] Siebelis, *Pr. de verb. compos. quæ quatuor partib. constant* (Budiss. 1832).

[2] Also abbreviated forms of proper names, which no doubt were previously used in the popular language, were admitted into the written; as Ἀλεξᾶς, Σπανία (for Ἰσπανία), &c. The derivatives of δίχεσθαι were but slightly altered, as πανδοχεύς, ξενοδοχεύς, for πανδοκεύς, &c. (Lob. p. 307).

[3] Many such words have been collected from the Fathers by Suicer, *Sacræ Observatt.* p. 311 sqq. (Tigur. 1665).

[4] In the written language ἐγκακεῖν alone was used ; see Winer, *Gal.* p. 131, and Meyer on 2 C. iv. 1. [Ἐκκ. occurs six times in *Rec.*, but Lachm., Tisch., Ellic., Westcott and Hort read ἐγκ. (ἐνκ.) in every case. The Fathers use ἐγκακεῖν. See Ellic. and Lightf. on G. vi. 9, Alf. on 2 C. iv. 1.]

[5] [See Ellicott on E. ii. 19. On καθώς, mentioned below, see Ellicott on G. iii. 6.]

SECT. II.] BASIS OF THE N. T. DICTION. 27

To these may be added the two presents formed from perfects, στήκω (see above), γρηγορῶ (Lob. p. 118). Compare also such adverbs as πάντοτε (διαπαντός, ἑκάστοτε, Sturz p. 187), παιδιόθεν (ἐκ παιδίου, Lob. p. 93), καθώς (Sturz p. 74), πανοικί (πανοικίᾳ, πανοικησίᾳ, Lob. p. 515).[1] Ἐσχάτως ἔχειν is a later phrase for κακῶς, πονηρῶς ἔχειν (Lob. p. 389), and καλοποιεῖν (see above) was used for the older phrase καλῶς ποιεῖν.

That this list contains many words which were coined by the Greek-speaking Jews or the N. T. writers themselves—especially Paul, Luke, and the author of the Ep. to the Hebrews, comp. Origen, *Orat.* § 27—according to the prevailing analogy of the time, will not be denied: compare particularly ὀρθρίζειν (הִשְׁכִּים), λιθοβολεῖν, αἱματεκχυσία, σκληροκαρδία, σκληροτράχηλος, ἀγαθοεργεῖν, ὀρθοποδεῖν, ὀρθοτομεῖν, μοσχοποιεῖν, μεγαλωσύνη, ταπεινοφροσύνη, παραβάτης, πατριάρχης, ἀγενεαλόγητος, ὑποπόδιον (Sturz p. 199), χρυσοδακτύλιος. And yet we cannot consider this point decided by the fact that no trace of these words has been found in the extant works of the Greek authors of the first centuries after Christ. Some of these works have not been examined:[2] besides, many words of the kind might be already current in the ordinary spoken language. Those words, however, which denote Jewish institutions, or which designate Gentile worship, etc., as idolatrous, naturally originated amongst the Greek-speaking Jews themselves: e.g. σκηνοπηγία, εἰδωλόθυτον, εἰδωλολατρεία. Lastly, many words received among the Jews a more specific meaning connected with Jewish usages and modes of thought; as ἐπιστρέφεσθαι and ἐπιστροφή, used absolutely, *be converted, conversion,* προσήλυτος, πεντηκοστή *Pentecost*, κόσμος (in a figurative sense), φυλακτήριον, ἐπιγαμβρεύειν of the levirate marriage. On the peculiarly Christian words and forms, e.g. βάπτισμα, see p. 36.

GRAMMATICAL PECULIARITIES.

These are in great measure limited to certain inflexions of nouns and verbs, which either were entirely unknown at an earlier period, or were not used in certain words, or at all events were foreign to written Attic,—for the mixture of the previously distinct dialects is seen in the inflexions as well as in the vocabulary of later Greek. The use of the dual became rare.

There are few peculiarities of syntax. Certain verbs are construed with cases different from those which they govern in classical Greek

---

[1] That this popular Greek should have adopted with slight alterations certain foreign words (appellatives) belonging to the other languages spoken in the different provinces, is very natural, but our present general inquiry is not further concerned with the fact. On the Egyptian words found in the LXX and elsewhere, see Sturz p. 84 sqq. Latin and Persian words have also been pointed out in the N. T. : comp. Olear. *de stylo N. T.* p. 366 sqq.; Georgi, *Hierocr.* I. 247 sqq. and II. (*de Latinismis N. T.*); Dresig, *de N. T. Gr. Latinismis merito et falso suspectis* (Lips. 1726); Schleiermacher, *Herm.* p. 62 sq.

[2] Most words of this kind appear later in the Byzantine writers, who abound in double compounds and lengthened forms of words. They especially delighted to revive in this way words which had been, as it were, worn out by use.

(§ 31. 1, 32. 4);[1] conjunctions which were formerly joined with the optative or conjunctive only are now found with the indicative; the use of the optative perceptibly declines, especially in the *oratio obliqua;* the future participle after verbs of *going, sending,* etc., gives place to the present participle or to the infinitive; active verbs with ἑαυτόν come into use instead of middle verbs, where no special emphasis is intended; and there is a general tendency to use the more expressive forms of speech without their peculiar force, and at the same time to strive after additional emphasis even in grammatical forms,—comp. μειζότερος, ἵνα in the place of the infinitive, &c. The later inflexions will be most appropriately noticed in § 4.

We cannot doubt that the late popular dialect had special peculiarities in different provinces. Critics have accordingly professed to find Cilicisms in Paul's writings, see Hieron. *ad Algasiam Quæst.* 10, Tom. IV. p. 204 (ed. Martianay); but the four examples which this Father adduces are not conclusive,[2] and, as we know nothing of Cilician provincialisms from any other source,[3] the inquiry should rather be abandoned than be founded on mere hypotheses. Comp. Stolberg, *De Cilicismis a Paulo usurpatis,* in his *Tr. de Solœc. N. T.* p. 91 sqq.

Section III.

HEBREW-ARAMAIC COLOURING OF THE N. T. DICTION.

The popular dialect of Greek was not spoken and written by the Jews without foreign admixture. The general characteristics of their mother-tongue—vividness and circumstantiality combined with great sameness of expression—were transferred from it to their Greek style, which also contains particular phrases and constructions derived from the same source. Both peculiarities, the general Hebraistic impress and the introduction of " Hebraisms," are more apparent in their direct translation from the Hebrew than in their original composition in Greek.[4]

The Hebraisms (and Aramaisms) are more frequently lexical than grammatical. The former consist partly of words used in an extended signification, partly of whole phrases imitated from the Hebrew, and partly of words newly framed in accordance

---

[1] Compare Boissonade, *Anecd.* III. 136, 154.
[2] Michaelis, *Introduction* I. 149 (Marsh's Transl.).
[3] Compare however Sturz p. 62, [who assigns a Cilician origin to such forms as ἴλαβα, ἔφαγα (see § 13. 1), and to the word σισόν, Lev. xix. 27. The Cilicisms of which Jerome speaks are καταναρκᾶν τινός, καταβραβεύειν τινά, ἀνθρώπινον λέγω, and the use of ἡμέρα in 1 C. iv. 3. See Schirlitz, *Grundz.* p. 26; Mullach, *Vulg.* p. 17].
[4] Herein lies an argument, hitherto little noticed, against regarding the N. T. text as a translation from the Aramaic,—a translation, too, for the most part unskilfully executed.

SECT. III.] HEBREW-ARAMAIC COLOURING OF THE N. T. DICTION. 29

with Hebrew analogy, to correspond with Hebrew words similarly formed. Thus arose a Jewish Greek, which was in part unintelligible to native Greeks,[1] and which they sometimes treated with contempt.

All the nations which after Alexander's death were subject to the Græco-Macedonian rule, and gradually accustomed themselves to the Greek language of their conquerors even in the ordinary intercourse of life,—and especially the Syrians and Hebrews,—spoke Greek less purely than native Greeks, imparting to it more or less the impress of their mother-tongue: see Salmas. *De ling. Hell.* p. 121, and compare Joseph. *Ant.* 20. 9.[2] As the Greek-speaking Jews are usually denominated Hellenists, this oriental dialect of Greek, known by us only from the writings of Jews, is not unsuitably called *Hellenistic;* see Buttm. I. 6.[3] By this name therefore,—first introduced by Scaliger (*Animadv. in Eus.* p. 134), not by Drusius (*ad Act.* vi. 6)—the language of the LXX and N. T. (with the *Libri Pseudepigraphi* and the apocryphal books of the N. T.) is specially designated.

The Hebraisms of the N.T. (for it is to these, and not to the oriental tone which is manifest in the structure of sentences and the arrange-

---

[1] Though L. de Dieu's opinion (*Præf. ad Grammat. Orient.*), "facilius Europæis foret Platonis Aristotelisque elegantiam imitari, quam Platoni Aristotelive N. T. nobis interpretari," is decidedly an exaggeration. The above-mentioned circumstances, however, serve to explain in general the liberty which learned Greek transcribers or possessors of MSS. often allowed themselves to make corrections for the sake of bringing the diction nearer to Grecian elegance: see Hug, *Introd.* I. § 24. II. [Tregelles, *Horne* IV. p. 54.]

[2] It is well known that Greek subsequently became *Latinised* to a certain extent, when the Romans began to write in that language. The Latin colouring, however, is not very marked before the time of the Byzantine writers, even in translations of Latin authors,—such as that of Eutropius by Pæanius, of Cicero's *Cato Maj.* and *Somn. Scip.* by Theodorus (edited by Götz: Nürnb. 1801),—partly because Greek and Latin are much more nearly allied in structure than Hebrew and Greek, and partly because these writers had *studied* Greek. [Specimens of Latinising are given by Mullach, p. 51 sq.]

[3] This designation is entirely appropriate, and should be resumed as a technical term, for ἑλληνιστής in the N. T. (A. vi. 1) denotes a Greek-speaking Jew. (Examples, of ἑλληνίζειν rather than of ἑλληνιστής, may be found in Wetstein II. 490, Lob. p. 379 sq.) The opinion of Salmasius, that in the N. T. a Hellenist means a proselyte to Judaism out of the Greek nation, is a hasty inference from A. vi. 5, and Eichstädt (*ad Mori Acroas. Herm.* I. 227) should not have adopted it. The controversy between D. Heinsius (*Exercit. de ling. Hellenist.*: Leyden, 1643) and Salmasius (*Hellenistica,* and *Funus ling. Hell.,* and *Ossilegium ling. Hell.*: Leyden, 1643) on the name *dialectus Hellenistica,* related even more to the word *dialectus* than to *Hellenistica:* for the former word Salmasius (*de Hellenist.* p. 250) wished to substitute *character* or *stylus idioticus.* Compare also Tittm. *Syn.* I. 259 sq. Yet dialect (διάλεκτος τοπική) is not inadmissible as a name for the Greek spoken by the Hellenistic Jews, especially if the wide meaning of the verb διαλέγεσθαι (*e.g.* Strabo 8. 514) be taken into consideration. Other writings on this title (*dial. Hellen.*) may be seen in Walch, *Biblioth. Theol.* IV. 278 sq., Fabric. *Biblioth. Gr.* IV. 893 sq. (ed. Harles). Thiersch and Rost have begun to call the language of the Greek Bible the "ecclesiastical dialect," but this name is too narrow for the Jewish Greek of which we are speaking: the word *dialect,* too, is not suitable. [See Mullach, p. 14; Roberts, *Discussions on the Gospels,* pp. 156-176.]

ment of words, that attention has usually been directed) have been frequently and copiously collected, especially by Vorst, Leusden, and Olearius;[1] but no one has executed the work with sufficient critical precision.[2] Almost all writers on the subject are more or less chargeable with the following faults:—

(*a*) Too little attention is paid to the Aramaic element in N. T. diction.[3] It is well known that the language ordinarily spoken by the Jews of Palestine in the time of Jesus was not the ancient Hebrew, but the Syro-chaldaic; and hence Jewish Greek would necessarily receive from this dialect many of the most common expressions of ordinary life.[4] Olearius, however, of the older writers, has a special section *de Chaldæo-Syriasmis N. T.* (p. 345 sqq.); comp. also Georgi, *Hierocr.* I. 187 sqq. More recently much relating to this subject has been collected by Boysen, Agrell, and Hartmann.[5] Some earlier writers had occasionally directed attention to Aramaisms: see Michaelis, *Introd.* I. 135 sqq. (Trans.), Fischer, *ad Leusd.* p. 140, Bertholdt, *Einleit.* Part I. p. 158.—Under this head come also the (few) Rabbinisms [6]—mostly school-terms, such as may have been current amongst Jewish doctors as early as the time of Jesus. For illustrating these very much material may still be extracted from Schœttgen's *Horæ Hebraicæ.*

(*b*) The difference between the styles of different authors was almost entirely lost sight of. To judge from the collections of these writers, every part of the N. T. would seem to be equally pervaded

---

[1] Leusden, *Philol. Hebr.*, from which the *Dissertat. de dialectis N. T. sing. de ejus Hebr.* was reprinted in a separate form by J. F. Fischer (Lips. 1754, 1792). Olearius, *De stylo N. T.* p. 232 sqq. Compare also Hartmann, *Linguist. Einl. in das Stud. des A. T.* p. 382 sqq. Anm.

[2] A complete work on this subject, executed with critical accuracy and on rational principles, is therefore greatly needed. Meanwhile, our thanks are due for the commencement recently made by D. E. F. Böckel, *De Hebraismis N. T.* Spec. I. (Lips. 1840).

[3] Many of the peculiarities adduced by the Hebraists might be either Hebraisms or Aramaisms: e.g. τἰς as indef. article, the frequent use of εἶναι with the partic. in the place of a finite verb. It is better, however, to regard these and similar expressions as Aramaisms, since they occur much more frequently and regularly in Aramaic, and in Hebrew are almost confined to those later writings whose style approaches the Aramaic. The N. T. alone is directly referred to in what has just been said, for there are but few Aramaisms in the LXX; comp. Olear. p. 308, Gesenius, *Isaiah* I. 63.

[4] To such expressions the Aramaic element in N. T. Greek is substantially confined. The religious expressions were derived from the sacred Hebrew, the sacred language, either directly or (in the case of most of the Jews out of Palestine) through the medium of the LXX. To the former category belongs also the use of θάνατος * for *pestilence*, Rev. vi. 8, xviii. 8 (מוּתָא ܡܰܘܬܳܐ): comp. Ewald, *Comm. in Apoc.* p. 122 [p. 139].

[5] Boysen, *Krit. Erläuterungen des Grundtextes d. N. T. aus der syr. Uebersetzung* (Quedlinb. 1761): Agrell, *Oratio de dict. N. T.* (Wexion. 1798), and *Otiola Syr.* pp. 53–58 (Lund. 1816); Hartmann, *l.c.* p. 382 sqq.

[6] See Olearius, *l.c.* p. 360 sqq.; Georgi, *l.c.* p. 221 sqq.

---

* Τὸ θανατικόν, in popular living Greek, is the ordinary term for the plague. E. M.

by Hebraisms. Such uniformity is far from existing in fact; and in this inquiry Matthew, Luke, John, Paul, James, and the author of the Ep. to the Hebrews, cannot possibly be considered together.[1] Another question left unnoticed is the relation between the diction of the N. T. and that of the LXX. With all their similarity they have also many points of difference; and, in general, the language of the N. T. is less Hebraistic than that of the LXX, which was a direct, and, in part, a literal translation from the Hebrew.

(c) They included in their lists of Hebraisms much that was not foreign to Greek prose, or is the common property of many languages; and, in general, had no clear definition of "Hebraism" to start from.[2] In fact, this word was used in three senses, to denote—

(1) Words, phrases, and constructions, which are peculiar to Hebrew or Aramaic, nothing corresponding to them being found in Greek prose; as σπλαγχνίζεσθαι, ὀφειλήματα ἀφιέναι, πρόσωπον λαμβάνειν, οἰκοδομεῖν (in a figurative sense), πλατύνειν τὴν καρδίαν, πορεύεσθαι ὀπίσω, οὐ ... πᾶς (for οὐδείς), ἐξομολογεῖσθαί τινι and ἔν τινι, &c.

(2) Words, phrases, and constructions, which are occasionally met with in Greek writers, but which were in the first instance suggested to the N. T. writers by their native language: as σπέρμα for *proles* (Schwarz, *Comm.* p. 1235), Hebr. זֶרַע; ἀνάγκη *distress* (comp. Diod. Sic. 4. 43, Schwarz *l.c.* p. 81), Hebr. מָצוֹק, צָר, מְצוּקָה, צָרָה; ἐρωτᾶν *request*, as שָׁאַל denotes both *request* and *interrogate*, comp. the Latin *rogare* (Babr. 97. 3, Apollon. *Synt.* p. 289); εἰς ἀπάντησιν (Diod. Sic. 8. 59, Polyb. 5. 26. 8), comp. לִקְרַאת; πέρατα τῆς γῆς (Thuc. 1. 69, Xen. *Ages.* 9. 4, Dio Chr. 62. 587), comp. אַפְסֵי אֶרֶץ; χεῖλος for *littus* (Her. 1. 191, Strabo, al.), comp. שָׂפָה; στόμα of a sword (פֶּה), comp., besides the poets, Philostr. *Her.* 19. 4. So also the phrase ἐνδύσασθαι Χριστόν—Dion. H. has Ταρκύνιον ἐνδύσ.—is formed on the model of לָבֵשׁ צֶדֶק, or the like. Comp. above, p. 17.

(3) Words, phrases, and constructions, which are equally common in Greek and in Hebrew, so that we may doubt whether they were used by the Jews as part of the popular Greek which they adopted, or because the corresponding words, &c., in their native language were so familiar; as φυλάσσειν νόμον, αἷμα *caedes*, ἀνήρ with appellatives (ἀνὴρ φονεύς), παῖς *slave*, μεγαλύνειν *praise*, διώκειν *strive after* (a virtue).[3]

(4) Lastly, it must be owned that Hebraisms (Aramaisms) were

---

[1] The style even of the same writer is not always uniform. Thus Luke in his Gospel, where he was dependent on the Gospel *paradosis*, has more Hebraisms than in the Acts; and the falling off in the diction after the preface to his Gospel was long ago pointed out. The hymns and discourses also are more Hebraistic than the narrative portions: comp. *e.g.* L. i. 13-20, 42-55, 68-79. The relation in which Luke stands to Matthew and Mark, as regards language and style, has not yet been clearly shown.

[2] See Tittmann, *Syn.* I. p. 269 sqq.; De Wette, *A. L. Z.* 1816, No. 39, p. 306.

[3] Many of the grammatical phenomena adduced in Haab's grammar are of this kind.

introduced into very many passages by the commentators themselves. Thus E. v. 26, ἐν ῥήματι ἵνα, עַל־דְּבַר אֲשֶׁר, see Koppe; Mt. xxv. 23, χαρά *convivium*, after the Aram. חֶדְוָה (see Fisch. *ad Leusd. Dial.* p. 52), or the Hebr. שִׂמְחָה Esth. ix. 17, al. (Eichhorn, *Einl. ins N. T.* I. 528); Mt. vi. 1, δικαιοσύνη *alms*, after the Chald. צְדָקָה ; Mt. xxi. 13, λῃσταί *traders* (Fisch. *l.c.* p. 48). Connected with this was considerable misuse of the LXX; e.g. L. xi. 22, σκῦλα *supellex*, comp. Esth. iii. 13; Acts ii. 24, ὠδῖνες *vincula*, comp. Ps. xvii. 6.[1] Πέραν has even been rendered *on this side of*, like עֵבֶר (?)! Compare further Fritz. *Rom.* I. 367.[2]

From what has been said it will be clear that the Hebraisms of the N. T. may be divided into two classes—*perfect* and *imperfect*. By perfect Hebraisms we understand those uses of words, those phrases and constructions, which belong exclusively to the Hebrew (Aramaic) language, and which therefore Hellenistic Greek (i.e., the language of the N. T.) has directly received from this source.[3] Imperfect Hebraisms are those uses of words, those phrases and constructions, which are also found in Greek prose, but which we may with very great probability suppose the N. T. writers to have immediately derived from the Hebrew or Aramaic—partly because these writers were most familiar with their mother-tongue, and partly because the phraseology in question was of more frequent occurrence in Hebrew than in Greek. This distinction has been noticed by De Wette, who says (*l.c.* p. 319): "Whether a phrase is absolutely un-Greek, or whether there exists in Greek a point of connexion to which the phrase can attach itself, makes an essential difference."

We must however carry the investigation farther back, and consider especially the *genesis* of the so-called Hebraisms. The language of the LXX[4] cannot be made the basis of this inquiry: as a translation, it affords no certain evidence respecting the Greek which was freely spoken and written by Jews, and which had been acquired by them from oral intercourse. Nor can we in the first instance deal with the doctrinal parts of the N. T., because the religious phraseology of the Jews in Greek naturally attached itself very closely to the Hebrew, and found a model already existing in the LXX. If we wish to ascer-

---

[1] [Since שָׁלָל (*spoils*) is translated by ὑπάρχοντα in Esth. iii. 13, it was said that σκῦλα, L. xi. 22, is used for *goods* "per Hebraismum;" and similarly that ὠδῖνες θαν., A. ii. 24, means *cords of death*, because in Ps. xviii. (xvii.) 5 חֶבְלֵי מָוֶת (which *has* this meaning) is rendered ὠδῖνες θαν. in the LXX.]

[2] In the title of Kaiser's *Diss. de ling. Aram. usu*, &c. (Norimb. 1831), the word *abusu* would be more in accordance with truth than *usu*.

[3] Such Hebraisms are thus defined by Blessig in the work cited above [p. 16, note [1]]: "Hebraismus est solius Hebræi sermonis propria loquendi ratio, cujusmodi in Græcam vel aliam linguam sine barbarismi suspicione transferre non licet."

[4] The most important work that has yet appeared on the linguistic element of the LXX is H. W. Jos. Thiersch, *De Pentateuchi versione Alex. libri* 3 (Erlang. 1840), from which, in the later editions of this grammar, many welcome illustrations have been received. But a complete examination of the language of the LXX is still very much needed.

tain as exactly as possible the influence which the mother-tongue exerted on the Greek spoken by Jews, we must examine especially the narrative style of the Apocrypha, the Gospels, and the Acts of the Apostles. In the first place, it is clear that it was the *general* character of Hebrew or Aramaic composition that was most naturally and unconsciously impressed—by original writers almost as much as by translators—on their Greek style. No one escapes without difficulty from this general influence, which is, as it were, born with him; only reflexion and practice can set him free from it. This general character consists:—

(1) In vividness—hence the use of a preposition instead of the simple case, the latter construction being rather the result of abstraction—and consequently circumstantiality of expression: e.g. φεύγειν ἀπὸ προςώπου τινός, ἐγράφη διὰ χειρός τινος, πάντες ἀπὸ μικροῦ ἕως μεγάλου, καὶ ἔσται . . . καὶ ἐκχεῶ, and the like; the accumulation of personal and demonstrative pronouns, especially after the relative, the narrative formula καὶ ἐγένετο, &c.

(2) In the simplicity and indeed monotony with which the Hebrew constructs sentences and joins sentence to sentence, preferring co-ordination to subordination: hence the very limited use of conjunctions (in which classical Greek is so rich), the uniformity in the use of the tenses, the want of the periodic compactness which results from the fusion of several sentences into one principal sentence, and along with this the sparing use of participial constructions, so numerous and diversified in classical Greek. In historical narrative there is this marked peculiarity, that words spoken by another are almost always quoted in the direct form, as uttered by him; whereas it is the indirect introduction of the speaker that gives so distinctive a colouring to the narrative style of classical authors, and that leads to the frequent and varied use of the optative, a mood which is almost unknown in Hellenistic Greek.

From this general Hebrew influence Jewish Greek necessarily received a strongly marked character. Many special peculiarities, however, were derived from the same source, and it is to these that the name of Hebraisms is usually given.

To begin with the simplest kind:—

(a) The Greek word which expressed the primary meaning of a Hebrew word often received in addition its secondary meanings also; compare ἐρωτᾶν, שָׁאַל, *interrogate* and *request*. Hence it would not be strange if the Jews had used δικαιοσύνη in the sense of *alms*, like צדקה. More certain examples are, ὀφείλημα *peccatum*, from the Aram. חוֹב; νύμφη (*bride*, also) *daughter-in-law*, Mt. x. 35, as כַּלָּה has both these meanings (Gen. xxxviii. 11, LXX); εἷς for *primus* in certain cases, like אֶחָד; ἐξομολογεῖσθαί τινι *to praise* (giving thanks), like הוֹדָה לְ (Ps. cv. 47, cxxi. 4, al., LXX); εὐλογεῖν *bless*, i.e. make happy, like בֵּרֵךְ; κτίσις *that which is created, creature*, compare the Chaldee בְּרִיָּה; δόξα in the sense of *brightness, splendour*, like כָּבוֹד; δυνάμεις *miracles*, גְּבוּרוֹת. The transference of a figurative sense is most frequent: as ποτήριον *sors, portio*, Mt. xx. 22 (כּוֹס); σκάνδαλον *stumbling block*, in a moral sense (מִכְשׁוֹל); γλῶσσα for *nation* (לָשׁוֹן); χεῖλος for *language* (שָׂפָה); ἐνώπιον τοῦ θεοῦ (לִפְנֵי יְהוָֹה) *according to God's judgment*; καρδία εὐθεῖα (יְשָׁרָה); περιπατεῖν *walk*, of a course of life; ὁδός (דֶּרֶךְ), comp. Schæfer, *Ind. ad Æsop.* p. 148; ἀνάθεμα, not merely *what is consecrated to God*, but (like the Hebrew חֵרֶם) what is *devoted to destruction*, Rom. ix. 3, Dt. vii. 26, Jos. vi. 17, al.; λύειν, Mt. xvi. 19, *declare lawful*, from the Rabbinical הִתִּיר.

(*b*) Certain very common vernacular phrases are literally translated into Greek: as πρόσωπον λαμβάνειν from נָשָׂא פָנִים; ζητεῖν ψυχήν from בִּקֵּשׁ נֶפֶשׁ; ποιεῖν ἔλεος (χάριν) μετά τινος from עָשָׂה חֶסֶד עִם; ἀνοίγειν τοὺς ὀφθαλμούς or τὸ στόμα τινός (פָּקַח); γεύεσθαι θανάτου, טְעַם מִיתָא (Talm.); ἄρτον φαγεῖν *coenare*, אָכַל לֶחֶם; αἷμα ἐκχέειν, שָׁפַךְ דָּם, *kill*; ἀνίστημι σπέρμα τινί from הֵקִים זֶרַע לְ: υἱὸς θανάτου from בֶּן־מָוֶת (οἱ υἱοὶ τοῦ νυμφῶνος); καρπὸς ὀσφύος from פְּרִי חֲלָצַיִם; καρπὸς κοιλίας from פְּרִי בֶטֶן; ἐξέρχεσθαι ἐκ τῆς ὀσφύος τινός from יָצָא מֵחַלְצֵי פ׳; ἐκ κοιλίας μητρός from מִבֶּטֶן אִמּוֹ;[1] ὀφείλημα ἀφιέναι from שָׁבַק חוֹבָא (Talm.); also στηρίζειν πρόσωπον αὐτοῦ from הֵשִׂים פָּנָיו; πᾶσα σάρξ from כָּל־בָּשָׂר.

(*c*) Reflexion and contrivance are more apparent in the formation of Greek derivatives, that vernacular words which belong to the same root may be similarly expressed in Greek: as ὁλοκαύτωμα (from ὁλοκαυτοῦν, Lob. p. 524) for עֹלָה; σπλαγχνίζεσθαι from σπλάγχνα, as רֶחֶם is connected with רַחֲמִים; σκανδαλίζειν, σκανδαλίζεσθαι, like נִכְשַׁל, הִכְשִׁיל; ἐγκαινίζειν from ἐγκαίνια, as חָנַךְ is connected with חֲנֻכָּה; ἀναθεματίζειν like הֶחֱרִים; ὀρθρίζειν like הִשְׁכִּים; and perhaps ἐνωτίζεσθαι like הֶאֱזִין, comp. Fisch. *ad Leus. Dial.* p. 27. This is carried still farther in προσωποληπτεῖν, for which the Hebrew itself has no single corresponding word.

All this easily accounts for the Hebrew-Aramaic colouring which is so distinctly apparent in the style of the N. T. writers, who were not (like Philo and Josephus[2]) acquainted with Greek literature, and who did not strive after a correct Greek style. The whole cast of their composition, and in particular the want of connexion (especially in narrative), could not but offend a cultivated Greek ear; and many expressions—such as ἀφιέναι ὀφειλήματα,[3] πρόσωπον λαμβάνειν, λογί-

---

[1] A similar Græcism in Latin is "a teneris unguiculis" (Cic. *Fam.* 1. 6. 3), which the Romans certainly understood, as καρπὸς χειλέων, for instance, would undoubtedly be understood by the Greeks, though it might seem a somewhat strange expression; comp. καρπὸς φρενῶν, Pind. *Nem.* 10. 22. Still less difficulty would be occasioned by καρπὸς κοιλίας, since *fruit* was used absolutely for *offspring* by the Greeks (Aristot. *Polit.* 7. 16, Eurip. *Bacch.* 1305) and others, where the meaning was made clear by the context: comp. Ruhnk. *ad* Hom. *in Cerer.* 23. [In Eurip. *Bacch.* 1305 (1307) the word is ἔρνος: this word and θάλος are not unfrequently used in this sense. On καρπός, see Hermann and Paley on Eurip. *Ion* 475 (καρποτρόφοι).]

[2] Though even Josephus, when narrating O. T. history after the LXX, is not altogether free from Hebraisms: see Scharfenberg, *De Josephi et LXX consensu*, in Pott, *Sylloge* vii. p. 306 sqq.

[3] In the sense of remitting *sins*, i.e. so far as ὀφιλήματα is concerned;

SECT. III.] HEBREW-ARAMAIC COLOURING OF THE N. T. DICTION. 35

ζεσθαι εἰς δικαιοσύνην, &c.—would convey to a native Greek either an erroneous meaning or no meaning at all.¹ At the same time, it is easy to explain the fact that such Hebraistic expressions are less numerous in the free composition of the N. T. than in the translation of the O. T., and that, in the N. T. itself, those writers whose education was Hellenistic—Paul, Luke (especially in the second part of the Acts), John, and the author of the Ep. to the Hebrews²—use fewer Hebraisms than those who properly belonged to Palestine (Matthew, Peter).³ It is also obvious that the Hebraisms which we find in the language of the Apostles were not all *unconsciously* adopted.⁴ The religious expressions—and these constitute by far the greatest portion of the N. T. Hebraisms—were necessarily retained, because these were, so to speak, completely imbued with the religious ideas themselves, and because it was designed that Christianity should in the first instance link itself to Judaism.⁵ Indeed there were no terms in the Greek language, as it then existed, by which the deep religious phenomena which apostolic Christianity made known could be expressed.⁶ But when it is maintained⁷ that the N. T. writers *always thought* in Hebrew or Aramaic what they afterwards wrote in Greek, this is an exaggeration. Such a habit belongs to beginners only. We ourselves, when we have had some practice in writing Latin, gradually (though never entirely) free ourselves from the habit of first thinking in our own language. Persons who, though not scientifically trained in Greek, yet constantly heard Greek spoken and very often—indeed regularly—spoke it themselves, could not but acquire in a short time a stock of words and phrases and a power of handling the language which would enable them, when writing, to command Greek expressions at once, without first thinking of verna-

for ἀφιέναι remit, even in reference to *offences*, occurs Her. 6. 30, in the phrase ἀφιέναι αἰτίαν, and ὀφειλήματα ἀφιέναι *debita remittere* (to remit what is due) is quite a common expression. In later Greek we find ἀφιέναι τινὶ τὴν ἀδικίαν, Plutarch, *Pomp.* 34, see Coraes and Schæf. *in loc.* A native Greek would also understand εὑρίσκειν χάριν, though it would sound strange to him in consequence of the use of the active for the middle εὑρίσκεσθαι.

¹ Comp. Gatak. *De stylo N. T.* cap. 5.
² Comp. Tholuck, *Commentar*, cap. 1. § 2. p. 25 sqq.
³ The Grecian training of particular writers shows itself especially in the appropriate use of *verba composita* and *decomposita*.
⁴ Van den Honert, *Synt.* p. 103.
⁵ Comp. Beza *ad* Act. x. 46. Rambach is not altogether wrong in saying (*Inst. Herm.* 1. 2. 2), "Lingua N. T. passim ad Ebræi sermonis indolem conformata est, ut hoc modo concentus scripturæ utriusque Test. non in rebus solum sed ipsis etiam in verbis clarius observaretur:" comp. Pfaff, *Nott. ad Matth.* p. 34; Olear. p. 341 sqq.; Tittm. *Syn.* I. p. 201 sq.—Compare further J. W. Schröder, *De causis quare dictio pure Græca in N. T. plerumque prætermissa sit* (Marb. 1768); also Van Hengel, *Comm. in Ep. ad Philipp.* p. 19.
⁶ Some good remarks on this point are to be found in Hvalstroem, *Spec. de usu Græcitatis Alex. in N. T.* p. 6 sq. (Upsal. 1794). Van den Honert even went so far as to assert, "Vel ipse Demosthenes, si eandem rem, quam nobis tradiderunt apostoli, debita perspicuitate et efficacia perscribere voluisset, Hebraismorum usum evitare non potuisset."
⁷ By Eichhorn and Bretschneider (*Præf. ad Lex. N. T.* II. 12, ed. 2); but the latter has retracted this opinion, at any rate so far as regards Paul (*Grundl. des ev. Pietism.* p. 179).

cular words and phrases to be afterwards translated into Greek.¹ The parallel drawn between the N. T. writers and our beginners in Latin composition, or the (uneducated) German-speaking Jews, is both unworthy and incorrect: comp. Schleierm. *Herm.* pp. 54, 59, 257. It is also forgotten that the Apostles found a Jewish Greek idiom already in existence, and that therefore they did not themselves construct most of their expressions by first thinking them out in Hebrew.

Many Greek words are used by the N. T. writers in a special relation to the Christian system of religion (and even in direct contrast to Judaism), as religious technical terms. These appear to constitute a third element of the N. T. diction—the peculiarly *Christian*.² Compare especially the words ἔργα (ἐργάζεσθαι, Rom. iv. 4), πίστις, πιστεύειν εἰς Χριστόν, or πιστεύειν absolutely, ὁμολογία, δικαιοσύνη and δικαιοῦσθαι, ἐκλέγεσθαι, οἱ κλητοί, οἱ ἐκλεκτοί, οἱ ἅγιοι (for *Christians*), οἱ πιστοί and οἱ ἄπιστοι, οἰκοδομή and οἰκοδομεῖν in a figurative sense, ἀπόστολος, εὐαγγελίζεσθαι and κηρύττειν used absolutely of Christian preaching, the appropriation of the form βάπτισμα to baptism, perhaps κλᾶν (τὸν) ἄρτον for *the holy repasts* (the Agape with the Lord's supper), ὁ κόσμος, ἡ σάρξ, ὁ σαρκικός in the familiar theological sense, and others. Most of these expressions and phrases, however, are found in the O. T. and in Rabbinical writings;³ hence it will always be hard to prove anything to be absolutely peculiar to the Apostles,—brought into use by them. This apostolic element, therefore, mainly consists in the meaning and the application given to words and phrases, and the subject scarcely lies within the limits of philological inquiry: compare, however, Schleierm. *Herm.* pp. 56, 67 sq., 138 sq. In the region of history, πάσχειν *suffer* and παραδίδοσθαι *be delivered up* (used absolutely) became established as technical expressions for the closing scenes of the life of Jesus on earth.⁴

Grammatical Hebraisms will be discussed in the next section.

---

¹ How easily do even we, who never hear Latin spoken by native Romans, attain the faculty of at once conceiving *in Latin* "dixit verum esse," or "quam virtutem demonstravit aliis præstare," and the like, without first mentally construing *dixit quod verum sit*, or *de qua virtute dem., quod ea etc.* Thinking in conformity with the genius of the mother-tongue shows itself particularly in phrases and figures which have become habitual, and which are unconsciously introduced into the foreign language. It was so with the Apostles, who regularly use, along with many Hebraistic expressions, numerous Greek idioms which are entirely foreign to the genius of Hebrew.

² See Olearius, *De stylo N. T.* p. 380 sqq. (ed. Schwarz), Eckard, *Technica Sacra* (Quedlinb. 1716).

³ To attempt to explain such expressions of the apostolical terminology by quotations from Greek authors (comp. Krebs, *Observ. Præf.* p. 4) is highly absurd. But, on the other hand, it is necessary to distinguish between the language of the Apostles, which still moved rather in the sphere of O. T. expressions, and the terminology of the Greek Church, which continually became more and more special in its meaning.

⁴ [On the Christian element see Westcott in Smith's *Dict. of Bible*, ii. p. 533; Fairbairn, *Hermen. Manual*, pp. 39–45; Schirlitz, *Grundzüge*, pp. 36–42; Webster, *Syntax*, p. 6 sq.; also Cremer, *Biblisch-theolog. Wörterbuch der*

Section IV.

THE GRAMMATICAL CHARACTER OF THE N. T. DICTION.

In examining the grammatical characteristics of the N. T. diction, the two elements of N. T. Greek must be carefully distinguished. In grammar, as in vocabulary, the peculiarities of the later common Greek are the basis; these however consist rather in certain forms of inflexion than in syntactical constructions. Mingled with these we find, but in very small proportion, Hebraistic expressions and constructions in connexion with all the parts of speech; the main peculiarity being a predilection for prepositions, where the Greeks would have used cases alone. On the whole, N. T. Greek obeys the ordinary laws of Greek grammar. Many peculiarly Greek idioms are familiarly used by the N. T. writers (e.g. the attraction of the relative and of prepositions), and several distinctions which are entirely alien to Hebrew—as that between the negatives οὐ and μή, etc.—are strictly observed, though by mere instinct.

The grammatical structure of a language is much less affected by time than the use and meaning of its words. This may be verified in the case of almost every language whose development we can trace historically; compare, for instance, the German of Luther's translation with that spoken at the present day.[1] Greek is no exception to this rule: the later common language is distinguished by few grammatical peculiarities, and these belong almost entirely to the accidence. We find in it especially a number of inflexions of nouns and verbs, which either did not exist at all in the earlier language, being formed later by shortening or lengthening the original inflexions, or which formerly belonged to particular dialects. The following are examples of the latter class:—

(a) Attic inflexions: τιθέασι, ἠβουλήθην, ἤμελλε, βούλει (βούλῃ), ὄψει.

(b) Doric: ἡ λιμός (for ὁ λ.), ἤτω (ἔστω), ἀφέωνται (ἀφεῖνται).

(c) Æolic: the 1 aor. opt. in εια,—which however was early admitted into Attic.

(d) Ionic: γήρει, σπείρης, εἶπα (1 aor.).

As forms entirely unknown in earlier Greek must be mentioned —such a dative as νοί, the imperative κάθου, perfects like ἔγνωκαν

---

neutest. *Gräcität* (2d ed. 1872,—translated by Urwick, 1878). Lünemann refers to Zezschwitz, *Profangräcität u. biblisch. Sprachgeist: eine Vorl. üb. d. bibl. Umbildung hellen. Begriffe, bes. der psychol.* (Leipz. 1859).]

[1] [On the relation of the English of our Auth. Ver. to that now spoken, see Max Müller, *Lectures on Language*, p. 35 sq. (1st series); Marsh, *Lectures on the Eng. Lang.* p. 443 sqq. (ed. Smith).]

(for ἐγνώκασι), second aorists and imperfects like κατελίποσαν, ἐδολιοῦσαν, second aorists like εἴδαμεν, ἔφυγαν, the future conjunctives (§ xiii. 1. e), the imperfect ἤμεθα. To this head specially belong many tense-forms which are regular in themselves, but for which the older language used others; as ἡμάρτησα for ἥμαρτον, αὔξω for αὐξάνω, ἧξα from ἥκω, φάγομαι for ἔδομαι: indeed the new tense- and mood-forms received by verbs from which earlier Greek, for the sake of euphony, used but few forms, constitute a special feature of the later language. It should be added that several nouns received a new gender, as ἡ βάτος (for ὁ β.), and some in consequence a twofold declension, e.g. πλοῦτος, ἔλεος: see § 9. Rem. 2.

The peculiarities of syntax in later Greek are less numerous, and consist mainly in a negligent use of the moods with particles. The following examples may be quoted from the N. T.: ὅταν with a past tense of the indicative, εἰ with the conjunctive, ἵνα with the present indicative, the construction of such verbs as γεύεσθαι, καταδικάζειν, with an accusative, of προςκυνεῖν and προςφωνεῖν with a dative of the person (Lob. p. 463, Matth. 402. c), the weakening of ἵνα in such phrases as θέλω ἵνα, ἄξιος ἵνα, etc., the extension of the genitive of the infinitive (τοῦ ποιεῖν) beyond its original and natural limits, the use of the conjunctive for the optative in narration after past tenses, and the consequent infrequency of the optative mood, which has entirely disappeared in modern Greek. Μέλλειν, θέλειν, etc., are more frequently followed by the aorist infinitive (Lob. p. 747). Neglect of declension is only beginning to show itself; thus we find μετὰ τοῦ ἕν and the like (but as the result of design), see § 10. Rem. Later still we find particular instances of entire misconception of the meaning of cases and tenses: thus σύν takes the genitive in Niceph. *Tact.* (Hase *ad Leon. Diac.* p. 38), ἀπό the accusative in Leo Gram. p. 232, and then in modern Greek; the aorist and present participles are interchanged in Leo Diac. and others. The dual (of nouns) is gradually superseded by the plural.

The grammatical character of the N. T. language has a very slight Hebraic colouring. It is true that in grammatical structure Hebrew (Aramaic) differs essentially from Greek; but this would rather tend to prevent the Greek-speaking Jews from intermingling with their Greek the constructions of their native language: a German would be in much greater danger of introducing German constructions into Latin or French. Besides, it is always easier to master the grammatical laws of a foreign language than to obtain a perfect command of its vocabulary and to acquire the general national complexion of the foreign idiom: comp. Schleierm. *Herm.* p. 73. The rules of syntax are but few in comparison with the multitude of words and phrases; these rules too—especially those fundamental laws on the observance of which depends correctness of style, not elegance merely—are much more frequently brought before the mind, particularly in speaking. Hence it was not difficult for the Jews to acquire such a knowledge of the grammatical framework of the Greek of their time (in which, indeed, some of the niceties of Attic Greek

SECT. IV.] GRAMMATICAL CHARACTER OF THE N. T. DICTION. 39

were unknown) as was quite sufficient for their simple style of composition. Even the LXX in most cases correctly represent a Hebrew construction by its counterpart in Greek.¹ Only certain expressions of frequent occurrence are either (when the laws of Greek syntax do not forbid) rendered literally, e.g. the expression of a wish by means of a question, 2 S. xv. 4 τίς με καταστήσει κριτήν; xxiii. 15, Num. xi. 29, Dt. v. 26, xxviii. 67, Cant. viii. 1;²—or translated, if possible, in a way which is at least in harmony with Greek analogy, as θανάτῳ ἀποθανεῖσθε Gen. iii. 4 (מוֹת תְּמֻתוּן), Dt. xx. 17, 1 S. xiv. 39, Is. xxx. 19;—or even translated by a construction in actual use in Greek (see however § 45), as Jud. xv. 2 μισῶν ἐμίσησας, for שָׂנֹא שְׂנֵאתָהּ, Gen. xliii. 2, Ex. xxii. 17, xxiii. 26, 1 S. ii. 25, al.; compare also the infinitive with τοῦ.³ Hebrew constructions which are altogether opposed to the genius of the Greek language are, as a rule, not retained in the LXX. Thus the feminine for the neuter is found in but few passages, where the translators have not sufficiently examined the original, or have anxiously sought for a literal rendering (e.g. Ps. cxviii. 50, cxvii. 23);⁴ and it is not probable that they consciously used the feminine to represent the neuter. In other passages it is clear that they understood the Hebrew feminine to relate to some feminine noun or pronoun indicated in the context, as in Jud. xix. 30: in Neh. xiii. 14, however, ἐν ταύτῃ is probably equivalent to the classical ταύτῃ, *in this respect, hoc in genere* (Xen. *Cyr.* 8. 8. 5), or *therefore*,—comp. ταύτῃ ὅτι *propterea quod*, Xen. *An.* 2. 6. 7 : see also 1 S. xi. 2. The combination of the Hebrew verb with prepositions is the construction most frequently imitated : as φείδεσθαι ἐπί τινι Dt. vii. 16, or ἐπί τινα Ez. vii. 4 [*Alex.*], οἰκοδομεῖν ἔν τινι Neh. iv. 10 (בָּנָה בְּ), ἐπερωτᾶν ἐν κυρίῳ (שָׁאַל בַּיהוָֹה) 1 S. x. 22, εὐδοκεῖν ἔν τινι (חָפֵץ בְּ, Fritz. *Rom.* II. 371). These imitations certainly sound harsh in Greek, but in each case some possible point of contact might be found in a language so flexible.⁵

¹ Various Greek idioms had become quite habitual to them, such as the use of the article with attributive words and phrases after a substantive (ὁ κύριος ὁ ἐν οὐρανῷ, and the like), the attraction of the relative, etc.: the negatives also are almost always correctly distinguished. The better translators furnish examples of the more extended use of the Greek cases, as Gen. xxvi. 10, μικροῦ ἐκοιμήθη *was within a little of* &c.
² Comp. Rom. vii. 24, and Fritz. *in loc.*, who adduces similar examples from Greek poets. The formula with πῶς (ἄν) and the optat. or conj. is discussed by Schæfer, *ad* Soph. *Œd. Col.* p. 523, and *Melet.* p. 100.
³ Hemsterhuis says (Lucian, *Dial. Mar.* 4. 3): "sæpenumero contingit, ut locutio quædam native Græca a LXX interpretibus et N. T. scriptoribus mutata paululum potestate ad Hebræam apte exprimendam adhibeatur."
⁴ The translator of the Psalms is, in general, one of the most careless; that of Nehemiah is little better.—Aquila, who translated syllable for syllable (and *e.g.* absurdly rendered אֵת, the sign of the accusative, by σύν), cannot at all be taken into consideration in any inquiry into the grammatical character of Hellenistic Greek. He violates the rules of grammar without hesitation for the sake of a literal rendering; as Gen. i. 5 ἐκάλεσεν ὁ θεὸς τῷ φωτὶ ἡμέρα. And yet he always uses the article correctly, and even employs the attraction of the relative,—so deeply were both rooted in the Greek language.
⁵ As in German, "bauen *an* etwas," "fragen *bei*," etc.

But even if the LXX presented more instances of servile imitation of Hebrew constructions, this would not come into consideration in our inquiry respecting the N. T. As we have already said, the style of these *translators*, who usually followed the words of the original with studious exactness, and in some cases did not even understand their meaning, does not furnish the type of that style which Jews would use in conversation or free composition. In point of *grammar*, so far as the particular rules of the language are concerned, the N. T. is altogether written in Greek; and the few real grammatical Hebraisms which it contains become hardly discernible. Amongst these we may with more or less certainty[1] include, in general, the use of prepositions in phrases in which a classical writer would have been content with the simple case, as ἀποκρύπτειν τι ἀπό τινος, ἐσθίειν ἀπὸ τῶν ψιχίων, ἀθῶος ἀπὸ τοῦ αἵματος, κοινωνὸς ἔν τινι, ἀρέσκειν and προςκυνεῖν ἐνώπιόν τινος, εὐδοκεῖν and θέλειν ἔν τινι. Many examples of this kind, however, belong to the simplicity of the ancient style, and hence are also found in classic writers, especially the poets; they are therefore not really discordant with the genius of the Greek language (*e.g.* παύειν ἀπό τινος). More special and certain examples of grammatical Hebraism are the following :—

(*a*) The verbal translation of Hebrew constructions which are opposed to the spirit of the Greek language; as ὁμολογεῖν ἔν τινι, βλέπειν ἀπό *sibi cavere a*, προςέθετο πέμψαι, the formula εἰ δοθήσεται to express a negative oath.

(*b*) The repetition of a word for the purpose of indicating distribution, as δύο δύο, *bini*, instead of ἀνὰ δύο.

(*c*) The imitation of the Hebrew infinitive absolute (see above).

(*d*) The use of the genitive of a noun expressing quality in the place of an adjective:—and probably also the remarkably frequent use of the infinitive with prepositions (and a subject in the accusative) in narration.

The constructions included under (*a*) and (*b*) may be considered *pure* Hebraisms.

When, however, we consider that by far the largest number of constructions in the N. T. are pure Greek, and that the N. T. writers have even appropriated peculiarities of Greek syntax[2] which are altogether alien to the genius of their native language—as the distinction of the different past tenses, the construction of verbs with ἄν, the attraction of the relative, such constructions as οἰκονομίαν πεπίστευμαι, the use of a singular verb with neuter plurals, etc.—we

---

[1] As imaginary Hebraisms may be mentioned—the supposed *plur. excellentiæ*, the ב *essentiæ*, the combinations which have been wrongly taken as periphrases for the superlative (e.g. σάλπιγξ τοῦ θεοῦ), the use of the feminine for the neuter, and the pretended hypallage τὰ ῥήματα τῆς ζωῆς ταύτης for ταῦτα τὰ ῥήμ. τ. ζωῆς. [See § 27. 3, § 29. Rem., § 36. 2 and 3, § 34. 3. Rem. 1, § 34. 3. *b.*]

[2] The more minute niceties of written Attic, it is true, are not found in the N. T., partly because they were unknown in the popular spoken language, which the N. T. writers always heard, partly because there was no place for these niceties in the simple style in which the N. T. is written.

shall not be inclined to join in the outcry respecting the innumerable grammatical Hebraisms of the N. T. We may naturally expect to find the diction of the N. T. much less Hebraistic grammatically than that of the LXX and the Palestinian Apocrypha. That this really is the case will clearly appear, if we mark in the LXX the constructions which have just been mentioned as Hebraistic, remembering at the same time that many Hebrew idioms retained in the LXX do not occur at all in the N. T., and others—as the expression of a wish by a question—only in isolated instances, in impassioned language. Such a periphrasis for the future as ἔσομαι διδόναι, Tob. v. 14, is nowhere found in the N. T., nor is a substantive ever doubled to indicate *each, every*, as in Num. ix. 10, 2 K. xvii. 29, 1 Chr. ix. 27.[1]

Of the peculiarities of particular N. T. writers very few are purely grammatical; the Apocalypse alone requires special (though not exceptional) notice in a N. T. Grammar.

It is evident that in the whole investigation of the grammatical character of the N. T. language differences of reading must be carefully considered. Conversely, a thorough knowledge of the various lexical peculiarities of individual writers is an indispensable requisite for successful textual criticism.[2]

---

[1] Yet in the better translated portions of the O. T. and in the Palestinian Apocrypha we sometimes find Greek constructions where a N. T. writer would use a Hebraism: thus in 3 (1) Esdr. vi. 10, Tob. iii. 8, the genitive is used with strict Grecian propriety. See further Thiersch, *De Pent. Alex.* p. 95 sq.

[2] [On the general character of N. T. Greek, see Ellicott, *Aids to Faith*, p. 457 sqq.; Westcott in Smith's *Dict. of Bible*, II. p. 531 sqq., and *Introd. to Gospels*, pp. 38–40; J. Donaldson in Kitto's *Cyclopædia*, II. p. 170 sq. (ed. 3); Scrivener, *Criticism of N. T.* c. viii.; Green, *Gram.* c. i.; Davidson, *Bibl. Crit.* p. 447 sqq.; Webster, *Synt.* c. 1; Tregelles in Horne's *Introd.* IV. pp. 8–23; Fairbairn, *Herm. Man.* pp. 12–45; Bleek, *Introd. to N. T.* I. pp. 58–83 (Transl.). To the German references may be added, A. Buttmann, *Gr.* p. xi, 1 sq.; Schirlitz, *Grundz.* Part I. The differences of opinion chiefly relate to the relative importance of the various elements which enter into the composition of N. T. Greek. Amongst the questions raised are the following: how much stress should be laid on the *direct* influence of the LXX (comp. Westcott in *Dict. of B., l. c.*),—whether some of the peculiarities commonly called Hebraistic should not rather be considered characteristics of the ordinary spoken language (see especially J. Donaldson *l. c.*),—whether we may admit that the N. T. *syntax* betrays the influence of the Latin (A. Buttm. *l. c.*). Many of the coincidences between Modern Greek and the Greek of the N. T. will be referred to in the following pages.]

PART II.

ACCIDENCE.

Section V.

ORTHOGRAPHY AND ORTHOGRAPHICAL PRINCIPLES.

1. The best MSS. of the N. T., like those of Greek authors generally,[1] exhibit extraordinary variations of orthography, especially in particular words and forms; and there are not always clear grounds for deciding which mode of spelling is correct. Editors of the text have to adopt some definite rule, and consistently adhere to it. On several points, however, though the work of collation has of late been executed with greater diplomatic exactness, a still more careful investigation of the MS. evidence is yet to be desired. To proceed to details :—

(*a*) The use of the apostrophe to prevent hiatus is, in general, much less frequent in the MSS. of the N. T. and of the LXX than in the texts of native Greek authors (especially the orators[2]). Ἅμα, ἄρα, ἆρα, γέ, ἐμέ, ἔτι, ἵνα, ὥστε, are never elided; δέ (before ἄν)[3] and οὐδέ very seldom: Mt. xxiii. 16, 18, xxiv. 21, Rom. ix. 7, 1 C. xiv. 21, H. viii. 4, L. x. 10, 2 C. iii. 16, xi. 21, Ph. ii. 18, 1 Jo. ii. 5, iii. 17. Only the prepositions ἀπό, διά, ἐπί, παρά, μετά, and the conjunction ἀλλά, regularly suffer elision; the prepositions especially before pronouns and in phrases of frequent occurrence, such as ἀπ᾽ ἀρχῆς,—ἀντί only in ἀνθ᾽ ὧν. Even here however MSS. vary, sometimes even the best, especially in regard to ἀλλά. Thus we find in A and

---

[1] See Poppo, *Thuc.* I. p. 214, Matth. 42.
[2] Comp. Benseler, *De hiatu in Script. Gr.* (Pt. I. : Friberg, 1841); *De hiatu in Demosth.* (ib. 1847).
[3] [Δί is always elided before ἄν in the N. T., and not, I believe, before any other word; for in Ph. ii. 18 we should probably read τὸ δὲ αὐτό.]

SECT. V.] ORTHOGRAPHY AND ORTHOGRAPHICAL PRINCIPLES. 43

several other MSS., ἀλλὰ ἀληθείας A. xxvi. 25, ἀλλὰ ἀπώσαντο A. vii. 39, ἀλλὰ ὄγδοον 2 P. ii. 5; also, in the best MSS., ἀλλὰ ὑμᾶς 2 C. xii. 14, ἀλλὰ υἱός G. iv. 7. MS. authority is also in favour of μετὰ ἀνδρός L. ii. 36, μετὰ εἴκοσι xiv. 31, μετὰ ἀπίστου 2 C. vi. 15, ἀπὸ ἀνατολῶν Rev. xxi. 13, ἀπὸ ἀσθενείας H. xi. 34, ἀπὸ Ἀδάμ Jude 14, διὰ εἴδους 2 C. v. 7. Compare also A. ix. 6, x. 20, xvi. 37, 2 C. iv. 2, v. 12, L. xi. 17 (ἐπὶ οἶκον), Mt. xxi. 5 (ἐπὶ ὄνον), etc. In L. iii. 2 ἐπὶ ἀρχιερέως, Mt. xxiv. 7 ἐπὶ ἔθνος, 1 C. vi. 11 ἀλλὰ ἀπελούσασθε, ἀλλὰ ἐδικαιώθητε, the weight of authority is against the elision: in Rom. vii. 13 ἀλλ᾽ and ἀλλά have equal support.¹ As the Ionic dialect is distinguished by indifference to hiatus, this peculiarity of N. T. Greek was formerly considered an Ionism: in Attic prose however elision is sometimes neglected, though all the instances which Georgi (*Hierocr.* I. 143) produces from Plato may not be trustworthy. See Buttm. I. 123 sqq. (Jelf 16 sq.).² It is possible that the variations may have been guided by some principle: Sintenis, for example, has reduced Plutarch's practice to rules (Plut. *Vit.* IV. 321 sqq.). So in the N. T. we might occasionally account for the absence of elision by reference to the writer's meaning; not imagining however that the Apostles would bestow attention on such matters as these, but regarding the choice as the result of a natural instinct. But the risk of trifling would here be very great (Bengel on 1 C. vi. 11).

In the poetical quotation from Menander, 1 C. xv. 33, even Lachmann reads χρῆσθ᾽ ὁμιλίαι κακαί (comp. Georgi, *Hier.* I. 186), although the best MSS. of the N. T. have the unelided form χρηστά, which Tischendorf has received.³

(*b*) In regard to the final ς of οὕτως, μέχρις, and the so-called ν ἐφελκυστικόν,⁴ the editors have for the most part followed the ordinary rule, which however has been limited by recent grammarians: see Buttm. I. 92 sqq. (Jelf 20). A more prudent course is to follow the best MSS. in each case: accordingly recent

---

¹ Comp. also Sturz p. 125.
² See also Heupel, *Marc.* p. 33; Benseler's excursus to his ed. of Isocr. *Areop.* p. 385 sqq.; Jacobs, *Præf. ad Æl. Anim.* p. 29 sq.; Poppo, *Thuc.* III. ii. p. 358.
³ [Lachm. reads χρῆσθ᾽, not χρῆσθ᾽ (*Rec.*): see Jelf 63. 2.]
⁴ See Voemel, *De ν et ς adductis literis* (Frankf. on M. 1853); Haake, *Beiträge z. griech. Grammat.* 1 Heft. [Lobeck, *Path. Elem.* II. pp. 158-218; Kühner I. 227-232; G. Meyer, *Griech. Gram.* pp. 259-264.]

editors of the N. T., following the uncial MSS.,[1] uniformly receive οὕτως and the ν ἐφελκυστικόν.[2] Classical philologers have endeavoured to discover some fixed principle which might determine the preference of one or the other form in Greek prose,[3] and it is not in itself improbable that the more careful writers would be guided by euphony (Franke in Jahn's *Jahrb.* 1842, p. 247) and other considerations;[4] though ancient grammarians affirm (Bekk. *Anecd.* III. p. 1400) that even in Attic Greek the ν was inserted before both consonants and vowels without distinction (Jacobs, *Præf. ad Æl. Anim.* p. 23 sq.), and the MS. evidence confirms this assertion.[5] On μέχρι and μέχρις, ἄχρι and ἄχρις, in particular, see Jacobs, *Achill. Tat.* p. 479. According to the grammarians μέχρι and ἄχρι are the

---

[1] Tisch. *Præf. ad N. T.* p. 23 (ed. 2): [p. 53, ed. 7.]
[2] [Of recent editors Tregelles and Alford adhere to the principle of writing οὕτως before consonants: Tregelles invariably, Alford except in Mt. vii. 17. Lachmann followed the evidence presented in each passage, but was often led astray by imperfect collations: he admitted οὕτω in A. xxiii. 11, Ph. iii. 17, H. xii. 21, Rev. xvi. 18, Rom. i. 15, vi. 19, 1 C. vii. 40. Tischendorf in ed. 7 admitted οὕτω once only (Rev. xvi. 18), but in ed. 8 agrees with Lachmann in the first four of the passages quoted above. Westcott and Hort omit the ς ten times; viz. in Mt. iii. 15, vii. 17, Mk. ii. 7, A. xiii. 47, xxiii. 11, Rom. i. 15, vi. 19, Ph. iii. 17, H. xii. 21, Rev. xvi. 18. In A. xxiii. 11 and in Ph. iv. 1 this word is followed by σ: in Ph. iv. 1, however, all recent editors (apparently) read οὕτως.—The ν ἐφελκυστικόν is naturally dealt with upon the same principles. Again we find very great uniformity in the texts of Tregelles and Alford, who almost invariably insert the ν. The few exceptions I have noted are nearly all found in plural datives. Thus δυσί is received by Tregelles in Mt. vi. 24 and L. xvi. 13, by Alford in L. xvi. 13 and A. xxi. 33; other examples in Alford's text will be found in A. xvii. 25, xxi. 33, Rom. ii. 8. Lachmann, Tischendorf, Westcott and Hort omit the ν somewhat more freely, following the evidence in each case. Thus Lachmann reads πᾶσι five times and δυσί four; Tisch. (ed. 8), πᾶσι five times and δυσί three. In the text of Westcott and Hort πᾶσιν occurs before a consonant forty times, πᾶσι fourteen; δυσίν and δυσί each three times. See also Mt. vii. 15, xx. 12, A. ii. 22, x. 41, xxi. 33, Rom. ii. 8, 2 Tim. iv. 8, where the ν is omitted in the dative plural by one or more of these editors. In verbs the omission is apparently very rare. In Lachmann's text examples will be found in L. i. 3, 9, A. ii. 6, vii. 25; in Tischendorf's, in L. i. 3, 9, Jo. x. 14. Westcott and Hort omit ν in these passages except A. vii. 25, and read ἀπέχουσι, ἐστί, in Mt. vi. 5, 25: in their text of Romans, if I mistake not, there are in all not more than eight instances of omission,—five in the dative plural, three in verbal inflexions (κατέκρινε, ἐτιμίνωσι, ἐξαπατῶσι). In many instances, however, the alternative reading is given in their Appendix. See Scrivener, *Criticism,* p. 486 sqq., *Cod. Sin.* p. liv, A. Buttm. *Gr.* p. 9.]
[3] Bornem. *De gem. Cyr. rec.* p. 89 (with whom Poppo agrees, *Ind. to Cyr.*); Frotscher, Xen. *Hier.* p. 9; Bremi, Æsch. *Ctes.* 3, 4; Schæf. *Dem.* I. 207; Mätzner, *Antiph.* p. 192.
[4] We are not here concerned with the much-disputed questions, whether οὕτως (Schæf. *Plut.* V. 219) or οὕτω (Buttm. II. 264) was the original form, and whether ν ἐφελκ. really belongs to the forms to which it is attached: see Rost, p. 47; Krüger, p. 31. [Don. pp. 53, 80, 193; Lobeck *u.s.* p. 203; Curtius, *Grundz.* p. 54, *Greek Verb,* p. 41 (Trans.).]
[5] Comp. also Bachmann, *Lycophr.* I. 156; Benseler, Isocr. *Areop.* p. 185.

Attic forms, even when a vowel follows (Th. M. p. 135, Phryn. p. 14, comp. Bornem. Xen. *Cyr.* 8. 6. 20); and though good MSS. of Attic authors are not unfrequently on the other side, this rule has been followed by modern editors. Comp. Stallb. Plat. *Phæd.* p. 183, *Sympos.* p. 128, Schæf. *Plut.* V. p. 268, and see on the whole Klotz, *Devar.* p. 231. In the N. T. the best MSS. have μέχρι invariably: ἄχρι before consonants and sometimes before vowels, A. xi. 5, xxviii. 15 ; but ἄχρις οὗ is best supported in Rom. xi. 25, 1 C. xi. 26, xv. 25, al. (also in A. vii. 18).[1]

The MSS. vary also between εἴκοσι and εἴκοσιν, but the best are said to omit the ν, see Tisch. *Præf. ad N. T.* p. 23. [*Proleg.* p. 54, ed. 7] ; the matter is but seldom noticed in the apparatus. In A. xx. 15 most authorities have ἄντικρυς, not ἀντικρύ; on this see Lob. p. 444, Buttm. II. p. 366.

(c) In compounds whose first part ends in ς, Knapp—after Wolf (*Lit. Analect.* I. 460 sqq., comp. Krüg. p. 11)—introduced the practice of writing ς instead of σ, as ὥςπερ, ὅςτις, δύςκολος, εἰςφέρειν : he has been followed by Schulz and Fritzsche. Matthiæ's objections (§ 1. Rem. 5), however, deserve all attention ; and no value should be attached to this orthographical rule, especially as it has no historical basis. Schneider in Plato and Lachmann in the N. T. write ὥσπερ, εἰσακούειν, &c.; Hermann prefers ς. That ς would be inadmissible in such words as πρεσβύτερος, βλασφημεῖν, τελεσφορεῖν, is obvious.[2]

(d) Of more importance than all this is the peculiar spelling of certain words and classes of words, which is found in the MSS. of the N. T., and has been received into the text by Lachmann and Tischendorf in almost every case. This includes peculiarities of the Alexandrian orthography and pronunciation.

1. For ἕνεκα we sometimes find in the MSS. (and in *Rec.*) the properly Ionic form εἵνεκα or εἵνεκεν (Wolf, Dem. *Lept.* p. 388, Georgi, *Hier.* I. 182), as L. iv. 18, 2 C. iii. 10, vii. 12 ; and elsewhere ἕνεκεν, as Mt. xix. 29, Rom. viii. 36. The authority of good MSS. must

---

[1] [Before a vowel μέχρι occurs in L. xvi. 16 (Tisch., al.), μέχρις in Mk. xiii. 30, H. xii. 4 (G. iv. 19): before a cons. μέχρι is always used. In Tisch. (ed. 8) ἄχρι occurs fourteen times before a vowel, ἄχρις twice only : ἄχρις οὗ is much less common than ἄχρι οὗ. On these words see Lob. *Path. El.* II. 210.]

[2] [In ed. 8, Tisch. writes σ even at the end of a word. See further Lipsius, *Grammat. Untersuchungen über die bibl. Gräcität,* p. 122 (Leipz. 1863).]

alone decide here, comp. Poppo, *Cyrop.* p. xxxix and *Index* s. v. with Buttm. II. 369; for the N. T., at any rate, no rule can be laid down for the distinctive use¹ of the two forms.²

2. For ἐννενήκοντα, Mt. xviii. 12, 13, L. xv. 4, 7, we should rather write ἐνενήκοντα, in accordance with good MSS. of Greek authors and of the N. T. (e.g. D) and with the *Etym. Magn.*: see Buttm. I. 277, Bornem. Xen. *Anab.* p. 47 (Don. p. 144). Ἔνατος also—a form very common in Greek prose,³ and also found in the Rosetta inscription (line 4)—is supported by good MSS. in Mt. xx. 5, xxvii. 45, L. xxiii. 44, A. x. 30, al.: compare also Rinck, *Lucub.* p. 33. Ἔνατος was preferred by as early a critic as Bengel (*Appar. ad* Mt. xx. 5).⁴

3. The Ionic forms (Matth. 10. 1) τέσσερες, τεσσεράκοντα, are sometimes found in good MSS., especially A and C (e.g. in A. iv. 22, vii. 42, xiii. 18, Rev. xi. 2, xiii. 5, xiv. 1, xxi. 17), and have been received into the text by Lachmann and Tischendorf. The same forms often occur in MSS. of the LXX (Sturz p. 118). In these documents, however, α and ε are frequently interchanged; and such readings as ἐκαθερίσθη Mt. viii. 3, ἐκαθερίσθησαν L. xvii. 14, κεκαθερισμένους H. x. 2 (A), will hardly be preferred by any one.⁵

4. Βαλάντιον. In all the places in which this word occurs (L. x. 4, xii. 33, xxii. 35, 36) good MSS. have βαλλάντιον, and this form is received by Lachm. and Tischendorf. In MSS. of classical authors also we find the doubled λ, both in βαλλάντιον itself (Bornem. Xen. *Conv.* p. 100) and in its derivatives, and Bekker has received it in Plato; see however Dindorf, Aristoph. *Ran.* 772, Schneider, Plat. *Civ.* I. p. 75, III. p. 38.—Κράββατος is but seldom written with a single β, and then usually κράβατος.⁶

5. On ὑποπιάζω (ὑποπιέζω), a various reading for ὑπωπιάζω (from ὑπώπιον), L. xviii. 5, 1 C. ix. 27, see Lob. p. 461. It is probably no more than an error of transcription; for the more characteristic ὑπωπιάζω certainly proceeds from Paul, and has long stood in the text.—Whether we should write ἀνώγαιον or ἀνάγαιον can hardly be decided, the authorities for each being nearly equal: the former is

---

¹ Weber, *Demosth.* p. 403 sq. On this see also Bremi, *Exc.* vi. *ad Lysiam*, p. 443 sqq. (Jelf 10. *Obs.* 2.)

² [Ἕνεκα is found three times in *Rec.*, twice in Tischendorf's 7th edition, five times in his 8th: for εἵνεκεν see L. iv. 18, 2 C. iii. 10, L. xviii. 29, A. xxviii. 20. Elsewhere ἕνεκεν is the form used, before both vowels and consonants: εἵνεκα is not mentioned in Tischendorf's apparatus.]

³ See Schæf. *Melet.* p. 32; Schol. ad Apoll. *Argon.* 2. 788.

⁴ [Of both these forms Tisch. (*Proleg.* p. 49, ed. 7) says, "plenissimam ubique auctoritatem habent:" ἐνενήκοντα indeed has the support of all the uncial MSS.]

⁵ [Tisch. in ed. 7 received ἐκαθέρ. in Mt. viii. 3, Mk. i. 42, L. iv. 27, A. x. 15; in the first two passages he retains this reading in ed. 8. See his notes on L. iv. 27, A. x. 15. ℵ never has this form; B in these two places only.—Tisch. receives τεσσεράκ. (on very strong authority) and τέσσερα throughout, but never τέσσερις or τέσσερας. In ed. 7 he admitted the latter form in Rev. iv. 4, vii. 1.]

⁶ [In the N. T. κράβαττος is now generally received.]

derived from the adverb ἄνω, the latter from ἀνά (Fritz. *Mark*, p. 611); see also Lob. p. 297.¹

6. Πανοικί, A. xvi. 34 (comp. Plat. *Eryx.* 392 c, Æsch. *Dial.* 2. 1, Joseph. *Ant.* 4. 4. 4, 3 Macc. iii. 27), is the only word in the N. T. connected with the well-known dispute respecting the adverbial ending ι or ει: see Herm. Soph. *Aj.* p. 183, Sturz, *Opusc.* p. 229 sqq. Perhaps Blomfield (*Glossar. in* Æsch. *Prom.* p. 131 sq.) is right in adopting ι for such adverbs, when derived from nouns in ος,—hence πανοικί (properly πανοικοί, which is the reading of some MSS. in this passage).² Yet the MSS. are almost always in favour of ει; see Poppo, *Thuc.* II. i. 1540, Lob. p. 515.

7. Should we write Δαυίδ or Δαβίδ? See Gersdorf, *Sprachch.* p. 44, who leaves the question undecided, but is in favour of Δαβίδ. The abbreviation Δᾱ̄δ is the most common form in the MSS.: where however the word is written in full, the oldest and best MSS. have Δαυίδ (Δαυείδ), and this orthography—which was long ago preferred by Montfaucon (*Palæogr. Gr.* 5. 1)—has been received by Knapp, Schulz, Fritzsche, and Tischendorf. Lachm. always writes Δαυείδ. Compare further Bleek on H. iv. 7.³

8. The name Moses is written Μωϋσῆς in the best MSS. of the N. T., as in the LXX. and Josephus; and this form has been adopted by Knapp, Schulz, Lachm.,⁴ and Tischendorf. Still it may be a question whether this properly Coptic form, which is naturally found in the LXX, should not in the N. T. give place to Μωσῆς (Scholz), which comes nearer to the Hebrew and was at all events the more usual form, which also passed over to the Greeks (Strabo 16. 760 sq.) and Romans. On the diæresis in Μωϋσῆς, which Lachm. omits, see Fritz. *Rom.* II. 313.

9. As to Κολοσσαί and Κολασσαί see the commentators on Col. i. 1. The first of these forms is found not only on the coins of this town (Eckhel, *Doctr. numor. vett.* I. iii. 147), but also in the best MSS. of classical authors (comp. Xen. *Anab.* 1. 2. 6); hence Valckenaer (on Her. 7. 30) declared himself in favour of it. In the N. T., however, Κολασσαί is better attested, and is received by Lachm. and Tisch.: it probably represents the popular pronunciation.⁵

---

¹ [The evidence which is now before us is strongly in favour of ἀνάγαιον, which is received by most recent editors. Comp. Mullach, *Vulg.* p. 21.]

² [Compare Kühner, I. 726 (Jelf 342. 2). In A. xvi. Lachm. and Treg. write -κί; Tisch., Westc. and Hort, -κεί.]

³ [For a full statement of the MS. evidence see Tisch. on Mt. i. 1 (ed. 8). Δαυείδ is adopted by Tisch., Tregelles, Alford, Westcott and Hort; see Alford, Vol. I. *Proleg.* p. 95.]

⁴ [Except in Rom. ix. 15. Most of the best MSS. have μωσῆς occasionally, but the form with ϋ (or υ) seems now generally received. Fritz. writes ωϋ because the Coptic original is a trisyllable, and τωὐτό, ἑωυτοῦ, &c., are not really parallel: Tisch. (*Proleg.* p. 62, ed. 7) quotes MS. authority on the same side. See also Lipsius, p. 140.]

⁵ [We now know that in Col. i. 2 B has Κολοσσαῖς *a prima manu*, so that א and B agree in this form here. In the title and subscription there is considerable authority for Κολασσαῖς. See Tischendorf's note, and especially Lightfoot on *Colossians*, pp. 16–18.]

10. For ἐννεός, A. ix. 7, it is better to write ἐνεός (comp. ἄνεως), according to the best MSS.

11. The un-Attic form οὐθείς, οὐθέν, is found in the N. T. in a few good MSS. only, L. xxiii. 14, 1 C. xiii. 2, 3, 2 C. xi. 8, A. xv. 9, xix. 27 ; μηθέν A. xxiii. 14, xxvii. 33 : see Lob. p. 181 [and *Path. El.* II. 344]. It is also found in the LXX (Bornem. *Act.* p. 115), and on Greek papyrus rolls.

12. Ἐθύθη, 1 C. v. 7 (*Elz.*), for which all the better MSS. have ἐτύθη (Buttm. I. 78, Jelf 31), is unusual, but rests on an unexceptionable retention of the radical θ where there is no reduplication, like λιθωθῆναι, καθορθῆναι [? καθαρθῆναι] ; though both θύειν and θεῖναι, the only verbal stems that begin with θ and form a 1 aor., change the radical θ into τ in this tense (Lob. *Paral.* p. 45). The partic. θυθείς, formed on the same analogy, occurs Dio Cass. 45. 17 ; in Æsch. *Choeph.* 242 the editions have τυθείς. It is not unlikely that ἐθύθη was written by Paul, and displaced by the transcribers.

13. For χρεωφειλέτης, L. vii. 41, xvi. 5, the best MSS. have χρεοφειλέτης, a form which Zonaras rejects, and which is found only once in MSS. of Greek authors : see Lob. p. 691.

14. The aspirate for the tenuis in ἔφιδε A. iv. 29, and ἀφίδω Ph. ii. 23, is received by Lachm. on MS. authority. Other examples of a similar kind are ἐφ᾽ ἐλπίδι 1 C. ix. 10, ἀφελπίζοντες L. vi. 35, οὐχ ὄψεσθε L. xvii. 22, οὐχ Ἰουδαϊκῶς G. ii. 14, οὐχ ὀλίγος A. xii. 18, al. : comp. Bornem. *Act.* p. 24. Analogous forms are found in the LXX (Sturz, p. 127) and in Greek inscriptions (Böckh, *Inscript.* I. 301, II. 774), and are explained by the fact that many of these words (as ἐλπίς, ἰδεῖν) had been pronounced with the digamma.[1]

15. Πραΰς and πραΰτης are the best attested forms in the N. T., though Photius (*Lexic.* p. 386, Lips.) gives the preference to πρᾶος : see however Lob. p. 403 sq.[2]

16. Ἐχθές (not χθές, Lob. *Path.* I. 47) was introduced into the text by Lachm. from the best MSS.[3]

---

[1] [Amongst other instances may be mentioned ἐφ᾽ ἐλπίδι Rom. viii. 20, A. ii. 26, ἐφεῖδεν L. i. 25, οὐχ ἰδού A. ii. 7. In some instances (as Ph. ii. 23, G. ii. 14, A. ii. 7, 26, Rom. viii. 20) the aspirate is well supported : it is received more or less frequently by Lachm., Meyer, Alf., Ellic., Westcott and Hort, and Tisch. (esp. in ed. 7). Conversely, οὐκ is found before an aspirate in Jo. viii. 44, οὐκ ἕστηκεν (Tisch., but see below, p. 106) ; so also L. xxiv. 3, A. iii. 6, in ℵ and C. Similar examples are found in the MSS. of the LXX, as οὐκ ὑπάρχει Job xxxviii. 26, καθ᾽ ὀφθαλμούς Ez. xx. 14. (In Mt. v. 33, ℵ has ἐφιορκήσεις, and Mullach, *Vulg.* p. 22, quotes ἐφιορκοῦντι from *Marm. Oxon.* II. 1. 69. 78 : ἐλπίς also occurs in inscriptions.) See Tisch. *Proleg.* p. 52 (ed. 7), *N. T. Vatic.* p. xxviii, and *Proleg. ad LXX.* p. 33 ; A. Buttm. *Gr.* p. 7 ; Mullach, *Vulg.* pp. 22, 146 ; Don. p. 17 ; Scrivener, *Coll. of Cod. Sin.* p. lv ; Lightfoot on G. ii. 14, and Ph. ii. 20 ; and compare Scrivener, *Criticism*, p. 491, where it is maintained that such forms are mere mistakes of the scribe.]

[2] [Tisch. has πραΰς, πραΰτης, in every case ; Lachm. πραότης twice, G. vi. 1, E. iv. 2 : see Tisch. *Proleg.* p. 50 (ed. 7), Lipsius p. 7, A. Buttm. p. 26.]

[3] [a. The Attic ττ for σσ is found in but few words. Κρείττων is much more common than κρείσσων. Ἥττων occurs twice in *Rec.*, but the true reading is

SECT. V.] ORTHOGRAPHY AND ORTHOGRAPHICAL PRINCIPLES. 49

2. Whether such words as διὰ τί, ἵνα τί, διά γε, ἀλλά γε, ἀπ' ἄρτι, τοῦτ' ἔστι should be written as two words or one, can scarcely be decided on any general principle; and the remarkable variations in the better MSS. make the question of less importance. In most instances Knapp has preferred to unite the words; and certainly in expressions of frequent occurrence two small words do naturally coalesce in pronunciation, as is shown by the crases, διό, διότι, καθά, ὥστε,—also by μηκέτι, etc. Schulz maintains the opposite view: but would he write εἴ γε, τοι νῦν, οὐκ ἔτι, etc.? How much the MSS., on the average, are in favour of uniting the words, may be seen from Poppo, *Thuc.* I. p. 455. Schulz himself writes διαπαντός in Mk. v. 5, L. xxiv. 53; and Schneider in Plato almost always joins the words.

ἥσσων; of ἐλάττων both forms are used. The derivatives from these last have ττ, except in 2 C. xii. 13 (ἡσσώθητε).

b. ρρ, ρσ. Both ἄρρην and ἄρσην occur in *Rec.*, and in Rom. i. 27 Tisch. now reads ἄρρην three times; but ἄρσην is probably the true reading throughout the N. T. Θαρρεῖν occurs frequently, and θάρσει also (in the Gospels and Acts); πυρρός, Rev. vi. 4; θάρσος, A. xxviii. 15.

c. For Ματθαῖος recent editors write Μαθθαῖος (comp. Jelf 22. 3), see Mt. i. 15, L. iii. 24, 29, A. i. 23, 26. Compare Scrivener, *Critic.* p. 488 sq.

d. Ἰωάννης is most frequently written by Tregelles and by Westcott and Hort with a single ν (comp. Scrivener, *l.c.*): on γένημα, which is very well supported in Mt. xxvi. 29, Mk. xiv. 25, L. (xii. 18) xxii. 18, 2 C. ix. 10, see Tisch. *Proleg.* p. 48 (ed. 7).

e. The MSS. frequently vary between ια and εια in the terminations of nouns. Tischendorf and Westcott and Hort write μεθοδία, ἀλαζονία, μαγία, κυβία, ἀρσκία, Ἀτταλία, Καισαρία, etc.; and the latter editors uniformly adopt the forms ἀπειθία, ἐριθία, ὠφελία, ἐπιεικία, εἰδωλολατρία. A similar variation is found in other words (as δανίζω, δανιστής), especially in proper names and foreign words; sometimes it is very difficult to decide between ι and ει. See Tisch. *Proleg.* p. 51 (ed. 7), Alford I. *Proleg.* p. 96 sq.

f. The breathings are often interchanged in proper names and foreign words; thus Tisch. writes Ἡσαΐας, Ὡσηέ, ἠλεί, Ἑρμογένης, ὡσαννά, etc.:—ἅλυσις is in the N. T. written with the aspirate, ἁλοάω without. See Lipsius, *Gr. Unt.* p. 18 sqq.

g. Miscellaneous examples: ἀνάπειρος L. xiv. 13, 21, ἀχρεόω Rom. iii. 12, ζβεννύω 1 Th. v. 19 (Tisch. ed. 7, comp. Shilleto, Dem. *Fals. Leg.* p. 130), συκομορέα and -μωρέα L. xix. 4 (see Tisch. *in loc.*), νηφάλιος (not -λεος), στιβάς Mk. xi. 8. On νοσσός L. ii. 24, νοσσίον Mt. xxiii. 37, ἡ νοσσιά L. xiii. 34, see Sturz p. 183, Lidd. and Scott s.vv. For σφυρίς the collateral form σφυρίς is a constant *v.l.* in one or more of the most ancient MSS.; it is received by Lachm. in Mt. xvi. 10, Mk. viii. 8, and always by Westcott and Hort. There is good authority for ἐραυνάω Jo. v. 39, al., πρόϊμος Ja. v. 7, μισσάομαι Rev. xvi. 10, Στοϊκός A. xvii. 18, πατροand μητρολῴας 1 Tim. i. 9, σιρικόν Rev. xviii. 12; Lachmann reads ῥάκκος in Mk. ii. 21. On λεγιών, λεγεών, see Tisch. *Proleg.* p. 50 (ed. 7) and note on Mt. xxvi. 53 (ed. 8), Alford *l.c.* p. 96; on ἁλιεῖς, ἁλεεῖς, Tisch. *Proleg. l.c.*, note on Mk. i. 16 (ed. 8), Alford *l.c.* p. 94: Tisch. reads λεγιών and ἁλεεῖς in ed. 8. For an example of the extreme fluctuation of the MSS. in certain proper names see the note on "Nazareth" in Alford *l.c.* p. 97, Scrivener, *Critic.* p. 488. It should be added that editors frequently differ in regard to the use of the diæresis, especially in proper names: thus we find Γάϊος and Γαιος, Καϊάφας and Καιάφας, etc.]

Many inconveniences, however, might arise from adopting either mode exclusively; and as the oldest and best N. T. MSS. are written continuously, and therefore give us no help here, the most prudent plan would be regularly to unite the words in the N. T. text in the following cases :—

(*a*) Where the language supplies an obvious analogy; thus οὐκέτι as μηκέτι, τοιγάρ as τοίνυν, ὅστις compare ὅτου.

(*b*) Where one of the words is not in use uncombined (in prose); hence εἴπερ, καίπερ.

(*c*) Where an enclitic follows a word of one or two syllables, in combination with which it usually expresses a *single* notion, as εἴτε, εὔγε, ἄραγε; but not διάγε τὴν ἀναίδειαν, L. xi. 8 (Lachm. διά γε).

(*d*) Where the two modes of writing are used to express two different meanings: thus ὁστισοῦν *quicumque*, but ὅς τις οὖν Mt. xviii. 4, *quisquis igitur* (Buttm. I. 308); ἐξαυτῆς the adverb, and ἐξ αὐτῆς;—not to mention οὐδείς and οὐδ᾽ εἷς. In the MSS., however, the οὖν (of ὁστισοῦν, etc.) usually stands alone, and the writers themselves sometimes separate it by a conjunction from the word to which it belongs: see Jacobs, *Præf. ad* Ælian. *Anim.* p. 25. In detail much must be left to the editor's judgment; but there can hardly be any sufficient reason for writing διαπαντός or ὑπερεγώ (2 C. xi. 23, Lachm.), and the like. Still we must bear in mind that in the Greek of the N. T., so closely related to the ordinary spoken language, orthographical combinations would be especially natural.[1]

The neuter of the pronoun ὅστις was formerly written ὅ,τι (with the hypodiastole) in editions of the N. T., as L. x. 35, Jo. ii. 5, xiv. 13, 1 C. xvi. 2, al. Lachmann, after Bekker, introduced ὅ τι (as ὅς τις, ἥ τις).[2] Others, as Schneider (Plat. *Civ.* I. *Præf.* p. 48 sq.),[3] even think it unnecessary to separate the words. Much may be said in favour of writing the pronoun ὅτι as one word; *inter alia*, that then the reader is not influenced in favour of a particular interpretation of the text. It has indeed been doubted in many passages of the N. T., *e.g.* in Jo. viii. 25, A. ix. 27, 2 C. iii. 14, whether this word should be regarded as the pronoun or as the conjunction. When however this question has been once decided, it is safest to

---

[1] [See Lipsius, *Gr. Unt.* pp. 124–134, where this subject is more minutely examined: see also Lob. p. 48.]

[2] [Lachmann writes ὅστις, ἥτις and follows Bekker in ὅ τι only.]

[3] Comp. *Jen. Lit. Z.* 1809. IV. 174.

SECT. V.] ORTHOGRAPHY AND ORTHOGRAPHICAL PRINCIPLES. 51

write ὅ τι (with a space between) or ὅ,τι (with the hypodiastole) in the case of the pronoun.[1]

3. *Crasis*[2] is on the whole rare, and is confined to certain expressions of frequent occurrence: in these, however, it is found almost without variation. It is most common in κἀγώ, κἄν, κἀκεῖ, κἀκεῖθεν, κἀκεῖνος: we find also κἀμοί, L. i. 3, A. viii. 19, 1 C. iii. 1 [κἀγώ], xv. 8; κἀμέ, Jo. vii. 28, 1 C. xvi. 4; τοὐναντίον, 2 C. ii. 7, G. ii. 7, 1 P. iii. 9; and once τοὔνομα, Mt. xxvii. 57. On the other hand, we always find τὰ αὐτά in good MSS.: see L. vi. 23, xvii. 30, 1 Th. ii. 14.[3] Τουτέστι, καθά, καθάπερ, and the like, are only improperly termed examples of crasis.

Contraction is but seldom neglected in the ordinary cases; see §§ 8 and 9 on ὄστεα, χειλέων, νοΐ, and the like. In L. viii. 38 the best MSS. have ἐδέετο, a form often found in Xenophon: see *Irr. V.* s. v., Lob. p. 220 (Jelf 239. 3).[4] The verb καμμύειν exhibits a contraction of a peculiar kind: comp. Lob. p. 340.

There is good authority for καὶ ἐκεῖ, Mt. v. 23, xxviii. 10, Mk. i. 35, 38; καὶ ἐκεῖθεν Mk. x. 1; καὶ ἐκείνοις Mt. xx. 4; [καὶ ἐγώ L. xvi. 9], etc.

4. In the earlier editions of the N. T. the ι subscript was too frequently introduced:[5] this abuse was first censured by Knapp. The ι must certainly be rejected—

(*a*) In a crasis with καί, when the first syllable of the second word does not contain ι (as κᾆτα from καὶ εἶτα); thus κἀγώ, κἀμοί, κἀκεῖνος, κἄν, κἀκεῖ, κἀκεῖθεν, etc.: see Herm. *Vig.* p. 526, Buttm. I. 114 (Jelf 13). The ι subscript is however defended by Thiersch (*Gr.* § 38 Anm. 1), and Poppo has retained it in Thucydides after the best MSS. (*Thuc.* II. i. p. 149).

---

[1] [See Lipsius p. 118 sq.]
[2] Ahrens, *De Crasi et Aphæresi* (Stollberg, 1845).
[3] [In these passages some of the oldest MSS. have ταυτα, which *may* be ταὐτά. Lachm. reads ταὐτά in L. xvii. 30 and (*in marg.*) L. vi. 23, but the accentuated MSS. are against this.]
[4] Compare Fritz. *De Conf. crit.* p. 32. [Uncontracted forms from δέομαι are frequently found in *the MSS. of* Xenophon, but in most instances they have been altered by the editors: see Veitch, *Gr. Verbs,* p. 159. In regard to L. viii. it should rather be said that *some of* the best MSS. have ἐδέετο. A similar example is ἰχύετι, Rev. xvi. 1.]
[5] [On the practice of Biblical MSS. in regard to ι subscript and ascript see Lipsius p. 3, Scrivener, *Critic.* pp. 41 sq., 160.]

(b) In the 2 perf. [? 1 perf.] and 1 aor. act. of the verb αἴρω and its compounds: thus ἦρκεν Col. ii. 14, ἆραι Mt. xxiv. 17, ἆρον Mt. ix. 6, ἦραν Mt. xiv. 12, ἄρας 1 C. vi. 15, etc.: see Buttm. I. 413, 439, and Poppo, *Thuc.* II. i. p. 150.

(c) In the infinitives ζῆν, διψῆν, πεινῆν, χρῆσθαι,[1]—properly Doric, but also commonly used in Attic (Matth. 48. Rem. 2). Some ancient grammarians[2] (later than the commencement of our era) affirm that the same rule should be followed in the infin. of contracted verbs in άω, as ἀγαπᾶν, ὁρᾶν, τιμᾶν; probably because these forms are immediately derived from (the Doric) τιμάεν, κ.τ.λ., as μισθοῦν from μισθόεν: see Wolf in the *Lit. Analekt.* I. 419 sqq. (Don. p. 256, Jelf 239). Bengel inclined towards this orthography, and it has been defended and adopted by several scholars.[3] Buttmann (I. 490) and Matth. (197. b. 5) speak doubtfully; and many editors—*e.g.* Lobeck, see his *Technol.* p. 188—retain the ι. It has however been removed from the N. T. by Schulz, Lachm., and Tisch.; comp. E. v. 28, Rom. xiii. 8, Mk. viii. 32, Jo. xvi. 19.[4]

(d) There is nothing decisive in favour of πρᾷος (Lob. *Phryn.* p. 403, *Pathol.* I. 442); yet see Buttm. I. 255. Πρωΐ also, from πρό, should not have ι subscript: see on this word generally Buttmann, Plat. *Crito*, p. 43, *Lexil.* 17. 2.

(e) On πάντῃ, A. xxiv. 3, see Buttm. II. 360: the ι, which is rightly found in ἄλλῃ, ταύτῃ, which are real datives, should be omitted in πάντη, which has no corresponding nominative. The ancient grammarians, however, are of a different opinion (Lob. *Paral.* p. 56 sq.), and Lachmann writes πάντῃ. Κρυφῇ (E. v. 12), Dor. κρυφᾶ—comp. Xen. *Conv.* 5. 8,—and εἰκῇ (Buttm. II. 342) are now the received forms in the N. T.; comp. Poppo, *Thuc.* II. i. 150. Lachmann still writes λάθρᾳ, though λάθρα is probably more correct.[5]

---

[1] [The last of these has surely no place here.]
[2] Comp. Vig. p. 220; see also Gregor. Chœrobosc. *Dictata* (ed. Gaisford), vol. ii. p. 721. See on the other side Herm. *Vig.* p. 748.
[3] Reiz, *Lucian* iv. p. 393 sq. (ed. Bip.); Elmsley, Eurip. *Med.* v. 69, and *Præf. ad* Soph. *Œdip. R.* p. 9 sq.; Ellendt, Arrian *Al.* i. p. 14 sq.
[4] [A. Buttm. remarks (p. 44) that such forms as κατασκηνοῖν, Mt. xiii. 32, may lead us to prefer ἀγαπᾶν, etc., in the N. T. See also Lipsius p. 6.]
[5] Schneider, Plat. *Civ.* I. p. 61 *Præf.;* Ellendt, *Lex. Soph.* II. p. 3 sq. [Lachmann and Westcott and Hort insert ι in κρυφῇ, εἰκῇ, πανταχῇ, as well as in πάντη, λάθρα (comp. Don. pp. 25, 149, Cobet, *N. T. Vatic.* p. xii); Tregelles rejects the ι in κρυφῇ, εἰκῇ, λάθρα; Tisch. and Alford in all these words. No

(f) In Mt. xxvii. 4, 24, Lachm. and subsequent editors have written ἀθῷον (ἀθώϊον, Elmsley, Eurip. *Med.* 1267),[1] but contrary to all grammatical traditions : Lob. *Path.* I. 440,[2] [and II. 377].

After the example of Bekker and others, Lachmann in his larger edition dropped the breathings over ρρ, as useless ; but he has no followers.[3] That the Romans heard an aspiration with ρ in the middle (as at the beginning) of words, is shown by the orthography of *Pyrrhus, Tyrrhenus,* etc. (Buttm. I. 28). Still less can the initial ρ be written without the aspirate, as is done by many : see Rost, *Gr.* p. 13. (Don. p. 16.)

The Alexandrians had, as is generally admitted (Sturz p. 116 sqq.), a special orthography of their own. They not only interchanged letters—as αι and ει, ε and η, ι and ει (comp. εἰδέα Mt. xxviii. 3),[4] γ and κ,—but even added superfluous letters, to strengthen the forms of words, as ἐκχθές, βασιλέαν, νύκταν, φθάννειν, ἐκχυννόμενον, ἔσσπειρε, ἀναβαίννον, ἤλλατο (A. xiv. 10, vii. 26, comp. Poppo, *Thuc.* I. 210) ; and rejected others that were really necessary (when a consonant was doubled), as δυσεβής, σάβασι, ἀντάλαγμα, φύλα, ἐρύσατο, ἄραφος (Jo. xix. 23). They also disregarded the expedients by which the Greeks avoided a harsh concurrence of many or dissimilar consonants (Buttm. I. 75 sqq., Jelf 22) ; thus λήμψομαι, ἀναλημφθείς, (*Irr. V.* p. 162), προςωπολημψία, ἀπεκτάνκασι, ἐνχώριον, συνκάλυμμα, συνρητεῖν [? συνζητεῖν], συνπνίγειν, συνμαθητής, πένπει.[5] These peculiarities are found more or less uniformly both in good MSS. of the LXX. and N. T. (Tisch. *Præf. ad N. T.* p. 20 sq., ed. 2) which are said to have been written in Egypt—as A, B, C (ed. Tisch. p. 21), D

---

editor (I believe) omits ι in πεζῇ, δημοσίᾳ, ἰδίᾳ. Jelf (324. 2) writes *all* these adverbs without ι subscript, and Rost (p. 318) inclines to the same side : see also Kühner, I. 728 (ed. 2).]

[1] Comp. also Weber, *Dem.* p. 231, [who defends ἀθῷος ; Paley, Eurip. *Med.* 1300 ; Lipsius p. 8 sq. Treg. writes ἀθῶος.]

[2] There will be no disposition to introduce the forms ᾠόν (Wessel on Her. 2. 68) and ζῷον (recently received by Jacobs in Æl. *Anim.* on the authority of a good MS.)—still less σῴζειν—into the N. T. text. Comp. Lob. *Path.* I. p. 442, [and II. p. 378. No editor (apparently) receives σώζειν ; but Lachm. and Cobet write ζῷον, ᾠόν, and Tisch. ᾠόν. See Lipsius p. 8 sq., Cobet, *N. T. Vatic.* p. xii, and A. Buttmann's review of the last-named work in *Stud. u. Krit.* 1862 (1. Heft, p. 154) : on πρῷρα (Lachm. and others), see A. Buttm. *Gr.* p. 11, and Cobet *l.c.* Lachm. and Tisch. write Τρῳάς : Winer and others, Τρωάς. West. and Hort insert the ι in all these words, except σώζειν.]

[3] [Tisch. writes ρρ in the N. T. : he says, "ῥῥ prorsus invita cdd. auctoritate edi consuevit" (*Proleg.* p. 276, ed. 7). See also Lipsius, p. 7, Jelf 7, Cobet, *N. T. Vatic.* p. xcvi.]

[4] [Εἰδία is received by Tisch., Treg., Westcott and Hort : see Tisch. *Proleg.* (p. 49, ed. 7). Ἄραφος also, Jo. xix. 23, is found in almost all the ancient MSS.]

[5] [Conversely, such forms as ἐμμέσῳ, ἐγκανᾶ (ἐν μέσῳ, ἐν Κανᾶ), are found in some of the oldest MSS. (Tisch. *Proleg.* p. 48, ed. 7) and in inscriptions (Don. p. 58).]

of Gospels, D of Paul's Epistles (Tisch. *Proleg. ad Cod. Clarom.* p. 18), K of Gospels,[1]—and in Coptic and Græco-Coptic documents (Hug, *Introd.* § 50). We cannot therefore, with Planck,[2] reject them at once as due to the caprice of copyists, especially as analogies may often be adduced from the older dialects. At the same time, many are not specially Alexandrian, as they occur in MSS. of Greek authors and in inscriptions which cannot be proved to be of Egyptian origin (*e.g.* ει for ι, εγ for εκ,—with λήμψομαι compare the Ionic λάμψομαι, Matth. 242); and, on the other hand, many Egyptian documents are tolerably free from the peculiarities in question.

These forms have been introduced into the text by Lachm. and Tischendorf, on the concurrent testimony of good (but usually few) MSS., in Mt. xx. 10, xxi. 22, Mk. xii. 40, L. xx. 47, A. i. 2, 8, 11, 38,[3] Ja. i. 7, Mk. i. 27, 2 C. vii. 3, Ph. ii. 25, al.; sometimes without citation of authorities, Mt. xix. 29, Jo. xvi. 14, 1 C. iii. 14, Ph. iii. 12, Rom. vi. 8, al. Without more decisive reasons, however, than those assigned by Tischendorf[4] (*Præf. ad N. T.* p. 19), we surely ought not to attribute to Palestinian writers—especially John, Paul, and James —all the peculiarities of the Alexandrian dialect, and particularly of the Alexandrian orthography; and it is not probable that the N. T. writers would follow this orthography in comparatively few instances only.[5] Codex B, too, is not yet thoroughly collated in this respect. Tischendorf has introduced these forms less frequently than the words of his preface (p. 21) would have led us to expect.

Hence before this orthography is introduced into the N. T. text —if the MSS. are to be followed in such points even in editions of

---

[1] See Hug, *Introd.* I. § 50 sqq.; Scholz, *Curæ Crit. in hist. text. Evangg.* pp. 40, 61.

[2] *De orationis N. T. indole*, p. 25, note. [*Bibl. Cab.* vol. ii. p. 129.]

[3] [This is no doubt intended for A. ii. 38.]

[4] [It will be remembered that Winer is speaking in this paragraph of Tischendorf's *second* edition (1849).—Happily we now possess a trustworthy edition of Cod. B. Many details respecting its peculiarities of orthography (so far as these were known from Mai's edition) will be found in the preface to Kuenen and Cobet's *N. T. Vaticanum.*]

[5] In several words, as συλλαμβάνειν, συλλαλεῖν, συμβούλιον, συμπίπτειν, we find no example of this orthography; in others, as συλλέγειν, συγκαλεῖν, συσταυροῦν, ἐγκαλεῖν, it is noted only in isolated instances. [Συμπίπτειν occurs in the N. T. once only, in the form συνίπεσιν; and of the first three words the irregular forms are sometimes found, see Tisch. *Proleg.* p. 47 (ed. 7). There are some interesting observations on this subject in the above-mentioned article in the *Stud. u. Krit.* 1862 (p. 179 sqq.). The writer (A. Buttmann) maintains (1) that ἐν is almost always assimilated before labials, comparatively seldom before gutturals:—(2) that those compounds in which the writer appears to have simply annexed the prepos. to another word in adverbial fashion, each part of the compound preserving its proper meaning, do not assimilate the ν; whilst in those compounds which were in regular and current use, and in which the two parts are fused together so as to express a single new idea, assimilation does take place. Compare συνκληρονόμος, συνμαρτυρεῖν, and similar words, with συμφέρει, συμβάλλειν, etc. The subject however still needs careful investigation.]

SECT. VI.] ACCENTUATION. 55

the N. T. designed for common use—the whole subject must receive a new and complete examination. One question to be considered will be, whether these peculiarities of spelling, which have been supposed to represent the true popular pronunciation, do not rather belong to a system of orthography adopted by the learned, somewhat as we find in Roman inscriptions on stone [1] the etymological spelling *adferre, inlatus,* etc.[2]

SECTION VI.

ACCENTUATION.

1. The accentuation of the N. T. text is to be regulated not so much by the authority of the oldest accentuated MSS. as by the regular tradition of the grammarians. Many points, however, have been left in doubt, and in the careful investigations of later scholars a tendency to excessive refinement is sometimes observable. We may notice specially the following points:—

(*a*) According to the ancient grammarians (Mœris p. 193) ἰδε should be written ἰδέ in Attic Greek only, ἴδε in other (later) Greek; the same distinction being made as between λαβέ

---

[1] Schneider, *Lat. Gr.* I. ii. p. 530 sq., 543 sq., 566 sq., al.
[2] [It is now admitted by most that we must, in general, follow the most ancient MSS. in regard to peculiarities both of inflexion and of orthography. "For a long time it has been most strangely assumed that the linguistic forms preserved in the oldest MSS. are *Alexandrine* and not in the widest sense *Hellenistic*. . . . In the case of St. Paul, no less than in the case of Herodotus, the evidence of the earliest witnesses must be decisive as to dialectic forms. Egyptian scribes preserved the characteristics of other books, and there is no reason to suppose that they altered those of the N. T." (Westcott in Smith's *Dict. of the Bible,* II. p. 531.) The following quotation refers directly to inflexions, but is equally applicable to orthography: "Our practical inference from the whole discussion will be, *not* that Alexandrian inflexions should be invariably or even usually received into the text, as some recent editors have been inclined to do, but that they should be judged separately in every case on their merits and the support adduced on their behalf; and be held entitled to no other indulgence than that a lower degree of evidence will suffice for them than when the sense is affected, inasmuch as idiosyncrasies in spelling are of all others the most liable to be gradually and progressively modernised even by faithful and painstaking transcribers." (Scrivener, *Critic.* p. 490.) See Tisch. *Proleg.* p. 43 sqq. (ed. 7); Alford, vol. I. *Proleg.* p. 94 sqq.; Tregelles, *Printed Text,* p. 178; and (against Kuenen and Cobet, who without hesitation substitute the ordinary forms of words) A. Buttm. in *Stud. u. Krit. l.c.* Comp. also Mullach, *Vulg.* p. 21; Lightfoot, *Clement,* p. 26. On the other hand, many peculiarities called Alexandrian by Sturz and others are no doubt mere errors in spelling: see Scrivener, *Critic.* p. 10.]

and λάβε : see Weber, *Demosth.* p. 173, and comp. Buttm. I. 448. This rule has been followed by Griesbach (except in G. v. 2), and by Lachmann[, Tischendorf, and others] in every case. Bornemann suggested [1] that the word should be written ἰδέ when it is used as a true imperative and followed by an accusative (as in Rom. xi. 22), ἴδε when it is a mere exclamation. But it is preferable to follow the ancient grammarians.

(*b*) Numerals compounded with ἔτος, according to some ancient grammarians (Th. M. p. 859, Moschopul. *in Sched.*), are paroxytone when they are predicated of time, and oxytone in all other cases. According to this we should have τεσσαρακονταέτης χρόνος in A. vii. 23, τεσσαρακονταέτη χρόνον in A. xiii. 18; but in Rom. iv. 19, ἑκατονταετής.[2] In the MSS., however, this distinction is not observed, and the rule is altogether doubtful (see Lob. p. 406): Ammonius (p. 136) exactly reverses it, see Bremi on Æschin. *Ctesiph.* 369 (ed. Goth.).[3]

(*c*) **Κῆρυξ** and **φοίνιξ** are by some written κήρυξ and φοῖνιξ,[4] on the ground that, according to some ancient grammarians, the **υ** and **ι** in the nomin. sing. were pronounced short (Bekker, *Anecd.* III. 1429). This rule is rejected by Hermann (Soph. *Œd. R.* p. 145), as contrary to all analogy. It is a question, however, whether we should not for later Greek follow the grammarians, and write κῆρυξ, φοῖνιξ (see Buttm. I. 167): this Lachmann has done.[5]

(*d*) For πούς, which is found in most of the older editions of the N. T., Knapp introduced πούς, because the penult. of the genitive ποδός is short: see Lob. *Phryn.* p. 765, *Paral.* p. 93.

(*e*) Griesbach and others wrongly write λαίλαψ: it must be λαῖλαψ, since the *a* is short. Similarly, θλῖψις is adopted by Schulz (though not invariably) and by Lachmann, because the vowel in the first syllable is long by nature and not by position, just as in λῆψις: so also κλῖμα, κρῖμα, χρῖσμα, μῦγμα, ψῦχος (comp. Reisig, *De constr. antistr.* p. 20, Lob. *Paral.* p. 418),

---

[1] Rosenmüller, *Exeg. Repert.* II. 267.
[2] Comp. Jacobs, *Anthol.* III. pp. 251, 253.
[3] [Tischendorf accentuates on the penult. in every instance; Tregelles and Westcott and Hort on the last syllable.]
[4] See Schæfer, *Gnom.* p. 215 sq., and on Soph. *Philoct.* 562 : comp. Ellendt, *Lex. Soph.* I. 956 sq.
[5] [Tisch. now writes κήρυξ (following MS. authority), see his note on 1 Tim. ii. 7 (ed. 7); also φοίνιξ, Ps. xci. 13. See Lidd. and Scott, s. vv.]

στῦλος (Lidd. and Scott s. v.), (ῥῖψις and) ῥῖψαν L. iv. 35. It is however rightly remarked by Fritzsche (*Rom.* I. 107) that, as we know from ancient grammarians [1] that a penultimate which was long in Attic was often shortened in later Greek, it is not so certain that we are justified in introducing the Attic accentuation into the N.T.[2] No editor has changed the regular θρῆσκος into θρησκός, though the latter is found in some MSS.; see Bengel, *Appar. Crit.* Ja. i. 26.[3]

(*f*) As the termination αι is considered short in reference to accentuation (Buttm. I. 54, Jelf 46), we must write θυμιᾶσαι L. i. 9, and κηρῦξαι L. iv. 19, A. x. 42, for θυμιάσαι and κηρύξαι, as the words are still written by Knapp: comp. Poppo, *Thuc.* II. i. 151, Bornem. *Schol.* p. 4. ʽΕστᾶναι, A. xii. 14 (Griesb., Knapp), is wrong, as the *a* is short. In Mk. v. 4 συντετρῖφθαι is already placed in the text.

(*g*) In older editions (and in Knapp's) ἐριθεία is written ἐρίθεια: as the word is derived from ἐριθεύειν, it is necessarily paroxytone (Buttm. I. 141, II. 401, Jelf 55). But for the same reason we must write ἀρεσκεία: as the word is derived from ἀρεσκεύειν, not from ἀρέσκειν, ἀρέσκεια (Lachmann, and with him Tischendorf [in earlier editions]) is incorrect.

(*h*) Κτιστῇ, 1 P. iv. 19 (Knapp, Griesb.), has already been changed by Lachmann into κτίστῃ, in accordance with the very

---

[1] Lob. *Phryn.* p. 107: comp. Dindorf, *Præf. ad* Aristoph. *Acharn.* p. 15.

[2] [Lipsius (*Gr. Unt.* pp. 31-46) examines most of these words and many others of a similar kind which occur in the LXX, dividing them into two classes, as the α, ι, or υ, is or is not long by position. He shows that *in the N. T.* θλῖψις, μῖγμα, χρῖσμα, κηρῦξαι, are to be preferred. "Lobeck (*Paral.* p. 400 sqq.) proves that it is not always safe to infer the quantity of derivatives from that of the root, and collects passages from the old grammarians which teach that the doubtful vowels were shortened before double consonants, especially before σσ, ζ, ξ, ψ. It is also very conceivable that the pronunciation would vary at different periods, and that the natural quantity of the vowels might possibly be retained in older Attic, whilst in later Greek the tendency might be towards shortening the doubtful vowels where they were long by position." Lipsius also receives (for the N. T.) κρῖμα, λῖνον, σπῖλος, στῦλος. Tisch. writes θλῖψις, κρῖμα, λῖνον, ἑλκύσαι (Jo. xxi. 6), μῖγμα, χρῖσμα, σπῖλος, στῦλος, κηρῦξαι, ψῦχος, usually following MS. authority specified in his notes (in ed. 7). In all these words, and also in συντετρίφθαι (Mk. v. 4), Westcott and Hort reject the circumflex accent. For a good defence of κρῖμα (in later Greek) see Cobet, *N. T. Vatic.* p. xlix. sqq., see also Vaughan on Rom. ii. 2; on σπῖλος, see Ellicott on E. v. 27; on στῦλος, Lightfoot on G. ii. 9. The quantity of the υ in κύπτω is disputed, Buttmann giving ῡ (*Irr. V.* s. v.), Lobeck (*Paral.* p. 414) ῠ; but παρακύψαι, ἀνακύψαι, are generally received in the N. T. Treg. writes σκύλα L. xi. 22, and συντρίβον L. ix. 39; some editors still write κράζον G. iv. 6.]

[3] [Tischendorf writes θρησκός (see his note, ed. 7); also Westcott and Hort.]

clear analogy presented by γνώστης, κλάστης, κ.τ.λ. Schott and Wahl retain κτιστῇ, though the true accentuation was long ago advocated by Bengel (*Appar.* p. 442).

(*i*) On μισθωτός see Schæf. *Demosth.* II. 88. Φάγος, Mt. xi. 19, L. vii. 34, is paroxytone in the N. T.,—and not in the N. T. only, see Lob. *Phryn.* p. 434. Analogy would lead us to expect φαγός: see Lob. *Paral.* p. 135, where Fritzsche's opinion [1] (*Mark* p. 790) is rejected.

(*k*) That the 1 aor. imper. of εἰπεῖν (A. xxviii. 26) should be written εἶπον, not εἰπόν, is maintained by Lobeck (*Phryn.* p. 348) and Buttmann (*Exc.* 1. *ad.* Plat. *Menon.*); but the counter-arguments of Wex (*Jahrb. für Philol.* VI. 169) deserve consideration. The accentuation εἶπον can only be claimed for Attic Greek: in favour of εἰπόν in the Greek Bible we have the express testimony of Charax (see Buttmann *l.c.*), who calls this accentuation Syracusan.[2] Recent editors have adopted εἰπόν: see further Bornem. *Act.* p. 234 sq.

(*l*) Personal names which were originally oxytone adjectives or appellatives throw back the accent, for the sake of distinction.[3] Thus Τύχικος not Τυχικός, Ἐπαίνετος not Ἐπαινετός (Lob. *Paral.* p. 481), Φίλητος not Φιλητός (see Bengel, *App. Crit.* 2 Tim. ii. 17), Ἔραστος not Ἐραστός, Βλάστος not Βλαστός, Κάρπος not Καρπός, Σωσθένης (like Δημοσθένης), and Διοτρέφης 3 Jo. 9. Similarly Τίμων instead of Τιμῶν, Ὀνησίφορος for Ὀνησιφόρος, Εὐμένης for Εὐμενής. Ὑμέναιος, however, remains unaltered, as in general it is not customary to throw the accent forward in proper names; hence also the proparoxytones —as Τρόφιμος, Ἀσύγκριτος—retain their accent [4] (Lob. *l.c.*). Yet the forms first mentioned are sometimes found in old grammarians and in good MSS. (comp. Tisch. *Proleg. Cod. Clarom.* p. 22) with their original accent: comp. also Φιλητός, Euseb. *Hist. Eccl.* 6. 21. 2. The name Χριστός has never been

---

[1] [That the *adjective* is φαγός, the *substantive* φάγος. See Lipsius *l.c.* p. 28.]
[2] [Charax informs us that εἰπόν was a Syracusan form of the *second* aorist imperative, and so Winer considers it (p. 103). See Fritz. *Mark* p. 517, A. Buttm. *Gr.* p. 57: comp. Curtius, *Gr. Verb*, pp. 303, 450 (Trans.). Tisch. receives εἰπόν in Mt. xviii. 17, xxii. 17, Mk. xiii. 4, L. x. 40, xx. 2, xxii. 67, Jo. x. 24, A. xxviii. 26. See also Mt. iv. 3, xxiv. 3.]
[3] So also geographical names; see Nobbe, *Sch. Ptol.* II. 17 sq. (Lips. 1842).
[4] ["In this case proper names sometimes become oxytone, as Συντυχή Ph. iv. 2 (Tisch.):" Lipsius p. 31. Lünemann adds Πύρρος, Ἑρμογένης, to the former list; Εὔτυχος to this.]

SECT. VI.] ACCENTUATION. 59

brought under the rule.¹ See in general Reiz, *De inclin. acc.* p. 116, Schæfer, *Dion. H.* p. 265, Funkhänel, Demosth. *Androt.* p. 108 sq., and especially Lehrs, *De Aristarchi studiis Homer.* p. 276 sqq.

On a similar principle the adverbs ἐπέκεινα, ἐπίταδε, ὑπερέκεινα (from ἐπ' ἐκεῖνα, etc.), have undergone a change of accent.

(*m*) Indeclinable oriental names have the accent, as a rule, on the last syllable; compare however Ἰούδα, Θάμαρ, Ζοροβάβελ, Ἰωάθαμ, Ἐλεάζαρ, and the segholate forms Ἐλιέζερ L. iii. 29, Ἰεζάβελ Rev. ii. 20 (according to good MSS.), Μαθουσάλα L. iii. 37. This accent is usually the acute, even when the vowel is long: as Ἰσαάκ, Ἰσραήλ, Ἰακώβ, Γεννησάρ, Βηθσαϊδά, Βηθεσδά, Ἐμμαούς, Καφαρναούμ. On the other hand, the MSS. have Κανᾶ, Γεθσημανῆ (though Γεθσημανεῖ, which Lachm. and Tisch. prefer, has more authority, see Fritz. *Mark* p. 626), also Βηθφαγῆ: comp. also Νινευῆ.² Words which in the Greek Bible are indeclinable and oxytone have their accent drawn back in Josephus, who usually prefers inflected forms: e.g. Ἀβία, in the N. T. Ἀβιά.³ The oldest MSS. are said to have Πιλᾶτος, not Πιλάτος, as the word is written by most editors and by Lachmann⁴ (also by Cardwell in his edition of Joseph. *Bell. Jud.*): see Tisch. *Proleg.* p. 36 (ed. 2). Yet even recent editors write, on MS. authority, Κοριολάνος, Plutarch, *Coriol.* c. 11, Dion. H. 6. p. 414 (ed. Sylb.); Κικιννάτος, Dion. H. 10. p. 650; Τορκουάτος, Plut. *Fab. Max.* c. 9, Dio C. 34. c. 34; Κοδράτος (Quadratus), Joseph. *Ant.* 20. 6; Ὀνοράτος, etc. As to Τίτος and Τῖτος see Sintenis, Plut. *Vit.* II. 190: on Φῆλιξ (not Φήλιξ) see Bornem. *Act.* p. 198.⁵

The accentuation ὁμοῖος, ἐρῆμος, ἑτοῖμος, μῶρος (Boisson. *Anecd.* V. 94), which according to the grammarians (Greg. Cor. pp. 12,

---

¹ [This rule is usually followed. Lachm. and Tischendorf however write Τυχικός (A. xx. 4, al.), Φιλητός (2 Tim. ii. 17); Tischendorf, Ἐπαινετός (Rom. xvi. 5), Διοτρεφής (3 Jo. 9). The MS. authority for the change is given by Tisch. *ll. cc.* and by Lipsius p. 30. See also Tisch. *Proleg.* p. 61 (ed. 7).]
² [Tisch. reads Μαθουσαλά, Γεθσημανεί, Βηθφαγή: Νινευή (L. xi. 32) is no longer in his text.]
³ [Josephus in *Ant.* 6. 3. 2 has Ἀβία (indecl.) as the name of Samuel's son; but for Ἀβιά, Mt. i. 7, he has Ἀβίας, genit. Ἀβία.]
⁴ [In his smaller edition: in the larger he uniformly writes Πιλᾶτος. Tischendorf in ed. 7 has Πιλᾶτος (see note on Mt. xxvii. 13); in ed. 8, Πειλᾶτος.]
⁵ [On Τίτος see Lipsius p. 42: on Φῆλιξ see Tisch. on A. xxiv. 3, Lipsius p. 37; Lachm. writes Φήλιξ. With Τίτος comp. Λίνος, which Tisch. and others read in 2 Tim. iv. 21, for Λῖνος (*Rec.*, Alf.).]

20 sqq.) belongs to Ionic and early Attic Greek, and which e.g. Bekker follows, is certainly not to be introduced even into Attic prose,[1] still less into the N. T. On the other hand, we must invariably write ἴσος; comp. Bornem. *Luc.* p. 4, Fritz. *Mark* p. 649. The N. T. MSS. have uniformly ἔσω for εἴσω, though they have always εἰς, never ἐς; *vice versa*, Thucydides, who mostly uses ἐς, has εἴσω 1. 134; see Poppo, I. 212. Recent editors reject ἔσω in Attic prose.[2] As to ἀποκνεῖ or ἀποκνεί in Ja. i. 15, see below, § 15.

On the accentuation of the diminutive τεκνίον as a paroxytone see Buttm. II. 441 (Jelf 56); comp. τεχνίον Athen. 2. 55, though recent editors prefer τέχνιον both here and in Plat. *Rep.* 6. 495 d: of τεκνίον, τεκνία is the only part that occurs in the N. T.[3] Ποίμνιον (contracted from ποιμένιον) should certainly be preferred to ποιμνίον. On ἁδροτής, βραδυτής, as oxytones, see Buttm. II. 417: this, according to the grammarians, is the old accentuation, an exception to the rule. Lachmann however writes ἁδρότητι 2 C. viii. 20, but βραδυτῆτα 2 P. iii. 9.[4] In later Greek these words seem to have been paroxytone, according to rule; see Reiz, *De incl. acc.* p. 109.[5]

On οὔκουν and οὐκοῦν, ἄρα and ἆρα, see §§ 57 and 61.

2. It is well known that many words were distinguished from one another solely by difference of accent: thus εἰμί *sum* and εἶμι *eo* (μύριοι *ten thousand* and μυρίοι *innumerable*, Buttm. I. 278). In such cases the accentuated MSS. and even the editors of the N. T. sometimes waver between the two modes of accentuation. Thus for μένει, 1 C. iii. 14, the future μενεῖ is read by Chrys., Theod., the Vulgate, etc., and this reading has been received into the text by Knapp and Lachmann; comp. 1 C. v. 13, H. i. 11. For τινές, H. iii. 16, several authorities have τίνες, and recent critics have almost unanimously accepted this reading. In 1 C. xv. 8 Knapp needlessly changed the article τῷ into τῳ (=τινι), which is the reading of some MSS.: there is however but little authority for τῳ, and it is certainly a cor-

---

[1] Poppo, *Thuc.* I. 213, II. i. 150, Buttm. I. 55.
[2] Schneider, Plat. *Civ.* I. *Præf.* p. 53: as to the poets, see Elmsley, Eurip. *Med.* p. 84 sq. (Lips.).
[3] See Janson, in *Jahns Archiv* VII. 487; and on ποιμνίον ib. p. 507.
[4] [Similarly Tischendorf, Alford, and others.]
[5] [The following words also are variously accentuated by the N. T. editors: πρῶρα A. xxvii. 41, see above (p. 53); Εὕα 1 Tim. ii. 13 Lach., Tisch., Εὔα Ellic., Alf.; in Mt. xiii. 30 Tisch. has the less usual δεσμή (for δέσμη), see Lob. *Paral.* p. 396; Ἀλεξανδρινός A. xxvii. 6 Tisch. (following MS. authority), for -ῖνος; ἀπόδεκτος 1 Tim. ii. 3 Tisch., al., ἀπόδεκτός Ellic., Alf.; in L. viii. 26 the accentuated MSS. are divided between ἀντιπέρα (Lach., Treg.) and ἀντίπερα (Tisch., Westc.), see Lob. *Path.* II. 206; οὐᾶ Mk. xv. 29 Tisch., for οὐά; σύρτις A. xxvii. 17 Lachm., for σύρτις. Griesbach and others have μαργαρῖται Rev. xxi. 21, for -ῖται; ὀσφῦν E. vi. 14 (ὀσφύν).

rection introduced by those who took offence at the use of the article. There is as little reason for reading ἕν τῷ πράγματι in 1 Th. iv. 6. In 1 C. x. 19 several recent editors (Knapp and Meyer) read, ὅτι εἰδωλόθυτον τί ἐστιν, ἢ ὅτι εἴδωλον τί ἐστιν; on the ground that τι is here emphatic (the opposite of οὐδέν), and that an ambiguity is occasioned by the other reading, εἰδωλόθυτόν τι ἔστιν (Lachm.), since this might be rendered, " that any offering to an idol exists,"—that there is such a thing as an offering to an idol. But even if we grant that Meyer's is certainly the true interpretation, the ordinary accentuation need not be changed; for with it we may translate, " that an offering to an idol *is* anything,"—in *reality*, and not in appearance merely.[1] In Jo. vii. 34, 36, critics are still divided between ὅπου εἰμὶ ἐγώ, and ὅπου εἶμι ἐγώ (the reading of several Fathers and versions); and in A. xix. 38 almost all recent editions have ἀγόραιοι (an adjective, in the sense *judicial*) instead of ἀγοραῖοι. In regard to the former passage, John's ordinary usage (comp. xii. 26, xiv. 3, xvii. 24) is sufficient proof that εἰμί is to be preferred :[2] in the latter ἀγόραιοι is probably correct, if we follow Suidas, and in Ammon. p. 4 read (with Kulencamp), ἀγόραιος μὲν γάρ ἐστιν ἡ ἡμέρα, ἀγοραῖος δὲ ὁ Ἑρμῆς ὁ ἐπὶ τῆς ἀγορᾶς. Comp. Lob. *Paral.* p. 340.[3]

In Rom. i. 30 some write θεοστύγεις, maintaining that the word is here used in an active sense, and that θεοστυγεῖς is passive, *Deo exosi*. But the analogy of such adjectives as μητρόκτονος and μητροκτόνος (Buttm. II. 482, Jelf 50) proves nothing for adjectives in ης; and Suidas says expressly that θεοστυγεῖς means both οἱ ὑπὸ θεοῦ μισούμενοι and οἱ θεὸν μισοῦντες, though he distinguishes between θεομισής and θεομίσης in signification. Hence θεοστυγεῖς, which alone is according to analogy (compound adjectives in ης being oxytone), is the only correct form. As regards the sense, it would seem that the active meaning which Suidas gives to the word was

---

[1] [That is, the same meaning may be obtained from εἰδωλόθυτόν τι ἔστιν through the emphasis laid on ἔστιν, as from εἰδωλ. τί ἐστιν through the emphasis on τί: "is *anything* at all" is practically equivalent to "*is* (really) anything."]

[2] See Lücke *in loc.*, after Knapp, *Comm. Isagog.* p. 32 sq.

[3] [Tisch. *in loc.* (ed. 8) remarks that the MSS. do not support the distinction, and reads ἀγοραῖοι: so Westcott and Hort. See Lipsius, p. 26.]

not derived by him from Greek usage, but was assumed for this very passage. The word, it is true, does not often occur, but no instance has been found in which a Greek author has certainly used it in an active sense: see Fritz. *in loc.* There is however good ground for the distinction between τροχός *wheel*, Ja. iii. 6 (in the text and the accentuated MSS.), and τρόχος *course*, the reading adopted by Grotius, Hottinger, Schulthess, and others; see Schæf. *Soph.* II. 307. The figure τροχὸς γενέσεως (in conjunction with φλογίζουσα) is neither incorrect nor, in James, particularly strange; hence no change of accent is required.

The alterations of accent which have been proposed in other passages—as ὁμῶς for ὅμως in 1 C. xiv. 7, πρωτοτόκος for πρωτότοκος in Col. i. 15 (see Meyer), and even φωτῶν for φώτων in Ja. i. 17 (πατὴρ τῶν φ.)—originated either in dogmatic prepossessions or in ignorance of the language. The last is altogether absurd.

3. It is still a disputed question whether in prose (for to poetry peculiar considerations apply, comp. e.g. Ellendt, *Lex. Soph.* I. 476) the pronoun should be joined as an enclitic to a preposition, where no emphasis is intended; that is, whether we should write παρά σου, ἔν μοι, εἴς με, rather than παρὰ σοῦ, ἐν ἐμοί, κ.τ.λ. In the editions of the N. T. (Lachmann's included), as in those of Greek authors in general, we regularly find πρός με, πρός σε, but ἐν σοί, ἐν ἐμοί, ἐπὶ σέ, εἰς ἐμέ, ἐπ' ἐμέ, etc. It is only in the case of πρός με, σε, that variants are noted, the orthotoned pronouns being sometimes found (L. i. 43, A. xxii. 8, 13, xxiii. 22, xxiv. 19) in B and other MSS., mostly at the end of a sentence or clause: see Bornem. on A. xxiv. 19. Partly on the authority of ancient grammarians, and partly for the reason assigned by Hermann (*De em. gr. Græc.* p. 75 sq.), that in such combinations the pronoun is the principal word, one must be disposed to decide generally in favour of retaining the accent of the pronoun: πρός με, however, is defended by a portion of the grammarians, and is often found in MSS. See Buttm. I. 285 sq., Jacobs, *Anth. Pal.* I. *Præf.* p. 32, Matth. Eurip. *Or.* 384 and *Sprachl.* 29, Krüg. p. 82, also Ellendt, *Arrian* I. 199. Yet Reisig (*Conj. in Aristoph.* p. 56) and Bornemann (Xen. *Conv.* p. 163) maintain the other view; and it must be confessed that—besides the case of πρός με—the enclitic forms are often found in good MSS. of Greek authors. The accent must of

course be retained when the pronoun is emphatic: thus Knapp and Schulz correctly write τί πρὸς σέ in Jo. xxi. 22.¹

As regards the inclination of the accent, the ordinary rules of the grammarians are in general observed in editions of the N. T. Hence even Fritzsche still writes ὁ παῖς μου Mt. viii. 6, ἐξ ὑμῶν τινες Jo. vi. 64, ὑπό τινων L. ix. 7; not παῖς μοῦ, ἐξ ὑμῶν τινές, ὑπὸ τινῶν, which are defended by Hermann (*De emend. gr. Gr.* I. 71, 73). Lachmann² introduced the accent in the last two cases, and also wrote ποῦ ἔστιν Mt. ii. 2, μετ' αὐτῶν ἔστίν Mk. ii. 19, but left παῖς μου unchanged: he has been followed by Tisch. (ed. 2). Compare however the cautious opinion of Buttmann (I. 65 sq.).³

SECTION VII.

PUNCTUATION.⁴

1. In the editions of the N. T. down to that of Griesbach inclusive, the punctuation was not only wanting in consistency, but was also excessive. To make the meaning clearer editors introduced a profusion of stops, especially commas; and in doing this often intruded on the text *their own* interpretation of it.⁵ Knapp was the first who bestowed closer attention on the subject, and attempted to reduce it to fixed principles. Schulz, Lachmann, and Tischendorf (who usually agrees with Lachmann), have followed in the same track,⁶ but with still greater reserve: no one of these, however, has given a general exposition of his principles.⁷

---

¹ [Most editors of the N. T. write πρός με, σε, in ordinary cases. In Tischendorf's 7th ed. we find regularly πρὸς μέ, σέ; but in ed. 8 he retains the accent of the pronoun (in this case) only when the pronoun is emphatic (as Mt. iii. 14). See further Lipsius pp. 59-67, Jelf 64, Don. p. 44.]

² Yet Lachm. writes ἐπί τινων A. xxvii. 44, ἐάν τινων Jo. xx. 23.

³ [This subject is examined by Lipsius in detail, as regards the usage of the LXX and the N. T. The principal departure from the ordinary rules is in the case of two enclitics, the first of which has one syllable, the second two; here, in editions of the LXX and the N. T., the second enclitic almost always retains its accent, as ἰσχυρότερός μου ἐστίν. Tischendorf usually follows this rule. He also writes (on MS. authority) ἥψατό μου τίς, not ἥψ. μού τις, and (once, Mk. xiv. 14) ποῦ ἐστίν. See his *Proleg.* p. 62 (ed. 7). Lipsius pp. 49-59, Jelf 64, Don. p. 43 sq. On "interpunctio cum enclisi conjuncta," see Lobeck, *Path.* II. 321-332, Lipsius p. 55 sq.]

⁴ Comp. especially Poppo in the *Allg. Lit. Zeit.* 1826, I. 506 sqq., and Matth. 59.

⁵ Comp. also Buttm. I. 68, Schleierm. *Hermen.* p. 76.

⁶ Among editors of Greek authors, I. Bekker has begun to punctuate with greater moderation and consistency, W. Dindorf with still more reserve: both however seem to carry the exclusion of the comma too far.

⁷ Rinck has proposed (*Stud. u. Krit.* 1842, p. 554 sq.) that in punctuation

There is a scientific necessity for punctuation, since any representation of oral discourse would manifestly be incomplete without it. It was however originally devised for a practical purpose—to aid the reader, especially in reading aloud, by marking the various pauses for the voice. And such its main object must still be,—to enable the reader to perceive at once what words are to be connected together, and, so far, to guide him to the correct perception of the meaning.[1] Punctuation must therefore be founded on an examination of the logical, or rather (since the thought is already clothed in language) of the grammatical and rhetorical relations of the words to one another. Hence it would be asking too much to require that an editor should *in no degree whatever* indicate his own interpretation of the passage by the punctuation, since he has to insert not merely commas but also the colon and the note of interrogation.

With respect to the proper use of the colon or of the full stop in the N. T. text there can scarcely be any doubt. Lachmann and Tischendorf[2] indeed have dropped the colon before a direct quotation, preferring to indicate the commencement of the quotation by a capital letter; but we can see no sufficient reason for this innovation.

There is much less uniformity in the use of the comma. So much as this is clear—that only a sentence which is itself grammatically complete,[3] and which also stands in close connexion with another sentence, should be marked off by a comma; and that the comma was, strictly speaking, invented for this purpose. But a grammatically complete sentence comprehends not merely subject, predicate, and copula (each of which three elements may be either expressed or understood), but also all qualifying words which are introduced into the sentence to define

---

we should return to the principles of the ancient Greek grammarians (Villoison, *Anecd.* II. 138 sqq.). This however would be hardly practicable.

[1] Buttmann, *loc. cit.*

[2] [In his 8th ed. Tisch. has returned to the old practice.]

[3] The grammatical sentence will, as a rule, coincide with the logical, but not always. In L. xii. 17, Jo. vi. 29 (see p. 65), for example, there are logically two sentences, but by means of the relative the second is incorporated in the first, so that the two form grammatically one whole. This is the case in every instance of breviloquence, where two sentences are contracted into one. Also in 1 Tim. vi. 3, εἴ τις ἑτεροδιδασκαλεῖ καὶ μὴ προσέρχεται ὑγιαίνουσι λόγοις, we have two logical propositions, but in this construction the two form one grammatical sentence: see below, p. 66.

these main elements more precisely, and without which the sense would be imperfect. Hence Griesbach, for instance, was wrong in separating the verb from its subject by a comma whenever the subject was accompanied by a participle, or consisted of a participle with its adjuncts; as in Mk. vii. 8, x. 49, Rom. viii. 5, 1 Jo. ii. 4, iii. 15. The comma is also wrongly inserted in 1 Th. iv. 9, περὶ δὲ τῆς φιλαδελφίας, οὐ χρείαν ἔχετε γράφειν ὑμῖν· Mt. vi. 16, μὴ γίνεσθε, ὥςπερ οἱ ὑποκριταί (for μὴ γίν. by itself gives no sense at all), Mt. v. 32, ὃς ἂν ἀπολύσῃ τὴν γυναῖκα αὐτοῦ, παρεκτὸς λόγου πορνείας (the last words contain the most essential part of the statement), Mt. xxii. 3, καὶ ἀπέστειλε τοὺς δούλους αὐτοῦ, καλέσαι τοὺς κεκλημένους· 1 Th. iii. 9, τίνα γὰρ εὐχαριστίαν δυνάμεθα τῷ θεῷ ἀνταποδοῦναι περὶ ὑμῶν, ἐπὶ πάσῃ τῇ χαρᾷ· 1 C. vii. 1, καλὸν ἀνθρώπῳ, γυναικὸς μὴ ἅπτεσθαι· A. v. 2 [?], καὶ ἐνοσφίσατο ἀπὸ τῆς τιμῆς, συνειδυίης καὶ τῆς γυναικός. But the notion of a complete sentence is still more comprehensive. Even a relative clause must be considered a part of the preceding sentence, when the relative (whether pronoun or adverb) includes the demonstrative, as Jo. vi. 29, ἵνα πιστεύσητε εἰς ὃν ἀπέστειλεν ἐκεῖνος· Mt. xxiv. 44, ᾗ οὐ δοκεῖτε ὥρᾳ ὁ υἱὸς τοῦ ἀνθρώπου ἔρχεται· L. xii. 17, ὅτι οὐκ ἔχω ποῦ συνάξω τοὺς καρπούς μου; or when there is an attraction of the relative, as L. ii. 20, ἐπὶ πᾶσιν οἷς ἤκουσαν;[1] or when the relative clause is so necessary a complement to the antecedent that the sense is not complete unless both are taken together, as L. xii. 8, πᾶς ὃς ἂν ὁμολογήσῃ· Mt. xiii. 44, πάντα ὅσα ἔχει; or when the preposition is not repeated before the relative, as A. xiii. 39, ἀπὸ πάντων ὧν οὐκ ἠδυνήθητε κ.τ.λ., L. i. 25.[2] Also when the subject, the predicate, or the copula of a sentence is composed of several words joined by καί (or οὐδέ), we must take all these words together, and regard them as one whole grammatically, though, logically considered, there are really several sentences: Mk. xiv. 22, λαβὼν ὁ Ἰησοῦς ἄρτον εὐλογήσας ἔκλασε καὶ ἔδωκεν αὐτοῖς· Jo. vi. 24, Ἰησοῦς οὐκ ἔστιν ἐκεῖ οὐδὲ οἱ μαθηταὶ αὐτοῦ· Mt. xiii. 6, ἡλίου ἀνατείλαντος ἐκαυματίσθη καὶ διὰ τὸ μὴ ἔχειν ῥίζαν ἐξηράνθη (so Lachm. correctly), 1 Tim. vi. 3, Mt. vi. 26.—(The case is

---

[1] Compare Schæf. *Demosth.* II. 657.
[2] It would be going too far to omit the comma before *every* relative sentence, as is done by Bekker, for instance, in his edition of Plato.

different in Mk. xiv. 27, πατάξω τὸν ποιμένα, καὶ διασκορπισθήσεται τὰ πρόβατα· Mt. vii. 7, αἰτεῖτε, καὶ δοθήσεται ὑμῖν : here two complete sentences are connected by καί, and therefore the comma cannot be omitted. When ἤ separates two sentences, the comma is always required before it.)

The comma must also be omitted between such sentences as σὺ μόνος παροικεῖς Ἰερουσ. καὶ οὐκ ἔγνως κ.τ.λ. (L. xxiv. 18), because they are so closely connected that they must be read without a pause, and only when thus joined together convey the proper sense. In Mk. xv. 25 also we must write ἦν ὥρα τρίτη καὶ ἐσταύρωσαν αὐτόν, and in Mt. viii. 8, οὐκ εἰμὶ ἱκανὸς ἵνα μου ὑπὸ τὴν στέγην εἰςέλθῃς, without any break. Lastly, the comma may be omitted before ἀλλά when the following sentence is incomplete, and therefore has its roots, so to speak, in what has gone before : thus Rom. viii. 9, ὑμεῖς δὲ οὐκ ἐστὲ ἐν σαρκὶ ἀλλ᾽ ἐν πνεύματι· and in ver. 4, τοῖς μὴ κατὰ σάρκα περιπατοῦσιν ἀλλὰ κατὰ πνεῦμα (here Fritzsche retains the comma).

2. On the other hand, we must not bring too much into a sentence grammatically complete, and thus omit commas when they are really necessary.

(*a*) The vocative is never a constituent part of the sentence with which it is connected, but it is to be regarded as a sort of announcement of it ; especially when the verb of the sentence is in the 1st or 3rd person. Hence the comma is required in Jo. ix. 2, ῥαββί, τίς ἥμαρτεν· Mk. xiv. 36, ἀββᾶ ὁ πατήρ, πάντα δυνατά σοι· 2 P. iii. 1, L. xv. 18, xviii. 11, al.

(*b*) A comma is correctly inserted after a word which is the subject both of a sentence immediately following it and beginning with a conjunction, and also of the principal sentence ; as Jo. vii. 31, ὁ Χριστός, ὅταν ἔλθῃ, . . . ποιήσει. Lachmann's practice is different.

(*c*) If a grammatically complete sentence is followed by a supplementary statement, which might properly form a sentence of itself, the two must be separated by a comma : thus Rom. xii. 1, παρακαλῶ ὑμᾶς παραστῆσαι τὰ σώματα ὑ. θ. ζ. . . . τῷ θεῷ, τὴν λογικὴν λατρείαν (that is, ἥτις ἐστὶν ἡ λογ. λατ.), 1 Tim. ii. 6, ὁ δοὺς ἑαυτὸν ἀντίλυτρον ὑπὲρ πάντων, τὸ μαρτύριον καιροῖς ἰδίοις. So also in the case of participles, &c. : Col. ii. 2, ἵνα παρακλ. αἱ καρδίαι αὐτῶν, συμβιβασθέντες ἐν ἀγάπῃ· Jo. ix. 13, ἄγουσιν αὐτὸν πρὸς τοὺς φαρισαίους, τόν ποτε τυφλόν· Rom. viii. 4, ἵνα τὸ δικαίωμα τοῦ νόμου πληρωθῇ ἐν ἡμῖν, τοῖς μὴ κατὰ σάρκα περιπατοῦσιν· ver. 20, E. i. 12.

(d) If a twofold construction is used in what is (logically) a single sentence,—as when an anacoluthon occurs,—the parts must be separated by a comma in writing, and in reading by a pause; as in Jo. xv. 2, πᾶν κλῆμα ἐν ἐμοὶ μὴ φέρον καρπόν, αἴρει αὐτό. By the addition of αὐτό the words πᾶν κλ. . . . καρπόν become a *casus pendens*, which is merely placed in front of the sentence; and hence no one would read the words without a pause. Similarly in Rev. iii. 12, ὁ νικῶν, ποιήσω αὐτὸν στύλον κ.τ.λ., H. ix. 23,[1] ἀνάγκη τὰ μὲν ὑποδείγματα τῶν ἐν τοῖς οὐρανοῖς, τούτοις καθαρίζεσθαι. It is obvious that, when complete sentences are introduced, they must be marked off by commas from the principal sentence, as L. ix. 28, A. v. 7, al. [see § 62. 2.]

(e) If in a sentence several words which stand in the same relation are joined to one another ἀσυνδέτως (without καί), or merely enumerated in succession, they must be separated from one another by commas : 1 P. v. 10, αὐτὸς καταρτίσει, στηρίξει, σθενώσει, θεμελιώσει· L. xiii. 14, ἀποκριθεὶς δὲ ὁ ἀρχισυνάγωγος, ἀγανακτῶν ὅτι . . . ὁ Ἰησοῦς, ἔλεγε.

If the use of the comma in all these cases is correct, one might wish that we had a subordinate stop—a half comma—that those words in a continuous grammatical sentence which a reader is in danger of connecting together, though they certainly do not form (so to speak) one grammatical group, might be exhibited to the eye as unconnected. Thus in L. xvi. 10, ὁ πιστὸς ἐν ἐλαχίστῳ καὶ ἐν πολλῷ πιστός ἐστι, any reader may go wrong, because καί naturally leads him to expect a second word parallel to πιστὸς ἐν ἐλαχίστῳ. The same may be said of the following passages : Rom. iv. 14, εἰ γὰρ οἱ ἐκ νόμου κληρονόμοι· Ja. v. 12, ἤτω δὲ ὑμῶν τὸ ναὶ ναὶ καὶ τὸ οὒ οὒ· 1 C. xv. 47, ὁ πρῶτος ἄνθρωπος ἐκ γῆς χοϊκός· H. v. 12, ὀφείλοντες εἶναι διδάσκαλοι διὰ τὸν χρόνον πάλιν χρείαν ἔχετε τοῦ διδάσκειν ὑμᾶς· Jo. v. 5, ἦν τις ἄνθρωπος ἐκεῖ τριάκοντα καὶ ὀκτὼ ἔτη ἔχων ἐν τῇ ἀσθενείᾳ· Rom. iii. 9, τί οὖν; προεχόμεθα; οὐ πάντως (οὐ, πάντως). A half comma would make all clear. As however no such stop exists, we might employ in its stead an ordinary comma, just as it is used in writing and print to distinguish ὅ,τι from ὅτι. But recent editors use no stop at all in such cases, and this is perhaps the most prudent course.[2]

---

[1] [This is probably misplaced, and should come in below, with Rom. iv. 14, etc.]
[2] [Lipsius (pp. 83-108) gives a detailed analysis of Lachmann's system of

3. It is in many respects desirable that an editor's view of a passage should not be introduced into the text by means of punctuation. This is easily avoided in cases where it is not necessary to punctuate at all, as in Rom. i. 17, vii. 21, Mt. xi. 11. There are passages, however, where a stop—full stop, colon, comma, or note of interrogation—is absolutely necessary, and yet cannot be introduced without the adoption of some particular interpretation. In Jo. vii. 21, 22, for instance, every editor must decide whether he will write, Ἐν ἔργον ἐποίησα καὶ πάντες θαυμάζετε· διὰ τοῦτο Μωσῆς δέδωκεν ὑμῖν περιτομήν κ.τ.λ. (with Chrysostom, Cyril, Euthymius Zigabenus, al.), or Ἐν ἔργον ... θαυμάζετε διὰ τοῦτο. Μωσῆς κ.τ.λ., with Theophylact and nearly all modern editors and commentators. The former punctuation might still be defended (not indeed on the ground that, as Schulz has shown, διὰ τοῦτο in John usually begins, but never ends a sentence,—but) if the connexion were understood thus: " I have done one work and ye all wonder : therefore (be it known to you) Moses has given you etc." That is : " I will put an end to your wonder : you yourselves perform circumcision on the Sabbath according to the law of Moses. If then this ceremony, which immediately affects only one part of the body, is not a violation of the Sabbath, surely the work of healing, which extends to the whole man, is also allowed." I confess, however, that (as also Lücke has shown) the explanation of the passage is far simpler if the ordinary punctuation is retained.[1] Heb. xi. 1 might be punctuated, ἔστι δὲ πίστις, ἐλπιζομένων ὑπόστασις κ.τ.λ. : the emphasis would thus fall on ἔστι, and the existence of πίστις of such a kind as the words in apposition describe would be indicated as an historical fact. I now think, however, that it is more appropriate to omit the comma, so that the words contain a definition of faith,—the accuracy of which definition is illustrated by the

---

punctuation, marking instances in which Tischendorf's practice is different. In his 7th ed. Tisch. punctuates more sparingly than before : " quod raritati studebamus, id eam commendationem habet, quod quo antiquiores cdd. sunt, eo rarior interpunctio est." (*Proleg.* p. 62.) On the traces of punctuation in the older MSS., see Lipsius pp. 67–76.]

[1] [Of recent commentators, Luthardt, Meyer, and Alford join διὰ τοῦτο to ver. 22, but do not assume an ellipsis. On the other side, the English reader may be referred to Stier, *Words of the Lord Jesus*, V. 259 ; Olshausen, *Comm.* III. 480, and the notes of Tholuck, Hengstenberg, and Wordsworth. Tisch. (ed. 8) omits διὰ τοῦτο, on very slender authority. Westcott and Hort join the words to ver. 22. See Westcott's note *in loc.*]

historical examples that follow: see Bleek *in loc.* In punctuating Jo. xiv. 30, 31, commentators vary between ἐν ἐμοὶ οὐκ ἔχει οὐδέν, ἀλλ' ἵνα ... ποιῶ. ἐγείρεσθε κ.τ.λ., and οὐδέν· ἀλλ' ἵνα ... ποιῶ, ἐγείρεσθε κ.τ.λ. It is impossible to avoid variations of this kind, if the N. T. text is punctuated at all. Compare further Rom. iii. 9, v. 16, vi. 21, viii. 33, ix. 5, xi. 31, 1 C. i. 13, vi. 4, xvi. 3, A. v. 35 (see Kühnöl), H. iii. 2, Ja. ii. 1, 4, 18, v. 3, 4.

The same reluctance to engage the reader in favour of any particular interpretation of the text is probably the main cause which has led to the entire disuse of the parenthesis (once so much abused) on the part of some recent editors, e.g. Tischendorf. It was retained by Lachmann. See below, § 62.

SECTION VIII.

UNUSUAL FORMS IN THE FIRST AND SECOND DECLENSIONS.

1. Masculine proper names in ᾶς of the 1st decl.—mostly oriental, but formed in accordance with a familiar Greek analogy—always make the genit. sing. in ᾶ: Ἰωαννᾶ L. iii. 27, Ἰωνᾶ Mt. xii. 39, Jo. i. 43, al., Κλωπᾶ Jo. xix. 25, Στεφανᾶ 1 C. i. 16, xvi. 15, Σκευᾶ A. xix. 14, Κηφᾶ 1 C. i. 12, Σατανᾶ Mk. i. 13, 2 Th. ii. 9, Ἐπαφρᾶ Col. i. 7 :[1] [comp. μαμωνᾶ L. xvi. 9].

Those also which end in unaccented ας make the genitive in α; as Καϊάφα Jo. xviii. 13, Ἄννα L. iii. 2, Ἀρέτα 2 C. xi. 32 (Joseph. *Ant.* 17. 3. 2, 18. 5. 1), Βαρνάβα G. ii. 1, Col. iv. 10, Ἀγρίππα[2] A. xxv. 23, comp. Joseph. *Ant.* 16. 2. 3, 16. 6. 7, 20. 7. 1, al. (Σίλα Joseph. *Vit.* 17, Ματθεία *Act. Apocr.* p. 133), Ἰούδα often.—The same forms are not unfrequently used by Attic writers in proper names; as Μασκᾶ Xen. *An.* 1. 5. 4, Γωβρύα Xen. *Cyr.* 5. 2. 14, Κομάτα Theocr. 5. 150, al.: comp. Krüg. p. 42[3] (Jelf 79, Don. p. 89), and on Βορρᾶ (L. xiii. 29, Rev. xxi. 13), in particular, Buttm. I. 147, 199, Bekker, *Anecd.* III. 1186.

---

[1] So Θωμᾶ in *Act. Thom.*, Λουκᾶ Euseb. *H. E.* 3. 24, Ἑρμᾶ *ib.* 3. 3.
[2] On the other hand, we find Ἀγρίππου occasionally in Josephus (*Ant.* 18. 7. 1 and 2, 18. 8. 8, al.) and Euseb. *H. E.* 2. 19. In the same way the MSS. of Xenophon vary between Γωβρύου and Γωβρύα.
[3] Georgi, *Hier.* I. 156, Ellendt on Arrian, *Al.* I. 83, V. Fritzsche, *Aristoph.* I. 566.

The genitive of nouns in ας pure ends in ου in the N. T., as usually in Attic writers (e.g. Αἰνείας);[1] as Ἀνδρέας Mk. i. 29, Jo. i. 45 (Joseph. *Ant.* 12. 2. 3, *Act. Apocr.* pp. 158, 159), Ἠλίας L. i. 17 [?], iv. 25, Ἡσαίας Mt. iii. 3, xiii. 14, A. xxviii. 25, al., Ἱερεμίας Mt. ii. 17, xxvii. 9, Ζαχαρίας Mt. xxiii. 35, L. i. 40, al., Λυσανίας L. iii. 1, Βαραχίας Mt. xxiii. 35. Similarly Ὀνί-ας -ου (so always in Josephus), Τωβί-ας -ου, Geo. Syncell. *Chronogr.* p. 164, though the usual genitive is Τωβία.[2]

Several names of places that might be declined as nouns of the 1st decl. are in the N. T. indeclinable: as Κανᾶ (dat. Jo. ii. 1, 11, accus. Jo. iv. 46), Βηθσαϊδά, Βηθφαγή, Γολγοθᾶ, Ῥαμᾶ.[3] Βηθαβαρᾶ, Jo. i. 28, must not be classed with these, for Origen treats it as a neuter plural: in this passage recent editors read ἐν Βηθανίᾳ. Λύδδα is certainly inflected as a fem. sing. in A. ix. 38 (Λύδδης); but in verses 32, 35, we find Λύδδα as a neut. accus. in good MSS.[4]

The compounds in αρχος[5] usually exchange this ending for αρχης (of the 1st decl.) in the N. T. and in later Greek:[6] as πατριάρχης H. vii. 4, plur. A. vii. 8, 9 (1 Chr. xxvii. 22); τετράρχης Mt. xiv. 1, L. iii. 19, ix. 7 (Joseph. *Ant.* 18. 7. 1, τετράρχαι Euseb. *H. E.* 1. 7. 4); πολιτάρχης A. xvii. 6; ἐθνάρχης 2 C. xi. 32 (1 Macc. xiv. 47, ἐθνάρχῃ 1 Macc. xv. 1, 2, ἐθνάρχην Joseph. *Ant.* 17. 11. 4, ἐθνάρχας Eus. *Const.* 1. 8); from ἀσιάρχης, ἀσιαρχῶν A. xix. 31 (ἀσιάρχην Euseb. *H. E.* 4. 15. 11, Asiarcha, *Cod. Theodos.* 15. 92); ἑκατοντάρχης A. x. 1, 22, xxi. 32, xxii. 26 (Joseph. *B. J.* 3. 6. 2), ἑκατοντάρχῃ A. xxiv. 23, xxvii. 31, Mt. viii. 13,—where however a few MSS. have

---

[1] Lobeck, *Proleg. Pathol.* p. 487 sqq.
[2] See in general Georg. Choerobosci *Dict. in Theod. Can.* (ed. Gaisf.), I. 42.
[3] [Βηθσαϊδάν may be the accus. of -δά in Mk. vi. 45, viii. 22, but is vocative in Mt. xi. 21. In Mt. xxvii. 33 we find εἰς Γολγοθά, but in Mk. xv. 22 (probably) ἐπὶ Γολγοθάν.]
[4] See Winer, *RWB.* II. 30. ["Λύδδα is feminine in 1 Macc. and in Pliny: Josephus uses both modes of inflexion." *RWB. l.c.* In A. ix. 38 we must read Λύδδας.—Compare Γομόρρων Mt. x. 15 (Gen. xiii. 10), Γομόρρας 2 P. ii. 6 (Gen. xiv. 2); Λύστραν A. xiv. 6, al., Λύστροις A. xiv. 8, al.; Θυατείρων A. xvi. 14, Θυάτειραν Rev. i. 11 (in good MSS.).—In the case of Μαρία, Μαριάμ, the variation between the inflected and the non-inflected forms is very perplexing.]
[5] It is true the MSS. of the older Greek writers also vary between αρχος and αρχης, but recent critics give the preference to αρχος (comp. Bornem. Xen. *Conv.* I. 4, Poppo, Xen. *Cyr.* 2. 1. 22, p. 109); this form also agrees best with the derivation of these words (from ἀρχός). Comp. τόπαρχος Æsch. *Choëph.* 662; but γυμνασιάρχης must be retained in Æschin. *Tim.* I. 23 (ed. Bremi).
[6] That αρχης was the usual termination in the apostolic age also seems a legitimate inference from the fact that the Romans, in translating these words into Latin, used this or a similar form, though it would have been as easy to use -archus. Thus we find *Tetrarches*, Hirt. *Bell. Al.* c. 67, Liv. *Epit.* 94, Horat. *Serm.* 1. 3. 12, Lucan 7. 227; *Alabarches*, Cic. *Attic.* 2. 17, Juven. *Sat.* 1. 130; *Toparcha*, Spartian. *in Hadrian.* 13; *Patriarcha*, Tertull. *de Anim.* c. 7. 55, al.: comp. Schæf. *Demosth.* II. 151. At a later period, we have the testimony of the Byzantine writers for the preponderance of this form.

SECT. VIII.] UNUSUAL FORMS IN THE FIRST DECLENSION. 71

ἑκατοντάρχῳ, as in Joseph. *B. J.* 2. 4. 3 ἑκατόνταρχον is read besides ἑκατοντάρχην. But ἑκατόνταρχος occurs almost without any variant in Mt. viii. 5, 8, L. vii. 6, A. xxii. 25 : ἑκατοντάρχου, L. vii. 2, may come from ἑκατοντάρχης ; so also may the gen. plur. A. xxiii. 23, if we write ἑκατονταρχῶν for -άρχων.¹ Lastly, for στρατοπεδάρχῃ A. xxviii. 16 (Const. Man. 4412, al.) the better MSS. have -άρχῳ. The following additional instances of the form -άρχης may be adduced from the Greek Bible and from writers of the first centuries after Christ: γενεσιάρχης Wis. xiii. 3,² κυπριάρχης 2 Macc. xii. 2, τοπάρχης Gen. xli. 34, Dan. iii. 2, 3, vi. 7, Euseb. *H. E.* 1. 13. 3, θιασάρχης Lucian, *Peregr.* 11, μεράρχης Arrian, *Tact.* p. 30, φαλαγγάρχης *ib.* p. 30, εἰλάρχης *ib.* p. 50, ἐλεφαντάρχης 2 Macc. xiv. 12, 3 Macc. v. 4, 45, ἀλαβάρχης Joseph. *Ant.* 19. 5. 1, γενάρχης Lycophr. 1307, Joseph. *Ant.* 1. 13. 4, ταξιάρχης Arrian, *Al.* 2. 16. 11, Euseb. *Const.* 4. 63 (though in 4. 51, 68, he uses ταξίαρχος, see Heinich. *Index* p. 585), ἱλάρχης Arrian, *Al.* 1. 12. 11, 2. 7. 5, συριάρχης *Act. Apocr.* p. 52, νομάρχης *Papyr. Taur.* p. 24, γειτονιάρχης Boisson. *Anecd.* V. 73. To quote from the Byzantines all the examples of compounds in -αρχης would be an endless work; they occur on almost every page.— Of some compounds -αρχος is the only form which occurs in the N.T.: thus we find χιλίαρχος in all the N. T. passages, 22 in number (on the other hand, χιλιάρχης Arrian, *Al.* 1. 22. 9, 7. 25. 11, see Ellendt, *Arrian* II. 267), and also in the LXX, Ex. xviii. 11,³ 25, Dt. i. 15, Num. i. 16, in which passages we also meet with δεκάδαρχος (δεκαδάρχαι Arrian, *Tact.* p. 98). In the Byzantines, κένταρχος Cedren. 1. 705, 708, νυκτέπαρχος Leo Diac. 6. 2, must be looked upon as isolated instances of this form.

We meet with dialectic inflexions of nouns of the 1st decl., in σπείρης the Ionic genit. of σπεῖρα, A. xxi. 31, xxvii. 1, and—with some variation in the MSS.—A. x. 1 (comp. Arrian, *Acies contra Alanos* pp. 99, 100, 102): good MSS. also have μαχαίρης Rev. xiii. 14, H. xi. 34, 37, and μαχαίρῃ Rev. xiii. 10, L. xxii. 49, A. xii. 2 (comp. Ex. xv. 9). Compare also Σαπφείρῃ A. v. 1 (Σαπφείρᾳ Lachm.), and συνειδυίης ver. 2, in good MSS.⁴ See Matth. 68. 2.⁵

---

¹ [In the received text -ος occurs 15 times, -ης 5; in Tisch. (ed. 7), -ος 6 times and -ης 13 ; in ed. 8 Tisch. reads -ος in A. xxii. 25 only, but in some passages there is little authority for the reading which he accepts. In the text of Westcott and Hort (who receive -ος 4 times, -ης 15), Matthew uses -ος in nomin., -ῃ in dative; Luke (in Gospel and Acts) -ης only, except in accus. sing. (A. xxii. 25).—For τετράρχης we should probably read τετραάρχης : so also τετρααρχεῖν.]
² [In ed. 7 Winer added κωμάρχης, Esth. ii. 3.]
³ [This should be xviii. 21: δεκάδαρχος occurs in *some of* these passages of the LXX, viz. Ex. xviii. 21, 25, Dt. i. 15.]
⁴ [Tischendorf (ed. 8) receives the η in all these instances; also πλημμύρης L. vi. 48, πρώρης A. xxvii. 30. On the Ionic forms in the N. T. see Cobet, *N. T. Vatic.* pp. xxxiii, lxxiii sq., xc: A. Buttmann (*Gr.* p. 11) maintains that these should not be called Ionisms, as we do not find the nomin. -ρη in the N. T. With συνειδυίης Tisch. compares ἐπιβεβηκυίης 1 S. xxv. 20, κυνομυίης Ex. viii. 21, 24: see his *Proleg.* p. 54 (ed. 7).]
⁵ [We have Μάρθης in Jo. xi. 1: comp. Ἄννᾳ 1 S. i. 2, 5, Λύδδας (Jelf 78. *Obs.*).]

2. In the 2nd declension we find the following forms:—

(a) Ἀπολλώ, accus. sing. of Ἀπολλώς (A. xviii. 24) A. xix. 1, 1 C. iv. 6 [?], instead of Ἀπολλῶν; comp. Buttm. I. 155, 199 (Jelf 86): the genitive is Ἀπολλώ, according to rule, 1 C. iii. 4, xvi. 12. In A. xxi. 1 we find in good MSS. τὴν Κῶ (1 Macc. xv. 23, Joseph. *Ant.* 14. 7. 2), see Buttm. I. 155, Krüg. p. 46: the common reading τὴν Κῶν is very weakly supported. For Κῶς, however, a collateral indeclinable form Κῶ occurs in Strabo 10. 489. Compare further Duker on Thuc. 8. 41.

(b) Νοΐ as dative of νοῦς, after the analogy of the 3rd decl., 1 C. i. 10, xiv. 15, Rom. vii. 25; νοός as genitive, for νοῦ, 1 C. xiv. 19. The usual form of the dative in Greek writers is νόῳ or νῷ: νοΐ occurs only in Simplic. *ad* Aristot. *Phys.* 31. 25, Philo I. 63 (Bekker, *Anecd.* III. p. 1196), the Byzantines,—e.g. Malalas, see the index in the Bonn ed., Theophan. 28,—and the Fathers: see Lob. p. 453, Boisson. *Marin.* p. 93 sq. Similarly πλοός, A. xxvii. 9, genit. for πλοῦ, as in Arrian, *Peripl.* p. 176, Malalas 5. p. 94, Cinnam. p. 86; comp. Lob. *l.c.*

(c) The vocative θεέ Mt. xxvii. 46, without variant (Jud. xxi. 3, Wis. ix. 1, *Act. Thom.* 25, 45, 57,—Τιμόθεε 1 Tim. i. 18, vi. 20): an instance of this form is hardly to be found in Greek writers, comp. Buttm. I. 151. Even in the LXX the voc. is usually θεός.[1]

(d) From ὀστέον we find the uncontracted plural ὀστέα L. xxiv. 39, and ὀστέων Mt. xxiii. 27, H. xi. 22, al. The latter is not very uncommon in Greek prose, see Lucian, *Necyom.* 15, Plat. *Locr.* 102 d.; comp. also Eurip. *Orest.* 404, *Troad.* 1177: ὀστέα is less common, but see Plat. *Locr.* 100 b., Aristot. *Anim.* 3. 7, Menand. p. 196 (ed. Meineke).[2]

The following instances of *metaplasmus* are found in the N. T.:

(1) Ὁ δεσμός has in the plural τὰ δεσμά, L. viii. 29, A. xvi. 26, xx. 23, and only once οἱ δεσμοί, Ph. i. 13;—in every instance without any variant. In Greek authors, too, δεσμοί is more rare than τὰ δεσμά: see Thom. M. p. 204, Buttm. I. 210[3] (Jelf 85).

(2) From σάββατον we find only the gen. sing. and plur. and

---

[1] [Krüger (p. 44) quotes θεί from Œnomaus in Euseb. *Præp. Ev.* 5. 33, p. 228; also Τιμόθεε Luc. *Harm.* 1, Φιλόθεε *Inscript.* 3175. 6, Ἀμφίθεε Aristoph. *Acharn.* 176.]

[2] [In Rev. ii. 1 Tisch. read χρυσίων in ed. 7; and in Rev. ix. 20 ℵ has χάλκεα, see Lob. p. 207: χρυσᾶν (for χρυσῆν) is strongly supported in Rev. i. 13.]

[3] Comp. Kühnöl, *Act.* p. 558.

SECT. IX.] UNUSUAL FORMS IN THE THIRD DECLENSION. 73

the dat. sing.¹ [and accus. plur.]: the dative plural is σάββασι (which occurs also in Meleag. 83, 4), formed according to Passow from a sing. σάββατ, -ατος.

(3) Ὁ σῖτος, plural (σῖτοι and) σῖτα A. vii. 12 *v. l.*, as often in Greek writers: a singular σῖτον was never in use, see Schæf. Soph. *Electr.* 1366. In A. vii., however, the best MSS. have σιτία, which now stands in the text.²

In regard to gender:—

(1) Λιμός is feminine (*Dorice*, Lob. p. 188) in L. xv. 14, A. xi. 28, on the testimony of a few good MSS.; in L. iv. 25 there is very little authority for the feminine. Comp. Malalas 3. p. 60, and see Bornem. on A. xi. 28.³

(2) In Mk. xii. 26 βάτος in masc., though not without *v. l.*; in L. xx. 37, A. vii. 35, feminine: see Fritz. *Mark* p. 532. See in general Lob. *Paral.* p. 174 sq., and comp. ἡ πηλός Const. Man. 2239, 2764, al.

(3) Instead of ὁ νῶτος, the later form, some MSS. in Rom. xi. 10 have τὸ νῶτον,⁴ the form used by the older writers: see Fritz. *in loc.*⁵

Section IX.

UNUSUAL FORMS IN THE THIRD DECLENSION.

Peculiar forms deserving attention are,

1. In the singular:—

(*a*) The genitive ἡμίσους Mk. vi. 23 (for the usual form ἡμίσεος) from the neuter ἥμισυ, used as a substantive; comp. Dio Chr. 7. 99, Schwarz, *Comm.* p. 652, Buttm. I. 191 (Jelf 122).

(*b*) The Ionic dative γήρει (contracted from γήρεϊ) L. i. 36,

---

¹ In the LXX we find (besides σάββασι) a dative plural from this form, σαββάτοις, 1 Chr. xxiii. 31, 2 Chr. ii. 4, viii. 13, Ez. xlvi. 3, as in Joseph. *Ant.* 16. 6. 4. In the N. T. σαββάτοις is occasionally found amongst the various readings, as Mt. xii. 1, 12, in good MSS. [Σαββάτοις does not seem to occur in the uncial MSS., except in Mt. xii. 1, 12, in B alone. With σάββασι compare ὀνείρασι, προσώπασι (Jelf 117).]

² [From στάδιον, στάδιοι L. xxiv. 13, Rev. xxi. 16; στάδια Jo. vi. 19 (Tisch. ed. 8) is doubtful: see Krüg. p. 58.]

³ [See also § 59. 4. *b*, on this word and on ληνός.]

⁴ [Fritz. quotes τὸ ν. from some early *editions* of the N. T., but adds: "Cdd. τὸν νῶτον." Neither Griesb. nor Tischendorf cites τὸ ν. from any MS.]

⁵ [For τὸ λιβανωτόν, Rev. viii. 5 *Rec.*, the true reading is τὸν λ.: for σάρδιος, Rev. xxi. 20 *Rec.*, we should read the usual form σάρδιον. In Mk. xiv. 3 *Rec.* has τὸ ἀλάβαστρον; Lachm., Fritz., and Tisch. (ed. 8) τὸν ἀ.; Treg., Westcott and Hort, τὴν ἀ.; in other places there is nothing to show the gender: the Attic form is ἀλάβαστος. In A. xxiii. 16 *Rec.* has τὸ ἔνεδρον (2 Chr. xiii. 13, al.), but the true reading is τὴν ἐνέδραν (A. xxv. 3, Jos. viii. 7, al.): τὸ ἔνεδρον seems not to occur in Greek authors. In A. xxviii. 8 we must read δυσεντέριον for (the Attic) δυσεντερία: see Lob. p. 518.]

where *Rec.* has γήρᾳ; comp. οὕδει from οὖδος in Homer. The same form occurs Ps. xci. 15, Ecclus. viii. 6, Theophan. p. 36, in the Fathers—e.g. Theodoret, *in Ps. cxix.* I. 1393 (ed. Hal.), —Fabric. *Pseudepigr.* II. 630, 747, Boisson. *Anecd.* III. 19.

(c) The accusative ὑγιῆ Jo. v. 11, 15, Tit. ii. 8 (Lev. xiii. 15). The Attic writers use another contraction ὑγιᾶ, but ὑγιῆ occurs Plat. *Phæd.* 89 d, and similar forms are found elsewhere (Matth. 113. Rem. 1, Jelf 129).

(d) In A. xxvii. 40, A and several other MSS. have ἀρτέμωνα as the accusative of ἀρτέμων (comp. γλήχωνι Hom. *Cerer.* 209); and Lachm. has received it into the text. Lobeck too (*Ajax* p. 171) prefers it to the common form ἀρτέμονα: " appellativi declinatio sine dubio eadem quæ proprii." See Anacr. *Fragm.* 27, and Fischer *in loc.*[1]

2. In the plural :—

(a) The accus. in εῖς instead of έας from nom. sing. in ευς; as γονεῖς Mt. x. 21, L. ii. 27, γραμματεῖς Mt. xxiii. 34, etc. The same form is also found in Attic writers, e.g. Xenophon (see Poppo, *Cyrop.* p. 32 sq., Weber, *Dem.* pp. 492, 513), though the Atticists reject it; see Matth. 83 a. Rem. 7 (Jelf 97).[2]

(b) Δυσίν for δυοῖν, the dative of the numeral δύο, Mt. xxii. 40, L. xvi. 13, A. xii. 6 (Th. M. p. 253), follows the analogy of the 3rd declension. It is found in Thuc. 8. 101 (δυσὶν ἡμέραις), in Plutarch, Aristotle, Hippocrates, and others: see Lob. p. 210 sq., Buttm. I. 276. In the genitive δύο is always indeclinable (Mt. xx. 24, xxi. 31, Jo. i. 41, 1 Tim. v. 19, al.), as sometimes in Greek authors, e.g. Lucian, *Dial. Mort.* 4. 1, Æsop. 145. 1 (Matth. 138, Jelf 166).

(c) The uncontracted forms ὀρέων Rev. vi. 15 (Ez. xi. 10, 1 K. xx. 28, Is. xiii. 4, al.) and χειλέων H. xiii. 15 (Pr. xii. 14, xxxi. 31, Wis. i. 6, Ecclus. xxii. 27, al.), for the usual ὀρῶν, χειλῶν, the other cases being regular. Such genitives, however, are not uncommon in Greek prose, comp. Poppo, Xen. *Cyr.* p. 213, Georgi, *Hier.* I. 145, Jacobs, *Achill. Tat.* 2. 1; as to the poets, see Ellendt, *Lex. Soph.* II. pp. x, xii.

---

[1] [From σπικουλάτωρ we find in *Rec.* σπικουλάτορα Mk. vi. 27: but -ατορα is now generally received. The same may be said of ἀρτέμωνα.]

[2] [The other form is not found in the N. T. In the plural of ἰχθύς, βοῦς, and similar words, the contracted forms do not occur in the N. T. (A. Buttm. p. 14).]

SECT. IX.] UNUSUAL FORMS IN THE THIRD DECLENSION. 75

(*d*) The contracted neuter plural ἡμίση (L. xix. 8), used as a subst.,—compare Theophr. *Ch.* 11: what has been said respecting ἡμίσους applies here also. The ordinary form is ἡμίσεα, which some MSS. have in this passage; Tisch. reads ἡμίσεια with B, L; comp. Buttm. I. 248.[1] See Fischer, *Prol.* p. 667, Buttm. I. 191.

(*e*) The contracted genitive πηχῶν Jo. xxi. 8, Rev. xxi. 17 (for πηχέων, which A has in the former passage): this is a later form (see Lob. p. 246), but it is found in Xen. *An.* 4. 7. 16, and frequently in Plutarch.[2]

For the Attic κλεῖν (Thom. M. p. 536, Lob. p. 460), the accus. of κλείς, we find the more "common" form κλεῖδα in L. xi. 52, and (in a few MSS.) Rev. iii. 7, xx. 1; in the LXX more frequently, Jud. iii. 25, Is. xxii. 22.[3] In the plural, κλεῖδας is the better reading in Mt. xvi. 19, but κλεῖς in Rev. i. 18. Of ἔρις also there are two plural forms, ἔριδες 1 C. i. 11, and ἔρεις (both nomin. and accus.) 2 C. xii. 20: in G. v. 20 we should probably read ἔρις.[4] Κρέας has in the plural the usual contracted form κρέα (Buttm. I. 196), Rom. xiv. 21, 1 C. viii. 13 (Ex. xvi. 8, 12), as in Xen. *Cyr.* 1. 3. 6, 2. 2. 2. On the other hand, κέρας has κέρατα Rev. v. 6, xiii. 1, 11, xvii. 12 (Am. iii. 14), κεράτων Rev. ix. 13, xiii. 1 (1 K. i. 50, ii. 29); and never the contracted κέρα, κερῶν (Buttm. *l.c.*, Bekker, *Anecd.* III. 1001). Lastly, τέρας has always τέρατα, Mt. xxiv. 24, A. ii. 43, v. 12, Jo. iv. 48, τεράτων Rom. xv. 19, instead of τέρα, τερῶν, which are considered the Attic forms (Moeris p. 339, Buttm. *l.c.*, Jelf 103).

Rem. 1. The nomin. sing. of ὠδῖνες occurs in 1 Th. v. 3 (Is. xxxvii. 3) in the form ὠδίν (for ὠδίς): comp. δελφίν, which is not

---

[1] [Tischendorf, Tregelles, Meyer, and Alford read ἡμίσεια; Westcott and Hort, ἡμίσια. Compare ἐξεῖα Hes. *Sc.* 348 (and Göttling *in loc.*), θήλεια Arat. 1068, for ἐξέα, θήλεα. Tischendorf (ed. 7) quotes ἡμίσεια from Antoninus Liberalis c. 2. p. 16, and Cleomed. *Theor. Cycl.* 1. 5. p. 23. A. Buttm. inclines to ἡμίση: see *Gr.* p. 14, *Stud. u. Krit.* 1862, p. 194.]

[2] [There is good authority for βαθέως L. xxiv. 1, πραέως 1 P. iii. 4, instead of βαθέος, πραέος (Lob. p. 247). Of comparatives in ων both the contracted and the uncontracted forms are found in the N. T.; from τίς, τὶς, ὅστις, only the uncontracted, with the single exception of ὅτου in the formula ἕως ὅτου (A. Buttm. pp. 26, 31). In Rev. xx. 8 ℵ has for τέσσαροι the poetical form τέτρασι, which is also a *v.l.* in A. x. 11, xi. 5.]

[3] [From χάρις we find the accus. χάριτα, A. xxiv. 27, Jude 4, as in Eur. *Hel.* 1378, Xen. *Hell.* 3. 5. 16, al.]

[4] [Tisch. (ed. 7) received the nomin. ἔρις in 2 C. *l.c.*, 1 Tim. vi. 4, but now reads ἔρις in both places: in Tit. iii. 9 authorities are divided between ἔρεις (Lachm., Treg.) and ἔριν (Tisch.). Similar to this is νήστεις, accus. plur. of νῆστις, Mt. xv. 32, Mk. viii. 3 (Lob. p. 326). Tisch. now (ed. 8) reads νήστις in Mk. viii.: Fritz. (*Mark*, Exc. 3, p. 796 sq.) examines the readings, and decides in favour of this Ionic form in both passages. Phrynichus (*App.* p. 52) says: νῆστις καὶ τὸ πληθυντικὸν νήστιδες καὶ νήστις: Lobeck (*Phryn.* p. 326) adds " leg. νήστεις." See also Tisch. on Mk. viii. 3 (ed. 8), and Wetstein *in loc.*]

uncommon in later writers; also κλειδίν, Constant. Porphyr. 14. 208. See Buttm. I. 162 (Jelf 104. 19).

Rem. 2. Πλοῦτος, which is usually masc., often appears in good MSS. as a neuter noun; see E. ii. 7, iii. 8, 16, Ph. iv. 19, Col. ii. 2 (*Act. Apocr.* p. 76).[1] This peculiarity is probably to be referred to the popular language, as indeed ὁ and τὸ πλ. are used promiscuously in modern Greek; see Coray, Plut. *Vit.* II. p. 58, *Isocr.* II. 103, 106. We find also τὸ ζῆλος 2 C. ix. 2 (in B), Ph. iii. 6 (in A, B),[2] see Clem. *Ep.* p. 17 (Ittig): perhaps also τὸ ἦχος L. xxi. 25, if ηχους (which is the reading of good MSS.) is accentuated ἤχους, as by Lachm. and others; comp. Malal. pp. 121, 436.[3] In later writers, comp. τὸ κλάδος Theophan. contin. p. 222 (ed. Bekker): see in general Benseler, Isocr. *Areop.* p. 106. Conversely, later writers use ὁ δεῖπνος (L. xiv. 16 in B, D)[4] and ὁ τεῖχος (Ducas p. 266, ed. Bonn, *Act. Apocr.* p. 84). The heteroclite σκότος (Poppo, *Thuc.* I. 225) is once masc. in the N. T., H. xii. 18 (where however σκότῳ is uncertain);[5] elsewhere it is always neuter (σκότους, -τει), without any difference of reading. Ἔλεος is sometimes masc. in the LXX, as also in Philo I. 284, but is usually neuter in the MSS. of the N. T.; the masc. form being noted as a variant in Mt. ix. 13, xii. 7, xxiii. 23, Tit. iii. 5, H. iv. 16,[6] only. In A. iii. 10 C has θάμβου as genitive of θάμβος.

Rem. 3. In the MSS. of the N. T. we find several examples of the ν appended to the accus. sing. in α or η (ἐλπίδαν, συγγενῆν);[7] as ἀστέραν Mt. ii. 10 (C), χεῖραν Jo. xx. 25 (A), ἄρσεναν Rev. xii. 13 (A), εἰκόναν xiii. 14 (A), μῆναν xxii. 2 (A), Δίαν A. xiv. 12 (in several MSS.), συγγενῆν Rom. xvi. 11 (A), ἀσφαλῆν H. vi. 19 (A, C, D), ποδήρην Rev. i. 13 (A). Such forms are met with in the Byzantine writers (see the index to Leo Gramm. p. 532, Boisson. *Anecd.* V. 102), and in the apocryphal writers (Tisch. *de Ev. Apocr.* p. 137): in the Apocalypse Lachm. has admitted the above-mentioned forms into the text.[8] This subjoined ν is probably to be considered, not (as by Ross) as an original ending propagated in the popular spoken language, but as an arbitrary extension of the familiar accusative ending (Matth. 73. 2) beyond its proper limits

---

[1] [The genitive is always πλούτου; the dative does not occur in the N. T. St. Paul uses both forms; the other N. T. writers ὁ πλ. only. Recent editors read τὸ πλ. in all the above passages, and in 2 C. viii. 2, E. i. 7, Col. i. 27: see Ellicott on E. i. 7, A. Buttm. p. 22.]

[2] [Τὸ ζ. is probably the true reading in both passages.]

[3] [Ὁ ἦχος occurs H. xii. 19.]

[4] On this word see Hase, *Leo Diac.* p. 239; Schæf. *Ind. Æsop.* pp. 128, 163; Boisson. Herod. *Epim.* p. 22, *Anecd.* I. 51. [It is a *v.l.* in Rev. xix. 9, 17.]

[5] [In this passage ζόφῳ is now generally received for σκότῳ.]

[6] [Ὁ ἔλεος is a variant in one or two other passages, but τὸ ἔλ. is now generally received in all instances.]

[7] Comp. Sturz, *Dial. Al.* p. 127; Lob. *Paral.* p. 142.

[8] [Except in Rev. i. 13 (ποδήρην). In his larger edition Lachm. reads ἀσφαλήν in H. vi. 19, receiving the ν, but regarding the word as inflected according to the 1st decl. (*metaplasmus*): see A. Buttm. p. 14 (Thayer's note).]

(Lobeck *l.c.*). In adjectives of two terminations in ης this form of the accus. is said to be Æolic (Matth. 113. Rem. 2):[1] see further Bornem. on A. xiv. 12.[2]

Section X.

DECLENSION OF FOREIGN WORDS: INDECLINABLE NOUNS.

1. A simple mode of declining certain Græcised oriental names was introduced by the LXX and the N. T. writers. In this, the genitive, dative, and vocative have usually one common form, and the accusative ends in ν. Thus Ἰησοῦς, genitive Ἰησοῦ Mt. xxvi. 69 ; dative Ἰησοῦ Mt. xxvi. 17 ;[3] vocative Ἰησοῦ Mk. i. 24; accusative Ἰησοῦν Mt. xxvi. 4, A. xx. 21 :—Λευΐ or Λευΐς (L. v. 29), accusative Λευΐν Mk. ii. 14 :—Ἰωσῆς, genitive Ἰωσῆ Mt. xxvii. 56, L. iii. 29, al.,—but in Mark B, D, L have always Ἰωσῆτος :[4] see Buttm. I. 199. The inflexion of the Egyptian word Θαμοῦς (Plat. *Phædr.* 274 d) presents a parallel to that of Ἰησοῦς (Matth. 70. 9).

The word Μωσῆς (Μωϋσῆς) is declined in two ways in the N. T. The genitive is invariably Μωσέως, as in the Greek Fathers and the Byzantine writers; comp. Diod. Sic. *Ecl.* 34. p. 194 (Lips.). In the dative even good MSS. vary between Μωσεῖ (which is also found in Eusebius and Theophanes) and Μωσῇ ; comp. Mt. xvii. 4, Mk. ix. 5, L. ix. 33, Jo. v. 46, ix. 29, A. vii. 44, Rom. ix. 15, 2 Tim. iii. 8.[5] The accusative is Μωσῆν A. vi. 11, vii. 35, 1 C. x. 2, H. iii. 3 (Diod. Sic. 1. 94) ; but in L.

---

[1] [Such forms as εὐσίβην, δυσμίνην (with accent thrown back), for ·εὐσεβῆ, δυσμενῆ, are said to be Æolic (Matth. 113. Rem. 2 ; Bekker, *Anecd.* p. 1233).]

[2] [In ed. 7 Tisch. received the final ν in the passages quoted above from the Apocalypse, and in ἀσφαλήν H. vi. 19, Δίαν A. xiv. 12 : see *Proleg.* p. 55. In ed. 8 he rejects the ν throughout, see his note on H. vi. 19. Similar forms are frequently found in ℵ, but not in any of these instances ; see Scrivener, *Collation* p. liv. See further A. Buttm. *Gr.* p. 14 ; also Mullach, *Vulg.* pp. 22, 162, where are given examples from inscriptions and analogies in modern Greek.]

[3] Besides these forms, the MSS. of the LXX have often Ἰησοῖ for the dative (Dt. iii. 21, 28, xxxi. 23), and even for the genitive (Ex. xvii. 14).

[4] [D has Ἰακώβου in Mk. xv. 47. Recent editors read Ἰησοῦ in L. iii. 29.]

[5] [Lachmann reads -σῇ in A. vii. 44, and in Rom. ix. 15 (-σεῖ *marg.*) : Tischendorf (ed. 7) in Mk. ix. 4, 5, A. vii. 44. In Mk. ix. Tisch. now (ed. 8) reads Μωϋσεῖ: Acts vii. 44 is probably influenced by the usage of the LXX.—Ἰωάννης is regularly inflected according to the 1st decl. ; but we find a dative -νει in L. vii. 18, 22.]

xvi. 29 (and here only) all the MSS. have Μωσέα, a form which occurs in Euseb. *H. E.* 1. 3, and often in Clem. Al., Georg. Syncell., Glycas, and others. All these forms, with the exception of Μωσέως, may clearly be derived from the nominative Μωσῆς; see the analogies in Buttm. I. 198, 210,[1] 221 (Jelf 116). Μωσέως has been referred to a form Μωσεύς, which however does not occur, and is after all unnecessary, for the genit. of Ἄρης is sometimes Ἄρεως (Ellendt, *Lex. Soph.* I. 224). No other forms are found in the N. T., but a genitive Μωσῆ occurs in the LXX and in Geo. Phranzes, and Μωσοῦ Bauer, *Glossar. Theodoret.* p. 269; a vocative Μωσῆ in Ex. iii. 4. Μανασσῆ [? -σσῆς] has in Mt. i. 10 the accusative Μανασσῆ, with the various reading -σσῆν.

In the received text the name Solomon is declined like Ξενοφῶν, -ῶντος; thus accus. Σολομῶντα Mt. i. 6, genit. Σολομῶντος Mt. xii. 42, L. xi. 31, Jo. x. 23, A. iii. 11, v. 12. The better MSS., however, have -ῶνα, -ῶνος;[2] see Wetst. I. 228. This latter inflexion, which is according to analogy, and is the received form in Josephus (ed. Havercamp), should therefore be admitted into the text: -ῶν, -ῶντος, would imply derivation from a participle (Buttm. I. 169, Lob. *Paralip.* p. 347). The nominative must then, in accordance with the best authorities,[3] be written Σολομών,[4] like Βαβυλών, &c.,—not Σολομῶν, as by Lachmann and others: Ποσειδῶν (-ῶνος) is not analogous, since it is a contraction of Ποσειδάων. In the LXX this name is indeclinable:[5] see 1 K. iv. 7, 29 (25), v. 12, 15, 16, vi. 18 [? v. 18], al.

2. Many Hebrew proper names which might have been inflected according to the 3rd decl. are treated as indeclinable in the LXX and the N. T.;[6] as Ἀαρών, genitive H. vii. 11, ix. 4, dative Ex. vii. 9, A. vii. 40, accusative Ex. vii. 8. Compare in particular Mt. i. and L. iii. 23 sqq.: also Συμεών L. iii. 30, Σαλ-

---

[1] [These two reff. are incorrect: perhaps Matth. pp. 198, 220 (§ 70, 78 a), Buttm. I. 221.]
[2] [That is, *usually*: -ῶντος is well supported in A. iii. 11, v. 12.]
[3] Comp. also Pappelb. *Cod. Diez.* p. 9. [The accentuated MSS. are strongly in favour of Σολομῶν, see Tisch. on Mt. vi. 29. Tisch., Treg., Westc. and Hort, write Σολομών; except in A. vii. 47, Σολομῶν, or (Tisch.) Σαλωμών.]
[4] In Glycas, Bekker still (in the new edition) writes Σολομῶντος, -ῶντα; but in the nomin. Σολομών.
[5] [Not always; e.g. Prov. xxv. 1, Σαλωμῶντος (Σολομῶντος *Alex.*).]
[6] [Sometimes we find two forms, one declined, the other not; as Μαρία, Μαριάμ; similarly, Σατᾶν 2 C. xii. 7 (*Rec.*, Meyer), Σατανᾶς L. xiii. 16, al. (Ecclus. xxi. 27,—not found in the LXX).]

SECT. X.]   FOREIGN WORDS: INDECLINABLE NOUNS.   79

μών L. iii. 32, Κεδρών Jo. xviii. 1 *v. l.* Similarly Ἱεριχῶ,¹ genit. Dt. xxxii. 49, Mt. xx. 29, H. xi. 30, accus. L. x. 30, xviii. 35 (Glyc. p. 304);² Ἱερουσαλήμ,—for which however the Græcised form Ἱεροσόλυμα should probably be preferred (on the authority of the MSS.) in Matthew, Mark, and John.³ Ἱεροσόλυμα is usually inflected as a neuter plural, as Mt. iv. 25, Mk. iii. 8, L. xxiii. 7, Jo. ii. 23; it is feminine in Mt. ii. 3 (iii. 5 ?) only.⁴ In the LXX we find Ἱερουσαλήμ always; Josephus has Ἱεροσόλυμα. Similarly, τὸ πάσχα L. ii. 41, Jo. ii. 23, as in the LXX:⁵ (τὸ) σίκερα L. i. 15, and in the LXX, Lev. x. 9, Num. vi. 3, Is. xxiv. 9, al.: Eusebius (*Præp. Ev.* 6. 10) has a genitive σίκερος.⁶ The Hebrew plural termination occurs only in Χερουβίμ H. ix. 5; but this word is construed like a neuter plural (as if πνεύματα), as in the LXX (Gen. iii. 24, 1 K. viii. 7, Ez. x. 3, al.).⁷

In Rev. i. 4, ἀπὸ ὁ ὢν καὶ ὁ ἦν καὶ ὁ ἐρχόμενος, a whole phrase (forming, as it were, a Greek equivalent for יְהֹוָה) is treated as an indeclinable noun,—probably by design, as expressing the name of the Unchangeable One. This resembles the use of ἕν, μηθέν, and similar words, in Greek philosophical writings, even as early as Aristotle; e.g. Aristot. *Polit.* 5. 3, Procl. *Theol. Plat.* 2 (ed. Hoeschel), μετὰ τοῦ ἕν, χωρὶς τοῦ ἕν (Stollberg, *de Sol. N. T.* p. 14 sqq.); but

---

¹ [Usually written Ἱεριχώ (-ειχώ Tisch.); so Winer in his *RWB.*]
² Elsewhere we find two modes of declining this word: (*a*) Genit. Ἱεριχοῦ 3 (1) Esdr. v. 22, dat. Ἱεριχῷ Procop. *de Ædif.* 5. 9, Theodoret V. p. 81 (Hal.), or Ἱεριχοῖ Joseph. *Bell. Jud.* 1. 21. 4, Suid. s. v. Ὠριγενής:—(*b*) From Ἱεριχοῦς (Ptol. 5. 16. 7), genit. Ἱερικοῦντος Strabo 16. 763, accus. Ἱερικοῦντα 16. 760, and usually in Josephus.
³ [In Mt. xxiii. 37 all the MSS. have Ἱερουσαλήμ; this is the only form of the word used in the Apocalypse. In St. Luke's Gospel Ἱεροσόλυμα occurs only 3 or 4 times, Ἱερουσαλήμ nearly 30 times; see the Preface to this Gospel in Bp. Wordsworth's Greek Testament. In the Acts (setting aside xv. 4 as somewhat doubtful) the inflected form occurs 24 times, the indeclinable 36. St. Paul has Ἱερουσαλήμ, except in Gal. i. 17, 18, ii. 1 (see Lightfoot on Gal. iv. 26); the same form is used in Heb. xii. 22.]
⁴ [A. Buttmann (p. 18) maintains that the word is here treated as indeclinable, and supposes an ellipsis of ἡ πόλις.]
⁵ So also in the Fathers; see Suicer, *Thes.* II. 607 sqq. Epiphanius (*Hær.* II. 19) inflects even the plural τὰ πάσχα.
⁶ Most of these are declined in Josephus, who, in conformity with the genius of the Greek language, gives Greek terminations and inflexions to almost all personal names, as Ἄδαμος, Ἰσμαῆλος, Νῶχος, Ἴσακος, al. The instances of undeclined foreign names which Georgi (*Hierocr.* I. 138) produces from Plato and Pausanias are not all in point, and can prove nothing against the tendency to inflexion. Even Ptolemy has some indeclinable names of places, by the side of a multitude of inflected names: see Nobbe, *Sched. Ptol.* I. 23 sq. (Lips. 1841). [In A. xvi. 11 the best MSS. have εἰς Νέαν Πόλιν (*Rec.* Νεάπολιν), see Cobet, *N. T. Vatic.* p. xiii, Lob. p. 604: in Col. iv. 13 we should read Ἱερᾷ Πόλει.]
⁷ [The LXX have sometimes οἱ Χερουβίμ (-βείν), Ex. xxv. 19, al.; Josephus, οἱ and αἱ Χερουβεῖς; Philo always τὰ Χερουβίμ: see Delitzsch on H. ix. 5. In this passage Lachm. and Tisch. read Χερουβείν.]

always ἐκ τοῦ ἑνός, ἐν τῷ ἑνί, in the writings of Proclus edited by Creuzer. Compare also τὸν ὁ δεῖνα Schæf. *Dem.* III. 282.

Section XI.

DECLENSION AND COMPARISON OF ADJECTIVES.

1. Adjectives of three terminations, particularly those in ιος, μιος, ειος, αιος, are not unfrequently used as if they had only two, especially by Attic writers (Matth. 117, Jelf 127).[1] Thus in the N. T. we find στρατιὰ οὐράνιος L. ii. 13, A. xxvi. 19, κόσμιος 1 Tim. ii. 9 : in Rev. iv. 3 also ὅμοιος is the best attested reading, though Ἶρις is feminine.[2] But in 1 Tim. ii. 8, ἐπαίροντας ὁσίους χεῖρας (where some MSS. have ὁσίας), ὁσίους may be joined with ἐπαίροντας ; though Fritzsche is wrong in maintaining that this *must* be the construction (*Rom.* III. 161). Compare also Tit. iii. 9, where μάταιοι is used in reference to feminine nouns; and Ja. i. 26, μάταιος ἡ θρησκεία.

In later writers we find instances of the converse, a feminine form being given to adjectives which in classical Greek have only two terminations, e.g. ἀργός; see Lob. p. 105, and *Paral.* p. 455 sqq., comp. Ellendt, Arr. *Al.* I. 242.[3] In this adjective, however, the feminine form occurs even in a citation from Epimenides, Tit. i. 12. From συγγενής, -ές, is formed a peculiar feminine, συγγενίς (as a substantive) L. i. 36; this is received by Lachm. on the authority of good MSS. (Lob. p. 451) : comp. Malal. pp. 95, 96.

Αἰώνιος is usually in the N. T. an adj. of two terminations, but αἰωνίαν occurs 2 Th. ii. 16, H. ix. 12,—in the latter passage without any variant; the same form is given by a single MS. in 2 P. i. 11, and also in A. xiii. 48 : comp. Num. xxv. 13, Plat. *Tim.* 38 b. Βεβαία, Rom. iv. 16, al., which the fastidious Thom. M. condemns (p. 149), is used by Isocrates, Demosthenes (Weber, *Dem.* p. 133), Xenophon, al. : comp. Duker on Thuc. 2. 43. Ἔρημος, which varies even in Attic writers,[4] has always two terminations in the N. T. As to ἀσφαλην H. vi. 19, i.e. ἀσφαλῆν, see § 9. Rem. 3.

In the N. T. Lexicons[5] γνήσιος is given as an adjective of two terminations (Ph. iv. 3 ?), but without sufficient reason, as no example of γνήσιος as a feminine form can be quoted.

---

[1] See Elmsley, Eurip. *Heracl.* p. 77 (Lips.) ; Monk, Eurip. *Hippol.* p. 56, and Eurip. *Alc.* 126, 548, 1043.
[2] See Winer, *Exeget. Stud.* I. 152 : [as to 1 Tim. ii. 8 see Ellicott *in loc.*]
[3] [See also Mullach, *Vulg.* p. 156.]
[4] Comp. Ellendt, Arr. *Al.* I. 262, Matth. 118. Rem. 1. [Ἕτοιμος varies in the N. T., as in classical Greek.]
[5] [Lünemann rightly adds, except Grimm's.]

2. On the comparison of adjectives we have only to observe that—

(*a*) The neuter comparative of ταχύς is τάχιον (Jo. xx. 4, 1 Tim. iii. 14, H. xiii. 19, 23, al., 1 Macc. ii. 40, Wis. xiii. 9), for which θᾶσσον, in Attic θᾶττον, was commonly used. Τάχιον is regularly used by Diod. Sic., Dion. H., Plutarch, al.; see Lob. p. 77, Meineke, *Menand.* p. 144.[1]

(*b*) In 3 Jo. 4 we find the double comparative μειζότερος, and in E. iii. 8 ἐλαχιστότερος, a comparative of a superlative; comp. ἐλαχιστότατος, Sext. Emp. 9. 406, and in Latin *minimissimus, pessimissimus*. Such forms belong mainly to poetry (Apoll. Rhod. 2. 368 μειότερος), or to the later language, which sought in this way to add fresh strength to the comparative, which had lost some of its significance: comp. κρειττότερος Ducas 27, 29, 37, μειζονότερος *ib.* c. 27 and Malal. 18. p. 490, μειζότερος Constant. Porph. III. 257, πλειότερος Theophan. p. 567. Some isolated examples of a similar kind are found in earlier writers (see Wetst. II. 247); these are not, however, introduced as words actually current, but are extemporised by the writers themselves, as ἐσχατώτερος Aristot. *Metaph.* 10. 4: see Buttm. I. 274, Lob. p. 136 (Jelf 140). Compare in German *mehrere* from *mehr*.

(*c*) The comparatives κατώτερος (E. iv. 9), ἀνώτερος (L. xiv. 10), ἐσώτερος (A. xvi. 24), from the adverbs κάτω, ἄνω, ἔσω, are groundlessly questioned by Buttmann (I. 271). They are certainly found in the N. T. and in the LXX; and not only occur frequently in later Greek (as Leo Diac. 10. 1), but are even used by Attic writers (Matth. 132).

On the comparative form of other adverbs derived from adjectives, as περισσοτέρως (2 C. i. 12, G. i. 14, Ph. ii. 28, al.), a form not unknown to classical writers, see Buttm. II. 345, Elmsley, Eurip. *Heracl.* p. 100 (Lips.).

The positive ἤρεμος, 1 Tim. ii. 2, is not found in the older Greek writers, see Buttm. I. 271, II. 343: Lobeck (*Path.* I. 158) has pointed it out in an inscription (*Inscript. Olbiopol.* 2059. 24).

---

[1] [From διπλοῦς we find the peculiar compar. διπλότερος Mt. xxiii. 15 (Appian, *Praef. Hist. Rom.* 10), as if from διπλός (which occurs in *Anthol. Pal.* 10. 101): see A. Buttm. p. 27, Lob. p. 234. The compar. of ἀγαθός in the N. T. is κρείσσων, superl. κράτιστος; βέλτιον occurs once as an adverb, 2 Tim. i. 18: χείρων is the usual compar. of κακός (A. Buttm. *l.c.*). Πλέων occurs much less frequently than πλείων.]

Section XII.

AUGMENT AND REDUPLICATION OF REGULAR VERBS.

1. The temporal instead of the syllabic augment occurs

(*a*) In the imperfect ἤμελλε, Jo. iv. 47, xi. 51, xii. 33, xviii. 32, L. x. 1, A. xvi. 27, xxvii. 33, Rev. x. 4, with decided preponderance of authority: in L. ix. 31, Jo. vi. 71, H. xi. 8, ἔμελλε is better attested.[1] See in general Böckh, Plat. *Men.* p. 148 sq.

(*b*) In the imperfect ἠδύνατο Mt. xxvi. 9, Mk. vi. 5, 19, xiv. 5, Jo. ix. 33, xi. 37, L. viii. 19, xix. 3, with preponderant authority; whilst there is good evidence for ἐδύνατο in L. i. 22, A. xxvi. 32, Rev. xiv. 3, and ἐδύνασθε 1 C. iii. 2. The aor. ἠδυνήθην is fully established Mt. xvii. 16, 19, Mk. ix. 28, L. ix. 40, 1 C. iii. 1.[2] On these common Attic forms see Buttm. I. 317[3] (Jelf 171), and comp. Bornem. *Act.* p. 278 [Veitch, *Gr. Verbs*, s. vv.].

(*c*) But neither ἠβουλόμην, A. xv. 37, xxviii. 18, nor ἠβουλήθην, 2 Jo. 12 (Matth. 162, Jelf 171) is sufficiently attested: see Bornem. *Act.* p. 233.

2. The syllabic augment in a verb beginning with a vowel occurs Jo. xix. 32, 33, in κατέαξαν, 1 aor. indic. of κατάγνυμι (comp. Thom. M. p. 498), and even in the other moods, as κατεαγῶσι[4] Jo. xix. 31 (Buttm. II. 97, Jelf 173. 8): comp. Thuc. 3. 89, Aristot. *Anim.* 9. 43, Plat. *Cratyl.* 389 b, c.[5] It is also inserted in the fut. κατεάξω Mt. xii. 20 (from the LXX),[6] to distinguish this from the future of κατάγω. But from ὠνέομαι, in which verb the syllabic augment is most commonly used in classical

---

[1] [Jo. xi. 51, Rev. x. 4, are somewhat doubtful; in H. xi. 8 we should probably read ἤμελλεν. For ἤμ. see also L. vii. 2, xix. 4, A. xii. 6; for ἔμ., Jo. vi. 6, vii. 39, A. xxi. 27, Rev. iii. 2.]

[2] [On the evidence now before us, we should probably read ἠδυν. seven times only, Mk. iv. 33, vi. 19, xiv. 5, L. viii. 19, xix. 3, Jo. ix. 33, xii. 39; and ἐδυν. (which occurs in *Rec.* twice only) twelve times. In the aorist we must read ἠδυνήθην (except in Mk. vii. 24, ἠδυνάσθη), but ἐδυν. is often a variant. From βούλομαι the forms with η are nowhere sufficiently attested.]

[3] Also Georgi, *Hierocr.* I. 32; Jacobs, *Achill. T.* p. 554; Ellendt, Arr. *Al.* II. 208; Boisson. *Æn. Gaz.* p. 173, and *Anecd.* V. 19.

[4] [Veitch quotes κατ-εαγῇ, -εαγείη, -εαγείς, from Hippocr. 4. 220, 128, 172. On this word see Cobet, *N. T. Vatic.* p. lxxix.]

[5] In Cinnam. p. 190 we find an unusual form of the perfect, κατέαγηκε.

[6] [This fut. does not occur in the LXX (κατάξω Hab. iii. 12); in Is. xlii. 3 the word is συντρίψει. Κατεάξω occurs Ps. xlvii. 8 Symm.]

SECT. XII.] AUGMENT AND REDUPLICATION OF REGULAR VERBS. 83

Greek, we find ὠνησάμην A. vii. 16 (as in Greek authors occasionally, Lob. p. 139): also ὦσα, ὠσάμην A. vii. 27, 39, 45, for ἔωσα, ἐωσάμην (§ 15). For similar instances see Poppo, *Thuc.* III. ii. p. 407, the Index to Leo Gr. p. 533. [Veitch, *Gr. V.* s. vv.]

3. In verbs beginning with ευ we find

(*a*) Without augment: εὐδόκησα usually, ηὐδ. being favoured by the MSS. in Mt. xvii. 5, 1 C. x. 5, Col. i. 19, H. x. 6, 8, only ;—εὐλόγησα more frequently than ηὐλ. (which is found Mt. xiv. 19, L. xxiv. 30, H. xi. 20, 21), and the perf. εὐλόγηκεν H. vii. 6 ;—εὔχοντο A. xxvii. 29 ;—εὐχαρίστησε A. xxvii. 35;—εὐπορεῖτο A. xi. 29 ;—and decidedly εὑρίσκειν [1] (except ηὕρισκον Mk. xiv. 55, in good MSS.; comp. further A. vii. 46, L. xix. 48).

(*b*) With augment: ηὐχόμην Rom. ix. 3 (the best reading), εὐχόμην occurs Xen. *Anab.* 4. 8. 25, *Cyr.* 3. 2. 15, but not without variants;—ηὐχαρίστησαν Rom. i. 21;—ηὐφόρησεν L. xii. 16 (doubtful);—ηὐκαίρουν Mk. vi. 31 (but doubtful in A. xvii. 21);—ηὐφράνθη A. ii. 26 (from the LXX). See in general Buttm. I. 321, Poppo, *Thuc.* I. 227, also Lehm. *Lucian* II. 456 (Jelf 173, Don. p. 196). Εὐαγγελίζ. has the augment after εὐ- (without any variant), A. viii. 35, 40, xvii. 18, 1 C. xv. 1, G. iv. 13, Rev. x. 7, al. (see Lob. p. 269),—even προευηγγελίσατο G. iii. 8 ; so also εὐαρεστεῖν H. xi. 5, though A and several other MSS. have εὐαρεστηκέναι, without augment. Προςεύχεσθαι almost always has the augment without any variant, as προςηύξατο Mt. xxvi. 44, A. viii. 15, προςηύχετο Mk. i. 35, L. xxii. 41, al.[2]

4. Οἰκοδομεῖν, the only verb beginning with οι which occurs

---

[1] Comp. Lob. p. 140, and *Ajax* p. 123 ; Herm. Eur. *Bacch.* p. 11 ; Boisson. Philostr. *Epp.* p. 75. Even in Attic Greek the augm. is defended by Elmsley, Eur. *Med.* 191, and it occurs frequently in the apocryphal writers (*Ev. Nic.* c. 20) and in the Fathers. [See Veitch, *Gr. V.* s. v.; compare Don. p. 196.]

[2] [The aor. of εὐδοκέω occurs 16 times : *Rec.* has εὐδόκ. once only, Lachm. 12 times, Treg. 8, Tisch. 9, Westc. and Hort 10. This diversity shows the difficulty of decision. The imperfect also is doubtful (1 Th. ii. 8). In εὐλογέω the augment should probably be rejected throughout. In Rom. ix. 3 we must read ηὐχόμην, but A. xxvii. 29 is doubtful. Εὐφόρησεν is the true reading in L. xii. 16 ; εὐκαίρουν in Mk. vi. 31, but ηὐκ. in A. xvii. 21. In A. vii. 41 we have εὐφραίνοντο ; in A. xvi. 11, Mt. xix. 12, εὐθυδρομέω and εὐνουχίζω reject the augment. From καθεύδω we have only ἐκάθευδον in the N. T. Ηὗρον and ηὑρέθην are not unfrequently *v. ll.*, but the evidence is against the augm. in this verb, except in ηὕρισκον, ηὑρισκόμην. Προςεύχομαι always has the augment, but -ευ- is often a variant. See Veitch, *Gr. V.* s. vv.]

in past tenses,¹ has the regular augment, not indeed without *v. ll.* but on greatly preponderating authority; as ᾠκοδόμησε Mt. vii. 24, xxi. 33, ᾠκοδόμητο L. iv. 29, ᾠκοδόμουν L. xvii. 28, ᾠκοδομήθη Jo. ii. 20: only in A. vii. 47 have good MSS. οἰκοδόμησε, on which later form see Lob. p. 153 (Jelf 173. 6).

5. In the verb προφητεύειν the augment is usually inserted after the preposition (Buttm. I. 335, Don. p. 199), and in Jude 14 the best reading is προεφήτευσε; but in all other passages in the N. T. the better MSS. have ἐπροφ.: thus ἐπροφήτευσαν Mt. xi. 13, ἐπροφητεύσαμεν Mt. vii. 22, ἐπροφήτευσε Mt. xv. 7, Mk. vii. 6, L. i. 67, Jo. xi. 51, ἐπροφήτευον A. xix. 6 (comp. Num. xi. 25, 26, Ecclus. xlviii. 13). Schulz (on Mt. vii. 22) urged that this form should be received into the text in every case, and this has been done by Lachm. and Tisch. In later writers the augm. is often put before the prepos., as ἐπρόςθηκεν, ἐσυμβούλευον (see the Index to Ducas, to Jo. Cananus, al., in the Bonn ed.), ἑκατήχουν Epiphan. Mon. 33. 16:² in προφητεύειν, however, this is less strange, since there is no simple verb φητεύειν.³

6. The augment of the form εἴληφα (for the unused λέληφα, Buttm. I. 316) is extended to the 1 aor. κατειλήφθην, which is found Jo. viii. 4 (though not without a *v. l.*) instead of κατελ.; see Maittaire, *Dialectt.* p. 58 (ed. Sturz). Traces of this form already existed in Ionic Greek.⁴

7. A double augment is found in

(*a*) ἀπεκατεστάθη Mt. xii. 13, Mk. iii. 5, L. vi. 10, now rightly admitted into the text: comp. ἀπεκατέστησε Lucian, *Philopatr.* c. 27, ἀπεκατέστησαν Ducas 29, ἀπεκατέστη⁵ Theophan. p. 374, ἀντεκατέστην Cinnam. p. 259: see Dindorf, *Diod. S.* p. 539, and Schæf. *Plutarch,* V. p. 198.⁶

---

¹ [The only *simple* verb,—there are several compounds: Tisch. now receives οἰκ. in Jo. ii. 20, ἐποικοδόμησιν 1 C. iii. 14 (Treg., Alf.), οἰκοδομήσθαι L. vi. 48 (see A. Buttm. in *Stud. u. Krit.* 1862, p. 164): Treg. reads οἰκ. in A. vii. 47. In these four places οἰκ. is received by Westc. and Hort. See Tisch. on A. vii. 47, and *Proleg.* p. 55 (ed. 7). Comp. οἰκοδόμησαν Ruth iv. 11 (*Alex.*), οἰκτείρησιν Ps. cii. 13, al.]
² *Epiphanii Mon. edita et inedita,* cura A. Dressel (Par. 1843).
³ [Lachm. reads προεφ. in Jude 14 only; Tisch., Treg., Westcott and Hort, ἐπροφ. always. The LXX use both forms.]
⁴ [Comp. εἰρήθην, Ionic for ἐρρήθην. But here κατειλ. has little support.]
⁵ [This is probably the true reading in Mk. viii. 25 (Ex. iv. 7).]
⁶ Comp. also ἐπροεφήτευον Leo Gramm. pp. 33, 35, 36, ἐκατεσκεύασαν Canan. 462, ἐσυνεμαρτύρουν ib. 478, ἠφώρισται Theophan. 112, ἐπροέταξα Theodor. *Gramm.* 40. 8. As to the Attic writers see V. Fritzsche, *Aristoph.* I. 55. [Comp. ἐπρονόμιυσα Jud. ii. 14, al. See also Mullach p. 246.]

SECT. XII.] AUGMENT AND REDUPLICATION OF REGULAR VERBS. 85

(b) In ἀνέῳξεν Jo. ix. 14, 30, ἀνεῴχθη L. i. 64 (*Irr. V.* s. v. οἴγω); once even in the infin. aor. ἀνεῳχθῆναι L. iii. 21. From this verb however several other forms are found in good MSS.: ἤνοιξεν Rev. xii. 16, al., ἠνοίχθησαν Rev. xx. 12, ἠνοίγην A. xii. 10, Rev. xi. 19, xv. 5,—as in the LXX and later writers (*Irr. V. l. c.*, Lob. p. 157); and with a threefold augment, ἠνεῴχθησαν Mt. ix. 30, Jo. ix. 10, A. xvi. 26, Rev. xx. 12 *v. l.* (Gen. vii. 11, Dan. vii. 10), ἠνεῳγμένον A. ix. 8, Rev. xix. 11 (Nicet. Eugen. 2. 84, 128, *v. l.*), ἠνέῳξε Jo. ix. 14 *v. l.* (Gen. viii. 6, 3 Macc. vi. 18): comp. Thilo, *Apocr.* I. 669.[1] [Jelf 173, 297, Veitch, *Gr. Verbs*, pp. 66, 67.]

(c) In ἠνείχεσθε 2 C. xi. 1 (*Elz.*), xi. 4 (*Rec.*)—compare Thuc. 5. 45, Herodian 8. 5. 9,—and ἠνεσχόμην A. xviii. 14, for ἀνεσχ. (comp. Her. 7. 159, Thuc. 3. 28): this is in exact conformity with classical usage, to which the forms with the single augment are almost unknown, see *Irr. V.* s. v. [Jelf 181, comp. Veitch, *Gr. Verbs*, s. v.] In 2 C. xi. 1, 4, however, the best MSS. have ἀνείχεσθε.[2]

8. From ἐργάζομαι we sometimes find in the MSS. ἤργ., instead of εἰργ., as in Mt. xxv. 16, xxvi. 10, Mk. xiv. 6, L. xix. 16, A. xviii. 3 (Ex. xxxvi. 4): this form occurs in a good MS. of Demosthenes (Schæf. *Appar.* V. 553), comp. Sturz p. 125.[3] Conversely, in L. xvi. 20 good MSS. have εἰλκωμένος (Lach., Tisch.) from ἑλκοῦν: comp. also Clem. Al. p. 348 (Sylb.).

9. The augment is usually omitted in the pluperfect, as δεδώκει Mk. xiv. 44, xv. 10, Jo. xi. 57, πεποιήκεισαν Mk. xv. 7, (ἐκβεβλήκει xvi. 9), τεθεμελίωτο L. vi. 48, μεμενήκεισαν 1 Jo. ii. 19, περιπεπατήκει A. xiv. 8 (see Valcken. *in loc.*), πεπιστεύκεισαν xiv. 23; and in the N. T. these forms should probably be preferred throughout.[4] In this tense the augment is often omitted by Ionic (Her. 1. 122, 3. 42, 9. 22) and Attic prose writers (e.g.

---

[1] [Some of these examples are doubtful, but all the forms given above are very well attested in some part of the N. T.: the following forms of this verb are also found, ἀνοίξω Mt. xiii. 35 (LXX), ἀνέῳγα 1 C. xvi. 9, ἀνεῳγμένος A. x. 11, διηνοιγμένος A. vii. 56 (ἀνοιχθήσομαι L. xi. 10), ἀνοιγήσομαι Mt. vii. 7.—Διακονέω has always διηκόνουν in the N. T.]

[2] [In 2 C. xi. 4 we must read either ἀνέχεσθε or ἀνέχεσθε; in A. xviii. 14, ἀνεσχόμην.]

[3] [This form is a variant wherever the imperf. or aor. (middle or passive) occurs, and is received more or less frequently by Lachm., Tisch., Alf., Treg., Westcott and Hort. Veitch (*Gr. V.* s.v.) quotes such forms from inscriptions. Comp. Mullach, *Vulg.* p. 27.]

[4] [Sometimes (as L. xvi. 20, Jo. ix. 22) no MS. omits the augment.]

Plato), especially when the augmented form would offend the ear (Buttm. I. 318); hence in compounds particularly (comp. A. xiv. 8).¹ Compare Thuc. 8. 92, Xen. *Cyr.* 3. 2. 24; and as to later writers see especially the Index to Joa. Cinnam. in the Bonn ed. (Jelf 171).²

10. Μνηστεύεσθαι receives the reduplication (after the analogy of μέμνημαι, Buttm. I. 315) in L. i. 27, ii. 5, μεμνηστευμένη; but some good MSS. read ἐμνηστ. [Lach., Tisch., and others]: comp. Dt. xx. 7, xxii. 23 sqq. On ῥεραντισμένοι H. x. 22, see § 13. 1. *b.*

In 2 Tim. i. 16, the aor. of the compound ἐπαισχύνομαι is in the best MSS. ἐπαισχύνθη, without the temporal augment, and recent editors have received this form into the text: similarly ἀνορθώθη L. xiii. 13.³

Section XIII.

UNUSUAL FORMS IN THE TENSES AND PERSONS OF REGULAR VERBS.

1. (*a*) Tenses which in other respects are formed entirely after the analogy of the 2 aor. have in the LXX the termination (of the 1 aor.) *a*, etc.:⁴ thus εἴδαμεν 1 S. x. 14, εἶδαν and ἔφυγαν 2 S. x. 14, εὗραν xvii. 20, ἐφάγαμεν xix. 42, ἐλθάτω Esth. v. 4 (Pr. ix. 5, Am. vi. 2, 2 Chr. xxix. 17), etc. In the N. T. recent editors have placed these forms in the text, following the best MSS.:⁵ ἤλθατε, ἐξήλθατε Mt. xxv. 36, xxvi. 55, παρελθάτω Mt. xxvi. 39, εἵλατο 2 Th. ii. 13, ἐξείλατο A. vii. 10, xii. 11, ἀνείλατο vii. 21, ἐξεπέσατε G. v. 4, ἔπεσαν Rev. vii. 11 (H. iii. 17, Jo.

---

¹ See Georgi, *Hierocr.* I. 179; Poppo, *Thuc.* I. 228; Bornem. Xen. *Anab.* p. 272; Jacob, Luc. *Tox.* p. 68; Ellendt, Arr. *Al.* I. pp. 265, 284; [Shilleto, Dem. *F. Leg.* p. 38. Compare Don. p. 201].
² [Mt. vii. 25 is more certain than L. vi. 48; in A. xiv. 8 the aorist is the best reading. Comp. δεδώκειν 2 S. xviii. 11, ἐπιβεβήκει Num. xxii. 22, and see Tisch. *Proleg.* p. 56 (ed. 7).]
³ [Similar examples are προορώμην A. ii. 25 (from LXX), διερμήνευεν or -νευσεν L. xxiv. 27, and (with less authority) ὁμοιώθημεν Rom. ix. 29, διηγείρετο Jo. vi. 18, ἀφωμοιωμένος H. vii. 3; see also 2 Chr. xxxv. 10, and Is. i. 9 in *Alex.*]
⁴ See Sturz p. 61; Valcken. *Herod.* p. 649, 91; D'Orville, *Charit.* p. 402; Wolf, Demosth. *Lept.* p. 216.
⁵ On the MSS. which have this form see Hug, *Introd.* § 50 sqq.; Scholz, *Curæ Crit.* p. 40; Rinck, *Lucubratt.* p. 37; Tisch. *Prolegg. ad Cod. Ephraemi* p. 21. [Scrivener, *Critic.* p. 489, *Cod. Sin.* p. liv.]

xviii. 6), ἀνέπεσαν Jo. vi. 10, εὐράμενος H. ix. 12, Epiph. *Opp.*
I. 619, Theodoret, *Opp.* II. 837 (Hal.). Comp. A. ii. 23, xvii.
6 [?], xii. 7, xvi. 37, xxii. 7, xxviii. 16, Mt. vii. 13, 25, xi. 7, 8,
xvii. 6, xxii. 22, L. ii. 16, xi. 52, xxii. 52, Rom. xv. 3, 1 C. x. 8,
2 C. vi. 17, 1 Jo. ii. 19, Rev. v. 8, 14, vi. 13.

There is indeed no consistency in the MSS., as regards either writers or words;[1] and in many passages, where such forms have the support of but few MSS., they may be due to transcribers,[2] particularly if similar inflexions in *a* precede or follow: see Elmsley, Eur. *Med.* p. 232 (Lips.), Fritz. *Mark*, p. 638 sqq. It is in the plural and in the 1st pers. sing. of the indic. that we usually meet with these forms; in the 2d sing. indic., the imper.,[3] and the participle, they occur very rarely. On the instances of such aorists in Greek authors (e.g. Orpheus) see Buttm. I. 404. In Eurip. *Troad.* 293, Seidler has changed προςέπεσα into -σον; and in *Alcest.* 477 (πέσειε), πέσοι is certainly the true reading, see Herm. *in loc.*[4] On the other hand, we find ἔπεσαν Theophan. p. 283, κατεπέσαμεν Achill. Tat. 3. 17, περιεπέσαμεν c. 19; and in Eustath. *Amor. Ism.* I. p. 4 we should read ἐκπέσειε on the authority of good MSS., see Jacobs p. 664. Compare further Lob. p. 183, Matth. 193. Rem. 5. In the Byzantine writers there are undeniably various examples of such forms; as ἦλθαν Malal. 18. p. 465, 12. p. 395, ἀνῆλθαν 15. p. 389, ηὕραμεν 18. p. 449, ἀπέλθατε Ducas 24, ἐξέλθατε Leo Gr. p. 343, ἐπεισέλθατε p. 337 : comp. in general the Index to Ducas p. 639, and to Theophan. p. 682 sq. (Bonn ed.).[5]

---

[1] They are mostly verbs which have not a 1 aorist in use.

[2] Ἀνάπισαι, which is found in good MSS. in L. xiv. 10, xvii. 7, would necessarily be the imper. of a similarly formed aor. middle ἀνεπισάμην. As, however, this tense nowhere occurs (though a trace of it appears in the v. l. ἐκπεισαμένοις Polyb. 6. 37. 4), ἀνάπισαι must probably be considered an error of transcription for ἀνάπισε, as ε and αι are often interchanged : indeed the best MSS. have -πισε, and this has recently been received into the text. Comp. also Rinck, *Lucubr.* p. 330, [Tisch. on L. xiv. 10, and *Proleg.* p. 56]. Besides, the 2 aor. active is the only tense of ἀναπίπτω that occurs in the N. T., Mt. xv. 35, Mk. vi. 40, L. xi. 37, xxii. 14, Jo. vi. 10, al. [The forms in α are now received in Mk. vi, Jo. vi.] Fritzsche (*Mark*, p. 641) considers ἀνάπισαι to be the 2d sing. fut. (like πίσαι) ; but the future would be unsuitable, especially as in L. xvii. 7 imperatives immediately follow.

[3] [In the 2d singular ; but the 3d sing. and 2d plur. are not rare.]

[4] But εὕριαν is distinctly found in a Greek inscription, Böckh II. 220. [In Eur. *Alc.* 477, ἴπεσα is received by Buttm. (II. 278) and by Mullach (*Vulg.* p. 226). Comp., however, Veitch, *Gr. V.* s.v. πίπτω.]

[5] [The forms in α are well attested in almost all the examples given above from the N. T. : in H. iii. 17, however, ἔπεσιν seems certainly the best reading. Rarer

(b) Augmented tenses of verbs beginning with ρ are found in the best MSS. with a single ρ (comp. § 5): as ἐραβδίσθην 2 C. xi. 25, ἐράντισε H. ix. 19 (ἐραντισμένοι x. 22), ἐράπισαν Mt. xxvi. 67, ἐρύσατο 2 Tim. iii. 11 (in A, D), ἐρύσθη iv. 17 (A, C): comp. 2 K. xxiii. 18, Ex. v. 23, vii. 10, Lev. xiv. 7, 51, Num. viii. 7. Such forms are recognised in poetry (Buttm. I. 84, Matth. 40, Jelf 176. 1), but also occur frequently in the MSS. of prose writers; see Bast, *Comm. Crit.* p. 788. In H. x. 22 the reduplicated perfect ῥεραντισμένοι is found in A. and C, compare ῥερυπωμένα Hom. *Odyss.* 6. 59; some examples of a similar kind are met with in late writers (Lob. *Paral.* p. 13). In Mt. ix. 36 also Lachm. reads ῥεριμμένοι [rather ῥεριμμ.] on the authority of D.[1]

(c) The futures of verbs in ιζω are sometimes found (with but slight variation in the MSS.) in the contracted form; as μετοικιῶ A. vii. 43, ἀφοριεῖ Mt. xxv. 32, ἀφοριοῦσι Mt. xiii. 49, γνωριοῦσι Col. iv. 9, καθαριεῖ H. ix. 14, διακαθαριεῖ Mt. iii. 12, ἐλπιοῦσι Mt. xii. 21, μακαριοῦσι L. i. 48, etc. This is an Atticism, though such forms are also found in Ionic Greek; comp. Georgi, *Hier.* I. 29, Fischer, *Weller* II. 355, Matth. 181. 2 (Jelf 203, Don. p. 182). From βαπτίζω we find only the common form βαπτίσει Mt. iii. 11: on στηρίζω see § 15. In the LXX verbs in αζω also form the future in the same way; as ἐργᾶται Lev. xxv. 40, ἁρπᾷ xix. 13, etc. Some have considered γεννᾶται Mt. ii. 4, θεωρεῖτε Jo. xvi. 17 (since ὄψεσθε follows), ποιῶ Mt. xxvi. 18, as similar Attic futures, from contracted verbs; but these are all present

---

forms are ἔπισα Rev. i. 17, xix. 10, al., ἴδα (or ἴδα) Rev. xvii. 6 (ἔπισας 2 S. iii. 34), ἀπῆλθα Rev. x. 9; and the imperfects εἶχαν Mk. viii. 7 (Rev. ix. 8), παρεῖχαν A. xxviii. 2, προσεῖχαν A. viii. 10 in ℵ. These forms are said to have been originally Cilician. See Jelf 192, Mullach p. 17 sq., 226, A. Buttm. p. 39 sq.]

[1] [*Augmented Tenses.* ℵ has the single ρ in the passages quoted in the text (except 2 Tim. iii. 11). In 2 C. xi. 25, H. ix. 19, 21, Mt. xxvi. 67, ἐρα. is no doubt correct: ῥίπτω occurs twice (Mt. xv. 30, A. xxvii. 19), and ῥύομαι five times (2 C. i. 10, Col. i. 13, 2 Tim. iii. 11, iv. 17, 2 P. ii. 7) with the augment, and in each case we should probably reject the double ρ. From ῥήσσω (and compounds) we find both forms: ἐρρ. Mt. xxvi. 65, L. ix. 42, ἐρ. L. v. 6, vi. 48, 49. Similarly after a preposition, ἐπιρίψαντες L. xix. 35 (1 P. v. 7, A. xxvii. 43), παραρυῶμεν H. ii. 1, διαρήσσων L. viii. 29 (A. xvi. 22, but διαρρ. A. xiv. 14,—Mk. xiv. 63 is more doubtful), ἐπιράπτει Mk. ii. 21.

Reduplicated Tenses. The ordinary form ἐρρ. is found in L. xvii. 2 (ἔρριπται), also in E. iii. 17, Col. ii. 7, A. xv. 29. In Mt. ix. 36 we should read ἐριμμένοι. In H. x. 22 the reduplication must certainly be received, whether we write ῥερ. (Tisch.), or ῥερ. (Lachm., Treg., Westc. and Hort), or ῥερρ. (Lobeck, *Paral.* p. 14). In Rev. xix. 13 ℵ has περιρεραμμένον, and (by a later hand) περιρεραντισμένον (Don. pp. 16, 195, Jelf 176).]

tenses, see § 40. 2, and comp. Fritz. on Mt. *ll. cc.*, Matth. 181. 2 a (Jelf 203).¹

(*d*) Of verbs in αινω, λευκαίνω has in the aor. the Attic form (Buttm. I. 439) λευκᾶναι Mk. ix. 3: in G. iii. 1 several MSS. have ἐβάσκηνα, from βασκαίνω,—also a correct form. Σημαίνω, however, has ἐσήμανα, A. xi. 28, Rev. i. 1; see below, § 15. The *a* is also retained in the aor. of μωραίνω 1 C. i. 20, and ξηραίνω Ja. i. 11, as it regularly is in verbs in *-ραίνω*: on φᾶναι see § 15. (Jelf 222.)²

(*e*) In particular passages future conjunctives are noted, as found in a greater or smaller number of MSS.: thus 1 C. xiii. 3 κανθήσωμαι (received into the text by Griesbach), 1 P. iii. 1 κερδηθήσωνται, 1 Tim. vi. 8 ἀρκεσθησώμεθα,—in the last two passages without much authority. In the better class of writers such forms are probably due to the transcribers (Lob. p. 721),³ but in later authors, especially the Scholiasts (as on Thuc. 3. 11 and 54), they cannot be set aside. In the N. T., however, there is very little in favour of these conjunctives. We find as isolated instances εὑρήσῃς Rev. xviii. 14, εὑρήσωσιν ix. 6 (yet an aor. εὑρῆσαι is sometimes met with, Lob. p. 721), γνώσωνται A. xxi. 24 (yet compare Lob. p. 735): ὄψησθε, L. xiii. 28, and δώσῃ, Jo. xvii. 2, are unquestionably aorists.⁴ [See § 15.]

2. Peculiar person-endings :—

(*a*) The 2 pers. sing. of the pres. and fut. passive and middle in ει instead of ῃ; as βούλει L. xxii. 42, παρέξει vii. 4 *v. l.*, ὄψει Mt. xxvii. 4 and Jo. xi. 40 *v. l.*: comp. also A. xvi. 31, xxiv. 8 *v. ll.* In the two verbs ὄπτεσθαι and βούλεσθαι this

---

¹ [A. Buttm. (p. 37) gives a list of verbs which have this future in the N. T.: ἀφορίζω, ἐλπίζω, παροργίζω, καθαρίζω, ἐδαφίζω, μακαρίζω, μετοικίζω, ἐγγίζω, χρονίζω, and sometimes κομίζομαι. To these will be added γνωρίζω, if we read γνωριοῦσιν in Col. iv. 9 ; the usual future is γνωρίσω. The fut. of χρονίζω, however, is probably χρονίσω (H. x. 37). On στηρίζω, σαλπίζω, see § 15. Contracted futures are very common in the LXX. On γεννᾶται and other presents which have been taken for futures, see A. Buttm. p. 38.]

² [In G. iii. 1 all the uncial MSS. have ἐβάσκανε. Add ποιμάνατε 1 P. v. 2 (ἐκκαθάρῃ 2 Tim. ii. 21). See Lob. p. 25; Veitch, *Gr. V.* pp. 305, 519.]

³ See Abresch in *Observatt. Misc.* III. p. 13 ; and as to the later writers Niebuhr, *Ind. ad Agath.* p. 418, and the Index to Theophan. p. 682.

⁴ [In 1 C. xiii. 3 the oldest MSS. have καυχήσωμαι ; Tisch. and Meyer καυθήσομαι: Alford and Treg. (*Printed Text* p. 191) with *Rec.* καυθήσωμαι: comp. Scriv. *Introd.* p. 547. In 1 P. iii. 1, 1 Tim. vi. 8, A. xxi. 24, Rev. xviii. 14 the fut. indic. is certainly the true reading ; in Rev. ix. 6 the oldest MSS. have either fut. indic. or 2 aor. subj.: even in Jo. xvii. 2 we should probably read the fut. indic. See below, p. 95 ; A. Buttm. p. 36 ; Lightfoot, *Clem. R.* pp. 188, 450.]

is the form always used by Attic writers (Buttm. I. 348, Jelf 196); in others it is of rare occurrence and is almost confined to the poets:[1] even in Attic prose, however, it is found in good MSS., see Buttmann *l. c.*, but compare Schneider, Plat. *Civ.* I. 49 sqq. *Præf.*[2]

(*b*) The original uncontracted form of the 2 pers. sing. is retained in δύνασαι (Mt. v. 36, viii. 2, Mk. i. 40), as usually in classical Greek (Buttm. I. 502): δύνῃ—Mk. ix. 22, Rev. ii. 2, and L. xvi. 2 *v. l.*[3]—was used by poets alone of earlier writers, but is found in later prose, as Polyb. 7. 11. 5, Ælian 13. 32; see Lob. p. 359. In the N. T. this ending appears also in contracted verbs; as ὀδυνᾶσαι L. xvi. 25 (Æschyl. *Choëph.* 354[4]), καυχᾶσαι Rom. ii. 17, 1 C. iv. 7, and κατακαυχᾶσαι Rom. xi. 18: comp. Georgi, *Hier.* I. 184, Buttm. I. 347, Boisson. *Anecd.* IV. 479 (Jelf 196). See § 15, s. v. πίνω.

(*c*) In the 3 pers. plur. of the perfect, αν (from the old ending αντι) instead of ασι; as ἔγνωκαν Jo. xvii. 7, τετήρηκαν xvii. 6, εἴρηκαν Rev. xix. 3, ἑώρακαν (in very good MSS.) L. ix. 36, Col. ii. 1,—similarly Rev. xxi. 6, Ja. v. 4: so also in the LXX, as Dt. xi. 7, Judith vii. 10 (*Act. Apocr.* p. 235). This form belongs to the Alexandrian dialect (comp. Sext. Empir. 1. 10. p. 261, and the *Papyri Taurin.* p. 24, κεκυρίευκαν), but occurs also in Lycophron (252, πέφρικαν), in inscriptions, and often in the Byzantine writers (comp. Index to Ducas p. 639, to Codinus, and to Leo Gramm.): see Buttm. I. 345 (Jelf 191, Don. p. 253). Tisch. has received it in all the above N. T. passages:[5] in Rev. ii. 3, however, he has rejected κεκοπίακες (Ex. v. 22 *Alex.*), the reading of A and C.

(*d*) The originally Æolic termination εια (ειας, ειε) instead of αιμι, in the 1 aor. opt.; as ψηλαφήσειαν A. xvii. 27, ποιήσειαν

---

[1] Comp. Valcken. Eur. *Phœn.* p. 216 sq. (261); Fischer, *Weller* I. 119, II. 399; Georgi, *Hier.* I. 34; Schwarz, *ad Olear.* p. 225.

[2] [L. xxii. 42 is the only passage in which this form is well supported.]

[3] On this form, for which some would substitute δύνᾳ, see Porson, Eur. *Hec.* 257; Schæf. and Herm. Soph. *Phil.* 787; Oudend. *ad Thom. M.* p. 252; Lob. p. 359. [Veitch, *Gr. V.* s. v. δύναμαι. In all these passages, and in Mk. ix. 23, δύνῃ is probably the true reading.]

[4] [Ὀδυνᾶσαι here is regarded as corrupt: Müller conjectured οὐ δύνασαι, Herm. δύνασαι. This form is in regular use in modern Greek: Mullach p. 229.]

[5] [In editions 7 and 8 he rightly retains these readings: A. xvi. 36, Rom. xvi. 7 may be added. He also receives the ending ες for ας in the 2 pers. sing. in Rev. ii. 3, ii. 4 (ἀφῆκες), and in the latter passage he has the support of ℵ: in Jo. xvii. 7, 8, B has ἔδωκες.]

L. vi. 11.[1] This form was very frequently used (in the 2 and 3 pers. sing. and 3 pers. plur.) in Attic Greek, as Thuc. 6. 19, 8. 6, Aristoph. *Plut.* 95, Plat. *Rep.* I. 337 c, *Gorg.* 500 c, Xen. *An.* 7. 7. 30, al. (Georgi, *Hier.* I. 150 sq., Buttm. I. 354 sq., Jelf 194), and still more frequently by later writers: see Ellendt, Arr. *Al.* I. 353.

(*e*) The 3 pers. plur. of the imperative in τωσαν occurs repeatedly in the N. T.; as γαμησάτωσαν 1 C. vii. 9, γαμείτωσαν vii. 36, μανθανέτωσαν 1 Tim. v. 4 (Tit. iii. 14); comp. A. xxiv. 20, xxv. 5.[2] Elmsley's opinion,[3] that this form was not in use before the time of Aristotle, is sufficiently refuted by Matth. (198) and Bornemann (Xen. *An.* p. 38).

(*f*) The 3 pers. plur. of the historical tenses often ends in οσαν in good MSS. (Buttm. I. 346); as εἴχοσαν (for εἶχον) Jo. xv. 22, 24, ἐδίδοσαν[4] (for ἐδίδουν) xix. 3, παρελάβοσαν 2 Th. iii. 6, and in Rom. iii. 13 (from LXX) ἐδολιοῦσαν. This termination is very common in the LXX and the Byzantine writers; as ἤλθοσαν Ex. xv. 27, ἐφάγοσαν Jos. v. 11, κατελίποσαν Ex. xvi. 24, ἐκρίνοσαν xviii. 26, εἴδοσαν Niceph. Greg. 6. 5. p. 113, κατήλθοσαν Nicet. Chon. 21. 7. p. 402, μετήλθοσαν Niceph. Bryenn. p. 165, Brunck, *Analect.* II. 47: comp. also 1 Macc. vi. 31, Cant. iii. 3, v. 7, vi. 8, Jos. ii. 1, iii. 14, v. 11, vi. 14, viii. 19, Jud. xix. 11, i. 6, Ruth i. 4, Lam. ii. 14, Ez. xxii. 11, Ex. xxxiii. 8, al.: see Fischer, *Weller* II. 336 sq., Georgi, *Hier.* I. 165 sq., Lob. *Phryn.* p. 349, *Pathol.* I. 485, Sturz p. 58 sqq. In the N. T., however, with the exception of Rom. *l. c.*, this form is found in a few MSS. only, and it may perhaps have originated with the Alexandrian transcribers in every case.[5]

3. From contracted verbs:—

(*a*) The future ἐκχεῶ A. ii. 17, 18 (from LXX), following the analogy of liquid verbs (Buttm. I. 469); comp. Ez. vii. 8, xxi. 31, Jer. xiv. 16, Hos. v. 10, Zech. xii. 10. If accentuated ἐκχέω, it would be, according to Elmsley, the Attic future: for ἐκχέω is

---

[1] [In L. vi. 11, recent editors read -αιεν.]
[2] [I believe the form in -ντων is not given by Tisch., even as a *v. l.* Similarly, in the passive we find -σθωσαν (not -σθων), as Ja. v. 14, L. xxi. 21.]
[3] Elmsley, Eurip. *Iph. Taur.* p. 232 (ed. Lips.).
[4] [In this verb, however, this is the regular form.]
[5] [This ending is received by Tisch., Alford, and others, in all these passages. See Mullach p. 16, who quotes ἔσχοσαν from Scymnus Chius, and the similar forms ἀφίλισαν, ἐλαμβάνοσαν, found in papyri in the Brit. Museum. Such forms as ἐδολιοῦσαν (in contr. verbs) are of regular occurrence in modern Greek.]

both pres. and fut. (Buttm. II. 325, Jelf 245). In the LXX, however, other persons occur, and these are circumflexed; as ἐκχεεῖς, ἐκχεεῖτε, Ex. iv. 9, xxix. 12, xxx. 18, Dt. xii. 16.

(*b*) From the two verbs διψάω, πεινάω, the forms in use in written (Attic) Greek were διψῆν, πεινῆν, in the infinitive, and διψῇς, διψῇ, κ.τ.λ., in the indicative (Buttm. I. 487, Jelf 239). In the N. T. we find instead διψᾶν, διψᾷ, Rom. xii. 20, Jo. vii. 37; πεινᾶν Ph. iv. 12, πεινᾷ Rom. xii. 20, 1 C. xi. 21: these forms in *a* are first found in Aristotle (*Anim.* 9. 21, comp. Sallier *ad Thom. M.* p. 699, Lob. p. 61). According to the same analogy we find the fut. πεινάσω (for πεινήσω) Rev. vii. 16, Jo. vi. 35 *v. l.* (Is. v. 27, Ps. xlix. 12), and 1 aor. ἐπείνασα Mk. ii. 25, xi. 12, Mt. xii. 1, 3, xxv. 35, L. iv. 2, al.: both these forms are peculiarities of later Greek, see Lob. p. 204.[1]

(*c*) Of the verbs in εω which retain ε in the future, etc. (Lob. *Paral.* p. 435, Jelf 233), καλέω and τελέω occur in the N. T.: thus we find καλέσω, τελέσω (Buttm. I. 386).[2] We find also φορέσω and ἐφόρεσα 1 C. xv. 49 (Ecclus. xi. 5, Palæph. 52. 4): in Greek writers φορήσω is the ordinary form (so εὐφόρησεν L. xii. 16), but φορέσαι is found as early as Isæus: see *Irr. V.* s. v. φέρω. On ἀπολέσω, ἐπαινέσω, see below [§ 15].[3]

---

[1] [In the fut. and aor. διψάω is regular; διψάσω very seldom occurs as a variant. In Ps. xlix. 12 πεινάσω is aor. subj. See Veitch, *Gr. V.* s. vv.]

[2] [These are not the only verbs of this class in the N. T., for tenses with ε occur from ἀρκέω (ἐπαρκέω), ἐμέω: of the verbs which have ε more partially (Jelf 233. 2. *c*), ἐπαινέω, ἀφ- and ἀναιρέω, δέω, are found in the N. T.: we might add κορέννυμι, σβέννυμι, (ἀμφιέννυμι). On φορέω see Veitch, *Gr. V.* s. v.]

[3] [The present infin. of verbs in όω sometimes ends in οῖν in good MSS. Tisch. receives this form in Mt. xiii. 32, H. vii. 5: Westcott and Hort read -οῖν in these passages, and in Mk. iv. 32, 1 P. ii. 15. On the occasional neglect of contraction see § 5. 3.]

Section XIV.

UNUSUAL INFLEXIONS OF VERBS IN μι AND IRREGULAR VERBS.

1. Verbs in μι:—
(*a*) Pluperf. active ἑστήκεσαν Rev. vii. 11 *v. l.*, for ἑστήκεισαν;[1] comp. ξυνεστήκεσαν Thuc. 1. 15, ἐφεστήκεσαν Xen. *An.* 1. 4. 4, ἐῴκεσαν Heliod. 4. 16, and see especially Jacobs, *Achill. Tat.* pp. 400, 622, Ellendt, Arr. *Al.* II. 77.

(*b*) The 3 pers. plur. present τιθέασι (for τιθεῖσι) Mt. v. 15, περιτιθέασι Mk. xv. 17, ἐπιτιθέασι Mt. xxiii. 4. This is the better and more usual form, comp. Thuc. 2. 34, Aristot. *Metaph.* 11. 1, Theophr. *Plant.* 2. 6 : see Georgi, *Hierocr.* I. 145 sq., where many examples are given, and Matth. 210, Schneider, Plat. *Civ.* II. 250 (Jelf 274). Similarly, διδόασι Rev. xvii. 13, in the best MSS. ; comp. Her. 1. 93, Thuc. 1. 42. The contracted forms τιθεῖσι and (more especially) διδοῦσι belong to later Greek : see Lob. p. 244.

(*c*) The 3 pers. plur. imperf. of (a compound of) δίδωμι is ἐδίδουν, instead of ἐδίδοσαν, A. iv. 33, xxvii. 1, after the analogy of contracted verbs ;[2] compare Hes. *ἔργ.* 123. In the singular ἐδίδουν is more common (Buttm. I. 509, Jelf 276).

(*d*) On the perf. infin. active ἑστάναι 1 C. x. 12 (a shortened form for ἑστηκέναι, but very common, and perhaps the only form in use), see *Irr. V.* s. v. ; comp. Georgi, *Hier.* I. 182 sq. (Jelf 309).[3]

(*e*) The imperative pres. passive περιΐστασο is found in several MSS. in 2 Tim. ii. 16, Tit. iii. 9 ; ἀφίστασο 1 Tim. vi. 5 *v. l. ;* περιΐστω, κ.τ.λ., were more usual, see Thom. M. p. 75, Matth. 213.[4]

(*f*) There is weighty authority for some forms from a present ἱστάω (Her. 4. 103, as ἀφιστάω Joa. Cinnam. p. 121, ἐφιστάω p. 65, καθιστάω p. 104) ; as ἱστῶμεν Rom. iii. 31, συνιστῶντες

---

[1] [No uncial MS. reads -ισαν in Rev. vii. 11. This person "always ends in εισαν, as πεποιήκεισαν Mk. xv. 7, al., even where in Attic Greek εσαν alone was in use, e.g. ᾔδεισαν. We find, however, ἀπ- ἐξῄεσαν A. xvii. 15, al." A. Buttmann p. 43.]

[2] [Similarly ἐτίθουν A. iii. 2, iv. 35, and perhaps Mk. vi. 56 (but ἐπετίθεσαν A. viii. 17) : this is confined to very late Greek (Veitch, *Gr. V.* p. 562).]

[3] [Veitch remarks that the longer form in the *simple* verb seems late (Æl. *Var. Hist.* 3. 18), but quotes ἀφεστηκέναι from Demosthenes. The later perfect ἕστακα occurs A. viii. 11 in the infin. ἐξεστακέναι (Jelf 278. 5, Veitch p. 300).]

[4] [Tisch. does not give ἵστω as a variant anywhere.]

2 C. vi. 4, x. 18 (Niceph. Bryenn. p. 41, comp. καθιστῶν Agath. 316. 2), ἀποκαθιστᾷ Mk. ix. 12 (Dan. ii. 21, 2 S. xviii. 12 [in some MSS.], Fabric. *Pseud.* II. 610, ξυνιστᾷ Plat. *Tim.* 33 a): see *Gram. Græci* (ed. Dindorf) I. 251, D'Orville, *Charit.* p. 542, Matth. 210 (Jelf 276). Similarly ἐμπιπλῶν (from ἐμπιπλάω) A. xiv. 17 ; comp. ἐμπιπρῶν Leo Diac. 2. 1.[1] [See Veitch p. 299.]

(*g*) The opt. pres. δῴη for δοίη, Rom. xv. 5, 2 Tim. i. 16, 18 (ii. 7), E. i. 17, iii. 16, Jo. xv. 16 ; ἀποδῴη 2 Tim. iv. 14 ;[2] see Gen. xxvii. 28, xxviii. 4, Num. v. 21, xi. 29, al., Themist. *Or.* 8. p. 174 d, Philostr. *Apoll.* 1. 34, Dio Chr. 20. 267, Aristeas p. 120 (Haverc.), al. This is a later form, rejected by the old grammarians (Phryn. p. 345, Mœris p. 117). In Plat. *Gorg.* 481 a, Lysias, *c. Andoc.* p. 215, t. iv, recent editors have restored δῷ; and in Xen. *Cyr.* 3. 1. 35, Schneider changed δῴης into δοίης: comp. Lob. p. 346, Sturz p. 52, Buttm. in *Mus. Antiq. Stud.* I. 238.[3]

(*h*) The 2 aor. imper. of βαίνω occurs in a contracted form; ἀνάβα Rev. iv. 1, κατάβα Mk. xv. 30 *v.l.;* comp. Eurip. *El.* 113, Aristoph. *Ach.* 262, *Vesp.* 979, and see Georgi, *Hier.* I. 153, *Irr. V.* s. v. The longer form is also found, as κατάβηθι Mt. xxvii. 40, Jo. iv. 49, μετάβηθι vii. 3: comp. Th. M. p. 495 and Oudendorp *in loc.* Quite analogous is ἀνάστα A. xii. 7, E. v. 14, comp. Theocrit. 24. 36, Menand. p. 48 (Mein.), Æsop. 62 (De Furia),— also ἀπόστα Protev. *Jac.* 2, παράστα Act. *Apocr.* 51: on the other hand, ἀνάστηθι A. ix. 6, 34, ἐπίστηθι 2 Tim. iv. 2.[4] (Jelf 302, 274.)

(*i*) The N. T. MSS. vary as to the form of the neuter perf. partic. of ἵστημι, but ἑστός (ἑστηκός) is the reading of the better MSS. in both Mt. xxiv. 15 and Mk. xiii. 14: this is the form found in the oldest and best MSS. of Greek authors (*Irr. V.* s.v.,

---

[1] [In *Rec.* the form in -αω occurs in Mk. ix. 12, A. viii. 9, xvii. 15, Rom. iii. 31, 2 C. iv. 2, vi. 4, x. 18; -ανω in A. i. 6, Rom. vi. 13, 16, 2 C. iii. 1, v. 12, x. 12, 1 C. xiii. 2. Lachm., Treg., and Tisch. read -ανω in all these places, except 2 C. iv. 2, vi. 4 (συνιστάντις), 1 C. xiii. 2 (μεθιστάναι), 2 Cor. iii. 1 (Tisch. συνιστάνειν, Lachm. and Treg. συνιστᾶν): they also read συνιστάνω in G. ii. 18. In all these fifteen passages Westcott and Hort adopt -ανω.]

[2] [We should read δώσει in 2 Tim. ii. 7, iv. 14, δῶ in E. iii. 16, Jo. xv. 16. In Rom. xv. 5, 2 Tim. i. 16, 18, we must certainly read the optative (δῴη). In E. i. 17, 2 Tim. ii. 25, Lachm. writes δώῃ (for δῴη), as a *subjunctive;* so also Tisch. (ed. 7) in Jo. xv. 16. See Fritz. *Rom.* III. 230, A. Buttm. p. 46, in favour of δῴη in these passages; on the other side, Meyer on E. i. 17, and below § 41. *b.* 1. On these forms see Veitch p. 168, Jelf 274.]

[3] This form in the N. T. is the more peculiar, since, wherever it occurs, ordinary N. T. usage would require the conjunctive.

[4] [Μετάβα Mt. xvii. 20: καταβάτω Mk. xiii. 15, al., ἀνάβατι Rev. xi. 12.]

Don. p. 124) and it is adopted by Bekker in Plato throughout. The uncontracted forms of this participle also occur not unfrequently in good MSS. of the N. T.; as ἑστηκότων Mt. xxvii. 47, Mk. ix. 1, xi. 5, ἑστηκώς Jo. iii. 29, vi. 22, παρεστηκόσιν Mk. xiv. 69 : these forms have been for the most part received into the text.[1]

The conjunctive δώσῃ is fairly supported in Jo. xvii. 2, Rev. viii. 3, (δώσωσιν xiii. 16). This according to some is a Doric form; it is found in Theocr. 27. 21, but has long been replaced there by the correction δώσει.[2] In later Greek, however, this form occurs frequently (Lob. p. 721, comp. Thilo, *Apocr.* I. 871, Index to Theophanes), and may probably have been one of the corrupt forms of the popular spoken language.[3] [Veitch, *Gr. V.* p. 169.]

2. From εἰμί we find

(*a*) The imperat. ἤτω for ἔστω (the usual form in the N. T., as elsewhere) 1 C. xvi. 22, Ja. v. 12, Ps. ciii. 31, 1 Macc. x. 31, comp. Clem. Al. *Strom.* 6. 275, *Acta Thom.* 3, 7 ; once only in Plato (*Rep.* 2. 361 d), see Schneider *in loc.*,—also *Irr. V.* s. v. εἰμί (Jelf 286, Don. p. 229). According to Heraclides (in Eustath. p. 1411. 22) this is a Doric inflexion. The other imperative form ἴσθι occurs Mt. ii. 13, v. 25, Mk. v. 34, L. xix. 17, 1 Tim. iv. 15 (Buttm. I. 527).[4]

(*b*) Ἤμην, 1 pers. sing. imperf. middle (*Irr. V. l. c.*, Jelf 286), is rejected by the Atticists, and is common in later writers only (who use it especially in conjunction with ἄν); see Lob. p. 152, Schæf. *Long.* 423, Valcken. *in N. T.* I. 478. In the N. T. it is the usual form ; see Mt. xxv. 35, Jo. xi. 15, A. x. 30, xi. 5, 17, 1 C. xiii. 11, al., and comp. Thilo, *Acta Thom.* p. 3: with ἄν it

---

[1] [Ἑστός is well attested in Mt. *l. c.*, Rev. xiv. 1, but ἱστώς has not much authority anywhere : in Mk. xiii. 14 we should probably read ἑστηκότα, and ἑστηκός is generally received in Rev. v. 6 (-κώς א). The uncontracted forms of this partic. (in the simple verb and its compounds) occur frequently, though much less frequently than the contracted: in Mk. xiv. 69 παριστῶσιν is the best reading.]

[2] [Tisch. still (but see § 13. 1. e) reads δώσῃ in Jo. xvii. 2, but δώσουσιν in Rev. iv. 9 : in Rev. viii. 3, xiii. 16, we should probably read δώσει and δῶσιν.]

[3] [In this verb some other peculiar forms deserve notice : the neuter partic. ἀποδιδοῦν Rev. xxii. 2 (Lachm., Westc. and Hort) ; pres. indic. διδῶ Rev. iii. 9 ; subj. pres. and aor. (3 sing.) διδοῖ, δοῖ, 1 C. xv. 24, Mk. iv. 29, al. (1 Macc. xi. 40, see below, p. 360): all these forms follow the present tense of contracted verbs. In A. iv. 35, 1 C. xi. 23, ἐδίδετο (for -οτο, in a compound) is strongly supported, and there is good authority for ἐξέδετο Mk. xii. 1, Mt. xxi. 33, al. In Mt. xxi. 41 *Rec.* has the peculiar future ἐκδόσεται, but with no uncial MS.]

[4] [So also ἵστωσαν L. xii. 35, 1 Tim. iii. 12.]

is found in G. i. 10 only. The plural ἤμεθα is found twice in Mt. xxiii. 30 in very good MSS., and was received into the text by Griesb.; in A. xxvii. 37 also Lachm. received it on the authority of A and B, but in G. iv. 3, E. ii. 3, it has not much support.[1] This form occurs in no good writer; see, however, Epiphan. *Opp.* II. 333, Malal. 16. p. 404.

(c) For ἦσθα, Mk. xiv. 67, MSS. of little weight have ἦς,[2] a form which in Attic Greek is unusual and indeed almost doubtful (Buttm. I. 528, Jelf 286). As to later usage see Lob. p. 149 [and *Pathol.* II. 267].

Rem. Ἔνι—G. iii. 28, Col. iii. 11, Ja. i. 17 (and in 1 C. vi. 5 doubtful[3]), comp. Ecclus. xxxvii. 2—is usually considered a contraction for ἔνεστι: this is the opinion of old grammarians (comp. Schol. Aristoph. *Nub.* 482), and it is defended by Fritzsche (*Mark* p. 642). Buttmann's view however is preferable (II. 375), that ἔνι is the preposition (ἐν, ἐνί) with the accent thrown back, used without εἶναι, in the same way as ἔπι, πάρα, etc. The contraction of ἔνεστι into ἔνι would be very harsh and also without example; whilst Buttmann's view is supported by the analogy of ἔπι and πάρα, the latter of which can hardly be considered a contraction of πάρεστι: see Krüger p. 25 (Jelf 63, 341). Ἔνι is very common in Attic Greek, both poetry and prose (Georgi, *Hier.* I. 152, Schwarz, *Comm.* 486): the poets use it for ἔνεισι, as ἔπι for ἔπεισι *Il.* 20. 248, *Odyss.* 9. 126; and πάρα is even joined with the 1 personal pronoun.[4]

3. The following forms are connected with the primitive verb ἵημι:—

(a) ἀφέωνται Mt. ix. 2, 5, Mk. ii. 5, L. v. 20, 23, vii. 47, 1 Jo. ii. 12 [Mk. ii. 9 *Rec.*, L. vii. 48, and perhaps Jo. xx. 23].[5] The ancient grammarians do not agree in their explanation of this word. Some, as Eustathius (*Iliad* 6. 590), consider it equivalent to ἀφῶνται, as ἀφέῃ is used by Homer for ἀφῇ. Others, e. g. Herodian, the *Etym. Mag.*, and Suidas, more correctly take it as the perfect indic. (for ἀφεῖνται). According to the *Etym. Mag.* it is

---

[1] [In all these passages ℵ has ἤμεθα: the other form ἦμεν is also found (Rom. vii. 5, al.). On ἤμην see Veitch p. 199.]

[2] [Ἦς occurs several times, as Mt. xxv. 21, 23, al., sometimes without any *v. l.*; ἦσθα, Mt. xxvi. 69, Mk. xiv. 67. The "MSS. of little weight" are some of the most important of the cursive MSS.]

[3] [Now generally received. See Ellicott and Lightfoot on G. iii. 28.]

[4] The *Etym. Mag.* (p. 357) regards ἔνι, not as a contraction for ἔνεστι, but as used elliptically, the proper person of εἶναι being supplied.—Whether ἔν is ever used for ἔνι is doubtful (Herm. Soph. *Trach.* 1020).

[5] [In Matthew and Mark ἀφίενται is probably the true reading.]

an Attic form, but Suidas is certainly right in ascribing it to the Doric dialect:[1] this perfect passive follows the analogy of the perf. act. ἀφέωκα. Comp. Fischer, *de Vitiis Lex.* p. 646 sqq., *Irr. V.* p. 145 (Jelf 284).

(*b*) Ἤφιε, Mk. i. 34, xi. 16 (Philo, *Leg. ad Cajum* p. 1021), is the imperfect (for ἀφίει), formed from a present ἀφίω (Eccl. ii. 18, ἀφίομεν Mt. vi. 12 *v. l.*); comp. ξύνιον for ξυνίεσαν Il. 1. 273, *Irr. V.* p. 147. In ἤφιε the augment is prefixed to the prepos., as in other forms of this verb, e.g. ἠφείθη Plutarch, *Sulla* 28. See Fischer, *Well.* II. 480.[2]

(*c*) Most MSS. have ἀφέθησαν in Rom. iv. 7[3] (from Ps. xxxi. 1) as 1 aor. pass. of ἀφίημι: in some MSS. however (of N. T. and LXX) we find the augmented form ἀφείθησαν, which is most commonly used by Greek authors (*Irr. V.* p. 146).

Ἀφείς (from a root ἀφέω) is now received into the text in Rev. ii. 20 (Ex. xxxii. 32), on the authority of good MSS.; comp. τιθείς for τίθης (Buttm. I. 506, Jelf 276).[4]

From συνίημι we have συνιοῦσι Mt. xiii. 13 (3 pers. plur.), 2 C. x. 12 (3 plur. or dative partic.), and the partic. συνιών Mt. xiii. 23 *v. l.* (Rom. iii. 11, from LXX, συνιῶν), instead of συνιείς which Lachm. and Tisch. have received into the text [in Mt. xiii. 23]. The first form (συνιοῦσι) belongs to a root συνιέω, from which we also find an infin. συνιεῖν in Theogn. 565: the participle, which is particularly common in the LXX (1 Chr. xxv. 7, 2 Chr. xxxiv. 12, Ps. xl. 2, Jer. xx. 12), is perhaps more correctly written συνίων, from συνίω; see above [on ἤφιε], and Buttm. I. 523. Lachmann accordingly writes συνίουσι in Mt. xiii. 13: see on the whole Fritz. *Rom.* I. 174 sq.[5]

---

[1] ["A Dorism not confined to the N. T. but somewhat widely diffused, and received even by Attic writers: see Ahrens, *Dial. Dor.* p. 344; Bredow, *Dial. Herod.* p. 395." A. Buttm. p. 49. Veitch (p. 293) quotes ἀνιῶσθαι from *Tab. Heracl.* 1. 105. See also Cobet, *N. T. Vatic.* p. lxxiv.]

[2] [The root -ιω is implied by the forms ἤφιεν, ἀφίομεν (L. xi. 4), ἀφίουσι (Rev. xi. 9), ἀφίονται (Jo. xx. 23, Westcott and Hort, and elsewhere as a *v. l.*). Under this head will come συνίουσι (Mt. xiii. 13), συνίων (Rom. iii. 11) if thus accentuated, as by Lachm., Treg., Westc. and Hort; also, according to the last-named editors, συνίωσι (Mk. iv. 12, L. viii. 10). In 2 C. x. 12 we should read συνιᾶσι, in Mt. xiii. 23 συνιείς: in Mk. iv., L. viii., most editors read συνιῶσι, the ordinary form. Tisch. treats several of these words as belonging to a root -ιεω: συνιῶν (Rom. iii. 11, and in LXX), συνιοῦσι (Mt. xiii. 13), συνιείς -εῖ -εῖν (Job xv. 9, Pr. xxi. 12, Jer. ix. 24, al.), ἀφιῶ -ῶν (Eccl. ii. 18, v. 11). See Veitch pp. 104, 291, 304, Jelf 283 sq.]

[3] [No uncial MS. inserts the augment here, or in ἀνέθη, A. xvi. 26.]

[4] [In Her. 2. 165 most MSS. have ἀνίονται, and ἀφίονται is sometimes a *v. l.* in good MSS. of the N. T.: in Mk. viii. 17, B has συνίετε. Mullach (*Vulg.* pp. 24, 38, 50) quotes the pres. ἀφῶ from a Nubian inscription of the 3d or 4th century (*Corp. Inscr.* III. p. 486), and from a MS. of the 7th century.]

[5] [In modern Greek, verbs in ω take the place of those in μι; thus δίδωμι,

4. The imper. of καθημαι is (not κάθησο, but) κάθου in Mt. xxii. 44, L. xx. 42, A. ii. 34, Ja. ii. 3 (1 S. i. 23, xxii. 5, 2 K. ii. 2, 6, al.) : only in Mk. xii. 36 Tisch. has received κάθισον on the authority of B. Κάθου never occurs in the earlier Greek authors, and is therefore reckoned a corrupt form by Mœris (p. 234) and Thom. Mag. (p. 485).[1] Similarly κάθῃ for κάθησαι A. xxiii. 3 ; see Lob. p. 395, Greg. Cor. p. 411 (ed. Schæf.). [Lob. *Pathol.* II. 129, Jelf 301.]

Section XV.

DEFECTIVE VERBS.

We find in the N. T. several verbal forms, framed indeed according to rule, but rejected as unclassical by the ancient grammarians because they do not occur in Greek authors, or occur only in the later. In particular, we often meet with the active form of the future in verbs which in better writers have the middle form instead, see Buttm. II. 84 sq., Monk, Eur. *Alc.* 159, 645 :[2] this point, however, needs closer examination. The following list contains all the forms which have been declared unclassical. Those in regard to which the grammarians, especially Thomas Magister and Mœris, have manifestly been too fastidious, are marked with an asterisk.[3]

ἀγγέλλω. The 2 aor. active and passive are rare in the better writers, and in many places doubtful (Buttm. II. 94 sq., *Irr. V.* s. v.) ; yet see Schæf. *Demosth.* III. 175, Schoem. *Isæus* p. 39. In the N. T. we find ἀνηγγέλη 1 P. i. 12 and Rom. xv. 21 (from LXX), διαγγελῇ Rom. ix. 17 (from LXX), κατηγγέλη A. xvii. 13. [See Veitch, *Gr. V.* p. 5.]

ἀφίημι, are replaced by δίδω, ἀφίνω, and similarly κάθημαι by κάθομαι (Mullach p. 261). Compare also στήνω with ἱστάνω (ἵστημι).]

[1] [Veitch (p. 307) quotes κάθου from comic writers (Meineke, *Fragm. Com.* 2. 1190, 3. 167, al.) and late prose. In L. xxii. 30 there is considerable authority for a future καθήσεσθε (1 S. v. 7, al.), which is quoted by the same writer from Eur. *Frag.* 77.]

[2] [Compare the lists in Jelf 321, Don. p. 270 sq. This reference is not repeated in each case. See also Veitch, *Greek Verbs*, s. vv.]

[3] [Winer incloses these words within brackets : the asterisk is here used instead, to avoid ambiguity. As κρίμαμαι and ἱλάω were manifestly placed within brackets for a different reason, the asterisk is not inserted before these verbs : possibly it should be omitted before μιαίνω also.]

SECT. XV.]   DEFECTIVE VERBS.   99

ἄγνυμι. On the fut. *κατεάξει* Mt. xii. 20, aor. *κατέαξα*, see § 12. 2.

*ἄγω. On the 1 aor. *ἦξα*, which occurs 2 P. ii. 5 in the compound *ἐπάξας*, see *Irr. V.* p. 9, Lob. pp. 287, 735 [Veitch, *Gr. V.* p. 13 sq.]. In compounds this tense is not rare (2 S. xxii. 35, 1 Macc. ii. 67, Index to Malal. s. v. *ἄγω*, Schæf. *Index ad Æsop.* p. 135), even in good prose writers, Her. 1. 190, 5. 34, Xen. *Hell.* 2. 2. 20, Thuc. 2. 97, 8. 25.

*αἱρέω. The fut. *ἑλῶ* (Rev. xxii. 19, in the compound *ἀφελῶ*[1]), is rare, see Buttm. II. 100; it is found however in Agath. 269. 5, and frequently in the LXX, as Ex. v. 8, Num. xi. 17, Dt. xii. 32, Job xxxvi. 7; comp. also Menand. Byz. p. 316. Against Reisig,[2] who claims this form for Aristophanes and Sophocles, see Herm. *Œd. Col.* 1454, and Eurip. *Hel.* p. 127.

*ἀκούω. Fut. *ἀκούσω* (for *ἀκούσομαι*) Mt. xii. 19, xiii. 14, Rom. x. 14 [*Rec.*], Jo. xvi. 13: *ἀκούσομαι*, however, is the more common future in the N. T., especially in Luke, see A. iii. 22 (vii. 37), xvii. 32, xxv. 22, xxviii. 28 (Jo. v. 28). *Ἀκούσω* occurs not only in poets (Jacobs, *Anthol. Gr.* III. 134, *Orac. Sibyll.* 8. 206, 345), but occasionally also in prose authors of the *κοινή*, as Dion. H. 980. 4 (Reiske).[3] In the LXX comp. Is. vi. 9, 2 S. xiv. 16.

ἅλλομαι varies in the aorist between *ἡλάμην* and *ἡλόμην* (*Irr. V.* s. v.). In A. xiv. 10 both these forms are found in the MSS. (and even with λ doubled), but *ἥλατο* has most authority.[4]

ἁμαρτάνω, *ἁμαρτέω*. The 1 aor. *ἡμάρτησα* for 2 aor. *ἥμαρτον*, Rom. v. 14, 16, Mt. xviii. 15, L. xvii. 4, Rom. vi. 15 (1 S. xix. 4, Lam. iii. 41),[5] Th. M. p. 420, Lob. p. 732; see however Diod. S. 2. 14 *ἁμαρτήσας*, Agath. 167. 18.[6] The fut. active also, *ἁμαρτήσω* (Mt. xviii. 21, Ecclus. vii. 36, xxiv. 22, Dio C.

---

[1] [L. xii. 18 καθελῶ, 2 Th. ii. 8 ἀνελεῖ; see Dion. H. *Ant.* 9. 26, Diod. S. 2. 25 (Veitch s. v.). On ἀναλοῖ, the reading of א in 2 Th. ii. 8, see Veitch, p. 61.]
[2] *Comm. Crit. in* Soph. *Œd. Col.* p. 365.
[3] Comp. Schæf. *Dem.* II. 232, Wurm, *Dinarch.* p. 153, Bachmann, *Lyc.* I. 92. [Mt. xii. 19, xiii. 14, A. iii. 22, xxviii. 26, are from the Old Testament. The best texts have -σω in John (v. 25, 28, x. 16), -σομαι in Acts (xvii. 32, xxi. 22, xxv. 22, xxviii. 28.]
[4] [In A. xix. 16 the best texts have ἐφαλόμενος.]
[5] Still the 2 aor. *ἥμαρτον* predominates in the LXX: see especially 1 K. viii. 47, ἡμάρτομεν, ἠνομήσαμεν, ἠδικήσαμεν.
[6] ["In the N. T. we find without exception the *second* aorist in the indic., the *first* aorist partic.; in the conj. both forms occur;" A. Buttm. p. 54.]

59. 20), is not very common: compare Monk, Eur. *Alc.* 159, Poppo, *Thuc.* III. iv. 361.¹

*ἀνέχομαι. Fut. ἀνέξομαι Mt. xvii. 17, Mk. ix. 19, L. ix. 41, 2 Tim. iv. 3,—for which Mœris from pure caprice would have ἀνασχήσομαι: ἀνέξομαι occurs very frequently, comp. e.g. Soph. *Electr.* 1017, Xen. *Cyr.* 5. 1. 26, Plat. *Phœdr.* 239 a.

ἀνοίγω. 1 aor. ἤνοιξα Jo. ix. 17 [*Rec.*], 21, al., for ἀνέῳξα (but comp. Xen. *Hell.* 1. 5. 13); 2 aor. pass. ἠνοίγην Rev. xv. 5. See § 12. 7.

ἀπαντάω. Fut. ἀπαντήσω (for ἀπαντήσομαι) Mk. xiv. 13 (Diod. S. 18. 15): see *Irr. V.* p. 33, Matth. Eur. *Supp.* 774.

ἀποκτείνω. The 1 aor. ἀπεκτάνθη, ἀποκτανθῆναι, Rev. ii. 13, ix. 18, 20, xi. 13, xiii. 10, xix. 21, Mt. xvi. 21, L. ix. 22, al.; comp. 1 Macc. ii. 9, 2 Macc. iv. 36. This form occurs indeed in Homer,² but belongs peculiarly to later prose, as Dio C. 65. c. 4, Menander, *Hist.* pp. 284, 304 (ed. Bonn); see Buttm. II. 227, Lob. pp. 36, 757.³ The un-Attic perf. ἀπέκταγκα occurs 2 S. iv. 11 (*Irr. V.* p. 200).

ἀπόλλυμι. Fut. ἀπολέσω Mt. xxi. 41, Mk. viii. 35, Jo. vi. 39, xii. 25 [*Rec.*]; comp. Lucian, *Asin.* 33, Long. *Pastor.* 3. 17 (Buttm. II. 254, *Irr. V.* p. 238); but see Lob. p. 746. In 1 C. i. 19 we find the ordinary form ἀπολῶ.⁴

---

¹ ['Αμφιέννυμι. In L. xii. 28 good MSS. have ἀμφιέζει (Plut. *C. Gracch.* 2) for -έννυσι. Lachmann, Westcott and Hort read ἀμφιάζει with B; comp. ἀπημφίαζε Plut. *Mor.* 340, Job xxix. 14, xl. 5: see A. Buttm. p. 49, Veitch p. 58.]

² [Not in Homer, see Lobeck on Buttmann *l. c.*, Lidd. and Scott s. v. : see also Veitch, *Gr. Verbs*, pp. 79, 349. In 2 Macc. *l. c.* we find the *perfect*, ἀπεκτάνθαι.]

³ In Rev. vi. 11 we find ἀποκτέννεσθαι (*v. l.* ἀποκτένεσθαι), and in 2 C. iii. 6 (Rev. xiii. 10) ἀποκτέννει (*v. l.* ἀποκτενεῖ). This form is considered Æolic, since the Æolians were accustomed to change σ into ε before λ, μ, ν, ρ, σ, doubling the following consonant, e.g. κτέννω for κτείνω, σπίρρω for σπείρω; see Koen, *Gregor. Cor.* pp. 587, 597 (ed. Schæf.), Matth. 14. 6, and comp. Dindorf, *Præf. ad Aristoph.* XII. p. 14. In Tob. i. 18 and Wis. xvi. 14 also we find this form amongst the variants. We must not (with Wahl) assume the existence of a present ἀποκτένω for Mt. x. 28, L. xii. 4, xiii. 34: ἀποκτενόντων (if we do not regard it as an aorist partic., see Fritz. *Matt.* p. 383) may be a corruption of ἀποκτεννόντων, which is the reading of a few good MSS., and which is received by Lachm. and in part by Tisch. See further Bornem. *Luc.* p. 81. [The form -εννω is received by Lachm., Tisch., Treg., Alford, in Mt. x. 28, Mk. xii. 5, L. xii. 4, 2 C. iii. 6, Rev. vi. 11 (except 2 C. iii. 6, Lachm.). In Rev. vi. 11 Westcott and Hort receive -εννω, but in Mk. xii. 5 they have the strange form ἀποκτέννυντες. None of these editors receive -ένω. In 2 C. iii. 6, Rev. xiii. 10, Lachm. adopts ("de conjectura," Tisch. *ll. cc.*) ἀποκταίνει, on which see A. Buttm. p. 61.]

⁴ [1 C. i. 19 is from the LXX. In Jo. vi. 39 ἀπολέσω is 1 aor. subj., but this future often occurs in the N. T. The fut. midd. is always ἀπολοῦμαι.]

ἁρπάζω.   Aor. ἡρπάγην 2 C. xii. 2, 4, for ἡρπάσθην (Rev. xii. 5), Th. M. p. 424, Moer. p. 50, Buttm. I. 372 (Jelf 212. 6): fut. ἁρπαγήσομαι 1 Th. iv. 17. (Also ἁρπάσω, for ἁρπάσομαι, Jo. x. 28: this is said to be a rare form, but it occurs as early as Xen. *Mag. Eq.* 4. 17.)

*αὐξάνω. The primitive form αὔξω, E. ii. 21, Col. ii. 19, is often found in Plato and Xenophon (Matth. 224).

βαρέω. From this root we find not only βεβαρημένος (Mt. xxvi. 43, L. ix. 32), but also, contrary to Attic prose usage (*Irr. V.* p. 51), βαρούμενοι 2 C. v. 4 (Mk. xiv. 40), βαρείσθω 1 Tim. v. 16, and the aor. ἐβαρήθην L. xxi. 34, 2 C. i. 8: for the last tense, ἐβαρύνθην (L. xxi. 34 *v. l.*) was used in the written language.[1]

βασκαίνω. The 1 aor. (G. iii. 1) is ἐβάσκανε in *Rec.*, but in many [cursive] MSS. ἐβάσκηνε (without ι subscript), comp. Buttm. I. 438: the latter occurs in Dio C. 44. 39, Herodian 2. 4. 11, and in later writers.

βιόω. 1 aor. infin. βιῶσαι 1 P. iv. 2, for which the 2 aor. βιῶναι is more usual in Attic Greek (Buttm. II. 129 sq., *Irr. V.* s. v.); βιῶσαι occurs however Aristot. *Nic.* 9. 8, Plutarch, *Opp.* II. 367 sq., and oftener in compounds (Steph. *Thes.* II. 260, ed. Hase). The other forms of the 1 aor. are more common, especially the partic. βιώσας.

βλαστάνω. Aor. ἐβλάστησα for ἔβλαστον Mt. xiii. 26, Ja. v. 18 (Gen. i. 11, Num. xvii. 8, al., *Acta Apocr.* p. 172); comp. Buttm. II. 131 (Jelf 255). From the time of Aristotle the 1 aor. is not uncommon in the written language (Steph. *Thes.* II. 273).[2]

*γαμέω. Aor. ἐγάμησα Mk. vi. 17, Mt. xxii. 25 [*Rec.*], 1 C. vii. 9, instead of the older form ἔγημα (from γάμω) L. xiv. 20, 1 C. vii. 28 (see Georgi, *Hier.* I. 29, Lob. p. 742): yet ἐγάμησα is found (if not in Xen. *Cyr.* 8. 4. 20) in Lucian, *Dial. Deor.* 5. 4, Apollodor. 3. 15. 3. Better attested is ἐγαμήθην Mk. x. 12 (where however the reading is doubtful), 1 C. vii. 39 (Lob. p. 742).

---

[1] [In Mk. xiv. 40 recent editors receive καταβαρυνόμενοι, the only instance in the N. T. of this form of the present.]

[2] ["Conj. pres. βλαστᾷ, Mk. iv. 27, from a cognate form βλαστάω, another example of which is hardly to be found; comp. Schol. Pind. *Py. θάλλει καὶ βλαστᾷ*:" A. Buttm. p. 48. Veitch quotes βλαστῶντα from Hermas, *Past.* p. 57 (p. 83, ed. Hilgenf.).]

γελάω. Fut. γελάσω (for γελάσομαι) L. vi. 21; see Buttm. II. 85, *Irr. V.* s. v.

γίγνομαι. Aor. pass. ἐγενήθην,[1] used for ἐγενόμην, A. iv. 4, Col. iv. 11, 1 Th. ii. 14, al.; comp. Th. M. p. 189. This form, originally Doric, is often found in writers of the κοινή (Lob. p. 109, *Irr. V.* p. 64).[2]

δίδωμι. The 1 aor. ἔδωκα is avoided by Attic writers in the 1 and 2 pers. plur., the 2 aor. being used instead (Buttm. I. 509, Jelf 277. 2). In the N. T., however, we find ἐδώκαμεν 1 Th. iv. 2, ἐδώκατε Mt. xxv. 35, G. iv. 15, al., as in Demosthenes. On δώσῃ see § 14. 1. Rem.[3]

*διώκω. Fut. διώξω (for διώξομαι) Mt. xxiii. 34, L. xxi. 12 (*Irr. V.* p. 89): comp. however Dem. *Nausim.* 633 c, Xen. *An.* 1. 4. 8 (and Krüg. *in loc.*), *Cyr.* 6. 3. 13.

δύναμαι. It is only necessary to remark that, beside ἐδυνήθην, the Ionic form ἠδυνάσθην (with augment η) is given amongst the variants in Mt. xvii. 16, as found in B; see Buttm. II. 155.[4]

δύω, δύνω. In Mk. i. 32 some good MSS. have the 1 aor. ἔδυσα, which in earlier Greek has only a causative signification (*Irr. V.* p. 92).[5] Another form of the 1 aor. is found L. iv. 40 (δύναντος) in some inferior authorities: this also occurs in Æl. 4. 1, Pausan. 2. 11. 7.[6]

εἴδω *know.* Perf. οἴδαμεν (for ἴσμεν) Mk. xi. 33, Jo. iii. 2, 1 C. viii. 1, al. (Poppo, Xen. *An.* 2. 4. 6); οἴδατε (ἴστε) Mk. x.

---

[1] [It has sometimes been maintained that ἐγενήθην has a passive *meaning;* against this see Meyer on 1 C. i. 30, Ellicott on Col. iv. 11.—In the N. T., as might be expected, γίνομαι is always found, not γίγν.; similarly γινώσκω.]

[2] [From ἔγνων, 2 aor. of γινώσκω, we find γνοῖ Mk. v. 43, ix. 30, L. xix. 15, in the best texts (Herm. *Mand.* 4, in א); this is variously regarded as subj. (A. Buttm. p. 46), or optative (Tisch. *Proleg.* p. 57, ed. 7): comp. δοῖ, p. 95, and see below, p. 360.—Δέομαι has the peculiar imperfect ἐδεῖτο L. viii. 38 in Lachmann's text; on this form (which is not well attested) see A. Buttm. p. 55.]

[3] [A. Buttm. remarks (p. 46) that the 2 aor. is only found once in the indic. (L. i. 2), but that the other moods are regularly formed from the 2 aor. Veitch quotes ἐδώκαμεν from Eur. *Cycl.* 296, Xen. *An.* 3. 2. 5, *Hell.* 6. 3. 6, al.]

[4] [Buttm. *l. c.* remarks that this form (with the augm. η) is confined to Hellenistic Greek: Tisch. now receives this form in Mk. vii. 24 (Jos. xv. 63). It is a *v. l.* in Her. 7. 106 (Veitch s. v.).]

[5] [B has παρεισεδύησαν in Jude 4. The present form ἐνδιδύσκω, Mk. xv. 17, L. xvi. 19 (L. viii. 27, Lachm.), 2 S. xiii. 18, al., is unknown in earlier Greek: see Fritz. *Mark,* p. 681.]

[6] [Ἐθέλω: in the N. T. we have always ἤθελον, ἠθέλησα, but in the present θέλω. (A. Buttm. p. 57.)]

SECT. XV.]   DEFECTIVE VERBS.   103

38, xiii. 33, 1 C. ix. 13, Ph. iv. 15 ; οἴδασιν (ἴσασι) L. xi. 44, Jo. x. 5 ; see Buttm. I. 546 (Jelf 314): comp. however Aristoph. *Av.* 599, Xen. *Œc.* 20. 14. The 2 pers. sing. οἶδας (for οἶσθα) 1 C. vii. 16, Jo. xxi. 15, is rather Ionic and Doric, yet it occurs Her. 4. 157, Xen. *Mem.* 4. 6. 6, Eurip. *Alc.* 790, and frequently in later Greek (Lob. p. 236). The 3 pers. plur. pluperf. is ᾔδεισαν Mk. i. 34, Jo. ii. 9, xxi. 4, al., for ᾔδεσαν (Buttm. I. 547).[1] [Veitch, *Gr. V.* s. v.]

εἰπεῖν (2 aor. εἶπον). The 1 aor. εἶπα occurs in the N. T. in the 2 pers. sing., Mt. xxvi. 25, Mk. xii. 32, and frequently. This person is also found in Attic writers, as Xen. *Œc.* 19. 14, Soph. *Œd. Col.* 1509 (along with εἶπες, which is often used by Plato), but is originally Ionic; see Greg. Cor. p. 481 (ed. Schæf.), Schæfer, *Dion. H.* p. 436 sq. The imperative εἴπατε Mt. x. 27, xxi. 5, Col. iv. 17, εἰπάτωσαν A. xxiv. 20, is also very common in Attic Greek (Plat. *Lach.* 187 d, Xen. *Cyr.* 3. 2. 28). Besides these forms, we find the following in good MSS.: 3 pers. plur. indic. εἶπαν Mt. xii. 2, xvii. 24, Mk. xi. 6, xii. 7, 16, L. v. 33, xix. 39, xx. 2, A. i. 11, 24, vi. 2, xxviii. 21, al. (Diod. S. 16. 44, Xen. *Hell.* 3. 5. 24, al., *v. l.*); partic. εἴπας (which is mainly Ionic) A. vii. 37, xxii. 24; and even the rarer 1 pers. εἶπα H. iii. 10 [Lachm.], A. xxvi. 15, for which εἶπον is generally used in the N. T.: see Sturz p. 61.[2] Recent editors have accepted these forms wherever they are attested by several MSS. In compounds we find ἀπειπάμην 2 C. iv. 2 (Her. 6. 100), and προείπαμεν 1 Th. iv. 6.[3] Εἰπόν—not εἶπον, see § 6. 1. *k.*—which occurs in good MSS. A. xxviii. 26, is to be regarded as a 2 aor. imper.; the same form now stands in the text in Mk. xiii. 4, L. x. 40, whilst in other passages εἰπέ has more authority.[4] The 1 aor. pass. of this verb, ἐρρήθην (from ῥέω, *Irr. V.* p. 112) is sometimes written ἐρρέθην in N. T. MSS., e.g. Mt. v. 21, 31, 33;[5] this form is often found in the MSS. of the later (non-Attic)

---

[1] [We find ἴσασι in A. xxvi. 4, ἴστε (indic. or imper.) E. v. 5, al. ; the 2 pers. sing. pluperf. is always ᾔδεις. For εἶδον, Tisch. sometimes reads ἴδον (Rev. vii. 1, al.), εἶδα (Rev. xvii. 6).]
[2] Εἶπαν also occurs in the well known Rosetta inscription, at the end of line 8.
[3] Comp. εἴπαμεν 1. *Turin. Papyr.* p. 10. [On εἴπαμεν and εἰπάτωσαν, see Veitch s. v.]
[4] [In most of the instances cited these forms are now generally received, and also in other passages, as εἶπα Mk. ix. 18, εἰπόν L. xx. 2, al. (see above, p. 58).]
[5] [Recent editors agree in reading ἐρρέθην in Rom. ix. 12, 26, G. iii. 16, Rev. vi. 11, ix. 4: in Mt. v. (six times) Lachm. and Treg. read ἐρρέθην, but Meyer,

writers, and here and there in Attic (Lob. p. 447),—but not in Plato, see Schneider, Plat. *Civ.* II. 5 sq. [Veitch, *Gr. V.* p. 509.]

ἐκχέω: later form ἐκχύνω [1] (Lob. p. 726). The future is ἐκχεῶ for ἐκχεύσω (Buttm. I. 396, *Irr. V.* p. 336): see § 13. 3.

(ἐλεάω for ἐλεέω occurs in certain good MSS. in several passages of the N. T., as ἐλεῶντος, ἐλεᾷ Rom. ix. 16, 18, ἐλεᾶτε Jude 23: also in Clem. Al. p. 54 (Sylb.) the Florentine edition has ἐλεᾷ. Compare further the *Etym. Mag.* 327. 30.[2] A similar form is ἐλλογᾶν Rom. v. 13, Phil. 18, which also is found in good MSS.: in Phil. 18 Lachmann has received it into the text, and after him Tischendorf. Fritzsche, *Rom.* I. 311, declares all these forms mistakes of transcription.[3])

ἕλκω. From this root we find a present and imperf., Ja. ii. 6, A. xxi. 30, as in Greek authors regularly; but instead of the fut. ἕλξω (Matth. 233), the less usual ἑλκύσω from the other form ἑλκύω, Jo. xii. 32; comp. Job xxxix. 10.

*ἐπαινέω. Fut. ἐπαινέσω 1 C. xi. 22, for ἐπαινέσομαι (Buttm. I. 388); comp. however Xen. *An.* 5. 5. 8, Himer. 20: in this verb indeed the fut. active is not uncommon. See Brunck, *Gnom.* pp. 10, 64, Schæf. *Dem.* II. 465, Stallb. Plat. *Symp.* p. 139. [Veitch, *Gr. V.* p. 226: comp. Shilleto, Dem. *F. L.* p. 31.]

*ἐπιορκέω. Fut. ἐπιορκήσω for ἐπιορκήσομαι Mt. v. 33: see Buttm. II. 85.

ἔρχομαι. The fut. ἐλεύσομαι, both in the simple verb and in its compounds, is of frequent occurrence in the N. T.: it is

---

Tisch., Westcott and Hort adopt ἐρρέθην, which ℵ and B have in every instance (except Mt. v. 21 in B). The partic. is uniformly ῥηθείς, without a variant.]

[1] [The best MSS. double the ν in the present, as ἐκχυννόμενον Mt. xxiii. 35, al., and this form is now generally received: comp. ἀποκτέννω above.]

[2] ["Ἐλεῶ κατὰ μὲν τοὺς Ἀττικοὺς πρώτης συζυγίας τῶν περισπωμένων, ἐλεεῖς, . . . κατὰ δὲ τὴν κοινήν, δευτέρας."]

[3] [Ἐλεάω is very strongly supported in Rom. ix. 16, but not in ver. 18. In ed. 7, Tisch. received -άω in both verses; Lachm., Treg., Alford (doubtfully), Tisch. (ed. 8), Westcott and Hort, read ἐλεεῖ in ver. 18. Fritzsche and Meyer retain -έω in both verses, urging that different forms would not be used in the same passage: see, however, page 107, note [1]. In favour of ἐλλογᾶν (Phil. 18, and probably Rom. v. 13) see Meyer and Ellicott on Phil. 18. Some instances of the substitution of -έω for -άω are found in good MSS. Tisch. and others receive ἠρώτουν Mt. xv. 23 (Mk. iv. 10); and the participle of νικέω in Rev. ii. 17 (see also ii. 7, xv. 2). Compare Mullach, *Vulg.* p. 252, and (A. Buttm. in) *Stud. u. Krit.* 1862, p. 188.]

SECT. XV.] DEFECTIVE VERBS. 105

principally met with in later prose (Arr. *Al.* 6. 12, Philostr. *Apoll.* 4. 4, Dio Chr. 33. 410, Max. Tyr. 24. p. 295), εἶμι being used instead in Attic Greek (Phryn. p. 37, Th. M. pp. 88, 336). In earlier writers, however, ἐλεύσομαι is not at all uncommon, as Her. 1. 142, 5. 125, Lys. *Dardan.* 12 (p. 233, Bremi). See in general Lob. p. 37 sq., Schæf. *Soph.* II. 323, and comp. Elmsl. Eur. *Heracl.* 210. For ἠρχόμην[1] (Mk. i. 45, ii. 13, Jo. iv. 30, vi. 17, al.), Attic writers commonly use the imperf. of εἶμι (*Irr. V.* p. 134)—but see Bornem. *Luc.* p. 106, and comp. Thuc. 4. 120, 121, Xen. *An.* 4. 6. 22; and for ἔρχου, ἔρχεσθε, Jo. i. 47, the imper. of εἶμι (ἴθι, ἴτε). The partic. ἐρχόμενος also is said to be rare in the earlier Attic writers (*Irr. V. l. c.*), yet it occurs in Plat. *Crit.* c. 15.[2]

ἐσθίω. From the poetical form ἔσθω (*Irr. V.* p. 136) we find ἔσθων amongst the *v. ll.* in Mk. i. 6, L. vii. 33, 34, x. 7, xx. 47, xxii. 30 [ἔσθητε]; and Tisch. has received it into the text on the authority of (a few) good MSS.: see his *Præf.* p. 21 (ed. 2).[3] In the LXX comp. Lev. xvii. 10, xix. 26, Ecclus. xx. 16.

εὑρίσκω. Aorist middle εὑράμην, for εὑρόμην, H. ix. 12 (Pausan. 7. 11. 1, 8. 30. 4, al., comp. Lob. p. 139 sq.): see § 13. 1. A 1 aor. εὕρησα seems implied in the conjunctives εὑρήσῃς Rev. xviii. 14, εὑρήσωσιν ix. 6 (as at least several MSS. read), unless we consider these to be future conjunctives (§ 13. 1). Lobeck however (p. 721) quotes a participle εὑρήσαντος.[4]

ζάω. Future ζήσω Rom. vi. 2, 2 C. xiii. 4, Jo. vi. 51, 57, 58 (συζήσω Rom. vi. 8, 2 Tim. ii. 11): ζήσομαι Mt. iv. 4, Mk. v. 23,[5] Jo. vi. 51, xi. 25, al.: 1 aor. ἔζησα Rev. ii. 8, L. xv. 24,

---

[1] [On ἠρχόμην see Don. *New Crat.* p. 651, but compare Veitch s. v. Εἶμι is not found in the N. T., and occurs once only in the LXX, ἴθι Pr. vi. 6; the compounds are sometimes found, chiefly in Acts (A. Buttm. p. 50).]
[2] Ἦλθε for ἐλήλυθε, G. iv. 4, Jo. xix. 39, al., is too hastily rejected by Thom. Mag. (p. 418); see Sallier *in loc.* [The note of Thom. Mag. which Winer thinks it worth while to notice is : ἦλθε κοινόν, ἐλήλυθε δὲ Ἀττικόν.]
[3] [Ἔσθω (found chiefly in B and D) is received by Tisch., Treg., Westc. and Hort, in Mk. i. 6, L. x. 7, xxii. 30: and by Westc. and Hort in L. vii. 33 (Treg.), 34, Mk. xii. 40 (Treg.). See Tisch. *Prol.* p. 49 (ed. 7).]
[4] [Veitch quotes this aorist from Maneth. 5. 137, Schol. Æsch. *Prom.* 59.]
[5] [Here we must read the aor. subj. : in Jo. vi. 51, quoted by Winer *twice*, ζήσει is probably the true reading. The fut. of ζάω (συζάω) occurs 22 times, 6 times in quotations from the LXX (ζήσεται). In 11 of the remaining 16 places we must read ζήσω (5 times in John, 6 times in the Epistles); ζήσομαι occurs in Mt. ix. 18, x. 28, Jo. xi. 25, Rom. viii. 13, x. 5. On ἔζησα (and on ἔζην, the reading of B in Rom. vii. 9) see Veitch p. 260.]

Rom. vii. 9, al., and often in the LXX. The futures are in the main later forms, which occur but seldom in the earlier writers (Buttm. II. 192); the aorist is confined to later Greek. Earlier writers used in the fut. and aor. the corresponding tenses of βιόω.

ἥκω. From the 1 aor. ἧξα, a later form (*Irr. V.* p. 153, Lob. p. 744), we find the conjunct. ἥξωσι in Rev. iii. 9, where however better MSS. have the fut. ἥξουσι. From the perf. ἧκα (Dt. xxxii. 17, Phot. *Biblioth.* 222, Malal. p. 136 sq., Leo Gramm. p. 98, al., Lob. p. 744) we find ἥκασι Mk. viii. 3, but on doubtful authority: Lachm.[1] however receives it.[2]

θάλλω. The 2 aor. ἀνεθάλετε[3] Ph. iv. 10,—a form never found in Greek prose, and seldom in poetry (*Irr. V.* p. 154).[4]

ἵστημι. The present ἱστάνω, which occurs Rom. iii. 31, and in compounds, e.g. συνιστάνω, 2 C. iii. 1 (iv. 2), v. 12, vi. 4, x. 12, 18, G. ii. 18, is found in Attic writers (Matth. 210), but more frequently in later Greek (as ἐφιστάνειν Cinnam. 214, 256).[5] On the later form ἱστάω see § 14 1. *f.*[6]

κατακαίω. Fut. κατακαήσομαι 1 C. iii. 15, 2 P. iii. 10 (from aor. κατεκάην,[7] Her. 1. 51, 4. 79): the Attic future is κατακαυθήσομαι, Rev. xviii. 8. See Thom. M. p. 511, Buttm. II. 211 [Veitch, *Gr. V.* s. v.].

καταλείπω. 1 aor. κατέλειψα A. vi. 2 (Lob. p. 714).[8]

---

[1] [Meyer, Treg., and Tisch. read ἥκασι. In L. xiii. 35 *Rec.* has ἥξῃ, but the best MSS. either omit the word or read ἥξει. The subj. ἥξω occurs Rev. ii. 25.]

[2] ['Ηττάομαι: in 2 C. xii. 13 recent editors receive ἡσσώθητε (for ἡττήθητε), as if from the Ionic ἑσσόομαι, the augment being added as in ἠδυνάσθην: see Cobet, *N. T. Vat.* p. xc.]

[3] [A. Buttmann (p. 59) quotes this aor. from Ps. xxvii. 7, Wis. iv. 4, Ecclus. xlvi. 12. Hermann reads θάλοιεν in Æsch. *Suppl.* 673, but see Paley *in loc.* Compare Lob. *Paral.* p. 557, and Lidd. and Scott s. v.]

[4] [Θνήσκω: the syncopated forms are not found in the N. T. In A. xiv. 19, τεθνηκέναι now stands in the place of τεθνάναι *Rec.*—From ἱλάσκομαι, the late aorist ἱλάσθην occurs L. xviii. 13: this aorist is used in modern Greek, see Mullach, *Vulg.* p. 288. Veitch quotes the compound ἐξιλασθὲν from Plat. *Legg.* p. 862.]

[5] [On ἱστάνω (a doubtful form in classic writers, Veitch s. v.) and ἱστάω see above, p. 94. Of στήκω we find the present (indic., imper., and subj.), and probably, if the reading οὐκ ἔστηκε is correct in Jo. viii. 44, the imperfect. See Mullach, *Vulg.* p. 299. In Mk. ix. 12 Westc. and Hort read ἀποκατιστάνει.]

[6] [Καθίζομαι: the 1 aor. partic. is well supported in L. x. 39. On this late aorist see Lob. p. 269, Veitch s. v.; and comp. Mullach pp. 25, 289.]

[7] [This aor. occurs Rev. viii. 7: κατακαήσομαι, Is. xlvii. 14 *Al.*]

[8] [In this verb the 1 aor. is frequently used in modern Greek (Mullach p. 258): the 2 aor. is used in the N. T., except in A. vi. 2.]

SECT. XV.] DEFECTIVE VERBS. 107

κεράννυμι. Perf. passive κεκέρασμαι Rev. xiv. 10, for the more usual κέκραμαι (*Irr. V.* p. 183): analogous to this is the partic. συγκεκερασμένους H. iv. 2, in very good MSS.

κερδαίνω. Aor. ἐκέρδησα Mt. xxv. 20, xviii. 15, κερδῆσαι A. xxvii. 21, κερδήσας L. ix. 25, κερδήσω conjunct. 1 C. ix. 19, 20, Mt. xvi. 26, and frequently; these forms belong to Ionic prose (*Irr. V.* p. 184, Lob. p. 740). In Attic Greek the verb is inflected regularly; comp. 1 C. ix. 21.[1]

κλαίω. Fut. κλαύσω (properly Doric), for κλαύσομαι, L. vi. 25, Jo. xvi. 20, Rev. xviii. 9; comp. Babr. 98. 9, Buttm. II. 85, *Irr. V.* p. 189 [Veitch, *Gr. V.* s. v.]. The LXX have always κλαύσομαι [Rev. xviii. 9, *Rec.*, Tisch.].

κλέπτω. Fut. κλέψω, for κλέψομαι,[2] Mt. xix. 18, Rom. xiii. 9 (Buttm. II. 85, 221): it occurs in Lucian, *Dial. Deor.* 7. 4,—never in the LXX.

κράζω. Fut. κράξω L. xix. 40, according to good authorities, for κεκράξομαι (which is always used in the LXX); aor. ἔκραξα for ἔκραγον, Mt. viii. 29, xx. 30, al. (Buttm. II. 223).[3] [Veitch, *Gr. V.* s. v.]

(κρέμαμαι. The form ἐξεκρέμετο L. xix. 48, in B,[4] is not even mentioned by Griesbach and Schulz, and undoubtedly is an error of transcription. Lachmann also has left it unnoticed.)

κρύπτω. The 2 aor. act. ἔκρυβον, L. i. 24 (Phot. *Biblioth.* I. 143, Bekk.); see *Irr. V.* p. 198 [Veitch, *Gr. V.* s. v.].

κύω (to be pregnant). The fut. and aor. are regularly κυήσω, ἐκύησα (*Irr. V.* p. 204); so ἀπεκύησε, Ja. i. 18. In the present κυέω also occurs, and not merely (as Eustathius asserts, p. 1548. 20) in the sense *bring forth*: see Lob. *Ajax* p. 182 sq., *Paral.* p. 556. Hence in Ja. i. 15 we may as correctly write ἀποκυεῖ as -κύει, but it is not necessary to prefer the former on account

---

[1] [Here κερδάνω is generally received (but written as fut. indic., κερδανῶ, by Griesb. and by Westc. and Hort), though κερδήσω precedes and follows. Comp. 1 C. vii. 28, where γαμήσῃς and γήμῃ are found in the same verse; Rom. ix. 16, 18, where the best MSS. have ἐλεῶντος and ἐλεεῖ; L. vii. 33, 34, in the texts of Lachm. and Tregelles. See Lobeck's essay *De orthographiæ Græcæ inconstantia* (*Path.* II. 341–355).]

[2] [So Buttmann, Lobeck, Jelf, and others. Veitch reverses the statement: "fut. κλέψω Arist. *Eccl.* 667, Xen. *Mag. Eq.* 4. 17, Luc., and rare κλέψομαι Xen. *Cyr.* 7. 4. 13." Κλέψω, not κλέψομαι, is the form used in the LXX.]

[3] [Also ἐκέκραξα A. xxiv. 21, as in the LXX frequently.]

[4] [Also in א; now received by Tisch., Westcott and Hort. Compare p. 95, note [3].]

of the form of the aorist in ver. 18. N. T. lexicons have κυέω only.

λάσκω. To this belongs the aor. ἐλάκησα A. i. 18, usually referred to the Doric present λακέω; Buttmann however (*Irr. V.* p. 208) maintains that it is immediately derived from the 2 aor. λακεῖν, which is in general use in Attic Greek.

*μιαίνω: in Tit. i. 15 good MSS. have the perf. partic. μεμιαμμένοι, instead of the usual μεμιασμένοι; comp. Lob. p. 35. [Veitch, *Gr. V.* s. v.]

νίπτω Jo. xiii. 6, 14, νίπτομαι Mt. xv. 2. Instead of this present earlier writers use νίζω; see Buttm. II. 249, Lob. p. 241.

οἰκτείρω. Fut. οἰκτειρήσω Rom. ix. 15 (as if from οἰκτειρέω), instead of οἰκτερῶ: comp. Ps. ci. 15, Jer. xxi. 7, Mic. vii. 19, al. This fut. also occurs in the Byzantine writers, see Lob. p. 741.

ὀμνύω for ὄμνυμι (Buttm. II. 255) Mt. xxiii. 20, 21, 22, xxvi. 74, H. vi. 16, Ja. v. 12: in Mk. xiv. 71, however, the better MSS. have ὀμνύναι for ὀμνύειν, and this was received into the text by Griesbach.[1]

*ὁράω. Imperf. middle ὡρώμην A. ii. 25 (from Ps. xv. 8), for which ἑωρώμην was used in Attic Greek (Buttm. I. 325). From ὄπτεσθαι we find in L. xiii. 28 (though not without variant) the 1 aor. conj. ὄψησθε, which occurs in Libanius and the Byzantines: see Lob. p. 734.[2]

παίζω. Aor. ἐνέπαιξα Mt. xx. 19, xxvii. 31 (Pr. xxiii. 35), for which in Attic Greek ἔπαισα was used (*Irr. V.* p. 251). But we find ἔπαιξα, παῖξαι, in Lucian, *Dial. Deor.* 6. 4, and *Encom. Demosth.* 15; comp. V. Fritzsche, *Aristoph.* I. 378, Lob. p. 240. The fut. παίξω[3] occurs Anacr. 24. 8.[4]

---

[1] [Compare δεικνύ-εις, -ειν, -οντος (Jo. ii. 18, Mt. xvi. 21, Rev. xxii. 8). See A. Buttm. p. 45, and Mullach p. 294, and Veitch on the particular verbs. The proper inflexions of verbs in υμι are by no means rare in the N. T.]

[2] [In A. ii. 25 προορώμην is strongly supported (§ 12. 10). In the perf. ἑόρακα is often a variant: see especially 1 C. ix. 1, Col. ii. 1, 18. Ὄψησθε is received by most in L. xiii. 28: comp. ἐπόψατο, Pindar, *Fr.* 58. 8, and ἐπιόψωνται, Plat. *Leg.* 947 c. See Veitch.]

[3] [See Mk. x. 34 (Is. xxxiii. 4): παίξομαι is the usual fut. in the Alex. dialect, as in later writers generally. In the N. T. the other tenses are similarly formed, as ἔπαιξα, ἐπαίχθην: see A. Buttm. p. 64, Veitch p. 450.]

[4] [Παύω: the fut. ἀναπαήσομαι (see above, κατακαίω) occurs Rev. xiv. 13, L. x. 6. Comp. also ἐπάην, Bekk. *An.* p. 1324: see Veitch. These forms (or else the gloss of Hesychius, ἀμπάζονται· ἀναπαύονται, pointing to a root παζ-) might lead us to regard ἀκαταπάστους, 2 P. ii. 14 (Lachm., Westc. and Hort) as a by-form

πέτομαι. The partic. πετώμενον (for πετόμενον), which occurs Rev. xiv. 6 [and viii. 13] in B, is from πετάομαι, which is used only by Ionic (e.g. Her. 3. 111) and later writers (e.g. Lucian, *Dial. Mort.* 15. 3, *v. l.*); see Buttm. II. 271, *Irr. V.* p. 262. [Veitch, *Gr. V.* p. 467.] The pres. πέταμαι, found as early as Pindar, is given by Wetstein and Matthäi amongst the variants in Rev. xii. 14 [see also Rev. xiv. 6].[1]

πίνω. From the fut. πίομαι the full form πίεσαι (Buttm. I. 347) occurs in L. xvii. 8, and in the same verse we have φάγεσαι from φάγομαι; both are found in Ez. xii. 18, Ruth ii. 9, 14. On the infin. πῖν Jo. iv. 9, received by Lachm. and Tisch. on the authority of good MSS., see Fritz. *De crit. conf.* p. 27 sq. Πεῖν only—not πῖν—occurs in later Greek; and this form (which is found in some MSS.) might perhaps be received here, if A had not distinctly πίειν in ver. 7 and 10, thus showing πῖν in ver. 9 to be an error of transcription.[2]

πίπτω. Aor. ἔπεσα: see § 13. 1.

ῥέω. Fut. ῥεύσω Jo. vii. 38, for ῥεύσομαι; in Attic Greek ῥυήσομαι is the usual form (Lob. p. 739, *Irr. V.* p. 281). The 1 aor. also (Cant. iv. 16 ῥευσάτωσαν) is confined to later Greek; comp. Lob. p. 739.[3] The 2 aor. ἐρρύην, which was in regular use, occurs in the compound παραρυῶμεν H. ii. 1.

σαλπίζω. Fut. σαλπίσω for σαλπίγξω, 1 C. xv. 52, comp. also *Mechan. Vett.* p. 201 (Num. x. 3; the 1 aor. ἐσάλπισα also —for ἐσάλπιγξα Xen. *An.* 1. 2. 17—is common in the LXX). See Phryn. p. 191, Th. M. p. 789.[4]

σημαίνω. 1 aor. ἐσήμανα A. xi. 28, xxv. 27 (Jud. vii. 21, Esth. ii. 22, Plutarch, *Aristid.* 19, Menand. Byz. *Hist.* p. 308,

---

of ἀκαταπαύστους. But the word (which is not found elsewhere) may also be derived from the root of πάσασθαι, πατέομαι, and rendered *insatiable:* compare Athen. i. 43, p. 24. The most obvious derivation—from καταπάσσω (στιφάνοις κατάπαστος, Arist. *Eq.* 502)—is excluded by the unsuitableness of the meaning, *unsprinkled.* The references to Athenæus and Hesychius I owe to the kindness of Dr. Hort. See A. Buttm. p. 65.]

[1] [Πιέζω: perf. partic. πεπιεσμένος L. vi. 38; elsewhere πιάζω (with 1 aor. ἐπίασα, not -ξα). See A. Buttm. p. 66, Mullach p. 296.]

[2] [Tisch. now writes πεῖν, and receives this form in the passages quoted above, and in 1 C. ix. 4, x. 7, Rev. xvi. 6: so (more or less frequently) Alford, Treg., Westc. and Hort. See also A. xxiii. 12, 21 (B), Rom. xiv. 21 (D), 1 P. v. 8 (ℵ). A. Buttm. (p. 66) regards this infin. as contracted from a form πίναι (as φῦν from φῦναι), not from πιεῖν. See Tisch. on Jo. iv. 7.]

[3] [See however Veitch s. v., where this aorist is quoted from Arist. *Eq.* 526, al.]

[4] [Σαλπιῶ is the form in Num. x. 3: ἐσάλπισα occurs Mt. vi. 2, Rev. ix. 1, al. Comp. σαλπιστής Rev. xviii. 22 (Polyb. 1. 45. 13 in some MSS.).]

309, 358, *Act. Thom.* p. 32), which occurs indeed in Xen. *Hell.* 2. 1. 28, but for which ἐσήμηνα was more commonly used by earlier Attic writers: see Buttm. I. 438, Lob. p. 24, and below s. v. φαίνω. [See § 13. 1. *d.*]

σκέπτομαι. The present (H. ii. 6, Ja. i. 27, comp. Ps. viii. 5, 1 S. xi. 8, xv. 4, al.) and the imperfect are seldom found in Attic writers (Buttm. II. 291, *Irr. V.* p. 288).

*σπουδάζω. Fut. σπουδάσω for the usual σπουδάσομαι, 2 P. i. 15 (Buttm. II. 85).

στηρίζω. The aor. imper. is in good MSS. στήρισον, L. xxii. 32, Rev. iii. 2; and in 2 Th. iii. 3, B has the fut. στηρίσει: the Greeks preferred στήριξον, στηρίξει (Buttm. I. 372).[1] Comp. in the LXX στήρισον Jud. xix. 5, Ez. xx. 46, and often; ἐστήρισα 1 Macc. xiv. 14, al. [also στηρίσει Jerem. xvii. 5].

τυγχάνω. The perf. τέτευχε (properly Ionic, then Attic, Buttm. II. 301)[2] is found in the received text of H. viii. 6: other MSS. however have the usual Attic perfect τετύχηκε, and A, D, etc., τέτυχε.[3] On the last see Lob. p. 395.

φαγεῖν. Fut. φάγομαι Ja. v. 3, Rev. xvii. 16 [L. xiv. 15, Jo. ii. 17], Gen. xxvii. 25, Ex. xii. 8 (and often), whence the 2 pers. φάγεσαι L. xvii. 8. For this Greek authors use ἔδομαι, the fut. of ἔδω (*Irr. V.* p. 136).

φαίνω. 1 aor. infin. ἐπιφᾶναι (for ἐπιφῆναι) L. i. 79,[4] contrary to the usage of the better writers. In later Greek however similar forms occur; see Lob. p. 26, Thilo, *Acta Thom.* p. 49 sq. (Ælian, *Anim.* 2. 11 and *Epil.* p. 396, ed. Jac.)

φαύσκω. From this we have the fut. ἐπιφαύσει E. v. 14; comp. Gen. xliv. 3, Jud. xvi. 2, 1 S. xiv. 36, Judith xiv. 2. This form does not occur in Greek writers, but is supported by the analogy of the subst. ὑπόφαυσις; see *Irr. V.* p. 318.

*φέρω. Aor. partic. ἐνέγκας A. v. 2, xiv. 13, ἐνέγκαντες L.

---

[1] [In the N. T. also the forms from the κ characteristic are more common.]

[2] [Buttmann's words are: "τίτυχα was the true Ionic perfect, which in a later period became frequent in the non-Attic writers." (*Irr. V.* p. 238.) Compare Veitch p. 578.]

[3] [Τέτυχε (which is also the reading of ℵ) is now generally received. This form was not known to the ancient grammarians, but is often found in MSS. of later authors: see Tisch. on H. viii. 6 (where no uncial MS. has τετύχηκε), Veitch p. 578, and especially Lobeck *l. c.*]

[4] [In Rev. viii. 12, xviii. 23, Tisch. and Westcott and Hort read φάνῃ, instead of φαίνῃ, φανῇ, of *Rec.*; and in A. xxi. 3, ἀναφάναντες.]

SECT. XV.]   DEFECTIVE VERBS.   111

xv. 23 v. l. for ἐνεγκών (*Irr. V.* p. 319); but see Xen. *Mem.* 1. 2. 53, Demosth. *Timoth.* 703 c, Isocr. *Paneg.* 40. The indic. ἤνεγκα is frequently used by Attic writers, as also the imperative forms with *a* (Jo. xxi. 10).[1]

*φθάνω. According to several Atticists, the 2 aor. ἔφθην is to be preferred to the 1 aor. ἔφθασα, which, however, often occurs even in Attic writers (*Irr. V.* p. 324), and is invariably used in the N. T., as Mt. xii. 28, Rom. ix. 31, 2 C. x. 14, Ph. iii. 16, 1 Th. ii. 16. In the last passage several MSS. have the perf. ἔφθακε.

φύω. 2 aor. passive ἐφύην, φυείς, L. viii. 6, 7, 8,—very common from the time of Hippocrates: for this Attic writers use the 2 aor. active ἔφυν, φύς (Buttm. II. 321). In Mt. xxiv. 32, Mk. xiii. 28, very good MSS. have ἐκφυῇ (conj. aor. passive) for ἐκφύῃ, and this may be the preferable reading; see Fritz. *Mark,* p. 578 sq.[2]

χαίρω. Fut. χαρήσομαι for χαιρήσω, L. i. 14, Jo. xvi. 20, 22, Ph. i. 18 (Hab. i. 16, Zach. x. 7, Ps. xcv. 12, and often); see Mœr. p. 120, Th. M. p. 910, Lob. 740,[3] Buttm. II. 322: it also occurs in Diod. *Exc. Vat.* p. 95.

*χαρίζομαι. Fut. χαρίσομαι, Rom. viii. 32, is the non-Attic form for χαριοῦμαι.

ὠθέω. Aor. ἀπώσατο,[4] A. vii. 27, 39 (Mic. iv. 6, Lam. ii. 7, and often,—Dion. H. II. 759), for which the better writers used ἐώσατο with the syllabic augment (Th. M. p. 403, Pol. 2. 69. 9, 15. 31. 12). 1 aor. pass. ἀπώσθην Ps. lxxxvii. 6, comp. Xen. *Hell.* 4. 3. 12, Dio C. 37. 47. Also aor. act. ἐξῶσεν[5] A. vii. 45, for which some MSS. have ἐξέωσεν (Ellendt, Arr. *Al.* I. 181). Strictly speaking, the rule for the use of the syllabic augment

---

[1] ["The partic. ἐνεγκών is in the N. T. entirely displaced by ἐνέγκας, whilst conversely, ἐνεγκεῖν has taken the place of ἐνέγκαι, which occurs once only." A. Buttm. p. 68. Tisch. reads ἐνέγκαι (not only in 1 P. ii. 5, but also) in L. xxii. 42. On these aorists see especially Veitch, *Gr. V.* pp. 592–4.]

[2] [The accentuated MSS. are divided between ἐκφυῇ (Lachm., Treg., Alf., Fritz., A. Buttm.) and ἐκφύῃ (Tisch., Meyer, Westc. and Hort): the latter may be either 2 aor. act. intransitive, or (Meyer) present and transitive.]

[3] [Lob. p. 740 refers to ἐχαίρησα solely. In Rev. xi. 10, *Rec.* has the fut. χαροῦσιν; this seems the only example of this form found in any writer.]

[4] From the fut. ὤσω (from ὤθω). The aorist form from the other future ὠθήσω occurs only in later authors; e.g. partic. εἰσωθήσας Cinnam. p. 193. [See Veitch, *Gr. V.* p. 614.]

[5] [Accentuated ἔξωσιν by Tischendorf and Meyer.]

in this verb applies to Attic writers only: see Poppo, *Thuc.* III. ii. 407.

*ὠνέομαι. 1 aor. ὠνησάμην A. vii. 16, as frequently in writers of the κοινή, e.g. Plutarch, Pausanias (Lob. p. 139). Attic writers prefer ἐπριάμην.

Rem. The later verbal forms are not always found in the N. T. where they might be expected. We have, for instance, πίομαι (not πιοῦμαι) as the 2 fut. of πίνω, Rev. xiv. 10, see Buttm. I. 395; aor. κοινῶσαι[1] Mk. vii. 15, 18, Mœris p. 434 (ed. Piers.), Locella, *Xen. Ephes.* p. 254; fut. φεύξομαι, θαυμάσομαι, not φεύξω, θαυμάσω (Buttm. II. 85). In H. iv. 15, we find amongst the various readings πεπειραμένον from the older πειράω (instead of πεπειρασμένον from πειράζω), and Tisch. has received this into the text.[2]

That the same forms are sometimes produced from different verbs by inflexion is well known: we shall only specify ἐξένευσε Jo. v. 13, which (grammatically) may belong equally well to ἐκνέω (*Irr. V.* p. 230) and to ἐκνεύω.

Section XVI.

FORMATION OF DERIVATIVE AND COMPOUND WORDS.[3]

The N. T. contains a number of words not used by Greek authors, which were either derived from the popular spoken language, or were newly coined: we find most examples of the latter class in the writings of Paul. The more numerous such words are, the more necessary is it to compare the established laws of derivation in Greek with these formations peculiar to the N. T. In connexion with this it will be useful to notice the analogies which, though not unknown to ordinary Greek, yet appear more prominently in the N. T. language. The following observations are based

---

[1] [For which later writers used κοινώσασθαι (Mœris *l.c.*).]

[2] [Most editors (including Tisch. in ed. 8) read πεπειρασμένον, since (1) this has more external support, and (2) the ordinary meaning of πεπειραμ., "experienced," is unsuitable here. Winer (apparently) and Tisch. (in ed. 7) considered the two equivalent in meaning; and Tisch. argued that there could be no motive for altering πεπειρασμ. (comp. H. ii. 18), but the ambiguous πεπειραμ. would naturally be changed into the more familiar word. See Delitzsch.]

[3] See Ph. Cattieri *Gazophylacium Grœcor.* (1651, 1708), ed. F. L. Abresch (Utr. 1757, Leyd. 1809); but especially Buttmann, *Ausf. Gr.* II. 382 sqq. (with Lobeck's additions), Lobeck, *Parerga to Phrynichus*, and Lobeck's other works quoted above p. 3. Amongst commentaries, *Selecta e scholiis Valckenarii* chiefly refers to this subject. Examples of the later formations are to be found in the Byzantine writers especially.

on Buttmann, whose lucid treatment of the subject (*Ausführl. Sprachl.* § 118 sqq.) embraces all points of importance. Comp. Krüger § 41 sq.[1]

A. DERIVATION BY TERMINATIONS.

1. VERBS.

The derivative verbs in οω and ιζω (mostly but not entirely from nouns) are peculiarly frequent. In some instances verbs in οω superseded others in ευω or ιζω; as δεκατόω (δεκατεύω Xen. *An.* 5. 3. 9, al.), ἐξουδενόω[2] (ἐξουδενίζω in Plutarch), σαρόω (for σαίρω, Lob. p. 89), κεφαλαιόω[3] (κεφαλίζω, Lob. p. 95), δυναμόω and ἐνδυναμόω (Lob. p. 605 note), ἀφυπνόω (ἀφυπνίζω, Lob. p. 224), ἀνακαινόω (ἀνακαινίζω, Isocr. *Areop.* c. 3); also μεστόω, δολιόω. From δεκατόω comes ἀποδεκατόω; with ἀφυπνόω comp. καθυπνόω Xen. *Mem.* 2. 1. 30. We find also κραταιόω for κρατύνω, σθενόω for σθενέω, ἀναστατοῦν for ἀνάστατον ποιεῖν; but χαριτόω is formed from χάρις, δυναμόω from δύναμις (Lob. p. 605).

Verbs in ιζω come from a great variety of roots; as ὀρθρίζω from ὄρθρος, αἰχμαλωτίζω from αἰχμάλωτος, δειγματίζω from δεῖγμα, πελεκίζω from πέλεκυς, μυκτηρίζω from μυκτήρ, σμυρνίζω, ἀνεμίζω, φυλακίζω, ἱματίζω, ἀναθεματίζω (found also in the Byz. writers), θεατρίζω (Cinnam. p. 213), σπλαγχνίζομαι, αἱρετίζω, συμμορφίζω (Ph. iii. 10, in good MSS.). Σκορπίζω (διασκορπίζω) has no evident root in the Greek written language; it was however a provincial, perhaps a Macedonian word (Lob. p. 218).—On verbs in ιζω from names of nations and persons, see Buttm. II. 385 (Jelf 330. *Obs.* 3): we have

---

[1] [See also Jelf 329–347, Donalds. *Gr.* pp. 310–340, *New Crat.* pp. 449 sqq., 524 sqq., 664 sqq., Webster, *Syntax of the N. T.* c. ii.]

[2] On this word see Lob. p. 182. [There are four forms of this word, ἐξου-θενέω, -θενόω, -θενέω, -θενόω: the last is quoted by Lobeck from Eustratius (also ἐξουθένωμα from Const. Porph.), and is received by Tisch. (ed. 8) in Mk. ix. 12; in this passage indeed each of the four forms is found in one or more of our best MSS. Ἐξουθενέω occurs frequently in the LXX and in the N. T.; -θενέω Mk. ix. 12 (Lachm., Treg., Westc. and Hort), 2 C. x. 10 (Lach.), Ez. xxi. 10; -θενόω Mk. ix. 12 *Rec.*, Jud. ix. 38, al.]

[3] [Κεφαλαιόω occurs once in the N. T. in the ordinary texts of Mk. xii. 4, but its proper meaning is altogether unsuitable in this passage. Tisch. (ed. 8) and Westcott and Hort adopt the very probable reading (of ℵBL) ἐκεφαλίωσαν: κεφαλιόω stands to κεφάλιον in the same relation as κεφαλαιόω to κεφάλαιον.]

only to mention ἰουδαΐζω, with which compare the later word δαυϊδίζω, Leo Gramm. p. 447.

There are also verbs in αζω that seldom or never occur elsewhere, as νηπιάζω, σινιάζω (σήθω); also in ευω, as μεσιτεύω, μαγεύω, ἐγκρατεύομαι, αἰχμαλωτεύω (Lob. p. 442), παγιδεύω, γυμνητεύω.[1] The last is from γυμνήτης, which (according to Buttm. II. 431) can only be vindicated as a collateral form of γυμνής. From γυμνός we should expect γυμνίτης, and thus we find γυμνιτεύω in 1 C. iv. 11, in the best MSS.:[2] we must not therefore, with Fritzsche (Conform. Crit. p. 21) and Meyer, regard this as a mistake in transcription.[3]

Amongst verbs in υνω which signify a *making to be* what the (concrete) root denotes (as ἱλαρύνειν = ἱλαρὸν ποιεῖν, Buttm. II. 387, Jelf 330. 2), σκληρύνω deserves mention; it is a collateral form of σκληρόω, which does not occur in the N. T.[4]

Verbs in αινω—λευκαίνω, ξηραίνω, εὐφραίνω (Buttm. II. 65 sq., Lob. *Prol. Path.* p. 37)—require no special remark.[5]

The formation of verbs in θω from primitives in εω, though not unknown to Attic writers (Buttm. II. 61, Lob. p. 151), may have been more frequently practised in later Greek; at all events νήθω, κνήθω, ἀλήθω [p. 22], are not used by the older writers. See however Lob. p. 254.

Verbs in σκω,[6] with the exception of εὑρίσκω and διδάσκω, are rare in the N. T., as elsewhere (Buttm. II. 59 sq., Jelf 330. 1). We find γηράσκω as an inchoative (Buttm. II. 393): μεθύσκω, causative of μεθύω, occurs in the passive only: γα-

---

[1] [To these should be added ζηλεύω, which is well supported in Rev. iii. 19, and ῥυπαρεύομαι Rev. xxii. 11 (Tisch. ed. 7): the latter verb is not found elsewhere, and the former is very rare, see Lidd. and Scott s. v.]

[2] [The best texts now have γυμνιτεύω: see Alf. *in loc.*]

[3] Comp. Lob. *Ajax*, p. 387. For ὀλοθρεύω, H. xi. 28, some good MSS. have ὀλεθρεύω (from ὄλεθρος); Lachm. and with him Tisch. have received this form into the text. I am not aware that the latter form of this Alexandrian word has been preserved elsewhere. [Recent editors receive ἐξολεθρεύω in A. iii. 23, with most of the uncial MSS. We find the same form in the Alex. MS. of the LXX (both in the simple verb and in the compound), as Ex. xii. 23, Jos. xxiii. 4, 5, al. In H. xi. Tisch. now reads ὀλεθρευών.]

[4] [Σκληρόω is very rare: σκληρύνω is not uncommon in the LXX and in medical writers (Hippocr., al.).]

[5] [To these verbs derived from adj. or subst. should be added εὐπροςωπέω G. vi. 12 ("not used by any earlier writer:" Ellic.), ἀκαιρέω Ph. iv. 10 (Diod. S. *Exc. Vat.* p. 30).]

[6] [On verbs in σκω, see Don. *New Cr.* p. 615; Curtius, *Elucidations*, p. 141 sqq., *Greek Verb*, chapters x. and xxii.]

μίσκω, equivalent in meaning to γαμίζω, is sufficiently attested in L. xx. 34 only.[1]

Γρηγορέω (from the perfect ἐγρήγορα) and its cognate ἐγρηγορέω are altogether singular in formation (Lob. p. 119, Buttm. II. 158); but with this formation from a reduplicated perfect [2] we may compare ἐπικεχειρέω *Papyri Taurin.* 7. line 7.

To derivative verbs in ευω belongs also παραβολεύεσθαι Ph. ii. 30, which Griesb., Lachm., al., have received into the text, in accordance with the weightiest critical authorities. From παράβολος a verb παραβολεῖσθαι might certainly have been formed directly; but the ending ευω is chosen to express the meaning παράβολον εἶναι, as in later Greek ἐπισκοπεύειν is used for ἐπίσκοπον εἶναι (Lob. p. 591), and, to give a still closer parallel, as we find περπερεύεσθαι from πέρπερος. It would not be right to make the admission of παραβολεύεσθαι depend on the assumption that there existed a verb βολεύεσθαι, which certainly is not to be found in any Greek writer.[3]

2. SUBSTANTIVES.[4]

a. From Verbs.[5] Of nouns in μος (Buttm. II. 398) from verbs in αζω, we have to mention ἁγιασμός, which does not occur in Greek authors, as also πειρασμός from πειράζω, ἐνταφιασμός from ἐνταφιάζω.[6] From verbs in ιζω we find μακαρισμός, ὀνειδισμός (Lob. p. 512), βασανισμός, παροργισμός, ῥαντισμός (ῥαντίζειν), σαββατισμός (σαββατίζειν), σωφρονισμός, ἀπελεγμός.

The most numerous formations, however, are those in μα (Lob. *Paral.* p. 391 sqq.) and σις, the former in great part peculiar to the N. T., but always framed in accordance with analogy; as βάπτισμα, ῥάπισμα (from βαπτίζειν, etc.), ψεῦσμα (from ψεύδεσθαι), ἱεράτευμα, κατάλυμα (καταλύειν), also ἐξέραμα (Lob. p. 64), ἀσθένημα, ἄντλημα, ἀντάλλαγμα, ἀπο-

---

[1] [This is the judgment of the best editors: γαμίζω, however, occurs not unfrequently. See Tisch. on Mt. xxii. 30.]
[2] Döderlein, *Ueber die Redupl. in der griech. und lat. Wortbildung*, in his *Reden und Aufsätzen* II. No. 2.
[3] [Mullach (p. 258) mentions that in modern Greek verbs in ιω have sometimes collateral forms in ινω, as ὠφιλινώ by the side of ὠφιλίω; and compares τυραννεύω, τυραννίω.]
[4] Compare G. Curtius, *De nomin. Gr. formatione linguar. cognat. ratione habita*: Berlin 1842 (*Zeitschr. für Alterth.* 1846, No. 68 sq.).
[5] Comp. Lobeck, *Paral.* p. 397 sqq., and especially *Technol.* lib. 3, p. 253 sqq.
[6] [On the rare noun ἁρπαγμός see Ellicott and Lightfoot on Ph. ii. 6, Donalds. *New Crat.* p. 451.]

σκίασμα, πρόσκομμα, ἀπαύγασμα, ἥττημα, αἴτημα, κατόρθωμα, στερέωμα (from contracted verbs, like φρόνημα, etc.).¹
These nouns mostly denote a product or state: only ἄντλημα
denotes an instrument (a meaning which nouns in μος often
have); and κατάλυμα, the place of καταλύειν (Eustath. *Odyss.*
p. 146. 33).

The nouns in σις, which are particularly numerous in the
Epistle to the Hebrews, are nearly all to be found in Greek
authors; only θέλησις, κατάπαυσις, πρόσχυσις,² ἀπολύτρωσις,
δικαίωσις, πεποίθησις (Lob. p. 295), βίωσις (ἐπιπόθησις), require mention. On παρασκευή, formed from the root of a verb
in αζω, see Buttm. II. 404; on οἰκοδομή, Lob. p. 490: and on
the very common word διαθήκη (from 1 aor. of τιθέναι), Buttm.
II. 401, Lob. *Paral.* p. 374.

To the abstract nouns belong also some in μονή; of these
we find in the N. T. πλησμονή (Buttm. II. 405). Ἐπιλησμονή,
however, is immediately derived from ἐπιλήσμων; πεισμονή
(found also in Pachym. II. 100, 120) is formed from πεῖσμα,
though it may be directly referred to πείθω, as πλησμονή to
πλήθω.³ Among abstract nouns from verbs in ευω should be
mentioned ἐριθεία.⁴

The concrete nouns have little that is peculiar. From verbs
in αζω, ιζω, υζω, we find in the N. T. the paroxytone κτίστης,
and the oxytone ⁵ βιαστής, βαπτιστής, μεριστής, εὐαγγελιστής,
γογγυστής, and ἑλληνιστής,⁶—all seldom or never found else-

---

¹ [In A. xxv. 7 αἰτίωμα (for αἰτίαμα) is very strongly supported: this word "is not found elsewhere, but Eustathius (p. 1422. 21) uses αἰτίωσις for αἰτίασις" (Meyer *in loc.*).—On the tendency of some nouns in μα to assume an active or abstract meaning, see Ellic. on Ph. iv. 6, Col. ii. 5.]

² The form χυσια seems to be used only when the first part of the compound is an appellative: the N. T. word αἱματεκχυσία (Leo Gr. p. 287) may be compared with αἱματοχυσία (Theophan. p. 510), φωτοχυσία, and ῥινεγχυσία.

³ [On πεισμονή see Ellic. on G. v. 8; and on the termination, *New Crat.* p. 457.]

⁴ The connexion of ἐριθεία with ἔρις is not precluded by the mere presence of the θ, for this letter is found in this family of words in ἐρέθειν, ἐρεθίζειν; but the whole form of the word shows that it can only be referred to ἐριθεύω. That moreover the N. T. word ἐριθεία is no other than the ἐριθεία (*labour for hire*) which was already in use among the Greeks, is convincingly shown by Fritzsche (*Rom.* I. 143 sqq.). Amongst earlier writers, see Stolberg, *De Solœc. N. T.* p. 136 sqq. [See also Ellicott and Lightfoot on G. v. 20; Alford on Rom. ii. 8.]

⁵ On the accentuation see Buttm. II. 408 (Jelf 59, Don. p. 315).

⁶ Ἑλληνίζειν has the general meaning *to deport oneself as a Greek* (Diog. L. I. 102). It is most frequently applied to *speaking Greek*, and especially to the use of the Greek language by foreigners (Strabo 14. 662); and in this case it is

where: only in the case of κολλυβιστής (which however is not peculiar to the N. T.) there exists no intermediate verb κολλυβίζειν.¹ From τελειοῦν we have τελειωτής, comp. ζηλωτής and λυτρωτής: from προσκυνεῖν, προσκυνητής (Constant. Man. 4670): on ἐπενδύτης see Buttm. II. 411 (Jelf 331). The older writers preferred διωκτήρ to διώκτης; similarly δοτήρ has the collateral form δότης.²

Κατάνυξις, Rom. xi. 8 (from the LXX), if derived from κατανυστάζω (as it was at one time supposed to be), would be a very strange formation. It is however clear from Dan. x. 9 (Theodot.) that this noun was regarded as cognate with κατανύσσειν; and thus it might denote *stupefaction* (תַּרְעֵלָה Ps. lx. 5), and thence *torpor*:³ see Fritz. *Rom.* II. 558 sqq.

Ταμεῖον (for ταμιεῖον, from ταμιεύω) is the reading of all good MSS. in L. xii. 24, and of many MSS. in Mt. vi. 6⁴ (see Lob. p. 493, *Paral.* p. 28): similarly we find the compound γλωσσόκομον for γλωσσοκομεῖον or γλωσσοκόμιον (from κομέω), without any variant (see Lob. p. 98 sq.). In each case the abbreviated form was the result of a careless pronunciation of the word.

β. *From Adjectives.* Under this head come

(1) Some abstract nouns in της, οτης; as ἁγιότης, ἁγνότης, ἀδελφότης (Leo Gramm. p. 464), ἁδρότης, ἁπλότης, ἱκανότης, ἀφελότης (ἀφέλεια in earlier writers), σκληρότης, τιμιότης, τελειότης, ματαιότης, γυμνότης, μεγαλειότης, κυριότης, αἰσχρότης, πιότης (ἀγαθότης, LXX), see Lob. p. 350 sqq.: ἀκαθάρτης, Rev. xvii. 4, is not well attested.

often used without implying disparagement, e.g. in Xen. *Anab.* 7. 3. 25, Strabo 2. 98: De Wette's assertion (*Bibel* p. 17,—reprinted from the *Hall. Encycl.*) is incorrect. Hence the substantive ἑλληνιστής (which never occurs in Greek authors) very naturally signifies *one who speaks Greek, though not a Greek by birth*, e.g. a Greek-speaking Jew. That in Christian Greek phraseology ἑλληνίζειν also meant *to be a heathen* (as in Malal. p. 449) has no further connexion with our subject. [See page 29, note³.]

¹ [This verb occurs Schol. Aristoph. *Ran.* 507; and in Schol. Aristoph. *Pax* 1196 we should probably read κεκολλυβισμένοι.]

² [In Rev. xii. 10 recent editors receive from A the strange form κατήγωρ, for κατήγορος. "This form of the word is Hebraic=קטיגור. A complete parallel is presented by the Rabbinical designation of Michael, the סניגור, ὁ συνήγωρ, i.e. συνήγορος (comp. Schöttg.). Similarly in later Greek διάκων for διάκονος; comp. Wetstein." Düsterd. *in loc.*]

³ [The Hebrew noun (תַּרְדֵּמָה) which the LXX render by κατάνυξις in Is. xxix. 10 (from which Rom. xi. 8 is freely quoted) is derived from the verb (נָרְדַּם) which Theodotion renders by κατανύσσω in Dan. x. 9.]

⁴ [Ταμεῖον is certainly the true reading in Mt. xxiv. 26, L. xii. 3, 24, and most probably in Mt. vi. 6.]

(2) Those in συνη, denoting non-material qualities: as ἐλεημοσύνη and ἀσχημοσύνη (from ἐλεήμων and ἀσχήμων, comp. σωφροσύνη from σώφρων); or ἁγιωσύνη, ἀγαθωσύνη, ἱερωσύνη, μεγαλωσύνη, with ω, since derived from adjectives with short penultimate;[1]—all later forms, found only in Hellenistic writers: see in general Lob. *Prol. Path.* p. 235 sqq.

Amongst nouns in ια also, derived from adjectives in ος, ρος (Buttm. II. 415), there are several later formations (Lob. p. 343), e.g. ἐλαφρία, like αἰσχρία (Eustathius) from αἰσχρός. In 2 P. ii. 16 we find παραφρονία from παράφρων (Lob. *Proleg. Path.* p. 238), like εὐδαιμονία from εὐδαίμων; but some [cursive] MSS. have the more usual παραφροσύνη.[2]

Lastly, the neuter of many adjectives in ιος is used as a substantive; as ὑποζύγιον, μεθόριον, ὑπολήνιον, σφάγιον (προσφάγιον), etc.: see Fritz. *Prälim.* p. 42.

γ. *From other substantives* (Buttm. II. 420 sqq., Jelf 335, Don. p. 319). Εἰδωλεῖον[3] (εἴδωλον), ἐλαιών (ἐλαία), μυλών Mt. xxiv. 41 *v. l.* (μύλος, μύλη), Buttm. II. 422 sq.; and the femin. βασίλισσα (Buttm. II. 427). Ἀφεδρών, which is peculiar to the N. T., comes from ἕδρα. The gentile femin. from Φοίνιξ is Φοίνισσα; hence we find Συροφοίνισσα Mk. vii. 26, as Κίλισσα from Κίλιξ (Buttm. II. 427). Perhaps however a femin. was also formed from Φοινίκη, the name of the country, for very many good MSS. have in this place Συροφοινίκισσα (comp. Fritz. *in loc.*):[4] this might be immediately derived from a simpler form Φοινικίς, as we find βασίλισσα by the side of βασιλίς, and as (in Latin at all events) Scythissa was used for Σκυθίς, or as in later Greek φυλάκισσα is found by the side of φυλακίς : see in general Lob. *Prol. Path.* p. 413 sq.

To the later and Latinising formation belong, of gentile nouns

---

[1] *Etym. Mag.* p. 275. 44. Yet we find μιγαλοσύνη in Glycas (p. 11), even in the later edition. That nearly all the nouns in ωσύνη belong to the later language, is shown by Buttm. (II. 420). On the termination συνη in general, see Aufrecht in the *Berl. Zeitschr. für vergleich. Sprachforsch.* 6. Heft. [Lünemann adds a reference to G. Bühler, *Das griech. Secundärsuffix της*: *ein Beitrag z. Lehre v. d. Wortbildung* (Gött. 1858).]

[2] Of substantives derived from adjectives in ης, some, as is well known, end in ια instead of υα (Buttm. II. 416, Jelf 334. *Obs.* 1). In others the spelling varies between ια and υα, e.g. κακοπαθία (comp. Poppo, *Thuc.* II. i. 154, Ellendt, *Præf. ad Arrian.* p. 30 sqq., Weber, *Demosth.* p. 511), the form υα however being best attested in this word. [See also p. 49.]

[3] [Written with -ι- (not -ει-) by Tischendorf, Westcott and Hort.]

[4] [So Lachm., Tisch., Westc. and Hort ; Tregelles, Σύρα Φοινίκισσα.]

and patronymics, Ἡρωδιανός, Mt. xxii. 16, and Χριστιανός, A. xi. 26, al.: comp. Καισαριανός Arr. Epict. 1. 19. 19, 3. 24. 117. In the earlier language the termination ανος was used only in forming gentile names for cities and countries out of Greece (Buttm. II. 429, Jelf 338. g).

Among diminutives deserves to be mentioned βιβλαρίδιον, formed immediately from βιβλάριον (which is mentioned by Pollux), and used instead of the older forms βιβλίδιον and βιβλιδάριον (like ἱματιδάριον from ἱματίδιον); see Lob. Pathol. I. 281. Γυναικάριον follows the ordinary analogy, but seems to have been of rare occurrence in Greek authors: the same may be said of ὠτάριον (Mk. xiv. 47, Jo. xviii. 10), κλινάριον, παιδάριον. Amongst diminutives in ιον, ψιχίον is decidedly a later form.[1]

The substantives in ηριον are properly neuter adjectives (Buttm. II. 412 sq.), as ἱλαστήριον, θυμιατήριον, φυλακτήριον. This termination became more common in the later language: e. g. ἀνακαλυπτήριον Niceph. Gregor. p. 667, δεητήριον Cedren. II. 377, θανατήριον ib. I. 679, ἰαματήριον ib. I. 190, al. Φυλακτήριος, formed immediately from φυλακτήρ, has like it an active meaning, *guarding, protecting*. Ἱλαστήριον is properly *something that propitiates*, but can be specially applied to the place where the propitiation is accomplished (as φυλακτήριον denotes a *guardhouse, outpost*), and hence to the covering of the ark of the covenant. For Rom. iii. 25 the signification *propitiatory offering* (Index to Theophan. cont.) is equally suitable: Philippi has lately denied this, but without sufficient reason. Ζευκτηρία is a femin. subst. of the same kind; comp. στυπτηρία. Σωτηρία is immediately connected with σωτήρ: besides this, σωτήριον also occurs as a substantive. Ὑπερῷον, i.e. ὑπερῷον, is in like manner to be regarded as the neuter of ὑπερῷος, which is formed from the prepos. ὑπέρ, as πατρῷος from πατήρ, for there is no intermediate adjective ὕπερος.[2]

3. ADJECTIVES.

a. From Verbs. To adjectives immediately derived from a verbal root belongs πειθός, which is fully established in 1 C. ii. 4: compare ἑδός from ἕδω, βοσκός from βόσκω, φειδός from

---

[1] On diminutives in ιον see Fritz. Prälim. p. 43, and Janson, *De vocibus in ιον trisyllabis*, in Jahn's Archiv VII. 485 sqq.

[2] [In L. xxi. 11 we should probably read φόβηθρον, for φόβητρον: compare κόρηθρον, κύκηθρον. See Lobeck in Buttm. II. 413. Here may also be mentioned the form συγγενεύς (συγγενεῦσι, Mk. vi. 4 and perhaps L. ii. 44): see A. Buttm. p. 25.]

(φείδω) φείδομαι, and see Lob. p. 434. These derivatives are as a rule oxytone; φάγος alone is also written as a paroxytone by the grammarians (Lob. *Paral.* p. 135), and this accentuation is followed in the N. T. Among those in ωλός, ἁμαρτωλός is most common (Buttm. II. 448); εἴδωλον, which is the neuter of εἴδωλος (Lob. *Path.* p. 134), belongs to the same class.

Verbals in τος [1] sometimes correspond to the Latin participle in *tus,* as γνωστός *notus,* σιτευτός *saginatus,* ἀπαίδευτος (*inept*), compare θεόπνευστος *inspiratus;* [2] sometimes to adjectives in *bilis,* as ὁρατός, δυσβάστακτος, ἀνεκτός, ἀκατάσχετος, ἀκαταπαυστός, ἀνεκδιήγητος, ἀνεκλάλητος. Some verbals have an active meaning (Fritz. *Rom.* II. 185), as ἄπταιστος *not stumbling,* i.e. *not sinning;* ἀλάλητος however (Rom. viii. 26) certainly does not belong to this class. Ἀπείραστος, Ja. i. 13, like the classical ἀπείρατος, is either *untried, untempted,* or—what amounts to the same in this passage—*incapable of being tried* [see p. 242]. Only παθητός has the meaning *one who is to suffer,* A. xxvi. 23; comp. φευκτός, πρακτός, Aristot. *De Anima* 3. 9, p. 64 (Sylb.), Cattier, *Gazophyl.* p. 34. The verbal προσήλυτος is immediately connected with such forms as ἔπηλυς, μέτηλυς, and is an extended formation of which we find no examples in Greek authors.

β. *From Adjectives.* Among adjectives derived from other adjectives (or from participles) a few deserve special notice: e.g. περιούσιος and ἐπιούσιος, like ἑκούσιος, ἐθελούσιος, (Lob. p. 4 sq.), which are formed from ἑκών and ἐθέλων in the same way as the feminines ἑκοῦσα, ἐθέλουσα. Ἐπιούσιος however has probably a direct connexion with the feminine (ἡ) ἐπιοῦσα, scil. ἡμέρα, so that ἄρτος ἐπιούσιος is *bread for the following day:* compare Stolberg, *Diss. de pane ἐπιουσίῳ* (*De Solœcismis N. T.* p. 220 sqq.), Valcken. *Select.* I. 190, and Fritz. *Matt.* p. 267 sq., where also the derivation of the word from οὐσία (which would be grammatically possible, comp. ἐνούσιος) is controverted.[3]

---

[1] See Buttm. I. 443 sqq., Lob. *Paral.* p. 478 sqq., Moiszisstzig, *De Adj. Græc. Verbal.* (Conitz 1844). [Don. p. 191; Curtius, *Gr. Verb,* p. 515. On the accentuation of compound verbals, see Lob. *Paral.* pp. 473-498, A. Buttm. *Gr.* p. 42.]

[2] The *passive* interpretation of this word in 2 Tim. iii. 16 can admit of no doubt, and is also supported by the analogy of ἐμπνευστος; though several derivatives of this kind have an active meaning, as εὔπνευστος, ἄπνευστος.

[3] [This word is most fully examined by Tholuck (*Serm. on the Mount,* pp. 341-348), Lightfoot (*Revision,* pp. 194-234), M'Clellan, *New Test.* pp. 632-647.

The meaning of περιούσιος in the Bible is not simply *proprius*, as opposed to what belongs to another, any more than περιουσιασμός in the LXX means simply *property*.

Πιστικός (Mk. xiv. 3, Jo. xii. 3), from πιστός, is explained by several ancient commentators as meaning *genuine*. In earlier writers the word signifies *convincing*, probably also *persuasive*, Plat. *Gorg.* 455 a, Diog. L. 4. 37, Dion. H. V. 631, Sext. Emp. *Math.* 2. 71, Theophrast. *Metaph.* 253 (Sylb.); in nearly all the passages, however, some MSS. have πειστικός, and this form has usually been preferred by the critics, see Bekker and Stallb. on Plat. *l. c.*, and compare Lob. *Ajax*, v. 151. In later Greek it signifies *faithful, trustworthy*, of persons; see Lücke, *Joh.* II. 496, Index to Cedrenus p. 950. A transition to the meaning *genuine*, as a material predicate, would not be impossible, particularly as technical expressions (and such νάρδος πιστική may very well have been), and mercantile terms especially, are often strange.[1] Others, after Casaubon, take πιστικός for *drinkable* (Fritz. *Mark*, p. 598 sqq.), from πιπίσκω or the root πίω, like πιστός *drinkable* (Æschyl. *Prom.* 480), πιστήρ, πίστρα, πίστρον, and other words quoted by the old lexicographers. That the ancients did sometimes drink the nard oil we know from Athenæus (15. 689). But I cannot clearly see why both evangelists applied this particular epithet: if the thin liquid nard-ointment which they used for pouring out (καταχέειν, Mk. *l. c.*) did not differ from that which was drinkable, it would be just as superfluous

---

Lünemann refers to articles by Leo Meyer (in Kuhn's *Zeitschr.* 1858, VII. 424 sq., 428), who maintains that the word is formed by the suffix ιο from ἐπί and ὄντ, and denotes "that which is ἐπί," so that ἄρτος ἐ. signifies "the bread which is serviceable or necessary for the support of life,—which answers to our necessities." Lightfoot's objection to all derivations from εἶναι (or οὐσία)—that the word would then be ἐπούσιος, not ἐπιούσιος, the ι never being retained *unless the second word was originally written with the digamma* (as in ἐπίορκος, ἐπιεικής, etc.)—appears decisive. His conclusion is that the phrase means *bread for the coming day*. M'Clellan refers the word to ὁ ἐπιών (scil. χρόνος, αἰών), " bread *for the future world*." In a second Appendix Bp. Lightfoot discusses περιούσιος.]

[1] They have this especial peculiarity, that words usually applied to persons only are transferred to articles of merchandise: compare the German *flau*, properly *weak, feeble* [but used for *dull, heavy*, in respect of sale], and such notices as "Sugar inactive, wheat unasked." Lobeck (*Paral.* p. 31) defends Scaliger's view, that πιστικός is derived from πτίσσω (Fritz. *Mark*, p. 595), since euphony leads to the omission of τ after π and in some other cases: comp. στέρνιξ, πέρνιξ, but especially πίτυρον and the Latin *pisso*. Meyer still adheres to the rendering *genuine*. [For other explanations see Alford on Mk. xiv. 3.]

to add the epithet πιστική as to speak of *fluid* nard. The νάρδος λεπτή of Dioscorides is properly only fluid nard, as opposed to the thick, viscid kind. In John's narrative, too, the mention of *drinkable* nard does not harmonise well with the manipulation indicated by ἀλείφειν. Lastly, Fritzsche's rendering of πιστ. by " qui *facile* bibi potest, *lubenter* bibitur " (p. 601) is not sufficiently supported; not to mention that it cannot be certainly shown that πιστικός anywhere has the meaning *drinkable*. Indeed πιστός itself was probably not much used—in Æschylus *l. c.* there is a play on words [οὐ χριστὸν οὔτε πιστόν]—being superseded by the unambiguous ποτός, πόσιμος.

γ. *From Substantives*. To adjectives derived from substantives belong amongst others σάρκινος and σαρκικός. The former signifies *fleshy*, i.e. *made of flesh* (2 C. iii. 3), as proparoxytone adjectives in ινος almost without exception denote the material of which a thing is made, e.g. λίθινος *of stone* (2 C. iii. 3), ξύλινος *wooden*, πήλινος *of clay*, ἀκάνθινος, βύσσινος, etc. (Buttm. II. 448): the latter is *fleshly*. There is however preponderant or considerable authority for σάρκινος in Rom. vii. 14, 1 C. iii. 1 (2 C. i. 12), H. vii. 16, where σαρκικός might have been expected; and even Lachmann has received it into the text.[1] But how easily might σαρκικός, a word found in the N. T. only,[2] be confounded in the MSS. with the familiar word σάρκινος (Fritz. *Rom.* II. 46 sq.). If Paul wrote σάρκινος, he must have intended some such special emphasis as Meyer attributes to the word in 1 C. iii. 1.[3] But in the doctrinal system of Paul we find no support for any description of the natural man which the merely material word σάρκινος would be sufficient to convey; whilst σαρκικός, in antithesis to πνευματικός, is all that is required even in these passages. Besides, 1 C. iii. 3, taken in connexion with ver. 2, shows that Paul used the same designation in both verses.[4]

---

[1] [Not in 2 C. i. 12: in the other passages recent editors read σάρκινος. On adj. in ινος see Donalds. *New Crat.* p. 458, Trench, *Syn.* s. v. σάρκινος.]

[2] [It occurs in *Anth. Pal.* 1. 107, Ps.-Arist. *Hist. An.* 10. 2. 7, and is a *v. l.* in 2 Chr. xxxii. 8.]

[3] [Meyer's view is that, to designate more emphatically the unspiritual nature of the Corinthians, Paul calls them *men of the flesh*—" men who had experienced so little of the Holy Spirit's operation, that the σάρξ appeared to constitute their whole being :" comp. Trench *l. c.*]

[4] [That is, in verses 1, 3 : σαρκικοί is undoubted in ver. 3. See Alford *in loc.*]

Such an expression as ἐντολὴ σαρκίνη, H. vii. 16, is hardly to be tolerated.¹

Among the oxytone adjectives in ινος which express notions of time (Buttm. II. 448, Jelf 338), καθημερινός, ὀρθρινός, πρωϊνός, are later forms, for which earlier writers used καθημέριος, κ.τ.λ. ; ταχινός belongs to the same class. Some adjectives derived from substantives end in εινός, as σκοτεινός, φωτεινός ; ἐλεεινός however—a form not uncommon in Attic Greek (V. Fritzsche, *Aristoph.* I. 456)—comes from the verb ἐλεέω, as ποθεινός from ποθέω (Buttm. II. 448). Κεραμικός (κεράμειος, κεράμιος) must also be reckoned with later adjectival formations.

Among adverbs derived from verbs, φειδομένως seems to be peculiar to the N. T.²

B. DERIVATION BY COMPOSITION.

4. *a. Substantives and Adjectives.* The compound nouns whose first part also is a noun are numerous in the N. T. Although many of these words are not to be found in Greek authors, yet there is nothing in their formation which is contrary to analogy. Compare in particular δικαιοκρισία (Leo Gr. p. 163), αἱματεκχυσία, ταπεινόφρων—like εὐσεβόφρων, κραταιόφρων Constant. Porphyr. II. 33, and in later writers even ἰουδαιόφρων, ἑλληνόφρων Cedren. I. 660, Theophan. I. 149—and ταπεινοφροσύνη (comp. ματαιοφροσύνη Constant. Man. 657), σκληροκαρδία, σκληροτράχηλος (from which we find σκληροτραχηλία and σκληροτραχηλιᾶν in Const. Man.), ἀκροβυστία,³ ἀκρογωνιαῖος, ἀλ-

---

¹ In general, we might perhaps assume that the later popular language confounded the forms, and used σάρκινος also in the sense of σαρκικός, especially as adjectives in ινος do not *always* denote substance or material (comp. ἀνθρώπινος); see Fritz. *Rom.* II. 47, Tholuck, *Hebr.* p. 301 sq. Somewhat similar in German is the use of *das Inwendige* (of a man) for *das Innere*: the former had at one time a more limited meaning. Since, however, σαρκικός had beyond doubt already established itself for the language of the N. T., there is no ground for such an assumption in this case. [Comp. Delitzsch on H. vii. 16 ; also Tisch. on 1 C. iii. 1, who maintains that the two words are synonymous in the N. T.]

² [It also occurs in Plutarch (*Alex.* 25). For κεραμικός see Plato, *Polit.* 288 a.]

³ That is, if (with the *Etym. Mag.*) we derive this word from βύζω, βύω. This derivation has been recently controverted by Fritzsche (*Rom.* I. 136), on the ground that βύω does not seem to have the meaning *tegere* (as this etymology assumes), and that the word, so derived, would contain no reference to any part of the body in particular, and would therefore be unintelligible from its vague-

λοτριοεπίσκοπος ¹ (comp. ἀλλοτριοπραγμοσύνη Plat. *Rep.* 4. 444 b), ἀνθρωπάρεσκος (Lob. p. 621), ποταμοφόρητος (comp. ὑδατοφόρητος Const. Man. 409), καρδιογνώστης (καρδιόπληκτος Theophan. I. 736, καρδιοκολάπτης Leo Gr. 441), σητόβρωτος, ὀφθαλμοδουλεία, εἰδωλολάτρης,² εἰδωλόθυτον (Cedren. I. 286, comp. the abstract εἰδωλοθυσία Theophan. 415), δεσμοφύλαξ (νωτοφύλαξ Theophan. I. 608), ὀρκωμοσία (comp. ἀπωμοσία, κατωμοσία), πατροπαράδοτος (θεοπαράδοτος Theophan. I. 627), ἰσάγγελος (Theoph. I. 16), εὐπερίστατος, πολυποίκιλος, the adverb παμπληθεί (the adjective παμπληθής is found in good writers), εἰλικρινής, εἰλικρίνεια (Fuhr, *Dicæarch.* p. 198). The nearest approach to the compound δευτερόπρωτος, L. vi. 1 (?), is found in δευτεροδεκάτη (Hieron. *in Ezech.* c. 45); as the one means *second-tenth*, the other means *second-first*.³ Δωδεκάφυλος, the neuter of which is used as a substantive in A. xxvi. 7, is supported by τετράφυλος (Her. 5. 66).—The first part of the compound is more rarely a verb, as in ἐθελοθρησκεία *self-imposed worship*: compare ἐθελοδουλία.

The adjectives whose first part is *a* privative exhibit nothing anomalous, though many of them may not have been used in the written language (ἀμετανόητος, ἀνεξερεύνητος, ἀνεξιχνίαστος). The only peculiar word is ἀνέλεος, which Lachm. has received in Ja. ii. 13 on good authority, in the place of ἀνίλεως; Greek writers used ἀνηλεής, or at any rate ἀνελεής (Lob. p. 710). Ἀνέλεος would be formed on the analogy of ἄνελπις, ἄπαις, and may have been chosen for its resemblance in sound to ἔλεος in the same clause. Buttmann (II. 467) maintains that the initial *a* of ἀτενίζειν (from the adj. ἀτενής) is the so-called "*a* in-

ness. The former argument seems to me to have more force than the latter. I am inclined however to think that ἀκροβυστία is not an unintentional corruption of ἀκροποσθία, but a euphemistic alteration of this word, made designedly in such a way that the latter part would convey the meaning *refertus, turgens* (βύω). It is in the nature of euphemistic expressions to be vague and general: those among whom they are current easily come to an understanding about their meaning.

¹ [Recent editors receive the more correct form ἀλλοτριεπίσκοπος.]
² Comp. ἀνθρωπολάτρης Ephraem. p. 743, πυρσολάτρης Pachym. 134, Geo. Pisid. *Heracl.* 1. 14. 182, ψευδολάτρης Theodos. *Acroas.* 2. 73; also χριστολάτρης, a common word in the Byzantine writers.
³ [On this word see Tischendorf's long note (ed. 8), and comp. Tregelles and Alford *in loc.*, Wieseler, *Syn.* pp. 203-215, Ellicott, *Hist. L.* p. 174, Scrivener, *Critic.* p. 515, M'Clellan, *New Test.* p. 690 sq. The word is retained by Tisch., bracketed by Lachm. and Alford, banished to the margin by Tregelles and by Westcott and Hort.—On ἐθελοθρησκεία see *Expositor*, xii. 295-297.]

tensive;" but it is better (with Lob. *Path.* I. 35) to take it for a *formativum*.¹ See further Döderlein, *De a intensivo sermonis Græci* (Erl. 1830).²

5. *Verbs.* When the last part of the compound is a verb (that is, in *verba composita*), the verbal root is retained unaltered, as a rule, only when the first part is one of the so-called old prepositions (Scaliger in Lob. *Phryn.* p. 266, Buttm. II. 469 sq.). In other cases the verb properly takes its termination from a noun derived from the root; as ἀδυνατεῖν, ὁμολογεῖσθαι, νουθετεῖν, εὐεργετεῖν, τροποφορεῖν,³ ὀρθοτομεῖν (comp. ὀρθοτομία Theophan. contin. p. 812), ἀγαθοεργεῖν and ἀγαθουργεῖν,⁴ μετριοπαθεῖν, etc.

It cannot however be denied that there are some isolated exceptions to this rule; Scaliger himself had discovered δυϛθνήσκω in Euripides, comp. Buttm. II. 472. Hence we must also derive εὐδοκεῖν from δοκεῖν directly, and not (as Passow maintained) through an intermediate noun δόκος, see Fritz. *Rom.* II. 370: the word originated in a mere union of εὖ and δοκεῖν in pronunciation, comp. Buttm. II. 470. The same applies to καραδοκεῖν, which must not be referred to δοκεύω (Fritzschior. *Opusc.* p. 151); a noun καραδόκος does not exist.⁵

Ὁμείρεσθαι also (the reading of the better MSS. in 1 Th. ii. 8, for ἱμείρεσθαι) would be admissible, even if derived from ὁμοῦ, ὁμός, and εἴρειν (Fritz. *Mark*, p. 792). We do not indeed meet with any other verb thus compounded with ὁμοῦ, for ὁμαδέω comes from ὅμαδος, and ὁμοδρομεῖν, ὁμοδοξεῖν, ὁμευνετεῖν, ὁμηρεύειν, ὁμοζυγεῖν, ὁμιλεῖν, and even ὁμονοεῖν (Buttm. II.

---

¹ [In favour of Buttmann's view see Don. *Gr.* p. 334, *New Cr.* p. 348 sq. Lobeck's words are: a χαίνω, τείνω, σκέλλω, σπέρχω, adjectiva in ης exeuntia fingi non potuerunt nisi accedente vel præpositione (διαχανής, ἐκτενής, περισπερχής), vel alia parte orationis (πολυχανής, εὐτενής), quarum nihil nulla conveniebat, decursum est ad præpositionem loquelarem ἀ, quæ, quia per se nihil significat, ideo ad formandum aptissima est. Curtius (*Gr. Etym.* pp. 195, 217) takes ἀτενής, ἀσπερχές, as standing for ἀν-τενής, ἀν-σπερχές. In Curtius, *Studien*, vol. viii, will be found a full investigation of the subject by Clemm, who arranges all examples of prefixed α under the four heads, α *protheticum, copulativum, privativum, præpositionale*, agreeing with Curtius in connecting the two words (and also ἀσελγής, ἀκραγγές) with the prepos. ἀνά.]

² [In Rev. viii. 1, we should probably read ἡμίωρον for ἡμιώριον.]

³ [For which several editors read τροφοφορεῖν, A. xiii. 18 (Dt. i. 31).]

⁴ On these forms see Buttm. II. 457. Against οἰκουργεῖν and οἰκουργός (Tit. ii. 5 v. l.), comp. Fritz. *De Crit. Conf.* p. 29. [In Tit. *l. c.* οἰκουργός is strongly supported, and is received by recent editors.]

⁵ [See Jelf 346, Don. p. 339 sq., *New Cr.* p. 666 sq., Curt. *Elucid.* pp. 167 sqq.]

473), are in like manner directly derived from nouns. A difficulty would also be presented by the genitive which is here governed by the verb; compare Matth. 405. The first objection, however, should perhaps not be pressed in regard to a word borrowed from the popular spoken language. If μείρεσθαι—which is found in Nicand. *Ther.* 400, for ἱμείρεσθαι—were the original form, μείρεσθαι and ὀμείρεσθαι might exist together as collateral forms, as easily as δύρεσθαι and ὀδύρεσθαι: indeed ὀμείρεσθαι may perhaps be the true reading here (Lob. *Path.* I. 72).[1]

A compound peculiar to Hellenistic Greek is προςωπολημπτεῖν,—προςωπολήπτης, προςωποληψία (Theodos. *Acroas.* 1. 32), ἀπροςωπολήπτως (*Acta Apocr.* p. 86). A corresponding verb is ἀκαταληπτεῖν, Sext. Emp. I. 201; with the concrete derivative compare δωρολήπτης and ἐργολήπτης (LXX); and with the abstract προςωποληψία compare ἐρωτοληψία, Ephraem. pp. 3104, 7890, Nicet. Eugen. 4. 251. Several nouns like προςωπολήπτης, θανατηφόρος,[2] in which the second part is derived from a verb, whilst the first denotes the object, etc. (Buttm. II. 478), are peculiar to the N. T.; as δεξιολάβος, *one who takes a place at the right of any one*, hence *an attendant*. From these compounds are again derived, not only abstract nouns—to which class σκηνοπηγία belongs, formed as if from σκηνοπηγός, according to a common analogy, like κλινοπηγία,—but also verbs, as λιθοβολεῖν from λιθοβόλος (comp. ἀνθοβολεῖν, θηροβολεῖν, ἡλιοβολεῖσθαι, etc.), ὀρθοποδεῖν from ὀρθόπους, δεξιολαβεῖν (Leo Gr. p. 175): see Buttm. II. 479.

In *verba decomposita* that preposition by means of which the compound became a double compound naturally stands first, as in ἀπεκδέχεσθαι, συναντιλαμβάνεσθαι. Διαπαρατριβή, 1 Tim. vi. 5, would be at variance with this rule if it signified *misplaced diligence* or

---

[1] [The form with ο is now generally received here, and is the reading of good MSS. in Job iii. 21. Ellicott considers it a late form of ἱμείρομαι : "as it seems probable that μείρομαι is not an independent verb, but only an apocopated form of ἱμείρομαι 'metri causa,' it seems safer to consider ὀμείρομαι a corrupted and perhaps strengthened form of the more usual verb." Similarly Jowett *in loc.*, who adds that the pseudo-form was supported perhaps by an imaginary derivation from ὁμοῦ and εἴρειν. Compare however Lobeck *l. c.:* "vocales autem longas deteri tam contra naturam est, ut pæne credam primitivum fuisse ἀμείρω amo vel ὀμείρω quod codd. optimi N. T. præbent." Westcott and Hort agree with Lobeck in writing ὀμ., not ὁμ.]

[2] A similar compound is αὐθάδης; from αὐτός, ἥδειν, ἥδεσθαι (Buttm. II. 458).

useless disputing. The only meaning which διαπαρατρ. can have is *continued* (endless) *enmities, collisions;* the other signification would require παραδιατριβή. As however most of the MSS. are in favour of διαπαρατρ., which Lachmann has received into the text, it has been supposed—even by Fritzsche (*Mark,* p. 796[1])— that in this particular instance the prepositions are transposed. But διαπαρατριβή, in the sense given above, is not unsuitable in this passage. The other compounds with διαπαρα, viz. διαπαρακύπτεσθαι 1 K. vi. 4, and διαπαρατηρεῖν [2] 2 S. iii. 30, are in accordance with the rule as regards their meaning : the former word however is doubtful, see Schleusner, *Thes. Phil.* s. v.

Παρακαταθήκη is equivalent in meaning to παραθήκη, see Lennep, Phalar. *Ep.* p. 198 (Lips.), Lob. p. 312 ; the latter is better supported in the N. T. The MSS. similarly vary between the two words in Thuc. 2. 72 (see the commentators), and also in Plutarch, *Ser. Vind.* (see Wyttenb. II. 530) : comp. also Heinichen, *Ind. ad Euseb.* III. 529.

In Biblical Greek we meet with many compounds and double compounds which do not occur in Greek authors.[3] In particular, we find the simple verbs of earlier writers strengthened through the addition of prepositions, which, so to speak, exhibit to the eye the mode of the action ; as indeed a love for what is vivid and expressive is a general characteristic of the later language. Thus we have καταλιθάζειν, *to stone down;* ἐξορκίζειν, as if *to extract an oath from a man, put on oath;* ἐξαστράπτειν, *to flash forth;* ἐκγαμίζειν, *to give away in marriage* (*out of* the family), *elocare;* διεγείρειν, ἐξανατέλλειν, ἐξομολογεῖν, and many others. See my 5 *Progr. de Verbor. cum Prepos. compositor. in N. T. usu* (Lips. 1834-43).

In the same way, and for the same reason, compound and doubly compound adverbs (and prepositions) came into use in later Greek, as ἐπάνω, κατενώπιον, κατέναντι. In the Byzantine writers such formations are carried to a still greater extent than in the Bible ; compare for instance κατεπάνω in Constantine Porphyrogenitus.

Rem. 1. Personal names, particularly such as are compound, are frequently found in the N. T. in the contracted forms which especially belong to the popular spoken language, and these abbreviations are sometimes very bold (Lob. p. 434, comp. Schmid on Horat. *Epp.* 1. 7. 55) ; as Ἀπολλώς for Ἀπολλώνιος, Ἀρτεμᾶς for Ἀρτεμίδωρος (Tit. iii. 12), Νυμφᾶς for Νυμφόδωρος (Col. iv. 15),[4]

---

[1] [All uncial MSS. have διαπαρατριβαί. No one now will agree with Fritzsche *l. c.*: " patet igitur voc. διατριβαί miris modis præpositione παρα- esse diremtum, quum exspectes παραδιατριβαί."]

[2] [To these Ellicott adds διαπαράγω Greg. Nyss. II. 177, διαπαρασύρω Schol. Lucian II. 796 (Hemst.). The Lexicons give also compounds of διαπαρα with σιωπάω, λαμβάνω, δοχή, ὀξύνω (?), but all from late writers.]

[3] [Comp. Ellicott's notes on Ph. iii. 11, E. i. 21.]

[4] Keil (*Philologus* II. 468) believes he has found this name in an inscription

Ζηνᾶς for Ζηνόδωρος (Tit. iii. 13), Παρμενᾶς for Παρμενίδης (A. vi. 5), Δημᾶς probably for Δημέας, Δημέτριος, or Δήμαρχος (Col. iv. 14, 2 Tim. iv. 10), probably also Ὀλυμπᾶς for Ὀλυμπιόδωρος (Rom. xvi. 15), Ἐπαφρᾶς for Ἐπαφρόδιτος (Col. i. 7, iv. 12), and Ἑρμᾶς for Ἑρμόδωρος (Rom. xvi. 14), Θευδᾶς for Θεύδωρος (i.e. Θεόδωρος), and Λουκᾶς for Lucanus. In Greek writers, compare Ἀλεξᾶς for Ἀλέξανδρος (Jos. *Bell. J.* 6. 1. 8), Μηνᾶς for Μηνόδωρος, Πυθᾶς for Πυθόδωρος, Μετρᾶς (Euseb. *H. E.* 6. 41).[1]

Many names in ας not circumflexed are abbreviated forms; as Ἀμπλίας for Ampliatus (Rom. xvi. 8),[2] Ἀντίπας for Ἀντίπατρος (Rev. ii. 13), Κλεόπας for Κλεόπατρος (L. xxiv. 18), and perhaps Σίλας for Σιλουανός, see Heumann, *Pœcile* III. 314. If Σώπατρος (A. xx. 4) is for Σωσίπατρος, which is found in some MSS., the contraction is nearer the commencement of the word, but is also very bold: Σώπατρος may however be an uncontracted name. On the other hand, those proper names which are compounds of λαος, and which by the Dorians (Matth. 49)—and probably by others also—were contracted into λας, appear in the N. T. in their uncontracted form, as Νικόλαος, Ἀρχέλαος. That at an earlier period also the Greeks contracted personal names on euphonic grounds is shown by examples in K. Keil's *Spec. Onomatolog. Gr.* p. 52 sqq. (Lips. 1840). In German there are numerous examples of similar abbreviations and contractions, sometimes very harsh; as Klaus from Nikolaus, Käthe (Kathi) from Katharina. Several of these have become independent names, occurring even in the written language; as Fritz (Friedrich), Heinz (Heinrich), Hans, Max: comp. Lobeck, *Prolegg. Path.* p. 504 sqq.[3]

Rem. 2. The Latin words taken up into the Greek of the N. T. —almost without exception substantives,[4] denoting Roman judicial institutions, coins, articles of clothing—have nothing peculiar in their form. Latin verbs in a Greek dress first appear at a later period, in the Greek of the *Libri Pseudepigraphi*, the Byzantine writers, etc. See Thilo, *Acta App. Petri et Pauli* I. 10 sq. (Hal. 1837).

in Böckh. [Lachm. writes Νύμφαν as the name of a woman (reading αὐτῆς for αὐτοῦ): so Westcott and Hort. See Lightfoot's note.]

[1] [See Mullach, *Vulg.* pp. 22, 165.]

[2] [In this passage Ἀμπλιᾶτος (Tisch., Ἀμπλίατος) is well supported.]

[3] On Greek personal names in general, see Sturz, *Progr. de Nominib. Græcor.* (included in his *Opuscula:* Lips. 1825), W. Pape, *Wörterb. der griech. Eigennamen* (Brschw. 1842), (*Hall. L. Z.* 1843, No. 106-108), and Keil, *Beiträge zur Onomatologie*, in Schneidewin, *Philologus* Vol. 2 and 3.

[4] [The only exception appears to be φραγελλόω. The remark here made as to the *meaning* of these substantives is hardly correct: see an article by Prof. Potwin in *Bibliotheca Sacra* 1875, pp. 703-714 (also 1880, p. 503). See further Mullach, *Vulg.* pp. 52, 54.]

PART III.
SYNTAX.

A.
SIGNIFICATION AND USE OF THE DIFFERENT PARTS OF SPEECH.

CHAPTER FIRST.
THE ARTICLE.[1]

Section XVII.

THE ARTICLE AS A PRONOUN.

1. The Article ὁ, ἡ, τό, was originally a demonstrative pronoun, and in epic poetry (to which belongs the quotation from Aratus in A. xvii. 28, τοῦ γὰρ γένος ἐσμέν) it is regularly used as such. Compare Soph. Œd. R. 1082, τῆς γὰρ πέφυκα μητρός (Matth. 286): for prose compare Athen. 2. p. 37. (Jelf 444, Don. p. 345.) This use of the article is not usual in prose, except—

---

[1] A. Kluit, *Vindiciæ Artic. in N. T.* (Traj. et Alcmar. 1768–1771; the book itself is written in Dutch); G. Middleton, *The Doctrine of the Greek Article applied to the criticism and the illustration of the N. T.* (London 1808). Compare Schulthess in the *Theol. Annal.* 1808, p. 56 sqq.; E. Valpy, *A short treatise on the doctrine of the Greek Article, according to Middleton, etc., briefly and compendiously explained as applicable to the criticism of the N. T.*,—prefixed to his *Greek Testament with English notes* (3 vols.: ed. 3, Lond. 1834). Emmerling's *Einige Bemerk. über den Artikel im N. T.* (in Keil and Tzschirner's *Analekt.* I. ii. 147 sqq.) are of no importance. On the other hand, Bengel has some brief but striking remarks on the subject in his note on Mt. xviii. 17. [See also A. Buttmann, *Gr.* pp. 85–103, Webster, *Syntax*, pp. 26–44, and especially Green, *Gr.* pp. 5–82, where the subject is very carefully treated. The references to Middleton in the following pages are made to the edition by Rose (Cambridge, 1841).]

(a) In the very common formulas ὁ μὲν . . . ὁ δέ, οἱ μὲν . . . . οἱ δέ,¹—sometimes standing in relation to a subject previously mentioned, *the one . . . . the other*, as in A. xiv. 4, xvii. 32, xxviii. 24, G. iv. 23 [?], H. vii. 20, 21 (Schæf. *Dion.* 421); sometimes simply partitive, without any such reference, as in E. iv. 11, ἔδωκεν τοὺς μὲν ἀποστόλους, τοὺς δὲ προφήτας, τοὺς δὲ κ.τ.λ., *some . . . . others.*

(b) In the course of a narration, when the simple ὁ δέ (οἱ δέ) is used for *but he*, etc., in opposition to some other subject; as ὁ δὲ ἔφη Mt. xiii. 29, οἱ δὲ ἀκούσαντες ἐπορεύθησαν ii. 9, ii. 14, ix. 31, L. iii. 13, viii. 21, xx. 12, Jo. i. 39, ix. 38, A. i. 6,² ix. 40, al.; Xen. *An.* 2. 3. 2, Æsch. *Dial.* 3. 15, 17, Philostr. *Ap.* 1. 21. 5, Diod. S. *Exc. Vat.* pp. 26, 29, al.

For οἱ μὲν . . . . οἱ δέ are used also οἱ μὲν . . . . ἄλλοι δέ Jo. vii. 12, οἱ μὲν . . . ἄλλοι δὲ . . . ἕτεροι δέ Mt. xvi. 14 (Plat. *Legg.* 2. 658 b, Æl. 2. 34, Palæph. 6. 5), τινὲς . . . . οἱ δέ A. xvii. 18, compare Plat. *Legg.* 1. 627 a, and Ast *in loc.* In Greek authors we find still greater variety in expressions of this kind (Matth. 288. Rem. 6, Jelf 764). The relative is sometimes used instead of the article in such opposed clauses: as 1 C. xi. 21, ὃς μὲν πεινᾷ, ὃς δὲ μεθύει· Mt. xxi. 35, ὃν μὲν ἔδειραν, ὃν δὲ ἀπέκτειναν κ.τ.λ., A. xxvii. 44, Rom. ix. 21, Mk. xii. 5; compare Polyb. 1. 7. 3, 3. 76. 4, Thuc. 3. 66, and see Georgi, *Hier.* I. 109 sqq., Herm. *Vig.* p. 706. Once, ὃς μὲν . . . ἄλλος δέ, 1 C. xii. 8 (Xen. *An.* 3. 1. 35); ὃ μὲν (neuter) . . . καὶ ἕτερον, L. viii. 5 sqq.:³ in 1 C. xii. 28 there is evidently an anacoluthon. See, in general, Bernh. p. 306 sq. (Jelf 816. 3. *b*).

In Rom. xiv. 2 ὁ δέ does not stand in relation to ὃς μέν; ὁ is simply the article, and belongs to ἀσθενῶν.

2. In Mt. xxvi. 67, xxviii. 17, we find the partitive οἱ δέ without a preceding οἱ μέν, so that only the second member of the partition is expressed. The former passage, ἐνέπτυσαν εἰς τὸ πρόςωπον αὐτοῦ καὶ ἐκολάφισαν αὐτόν, οἱ δὲ ἐρράπισαν, would be more regular if οἱ μέν were inserted before ἐκολάφισαν. When however Matthew wrote this word, a second member of the sentence was not as yet definitely before his mind; but when he adds οἱ δὲ ἐρρ. it becomes evident that the ἐκολάφ.

---

¹ On the accentuation see Herm. *Vig.* p. 700, and on the other side Krüger p. 97. [Jelf 444. Obs. 6, Lidd. and Scott s. v.]

² [A mistake: perhaps Jo. xxi. 6. In Jo. v. 11 we find ὃς δέ without ὃς μέν.]

³ [Also ὁ μὲν . . . καὶ ἄλλο, Mk. iv. 4, 5. A. Buttmann (p. 102) remarks that ὁ, ἡ, οἱ, αἱ, are the only forms of the article which are used with μέν and δέ in the N. T., if we except E. iv. 11.]

applied to a part only of the mockers. Compare Xen. *Hell.* 1. 2. 14, οἱ αἰχμάλωτοι . . . ᾤχοντο ἐς Δεκέλειαν, οἱ δ᾽ ἐς Μέγαρα· *Cyr.* 3. 2. 12; and see Poppo, Xen. *Cyr.* p. 292, Bremi, *Demosth.* p. 273 (Jelf 767. 2). Similarly, in Mt. xxviii. 17 we have first the general statement, οἱ ἕνδεκα μαθηταὶ . . . . ἰδόντες αὐτὸν προςεκύνησαν: that this, however, refers only to the greater part, is clear from the words which follow, οἱ δὲ ἐδίστασαν.¹

In L. ix. 19, οἱ δέ would regularly refer to the μαθηταί mentioned in the preceding verse, and would indicate that *all* returned the answer which follows; but from ἄλλοι δὲ . . . ἄλλοι δέ, it is clear that it was given by a part only. The corresponding verse in Matthew (xvi. 14) is expressed with more exactness: οἱ δὲ εἶπον· οἱ μὲν Ἰωάννην . . . . ἄλλοι δὲ . . . . ἕτεροι δέ.

Section XVIII.

THE ARTICLE BEFORE NOUNS.

1. When ὁ, ἡ, τό, stands before a noun as a true article, it indicates that the object is conceived as definite,² either from its nature, or from the context, or by reference to a circle of ideas which is assumed to be familiar to the reader's mind:³ Mk. i. 32, ὅτε ἔδυ ὁ ἥλιος· Jo. i. 52, ὄψεσθε τὸν οὐρανὸν ἀνεῳγότα· 1 C. xv. 8, ὡςπερεὶ τῷ ἐκτρώματι ὤφθη κἀμοὶ (he is the only abortion among the apostles); A. xxvii. 38, ἐκβαλλόμενοι τὸν σῖτον εἰς τὴν θάλασσαν, *the wheat* (the ship's store of provisions); L. iv. 20, πτύξας τὸ βιβλίον (which had been handed to him, ver. 17) ἀποδοὺς τῷ ὑπηρέτῃ, *the synagogue-attendant;* Jo. xiii. 5, βάλλει ὕδωρ εἰς τὸν νιπτῆρα, *the basin* (which, as usual, was standing by), comp. Mt. xxvi. 26 sq.;⁴ Jo. vi. 3,

---

¹ [So Bengel (as an alternative) and Meyer: Alford, Ellicott (*Hist. Lect.* p. 411), Ebrard (*Gospel Hist.* p. 462, Trans.), Stier (*Words of the Lord Jesus*, VIII. 278, Trans.), object to this interpretation, though not on grammatical grounds.]

² Compare Epiphan. *Hær.* 1. 9. 4.—Herm. *Præf. ad* Eurip. *Iphig. Aul.* p. 15: "Articulus quoniam origine pronomen demonstrativum est, definit infinita idque duobus modis, aut designando certo de multis aut quæ multa sunt, cunctis in unum colligendis."

³ [See Jelf 446 sq., Don. p. 350, Middleton p. 32 sqq., Madvig 8: for the N. T. see especially Green, *Gr.* ch. II., sections 1 and 2.]

⁴ [The article should probably be rejected in these two verses: comp. L. xxiv. 30, 1 C. xi. 25.]

ἀνῆλθεν εἰς τὸ ὄρος, *into the mountain* (which was situated on the farther shore, ver. 1); 1 C. v. 9, ἔγραψα ἐν τῇ ἐπιστολῇ (which Paul had written to the Corinthians before this present epistle); A. ix. 2, ᾐτήσατο ἐπιστολὰς εἰς Δαμασκὸν πρὸς τὰς συναγωγάς, *to the synagogues* (which were in Damascus); Rev. xx. 4 [*Rec.*], ἐβασίλευσαν μετὰ Χριστοῦ τὰ χίλια ἔτη, *the thousand years* (the known duration of Messiah's kingdom); Ja. ii. 25, Ῥαὰβ ἡ πόρνη ὑποδεξαμένη τοὺς ἀγγέλους, *the spies* (familiarly known from the history of Rahab); H. ix. 19, λαβὼν τὸ αἷμα τῶν μόσχων καὶ τῶν τράγων, with allusion to Ex. xxiv. 8. So in 1 C. vii. 3, τῇ γυναικὶ ὁ ἀνὴρ τὴν ὀφειλὴν ἀποδιδότω, *the debt* (of marriage); vii. 29, ὁ καιρὸς συνεσταλμένος ἐστίν, comp. ver. 26, διὰ τὴν ἐνεστῶσαν ἀνάγκην.

The article thus refers to well-known facts, arrangements, or doctrines (A. v. 37, xxi. 38, H. xi. 28, 1 C. x. 1, 10, 2 Th. ii. 3, Jo. i. 21, ii. 14, xviii. 3, Mt. viii. 4, 12); or to something previously mentioned, Mt. ii. 7 (ver. 1), L. ix. 16 (ver. 13), A. ix. 17[1] (ver. 11), Jo. iv. 43 (ver. 40), A. xi. 13 (x. 3, 22), Ja. ii. 3 (ver. 2), Jo. xii. 12 (ver. 1), xx. 1 (xix. 41), H. v. 4 (ver. 1), Rev. xv. 6 (ver. 1). Thus ὁ ἐρχόμενος signifies *the Messiah*, ἡ κρίσις *the (Messianic) universal judgment*, ἡ γραφή *the Scriptures*, ἡ σωτηρία *the salvation of Christ*, ὁ πειράζων *the tempter* (Satan), etc. So also of geographical designations: ἡ ἔρημος, *the* wilderness *par excellence*, הַמִּדְבָּר,—i. e., according to the context, either the Arabian wilderness (of Mount Sinai), Jo. iii. 14, vi. 31, A. vii. 30, or the wilderness of Judah (Mt. iv. 1, xi. 7).

Another case deserving mention is the use of a singular noun with the article to denote, in the individual which it particularises, the whole class,[2]—as we ourselves say, *The soldier must be trained to arms:* 2 C. xii. 12, τὰ σημεῖα τοῦ ἀποστόλου· Mt. xii. 35, ὁ ἀγαθὸς ἄνθρωπος . . . . ἐκβάλλει ἀγαθά· xv. 11, xviii. 17, L. x. 7, G. iv. 1, Ja. v. 6. Akin to this is the use of the singular in parables and allegories: Jo. x. 11, ὁ ποιμὴν ὁ καλὸς τὴν ψυχὴν αὐτοῦ τίθησιν (it is the *ideal* Good Shepherd that is spoken of), Mt. xiii. 3, ἐξῆλθεν ὁ σπείρων τοῦ σπείρειν, where Luther incorrectly has *a sower*. See Krüger p. 103 sq.

---

[1] [Corrected (for ix. 7) from ed. 5, where the words of the verse are quoted.]
[2] [Jelf 446. β, Green p. 21, where the very common use of the *plural* to denote a class is also noticed.]

SECT. XVIII.]   THE ARTICLE BEFORE NOUNS.   133

Rem. According to Kühnöl, the article sometimes includes the pronoun *this;*[1] e.g. in Mt. i. 25 [*Rec.*], τὸν υἱόν for τοῦτον τὸν υἱόν· Jo. vii. 17, γνώσεται περὶ τῆς διδαχῆς· ver. 40, ἐκ τοῦ ὄχλου· A. xxvi. 10, τὴν παρὰ τῶν ἀρχιερέων ἐξουσίαν λαβών· Mk. xiii. 20, A. ix. 2. In all these instances, however, the definite article is quite sufficient. Heumann has been still more liberal in this doctrine of the article, and he has been followed by Schulthess (*N. Krit. Journ.* I. 285) : both Schulthess and Kühnöl refer most incorrectly to Matth. § 286, where such a use of the article (which indeed is hardly to be found in prose, except Ionic) is not the subject of discussion. As to Col. iv. 16, ὅταν ἀναγνωσθῇ παρ' ὑμῖν ἡ ἐπιστολή, we too say *when the letter is read*, and nothing more than the article was required, since no other epistle than the present could be thought of : some authorities annex αὕτη, but the ancient versions must not be reckoned with these.[2] In 1 Tim. i. 15 the demonstrative pronoun is not required even in German [or English], any more than in vi. 13 [? 14]. In 2 C. v. 4 τῷ is not put δεικτικῶς for τούτῳ ; the article simply points to the σκῆνος spoken of in ver. 1. In Col. iii. 8 τὰ πάντα is not "*these, all* of them" (intensive), but *the whole*, viz. the sins which are (a second time) specified in the words which immediately follow. In Rom. v. 5, too, ἡ (ἐλπίς) is simply the article ; see Fritz. *in loc.* Least of all can ὁ κόσμος be taken for οὗτος ὁ κόσμος : it is *the world* as opposed to *heaven*, *the kingdom of heaven*, not *this world* as opposed to another κόσμος. The passages in Greek authors which might be claimed as instances of this idiom (Diog. L. 1. 72, 86) are to be judged of in the same way. Indeed one cannot see what could induce the apostles to avoid *expressing* the demonstrative pronoun in certain passages, in which it was present to their *thought*, and to substitute for it the article, which in any case has much less force : mere instinct would revolt at this. Besides, expressiveness of language is a characteristic of N. T. Greek, and of later Greek in general.

In Greek authors, especially the Ionic and Doric,[3] and afterwards in the Byzantine writers (Malal. pp. 95, 102), the article is sometimes used for the relative. In the N. T., Σαῦλος ὁ καὶ Παῦλος (A. xiii. 9) has been regarded as an example of this usage (see Schleusner s. v. ὁ), but wrongly : ὁ καὶ Π. is here equivalent to ὁ καὶ καλούμενος Παῦλος (Schæfer, *L. Bos.* p. 213), and the article retains its ordinary meaning, just as in Σαῦλος ὁ Ταρσεύς. Comp. the similar phrase Πῖκος ὁ καὶ Ζεύς, Malal. p. 19 sq. (ed. Bonn), *Act. Thom.* p. 34. One example however may be quoted from Hellenistic writers, viz. *Psalt. Sal.* 17. 12, ἐν τοῖς κρίμασι, τὰ

---

[1] Compare Siebelis, *Pausan.* I. 50, Boisson. *Babr.* p. 207. Compare the German *das* when emphasised.
[2] ["The genius of the language into which the translation is made may require the introduction of connecting particles or words of reference, as can be seen from the italicised words in the Authorised Version." Westcott in Smith's *Dict. of Bible*, II. 528.]
[3] Matth. 292 : comp. Ellendt, *Lex. Soph.* II. 204 (Jelf 445).

ποιεῖ ἐπὶ τὴν γῆν, if the reading is correct.¹ In Wisd. xi. 15, where ὄν (*Alex.*) is probably a correction, τόν must be regarded as the article.

2. So far, Greek usage agrees with that of all languages which possess an article. In the following cases, in which the definite article would not be employed in German [or English], the use of the Greek article is idiomatic:—

(*a*) Rev. iv. 7, τὸ ζῶον ἔχον τὸ πρόςωπον ὡς ἀνθρώπου (Xen. *Cyr.* 5. 1. 2, ὁμοίαν ταῖς δούλαις εἶχε τὴν ἐσθῆτα· Theophr. *Ch.* 12 (19), τοὺς ὄνυχας μεγάλους ἔχων· Polyæn. 8. 10. 1, al.) ; A. xxvi. 24 [*Rec.*], μεγάλῃ τῇ φωνῇ ἔφη· xiv. 10 [*Rec.*], 1 C. xi. 5 (Aristot. *Anim.* 2. 8, 10, Lucian, *Catapl.* 11, Diod. S. 1. 70, 83, Pol. 15. 29. 11, Philostr. *Ap.* 4. 44). We say, *He had eyes as, He spoke with a loud voice,* etc. By the use of the article here something which belongs to the individual is pointed out as possessed of a certain quality.² This is shown still more clearly by H. vii. 24, ἀπαράβατον ἔχει τὴν ἱερωσύνην, *He hath the priesthood as unchangeable* (predicate), Mk. viii. 17, 1 P. ii. 12, iv. 8, E. i. 18 ; and by Mt. iii. 4, εἶχε τὸ ἔνδυμα αὐτοῦ ἀπὸ τριχῶν καμήλου· Rev. ii. 18 (which differ from the previous examples through the addition of the pronoun). With the former examples compare further Thuc. 1. 10, 23, Plat. *Phædr.* 242 b, Lucian, *Dial. Deor.* 8. 1, *Fugit.* 10, *Eun.* 11, Diod. S. 1. 52, 2. 19, 3. 34, Æl. *Anim.* 13. 15, Pol. 3. 4. 1, 8. 10. 1 ; and see Lob. p. 265, Krüg. *Dion. H.* 126. (The article is sometimes omitted, e.g. in 2 P. ii. 14: comp. Aristot. *Anim.* 2. 8, 10, with 2. 11.)

(*b*) 1 C. iv. 5, τότε ὁ ἔπαινος γενήσεται ἑκάστῳ, *the praise* (that is due to him); Rom. xi. 36, αὐτῷ ἡ δόξα εἰς τ. αἰῶνας· xvi. 27, E. iii. 21, G. i. 5, 1 P. iv. 11, Rev. v. 13 ; Rev. iv. 11, ἄξιος εἶ λαβεῖν τὴν δόξαν κ. τὴν τιμήν· Ja. ii. 14 [*Rec.*], τί τὸ ὄφελος ἐὰν πίστιν λέγῃ τις ἔχειν, *the advantage* (to be expected), 1 C. xv. 32 ; 1 C. ix. 18, τίς μοί ἐστιν ὁ μισθός (Ellendt, *Lex. Soph.* II. 212). In all these cases the article denotes that

---

¹ [The Vienna MS. reads οἷς ποιεῖ.]
² ["Something is assumed as belonging to the subject, and a quality is then predicated of that something." Clyde, *Syntax* p. 22. We must use the personal pronoun, or change the construction of the sentence : e.g. in H. vii. 24, *He hath His priesthood unchangeable,* or *The priesthood which He hath is unchangeable.* See Don. p. 528, Green, *Gr.* p. 50 sq.]

which is due, requisite (Krüg. p. 98, Jelf 477. 1). And thus the article is often found where we should use a personal pronoun; as Rom. iv. 4, τῷ ἐργαζομένῳ ὁ μισθὸς οὐ λογίζεται *his reward*, ix. 22, L. xviii. 15 ; compare Fritzsche, Aristot. *Amic.* pp. 46, 99.

No example occurs of the use of the article in appellations (Matth. 268, Rost p. 428, Schæf. *Dem.* IV. 365); for in Rev. vi. 8, ὄνομα αὐτῷ ὁ θάνατος· viii. 11, τὸ ὄνομα τοῦ ἀστέρος λέγεται ὁ ἄψινθος·[1] xix. 13, κέκληται τὸ ὄνομα αὐτοῦ ὁ λόγος τοῦ θεοῦ, a name is in each case mentioned which belongs individually and exclusively to the object spoken of.

3. Adjectives and participles when used as substantives are, like substantives, made definite by the article : 1 C. i. 27, οἱ σοφοί· E. vi. 16, βέλη τοῦ πονηροῦ· G. i. 23, ὁ διώκων ὑμᾶς· Tit. iii. 8, οἱ πεπιστευκότες τῷ θεῷ· 1 C. ix. 13, οἱ τὰ ἱερὰ ἐργαζόμενοι· Mt. x. 20, 2 C. ii. 2, x. 16, 1 C. xiv. 16, H. xii. 27. Instead of a noun we may have an indeclinable word, as an infinitive or an adverb (2 C. i. 17), or a phrase, as Rom. iv. 14, οἱ ἐκ νόμου· H. xiii. 24, οἱ ἀπὸ τῆς Ἰταλίας (Diod. S. 1. 83), A. xiii. 13, οἱ περὶ Παῦλον· Ph. i. 27, τὰ περὶ ὑμῶν κ.τ.λ., 1 C. xiii. 10 (Krüg. p. 106 sq., Jelf 436, 457). Even a complete sentence may have the article (τό) prefixed to it; e.g. A. xxii. 30, γνῶναι τὸ τί κατηγορεῖται (iv. 21, 1 Th. iv. 1, L. xxii. 2, 23, 37), Mk. ix. 23, εἶπεν αὐτῷ τό· εἰ δύνῃ; G. v. 14, ὁ πᾶς νόμος ἐν ἑνὶ λόγῳ πεπλήρωται, ἐν τῷ· ἀγαπήσεις τὸν πλησίον σου, Rom. viii. 26, xiii. 9, L. i. 62:[2] these sentences are for the most part quotations or interrogations, which are in this way rendered more prominent. Compare Plat. *Gorg.* 461 e, *Phœd.* 62 b, *Rep.* 1. 352 d, Demosth. *Con.* 728 c, Lucian, *Alex.* 20, Matth. 280, Stallb. Plat. *Euthyph.* p. 55, and *Men.* 25. When a mere adverb or a genitive thus receives the article (especially the neuter τό), it becomes a virtual substantive :[3] L. xvi. 26 [*Rec.*], οἱ ἐκεῖθεν· Jo. viii. 23, τὰ κάτω, τὰ ἄνω· Jo. xxi. 2, οἱ τοῦ Ζεβεδαίου· L. xx. 25, τὰ Καίσαρος· Ja. iv. 14, τὸ τῆς αὔριον· 2 P. ii. 22, τὸ τῆς ἀληθοῦς παροιμίας· 1 C. vii. 33, τὰ τοῦ κόσμου· 2 P. i. 3, 2 C. x. 16, Ph. i. 5, Jo. xviii. 6, al. (Krüg. pp. 32, 107 sq.). We are often obliged to use a periphrasis, *the import of the true proverb, what*

---

[1] [The article is somewhat doubtful in Rev. vi. 8.]
[2] [Lünemann adds Mt. xix. 18. The use of τό with indirect questions is most common in St. Luke (A. Buttm. p. 96).]
[3] Ellendt, Arr. *Al.* I. 84, Weber, *Dem.* p. 237.

is due to Cæsar.[1] In 1 P. iv. 14, Huther (in ed. 1) wrongly takes τὸ τῆς δόξης as a mere periphrasis for ἡ δόξα: such a use of the neuter article is not found in the N. T.

The neuter τό is sometimes prefixed to nouns in order to designate them materially, as sounds or combinations of sounds: G. iv. 25, τὸ γὰρ Ἄγαρ κ.τ.λ., the word *Hagar*.[2]
The substantivised participle with the article occurs in several combinations in which our idiom will not allow the article; viz. as a definite predicate of an indefinite subject, e.g. G. i. 7, τινές εἰσιν οἱ ταράσσοντες ὑμᾶς· Col. ii. 8, μή τις ὑμᾶς ἔσται ὁ συλαγωγῶν· and also Jo. v. 32, L. xviii. 9,—or as a definite subject where logically an indefinite might have been expected, e.g. Rom. iii. 11, οὐκ ἔστιν ὁ συνιῶν (Jo. v. 45), 2 C. xi. 4, εἰ ὁ ἐρχόμενος ἄλλον Ἰησοῦν κηρύσσει. In all these cases, however, the quality is conceived as a definite concrete, only the person who really acts as this concrete remains undefined. The ταράσσοντες ὑμᾶς actually exist, but they are not particularised:[3] *if he that cometh* (the preacher appearing among you, who will certainly come,—person and name are of no consequence), etc.; *the man of understanding does not exist*, etc. The following examples are similar: Lucian, *Abdic.* 3, ἦσάν τινες οἱ μανίας ἀρχὴν τοῦτ᾽ εἶναι νομίζοντες· Lysias, *Bon. Aristoph.* 57, εἰσί τινες οἱ προσαναλίσκοντες· Dio Chr. 38. 482, ἤδη τινές εἰσιν οἱ καὶ τοῦτο δεδωκότες·[4] and the common phrase εἰσὶν οἱ λέγοντες (Matth. 268 *init.*, Jelf 817, *Obs.* 3); also Xen. *An.* 2. 4. 5, ὁ ἡγησόμενος οὐδεὶς ἔσται· Thuc. 3. 83, οὐκ ἦν ὁ διαλύσων· Porphyr. *Abst.* 4. 18, οὐδείς ἐστιν ὁ κολάσων· Gen. xl. 8, xli. 8, Dt. xxii. 27, 1 S. xiv. 39: see Bernh. p. 318 sq. (Jelf 451. 2).[5] In A. ii. 47, ὁ κύριος προσετίθει τοὺς σωζομένους τῇ ἐκκλησίᾳ means, *He added to the church those who became saved* (through becoming believers); He increased the church by the addition of those in the case of whom the preaching proved effectual: comp. Krüg. p. 103 sq.

Between πολλοί and οἱ πολλοί, used as a substantive, the usual distinction is observed. Οἱ πολλοί, which is very rare in the N. T., means *the* well-known *many* (2 C. ii. 17) in marked contrast

---

[1] We might however say in German *das droben, das des morgenden Tags* (*the morrow's* = what will happen on the morrow), *die des Zebedäus* (those who belong to Zebedee, e.g. his sons): see § 30. 3.

[2] ["Τό denotes that 'Hagar' is regarded not as a person, but as an object of thought or of speech. It need not necessarily mean 'the *word* Hagar;' compare for instance E. iv. 9, τὸ δὲ ἀνέβη τί ἐστιν; where τό is the *statement*, for the preceding *word* was not ἀνέβη, but ἀναβάς." Lightfoot, *Gal.* p. 193 (ed. 6).]

[3] Compare in Latin *sunt qui existimant*, as distinguished from *sunt qui existiment*: see Zumpt § 563. [Don. *Lat. Gr.* p. 353, Madvig, *Lat. Gr.* § 365.]

[4] [Also Demosth. *De Cor.* p. 330, ἦσάν τινες οἱ διασύροντες· Xen. *De Re Eq.* 9. 2, ἥκιστ᾽ ἂν ὀργίζοι τις ὁ μήτε λέγων κ.τ.λ. (where some omit ὁ): these examples are given by Bernhardy, *l.c.*]

[5] Herm. Soph. *Œd. R.* 107, Doederl. Soph. *Œd. C.* p. 296, Dissen, Dem. *Cor.* p. 238.

with a unity (Rom. xii. 5, οἱ πολλοὶ ἓν σῶμά ἐσμεν· 1 C. x. 17) or with a particular individual (Rom. v. 15, 19), or, without such contrast, *the multitude, the great mass, vulgus* (with the exception of a few individuals), Mt. xxiv. 12 : compare Schæf. *Melet.* pp. 3, 65.

4. A noun defined by οὗτος, ἐκεῖνος, as attributives,[1] always takes the article, as denoting a particular individual singled out from a class; in this respect the Greek idiom differs from our own : L. ii. 25 ὁ ἄνθρωπος οὗτος, L. xiv. 30 οὗτος ὁ ἄνθρωπος, Mt. xiii. 44 [2] τὸν ἀγρὸν ἐκεῖνον, Mt. vii. 22 ἐν ἐκείνῃ τῇ ἡμέρᾳ, Mt. xxiv. 48 ὁ κακὸς δοῦλος ἐκεῖνος. In L. vii. 44, too, the correct reading is βλέπεις ταύτην τὴν γυναῖκα, though—according to Wolf, Dem. *Lept.* p. 263, Ellendt, *Lex. Soph.* II. 243, Krüg. p. 126 (Jelf 655. 4)—there would be no reason for rejecting ταύτην γυναῖκα, since the woman was present. Names of persons also with which οὗτος is joined usually take the article : see H. vii. 1, A. i. 11, ii. 32, xix. 26 (vii. 40).

The noun with which πᾶς is joined may either have the article or not. Πᾶσα πόλις is *every city,* πᾶσα ἡ πόλις *the whole city* (Mt. viii. 34), compare Rom. iii. 19, ἵνα πᾶν στόμα φραγῇ καὶ ὑπόδικος γένηται πᾶς ὁ κόσμος : πᾶσαι γενεαί *all* generations, whatever their number, πᾶσαι αἱ γενεαί (Mt. i. 17) *all the* generations,—those which (either from the context or in some other way) are familiar as a definite number. Compare for the singular Mt. iii. 10, vi. 29, xiii. 47, Jo. ii. 10, L. vii. 29, Mk. v. 33, Ph. i. 3 ; for the plural, Mt. ii. 4, iv. 24, L. xiii. 27, A. xxii. 15, G. vi. 6, 2 P. iii. 16 (where there is not much authority for the article). This rule is not violated[3] in Mt. ii. 3, πᾶσα Ἱεροσόλυμα *all Jerusalem,* for Jerusalem is a proper name (see below, no. 5); or in A. ii. 36, πᾶς οἶκος Ἰσραήλ *the whole house of Israel,* for this too is treated as a proper name (1 S. vii. 2 sq., Neh. iv. 16, Judith viii. 6). E. iii. 15, πᾶσα πατριά, is obviously

---

[1] It is otherwise when these pronouns are predicates, as in Rom. ix. 8, ταῦτα τέκνα τοῦ θεοῦ· L. i. 36, οὗτος μὴν ἕκτος ἐστίν· Jo. iv. 18, τοῦτο ἀληθὲς εἴρηκας· Jo. ii. 11, al. ; compare Fritz. *Matt.* p. 663, Schæf. *Plut.* IV. 377 (Don. p. 352).

[2] [Corrected for L. ii. 35, xiv. 13, Mt. xiii. 14.]

[3] Such nouns as those specified in § 19. 1 may dispense with the article even with πᾶς *all, whole,* as πᾶσα γῆ ; comp. Poppo, *Thuc.* III. ii. p. 224. In the N. T. this particular word always has the article, as Mt. xxvii. 45, ἐπὶ πᾶσαν τὴν γῆν· Rom. x. 18, al. Most of the passages quoted by Thiersch (*de Pentat. Alex.* p. 121) to prove that the LXX omit the article with πᾶς (*all*) are quite unsuitable.

every race; Col. iv. 12, ἐν παντὶ θελήματι τοῦ θεοῦ, *in every will of God*, in everything that God wills ; 1 P. i. 15, ἐν πάσῃ ἀναστροφῇ, *in omni vitæ modo*. Still less can Ja. i. 2 πᾶσαν χαρὰν ἡγήσασθε, E. i. 8 ἐν πάσῃ σοφίᾳ (2 C. xii. 12, A. xxiii. 1), in the sense of *all* (full) *joy, in all* (full) *wisdom*, be considered exceptions ; the nouns here are abstracts denoting a whole, and hence the meaning is the same whether we say *every wisdom* or *all wisdom* (Krüg. p. 124). In E. ii. 21, however, the weight of authority is in favour of πᾶσα οἰκοδομή, though, as the subject is the church of Christ as a whole, *the whole building* is the correct translation :[1] yet the article is actually found in A and C, and it might easily be left out through itacism.

Πᾶς with the participle—which is not in itself equivalent to a noun —deserves special notice. Πᾶς ὀργιζόμενος means *every one being angry* (if, or when he is angry, in being angry), comp. 1 C. xi. 4 ; but πᾶς ὁ ὀργιζόμ., Mt. v. 22, is *every angry man*, = πᾶς ὅστις ὀργίζεται. Compare L. vi. 47, xi. 10, Jo. iii. 20, xv. 2, 1 C. ix. 25, 1 Th. i. 7, al. (Krüg. p. 103). The same remarks apply to the two readings in L. xi. 4, παντὶ ὀφείλοντι, παντὶ τῷ ὀφ. ; see Meyer.[2]

Τοιοῦτος[3] is joined to an anarthrous noun in the sense of *any such, of such a kind;* Mt. ix. 8 ἐξουσία τοιαύτη, Mk. iv. 33 τοιαῦται παραβολαί, A. xvi. 24 παραγγελία τοιαύτη, 2 C. iii. 12. But if a particular object is pointed out as *such* or *of such a sort*, the noun naturally takes the article : Mk. ix. 37 ἓν τῶν τοιούτων παιδίων (in allusion to the παιδίον mentioned in ver. 36, which as it were represented the world of children), Jo. iv. 23, 2 C. xii. 3 (comp. ver. 2), 2 C. xi. 13 (Schæf. *Demosth.* III. 136, Schneider, Plat. *Civ.* II. p. 1).

Ἕκαστος, which is seldom used as an adjective in the N. T., is always joined to an anarthrous noun ;[4] as L. vi. 44 ἕκαστον δένδρον, Jo. xix. 23 ἑκάστῳ στρατιώτῃ, H. iii. 13 καθ' ἑκάστην ἡμέραν (Bornem.

---

[1] [See Ellicott *in loc.* As however this rendering is altogether opposed to the usage of the N. T., it is surely preferable to regard St. Paul as speaking of the many οἰκοδομαί which together make up the temple : Vaughan quotes Mt. xxiv. 1, Mk. xiii. 1, 2, as aptly illustrating this meaning of the word. On itacism see Scrivener, *Crit.* p. 10.]

[2] [On πᾶς see Jelf 454. 1, Don. p. 354, Green p. 54 sq., Middleton p. 102 sqq. Πᾶς rarely comes between the art. and the noun, as in A. xx. 18, G. v. 14, 1 Tim. i. 16 (ἅπας) ; plural A. xix. 7, xxvii. 37 : see Green p. 55, Jelf *l. c.* On the meaning of πᾶς when used with abstracts, see Ellicott on E. i. 8 ; comp. Shilleto, Dem. *Fals. Leg.* pp. 49, 100.]

[3] ["The article with τοιοῦτος denotes a known person or thing, or the whole class of such, but not an undefined individual out of the class ; as in that case τοιοῦτος is anarthrous : see Kühner on Xenoph. *Mem.* I. 5. 2, and Krüger, *Sprachl.* § 50. 4. 6." Ellicott (on G. v. 21). Compare Buttm. *Griech. Gr.* p. 337, Jelf 453. β.]

[4] Orelli, Isocr. *Antid.* p. 255 (9).

Xen. *An*. p. 69). In Greek authors the article is not uncommon ; see Stallb. Plat. *Phileb.* p. 93, *Hipp. Maj.* 164 (Jelf 454. 2, Don. p. 354).

Τὸ αὐτὸ πνεῦμα is *the same Spirit ;* αὐτὸ τὸ πνεῦμα, *He Himself* (of Himself) *the Spirit* (Krüg. p. 125). For the former, comp. Rom. ix. 21, Ph. i. 30, L. vi. 38 [*Rec.*], xxiii. 40, 2 C. iv. 13 ; for the latter, Rom. viii. 26, 1 C. xv. 28, 2 C. xi. 14, Jo. xvi. 27. In both cases the article is always inserted in the N. T. with appellatives.[1] In Greek authors it is sometimes omitted ; in the former case chiefly in epic poetry (Herm. *Opusc.* I. 332 sqq.) and later prose (Index to Agath. p. 411, Bonn ed.) ; in the latter, in the better prose writers also.[2]

5. Proper names, as they already denote definite individuals, do not need the article, but they frequently receive it as the existing symbol of definiteness. First, in regard to geographical names :[3]—

(*a*) The names of countries (and rivers) take the article more frequently than those of cities : comp. in German *die Schweiz, die Lausitz, die Lombardei, das Elsass, das Tyrol,* etc. [in English, *the Tyrol, the Morea*]. The article is never or very seldom omitted with Ἰουδαία, Ἀχαΐα, Ἰορδάνης, Ἰταλία, Γαλιλαία, Μυσία, Ἀσία (A. ii. 9, yet see vi. 9, 1 P. i. 1), Σαμάρεια (L. xvii. 11), Συρία (A. xxi. 3), Κρήτη (yet see Tit. i. 5). Αἴγυπτος never takes the article ;[4] in regard to Μακεδονία the usage varies.

(*b*) With names of cities the omission of the article is most common when a preposition precedes (Locella, *Xen. Eph.* pp. 223, 242), especially ἐν, εἰς, or ἐκ ; see the Concordance under the words Δαμασκός, Ἱερουσαλήμ, Ἱεροσόλυμα, Τάρσος, Ἔφεσος, Ἀντιόχεια, Καπερναούμ: only Τύρος[5] and Ῥώμη vary strangely.

(*c*) Sometimes a geographical name, when it first occurs in the narration, is without the article, but takes it on renewed mention. Thus we find ἕως Ἀθηνῶν in A. xvii. 15, on the first mention of the city, but in ver. 16 and in xviii. 1 the article is

---

[1] Hence L. xx. 42, xxiv. 15 [where the article is omitted *with proper names*], are not exceptional instances : see Bornem. *Schol.* p. 158. In Mt. xii. 50 it is quite unnecessary (with Fritzsche) to take αὐτός for ὁ αὐτός.

[2] Krüg. *Dion. H.* 454 sq., Bornem. Xen. *An.* p. 61, Poppo, *Ind. ad Cyr.* s. v.

[3] [Jelf 450. 2, Don. p. 347, Green p. 29, Middleton p. 82. In the N. T. names of rivers *always* have the article, except perhaps in Rev. xvi. 12.]

[4] [Lachmann, Tregelles, Westcott and Hort, accept the article in A. vii. 36.]

[5] [Τύρος never has the article in the N. T. In the 7th edition Winer substitutes for Τύρος Καισάρεια and Τρωάς.]

inserted; εἰς **Βέροιαν** A. xvii. 10, but ἐν τῇ **B.** ver. 13 ; διαβὰς εἰς **Μακεδονίαν** A. xvi. 9, and then ἡ **Μακ.** six times, the article being omitted in xx. 3 only ;[1] ἤλθομεν εἰς **Μίλητον** A. xx. 15, ἀπὸ τῆς **Μιλ.** ver. 17.

Ἱερουσαλήμ has the article only four times, G. iv. 25, 26, Rev. iii. 12 (in which passages it is accompanied by an attributive), and A. v. 28 (τὴν Ἱ.,—contrast with this L. xxiv. 18, A. i. 19, al.). With Ἱεροσόλυμα the article is used by John only,—in v. 2, x. 22, xi. 18 [and ii. 23]; in each instance the word is in an oblique case.

6. The use of the article with names of persons can hardly be reduced to any rule ; see Bernh. p. 317, Madv. 13 (Don. p. 347, Jelf 450. 1) : a comparison of passages will readily show that the practice of the writers in this respect is very irregular.[2] The rule[3] that a proper name has not the article when first introduced, but receives it on repeated mention, will not go far in explaining the actual usage : comp. Matt. xxvii. 24, 58, with ver. 62 ; Mk. xv. 1, 14, 15, with ver. 43 ; L. xxiii. 1 sqq. with verses 6 and 13 ; Jo. xviii. 2 with ver. 5; A. vi. 5 with ver. 8 sq.; viii. 1 with ver. 3 and ix. 8; viii. 5 with verses 6, 12.[4] The same may be said of the remark of Thilo (*Apocr.* I. 163 sq.), that proper names are usually without the article in the nominative, but often take it in oblique cases.[5] Hence the authority of the best MSS. must in the main decide whether the article shall be inserted or not.[6] Proper names which are rendered definite by

---

[1] [The best texts omit the article in A. xvi. 10, 12, xx. 1.]

[2] It is well known that in German the use of the article with names of persons is peculiar to certain provinces; *Der Lehmann*, which is the regular form in the South of Germany, would in the North be considered incorrect.

[3] Herm. *Præf. ad Iph. Aul.* p. 16, Fritz. *Matt.* p. 797, Weber, *Dem.* p. 414.

[4] A person mentioned for the first time may take the article as being well known to the reader, or as being in some other way sufficiently particularised. [A combination of these rules (Middleton p. 80) will perhaps explain most cases. We may at least say (with A. Buttmann, p. 86) that when a writer wishes simply to name a person he may omit the article ; but he may use it to indicate notoriety or previous mention, or for the sake of perspicuity, e. g. to point out the case of an indeclinable noun : see further Green p. 29. In the examples which follow Winer sometimes quotes readings which are now doubtful, but the fluctuation is quite sufficient to establish the truth of his remarks.]

[5] Compare especially the want of uniformity in the use of the article with Παῦλος and Πέτρος in the Acts of the Apostles. Πιλᾶτος always has the article in John [except (probably) in xviii. 31], and almost always in Matthew and Mark ; but in the Acts never. Τίτος never takes the article.

[6] That in the superscriptions of letters the names of persons are without the article, may be seen from the collections of Greek letters, from Diog. L. (e.g., 3. 22, 8. 49, 80, 9. 13), from Plutarch, *Apophth. Lac.* p. 191, from Lucian, *Parasit.* 2, al. Compare 2 Jo. 1. To this rule we should probably refer the superscrip-

explanatory appositions, denoting kindred or office, do not usually take the article, since it is only by means of the apposition that they are made definite: the practice of Greek authors agrees with this (Ellendt, Arr. *Al.* I. 154,—see however Schoem. *Isæus* p. 417 sq., Diod. S. *Exc. Vat.* p. 37). Thus we find ʼΙάκωβον τὸν ἀδελφὸν τοῦ κυρίου G. i. 19, ʼΙούδας ὁ ʼΙσκαριώτης Mt. x. 4, ii. 1, 3, iv. 21, xiv. 1, Mk. x. 47, xvi. 1, Jo. xviii. 2, 1 Th. iii. 2, Rom. xvi. 8 sqq., A. i. 13, xii. 1, xviii. 8, 17: so also Pausan. 2. 1. 1, 3. 9. 1, 7. 18. 6, Æschin. *Tim.* 179 c, Diog. L. 4. 32, 7. 10, 13, 8. 58, 63, Demosth. *Theocr.* 511 c, *Apatur.* 581 b, *Phorm.* 605 b, al., *Conon.* 728 b, Xen. *Cyr.* 1. 3. 8, 2. 1. 5, Diod. S. *Exc. Vat.* pp. 20, 22, 39, 41, 42, 51, 69, 95, al. When however the personal name is indeclinable, and its case is not at once made evident by a preposition or by an appositional phrase (as in Mk. xi. 10, L. i. 32, Jo. iv. 5, A. ii. 29, vii. 14, xiii. 22, Rom. iv. 1, H. iv. 7), the insertion of the article was more necessary, for the sake of perspicuity: Mt. i. 18, xxii. 42, Mk. xv. 45, L. ii. 16, A. vii. 8, Rom. ix. 13, xi. 25, G. iii. 8, H. xi. 17, al. (Hence in Rom. x. 19 [1] Paul would certainly have written μὴ τὸν ʼΙσραὴλ οὐκ ἔγνω; had he intended ʼΙσραήλ to be the object of ἔγνω: comp. 1 C. x. 18, L. xxiv. 21.) In the genealogical tables of Mt. i. and L. iii. this principle is observed throughout, and even extended to the declinable names. It should be observed that the MSS. frequently vary in regard to the use of the article with proper names.

We may remark in passing that the proper name ʼΙούδα, where it is to be characterised as the name of a territory, never occurs in the LXX in the form ἡ ʼΙούδα, τῆς ʼΙ., κ.τ.λ.: we always find either ἡ γῆ ʼΙούδα (1 K. xii. 32, 2 K. xxiv. 2), or the inflected form ἡ ʼΙουδαία (2 Chr. xvii. 19). Hence the conjecture of τῆς ʼΙούδα in Mt. ii. 6 is destitute of probability even on philological grounds.

7. The substantive with the article may as correctly form the predicate as the subject of a sentence (though from the nature of the case it will more frequently be the subject), since the predicate may be conceived as a definite individual. In the N. T. the predicate has the article much more frequently than

---

tion 1 P. i. 1, Πέτρος . . . . ἐκλεκτοῖς παρεπιδήμοις· and also Rev. i. 4. Even those predicates which are characteristic of the subject dispense with the article in addresses, Diog. L. 7. 7, 8.

[1] Fritzsche *in loc.* has adduced dissimilar passages; and for G. vi. 6 he must have meant vi. 16.

is commonly supposed¹ (Krüg. p. 106): Mk. vi. 3, *οὐχ οὗτός ἐστιν ὁ τέκτων, is not this the* (well-known) *carpenter?* vii. 15, *ἐκεῖνά ἐστι τὰ κοινοῦντα τὸν ἄνθρωπον, those are the things that defile the man;* xii. 7, *οὗτός ἐστιν ὁ κληρονόμος·* xiii. 11, *οὐ γάρ ἐστε ὑμεῖς οἱ λαλοῦντες·* Mt. xxvi. 26, 28, *τοῦτό ἐστι τὸ σῶμά μου, τοῦτό ἐστι τὸ αἷμά μου·* Jo. iv. 42, *οὗτός ἐστιν ὁ σωτὴρ τοῦ κόσμου·* 1 C. x. 4, *ἡ δὲ πέτρα ἦν ὁ Χριστός·* xi. 3, *παντὸς ἀνδρὸς ἡ κεφαλὴ ὁ Χριστός ἐστι·* xv. 56, *ἡ δύναμις τῆς ἁμαρτίας ὁ νόμος·* 2 C. iii. 17, *ὁ κύριος τὸ πνεῦμά ἐστιν·* 1 Jo. iii. 4, *ἡ ἁμαρτία ἐστὶν ἡ ἀνομία·* Ph. ii. 13, *ὁ θεός ἐστιν ὁ ἐνεργῶν·* E. ii. 14, *αὐτὸς γάρ ἐστιν ἡ εἰρήνη ἡμῶν.* Compare also Mt. v. 13, vi. 22, xvi. 16, Mk. viii. 29, ix. 7, xv. 2, Jo. i. 4, 8, 50, iii. 10, iv. 29,² v. 35, 39, vi. 14, 50, 51, 63, ix. 8, 19, 20, x. 7, xi. 25, xiv. 21, A. iv. 11, vii. 32, viii. 10, ix. 21, xxi. 28, 38, Ph. iii. 3, 19, E. i. 23, 1 C. xi. 3, 2 C. iii. 2, 1 Jo. iv. 15, v. 6, Jude 19, Rev. i. 17, iii. 17, iv. 5, xvii. 18, xviii. 23, xix. 10, xx. 14. In the following passages the MSS. vary more or less: Rev. v. 6, 8, A. iii. 25, 1 Jo. ii. 22, 1 C. xv. 28, Jo. i. 21. In one instance two substantives, one of which has the article and the other not, are combined in the predicate: Jo. viii. 44, *ὅτι ψεύστης ἐστὶ καὶ ὁ πατὴρ αὐτοῦ (ψεύδους), he is a liar and the father of it.* In Greek authors also the predicate frequently has the article: compare Xen. *Mem.* 3. 10. 1, Plat. *Phædr.* 64 c, *Gorg.* 483 b, Lucian, *Dial. M.* 17. 1, and see Schæf. *Demosth.* III. 280, IV. 35, Matth. 264. Rem.

Hence the rule often laid down, that the subject of a sentence may be known from its having the article, is incorrect; as was already perceived by Glass and Rambach (*Instit. Hermen.* p. 446).³

---

¹ [These exceptions may be classified and explained without giving up the general rule that the article usually distinguishes the subject from the predicate (Don. p. 346, Jelf 460). When the predicate receives the article, it is usually in reference to a previous mention of the word, or because the proposition is such that the subject and predicate are convertible (Middl. p. 54, Don. *New Crat.* p. 522). Compare Green's remarks (p. 35 sq.), which perhaps will explain most of the examples: "When the article is inserted after a verb of existence, the real predicate of the sentence is a simple identity, the identity of the subject with something else, the idea of which is a familiar one. But when the word or combination of words following the verb of existence is anarthrous, then the circumstances or attributes signified by it form the predicate, instead of a mere identity." See Don. p. 348 sq., Ellicott on 1 Th. iv. 3 and 1 Tim. vi. 10. Lünemann refers to Dornseiffen, *De articulo apud Græcos ejusque usu in prædicato* (Amstel. 1856), as affording a copious collection of examples, without any real enlargement of the theory.]

² Probably also Jo. iv. 37; see Meyer. [The article before ἀληθινός is probably spurious.]

³ Compare also *Jen. Lit. Z.* 1834: No. 207.

8. In the language of living intercourse it is utterly impossible that the article should be omitted where it is absolutely necessary (compare on the other hand § 19), or inserted where it is not required:[1] ὄρος can never be *the mountain*, nor can τὸ ὄρος ever mean *a mountain*.[2] The very many passages of the N. T. in which older commentators—professedly following the analogy of the Hebrew article (Gesen. *Lg.* p. 655)[3]—supposed ὁ, ἡ, τό, to stand for the indefinite article,[4] will be easily disposed of by the careful reader. 1 Th. iv. 6, πλεονεκτεῖν ἐν τῷ πράγματι, means to *overreach in business* (in business affairs):[5] Jo. ii. 25, ἐγίνωσκεν τί ἦν ἐν τῷ ἀνθρώπῳ, in *the* man with whom he (on each occasion) had to do,—in every man (Krüg. p. 98); compare Diog. L. 6. 64, πρὸς τὸν συνιστάντα τὸν παῖδα καὶ λέγοντα ὡς εὐφυέστατός ἐστι ... εἶπε κ.τ.λ., *to him who recommended the boy*, i.e. to every one who did this. In Jo. iii. 10, σὺ εἶ ὁ διδάσκαλος τοῦ Ἰσραήλ, Nicodemus is regarded as *the* teacher of Israel κατ' ἐξοχήν, as the man in whom all erudition was concentrated, in order that more force may be given to the contrast expressed in καὶ ταῦτα οὐ γινώσκεις; compare Plat. *Crit.* 51 a, καὶ σὺ φήσεις ταῦτα ποιῶν δίκαια πράττειν ὁ τῇ ἀληθείᾳ τῆς ἀρετῆς ἐπιμελόμενος (Stallb. Plat. *Euth.* p. 12, Valcken. Eur. *Phœn.* p. 552, Krüg. p. 101, Jelf 447). In H. v. 11, ὁ λόγος is *the* (our) *discourse*, that which we have to say: comp. Plat. *Phædr.* 270 a.

On the other hand, there are cases in which the article may be either inserted or omitted with equal objective correctness[6]

---

[1] Sturz, in his *Lexic. Xenoph.* III. 232, even quotes passages from Xenophon as containing examples of the use of ὁ for τὶς. To all this applies what Schæfer (*ad Plutarch.*) somewhere says: Tanta non fuit vis barbaræ linguæ, ut Græcæ ipsa fundamenta convellere posset.

[2] Kuinoel on Mt. v. 1, Jo. xix. 32, iii. 10.

[3] [In his *Lehrgeb. l. c.* Gesenius thus explained several passages in the O. T. (as 1 S. xvii. 34, Gen. xiv. 13, al.), but he afterwards entirely retracted this opinion; see his *Thesaur.* p. 361, *Hebr. Gramm.* p. 185 (Bagst.): see also Ewald, *Ausf. Lehrb.* p. 686, Kalisch, *Hebr. Gr.* I. 238 sq.]

[4] This frivolous principle is not justified by reference to commentators who in particular passages have attributed a *false* emphasis to the article (Glass 138 sqq.), or have pressed it unduly. Böhmer has discovered an extraordinary mode of mediating between the old view and the new (*Introd. in Ep. ad Coloss.* p. 291).

[5] [See Ellicott, Alford, and Jowett *in loc.*, who agree in the rendering, "in the matter" (of which we are speaking): see also Green p. 26 sq.]

[6] Thus it is easy to explain how one language even regularly employs the article in certain cases (οὗτος ὁ ἄνθρωπος, τοὺς φίλους ποιεῖσθαι), in which another does not (*this man, Götter glauben*). Compare Sintenis, Plut. *Themist.* p. 190:

(Förtsch, *ad Lys.* p. 49 sq.). In Ja. ii. 26, τὸ σῶμα χωρὶς πνεύματος νεκρόν means *the body without spirit;* χωρὶς τοῦ πν. would be, *without the spirit* belonging to this particular body. In L. xii. 54, good MSS. have ὅταν ἴδητε νεφέλην ἀνατέλλουσαν ἀπὸ δυσμῶν, whereas the received text has τὴν νεφ. Both expressions are correct: with the article the words mean *when ye see the cloud* (which appears in the sky) *rising from the west*,—when the course of the cloud is from the west. In Col. i. 16, ἐν αὐτῷ ἐκτίσθη τὰ πάντα, the meaning of τὰ πάντα is *the (existing) all, the totality of creation, the universe:* πάντα would mean *all things,* whatever exists. The article but slightly affects the sense, yet the two expressions are differently conceived: comp. Col. iii. 8, where the two are combined. In Mt. xxvi. 26 [*Rec.*] we have λαβὼν ὁ Ἰησοῦς τὸν ἄρτον (which lay before him); but in Mk. xiv. 22, L. xxii. 19, 1 C. xi. 23, the best MSS. have ἄρτον, *bread,* or *a loaf.* Compare further Mt. xii. 1 with Mk. ii. 23 and L. vi. 1; Mt. xix. 3 with Mk. x. 2; L. ix. 28 with Mk. ix. 2. So also in parallel members: L. xviii. 2, τὸν θεὸν μὴ φοβούμενος καὶ ἄνθρωπον μὴ ἐντρεπόμενος· xviii. 27, τὰ ἀδύνατα παρὰ ἀνθρώποις δυνατά ἐστι παρὰ τῷ θεῷ· xvii. 34, ἔσονται δύο ἐπὶ κλίνης μιᾶς· εἷς[1] παραληφθήσεται καὶ ὁ ἕτερος ἀφεθήσεται (*one ... the other;* contrast Mt. vi. 24, xxiv. 40 sq.); 1 Jo. iii. 18, μὴ ἀγαπῶμεν λόγῳ μηδὲ τῇ γλώσσῃ (according to the best MSS.; comp. Soph. *Œd. Col.* 786, λόγῳ μὲν ἐσθλά, τοῖσι δ' ἔργοισιν κακά); 2 Tim. i. 10, 1 C. ii. 14, 15, Rom. ii. 29, iii. 27, 30, H. ix. 4, xi. 38, Jude 16, 19, Jo. xii. 5, 6, Ja. ii. 17, 20, 26, Rev. xx. 1.[2] Compare Plat. *Rep.* I. 332 c and d, Xen. *An.* 3. 4. 7, Galen. *Temper.* 1. 4, Diog. L. 6. 6, Lucian, *Eunuch.* 6, Porphyr. *Abstin.* 1. 14. (The antithesis ἐν οὐρανῷ καὶ ἐπὶ τῆς γῆς is not fully established in any passage, see Mt. xxviii. 18, 1 C. viii. 5;[3] in E. iii. 15 the article is omitted in both members, without any variant.)

There is however a clear necessity for the respective omission

---

"Multa, quæ nos indefinite cogitata pronuntiamus, definite proferre soliti sunt Græci, ejus, de quo sermo esset, notitiam animo informatam præsumentes." Kühnöl misuses such remarks (*ad Matt.* p. 123).

[1] This lends support to my exposition of G. iii. 20, to which it has always been objected that I have taken εἷς for ὁ εἷς. [The reading is doubtful in L. xvii. 34.]

[2] See Porson, Eurip. *Phœn.* p. 42 (ed. Lips.), Ellendt, Arr. *Al.* I. 58, *Lex. Soph.* II. 247.

[3] [In Mt. xviii. 18, Tisch. (ed. 8) and others read ἐπὶ τῆς γ. and ἐν οὐρ. in contrasted clauses. In xxviii. 18 the reading is uncertain.]

or insertion of the article in L. ix. 13, οὐκ εἰσὶν ἡμῖν πλεῖον ἢ πέντε ἄρτοι καὶ ἰχθύες δύο· and ver. 16, λαβὼν τοὺς π. ἄρτους καὶ τοὺς δ. ἰχθύας. Also in Rom. v. 7, μόλις ὑπὲρ δικαίου τις ἀποθανεῖται, ὑπὲρ γὰρ τοῦ ἀγαθοῦ τάχα τις καὶ τολμᾷ ἀποθανεῖν, for *a* righteous man (one who is upright, without reproach), for *the* kind man (i.e., for the man who has shown himself such to him,—for his benefactor); Rückert has unquestionably misunderstood the passage. In Col. iii. 5 we find four nouns in apposition without the article, and then a fifth, πλεονεξία, marked by the article as a notorious immorality, especially to be avoided,[1] further characterised by the Apostle in the words which follow,—for I cannot regard ἥτις κ.τ.λ. as referring to all the preceding nouns. In 2 C. xi. 18 there is no doubt that Paul designedly wrote (καυχῶνται) κατὰ τὴν σάρκα, as differing from κατὰ σάρκα (a kind of adverb), though all recent commentators consider the two expressions identical in meaning. See also Jo. xviii. 20, Rev. iii. 17; also Rom. viii. 23, where a noun which has the article stands in apposition to an anarthrous noun, υἱοθεσίαν ἀπεκδεχόμενοι, τὴν ἀπολύτρωσιν τοῦ σώματος, *waiting for adoption* (namely) *the redemption of the body*.

9. The indefinite article (for which, where it seemed necessary to express it, the Greeks used τὶς) is in particular instances expressed by the (weakened) numeral εἷς: this usage is found mainly in later Greek.[2] In the N. T., see Mt. viii. 19, προςελθὼν εἷς γραμματεύς· Rev. viii. 13, ἤκουσα ἑνὸς ἀετοῦ. In Jo. vi. 9 ἕν is probably not genuine (comp. Mt. ix. 18); and in Mt. xxi. 19 μίαν συκῆν perhaps signifies *one fig-tree*, standing by itself. Εἷς τῶν παρεστηκότων, Mk. xiv. 47, is like the Latin *unus adstantium*: compare Mt. xviii. 28, Mk. xiii. 1, L. xv. 26 (Herod. 7. 5. 10, Plutarch, *Arat*. 5, *Cleom*. 7, Æschin. *Dial*. 2. 2,[3] Schoem. *Isæus* p. 249). The numeral retains its proper meaning in Ja. iv. 13 [*Rec.*], ἐνιαυτὸν ἕνα; and still more distinctly in 2 C. xi. 2, Mt. xviii. 14, Jo. vii. 21. See, in general, Boisson. *Eunap.* 345, Ast, Plat. *Legg.* 219, Jacobs, *Achill. Tat.* p. 398, Schæf. *Long.*

---

[1] Weber, *Dem.* p. 327. Another case, in which, of several connected nouns the last only has the article, for the sake of emphasis, is discussed by Jacobitz, Luc. *Pisc.* p. 209 (ed. min.).

[2] So also sometimes the Hebrew אֶחָד, see Gesen. *Lg.* p. 655, [*Heb. Lex.* s. v., Ewald, *Ausf. L.* p. 693]. The use of εἷς in this sense arises from that love of expressiveness which has already been noticed as a peculiarity of later Greek.

[3] Τὶς τῶν παρ. might indeed have been used instead (compare L. vii. 36, xi. 1, al.), as in Latin *suorum aliquis*, etc. Both expressions are logically correct, but they are not identical. *Unus adstantium* really suggests a numerical unity,— *one* out of several. [Meyer (on Mt. viii. 19) denies that εἷς is ever used in the N. T. in the sense of τὶς: on the other side see A. Buttm. p. 85.]

399.[1]—An antithesis is probably designed in Mt. xviii. 24, εἷς ὀφειλέτης μυρίων ταλάντων. In εἷς τις also, *unus aliquis* (Mk. xiv. 51 *v. l.*, and, in a partitive sense, Mk. xiv. 47,[2] L. xxii. 50, Jo. xi. 49), τὶς does not destroy the arithmetical force of εἷς.[3]

Rem. 1. In some few instances the use or omission of the article is also a mark of the distinctive style of the writer. Thus Gersdorf has shown (*Sprachchar.* pp. 39, 272 sqq.,) that the four evangelists almost always write ὁ Χριστός—*the* expected *Messiah*, like ὁ ἐρχόμενος,—while Paul and Peter write Χριστός, when this appellation had become more of a proper name. In the Epistles of Paul and Peter, however, those cases are to be excepted in which Χριστός is dependent on a preceding noun [which has the article],[4] as τὸ εὐαγγέλιον τοῦ Χριστοῦ, ἡ ὑπομονὴ τοῦ Χριστοῦ, τῷ αἵματι τοῦ Χριστοῦ, for in these Χριστός always receives the article: see Rom. vii. 4, xv. 19, xvi. 16, 1 C. i. 6, 17, vi. 15, x. 16, 2 C. iv. 4, ix. 13, xii. 9, G. i. 7, E. ii. 13, 2 Th. iii. 5, al. But besides these instances, the article is not unfrequently used by Paul with this word, not only after prepositions, but even in the nominative, e.g. Rom. xv. 3, 7, 1 C. i. 13, x. 4, xi. 3, al. There is no less variation in the Epistle to the Hebrews: see Bleek on H. v. 5.

Rem. 2. MSS. vary extremely in regard to the article, especially where its insertion or omission is a matter of little consequence; and critics must be guided more by the value of the MSS. than by any supposed peculiarity of a writer's style. Compare Mt. xii. 1, στάχυας· Mk. vi. 17, ἐν φυλακῇ (better attested than ἐν τῇ φ.), vii. 37, ἀλάλους· x. 2, Φαρισαῖοι· x. 46, υἱός· xi. 4, πῶλον· xii. 33, θυσιῶν· xiv. 33,

---

[1] Bretschneider makes an unfortunate attempt to bring under this head 1 Tim. iii. 2, 12, Tit. i. 6, μιᾶς γυναικὸς ἀνήρ· translating, *He must be the husband of a wife*, i.e. he must be married. But, not to mention that 1 Tim. iii. 4 sq. would not assign a sufficient reason for an injunction that only married men should be admitted to the office of ἐπίσκοπος, no careful writer could use εἷς for the indefinite article where his doing so would give rise to any ambiguity, for we speak and write that we may be *understood* by others. It is true that in the expression "there came a man" numerical unity is implied, and *homo aliquis* suggests to every one *homo unus;* but μίαν γυναῖκα ἔχειν cannot be used for γυναῖκα ἔχειν, as it is possible for a man to have *several* wives (at the same time or successively), and hence the expression necessarily conveys the notion of numerical unity. Besides, one who wished to say *a bishop must be married*, would hardly say, *a bishop must be husband of a wife*.

[2] [Quoted above without τὶς, which is omitted by some recent editors.]

[3] Heindorf, Plat. *Soph.* 42, Ast *l. c.*, and on Plat. *Polit.* 532, Boisson. *Marin.* p. 15.

[4] [I have inserted these words from the 5th edition of the German work; in the 6th and 7th they are omitted, no doubt by accident. In a single Epistle for instance, 2 Corinthians, we find ten examples of τοῦ Χριστοῦ after a noun with the article, and nearly as many of Χριστοῦ after an anarthrous noun. Such instances as κεφαλὴ τοῦ Χρ. 1 C. xi. 3 (Col. i. 7), or τὸ ἔργον Χριστοῦ Ph. ii. 30 Lachm. (1 P. i. 11), are very rare. The copious tables given by Rose in his edition of Middleton (pp. 486-496) cannot be fully relied on, as in many instances doubtful readings are followed.]

Ἰάκωβον· xiv. 60, εἰς μέσον· L. ii. 12, ἐν φάτνῃ· iv. 9, ὁ υἱός· iv. 29, ἕως ὀφρύος τοῦ ὄρους· vi. 35, ὑψίστου· Jo. v. 1, Rom. x. 15, xi. 19, G. iv. 24, 2 P. ii. 8, al.

Rem. 3. It is singular that commentators (with the exception indeed of Bengel), when, contrary to their usual practice, they have noticed the article in any passage, have in most instances explained it wrongly. Thus Kühnöl, after Krause (a very poor authority), supposes that the use of the article with ἐκκλησίᾳ in A. vii. 38 requires us to understand this word as meaning *certa populi concio.* The context may indeed render this probable, but in point of mere grammar it is just as correct to render ἡ ἐκκλ. (with Grotius and others) *the congregation,* קְהַל יִשְׂרָאֵל, and this would be as regular an example as any other of the use of the article. Nor are Kühnöl's remarks on A. viii. 26 more than half true. Luke must have written ἡ ἔρημος (ὁδός), if he had wished to distinguish one particular road, well known to his readers, from the other road: if however he meant to say, *this* (*road*) *is* (now) *desert, unfrequented, lies waste,* the article would be as inadmissible in Greek as in our own language. In 2 Th. iii. 14 also (διὰ τῆς ἐπιστολῆς) the commentators have noticed the article, and have maintained that its presence makes it impossible to join this clause with the following verb σημειοῦσθε. This may perhaps afford an explanation of the omission of the article in two MSS. But Paul might very well say διὰ τῆς ἐπιστολῆς σημειοῦσθε, if he at that time assumed an answer on the part of the Thessalonians: "Note him to me in *the* letter,"—that which I hope to receive from you, or which you have then to send to me. See however Lünemann.[1]

Rem. 4. The article properly stands immediately before the noun to which it belongs. Those conjunctions however which cannot stand first in a sentence are regularly placed between the article and the noun: Mt. xi. 30, ὁ γὰρ ζυγός μου· iii. 4, ἡ δὲ τροφή· Jo. vi. 14, οἱ οὖν ἄνθρωποι, etc. This is a well-known rule, which needs no further illustration by examples. See Rost p. 427, and compare Herm. Soph. *Antig.* p. 146.

SECTION XIX.

OMISSION OF THE ARTICLE BEFORE NOUNS.

1. Appellatives which, as denoting definite objects, should naturally have the article, are in certain cases used without it, not only in the N. T., but also in the best Greek writers: see Schæfer, *Melet.* p. 4. Such an omission, however, takes place

---

[1] [Most commentators connect these words with λόγῳ: see Ellicott and Jowett.]

only when it occasions no ambiguity, and does not leave the reader in doubt whether he is to regard the word as definite or indefinite. Hence

(*a*) The article is omitted before words which denote objects of which there is but one in existence, and which therefore are nearly equivalent to proper names.[1] Thus ἥλιος is almost as common as ὁ ἥλιος, and γῆ is not unfrequently used for ἡ γῆ, in the sense of *the earth* (Poppo, *Thuc.* III. iii. 46). Hence also abstract nouns denoting virtues, vices, etc.,[2] as ἀρετή, σωφροσύνη, κακία, and the names of the members of the animal body,[3] very often dispense with the article. The same may be said of a number of other appellatives—as πόλις, ἄστυ, ἀγρός, δεῖπνον, and even πατήρ, μήτηρ, ἀδελφός,[4]—when the context leaves no room for doubt as to the particular town, field, etc., intended. This omission, however, is more frequent in poetry than in prose (Schæfer, *Demosth.* I. 329), and is again more common in Greek prose generally than in the N. T.[5]

Of anarthrous abstracts [6] in the N. T., 1 Tim. vi. 11, Rom. i.

---

[1] [Jelf 447. 2, Don. p. 348, Green p. 42 sq.]

[2] To which must be added the names of sciences and arts (as ἱππική, see Jacob on Lucian, *Toxar.* p. 98), of magistracies and offices of state (Schæf. *Demosth.* II. 112, Held, Plut. *Æm. P.* p. 138), of seasons of the year, of corporations (Held *l. c.* p. 238), with many other names (Schoem. *Isæus*, p. 303, and on Plutarch, *Cleom.* p. 199). See also Krüg. p. 101 sq. As to abstract nouns, see Schæf. *Demosth.* I. 329, Bornem. Xen. *Conv.* p. 52, Krüg. p. 101.

[3] Held, Plut. *Æm. P.* p. 248. On πόλις, ἄστυ, see Schæf. *Plutarch*, p. 416, Poppo, *Thuc.* III. i. 111, Weber, *Dem.* p. 235; on ἀγρός, Schæf. Soph. *Œd. R.* 630; and on δεῖπνον, Jacobs, *Achill. Tat.* p. 490, Bornem. Xen. *Conv.* p. 57.

[4] Schæf. *Melet.* p. 4, *Demosth.* 1. 328, Eur. *Hec.* p. 121, *Plutarch l. c.*, Stallb. Plat. *Crit.* p. 134.

[5] Thus in Greek authors we usually find γένει *by nation*, πλήθει, etc.: in the N. T. always τῷ γένει, A. iv. 36, xviii. 2, 24: also τῷ πλήθει, H. xi. 12. In Greek authors the omission of the article with the nominative case of the noun is not uncommon, e.g. ἥλιος ἐδύετο, Xen. *An.* 1. 10. 15, Lucian, *Scyth.* 4: with this contrast Mk. i. 32, ὅτε ἔδυ ὁ ἥλιος· L. iv. 40, δύνοντος τοῦ ἡλίου· E. iv. 26, ὁ ἥλιος μὴ ἐπιδυέτω. Σελήνη also and other similar words always have the article in the N. T., when they are in the nominative case.

[6] Harless (*Ephes.* p. 320) maintains that the article is not omitted with abstracts unless they denote virtues, vices, etc., as properties of a subject: but this assertion has not been proved, and cannot be proved on rational principles. Compare also Krüger in Jahn's *Jahrb.* 1838. I. 47. [Middleton (p. 91) says that the article is usually omitted with an abstract noun, except in the following cases: (1) When the noun is used in its most abstract sense (see Ellicott on Phil. 9, E. iv. 14); (2) When the attribute, etc., is personified (Rom. vi. 12); (3) When the article is employed in the sense of a possessive pronoun (G. v. 13); (4) Where there is reference of any kind (E. ii. 8, comp. ver. 5). Of *special* omissions of the article with these nouns, that with the adverbial dative (E. ii. 5) is the most important. See further Green p. 16 sq., Jelf 448, Ellicott on G. ii. 5, Ph. ii. 3.]

SECT. XIX.] OMISSION OF THE ARTICLE BEFORE NOUNS. 149

29, and Col. iii. 8 will serve as general examples. Passing to particular words, we have δικαιοσύνη, Mt. v. 10, A. x. 35, Rom. viii. 10, H. xi. 33, al.; ἀγάπη, G. v. 6, 2 C. ii. 8; πίστις, A. vi. 5, Rom. i. 5, iii. 28, 2 C. v. 7, 1 Th. v. 8, al.; κακία, 1 C. v. 8, Tit. iii. 3, Ja. i. 21; πλεονεξία, 1 Th. ii. 5, 2 P. ii. 3; ἁμαρτία, G. ii. 17, 1 P. iv. 1, Rom. iii. 9, vi. 14, al.; σωτηρία, Rom. x. 10, 2 Tim. iii. 15, H. i. 14, vi. 9. To these should be added ἀγαθόν Rom. viii. 28 (comp. Fritz. *in loc.*), πονηρόν 1 Th. v. 22, καλόν τε καὶ κακόν H. v. 14. The article is also frequently omitted in the N. T. with the concretes ἥλιος, γῆ (*Earth*), θεός, πρόςωπον, νόμος, etc., and also with a number of other words, at all events when, in combination with prepositions, etc., they form certain phrases of very frequent occurrence.[1] We subjoin a list of anarthrous concretes in the N. T., following the best attested readings.

ἥλιος (Held, Plut. *Timol.* p. 467), e. g. Mt. xiii. 6, ἡλίου ἀνατείλαντος (Polyæn. 6. 5, Lucian, *Ver. Hist.* 2. 12, Ælian 4. 1): especially when it is joined in the genitive to another noun, and a single notion is expressed by the combination, as ἀνατολὴ ἡλίου *sunrise*, Rev. vii. 2, xvi. 12 (Her. 4. 8), φῶς ἡλίου *sunlight*, Rev. xxii. 5 *v. l.* (Plat. *Rep.* 5. 473 e), δόξα ἡλίου *sun-glory*, 1 C. xv. 41; or where the sun is mentioned in an enumeration[2] (in connexion with moon and stars), L. xxi. 25, ἔσται σημεῖα ἐν ἡλίῳ καὶ σελήνῃ καὶ ἄστροις, *in sun, moon, and stars*, A. xxvii. 20 (Æsch. *Dial.* 3. 17, Plat. *Crat.* 397 d).

γῆ (*Earth*), 2 P. iii. 5, 10, A. xvii. 24; ἐπὶ γῆς, L. ii. 14, 1 C. viii. 5, E. iii. 15, (H. viii. 4); ἀπ' ἄκρου γῆς, Mk. xiii. 27.[3] In this signification, however, γῆ usually has the article: when used for *country* it is anarthrous, as a rule, if the name of the country follows: e. g. Mt. xi. 24, γῇ Σοδόμων· A. vii. 29, ἐν γῇ Μαδιάμ· vii. 36, ἐν γῇ Αἰγύπτου· xiii. 19, ἐν γῇ Χαναάν, al.; but in Mt. xiv. 34, εἰς τὴν γῆν Γεννησαρέτ.[4] See below, (*b*). Van Hengel's observations (1 *Cor. xv.* p. 199) are not to the point.

οὐρανός (οὐρανοί) is seldom anarthrous.[5] In the Gospels the article

---

[1] Kluit II. 377, Heindorf, Plat. *Gorg.* p. 265.
[2] [This is an example of irregularity noticed by Bp. Middleton (p. 99),—that nouns coupled together by conjunctions very frequently reject the article though they would require it if they stood singly: he refers to this under the name of omission "in Enumeration," and gives Mt. vi. 19, x. 28, 1 C. iv. 9, al., as examples. See also Krüg. p. 100, Jelf 447. 2. *b*, Green p. 45.]
[3] Compare Jacobs, Philostr. *Imag.* p. 266, Ellendt on Arrian, *Al.* I. 91, Stallb. Plat. *Gorg.* p. 257.
[4] [In A. vii. 36 we should probably read ἐν τῇ Αἰγύπτῳ, and in Mt. xiv. 34 ἐπὶ τὴν γῆν εἰς Γεννησαρέτ. Lünem. adds Mt. iv. 15.]
[5] Compare Jacobs in the *Schulzeit.* 1831. No. 119, and Schoem. Plut. *Agis* p. 135.

is omitted only in the phrases ἐν οὐρανῷ, ἐν οὐρανοῖς, ἐξ οὐρανῶν, ἐξ οὐρανοῦ,[1] and in these by no means invariably (comp. Mt. vi. 1, 9, xvi. 19, Mk. xii. 25, L. vi. 23); John also always writes ἐκ τοῦ οὐρανοῦ, except in i. 32 [and vi. 58]. By Paul the article is omitted, as a rule, in such phrases as ἀπ' οὐρανοῦ, ἐξ οὐρανοῦ;[2] and in 2 C. xii. 2 we find ἕως τρίτου οὐρανοῦ (Lucian, *Philopatr.* 12), see below, (*b*). Peter omits the article even with the nominative οὐρανοί, 2 P. iii. 5, 12. In the Apocalypse the article is always inserted.[3]

θάλασσα: e. g. A. x. 6, 32, παρὰ θάλασσαν· L. xxi. 25 [*Rec.*], ἠχούσης θαλάσσης καὶ σάλου; comp. Demosth. *Aristocr.* 450 c, Diod. S. 1. 32, Dio Chr. 35. 436, 37. 455, Xen. Eph. 5. 10, Arrian, *Al.* 2. 1, 2, 3, Held in *Act. Philol. Monac.* II. 182 sqq. In A. vii. 36 we even find ἐν ἐρυθρᾷ θαλάσσῃ (but in H. xi. 29, τὴν ἐρ. θάλ.). As a rule, however, θάλασσα has the article, especially when opposed to ἡ γῆ.[4]

μεσημβρία, in the phrases κατὰ μεσημβρίαν *southwards*, A. viii. 26, and περὶ μεσημβρίαν, xxii. 6 : compare Xen. *An.* 1. 7. 6, πρὸς μεσημβρίαν· Plat. *Phædr.* 259 a, ἐν μεσημβρίᾳ. The article is also omitted with the other words which denote the cardinal points, e. g. Rev. xxi. 13, ἀπὸ ἀνατολῶν, ἀπὸ βορρᾶ, ἀπὸ νότου, ἀπὸ δυσμῶν; similarly πρὸς νότον Strabo 16. 719, πρὸς ἑσπέραν Diod. S. 3. 28, πρὸς ἄρκτον Strabo 15. 715, 719, 16. 749, πρὸς νότον Plat. *Crit.* 112 c. (Compare Mt. xii. 42, βασίλισσα νότου; here however νότος is a kind of proper name.) The same may be said of the words which denote the divisions of the day; see L. xxiv. 29, A. xxviii. 23 (Krüg. p. 99).

ἀγορά :[5] Mk. vii. 4, καὶ ἀπ' ἀγορᾶς, ἐὰν μὴ βαπτίσωνται, οὐκ ἐσθίουσι.[6] This word is often anarthrous in Greek authors (Her. 7. 223, 3. 104, Lys. *Agor.* 2, Dion. H. IV. 2117. 6, 2230. 2, Theophr. *Ch.* 19, Plat. *Gorg.* 447 a, Lucian, *adv. Ind.* 4, *Eunuch.* 1), especially in the phrase πληθούσης ἀγορᾶς, Her. 4. 181, Xen. *Mem.* 1. 1. 10, *An.* 1. 8. 1, Ælian 12. 30, Diod. S. 13. 48, al.

ἀγρός: Mk. xv. 21, ἐρχόμενον ἀπ' ἀγροῦ (L. xxiii. 26), L. xv. 25, ἦν ὁ υἱὸς ἐν ἀγρῷ. Here however there is no reference to any particular field (ἀπὸ τοῦ ἀγροῦ); the expression is general, *from the country* (as opposed to the town, etc.). Similarly, εἰς ἀγρόν Mk. xvi. 12, Jud. ix. 27, ἐξ ἀγροῦ Gen. xxx. 16, 1 S. xi. 5, al., Plat. *Theæt.* 143 a, *Legg.* 8. 844 c.

θεός is frequently anarthrous,[7]—most frequently by far in the

---

[1] [Add to these ἀπ' οὐρ. L. xvii. 29, xxi. 11, ὑπ' οὐρανόν L. xvii. 24, ἕως οὐρ. Mt. xi. 23, L. x. 15, ἕως ἄκρου οὐρ. Mk. xiii. 27, ἀπ' ἄκρων οὐρ. Mt. xxiv. 31.]
[2] 'Εκ τοῦ οὐρ. (Van Hengel, 1 *Cor. xv.* p. 199) is not used by Paul. [After ἐν the article is as frequently inserted as omitted.]
[3] [*Rec.* wrongly omits the article in vi. 14: xxi. 1 is of course no exception.]
[4] [The two words have a common article in Rev. xiv. 7.]
[5] Compare Bremi, *Lys.* p. 9, Sintenis, Plut. *Pericl.* p. 80.
[6] [This and L. vii. 32 are the only certain examples of ἀγορά anarthrous.]
[7] Compare Herm. Arist. *Nub.* 816, Bornem. Xen. *Conv.* p. 142, Jacob on Lucian, *Toxar.* p. 121.

Epistles.¹ In the following cases especially the article is omitted with this word :—

(1) When the genitive θεοῦ is dependent on another (anarthrous) noun : L. iii. 2, Rom. iii. 5, viii. 9, xv. 7, 8, 32 [*Rec.*], 1 C. iii. 16, xi. 7, 2 C. i. 12, viii. 5, E. v. 5, 1 Th. ii. 13.²

(2) In the phrases θεὸς πατήρ, 1 C. i. 3, 2 C. i. 2, G. i. 1, Ph. i. 2, ii. 11, 1 P. i. 2 ; υἱοὶ or τέκνα θεοῦ, Mt. v. 9, Rom. viii. 14, 16, G. iii. 26, Ph. ii. 15, 1 Jo. iii. 1, 2 (where these governing nouns also are without the article ³).

(3) With prepositions : as ἀπὸ θεοῦ, Jo. iii. 2, xvi. 30, Rom. xiii. 1 [*Rec.*], 1 C. i. 30, vi. 19 ; ἐν θεῷ, Jo. iii. 21, Rom. ii. 17 ; ἐκ θεοῦ, A. v. 39, 2 C. v. 1, Ph. iii. 9 ; κατὰ θεόν, Rom. viii. 27 ; παρὰ θεῷ, 2 Th. i. 6, 1 P. ii. 4. Similarly with an adjective in 1 Th. i. 9, θεῷ ζῶντι καὶ ἀληθινῷ.—In Jo. i. 1 (θεὸς ἦν ὁ λόγος), the article could not have been omitted if John had wished to designate the λόγος as ὁ θεός, because in such a connexion θεός without the article would be ambiguous. It is clear, however, both from the distinct antithesis πρὸς τὸν θεόν, ver. 1, 2, and from the whole description (*Characterisirung*) of the λόγος, that John wrote θεός designedly.⁴ Similarly, in 1 P. iv. 19 we find πιστὸς κτίστης without the article.

πνεῦμα ἅγιον (rarely πνεῦμα θεοῦ), A. viii. 15, 17, Rom. viii. 9, 14, H. vi. 4, 2 P. i. 21, 1 C. xii. 3 ; πνεῦμα Ph. ii. 1 ; also ἐν πνεύματι E. ii. 22, vi. 18, Col. i. 8 ; ἐν πνεύματι ἁγίῳ Jude 20. (The baptismal formula, εἰς τὸ ὄνομα τοῦ πατρὸς κ. τοῦ υἱοῦ κ. τοῦ ἁγίου πνεύματος, is thus quoted in *Acta Barn.* p. 74, εἰς ὄνομα πατρὸς κ. υἱοῦ κ. ἁγίου πνεύματος.⁵)

πατήρ : H. xii. 7, υἱὸς ὃν οὐ παιδεύει πατήρ· Jo. i. 14, μονογενοῦς παρὰ πατρός ; ⁶ also in the phrase θεὸς πατήρ (ἡμῶν). With μήτηρ

---

¹ [That is, the article is much more frequently omitted in the Epistles than elsewhere in the N. T. : even in the Epistles the instances in which the article is used with this word are twice as numerous as those in which it is omitted.]

² [E. v. 5 is remarkable on other grounds (τοῦ Χρ. καὶ θεοῦ), but has no place here since the governing noun has the article. In Rom. xv. 7 τοῦ θ. is the best reading : in 2 C. i. 12 θεοῦ is used both with and without the article after an anarthrous noun. In 1 Th. i. 9, 1 P. iv. 19 (quoted below), the renderings *a living and true God, a faithful Creator*, are clearly to be preferred.]

³ [So that this case coincides with that first mentioned.]

⁴ [" Even ὕψιστος, which, when it is used for *God*, ought as an adjective to have the article, is anarthrous in L. i. 32, 35, 76, vi. 35." (A. Buttm. p. 89.)]

⁵ [Middleton's canon is, that the article is never omitted when the Person of the Holy Spirit is signified, " except indeed in cases where other terms, confessedly the most definite, lose the article "—i.e., according to his theory, after a preposition or an anarthrous noun. Similarly Westcott (on Jo. vii. 39) : " When the term occurs in this form " (i.e., without the article), " it marks an operation, or manifestation, or gift of the Spirit, and not the personal Spirit." See also Vaughan's note on Rom. v. 5. In favour of Winer's view see Fritzsche and Meyer on Rom. viii. 4, Ellicott on G. v. 5, Alford on Mt. i. 18, G. v. 16.]

⁶ [If St. John's usage be examined, it will appear very doubtful whether we have a right to take πατρός as simply equivalent to τοῦ πατρός in this passage. The true rendering must surely be : "as of an only son from a father." See Westcott *in loc.*]

the article is omitted only in the phrase ἐκ κοιλίας μητρός (Mt. xix. 12).¹

ἀνήρ (*husband*): 1 Tim. ii. 12, γυναικὶ διδάσκειν οὐκ ἐπιτρέπω, οὐδὲ αὐθεντεῖν ἀνδρός· E. v. 23; contrast 1 C. xi. 3. L. xvi. 18, πᾶς ὁ ἀπολύων τὴν γυναῖκα αὐτοῦ ... πᾶς ὁ ἀπολελυμένην ἀπὸ ἀνδρὸς γαμῶν, does not necessarily come under this head, though γυνή has the article in the first clause; for the last words should be translated, *he who marries a woman dismissed by a man*. In A. i. 14, however, we might have expected the article before γυναιξί (see De Wette *in loc.*); not so much in A. xxi. 5; but compare what is said above.

πρόςωπον: L. v. 12, πεσὼν ἐπὶ πρόςωπον· xvii. 16, 1 C. xiv. 25; comp. Ecclus. l. 17, Tob. xii. 16, Heliod. 7. 8, ῥίπτει ἑαυτὸν ἐπὶ πρόςωπον· Achill. Tat. 3. 1, Eustath. *Amor. Ismen.* 7. p. 286 (Heliod. 1. 16); κατὰ πρόςωπον, A. xxv. 16, 2 C. x. 7 (Ex. xxviii. 27, xxxix. 13, al.).

δεξιά, ἀριστερά, and similar words, in the phrases ἐκ δεξιῶν, Mt. xxvii. 38, xxv. 41,² L. xxiii. 33; ἐξ εὐωνύμων, Mat. xx. 21, xxv. 33, Mk. x. 37 (Krüg. p. 100).

ἐκκλησία: 3 Jo. 6, οἳ ἐμαρτύρησάν σου τῇ ἀγάπῃ ἐνώπιον ἐκκλησίας· 1 C. xiv. 4 (ἐν ἐκκλησίᾳ, 1 C. xiv. 19, 35 ?).

θάνατος: Mt. xxvi. 38, ἕως θανάτου (Ecclus. xxxvii. 2, li. 6); Ph. ii. 8, 30, μέχρι θανάτου (Plat. *Rep.* 2. 361 c, Athen. 1. 170); Ja. v. 20, ἐκ θανάτου (Job v. 20, Pr. x. 2, Plat. *Gorg.* 511 c); L. ii. 26, μὴ ἰδεῖν θάνατον· Rom. vii. 13, κατεργαζομένη θάνατον; Rom. i. 32, ἄξιοι θανάτου; 2 C. iv. 11, εἰς θάνατον παραδιδόμεθα, etc.: comp. Himer. 21, μετὰ θάνατον· Dion. H. IV. 2112, 2242, and also Grimm on *Wisdom*, p. 26.

θύρα, in the plural, ἐπὶ θύραις *ad fores*, Mt. xxiv. 33, Mk. xiii. 29; compare Plutarch, *Themist.* 29, Athen. 10. 441, Aristid. *Orat.* II. 43: but in the singular ἐπὶ τῇ θύρᾳ A. v. 9.³ See Sintenis, Plut. *Them.* p. 181.

νόμος, of the *Mosaic law:* Rom. ii. 12, 23, iii. 31, iv. 13, 14, 15, v. 13, 20, vii. 1, x. 4, xiii. 8, 1 C. ix. 20, G. ii. 21, iii. 11, 18, 21, iv. 5, Ph. iii. 6, H. vii. 12, al. The genitive is always anarthrous when the governing noun has no article, as in ἔργα νόμου, etc. In the Gospels this word always has the article, except in L. ii. 23, 24 [*Rec.*], where however a defining genitive follows. As to the Apocrypha see Wahl, *Clav.* p. 343. Compare further Bornem. *Acta* p. 201.⁴

---

¹ [See Mt. xix. 29 (xv. 4), Luke xii. 53, al.]
² [This should be xxv. 34 : xxv. 41 is an example of ἐξ εὐωνύμων.]
³ [The article should probably be omitted with the singular in Mk. xi. 4.]
⁴ [There is still difference of opinion on the proper interpretation of νόμος without the article. De Wette, Fritzsche, Meyer, Alford (see their notes on Rom. ii. 12), Ellicott (on G. ii. 19, al.), Jowett (on Rom. i. 2), and others agree with Winer. On the other side (i.e. against the view that νόμος without the

ῥῆμα, of the *word of God:* followed by θεοῦ, Rom. x. 17 [*Rec.*], E. vi. 17, H. vi. 5; without θεοῦ, E. v. 26.

νεκροί (the *dead*) is always anarthrous (except in E. v. 14) in the phrases ἐγείρειν, ἐγείρεσθαι, ἀναστῆναι ἐκ νεκρῶν, Mt. xvii. 9, Mk. vi. 14, 16 [*Rec.*], ix. 9, 10, xii. 25, L. ix. 7, xvi. 31, xxiv. 46, Jo. ii. 22, xii. 1, 9, 17, xx. 9, xxi. 14, A. iii. 15, iv. 2, x. 41, xiii. 30, xxvi. 23, Rom. iv. 24, 1 C. xv. 20, al.; so also in ἀνάστασις νεκρῶν (both words without the article), A. xvii. 32, xxiv. 21, Rom. i. 4, 1 C. xv. 12, 13, 21, 42,[1] al.: in Col. ii. 12 and 1 Th. i. 10 only is a variant noted.[2] On the other hand, we almost always find ἐγείρεσθαι, ἀναστῆναι ἀπὸ τῶν νεκρῶν, Mt. xiv. 2, xxvii. 64, xxviii. 7. Elsewhere νεκροί denotes *dead persons* (L. vii. 22, 1 C. xv. 15, 29, 32, also 1 P. iv. 6, al.), but οἱ νεκροί *the dead*, as a definitely conceived whole (Jo. v. 21, 1 C. xv. 52, 2 C. i. 9, Col. i. 18).[3] Greek authors, too, regularly omit the article with this word.[4]

μέσον, in the phrases (ἔστησεν) ἐν μέσῳ Jo. viii. 3 (Schoem. Plut. *Agis* p. 126), εἰς μέσον Mk. xiv. 60 (but εἰς τὸ μέσον Jo. xx. 19, 26, L. iv. 35, vi. 8), ἐκ μέσου 2 Th. ii. 7: the omission of the article is still more common when a defining genitive follows, as Mk. vi. 47, ἐν μέσῳ τῆς θαλάσσης· L. viii. 7, ἐν μέσῳ τῶν ἀκανθῶν· A. xxvii. 27, κατὰ μέσον τῆς νυκτός (Theophr. *Ch.* 26). See Wahl, *Clav. Apocr.* p. 326.

κόσμος is always anarthrous in the phrases ἀπὸ καταβολῆς κόσμου L. xi. 50, H. iv. 3, πρὸ καταβ. κόσ. J. xvii. 24, 1 P. i. 20, ἀπὸ κτίσεως κόσ. Rom. i. 20, ἀπ' ἀρχῆς κόσ. Mt. xxiv. 21: in the Epistles we find also ἐν κόσμῳ, Rom. v. 13, 1 C. viii. 4, xiv. 10, Ph. ii. 15, 1 Tim. iii. 16, 1 P. v. 9 [*Rec.*]. The nominative is but seldom found without the article, as in G. vi. 14 ἐμοὶ κόσμος ἐσταύρωται: in Rom. iv. 13 the reading of the best MSS. is κληρονόμον εἶναι κόσμου.

κτίσις, *creation* (i. e. what has been created, the world), in the phrase ἀπ' ἀρχῆς κτίσεως, Mk. x. 6, xiii. 19, 2 P. iii. 4. But there is always a distinction in meaning between πᾶσα κτίσις 1 P. ii. 13, Col. i. 15 (see Meyer), and πᾶσα ἡ κτίσις Mk. xvi. 15, Rom. viii. 22, Col. i. 23 [*Rec.*].[5]

---

article is used for *the Mosaic law*), see Middleton p. 303 sq., Lightfoot on G. ii. 19, iv. 5, Ph. iii. 5, *Rev. of N. T.* p. 99, Vaughan on Rom. ii. 13; and Dr. Gifford's full discussion in *Speaker's Comm.* Vol. III. pp. 41-48.]

[1] [In ver. 42 both words have the article.]
[2] [Ἐκ τῶν ν. is a variant in some other passages, but is strongly supported in 1 Th. i. 10, and well in Col. ii. 12.]
[3] The distinction made by Van Hengel (*on* 1 *Cor.* xv. p. 135) between νεκροί and οἱ ν. has no foundation either in principle or in usage.
[4] ["This remark needs considerable limitation: e.g., in Thucydides the article is much more frequently inserted than omitted." A. Buttm. p. 89.]
[5] [See Ellicott and Lightfoot on Col. i. 15.]

ὥρα: as 1 Jo. ii. 18, ἐσχάτη ὥρα ἐστί; especially with numerals, as ἦν ὥρα τρίτη Mk. xv. 25, Jo. xix. 14, περὶ τρίτην ὥραν Mt. xx. 3, A. x. 9, ἕως ὥρας ἐννάτης Mk. xv. 33, ἀπὸ ἕκτης ὥρας Mt. xxvii. 45, etc.; compare Diod. S. 4. 15, Held, Plut. *Æm. P.* p. 229. (So also in a different sense, ὥρα χειμέριος Ælian 7. 13, ὥρα λούτρου Polyæn. 6. 7.) The article is however omitted with other words when they have an ordinal numeral joined with them; as πρώτη φυλακή Heliod. 1. 6, Polyæn. 2. 35 (comp. Ellendt, Arr. *Al.* I. 152), and ἀπὸ πρώτης ἡμέρας Ph. i. 5 [*Rec.*].

καιρός: in the phrases πρὸ καιροῦ *before the time*, Mt. viii. 29, 1 C. iv. 5, κατὰ καιρόν Rom. v. 6 (Lucian, *Philops.* 21), and ἐν καιρῷ L. xx. 10[1] (Xen. *Cyr.* 8. 5. 5, Polyb. 2. 45, 9. 12, al.); also ἐν καιρῷ ἐσχάτῳ 1 P. i. 5, like ἐν ἐσχάταις ἡμέραις 2 Tim. iii. 1, Ja. v. 3.

ἀρχή:[2] especially in the common phrases ἀπ' ἀρχῆς Mt. xix. 8, A. xxvi. 4, 2 Th. ii. 13, 1 Jo. i. 1, ii. 7, al. (Her. 2. 113, Xen. *Cyr.* 5. 4. 12, Ælian 2. 4), ἐξ ἀρχῆς Jo. vi. 64, xvi. 4 (Theophr. *Ch.* 28, Lucian, *Dial. Mort.* 19. 2, *Merc. Cond.* 1), and ἐν ἀρχῇ Jo. i. 2, A. xi. 15 (Plat. *Phædr.* 245 d, Lucian, *Gall.* 7). The same is of regular occurrence in the LXX.

κύριος—which in the Gospels is commonly used for *God* (the *Lord* of the O. T.[3]), but which in the Epistles (especially those of Paul) most frequently denotes *Christ*, the *Lord* (Ph. ii. 11, comp. 1 C. xv. 24 sqq., Krehl, *N. T. Wörterb.* p. 360), in accordance with the progress of Christian phraseology—is, like θεός, often used without the article. This is the case particularly where κύριος is governed by a preposition (especially in frequently recurring phrases, such as ἐν κυρίῳ), or when it is in the genitive case (1 C. vii. 22, 25, x. 21, xvi. 10, 2 C. iii. 18, xii. 1), or when it precedes Ἰησοῦς Χριστός, as in Rom. i. 7, 1 C. i. 3, G. i. 3, E. vi. 23, Ph. ii. 11,[4] iii. 20: the word had already become almost a proper name. It has been erroneously maintained[5] that the meaning of κύριος depends on the insertion or omission of the article: it was to Christ, the Lord, whom all knew as Lord, and who so often received this appellation, that the Apostles could most easily give the name κύριος, just as θεός is nowhere more frequently anarthrous than in the Bible.[6] Still the use of the article with κύριος is more common than its omission, even in Paul.

διάβολος (*the devil*) usually has the article: 1 P. v. 8, ὁ ἀντί-

---

[1] [The best reading is καιρῷ, without ἐν.]
[2] Schæf. *Demosth.* III. 240.
[3] Compare Thilo, *Apocr.* I. 169.
[4] [Ph. ii. 11 has no place in this list: κύριος is the predicate.]
[5] By Gabler in his *Neuest. Theol. Journ.* IV. pp. 11-24.
[6] Compare my *Progr. de sensu vocum κύριος et ὁ κύριος in Actis et Epist. Apostolor.* (Erlang. 1828).

δικος ὑμῶν διάβολος (where this word is in apposition), and A. xiii. 10, υἱὲ διαβόλου,[1] are the only exceptions.[2] That in titles and superscriptions appellatives (especially when in the nominative case) dispense with the article, may be easily explained: compare Mt. i. 1, βίβλος γενέσεως Ἰησοῦ Χριστοῦ· Mk. i. 1, ἀρχὴ τοῦ εὐαγγελίου· Rev. i. 1, ἀποκάλυψις Ἰησοῦ Χριστοῦ.

2. (b) The article is often omitted with a noun that is followed by a genitive which indicates the singly existing object as belonging[3] to this individual.[4] Thus[5] Mt. xvii. 6, ἔπεσον ἐπὶ πρόςωπον αὐτῶν· comp. xxvi. 39 (Is. xlix. 23, ἐπὶ πρόςωπον τῆς γῆς; contrast Mt. xxvi. 67, εἰς τὸ πρόςωπον αὐτοῦ· Rev. vii. 11), L. i. 51, ἐν βραχίονι αὐτοῦ· Rom. i. 1, εἰς εὐαγγέλιον θεοῦ (where Rückert still raises needless difficulties), E. i. 20, ἐν δεξιᾷ αὐτοῦ (H. i. 3, Mt. xx. 21), L. xix. 42, ἐκρύβη ἀπὸ ὀφθαλμῶν σου· 1 C. ii. 16, τίς γὰρ ἔγνω νοῦν κυρίου;[6] 1 P. iii.

---

[1] [Compare Rev. xii. 9, ὁ καλούμενος διάβολος καὶ ὁ σατανᾶς· and xx. 2, ὅς ἐστι διάβολος καὶ ὁ σατανᾶς (the most probable reading). Σατανᾶς always has the article, except in Mk. iii. 23, L. xxii. 3.]

[2] Ἄγγελος does not belong to this class of words. When it is used without the article, the singular always signifies *an angel* (one of the many), and the plural ἄγγελοι, *angels*, e. g. in 1 Tim. iii. 16, G. iii. 19, al.: on the other hand, οἱ ἄγγελοι denotes *the angels*, as an order of beings. Hence 1 C. vi. 3, ὅτι ἀγγέλους κρινοῦμεν, must be rendered, *that we shall judge angels*,—not *the angels*, the whole community of angels, but all angels for whom the κρίσις is reserved. On υἱοθεσία Rom. viii. 23, see Fritz. against Rückert. That the word in apposition sometimes has the article, when the principal noun is anarthrous, has been remarked by Geel (Dio Chr. *Olymp.* p. 70).

[3] Thus in Jo. v. 1, ἑορτὴ τῶν Ἰουδαίων could not be rendered *the feast of the Jews* (the Passover): there is however much authority for the article, and Tisch. has received it into the text. [Tisch. received ἡ in his 2d edition, and again in ed. 8. By most editors (and by Tisch. in ed. 7) the article is rejected: see Alf. *in loc.*, Ellicott, *Hist. L.* p. 136.]

[4] Schæf. Soph. *Œd. C.* 1468, Bornem. Xen. *Cyr.* p. 219, Schoem. *Isæus* p. 421, and Plut. *Agis* p. 105, Engelhardt, Plat. *Menex.* p. 277, Herm. Luc. *Conscr. Hist.* p. 290.—In Hebrew, as is well known, the governing noun has no article in this construction. On this Hengstenberg (*Christol.* II. 565) founded a new discovery, which Lücke (on Jo. v. 1) has estimated as it deserves. [In his 2d edition Hengst. omitted the observations to which Winer here refers.]

[5] [Take Ja. i. 26, καρδίαν ἑαυτοῦ, as an example. Καρδία denotes an object which exists singly in the case of any particular individual: the genitive ἑαυτοῦ points out this individual; hence καρδία ἑαυτοῦ is (Winer maintains) as definite as a proper name, and may therefore dispense with the article.]

[6] [The above rule is more questionable than any other given by Winer; certainly none of his rules differ so widely as this from those which apply to classical Greek. In some of the examples which he quotes from the N. T. (as L. xix. 13, 1 Th. v. 8, al.) most will admit that the governing noun is really indefinite in meaning. If we analyse the remainder (to which Lünemann adds Mt. xvi. 18, πύλαι ᾅδου) we shall find that they are represented by the following types: (1) ἀπὸ προςώπου τοῦ κυρίου (2 Th. i. 9); (2) ἐστὶν ἀπαρχὴ τῆς Ἀχαίας (1 C. xvi. 15); (3) νοῦν κυρίου (1 C. ii. 16); (4) καρδίαν ἑαυτοῦ (Ja. i. 26). The

12, 20, Ja. i. 26, Mk. viii. 3, xiii. 27, Rom. i. 20, ii. 5, L. i. 5, ii. 4, 11, xiii. 19, xix. 13, H. xii. 2, 1 C. x. 21, xii. 27, xvi. 15, Ph. ii. 16, iv. 3, E. i. 4, 6, 12, iv. 30, 1 Th. v. 8, 2 Th. i. 9, 2 Th. ii. 2,[1] 2 P. ii. 6, iii. 10, Jude 6 (A. viii. 5), al. This is a very common usage in the LXX: 1 S. i. 3, 7, iv. 6, v. 2, Ex. iii. 11, ix. 22, xvii. 1, Cant. v. 1, viii. 2, Judith ii. 7, 14, iii. 3, 9, iv. 11, v. 8, vi. 20, 1 Macc. ii. 50, v. 66, 3 (1) Esdr. i. 26. But in 1 C. iv. 14, ὡς τέκνα μου ἀγαπητά, the article was necessarily omitted, since the Corinthians were not *the* only beloved children of Paul: in L. xv. 29, οὐδέποτε ἐντολήν σου παρῆλθον, the meaning is *a command of thine*; and A. i. 8, λήψεσθε δύναμιν ἐπελθόντος τοῦ ἁγίου πνεύματος, must be rendered, *Ye shall receive power when the Holy Ghost shall have come down*.[2]

The article is also sometimes omitted when a noun is defined by a numeral: A. xii. 10, διελθόντες πρώτην φυλακὴν καὶ δευτέραν· Mk. xv. 25, ἦν ὥρα τρίτη καὶ ἐσταύρωσαν αὐτόν· xv. 33, ἕως ὥρας ἐννάτης· L. iii. 1, ἐν ἔτει πεντεκαιδεκάτῳ τῆς ἡγεμονίας κ.τ.λ., 2 C. xii. 2, E. vi. 2 (Ph. i. 5 *v.l.*). From Greek authors compare Lysias 7. 10, τρίτῳ ἔτει· Plat. *Min.* 319 c, *Hipp. Maj.* 286 b, Antiph. 6. 42, Andoc. 4. 17, Diog. L. 7. 135, 138, 141 sqq. (contrast 7. 150, 151, 153). See above 1. (*a*), under

---

first of these seems merely an extension of a common usage beyond its ordinary limits. The article is naturally omitted in an adverbial phrase, such as πρὸ προσώπου: the peculiarity in these examples is, as A. Buttmann well remarks (p. 90), that the article is not inserted when a defining genitive limits the general phrase to a particular case. This extension was the more natural as the phrase is often a literal translation of a Hebrew combination which almost plays the part of an ordinary preposition. As to (2), where the article is omitted after ἐστί (Madvig 10. Rem. 2), see above, page 142. In such examples as (3) we may often trace the influence of the principle of "correlation" (see below, § 20. 4, note). In (4), however, we must recognise a peculiarity of the N. T. language—the occasional omission of the article with nouns definite in sense when they are accompanied by the genitive of a personal pronoun (see A. Buttm. p. 119). Madvig's rule (*loc. cit.*), "The governing noun is sometimes anarthrous when the writer wishes to express a notion that in itself is definite, in a general manner," will not apply to many of these examples; and it may perhaps be doubted whether the examples he gives (e. g. ὑπὸ πλήθους τῶν νεῶν, Thuc. 8. 105) and most of those quoted by Winer from classical Greek are not best explained by reference to the nature and meaning of the particular words (as πλῆθος, μέγεθος) by which the genitive is governed: comp. Krüger p. 100.]

[1] [This passage has no place here: in his 4th and 5th editions Winer has "2 Th. ii. 2, ἐν ἡμέρᾳ τοῦ Χριστοῦ." These words however are not found in this verse (ἡ ἡμέρα τοῦ κυρίου), nor does the article appear to be ever omitted with ἡμέρα in this and similar phrases, unless the following word (Χριστοῦ, κυρίου) is also anarthrous.]

[2] Gersdorf (p. 316 sqq.) has not properly distinguished the cases. In L. xxiii. 46, εἰς χεῖράς σου παρατίθεμαι τὸ πνεῦμά μου, the article is both inserted and omitted in the same clause: similarly in other passages.

ὥρα.¹—This usage enables us to justify Mt. xii. 24, ἐν τῷ Βεελζεβούλ, ἄρχοντι τῶν δαιμονίων (the reading of all the MSS.): Fritzsche, who usually finds a difficulty in such omissions of the article, substitutes ἐν Β. τῷ ἄρχ. τ. δ., without any support from the MSS. (*Matt.* p. 774).²

In Greek authors such an omission of the article is by no means rare, especially if the noun is preceded by a preposition: compare Xen. *Cyr.* 6. 1. 13, περὶ καταλύσεως τῆς στρατιᾶς· *Apol. Socr.* 30, ἐν καταλύσει τοῦ βίου· *Mem.* 1. 5. 2, ἐπὶ τελευτῇ τοῦ βίου· 4. 3. 16, Plat. *Phœdr.* 237. c. Lys. *Agorat.* 2, ἐπὶ καταλύσει τοῦ δήμου τοῦ ὑμετέρου· and farther on, πατρίδα σφετέραν αὐτῶν καταλιπόντες· Lucian, *Scyth.* 4, βίον αὐτῶν· Dio. Chr. 38. 471, ὑπὲρ γενέσεως αὐτῆς· Strabo 15. 719, ὑπὸ μήκους τῶν ὁδῶν (17. 808), Thuc. 2. 38, διὰ μέγεθος τῆς πόλεως· 7. 72. In German also the article is commonly omitted in such cases, if a preposition precedes: e.g. *über Auflösung des Räthsels, Stärke des Körpers*, etc. In Greek authors, however, the genitive also frequently loses the article, or the genitive with the article *precedes* the governing noun, as τῶν χωρίων χαλεπότης : see Xen. *Cyr.* 8. 6. 16, *Mem.* 1. 4. 12, Thuc. 1. 1, 6. 34, 8. 68.³

3. (*c*) When the conjunction καί joins together two or more nouns⁴ (denoting different objects⁵) which agree in case and number but differ in gender, the article is, as a rule, repeated with each substantive. This rule holds good not merely when the nouns denote persons (as in A. xiii. 50, τὰς σεβομένας γυναῖκας ... καὶ τοὺς πρώτους τῆς πόλεως· L. xiv. 26, E. vi. 2, A. xxvi. 30), but also when they signify objects without life : as Col. iv. 1, τὸ δίκαιον καὶ τὴν ἰσότητα τοῖς δούλοις παρέχεσθε· Rom. viii. 2, ἀπὸ τοῦ νόμου τῆς ἁμαρτίας καὶ τοῦ θανάτου· Mt. xxii. 4, L. x. 21, Rom. xvi. 17, Ph. iv. 7, 1 C. ii. 4, E. ii. 1, Rev.

---

¹ [Krüg. p. 100, Middleton p. 100, Green p. 42, Ellicott on E. vi. 2, Shilleto, Dem. *F. L.* p. 38. The article is sometimes omitted with superlative expressions, as in 1 P. i. 5 (Krüg. p. 92, Middleton p. 101).]
² [Meyer renders, "by Beelzebul, as ruler over the devils."]
³ Compare Krüg. *Dion. H.* p. 168, Jacobs, *Athen.* p. 18 sq., Poppo, *Thuc.* III. i. 130.
⁴ Benseler (Isocr. *Areop.* p. 290 sqq.) has collected much from Isocrates on the repetition and non-repetition of the article with nouns (substantives, adjectives, participles,—also infinitives) which are thus connected by conjunctions, but does not succeed in presenting the subject very clearly. Compare also Tholuck, *Literar. Anzeig.* 1837. No. 5. [Middleton pp. 56-70, Green pp. 67-75, A. Buttmann p. 97 sqq., Webster, *Gr.* p. 36, Jelf 459. 9.]
⁵ For if the connected nouns are, for instance, only predicates of one and the same person, as in Col. iii. 17 [*Rec.*], τῷ θεῷ καὶ πατρί· 2 P. i. 11, τοῦ κυρίου ἡμῶν καὶ σωτῆρος 'Ι. Χρ., E. vi. 21, Mk. vi. 3, A. iii. 14, the article cannot be repeated. [So even with ἀλλά, 2 Th. ii. 12 (A. Buttm. p. 99); and with δέ L. xii. 48.]

i. 2, xiv. 7, H. iii. 6. Compare Xen. *Cyr.* 2. 2. 9, σὺν τῷ θώρακι κ. τῇ κοπίδι· Plut. *Virt. Mul.* p. 210, διὰ τὸν ἄνδρα κ. τὴν ἀρετήν· Dion. H. IV. 2245. 4, ἐπὶ τοῦ τόκου καὶ τῆς λοχείας· 2117. 17, τὰς ψυχὰς καὶ τὰ ὅπλα· 2089. 14, Diod. S. 1. 50, 51, 86, Philostr. *Her.* 3. 2, Diog. L. 3. 18, 5. 51, Herod. 2. 10. 15, Strabo 3. 163, 15. 712, Plut. *Aud. Poët.* 9. *init.*, *Themist.* 8, Isocr. *Areop.* p. 334, Plat. *Charm.* p. 160 b, Sext. Emp. *adv. Math.* 2. 58.

In these combinations the repetition of the article appeared *grammatically* necessary, but at the same time the nouns joined for the most part express notions which must be apprehended separately; see below, no. 4. When however the notions are not to be sharply distinguished, or when there is joined to the first noun an adjective which belongs to the second also, the article is not repeated (although the nouns differ in gender), the single article belonging to all the nouns in common: Col. ii. 22, τὰ ἐντάλματα καὶ διδασκαλίας τῶν ἀνθρώπων· L. xiv. 23, ἔξελθε εἰς τὰς ὁδοὺς καὶ φραγμούς· i. 6, ἐν πάσαις ταῖς ἐντολαῖς καὶ δικαιώμασι τοῦ κυρίου· Mk. xii. 33, Rev. v. 12. Similar examples are furnished in much greater numbers by Greek authors— both poets (Herm. Eur. *Hec.* p. 76) and prose-writers—without anxious regard to the meaning of the words; e.g. Plat. *Rep.* 9. 586 d, τῇ ἐπιστήμῃ καὶ λόγῳ· *Legg.* 6. 784, ὁ σωφρονῶν καὶ σωφρονοῦσα· 6. 510 c, *Apol.* 18 a, *Crat.* 405 d, Aristot. *Anal. Post.* 1. 26, Thuc. 1. 54, Lycurg. 30, Lucian, *Parasit.* 13, Herod. 8. 6. 11, Æl. *Anim.* 5. 26.[1] When the nouns are separated by ἤ, the article is invariably repeated: Mt. xv. 5, τῷ πατρὶ ἢ τῇ μητρί· Mk. iv. 21, ὑπὸ τὸν μόδιον ἢ ὑπὸ τὴν κλίνην· Rev. xiii. 17.

When the connected nouns do not agree in number, the repetition of the article was natural, and in point of grammar is almost indispensable: as Col. ii. 13, ἐν τοῖς παραπτώμασι καὶ τῇ ἀκροβυστίᾳ· E. ii. 3, τὰ θελήματα τῆς σαρκὸς καὶ τῶν διανοιῶν· 1 Tim. v. 23, Tit. ii. 12, A. xv. 4, 20,[2] xxviii. 17, Mt. v. 17, Rev. ii. 19. Compare Plat. *Crito* 47 c, τὴν δόξαν καὶ τοὺς ἐπαίνους· Dion. H. IV. 2238. 1, ὑπὸ τῆς παρθένου καὶ τῶν περὶ αὐτὴν γυναικῶν; on the other hand, Xen. *An.* 2. 1. 7, ἐπιστήμων τῶν περὶ τὰς τάξεις τε καὶ ὁπλομαχίαν· Agath. 14. 12, τὰς δυνάμεις καὶ πόλεμον.—1 C. iv. 9,

---

[1] Compare also Krüg. *Dion.* p. 140, and Xen. *Anab.* p. 92, Bornem. *Cyr.* p. 668.

[2] [The article before πηκτοῦ should probably be omitted.]

SECT. XIX.] OMISSION OF THE ARTICLE BEFORE NOUNS. 159

θέατρον ἐγενήθημεν τῷ κόσμῳ καὶ ἀγγέλοις καὶ ἀνθρώποις, does not come under this head : the two anarthrous nouns specialise τῷ κόσμῳ, *the world, as well angels as men.*

4. (*d*) If the nouns connected by καί agree in gender, the article is *not* repeated,

(1) If the nouns are regarded only as parts of one whole, or members of one community :[1] Mk. xv. 1, συμβούλιον ποιήσαντες οἱ ἀρχιερεῖς μετὰ τῶν πρεσβυτέρων καὶ γραμματέων (where the elders and scribes, as distinguished from the chief priests, are indicated as a single class of individuals), L. xiv. 3, 21, Col. ii. 8, 19,[2] E. ii. 20, v. 5, Ph. i. 7, ii. 17, A. xxiii. 7, 2 P. i. 10 ; Xen. *An.* 2. 2. 5, 3. 1. 29, Plat. *Phil.* 28 e, Dion. H. IV. 2235. 5, Plut. *Aud. Poët.* 1. *in.*, 12. *in.*

(2) When a genitive or some other attributive belonging to both nouns is inserted between the first noun and its article : 1 Th. ii. 12, εἰς τὴν ἑαυτοῦ βασιλείαν καὶ δόξαν· iii. 7, ἐπὶ πάσῃ τῇ θλίψει καὶ ἀνάγκῃ ἡμῶν· Rom. i. 20, ἥ τε ἀΐδιος αὐτοῦ δύναμις κ. θειότης· Ph. i. 25, E. iii. 5. Compare Dion. H. IV. 2246. 9, τὰς αὐτῶν γυναῖκας καὶ θυγατέρας· 2089. 4, Diod. S. 1. 86, τὴν προειρημένην ἐπιμέλειαν καὶ τιμήν· 2. 18, Æl. *Anim.* 7. 29, Aristot. *Eth. Nicom.* 4. 1. 9, 7. 7. 1.[3] So also when the common genitive follows the second noun, as in Ph. i. 20, κατὰ τὴν ἀποκαραδοκίαν καὶ ἐλπίδα μου· i. 7, ἐν τῇ ἀπολογίᾳ κ. βεβαιώσει τοῦ εὐαγγελίου· 1 P. ii. 25 : on Ph. i. 19 see Meyer.[4] Compare Benseler p. 293 sq.

Under (1) it should be noted, that in a series of nouns which belong to one category the first only has the article : as A. xxi. 25 φυλάσσεσθαι αὐτοὺς . . . . τό[5] αἷμα καὶ πνικτὸν καὶ πορνείαν· E. iii. 18, τί τὸ πλάτος κ. μῆκος κ. βάθος κ. ὕψος· Jo. v. 3, 1 C. v. 10 :

---

[1] Engelhardt, Plat. *Menex.* p. 253, Held, Plut. *Timol.* p. 455.
[2] [The nouns here differ in gender, though the same form of the article suits both.]
[3] In this case we find the article omitted even when the nouns differ in gender: Lysias, *in Andoc.* 17, περὶ τὰ ἀλλότρια ἱερὰ καὶ ἑορτὰς ἠσέβει. Compare above, 3.
[4] [In the edition referred to (the 1st) Meyer regards ὑμῶν as connected with both δεήσεως and ἐπιχορηγίας : in ed. 5 Winer had taken the same view. In Meyer's later editions (1859, 1865) the absence of the article is differently explained, viz. as arising from the manner in which ἐπιχορ. is conceived,— "supply, not *the* supply." Winer gives another explanation below—see 5 (*b*), and with this Ellicott agrees. Alford and A. Buttmann join ἐπιχορ. with ὑμῶν.]
[5] [This article should be omitted, but the passage still illustrates the rule. Jo. v. 3, however, is of a different kind.]

compare Her. 4. 71, θάπτουσι καὶ τὸν οἰνοχόον κ. μάγειρον κ. ἱπποκόμον κ. διήκονον κ. ἀγγελιηφόρον κ.τ.λ., Plat. *Euthyph.* p. 7 c. For examples of proper names thus connected, see A. i. 13, xv. 23.

5. On the other hand, it is usual to repeat the article

(*a*) Where each of the nouns is to be regarded as having an independent existence :[1] 1 C. iii. 8, ὁ φυτεύων καὶ ὁ ποτίζων ἕν εἰσιν· A. xxvi. 30, ἀνέστη ὁ βασιλεὺς καὶ ὁ ἡγεμών κ.τ.λ., Mk. ii. 16 [*Rec.*], οἱ γραμματεῖς καὶ οἱ Φαρισαῖοι (the two distinct classes of Christ's adversaries united together for one object), Jo. xix. 6, οἱ ἀρχιερεῖς καὶ οἱ ὑπηρέται (*the chief priests and the attendants* belonging to them,—with their attendants), ii. 14, xi. 47, Mk. ii. 18, vi. 21, xi. 9, 18, 27, xii. 13, xiii. 17, xiv. 43, L. i. 58, viii. 24, xi. 39, 42, xii. 11, xv. 6, 9,[2] xx. 20, xxi. 23, xxiii. 4, A. iv. 23, vi. 4, 13, xiii. 43, xv. 6, xxiii. 14, xxv. 15, Rom. vi. 19, E. iii. 10, 12 [*Rec.*], 2 C. xiii. 2, Ph. iv. 6, 1 Tim. iv. 6, Ja. iii. 11, 1 Jo. ii. 22, 24, iv. 6, v. 6, Rev. vi. 15, vii. 12, xiii. 10, 16, xxii. 1. Compare Xen. *Athen.* 1. 4, Lys. *Agorat.* 2, adv. *Nicom.* 3, Isocr. *Areop.* p. 352, *Permut.* 736, Diod. S. 1. 30 (διὰ τὴν ἀνυδρίαν καὶ τὴν σπάνιν τῆς ἁπάσης τροφῆς), 3. 48, 5. 29, 17. 52, Plut. *Virt. Mul.* p. 214 (ἔπεμψε τὴν γυναῖκα καὶ τὴν θυγατέρα), Æl. *Anim.* 7. 29, Diog. L. 5. 52,[3] Weber, *Demosth.* p. 395.

This rule holds particularly when the two nouns are connected by τε . . . καί, or καὶ . . . καί, and in this way are still more prominently exhibited as independent :[4] see L. xxiii. 12, A. v. 24, xvii. 10, 14, xviii. 5, Ph. iii. 10 [*Rec.*], H. ix. 2, and compare Æl. *Anim.* 7. 29, Theophr. *Char.* 25 (16), Thuc. 5. 72, Xen. *Cyr.* 7. 5. 41, *Mem.* 1. 1. 4, Aristot. *Pol.* 3. 5, Isocr. *Demon.* pp. 1, 12, *Permut.* 738, Diod. S. 1. 69, 4. 46, Lucian, *Fug.* 4, Arrian, *Ind.* 34. 5, al. Even in this case, however, the article is sometimes omitted in (good MSS. of) Greek authors, where there is no proper anti-

---

[1] Schæf. *Dem.* V. 501, Weber, *Dem.* p. 268.

[2] [Recent editors read τὰς φίλας καὶ γείτονας ; contrast ver. 6.]

[3] We find the article both inserted and omitted before nouns of the same gender in Arrian, *Epict.* 1. 18. 6, τὴν ὄψιν τὴν διακριτικὴν τῶν λευκῶν καὶ μελάνων . . . . τῶν ἀγαθῶν καὶ τῶν κακῶν. The case is somewhat different in A. vi. 9, τινὲς τῶν ἐκ τῆς συναγωγῆς τῆς λεγομένης Λιβερτίνων καὶ Κυρην. καὶ Ἀλεξανδρ., καὶ τῶν ἀπὸ Κιλικίας καὶ Ἀσίας : here two parties are intended, each possessing a common synagogue ; Κυρην. and Ἀλεξ. combined with Λιβερτ. constitute the first, the Jews of Cilicia and Asia the second. [See Meyer, who supposes that *five* synagogues were referred to. See also Alford *in loc.* for a good explanation of the second τῶν.]

[4] Schæf. *Demosth.* III. 255, IV. 68.

SECT. XIX.] OMISSION OF THE ARTICLE BEFORE NOUNS. 161

thesis :[1] compare Xen. *Mem.* 1. 1. 19, τά τε λεγόμενα καὶ πραττόμενα (where there immediately follows, as an antithesis to these two participles, καὶ τὰ σιγῇ βουλευόμενα), Thuc. 5. 37, Plat. *Rep.* 6. 510 c, *Phæd.* 78 b, Dion. H. IV. 2242. 2, Diod. S. 1. 50, 2. 30, Arrian, *Ind.* 5. 1, Dio Chr. 7. 119, Marc. Ant. 5. 1; see also Matth. 268. Rem. 1.

A disjunctive particle obviously requires the repetition of the article : L. xi. 51, μεταξὺ τοῦ θυσιαστηρίου καὶ τοῦ οἴκου· Mt. xxiii. 35, 1 C. xiv. 7, πῶς γνωσθήσεται τὸ αὐλούμενον ἢ τὸ κιθαριζόμενον; Mt. x. 14, xvii. 25, xxiii. 17, 19, Mk. xiii. 32, L. xiii. 15, xxii. 27, Jo. iii. 19, A. xxviii. 17, Rom. iv. 9, 1 C. xiv. 5. Compare Isocr. *Permut.* p. 746.

(*b*) When the first noun is followed by a genitive, and the second is thus annexed to a completed group of words ; as in 1 C. i. 28, τὰ ἀγενῆ τοῦ κόσμου καὶ τὰ ἐξουθενημένα· v. 10. If each of the nouns has its own genitive, they are already sufficiently disjoined, and therefore the repetition of the article is not necessary : Ph. i. 19, διὰ τῆς ὑμῶν δεήσεως καὶ ἐπιχορηγίας τοῦ πνεύματος κ.τ.λ.[2]

Rem. 1. We find various readings in very many passages : e. g. Mt. xxvii. 3, Mk. viii. 31, x. 33, xi. 15, L. xxii. 4, A. xvi. 19, Rom. iv. 2, 11, 19, 1 C. xi. 27, 1 Th. i. 8.
It may not unfrequently be a matter of indifference what particular

---

[1] See Poppo, *Thuc.* I. 196 sq., III. i. 395, Geel on Dio Chr. *Ol.* p. 295.
[2] [It will be useful to compare with the last two sections A. Buttmann's careful classification of examples (pp. 97–101).
1. When the nouns (which agree in gender and number) have no attributives, the article is
(*a*) not repeated, when the nouns may be regarded as parts of one whole, as expressing ideas which are kindred or necessarily connected, or which supplement one another ;
(*b*) repeated, when they represent contrasted or independent notions.
There are, however, many exceptions to (*a*), as the writer without any risk of ambiguity may name the parts for themselves, *as parts:* comp. Mt. xx. 18 with xxi. 15, A. xiii. 43 with xv. 22.
2. (*a*) If any one of the nouns has an attributive which belongs to all, the article is not repeated.
(*b*) if the attributive belongs to this noun only, the article is repeated ;
(*c*) if each noun has its own attributive, the case is substantially the same as (1), and the same rules apply.
As examples of 2. (*a*) he gives Rom. i. 20, Ph. i. 20 : as exceptions, E. iii. 10, 1 C. xi. 27, A. xxv. 15, Rev. xiii. 10. For 2. (*b*) see Mk. vi. 21, 1 C. v. 10, 1 Tim. iv. 6 : Col. ii. 8 is an exception. For 2. (*c*) he quotes 1 Th. iii. 11, —also 2 Th. i. 12, Tit. ii. 13, 2 C. i. 3.
In applying these rules we must always bear in mind that regard for perspicuity will often influence the writer's choice ; and also that the repetition of the article gives emphasis and weight (Green p. 74, Ellicott on E. iii. 10, Tit. iii. 4).]

view shall be taken of the mutual relation of the connected nouns, so that the choice is left entirely to the writer's preference : in 1 Th. i. 7, for instance, we read ἐν τῇ Μακεδον. καὶ ἐν τῇ Ἀχαΐᾳ ; but in ver. 8, καὶ Ἀχαΐᾳ. Hence there are passages in which the reader would not feel the want of the article if it were omitted (e. g. 1 Tim. v. 5[1]), and others in which it might perhaps have been inserted, as E. ii. 20 (see Meyer *in loc.*). See, in general, Engelhardt on Plat. *Menex.* p. 253, Poppo, *Thuc.* III. i. 395.

In Tit. ii. 13, ἐπιφάνεια τῆς δόξης τοῦ μεγάλου θεοῦ καὶ σωτῆρος ἡμῶν Ἰησοῦ Χριστοῦ, considerations derived from Paul's system of doctrine lead me to believe that σωτῆρος is not a second predicate, co-ordinate with θεοῦ,—Christ being first called ὁ μέγας θεός, and then σωτήρ. The article is omitted before σωτῆρος, because this word is defined by the genitive ἡμῶν, and because the apposition *precedes* the proper name : *of the great God and of our Saviour Jesus Christ.*[2] Similarly in 2 P. i. 1, where there is not even a pronoun with σωτῆρος. So also in Jude 4 we might suppose two different subjects to be referred to, for κύριος, being defined by ἡμῶν, does not need the article : κύρ. ἡμῶν Ἰησ. Χρ. is equivalent to Ἰησ. Χρ. ὅς ἐστι κύριος ἡμῶν. (In 2 Th. i. 12 we have simply an instance of κύριος for ὁ κύριος.[3])

---

[1] As the words stand, προςμένει ταῖς δεήσεσι καὶ ταῖς προςευχαῖς, prayer is subdivided into its two kinds : if the article were not repeated, prayer and intercession would be taken together as forming one whole.

[2] In the above remarks it was not my intention to deny that, in point of *grammar*, σωτῆρος ἡμῶν may be regarded as a second predicate, jointly depending on the article τοῦ ; but the dogmatic conviction derived from Paul's writings that this apostle cannot have called Christ *the great God* induced me to show that there is no grammatical obstacle to our taking the clause καὶ σωτ. . . . Χριστοῦ by itself, as referring to a second subject. As the anonymous writer in Tholuck's *Lit. Anz.* (1837, No. 5) has not proved that my explanation of this passage would *require* a second article before σωτῆρος (the parallels adduced are moreover dissimilar, see Fritz. *Rom.* II. 268), and still less that to call Christ ὁ μέγας θεός would harmonise with Paul's view of the relation of Christ to God, I adhere to the opinion expressed above. Any unprejudiced mind will at once perceive that such examples as are adduced in § 19. 2 prove that the article was *not* required with σωτῆρος, and the question whether σωτήρ *is elsewhere* applied to God is nothing to the purpose. It is sufficient that σωτὴρ ἡμῶν, our *Saviour*, is a perfectly definite predicate,—as truly so as "*his face:*" πρόςωπον indeed is applied to many more individuals than σωτήρ is ! The words on p. 38, "If σωτὴρ ἡμῶν were used in the N. T. of one definite individual only, etc.," contain an arbitrary assumption. Matthies has contributed nothing decisive towards the settlement of the dispute. [This passage is very carefully examined by Ellicott and Alford *in loc.* ; and though these writers come to different conclusions (the latter agreeing with Winer, the former rendering the words, "of our great God and Saviour Jesus Christ "), they are entirely agreed as to the admissibility of both renderings in point of *grammar*. See also Green, *Gr.* p. 75, Scholefield, *Hints*, Middleton p. 393 sq.]

[3] ["Granville Sharp's first rule," so often referred to in discussions on these texts, is as follows : "When the copulative καί connects two nouns of the same case (viz. nouns—either substantive, or adjective, or participles—of personal description respecting office, dignity, affinity, or connexion, and attributes, properties or qualities good or ill), if the article ὁ, or any of its cases, precedes the first of the said nouns or participles, and is not repeated before the second noun

Rem. 2. We find a singular omission of the article in L. x. 29, τίς ἐστί μου πλησίον; and ver. 36, τίς τούτων . . . πλησίον δοκεῖ σοι γεγονέναι τοῦ ἐμπ.; here ὁ πλησίον might have been expected (see Markland, Eur. *Suppl.* 110), since πλησίον is also an adverb. Döderlein (*Synon.* I. 59) has adduced a similar example, Æschyl. *Prom.* 938, ἐμοὶ δ᾽ ἔλασσον Ζηνὸς ἢ μηδὲν μέλει, where μηδέν appears to stand for τοῦ μηδέν. In the above passages, however, it would be admissible to take πλησίον as an adverb, *who* (is) *stands near me?* See Bornem. *in loc.*

Section XX.

THE ARTICLE WITH ATTRIBUTIVES.

1. When attributives—consisting of adjectives, genitive cases, or prepositional clauses [1]—are joined to a noun which has the article, they are placed either—

(*a*) Between the article and the noun; as ὁ ἀγαθὸς ἄνθρωπος Mt. xii. 35, τὸ ἐμὸν ὄνομα Mt. xviii. 20, τὸ ἅγιον πνεῦμα, ἡ τοῦ θεοῦ μακροθυμία 1 P. iii. 20, ἡ ἄνω κλῆσις Ph. iii. 14, ἡ ἐν φόβῳ ἁγνὴ ἀναστροφή 1 P. iii. 2, ἡ παρ᾽ ἐμοῦ διαθήκη Rom. xi. 27, ἡ κατ᾽ ἐκλογὴν πρόθεσις Rom. ix. 11, τὸ καινὸν αὐτοῦ μνημεῖον Mt. xxvii. 60; compare 2 P. ii. 7, H. v. 14, vi. 7:—or

(*b*) After the noun,—with or without a second article according to the nature of the attributive.

(*a*) If the attributive consists of an adjective [2] or a prepositional clause, the article is, as a rule, repeated.

---

or participle, the latter always relates to the same person that is expressed or described by the first noun or participle; i. e. it denotes a further description of the first-named person." *Remarks on the uses of the definitive article in the Greek text of the N. T.*, p. 3 (2d ed. 1802). He adduces the following examples: A. xx. 28 (with the reading κυρ. καὶ θεοῦ), E. v. 5, 2 Th. i. 12, 1 Tim. v. 21 *Rec.*, 2 Tim. iv. 1 (*Rec.*, but κυρ. instead of τοῦ κ.), Tit. ii. 13, 2 P. i. 1, Jude 4 *Rec.* "The rule is sound in principle, but, in the case of proper names or quasi-proper names, cannot safely be pressed:" Ellicott in *Aids to Faith*, p. 462. See also Ellicott *in locc.*, Middleton p. 60 sqq., Green, *Gr.* p. 73 sqq.]

[1] Genitives of personal pronouns are joined to the noun without a second article, as ὁ παῖς μου: they blend, so to speak, with the substantive.

[2] Of course this only applies to adjectives which are used as attributives of substantives. In L. xxiii. 45, ἐσχίσθη τὸ καταπέτασμα τοῦ ναοῦ μέσον, the adjective μέσον belongs to the verb, . . . *was rent in the middle:* τὸ μέσον καταπέτ. would have a different meaning. The other adjectives of this kind, defining

(β) If however the attributive is the genitive case of a noun, the repetition of the article is usually restricted to the following cases:—

(aa) When the writer desires to give the adjunct more emphasis or prominence (as in 1 C. i. 18, ὁ λόγος ὁ τοῦ σταυροῦ· Tit. ii. 10, τὴν διδασκαλίαν τὴν τοῦ σωτῆρος ἡμῶν· see Schæf. *Melet.* pp. 8, 72 sq., Matth. 278. Rem. 1) ; [1] and especially when a relation of kindred or affinity is appended for the sake of *distinction,* as in Jo. xix. 25, Μαρία ἡ τοῦ Κλωπᾶ.[2] A. xiii. 22, Δαβὶδ ὁ τοῦ Ἰεσσαί· Mt. iv. 21, x. 2, Mk. iii. 17.

(ββ) When the noun already has its own (personal) genitive, as in Mt. xxvi. 28, τὸ αἷμά μου τὸ τῆς καινῆς διαθήκης ; in this passage, however, the article is not firmly established.[3]

(c) Such attributives—especially if adjectives—are sometimes, though rarely, placed before the noun and its article: as A. xxvi. 24, μεγάλῃ τῇ φωνῇ ἔφη (see above, p. 134), Mt. iv. 23, περιῆγεν ἐν ὅλῃ τῇ Γαλιλαίᾳ.

In case (a), more than one attributive may be inserted between the article and the noun, as ὁ ἅγιος καὶ ἄμωμος ἄνθρωπος: as a rule, the article is not repeated. When however the attributives

---

place or number—ἔσχατος, ὅλος, μόνος, ὀλίγος—appear in the sentence without an article whenever they are not true epithets ; and are placed either

(a) After their noun, as in Mt. xvi. 26, ἐὰν τὸν κόσμον ὅλον κερδήσῃ, *if he should gain the whole world* (the world wholly) ; Mt. x. 30, αἱ τρίχες τ. κεφαλῆς πᾶσαι ἠριθμημέναι εἰσίν (ix. 35, Jo. v. 22, Rev. vi. 12, Plat. *Epin.* 983 a), Mt. xii. 4, οὐκ ἐξὸν ἦν φαγεῖν ... εἰ μὴ τοῖς ἱερεῦσιν μόνοις :—or

(b) Before it, as in Mt. iv. 23, H. ix. 7, μόνος ὁ ἀρχιερεύς Jo. vi. 22.—See Gersdorf p. 371 sqq., though his collection of examples is for the most part uncritical. Comp. Jacob on Lucian, *Al.* p. 51, Krüg. p. 123, Rost p. 425 (Don. p. 462, Jelf 459).

[1] Stallb. Plat. *Gorg.* p. 55, Madvig 9. This construction however gradually lost its force, and with many writers,—Demosthenes, Isocrates, Xenophon Ephes., in particular,—it is almost a rule to insert the article before such a genitive, even when no emphasis is intended. The orators may have had reasons for doing this in *spoken* discourses. Compare Siebelis, *Pausan.* I. 17.

[2] The proper meaning of this phrase is : among the women whose name is Mary the (particular Mary) of Clopas,—the wife of Clopas.—The article is not introduced if the writer, in appending the genitive, does not aim at any precise distinction : L. vi. 16, Ἰούδαν Ἰακώβου· A. i. 13, Ἰάκωβος Ἀλφαίου· just as in Her. 1. 59, Λυκοῦργος Ἀριστολαΐδεω· and Dion. H. *Comp.* 1, Διονυσίου Ἀλεξάνδρου (though in both places Schæfer would insert the article), or in Aristot. *Polit.* 2. 6, Ἱππόδαμος Εὐρυφῶντος· and Thuc. 1. 24, Φάλιος Ἐρατοκλείδου (Poppo, *Thuc.* I. 195), Thilo, *Act. Thom.* p. 3: comp. Herm. *Vig.* p. 701. In L. xxiv. 10, however, we must certainly read Μαρία ἡ Ἰακώβου, with the best MSS. See further Fritz. *Mark,* p. 696 sq. Such a collocation of words as τῆς Φορωνέως Νιόβης (Pausan. 2. 22. 6) is not found in the N. T.

[3] [It is omitted by recent editors.]

consist of genitives or prepositional adjuncts, the article may be repeated; as in L. i. 70, διὰ στόματος τῶν ἁγίων τῶν ἀπ' αἰῶνος προφητῶν[1] 1 P. iv. 14, τὸ τῆς δόξης καὶ τὸ τοῦ θεοῦ πνεῦμα, that is, *the Spirit of glory and* (therefore) *the Spirit of God,*—the Spirit of glory, who is no other than the Spirit of God Himself. Of a similar kind are Thuc. 1. 126, ἐν τῇ τοῦ Διὸς τῇ μεγίστῃ ἑορτῇ· Plat. *Rep.* 8. 565 d, περὶ τὸ ἐν Ἀρκαδίᾳ τὸ τοῦ Διὸς ἱερόν; except that in these examples καί is wanting (Jelf 459. 5).—In case (*b*) also there is nothing to prevent an accumulation of adjuncts: see H. xi. 12, ἡ ἄμμος ἡ παρὰ τὸ χεῖλος τῆς θαλάσσης, ἡ ἀναρίθμητος· Rev. ii. 12, τὴν ῥομφαίαν τὴν δίστομον τὴν ὀξεῖαν (Krüg. p. 119): when however the attributives are not connected by καί (§ 19. 4), the article must be repeated.[2]

The first of the cases mentioned under (*b*),—that of adjectives and prepositional clauses placed after the noun which they qualify,—requires further explanation and illustration by examples.

a. Adjectives and possessive pronouns (with the article) following their noun:—

(1) For the simple case see Jo. x. 11, ὁ ποιμὴν ὁ καλός· A. xii. 10, ἐπὶ τὴν πύλην τὴν σιδηρᾶν· Jo. vii. 6, ὁ καιρὸς ὁ ἐμός· i. 9, iv. 11, xv. 1, L. ii. 17, iii. 22, viii. 8, A. xix. 16, E. vi. 13, Col. i. 21, 2 Tim. iv. 7 [*Rec.*], 1 C. vii. 14, xii. 2, 31, 1 Jo. i. 3, Ja. i. 9, iii. 7. In some of these instances the writer appends the adjective for the sake of adding some closer specification (comp. especially Ja. iii. 7); in others, that he may give to the adjective more emphatic prominence (Bornemann, *Luc.* p. xxxvi, Madvig 9 [3]).

(2) We also find this arrangement chosen when the noun is already qualified by a genitive or some other attributive: Mt. iii. 17, ὁ υἱός μου ὁ ἀγαπητός· 2 C. vi. 7, διὰ τῶν ὅπλων τῆς δικαιοσύνης τῶν δεξιῶν καὶ ἀριστερῶν· Jo. vi. 13, τῶν πέντε ἄρτων τῶν κριθίνων· Mt. vi. 6, L. vii. 47, Tit. ii. 11 [*Rec.*], H. xiii. 20, al. The N. T. writers usually avoid such a combination

---

[1] [The second article is omitted in the best texts. (Jelf 459. 5).]
[2] A rare reiteration of the article, in full accordance with the above rules, is found in Rev. xxi. 9, ἦλθεν εἷς ἐκ τῶν ἑπτὰ ἀγγέλων τῶν ἐχόντων τὰς ἑπτὰ φιάλας (τὰς) γεμούσας (τῶν) ἑπτὰ πληγῶν τῶν ἐσχάτων.
[3] [Jelf 458. 2, Green p. 33.]

as τὸν μονογ. θεοῦ υἱόν, as more intricate; compare Jo. iii. 16 [*Rec.*], 1 Jo. iv. 9.

In 1 Jo. v. 20 *Rec.*, ἡ ζωὴ αἰώνιος, the adjective is appended without a second article; but the better MSS. omit the article before ζωή. No exception could however be taken to the common reading in itself, for the later writers begin to omit the article in such cases (Bernh. p. 323),[1] though the examples adduced from Long. *Past.* 1. 16, Heliod. 7. 5, Diod. S. 5. 40, are not exactly parallel with the passage of which we are speaking. Besides, ζωὴ αἰώνιος had already come to be regarded as a single notion: comp. Jo. iv. 36. In L. xii. 12, Griesbach and Schott read τὸ γὰρ πνεῦμα ἅγιον; but Knapp and all recent editors, τὸ γὰρ ἅγιον πνεῦμα, without noting any variant. In 1 C. x. 3 [*Rec.*], τὸ βρῶμα πνευματικόν, and G. i. 4,[2] ὁ αἰὼν πονηρός, we must look upon the adjective and substantive as coalescing to express one main idea, and αὐτό and ἐνεστ. are (as often) inserted as epithets between the article and the noun: compare 1 P. i. 18.[3] See also H. ix. 1, τὸ ἅγιον κοσμικόν.[4] With Jo. v. 36, ἐγὼ ἔχω τὴν μαρτυρίαν μείζω τοῦ Ἰωάννου,—in which μείζω is the predicate, "*the* testimony which I have is greater than, etc." (Rost p. 425, Don. p. 528 sq.),—may be compared Isocr. *Philipp.* c. 56, τὸ σῶμα θνητὸν ἅπαντες ἔχομεν. See further Schæf. *Plut.* V. 30.

b. The following are examples of attributive prepositional

---

[1] The earlier writers did the same in certain cases, according to good MSS.: compare Schneider, Plat. *Civ.* II. 319, and Krüger in *Jahns Jahrb.* 1838. I. 61.

[2] [In 1 C. x. 3, πνευματικόν should probably precede βρῶμα: in G. i. 4, Lachm., Alford, Lightfoot, Westcott and Hort, read ἐκ τοῦ αἰῶνος τοῦ ἐνεστῶτος πονηροῦ.]

[3] [1 C. x. 3 *Rec.*, G. i. 4 *Rec.*, 1 P. i. 18, fall directly under a rule thus given by Krüger (p. 121): "When an attributive is inserted between the article and the noun, a second attributive sometimes follows the noun without a second article:" similarly Madvig 10. Rem. 6, A. Buttm. p. 91, Jelf 459. 3, Green p. 59 (who adds E. ii. 11, Rom. ix. 5, A. xiii. 32): see also Rost p. 426, Riddell, Plat. *Apol.* p. 128. Donaldson (p. 369 sqq.) seems to regard such examples as instances of apposition: see also Ellicott on G. i. 4.]

[4] [This is a different case, since there is only one attributive. As the ordinary rule is so carefully observed by the N. T. writers,—St. John, for instance, uses ζωὴ αἰώνιος (in this order and without article) 20 times, but whenever the article comes in we find either ἡ αἰ. ζ. (Jo. xvii. 3), or ἡ ζ. ἡ αἰ. (1 Jo. i. 2, ii. 25), see A. Buttm. p. 91—it is far preferable to consider κοσμικόν as an apposition, or even as a substantive (Middl. p. 414, Green p. 53), than to render, "*the worldly sanctuary.*" The word, however, is best taken as predicative (comp. Delitzsch *in loc.*). In Jo. xii. 9 Tisch. and Westcott and Hort read ὁ ὄχλος πολύς: this is a simpler case, since the two words easily coalesce to express one idea.]

clauses with the article: 1 Th. i. 8, ἡ πίστις ὑμῶν ἡ πρὸς τὸν θεόν· 2 C. viii. 4, τῆς διακονίας τῆς εἰς τοὺς ἁγίους· Ja. i. 1, ταῖς φυλαῖς ταῖς ἐν τῇ διασπορᾷ· A. xv. 23, τοῖς κατὰ τὴν Ἀντιόχειαν . . . . ἀδελφοῖς, τοῖς ἐξ ἐθνῶν· xxiv. 5, πᾶσι τοῖς Ἰουδαίοις τοῖς κατὰ τὴν οἰκουμένην· iii. 16, iv. 2, viii. 1, xi. 22 [*Rec.*], xxvi. 4, 12, 22,[1] xxvii. 5, Mk. iv. 31, xiii. 25, Jo. i. 46, L. xx. 35, Rom. iv. 11, vii. 5, 10, viii. 39, x. 5, xiv. 19, xv. 26, 31, xvi. 1, 1 C. ii. 11 sq., iv. 17, xvi. 1, 2 C. ii. 6, vii. 12, ix. 1, xi. 3, Ph. i. 11, iii. 9, 1 Th. ii. 1, iv. 10, 1 Tim. i. 14, 2 Tim. ii. 1, E. i. 15, Rev. xiv. 17, xvi. 12, xix. 14, xx. 13. (There are variants in A. xx. 21, L. v. 7, Jo. xix. 38, Rom. x. 1.) Every page of Greek prose furnishes illustrations of this usage: examples from Arrian are given by Ellendt (Arr. *Al.* I. 62). This mode of attaching such attributives to the substantive (by which, strictly speaking, that which defines the noun is brought in afterwards as a supplement) is, from its greater simplicity, much more common in the N.T. than the insertion of the prepositional clause between the article and the noun.—That the LXX regularly insert the article in this case, a very slight examination will show.

c. Participles, as attributives, do not here stand on exactly the same footing as adjectives, inasmuch as they have not entirely laid aside the notion of time. They receive the article only where reference is made to some relation which is already known, or which is especially worthy of remark (*is qui, quippe qui*), and where consequently the participial notion is to be brought into greater prominence:[2] 1 P. v. 10, ὁ θεὸς . . . . ὁ καλέσας ἡμᾶς εἰς τὴν αἰώνιον αὐτοῦ δόξαν . . . . ὀλίγον παθόντας, αὐτὸς καταρτίσαι, *God . . . . He who called us unto His eternal glory, after we should have suffered a while*, etc.; E. i. 12, εἰς τὸ εἶναι ἡμᾶς εἰς ἔπαινον . . . . τοὺς προηλπικότας ἐν τῷ Χρ., *we, those who* (*quippe qui*) *have hoped* (as those who have hoped); compare ver. 19, H. iv. 3, vi. 18, Rom. viii. 4, 1 C. viii. 10, Jo. i. 12, 1 Jo. v. 13, 1 Th. i. 10, iv. 5, 1 P. i. 3, iii. 5, Ja. iii. 6, A. xxi. 38. Compare Dion. H. III. 1922, Polyb. 3. 45. 2, 3. 48. 6, Lucian *Dial. M.* 11. 1, al.

---

[1] [In A. xxvi. 4 the article is not certain; in ver. 12 we must omit παρά; ver. 4 is quoted below as an example of the *omission* of the article. In ver. 22 the main noun is anarthrous.]
[2] [Compare Ellicott on E. i. 12, 2 Tim. i. 10, Don. *Gr.* p. 532, *New Crat.* p. 521, Jelf 451, 695 sqq.; and see below, § 45. 2.]

On the other hand, the participle is without the article in A. xxiii. 27, τὸν ἄνδρα τοῦτον συλληφθέντα ὑπὸ τῶν Ἰουδαίων, *hunc virum comprehensum*, who has been apprehended, after he had been apprehended ; 2 C. xi. 9, ὑστέρημά μου προςανεπλήρωσαν οἱ ἀδελφοὶ ἐλθόντες ἀπὸ Μακεδονίας, *the brethren when they had come;* A. iii. 26, ἀναστήσας ὁ θεὸς τὸν παῖδα αὐτοῦ ἀπέστειλεν αὐτόν κ.τ.λ., *God, raising up*[1] *his Son, sent him*, etc. (contrast H. xiii. 20); Rom. ii. 27, κρινεῖ ἡ ἐκ φύσεως ἀκροβυστία τὸν νόμον τελοῦσα σέ κ.τ.λ., *if it fulfil*, or *by fulfilling :* compare L. xvi. 14, Jo. iv. 6, 39, 45, 1 C. i. 7, xiv. 7, 2 C. iii. 2, H. x. 2, xii. 23, 1 P. i. 12 (Fritz. *Matt.* p. 432, Stallb. Plat. *Apol.* p. 14). So also in A. xxi. 8, εἰς τὸν οἶκον Φιλίππου τοῦ εὐαγγελιστοῦ, ὄντος ἐκ τῶν ἑπτά, the correct translation is *qui erat,—as one of the seven ;* τοῦ ὄντος, the reading of several [cursive] MSS., gives a false emphasis to the clause : Rom. xvi. 1 is a similar instance. Compare Demosth. *Con.* 728 c, Εὐξίθεον τουτονὶ ὄνθ' ἡμῖν συγγενῆ· Diod. S. 17. 38, ὁ παῖς ὢν ἐξ ἐτῶν 3. 23, τὸν πίπτοντα καρπὸν ὄντα καλόν· Philostr. *Apoll.* 7. 16, ἐν τῇ νήσῳ ἀνύδρῳ οὔσῃ πρέτερον· Thuc. 4. 3, 8. 90, Demosth. *Polycl.* 710 b, Isocr. *Trap.* 870, Lucian, *Hermot.* 81, *Dial. M.* 10. 9, Alciphr. 3. 18, Strabo 3. 164, Long. 2. 2, Philostr. *Her.* 3. 4, *Sophist.* 1. 23. 1.

In E. vi. 16, τὰ βέλη τὰ πεπυρωμένα, the second τά is of doubtful authority : if we omit it (with Lachm.) the words must be rendered, *the darts, when* or *though they are fiery* (quench Satan's darts burning). In 2 Jo. 7 ἐρχόμενον belongs to the predicate. In G. iii. 1, Ἰησοῦς Χρ. προεγράφη ἐν ὑμῖν ἐσταυρωμένος, we must translate, *Jesus Christ as crucified*, compare 1 C. i. 23 ; it is otherwise in Mt. xxviii. 5.

The passage first quoted, 1 P. v. 10, ὁ θεός, ὁ καλέσας ἡμᾶς . . . . ὀλίγον παθόντας· is an instructive illustration of the use of the participle with and without the article. Sometimes the insertion or omission of the article with the participle depends entirely on the aspect under which the writer chooses to regard the subject. Thus in Rom. viii. 1, τοῖς ἐν Χρ. Ἰησοῦ, μὴ κατὰ σάρκα περιπατοῦσιν κ.τ.λ. (with a comma after Ἰησοῦ), would be, *to those who are in Christ, since they walk not according to the flesh:* τοῖς μὴ κ. σ. περ. would give greater prominence to the apposition,—*to those who are in Christ, as men who* etc., *to them, who* etc. : compare Matth. 271. Rem. But the whole clause μὴ . . . . πνεῦμα is certainly not genuine.

---

[1] [This English expression is ambiguous. The word used by Winer does not signify "raising *from the dead :*" he takes ἀναστήσας in the same sense as ἀναστήσει, ver. 22.]

When a participle with the article is placed in apposition to a noun, or used as a vocative (as if in apposition to σύ), it sometimes expresses derision or indignation, or gives prominence to some property which is pointed at with derision or indignation. Commentators on Greek authors have often attributed a derisive force to the article itself,[1] but this force lies only in the *thought* and the special prominence with which it is expressed; in speaking, it would also be indicated by the voice. From the N. T. may be adduced Rom. ii. 1, τὰ γὰρ αὐτὰ πράσσεις ὁ κρίνων· Mt. xxvii. 40, ὁ καταλύων τὸν ναόν . . . κατάβηθι ἀπὸ τοῦ σταυροῦ. See Herm. Eur. *Alc.* 708, Matth. 276.

2. To the general rule explained above [p. 167. b.] there are certain undoubted, indeed almost established exceptions. In these a prepositional clause which with the noun it qualifies expresses in the main *one* idea is to be connected with this noun by the voice alone, the grammatical sign of union (the article) being absent:[2] Col. i. 8, δηλώσας ἡμῖν τὴν ὑμῶν ἀγάπην ἐν πνεύματι, *your love in the Spirit* (see Huther); 1 C. x. 18, βλέπετε τὸν Ἰσραὴλ κατὰ σάρκα (the opposite of Ἰσρ. κατὰ πνεῦμα); 2 C. vii. 7, τὸν ὑμῶν ζῆλον ὑπὲρ ἐμοῦ· E. ii. 11. These exceptions are found chiefly—

(*a*) In the oft-recurring apostolic (Pauline) phrases ἐν Χριστῷ Ἰησοῦ, ἐν κυρίῳ, κατὰ σάρκα: as Col. i. 4 [*Rec.*], ἀκούσαντες τὴν πίστιν ὑμῶν ἐν Χρ. Ἰ. καὶ τὴν ἀγάπην τὴν εἰς πάντας τοὺς ἁγίους· E. i. 15, ἀκούσας τὴν καθ᾽ ὑμᾶς πίστιν ἐν τῷ κυρίῳ Ἰ. καὶ τὴν ἀγάπην τὴν εἰς πάντας τοὺς ἁγίους· Rom. ix. 3, τῶν συγγενῶν μου κατὰ σάρκα· 1 Th. iv. 16, οἱ νεκροὶ ἐν Χριστῷ ἀναστήσονται πρῶτον, *the dead in Christ* (1 C. xv. 18), the antithesis to which is ἡμεῖς οἱ ζῶντες (ver. 17), for these are ζῶντες ἐν Χριστῷ (of the resurrection of those who are not Christians Paul has here no occasion to speak); Ph. iii. 14, E. iv. 1 (here ἐν κυρίῳ would have been placed after ὑμᾶς if Paul had intended that it should be joined with παρακαλῶ, and moreover it is δέσμιος ἐν κυρίῳ which gives the true emphasis to the exhortation which follows), ii. 21, vi. 21. Not unlike these examples

---

[1] "Articulus irrisioni inservit," Valcken. Eur. *Phœn.* 1637: Markland, Eur. *Suppl.* 110, Stallb. Plat. *Euthyphr.* p. 12, *Apol.* p. 70.
[2] [Several of the instances quoted in this section are examples of the rule given on p. 166, note 3, the prepositional clause being connected with a noun which already has an attributive (prefixed or subjoined): comp. Thuc. 1. 18, μετὰ τὴν τῶν τυράννων κατάλυσιν ἐκ τῆς Ἑλλάδος. See Krüg. p. 121, A. Buttm. p. 91.]

are 1 Th. i. 1, 2 Th. i. 1, τῇ ἐκκλησ. Θεσσαλον. ἐν θεῷ πατρὶ καὶ κυρίῳ κ.τ.λ.: in 1 Tim. vi. 17, also, the words τοῖς πλουσίοις ἐν τῷ νῦν αἰῶνι must be connected together.[1] Compare further A. xxvi. 4, Rom. xvi. 3, 8, 10, E. ii. 15, Ph. i. 1.

(b) When the verb from which the substantive is derived is construed with a particular preposition, or when the appended clause forms the natural complement to the meaning of the substantive[2] (Held, Plut. *Timol.* p. 419, Krüg. p. 121): E. iii. 4, δύνασθε νοῆσαι τὴν σύνεσίν μου ἐν τῷ μυστηρίῳ (Jos. i. 7, 2 Chr. xxxiv. 12, 1 Esdr. i. 31), compare Dan. i. 4, συνιέντες ἐν πάσῃ σοφίᾳ; Rom. vi. 4, συνετάφημεν αὐτῷ διὰ τοῦ βαπτίσματος εἰς τὸν θάνατον (ver. 3, ἐβαπτίσθημεν εἰς τὸν θάνατον αὐτοῦ); Ph. i. 26, διὰ τῆς ἐμῆς παρουσίας πάλιν πρὸς ὑμᾶς·[3] 2 C. ix. 13, ἁπλότητι τῆς κοινωνίας εἰς αὐτοὺς καὶ εἰς πάντας· Col. i. 12 (Job xxx. 19), comp. Bähr *in loc.;* E. iii. 13, ἐν ταῖς θλίψεσι μου ὑπὲρ ὑμῶν (compare ver. 1); 2 C. i. 6 [?], Col. i. 24. So also Polyb. 3. 48. 11, τὴν τῶν ὄχλων ἀλλοτριότητα πρὸς Ῥωμαίους· Diod. S. 17. 10, τῆς Ἀλεξάνδρου παρουσίας ἐπὶ τὰς Θήβας· Her. 5. 108, ἡ ἀγγελία περὶ τῶν Σαρδίων· Thuc. 5. 20, ἡ ἐσβολὴ ἐς τὴν Ἀττικήν· 2. 52, ἡ συγκομιδὴ ἐκ τῶν ἀγρῶν ἐς τὸ ἄστυ· 1. 18, Plutarch, *Coriol.* 24, ἡ τῶν πατρικίων δυσμένεια πρὸς τὸν δῆμον· *Pomp.* 58, αἱ παρακλήσεις ὑπὲρ Καίσαρος. In the LXX compare Ex. xvi. 7, τὸν γογγυσμὸν ὑμῶν ἐπὶ τῷ θεῷ, which Thiersch considered *pœne vitiosum!*

The case (a) is probably to be referred to the spoken language, which, possessing the living medium of the voice, would hardly insert the article in every case; whilst the written language, in the interests of precision, could less easily dispense with it. Yet even for this case some parallel examples might be quoted from Greek writers: compare Polyb. 5. 64. 6, διὰ τὴν τοῦ πατρὸς δόξαν ἐκ

---

[1] In the O. T. quotation which occurs in Rom. i. 17 and G. iii. 11, Paul probably connected ἐκ πίστεως with ὁ δίκαιος. In the first passage he adduces the words of the prophet to establish the proposition δικαιοσύνη θεοῦ ἐκ πίστεως κ.τ.λ., not ἡ ζωὴ ἐκ δικαιοσύνης: compare Rom. x. 6, ἡ ἐκ πίστεως δικαιοσύνη. In H. x. 38, however, ἐκ πίστεως certainly belongs to ζήσεται; see Bleek. [In favour of connecting ἐκ π. with ζήσεται in Rom. i. 17, Gal. iii. 11 (Ewald, De Wette, al.) see the notes of Wieseler and Ellicott on the latter passage; see also Delitzsch *on Habakkuk* p. 50 sqq.]

[2] ["Liegt in der Tendenz des Subst."—See Ellicott on E. i. 15.]

[3] Hence in Rom. v. 2 the absence of the article before εἰς τὴν χάριν ταύτην would be no obstacle to our connecting this clause with τῇ πίστει (which words, however, are omitted by Lachm. and Tisch.); but there are other difficulties. [Tisch. retains the words in his last edition.]

τῆς ἀθλήσεως· Sext. Emp. *Hypot.* 3. 26, ζητοῦμεν περὶ τοῦ τόπου πρὸς ἀκρίβειαν (for τοῦ πρὸς ἀκρ., as is clear from what precedes), Thuc. 6. 55, ὡς ὅ τε βωμὸς σημαίνει καὶ ἡ στήλη περὶ τῆς τῶν τυράννων ἀδικίας (where Bekker from conjecture inserts ἡ before περί): compare Krüg. *Dion.* p. 153, Poppo, *Thuc.* III. i. 234.

We must however be cautious in dealing with particular passages:[1] several which might at first seem to come under this head, a closer examination will show to be of a different kind; comp. Ellendt, Arr. *Al.* I. 315.

(*a*) Sometimes there may have been a slight transposition of the words. Thus in 1 Tim. i. 2, **Τιμοθέῳ γνησίῳ τέκνῳ ἐν πίστει**, the words ἐν πίστει, if construed in sense with γνησίῳ, will give the meaning *genuine in faith*: compare Xen. *An.* 4. 3. 23, κατὰ τὰς προσηκούσας ὄχθας ἐπὶ τὸν ποταμόν, that is, κατὰ τὰς ἐπὶ τ. π. προσηκ. ὄχθας. But it is preferable on several grounds to consider ἐν πίστει here as an adjunct to the compound idea *genuine son*. In 1 P. i. 2, however, the qualifying clauses κατὰ πρόγνωσιν θεοῦ . . . . εἰς ὑπακοὴν καὶ ῥαντισμόν κ.τ.λ. are probably to be joined with ἐκλεκτοῖς in ver. 1.

(*b*) In other instances the prepositional clause really qualifies the verb: Col. i. 6, ἀφ᾽ ἧς ἡμέρας ἠκούσατε καὶ ἐπέγνωτε τὴν χάριν τοῦ θεοῦ ἐν ἀληθείᾳ (see Bähr and Meyer *in loc.*); Rom. iii. 25, ὃν προέθετο ὁ θεὸς ἱλαστήριον διὰ πίστεως ἐν τῷ αὐτοῦ αἵματι (see Fritz. and De Wette *in loc.*); Rom. viii. 2, ὁ νόμος τοῦ πνεύματος τῆς ζωῆς ἐν Χριστῷ Ἰ. ἠλευθέρωσέ με ἀπὸ τοῦ νόμου τῆς ἁμαρτίας καὶ τοῦ θανάτου, where it is evident from the antithesis νόμ. τοῦ θαν. (to which νόμος τῆς ζωῆς accurately corresponds), and also from ver. 3, that ἐν Χρ. must be connected with ἠλευθ. (so Koppe); Ph. i. 14, τοὺς πλείονας τῶν ἀδελφῶν ἐν κυρίῳ πεποιθότας τοῖς δεσμοῖς μου (compare a

---

[1] Harless (on E. i. 15) and Meyer (on Rom. iii. 25, al.) have expressed their concurrence with the view maintained above. Fritzsche, too, who in his *Letter to Tholuck* (p. 35) had declared that such a combination as διὰ τῆς πίστεως ἐν τῷ αὐτοῦ αἵματι would be a solecism, has since expressed his change of view (*Rom.* I. 195, 365): in his note on Rom. vi. 4 also he maintains that the only admissible construction of the words is that which joins εἰς τὸν θάνατον with διὰ τοῦ βαπτίσματος,—a combination which he had previously (*Letter*, p. 32) pronounced grammatically incorrect. [Fritzsche himself does not connect ἐν τῷ αὐτ. αἵμ. with πίστεως in Rom. iii. 25; he acknowledges, however, that such a connexion is grammatically admissible.]

similar construction in G. v. 10, πέποιθα εἰς ὑμᾶς ἐν κυρίῳ· and in 2 Th. iii. 4), as it is only when joined to πεποιθότας that ἐν κυρίῳ has real significance ; Ja. iii. 13, δειξάτω ἐκ τῆς καλῆς ἀναστροφῆς τὰ ἔργα αὐτοῦ ἐν πραΰτητι σοφίας, where the added clause ἐν πραΰτ. σοφ. is an explanatory adjunct to ἐκ τῆς καλ. ἀναστροφῆς. Compare also Rom. v. 8, 1 C. ii. 7, ix. 18, Ph. iii. 9,[1] iv. 19, 21, Col. i. 9, E. ii. 7, iii. 12, 1 Th. ii. 16, Phil. 20, H. xiii. 20, Jo. xv. 11 (see Lücke *in loc.*), 1 Jo. iv. 17, Jude 21. So also A. xxii. 18 [*Rec.*], οὐ παραδέξονταί σου τὴν μαρτυρίαν περὶ ἐμοῦ, may be rendered, *thy testimony they will not receive concerning me,* i.e. in reference to me they will not receive any testimony from thee : τὴν μαρτ. τὴν περὶ ἐμοῦ would be, *the testimony which thou wilt bear* or *hast borne concerning me.* In E. v. 26, ἐν ῥήματι does not belong to τῷ λουτρῷ τοῦ ὕδατος : the verse should probably be divided thus,—ἵνα αὐτὴν ἁγιάσῃ, καθαρίσας τῷ λ. τ. ὕδ., ἐν ῥήματι. The καθαρίζειν precedes the ἁγιάζειν, and denotes something negative, as ἁγιάζειν something positive : see Rückert and Meyer *in loc.*[2] In H. x. 10 it was not necessary to write διὰ τῆς προσφορᾶς τοῦ σώματος . . . . τῆς ἐφάπαξ : the last word relates just as well to ἡγιασμένοι, see Bleek *in loc.* On E. ii. 15, Col. ii. 14, see § 31. Rem. 1.

In E. vi. 5, for τοῖς κυρίοις κατὰ σάρκα, Lachm. has received τοῖς κατὰ σάρκα κυρίοις, on the authority of good MSS.

3. (*a*) An appellative in apposition to a proper name usually has the article : A. xxv. 13, Ἀγρίππας ὁ βασιλεύς· L. ix. 19, Ἰωάννην τὸν βαπτιστήν· A. xii. 1, xiii. 8, xxiii. 24, xxvi. 9, 2 C. xi. 32, Mt. xxvii. 2, al. In all these instances the appellative denotes a rank, office, or the like, which is already well known ; and it is only by means of the apposition that the proper name, which may be common to many persons, becomes definite. " Agrippa the king," is properly, " that Agrippa, out of all those who bear the name Agrippa, who is king: " compare § 18. 6.

(*b*) But the apposition has no article in A. x. 32, Σίμων βυρσεύς, *Simon a tanner* (a certain Simon, who was a tanner); L. ii. 36, Ἄννα προφῆτις, *Anna, a prophetess ;* viii. 3, Ἰωάννα,

---

[1] [So Meyer : on the other side see Alford and Ellicott *in loc.*]
[2] [Ellicott, Alford, and Eadie join ἐν ῥήματι and καθαρίσας.]

γυνὴ Χουζᾶ, ἐπιτρόπου Ἡρώδου· A. xx. 4, Γάϊος Δερβαῖος, *Gaius of Derbe* (not *the* well-known *inhabitant of Derbe*), x. 22. In all these instances the writer simply annexes an appositional predicate, without any special design to distinguish the subject from others of the same name.

In L. iii. 1 also, ἐν ἔτει πεντεκαιδεκάτῳ τῆς ἡγεμονίας Τιβερίου Καίσαρος, the proper translation is, *of Tiberius as emperor.*[1] A. vii. 10, ἐναντίον Φαραὼ βασιλέως Αἰγύπτου is not, *before Pharaoh, the* well-known *king*, or *the* then *king of Egypt*; but *before Pharaoh, king of Egypt*, i. e. before Pharaoh, who was king of Egypt. Compare Plutarch, *Parallel.* 15, Βρέννος Γαλατῶν βασιλεύς· c. 30, Ἀτεπόμαρος Γάλλων βασιλεύς· etc., etc.

The general rule must also determine the use of the article with other words in apposition, and it is strange that any one should assert absolutely that a word in apposition never has the article. A Greek would use no article in expressing *your father, an unlearned man*; whilst in *your father the general*, the article would be quite in place. This applies to Jo. viii. 44, *grammatically* considered.[2]

In general, we may consider that the article is more frequently present than absent before the word in apposition (Rost p. 430, Jelf 450). In accordance with the principles explained in § 19, the article may at times be omitted, even when the predicate is characteristic, distinguishing the individual from others: Rom. i. 7, ἀπὸ θεοῦ πατρὸς ὑμῶν· 1 Tim. i. 1, κατ' ἐπιταγὴν θεοῦ σωτῆρος ἡμῶν· 1 P. v. 8, ὁ ἀντίδικος ὑμῶν διάβολος. So also when the appellative predicate precedes the proper name, as κύριος Ἰησοῦς Χριστός (2 C. i. 2, G. i. 3, Ph. iii. 20, al.); though in this case the article is commonly inserted, as 1 C. xi. 23, ὁ κύριος Ἰησοῦς· 2 Tim. i. 10, τοῦ σωτῆρος ἡμῶν Χριστοῦ· Tit. iii. 4, 1 Th. iii. 11, Phil. 5, al.

4. An epithet joined to an anarthrous noun (appellative), is itself anarthrous, as a rule: Mt. vii. 11, δόματα ἀγαθά· Jo.

---

[1] Gersdorf (p. 167) is wrong. [Gersdorf appears to regard the presence or absence of the article before the word in apposition as a mere characteristic of style, not affecting the sense in any degree.]

[2] [It had been maintained (by Hilgenfeld) that τοῦ διαβόλου here is not in apposition to πατρός, but is *dependent* upon it.]

ix. 1, εἶδεν ἄνθρωπον τυφλὸν ἐκ γενετῆς· 1 Tim. iv. 3, ἃ ὁ θεὸς ἔκτισεν εἰς μετάληψιν μετὰ εὐχαριστίας· i. 5, ἀγάπη ἐκ καθαρᾶς καρδίας· Tit. i. 6, τέκνα ἔχων πιστά, μὴ ἐν κατηγορίᾳ ἀσωτίας ἢ ἀνυπότακτα· Rom. xiv. 17, δικαιοσύνη καὶ εἰρήνη καὶ χαρὰ ἐν πνεύματι ἁγίῳ. Compare Plat. *Rep.* 2. 378 d, "Ἥρας δὲ δεσμοὺς ὑπὸ υἱέος καὶ Ἡφαίστου ῥίψεις ὑπὸ πατρός, μέλλοντος τῇ μητρὶ τυπτομένῃ ἀμύνειν, καὶ θεομαχίας, ὅσας Ὅμηρος πεποίηκεν, οὐ παραδεκτέον εἰς τὴν πόλιν· Theophr. *Ch.* 29, ἔστι δὲ ἡ κακολογία ἀγὼν τῆς ψυχῆς εἰς τὸ χεῖρον ἐν λόγοις· Ælian, *Anim.* 11. 15, ἔοικα λέξειν ἐλέφαντος ὀργὴν εἰς γάμον ἀδικουμένου.[1] Compare Stallb. Plat. *Rep.* I. 91, 110, 152, Krüg. p. 118.

Not unfrequently however such attributives have the article though the noun is anarthrous; and that not merely when the noun belongs to the class noticed in § 19. 1 (e. g. 1 P. i. 21), but also in other cases,—though never without sufficient reason. Thus 1 P. i. 7, τὸ δοκίμιον ὑμῶν τῆς πίστεως πολυτιμότερον χ ρ υ σ ί ο υ, τ ο ῦ ἀ π ο λ λ υ μ έ ν ο υ, must be resolved into, *is more precious than gold, which is perishable;* A. xxvi. 18, πίστει τῇ εἰς ἐμέ, *through faith,* namely, *that in me;* 2 Tim. i. 13, ἐν ἀγάπῃ τῇ ἐν Χριστῷ Ἰησοῦ· Tit. iii. 5, οὐκ ἐξ ἔργων τῶν ἐν δικαιοσύνῃ· Rom. ii. 14, ἔθνη τὰ μὴ νόμον ἔχοντα, *gentiles, those that have not the law,* see Fritz. *in loc.* (contrast 1 Th. iv. 5) ; Rom. ix. 30, G. iii. 21 (comp. Liban. *Oratt.* p. 201 b), H. vi. 7, Ph. iii. 9. In such cases the noun (strictly speaking) is first conceived indefinitely,[2] and is then more closely defined by the attributive, whose import receives special prominence in this construction.[3] See also A. x. 41, xix. 11, 17, xxvi. 22, Ph. i. 11, iii. 6, 1 Tim.

---

[1] So κλέπτης ἐν νυκτί might signify *a nocturnal thief;* but in 1 Th. v. 2 after ὡς κλ. ἐν ν. we must supply ἔρχεται from what follows, *that the day of the Lord, as a thief* (cometh) *in the night, so cometh.* Even adverbs are joined (i. e. prefixed) without the article to such anarthrous nouns ; as μάλα χειμών, Xen. *Hell.* 5. 4. 14, *a severe winter.* See Krüg. in *Jahns Jahrb.* 1838, I. 57.

[2] This appears most plainly in such sentences as Mk. xv. 41, ἄλλαι πολλαὶ αἱ συναναβᾶσαι αὐτῷ εἰς Ἱεροσόλυμα.

[3] ["The anarthrous position of the noun may be regarded as employed to give a prominence to the peculiar meaning of the word without the interference of any other idea, while the words to which the article is prefixed limit by their fuller and more precise description the general notion of the anarthrous noun, and thereby introduce the determinate idea intended." (Green p. 34.) See also Ellicott on G. iii. 21, 1 Tim. iii. 13.]

SECT. XX.] THE ARTICLE WITH ATTRIBUTIVES. 175

i. 4, iii. 13, iv. 8, 2 Tim. i. 14, ii. 10, H. ix. 2, 2 Jo. 7, Jude 4, Ja. i. 25, iv. 14 [*Rec.*], 1 P. v. 1. Compare Her. 2. 114, ἐς γῆν τὴν σήν· Xen. *Mem.* 2. 1. 32, ἀνθρώποις τοῖς ἀγαθοῖς (*men,* that is to say, *the good*), *Hiero* 3. 8, ὑπὸ γυναικῶν τῶν ἑαυτῶν· *Mem.* 1. 7. 5, 4. 5. 11, Dion. H. IV. 2219. 4, εὐνοίᾳ τῇ πρὸς αὐτόν· 2221. 5, ὁπλισμὸς ὁ τοῖς τηλικούτοις πρέπων· Ælian, *Anim.* 3. 23, οὐδὲ ἐπὶ κέρδει τῷ μεγίστῳ· 7. 27, Her. 5. 18, 6. 104, Plat. *Rep.* 8. 545 a, *Legg.* 8. 849 b, Demosth. *Neær.* 517 b, Theophr. *Ch.* 15, Schneid. Isocr. *Paneg.* c. 24, Arr. *Ind.* 34. 1, Xen. Ephes. 2. 5, 4. 3, Heliod. 7. 2, 8. 5, Strabo 7. 302, Lucian, *Asin.* 25, 44, *Scyth.* 1, Philostr. *Apol.* 7. 30 [1] (Madvig 9).

In Ph. ii. 9 *Rec.* we read, ὄνομα τὸ ὑπὲρ πᾶν ὄνομα, *a name, which is above every name:* good MSS. however have τὸ ὄνομα, *the name* (which he now possesses), *which* etc.,—the (well known) dignity, which etc.[2]

---

[1] Compare Held, Plut. *Timol.* p. 409, Hermann. on Luc. *Conscr. Hist.* p. 106, Ellendt, *Lex. Soph.* II. 241, Schoem. Plut. *Cleom.* p. 226.

[2] [On most of the points discussed in this and the preceding sections the best writers on the N. T. are in the main agreed. The chief differences of opinion relate to the extent to which the following principles are to be carried.
  (1) The laws of "correlation" (Middleton pp. 36, 48 sq.) :—
    (α) "As a general rule, if a noun in the genitive is dependent on another noun, and if the main noun has the article, the genitive has it likewise" (Don. p. 351) ; see Bernhardy p. 321, Ellicott on Col. ii. 22, Alford on Jo. iii. 10.
    (β) If the governed noun is anarthrous, the governing noun is not unfrequently anarthrous also, and *vice versâ ;* see Bernhardy *l. c.,* Ellicott on E. iv. 12, v. 8, and comp. Green p. 46. Winer mentions some particular examples which illustrate both parts of this rule (for α, see p. 146, Rem. 1 ; for β, his observations on νόμος and θεός,—compare also p. 157) ; but lays down no general rule of this kind.
  (2) The omission of the article after a preposition. Middleton carries this principle much farther than Winer (see above pp. 157, 149), and indeed to a perilous extent, maintaining that the absence of the article "with nouns governed by prepositions" affords no presumption that the nouns are used indefinitely (p. 99) : see Alford on H. i. 1, 1 C. xiv. 19, Ellicott on 1 Tim. iii. 7, Krüg. p. 100.
  (3) The omission of the article with nouns which are made definite by a dependent genitive : on this see p. 155, note 6. See further Ellicott, *Aids to Faith,* p. 461 sq.]

CHAPTER SECOND.
PRONOUNS.
Section XXI.
THE PRONOUNS IN GENERAL.

1. In the use of the pronouns the language of the N. T. agrees in most respects with the older Greek prose, and with Greek usage in general. The only peculiarities are

(1) The more frequent use of personal and demonstrative pronouns, for the sake of greater clearness (or emphasis),—see § 22 sq.:

(2) The comparative neglect of several forms, which belonged rather to the luxuries of the language, or of which an Oriental would not feel the need, as the correlatives, ὅστις, ὁπόσος, ὁποῖος, πηλίκος [? ὁπηλίκος], in the indirect construction; indeed these forms are used in the N. T. even less frequently than by the later Greeks. On the other hand, those modes of expression by which the Greeks consolidated their sentences (attraction) had become very familiar to the N. T. writers (§ 24). The assertion that αὐτός is used in the N. T. for the unemphatic *he*, is incorrect; and the Hebraistic separation of οὐδείς into οὐ . . . . πᾶς is almost confined to sententious propositions or phrases.

2. The gender of pronouns,—personal, demonstrative, and relative,—is not unfrequently different from that of the noun to which they refer, the meaning of the noun being considered rather than its grammatical gender (*constructio ad sensum*). This construction is most common when an animate object is denoted by a neuter substantive or a feminine abstract, in which case the masculine or feminine pronoun is used, according to the sex of the object: Mt. xxviii. 19, μαθητεύσατε πάντα τὰ ἔθνη, βαπτίζοντες αὐτούς, Rev. xix. 15 (compare Ex. xxiii. 27, Dt. iv. 27, xviii. 14, al.), Rom. ii. 14, A. xv. 17, xxvi. 17, G. iv. 19, τεκνία μου, οὓς πάλιν ὠδίνω·[1] 2 Jo. 1, Rev. iii. 4 (like Eur. *Suppl.* 12, ἑπτὰ γενναίων τέκνων, οὕς· Aristoph. *Plut.* 292), Jo. vi. 9, ἔστι παιδάριον ἓν

---

[1] [In A. xxiv. 18, if we retain the more difficult reading ἐν οἷς, we should have an example of a *constr. ad sensum* of a somewhat different kind : compare Mk. iii. 28, βλασφημίαι ὅσα ἂν βλασφημήσωσιν, Dt. iv. 2, v. 28 (Tisch. *Prol.* p. 58).]

ὧδε, ὃς ἔχει (as most of the better MSS. read, for ὅ of *Rec.*), Mk. v. 41 (Esth. ii. 9), Col. ii. 15, τὰς ἀρχὰς κ. τ. ἐξουσίας . . . θριαμβεύσας αὐτούς· Col. ii. 19, τὴν κεφαλήν (Χριστόν), ἐξ οὗ πᾶν τὸ σῶμα κ.τ.λ. Jo. xv. 26, however, is not an example of this kind, as πνεῦμα is only an apposition. For examples from Greek authors see Matth. 434, Wurm, *Dinarch.* 81 sq., Ellendt, *Lex. Soph.* II. 368 (Jelf 379, 819, Don. p. 362): comp. Drakenborch on Liv. 29. 12. In Rev. iii. 4, xiii. 14, al., the readings vary.

Under this head comes also Rev. xvii. 16, καὶ τὰ δέκα κέρατα ἃ εἶδες καὶ τὸ θηρίον, οὗτοι μισήσουσι; where, in accordance with the prophetic symbolism, κέρατα and θηρίον are to be understood as signifying persons.

3. On the same principle we find the plural of these pronouns used in relation to a singular noun, if this noun has a collective signification or is an abstract used for a concrete: Mt. i. 21, τὸν λαὸν . . . . αὐτῶν· xiv. 14, Ph. ii. 15, γενεά, ἐν οἷς· 3 Jo. 9, ἡ ἐκκλησία . . . . αὐτῶν· E. v. 12, σκότος (ἐσκοτισμένοι) . . . . ὑπ' αὐτῶν· Mk. vi. 45 sq., ... τὸν ὄχλον, καὶ ἀποταξάμενος αὐτοῖς· Jo. xv. 6 (see Lücke *in loc.*), L. vi. 17 (comp. § 22. 3): A. xxii. 5 does not come in here. Compare Soph. *Trach.* 545, Thuc. 6. 91, 1. 136, Plat. *Tim.* 24 b, *Phædr.* 260 a, Xen. *Cyr.* 6. 3. 4, Diod. S. 18. 6: in the LXX this is very common, see Is. lxv. 1, Ex. xxxii. 11, 33, Dt. xxi. 8, 1 S. xiv. 34; comp. Judith ii. 3, iv. 8, Ecclus. xvi. 8, Wis.[1] v. 3, 7.[2] Some have supposed that Ph. iii. 20, ἐν οὐρανοῖς ἐξ οὗ, is an example of the inverse construction, the use of a singular pronoun in reference to a plural noun (Bernh. p. 295); but ἐξ οὗ had in usage become a mere adverb, exactly equivalent to *unde*. On the other hand, in 2 Jo. 7, οὗτός ἐστιν ὁ πλάνος κ.τ.λ., there is a transition from the plural μὴ ὁμολογοῦντες κ.τ.λ. to the collective singular.

Different from these examples are A. xv. 36, κατὰ πᾶσαν πόλιν, ἐν αἷς (where πᾶσα πόλις, in itself,—without considering the inhabitants,—implies a plurality, πᾶσαι πόλεις; comp. Poppo, *Thuc.* I. 92), and 2 P. iii. 1, ταύτην ἤδη δευτέραν ὑμῖν γράφω ἐπιστολήν, ἐν αἷς κ.τ.λ., where δύο is implied in δευτέραν. I do not know any exact parallel to this, but we may compare with it the converse πάντες ὅστις, which is not at all uncommon (Rost p. 460, Jelf 819. 2. β, Don. p. 362).

[1] [A mistake. We may substitute Judith v. 3, 7, or Wis. xvi. 3, 20.]
[2] Some commentators (e.g. Reiche) thus explain Rom. vi. 21, τίνα καρπὸν εἴχετε τότε ἐφ' οἷς (i.e. καρποῖς) νῦν ἐπαισχύνεσθε; see however § 23. 2.

Rem. 1. According to some commentators (e.g. Kühnöl) the pronoun occasionally refers to a noun which is not expressed until afterwards; e.g. Mt. xvii. 18, ἐπετίμησεν αὐτῷ (namely τῷ δαιμονίῳ), A. xii. 21, ἐδημηγόρει πρὸς αὐτούς (compare ver. 22, ὁ δῆμος).[1] But neither of these passages proves anything in regard to N. T. usage. In the first, αὐτῷ refers to the demoniac himself, for in the Gospels, as is well known, the person possessed and the possessing demon are often interchanged; and the fact that Mark (ix. 25) has ἐπετ. τῷ πν. τῷ ἀκαθάρτῳ is of no weight against this. In the other passage, αὐτούς refers to the Tyrian and Sidonian ambassadors mentioned in ver. 20, as Kühnöl himself has admitted (comp. Georgi, *Vind.* p. 208 sq.): the verb δημηγορεῖν does not stand in the way of this explanation, for the king's answer was given in a full assembly of the people.

Rem. 2. The neuter of the interrogative pronoun τίς and of the demonstrative οὗτος (αὐτός) are often used adverbially to denote *why* (*wherefore*) and *therefore*. There is a similar use of the interrogative pronoun in Latin and German, *quid cunctaris? was zögerst du?* As originally conceived, these words were true accusatives: see Herm. *Vig.* p. 882, Bernh. p. 130 (Jelf 580. *Obs.* 5). For the strengthened demonstrative αὐτὸ τοῦτο compare 2 P. i. 5, καὶ αὐτὸ τοῦτο σπουδὴν πᾶσαν παρεισενέγκαντες (Xen. *An.* 1. 9. 21, Plat. *Protag.* 310 e, αὐτὰ ταῦτα νῦν ἥκω παρά σε): see Matth. 470. 8, Ast, Plat. *Legg.* pp. 163, 169, 214.[2] G. ii. 10 does not come in here; see § 22. 4. For examples of τί, classified according to the very varied relations expressed, see Wahl, *Clav.* 483. Greek writers also use ὅ and ἅ for δι' ὅ and δι' ἅ (Matth. 477. e); but Meyer is wrong in introducing this mainly poetic use of ἅ into A. xxvi. 16 (see § 39. Rem. 1): in G. ii. 10 Meyer himself rejects on this very ground Schott's proposal to take ὅ for δι' ὅ.

The demonstrative is also used adverbially in the distributive formula τοῦτο μὲν . . . τοῦτο δέ, *partly* . . . *partly* (H. x. 33, Her. 1. 30, 3. 132, Lucian, *Nigr.* 16); compare Wetstein II. 423, Matth. 288. Rem. 2 (Jelf 579. 6).—On 1 C. vi. 11, ταῦτά τινες ἦτε, where there is a mixture of two constructions, see § 23. 5.[3]

Section XXII.

PERSONAL AND POSSESSIVE PRONOUNS.

1. The personal pronouns are used much more frequently in the N. T. than in ordinary Greek.[4] This peculiarity, which has

---

[1] Fritz. *Conj.* I. p. 18 sq.—See Gesen. *Lehrg.* p. 740, Bornem. Xen. *Conv.* p. 210.

[2] [See Alford *in loc.*, Ellicott on E. vi. 22, Jelf *l.c.*, Riddell, Plat. *Apol.* p. 119 sq.]

[3] [Lünemann here adds a note on the use of τί in an exclamation (*how*), in Mt. vii. 14 (Lachm.), L. xii. 49, 2 S. vi. 20: on these passages, however, see p. 562.]

[4] We find however a complete parallel in the Homeric use of the possessive

its origin in Hebrew circumstantiality of expression, appears particularly in the use

(a) Of αὐτοῦ, σοῦ, etc., with substantives (especially in connexion with the middle voice, § 38. 2): Jo. ii. 12, L. vi. 20, vii. 50, xi. 34, xxiv. 50, Mt. vi. 17, xv. 2, Mk. xii. 30, 1 P. iii. 11,[1] Rom. ix. 17, xvi. 7, A. xxv. 21, al.; compare 1 Macc. i. 6, Jos. xxiii. 2, xxiv. 1, Neh. ix. 34.

(b) Of the accusative of the subject, in combination with the infinitive: L. x. 35, ἐγὼ ἐν τῷ ἐπανέρχεσθαί με ἀποδώσω· Jo. ii. 24, H. vii. 24, A. i. 3.

(c) Of the oblique cases of pronouns with both participle and principal verb: Mk. x. 16, ἐναγκαλισάμενος αὐτὰ κατευλόγει τιθεὶς τὰς χεῖρας ἐπ᾽ αὐτά· ix. 28, A. vii. 21, L. xvi. 2, 2 P. iii. 16 (compare below, no. 4). So especially in the Apocalypse.

In Mt. xxii. 37, Rev. ix. 21, the repetition of the pronoun is probably to be ascribed to rhythm.

Along with this general tendency towards the accumulation of pronouns, we meet with some instances (though but few) in which a pronoun is not inserted where it might have been expected: A. xiii. 3, καὶ ἐπιθέντες τὰς χεῖρας αὐτοῖς ἀπέλυσαν (αὐτούς), Mk. vi. 5, E. v. 11, Ph. i. 6, 2 Thess. iii. 12, H. iv. 15, xiii. 17, 1 Tim. vi. 2, Jo. x. 29, L. xiv. 4; compare Demosth. *Conon* 728 b, ἐμοὶ περιπεσόντες .... ἐξέδυσαν.[2] In Mt. xxi. 7, however, the better reading is ἐπεκάθισεν, and in 1 C. x. 9 πειράζειν may be taken absolutely: in 2 Tim. ii. 11, σὺν αὐτῷ would be heavy in a sententious saying. In 1 P. ii. 11 ὑμᾶς (found in some MSS. after παρακαλῶ, in others after ἀπέχεσθαι) is certainly not genuine. In acclamations, such as Mt. xxvii. 22, σταυρωθήτω, the omission of the pronoun is very natural (here a German would use the infinitive without a pronoun, *kreuzigen!*); yet in the parallel passage, Mk. xv. 13, we find

---

pronoun ὅς. In later (and sometimes in older) prose αὐτός also is thus used *abundanter*: see Schæf. *Ind. Æsop.* p. 124, Schoem. *Isæus* p. 382.

[1] [This should be 1 P. iii. 10; but the pronouns have not much authority. In Mt. xv. 2 also the reading is doubtful. The same redundancy is common in modern Greek: according to Mullach (*Vulg.* p. 315) this is to be ascribed to the influence of the LXX and N. T. But is it not natural to suppose that the free use of these pronouns would be a characteristic of the *colloquial* language of all periods?]

[2] In Latin compare Sallust, *Jug.* 54. 1, universos in concione laudat atque agit gratias (iis); Cic. *Orat.* 1. 15, si modo erunt ad eum delata et tradita (ei); Liv. 1. 11, 20. Compare Kritz on the first passage.

σταύρωσον αὐτόν. The omission of the pronoun is carried much farther in Greek authors.[1]

In E. iii. 18, τί τὸ πλάτος κ.τ.λ., we can hardly help out the meaning by supposing an ellipsis of αὐτῆς (ἀγάπης): see Meyer. Some (e.g. Kühnöl) have maintained that αὐτούς is redundant in Mt. xxi. 41, κακοὺς κακῶς ἀπολέσει αὐτούς,—but altogether without reason. Without αὐτούς the words would be quite general; it is the pronoun that connects them with the case in question, with the γεωργοί mentioned in the parable.

2. Instead of personal pronouns the nouns themselves are sometimes used. In some cases this arises from a certain inadvertency on the writer's part; in others, where there are several nouns to which the pronoun might possibly be referred, or where the noun stands at some distance, the design is to save the reader from uncertainty as to the meaning: see Jo. iii. 23 sq., x. 41, L. iii. 19, E. iv. 12, and compare 1 K. ix. 1, xii. 1, Xen. Eph. 2. 13, Thuc. 6. 105, Diod. S. *Exc. V.* p. 29 (Ellendt, *Arrian* I. 55).

In Jo. iv. 1, however, Ἰησοῦς is repeated because the apostle wishes to quote the very words which the Pharisees had heard: compare 1 C. xi. 23. Those passages also in the discourses of Jesus in which the name of the person or office is repeated for the sake of emphasis, must not be referred to this head: Mk. ix. 41, ἐν ὀνόματι ὅτι Χριστοῦ ἐστέ· L. xii. 8, πᾶς ὃς ἂν ὁμολογήσῃ ἐν ἐμοὶ . . . καὶ ὁ υἱὸς τοῦ ἀνθρώπου ὁμολογήσει ἐν αὐτῷ· Jo. vi. 40, 1 C. i. 8, 21, 1 Jo. v. 6, Col. ii. 11, etc., etc.: compare Plat. *Euthyphr.* p. 5 e, Æschyl. *Prom. Vinct.* 312, Cic. *Fam.* 2. 4. In all these instances the pronoun would be out of place, and would mar the rhetorical effect. Least of all can the well-known appellation ὁ υἱὸς τοῦ ἀνθρώπου, under which Jesus in the Synoptic Gospels speaks of himself, as of a third person, be regarded as standing for ἐγώ. Elsewhere we find the noun repeated for the sake of an emphatic antithesis: Jo. ix. 5, ὅταν ἐν τῷ κόσμῳ ὦ, φῶς εἰμὶ τοῦ κόσμου· xii. 47, οὐκ ἦλθον ἵνα κρίνω τὸν κόσμον ἀλλ' ἵνα σώσω τὸν κόσμον (Xen. *An.* 3. 2. 23, οἳ βασιλέως ἄκοντος ἐν τῇ βασιλέως χώρᾳ . . . . οἰκοῦσι), Arrian, *Al.* 2. 18. 2, Krüg. p. 134 (Liv. 1. 10. 1, 6. 2. 9, 38. 56. 3). Accordingly, no one will find an unmeaning repetition of the noun in Rom. v. 12, δι' ἑνὸς ἀνθρ. ἡ ἁμαρτία εἰς τὸν κόσμ.

---

[1] See Jacobs, *Anth. Pal.* III. 294, Bremi, *Lys.* p. 50. Schæf. *Demosth.* IV. 78, 157, 232, V. 556, 567.

εἰσῆλθε, καὶ διὰ τῆς ἁμαρτίας ὁ θάνατος; or in Jo. x. 29, ὁ πατήρ μου, ὃς δέδωκέ μοι, μείζων πάντων ἐστί· καὶ οὐδεὶς δύναται ἁρπάζειν ἐκ τῆς χειρὸς τοῦ πατρός μου: compare also A. iii. 16. See § 65.

In A. x. 7 the better MSS. have the personal pronoun (see Kühnöl *in loc.*), and τῷ Κορνηλίῳ is evidently a gloss. The passages which Bornemann (Xen. *An.* p. 190) quotes from Greek authors are not all of the same description, nor is the reading certain in every case.

It is not altogether correct to say[1] that the use of the noun in the place of αὐτός or ἐκεῖνος is a special peculiarity of Mark's style. In Mk. ii. 18 the nouns could not be dispensed with, for the writer could not put into the mouth of the inquirers an ἐκεῖνοι which would point back to *his own* words. In vi. 41, and also in xiv. 67, the pronoun would have been very inconvenient. In ii. 27 the nouns are used for the sake of antithesis: i. 34, iii. 24, v. 9, x. 46, are instances of circumstantiality in expression (so common in Cæsar), and not properly of the substitution of nouns for pronouns; comp. Ellendt *loc. cit.*

3. Through some negligence on the part of the writer, the pronoun αὐτός[2] is not unfrequently used when the sentences immediately preceding contain no noun to which it can be directly referred. Such cases may be arranged in four classes:—

(1) Most frequently the plural of this pronoun is used in reference to a collective noun,—particularly the name of a place or country (compare § 21. 3), in which the notion of the inhabitants is implied: Mt. iv. 23, ἐν ταῖς συναγωγαῖς αὐτῶν, i.e. Γαλιλαίων (implied in ὅλην τὴν Γαλιλαίαν), ix. 35 (L. iv. 15), Mt. xi. 1, 1 Th. i. 9 (compare ver. 8), A. viii. 5, xx. 2; 2 C. ii. 12, 13, ἐλθὼν εἰς τὴν Τρωάδα . . . ἀποταξάμενος αὐτοῖς· v. 19, θεὸς ἦν ἐν Χριστῷ κόσμον καταλλάσσων ἑαυτῷ, μὴ λογιζόμενος αὐτοῖς τὰ παραπτώματα· Jo. xvii. 2. This usage is sufficiently common in Greek writers; compare Thuc. 1. 27, 136, Lucian, *Tim.* 9. *Dial. Mort.* 12. 4, Dion. H. IV. 2117, Jacob, Luc. *Toxar.* p. 59.[3]—Akin to this case is the following:—

(2) Αὐτός refers to an abstract noun which must be supplied from a preceding concrete, or *vice versâ*: Jo. viii. 44, ψεύστης ἐστὶ καὶ ὁ πατὴρ αὐτοῦ (ψεύδους), see Lücke *in loc.*;[4] Rom.

---

[1] Schulze in *Keils Analect.* II. ii. 112.
[2] On the whole subject compare Hermann, *Diss. de pronom.* αὐτός, in the *Acta Seminar. philol. Lips.* Vol. I. 42 sqq., and in his *Opusc.* I. 308 sqq. [A. Buttm. *Gr.* p. 106.]
[3] It is a simpler case when αὐτός in the plural refers to an abstract noun which in itself merely signifies a community of men, e.g. ἐκκλησία: on this see § 21. 3. On Col. iv. 15, with the reading αὐτῶν, see Meyer. [See also Alford, who adopts this reading on good authority, and Lightfoot, *Col.* pp. 309, 322.]
[4] The other explanation, *father of the liar*, appears to be neither simpler in

182   PERSONAL AND POSSESSIVE PRONOUNS.   [PART III.

ii. 26, ἐὰν ἡ ἀκροβυστία τὰ δικαιώματα τοῦ νόμου φυλάσσῃ, οὐχὶ ἡ ἀκρ. αὐτοῦ (of such an ἀκρόβυστος) εἰς περιτομὴν λογισθήσεται; comp. Theodoret I. 914, τοῦτο τῆς ἀποστολικῆς χάριτος ἴδιον· αὐτοῖς γὰρ (ἀποστόλοις) κ.τ.λ.[1] In L. xxiii. 51, αὐτῶν refers to the Sanhedrin, suggested by the predicate βουλευτής, ver. 50 : compare Jon. i. 3, εὗρε πλοῖον βαδίζον εἰς Θαρσίς . . . καὶ ἀνέβη εἰς αὐτὸ τοῦ πλεῦσαι μετ' αὐτῶν κ.τ.λ.,—see above, no. 2 [21. 2]; Sallust, *Cat.* 17. 7, simul confisum, si conjuratio valuisset, facile apud illos (i.e. conjuratos) principem se fore. Similar to this would be Mt. viii. 4, εἰς μαρτύριον αὐτοῖς (Mk. i. 44, L. v. 14), if the pronoun related to ἱερεῖ in the preceding clause, the plural ἱερεῦσι being supplied with αὐτοῖς. But if the man who has been healed has already received from the priests permission to bring the prescribed purification-offering, the priest needs no further μαρτύριον that he is clean: see below, no. 4.

(3) Αὐτός has a reference which is at least suggested by some previous word, or by the verb of the sentence itself: 1 P. iii. 14, τὸν δὲ φόβον αὐτῶν μὴ φοβηθῆτε· i.e. τῶν κακούντων ὑμᾶς, or of those from whom ye are to suffer (πάσχειν),[2] see Herm. *Vig.* p. 714;[3] E. v. 12, τὰ κρυφῇ γινόμενα ὑπ' αὐτῶν, that is, τῶν τὰ ἔργα τοῦ σκότους ποιούντων (ver. 11);[4] A. x. 10. Compare Aristoph. *Plut.* 566, Thuc. 1. 22. 1, and Poppo *in loc.*, Heinichen, *Ind. ad Euseb.* III. 539.   On A. xii. 21 see § 21. Rem. 1.

(4) Αὐτός has no reference grammatically indicated in the previous context, but must be understood of a subject which is supposed to be familiar: L. i. 17, αὐτὸς προελεύσεται αὐτοῦ, i.e.

---

point of grammar nor preferable in sense ; indeed *father of falsehood* is a fuller conception for John, who loves what is abstract. [See Brückner *in loc.*, who reviews the various explanations, and decides in favour of referring αὐτοῦ—not to an abstract implied in ψεύστης (Winer, De Wette), but—to ψεῦδος in the preceding clause. See however p. 736, note [3].]

[1] For a similar example with a relative see *Testam. Patr.* p. 608, ἀπεκάλυψα τῇ Χανανίτιδι Βησουέ, οἷς (Χαναναίοις) εἶπεν ὁ θεὸς μὴ ἀποκαλύψαι. Compare also the passage cited from an old poet by Cicero (*Orat.* 2. 46. 193): neque paternum adspectum es veritus, quem (patrem) ætate exacta indigem Liberum lacerasti ; and Gell. 2. 30. 6.

[2] [That is, the subject of αὐτῶν must be supplied either from ὁ κακώσων in ver. 13, or πάσχοιτε in ver. 14.]

[3] Otherwise in Epiphan. II. 368 a : εὐξαί μοι, πάτερ, ὅπως ὑγιαίνω· . . . πίστευε, τέκνον, τῷ ἐσταυρωμένῳ, καὶ ἕξεις ταύτην (ὑγείαν).

[4] [Winer gives a somewhat different explanation on p. 177 : Meyer and Ellicott refer the pronoun to τοὺς υἱοὺς τῆς ἀπ. in ver. 6.]

before the Messiah[1] (see Kühnöl *in loc.*), αὐτός being used as in αὐτὸς ἔφα, in reference to one who is recognised within a certain circle as head or leader: in 1 Jo. ii. 12, 2 Jo. 6, 2 P. iii. 4, the pronoun is thus used of Christ. In L. v. 17, εἰς τὸ ἰᾶσθαι αὐτούς, the pronoun expresses the general notion, *the sick, those who required healing* (amongst the persons present in the synagogue): the pronoun cannot refer back to ver. 15, though even Bengel so explains it. On the other hand, in A. iv. 5 αὐτῶν refers to the Jews, among whom the events recorded occurred; their priests, etc., are however mentioned in ver. 1, and λαός is used more than once in ver. 1 sq. of the Jewish people. In Mt. xii. 9 the pronoun refers to those amongst whom Jesus then was, the Galileans. In H. iv. 8, viii. 8, xi. 28, it refers to the Israelites, suggested to the reader's mind by the circumstances just spoken of. The above-mentioned εἰς μαρτύριον αὐτοῖς, Mt. viii. 4, comes in here: those meant by αὐτοῖς are the Jews (the Jewish public),—the circle in which the injunctions of Moses (ὁ προσέταξε Μωϋσῆς) are binding. In Jo. xx. 15, αὐτόν supposes that the inquirer must know who is spoken of, inasmuch as he has taken Him away; or else Mary, herself engrossed with the thought of the Lord, attributes her own ideas to the person whom she is addressing.[2]

In L. xviii. 34 αὐτοί points back to τοὺς δώδεκα and αὐτούς in ver. 31 (the intervening words are a saying of Jesus); in H. iv. 13 αὐτοῦ refers to τοῦ θεοῦ in ver. 12; and in L. xxi. 21 αὐτῆς refers to Ἰερουσαλήμ, ver. 20. In 2 C. vi. 17, ἐκ μέσου αὐτῶν, in a somewhat transformed quotation from the O. T., relates to ἄπιστοι, ver. 14; and in Rom. x. 18 αὐτῶν suggests to every reader the preachers mentioned *in concreto* in ver. 15. On A. xxvii. 14, where some refer αὐτῆς to *the ship*, see Kühnöl.[3] In L. ii. 22, by αὐτῶν we are to understand mother and child (Mary and Jesus). The commentators on H. xii. 17 are in doubt whether αὐτήν refers to μετάνοιαν or to εὐλογίαν; but the correlation of εὑρίσκειν and ἐκζητεῖν of itself renders the former the more probable reference. In Mt. iii. 16 αὐτῷ and ἐπ' αὐτόν unquestionably relate to Jesus.

A slight negligence of another kind appears in Mt. xii. 15, xix. 2, ἠκολούθησαν αὐτῷ ὄχλοι πολλοὶ καὶ ἐθεράπευσεν αὐτοὺς πάντας. Here

---

[1] [Against this, see Meyer and Alford *in loc.* In L. v. 17 αὐτόν is probably the true reading.]
[2] Compare also Poppo, Xen. *Cyr.* 3. 1. 31, 5. 4. 42, *Thuc.* III. i. 184, Lehmann, *Lucian* II. 325, IV. 429, Stallb. Plat. *Rep.* II. 286; and on the whole subject see Van Hengel, *Annotat.* p. 195 sqq.
[3] [Meyer, Alford, and others with good reason refer αὐτῆς to Κρήτην, ver. 13.]

the pronoun grammatically refers to ὄχλοι, but this reference is of course loose in point of logic,—*he healed them* (i.e. the sick who were in the crowds) *in a body:* in xiv. 14, ἐθερ. τοὺς ἀρρώστους αὐτῶν. Compare also L. v. 17.

According to some commentators the demonstrative οὗτος is similarly construed *ad sensum* in 2 C. v. 2, τούτῳ being supposed to agree with σώματι implied in ἡ ἐπίγειος ἡμῶν οἰκία τοῦ σκήνους; but it is much simpler to supply σκήνει (ver. 4). That however the Greeks did use the demonstrative as well as αὐτός with some looseness of reference is well known; compare Mätzner, *Antiph.* p. 200 : A. x. 10 would be an instance of this, if the reading ἐκείνων for αὐτῶν were correct.

4. (*a*) When the principal noun is followed by several other words, we often find αὐτός and the other personal pronouns introduced into the same sentence, for the sake of perspicuity : Mk. v. 2, ἐξελθόντι αὐτῷ ἐκ τοῦ πλοίου εὐθέως ἀπήντησεν αὐτῷ· ix. 28, Mt. iv. 16, v. 40, viii. 1, xxvi. 71, A. vii. 21,[1] Ja. iv. 17, Rev. vi. 4 ; Col. ii. 13, καὶ ὑμᾶς νεκροὺς ὄντας ἐν τοῖς παραπτώμασιν καὶ τῇ ἀκροβυστίᾳ τῆς σαρκὸς ὑμῶν συνεζωοποίησεν ὑμᾶς κ.τ.λ.; Ph. i. 7. In most of these instances a participial clause having the force of a sentence proper has preceded : in this case Greek authors often add the pronoun, as Paus. 8. 38. 5, Herod. 3. 10. 6. Compare further Plat. *Apol.* 40 d, *Symp.* c. 21, Xen. *Cyr.* 1. 3. 15, *Œc.* 10. 4, Paus. 2. 3. 8, Arrian, *Epict.* 3. 1, Cic. *Catil.* 2. 12. 27, Liv. 1. 2, Sall. *Catil.* 40. 1, Herm. Soph. *Trach.* p. 54, Schwarz, *Comment.* p. 217.[2] In Jo. xviii. 11, τὸ ποτήριον ὃ δέδωκέν μοι ὁ πατήρ, οὐ μὴ πίω αὐτό ; the pronoun is used for emphasis : so also in Mt. vi. 4, 1 P. v. 10 (A. ii. 23), Rev. xxi. 6.—After a case absolute the pronoun is almost necessarily added, in the case required by the verb : Rev. iii. 12, ὁ νικῶν, ποιήσω αὐτόν· Jo. xv. 2, Mt. xii. 36, A. vii. 40 ; compare Plat. *Theæt.* 173 d, Æl. *Anim.* 5. 34, 1. 48, al.

(*b*) A redundancy of this kind is still more common in relative sentences : Mk. vii. 25, γυνή, ἧς εἶχε τὸ θυγάτριον αὐτῆς πνεῦμα ἀκάθαρτον· i. 7, Rev. vii. 2, οἷς ἐδόθη αὐτοῖς ἀδικῆσαι τὴν γῆν κ.τ.λ., iii. 8, vii. 9, xiii. 8, xx. 8 ; similarly in Mk. xiii. 19, θλῖψις, οἵα οὐ γέγονε τοιαύτη ἀπ' ἀρχῆς κτίσεως. So also with a relative adverb : Rev. xii. 6, 14, ὅπου ἔχει ἐκεῖ τόπον κ.τ.λ.

---

[1] [There is considerable authority for the genitive absolute in Mk. v. 2, ix. 28, A. vii. 21 ; and for the omission of αὐτός in Mt. vi. 4, Rev. xxi. 6.]

[2] [Comp. Jelf 658. 2, 699. *Obs.* 3, Green p. 118 sq.]

Such instances of pleonasm occur much more frequently in the LXX, in accordance with the Hebrew idiom:[1] Ex. iv. 17, Lev. xi. 32, 34, xiii. 52, xv. 4, 9, 17, 20, 24, 26, xvi. 9, 32, xviii. 5, Num. xvii. 5, Dt. xi. 25, Jos. iii. 4, xxii. 19, Jud. xviii. 5, 6, Ruth i. 7, iii. 2, 4, 1 K. xi. 34, xiii. 10, 25, 31, 2 K. xix. 4, Bar. ii. 4, iii. 8, Neh. viii. 12, ix. 19, Is. i. 21, Joel iii. 7, Ps. xxxix. 5, Judith v. 19, vii. 10, x. 2, xvi. 3, 3 (1) Esdr. iii. 5, iv. 54, vi. 32, al.: see Thiersch, *De Pentat. Alex.* p. 126 sq. In Greek prose, however, αὐτός[2] and the demonstrative pronouns are sometimes superadded in a relative sentence, as Xen. *Cyr.* 1. 4. 19, Diod. S. 1. 97, 17. 35, Paus. 2. 4. 7, Soph. *Philoct.* 316 (compare in Latin, Cic. *Fam.* 4. 3, *Acad.* 2. 25, *Philipp.* 2. 8); but the demonstrative is probably very seldom found so near the relative[3] as in most of the examples quoted above,—almost all of which are found in passages which are Hebraistic in style.[4]

In A. iii. 13 [*Rec.*] the relative construction is dropped in the second sentence (see below p. 186): in Rom. vii. 21 the first and second ἐμοί seem to me to belong to different sentences, see § 61. 5. Those passages also are of a different kind in which the personal pronoun is accompanied by some other word, by means of which the relative is more closely defined and explained: G. iii. 1, οἷς κατ' ὀφθαλμοὺς Ἰησοῦς Χρ. προεγράφη ἐν ὑμῖν (*in animis vestris*) ἐσταυρωμένος (Lev. xv. 16, xxi. 20, xxii. 4, Ruth ii. 2); Rev. xvii. 9, ὅπου ἡ γυνὴ κάθηται ἐπ' αὐτῶν· xiii. 12; compare Gen. xxiv. 3, 37, Jud. vi. 10, Ex. xxxvi. 1, Lev. xvi. 32, Judith ix. 2. Likewise in G. ii. 10, ὃ καὶ ἐσπούδασα αὐτὸ τοῦτο ποιῆσαι, the emphasis which is given by the annexed αὐτό, strengthened by τοῦτο, is unmistakeable[5] (Bornem. *Luc.* p. liv).

1 P. ii. 24, ὃς τὰς ἁμαρτίας ἡμῶν αὐτὸς ἀνήνεγκεν κ.τ.λ., certainly cannot be brought in here: it is obvious that αὐτός must be taken by itself, and that it brings out more forcibly the antithesis with ἁμαρτ. ἡμῶν. In Mt. iii. 12, οὗ τὸ πτύον ἐν τῇ χειρὶ αὐτοῦ, the relative serves instead of τούτου to connect this sentence with the preceding one, and the two pronouns are to be taken separately,—as if the words ran, *He has his winnowing shovel in his hand.* In E. ii. 10, however, οἷς

---

[1] See Gesen. *Lg.* p. 734. [Gesen. *Hebr. Gr.* p. 200 (Bagst.), Kalisch, *Hebr. Gr.* I. 226.]
[2] Göttling, *Callim.* p. 19 sq., Ast, Plat. *Polit.* p. 550.
[3] In Aristoph. *Av.* 1238, the Cod. Rav. has οἷς θυτέον αὐτοῖς, for the ordinary reading οἷς θυτέον αὐτούς. On another accumulation of the pronoun see § 23. 3.
[4] See also Herm. Soph. *Philoct.* p. 58, Vc. Fritzsche, *Quæst. Lucian.* p. 109 sq. Jelf 833. *Obs.* 2, Green p. 121.]
[5] ["Which, namely this very thing:" Ellicott *in loc.*]

προητοίμασεν is for ἃ προητοίμασεν, by attraction. Lastly, ἐν κυρίῳ in E. ii. 21 probably belongs to εἰς ναὸν ἅγιον.

We sometimes find αὐτός repeated within a brief space, though different objects are referred to : Mk. viii. 22, φέρουσιν αὐτῷ (Χριστῷ) τυφλὸν κ. παρακαλοῦσιν αὐτόν (Χριστόν), ἵνα αὐτοῦ (τυφλοῦ) ἅψηται· Mk. ix. 27, 28 : so also οὗτος in Jo. xi. 37. Compare § 67.

After a relative sentence, where we might expect a repetition of ὅς or a continuance of the relative construction, Greek writers not unfrequently, indeed almost regularly (Bernh. p. 304, Jelf 833. 2), change the structure of the sentence and substitute καὶ αὐτός (οὗτος).[1] From the N. T. may be quoted 2 P. ii. 3, οἷς τὸ κρίμα ἔκπαλαι οὐκ ἀργεῖ, καὶ ἡ ἀπώλεια αὐτῶν οὐ νυστάζει· A. iii. 13 [Rec.], 1 C. viii. 6 : it is less correct to bring in here Rev. xvii. 2, μεθ' ἧς ἐπόρνευσαν . . . καὶ ἐμεθύσθησαν ἐκ τοῦ οἴνου τῆς πορνείας αὐτῆς, for the relative construction was here necessarily avoided on account of the nouns to be connected with the pronoun. In Hebrew, owing to the simplicity of its structure, the continuation of the construction without the relative is very common; but we must not, by supplying אֲשֶׁר with the subsequent clause, give to the sentence a turn which is foreign to the character of the language.—To require the relative instead of αὐτός or οὗτος in such passages as Jo. i. 6, A. x. 36, L. ii. 36, xix. 2, is to misapprehend the simplicity of the N. T. diction, especially as similar examples are not unfrequently to be found in Greek authors (Ælian 12. 18, Strabo 8. 371, Philostr. Soph. 1. 25) ; comp. Kypke I. 347. In 1 C. vii. 13, however, for ἥτις ἔχει ἄνδρα ἄπιστον καὶ αὐτὸς [2] συνευδοκεῖ κ.τ.λ., Paul might also have written ὃς συνευδοκεῖ.

In the N. T., as elsewhere, ὁ αὐτός the same is followed by a dative of the person, in the sense of the same with, as in 1 C. xi. 5 ; compare Her. 4. 119, Xen. Mem. 1. 1. 13, 2. 1. 5, Cyr. 3. 3. 35, 7. 1. 2, Isocr. Paneg. c. 23, Plat. Menex. 244 d, Dio C. 332. 97.

Rem. In classical Greek, as is well known, the nominative of αὐτός is not used for the unemphatic he (Krüg. pp. 128, 135). Nor can any decisive instance of such a usage be adduced from the N. T.[3] (compare Fritz. Matt. p. 47) : even in Luke, who uses αὐτός most

---

[1] See Herm. Vig. p. 707, Ast, Plat. Legg. p. 449, Boisson. Nic. p. 32, Bornem. Xen. Conv. p. 196, Stallb. Plat. Protag. p. 68, Rep. I. 197, Foertsch, Obs. in Lysiam, p. 67, Weber, Dem. p. 355 ; Teipel, Scriptores Grœc., Germ., Lat. a relativa verbor. construct. sœpe neque injuria semper discessisse (Coesfeld 1841): compare Grotefend, Lat. Gram. § 143. 5, Kritz, Sallust II. 540.

[2] [Here the true reading is certainly καὶ οὗτος : hence we must read καὶ αὕτη in the preceding verse.]

[3] According to Thiersch (De Pentat. Vers. Alex. p. 98), the LXX use the masc. αὐτός for the simple pronoun (he), but not αὐτή or αὐτό, the demonstrative being regularly used instead of these. As regards the Apocrypha, Wahl denies this usage altogether (Clav. p. 80). [In the N. T. passages editors are divided between αὐτή and αὕτη (as in L. ii. 37, vii. 12) : L. xi. 14 might be an example of αὐτό so used, if the words καὶ αὐτὸ ἦν were genuine. See A. Buttm. p. 109,— also Mullach, Vulg. p. 192 sq.]

frequently (compare especially L. v. 16, 17, xix. 2), it never occurs without a certain degree of emphasis. It denotes

a. Self, in antitheses of various kinds, and for all three persons : Mk. ii. 25, ἐπείνασεν αὐτὸς καὶ οἱ μετ' αὐτοῦ· A. xviii. 19, ἐκείνους κατέλιπεν αὐτὸς δὲ εἰσελθών κ.τ.λ., L. v. 37, x. 1, xviii. 39, 1 C. iii. 15, Mk. i. 8, Jo. iv. 2, vi. 6, ix. 21, L. vi. 42, πῶς δύνασαι λέγειν . . . αὐτὸς τὴν ἐν τῷ ὀφθαλμῷ σοῦ δοκὸν οὐ βλέπων· H. xi. 11, πίστει καὶ αὐτὴ Σάρρα δύναμιν εἰς καταβολὴν σπέρματος ἔλαβεν, even *Sarah herself* (who had been unbelieving), Jo. xvi. 27, αὐτὸς ὁ πατὴρ φιλεῖ ὑμᾶς, *He himself*, of himself (without entreaty on my part, ver. 26), Rom. viii. 23. Αὐτός is thus used by the disciples in speaking of Christ (compare the familiar αὐτὸς ἔφα), Mk. iv. 38, L. v. 16, ix. 51 (xxiv. 15), xxiv. 36 ; compare Fischer, *Ind. Theophan.* s. v. αὐτός. See the lexicons.

b. He, with emphasis,—*he* and no other : Mt. i. 21, καλέσεις τὸ ὄνομα αὐτοῦ Ἰησοῦν· αὐτὸς γὰρ σώσει τὸν λαόν· xii. 50, Col. i. 17. Αὐτός does not stand for the unemphatic *he* in L. i. 22 (*he* himself, as contrasted with the others : ἐπέγνωσαν), ii. 28 (*he*, Simeon, as contrasted with the parents of Jesus, ver. 27), iv. 15, vii. 5 (*he* by himself, at his own expense), A. xiv. 12 (*he*, Paul, as the principal person, ver. 11),[1] Mk. vii. 36 [*Rec.*].[2] (On the antithesis αὐτοὶ . . . ἐν ἑαυτοῖς, Rom. viii. 23, see Fritz. *in loc.*)

5. The reflexive pronoun ἑαυτοῦ, which, as compounded of ἕ and αὐτός, naturally belongs to the third person, is regularly so used in the N. T.,—not unfrequently in antithesis and with emphasis (1 C. x. 29, xiv. 4, E. v. 28, al.). Where however no ambiguity is to be apprehended, it is used for the other persons :—

a. In the plural. For the 1st person : Rom. viii. 23 (ἡμεῖς) αὐτοὶ ἐν ἑαυτοῖς στενάζομεν· 1 C. xi. 31, 2 C. i. 9, x. 12, A. xxiii. 14, al. For the 2d person : Jo. xii. 8, τοὺς πτωχοὺς πάντοτε ἔχετε μεθ' ἑαυτῶν· Ph. ii. 12, τὴν ἑαυτῶν σωτηρίαν

---

[1] [Lünemann adds 1 Th. iii. 11, iv. 16, v. 23, 2 Th. ii. 16, iii. 16 ; but these should rather come under (*a*).]

[2] [The same view of the N. T. use of the nominative of αὐτός is taken by Fritzsche, Meyer, Lünemann, and others. On the other side see A. Buttmann (*Gr.* p. 106 sqq.), who maintains, (1) that, even if Winer's assertions are correct, they do not prove that N. T. usage agrees in this point with that of the classic writers : (2) that there are not a few passages in which αὐτός is used though there is neither emphasis nor contrast. Compare also Ellicott on Col. i. 17 : "Though αὐτός appears both in this and the great majority of passages in the N. T. to have its proper classical force ('ut rem ab aliis rebus discernendam esse indicet,' Hermann, *Dissert.* αὐτός, 1), the use of the corresponding Aramaic pronoun should make us cautious in pressing it *in every case*." Similarly Green, *Gr.* p. 117. On the classical usage see Don. pp. 375, 462, and Jelf 654. 1, 656 ; and as to modern Greek (in which the nomin. of αὐτός is used for *he*) see Mullach p. 317.]

κατεργάζεσθε· Mt. iii. 9, xxiii. 31, A. xiii. 46, H. iii. 13, x. 25, al. (Jelf 654. 2. *b*.)

b. In the singular,—though far less frequently (Bernh. p. 272). For the 2d person : Jo. xviii. 34, ἀφ' ἑαυτοῦ σὺ τοῦτο λέγεις, where σεαυτοῦ in B and other MSS. is certainly a correction : in Rom. xiii. 9, Mt. xxii. 39 (from the LXX), and G. v. 14, σεαυτόν is the better reading.

This usage is also found in Greek writers :[1] for (*b*) compare Xen. *Mem.* 1. 4. 9, *Cyr.* 1. 6. 44, Aristot. *Nicom.* 2. 9, 9. 9, Ælian 1. 21, Arrian, *Epict.* 4. 3. 11.[2] On ἑαυτῶν for ἀλλήλων see the lexicons : compare Döderlein, *Synon.* III. 270 (Jelf 654. 3).

Αὐτοῦ is frequently used by (Attic) Greek writers as a reflexive :[3] the MSS. however often vary between αὐτοῦ and αὑτοῦ.[4] To decide between the two on internal grounds is the more difficult because the Greeks use the reflexive pronoun even when the principal subject is remote,[5] and because in many cases it depended entirely on the writer's preference whether the reflexive pronoun should be used or not.[6] In the N. T. also—where from the time of Griesbach αὐτοῦ has

---

[1] See Locella, *Xen. Eph.* 164, Bremi, Æschin. *Oratt.* I. 66, Herm. Soph. *Trach.* 451, Boisson. Philostr. *Her.* p. 326, Jacobs, *Achill. Tat.* p. 932, Held, Plut. *Æm. Paul.* p. 130. Compare however the assertion of an ancient grammarian, Apollonius, in Wolf and Buttmann's *Mus. Antiq. Studior.* I. 360, and Eustath. *ad Odyss.* ι', p. 240.

[2] [In Jo. xviii. 34, Lachmann, Tregelles, Alford, Westcott and Hort, read σεαυτοῦ, with the best MSS. : Rom. xiii. 9, Mt. xxii. 39, G. v. 14, are *all* from the LXX (Lev. xix. 18, also quoted in Mt. xix. 19, Mk. xii. 31, L. x. 27, Ja. ii. 8), and here also the best MSS. have σεαυτόν. "It is worthy of notice that, in those passages of the classics in which the singular of ἑαυτοῦ is thus used, there is almost always considerable uncertainty of reading : this is not the case with the examples of the plural. And since it is often in the inferior and later MSS. that we find these examples, we may at any rate assume it as certain that this usage was in later times tolerably general (indeed almost universal in the case of the plural), and was therefore *very familiar to the transcribers.* Hence the common assumption that *through ignorance of this idiom* the transcribers altered the 3d person into the 1st or 2d, must be given up in regard to the passages in the N. T., and to many of those in earlier writers." A. Buttm. *Gr.* p. 114. In modern Greek ἑαυτοῦ is used for all three persons ; the popular language expresses ἐμαυτοῦ by τοῦ ἑαυτοῦ μου : see Mullach, *Vulg.* pp. 207, 320 sq., J. Donaldson, *Gr.* p. 17. See further Lightfoot on G. v. 14, Jelf 654. 2. *b*, Jebb, Soph. *Electra*, p. 30.]

[3] Arndt, *De pronom. reflex. ap. Græc.* (Neobrandenb. 1836).

[4] In later writers (as Æsop, the Scholiasts, al.) αὑτοῦ seems to predominate ; see Schæf. *Ind. ad Æsop.* p. 124, and comp. Thilo, *Apocr.* I. 163.

[5] Compare however Held, Plut. *Timol.* p. 373.

[6] See Buttm. Demosth. *Midias*, Exc. x. p. 140 sqq., F. Hermann, *Comm. Crit. ad Plutarch. superst.* p. 37 sq., Benseler, Isocr. *Areopag.* p. 220.—Bremi (in the *Jahrb. der Philol.* IX. p. 171) says : "On the use of αὐτοῦ and αὑτοῦ certain

been frequently introduced—careful editors have often been in doubt which of these two pronouns to prefer. In some passages either would be appropriate. In Mt. iii. 16, for instance, εἶδε τὸ πνεῦμα τοῦ θεοῦ ... ἐρχόμενον ἐπ᾽ αὐτόν would be said from the narrator's point of view, whilst ἐφ᾽ αὑτόν would refer directly to the subject of the verb εἶδε, namely Jesus (Krüg. p. 130). In general, it is improbable that the N. T. writers, whose style of narration is so simple (who, to quote a similar case, drop the relative construction, instead of carrying it on to a second clause, see p. 186), would use the reflexive pronoun when the subject is remote, i.e. when the subject and pronoun are not in the same clause. Accordingly, in Mt. *l.c.*,[1] E. i. 17, we should unhesitatingly write αὐτόν, αὐτοῦ; but in A. xii. 11, H. v. 7, Rom. xiv. 14, αὑτοῦ : see Fritz. *Matt.* Exc. 5, p. 858 sqq.—where also Matthiæ's view (Eur. *Iphig. Aul.* 800, and *Gr.* 148. Rem. 3) is examined,—and Poppo, *Thuc.* III. i. 159 sq. On the other hand, the fact noticed by Bengel (*Appar. ad* Mt. i. 21) deserves attention—that in the MSS. of the N. T. the prepositions ἀπό, ἐπί, ὑπό, κατά, μετά, are never written ἀφ᾽, ἐφ᾽, etc., when they come before αυτοῦ; from which we might conclude with Bleek (*Hebr.* II. 69) that the N. T. writers were not acquainted with the form αὑτοῦ, but always used ἑαυτοῦ instead where the reflexive pronoun was needed. And as those uncial MSS. of the N. T. and the LXX which possess diacritical marks have for the most part αὐτοῦ exclusively,[2]—though, it is true, these MSS. are not older than the eighth century, and the "*fere* constanter" leaves us to wish for a more accurate collation,—recent editors almost always write αὐτοῦ. In most of the passages there is no need whatever of a reflexive pronoun ; but it is difficult to believe that in Rom. iii. 25 Paul wrote εἰς ἔνδειξιν τῆς δικαιοσύνης αυτοῦ (over against ἐν αἵματι αὐτοῦ), or that John wrote αὐτὸς περὶ αυτοῦ in ix. 21: compare also E. i. 9, Rom. xiv. 14, L. xix. 15, xiii. 34, Mk. viii. 35, Rev. xi. 7, xiii. 2. For these reasons, the decision between αὐτοῦ and αὑτοῦ in the N. T. must (as in classical Greek) be left to the *cautious* judgment of editors.[3]

---

rules may be easily and safely laid down, but there are cases in which the decision between the two words will always remain doubtful, and it is much more difficult to hit the mark in Greek than in Latin .... When in the mind of the writer the reference to the subject predominates, the reflexive is used ; when the subject is viewed as more remote, the 3d personal pronoun. In Greek one must give oneself up to his own personal feeling,—to the mood of the moment, if you will." On reciprocation in general, see some good observations by Hoffmann in the *Jahrb. der Philol.* VII. p. 38 sqq. [Jelf 653, Frost, *Thucyd.* pp. 269, 296, 317.]

[1] [Even if the question were not decided here by the preceding ἐπ᾽ (not ἐφ᾽). To the prepositions mentioned below Lünemann adds ἀντί.]

[2] Tischend. *Præf. N. T.* p. 26 sq., [p. 58, ed. 7].

[3] [A. Buttmann (*Gr.* p. 111) urges the following additional reasons in favour of the opinion that ἑαυτοῦ is almost always the form used by the N. T. writers when they wish to employ the reflexive pron. of the 3d pers., and that therefore αυτοῦ must in most cases be written without the aspirate. (1) In the 2d person we always find σεαυτοῦ, not σαυτοῦ. (2) The ordinary rule for the *position* of

6. The personal pronouns ἐγώ, σύ, ἡμεῖς, etc., cannot be dispensed with in the oblique cases; but in the nominative they are regularly omitted, unless there belongs to them (usually in consequence of antithesis) some emphasis, manifest or latent: Ph. iv. 11, ἐγὼ ἔμαθον ἐν οἷς εἰμὶ αὐτάρκης εἶναι· Jo. ii. 10, πᾶς ἄνθρωπος . . . . σὺ τετήρηκας κ.τ.λ., Rom. vii. 17, L. xi. 19, A. x. 15, Mk. xiv. 29, Jo. xviii. 38 sq., G. ii. 9; A. xi. 14, σωθήσῃ σὺ καὶ ὁ οἶκός σου· Jo. x. 30, A. xv. 10, 1 C. vii. 12, L. i. 18; Mt. vi. 12, ἄφες ἡμῖν τὰ ὀφειλήματα ἡμῶν ὡς καὶ ἡμεῖς ἀφήκαμεν κ.τ.λ.; Jo. iv. 10, σὺ ἂν ᾔτησας αὐτόν (whereas *I* asked of thee, ver. 7, 9), Mk. vi. 37, δότε αὐτοῖς ὑμεῖς φαγεῖν (*ye*, since they themselves have no provisions with them, ver. 36), Jo. vi. 30, xxi. 22, Mk. xiii. 9, 23, 1 C. ii. 3 sq., Mt. xvii. 19, 2 Tim. iv. 6. So where the person is characterised by a word in apposition, as in Jo. iv. 9, πῶς σὺ Ἰουδαῖος ὢν κ.τ.λ., Rom. xiv. 4, σὺ τίς εἶ ὁ κρίνων ἀλλότριον οἰκέτην· Jo. x. 33, A. i. 24, iv. 24, L. i. 76, E. iv. 1 : or where there is reference to some description contained in the previous context, as in Jo. v. 44 (ver. 42, 43), Rom. ii. 3 ; or where it is supposed that such a description will suggest itself, as in Jo. i. 30, L. ix. 9 (I, who as king cannot be mistaken as to what has taken place), E. v. 32 (I, as apostle), Jo. ix. 24, G. vi. 8,[1] 1 C. xi. 23. In an address σύ is found particularly when one out of many is indicated (Jo. i. 43, Ja. ii. 3), or where the person addressed is made prominent by an attributive, as in 2 Tim. iii. 1 [ii. 1 ?], Mt. xi. 23.

In no instance do we find these pronouns expressed where no emphasis rests upon them, and where consequently they might have been omitted[2] (Bornem. Xen. *Conv.* 187). If, for instance, we find in E. v. 32, ἐγὼ δὲ λέγω εἰς Χριστόν, but

---

αὑτοῦ and ἑαυτοῦ, in a possessive sense (ὁ ἑαυτοῦ πατήρ, ὁ πατὴρ αὐτοῦ, see Jelf 652. 3), is commonly observed in the N. T. (3) The 1st and 2d personal pronouns are *very* frequently used in the N. T. instead of the reflexive, unless the pronoun is immediately dependent on the verb. On the principle of the exception just named, Buttmann would write αὑτ. in Jo. ii. 24, xix. 17, A. xiv. 17, Rev. viii. 6, xviii. 7 ; unless indeed the full form ἑαυτ. be received. See Ellicott on E. i. 9.—Winer often writes αὑτοῦ where all recent editors have αὐτοῦ.]

[1] [A mistake, probably for G. vi. 17 (a passage quoted in ed. 5, as illustrating the use of the pronoun without *direct* antithesis), or for 1 C. vi. 8. A few lines above I have written 2 Tim. for 1 Tim. (iv. 6), on the authority of ed. 5.]

[2] [See Green, *Gr.* pp. 113-116. The opposite view, that the nominative of the pronoun is often expressed in the N. T. where no particular emphasis is intended, is maintained by A. Buttmann (p. 132). In modern Greek the classical usage is observed (Mullach p. 311).]

SECT. XXII.]   PERSONAL AND POSSESSIVE PRONOUNS.   191

simply λέγω δέ in 1 C. i. 12, Rom. xv. 8, there is an emphasis designed in the first passage and none in the others. In regard to the omission or insertion, and also the position, of these pronouns, the MSS. vary very greatly: the decision must not be made to depend on any fancied peculiarity of a writer's style (Gersdorf p. 472 sq.), but on the nature of the sentence.

The personal pronoun is inserted and omitted in two consecutive sentences in L. x. 23 sq., οἱ βλέποντες ἃ βλέπετε . . . . πολλοὶ προφῆται . . . . ἠθέλησαν ἰδεῖν, ἃ ὑμεῖς βλέπετε. But it is only in the latter case that there is any real antithesis (ὑμεῖς in contrast with προφῆται, βασιλεῖς, etc.): in ver. 23, the ὀφθαλμοὶ βλέποντες ἃ βλέπετε are, properly speaking, none other than those of whom the βλέπετε is predicated. Compare 2 C. xi. 29, τίς ἀσθενεῖ καὶ οὐκ ἀσθενῶ; τίς σκανδαλίζεται καὶ οὐκ ἐγὼ πυροῦμαι:[1] here we must not overlook the fact that in the second member πυροῦμαι (which the apostle attributes to *himself*) is a stronger word than σκανδαλίζεσθαι. In 1 C. xiii. 12, τότε ἐπιγνώσομαι καθὼς καὶ ἐπεγνώσθην, some authorities add ἐγώ to the latter verb, but improperly, since the contrast is expressed by the voice of the verb.

It may be remarked in passing that, in some books of the O. T., the expressive אָנֹכִי with a verb is rendered in the LXX by ἐγώ εἰμι, accompanied by the 1st person of the verb; e. g. Jud. xi. 27, וְאָנֹכִי לֹא חָטָאתִי, καὶ νῦν ἐγώ εἰμι οὐχ ἥμαρτον: compare v. 3, vi. 18, 1 K. ii. 2.

On αὐτὸς ἐγώ (in A. x. 26, ἐγὼ αὐτός) see Fritz. *Rom*. II. 75.

7. The possessive pronouns are sometimes to be taken objectively: L. xxii. 19, ἡ ἐμὴ ἀνάμνησις, *memoria mei* (1 C. xi. 24), Rom. xi. 31, τῷ ὑμετέρῳ ἐλέει· xv. 4, 1 C. xv. 31, xvi. 17; but not Jo. xv. 10.[2] So also in Greek writers, especially in poetry: Xen. *Cyr*. 3. 1. 28, εὐνοίᾳ καὶ φιλίᾳ τῇ ἐμῇ· Thuc. 1. 77, τὸ ἡμέτερον δέος· 6. 89, Plat. *Gorg*. 486 a, Antiphon 6. 41, al.[3] As to Latin, compare Kritz on Sallust, *Cat*. p. 243.

The N. T. writers occasionally employ ἴδιος instead of a personal pronoun, by the same kind of misuse as when in later Latin *proprius* takes the place of *suus* or *ejus* (compare also οἰκεῖος in the Byzantine writers[4]). Thus in Mt. xxii. 5 we have

---
[1] ["Who is made to stumble without my being the one who burns? Of the offence which another takes, I have the pain." Meyer.]
[2] [This should be xv. 9 (or 11).]
[3] [Jelf 652. *Obs*. 6: for the N. T. see Green, *Gr*. p. 124, where the limited use of possessive pronouns in the N. T. is also noticed.]
[4] See for example the Indices to Agathias, Petr. Patricius, Priscus, Dexippus, Glycas, and Theophanes, in the Bonn edition. [Mullach, *Vulg*. p. 53.]

ἀπῆλθεν εἰς τὸν ἴδιον ἀγρόν, though there is no emphasis, i.e., no contrast with κοινός or ἀλλότριος; the parallel words in the second member are ἐπὶ τ. ἐμπορίαν αὐτοῦ· Mt. xxv. 14, ἐκάλεσε τοὺς ἰδίους δούλους· Tit. ii. 9, Jo. i. 42. Similarly, οἱ ἴδιοι ἄνδρες is used for *husbands* in E. v. 22, Tit. ii. 5, 1 P. iii. 1, 5; where οἱ ἄνδρες, with or without a personal pronoun, would have been sufficient (comp. 1 C. vii. 2).[1] But this usage is on the whole rare. Greek writers probably furnish no similar example,—for the instances quoted by Schwarz and Weiske[2] are all unsatisfactory, or at most only apparently similar: the same may be said of Diod. S. 5. 40. Conversely, σφέτερος is occasionally taken for ἴδιος, see Wessel. *Diod. S.* II. 9. By the Fathers, however, ἴδιος is certainly sometimes used for a personal pronoun; compare Epiphan. *Opp.* II. 622 a.

In by far the greater number of passages there is an antithesis, open or latent: Jo. x. 3, v. 18, Mt. xxv. 15, A. ii. 6, Rom. viii. 32, xi. 24, xiv. 4, 5, 1 Th. ii. 14, H. ix. 12, xiii. 12, also Mt. ix. 1. The parallel clauses in 1 C. vii. 2, ἕκαστος τὴν ἑαυτοῦ γυναῖκα ἐχέτω, καὶ ἑκάστη τὸν ἴδιον ἄνδρα ἐχέτω, we may render, *Let every man have his wife, and let every woman have her own husband:* Isocr. Demon. p. 18, σκόπει πρῶτον, πῶς ὑπὲρ τῶν αὐτοῦ διῴκησεν· ὁ γὰρ κακῶς διανοηθεὶς ὑπὲρ τῶν ἰδίων κ.τ.λ. In H. vii. 27, Böhme, Kühnöl, and others wrongly take ἴδιος for the mere possessive pronoun; to the ἴδιαι ἁμαρτίαι are expressly opposed αἱ τοῦ λαοῦ (as ἀλλότριαι): comp. also iv. 10. When ἴδιος has a personal pronoun joined with it, as in Tit. i. 12, ἴδιος αὐτῶν προφήτης (Wis. xix. 12), the pronoun merely expresses the notion of *belonging to* (*their poet*), whilst ἴδιος gives the antithesis *their own poet*,—not a foreigner. For similar instances see Æschin. *Ctesiph.* 294 c, Xen. *Hell.* 1. 4. 13, Plat. *Menex.* 247 b: see Lob. p. 441, Wurm, *Dinarch.* p. 70.

---

[1] Meyer introduces into these passages an emphasis, which either is altogether remote (Mt. xxv. 14), or would have been fully expressed by the pronoun. This very use of ἴδιος for the sake of emphasis, where there is no trace of an antithesis, is unknown to Greek writers. [See Ellicott on E. iv. 28, v. 22. It may be mentioned that in modern Greek ὁ ἴδιος is equivalent to ὁ αὐτός, and also to αὐτὸς ὁ; and that the ordinary possessive pronouns are formed by joining μου etc. to ὁ ἰδικός, which is by some derived from ἴδιος (Mullach, *Vulg.* p. 188 sq., 313, J Donalds. *Gr.* p. 18 sq.).]

[2] Schwarz, *Comment.* p. 687, Weiske, *De Pleon.* p. 62.

SECT. XXII.] PERSONAL AND POSSESSIVE PRONOUNS. 193

Κατά joined with the accusative of a personal pronoun has been regarded as forming a periphrasis for a possessive pronoun: E. i. 15, ἡ καθ' ὑμᾶς πίστις, *your faith*, A. xvii. 28, οἱ καθ' ὑμᾶς ποιηταί· xviii. 15, νόμος ὁ καθ' ὑμᾶς· xxvi. 3, al. This view is correct on the whole, but the possessive meaning follows very simply from the signification of κατά. Ἡ καθ' ὑμᾶς πίστις is strictly *fides quæ ad vos pertinet, apud vos (in vobis) est*: comp. Ælian 2. 12, ἡ κατ' αὐτὸν ἀρετή· Dion. H. I. 235, οἱ καθ' ἡμᾶς χρόνοι. Compare § 30. 3. Rem. 5.

Rem. 1. The genitive of the personal pronouns, especially μοῦ and σοῦ (more rarely ὑμῶν, ἡμῶν, αὐτοῦ), is very frequently [1] placed *before* the governing noun (and its article), though no special emphasis is laid on the pronoun: Mt. ii. 2, vii. 24, viii. 8, xvi. 18, xvii. 15, xxiii. 8, Mk. v. 30, ix. 24, Rom. xiv. 16, Ph. ii. 2, iv. 14, Col. ii. 5, iv. 18, 1 C. viii. 12, 1 Th. ii. 16, iii. 10, 13, 2 Th. ii. 17, iii. 5, 1 Tim. iv. 15, 2 Tim. i. 4, Phil. 5, L. vi. 47, xii. 18, xv. 30, xvi. 6, xix. 35, al.; Jo. ii. 23, iii. 19, 21, 33, iv. 47, ix. 11, 21, 26, xi. 32, xii. 40, xiii. 1, al.; 1 Jo. iii. 20, Rev. iii. 1, 2, 8, 15, x. 9, xiv. 18, xviii. 5, al. So also when the noun has a preposition: Jo. xi. 32, ἔπεσεν αὐτοῦ εἰς τοὺς πόδας. In many passages of this kind, however, variants are noted. See on the whole Gersdorf p. 456 sqq.

The genitive is *designedly* placed before the noun

(*a*) In E. ii. 10, αὐτοῦ γάρ ἐσμεν ποίημα (more emphatic than ἐσμὲν γάρ π. αὐτοῦ), L. xii. 30, xxii. 53.

(*b*) In 1 C. ix. 11, μέγα, εἰ ἡμεῖς ὑμῶν τὰ σαρκικὰ θερίσομεν, on account of the antithesis; Ph. iii. 20.

(*c*) In Jo. xi. 48, ἡμῶν καὶ τὸν τόπον καὶ τὸ ἔθνος, where the genitive belongs to two nouns;[2] A. xxi. 11, L. xii. 35, Rev. ii. 19, 2 C. viii. 4,[3] 2 Tim. iii. 10, Tit. i. 15, 1 Th. i. 3, ii. 19 (Diod. S. 11. 16).

The form ἐμοῦ, dependent on a noun and placed after it, appears only in such combinations as πίστεως ὑμῶν τε καὶ ἐμοῦ Rom. i. 12, μητέρα αὐτοῦ καὶ ἐμοῦ Rom. xvi. 13.

The insertion of the personal pronoun between the article and the noun (as in 2 C. xii. 19, ὑπὲρ τῆς ὑμῶν οἰκοδομῆς· xiii. 9, i. 6) occurs on the whole but rarely.[4] Compare, in general, Krüger on Xen. *Anab.* 5. 6. 16. When an attributive precedes the noun, the prefixed

---

[1] The usual order in the N. T., as elsewhere, is ὁ πατήρ μου, ὁ υἱός μου ὁ ἀγαπητός. The genitive of αὐτός also is, as a rule, placed after the noun: see however Rost p. 453 (Jelf 652. 3).
[2] Where this order was not adopted, the pronoun was necessarily repeated for the sake of perspicuity: A. iv. 28, ὅσα ἡ χείρ σου καὶ ἡ βουλή σου προώρισε κ.τ.λ., Mt. xii. 47; also (from the LXX) L. xviii. 20, A. ii. 17. [The second σοῦ is probably not genuine in A. iv. and L. xviii.]
[3] [This is not an example: see § 30. 7. *a*.]
[4] [A. Buttmann adds: "In Paul only, and with no other pronoun than ὑμῶν."]

genitive of the personal pronoun has its place between the attributive and the noun: 2 C. v. 1, ἡ ἐπίγειος ἡμῶν οἰκία· 2 C. iv. 16, ὁ ἔξω ἡμῶν ἄνθρωπος.

Rem. 2. In both Greek and Hebrew we sometimes find an apparently pleonastic use of the dative of the personal pronouns in easy and familiar language (*dativus ethicus*[1]). Of this usage, which certainly might have been expected to occur in the N. T., Mt. xxi. 5 (a quotation from the O. T.), and also Mt. xxi. 2, Rev. ii. 5, 16, H. x. 34, have been considered examples. In Mt. xxi. 2, however, ἀγάγετέ μοι means *bring it [them] to me*, and ἀγάγετε by itself would have been incomplete. In Rev. ii. ἔρχομαί σοι ταχύ is *I will come upon thee* (ἐπὶ σέ, iii. 3) *quickly*,—for punishment; compare ver. 14, ἔχω κατὰ σοῦ ὀλίγα, and ver. 16, μετανόησον.[2] In the last passage, ἔχειν ἑαυτοῖς ὕπαρξιν means *repositam* or *destinatam sibi habere*,—*for themselves*, as belonging to themselves. In Mt. xxi. 5 also σοί is not without force.

Rem. 3. It is usual to take ἡ ψυχή μου, σου, etc., as periphrases for personal pronouns (Weiske, *Pleon.* p. 72 sq.),—both in quotations from the O. T. (e.g. Mt. xii. 18, A. ii. 27, H. x. 38), and in the N. T. language proper; and this usage is regarded as being in the first instance a Hebraism.[3] In no passage of the N. T., however, is ψυχή entirely without meaning, any more than נֶפֶשׁ in the O. T.,—see my edition of *Simonis*. It signifies *the soul* (the spiritual principle on which the influence of Christianity is exerted, 1 P. i. 9) in such expressions as ἐκδαπανηθήσομαι ὑπὲρ τῶν ψυχῶν ὑμῶν 2 C. xii. 15, ἐπίσκοπος τῶν ψυχῶν ὑμῶν 1 P. ii. 25, H. xiii. 17;—or *the heart* (the seat of the feelings and desires), as Rev. xviii. 14, ἐπιθυμίαι τῆς ψυχῆς σου· Mt. xxvi. 38, περίλυπός ἐστιν ἡ ψυχή μου· A. ii. 43, ἐγίνετο πάσῃ ψυχῇ φόβος. Nor is ψυχή redundant in Rom. ii. 9; it denotes that in man which *feels* the θλῖψις and the στενοχωρία, even though these may affect the body. In Rom. xiii. 1, πᾶσα ψυχὴ ἐξουσίαις ὑπερεχούσαις ὑποτασσέσθω, the simple πᾶσα ψυχή (compare 1 P. iii. 20) may be *every soul*, i.e. *every one;* but even in estimates of population "so many souls" (in Latin *capita*) is not precisely identical with "so many men." Compare also A. iii. 23 (from the LXX). Hence the use of ψυχή must in every instance be referred to vividness or to circumstantiality of language, which is altogether different from pleonasm. It is not at all uncommon to find this use of the word

---

[1] Buttm. *Gr.* 120. 2, and on Dem. *Midias* p. 9; Jacob, Luc. *Toxar.* p. 138. In German the dative is used in exactly the same way, as *das war dir schön!* [See Donalds. p. 495 sq., Jelf 600. 2; and as to English, Latham, *Eng. Lang.* II. 341, Craik, *Engl. of Shakesp.* p. 113 (ed. 3), Clyde, *Greek Synt.* p. 38, Farrar, *Gr. Synt.* p. 74.]

[2] On the similar phrase ἥκω σοι (e.g. Luc. *Pisc.* 16, ἥξω ὑμῖν ἐκδικάσασα τὴν δίκην) see Hermann, Luc. *Conscr. Hist.* p. 179. It is a kind of *dativus incommodi* (§ 31. 4. *b*): comp. 1 K. xv. 20 (LXX). [In H. x. 34 the best texts have ἑαυτούς.]

[3] Gesen. *Lg.* p. 752 sq., [*Hebr. Gr.* p. 202 (Bagst.), Kalisch, *Hebr. Gr.* I. 221], Vorst, *Hebr.* p. 121 sq., Rückert on Rom. xiii. 1.

in Greek writers (compare Xen. *Cyr.* 5. 1. 27, Ælian 1. 32), especially the poets, e. g. Soph. *Philoct.* 714, *Œd. Col.* 499, 1207:[1] it is no Hebraism, but an example of antique vividness of expression. See further Georgi, *Vind.* p. 274, Schwarz *ad Olear.* p. 28, *Comment.* p. 1439.[2]

Section XXIII.

DEMONSTRATIVE PRONOUNS.

1. The pronoun οὗτος sometimes refers, not to the noun which stands nearest to it, but to one more remote, which is to be regarded as the principal subject, and which therefore was to the writer the nearest *psychologically*,—was more vividly present to his mind than any other:[3] A. iv. 11, οὗτός ('Ιησοῦς Χριστός in ver. 10, though ὁ θεός is the nearest noun) ἐστιν ὁ λίθος. So in 1 Jo. v. 20, οὗτός ἐστιν ὁ ἀληθινὸς θεός, the pronoun refers to ὁ θεός—not Χριστός (which immediately precedes), as the older theologians maintained on dogmatic grounds; for, in the first place, ἀληθινὸς θεός is a constant and exclusive epithet of the Father; and, secondly, there follows a warning against idolatry, and ἀληθινὸς θεός is always contrasted with εἴδωλα.[4]

A. viii. 26, αὕτη ἐστὶν ἔρημος, is doubtful, some supplying the nearest subject Γάζα, others ὁδός. See Kühnöl *in loc.*, and my

---

[1] In these passages it is not hard to discover the notion which is expressed by the Latin *anima*, and I do not know why Ellendt (*Lex. Soph.* II. 979) takes ψυχή as a mere circumlocution. The passages of Plato quoted by Ast (*Lex. Plat.* III. 575) would really lose their distinctive colouring, if the canon "orationem amplificat" were applied to them.

[2] Mt. vi. 25, where ψυχή is contrasted with the σῶμα, can present no difficulty to any one who is familiar with the anthropological notions of the Jews.—Nor is καρδία a mere circumlocution in A. xiv. 17, ἐμπιπλῶν τροφῆς καὶ εὐφροσύνης τὰς καρδίας ὑμῶν· or in Ja. v. 5, ἐθρέψατε τὰς καρδίας ὑμῶν; for, if so, it must be possible to say *he struck his heart,* instead of *he struck him,* etc. In these verses, however, καρδία is probably not used (as לֵב sometimes is) in a merely material sense, in accordance with the physiological notions of antiquity,—*to strengthen the heart,* i. e. in the first instance *the stomach* and by means of this *the heart* (even in Greek the meaning *stomach* is not entirely effaced in καρδία); but the idea of *enjoyment* is included. See Baumgarten on the last passage.

[3] Schæf. *Dem.* V. 322, Stallb. Plat. *Phædr.* pp. 28, 157, Foertsch, *Obs. in Lysiam* p. 74. (Jelf 655. *Obs.* 1.)

[4] [So Alford (who also urges the parallelism with Jo. xvii. 3), Lücke (*Bibl. Cat.* vol. xv. p. 288 sqq.), Haupt *in loc.*: on the other side see Ebrard, *Comment.* p. 345 sqq. (Clark), and Wordsworth *in loc.*]

RWB. I. 395: I decidedly prefer ὁδός.¹ There is less difficulty in A. vii. 19, 2 Jo. 7. For examples from Greek prose writers see Ast, Plat. *Polit.* 417, *Legg.* p. 77.

Conversely, in A. iii. 13 ἐκεῖνος is to be referred to the nearest subject (Krüg. p. 138,² Jelf 655. 7): so also in Jo. vii. 45, where ἐκεῖνοι refers to the members of the Sanhedrin, ἀρχιερεῖς καὶ φαρισαίους, regarded (as the single article shows) as forming one body. For an example of οὗτος and ἐκεῖνος so combined that the former belongs to the more distant and the latter to the nearer subject, see Plutarch, *Vit. Demosth.* 3; and for examples of ἐκεῖνος where there is only one subject, and where we might have expected οὗτος or simply αὐτός, see 2 C. viii. 9, Tit. iii. 7.³

In Ph. i. 18, καὶ ἐν τούτῳ χαίρω, the demonstrative simply refers to the main thought Χριστὸς καταγγέλλεται: in 2 P. i. 4, διὰ τούτων refers to ἐπαγγέλματα.

The relative also is supposed sometimes to refer to a remote subject (compare Bernh. p. 297).⁴ Thus in 1 C. i. 8 (see Pott *in loc.*) it has been maintained that ὅς relates to θεός in ver. 4, as the principal subject, though Ἰησ. Χριστ. immediately precedes. This however is not necessary, either on account of τοῦ κυρίου ἡμῶν Ἰησοῦ Χρ. at the end of this verse (compare Col. ii. 11, E. iv. 12), or on account of πιστὸς ὁ θεός which immediately follows; for that which is here ascribed to God, the calling εἰς κοινωνίαν Ἰ. Χρ., is at the same time a calling to the βεβαιοῦσθαι through Christ, which (βεβαιοῦσθαι) indeed can only be effected in the fellowship of Christ. This canon has been applied to H. ix. 4 (see Kühnöl *in loc.*), to evade antiquarian difficulties, and to Rom. v. 12 (ἐφ' ᾧ) on dogmatic grounds; in both instances quite erroneously. There is no difficulty in H. v. 7 and 2 Th. ii. 9. In 2 P. iii. 12 δι' ἥν may very well be referred to the nearest word ἡμέρας; in 1 P. iv. 11 ᾧ points back to the principal subject ὁ θεός. Of H. iii. 6 (οὗ οἶκος) recent expositors have taken the correct view.⁵

2. Where no special emphasis is intended, the demonstrative pronoun which precedes a relative sentence is usually included

---

¹ [See Meyer and Alford *in loc.*, Smith, *Dict. of B.* I. 657, Kitto, *Cycl.* II. 77, Greswell, *Diss.* I. 177 sqq., Robinson, *Bibl. Res.* II. 514, in support of this view.]
² Bremi, *Lys.* p. 154, Schoem. Plut. *Agis* p. 73, Foertsch *l. c.*
³ [On the question whether αὐτός and ἐκεῖνος can be used in the same passage with reference to *the same subject*, see Ellicott and Alford on 2 Tim. ii. 26, Riddell, Plat. *Apol.* p. 135.]
⁴ Göller, *Thuc.* II. 21, Siebelis, *Pausan.* III. 52, Schoem. *Isaeus* p. 242 sq., Ellendt, *Lex. Soph.* II. 369; and as to Latin, Kritz, *Sallust* II. 115.
⁵ [Of recent writers, Bleek, De Wette, Ebrard refer αὐτοῦ and οὗ to Χριστός; Lünemann, Delitzsch, Alford, Kurtz, Hofmann, and others, to *God.*]

in the relative pronoun (Krüg. p. 145 sq., Jelf 817):—not only

(*a*) Where, in accordance with the laws of government or of attraction, the demonstrative would have been in the same case as the relative; as

(α) A. i. 24, ἀνάδειξον ὃν ἐξελέξω (for τοῦτον ὅν), Rom. viii. 29, Jo. xviii. 26, συγγενὴς ὢν οὗ ἀπέκοψεν Πέτρος τὸ ὠτίον· 1 C. vii. 39, 2 C. xi. 12, Ph. iv. 11;

(β) A. viii. 24, ὅπως μηδὲν ἐπέλθῃ ἐπ᾽ ἐμὲ ὧν εἰρήκατε (for τούτων ἃ εἰρ.), xxi. 19, xxii. 15, xxvi. 16, 22, L. ix. 36, Rom. xv. 18, E. iii. 20, 1 C. [2 C.] xii. 17; compare Is. ii. 8, Wis. xii. 14, Tob. i. 8, xii. 2, 6, Plat. *Gorg.* 457 e, *Phæd.* 94 c, Isocr. *Phil.* p. 226, *De Pace* 388, Plut. *Virt. Mul.* p. 202, Xen. *An.* 1. 9. 25, Demosth. *Ep.* 5. *in.*, *Olynth.* I. p. 2, al., and Ellendt, *Lex. Soph.* II. 368:—but also

(*b*) Where the case of the demonstrative would have been different, as in Jo. xiii. 29, ἀγόρασον ὧν χρείαν ἔχομεν (for ταῦτα ὧν), Rom. vi. 16, Mt. xix. 11, A. viii. 19, xiii. 37, 1 C. xv. 36, 2 P. i. 9; compare Xen. *Cyr.* 6. 2. 1, ἀπήγγειλας ὧν ἐδέου· Eurip. *Med.* 735, ἐμμένειν ἅ σου κλύω (i.e. τούτοις ἅ, see Elmsley *in loc.*), Lysias p. 152 (Steph.), μὴ καταγιγνώσκετε ἀδικίαν τοῦ . . . δαπανῶντος ἀλλ᾽ ὅσοι . . . εἰθισμένοι εἰσὶν ἀναλίσκειν (for τούτων ὅσοι): see Stallb. Plat. *Rep.* I. 139, and compare Kritz, *Sallust* II. 301. In this case even the preposition on which the case of the demonstrative depends is omitted: Rom. x. 14, πῶς πιστεύσουσιν οὗ οὐκ ἤκουσαν· that is, εἰς τοῦτον οὗ κ.τ.λ.[1]

If a preposition precedes a relative before which the demonstrative is suppressed, this preposition logically belongs either

a. To the relative clause: Rom. x. 14, πῶς ἐπικαλέσονται εἰς ὃν οὐκ ἐπίστευσαν· vi. 21, τίνα καρπὸν εἴχετε τότε (that is, τούτων) ἐφ᾽ οἷς νῦν ἐπαισχύνεσθε·[2] xiv. 21, Jo. xix. 37 (from the

---

[1] Similar to this would be 1 Tim. ii. 10, ἀλλ᾽ ὃ πρέπει γυναιξὶν ἐπαγγελλομέναις θεοσέβειαν, if (with Matthies) we resolved ὃ πρέπει into ἐν τούτῳ ὃ πρέπει. But it is simpler and easier to join δι᾽ ἔργων with κοσμεῖν, ver. 9. The former meaning would have been more distinctly expressed by ἐν ᾧ πρέπει.

[2] Reiche evidently goes too far when he says that, in all other examples, it is only the demonstrative which would have been governed by the *verb* that is omitted, and never one governed by a *noun* (compare Jo. xviii. 26, L. xxiii. 41): even if the remark were true, it would not set aside the above explanation, see Fritzsche.—Perhaps also we might give to ἐφ᾽ οἷς the meaning which is discussed

LXX), L. v. 25, 2 P. ii. 12 ;¹ Soph. *Phil.* 957, Aristot. *Rhet.* 2. 1. 7, *Demon.* p. 2 :—or

    b. To the demonstrative understood : Jo. vi. 29, ἵνα πιστεύσητε εἰς ὃν ἀπέστειλεν ἐκεῖνος· xvii. 9, Rom. xiv. 22, 2 C. v. 10, xii. 6, G. i. 8 sq., H. v. 8 (Num. vi. 21). In H. ii. 18 also, ἐν ᾧ πέπονθεν αὐτὸς πειρασθείς, δύναται τοῖς πειραζομένοις βοηθῆσαι, should probably be resolved into ἐν τούτῳ ὃ πέπονθεν .... δύναται ... βοηθῆσαι. Compare Xen. *Mem.* 2. 6. 34, ἐγγίγνεται εὔνοια πρὸς οὓς ἂν ὑπολάβω εὐνοϊκῶς ἔχειν πρὸς ἐμέ. *Anab.* 1. 9. 25, *Hell.* 4. 8. 33, Demosth. *Con.* p. 729 a, *Olynth.* I. p. 2, *Ep.* 4. p. 118 b, Plat. *Rep.* 2. 375 d, *Phœd.* 61 c, Arrian, *Alex.* 6. 4. 3, Diog. L. 9. 67, 6. 74 :—or

    c. To both clauses : 2 C. ii. 3, ἵνα μὴ λύπην ἔχω ἀφ᾽ ὧν ἔδει με χαίρειν· 1 C. vii. 39, x. 30, Jo. xi. 6, Rom. xvi. 2 ; compare Isocr. *Evag.* p. 470, πλείους ἐν τούτοις τοῖς τόποις διατρίβειν, ἢ παρ᾽ οἷς πρότερον εἰωθότες ἦσαν (Cic. *Agrar.* 2. 27). 1 C. vii. 1 and Ph. iv. 11 may be thus explained.²

    In the same way, relative adverbs include the demonstrative : Jo. xi. 32, ἦλθεν ὅπου ἦν ὁ Ἰησοῦς (i.e. ἐκεῖσε ὅπου), vi. 62, Mk. v. 40, εἰσπορεύεται ὅπου ἦν τὸ παιδίον (compare Buttm. *Philoct.* p. 107), 1 C. xvi. 6, Mt. xxv. 24, συνάγων ὅθεν οὐ διεσκόρπισας (for ἐκεῖθεν ὅπου) ; compare Thuc. 1. 89. Still freer is the construction in Jo. xx. 19, τῶν θυρῶν κεκλεισμένων ὅπου ἦσαν οἱ μαθηταί κ.τ.λ.—That in condensed sentences of this kind (in which the Greek did not really supply a demonstrative in thought, see Krüg. p. 145) no comma should be inserted before the relative, has been already remarked : such punctuation would make Jo. vi. 29 quite meaningless.

    3. In emphatic passages the demonstrative may be frequently repeated in connected sentences : A. vii. 35 sqq., τοῦτον τὸν Μωϋσῆν.... τοῦτον ὁ θεὸς ἀπέσταλκεν.... οὗτος ἐξήγαγεν .... οὗτός ἐστιν ὁ Μωϋσῆς ὁ εἴπας .... οὗτός ἐστιν ὁ γενόμενος ἐν τῇ ἐκκλησίᾳ κ.τ.λ. ; and in a different spirit Jo. vi.

---

by Weber, *Dem.* p. 492 [viz. as representing ἐπὶ τούτοις, ἐφ᾽ οἷς, in the things in which (Dem. *Aristocr.* p. 684, *Phil.* 3. p. 119, al.).]

[1] Ἀγνοεῖν ἐν, Porphyr. *Abst.* 2. 53. Some would bring in here Rom. vii. 6, supplying ἐκείνῳ (νόμῳ) before ἐν ᾧ ; but ἐν ᾧ points back to ἀπὸ τοῦ νόμου, and ἀποθαν. is annexed absolutely to κατηργ., as a designation of manner : see Philippi.

[2] [See Jelf 822. *Obs.* 3 sq., Don. p. 363 ; and on the attraction of adverbs Jelf 822. *Obs.* 10.]

SECT. XXIII.]   DEMONSTRATIVE PRONOUNS.   199

42 [Rec.], οὐχ οὗτός ἐστιν Ἰησοῦς ὁ υἱὸς Ἰωσήφ . . . . πῶς οὖν λέγει οὗτος κ.τ.λ.[1] Amongst other passages, Bornemann quotes as parallel Xen. Mem. 4. 2. 28, καὶ οἵ τε ἀποτυγχάνοντες τῶν πραγμάτων ἐπιθυμοῦσι τούτους ὑπὲρ αὐτῶν βουλεύεσθαι, καὶ προΐστασθαί τε ἑαυτῶν τούτους, καὶ τὰς ἐλπίδας τῶν ἀγαθῶν ἐν τούτοις ἔχουσι καὶ διὰ πάντα ταῦτα πάντων μάλιστα τούτους ἀγαπῶσιν. In Latin, compare Cic. Verr. 3. 9. 23 : hunc in omnibus stupris, hunc in fenorum expilationibus, hunc in impuris conviviis principem adhibebat (Verres). With a relative adjective this *anaphora* occurs in Ph. iv. 8, ὅσα ἐστὶν ἀληθῆ, ὅσα σεμνά, ὅσα δίκαια, ὅσα ἁγνά, ὅσα προσφιλῆ, ὅσα εὔφημα. Compare further § 65. 5.

4. Another use of these pronouns is far more common. When the subject of a sentence or the predicate placed early in the sentence consists of several words, we find οὗτος or ἐκεῖνος introduced immediately before (more rarely *after*) the verb, that the subject or predicate may stand out more clearly or with greater prominence : Mt. xxiv. 13, ὁ ὑπομείνας εἰς τέλος, οὗτος σωθήσεται· Jo. i. 18, ὁ μονογενὴς υἱὸς ὁ ὢν εἰς τὸν κόλπον τοῦ πατρός, ἐκεῖνος ἐξηγήσατο· Mk. vii. 15, τὰ ἐκπορευόμενα ἀπ' αὐτοῦ, ἐκεῖνά ἐστι τὰ κοινοῦντα τὸν ἄνθρωπον· vii. 20, xii. 40, 1 C. vi. 4, τοὺς ἐξουθενημένους ἐν τῇ ἐκκλησίᾳ, τούτους καθίζετε· Rom. vii. 10, 15 sq., 19 sq., ix. 6, 8, xiv. 14, Jo. v. 11, xii. 48, Ph. i. 22, al. Compare Thuc. 4. 69, Xen. Conv. 8. 33, Ages. 4. 4, Plat. Protag. p. 339 d, Isocr. Evag. c. 23, Paus. 1. 24. 5, Lucian, Fug. 3, Æl. 12. 19, al.[2] Of the use of δέ to add strength to this emphasis [3] no example is found in the N. T. ; nor is there any trace here of the anacoluthon which is not uncommon in Greek writers in such cases,[4]—unless we bring under this head the attraction in 1 P. ii. 7.

Still more frequently are these pronouns so used after an antecedent clause beginning with a conjunction or a relative:

---

[1] See Bornemann, Bibl. Stud. der sächs. Geistl. I. 66 sq.
[2] See Schæf. Melet. p. 84, Jacob, Luc. Toxar. pp. 78, 144, and Luc. Alex. p. 7, Siebelis, Pausan. I. 63, Weber, Dem. p. 158. As to Latin see Kritz, Sallust I. 171. [Jelf 658. 1. On the frequency with which St. John thus uses ἐκεῖνος see Alford on Jo. vii. 29 : in classical Greek οὗτος is more common.]
[3] Buttm. Demosth. Mid. p. 152, Engelhardt, Plat. Menex. p. 252, [Jelf 770, 1. a; compare Don. p. 577. Some regard 2 P. ii. 20 as an example of this kind, but see Alford in loc: δέ is similarly used in A. xi. 17 Rec., see § 53. 7. b].
[4] Schwarz, De discipulor. Chr. solœcism. p. 77.

Jo. ix. 31, ἐάν τις θεοσεβὴς ᾖ καὶ τὸ θέλημα αὐτοῦ ποιῇ τούτου ἀκούει· Ja. i. 23, Mt. v. 19, xii. 50, Ph. iii. 7, iv. 9, 2 Tim. ii. 2.

We have a remarkable repetition of the demonstrative in L. xix. 2, καὶ αὐτὸς ἦν ἀρχιτελώνης καὶ οὗτος ἦν πλούσιος; the meaning is, *He was a chief publican and indeed* (as such) *a rich man,—isque* dives fuit (Matth. 470. 6, Jelf 655. 6. *Obs.* 2). Lachmann reads (with B) καὶ αὐτὸς (ἦν) πλούσιος; but this reading has less to recommend it.[1] Compare Xen. *Cyr.* 8. 3. 48.

It is a different case when in a lengthened sentence the substantive is taken up again by a pronoun, for the sake of clearness: 2 C. xii. 2, οἶδα ἄνθρωπον ἐν Χριστῷ ... πρὸ ἐτῶν δεκατεσσάρων ... εἴτε ἐν σώματι ... ἁρπαγέντα τὸν τοιοῦτον κ.τ.λ. (Plat. *Rep.* 3. 398, Xen. *Cyr.* 1. 3. 15), 1 C. v. 3, 5, A. i. 21 sq.: compare § 22. 4.

5. Before ὅτι, ἵνα, and similar particles, a demonstrative pronoun is often inserted (particularly in Paul and John) when the clause which follows is to receive special prominence. See 1 Tim. i. 9, εἰδὼς τοῦτο, ὅτι κ.τ.λ., A. xxiv. 14, ὁμολογῶ τοῦτό σοι, ὅτι κ.τ.λ., Rom. vi. 6,[2] 1 C. i. 12, xv. 50, 2 C. v. 15, x. 7, 11, 2 Th. iii. 10, Ph. i. 6, 25, Jo. xvii. 3, 2 P. i. 20, 1 Jo. i. 5, iii. 11, 23, iv. 9, 10, v. 3, 11, 14, 2 Jo. 6; compare Plat. *Soph.* 234 b. So εἰς τοῦτο before ἵνα, A. ix. 21, Rom. xiv. 9, 2 C. ii. 9, E. vi. 22, 1 P. iii. 9, 1 Jo. iii. 8; ἐν τούτῳ ὅτι, 1 Jo. iv. 13; ἐν τούτῳ ἵνα, Jo. xv. 8,[3] 1 Jo. iv. 17 (see Lücke *in loc.*); ἐν τούτῳ ἐάν, 1 Jo. ii. 3; ἐν τούτῳ ὅταν, 1 Jo. v. 2. Compare Ellendt, *Lex. Soph.* II. 461, Franke, *Demosth.* p. 40 (Jelf 657).

The demonstrative is also introduced for the sake of emphasis when an infinitive[4] or a noun follows as predicate. 2 C. ii. 1, ἔκρινα ἐμαυτῷ τοῦτο, τὸ μὴ πάλιν ἐν λύπῃ πρὸς ὑμᾶς ἐλθεῖν· vii. 11, αὐτὸ τοῦτο τὸ κατὰ θεὸν λυπηθῆναι· 1 C. vii. 37, E. iv. 17, Ja. i. 27: compare Xen. *Hell.* 4. 1. 2, *Ages.* 1. 8, Plat. *Hipp. Maj.* 302 a, *Gorg.* 491 d, Isocr. *Evag.* c. 3, Porphyr. *Abstin.* 1. 13, Dion. H. VI. 667, *de Thuc.* 40. 3, Epict. *Enchir.* 31. 1, 4, Stallb. Plat. *Rep.* II. 261. 2 C. xiii. 9, τοῦτο καὶ εὐχόμεθα, τὴν ὑμῶν κατάρτισιν· 1 Jo. iii. 24, v. 4: compare Achill. Tat. 7. 2, φάρμακον αὐτῷ τοῦτο τῆς ... λύπης ἡ πρὸς

---

[1] [Recent editors either read αὐτός or omit the pronoun.]
[2] In Rom. ii. 3 an extended vocative is inserted between τοῦτο and the clause beginning with ὅτι.
[3] [Here the connexion of ἐν τούτῳ with ἵνα may well be doubted. "The pronoun looks back, while at the same time the thought already indicated is developed in the words which follow:" Westcott *in loc.*]
[4] Matth. Eurip. *Phœn.* 520, Sprachl. 472. 2.

ἄλλον εἰς τὸ παθεῖν κοινωνία· Plat. *Rep.* 3. 407 a, Lucian, *Navig.* 3, Eurip. *Suppl.* 510, and also Jacob, Luc. *Toxar.* p. 136, Ast, Plat. *Polit.* p. 466. Even εἰς τοῦτο is so used in A. xxvi. 16, εἰς τοῦτο γὰρ ὤφθην σοι προχειρίσασθαί σε ὑπηρέτην καὶ μάρτυρα κ.τ.λ.; οὕτως in 1 P. ii. 15 (1 C. iv. 1); and ἐντεῦθεν in Ja. iv. 1.

Lastly, the demonstrative is thus placed before a participial clause in Mk. xii. 24, οὐ διὰ τοῦτο πλανᾶσθε, μὴ εἰδότες τὰς γραφάς κ.τ.λ., *on account of this . . . because ye know not*, etc.: comp. Antiphon 6. 46, οὐκ ἀπεγράφοντο τούτου αὐτοῦ ἕνεκα, οὐχ ἡγούμενοί με ἀποκτεῖναι κ.τ.λ.[1] (Jelf 657.)

The use of the demonstrative pronoun in such phrases as οὐ μετὰ πολλὰς ταύτας ἡμέρας, *after (in) a few days* (A. i. 5), presents no difficulty. It is not based (as is still maintained by Kühnöl) upon a transposition of πολύς, but is to be explained in the same way as the Latin phrase "ante *hos* quinque dies:" in Greek compare Achill. Tat. 7. 14, ὡς ὀλίγων πρὸ τούτων ἡμερῶν· Heliod. 2. 22, 97, οὐ πρὸ πολλῶν τῶνδε ἡμερῶν. Αὗται ἡμέραι are these days just now past, and "ante *hos* quinque dies" properly means *before the five days just past* —reckoned back from the present time. Thus the pronoun connects the note of time with the *present*.[2]

The demonstrative in Ja. iv. 13, πορευσώμεθα εἰς τήνδε τὴν πόλιν, *into this and that town*, the commentators and lexicographers are able to illustrate only by reference to the familiar expression ὁ δεῖνα; but ὅδε is used by Greek writers in exactly the same way, e. g. Plutarch, *Symp.* 1. 6. 1, τήνδε τὴν ἡμέραν, *this and that day*.[3]

The plural of the demonstrative pronoun, ταῦτα, is not unfrequently used in Greek in reference to a single object, and thus, strictly speaking, stands for τοῦτο: Plat. *Apol.* 19 d, *Phædr.* 70 d, Xen. *Cyr.* 5. 3. 19.[4] We find examples of this in 3 Jo. 4 (where some MSS. have the correction ταύτης,—see Lücke *in loc.*) and Jo. i. 51; but certainly not in Jo. xix. 36, see Van Hengel, *Annotat.* p. 85 sq. In L. xii. 4 μετὰ ταῦτα is *afterwards*, this formula having become simply

---

[1] See Maetzner, *Antiph.* p. 219, Schoem. *Isæus* p. 370.
[2] [On the position of οὐ see Jelf 738. 2. *Obs.* 3 (*not after many*, but after few: Meyer); and on that of ταύτας, Jelf 453. *Obs.* 2, Don. p. 352.]
[3] [It is not easy to see why τήνδε should not have its full force "as implying an object in immediate prospect; *we will travel to this city here*" (Green p. 125): see also Alford *in loc.*, A. Buttm. p. 103, and compare Grant, Aristot. *Ethics*, I. 372. The passage from Plutarch admits of a similar explanation.]
[4] See Schæf. *Dion.* p. 80; comp. also Jacobs, *Achill. Tat.* p. 524, Stallb. Plat. *Apol.* p. 19 d, Maetzner, *Antiphon* p. 153. Fritzsche (*Quæst. Lucian.* p. 126) thus qualifies this observation: plur. poni de una re tantummodo sic, si neque ulla emergat ambiguitas et aut universe, non definite quis loquatur, aut una res plurium vi sit prædita. [See Riddell, Plat. *Apol.* p. 131 sq., Jelf 381. *Obs.* 1.]

adverbial. Nearly the same is to be said of the familiar phrase καὶ ταῦτα idque, H. xi. 12. On 1 C. ix. 15 [1] see Meyer.[2]

In 1 C. vi. 11, καὶ ταῦτά τινες ἦτε, ταῦτα may be used with an implication of contempt, *of such a sort, talis farinæ homines* (Bernh. p. 281, Stallb. Plat. *Rival.* p. 274). Yet this was perhaps remote from the Apostle's thought, and ταῦτα is often used with reference to a series of predicates, *of such a description, ex hoc genere fuistis.* Kypke and Pott *in loc.* have confounded usages which are quite dissimilar.

In 1 Jo. v. 20 Lücke [3] thinks there is a *prozeugma* of the demonstrative pronoun, οὗτός ἐστιν ὁ ἀληθινὸς θεός, καὶ (αὕτη) ζωὴ αἰώνιος: this is not impossible in itself, but, as I think, it is unnecessary.

Rem. As regards the position of οὗτος and ἐκεῖνος, it should be remarked that the former, from the nature of the case, usually stands *before*, the latter *after* the noun,—οὗτος ὁ ἄνθρωπος, ὁ ἄνθρωπος ἐκεῖνος. We find however the opposite order: in the case of οὗτος (Mt. xxviii. 15 ὁ λόγος οὗτος, L. i. 29, al.) without any substantial difference of meaning; in the case of ἐκεῖνος (L. xii. 47, H. iv. 11) especially in the connective formulas ἐν ἐκείναις ταῖς ἡμέραις, ἐν ἐκείνῃ τῇ ἡμέρᾳ or ὥρᾳ, ἐν ἐκείνῳ τῷ καιρῷ (Gersdorf p. 433). But it must not be supposed that any writer has so bound himself to one particular arrangement that we are justified in altering the other when it is supported by good MSS. or by the sense of the passage.[4]

SECTION XXIV.

RELATIVE PRONOUNS.

1. According to the law of attraction,[5] the relative pronoun ὅς (never ὅστις [6] in the N. T.), when required by the governing

---

[1] [Meyer refers τούτων to the ἐξουσία, the plural having reference to the *various forms* of this power: so also Alford.]

[2] In the same way, ἐφ' οἷς and ἀνθ' ὧν are used in Greek where the singular would be sufficient (Fritz. *Rom.* I. 299).

[3] Compare also *Studien und Kritik.* II. p. 147 sqq.

[4] [The demonstrative pronouns in -δε are very seldom used in the N. T. In the best texts ὅδε occurs 10 times (7 times in Rev. ii. and iii.), and τοιόσδε once: in most instances ὅδε has its usual reference to what *follows* (Jelf 655. 6).]

[5] See Herm. *Vig.* p. 891 sqq., Bernh. p. 299 sqq. Compare also G. T. A. Krüger's thorough examination of the subject (with immediate reference to Latin) in his *Untersuch. a. d. Gebiete der lat. Sprachlehre* (3 Hefte: Braunschw. 1827). K. W. Krüger prefers the term *assimilation* (*Sprachl.* p. 141). [Jelf 822, Don. p. 362, Green p. 120 sqq.]

[6] Ὅστις occurs in the N. T. in no other case than the nominative, [the neuter accusative, and the contracted genitive,—the last only in ἕως ὅτου (p. 75).]

verb to stand in the accusative, is so attracted by the oblique case (the genitive or dative) of the preceding noun with which it is logically connected (as secondary clause with principal) that it itself assumes this case. This peculiarity, which gives to the sentences a closer internal connexion and a certain roundness, was quite familiar to the LXX, and is of regular occurrence in the N. T. (though variants are sometimes found): L. ii. 20, ἐπὶ πᾶσιν οἷς ἤκουσαν Jo. ii. 22 (iv. 50), ἐπίστευσαν τῷ λόγῳ ᾧ εἶπεν· A. iii. 21, 25, vii. 17, x. 39, xvii. 31, xx. 38, xxii. 10, Ja. ii. 5, 1 P. iv. 11, Jo. vii. 31, 39, xv. 20, xvii. 5, Mk. vii. 13, L. v. 9, xix. 37, Mt. xviii. 19, 1 C. vi. 19, 2 C. x. 13, xii. 21, 2 Th. i. 4, Tit. iii. 6, H. vi. 10 (ix. 20), x. 1,[1] E. i. 8, ii. 10, Rev. xviii. 6, al. Here the comma before the relative is in every case to be struck out; see § 7. 1. Jude 15, περὶ πάντων τῶν ἔργων ἀσεβείας αὐτῶν ὧν ἠσέβησαν, deserves special notice: see § 32. 1.

There are passages however in which this usage is neglected, as H. viii. 2, τῆς σκηνῆς τῆς ἀληθινῆς, ἣν ἔπηξεν ὁ κύριος· and according to good MSS. Mk. xiii. 9, Jo. vii. 39, iv. 50, Tit. iii. 5 :[2] compare also the variants in Jo. xvii. 11, H. vi. 10, A. vii. 16, Rev. i. 20. Similar instances are frequently met with in the LXX and the Apocrypha :[3] for examples from Greek writers see Bornem. Xen. *An.* p. 30, Weber, *Dem.* p. 543, Krüg. p. 142 (Jelf 822. *Obs.* 9).

Some passages appear to go beyond the rule as laid down above: thus in E. i. 6, τῆς χάριτος ἧς ἐχαρίτωσεν (*v.l.* ἐν ᾗ), iv. 1, τῆς κλήσεως ἧς ἐκλήθητε· 2 C. i. 4, διὰ τῆς παρακλήσεως ἧς παρακαλούμεθα,[4] the genitive ἧς seems to stand for the dative ᾗ. But all these passages may be explained by reference to the well-known phrases κλῆσιν καλεῖν, παράκλησιν παρακαλεῖν, χάριν χαριτοῦν, ἀγάπην ἀγαπᾶν (§ 32. 2), and to the equally familiar construction of the passive.[5] In A. xxiv. 21 also, φωνῆς ἧς ἔκραξα ἑστώς κ.τ.λ., ἧς probably is not put for ᾗ (φωνῇ κράζειν, Mt. xxvii. 50, Mk. i. 26, Rev. vi. 10, al.) :[6] φωνή is

---

[1] [Jo. ii. 22, iv. 50, H. x. 1, are doubtful.]
[2] [Mk. xiii. 9 should be xiii. 19 (as in ed. 5) : on Tit. iii. 5 see Ellicott.]
[3] Wahl, *Clav.* p. 360.
[4] Here however we might (with Wahl) consider the genitive to be governed by the omitted preposition διά : see § 50. 7 (Jelf 650. 3).
[5] See Gieseler in Rosenm. *Repertor.* II. 124 : Aristoph. *Plut.* 1044, πάλαι ἐγὼ τῆς ὕβριως ἧς ὑβρίζομαι, is probably to be explained in the same way.
[6] Compare Boisson. *Nicet.* p. 33.

used in the sense of *cry, exclamation* (loud utterance), so that the construction resolves itself into φωνὴν κράζειν (Rev. vi. 10 *v. l.*),—an unusual, but not an inadmissible expression : compare Is. vi. 4, φωνῆς ἧς ἐκέκραγον.—In E. i. 8, ἧς ἐπερίσσευσεν, the verb is to be taken transitively, as is shown by γνωρίσας, ver. 9.

That however attraction *may* affect the dative of the relative, so as to change it into a genitive, is shown by G. Krüger *l.c.* p. 274 sq. : [1] thus in 1 Tim. iv. 6, A has τῆς καλῆς διδασκαλίας ἧς παρηκολούθηκας. In Rom. iv. 17 also many commentators (and recently Fritzsche) resolve κατέναντι οὗ ἐπίστευσεν θεοῦ into κατέναντι θεοῦ ᾧ ἐπίστευσεν,[2] but this explanation is not necessary : see below, no. 2.[3] On the other hand, Mt. xxiv. 38, ἦσαν . . . γαμοῦντες καὶ ἐκγαμίζοντες ἄχρι ἧς ἡμέρας εἰςῆλθε Νῶε εἰς τὴν κιβωτόν, is probably a condensation of ἄχρι τῆς ἡμ. ᾗ εἰςῆλθεν : similarly in L. i. 20, A. i. 2, 22.[4] We find the same attraction of the dative of the relative (without a condensation of the two clauses into one) in Lev. xxiii. 15, ἀπὸ τῆς ἡμέρας ἧς ἂν προςενέγκητε· Bar. i. 19 : the phrase ἧς ἡμέρας, it is true, is also used (*on which day*), but in the LXX the dative of time predominates.

2. We sometimes meet with instances of an inverse attraction, the noun to which the relative refers being attracted into the construction of the relative clause, and assuming the case in which the governing verb requires the relative to stand (Jelf 824, Don. p. 364). When this occurs, either

a. The noun precedes the relative clause : 1 C. x. 16, τὸν ἄρτον ὃν κλῶμεν, οὐχὶ κοινωνία τοῦ σώματος ; Mt. xxi. 42 (from the LXX), λίθον ὃν ἀπεδοκίμασαν οἱ οἰκοδομοῦντες, οὗτος ἐγενήθη (1 P. ii. 7) ;[5] L. xii. 48, παντὶ ᾧ ἐδόθη πολύ, πολὺ ζητη-

---

[1] Comp. Heinichen, *Euseb.* II. 98 sq. [Jelf 822. *Obs.* 8, Madvig 103, Krüg. p. 142.]

[2] [So also Tholuck, A. Buttm. (p. 287), Jowett, Vaughan, Webster and Wilkinson. Meyer and Alford agree with Winer: see also Ellicott on E. i. 8. On A. xxvi. 16 see § 39. 3. Rem. 1. In 2 Th. i. 4, αἷς ἀνέχεσθε, some consider αἷς to stand for ὧν, as in the N. T. ἀνέχεσθαι governs the genitive in every other instance. Such an attraction as this, however, would be unexampled : see Jelf 822. *Obs.* 8, and Ellicott *in loc.*—From the LXX, Thiersch quotes Gen. xxiv. 7 as an example of ἧς for ᾗ (*De Pent. Al.* p. 105).]

[3] Compare Schmid in the *Tübing. Zeitschr. f. Theol.* 1831. II. 137 sqq.

[4] [Ἄχρι ἧς ἡμ. (comp. ἄχρις οὗ, ἕως οὗ, ἕως ὅτου) occurs Mt. xxiv. 38, L. i. 20, xvii. 27, A. i. 2 : ἀφ' ἧς ἡμ. (comp. ἀφ' οὗ), Col. i. 6, 9 ; ἀφ' ἧς (scil. ἡμέρας or ὥρας, see §. 64. 5), L. vii. 45, 2 P. iii. 4 ; in A. xxiv. 11, ἡμέρας may be supplied from the preceding ἡμέραι. In A. xx. 18, ἀφ' ἧς is most simply explained in the same way : Jelf (822. *Obs.* 5) considers this an example of the repetition of the prepos. which belongs to the antecedent (Thuc. 3. 64). With these examples compare Dem. *De Cor.* 233. 27, οὐκ ἀφ' ἧς ὠμόσατε ἡμέρας, ἀλλ' ἀφ' ἧς ἠλπίσατε κ.τ.λ., Xen. *An.* 5. 10. 12, ἡμέρᾳ ἕκτῃ ἀφ' ἧς ᾑρέθη. In A. i. 22, ἕως τῆς ἡμ. ἧς, Meyer explains ἧς as a genitive of time. See Madvig *l. c.*]

[5] [In 1 P. ii. 7, λίθος is probably the true reading.]

θήσεται παρ' αὐτοῦ: probably also L. i. 72, 73, μνησθῆναι διαθήκης ἁγίας αὐτοῦ, ὅρκον ὃν ὤμοσε πρὸς Ἀβραάμ· but probably not A. x. 36, see below § 62. 3.[1]—Or

b. In position, as in construction, the noun is completely incorporated with the relative clause: Mk. vi. 16, ὃν ἐγὼ ἀπεκεφάλισα Ἰωάννην, οὗτός ἐστι· Phil. 10, L. xix. 37. Rom. vi. 17, ὑπηκούσατε εἰς ὃν παρεδόθητε τύπον διδαχῆς, is an example of this kind,—whether it be resolved into εἰς τὸν τύπον διδαχῆς ὃν παρεδόθητε, an accusative with a passive, for ὃς παρεδόθη ὑμῖν (for a similar attraction, by which the accusative of the more remote object is affected, see Demosth. *Mid.* 385 c, δίκην ἅμα βουλόμενοι λαβεῖν, ὧν ἐπὶ τῶν ἄλλων ἐτεθέαντο θρασὺν ὄντα· where ὧν is for ἅ, i.e. ἐν οἷς, as a complement of θρασὺν ὄντα,—and Dion. Hal. 9. 565, ἀγανάκτησις ὑμῶν περὶ ὧν ὑβρίζεσθε ὑπὸ τῶν πολεμίων· Demosth. *Ep.* 4. p. 118 b);—or more simply (as by Bornemann, Rückert, Fritzsche, al.) into ὑπηκούσατε (τῷ) τύπῳ διδαχῆς εἰς ὃν παρεδόθητε, since the construction ὑπακούειν τινί[2] is the only one that is suitable here. Even A. xxi. 16, ἄγοντες παρ' ᾧ ξενισθῶμεν Μνάσωνι, is explained by some as an example of attraction,—ἄγοντες παρὰ Μνάσωνα ... παρ' ᾧ ξενισθῶμεν; but see § 31. 5. On 2 C. x. 13 see § 59. 7.

Examples parallel to (*a*): Hippocr. *Morb.* 4. 11, τὰς πηγὰς ἃς ὠνόμασα, αὗται τῷ σώματι κ.τ.λ., Lysias, *Bon. Arist.* p. 649, Ælian, *Anim.* 3. 13, Her. 2. 106, Soph. *El.* 653, *Trach.* 283, Eurip. *Bacch.* 443 sqq., Aristoph. *Plut.* 200, Alciphr. 3. 59: the well-known passage in the *Æneid* (1. 577), urbem quam statuo vestra est; Terent. *Eunuch.* 4. 3. 11, Sen. *Ep.* 53. See Wetstein I. 468. From the LXX may be quoted Gen. xxxi. 16, τὴν δόξαν ἣν ἀφείλετο ὁ θεὸς .... ἡμῖν ἔσται· and Num. xix. 22: from the *Acta Petri et Pauli* (Thilo, *Cod. Ap.* I. 7), ἀρκεῖ ἡμῖν τὴν θλῖψιν ἣν ἔχομεν παρὰ Πέτρου. (Jelf 824. I.)

To (*b*): Xen. *An.* 1. 9. 19, εἴ τινα ὁρῴη κατασκευάζοντα ἧς ἄρχοι χώρας (χώραν ἧς ἄρχοι), Soph. *Œd. Col.* 907, *El.* 1029, Eurip. *Orest.* 63, *Electr.* 860, *Hec.* 986, Plat. *Tim.* 49 e, Demosth. *Ep.* 4. p. 118 c, Plut. *Coriol.* 9 (*Evang. Apocr.* p. 414,

---

[1] Comp. Gieseler *l. c.* p. 126, Krüg. 224 sq.
[2] On ὑπακούειν εἰς, especially in Josephus, see Kypke, *Observatt.* II. 167, though exception may be taken to some of his examples.

Acta Apocr. p. 69): compare Liv. 9. 2, Terent. *Andr.* prol. 3 (Jelf 824. II.).—On the whole subject see Matth. 474, Lob. *Ajax* p. 354.

To (*b*) would also belong Rom. iv. 17, κατέναντι οὗ ἐπίστευσε θεοῦ, if resolved into κατέναντι θεοῦ, ᾧ ἐπίστευσε. On this supposition, the law of attraction (so familiar had the construction become) is here extended so as to include the dative. Instances of this kind certainly do occur here and there (Krüg. 247 sq., Jelf 822. *Obs.* 8), e.g. Xen. *Cyr.* 5. 4. 39, ἤγετο τῶν ἑαυτοῦ τῶν τε πιστῶν, οἷς ἥδετο καὶ ὧν (i.e. τούτων οἷς) ἠπίστει πολλούς : see Fritz. *Rom.* I. 237. Still, κατέναντι θεοῦ, κατέναντι οὗ ἐπίστευσε (see above, 1) is a simpler resolution of the words. The explanation proposed by Bretschneider (*Lex. Man.* p. 220) is far-fetched in more respects than one.

In the following examples the antecedent is merely incorporated with the relative clause, without change of case : Mt. xxiv. 44, ᾗ ὥρᾳ οὐ δοκεῖτε, ὁ υἱὸς τοῦ ἀνθρώπου ἔρχεται (Gen. ii. 17, Ex. x. 28, xxxii. 34, Num. vi. 13, xxx. 6), Mt. vii. 2, ἐν ᾧ μέτρῳ μετρεῖτε, μετρηθήσεται ὑμῖν· Jo. xi. 6, Mk. xv. 12 (H. xiii. 11), L. i. 4 ; also Rom. iv. 17, see above. When the clause containing the relative and the noun stands first, Greek writers usually insert in the principal clause a demonstrative corresponding to the noun, and also keep relative and noun apart by placing some word between them (Krüg. p. 144, Jelf 824. II.).

The following are examples of attraction, with omission of the attracting word (demonstrative) :—

a. Where a preposition is present : H. v. 8, ἔμαθεν ἀφ' ὧν ἔπαθε, i.e. ἀπὸ τούτων ἃ (ὧν) ἔπαθε· Rom. x. 14, Jo. vi. 29, xvii. 9, 1 C. vii. 1 ; Demosth. *Euerg.* 684 b, ἀγανακτήσασα ἐφ' οἷς ἐγὼ ἐπεπόνθειν· Plat. *Cratyl.* 386 a, Xen. *An.* 1. 9. 25, Arrian, *Al.* 4. 10. 3, Lysias II. 242 (ed. Auger.): see § 23. 2.

b. Without a preposition : Rom. xv. 18, οὐ τολμήσω λαλεῖν τι ὧν οὐ κατειργάσατο κ.τ.λ., A. viii. 24, xxvi. 16 ; Soph. *Phil.* 1227, *Œd. R.* 855. On this, and on attraction with a local adverb (G. Krüg. 302 sqq.), see § 23. 2.

3. The noun which forms the predicate in a relative sentence, annexed for the purpose of explanation (ὅς—ἐστί), sometimes gives its own gender and number to the relative, by a kind of attraction (Herm. *Vig.* p. 708, Jelf 821. 3, Don. p. 362): Mk. xv. 16, τῆς αὐλῆς, ὅ ἐστι πραιτώριον· G. iii. 16, τῷ σπέρματί σου, ὅς ἐστι Χριστός· 1 Tim. iii. 15, ἐν οἴκῳ θεοῦ, ἥτις ἐστὶν ἐκκλησία θεοῦ· E. vi. 17, i. 14, Ph. i. 28, E. iii. 13, μὴ ἐκκακεῖν ἐν ταῖς θλίψεσί μου ὑπὲρ ὑμῶν, ἥτις ἐστὶ δόξα ὑμῶν (for ὅ) ; also 1 C. iii. 17, where Meyer needlessly finds a difficulty in

οἵτινες. Compare also the variants in Rev. iv. 5, v. 6, 8. On the other hand, see E. i. 23, τῇ ἐκκλησίᾳ, ἥτις ἐστὶ τὸ σῶμα αὐτοῦ· 1 C. iv. 17, Col. i. 24, ii. 17. Some have wrongly referred to this head Col. iii. 5, ἥτις ἐστὶν εἰδωλολατρεία, taking ἥτις for ἅτινα (μέλη); the relative refers to πλεονεξία alone, see Huther *in loc.* In Col. iii. 14, ὅ seems the best reading,—a pure neuter, used without reference to the gender of the preceding or of the following noun:[1] on E. v. 5 see Rem. 1. In Mt. xxvii. 33 and similar passages ὅ is *quod* (scil. *vocabulum*). The commentators on H. ix. 9 are not agreed, but most now refer ἥτις to ἡ πρώτη σκηνή in ver. 8, so that the passage does not fall under this rule. There is greater difference of opinion in regard to Col. i. 27, but it is better to connect ὅς with ὁ πλοῦτος, as the principal word, than with μυστήριον.[2]

It would seem that the relative usually takes the gender of the noun which follows

(1) Where this is regarded as the principal noun; as when the relative clause gives the proper names of things which in the principal clause were mentioned in general terms (Mk. xv. 16, 1 Tim. iii. 15; compare Pausan. 2. 13. 4, Cic. *pro Sest.* 42. 91, domicilia conjuncta quas urbes dicimus)—especially in the case of personal names (G. iii. 16,—compare Cic. *Legg.* 1. 7. 22, animal, *quem* vocamus hominem).

(2) Where the relative should strictly have been a neuter, used absolutely, as in E. iii. 13.

On the other hand, the relative retains the gender of the noun in the principal clause when the relative sentence serves to expand and illustrate the principal subject, containing some predicate of it (E. i. 23, 1 C. iv. 17).[3]—See on the whole G. Krüg. *l.c.* 90 sqq.;[4] and as to Latin, Zumpt, *Gramm.* § 372, Kritz, *Sallust* I. 292, [Madvig, *Lat. Gr.* § 316.]

4. The relative pronoun appears to stand for the interrogative in a *direct*[5] question in Mt. xxvi. 50, ἑταῖρε, ἐφ' ὃ (that

---

[1] [See Ellicott *in loc.*, Jelf 820. 1.]
[2] [The most recent editors read τὸ πλοῦτος, so that, whether we take this word (Mey.) or μυστηρίου (Ellicott) as the antecedent, the gender would result from attraction. The best texts, however, have ὅ instead of ὅς.]
[3] Comp. Bremi on Nep. *Thrasyb.* 2.
[4] [See Ellicott on E. i. 14, Madvig 98.]
[5] Ὅς occurs in an indirect question in Soph. *Œd. R.* 1068; see Ellendt, *Lex. Soph.* II. 372. Compare also Passow s. v. [For examples of ὅς after verbs of

is, ἐπὶ τί, Aristoph. *Lysistr.* 1101) πάρει. This misuse of the relative belongs to declining Greek (Schæf. *Dem.* V. 285), and similar examples with other relative pronouns are given by Lobeck (*Phryn.* p. 57),—see also Plat. *Alcib.* I. p. 110 c: there is however nothing very strange in such a usage if we consider how closely *qui* and *quis* are connected in meaning. It is not known in good prose. In Plat. *Men.* 74 d, τί has been substituted, apparently without MS. authority: on Plat. *Rep.* 8. 559 a see Stallbaum. But it is not necessary on this account to assume an aposiopesis in Mt. xxvi. 50 (Meyer),[1] or with Fritzsche to regard the sentence as an exclamation, " Vetus sodalis, ad qualem rem perpetrandam ades ! " By the question itself Jesus could fully set before the mind of Judas the wickedness of his purpose.

There would be less difficulty in supposing (with Lachmann) that ὅ,τι stands for τί, i.e. διὰ τί, in Mk. ix. 11, λέγοντες· ὅ,τι λέγουσιν οἱ γραμματεῖς κ.τ.λ.; as in Heliod. 4. 16, 7. 14 (quoted by Lobeck, *l. c.*), ὅστις appears in a direct question. In the N. T. however ὅ,τι is never used as an interrogative pronoun (certainly not in Jo. viii. 25, see § 54. 1), even in an indirect question [§ 25. 1]; and as another ὅτι immediately follows, the first may be an error of transcription for τί: see Fritzsche.[2]

---

knowing, declaring, etc., see Mt. vi. 8, Mk. v. 33, Jo. xviii. 21, A. xxii. 24, L. vi. 3 (ἀνέγνωτε δ'· compare Mt. xii. 3, ἀνέγν. τί), Mt. xi. 4, L. viii. 47 (Her. 4. 131, Plat. *Men.* 80 c, Her. 6. 124, Thuc. 1. 136, 137). With L. viii. 47, δι' ἣν αἰτίαν ἥψατο αὐτοῦ ἀπήγγειλεν, compare especially Plat. *Tim.* 67, δι' ἃς αἰτίας τὰ περὶ αὐτὰ ξυμβαίνει παθήματα, λεκτέον. See Madvig 198 b, Jelf 877. *Obs.* 3 sq., A. Buttm. p. 250.]

[1] [Similarly Alford, Lightfoot, and others: against Fritz., Meyer urges that an exclamation would naturally have been expressed in an interrogative form. A. Buttm. (p. 253) agrees with Fritz.: comp. *Vulg.* (Cod. Amiat.), "ad quod venisti?" (*Clem.*; "ad *quid* venisti?"). Most of those who read ὅτι in Mt. vii. 14 (on τί see § 53. 8. c) take the word in the sense of *because*: A. Buttm. is inclined to regard the clause as an exclamation, but it is doubtful whether he is justified in quoting Jer. ii. 36 (where ὅτι corresponds to the Hebrew מָה) as a parallel case.]

[2] ["Οτι (ὅ,τι) is received by almost all editors in Mk. ix. 11, 28: it is taken in the sense of *why?* by Meyer, De Wette, A. Buttm., Alford, Webster and Wilk.,—either as being the pronoun ὅ,τι used for τί (Meyer, A. Buttm., Alf.), or through an ellipsis (as in τί ὅτι, De W., Jelf 905 8. κ). In Mk. ii. 16, ὅτι (ὅ,τι) is received by Tisch., Treg., A. Buttm., who also regard the word as interrogative. Tisch. quotes Barnab. *Ep.* 10. 1, ὅτι δὲ Μωϋσῆς εἴρηκεν; (Hilgenf. εἴρηκεν·), rendered in the *Vet. interp.*, " Quare autem Moyses dicit ? " See also Barnab. *Ep.* 7. 9, 8. 5. In 1 Chr. xvii. 6 (cited by A. Buttm. p. 254) we find ὅτι corresponding with לָמָּה in the Hebrew: comp. Jer. ii. 36. Lachmann (*Præf.* p. 43) compares this use of ὅ,τι with the introduction of a direct question by εἰ (§ 57. 2). See Tisch. on Mk. ii. 16, Meyer on Mk. ix. 11,

If ὅτι were the true reading, it might rather be taken as ὅτι *because*: see § 53. 8, 10.

Rem. 1. It is peculiar to Paul to connect sometimes two, three, or more sentences by the repetition of the relative pronoun, even when it refers to different subjects: Col. i. 24 sq., 28, 29, E. iii. 11, 12, 1 C. ii. 7; compare 1 P. ii. 22.—In other passages the singular relative has been supposed to refer to a series of nouns, and to have, as it were, a collective force: e.g. E. v. 5, ὅτι πᾶς πόρνος ἢ ἀκάθαρτος ἢ πλεονέκτης, ὅς ἐστιν εἰδωλολάτρης κ.τ.λ.[1] But this is arbitrary, and would presuppose a similar forced explanation of Col. iii. 5 (see above, p. 207).

Rem. 2. The relative clause beginning with ὅς or ὅστις commonly follows the clause containing the noun, but takes the first place if it is to be brought into prominence (Krüg. p. 144): 1 C. xiv. 37, ἃ γράφω ὑμῖν ὅτι κυρίου ἐστίν· H. xii. 6, ὃν ἀγαπᾷ κύριος παιδεύει· Rom. vi. 2, οἵτινες ἀπεθάνομεν τῇ ἁμαρτίᾳ, πῶς ἔτι ζήσομεν ἐν αὐτῇ; Mk. viii. 34, al. With a demonstrative in the second clause: Ph. iii. 7, ἅτινα ἦν μοι κέρδη, ταῦτα ἥγημαι κ.τ.λ., Ja. ii. 10,[2] Jo. xxi. 25, xi. 45, Mt. v. 39, L. ix. 50, A. xxv. 18, 1 C. iv. 2, H. xiii. 11 (Jelf 817. *Obs.* 10).

Rem. 3. The neuter ὅ is prefixed to a whole sentence in the sense of *as concerns, as regards*, etc. (as *quod* in Latin): Rom. vi. 10, ὃ δὲ ζῇ, ζῇ τῷ θεῷ· G. ii. 20, ὃ δὲ νῦν ζῶ ἐν σαρκί, ἐν πίστει ζῶ κ.τ.λ.; compare Matth. 478 (Jelf 579. 6). In both these passages, however, ὅ may be taken as the object, *quod vivit,—vita quam vivit.* See Fritz. *Rom.* I. 393. (Jelf 905. 7.)

Rem. 4. That ὅς is used in prose for the demonstrative (i. e. in other cases than those which are familiar to all, Matth. 288 sq.) was believed by many commentators during the reign of empiricism. Now every beginner knows how to take the passages which were so explained; e.g. 2 C. iv. 6, ὁ θεὸς ὁ εἰπὼν ἐκ σκότους φῶς λάμψαι, ὃς ἔλαμψεν ἐν ταῖς καρδίαις κ.τ.λ. In 1 C. ii. 9, Rom. xvi. 27, there is an anacoluthon.[3]

A. Buttm. *l. c.*, Grimm's *Clavis* s. v. As regards these three passages of St. Mark, however, it seems probable that ὅτι should rather be taken as the conjunction, introducing an assertion or exclamation (so Alford in ii. 16): see § 53. 10. 5.]

[1] Compare Fritzsche, *De Conformat. Crit.* p. 46.

[2] [In Ja. ii. 10, L. ix. 50, there is no demonstrative: indeed none of the following examples, except Mt. v. 39, H. xiii. 11, are really in point.]

[3] [On the distinction between ὅς and the indefinite relative ὅστις, see Krüger p. 139 (who calls ὅς objective, ὅστις qualitative and generic), Jelf 816, Madvig 105, Clyde, *Syntax* p. 58; for the N. T., A. Buttm. p. 115, Green p. 122 sq., Webster, *Gr.* p. 55, Lightfoot, *Gal.* pp. 177 sq., 207, and especially Ellicott on G. iv. 24. Ὅστις properly indicates the class or kind to which an object belongs, and hence its most common meaning is *whoever;* elsewhere it may usually be rendered, *a man who* (*a thing which*), *a class of men who, such as, of such a kind as* (Mk. xii. 18, Col. ii. 23, Ph. ii. 20, L. xxiii. 19). Hence ὅστις often brings in an explanation or the statement of a cause (Æsch. *Prom.*

Section XXV.

THE INTERROGATIVE AND INDEFINITE PRONOUN τις.

1. The use of the interrogative pronoun τίς, τί, is in the N. T. extended somewhat beyond its ordinary limits. Not only is τίς of very common occurrence in the *indirect* question and after verbs of *knowing, inquiring*, etc. (whilst ὅςτις, ὅ,τι, is never so used in the N. T.), but—especially in the neuter (τί)—it is sometimes found where a Greek writer would certainly have employed ὅ,τι, so that the interrogative is weakened into our *what*. For examples of the former kind see Mt. xx. 22, L. xxiii. 34 (Mk. xiv. 36), Jo. x. 6, A. xxi. 33, Rom. viii. 26, Col. i. 27, al.: compare Xen. *Cyr.* 1. 1. 6, 1. 3. 17, *Mem.* 1. 6. 4, al.[1] (Jelf 877. *Obs.* 2). Of the latter kind are Mt. x. 19, δοθήσεται ὑμῖν . . . τί λαλήσετε, *quod dicatis*, and L. xvii. 8, ἑτοίμασον, τί δειπνήσω, *para, quod comedam* (not *quid comedam*, which would hardly be allowable in Latin in this connexion): compare Bernh. p. 443. Only once do we find ὅ,τι,—in A. ix. 6.[2] The transition to this use of τί is formed by such a construction as τί φάγωσιν οὐκ ἔχουσι, Mk. vi. 36 (Mt. xv. 32), for which ὅ,τι φάγωσιν οὐκ ἔχουσι might be substituted with but slight change of meaning; just as in Latin both "non habent *quid* comedant" and "non habent *quod* comedant" are correct (Ramshorn, *Lat. Gramm.* 368).[3] In the latter formula, ἔχειν and *habere* simply

---

V. 38, ὅςτις προὔδωκεν), as in Col. iii. 5, "covetousness, a thing which is idolatry "= " seeing it is idolatry,"—the reader at once perceiving that St. Paul introduces this statement of the *quality* of ἡ πλεονεξία, that he may enforce his exhortation. See also Jo. viii. 53, H. x. 35, E. iii. 13, Ph. iv. 3. On the use of ὅςτις to denote "that which is to be regarded as the *especial* attribute of the individual" (1 C. v. 1, L. ii. 4), see Jelf 816. 6. The two pronouns were confounded in late Greek (see Lidd. and Sc. s. v., Ellic. *l.c.*): but in the N. T. the distinctive use of each is almost always, if not always, maintained. See Fritz. *Opusc.* p. 182, Grimm's *Clavis* s. v., A. Buttm. *l.c.* In modern Greek ὅςτις (which is commonly used in the nominative only) almost always has the meaning *qui*; ὅς is extremely rare in the popular language: see Mullach, *Vulg.* p. 201.—Ὅσος, οἷος, ὁποῖος, ἡλίκος, occur in the N. T. as indirect interrogatives (see 2 Tim. i. 18, 1 Th. i. 5, 1 C. iii. 13, Col. ii. 1), and also—with the exception of ἡλίκος—as relatives. In H. i. 4, vii. 20 sqq., Rev. xviii. 7, ὅσος is accompanied by its correlative τοσοῦτος: οἷος follows τοιοῦτος in 1 C. xv. 48, al. (τηλικοῦτος, Rev. xvi. 18 ?): ὁποῖος follows τοιοῦτος in A. xxvi. 29.—It may be mentioned here that of the neuter of τοσοῦτος, τοιοῦτος, both forms occur in the N. T., according to the best MSS.]

[1] Herm. *Æschyl.* p. 461, Ellendt, *Lex. Soph.* II. 823.
[2] ["Ο,τι is received here by the best editors.]
[3] [Zumpt § 562, Madvig, *Lat. Gr.* § 363.]

express the notion of *having* or *possessing*,—" that which they might eat, they have not:" in the former, the notion of an inquiry is also conveyed (and hence *habeo quid* must sometimes be rendered *I know what*),—" inquiring what they are to eat, they have not (anything to eat)." Similar examples are Xen. *Cyr.* 6. 1. 48, οὐκ ἔχω τί μεῖζον· *Hell.* 1. 6. 5, Soph. *Œd. Col.* 317, οὐκ ἔχω τί φῶ: see on the whole Heindorf, Cic. *Nat. D.* p. 347.

The relative and interrogative are combined in 1 Tim. i. 7, μὴ νοοῦντες μήτε ἃ λέγουσι μήτε περὶ τίνων διαβεβαιοῦνται, *non intelligentes nec quod dicunt nec quid asserant*. Similarly in Greek writers we find τί and ὅ,τι in parallel clauses: compare Stallb. Plat. *Rep.* I. 248, II. 261, Bornem. Xen. *Cyr.* p. 641.[1]

Schleusner, Haab (p. 82 sq.), and others refer to this head many examples which are of an entirely different kind:—

(a) In some of these τίς retains its meaning as an interrogative pronoun, and must be rendered in Latin by *quis* or *quid:* Mt. vii. 9, τίς ἔσται [ἐστιν] ἐξ ὑμῶν ἄνθρωπος κ.τ.λ., *quis erit inter vos homo*, etc.; compare Mt. xii. 11, L. xiv. 5, xi. 5 sq.

(b) In others τις is not an interrogative at all, but the pronoun *aliquis:* 1 C. vii. 18, περιτετμημένος τις ἐκλήθη, μὴ ἐπισπάσθω, *some one who is circumcised is called* (I suppose the case), *let him not become uncircumcised;* Ja. v. 13, κακοπαθεῖ τις, προσευχέσθω (Jelf 860. 8). It is not correct to say that here τις stands for εἴ τις, see § 64. 5. Rem., [and § 60. 4]. Ja. iii. 13 should be thus punctuated (as by Pott, Schott, al.): τίς σοφὸς . . . ἐν ὑμῖν; δειξάτω κ.τ.λ. In A. xiii. 25 also we might write τίνα με ὑπονοεῖτε εἶναι; οὐκ εἰμὶ ἐγώ· though I do not consider the ordinary view (that τίνα is for ὅντινα) inadmissible:[2] compare Soph. *El.* 1167, Callim. *Epigr.* 30. 2.

Τίς is sometimes used where only two persons or things are spoken of, in the place of the more precise πότερος (which never occurs as an adjective in the N. T.): Mt. ix. 5, τί γάρ ἐστιν εὐκοπώτερον; xxi. 31, τίς ἐκ τῶν δύο ἐποίησε; L. vii. 42, xxii. 27, Ph. i. 22. Similar examples are to be found in Greek writers,[3] who are not so accurate in

---

[1] [On the passages in which τίς has been supposed to stand for the relative pronoun in the N. T., see A. Buttmann p. 251 sq.: see also Jelf 877, and Rost and Palm, *Lex.* s. v. Compare Demosth. *Dionys.* p. 1290, ἐκλεγόμενοι τίνων αἱ τιμαὶ ἐπετέταντο· *Fals. Leg.* p. 433 sq., τί παρ' ὑμῖν ἐψήφισται, τοῦτ' ἐπετήρουν κ.τ.λ.]

[2] [De Wette and Meyer treat the first clause as a question: Ewald and A. Buttmann regard τίνα (or τί) as used for the relative, and Meyer allows that this is grammatically admissible. Compare Ecclus. vi. 34, Ps. xxxix. 6, Lev. xxi. 17, Dt. xxix. 18 (Tisch. *N. T.* p. lix, ed. 7; Field, *LXX* p. xxv). See Jebb, Soph. *Electr.* pp. 32, 116.]

[3] Stallb. *Phileb.* p. 168 (Jelf 874. Obs. 4).

the distinctive use of τίς and πότερος as the Romans are in regard to their *quis* and *uter*,—though even in Latin the distinction is not always observed.[1]

It is a mistake to say that the singular of the interrogative is used for the plural in such expressions as τί εἴη ταῦτα L. xv. 26, Jo. vi. 9, A. xvii. 20. Here the various objects referred to (ταῦτα) are included under one general expression (τί), *what (of what kind) are these things* (hence also *quid sibi volunt*); whereas in τίνα ἐστί κ.τ.λ. (compare H. v. 12) there is definite reference to the plurality, *quæ (qualia) sunt:* compare Plat. *Theæt.* 154 e, 155 c.[2]

The interrogative τί sometimes stands at the end of the sentence, as in Jo. xxi. 21, οὗτος δὲ τί; in the orators πῶς is often so placed (Weber, *Dem.* p. 180 sq., Jelf 872).

Both in the N. T. and in the LXX we meet with ἵνα τί, *for what purpose, wherefore*, as a formula of interrogation: Mt. ix. 4, ἵνα τί ὑμεῖς ἐνθυμεῖσθε πονηρά; xxvii. 46, L. xiii. 7, al. This expression is elliptical, like the Latin *ut quid*, and stands for ἵνα τί γένηται (or γένοιτο, after a past tense); see Herm. *Vig.* p. 849, Lob. *Ajax* p. 107 (Jelf 882): it is not uncommon in Greek writers, particularly the later; see Plat. *Apol.* 26 d, Aristoph. *Eccles.* 718, Arrian, *Epict.* 1. 24, al., and compare Ruth i. 11, 21, Ecclus. xiv. 3, 1 Macc. ii. 7.

2. The indefinite pronoun τις, τι, is joined

(*a*) To abstract nouns, for the purpose (*inter alia*) of softening their meaning in some degree; as in Xen. *Cyr.* 8. 1. 16, τούτους ἡγεῖτο ἢ ἀκρατείᾳ τινὶ ἢ ἀδικίᾳ ἢ ἀμελείᾳ ἀπεῖναι, *from a certain* (a kind of) *weakness or injustice*, etc., Plut. *Coriol.* 14. Hence we meet with it when a writer is using a figure which is uncommon or too bold; as in Ja. i. 18, ἀπαρχή τις *quædam* (quasi) *primitiæ* (Buttm. I. 579, Schoem. Plut. *Agis* p. 73).

(*b*) To numerals, when the number is to be taken approximately and not exactly: A. xxiii. 23, δύο τινάς *about two*, xix. 14; see Schæf. *Dem.* III. 269, Matth. 487. 4 (Jelf 659, Don. p. 380).

(*c*) To adjectives of quality and quantity, with rhetorical emphasis: H. x. 27, φοβερά τις ἐκδίκησις *terribilis quædam*,[3]

---

[1] [Τίς is sometimes used in the sense of ποῖος both in the N. T. (as L. iv. 36) and in classical Greek: see Herm. *Vig.* p. 731, Shilleto, Dem. *Fals. Leg.* p. 14. It was at one time supposed that ποῖος frequently stands for τίς in the N. T., but in most of the passages quoted in proof of this (e. g. Rom. iii. 27, A. iv. 7), if not in all, the qualitative force of ποῖος may be traced with more or less distinctness. In modern Greek ποῖος is frequently used in the same sense as τίς : see Mullach, *Vulg.* pp. 53, 209.]
[2] Stallb. Plat. *Euthyphr.* p. 101, Weber, *Dem.* p. 192.
[3] Klotz, Cic. *Læl.* p. 142, Nauck in *Jahns Jahrb.* vol. 52. p. 183 sq.

a right terrible (very terrible) punishment;[1] compare Lucian, *Philop.* 8, φοβερόν τι θέαμα· Diod. S. 5. 39, ἐπίπονός τις βίος· Æschin. *Dial.* 3. 17, Xen. *Cyr.* 1. 6. 14, 6. 4. 7, Heliod. 2. 23. 99, Lucian, *Dial. M.* 5. 1, Plutarch, *Phoc.* c. 13.[2] So of persons in A. viii. 9, μέγας τις *a very great man* (Xen. *Eph.* 3. 2, Athen. 4. 21, al.).[3] Compare A. v. 36, λέγων εἶναί τινα ἑαυτόν *that he is some one* (of consequence,—really something): see Bernh. p. 440, Krüg. p. 151, Jelf *l. c. Obs.* 1. In Latin *quidam* is similarly used, and also—where there is no substantive or adjective to be strengthened—*aliquis,* e. g. " aliquem esse," Cic. *Att.* 3. 15.

Πᾶς τις does not occur in the N. T.; some would introduce it in 1 C. ix. 22 (for πάντως τινάς)[4] on the testimony of a few authorities, but without necessity, and even without any critical probability. Εἷς τις, *unus aliquis,* may be emphatic in Jo. xi. 49.

The neuter τι, *aliquid,* may be used with emphasis in Mt. xx. 20, for *aliquid magni* (see Fritz. *in loc.*), but this is not probable. The pronoun must however be so taken in the formula εἶναί τι, G. ii. 6, vi. 3, al., as in the familiar Latin phrase *aliquid esse.* In every case it is the connexion that gives the emphasis (compare Herm. *Vig.* p. 731), and hence the subject belongs to the province of rhetoric: τὶ λέγειν, τὶ πράσσειν, are particularly common in Greek writers.

Rem. Τὶς may stand either before or after its substantive, as τὶς ἀνήρ A. iii. 2, ἀνήρ τις A. v. 1, x. 1: the latter is the more usual position in the N. T. It has been doubted (Matth. 487. 6, Jelf 660) whether τὶς can be the first word of a sentence; Hermann however (*Emend. Rat.* p. 95) sees nothing objectionable in this position of the pronoun. In the N. T. compare 1 Tim. v. 24, τινῶν ἀνθρώπων αἱ ἁμαρτίαι πρόδηλοί εἰσιν . . . τισὶν δὲ κ.τ.λ., A. xvii. 18, xix. 31.

The abbreviated forms του, τῳ (Buttm. I. 301, Jelf 156) are not found in the N. T.: they have been introduced by some into 1 C. xv. 8, 1 Th. iv. 6, but wrongly.

---

[1] [" Bernhardy's account of this usage (*Syntax* p. 442) seems to be the true one, that it has the power of a doubled adjectival sense, and generalises the quantity predicated, indicating *some one* of that kind, it may be *any one.* . . The indefiniteness makes the declaration more awful." Alford on H. x. 27. See also Delitzsch *in loc.*, Jelf *l. c.*—The word ἐκδίκησις above should be ἐκδοχή: it is curious that this mistake should have escaped correction in all the German editions.]

[2] Compare Boisson. *Nicet.* p. 268.

[3] In these cases τις is our [indefinite article] *ein* emphasised; as we can say in German, *das war eine Freude,* that was a joy (a great joy), *das ist ein Mann,* that is a man (a strong, able man).

[4] See Boisson. *Eunap.* p. 127.

Section XXVI.

HEBRAISTIC MODES OF EXPRESSING CERTAIN PRONOUNS.

1. In accordance with the Hebrew idiom,[1] the N. T. writers sometimes use οὐ (μή) . . . πᾶς in the place of οὐδείς, μηδείς, always however placing the negative in direct connexion with the verb of the sentence: Mt. xxiv. 22, οὐκ ἂν ἐσώθη πᾶσα σάρξ· Rom. iii. 20, ἐξ ἔργων νόμου οὐ δικαιωθήσεται πᾶσα σάρξ· L. i. 37, οὐκ ἀδυνατήσει παρὰ τοῦ θεοῦ πᾶν ῥῆμα· 1 C. i. 29, ὅπως μὴ καυχήσηται πᾶσα σάρξ κ.τ.λ.; compare also Rev. xxi. 27, οὐ μὴ εἰςέλθῃ εἰς αὐτὴν πᾶν κοινόν· A. x. 14, οὐδέποτε ἔφαγον πᾶν κοινόν· Rev. ix. 4 (Jud. xiii. 4, Sus. 27).

On the other hand, when οὐ (μή) and πᾶς are joined together, without an intervening word, the meaning is *not every* (like *non omnis*): 1 C. xv. 39, οὐ πᾶσα σὰρξ ἡ αὐτὴ σάρξ· Mt. vii. 21, οὐ πᾶς ὁ λέγων· κύριε, κύριε, εἰςελεύσεται εἰς τὴν βασ. . . . ἀλλ' ὁ ποιῶν κ.τ.λ., *Not every one who* (willingly) *calls me Lord, but* (amongst those who do this) *only he who does the will*, etc.,[2]— it is not the (mere) saying "Lord" that gives an entrance into the kingdom of heaven, but, etc.: A. x. 41 is similar. So also οὐ πάντες is *non omnes*: Mt. xix. 11, Rom. ix. 6, x. 16.

This distinction has its foundation in the nature of the case. In οὐ . . . πᾶς, οὐ negatives the notion of the verb,—a negative assertion being made in reference to πᾶς: thus in Rom. iii. 20, *every man shall not-be-justified*, the "not-being-justified" is asserted of every man, and hence the meaning is, *no man shall be justified*.[3] In οὐ πᾶς, it is πᾶς that is negatived.—On the whole, however, the formula οὐ . . . πᾶς occurs but rarely: in

---

[1] Leusden, *Diall.* p. 107, Vorst, *Hebr.* p. 529 sq., Gesen. *Lg.* 831 [Gesen. *Hebr. Gr.* p. 236 (Bagst.), Kalisch, *Hebr. Gr.* I. 236. For the N. T., see Green, *Gr.* p. 190, Jelf 905. *Obs.* 9.]

[2] I cannot agree with Fritzsche (see also *Prälim.* p. 72 sq.) in joining οὐ with the verb and rendering the words "no Lord-sayer." The "saying Lord, Lord," is by no means excluded by the second member of the verse (ἀλλ' ὁ ποιῶν); indeed ποιεῖν τὸ θέλημα τοῦ πατρός μου involves the acknowledgment of Jesus as the Lord.

[3] Gesenius *l. c.* merely mentions this peculiarity of the Hebrew language, without making any effort to explain it: Ewald, on the other hand (p. 657) [*Lehrb.* p. 790: ed. 7], has at least indicated the correct explanation. See Drusius on G. ii. 16, and Beza on Mt. xxiv. 22, Rom. iii. 20. I have never been able to see what Gesenius means by his distinction between οὐ πᾶς and μὴ πᾶς.

SECT. XXVI.] HEBRAISTIC MODES OF EXPRESSING PRONOUNS. 215

the examples quoted above (which are for the most part sentences of a proverbial character) it seems to have been used designedly, as being more expressive. The N. T. use of this construction is almost confined to those passages in which the O. T. phrase כָּל־בָּשָׂר is introduced: in the LXX, as a translation, the idiom is of frequent occurrence.¹ All Georgi's quotations (*Vind.* p. 317) to prove that this construction is pure Greek, are beside the mark: in every instance πᾶς belongs to the noun, signifying either *whole* (as in μηδὲ τὸν ἅπαντα χρόνον), or *full, complete* (as in πᾶσα ἀνάγκη).²

This Hebraism should in strictness be limited to the expression οὐ (μή) . . . πᾶς; for in sentences with πᾶς . . . οὐ (μή)³ there is usually nothing that is alien to Greek usage,⁴ or else the writer's reason for choosing this particular mode of expression is evident of itself. 1 Jo. ii. 21, πᾶν ψεῦδος ἐκ τῆς ἀληθείας οὐκ ἔστιν, *all falsehood (every lie) is not of the truth*, is a sentence which any Greek might have written: Jo. iii. 16, ἵνα πᾶς ὁ πιστεύων εἰς αὐτὸν μὴ ἀπόληται, ἀλλ᾽ ἔχῃ κ.τ.λ. (v. l.),⁵ *that every believer in Him may not perish, but*, etc. In E. v. 5, πᾶς πόρνος ἢ ἀκάθαρτος ἢ πλεονέκτης . . . οὐκ ἔχει κληρονομίαν ἐν τῇ βασιλείᾳ τοῦ Χριστοῦ, the apostle may have had an

---

¹ For instance, Ex. xii. 16, 44, xx. 10, Dt. v. 14, xx. 16, Jud. xiii. 4, 2 S. xv. 11, Ps. xxxiii. 11, cxlii. 2, Ex. xxxi. 14 (Tob. iv. 7, 19, xii. 11). Yet they just as frequently use the classical οὐ . . . οὐδείς or οὐδέν (see Ex. x. 15, Dt. viii. 9, Jos. x. 8, Pr. vi. 35, xii. 21), or even the simple οὐδείς (Jos. xxiii. 9).

² If Schleusner means to prove from Cic. *Rosc. Amer.* 27, and *ad Famil.* 2. 12, that "non omnis" is used for "nullus," he cannot have looked at these passages.

³ That is, in the singular; when πᾶς is plural (e. g. *all men love not death*), that is the ordinary mode of expression in Greek. Of this kind is the passage quoted by Weiske (*Pleon.* p. 58) in illustration of this Hebraism, Plat. *Phæd.* 91 e, πότερον, ἔφη, πάντας τοὺς ἔμπροσθεν λόγους οὐκ ἀποδέχεσθε, ἢ τοὺς μέν, τοὺς δ᾽ οὔ; "is it *all* . . . that you do not receive, or do you receive part and reject part?" In what other way could this have been (simply) expressed? In the LXX compare Num. xiv. 23, Jos. xi. 13, Ez. xxxi. 14, Dan. xi. 37.

⁴ If a writer joins the negative to the verb at the beginning of the sentence (οὐ δικαιωθήσεται), it may be supposed that he has the subject already before his mind (πᾶς), and therefore might say οὐδείς. If however he begins with πᾶς, either he has not yet decided whether he will use an affirmative or a negative verb, or else it seems to him more appropriate to make a negative assertion in reference to *every one* (πᾶς ὁ πιστεύων . . . οὐ μὴ ἀπόληται), than to make an affirmative assertion in reference to *no one*. Such an assurance as " *no believer* shall perish" would seem to presuppose that there existed some apprehension which it was the object of the assurance to remove.

⁵ [This is a *v. l.* in ver. 15, but in ver. 16 there is no doubt about the reading.]

affirmative predicate before his mind when he began the sentence (Ez. xliv. 9). Only in E. iv. 29, Rev. xviii. 22, and perhaps in Rev. xxii. 3, οὐδέν would have been more pleasing to a Grecian ear.

In Mt. x. 29 (L. xii. 6), we find ἓν ἐξ αὐτῶν οὐ πεσεῖται, (vel) unum non, ne unum quidem (in contrast with δύο, "*two* for an assarion, and not even *one*, etc."); similarly in Mt. v. 18. Such expressions (with a negative) are also found in Greek writers: Dion. H. *Comp.* 18 (V. 122), μίαν οὐκ ἄν εὕροι τις σελίδα· *Antiqq.* II. 980. 10, μία τε οὐ κατελείπετο (according to Schæfer's emendation), Plutarch, *Gracch.* 9:[1] in Hebrew compare Ex. x. 19, Is. xxxiv. 16. This construction cannot be called either a Græcism or a Hebraism; in every case the writer aims at greater emphasis than would be conveyed by οὐδείς,—which properly expresses the same thing, but had become weakened by usage.[2]

L. i. 37, οὐκ ἀδυνατήσει παρὰ [τῷ] θεῷ πᾶν ῥῆμα [3]—*nothing, no thing* (compare דָּבָר, and in Greek ἔπος)—is probably taken from Gen. xviii. 14 (LXX). Mt. xv. 23, οὐκ ἀπεκρίθη αὐτῇ λόγον, is simply, *He answered her not a word:* there was no need of ἕνα here,—we also say "a word," not "*one* word."[4] The Greeks could use the same expression, and its occurrence in 1 K. xviii. 21 does not make it a Hebraism.

2. *The one, the other,* is sometimes expressed by the repetition of εἷς:—

(*a*) In antithetical clauses, εἷς ... καὶ εἷς: Mt. xx. 21, xxiv. 40, xxvii. 38, xvii. 4, Mk. x. 37, Jo. xx. 12, G. iv. 22,—but in L. xvii. 34, ὁ εἷς ... [καὶ] ὁ ἕτερος,[5] compare xvi. 13, xviii. 10, Æsop 119 (De Fur.): so in Hebrew אֶחָד, Ex. xvii. 12, Lev. xii. 8,

---

[1] See Schæfer on Plutarch *l. c.*, and on Dionys. *Compos.* p. 247, Erfurdt, Soph. *Antig.* p. 121. [Jelf 738. Obs. 3.]

[2] Hence also the combination οὐδὲ εἷς *nemo quisquam, nemo unus,* Mt. xxvii. 14, οὐδὲ ἓν ῥῆμα *ne unum quidem,* Jo. i. 3, Rom. iii. 10, 1 C. vi. 5 [*Rec.*]: see Herm. *Vig.* p. 467, Weber, *Dem.* p. 501 (Xen. *Cyr.* 2. 3. 9, 4. 1. 14). This is frequently found in the LXX (especially as a rendering of לֹא אֶחָד), as Ex. xiv. 28, Num. xxxi. 49. Compare also οὐ ... ποτέ, 2 P. i. 21.

[3] [This passage is quoted above with the reading παρὰ τοῦ θεοῦ, which is received by recent editors. In favour of taking ῥῆμα as *word* (not *thing*), see Meyer and Alford *in loc.,* Ellic. *Hist. L.* p. 49.]

[4] No one who has learnt to make distinctions in language will require ἕνα here, on the ground that εἷς is expressed elsewhere (Mt. xxi. 24, ἐρωτήσω ὑμᾶς κἀγὼ λόγον ἕνα).

[5] [Besides these two forms of expression, we find the following in the N. T.: εἷς ... καὶ ὁ ἕτερος (Mt. vi. 24, L. xvi. 13), ὁ εἷς ... ὁ δὲ ἕτ. (L. vii. 41, A. xxiii. 6), εἷς ... ὁ δὲ ἕτ. (L. xvii. 35, Tisch. ed. 7), ὁ εἷς ... ὁ ἄλλος (Rev. xvii. 10). In L. xvii. 34, xviii. 10 (quoted above), it is doubtful whether we should read εἷς or ὁ εἷς. In G. iv. 24 we find μία μέν, not followed by a second clause. In Mk. ix. 5, Mt. xvii. 4, L. ix. 33, there are *three* members (εἷς ... καὶ εἷς ... καὶ εἷς). See A. Buttm. p. 102.]

xv. 15, 1 S. x. 3, al. The Greek said εἷς μὲν ... εἷς δέ, or εἷς μὲν ... ὁ δέ;[1] for the examples which Georgi and Schwarz[2] have quoted as parallel to the N. T. formula are rather enumerations proper, reckonings of a sum total (e.g. *eight in all, one .... one .... one ....* etc.).

(*b*) With a reciprocal meaning : 1 Th. v. 11, οἰκοδομεῖτε εἷς τὸν ἕνα· 1 C. iv. 6. This would rather be an Aramaism[3] (hence the Peshito repeats ܐ to express ἀλλήλ., e.g. in Mt. xxiv. 10, Jo. xiii. 35), but is not in discordance with Greek syntax ; see Her. 4. 50, ἓν πρὸς ἓν συμβάλλειν· Lucian, *Conscr. Hist.* 2, ὡς οὖν ἕν, φασίν, ἑνὶ παραβαλεῖν· *Asin.* 54. Compare also the phrase ἓν ἀνθ' ἑνός (Ast, Plat. *Polit.* p. 339, Bernhardy, *Dionys. Perieg.* p. 853), and Kypke II. 339.

Mt. xii. 26, ὁ σατανᾶς τὸν σατανᾶν ἐκβάλλει, is rendered by some (on the principle of *cuneus cuneum trudit*), " *the one* Satan casts out *the other* Satan ;" but the true translation is, *Satan casts out Satan.* Compare, on the other hand, L. xi. 17.

The Hebrew idiom, *the man .... to his friend,* or *brother,* is retained by the LXX (Gen. xi. 3, xiii. 11, Jud. vi. 29, Ruth iii. 14, Jer. ix. 20, al.), but does not occur in the N. T. : compare however H. viii. 11 (a quotation from the LXX), οὐ μὴ διδάξωσιν ἕκαστος τὸν πλησίον (or better πολίτην) αὐτοῦ καὶ ἕκαστος τὸν ἀδελφὸν αὐτοῦ.

On a Hebraistic mode of expressing *every,* by repeating the noun, e.g. ἡμέρᾳ καὶ ἡμέρᾳ, see § 54. 1.

CHAPTER THIRD.

THE NOUN.

SECTION XXVII.

NUMBER AND GENDER OF NOUNS.

1. The singular of a masculine noun, with the article, is not unfrequently used in a collective sense to denote the whole class : Ja. ii. 6, ἠτιμάσατε τὸν πτωχόν (in 1 C. xi. 22 we find the plural), Ja. v. 6, Rom. xiv. 1, 1 P. iv. 18, Mt. xii. 35. This usage is especially common in the case of national names, as

---

[1] See Fischer *ad* Leusden. *Diall.* p. 35, Matth. 288. Rem. 6.
[2] Georgi, *Vind.* p. 159 sq., Schwarz, *Comment.* p. 421.
[3] Hoffmann, *Gramm. Syr.* p. 330. [Cowper, *Syr. Gr.* p. 112.]

ὁ Ἰουδαῖος Rom. iii. 1; so *Romanus* often stands for *Romani* (Markland, Eur. *Suppl.* 659). This quality is brought out more purely and sharply by the singular than by the plural, which points to the multitude of the individuals [§ 18. 1]. Akin to this is the use of the singular in reference to a plurality of objects, to denote something which belongs to each of the objects: 1 C. vi. 19, ὅτι τὸ σῶμα ὑμῶν ναὸς τ. ἁγ. πνεύματος (the reading of the best MSS.); Mk. viii. 17, πεπωρωμένην ἔχετε τὴν καρδίαν (Ja. iii. 14, L. i. 66, 2 P. ii. 14, al.); Mt. xvii. 6, ἔπεσαν ἐπὶ πρόςωπον αὐτῶν (L. ii. 31, 2 C. iii. 18, viii. 24);[1] Rev. vi. 11, ἐδόθη αὐτοῖς στολὴ λευκή (L. xxiv. 4, A. i. 10 ?); E. vi. 14, περιζωσάμενοι τὴν ὀσφὺν ὑμῶν κ.τ.λ. (Jelf 354). This distributive singular, as it may be called, is common in Greek writers: Xen. *An.* 4. 7. 16, εἶχον κνημῖδας καὶ κράνη καὶ μαχαίριον .... δόρυ κ.τ.λ., *Cyr.* 4. 3. 11, Eurip. *Cycl.* 225, Thuc. 3. 22, 4. 4, 6. 58, Pol. 3. 49. 12, Æl. *Anim.* 5. 4; compare Cic. *Rab.* 4. 11, Sen. *Ep.* 87. In the LXX compare Gen. xlviii. 12, Lev. x. 6, Jud. xiii. 20, Lam. ii. 10, 2 Chr. xxix. 6: see also *Testam. Patr.* p. 565.[2] In the N. T., as elsewhere, the plural is the form ordinarily used (so also in L. xxiv. 5, A. i. 10[3]). See, in general, Elmsley on Eur. *Med.* 264, Bornem. Xen. *Cyr.* p. 158.

The *collective* use of the singular must not be extended beyond its natural limits. In 1 C. vi. 5, διακρῖναι ἀνὰ μέσον τοῦ ἀδελφοῦ, τοῦ ἀδ. does not stand for τῆς ἀδελφότητος: nor would anything be gained by such a supposition, for ἀνὰ μέσον *between* should be followed by the mention of particular individuals, not of a collective whole. (Mt. xiii. 25 is a different case.) We should have ἀνὰ μέσον ἀδελφοῦ καὶ ἀδελφοῦ (Gen. xxiii. 15), or τῶν ἀδελφῶν αὐτοῦ (see Grotius,—compare Pol. 10. 48. 1), or else the structure is faulty through excessive conciseness. Even in Meyer's explanation it is implied that the expression is incorrect, as it is also without example.

2. Conversely, the plural of the class (masculine or feminine) is used where the writer wishes to express himself *gene-*

---

[1] I cannot bring in here ἀπὸ or πρὸ προςώπου αὐτῶν or ὑμῶν, κατὰ πρ. πάντων, etc. (L. ii. 31, A. vii. 45, Ex. xxxiv. 11, Dt. iii. 18, vii. 19, viii. 20, al.), as these phrases had already become mere adverbs.

[2] In 1 Th. i. 7, ὥστε γινέσθαι ὑμᾶς τύπον πᾶσι τοῖς πιστεύουσιν, the singular is quite regular, because Paul is thinking of the church as a whole. 1 C. x. 6, 11 [*Rec.*], 1 P. v. 3, are of a different kind; here the singular would be inappropriate.

[3] [In these two passages *Rec.* has the singular, the best MSS. the plural.]

rally, though the predicate directly refers to one individual only: Mt. ii. 20, τεθνήκασιν οἱ ζητοῦντες τὴν ψυχὴν τοῦ παιδίου, though Herod the Great alone is meant (ver. 19); comp. Ex. iv. 19, and see Æschyl. *Prom.* 67, Eurip. *Hec.* 403, Æschin. *adv. Timarch.* 21, and Bremi *in loc.*[1] On the other hand, in Mt. ix. 8, ἐδόξασαν τὸν θεὸν τὸν δόντα ἐξουσίαν τοιαύτην τοῖς ἀνθρώποις, the reference is certainly not to Christ alone; the words must be taken quite generally, as in H. ix. 23. In Mt. xxvii. 44, οἱ λῃσταί, we must recognise a different tradition from that followed in L. xxiii. 39.[2] In 1 C. xv. 29, ὑπὲρ τῶν νεκρῶν can hardly refer to (the dead) Christ,—in that case we should have had εἰς τοὺς νεκρούς,—but must be understood of (unbaptised) dead men.

In A. xiii. 40, τὸ εἰρημένον ἐν τοῖς προφήταις (Jo. vi. 45), we have merely a general form of quotation (A. vii. 42, ἐν βιβλίῳ τῶν προφητῶν), just as we ourselves say "in Paul's Epistles," etc., when we either do not wish or are not able to give the exact reference. Mt. xxiv. 26, ἐν τοῖς ταμείοις (opposed to ἐν τῇ ἐρήμῳ) is essentially of the same kind: compare Liv. 1. 3, Silvius casu quodam in *silvis* natus.

In Mt. xxi. 7, ἐπάνω αὐτῶν probably refers to the ἱμάτια; but there would be nothing absurd in the words even if they referred to the two animals, any more than in ἐπιβεβηκὼς ἐπὶ ὄνον καὶ πῶλον, ver. 5. We ourselves say loosely, "he sprang from the horses," although only one of the team, the saddle-horse, is meant.

It is quite erroneous to suppose that in 1 C. xvi. 3 the plural ἐπιστολαί is used for the singular (Heumann *in loc.*). Though ἐπιστολαί may be used of a single letter,[3] yet in this passage the words δι' ἐπιστ. must certainly be joined with πέμψω, and it is in itself not at all improbable that Paul might send several letters to different persons.

3. Not a few nouns which in German [and English] are used in the singular are either always or usually plural in the N. T. These nouns denote objects which—from a general, or a Grecian, or a Biblical point of view—present to the senses or to the mind something plural or comprehensive (Krüg. p. 12, Jelf 355, Don. p. 367). Thus we find αἰῶνες H. i. 2, *the world*

---

[1] Porson, Eur. *Phœn.* 36, Reisig, *Conject. in Aristoph.* p. 58, and C. L. Roth, *Grammat. Quæst. e C. Tacito* (Norimb. 1829), § 1. [Green, *Gr.* p. 83 sq.]

[2] [On the other side, see Smith, *Dict. of Bible* III. 1488; Lange, *Life of Christ* IV. 397 (Transl.); Farrar, *Life of Christ*, p. 410 sq., and note on L. xxiii. 39. Compare Green p. 84.]

[3] Schæf. *Plutarch* V. 446, Poppo on Thuc. 1. 132.

(עוֹלָמִים); οὐρανοί *cœli*,[1] compare 2 C. xii. 2 ; τὰ ἅγια the sanctuary, H. viii. 2, ix. 8, 12, al. ; ἀνατολαί, δυσμαί, *the regions of the East, West*, Mt. viii. 11, xxiv. 27 (Plat. *Def.* 411 b, *Epin.* 990 a, Diod. S. 2. 43, Dio C. 987. 32, Lucian, *Peregr.* 39); τὰ δεξιά, ἀριστερά, εὐώνυμα, *the right, left side* (frequently); θύραι *fores, folding doors* (so also πύλαι in Greek writers), A. v. 19, Jo. xx. 19,—but not A. xvi. 26 sq., Mt. xxiv. 33, for here θύραι is a real plural ; κόλποι *bosom*, L. xvi. 23 (κόλπος in ver. 22), compare Paus. 6. 1. 2, Æl. 13. 31 ; τὰ ἱμάτια of the (single) *upper-garment*, Jo. xix. 23, xviii. 4, A. x. 6 ;[2] the names of the festivals ἐγκαίνια, γενέσια, ἄζυμα (Παναθήναια, *Saturnalia*[3]); γάμοι *nuptials*, Mt. xxii. 2, L. xii. 36 (compare Tob. xi. 20[4]); ὀψώνια *wages*, Rom. vi. 23 (Fritz. *Rom.* I. 428), and ἀργύρια *pieces of money, shekels*, Mt. xxvi. 15, xxviii. 12.

When the names of countries or cities are plural, the cause must be sought in the (original) plurality of the provinces (*Galliæ*) or of the distinct parts of the city, as Ἀθῆναι, Πάταρα, Φίλιπποι, and probably τὰ Ἱεροσόλυμα.[5] Lastly, the plural of those nouns which denote a feeling, a disposition, or a state, expresses the forms or acts in which these are manifested : 1 P. ii. 1, ἀποθέμενοι πᾶσαν κακίαν ... κ. ὑποκρίσεις κ. φθόνους κ. πάσας καταλαλιάς· 2 C. xii. 20, ἔρις, ζῆλος, θυμοί, ἐριθεῖαι, καταλαλιαί, ψιθυρισμοί, φυσιώσεις, ἀκαταστασίαι· 2 C. xi. 23, ἐν θανάτοις πολλάκις· E. vi. 11, G. v. 20, 1 P. iv. 3, Ja. ii. 1 (2 C. ix. 6), Jude 13, 1 C. vii. 2.[6] Thus the plural οἰκτιρμοί, רַחֲמִים, is more common than the singular, which is found once only (Col. iii. 12 *v. l.*[7]): E. ii. 3, θελήματα τῆς σαρκός, also comes in here.[8]

The plural of αἷμα *blood* occurs Jo. i. 13 (with reference to natural generation): the only direct parallel to this is found in a poetical

---

[1] Schneider, *Lat. Gr.* II. 476.
[2] [These two references are wrong. In ed. 5, Winer gives Mt. xxvii. 31, Mk. v. 30, Jo. xiii. 4, 12, A. xviii. 6 : hence we should probably read here Jo. xix. 23, xiii. 4, A. xviii. 6.]
[3] Poppo, *Thuc.* III. iv. 20.
[4] [A mistake, probably for viii. 20, or xi. 18.]
[5] Comp. Nobbe, *Schedæ Ptolem.* I. 22. [See also Smith, *Dict. of Bible* I. 982.]
[6] Fritz. *Rom.* III. 6, Kritz, *Sallust* I. 76.
[7] [Here the plural has the support of one only (K) of the uncial MSS.]
[8] On the whole subject see Jacobs, *Act. Philol. Monac.* I. 154 sq., Schoem. Plut. *Agis* p. 75 sq., Stallb. Plat. *Rep.* II. 368, Heinichen, *Euseb.* III. 18 sq., Bernh. p. 62 sq. (Jelf 355, Don. p. 367).

SECT. XXVII.] NUMBER AND GENDER OF NOUNS. 221

passage, Eur. *Ion* 693, but the plural in itself presents no more difficulty in the case of αἷμα than in that of other fluids, as τὰ ὕδατα and τὰ γάλακτα, Plat. *Legg.* 10. 887 d (Jelf 355). In Rev. xviii. 24 αἵματα is a real plural. The plural is not used for the singular in αἱ γραφαί, τὰ ἱερὰ γράμματα; or in αἱ διαθῆκαι Rom. ix. 4, E. ii. 12, *the covenants* which God repeatedly made in the patriarchal age, with Abraham, with Jacob, through Moses (compare Wis. xii. 21, 2 Macc. viii. 15). Ἐπαγγελίαι, H. vii. 6, must be similarly explained. Neither in these words, nor in Jo. ix. 3, 2 C. xii. 1, 7, nor in H. ix. 23 (where the language is general), can we assume the existence of a Hebraistic *pluralis majestatis*.

Τὰ σάββατα, where the weekly day of rest is meant (Mt. xii. 1, L. iv. 16, al.), either is a transcript of the Aramaic שַׁבְּתָא, or is formed according to the analogy of names of festivals. With more reason might ἅγια ἁγίων, used in H. ix. 3 for the *most holy place* of the temple of Jerusalem, be regarded as a *pluralis excellentiæ*; unless indeed (with Erasmus and others) we prefer the accentuation ἁγία ἁγίων (compare δειλαία δειλαίων, Soph. *El.* 849). But though in the Pentateuch this part of the Israelitish sanctuary is called τὸ ἅγιον τῶν ἁγίων (Ex. xxvi. 33, Num. iv. 4, compare Joseph. *Antt.* 3. 6. 4), yet in 1 K. viii. 6 this very (plural) form τὰ ἅγια τῶν ἁγίων is used in the same sense.[1] We may compare the Latin *penetralia, adyta* (Virg. *Æn.* 2. 297).

As to Ph. ii. 6, τὸ εἶναι ἴσα θεῷ, where ἴσα is used adverbially, compare the classical usage of the word, *Il.* 5. 71, *Odyss.* 1. 432, 15. 520, Soph. *Œd. R.* 1179, Thuc. 3. 14, Philostr. *Ap.* 8. 26, al.; and see Reisig, *Œd. Col.* 526 (Jelf 382. 1).

4. The dual of the noun is not found in the N. T.[2] (except in the numeral δύο), the plural being used in its place,—even with δύο, see Mt. iv. 18, xviii. 9, xxvi. 37, Jo. iv. 20 [40 ?], A. xii. 6, al. Indeed in later Greek generally the dual form is rare. In Rev. xii. 14, τρέφεται καιρὸν καὶ καιροὺς καὶ ἥμισυ καιροῦ, the plural by itself denotes *two years*: this is an imitation of the Chaldee עִדָּנִין in the Greek versions of Dan. vii. 25.[3] Standing thus between *a year* and *half a year*, the plural was allowably made to signify *two years*. The use of χρόνος, χρόνοι, in the sense of *year, years*, becomes more and more common

---

[1] [Not in this passage only: see Num. iv. 19, 2 Chr. iv. 22, v. 7 (quoted by Bleek *in loc.*).]
[2] [It is not found in the LXX, or in modern Greek: see Mullach, *Vulg.* p. 149 sq.]
[3] It should be noticed that the Chaldee has (as a rule) no dual: see my *Chaldee Grammar* p. 77. ["As a rule"—because "the few dual forms are borrowed from the Hebrew, and are found only in Biblical Chaldee."]

in later Greek: see also *Evang. Apocr.* pp. 60, 61, Epiphan. *Mon.* 29. 28.

Bornemann discovers a trace of the dual in A. xv. 12, in a reading ἐξηγουμένω (with ν added above the line) found in a single MS.,—from which Tischendorf quotes the reading ἐξηγούμενοι,—and is ready to greet this number *læto animo!*

5. The neuter singular or plural is sometimes found where persons are referred to, the writer wishing to make his statement altogether general (Jelf 436. 2): 2 Th. ii. 6, τὸ κατέχον οἴδατε (in ver. 7, ὁ κατέχων); H. vii. 7, τὸ ἔλαττον ὑπὸ τοῦ κρείττονος εὐλογεῖται (Theodor. *in loc.*); L. i. 35, 1 C. i. 27, 28, τὰ μωρὰ τοῦ κόσμου ... τὰ ἀσθενῆ τὰ ἐξουθενημένα (in ver. 26 οἱ σοφοί); Jo. vi. 37, 1 Jo. v. 4 (compare ver. 1): so also in 1 C. xi. 5, but not in Col. i. 20, H. vii. 19, Jo. iii. 6, see the more recent commentators. In Rom. xi. 32 τοὺς πάντας is the established reading. Similarly in Thuc. 3. 11, τὰ κράτιστα ἐπὶ τοὺς ὑποδεεστέρους ξυνεπῆγον· Xen. *An.* 7. 3. 11, τὰ μὲν φεύγοντα καὶ ἀποδιδράσκοντα ἡμεῖς ἱκανοὶ ἐσόμεθα διώκειν καὶ μαστεύειν, ἢν δέ τις ἀνθίστηται κ.τ.λ.[1]

6. The neuter seems to be used for the feminine in Mk. xii. 28, ποία ἐστὶν ἐντολὴ πρώτη πάντων (for πασῶν, which is a correction). Here however πάντων stands without any generic relation to the noun which precedes, for the general expression *omnium (rerum)*:[2] comp. Lucian, *Piscat.* 13, μία πάντων ἤγε ἀληθὴς φιλοσοφία (according to the common text; al. πάντως), Thuc. 4. 52, τάς τε ἄλλας πόλεις καὶ πάντων μάλιστα τὴν Ἄντανδρον: see D'Orville, *Charit.* p. 549 sq., Porson, Eur. *Phœn.* 121, Fritz. on Mk. *l. c.* We cannot however say (with D'Orville *l. c.* p. 292 sq.) that in A. ix. 37, λούσαντες αὐτὴν ἔθηκαν, the masculine λούσαντες is used for λούσασαι, because the *women* attended to the washing of the corpse. The writer's language is quite general[3] and impersonal: *they washed and laid.* If Luke had wished to notice the custom with historical precision, he must have expressed himself more circumstantially. Compare Xen. *Mem.* 2. 7. 2, συνεληλύθασιν ...

---

[1] Poppo, *Thuc.* I. 104, Seidler, Eur. *Troad.* p. 61, Kritz, *Sall.* II. 69.
[2] [A. Buttm. p. 374, Green p. 109: A. Buttmann compares ἐν τοῖς, which is joined to a superlative without change of gender (Don. p. 396), as ἐν τοῖς πλεῖσται Thuc. 3. 17. See further Alford on Mk. *l. c.*]
[3] Herm. Soph. *Trachin.* p. 39 (Jelf 379. *Obs.* 1).

ἀδελφαί τε καὶ ἀδελφιδαὶ καὶ ἀνεψιαὶ τοσαῦται, ὥςτ' εἶναι ἐν τῇ οἰκίᾳ τεσσαρακαίδεκα τοὺς ἐλευθέρους, *fourteen free persons*, where the masculine is used, although, as it appears, these free persons are women: Suet. *Ner.* 33, acceptum a quadam Locusta, venenariorum inclita. (In L. xxii. 58 and Mt. xxvi. 71 we have two different accounts; see Meyer.[1])

The masculine does not stand for the feminine in Gen. xxiii. 3, ἀνέστη Ἀβραὰμ ἀπὸ τοῦ νεκροῦ αὐτοῦ· or in ver. 4, θάψω τὸν νεκρόν μου (ver. 15), though Sarah is meant; or in Susan. 61, ἐποίησαν αὐτοῖς ὃν τρόπον ἐπονηρεύσαντο τῷ πλησίον, though Susanna is meant. With Gen. xxiii.[2] compare Soph. *Antig.* 830, φθιμένῳ (vulg. φθιμένᾳ) τοῖς ἰσοθέοις ἔγκληρα λαχεῖν μέγα: for *a corpse* the Greeks always use ὁ νεκρός, never the feminine. See further Herm. Soph. *Antig.* pp. 114, 176. (Jelf 390. 1. c.)

Rem. 1. In Rom. xi. 4, a quotation from the O. T. (1 K. xix. 18), we meet with the feminine ἡ Βάαλ (Hos. ii. 8, Zeph. i. 4). It is not probable that this form was chosen for the sake of expressing contempt, in the same way as the feminine forms of the names of idols are said to be used in Arabic and by Rabbinical writers (?).[3] In this particular passage the LXX has τῷ Βάαλ, but Paul, who is quoting from memory, might easily write ἡ Βάαλ, a form which he had found in some passages of the LXX (though the MSS. vary now): Rückert is in perplexity, as he often is. It was after all a matter of indifference whether the male or the female Baal should be mentioned.—The feminine μοιχαλίδες, Ja. iv. 4, in the midst of a general address, is explained by Theile by reference to O. T. usage: against this see De Wette. There is no decisive external evidence for the omission of μοιχοὶ καί; and to refuse to admit an error of transcription, even when similar words come together, is to carry reverence for the (remaining) principal MSS. too far.[4]

Rem. 2. When a noun of any gender is taken in a material sense, as a *word*, it is joined with the neuter article: as G. iv. 25, τὸ Ἄγαρ, *the* (word) *Hagar*.[5] The feminine may seem to be used for the neuter in ἡ οὐαί, Rev. ix. 12, xi. 14; but the writer probably had some such word as θλῖψις or ταλαιπωρία before his mind.

Rem. 3. On the adverbial use of the feminine adjective (as in ἰδίᾳ, κατ' ἰδίαν, etc.), see § 54.

---

[1] [See however Alford on Mt. xxvi. 69; but especially Westcott, *St. John* pp. 263-266.]

[2] We ourselves say, *Er begrub seinen Todten.* [That is, *He buried his dead,* —the last word being masculine.]

[3] See Gesenius in Rosenm. *Repertor.* I. 139, Tholuck on Rom. *l. c.*; and on the other side Fritz. *Rom.* II. 442.

[4] [ℵ agrees with A and B in omitting μοιχοὶ καί, and the testimony of these MSS. is rightly followed by recent editors. See Alford's note for a good defence of Theile's view.]

[5] [See above § 18. 3.]

Section XXVIII.

THE CASES IN GENERAL.[1]

1. It was not difficult for foreigners to understand the general import of the Greek cases. Even in the language of the Jews the ordinary case-relations are exhibited clearly enough, though they are not marked by special terminations; and, in particular, the Aramaic approaches the Western languages in the mode of expressing the genitive. To learn to *feel*, as a Greek would feel, the force of the oblique cases in *all* their varied applications, remote as some of these applications were, was a matter of great difficulty; and in this particular Greek usage did not accord with the vivid and expressive style of the Oriental tongues. Hence we find that the N. T. writers, in accordance with the Oriental idiom, and partly in direct imitation of it, not unfrequently use a preposition where a Greek writer, even in prose, would have used the case alone. Thus we have διδόναι ἐκ, ἐσθίειν ἀπό, μετέχειν ἐκ, in the place of διδόναι, ἐσθίειν, μετέχειν τινός (comp. § 30); πολεμεῖν μετά τινος, instead of τινί; κατηγορεῖν and ἐγκαλεῖν κατά τινος (L. xxiii. 14, Rom. viii. 33), for τινί;[2] ἐγείρειν τινὰ εἰς βασιλέα, A. xiii. 22 (§ 32); βασιλεύειν ἐπί τινι or τινά (מָלַךְ עַל), for τινός; ἀθῶος with ἀπό, in the place of the simple genitive.[3] In the LXX compare φείδεσθαι ἐπί τινι, or τινος, or ὑπέρ τινος (חוּס עַל).

This use of prepositions in the place of cases is, however, a general feature of (antique) simplicity, and is therefore found not only in the earlier Greek poets (as Homer), but also in the prose writers (as Lucian).[4] Hence also for several expressions of this kind parallels may be produced even from good writers,—e. g. for παύειν ἀπό, compare Matth. 355. Rem. 1.[5]

---

[1] Hermann, *De Emend. Rat.* I. 137 sqq., Bernhardy p. 74 sqq. There is a monograph on the subject by J. A. Hartung, *Ueber die Casus, ihre Bildung und Bedeutung in der griech. u. lat. Sprache* (Erlang. 1831): and another by Rumpel, *Ueber die Casuslehre in Beziehung auf die griech. Sprache* (Halle 1845). [Donalds. *New Crat.* p. 428 sqq., *Gramm.* p. 464 sqq., Clyde, *Greek Synt.* pp. 23 sqq., 38 : compare Jelf 471 sqq.]

[2] Somewhat as the Byzantines say ἀγανακτεῖν or ὀργίζεσθαι κατά τινος, or like ὀργίζεσθαι πρός τινα Dio. Chr. 38. 470.

[3] Krebs, *Obs. e Josepho* p. 73 sq. [Lünemann adds μυιῖσθαι ἐν, Ph. iv. 12.]

[4] See Jacob, *Quæst. Lucian.* p. 11 sq.

[5] [This excessive use of prepositions may have been then, as now, a characteristic of the popular spoken language; see J. Donaldson in Kitto, *Cycl.* II. 171. For many examples of this kind in modern Greek see Mullach, *Vulg.* p. 323 sqq., Sophocles, *Gramm.* p. 152 sqq.]

2. There is in reality no such thing as the use of one case in the place of another (*enallage casuum*); but sometimes two cases may be used in the same connexion with equal correctness, if the relation is such that it can be viewed in two different ways. Thus we may have Ἀσσύριος τῷ γένει and Ἀσσύριος τὸ γένος, προςκυνεῖν τινί *to show reverence to*, and προςκυνεῖν τινά *to reverence*, καλῶς ποιεῖν τινά and τινί (Thilo, *Act. Thom.* 38), ἔνοχός τινι and τινος (Fritz. *Matt.* p. 223),[1] ὅμοιός τινος and τινι, πληροῦσθαί τινος (*from* or *of* something) and τινι (*with, by means of*). So also μιμνήσκεσθαί τι and τινος (like *recordari rei* and *rem*); in the former case (μιμν. τι, *to remember* a thing) I regard the remembrance as directed (transitively) on the object; in the latter (μιμν. τινος, *to bethink oneself of* a thing, *meminisse rei*) the remembrance is regarded as proceeding from the object (Jelf 473). Hence we cannot say that the dative or accusative is ever used for the genitive or *vice versâ*: logically, both cases are equally correct, and we have only to observe which of the constructions was more commonly used in the language, or whether any one of them may have especially belonged to the later language (or to some particular writer), as εὐαγγελίζεσθαί τινα, προςκυνεῖν τινί.

Perhaps the most absurd instance of this kind of enallage would be 2 C. vi. 4, συνιστῶντες ἑαυτοὺς ὡς θεοῦ διάκονοι, if διάκονοι stood for διακόνους. Here either the nominative or the accusative might be used, but they would express different relations. *I recommend myself as a teacher* (nominative) means, "I, in the office of teacher undertaken by me, recommend myself:" *I recommend myself as a teacher* (objective) is, "I recommend myself as one who wishes or who is able to be a teacher."

3. Every case, as such, stands according to its nature in a necessary connexion with the construction of the sentence to which it belongs. The nominative and accusative cases, denoting respectively the subject and the object, have the most direct connexion with the sentence; the genitive and dative express secondary relations. There are however *casus absoluti*, i. e. cases which are not interwoven with the grammatical texture of the sentence,—which, so to speak, hover near the grammatical

---

[1] The distinction which Schæfer makes between these two constructions (*Dem.* V. 323) receives no confirmation from the N. T. Compare further Matth. 370. Rem. 4.

sentence, and are only connected logically with the proposition it expresses. Of these the most frequent and the most decided examples are the *nominativi absoluti* (Bengel on Mt. xii. 36). Real *accusativi absoluti* (§ 63. I. 2. d)[1] are more rare; for what is called an accusative absolute is often dependent, though loosely, on the construction of the sentence. The *genitivi* and *dativi absoluti* are more regular members of the sentence, as a consideration of the meaning of these cases will show.[2] The whole subject of the nominative absolute, however, must be treated in connexion with the structure of sentences [see § 63].

Section XXIX.

NOMINATIVE AND VOCATIVE.

1. A noun considered directly and purely in itself is represented by the nominative, either as subject or as predicate, according to the structure of the sentence: Jo. i. 1, ἐν ἀρχῇ ἦν ὁ λόγος· E. ii. 14, αὐτός ἐστιν ἡ εἰρήνη ἡμῶν.

Sometimes, however, we meet with a nominative which is not comprised in the structure of the sentence to which it belongs; but either

(*a*) Stands at the head of a sentence, as a kind of *thema* (nominativus absolutus), as in A. vii. 40, ὁ Μωϋσῆς οὗτος ... οὐκ οἴδαμεν τί γέγονεν αὐτῷ (see § 28. 3):[3]—or

(*b*) Is simply inserted in the sentence as a name (nominativus tituli), as if a mere (indeclinable) sound: Jo. xviii. 10, ἦν ὄνομα τῷ δούλῳ Μάλχος· Rev. vi. 8, viii. 11, xix. 13 (Demosth.*Macart.* 669 b), L. xix. 29, πρὸς τὸ ὄρος τὸ καλούμενον Ἐλαιών:[4]

---

[1] Compare Fritz. *Rom.* III. 11 sq.
[2] See on the whole A. de Wannowski, *Syntaxeos anomalæ Græcæ pars de constructione, quæ dicitur, absoluta* etc. (Lips. 1835); F. W. Hoffmann, *Observata et monita de casibus absol. apud Græcos et Lat. ita positis ut videantur non posse locum habere* (Budiss. 1836),—the author treats only of the genitive and dative absolute; also J. Geisler, *De Græcorum nominativis absol.* (Vratisl. 1845); and E. Wentzel, *De genitivis et dat. absol.* (Vratisl. 1828). [See Jelf 477, 695, 699 sq., Clyde, *Greek. Synt.* p. 144 sqq.]
[3] [See § 63, I. 2. d, Jelf 477.]
[4] In all the earlier editions and in Lachmann's we find ἐλαιῶν. I cannot agree with Fritzsche [*Mark*, p. 794 sq.] in pronouncing this accentuation *decidedly* incorrect. By Luke, who designed his Gospel for foreign readers, the Mount of Olives, sufficiently well known in Palestine, might very well be mentioned for the first time as *the so called Mount of Olives*, just as in A. i. 12: the phrase πρὸς τὸ ὄρος τὸ λεγ. ἐλαιῶν when resolved becomes τὸ λεγ. ὄρος ἐλαιῶν,

SECT. XXIX.]   NOMINATIVE AND VOCATIVE.   227.

compare 1 S. ix. 9, τὸν προφήτην ἐκάλει ὁ λαὸς ἔμπροσθεν ὁ βλέπων· Malal. 18. 482, 10. 247; see Lob. p. 517.¹ Contrast A. i. 12, ἀπὸ ὄρους τοῦ καλουμένου Ἐλαιῶνος. (Jelf 475. Obs. 1.)

Usually however, when the construction requires an oblique case, the writer expresses the name in this case (simply interposing ὀνόματι), and thus brings the name into the regular construction of the sentence. See A. xxvii. 1, ἑκατοντάρχῃ ὀνόματι Ἰουλίῳ· ix. 11, 12, ἄνδρα Ἀνανίαν ὀνόματι εἰσελθόντα (xviii. 2, Mt. xxvii. 32, L. v. 27), A. xviii. 7, οἰκία τινὸς ὀνόματι Ἰούστου ; also Mt. i. 21, 25, καλέσεις τὸ ὄνομα αὐτοῦ Ἰησοῦν, L. i. 13 (in apposition to ὄνομα) ; and even Mk. iii. 16, ἐπέθηκεν ὄνομα τῷ Σίμωνι Πέτρον.—In Plut. Coriol. 11, different modes of expression are combined.

In Rev. i. 4, the nominative ὁ ὢν κ. ὁ ἦν κ. ὁ ἐρχόμενος (יְהֹוָה, the Unchangeable One!), is designedly treated as an indeclinable noun ; see § 10.

2. The nominative (with the article) is sometimes used in an address, particularly in calling or commanding, thus taking the place of the vocative, the case framed for such purposes.² Examples of this usage, which really coincides with that mentioned in 1 (a), are found in the N. T.: Mt. xi. 26, ναί, ὁ πατήρ (ἐξομολογοῦμαί σοι, ver. 25), ὅτι οὕτως ἐγένετο· H. i. 8, x. 7 (in the LXX compare Ps. xlii. 2, xxi. 2); especially with an imperative, L. viii. 54, ἡ παῖς ἔγειρε· Mt. xxvii. 29, χαῖρε ὁ βασιλεὺς τ. Ἰουδ., Jo. xix. 3, Mk. v. 41, ix. 25, E. vi. 1, Col. iii. 18, Rev. vi. 10. This mode of expression may have originally been some-

---

ad montem qui dicitur olivarum, and hence the article would very naturally be omitted with ἐλαιῶν. Perhaps, however, the translator of the Peshito Syriac read Ἐλαιών: in this passage his reading is ܚܕ ܕܡܬܩܪܐ ܙܝܬܐ, as in A. i. 12; but in Mt. xxi. 1, xxiv. 3, al., for ὄρος τῶν ἐλαιῶν, he has simply ܛܘܪ ܙܝܬܐ. [What is here said of L. xix. 29 is also true of L. xxi. 37: the latter verse is thus quoted by Tertullian (adv. Marc. 4. 39), "Sed enim per diem in templo docebat ; ad noctem vero in elæonem secedebat." The argument from the Syriac Version is somewhat weakened by the fact that the translator introduces ܒܝܬ ("mons loci olivarum," instead of "mons olivarum") not only in L. xix. 29, xxi. 37, A. i. 12, but also in L. xix. 37, xxii. 39 (τ. ὄρ. τῶν ἐλαιῶν). Lachmann is wrongly quoted above in favour of ἐλαιῶν : in both editions he reads -ών, which form most editors (but not Westcott and Hort) now receive in the two passages referred to. With A. i. 12 compare Joseph. Ant. 7. 9. 2 ; with L. xix. 29, Ant. 20. 8. 6, Bell. Jud. 2. 13. 5 (Grimm, Clavis s. v.).—A striking example of the nominat. tituli is found in Jo. xiii. 13 ; see also Rev. ix. 11.]

¹ So even τὴν ἀνθρωποτόκος φωνήν, Theodoret IV. 1304 ; τὴν θεὸς προσηγορίαν, III. 241, IV. 454. In such cases the Romans always use the genitive,—a fact which is usually overlooked by modern writers of Latin.
² Fischer, Weller III. 1. 319 sq. ; Markland, Eur. Iph. Aul. 446. [Jelf 76. b, Green pp. 9, 85.]

what rough and harsh (Bernh. p. 67), and may even retain this character wherever it is used by the Greek prose writers; but in later Greek it is found where there is no special emphasis, even in very gentle address (L. xii. 32, μὴ φοβοῦ, τὸ μικρὸν ποιμνίον· viii. 54, Bar. iv. 5), and in prayers (L. xviii. 11, H. x. 7). Jo. xx. 28, however, though directed to Jesus (εἶπεν αὐτῷ), is yet rather an exclamation than an address:[1] such nominatives appear early and very distinctly in Greek writers (Bernh. l.c., Krüg. p. 14, Jelf 476. Obs.). Similarly in L. xii. 20 (with the reading ἄφρων,—also 1 C. xv. 36, where there is not much authority for ἄφρον); in Ph. iii. 18, 19, πολλοὶ γὰρ περιπατοῦσιν, οὓς πολλάκις ἔλεγον . . . τοὺς ἐχθροὺς τοῦ σταυροῦ τοῦ Χριστοῦ, ὧν τὸ τέλος ἀπώλεια . . . οἱ τὰ ἐπίγεια φρονοῦντες;[2] and perhaps in Mk. xii. 38–40, βλέπετε ἀπὸ τῶν γραμματέων, τῶν θελόντων . . . καὶ ἀσπασμοὺς . . . καὶ πρωτοκαθεδρίας . . . οἱ κατεσθίοντες τὰς οἰκίας· . . . . οὗτοι λήψονται περισσότερον κρίμα· though here οἱ κατεσθίοντες might be joined with οὗτοι λήψονται.[3] In Rev. xviii. 20 the vocative and the nominative are found in connexion.

3. The vocative however is used by the N. T. writers in addresses much more frequently than the nominative. It is sometimes accompanied by ὦ, but more commonly stands alone. Ὦ occurs only in addresses (A. i. 1, xxvii. 21, xviii. 14, 1 Tim. vi. 11), mostly in connexion with an adjuration or an expression of blame[4] (Rom. ii. 1, 3, ix. 20, 1 Tim. vi. 20, Ja. ii. 20, G. iii. 1), or in exclamations, as L. xxiv. 25, A. xiii. 10. A simple call or summons is expressed by the vocative without ὦ: L. xiii. 12, xxii. 57, [Acts] xxvii. 10, Mt. ix. 22, Jo. iv. 21, xix. 26, A. xiii. 15, xxvii. 25. Even at the beginning of a speech, where

---

[1] On this verse see Alford and Westcott : see also Green p. 86.]
[2] [Compare Ellicott *in loc.*, who explains this "as an emphatic return to the primary construction of the sentence (πολλοὶ γὰρ περιπ.):" see further Alford *in loc.*, and below § 63 I. 2. In Mk. xii. 40 Bengel, Meyer, Lachm., Tisch., Treg., Westcott and Hort, join οἱ κατεσθίοντες with οὗτοι: the other connexion is defended by Alford and A. Buttmann (p. 79).]
[3] Hermann says (*Præf. ad* Eurip. *Androm.* p. 15 sq.): mihi quidem ubique nominativus, quem pro vocativo positum volunt, non vocantis sed declarantis esse videtur: o tu, qui es talis. This would apply to some of the above passages, but not to all, and the remark is probably intended to refer directly to the poets only.
[4] Lob. *Ajax* 451 sq.: see Fritzsche, *Aristoph.* I. 4.

the Greeks regularly prefix ὦ, the vocative commonly stands by itself in the N. T.: as A. i. 16, ii. 14, iii. 12, xiii. 16, xv. 13. (See however Franke, *Demosth.* p. 193.)¹

An adjective joined to a vocative stands in the same case, as Ja. ii. 20, ὦ ἄνθρωπε κενέ· Jo. xvii. 11, Mt. xviii. 32.² On words in apposition to a vocative see § 59. 8 (Jelf 476. *c, d*).³

Rem. It has been supposed, but erroneously, that the N. T. writers sometimes use Hebraistic periphrases for the nominative case: namely,

a. Εἰς with the accusative, in the phrase εἶναι or γίνεσθαι εἴς τι (Leusden, *Diall.* p. 132). By far the greater number of the examples adduced occur in quotations from the O. T., or in O. T. expressions which had become established formulas (Mt. xix. 5, 1 C. vi. 16, E. v. 31, H. viii. 10, al.). Two facts, moreover, have been overlooked. In the first place, γίνεσθαι εἴς τι, *fieri* i.e. *abire (mutari) in aliq.* (A. v. 36, Jo. xvi. 20, Rev. viii. 11) is a correct expression in Greek⁴ (as in German), and is used, at all events by later writers, even in reference to persons (Geo. Pachymer. I. 345, εἰς συμμάχους αὐτοῖς γίνονται). Again, in the Hebrew phrase rendered by εἶναι εἴς τι, the preposition ל is not really an indication of the nominative, but answers to our *to* or *for (to serve for, turn to)*: see H. viii. 10, 1 C. xiv. 22, and compare Wis. ii. 14, *Acta Apocr.* 169. In 1 C. iv. 3, ἐμοὶ εἰς ἐλάχιστόν ἐστιν means, *to me, for me, it belongs to the least, the most insignificant thing* (with such a thing I associate it): A. xix. 27, εἰς οὐδὲν λογισθῆναι, is similar, *to be reckoned for nothing* (Wis. ix. 6⁵). In L. ii. 34, κεῖται εἰς πτῶσιν, the preposition is similarly used to express *destination*, and there is no departure from Greek analogy, see Ph. i. 17 (16), 1 Th. iii. 3: compare Æsop 24. 2, εἰς μείζονά σοι ὠφέλειαν ἔσομαι· and the Latin *auxilio esse.*⁶ See further § 32. 4. b.

---

¹ On ὦ before the vocative see, in general, Doberenz, *Prog. Hildburgh.* (1844). ["Not only is ὦ rarely joined to the vocative in the N. T. (only 16 times in all), but in most of these instances it is more than a mere sign of the vocative, inasmuch as the expression has an emphatic character, and is therefore rather an exclamation, than a simple address." A. Buttm. p. 140. The same writer refers to this peculiarity as a result of *Latin* influence (*Index*, s. v. *Latinismen*). Jelf 479. 2.]

² But compare Jacobs, *Achill. Tat.* p. 466.

³ ["The interjections ἰδού and (especially in John) even ἴδε, answering to the Latin *ecce* and *en*, are joined with a nominative. The frequent occurrence of these words in narration and in argument must not be attributed to the influence of the O. T. alone, but was a feature of the popular language; hence they become more and more common at a later period." A. Buttm. p. 139.]

⁴ Georgi, *Vind.* 337, Schwarz, *Comm.* 285. [Liddell and Scott, s. v. γίγνομαι: compare Jelf 625. 3. *c.*]

⁵ Xen. *Cyr.* 3. 1. 33, χρήματα εἰς ἀργύριον λογίζεσθαι, is of a different kind (Jelf 625. 3. *c.*).

⁶ Zumpt, *Gr.* § 664. Note 1. [Madvig, *Lat. Gr.* 249, Roby, *Lat. Gr.* II. xxv–lvi.]

b. Ἐν with the dative, as an imitation of the Hebrew *Beth essentiæ*,[1] in the following passages: Mk. v. 25, γυνή τις οὖσα ἐν ῥύσει αἵματος; Rev. i. 10, ἐγενόμην ἐν πνεύματι ἐν τῇ κυριακῇ ἡμέρᾳ (Glass I. 31); E. v. 9, ὁ καρπὸς τοῦ φωτὸς ἐν πάσῃ ἀγαθωσύνῃ (Hartmann, *Linguist. Einl.* 384); and Jo. ix. 30, ἐν τούτῳ θαυμαστόν ἐστι (Schleusner, s. v. ἐν). But in Mk. v. εἶναι ἐν ῥύσει is *to be in the condition* or *state of an issue;* in Rev. i. γίνεσθαι ἐν πνεύματι means *in the spirit*[2] *to be present somewhere;* in E. v. εἶναι ἐν is equivalent to *contineri, positum esse in* (see the commentators); and Jo. ix. may be very appropriately rendered, *herein is this marvellous,* etc. Gesenius has attributed the same construction to Latin and Greek writers, but without reason; εἶναι ἐν σοφοῖς, *in magnis viris (habendum) esse,* cannot be brought in here, for this combination is perfectly natural, and must be rendered *to belong to the number of.* If ἐν σοφῷ or *in sapienti viro* were used for σοφός or *sapiens,* then and then only could ἐν or *in* be said to represent a *Beth essentiæ.* But no rational being could use words thus, and indeed the whole doctrine of the Hebrew *Beth essentiæ* is a mere figment, an invention of empirical grammarians:[3] see my edition of *Simonis* p. 109, and Fritz. *Mark,* p. 291 sq.[4]

SECTION XXX.

THE GENITIVE.

1. The genitive is unquestionably the *whence-case,* the case of *proceeding from* or *out of:*[5] it is most clearly recognised as such when joined with words which denote an activity, consequently with verbs. Its most common and familiar application in prose, however, is in connecting two substantives, where (with a gradually increased latitude of meaning) it denotes any

---

[1] Gesen. *Lgb.* p. 838, Knobel on Is. xxviii. 16. [Gesen. *Hebr. Gr.* p. 241, *Thesaur.* p. 174, Kalisch, *Hebr. Gr.* II. 296.]

[2] [Or *in the Spirit.* Winer connects ἐγενόμην with ἐν τῇ κυριακῇ ἡμέρᾳ, probably in the sense, "Diem judicii vidi in spiritu." Against this, see Düsterdieck and Alford *in loc.*]

[3] With the entirely misunderstood בְּרָע הוּא, Ex. xxxii. 22, compare Æl. 10. 11, ἀποθανεῖν ἐν καλῷ ἐστίν: should this too be taken for καλόν ἐστιν? [Winer renders Ex. *l. c.,* "*in malo* (in wickedness) *est,* h. e. *malus est:*" similarly Ewald.]

[4] Haab's other examples (p. 337 sq.) are so manifestly untenable that we cannot give them a moment's notice.

[5] Compare Hartung, *Casus* p. 12. [Don. p. 464, Clyde, *Gr. Synt.* pp. 30 sq. On the name of this case see Max Müller, *Lectures on Language,* I. 105 sq.]

kind of *dependence on* or *belonging to*,¹ as in ὁ κύριος τοῦ κόσμου, Ἰούδας Ἰακώβου: here a pronoun or the article may take the place of the governing noun, compare § 18. 3. This use of the genitive, associated even in plain prose with a great variety of meanings,² we shall consider first. Besides the ordinary cases—amongst which the genitive of quality (Rom. xv. 5, 13, al.) and the partitive genitive (Rom. xvi. 5, 1 C. xvi. 15) should be specially mentioned³—we have to notice

a. The genitive of the object, after substantives which denote an internal or external activity,—a feeling, expression, action (Krüg. p. 36, Don. p. 482, Jelf 542. ii.): Mt. xiii. 18, παραβολὴ τοῦ σπείροντος *the sower-parable*, i.e. the parable *about* the sower; 1 C. i. 6, μαρτύριον τοῦ Χριστοῦ, witness *concerning* Christ (ii. 1, compare xv. 15); viii. 7, ἡ συνείδησις τοῦ εἰδώλου, their consciousness of the idol; i. 18, ὁ λόγος ὁ τοῦ σταυροῦ; Mt. xxiv. 6, ἀκοαὶ πολέμων *war-rumours* (rumours *about* wars), compare Matth. 342. 1; A. iv. 9, εὐεργεσία ἀνθρώπου, *towards* or *to* a man (Thuc. 1. 129, 7. 57, Plat. *Legg.* 8. 850 b); Jo. vii. 13, xx. 19, φόβος Ἰουδαίων, fear of the Jews (Eur. *Andr.* 1059); xvii. 2, ἐξουσία πάσης σαρκός, *over* all flesh (Mt. x. 1, 1 C. ix. 12); 2 P. ii. 13, 15, μισθὸς ἀδικίας, reward *for* unrighteousness; Rom. x. 2, ζῆλος θεοῦ, zeal *for* God (Jo. ii. 17, 1 Macc. ii. 58,—otherwise in 2 C. xi. 2); H. ix. 15, ἀπολύτρωσις τῶν παραβάσεων, *sin-redemption*, i.e. redemption *from* sins (Plat. *Rep.* 1. 329 c). Compare also Mt. xiv. 1 (Joseph. *Antt.* 8. 6. 5), L. vi. 12 (Eurip. *Troad.* 895), E. ii. 20 [?], Rom. xv. 8, 2 P. i. 9, Ja. ii. 4,⁴ 1 C. xv. 15, H. x. 24.⁵

---

¹ If we consider the genitive with reference to its abstract meaning rather than to its origin, its nature may be thus defined (Herm. *Opusc.* I. 175, and *Vig.* p. 877): "Genitivi proprium est id indicare, cujus quid aliquo quocumque modo accidens est;" compare *De Emend. Rat.* p. 139. Similarly Madvig, § 46. See further Schneider on Cæsar, *Bell. Gall.* 1. 21. 2. [Rost's definition resembles Hermann's: Jelf regards the genitive as the case which expresses "the *antecedent notion*" (471, 480).]

² Schæfer, Eurip. *Or.* 48.

³ [On the genitive of *quality* see Don. p. 482, Jelf 435; on the *partitive* genitive, Don. p. 470 sq., Jelf 533 and 542. vi.: on the *objective* genitive in the N. T., Green, *Gr.* p. 87 sq., Webster, *Syntax* p. 72.]

⁴ [This passage is also noticed below, p. 233. In ed. 5 Winer maintained the simpler view that διαλ. is a genitive of quality ("ill-bethinking judges," Green p. 91); see Alford, Webster and Wilk., *in loc.*]

⁵ For examples from Greek authors see Markland, Eur. *Suppl.* 838, D'Orville,

The following phrases are of frequent recurrence in the N. T.: ἀγάπη τοῦ θεοῦ or Χριστοῦ, love *to* God, *to* Christ, Jo. v. 42, 1 Jo. ii. 5, 15, iii. 17, 2 Th. iii. 5 (but not Rom. v. 5, viii. 35, 2 C. v. 14, E. iii. 19 [1]); φόβος θεοῦ or κυρίου, A. ix. 31, Rom. iii. 18, 2 C. v. 11, vii. 1, E. v. 21; πίστις τοῦ θεοῦ, Χριστοῦ, or Ἰησοῦ, Mk. xi. 22, Rom. iii. 22, G. ii. 16, iii. 22, E. iii. 12, Ph. iii. 9, Ja. ii. 1, Rev. xiv. 12 (πίστις ἀληθείας, 2 Th. ii. 13); ὑπακοὴ τοῦ Χριστοῦ or τῆς πίστεως κ.τ.λ., 2 C. x. 5, Rom. i. 5, xvi. 26, 1 P. i. 22 (2 C. ix. 13). But δικαιοσύνη θεοῦ in the dogmatic language of Paul (Rom. i. 17, iii. 21 sq., x. 3, al.) is, in accordance with his doctrine of θεὸς ὁ δικαιῶν (compare iii. 30, iv. 5), *God's righteousness*, i.e. righteousness which God bestows (on man); and, the meaning once fixed, δικαιοσύνη θεοῦ could even be used (in 2 C. v. 21) as a predicate of the believers themselves. Others, with Luther, understand the phrase to mean *righteousness which avails before God* (quæ Deo satisfacit, Fritz. *Rom.* I. 47), δικαιοσύνη παρὰ τῷ θεῷ. The possibility of this interpretation is implied in δίκαιος παρὰ τῷ θεῷ, Rom. ii. 13 (set over against δικαιοῦσθαι), and still more directly in δικαιοῦσθαι παρὰ τῷ θεῷ G. iii. 11, or ἐνώπιον τοῦ θεοῦ Rom. iii. 20. From the nature of the δικαιοῦσθαι both expressions are correct; but δικαιοῖ ὁ θεὸς τὸν ἄνθρωπον is the more stringent of the two, and in Rom. x. 3 we obtain a better antithesis if δικ. θεοῦ is *righteousness which God grants*: compare also Ph. iii. 9, ἡ ἐκ θεοῦ δικαιοσύνη.[2]

From what has just been said it will be clear that in many passages the decision between the subjective and the objective genitive belongs to exegesis, not to grammar: the question especially requires a cautious use of parallel passages. In Ph. iv. 7, εἰρήνη θεοῦ can probably have no other meaning than *peace* (peace of soul) *which God gives*, as the wish which the apostles express for their readers is that they may have εἰρήνην ἀπὸ θεοῦ: this parallelism is more decisive here than that of Rom. v. 1, εἰρήνην ἔχομεν πρὸς τὸν θεόν, which would lead us to render εἰρήνη θεοῦ *peace with God*. In Col. iii. 15 also (εἰρήνη Χριστοῦ) I consider the genitive to be subjective; compare Jo. xiv. 27. That in Rom. iv. 13 δικαιοσύνη πίστεως (*one notion*,—

Char. p. 498, Schæf. *Soph.* II. 300, Stallb. Plat. *Rep.* II. 201, *Apol.* p. 29, Poppo, *Thuc.* III. i. 521.

[1] [See Alford's note on 2 C. v. 14. On the nature of the genitive after πίστις, see Ellicott and Lightfoot on Col. ii. 12.]

[2] [See Alford and Vaughan on Rom. i. 17.]

faith-righteousness) means *righteousness which faith brings*, is manifest from the expression more frequently used, ἡ δικαιοσύνη ἡ ἐκ πίστεως (Rom. ix. 30, x. 6). In E. iv. 18 (ἀπηλλοτριωμένοι) τῆς ζωῆς τοῦ θεοῦ is *God's life*: the life of Christian believers is so called, as being a life imparted by God, excited within the soul by Him.

In the phrase εὐαγγέλιον τοῦ Χριστοῦ it may appear doubtful whether the genitive should be considered subjective (the Gospel preached by Christ) or objective (the Gospel *concerning* Christ). I prefer the latter, because we find in some passages (e. g. Rom. i. 3 [1]) the complete expression εὐαγγέλιον τοῦ θεοῦ περὶ τοῦ υἱοῦ αὐτοῦ, of which this may be merely an abridgment: compare also εὐαγγέλιον τῆς χάριτος τοῦ θεοῦ A. xx. 24, and εὐαγγέλιον τῆς βασιλείας τοῦ θεοῦ Mt. iv. 23, ix. 35. Meyer (on Mk. i. 1) regards the genitive in this phrase as sometimes subjective, sometimes objective.[2] In Col. ii. 18 also it is a matter of dispute amongst the commentators whether (θρησκεία) ἀγγέλων is a genitive of the subject or of the object. The latter view is preferable, *reverence of angels, angel-worship*: compare Euseb. *H. E.* 6. 41 *v. l.*, θρησκεία τῶν δαιμόνων· Philo II. 259, θρησ. θεῶν, (ἡ τοῦ θεοῦ λατρεία, Plat. *Apol.* 23. c). In 1 Tim. iv. 1 δαιμονίων is certainly a subjective genitive: in H. vi. 2 however, βαπτισμῶν διδαχῆς, if the latter be regarded as the principal noun (see below, 3. Rem. 4), βαπτισμῶν can only be the object of the διδαχή. In Rom. viii. 23 it seems better, according to the mode in which Paul presents the subject, to regard ἀπολύτρωσις τοῦ σώματος as *liberation of the body* (namely from the δουλεία τῆς φθορᾶς spoken of in ver. 21), than as *liberation from the body*. Likewise in H. i. 3, 2 P. i. 9, καθαρισμὸς τῶν ἁμαρτιῶν might signify *purification of sins* (removal of sins, compare Dt. xix. 13), as the Greeks could say καθαρίζονται αἱ ἁμαρτίαι (comp. καθαίρειν αἷμα *to remove through cleansing*, Iliad 16. 667); but it is simpler to take τῶν ἁμ. as a genitive of the object.[3] Rom. ii. 7, ὑπομονὴ ἔργου ἀγαθοῦ, and 1 Th. i. 3, ὑπομονὴ τῆς ἐλπίδος, mean very simply, *constancy* or *steadiness of good work, of hope*. Ja. ii. 4 is probably an indignant question: *then . . . would ye not become judges of evil thoughts* (your own)?

---

[1] [This is the only passage in which this expression occurs, and here it is probable that περὶ τ. υἱ. αὐ. belongs to the verb προσπ. in ver. 2 : so Meyer, Fritz., Alford, al.]
[2] ["When the genitive with εὐαγγέλιον does not denote a *person*, this genitive is always that of the object; in εὐαγγ. θεοῦ, εὐαγγ. μου, the genitive expresses the subject. In εὐαγγ. Χριστοῦ the genitive may be either subjective (*genitivus auctoris*) or objective; the context alone can decide." (Meyer *l.c.*) I cannot however find any passage in which Meyer does not regard this phrase as meaning "the gospel *concerning* Christ" (*genit. obj.*).]
[3] [In H. i. 3 the rendering "purification of sins" (where the genitive is surely objective) is adopted by Bleek, Delitzsch, Alford, and was preferred by Winer in ed. 5 : compare Mt. viii. 3. Lünemann (ed. 3) and Kurtz render the words "purification from sins," comparing the use of καθαρός with a genitive (Don. p. 468, Jelf 529).]

2. *b.* But the genitive is also used to express more remote relations of dependence,¹ and in this way are formed, by a kind of breviloquence, various composite terms (such as *blood-of-the-cross, repentance-baptism, damage-law*), the resolution of which will vary according to the nature of the component notions. We notice

a. The genitive which expresses relations merely external (relations of place or of time) : Mt. x. 5, ὁδὸς ἐθνῶν *Gentiles' road,* i. e. *road to the Gentiles* (H. ix. 8, compare Gen. iii. 24, ἡ ὁδὸς τ. ξύλου τῆς ζωῆς· Jer. ii. 18, Judith v. 14) ;² Jo. x. 7, θύρα τῶν προβάτων, *door to the sheep* (Meyer); Mt. i. 11, 12, μετοικεσία Βαβυλῶνος, *removal to Babylon* (Orph. 200, ἐπὶ πλόον Ἀξείνοιο, *ad expeditionem in Axinum ;* 144, νόστος οἴκοιο, *domum reditus ;* Eurip. *Iph. T.* 1066 ³) ; Jo. vii. 35, ἡ διασπορὰ τῶν Ἑλλήνων, *the dispersion* (the dispersed) *among the Greeks ;* Mk. viii. 27, κῶμαι Καισαρείας τῆς Φιλίππου, *villages around Cæsarea Philippi,* villages which are situated on its territory ⁴ (Is. xvii. 2 ⁵) ; Col. i. 20, αἷμα τοῦ σταυροῦ, *blood of the cross,* i. e. blood shed on the cross ; 1 P. i. 2, ῥαντισμὸς αἵματος, *sprinkling* (purifying) *with blood ;* 2 C. xi. 26, κίνδυνοι ποταμῶν, *perils on rivers* (soon followed by κινδ. ἐν πόλει, ἐν θαλάσσῃ, κ.τ.λ.), compare Heliod. 2. 4. 65 κίνδυνοι θαλασσῶν.

Designations of time : Rom. ii. 5 (Zeph. ii. 2) ἡμέρα ὀργῆς, *day of wrath,* i. e. day on which the wrath (of God) will manifest itself in punishment : Jude 6, κρίσις μεγάλης ἡμέρας, *judgment on the great day ;* L. ii. 44, ὁδὸς ἡμέρας, *a day's journey* (distance traversed in a day, compare Her. 4. 101, Ptol. 1. 11. 4) ; H. vi. 1, ὁ τῆς ἀρχῆς τοῦ Χριστοῦ λόγος, *the elementary in-*

---

¹ Compare Jacob, Luc. *Alex.* p. 108 sq., Stallb. Plat. *Tim.* p. 241 sq., Bernh. p. 160 sqq.
² In Mt. iv. 15, however, ὁδὸς θαλάσσης certainly means *way by the sea* (of Tiberias). [See below, p. 289.]
³ Compare Schæf. *Melet.* p. 90, Seidler, Eur. *Electr.* 161, Spohn, Isocr. *Paneg.* p. 2, Buttm. Soph. *Philoct.* p. 67. The genitive has the opposite meaning in Plat. *Apol.* 40 c, μετοίκησις τῆς ψυχῆς τοῦ τόπου τοῦ ἐνθένδε (*away from this place*).
⁴ This reduces itself finally to the common topographical genitive (Krüg. p. 32 sq.),—which is simply a genitive of *belonging to :* Jo. ii. 1, Κανᾶ τῆς Γαλιλαίας· A. xxii. 3, Ταρσὸς τῆς Κιλικίας· xiii. 13, 14 [*Rec.*], xxvii. 5, L. iv. 26 ; compare Xen. *Hell.* 1. 2. 12, Diod. S. 16. 92, 17. 63, Diog. L. 8. 3, Arrian, *Al.* 2. 4. 1 ; and see Ellendt, Arr. *Al.* I. 151, Ramshorn, *Lat. Gr.* I. 167. (Don. p. 482, Jelf 542. vi.)
⁵ [This reference is incorrect : probably, Jos. xvii. 11.]

struction *of Christ* ; so also τεκμήρια ἡμερῶν τεσσαράκοντα, A. i. 3, according to the reading of D.[1]

An external relation (of place) is also indicated in ἀλάβαστρον μύρου Mk. xiv. 3, and κεράμιον ὕδατος ver. 13 ; compare 1 S. x. 3, ἀγγεῖα ἄρτων, ἀσκὸς οἴνου· Soph. *El.* 758, χαλκὸς σποδοῦ·[2] Dion. H. IV. 2028, ἀσφάλτου καὶ πίσσης ἀγγεῖα· Theophr. *Ch.* 17, Diog. L. 6. 9, 7. 3, Lucian, *Asin.* 37, *Fugit.* 31, Diod. S. *Vatic.* 32. 1. To the same class belongs Jo. xxi. 8, τὸ δίκτυον τῶν ἰχθύων (in ver. 11, μεστὸν ἰχθύων), and even ἀγέλη χοίρων Mt. viii. 30, and ἑκατὸν βάτοι ἐλαίου L. xvi. 6. On this genitive of *content,* see Krüg. p. 37 sq. (Don. p. 468, Jelf 542. vii.)

In no passage of the N. T. is ἀνάστασις νεκρῶν equivalent to ἀνάστ. ἐκ νεκρῶν : even in Rom. i. 4 it signifies the *resurrection of the dead* absolutely and generically, though this resurrection is actually realised in one individual only. Philippi's dogmatic inference from this expression is mere trifling.

β. The genitive is used, especially by John and Paul, to express an inner reference of a remoter kind : Jo. v. 29, ἀνάστασις ζωῆς, κρίσεως, *resurrection of life, resurrection of judgment,* i. e. resurrection to life, to judgment (genitive of destination, Theodor. IV. 1140, ἱερωσύνης χειροτονία *to the priesthood ;* compare Rom. viii. 36, from the LXX, πρόβατα σφαγῆς) ; Rom. v. 18, δικαίωσις ζωῆς, *justification to life ;* Mk. i. 4, βάπτισμα μετανοίας, *repentance-baptism,* i. e. baptism which binds to repentance ; Rom. vii. 2, νόμος τοῦ ἀνδρός, *the law of the husband,* i. e. the law which determines the relation to the husband (compare Dem. *Mid.* 390 a, ὁ τῆς βλάβης νόμος, *the law of damage,* and many examples in the LXX, as Lev. xiv. 2, ὁ νόμος τοῦ λεπροῦ· vii. 1, xv. 32, Num. vi. 13, 21, see Fritz. *Rom.* II. 9) ; vi. 6, σῶμα τῆς ἁμαρτίας, *sin-body,* i. e. body which belongs to sin, in which sin has being and dominion (in which sin carries itself into effect), almost like σῶμα τῆς σαρκός, Col. i. 22, body in which fleshliness has its being and its hold; Rom. vii. 24, σῶμα τοῦ θανάτου τούτου, *body of this death,* i. e. which (in the way described in ver. 7 sqq.) leads to death, ver. 5, 10, 13. See further Tit. iii. 5.

---

[1] Others with less probability take the words ἡμερῶν τεσσαρ. by themselves, *throughout forty days* (Jacobs, *Achill. Tat.* p. 640 sq.) ; but see below, no. 11.

[2] See Schæfer on Long. *Past.* p. 386.

In L. xi. 29, τὸ σημεῖον Ἰωνᾶ is nothing else than *the sign which was once exhibited in Jonah* (which is now to be repeated in the person of Christ). Jude 11 must be similarly explained. In Jo. xix. 14, however, παρασκευὴ τοῦ πάσχα does not mean "preparation-day *for* the passover," but quite simply "the preparation-day[1] of the passover" (that which belongs to the paschal feast). In H. iii. 13, ἀπάτη τῆς ἁμαρτίας, the genitive is subjective and ἁμαρτία is personified (Rom. vii. 11, al.). But in 2 Th. ii. 10 ἀπάτη τῆς ἀδικίας is *deceit which leads to unrighteousness.* On E. iv. 18 see Meyer; on Ja. i. 17, De Wette.[2]

In E. iii. 1, 2 Tim. i. 8, Phil. i. 9, δέσμιος Χριστοῦ is *a prisoner of Christ,* i. e. one whom Christ (the cause of Christ) has brought into captivity and retains in it;[3] compare Wis. xvii. 2. In Ja. ii. 5, οἱ πτωχοὶ τοῦ κόσμου (if the reading is correct) signifies *the poor of the world,* i. e. those who in their position towards the κόσμος are poor, hence *poor in earthly goods* (though it does not follow from this that κόσμος itself denotes earthly goods). In Jo. vi. 45, διδακτοὶ τοῦ θεοῦ means *God's instructed ones,* i.e. instructed by God, like οἱ εὐλογημένοι τοῦ πατρός Mt. xxv. 34, *the Father's blessed ones,* i.e. those blessed by the Father (Jelf 483. *Obs.* 3). In E. vi. 4, 11, 13, κυρίου and θεοῦ are *genitivi auctoris,* as also τῶν γραφῶν Rom. xv. 4. Likewise in Ph. i. 8, ἐν σπλάγχνοις Χριστοῦ Ἰ., the genitive is to be taken as sub-

---

[1] [I venture to substitute "Rüst-tag" *day of preparation,* for "Ruhetag" *day of rest,* as this latter word—though found in four editions of the German work—must surely be a misprint. In his *RWB.* (II. 341), Winer renders παρασκευὴ τοῦ πάσχα "Rüsttag auf Ostern," *preparation-day for the passover* ("14th of Nisan"), and on p. 205 of the same work says that this is the only meaning which the words could of themselves convey to a Greek reader: similarly in his tract on the δεῖπνον of Jo. xiii. (p. 12). The object of the remarks in the text seems to be to show that, whilst this is the *meaning,* τοῦ πάσχα is simply a possessive genitive.]

[2] ["It seems now generally agreed that by τὰ φῶτα here is meant the *heavenly bodies,* and by πατήρ the creator, originator:" Alford *in loc.*]

[3] As in Phil. 13 δεσμοὶ τοῦ εὐαγγελίου means *bonds which the Gospel has brought.* Without reference to this parallel passage, δέσμιος Χρ. might be rendered *a prisoner who belongs to Christ.* Others render, *a prisoner for Christ's sake:* this mode of resolving the genitive (Matth. 371 c, Krüg. p. 37, Jelf 481) has been applied to many N. T. passages, but in every case incorrectly. In H. xiii. 13, τὸν ὀνειδισμὸν Χριστοῦ φέροντες means, *bearing the reproach which Christ bore* (and still bears). So also in 2 C. i. 5, περισσεύει τὰ παθήματα τοῦ Χρ. εἰς ἡμᾶς, *the sufferings which Christ had to endure,* namely, from the enemies of the Divine truth, *abundantly come* (anew) *on us;* for the sufferings which believers endure (for the sake of the Divine truth) are essentially one with the sufferings of Christ, and but a continuation of them: compare Ph. iii. 10. Col. i. 24, αἱ θλίψεις τοῦ Χριστοῦ, and 2 C. iv. 10, are probably to be explained in the same way. On the former passage, which has been very variously explained, see Lücke, *Progr. in loc.* Col. i. 24 (Götting. 1833) p. 12 sq., also Huther and Meyer *in loc.* [Lücke takes Χριστοῦ here as *genit. auctoris;* Meyer and Lightfoot consider the genitive *possessive,* in the sense explained above. Ellicott and Alford agree with De Wette and Olshausen in explaining *the afflictions of Christ* to mean, the afflictions which he endures *in His Church.*]

jective, though opinions may differ as to the more precise nature of the relation. Compare also E. vi. 4, and Meyer *in loc.*¹ In 1 P. iii. 21 the correct explanation does not depend so much on the genitive συνειδήσεως ἀγαθῆς as on the meaning of ἐπερώτημα :² the rendering *sponsio* may suit the context very well, but neither De Wette nor Huther has shown that it is philologically admissible. On H. ix. 11 see Bleek.³ In 1 C. i. 27 τοῦ κόσμου is a subjective genitive : see Meyer. In 1 C. x. 16 τὸ ποτήριον τ. εὐλογίας very simply means *cup of the blessing,* i.e. over which the blessing is pronounced; and in ver. 21 ποτήριον κυρίου is *cup of the Lord,* where the more exact reference of the genitive is supplied by ver. 16, as in Col. ii. 11 (Χριστοῦ) by ver. 14.⁴ On Col. i. 14 Meyer's decision is correct. In A. xxii. 3 νόμου depends on κατὰ ἀκρίβειαν.

In H. iii. 3, some join the genitive οἴκου to τιμήν, *greater honour of the house* (i.e. in the house): this is not in itself impossible, but for this Epistle it is harsh, and it is certainly opposed to the writer's aim; see Bleek *in loc.*

On the genitive of apposition, as πόλεις Σοδόμων καὶ Γομόρρας 2 P. ii. 6 (urbs *Romœ*), σημεῖον περιτομῆς Rom. iv. 11, see § 59. 8 (Jelf 435. *d*).

3. For a long time it was usual to regard the genitive of *kindred* (Μαρία Ἰακώβου, Ἰούδας Ἰακώβου, Δαυὶδ ὁ τοῦ Ἰεσσαί) as involving an ellipsis. As however the genitive is the case of dependence, and as every relationship is a kind of dependence, there is no essential notion wanting (Herm. *Ellips.* p. 120): only it is left to the reader to define more exactly, in accordance with the actual fact, that which the genitive expresses quite generally (Plat. *Rep.* 3. 408 b). This genitive is most commonly to be understood of *son* or *daughter,* as in Mt. iv. 21, Jo. vi. 71, xxi. 2, 15, A. xiii. 22. In L. xxiv. 10, Mk. xv. 47, xvi. 1, μήτηρ must be supplied,—compare Mt. xxvii. 56, Mk. xv. 40 (Ælian 16. 30, Ὀλυμπιὰς ἡ Ἀλεξάνδρου, sc. μήτηρ). Πατήρ, in A. vii. 16 [*Rec.*], Ἐμμὼρ τοῦ Συχέμ (compare Gen. xxxiii. 19): similarly Steph. Byz. (s. v. Δαίδαλα), ἡ πόλις ἀπὸ Δαιδάλου τοῦ Ἰκάρου. Γυνή, in Mt. i. 6, ἐκ τῆς τοῦ Οὐρίου,

---

¹ [Meyer regards the genitive in Ph. i. 8 as *possessive;* in E. vi. 4 (παιδείᾳ καὶ νουθεσίᾳ κυρίου), as *genit. subjecti:* see Ellic. *ll. cc.*, who takes the same view of each passage.]
² [Winer renders this (in ed. 5) "the inquiry of a good conscience after God:" comp. below, 3. Rem. 5. See Alford *in loc.*]
³ [Bleek takes τ. μελλ. ἀγ. as a genitive of *reference* or *dependence;* Delitzsch, Hofm., Alf., as *genitivus objecti.*]
⁴ [This reference and the next seem incorrect: perhaps we should read ver. 12, and Col. iii. 14.]

and in Jo. xix. 25 :[1] compare Aristoph. *Eccl.* 46, Plin. *Epp.* 2. 20, *Verania Pisonis.* Ἀδελφός is perhaps to be supplied in L. vi. 16, A. i. 13, Ἰούδας Ἰακώβου, if the same apostle is mentioned in Jude 1: compare Alciphr. 2. 2, Τιμοκράτης ὁ Μητροδώρου, scil. ἀδελφός. Such a designation might arise in the apostolic circle from the circumstance that James, the brother of Judas, was better known or of higher position than the father of Judas.[2]

Accordingly οἱ Χλόης, 1 C. i. 11, are *those who are connected with Chloe*, like οἱ Ἀριστοβούλου, οἱ Ναρκίσσου, Rom. xvi. 10 ; a more definite explanation the history alone could supply. Perhaps, with most interpreters, we should understand the *households* of these persons : others suppose the slaves to be referred to. To the original readers of the Epistles the expression was clear. See further Valcken. *l. c.* (Don. pp. 356, 468, Jelf 436).

Rem. 1. Not unfrequently, especially in Paul's style, *three* genitives are found connected together, one governed grammatically by another. In this case one of the substantives often represents an adjectival notion : 2 C. iv. 4, τὸν φωτισμὸν τοῦ εὐαγγελίου τῆς δόξης τοῦ Χριστοῦ· E. i. 6, εἰς ἔπαινον δόξης τῆς χάριτος αὐτοῦ· iv. 13, εἰς μέτρον ἡλικίας τοῦ πληρώματος τοῦ Χριστοῦ (where the last two genitives are connected together), i. 19, Rom. ii. 4, Col. i. 20, ii. 12, 18, 1 Th. i. 3, 2 Th. i. 9, Rev. xviii. 3, xxi. 6, H. v. 12, 2 P. iii. 2.[3] In Rev. xiv. 10 (xix. 15), οἶνος τοῦ θυμοῦ must be closely joined together,—*wrath-wine, wine of burning*, according to an O. T. figure. Four genitives are thus connected in Rev. xiv. 8, ἐκ τοῦ οἴνου τοῦ θυμοῦ τῆς πορνείας αὐτῆς· xvi. 19, xix. 15 (Judith ix. 8, x. 3, xiii. 18, Wis. xiii. 5, al.). But in 2 C. iii. 6, διακόνους καινῆς διαθήκης οὐ γράμματος ἀλλὰ πνεύματος, the last two genitives depend on διακόνους, as the following verse shows. Similarly in Rom. xi. 33 all three genitives depend on βάθος.

Rem. 2. Sometimes, especially in Paul's Epistles, the genitive, when placed after the governing noun, is separated from it by some other word : Ph. ii. 10, ἵνα πᾶν γόνυ κάμψῃ ἐπουρανίων καὶ ἐπιγείων καὶ καταχθονίων (explanatory genitives appended to πᾶν γόνυ), Rom. ix. 21, ἢ οὐκ ἔχει ἐξουσίαν ὁ κεραμεὺς τοῦ πηλοῦ ; 1 Tim. iii. 6, ἵνα μὴ εἰς κρίμα ἐμπέσῃ τοῦ διαβόλου (probably for emphasis), 1 Th. ii. 13, 1 C. viii. 7, H. viii. 5, Jo. xii. 11, 1 P. iii. 21 : we find again a different arrangement in Rev. vii. 17. On the other hand, in E. ii. 3, ἦμεν

---

[1] See Winer, *RWB.* II. 57 sq. [Smith, *Dict. of Bible* II. 254. On this example and the next see Lightfoot on *Galatians,* Dissert. 2.]
[2] See on the whole Bos, *Ellips.* (ed. Schæf.) s. vv., Boisson. Philostr. *Her.* p. 307.
[3] Comp. Krüger, Xen. *An.* 2. 5. 38, Bornem. Xen. *Apol.* p. 44, Boisson. *Babr.* p. 116.

τέκνα φύσει ὀργῆς, the words could scarcely be arranged differently without laying undue emphasis on φύσει (ἦμεν φύσει τέκνα ὀργῆς).[1]

Rem. 3. Sometimes, but not frequently, we find one noun connected with two genitives of different reference,—usually separated from each other in position; the chief case is when one genitive refers to a person, the other to a thing (Krüg. p. 40) : A. v. 32, ἡμεῖς ἐσμὲν αὐτοῦ (Χριστοῦ) μάρτυρες τῶν ῥημάτων τούτων· 2 C. v. 1, ἡ ἐπίγειος ἡμῶν οἰκία τοῦ σκήνους· Ph. ii. 30, τὸ ὑμῶν ὑστέρημα τῆς λειτουργίας· 2 P. iii. 2, τῆς τῶν ἀποστόλων ὑμῶν ἐντολῆς τοῦ κυρίου· H. xiii. 7.[2] Compare Her. 6. 2, τὴν Ἰώνων τὴν ἡγεμονίην τοῦ πρὸς Δαρεῖον πολέμου· Thuc. 3. 12, τὴν ἐκείνων μέλλησιν τῶν εἰς ἡμᾶς δεινῶν· 6. 18, ἡ Νικίου τῶν λόγων ἀπραγμοσύνη· Plat. Legg. 3. 690 b, τὴν τοῦ νόμου ἑκόντων ἀρχήν· Rep. 1. 329 b, τὰς τῶν οἰκείων προπηλακίσεις τοῦ γήρως· Diog. L. 3. 37, and Plat. Apol. 40 c, μετοίκησις τῆς ψυχῆς τοῦ τόπου τοῦ ἐνθένδε (a very harsh instance). See Bernh. p. 162, Matth. 380. Rem. 1 (Jelf 466).[3]

We may also bring in here 1 P. iii. 21, σαρκὸς ἀπόθεσις ῥύπου, *the flesh's putting away of filth* (σὰρξ ἀποτίθεται ῥύπον), unless there is a trajection in these words.

Two genitives are connected in a different way in Jo. vi. 1, ἡ θάλασσα τῆς Γαλιλαίας, τῆς Τιβεριάδος, *the lake of Galilee, of Tiberias*. This lake is only once besides mentioned under the latter name (Jo. xxi. 1). It may be that John added the more definite to the general designation (compare Pausan. 5. 7. 3) for the sake of foreign readers, in order to give them more certain information of the locality. Beza *in loc.* gives a different explanation. Kühnöl's suspicion that the words τῆς Τιβ. are a gloss is too hasty. Paulus understands the words to mean that Jesus crossed over *from Tiberias;* but this is at variance, if not with Greek prose usage, yet certainly with that of the N. T. writers (compare Bornem. *Acta* p. 149), who in such instances insert a preposition, as expressing the meaning more vividly than the simple case. The genitive Τιβ. cannot be made to depend on the ἀπό in ἀπῆλθεν.

Rem. 4. When the genitive stands *before* the governing noun, either

(*a*) It belongs equally to two nouns as in A. iii. 7 [*Rec.*], αὐτοῦ αἱ βάσεις καὶ τὰ σφυρά· Jo. xi. 48 :—or

(*b*) It is emphatic :[4] 1 C. iii. 9, θεοῦ γάρ ἐσμεν συνεργοί, θεοῦ γεώργιον, θεοῦ οἰκοδομή ἐστε· A. xiii. 23, τούτου (Δαυὶδ) ὁ θεὸς ἀπὸ τοῦ σπέρματος . . . . ἤγαγε σωτῆρα Ἰησοῦν· Ja. i. 26, εἴ τις . . . . τούτου μάταιος ἡ θρησκεία· iii. 3, H. x. 36, E. ii. 8. This em-

---

[1] See on the whole Jacob, Luc. *Tox.* p. 46, Ellendt, Arr. *Al.* I. 241, Fritz. *Rom.* II. 331.

[2] [Lünem. adds Mt. xxvi. 28, τὸ αἷμά μου τῆς διαθήκης.]

[3] See Ast, Plat. *Polit.* p. 329, and *Legg.* p. 84 sq., Lob. *Ajax* p. 219, Buttm. Dem. *Mid.* p. 17, and Soph. *Phil.* 751, Fritz. *Quæst. Luc.* p. 111 sq. (Kritz, *Sallust* II. 170).

[4] Stallb. Plat. *Protag.* p. 118, Madvig 10.

phasis not unfrequently arises from an express antithesis : Ph. ii. 25, τὸν συστρατιώτην μου, ὑμῶν δὲ ἀπόστολον καὶ λειτουργὸν τῆς χρείας μου· Mt. i. 18, H. vii. 12, 1 P. iii. 21, E. ii. 10, vi. 9, G. iii. 15, iv. 28, 1 C. vi. 15, Rom. iii. 29, xiii. 4. Most commonly, however, the genitive contains the principal notion : Rom. xi. 13, ἐθνῶν ἀπόστολος, *apostle of Gentiles;* 1 Tim. vi. 17, ἐπὶ πλούτου ἀδηλότητι, *on riches, which yet are fleeting;* Tit. i. 7, H. vi. 16, 2 P. ii. 14. That this position of the genitive may belong to the peculiarities of a writer's style (Gersdorf p. 296 sqq.) is not in itself impossible (since particular writers use even emphatic combinations with a weakened force), but at all events cannot be made probable. See further Poppo, *Thuc.* III. i. 243.

There is difficulty in H. vi. 2, βαπτισμῶν διδαχῆς (in dependence on θεμέλιον),—for, though some commentators, and recently Ebrard,[1] strangely detach διδαχῆς from βαπτ., making it the governing noun for the four genitives, these two words must certainly be taken together. The only question is, whether (with most recent writers) we should assume a trajection, and take βαπτ. διδ. as put for διδαχῆς βαπτισμῶν. Such a trajection, however, would disturb the whole structure of the verse. If on the other hand we render βαπτισμοὶ διδαχῆς *baptisms of doctrine* or *instruction,* as distinguished from the legal baptisms (washings) of Judaism, we find a support for this designation, as characteristically Christian, in Mt. xxviii. 19, βαπτίσαντες[2] αὐτούς .... διδάσκοντες αὐτούς : Ebrard's objection, that that which distinguishes Christian baptism from mere lustrations is not doctrine but forgiveness of sins and the new birth, is of no weight whatever, for in Mt. xxviii. 19 nothing is said respecting forgiveness of sins. As regards the writer's use of the word βαπτισμός here, and that in the plural, what Tholuck has already remarked may also be employed in favour of the above explanation.

Rem. 5. In Mk. iv. 19, αἱ περὶ τὰ λοιπὰ ἐπιθυμίαι, Kühnöl and others regard περί with the accusative as a periphrasis for the genitive. But though Mark might very well have written αἱ τῶν λοιπῶν ἐπιθ., the other form of expression not only is more definite but also preserves the proper meaning of περί, cupiditates quæ *circa reliqua* (reliquas res) *versantur* (Heliod. 1. 23. 45, ἐπιθυμία περὶ τὴν Χαρίκλειαν· Aristot. *Rhet.* 2. 12, αἱ περὶ τὸ σῶμα ἐπιθυμίαι), just as fully as the meaning of περί with the genitive is preserved in Jo. xv. 22. The instances in Greek authors in which περί with the accusative forms a periphrasis for the genitive of the object to which a

---

[1] [So also Delitzsch and Alford: Bleek considers βαπτ. and ἐπιθ. as governed by διδαχῆς, but is undecided in regard to the other genitives. Winer's objections are examined by Delitzsch (p. 214), who argues that teaching could not be assigned as the characteristic of Christian baptism, inasmuch as the Jewish baptism of proselytes was accompanied by instruction. Besides, the point of Mt. xxviii. 20 surely lies in πάντα ὅσα ἐνετειλάμην, not in διδάσκ. alone.]

[2] [Quoted above (§ 21. 2) with the reading βαπτίζοντες, which is found in almost all the MSS.]

certain property is ascribed (as Diod. Sic. 11. 89, ἡ περὶ τὸ ἱερὸν ἀρχαιότης· *ib.*, τὸ περὶ τοὺς κρατῆρας ἰδίωμα[1]), are of a somewhat different kind. We might rather say that περί with the genitive stands for the simple case in 1 C. vii. 37, ἐξουσία περὶ τοῦ ἰδίου θελήματος, as the genitive might here have been used alone ; but *power in regard to his will* is at all events the more definite and the fuller expression. A similar use of ἀπό and ἐκ to form a periphrasis for the genitive is discovered by the commentators in A. xxiii. 21, τὴν ἀπὸ σοῦ ἐπαγγελίαν· and in 2 C. viii. 7, τῇ ἐξ ὑμῶν ἀγάπῃ ; but these strictly mean *amor qui a vobis proficiscitur*, *promissio a te profecta :* τῇ ὑμῶν ἀγάπῃ would be less precise, as this might also mean *amor in vos.*[2] Similarly in Thuc. 2. 92, ἡ ἀπὸ τῶν Ἀθηναίων βοήθεια· Dion. H. IV. 2235, πολὺν ἐκ τῶν παρόντων κινήσας ἔλεον· Plat. *Rep.* 2. 363 a, τὰς ἀπ' αὐτῆς εὐδοκιμήσεις· Dem. *Pac.* 24 b, Polyæn. 5. 11, Diod. S. 1. 8, 5. 39, *Exc. Vat.* p. 117, Lucian, *Conscr. Hist.* 40[3] (Jelf 483. *Obs.* 4). Rom. xi. 27, ἡ παρ' ἐμοῦ διαθήκη, requires the same explanation : compare Xen. *Cyr.* 5. 5. 13, Isocr. *Demon.* p. 18, Arr. *Al.* 5. 18. 10, and see Fritz. *in loc.*, Schoem. *Isæus* p. 193. On Jo. i. 14 see Lücke. In no passage is there a meaningless periphrasis.[4] In 1 C. ii. 12, in parallelism with οὐ τὸ πνεῦμα τοῦ κόσμου ἐλάβομεν, Paul designedly writes, ἀλλὰ τὸ πνεῦμα τὸ ἐκ θεοῦ, not τὸ πνεῦμα θεοῦ, or τὸ θεοῦ. The assertion that ἐν with its case stands for the genitive[5] (in 1 C. ii. 7, E. ii. 21, Tit. iii. 5, 2 P. ii. 7) is altogether futile, as any one who reads with even moderate attention will perceive. Nor can we regard κατά with the accusative, in the examples commonly quoted, as a mere periphrasis for the genitive. In Rom. ix. 11, ἡ κατ' ἐκλογὴν πρόθεσις means *the predestination according to election*, *in consequence of an election ;* xi. 21, οἱ κατὰ φύσιν κλάδοι are *the branches according to nature*, i.e. the natural branches ; similarly, H. xi. 7, ἡ κατὰ πίστιν δικαιοσύνη. In H. ix. 19, also, κατὰ τὸν νόμον, if joined with πάσης ἐντολῆς, would not (as was clearly seen by Bleek) stand in the place of τοῦ νόμου. See however above, § 22. 7. More suitable examples may be found in Greek writers ; as Diod. S. 1. 65, ἡ κατὰ τὴν ἀρχὴν ἀπόθεσις, *resignation of government* (strictly, *in respect of government*), 4. 13, *Exc. Vat.* p. 103, Arr. *Al.* 1. 18. 12, Matth. 380. Rem. 5. On εὐαγγέλιον κατὰ Ματθαῖον, κ.τ.λ., see Fritzsche.[6] It is altogether

---

[1] Compare Schæf. *Julian* p. vi, and on Dion. *Comp.* p. 23.
[2] 2 C. ix. 2, ὁ ἐξ ὑμῶν ζῆλος ἠρέθισε τοὺς πλείονας, is an instance of attraction. [This reading is doubtful : good MSS. omit ἐξ.]
[3] Compare Jacobs, *Athen.* 321 sq., *Anth. Pal.* I. 1, 159, Schæf. Soph. *Aj.* p. 228, Ellendt, Arr. *Al.* I. 329.
[4] [A. Buttmann (p. 156), acknowledging that Winer's view is critically exact, maintains that in many of these instances the term " periphrasis for the genitive " is convenient and substantially correct. In the same way the partitive genitive is often supported by ἐκ (Jo. vi. 60, al.) : compare Jelf 621. 3. *i*, and Mullach, *Vulg.* p. 324.]
[5] See Koppe, *Eph.* p. 60.
[6] Compare examples in the *Nova Biblioth. Lubec.* II. 105 sq. [See Westcott, *Introd. to Gospels*, p. 210.]

wrong to take τὰ εἰς Χριστὸν παθήματα, 1 P. i. 11, for τὰ Χριστοῦ παθήματα (v. 1): they are (like περὶ τῆς εἰς ὑμᾶς χάριτος, ver. 10) *the sufferings* (destined, intended) *for Christ*.

It is a different matter when a preposition with its case takes the place of a genitive in dependence on a noun through the preference of the *root-verb* for this preposition, as κοινωνία ὑμῶν εἰς τὸ εὐαγγέλιον Ph. i. 5; compare iv. 15. So probably ἐπερώτημα εἰς θεόν (*after God*) 1 P. iii. 21; compare 2 S. xi. 7, ἐπερωτᾶν εἰς θεόν.

4. The same type of immediate dependence is also presented when the genitive is joined with verbal adjectives and participles, whose meaning is not such that they (the root-verbs) would regularly govern the genitive (as in 2 P. ii. 14, μεστοὺς μοιχαλίδος· Mt. x. 10, ἄξιος τῆς τροφῆς· H. iii. 1, κλήσεως μέτοχοι, etc., see no. 8; E. ii. 12, ξένοι τῶν διαθηκῶν; etc.). Thus we have in 1 C. ii. 13, λόγοι διδακτοὶ πνεύματος ἁγίου (see above, page 236); 2 P. ii. 14, καρδίαν γεγυμνασμένην πλεονεξίας.[1] Compare *Iliad* 5. 6, λελουμένος ὠκεάνοιο· Soph. *Aj*. 807, φωτὸς ἠπατημένη· *ib.* 1353, φίλων νικώμενος: with 1 C. ii. 13 in particular, compare Soph. *El.* 344 κείνης διδακτά; and with 2 P. ii. 14, Philostr. *Her.* 2. 15 θαλάττης οὔπω γεγυμνασμένοι· 3. 1, Νέστορα πολέμων πολλῶν γεγυμνασμένον· 10. 1, σοφίας ἤδη γεγυμνασμένον; see Boisson. Philostr. *Her.* p. 451.[2] In German [and English] we resolve the genitive in all these instances by means of a preposition, *taught by the Holy Spirit, bathed in the ocean, practised on sea*, etc. And perhaps in the simple language of ancient times the genitive in combinations of this kind was conceived as the *whence*-case: see Hartung, *Casus*, p. 17 (Jelf 540. *Obs.*). The two following passages also may be easily explained on the same principle: H. iii. 12, καρδία πονηρὰ ἀπιστίας, *a heart evil in respect of unbelief*, where it is ἀπιστία that proves the πονηρία; if the substantive were used, πονηρία ἀπιστίας, the genitive (of apposition) would present no difficulty whatever. A similar example is Wis. xviii. 3, ἥλιον ἀβλαβῆ φιλοτίμου ξενιτείας παρέσχες: see Monk, Eur. *Alc.* 751, Matth. 339, 345.

The second passage is Ja. i. 13, where most commentators render ἀπείραστος κακῶν *untempted*—incapable of being tempted

---

[1] [The reading of *Rec.*, πλεονεξίαις, is found in no uncial MS.]
[2] [Compare Jelf 483. *Obs.* 3, Green, *Gr.* p. 96 sq.]

—*by evil* (compare Soph. *Ant.* 847, ἄκλαυτος φίλων· Æschyl. *Theb.* 875, κακῶν ἀτρύμονες· and Schwenck, Æschyl. *Eumen.* 96); but Schulthess, *unversed in evil.*[1] The parallelism with πειράζει is unfavourable to the latter explanation. The active meaning given to the word in the Æthiopic version, *not tempting to evil*, is inadmissible, but rather because it would render the following words πειράζει δὲ αὐτὸς οὐδένα tautological (whereas the use of δέ shows that the apostle wished to make some new assertion, and not merely to repeat ἀπείραστος), and also because ἀπείραστος does not occur in an active sense, than (as Schulthess thinks) because of the genitive κακῶν.[2] The genitive is used, at all events by poets and by writers whose language has to some extent a poetic or rhetorical colouring, with great latitude of meaning: ἀπείραστος κακῶν, in the sense of *not tempting in reference to evil*, would be as correct an expression as Soph. *Aj.* 1405, λουτρῶν ὁσίων ἐπίκαιρος, *convenient for holy washings*, or Her. 1. 196, παρθένοι γάμων ὡραῖαι, *ripe for marriage.* (Don. 478, Jelf 518. 4.)

The Pauline expression κλητοὶ Ἰησοῦ Χριστοῦ, Rom. i. 6, cannot be brought under the above rule (as is still done by Thiersch): in accordance with the view of the κλῆσις which the apostles take in other places, the words must be rendered *Christ's called ones*, i.e. men *called* (by God), who are *Christ's*,—who belong to Christ. On the other hand, we may bring in here ὅμοιός τινος, Jo. viii. 55 (ὅμοιός τινι being the regular construction),[3] and also ἐγγύς with the genitive, Jo. xi. 18, Rom. x. 8, xiii. 11, H. vi. 8, viii. 13, al. With ἐγγύς this is the ordinary construction, but ἐγγύς τινι also occurs, see Bleek, *Hebr.* II. ii. 209, Matth. 339 (Jelf 592. 2). Even adjectives compounded with σύν sometimes take the genitive, as σύμμορφος τῆς εἰκόνος Rom. viii. 29 (Matth. 379. Rem. 2, Jelf 507).

5. Most closely akin to the simple genitive of dependence with nouns, and in fact only a resolution of this genitive into a sentence, is the very common construction εἶναί or γίνεσθαί τινος, which is used in Greek prose (Krüg. p. 34 sq., Madvig 54,

---

[1] [So De W., Brückner, Huther, Alford (see his note *in loc.*). A. Buttmann (p. 170) defends the rendering *untempted by evil.*]
[2] On the active and passive meaning of verbals see Wex, Soph. *Ant.* I. 162 (Jelf 356. *Obs.* 2, Don. p. 191.)
[3] See Matth. 386. Rem. 2, Schneider, Plat. *Civ.* II. 104, III. 46 (Jelf 507). On *similis alicujus* and similar expressions, see Zumpt, *Lat. Gr.* § 411. [Comp. Madvig, *Lat. Gr.* § 247. *Obs.* 2, Don. *Lat. Gr.* p. 287. In Jo. viii. 55, we should probably read ὑμῖν (Lachm., Treg., Westcott), not ὑμῶν (Tisch., Lünem.).]

Ast, *Lex. Plat.* I. 621, Don. p. 473 sq.) with yet greater variety of meaning than in the N. T. This construction was formerly explained as arising from the ellipsis either of a preposition or of a substantive. In the N. T. we may distinguish

(*a*) The genitive of the *whole*, of the *class* (plural), and of the *sphere* (singular), to which a man belongs: 1 Tim. i. 20, ὧν ἐστὶν Ὑμέναιος, *of whom is* (to whom belongs) *Hymenæus;* 2 Tim. i. 15, A. xxiii. 6 (1 Macc. ii. 18, Plat. *Protag.* 342 e, Xen. *An.* 1. 2. 3); 1 Th. v. 5, 8, οὐκ ἐσμὲν νυκτὸς οὐδὲ σκότους .... ἡμεῖς ἡμέρας ὄντες, *belonging to the night, to the day;* A. ix. 2. (Jelf 533.)

(*b*) The genitive of the *ruler, lord, possessor,* etc.: Mt. xxii. 28, τίνος τῶν ἑπτὰ ἔσται γυνή; 1 C. iii. 21, πάντα ὑμῶν ἐστίν (Xen. *An.* 2. 1. 4, Ptol. 1. 8. 1); vi. 19, οὐκ ἐστὲ ἑαυτῶν, *ye belong not to yourselves;* 2 C. iv. 7, ἵνα ἡ ὑπερβολὴ τῆς δυνάμεως ᾖ τοῦ θεοῦ καὶ μὴ ἐξ ἡμῶν, *that ... may be God's and not from us;* x. 7, Χριστοῦ εἶναι· Rom. viii. 9 (similarly in 1 C. i. 12 of the heads of parties, ἐγώ εἰμι Παύλου· compare Diog. L. 6. 82). Akin to this are A. i. 7, οὐχ ὑμῶν ἐστί γνῶναι κ.τ.λ., *it does not appertain to you, it is not in your power to know* (Plat. *Gorg.* 500 a, Xen. *Œc.* 1. 2), Mk. xii. 7, ἡμῶν ἔσται ἡ κληρονομία (Mt. v. 3), 1 P. iii. 3 ; also H. v. 14, τελείων ἐστὶν ἡ στερεὰ τροφή, *belongs to* (is suitable for) *those who are perfect* (Jelf 518).

(*c*) The genitive of a property [1] (expressed by the singular of an abstract noun) in which any one participates, as in 1 C. xiv. 33, οὐκ ἔστιν ἀκαταστασίας ὁ θεός· H. x. 39, ἡμεῖς οὐκ ἐσμὲν ὑποστολῆς .... ἀλλὰ πίστεως κ.τ.λ. (Plat. *Apol.* 28 a): the application of this idiom is very varied. We also find the genitive of a concrete noun, as in A. ix. 2, τινὰς τῆς ὁδοῦ ὄντας ; [2] especially of the years of a person's age, Mk. v. 42, ἦν ἐτῶν δώδεκα· L. ii. 42, iii. 23, A. iv. 22, Tob. xiv. 2, 11, Plat. *Legg.* 4. 721 a. In these examples the subject is a person, in the following a thing: H. xii. 11, πᾶσα παιδεία οὐ δοκεῖ χαρᾶς εἶναι, *is not* (matter) *of joy, something joyous,*—though this might be

---

[1] [A. Buttmann (p. 163) adds the remark that the use of the genitive with εἶναι to denote a *permanent* property or quality (as in H. xii. 11, x. 39, 2 P. i. 20) is almost unknown to Greek prose (Madvig 54. Rem. 1): compare below § 34. 3. b.—He refers to this head the genitive πηχῶν in Rev. xxi. 17 (as having arisen out of τὸ τεῖχος ἦν τ. πηχῶν); similarly χιλιάδων in ver. 16.]

[2] [A. ix. 2 is also quoted above, under (*a*).]

referred to (a); 2 P. i. 20, πᾶσα προφητεία γραφῆς ἰδίας ἐπιλύσεως οὐ γίνεται. When persons are spoken of, this construction of εἰμί is sometimes made more animated, after the oriental manner, by the insertion of υἱός or τέκνον; compare 1 Th. v. 5, ὑμεῖς υἱοὶ φωτός ἐστε καὶ υἱοὶ ἡμέρας.[1] (Jelf 518.)

The verb εἶναι is sometimes omitted, the same relations being expressed by the genitive; as in Ph. iii. 5, ἐγὼ ..... φυλῆς Βενιαμίν.

6. The genitive appears in the N. T. with verbs (and adjectives) as a clearly conceived case of *proceeding from, motion whence,* with a variety of application natural to this relation: Greek prose however is still richer than the N. T. in such applications, and in the N. T. the genitive is frequently supported by prepositions. Since *separation from* is closely related to *proceeding from,* and that which *proceeds from* and *is separated from* may in many cases be regarded as *a part of* the whole which remains behind, the genitive, as the case of *proceeding from,* is also the regular case of *separation* and of *partition.* We shall first consider the genitive of *separation* and *removal,* as the more limited.

Words which express the notion of separation or removal are ordinarily construed by Greek writers with a simple genitive, even in prose; as ἐλευθεροῦν τινός *to free from something,* κωλύειν, ὑποχωρεῖν, παύειν, διαφέρειν, ὑστερεῖν τινός (see Matth. 353 sqq., 366, Bernh. p. 179 sq., Don. p. 466, Jelf 530 sq.[2]), though it is not at all uncommon to find suitable prepositions used in such cases. Accordingly, in the N. T. the simple genitive is found with μετασταθῆναι, L. xvi. 4;[3] ἀστοχεῖν, 1 Tim. i. 6;[4] παύεσθαι, 1 P. iv. 1; κωλύειν, A. xxvii. 43 (compare Xen. *Cyr.* 2. 4. 23, *An.* 1. 6. 2, Pol. 2. 52. 8, al.); διαφέρειν, Mt. x. 31, 1 C. xv. 41, al. (Xen. *Cyr.* 8. 2. 21, compare Krüg. *Dion. H.* p. 462); ἀποστερεῖσθαι, 1 Tim. vi. 5;[5] also ὑστερεῖν, *to be*

---

[1] We also use both modes of expression, *thou art Death's,* and *thou art a child of Death;* but it does not follow from this that there is an ellipsis in the former phrase (Kühnöl on H. x. 39).

[2] [For verbs of *missing* (ἀστοχεῖν) see Don. p. 466, Jelf 514; for διαφέρειν, Don. p. 476, Jelf 503 sq.; ὑστερεῖν, Don. p. 476, Jelf 506.]

[3] [The best texts insert ἐκ here.]

[4] [That is, if ὧν is governed by ἀστοχήσαντες (Huther, Grimm, Alford), and not by ἐξετράπησαν (Ellicott).]

[5] In A. xix. 27 good MSS. have μέλλειν τε καὶ καθαιρεῖσθαι τῆς μεγαλειότητος αὐτῆς, and Lachmann has received this reading; but I agree with

behind, fall short of, 2 C. xi. 5, xii. 11 (see Bleek on H. iv. 1), and ξένοι τῶν διαθηκῶν, E. ii. 12. Yet the use of the preposition has the preponderance :—

(a) With verbs of *separating, freeing,* and *being free* (Matth. 353 sq., Bernh. p. 181, Jelf 531. *Obs.* 3), invariably: χωρίζειν ἀπό, Rom. viii. 35, 1 C. vii. 10, H. vii. 26 (Plat. *Phæd.* 67 c,— contrast Polyb. 5. 111. 2); λύειν ἀπό, L. xiii. 16, 1 C. vii. 27 ; ἐλευθεροῦν ἀπό, Rom. vi. 18, 22, viii. 2, 21 (Thuc. 2. 71: found also with ἐκ, Matth. 353. Rem.); ῥύεσθαι ἀπό, Mt. vi. 13 (2 S. xix. 9, Ps. xvi. 13 sq.), with ἐκ L. i. 74, Rom. vii. 24, al., Ex. vi. 6, Job xxxiii. 30, Ps. lxviii. 15 ; σώζειν ἀπό, Rom. v. 9 (Ps. lxviii. 15), and more frequently with ἐκ, Ja. v. 20, H. v. 7 (2 S. xxii. 3 sq., 1 K. xix. 17); λυτροῦν ἀπό, Tit. ii. 14, Ps. cxviii. 134 (λυτροῦν τινός, Fabric. *Pseudepigraph.* 1. 710) ; καθαρίζειν ἀπό, 1 Jo. i. 7, 2 C. vii. 1, H. ix. 14,—and accordingly καθαρὸς ἀπό A. xx. 26, compare Tob. iii. 14, Demosth. *Neær.* 528 c (with ἐκ Appian, *Syr.* 59), ἀθῷος ἀπό (נקי מ) Mt. xxvii. 24, comp. Krebs, *Observ.* 73, Gen. xxiv. 41, Num. v. 19, 31 (ἀθῷός τινι, Jos. ii. 17, 19 sq.): similarly λούειν ἀπό (a pregnant construction, *by means of washing cleanse from*), A. xvi. 33, Rev. i. 5.[1]

(b) Where the construction with the simple genitive is also used : Rev. xiv. 13, ἀναπαύεσθαι[2] ἐκ τῶν κόπων· 1 P. iii. 10, παυσάτω τὴν γλῶσσαν ἀπὸ κακοῦ (Esth. ix. 16, Soph. *El.* 987, Thuc. 7. 73): ὑστερεῖν ἀπό, H. xii. 15, is probably a pregnant construction.

The notion of separation and removal is also the foundation of the Hellenistic construction κρύπτειν (τι) ἀπό τινος, L. xix. 42 (for which the Greeks said κρύπτειν τινά τι) ; this too is properly a pregnant construction. In the LXX compare Gen. iv. 14, xviii. 17, 1 S. iii. 18, al. To the construction of verbs of *remaining behind anything* (ὑστερεῖν τινός) may be referred the genitive in 2 P. iii. 9, οὐ βραδύνει ὁ κύριος τῆς ἐπαγγελίας (οὐ βραδύς ἐστι τῆς ἐπαγγελίας) : compare

---

Meyer, who considers this reading (which probably is due to an error of transcription, see Bengel) too weak for the character of the passage. [The genitive is received by recent editors. A. Buttmann (p. 158) considers the genitive partitive : Alford with better reason translates "deposed from her greatness." In 2 P. i. 4 ἀποφεύγειν is followed by a genitive : see Alford's note.]

[1] [In Rev. i. 5 λύσαντι is strongly supported, and is received by Lachm., Tisch., Treg., Westcott and Hort. With καθαρὸς ἀπό compare ἄσπιλος ἀπό, Ja. i. 27 (A. Buttm.) ; unless ἀπό here belongs to τηρεῖν (De W., Alford).—In modern Greek verbs of *liberating,* etc., are always followed by ἀπό (Mullach p. 324).]

[2] [Ἀναπαύεσθαι *itself* is not joined with a simple genitive in the N. T.]

ὑστεροῦν τῆς βοηθείας, Diod. S. 13. 110. Even as early as the Syriac version we find ἐπαγγ. joined with βραδύνει.

7. The simplest examples in prose of the genitive of *proceeding from* and of derivation are presented by ἄρχομαί τινος *I begin from* (with) *something* (Hartung p. 14), δέχομαί τινος *I receive from some one* (Herm. *Vig.* p. 877), δέομαί τινος (genitive of person) *I supplicate from some one* (Matth. 355. Rem. 2), ἀκούω τινός *I hear from some one*: then we find γεύομαι, ἐσθίω τινός (e.g. ἄρτου, μέλιτος) *I taste, eat of something*, ὀνίναμαί τινος *I derive advantage, enjoyment, from something*; and, lastly, δίδωμί, λαμβάνω τινός, *I give, take, of something* (Herm. *Opusc.* I. 178). In all these instances the genitive denotes the object from which the *hearing, eating, giving*, proceeds,—from which is derived what is eaten, tasted, given, etc. In the last examples the genitive also denotes the mass, the whole, a part of which is enjoyed, tasted, given, etc., and therefore these genitives may also be regarded as partitive; for where the reference is to the whole, or to the object absolutely, the accusative is used, as the case of the simple object. In the language of the N. T., however, the genitive is supported by a preposition in many of these constructions. To come to particulars :—

(*a*) Δέομαι takes without exception the genitive of the person (Mt. ix. 38, L. v. 12, viii. 28, A. viii. 22, al.), the thing requested being subjoined in the accusative, as in 2 C. viii. 4, δεόμενοι ἡμῶν τὴν χάριν κ.τ.λ.[1] (Don. p. 468, Jelf 529.)

(*b*) Of the genitive with verbs of *giving* there is only one example, Rev. ii. 17, δώσω αὐτῷ τοῦ μάννα; where some MSS. have the correction δώσω αὐτῷ φαγεῖν ἀπὸ τοῦ μάννα.[2] On the other hand, in Rom. i. 11 and 1 Th. ii. 8 the apostle could not have written μεταδιδόναι χαρίσματος or εὐαγγελίου (Matth. 326. 3); for in the first passage he means some particular charisma (in fact he says χάρισμά τι) as a whole, and in the latter the gospel is referred to as something indivisible. Paul did not purpose to impart *something from* a spiritual gift, or *something from* the Gospel. (Don. p. 473, Jelf 535.)

---

[1] Weber, *Dem.* p. 163. [Once we find δεῖσθαι πρὸς τὸν κύριον ὅπως κ.τ.λ. (A. viii. 24).]
[2] This very passage clearly shows the distinction between the genitive and the accusative, as καὶ δώσω ψῆφον λευκήν immediately follows: compare Heliod. 2. 23. 100, ἐπιρρόφουν ὁ μὲν τοῦ ὕδατος, ὁ δὲ καὶ οἶνον.

(c) Verbs of *enjoying* or *partaking*: προςλαμβάνεσθαι τροφῆς A. xxvii. 36, μεταλαμβάνειν τροφῆς A. ii. 46, xxvii. 33 sq., γενέσθαι τοῦ δείπνου L. xiv. 24 (figuratively in H. vi. 4 γενέσθαι τῆς δωρεᾶς τῆς ἐπουρανίου, γενέσθαι θανάτου Mt. xvi. 28, L. ix. 27, H. ii. 9, al.): also with the genitive of a person, Phil. 20, ἐγώ σου ὀναίμην ἐν κυρίῳ (so as early as *Odyss.* 19. 68), Rom. xv. 24, ἐὰν ὑμῶν . . . . ἐμπλησθῶ. But γενέσθαι governs the accusative in Jo. ii. 9 ἐγεύσατο τὸ ὕδωρ, and in H. vi. 5,[1] as it frequently does in Jewish Greek (Job xii. 11, Ecclus. xxxvi. 24, Tob. vii. 11), but probably never in Greek writers.[2] Verbs of *eating of*, as also those of *giving* and *taking of* or *from*, are in all other N. T. passages accompanied by prepositions:—

a. By ἀπό: L. xxiv. 42 [*Rec.*], ἐπέδωκαν αὐτῷ . . . ἀπὸ μελισσίου κηρίου, xx. 10 ; Mt. xv. 27, τὰ κυνάρια ἐσθίει ἀπὸ τῶν ψιχίων τῶν παιδίων,—compare אָכַל מִן, and φαγεῖν ἀπό Fabric. *Pseudep.* I. 706 ; L. xxii. 18, οὐ μὴ πίω ἀπὸ τοῦ γεννήματος τῆς ἀμπέλου, Jer. li. (xxviii.) 7; A. ii. 17, ἐκχεῶ ἀπὸ τοῦ πνεύματός μου (from the LXX); v. 2, καὶ ἐνοσφίσατο ἀπὸ τῆς τιμῆς· Jo. xxi. 10, ἐνέγκατε ἀπὸ τῶν ὀψαρίων· Mk. xii. 2, ἵνα . . . . λάβῃ ἀπὸ τοῦ καρποῦ τοῦ ἀμπελῶνος.

b. By ἐκ: 1 C. xi. 28, ἐκ τοῦ ἄρτου ἐσθιέτω· ix. 7 (2 S. xii. 3, 2 K. iv. 40, Ecclus. xi. 19, Judith xii. 2): Jo. iv. 14, ὃς ἂν πίῃ ἐκ τοῦ ὕδατος·[3] v. 50, ὁ ἄρτος . . . ἵνα τις ἐξ αὐτοῦ φάγῃ·

---

[1] Bengel (on H. vi. 4) seems to trifle, in making a distinction in this passage between γιύεσθαι with a genitive and with an accusative. ["The change of construction from the genitive to the accusative in the small compass of this passage cannot be mere looseness of language. . . . This construction must be viewed as an indication of a change of meaning, resulting from the presence of an epithet, not as a mere epithet, but as entering into the predicate ; the action signified being now no longer the bare process of tasting, but of becoming cognisant by that means of a quality or condition of the object of taste. The epithet καλόν must be regarded as belonging to δυνάμεις as well as ῥῆμα."—Green, *Gr.* p. 94. Other explanations (less probable) will be found in the notes of Delitzsch and Alford. Comp. Jo. iv. 23 (p. 263, note [3]).]

[2] In the sense of *eating up, consuming*, φαγεῖν and ἐσθίειν of course take an accusative (Mt. xii. 4, Rev. x. 10); 1 C. ix. 7 [τὸν καρπὸν] is a characteristic example. They also have the accusative when there is merely a general reference to the food which a man (ordinarily) takes, on which he supports himself: Mk. i. 6, ἦν Ἰωάννης . . . ἐσθίων ἀκρίδας καὶ μέλι ἄγριον· Rom. xiv. 21, Mt. xv. 2, 1 C. viii. 7, x. 3, 4 (Jo. vi. 58) ; compare Diog. L. 6. 45. Probably in no instance would ἐσθίειν τι (compare also 2 Th. iii. 12) be entirely indefensible, and hence the non-occurrence of ἐσθίειν τινός (by the side of ἀπό or ἔκ τινος) ceases to appear strange. L. xv. 16, ἀπὸ τῶν κερατίων ὧν ἤσθιον οἱ χοῖροι, is most likely an example of attraction. In the LXX we regularly find ἐσθίειν, πίνειν τι : the only exception is Num. xx. 19, ἐὰν τοῦ ὕδατός σου πίωμεν.

[3] It is otherwise in 1 C. x. 4, ἔπινον ἐκ πνευματικῆς ἀκολουθούσης πέτρας : Flatt's explanation is a complete failure.

1 Jo. iv. 13, ἐκ τοῦ πνεύματος αὐτοῦ δέδωκεν ἡμῖν. But H. xiii. 10, φαγεῖν ἐκ θυσιαστηρίου, is not an example of this kind, as if the words were tantamount to φαγεῖν ἐκ θυσίας, for θυσιαστήριον means *altar*: it is only in sense that *eat from the altar* is equivalent to *eat of the sacrifice* (offered on the altar). There is probably no example of ἐσθίειν ἀπό or ἐκ to be found in Greek authors, but ἀπολαύειν ἀπό τινος, Plat. *Rep.* 3. 395 c, 10. 606 b, *Apol.* 31 b, is a kindred expression.

(*d*) Of verbs of *perception*, ἀκούω is construed with the genitive of the person (to hear *from* some one), *to hear some one*, as in Mt. xvii. 5, Mk. vii. 14, L. ii. 46, Jo. iii. 29, ix. 31, Rev. vi. 1, 3, Rom. x. 14;[1] the object is expressed by the accusative, as in A. i. 4, ἣν ἠκούσατέ μου· Lucian, *Dial. Deor.* 20. 13 (Don. p. 469 sq., Jelf 485 sqq.). Besides this construction, however, we also find ἀκούειν τι ἀπό, 1 Jo. i. 5; ἐκ, 2 C. xii. 6 (this occurs as early as *Odyss.* 15. 374); παρά, A. x. 22: here Greek authors would have been content with a simple genitive.[2] A genitive of the thing is joined to ἀκούειν in Jo. v. 25, H. iv. 7, ἀκ. φωνῆς· L. xv. 25, ἤκουσε συμφωνίας καὶ χορῶν· Mk. xiv. 64, ἠκούσατε τῆς βλασφημίας· 1 Macc. x. 74, Bar. iii. 4 (Lucian, *Halc.* 2, *Gall.* 10, Xen. *Cyr.* 6. 2. 13, al.); an accusative in L. v. 1, ἀκούειν τὸν λόγον τοῦ θεοῦ· Jo. viii. 40, τὴν ἀλήθειαν, ἣν ἤκουσα παρὰ τ. θεοῦ κ.τ.λ. In the latter examples the object is regarded as one coherent whole, and the hearing is an act of the intellect: in the former, the reference is in the first instance to the particular tones or words which are heard (with the physical ear): compare Rost p. 535.[3]

The genitive after τυγχάνειν (ἐπιτυγχάνειν) is perhaps, in its origin, to be explained by the above rule; yet we also find it where the

---

[1] By others (Rückert and Fritzsche) the personal genitive in οὗ οὐκ ἤκουσαν is understood to mean *of whom* (de quo) *they have not heard*, as we find ἀκούειν τινός in *Iliad* 24. 490. This does not seem to me probable (for the construction in this sense is confined to poetry), and still less is it necessary: we hear Christ when we hear the Gospel in which He speaks, and accordingly Χριστὸν ἀκούειν is in E. iv. 21 predicated of those who had not heard Christ in person. Philippi's note *in loc.* is superficial.

[2] [These prepositions are sometimes inserted in classical Greek (Don. p. 470, Jelf 485): e. g., ἀπό, Thuc. 1. 125; παρά, Xen. *An.* 1. 2. 5; ἐκ, Her. 3. 62.]

[3] [A. Buttmann (p. 167) considers Jo. xii. 47, A. xxii. 1, al., as examples of another construction of ἀκούω,—with *two* genitives, of person and thing.—He remarks that all other verbs of this class have in the N. T. an accusative of the object, and take παρά or ἀπό before the genitive of the person.]

whole object is referred to. This verb always takes the genitive in the N. T.¹ (L. xx. 35, A. xxiv. 3, xxvii. 3, al.) : on the accusative see Herm. *Vig.* p. 762, Bernh. p. 176 (Jelf 512. *Obs.*). In the same way earlier writers almost always construe κληρονομεῖν (*inherit*, also *participate in*) with a genitive (Kypke II. 381) ; in the later writers and in the N. T. it takes the accusative of the thing, e. g. in Mt. v. 4 [v. 5 *Rec.*], xix. 29, G. v. 21 (Polyb. 15. 22. 3) : see Fischer, *Well.* III. i. 368, Lob. p. 129, Matth. 329.

Λαγχάνειν has an accus. in A. i. 17, and in 2 P. i. 1, ἰσότιμον ἡμῖν λαχοῦσι πίστιν (where πίστις is not the faith, in the ideal sense, in which every Christian participates through his personal conviction, but the subjective faith belonging to the Christians immediately addressed) : see Matth. 328. Rem. In L. i. 9 this verb (in the sense of *obtain by lot*) is joined with a genitive.² (Jelf 512.)

8. In the foregoing examples we have already perceived the notion of *proceeding from* glide into that of *participation in* : this partitive signification of the genitive is still more distinctly apparent in such combinations as μετέχειν τινός, πληροῦν τινός, θιγγάνειν τινός. With the genitive are construed

(*a*) Words that express the notion of *sharing in, participating in, wanting* (wishing to participate), see Matth. 325 (Don. p. 472, 468, Jelf 535, 529) : κοινωνεῖν, H. ii. 24 ; κοινωνός, 1 C. x. 18, 1 P. v. 1 ; συγκοινωνός, Rom. xi. 17 ; μετέχειν, 1 C. ix. 12, x. 21, H. v. 13; μεταλαμβάνειν, H. vi. 7, xii. 10; μέτοχος, H. iii. 1: also χρήζειν,³ Mt. vi. 32, 2 C. iii. 1, al.; προσδεῖσθαι, A. xvii. 25. But κοινωνεῖν is also found with a dative of the thing, and indeed this is the more common construction in the N. T. ;⁴ 1 Tim. v. 22, μὴ κοινώνει ἁμαρτίαις ἀλλοτρίαις· Rom. xv. 27, 1 P. iv. 13, 2 Jo. 11 (Wis. vi. 25). In a transitive sense it is joined with εἰς in Ph. iv. 15, οὐδεμία μοι ἐκκλησία ἐκοινώνησεν εἰς λόγον δόσεως : compare Plat. *Rep.* 5. 453 b, δυνατὴ φύσις ἡ θήλεια τῇ τοῦ ἄρρενος γένους κοινωνῆσαι εἰς ἅπαντα τὰ ἔργα· *Act. Apocr.* p. 91. The dative of the thing with κοινωνεῖν and μετέχειν is sometimes found in Greek writers (Thuc. 2. 16, De-

---

¹ In good MSS. ἐπιτυγχάνειν has the accus. once, Rom. xi. 7 ; see Fritz. *in loc.*
² Compare Brunck, Soph. *El.* 364, Jacobs, *Anth. Pal.* III. 803.
³ In L. xi. 8 several MSS. have ὅσον χρῄζει, but we cannot (with Kühnöl) infer from this, any more than from the construction χρῄζειν τι (Matth. 355. Rem. 2), that χρῄζειν takes an accusative, in the sense of *desiring, craving.* [Compare Green p. 95, and see below, § 32. 4.]
⁴ [On the constructions of κοινωνεῖν in the N. T. see Ellicott's note on G. vi. 6 : he maintains that this verb is always intransitive in the N. T. Κοινωνός also takes a dative of the person (L. v. 10).]

mosth. *Cor.* c. 18), see Poppo, *Thuc.* III. ii. 77 : in the case of κοινωνεῖν this construction is explained by the notion of *association* which lies in the word. (1 Tim. v. 22 cannot be resolved into μηδέν σοι καὶ ταῖς ἁμαρτίαις ἀλλοτρ. κοινὸν ἔστω.) Once we find μετέχειν joined with ἐκ: 1 C. x. 17, ἐκ τοῦ ἑνὸς ἄρτου μετέχομεν : I know of no example of the kind in Greek writers.

(*b*) Words of *fulness, filling,*[1] *emptiness,* and *deficiency* (Matth. 351 sq., Don. p. 468, Jelf 539, 529) : Rom. xv. 13, ὁ θεὸς πληρώσαι ὑμᾶς πάσης χαρᾶς καὶ εἰρήνης· L. i. 53, πεινῶντας ἐνέπλησεν ἀγαθῶν· A. v. 28, πεπληρώκατε τὴν Ἱερουσαλὴμ τῆς διδαχῆς ὑμῶν (A. ii. 28, from the LXX), Jo. ii. 7, γεμίσατε τὰς ὑδρίας ὕδατος (vi. 13), Mt. xxii. 10, ἐπλήσθη ὁ γάμος ἀνακειμένων (A. xix. 29), Jo. i. 14, πλήρης χάριτος· 2 P. ii. 14, ὀφθαλμοὶ μεστοὶ μοιχαλίδος· L. xi. 39, τὸ ἔσωθεν ὑμῶν γέμει ἁρπαγῆς καὶ πονηρίας· Ja. i. 5, εἴ τις ὑμῶν λείπεται σοφίας.[2] Rom. iii. 23, πάντες ὑστεροῦνται τῆς δόξης τοῦ θεοῦ (compare Lob. p. 237) ; see also A. xiv. 17, xxvii. 38, L. xv. 17, xxii. 35, Jo. xix. 29, Rom. xv. 14, 24, Rev. xv. 8. Only seldom are verbs of fulness joined with ἀπό[3] (L. xv. 16, ἐπεθύμει γεμίσαι τὴν κοιλίαν αὐτοῦ ἀπὸ τῶν κερατίων xvi. 21), or with ἐκ, as in Rev. viii. 5 (γεμίζειν ἐκ), Rev. xix. 21 (χορτάζ. ἐκ, contrast χορτάζειν τινός Lam. iii. 15, 29), Rev. xvii. 2, 6 (μεθύειν, μεθύσκεσθαι ἐκ), compare Lucian, *Dial. D.* 6. 3.[4] Altogether solecistic is γέμον τὰ ὀνόματα, Rev. xvii. 3 (compare ver. 4).[5] The use of the dative with πληροῦν, μεθύσκεσθαι, etc., rests on an essentially different view of the relation ; see § 31. 7. In 1 C. i. 7 ὑστερεῖσθαι ἐν

---

[1] To this head belongs also πλούσιος with the genitive, Eur. *Or.* 394. In the N. T. the preposition ἐν is always used : E. ii. 4, πλούσιος ἐν ἐλέει (*rich in compassion*), Ja. ii. 5. Compare πλουτεῖν, πλουτίζεσθαι ἔν τινι, 1 Tim. vi. 18, 1 C. i. 5, al.

[2] Matthiæ, Eurip. *Hippol.* 323.

[3] [These verbs are followed by ἀπό in modern Greek (Mullach, *Vulg.* p. 325).]

[4] On πληθύνειν ἀπό, Athen. 13. 569, see Schweighäus. *Add. et Corrig.* p. 478.—Mt. xxiii. 25, ἔσωθεν γέμουσιν (the cup and platter) ἐξ ἁρπαγῆς καὶ ἀκρασίας, must probably be rendered, *are filled from robbery ;* they have contents which are derived from robbery. Luke however transfers the *fulness* to the Pharisees themselves, and hence writes τὸ ἔσωθεν ὑμῶν γέμει ἁρπαγῆς κ.τ.λ. So also in Jo. xii. 3, ἡ οἰκία ἐπληρώθη ἐκ τῆς ὀσμῆς τοῦ μύρου, we must not take ἐκ τῆς ὀσμῆς as standing for a genitive ; these words indicate that *out of which* the filling of the house arose,—*it was filled* (with fragrance) *from* (by) *the odour of the ointment.*

[5] [Lünemann rightly points to πληροῦσθαι καρπόν (Ph. i. 11) as a similar construction. See below, p. 287.]

μηδενὶ χαρίσματι, it is easy to perceive the writer's conception and meaning: compare Plat. *Rep.* 6. 484 d.[1]

(*c*) Verbs of *touching* (Matth. 330, Jelf 536 [2]), inasmuch as the touching affects only a *part* of the object: Mk. v. 30, ἥψατο τῶν ἱματίων (vi. 56, L. xxii. 51, Jo. xx. 17, 2 C. vi. 17, al.), H. xii. 20, κἂν θηρίον θίγῃ τοῦ ὄρους (xi. 28). The construction βάπτειν ὕδατος, L. xvi. 24, comes under the same head.[3]

(*d*) Verbs of *taking hold of*, where the action is limited to a *part* of the whole object: Mt. xiv. 31, ἐκτείνας τὴν χεῖρα ἐπελάβετο αὐτοῦ, compare Theophr. *Ch.* 4 (with the hand He could grasp the sinking man only by a part of the body, possibly by the arm), L. ix. 47:—somewhat differently in Mk. ix. 27 [*Rec.*], κρατήσας αὐτὸν τῆς χειρός· A. iii. 7, πιάσας αὐτὸν τῆς δεξιᾶς χειρός (*by the hand*), compare Plat. *Parm.* 126, Xen. *An.* 1. 6. 10. Hence these verbs are commonly used with the genitive of a limb, as in L. viii. 54, κρατήσας τῆς χειρὸς αὐτῆς· A. xxiii. 19 (Is. xli. 13, xlii. 6, Gen. xix. 16). On the other hand, κρατεῖν, λαμβάνειν, or ἐπιλαμβάνεσθαί τινα, always means to *seize a man*, i. e. his whole person, to *apprehend*:[4] Mt. xii. 11, xiv. 3, xviii. 28, A. ix. 27, xvi. 19. The same distinction is observed in the figurative use of these verbs: genitive,—H. ii. 16, L. i. 54, 1 Tim. vi. 2 (Xen. *Cyr.* 2. 3. 6); accusative,— 2 Th. ii. 15, Col. ii. 19, al. But κρατεῖν *cling to*, H. iv. 14, vi. 18, and ἐπιλαμβάνεσθαι *lay hold of*, 1 Tim. vi. 12, 19 (Æl. 14. 27), are construed with a genitive: in each case, however, the reference is to a possession (ὁμολογία, ἐλπίς) designed for many, which each man for his own part holds fast or attains. See on the whole Matth. 330 sq. Ἐπιλαμβάνεσθαι, used in a

---

[1] [To this class belongs also περισσεύειν *abound in*, L. xv. 17: in its strictly comparative sense (Xen. *An.* 4. 8. 11) this word does not directly govern a case in the N. T. Here may be mentioned the genitive with verbs which express a notion of comparison,—the genitive of relation (Don. p. 476, Jelf 505 sq.): ὑπερβάλλειν, E. iii. 19; ὑπερέχειν, Ph. ii. 2; προΐστασθαι, 1 Tim. iii. 4; ὑστερεῖν and διαφέρειν, which however Winer places in a different class. On the genitive after verbs compounded with πρό, etc., see § 52. 2. 4. (A. Buttm. p. 168 sq.).]

[2] [Donaldson takes a different view of this genitive, see p. 483.]

[3] Bernhardy p. 168 (Jelf 540, *Obs.*). Compare βάπτειν εἰς ὕδωρ, Plat. *Tim.* 73 e, Æl. 14. 39.

[4] [A. Buttmann (p. 160) maintains that ἐπιλαμβάνεσθαι never really governs an accusative. "In all the instances (either in the N. T. or in Greek authors) in which such an accusative seems to occur, ἐπιλαμβάνεσθαι stands connected with another transitive verb, so that the accusative (by the σχῆμα ἀπὸ κοινοῦ) is *jointly* dependent on both predicates." Similarly Meyer (on A. ix. 27). Lünemann, in a note introduced in this place, takes the same view, and quotes A. xviii. 17 as an additional example.]

metaphysical sense, is followed by two genitives in L. xx. 20, ἵνα ἐπιλάβωνται αὐτοῦ λόγου, *that they might lay hold of him by a word*, and in ver. 26, ἐπιλαβέσθαι αὐτοῦ ῥήματος : so in its proper sense Xen. *An.* 4. 7. 12. Lastly, we must bring in here the construction ἔχεσθαί τινος *to cling to, hang on something*, pendere ex (see Bleek, *Hebr.* II. ii. 220 sq., Matth. 330, Jelf 536, Don. p. 483), and ἀντέχεσθαί τινος. In the N. T. these two verbs are so used only in the figurative sense : H. vi. 9, τὰ κρείσσονα καὶ ἐχόμενα σωτηρίας· Mt. vi. 24, τοῦ ἑνὸς ἀνθέξεται καὶ τοῦ ἑτέρου καταφρονήσει· 1 Th. v. 14, ἀντέχεσθε τῶν ἀσθενῶν· Tit. i. 9, ἀντεχόμενος τοῦ κατὰ τὴν διδαχὴν πιστοῦ λόγου. Akin to these is ἀνέχεσθαί τινος, *to endure anything* or *any one*, since it properly signifies *to hold to something*[1] (Mt. xvii. 17, H. xiii. 22, E. iv. 2), compare Kypke II. 93 : so also ἔνοχός (ἐνεχόμενός) τινος, as in Mt. xxvi. 66, ἔνοχος θανάτου, or 1 C. xi. 27, ἔνοχος τοῦ σώματος καὶ τοῦ αἵματος τοῦ κυρίου (Ja. ii. 10), for in all these instances there is denoted a *being bound to* (something),—in the first example, to a punishment which must be suffered,—in the second, to a thing to which satisfaction must be given. See Fritz. *Matt.* p. 223, Bleek, *Hebr.* II. i. 340 sq.: compare § 31. 1.

Rem. 1. The partitive genitive is sometimes governed by an adverb : H. ix. 7, ἅπαξ τοῦ ἐνιαυτοῦ *once in the year*,[2] L. xviii. 12, xvii. 4 (Ptol. *Geogr.* 8. 15. 19, 8. 29. 31, 8. 16. 4, al.) : compare Madv. 50 (Jelf 523).

Rem. 2. The partitive genitive is not always under the government of another word : it sometimes appears as the subject of the sentence, as in Xen. *An.* 3. 5. 16, ὁπότε . . . σπείσαιντο καὶ ἐπιμίγνυσθαι σφῶν τε πρὸς ἐκείνους καὶ ἐκείνων πρὸς αὐτούς, *and of them* (some) *hold intercourse with the Persians, and* (some) *of the Persians with them;* Thuc. 1. 115 (Theophan. I. 77). An example from the N. T. is A. xxi. 16, συνῆλθον καὶ τῶν μαθητῶν σὺν ἡμῖν; compare Pseud-Arist. p. 120 (Haverc.), ἐν οἷς καὶ βασιλικοὶ ἦσαν καὶ τῶν τιμωμένων ὑπὸ τοῦ βασιλέως. As a rule, however, the genitive is accompanied by a preposition in such cases ; e.g. Jo. xvi. 17,[3] εἶπον ἐκ τῶν μαθητῶν αὐτοῦ κ.τ.λ. (Jelf 893. *e*).

9. It is not difficult to recognise the genitive as the *whence-case* when it is joined with

---

[1] [Compare Jelf I. p. 454, Note ; and on ἔνοχος, Jelf § 501.]
[2] [Lünemann adds Mt. xxviii. 1, ὀψὲ σαββάτων.]
[3] [Compare also Rev. xi. 9, Jo. vii. 40 (Tisch., al.) : in several passages ἐκ with its case occupies the place of the *object*, as 2 Jo. 4, Rev. ii. 10, Mt. xxiii. 34, L. xxi. 16 ; compare also Rev. v. 9, if ἡμᾶς be omitted. A. Buttm. p. 158 sq., Schirlitz, *Grundz.* p. 250.]

(a) Verbs of *accusing* and *impeaching* (*condemning*), as the genitive of the thing (Matth. 369, Don. p. 479, Jelf 501); for the crime of which one is accused is that *from which* the κατηγορεῖν proceeds. See A. xix. 40, κινδυνεύομεν ἐγκαλεῖσθαι στάσεως· xxv. 11, οὐδέν ἐστιν ὧν οὗτοι κατηγοροῦσί μου· L. xxiii.14, οὐδὲν εὗρον ἐν τῷ ἀνθρώπῳ τούτῳ αἴτιον ὧν κατηγορεῖτε κατ' αὐτοῦ. (On the other hand, we find περί τινος *de aliqua re*, A. xxiii. 29, xxiv. 13,[1] compare Xen. *Hell.* 1. 7. 2; as also κρίνεσθαι περί τ., A. xxiii. 6, xxiv. 21.) Yet it must not be concealed that the two verbs just mentioned have commonly a different construction in Greek authors, viz. κατηγορεῖν τινός τι (of which construction Mk. xv. 3 cannot well be considered an example, compare Lucian, *Necyom.* 19), and ἐγκαλεῖν τινί τι (Matth. 370, Jelf 589. 3).[2]

(b) Κατακαυχᾶσθαι, to *glory in a thing* (derive glory *from* a thing), Ja. ii. 13. The combination ἐπαινεῖν τινά τινος (4 Macc. i. 10, iv. 4, Poppo, *Thuc.* III. i. 661) does not occur in the N. T.; for in L. xvi. 8 τῆς ἀδικίας must undoubtedly be joined with οἰκονόμος, and the object of ἐπαινεῖν is only expressed in the clause ὅτι φρονίμως ἐποίησεν.[3] In later writers μισεῖν also has the genitive of the thing, like ἐπαινεῖν; see Liban. *Oratt.* p. 120 d, Cantacuz. I. 56. (Don. p. 479, Jelf 495.)

(c) Verbs of *exhaling* (*smelling*, *breathing*), Matth. 376 (Don. p. 469, Jelf 484); for in ὄζειν τινός the genitive denotes the material or the substance *from which* the ὄζειν emanates.

---

[1] [The constructions of κατηγορεῖν in the N. T. are as follows:—
a. Genitive of person, the charge being either expressed by περί (A. xxiv. 13 only), or left unexpressed; this is the most common construction.
b. Κατηγορεῖν τινά, Rev. xii. 10 (probably).
c. Two genitives *apparently* in A. xxiv. 8, xxv. 11 (compare Dem. *Mid.* 3, παρανόμων αὐτοῦ κατηγορεῖν); but it is probable that ὧν stands for τούτων ἅ (by attraction), so that we have the regular construction κατηγορεῖν τί τινος: hence we need not take πολλά and πόσα in Mk. xv. 3, 4, as semi-adverbial accusatives, but may consider them examples of the same kind.
d. Κατηγορεῖν τι κατά τινος, L. xxiii. 14 (ὧν for τούτων ἅ). In several passages this verb is used absolutely.—Καταμαρτυρεῖν is followed by a genitive of the person,—with τί (Mt. xxvi. 62, Mk. xiv. 60), πόσα Mt. xxvii. 13: καταγινώσκειν by a genitive of the person only. (In part, from A. Buttmann p. 165.)]

[2] How κατηγορεῖν (properly, to affirm or maintain *against* some one) comes to have a genitive of the *person* (Mt. xii. 10, L. xxiii. 2, al.) is obvious; but καταγινώσκειν τινός 1 Jo. iii. 20, 21, is exactly similar (Matth. 378). For ἐγκαλεῖν τινί (Ecclus. xlvi. 19) we find in Rom. viii. 33 ἐγκαλεῖν κατά τινος, which is as easily explained as κατηγορεῖν τίς τινα Maetzn. *Antiph.* 207. ['Εγκαλεῖν τινί occurs in the N. T. also, A. xix. 38, xxiii. 28.]

[3] On this construction see (Sintenis, in the) *Leipz. L. Z.* 1833, I. 1135.

SECT. XXX.] THE GENITIVE. 255

The only N. T. example is one in which the verb is used figuratively, viz. A. ix. 1, ἐμπνέων ἀπειλῆς καὶ φόνου, *breathing of threatening and murder*: compare Aristoph. *Eq.* 437, οὗτος ἤδη κακίας καὶ συκοφαντίας πνεῖ Heliod. 1. 2, Ephraem. 2358. Different from this are φόνον πνέοντες Theocr. 22. 82, and θυμὸν ἐκπνέων Eur. *Bacch.* 620; here the simple object is expressed (*breathing murder, courage*), and the verbs are treated as transitive. (Jelf 540. *Obs.*)

10. There appears to be a somewhat wider departure from the nature of the genitive, when this case is used with

(*a*) Verbs of *feeling*, to denote the object *towards* which the feeling is directed; as σπλαγχνίζεσθαί τινος Mt. xviii. 27. In German, however, we have the genitive construction (*sich jemandes erbarmen*), and in Greek the object was certainly regarded as exerting an influence on the person who feels, and consequently as the point *from which* the feeling proceeds, i.e. from which it is excited. Yet most of these verbs take the accusative, the relation being differently conceived: see § 32. 1, and Hartung p. 20 (Jelf 488).

(*b*) Verbs of *longing* and *desiring* (Matth. 350, Jelf 498 [1]). With these verbs we commonly express the object *towards* or *on* which the desire is fixed. But in ἐπιθυμεῖν τινός, as conceived by the Greeks (if we except those combinations in which the genitive may be considered partitive, as ἐπιθυμεῖν σοφίας, *to desire of wisdom*), the longing and the desire were regarded as proceeding from the object desired, the object sending forth from itself to the subject the incitement to desire. In the N. T. ἐπιθυμεῖν always takes the genitive (a variant being noted in Mt. v. 28 only [2]), as A. xx. 33, ἀργυρίου ἢ χρυσίου ἢ ἱματισμοῦ οὐδενὸς ἐπεθύμησα (1 Tim. iii. 1): so also ὀρέγεσθαι, 1 Tim. iii. 1, εἴ τις ἐπισκοπῆς ὀρέγεται, καλοῦ ἔργου ἐπιθυμεῖ (Isocr. *Demon.* p. 24, ὀρεχθῆναι τῶν καλῶν ἔργων Lucian, *Tim.* 70), H. xi. 16; and ἱμείρεσθαι, 1 Th. ii. 8 [*Rec.*]. In the LXX, also, and in the Apocrypha (Wis. vi. 12, 1 Macc. iv. 17, xi. 11, al.) ἐπιθυμεῖν τινός (ὀρέγεσθαι does not occur) is the usual con-

---

[1] [Compare Don. p. 484, where reasons are given for taking a different view of the nature of this genitive.]
[2] [Here αὐτήν is much better supported than αὐτῆς. Tisch. in ed. 8 omits the pronoun, which is placed within brackets by Westcott and Hort.]

struction; but the verb is already beginning to take an accusative, as a transitive verb, e.g. Ex. xx. 17, Dt. v. 21, vii. 25, Mic. ii. 2, Job xxxiii. 20,—compare Wis. xvi. 3, Ecclus. xvi. 1. Even in earlier Greek the verb ἐπιποθεῖν is always followed by an accusative (because the verb was in thought resolved into ποθεῖν or πόθον ἔχειν ἐπί τι, *towards something*, compare Fritz. *Rom.* I. 31), Plat. *Legg.* 9. 855 e, Diod. S. 17. 101 ; compare 2 C. ix. 14, Ph. i. 8, 1 P. ii. 2 (Jelf *l.c. Obs.* 2). Πεινῆν and διψῆν also, which in Greek writers are regularly followed by a genitive, take an accusative in the N. T. (in a figurative sense, with reference to spiritual blessings); see Mt. v. 6, πεινῶντες καὶ διψῶντες τὴν δικαιοσύνην,[1] and compare φιλοσοφίαν διψ. *Epist. Socr.* 25, 53 (Allat.). The distinction between the two constructions is obvious: διψῆν φιλοσοφίας is *to thirst towards philosophy*, whilst in διψῆν φιλοσοφίαν philosophy is regarded as an indivisible whole, into the possession of which one desires to come. Most closely connected with these verbs are

(c) Verbs of *thinking of, remembering* (Matth. 347, Don. p. 468, Jelf 515): L. xvii. 32, μνημονεύετε τῆς γυναικὸς Λώτ· i. 72, μνησθῆναι διαθήκης· A. xi. 16, 1 C. xi. 2, L. xxii. 61, H. xiii. 3, Jude 17, 2 P. iii. 2. (On the other hand ὑπομιμνήσκειν τινὰ περί τινος, 2 P. i. 12.) We also use the genitive in German to express thinking *of* a thing, for this operation is no other than grasping, taking hold of something with the memory. Analogous to this is *to be forgetful of* a thing: H. xii. 5, ἐκλέλησθε τῆς παρακλήσεως· vi. 10, ἐπιλαθέσθαι τοῦ ἔργου ὑμῶν· xiii. 2, 16. Yet we often find the accusative with ἀναμιμνήσκεσθαι, H. x. 32, 2 C. vii. 15, Mk. xiv. 72, and with μνημονεύειν, Mt. xvi. 9, 1 Th. ii. 9, Rev. xviii. 5 (Matth. *l. c.* Rem. 2, Jelf 515); but rather in the sense of *having a thing present to the mind, holding in remembrance* (Bernh. p. 177). Ἐπιλανθάνεσθαι also takes an accusative in Ph. iii. 14, as sometimes in the LXX (Dt. iv. 9, 2 K. xvii. 38, Is. lxv. 16, Wis. ii. 4, Ecclus. iii. 14 [2]) and even in Attic Greek (Matth. *l. c.*, Jelf 515). This twofold construction rests on a difference in the view which is taken of the

---

[1] In the LXX this verb is found with a dative, Ex. xvii. 3, ἐδίψησεν ὁ λαὸς ὕδατι (*towards* water). In Ps. lxii. 2 also *Vat.* has ἐδίψησί σοι (θεῷ, al. σε) ἡ ψυχή μου.

[2] [In Wis. ii. 4 and Ecclus. iii. 14 ἐπιλ. does not govern an accusative.]

relation, a difference which also shows itself in Latin. Verbs of *making mention of* do not take a genitive in the N. T. :[1] we find instead μνημονεύειν περί, H. xi. 22 ; compare μιμνήσκεσθαι περί Xen. *Cyr.* 1. 6. 12, Plut. *Pœdag.* 9. 27, Tob. iv. 1.

(*d*) The transition is easy to verbs which signify *to care for* or *to neglect* anything (Matth. 348, Jelf 496) : L. x. 34, ἐπεμελήθη αὐτοῦ (1 Tim. iii. 5), 1 C. ix. 9, μὴ τῶν βοῶν μέλει τῷ θεῷ ; (A. xviii. 17,[2] Plut. *Pœdag.* 17. 22), Tit. iii. 8, ἵνα φροντίζωσι καλῶν ἔργων·[3] 1 Tim. v. 8, τῶν ἰδίων οὐ προνοεῖ· 1 Tim. iv. 14, μὴ ἀμέλει τοῦ ἐν σοὶ χαρίσματος (H. ii. 3), H. xii. 5, μὴ ὀλιγώρει παιδείας κυρίου. To this head belongs also φείδεσθαι[4] (Matth. 348, Jelf *l. c.*): A. xx. 29, μὴ φειδόμενοι τοῦ ποιμνίου, *not sparing the flock ;* 1 C. vii. 28, 2 P. ii. 4, al. But μέλει is also used with περί, Mt. xxii. 16, Jo. x. 13, xii. 6, al. (Her. 6. 101, Xen. *Cyr.* 4. 5. 17, *Hiero* 9. 10, al., Wis. xii. 13, 1 Macc. xiv. 43).[5]

(*e*) Lastly, verbs of *ruling* (Matth. 359, Don. p. 476, Jelf 505) take the genitive, as the simple case of dependence,—for the notion of *going before* or *leading* (Hartung p. 14) reduces itself to this : Mk. x. 42, οἱ δοκοῦντες ἄρχειν τῶν ἐθνῶν κατακυριεύουσιν αὐτῶν· Rom. xv. 12 (from the LXX). Compare also κυριεύειν Rom. xiv. 9, 2 C. i. 24, αὐθεντεῖν 1 Tim. ii. 12, καταδυναστεύειν Ja. ii. 6, ἀνθυπατεύειν A. xviii. 12, etc. ; these verbs are merely derivatives from nouns, and the construction resolves itself into κύριόν τινος εἶναι, ἀνθύπατόν τινος εἶναι.[6] Yet βασιλεύειν τινός (Her. 1. 206 and LXX) never occurs in the N. T. ;[7] in its stead we find the Hebraistic expression (על being used with verbs of ruling, Ps. xlvii. 9, Prov. xxviii. 15, Neh. v. 15) βασιλεύειν ἐπί τινος, Mt. ii. 22, Rev. v. 10, or βασ. ἐπί τινα, L. i. 33, xix. 14, 27, Rom. v. 14 : compare Lob. p. 475.

---

[1] [This is a question of interpretation : some of the best commentators take μνημονεύειν in this sense in H. xi. 15, where the verb governs a genitive.]
[2] [If οὐδέν be taken adverbially : but it is surely simpler to consider οὐδέν the subject of ἔμελεν, and τούτων dependent on οὐδέν (Jelf 496. *Obs.* 2).]
[3] [Similarly μεριμνήσει ἑαυτῆς, Mt. vi. 34.]
[4] In Latin, parcere *alicui.* In the Greek φείδεσθαι, if we may judge from the construction, there is rather the notion of restraining oneself *from*, sibi temperare a. In the LXX, however, this verb is also construed with the dative and with prepositions.
[5] Compare Strange in *Jahns Archiv* II. 400.
[6] [In A. xviii. 12, just quoted, the preferable reading is ἀνθυπάτου ὄντος.]
[7] [In Mt. ii. 22 we should probably read βασιλεύει τῆς Ἰουδαίας.]

Verbs of *buying* and *selling* take the genitive of the price (Bernh. p. 177 sq., Madv. 65, Don. p. 478, Jelf 519): Mt. x. 29, οὐχὶ δύο στρουθία ἀσσαρίου πωλεῖται· xxvi. 9, ἠδύνατο τοῦτο πραθῆναι πολλοῦ· xx. 13, Mk. xiv. 5, A. v. 8 (Plat. *Apol.* 20 b), 1 C. vi. 20 (compare Rev. vi. 6), Bar. i. 10, iii. 30 (but in Mt. xxvii. 7, ἠγόρασαν ἐξ αὐτῶν, scil. ἀργυρίων· A. i. 18), A. vii. 16, ὠνήσατο τιμῆς ἀργυρίου (with ἐκ in Palæph. 46. 3, 4). Under this head comes also Jude 11, τῇ πλάνῃ τοῦ Βαλαὰμ μισθοῦ ἐξεχύθησαν, *for reward* (Xen. *Cyr.* 3. 2. 7, Plat. *Rep.* 9. 575 b). This construction with ἐκ, and still more a consideration of the primary meaning of the genitive, might lead us to refer this genitive of price to the notion of *proceeding from*, since that which is bought etc. for a price, proceeds for us, so to speak, out of the price (or equivalent) which is given for it. But it is probably nearer the truth to think of the genitive of exchange, and of such expressions as ἀλλάσσειν τί τινος (Hartung p. 15, Matth. 364, Don. *l. c.*, Jelf 520); for the object bought or sold is set over against so much money,[1] and hence in Greek ἀντί is the preposition of price.[2] The construction ἀλλάσσειν, διαλλάσσειν τί τινος, does not itself occur in the Greek Bible: in Rom. i. 23 we find instead the more vivid phrase ἀλλάσσειν τι ἔν τινι, by which in Ps. cv. 20 the LXX render the Hebrew בְּ הֵמִיר. The nearest approach to this is found in ἀλλάσσειν τί τινι, which occurs Her. 7. 152 and often in the LXX (Ex. xiii. 13, Lev. xxvii. 10, al.). Words of *valuing, estimation*, etc., belong to the same category as verbs of buying and selling, and, like them, govern the genitive,—*to esteem worthy of* a thing (Krüg. p. 53, Don. *l. c.*, Jelf 521): compare ἄξιος Mt. iii. 8, x. 10, Rom. i. 32; ἀξιοῦν 2 Th. i. 11, 1 Tim. v. 17, H. iii. 3, and frequently.

11. The genitive of place and of time: as Æsch. *Prom.* 714 λαιᾶς χειρὸς σιδηροτέκτονες οἰκοῦσι Χάλυβες, *on the left hand*[3] (Her. 5. 77), Xen. *Eph.* 5. 13 ἐκείνης τῆς ἡμέρας, *on that day*, Philostr. *Her.* 9. 3 sq. χειμῶνος *in winter*, Thuc. 3. 104 (Matth. 377, Don. p. 471, Jelf 522 sq.). This genitive is not governed directly by any particular word, but its relation to the construction of the sentence is quite clear; and there is in it nothing alien to the primary meaning of the genitive case.[4] The N. T. writers almost always insert a preposition: their use of

---

[1] [The German preposition *gegen* (over against) is used with verbs of buying, etc., in the sense *for, in exchange for*, and thus closely resembles ἀντί.]

[2] A different view will be found in Herm. *Opusc.* I. 179. See on the other hand Prüfer, *De Græca et Lat. Declinatione* 98 sq. [Lünemann adds: compare H. xii. 2, 16.]

[3] [In the phrases which are translated in this section Winer is able to imitate the Greek construction by using the German genitive: with τοῦ λοιποῦ he compares the German *des weitern*.—Compare Mätzner, *Eng. Lang.* I. 389 sqq., Morris, *Hist. Outl.* pp. 193, 196.]

[4] Herm. *Vig.* p. 881, Hartung p. 32 sqq.

the simple genitive of place or time (which is properly a partitive genitive) is almost confined to certain standing formulas: thus we often meet with νυκτός *by night*, also μέσης νυκτός Mt. xxv. 6, ἡμέρας καὶ νυκτός L. xviii. 7, A. ix. 24 (Xen. *An.* 2. 6. 7); χειμῶνος Mt. xxiv. 20 (connected with σαββάτῳ); ὄρθρου βαθέος L. xxiv. 1; μὴ εὑρόντες, ποίας (ὁδοῦ) εἰςενέγκωσιν αὐτόν, L. v. 19, *by what way*, ἐκείνης (scil. ὁδοῦ) L. xix. 4; τοῦ λοιποῦ G. vi. 17 (Thuc. 4. 98). For this reason—because the use of the genitive of time is limited in the N. T. to simple and familiar formulas—we cannot render ἡμερῶν τεσσαράκοντα in A. i. 3 (with the reading of D) *within forty days* (Matth. 377. 2. b): see above 2. *a.* To express this meaning Luke would certainly have used a preposition.

Rev. xvi. 7, ἤκουσα τοῦ θυσιαστηρίου λέγοντος, must certainly not be brought in here (*I heard one speaking from the altar*,—compare Soph. *El.* 78, Bernh. p. 137).[1] In accordance with analogous sentences in ver. 5 and vi. 3, 5, the words must be rendered, *I heard the altar speak* (see Bengel *in loc.*); and this prosopopœia well suits the strangely mysterious character of these visions: see De Wette. The other reading, ἤκουσα ἄλλου ἐκ τοῦ θυσιαστ. λέγοντος, is a palpable correction. On Τιβεριάδος, Jo. vi. 1, see above, page 239.

Rem. The genitive absolute is of frequent occurrence in the historical style of the N. T. In its original application this is not an absolute case in the proper sense of the word, but depends on the use of the genitive for definitions of time (compare Hartung p. 31 [2]): hence the corresponding absolute case in Latin is the ablative. It is however used with a more extended reference, especially to assign the cause and the condition,—both relations which are expressed by the genitive. The only point needing remark here is, that a genitive absolute is sometimes used where the nature of the following verb would lead us to expect a different oblique case: L. xvii. 12 [*Rec.*], εἰσερχομένου αὐτοῦ . . . ἀπήντησαν αὐτῷ, xxii. 10, 53, xviii. 40, ἐγγίσαντος αὐτοῦ ἐπηρώτησεν αὐτόν· Mk. xi. 27, A. iv. 1, xxi. 17, 2 C. xii. 21,[3] Jo. iv. 51. Examples of this kind are also common in Greek authors, partly because when the sentence was commenced the principal verb was not yet determined on, partly because the more regular construction would in many cases render the expression clumsy: compare Her. 1. 41, Thuc. 1. 114, 3. 13, Xen. *An.* 2. 4.

---

[1] Erfurdt, Soph. *Œd. R.* 142, Buttm. *Philoct.* 115.
[2] [Compare Jelf 541, Don. p. 485.]
[3] [With the reading ἐλθόντος μου ταπεινώσῃ με: in the later MSS. the construction is made regular. So in Rev. xvii. 8, quoted below, *Rec.* has the more regular βλέποντες, for βλεπόντων (Tisch., al.). On this irregularity see Jelf 710, and especially A. Buttmann p. 314 sqq.]

24, *Mem.* 4. 8. 5, Pol. 4. 49. 1, Xen. Eph. 4. 5, Heliod. 2. 30. 113.[1] In 2 C. iv. 18 also, for αἰώνιον βάρος δόξης κατεργάζεται ἡμῖν, μὴ σκοπούντων ἡμῶν τὰ βλεπόμενα, Paul might have written μὴ σκοποῦσι τὰ βλ. ; but the former construction brings out the participial member with more prominence and force : compare Xen. *Cyr.* 6. 1. 37. Lastly, we find exceptional instances of the use of a genitive absolute where the principal sentence has the same subject (in the nominative) as the subordinate sentence ; as Mt. i. 18, μνηστευθείσης τῆς μητρὸς αὐτοῦ Μαρίας τῷ Ἰωσήφ, πρὶν ἢ συνελθεῖν αὐτούς, εὑρέθη ἐν γαστρὶ ἔχουσα, where the writer probably had in his mind another mode of finishing the sentence. So perhaps in Rev. xvii. 8. Such instances as *these* are rare in Greek authors : see however Her. 5. 81, Plat. *Rep.* 8. 547 b, Pol. 31. 17. 1 ; and compare Poppo, *Thuc.* I. 119 sq., Wannowski p. 61 sqq. In the LXX see Gen. xliv. 4, Ex. iv. 21, v. 20, xiv. 18 : compare *Acta Apocr.* pp. 68, 69, Epiphan. *Vit.* pp. 326, 340, 346 (in the 2d volume of Epiphan. *Opp.:* ed. Colon.), and in Latin, Suet. *Tib.* 31. In all these examples the genitive absolute is employed as a regularly established construction, the grammatical origin of which was no longer considered.[2]

Section XXXI.

THE DATIVE.

In Greek the dative is a more comprehensive case than in Latin, representing, as it does, the Latin ablative as well as the Latin dative.[3] In general, however, its connexion with the sentence is not so close and necessary as that of the accusative or even of the genitive : its office is merely to complete and

---

[1] Wyttenbach, Plut. *Mor.* II. 21, Schæf. *Apollon. Rh.* II. 171, and *Demosth.* II. 202, Poppo, *Thuc.* I. 2, 119, Siebelis, *Pausan.* II. 8, Hoffmann, *Pr. de Casib. Absol.* p. 1. Compare the Latin ablatives absolute in Cic. *Phil.* 11. 10, *Fam.* 15. 4. 18, Cæsar, *Bell. Gall.* 5. 4, *Civ.* 1. 36, 2. 19, 3. 21.

[2] [Bp. Ellicott has some general remarks on the N. T. use of the genitive with the noun, in his Essay on " Scripture, and its interpretation " (*Aids to Faith*, p. 462 sq.). Besides the genitive of apposition or identity (§ 59. 8. a), of remoter reference (§ 30. 2), of quality (§ 34. 3. b), he specifies "a widely extended use" of this case "to denote the ideas of origination (Rom. iv. 13, δικαιοσύνη πίστεως), and not unfrequently of definite agency (2 Th. ii. 13, ἁγιασμὸς Πνεύματος),"—upon this see especially his note on 1 Th. i. 6 ; and a smaller class of examples " in which ideas, so to speak, of ethical substance or contents appear to predominate (E. i. 13, ἀληθείας and σωτηρίας)." See also Green, *Gr.* pp. 87-98, Webster, *Synt.* pp. 67-77, for notices of many passages.]

[3] Compare Herm. *Emend. Rat.* p. 140. [On the radical force of the dative see Don. p. 486, Jelf 471, 586, Clyde, *Gr. Synt.* p. 35. On the dative in the N. T. see Green pp. 98-102, Webster, *Synt.* pp. 76-79, Ellicott *u.s.*]

extend, by indicating the object (in most cases the *personal* object) at which an action is aimed, which an action concerns, but which is not directly affected by the action. Hence we often find this case in conjunction with the accusative of the object, as in 2 C. ix. 2, προθυμία ἦν καυχῶμαι Μακεδόσιν A. xxii. 25, προέτειναν αὐτὸν τοῖς ἱμᾶσιν (see Kühnöl),[1] xxiv. 5, Jo. vi. 13. In a loose application the dative is used (of *things*) to denote whatever accompanies the action, as motive, power, circumstance (of time or place), etc.

1. We first consider the dative as the case of reference (of the more remote object, as it is usually expressed), both in its connexion with transitive verbs—as διδόναι (δωρεῖσθαί) τί τινι, γράφειν τί τινι (2 C. ii. 3), εὐαγγελίζεσθαί τινί τι (L. ii. 10, 2 C. xi. 7), ὀφείλειν τινί τι (Mt. xviii. 28, Rom. xiii. 8, compare Rom. i. 14, viii. 12, but contrast xv. 27), ὁμοιοῦν τινά τινι (Mt. vii. 24, xi. 16), καταλλάσσειν τινά τινι (2 C. v. 18), ἐγείρειν θλῖψιν τοῖς δεσμοῖς (Ph. i. 17), all which instances are entirely free from difficulty;—and especially as joined with intransitive verbs and adjectives allied to these. The force of the dative is more or less clear.[2]

(*a*) In ἀκολουθεῖν τινί, ἐγγίζειν, κολλᾶσθαί, στοιχεῖν (Rom. iv. 12, al.), δεδέσθαι (Rom. vii. 2, 1 C. vii. 27), ἐντυγχάνειν τινί, etc.; also in εὔχεσθαί τινι, A. xxvi. 29. (Jelf 522 sq.)

(*b*) In μεριμνᾶν τινί[3] (Mt. vi. 25), ὀργίζεσθαί (Mt. v. 22), μετριοπαθεῖν τινί (H. v. 2), μέμφεσθαί (H. viii. 8,[4] see Krüg. p. 25, Jelf 589), φθονεῖν G. v. 26. (Jelf 596, 601.)

(*c*) In πιστεύειν τινί, πεποιθέναι,[5] ἀπιστεῖν, ἀπειθεῖν, ὑπακούειν, ὑπήκοός, ἐναντίος, etc. (Jelf 593.)

(*d*) In προςκυνεῖν τινί, λατρεύειν (not in Ph. iii. 3), δουλοῦν. (Jelf 596.)

---

[1] [Unless τοῖς ἱμᾶσιν be taken as instrument, see Alford. Against Kühnöl's rendering of προτείνειν (*tradere*) see Bornem. *Luc*. p. 181 sq., Meyer *in loc*.]

[2] [The references in the text to Jelf's *Gr*. apply to most of the words in the various classes; for εὔχεσθαι, ἐντυγχάνειν, see 589; ἐναντίος, 601; ξενίζεσθαι, 607; κοινωνεῖν, 588; ὁμιλεῖν, 590. In Donaldson's classification, *c*, *d*, *e* (with εὔχεσθαι, but not ἐναντίος), would come under the "dative of the recipient" (pp. 493–495); χρῆσθαι, "instrumental dative" (p. 491); most of the other words under the "dative of coincidence or contingency" (p. 486 sqq.).]

[3] [Also μεριμνήσει τὰ περὶ ὑμῶν, Ph. ii. 20 (1 C. vii. 32); μεριμνήσει ἑαυτῆς, Mt. vi. 34, like φροντίζειν τινός, § 30. 10. (A. Buttm. p. 186.)]

[4] [Here αὐτούς is strongly supported: some (e. g. Bleek, Kurtz) who read αὐτοῖς join it with λέγει.—The dative is similarly used with ἐπιτιμᾶν, ἐγκαλεῖν, ἐμβριμᾶσθαι: A. Buttm. p. 177.]

[5] [The dative with ἐλπίζειν in Mt. xii. 21 either follows the analogy of these verbs (A. Buttm. p. 176), or belongs to No. 6 *c* (so Meyer).]

(e) In ἀρέσκειν τινί [εὐαρεστεῖν, H. xi. 5], ἀρκεῖν (Mt. xxv. 9, 2 C. xii. 9), ἀρκετός and ἱκανός, Mt. vi. 34, 1 P. iv. 3, 2 C. ii. 6. (Jelf 594, 596.)

(f) Then in ξενίζεσθαί τινι, 1 P. iv. 12 (Thuc. 4. 85), *be astonished at a thing* (the astonishment is directed towards the thing); ἀπολογεῖσθαί (2 C xii. 19, A. xix. 33, compare 1 P. iii. 15), and διαλέγεσθαί τινι, A. xvii. 2, xviii. 19; διακατελέγχεσθαί τινι, A. xviii. 28 (δογματίζειν τινί, compare Col. ii. 20); where the dative indicates the person to whom the conversation or defence is addressed. Likewise ὁμολογεῖν and ἐξομολογεῖσθαί τινι (Ja. v. 16), even with the signification *praise* (הוֹדָה לְ), L. x. 21, Rom. xiv. 11, H. xiii. 15; for every act of praise to God is a confession made to Him that we acknowledge Him as the High and Glorious One. (Jelf 589, 594.)

Once, in Rev. xix. 5, the best MSS. have the construction αἰνεῖν τινί (compare Ecclus. li. 12): probably הוֹדָה לְ was before the writer's mind,—unless indeed αἰνεῖν is here construed *ad sensum*, as equivalent to εἰπεῖν αἴνεσιν.

(g) In κρίνεσθαί (Mt. v. 40) and διακρίνεσθαί τινι Jude 9 (Jer. xv. 10), *go to law, contend against* or *with*. (Jelf 601.)

(h) Somewhat differently in the verbs of *equality* or *likeness*; as Mt. xxiii. 27, ὁμοιάζετε τάφοις κεκονιαμένοις· vi. 8, H. ii. 17, 2 C. x. 12; compare ὅμοιός, ἴσος τινί, Mt. xi. 16, Jo. ix. 9, 1 Jo. iii. 2, A. xiv. 15, Mt. xx. 12, Ph. ii. 6[1] (once ὅμοιός τινος, Jo. viii. 55,—Matth. 386, comp. § 30. 4): also in verbs of *participating in*, 1 Tim. v. 22, 1 P. iv. 13 (compare L. v. 10, Rom. xv. 27), though these verbs more commonly take the genitive (§ 30.8): similarly ὁμιλεῖν τινί, A. xxiv. 26. (Jelf 594.)

(i) In the verbs of *using*, as χρῆσθαι, A. xxvii. 17, 1 C. ix. 12, 15. Once however (in 1 C. vii. 31) this verb has an accusative in the best MSS.,[2] as sometimes in the later writers, e.g. Malal. p. 5, Theophan. p. 314, Böckh, *Corp. Inscript.* II. 405, (but not Xen. *Ages.* 11. 11), compare Bornem. *Acta* p. 222: in A. xxvii. 17 there is little authority for the accusative. (Jelf 591.)

---

[1] Comp. Fritzsche, Arist. *Amic.* p. 15: [on κοινωνεῖν, Green, *Gr.* p. 102.]
[2] [A. Buttm. (p. 181 sq.) suggests that the accusative may have been occasioned by the verb which immediately follows (καταχρώμενοι), κόσμον being regarded as in some measure dependent on both verbs (ἀπὸ κοινοῦ): similarly Meyer. Καταχρῆσθαι takes an accusative in later writers.]

(*k*) In στήκειν (ἑστηκέναι) τινί, *stand fast to a thing* (2 C. i. 24, G. v. 1 *v. l.*), or to a person, Rom. xiv. 4.[1] (Jelf 590.[2])

Προσκυνεῖν (*reverence, worship*) is always followed by a dative in Matthew, Mark, and Paul[3] (for Mt. iv. 10 is a quotation from Dt. vi. 13); in the rest of the N. T. we find sometimes the dative (Jo. ix. 38, A. vii. 43, H. i. 6, Rev. iv. 10, vii. 11, xiii. 4, al.), sometimes the accusative (L. iv. 8, xxiv. 52, Jo. iv. 23, Rev. ix. 20, xiv. 11): similarly γονυπετεῖν τινά in Mk. (i. 40) x. 17, Mt. xvii. 14 (and sometimes λατρεύειν τινά: Matth. 392. Rem., Jelf 553. *c*). The construction of προσκυνεῖν with a dative is peculiar to later Greek (Lob. p. 463).[4]— Χαίρειν, which by the Greeks is more frequently construed with the dative (Fritz. *Rom.* III. 78 sq.), as it is sometimes in the LXX (Pr. xvii. 19, compare Bar. iv. 37), has never this construction in the N. T., being usually accompanied by ἐπί *over*: on Rom. xii. 12 see below, no. 7: in 1 C. xiii. 6 the dative depends on σύν.—The phrases ἀποθανεῖν τῇ ἁμαρτίᾳ, τῷ νόμῳ (Rom. vi. 2, G. ii. 19), θανατοῦσθαι τῷ νόμῳ (Rom. vii. 4), νεκρὸν εἶναι τῇ ἁμ. (vi. 11), opposed to ζῆν τινί (τῷ θεῷ Rom. vi. 10, compare 1 P. iv. 10[5]), signify *to have died* or *to be dead to sin, to the law* (for sin, for the law); compare Rom. vii. 4, εἰς τὸ γενέσθαι ὑμᾶς ἑτέρῳ· 1 P. ii. 24, ἀπογενέσθαι τῇ ἁμαρτίᾳ. In the same way we find in Rom. vi. 20 ἐλεύθεροι τῇ δικαιοσύνῃ, in antithesis to δουλοῦσθαι τῇ δικ. (ver. 18, compare ver. 19, 20): *when ye were servants of sin ye were free with reference to righteousness,* to righteousness ye were in the relation of free men. (Jelf 599.)

We must also recognise a *dativus rei* of direction in the phrase κατακρίνειν τινὰ θανάτῳ, Mt. xx. 18 (compare 2 P. ii. 6[6]), *to sentence some one to death*, i. e. to assign to death by a sentence. This con-

---

[1] [The reading of G. v. 1 is most fully discussed by Lightfoot (*Gal.* p. 197), who—with most recent editors—rejects ᾖ, and takes στήκετε absolutely. If ᾖ be retained, it is probably a dative of *reference to* (no. 6), see Ellicott *in loc.*: similarly in 2 C. i. 24 (Meyer). In Rom. xiv. 4 the dative appears rather to come under no. 4. *b*, than to stand in close connexion with the verb.]

[2] [On the dative with compound verbs, see § 52.]

[3] [Excluding O. T. quotations (with which A. vii. 43 may be reckoned, for the words προσκυνεῖν αὐτοῖς, though not found in Am. v. 26, seem to be a reminiscence of other familiar passages), we find 56 examples of this word in the N. T. In 16 the word is used absolutely; in two (Jo. iv. 22) the omission of the demonstrative makes the construction doubtful. In the remaining passages, the dative (probably) occurs 28, the accusative 10 times. Hence in the N. T., as in the LXX, the dative construction is the more common. Προσκυνεῖν occurs most frequently in St. Matthew's Gospel and the Revelation. In the former book we find the dative only; in the latter the dative seems to occur 13, the accusative 6 times. The remaining examples are Mk. xv. 19, Jo. iv. 21, 23, ix. 38, 1 C. xiv. 25 (dative); Mk. v. 6, L. xxiv. 52, Jo. iv. 23, 24 (accusative). It seems almost impossible to believe that in a single verse (Jo. iv. 23) this word can have both constructions without any variation of meaning: at all events we may recognise that the accusative expresses a connexion between verb and object closer than that expressed by the dative construction. Compare p. 248, note [1], p. 263, note [3].]

[4] Compare Bos, *Exercitatt. Philol.* p. 1 sqq., Kypke, *Obs.* I. 7 sq.

[5] [Perhaps intended for 1 P. iv. 6: the reference is wrong as it stands.]

[6] [That is "condemned them *to* overthrow" (Huther, Alford, al.).]

struction is not found in Greek writers, who use κατακρίνειν τινὰ θανάτου, or θάνατον (Matth. 370. Rem. 3, Heupel, Mark. 285), or κατακρ. τινὶ θάνατον, Her. 6. 85 (to adjudge death to).[1] An analogous phrase is καταδικάζειν τινὰ θανάτῳ (Lob. p. 485). Compare also ἔνοχος τῇ κρίσει, Mt. v. 21, 22, *subject to the judgment* (§ 30. 8): compare Bleek, *Hebr.* II. i. 340.

2. Most closely connected with this is the dative which is dependent on εἶναι (ὑπάρχειν) and γίνεσθαι,—not on any predicate joined with these verbs; for ἐστί or γίνεταί μοι φόβος can only mean, that the φόβον εἶναι or γίνεσθαι applies to or concerns me.

(*a*) Without a predicate εἶναί τινι expresses *belonging to* (possession), γίνεσθαί τινι denotes *becoming the property of*: L. ii. 7, οὐκ ἦν αὐτοῖς τόπος, *they had not room;* A. viii. 21, x. 6, iii. 6, xxi. 23, Mt. xviii. 12, L. i. 14, ἔσται χαρά σοι· Mt. xvi. 22, οὐ μὴ ἔσται σοι τοῦτο, *this will not befall thee;* A. xx. 3, 16, ii. 43, ἐγένετο πάσῃ ψυχῇ φόβος, *fear fell on;* Rom. xi. 25. With an ellipsis, 1 C. vi. 13, v. 12, 2 C. vi. 14, Jo. ii. 4 (Krüg. p. 69, Jelf 597).

(*b*) With a predicate (usually a substantive) εἶναι or γίνεσθαί τινι denotes what quality the thing spoken of has or receives *for some one*, either objectively or subjectively (in his opinion): 1 C. viii. 9, μήπως ἡ ἐξουσία . . . . πρόσκομμα γένηται τοῖς ἀσθενέσιν· i. 18, ὁ λόγος ὁ τοῦ σταυροῦ τοῖς μὲν ἀπολλυμένοις μωρία ἐστίν κ.τ.λ., ix. 2, xiv. 22, Rom. ii. 14, vii. 13, 1 C. iv. 3, ix. 3, Ph. i. 28 (Jelf 600, 602). But to express *turn to, prove* (Krüg. p. 69), the N. T. writers commonly use εἶναι or γίνεσθαι εἴς τι.

3. Substantives derived from verbs which govern a dative are sometimes followed by this case, instead of the ordinary genitive: 2 C. ix. 12, εὐχαριστίαι τῷ θεῷ (but not in ver. 11), somewhat like εὐχαὶ τοῖς θεοῖς Plat. *Legg.* 7. 800 a[2] (Jelf 588, 597, Don. p. 495). Compare also τὸ εἰωθὸς αὐτῷ, L. iv. 16, A. xvii. 2 (Plat. *Legg.* 658 e, τὸ ἦθος ἡμῖν), and τὸ εὐπάρεδρον τῷ κυρίῳ, 1 C. vii. 35.[3] A different case from this is L. vii. 12, υἱὸς μονογενὴς τῇ μητρί, *a son who for the mother was the only*

---

[1] In the O. T. also this construction is unknown. One of the parallels cited by Bretschneider is Sus. 41, κατέκριναν αὐτὴν ἀποθανεῖν; in the other, ver. 48, the verb is used absolutely, κατεκρίνατε θυγατέρα Ἰσραήλ.

[2] See Wyttenb. Plut. *Mor.* I. 154 (Lips.); Stallb. Plat. *Euthyphr.* 101, *Rep.* I. 372; Ast, Plat. *Polit.* 451; Bornem. Xen. *Cyr.* 374; Fritz. *Mark* p. 63.

[3] [Also Jo. xii. 13, 2 C. xi. 28 (probably).]

SECT. XXXI.]   THE DATIVE.   265

son (thus not strictly for the genitive: compare Tob. iii. 15, μονογενὴς τῷ πατρί· Jud. xi. 34): this must not be confounded with the dative of relationship (compare L. v. 10, Rom. iv. 12).[1] On Rom. iv. 12 see § 63. II. 1.

In Mt. xxvii. 7 also, ἠγόρασαν τὸν ἀγρὸν . . . . εἰς ταφὴν τοῖς ξένοις, *for burial for strangers*, the dative belongs to the substantive: comp. Strabo 17. 807, πρὸς ἐπίδειξιν τοῖς ξένοις.[2] But in 1 C. vii. 28 the dative may be joined with the verb of the sentence. See however Bernhardy p. 88.

4. Without direct dependence on the notion of a verb or noun, the dative may indicate the *reference* which an action has *to* some one; as in 2 C. ii. 13, οὐκ ἔσχηκα ἄνεσιν τῷ πνεύματί μου *for my spirit* (1 C. vii. 28), or in L. xviii. 31, πάντα τὰ γεγραμμένα . . . τῷ υἱῷ τοῦ ἀνθρώπου *what was written for Him* (that it should be fulfilled in Him),[3] Mt. xiii. 14, Jude 14: compare also Mt. xiii. 52, Ph. i. 27, 1 Tim. i. 9, Rev. xxi. 2.

Especially deserving of notice are

(*a*) The dative of *opinion* or *judgment* (compare above, no. 2), as in Plat. *Phæd.* 101 d, εἴ σοι ἀλλήλοις ξυμφωνεῖ ἢ διαφωνεῖ; Soph. *Œd. Col.* 1446. So in the phrases ἀστεῖος τῷ θεῷ A. vii. 20, and δυνατὰ τῷ θεῷ 2 C. x. 4;[4] see also 1 C. ix. 2. Compare Krüg. p. 71 sq.[5] (Don. p. 495, Jelf 600).

(*b*) The dative of *interest*,—2 C. v. 13, εἴτε ἐξέστημεν, θεῷ· εἴτε σωφρονοῦμεν, ὑμῖν (Rom. xiv. 6, 1 C. xiv. 22),—or more definitely, the *dativus commodi* and *incommodi*: Jo. iii. 26, ᾧ σὺ μεμαρτύρηκας, *for whom*, in favour of whom (L. iv. 22, Rom. x. 2, 2 C. ii. 1, comp. Xen. *Mem.* 1. 2. 21); on the other hand, Mt. xxiii. 31, μαρτυρεῖτε ἑαυτοῖς, ὅτι υἱοί ἐστε κ.τ.λ., *against yourselves* (compare Ja. v. 3). Compare further H. vi. 6, Jude 1, Rom. xiii. 2:[6] on Rev. viii. 3 see Ewald. In E. v. 19, however,

---

[1] Buttm. *Philoct.* p. 102 sq., Boisson. *Nic.* p. 271, Ast, Plat. *Polit.* 451, 519, and *Legg.* p. 9. [Comp. Riddell, Plat. *Apol.* p. 126 sq.]
[2] See Schoem. *Isæus* p. 264, Krüg. p. 80.
[3] [Jelf (588. 2) refers this to the construction of verbs which denote that "something is allotted to any one, awaits any one, etc." (Green p. 100): A. Buttmann (p. 178) joins the dative with both verbs: "if the word belonged to γίγραμ. only, we should have had ἐπὶ τῷ υἱῷ, as in Jo. xii. 16." Bleek, Meyer, and others agree with Winer.]
[4] We should have a similar example in Ja. ii. 5, if (with Lachmann and Tischendorf) we read τοὺς πτωχοὺς τῷ κόσμῳ.
[5] Compare Wyttenb. *Phæd. l. c.*, Erfurdt, Soph. *Œd. R.* 615.
[6] [Jelf 598, 601, Don. p. 494.]

λαλοῦντες ἑαυτοῖς (ἀλλήλοις) ψαλμοῖς κ.τ.λ., we have a simple dative of direction, *speaking to one another* etc.

5. From these examples it is obvious that the dative is akin to the prepositions εἰς (Engelhardt, Plat. *Menex.* p. 360 [1]) and πρός (compare Ast, Plat. *Legg.* p. 558), just as the genitive to the prepositions ἐκ and ἀπό. Hence in many phrases εἰς or πρός with an accusative is used instead of the dative. Thus we find not only the familiar example λέγειν τινί and πρός τινα (the former is usually, almost constantly, preferred by Matthew and Mark [2]),—compare κράζειν τινί, Rev. vii. 2, xiv. 15, φωνεῖν τινί, Rev. xiv. 18,—but also εὔχεσθαι θεῷ A. xxvi. 29 (Xen. *Cyr.* 5. 2. 12, Demosth. *Conon* 729 c, Plut. *Coriol.* 9, Xen. *Eph.* 4. 3), and εὔχεσθαι πρὸς θεόν 2 C. xiii. 7 (Xen. *Mem.* 1. 3. 2), compare Ph. iv. 6 ; βοᾶν τινί L. xviii. 7, and βοᾶν πρός τινα Hos. vii. 14; ψεύδεσθαί τινι [3] A. v. 4, Ps. xvii. 45, lxxvii. 36, Jer. v. 12 (not in Greek authors), and ψεύδ. πρός τινα (*to lie towards, belie, some one*) Xen. *An.* 1. 3. 5 ; καταλλάττειν τινί and πρός τινα, Xen. *Vectig.* 6. 8, Joseph. *Antt.* 14. 11. 3 ; [4] εὐδοκεῖν εἴς τινα 2 P. i. 17, and εὐδ. τινί in Greek authors [5] (Pol. 4. 22. 7, 1 Macc. i. 43) ; μάχεσθαί τινι Xen. *An.* 4. 5. 12, Plat. *Rep.* 3. 407 a, and πρός τινα Jo. vi. 52, *Iliad* 17. 98, Plat. *Lach.* 191 d, Luc. *Conv.* 42, and often (also in the LXX) ; [6] ὁμιλεῖν τινί and πρός τινα, L. xxiv. 14, Xen. *Mem.* 4. 3. 2. To the N. T. writers the prepositional construction was also naturally suggested by the more expressive and vivid phraseology of their mother tongue ; and hence we sometimes find εἰς where Greek writers would have been content with the simple *dativus commodi* or

---

[1] In modern Greek the accusative with εἰς very commonly serves as a periphrasis for the dative, even in its simplest relations ; as λέγω εἰς τὸν φίλον μου, *dico amico meo* (towards my friend): see Von Lüdemann, *Lehrb.* p. 90. [Sophocles, *Gr.* p. 151, Mullach, *Vulg.* p. 332. The dative has in great measure disappeared from modern Greek: see Mullach pp. 151, 327 sq., Clyde, p. 30 sq.]

[2] See Schulz, *Parab. v. Verwalt.* p. 38. [I have substituted "former" for "latter," which is a manifest mistake. The use of πρός with the accus. after λέγειν and other verbs of speaking is very common in St. Luke and St. John : see Gersdorf pp. 180, 186, Davidson, *Introd.* p. 194.]

[3] [On ψεύδεσθαί τινα (" actual deception by falsehood ") and ψ. τινι (" address directed to a person in terms of falsehood ") see Green, *Gr.* p. 100.]

[4] Col. i. 20, ἀποκαταλλ. εἰς, would be an analogous example, if this were not a pregnant construction, used designedly : see Meyer *in loc.*

[5] [And in 2 Thess. ii. 12, according to the best MSS.]

[6] Thus besides παραβάλλειν τί τινι (Her. 4. 198) we also find παρ. τι πρός τι (Joseph. *Ap.* 2. 15). Different still is Mk. iv. 30, ἐν ποίᾳ παραβολῇ παραβάλωμεν τὴν βασιλείαν τοῦ θεοῦ (see Fritz.), but the readings vary. ['Εν τίνι αὐτὴν παραβολῇ θῶμεν is adopted by Fritz. and by recent editors.]

incommodi: A. xxiv. 17, ἐλεημοσύνας ποιήσων εἰς τὸ ἔθνος μου· L. vii. 30, τὴν βουλὴν τοῦ θεοῦ ἠθέτησαν εἰς ἑαυτούς, *to their own detriment* (as indeed εἰς also signifies *contra*[1]). On the other hand, κηρύττειν or εὐαγγελίζ. εἰς (Mk. xiii. 10, 1 P. i. 25, L. xxiv. 47,—Paus. 8. 5. 8) must be rendered *proclaim* or *preach amongst them*, since a plural noun always follows : in Mt. xx. 1, μισθοῦσθαι εἰς τὸν ἀμπελῶνα is not *hire for* but *hire into* the vineyard ; and there is the same pregnancy of expression in Mk. viii. 19, τ. ἄρτους ἔκλασα εἰς τοὺς πεντακισχιλίους, *have broken* (and divided) *amongst* etc. Similarly in Mt. v. 22, ἔνοχος εἰς τὴν γέενναν, *liable* (to come, to be cast) *into the Gehenna*: contrast τῇ κρίσει, τῷ συνεδρίῳ.[2] In Rom. viii. 18 also τὴν μέλλουσαν δόξαν ἀποκαλυφθῆναι εἰς ἡμᾶς is an abbreviated expression (see Fritz. *in loc.*[3]), like the Hebrew נִגְלָה אֶל־, 1 S. iii. 7. Lastly, we cannot say that a preposition is used instead of a dative in the phrase ὠφέλιμος πρός τι 1 Tim. iv. 8, 2 Tim. iii. 16 (ὠφέλιμος εἰς Xen. *Œc.* 5. 11, compare χρήσιμος εἰς Wis. xiii. 11), or in εὔθετος εἴς τι L. xiv. 35 (Dion. H. *De Thuc.* 55. 3, εὔθετος πρός Pol. 26. 5. 6, Diod. S. 5. 37); the expressions *useful*, *suitable to* or *for a thing*, are perfectly correct, as the dative would be more fitly used in reference to the *person*: compare however L. ix. 62 *v. l.*[4]

The combination πιστεύειν εἰς or ἐπί τινα (A. ix. 42, xxii. 19) obviously means in Christian phraseology more than πιστεύειν τινι (credere, confidere alicui), and must be taken as a pregnant expression,—*believing, to give oneself up to some one, with faith to declare adherence to some one,* fide se ad aliquem applicare.[5] Also

---

[1] In L. viii. 43 *Rec.* has εἰς ἰατροὺς προσαναλώσασα ὅλον τὸν βίον, but the best MSS. have ἰατροῖς, and this reading is to be preferred, as εἰς ἰατροὺς is an evident correction : this verb, indeed, is commonly construed with εἰς in Greek writers (Xen. *Cyr.* 2. 4. 9, Æl. 14. 32).

[2] [A. Buttmann (p. 170) maintains that it is most natural to regard εἰς τήν here as a periphrasis for the dative, the change from τῇ κρίσει, τῷ συνεδρίῳ, to this construction being occasioned by the transition from the abstract and quasi-abstract words (κρίσις, συνέδριον) to the more material γέεννα.]

[3] [Fritzsche explains ἀποκαλύπτεται εἰς ἐμέ thus : manifestatur res *ad me* (ita, ut ad me perferatur).]

[4] [Here εὔθ. τῇ βασιλείᾳ is generally received. For ὠφέλιμος with *dat. pers.* see Tit. iii. 8. Compare Clyde, *Synt.* p. 163.]

[5] Πιστεύειν ἐν Χριστῷ would be explained in the same way, but the existence of this formula is not fully proved by G. iii. 26, E. i. 13 ; in Mk. i. 15, however, we find πιστ. ἐν τῷ εὐαγγελίῳ, which is not essentially different.—Such phrases as ἡ πρός τινα πίστις do not prove the construction πιστεύειν πρός or εἰς τινα to be pure Greek (Schwarz, *Comment.* p. 1102). [We should probably read ἐν αὐτῷ in Jo. iii. 15, but (with Meyer) connect the words with ἔχῃ, not πιστεύων. The

παραδιδόναι εἰς is not simply equivalent to παραδιδόναι τινί, but has rather the meaning *give into the power of* (Mt. x. 17); hence it is used with θάνατος Mt. x. 21, 2 C. iv. 11, with θλῖψις Mt. xxiv. 9, with ἀκαθαρσία Rom. i. 24, etc.: compare Xen. *Hell.* 1. 7. 3. The combination in E. iv. 19, ἑαυτοὺς παρέδωκαν τῇ ἀσελγείᾳ εἰς ἐργασίαν ἀκαθαρσίας πάσης κ.τ.λ., needs no explanation.

Rem. The preposition μετά also is akin to the dative. Thus for πολεμεῖν τινί we find in the N. T. πολεμεῖν μετά τινος, Rev. xii. 7, xiii. 4; also κρίνεσθαι μετά τινος, 1 C. vi. 6 (7). With a different reference, the dative is replaced

(*a*) By ἐνώπιόν τινος: A. vi. 5, ἤρεσεν ἐνώπιον παντὸς τοῦ πλήθους (Gen. xxxiv. 18, xli. 37,[1] 2 S. iii. 36, al.); compare 1 Jo. iii. 22, προσκυνεῖν ἐνώπιον τοῦ θεοῦ (L. iv. 7, Rev. xv. 4). This belongs to the Hebraic colouring of the language, as indeed the preposition ἐνώπιον itself (לִפְנֵי) may almost be said to do.

(*b*) After πέποιθα—by ἐν, Ph. iii. 3; by ἐπί with the dative, Mk. x. 24, 2 C. i. 9; or by ἐπί with the accusative, Mt. xxvii. 43, 1 Macc. x. 77 (*Alex.*). [See below, p. 292.]

(*c*) After ἀκολουθεῖν by ὀπίσω, Mt. x. 38; see § 33.

That the dative may stand for the *local* πρός or εἰς with an accusative, has been denied by Bornemann,[2] and after him by Meyer (on A. ii. 33). It is true that the examples which Fritzsche (*Conject.* I. 42) has quoted from Greek poets do not prove the point (for prose), and also that the N. T. passages may be otherwise explained. In A. ii. 33 and v. 31 (ὑψοῦν) τῇ δεξιᾷ may mean *by (His) right hand;* and in Rev. ii. 16 σοι is simply a *dativus incommodi.* Even A. xxi. 16 might be rendered (as by Beza and Glass) *adducentes secum, apud quem hospitaremur Mnasonem,*—the word which should have been in the accus. case, as the object of ἄγοντες (viz. Μνάσωνα κ.τ.λ.), being brought into the construction of the relative sentence (Μνάσωνι): but this explanation has but little probability.[3] A better course

---

constructions of this verb in the N. T. are fully examined by A. Buttmann (p. 173), and more succinctly by Bp. Ellicott (on 1 Tim. i. 16).]

[1] [In Genesis *ll. cc.* we have ἐναντίον, not ἐνώπιον.]
[2] In Rosenm. *Repertor.* II. 253, and in the *Neu. krit. Journ. der theol. Literat.* VI. 146 sq.: compare also *ad Anab.* p. 23.
[3] Not exactly because the predicate ἀρχαίῳ μαθητῇ is annexed (Bengels *N. Archiv* III. 175), for this description of Mnason is added in order to show that Paul might fully trust himself to him; but rather because it is not very likely that those who accompanied Paul from Cæsarea would have brought with them a host for him, since there were in Jerusalem itself so many trustworthy Christians. Hence we should have to assume, either that this Mnason was in Cæsarea by mere accident, or that he had a residence in both places at the same time. If we were to drop the *secum*, which certainly is not necessarily implied in ἄγοντες, it would simplify the matter (after their arrival in Jerusalem they brought Mnason forward), but then the words would not be suitably arranged.

would be to adopt Bornemann's more recent suggestion (*Luc.* p. 177 sq.) and resolve the attraction thus : ἄγοντες (ἡμᾶς) παρὰ Μνάσωνά τινα . . . παρ' ᾧ ξενισθῶμεν¹ (for ἄγειν παρά τινα compare Her. 1. 86, 3. 15). Even this however is not the simplest explanation. The construction ἄγειν τινί, *lead to some one* (but see the note below), may indeed be uncommon in Attic prose, but later prose writers use expressions which are entirely similar, as φοιτᾶν τινί Philostr. *Soph.* 2. 1. 14,² ἥκειν τινί Plut. *Æm.* 16. 1, εἰςφέρειν τινά τινι Malal. 10. p. 231 : with A. xxi. 16, in particular, compare Xen. *Eph.* 3. 6. p. 63, πότερον ἡγόμην 'Αβροκόμῃ· Epiph. *Vit.* p. 340 d, ἤγαγεν αὐτὸν 'Αθανασίῳ τῷ πάππᾳ.³ See also Bernh. p. 95, Held, Plut. *Æm. P.* p. 200. Hence we may without hesitation render ὑψοῦν τῇ δεξιᾷ, *exalt to the right hand;* compare ver. 34, κάθου ἐκ δεξιῶν μοῦ· see also Luc. *Asin.* 39.

L. ii. 41, ἐπορεύοντο . . . εἰς 'Ιερουσαλὴμ τῇ ἑορτῇ, must not be rendered (as by Luther) *to the feast*, but either *on account of the feast* (see below 6. *c*), or as a loose expression, *at the feast*.⁴ With more reason might Mk. xiv. 53 συνέρχονται αὐτῷ (*convenerant eum*), and Jo. xi. 33 τοὺς συνελθόντας αὐτῇ 'Ιουδαίους, be brought in here (Fritz. *Mark* p. 648). In my opinion, however, the dative in both passages is really governed by σύν ; the latter simply meaning *who had come with her*, the former, *they came with Him*, namely, with Jesus (ver. 54) ; see Baumg.-Crusius. (Jelf 592.)

The use of the dative with verbs of coming in a non-local and non-material sense (as in A. xxi. 31, ἀνέβη φάσις τῷ χιλιάρχῳ), is also a different construction from that noticed above.⁵ To this unquestioned parallels occur frequently in Greek writers : e. g. Plut. *Brut.* 27, μέλλοντι αὐτῷ διαβαίνειν . . . ἧκεν ἀγγελία περὶ τῆς μεταβολῆς· *Pomp.* 13, τῷ Σύλλᾳ πρώτῃ μὲν ἦλθεν ἀγγελία ; compare also ἀνάγειν τί τινι, *to bring something before some one* (notify to), Malal. 3. p. 63, 10. p. 254 (Jelf 592).

6. The dative is used with still greater latitude, in reference

---

¹ [So Meyer, De Wette, Alford, and others. The rarity of such (local) datives is not the only objection to Winer's view : the order of the words would surely have been different, ἄγοντες Μν. τινι Κ., παρ' ᾧ ξεν. (A. Buttm. p. 284).]
² Wyttenbach, Plut. *Mor.* IV. 339.
³ In none of these instances, however, has ἄγειν τινί (comp. προςάγειν τινί § 52. 4) a purely local or material meaning : it is used rather in the sense of *introducing*, bringing into connexion with, into the society of some one. Similarly φοιτᾶν τινί (to go to some one as teacher), different from φοιτᾶν πρός τινα Epict. *Ench.* 33. 13. ["In Plut. *Æm. l. c.* the dative depends on the whole expression ἧκε μηνύων :" A. Buttm. p. 179.]
⁴ We also should say in German : sie machten jährlich *zu Ostern* eine Reise nach . . . um dem Gottesdienste beizuwohnen.
⁵ Compare our "es kam *ihm* die Kunde, die Anzeige."

to things, to denote that *in which* or *in reference to which* an action or a state exists. Hence it indicates

(*a*) The *sphere* to which a general predicate is to be limited (compare Bernh. p. 84, Krüg. p. 86 [1]) : 1 C. xiv. 20, μὴ παιδία γίνεσθε ταῖς φρεσίν, ἀλλὰ τῇ κακίᾳ νηπιάζετε, children in understanding, children as regards malice (Plat. *Alcib. pr.* 122 c) ; Rom. iv. 20, ἐνεδυναμώθη τῇ πίστει, *he grew strong in faith*; Ph. ii. 8, σχήματι εὑρεθεὶς ὡς ἄνθρωπος· iii. 5,[2] Mt. v. 8, xi. 29, A. vii. 51, xiv. 8, xvi. 5, xviii. 2, xx. 22, Rev. iv. 3, 1 C. vii. 34, H. v. 11, xi. 12, xii. 3, 1 P. iii. 18, v. 9 (Pol. 20. 4. 7), G. i. 22, Rom. xii. 10, 11, Col. ii. 5, E. iv. 18, 23 (Matth. 400. 7, Fritz. *Rom.* III. 68). A dative of this kind comes between two connected nouns in E. ii. 3, ἦμεν τέκνα φύσει ὀργῆς, *natural children-of-wrath*.

(*b*) The *norm* or *rule* in accordance with which something takes place: A. xv. 1, ἐὰν μὴ περιτέμνησθε τῷ ἔθει Μωϋσέως (but in xvii. 2 κατὰ τὸ εἰωθός, and more frequently κατὰ ἔθος); compare Xen. *Cyr.* 1. 2. 4, Sext. Emp. 2. 6, Strabo 15. 715, Tob. iii. 8 [3 ?], 2 Macc. vi. 1.[3]

(*c*) The *occasion* or *cause* (on account of): Rom. xi. 20, τῇ ἀπιστίᾳ ἐξεκλάσθησαν, *on account of unbelief* (compare ver. 30, ἠλεήθητε τῇ τούτων ἀπειθείᾳ), G. vi. 12, Col. i. 21.[4] Also the *motive* (from, in consequence of) : 1 C. viii. 7, τῇ συνειδήσει τοῦ εἰδώλου ὡς εἰδωλόθυτον ἐσθίουσι· 2 C. i. 15, Rom. iv. 20. See Diog. L. 2. 57, Heliod. 1. 12. 33, Paus. 3. 7. 3, Joseph. *Antt.* 17. 6. 1 [5] (Matth. 398 sq., Bernh. p. 102 sq., Krüg. p. 84).

More singular is the use of the dative in Rev. viii. 4, ἀνέβη ὁ καπνὸς τῶν θυμιαμάτων ταῖς προσευχαῖς τῶν ἁγίων κ.τ.λ., and many conjectures have been made respecting it. The simplest translation is, *the smoke of the* (angels')[6] *incense ascended to the prayers,* i. e., the ascending smoke had reference to the prayers, was designed to accompany them and render them more acceptable : on the idea see

---

[1] [" A *local* dative ethically used : " Ellic. on G. i. 22. See Don. p. 488, Jelf 605. 4, Green p. 99.]

[2] [Reading of course περιτομῇ. Lünemann adds Mt. v. 3.]

[3] [Jelf 603, Green p. 99 : the dative with πορεύεσθαι (below, no. 9) should perhaps come in here.]

[4] [So Meyer, taking ἐχθρούς passively, *invisos Deo* : if ἐχθρούς is active (Alford, Ellicott) τῇ διανοίᾳ will be a dative of *reference*.]

[5] Compare Ast, Plat. *Polit.* p. 392, Goeller, *Thuc.* pp. 157, 184, al. (Don. p. 493).

[6] [Or rather "angel's."—Compare Green p. 102 : " The dative may be regarded as dependent on an unexpressed, but implied, idea of bestowal, since the incense is to be viewed as the accompaniment which gave to the prayers a passport into the divine presence."]

Ewald *in loc.* That this is the meaning was felt by those who supplied σύν: the rendering *inter preces sanctorum* is altogether untenable. —In 2 C. vii. 11 τῷ πράγματι would certainly be admissible, but for the language of the N. T. the construction would be harsh. There are good authorities in favour of prefixing ἐν ; and the omission of this word may have arisen either from the absorption of ἐν in the preceding word εἶναι or from the reader's connecting πράγματι with ἐν παντί.

7. In the various usages noticed in no. 6 we can discern more or less clearly the dative of *direction*, that is (according to the Greek conception), the true dative. The case is however extended farther still in its application to what is external, to what accompanies the action, and passes over entirely into the ablative, denoting

(*d*) The *mode* and *manner*, as the *casus modalis* (Bernh. p. 100 sq., Don. p. 487, Jelf 603); 1 C. xi. 5, προςευχομένη ἀκατακαλύπτῳ τῇ κεφαλῇ *with uncovered head*, x. 30, Col. ii. 11, Ph. i. 18, 2 P. ii. 4 (Jude 6) ; also Rom. viii. 24, τῇ ἐλπίδι ἐσώθημεν (and E. v. 19 [1]):—or the (material) *means, instrument*, as the *casus instrumentalis* (Madv. 39, but comp. Krüg. p. 83 [2]); 1 P. i. 18, οὐ φθαρτοῖς, ἀργυρίῳ ἢ χρυσίῳ, ἐλυτρώθητε· G. ii. 13, ὥστε . . . συναπήχθη αὐτῶν τῇ ὑποκρίσει (2 P. iii. 17, compare Zosim. 5. 6), E. i. 13, Col. ii. 7, Ph. iii. 3, 1 C. ix. 7, τίς στρατεύεται ἰδίοις ὀψωνίοις ποτέ, *by means of his own expenditure ;* H. vi. 17, ἐμεσίτευσεν ὅρκῳ· iii. 1,[3] Rom. xv. 18 :—further A. i. 5, ἐβάπτισεν ὕδατι (xi. 16), Jo. xxi. 8, τῷ πλοιαρίῳ ἦλθον· Mk. vi. 32 [4] (though elsewhere we find ἐν πλοίῳ· Mt. xiv. 13, A. xxviii. 11, Diod. S. 19. 54), A. xii. 2, Rom. i. 20, iii. 24, Tit. iii. 7, E. v. 19, al. H. xii. 18, ὄρος κεκαυμένον πυρί, *igni ardens, burning in fire, with fire* (Ex. iii. 2, Dt. iv. 11, ix. 15, compare Lob. *Paral.* p. 523 sq.), may also be brought in here. In Rom. xii. 12 τῇ ἐλπίδι χαίροντες is *through hope, in hope rejoicing :* in regard to 2 C. ix. 14, δεήσει, I now agree with Meyer.[5] We frequently find ἐν or διά (especially of persons)

---

[1] [This passage is again quoted below. On a peculiar use of the modal dative in the LXX and N. T. see § 54. 3.]

[2] [Krüger prefers the term *dynamic* dative, since "it does not properly denote the mere instrument or tool, though it is often improperly used of this." On the *dativ. instrum.* see Don. p. 490, Jelf 607.]

[3] [This reference is wrong : perhaps i. 3.]

[4] [The reading is not certain : Lachm., Westc. and Hort insert ἐν.]

[5] [In ed. 5 Winer had taken δεήσει as dependent on περισσεύουσα (ver. 12), and consequently as parallel with the prepositional clause διὰ π. εὐχ. : so Alford. Meyer takes καὶ αὐτῶν . . . ἐπιποθ. as a genitive absolute, δεήσει as a modal dative : Stanley takes a similar view.]

in parallelism with the instrumental dative: see Rom. xv. 18, 2 C. xi. 23, 26 sq.

The ablative is also to be recognised in the construction μεθύσκεσθαι οἴνῳ, E. v. 18 (Pr. iv. 17), and πληροῦσθαί τινι, Rom. i. 29,[1] 2 C. vii. 4, Eurip. *Herc. Fur.* 372; compare πλήρης τινί Eurip. *Bacch.* 18 (though this word more frequently takes a genitive), and see Bernh. p. 168. In later Greek compare πλησθέντες ἀγνοίᾳ Malal. p. 54. (In E. iii. 19 εἰς with the accusative does not stand for an ablative: this preposition rather expresses, *be filled up to the fulness* etc.)

8. All these relations however are not unfrequently (in some cases, more frequently) expressed by means of prepositions, with or without a modification of the meaning. This remark applies to Greek prose generally, but is especially illustrated by N. T. Greek. Thus we find

For (*a*), ἐν: 1 P. iv. 1, ἐν σαρκὶ παθών[2] (in connexion with σαρκὶ παθών), Tit. i. 13, compare ii. 2; διαφέρειν ἔν τινι 1 C. xv. 41, Soph. *Œd. Col.* 1112, Dion. H. *Ep.* p. 225 (Krüg.).

For (*b*), κατά: as almost always κατὰ τὸ ἔθος εἰωθός, L. iv. 16, A. xvii. 2.

For (*c*), διά with the accusative: see § 49. c.

For (*d*), διά or ἐν,—also μετά. Thus for βαπτίζεσθαι ὕδατι we commonly[3] find βαπτίζεσθαι ἐν ὕδατι (*in* water), Mt. iii. 11, Jo. i. 26, 31 (but also ἐν πνεύματι); for βίᾳ, always μετὰ βίας, A. v. 26, xxiv. 7; for πίστει, sometimes διὰ πίστεως, etc. But in E. ii. 8, τῇ χάριτί ἐστε σεσωσμένοι διὰ τῆς πίστεως, and in Rom. iii. 24, the dative expresses the motive, and διὰ πίστεως the subjective means. In 2 P. iii. 5 also we find a twofold expression of the means, διά indicating what is external, the dative what is not material. For παντὶ τρόπῳ (Ph. i. 18) we find in 2 Th. iii. 16 ἐν παντὶ τρόπῳ. On the other hand, in 2 P. ii. 3 the dative denotes the means, ἐν the state (the disposition).

When however the commentators on the N. T. explained ἐν as a simple *nota dativi*,[4] even in cases where a dative proper (not an ablative) is required, they took an exaggerated view which cannot in the least be justified by appealing to the Hebrew idiom. Most of the examples quoted owe all their plausibility to the circumstance that elsewhere the dative of the person is commonly found in similar

---

[1] [See Green, *Gr.* p. 101.]
[2] ['Ἐν is omitted by the best editors on strong MS. authority.]
[3] [The two expressions are about equally frequent: ἐν is inserted in the passage quoted in the text and in Jo. i. 33, Mk. i. 8 *Rec.*, but omitted in L. iii. 16, A. i. 5, xi. 16, Mk. i. 8 (Tisch. ed. 8, Westcott and Hort).]
[4] Comp. Blomfield, Æschyl. *Agam.* 1425, and Eurip. *Med.* p. 628.

SECT. XXXI.]   THE DATIVE.   273

combinations (compare 1 C. xiv. 11, iii. 1, i. 18); in reality, they are quite unsatisfactory. In A. iv. 12, δεδομένον ἐν ἀνθρώποις is most certainly equivalent to *given* (set forth) *amongst men* (compare 2 C. viii. 1 [1]); G. i. 16, ἀποκαλύψαι τὸν υἱὸν αὐτοῦ ἐν ἐμοί, is *to reveal in me* (ἐν τῷ πνεύματί μου); 1 Jo. iv. 9, ἐφανερώθη ἡ ἀγάπη τοῦ θεοῦ ἐν ἡμῖν, *the love of God manifested itself on* or *in us*, which undoubtedly is different from "manifested itself *to us;*" 1 C. xiv. 11, ὁ λαλῶν ἐν ἐμοὶ βάρβαρος, *in my estimation, meo judicio;*[2] 1 C. ii. 6, σοφίαν λαλοῦμεν ἐν τοῖς τελείοις, is *we set forth wisdom amongst*—or *with, before* (*coram*, Plat. *Symp.* 175 e, as often in the orators, see § 48. a) —*the perfect*, that is, when we have to do with the perfect, compare Judith vi. 2. 2 C. iv. 3, ἐν τοῖς ἀπολλυμένοις ἐστὶ κεκαλυμμένον, is in the main rightly explained by Baumgarten,—*is hidden in* (*amongst, with*) *those who are lost*. On ὁμολογεῖν ἔν τινι see § 32. 3. *b.* A. xiii. 15 and Col. ii. 13 need no explanation; and E. ii. 5, νεκροὺς τοῖς παραπτώμασι, is not grammatically parallel to the latter passage. In E. i. 20, ἐνήργησεν ἐν Χριστῷ is quite regular, (*power*) *which He manifested on Christ* (in raising Him from the dead). In Mt. xvii. 12, ἐποίησαν ἐν αὐτῷ ὅσα ἠθέλησαν (in Mk. ix. 13, ἐποίησαν αὐτῷ) means, *they did, perpetrated, on him;* compare Mk. xiv. 6, Jo. xiv. 30, L. xxiii. 31, 1 C. ix. 15 (Gen. xl. 14, Judith vii. 24). Equally correct is 2 C. x. 12, μετρεῖν ἑαυτοὺς ἐν ἑαυτοῖς, *measure themselves on themselves*, though Greek writers use the simple dative (Aristot. *Rhet.* 2. 12, Herod. 1. 6. 2).

9. Time, as the substratum connected with actions in general, is expressed in the dative, in answer to the question *when*. This temporal dative denotes

a. A space of time: L. viii. 29, πολλοῖς χρόνοις συνηρπάκει αὐτόν, *within* (*during*) *a long time*, A. viii. 11, xiii. 20, Rom. xvi. 25, Jo. ii. 20 (not E. iii. 5[3]); compare Joseph. *Antt.* 1. 3. 5, τὸ ὕδωρ ἡμέραις τεσσαράκοντα ὅλαις κατεφέρετο· Soph. *Trach.* 599, μακρῷ χρόνῳ· Æschin. *Ep.* 1. p. 121 c, Diod. S. 19. 93.

b. More frequently, a point of time *at* which something happens,—either with words which directly express the notion of time or of a division of time (accompanied by a numeral or

---

[1] So in Diog. L. 1. 105, τί ἐστιν ἐν ἀνθρώποις ἀγαθόν τε καὶ φαῦλον, where also the Latin translator has *quidnam esset hominibus bonum*, etc. Compare also Fabric. *Pseudepigr.* I. 628, δουλεύσουσιν ἐν τοῖς ἐχθροῖς αὐτῶν· Arrian, *Epict.* 1. 18. 8. [The "also" refers to the fact that in A. iv. 12 the *Vulgate* has "datum hominibus."]

[2] Comp. Jacobs, *Athen.* p. 183, Döderlein, *Œdip. Col.* p. 529, Wex, Soph. *Antig.* v. 549.

[3] [Winer apparently agrees with Meyer (ed. 2, 3) in regarding ἑτέραις γενεαῖς as an ordinary transmissive dative. De W., Ellicott, and Alford take γενεά in its *temporal* sense, and the dative as a dative of time: so also A. Buttmann and Meyer in ed. 4.]

18

274   THE DATIVE.   [PART III.

by a genitive, Krüg. p. 67), as L. xii. 20, ταύτῃ τῇ νυκτί· Mk. vi. 21, Ἡρώδης τοῖς γενεσίοις αὐτοῦ δεῖπνον ἐποίησε[1] Mt. xx. 19, τῇ τρίτῃ ἡμέρᾳ ἀναστήσεται· xxvi. 17, L. xiii. 16, A. vii. 8, xii. 21, xxi. 26, xxii. 13, xxvii. 23 ;—or with the name of a festival (Wannowski p. 86), L. xiii. 14, τῷ σαββάτῳ ἐθεράπευσε (xiv. 1), Mt. xii. 1, τοῖς σάββασι, al. Compare Plat. *Conv.* 174 a, Madvig 45. As a rule, however, ἐν is added to the dative in the latter case, as it frequently is in the former (especially with ἐσχάτη ἡμέρα or ἡμέρα τῆς κρίσεως), even in Luke (iii. 1, i. 26), compare Krüg. p. 67 (Don. p. 487, Jelf 606). In Greek authors also the use of τῇ ἑορτῇ or ταῖς ἑορταῖς without ἐν is rare (Wannowski p. 88).

The dative of *place* has not taken deep root in the N. T. Before names of towns ἐν is always inserted, as ἐν Ῥώμῃ, ἐν Τύρῳ, A. xvii. 6 [? xvii. 16], xix. 1, Rom. i. 7, 2 Tim. i. 17, iv. 20, al. Ὁδός occasionally dispenses with the preposition, as in Ja. ii. 25, ἑτέρᾳ ὁδῷ ἐκβαλοῦσα (where however a preposition was hardly needed), compare Xen. *Cyr.* 1. 2. 16 ; ὁδῷ πορεύεσθαι 2 P. ii. 15, A. xiv. 16 (in a figurative sense), comp. Lucian, *Tim.* 5, ὁδῷ βαδίζειν (Fritz. *Rom.* III. 140 sq.) ; στοίχειν τοῖς ἴχνεσι Rom. iv. 12 (βαίνειν ἴχνεσι Plut. *Sol.* 30). To this usage should also be referred the figurative phrases πορεύεσθαι τῷ φόβῳ A. ix. 31, xiv. 16, Pr. xxviii. 26, 2 S. xv. 11,[2] 1 Macc. vi. 23, Bar. i. 18, ii. 10, iv. 13, Tob. i. 2, iv. 5 (also πορεύεσθαι ἐν 1 P. iv. 3, al.), and even περιπατεῖν τοῖς ἔθεσι A. xxi. 21, 2 C. xii. 18, G. v. 16, Rom. xiii. 13. In Greek prose generally the use of the *dativus localis* is very limited: see Madvig 45, Poppo on Thuc. 1. 143. (Jelf 605.)

10. Sometimes, though rarely, the dative (of a person) accompanies a passive verb (usually in the perfect tense), instead of ὑπό, παρά, etc., with the genitive : L. xxiii. 15, οὐδὲν ἄξιον θανάτου ἐστὶ πεπραγμένον αὐτῷ (Isocr. *Paneg.* c. 18). Yet there is some difference between these constructions: the dative does not indicate *by whom* something is done, but *to whom* that which is done belongs (Madv. 38. g, Krüg. p. 84[3]). This construction is found with εὑρίσκεσθαι especially, as 2 C. xii. 20, 2 P. iii. 14,[4] Rom. x. 20 (from the LXX): compare also L.

---

[1] [Lünemann adds Mt. xiv. 6. On this see p. 276.]
[2] [This is surely not an example. Many of these examples may well be referred to 6. *b*, above. For 2 Pet. ii. 15 above read Jude 11.]
[3] Benseler, Isocr. *Evag.* p. 13 (Don. p. 492, Jelf 611).
[4] [In ed. 5 Winer regarded the dative in these two passages as a dative of opinion or judgment (no. 4. *a*): so Meyer in 2 C. *l. c.*, and Alford, Huther, A. Buttmann, in 2 P. iii. 14.]

SECT. XXXI.]　　　　THE DATIVE.　　　　　　275

xxiv. 35 (Ja. iii. 18), Ph. iv. 5 (A. xxiv. 14 [*Rec.*]), and 2 P. ii. 19, where ᾧ τις ἥττηται means, *to whom any one is inferior, succumbs* (like ἡττᾶσθαί τινος in Greek writers). But in A. xvi. 9 ὤφθη ὅραμα τῷ Παύλῳ signifies *became visible to him*, as ὀφθῆναί τινι often means *to appear to some one*. In Ja. iii. 7, τῇ φύσει τῇ ἀνθρωπίνῃ is rather *through the nature of man*, ingeniis hominum. In general, the dative of the thing with passive verbs (as probably in Rom. xii. 16, see Fritz. *in loc.*[1]) is less strange, as it coincides with the dative of the *means*. In H. iv. 2, τοῖς ἀκούσασιν probably indicates the persons in whose case the μὴ συγκεκ. τῇ πίστει existed. Lastly, in Mt. v. 21 sqq. ἐρρήθη τοῖς ἀρχαίοις signifies *was said to the ancients*: see Tholuck *in loc.*[2] This dative (of the person) is similarly used in Greek prose, but is especially common after a participle: compare Dem. *Olynth.* 3. p. 12 c, *Theocrin.* 507 c, *Coron.* 324 a, *Conon* 731 b, Diog. L. 8. 6, Philostr. *Her.* 4. 2.

　　Rem. 1. The dative in Col. ii. 14, ἐξαλείψας τὸ καθ' ἡμῶν χειρόγραφον τοῖς δόγμασι, is worthy of notice. The explanation given by some of the commentators, ὃ ἦν ἐν τοῖς δόγμασι, *quod constabat placitis* (*Mos.*)—in accordance with E. ii. 15, τὸν νόμον τῶν ἐντολῶν ἐν δόγμασι καταργήσας,—is correct indeed as regards the sense, but ungrammatical: to express this Paul must have written χειρόγραφον τὸ ἐν τοῖς δόγμασι. To take E. ii. 15 first: τῶν ἐντολῶν ἐν δόγμασι must certainly be regarded as expressing a single notion, *the commandments in* (particular) *decrees;*[3] compare § 20. 2. In Col. ii. 14 however, all things considered, we cannot but join δόγμασι closely with τὸ καθ' ἡμ. χειρ., *the bond* (in force) *against us through the decrees;* and perhaps Paul chose this position for δόγμασι in order to give the word prominence. Meyer's explanation, *that which was written with the commandments* (the dative being used as in the phrase *written with letters*), is the more harsh as χειρόγραφον has so completely established itself in usage as an independent word that it is hardly capable of governing (like γεγραμμένον) such a dative as this.

　　Rem. 2. Kühnöl's remark in his note on Mt. viii. 1, that datives absolute sometimes take the place of absolute genitives (e.g., καταβάντι

---

[1] [Fritzsche takes τοῖς ταπεινοῖς as neuter, and renders *per miseram rem.*]
[2] [See Alford *in loc.* for a clear summary of the arguments on this side.]
[3] [This is more fully examined in ed. 5. "If, in accordance with grammatical rule, ἐν δόγμασι be connected with καταργήσας, we must either understand δόγματα to mean *Christian doctrines* (which would stand in the same relation to ἐντολαί as πίστις to ἔργα); or we must translate (with Harless), *He has abolished the law of the commandments in decrees* (abolished it on the side of decrees). N. T. usage however does not support the former interpretation of δόγματα; and on Harless's view I should expect τοῖς δόγμασι, since a definite side of a definite law is spoken of." See Ellicott and Lightfoot *in loc.*]

αὐτῷ for καταβάντος αὐτοῦ, and ἐλθόντι αὐτῷ Mt. xxi. 23), expresses what was formerly the general belief of philologers as well as of N. T. commentators.[1] In reality, however, all such datives (at any rate in the better writers, Wannowski p. 91 sqq.) are as easily explained from the nature of this case as the genitive absolute from the nature of the genitive:[2] see Bernh. p. 82, Stallb. Plat. *Protag.* 60, Rost p. 721 (Jelf 699). Kühnöl's remark cannot with even the least show of reason be applied to the passages he has quoted, for in them καταβάντι and ἐλθόντι are connected with the verb ἀκολουθεῖν; though it cannot be denied that Matthew might have written καταβάντος αὐτοῦ ἠκολούθησαν αὐτῷ ὄχλοι πολλοί, compare Mt. viii. 28, Mk. v. 2 *v. l.*[3] The only peculiarity of this construction is, that αὐτῷ is uniformly repeated,—because the dative participle and the governing verb are separated by several other words. In the examples cited by Kypke (I. 47) from Pausanias and Josephus, either there is simply a pronoun joined to the participle, or the pronoun comes in only in immediate connexion with the verb (Joseph. *Antt.* 8. 13. 4); hence they prove nothing for the main point. Nor is there a real dative absolute in A. xxii. 6 or 17: in the latter passage, just as in ver. 6, μοι ὑποστρέψαντι belongs to ἐγένετο, but a different construction (with the genitive absolute) then commences: accidit mihi reverso, cum precabar in templo, etc. Compare Paus. 3. 10, 7, and 25. 3.

Rem. 3. We find a double dative, one of the person, the other (a dative of explanation, of more exact definition) of the thing, in 2 C. xii. 7, ἐδόθη μοι σκόλοψ τῇ σαρκί, *there was given me a stake for the (in the) flesh*[4] (Ex. iv. 9, Gen. xlvii. 24): compare the Homeric δίδου οἱ ἡνία χερσίν.[5] It is otherwise with the double datives in E. iii. 5, Rom. vii. 25, H. iv. 2, Rev. iv. 3: these need no remark.

Rem. 4. We meet with a very singular dative in 2 C. vi. 14, μὴ γίνεσθε ἑτεροζυγοῦντες ἀπίστοις: here some would even supply σύν, whilst others seek for the same meaning in the dative itself. The dative may indeed be sometimes resolved by *with* (Reitz, *Lucian*

---

[1] Fischer, *Well.* III. a. p. 391, Wyttenbach, Plut. *Mor.* II. 304, Heupel, *Mark.* p. 79.

[2] [With Mt. xiv. 6, γενεσίοις γενομένοις, compare the examples quoted by Kühner II. 371 (ed. 2): see also Jelf 699, A. Buttm. p. 317.]

[3] [There is a great difference of opinion as to the reading in the four passages quoted in this paragraph. The MSS. are divided, and internal arguments may be adduced on both sides, since both constructions are grammatically inexact (on the redundancy of the pronoun see § 22. 4, and on the combination of genitive and dative § 30. Rem.), and yet the transcribers were certainly familiar with both. Tischendorf receives the dative in Mt. viii. 1, but the genitive in Mt. viii. 28, xxi. 23, Mk. v. 2. Westcott and Hort have the genitive in each case.]

[4] [So Alford, referring to G. iv. 14; Meyer prefers to connect τῇ σαρκί closely with σκόλοψ, *a thorn for the flesh.* As regards the *meaning* of σκόλοψ, see Meyer and Alford *in loc.* in defence of "thorn," and on the other side Stanley p. 539 sq. (ed. 3).]

[5] Reisig, Soph. *Œd. Col.* 266, Elmsley, Eur. *Bacch.* pp. 49, 80 (ed. Lips.), Bornem., Xen. *Conv.* p. 214, Jacobs, *Achill. Tat.* p. 811, Ast, Plat. *Legg.* p. 278.

VI. 599. Bip., Matth. 405, compare Polyæn. 8. 28), but this is quite a different case. The apostle's language seems abbreviated, and the dative appears to be adapted rather to the thoughts than to the words. His meaning obviously is: μὴ γίν. ἑτεροζυγοῦντες καὶ οὕτως ὁμοζυγοῦντες (συζυγοῦντες) ἀπίστοις, *do not let yourselves be yoked in a strange yoke*, i.e., in the same yoke with unbelievers.

Section XXXII.

THE ACCUSATIVE.

1. The accusative appears in connexion with transitive verbs, active, middle, and deponent, as the proper object-case: κόπτειν τὴν θύραν, κόπτεσθαι τὴν κεφαλήν, φυλάσσειν τὸν κῆπον, φυλάσσεσθαι τὰς ἐντολάς. It must however be borne in mind—not only

a. That in later, and particularly in Biblical Greek, several neuter verbs have acquired a transitive (causative) meaning, as μαθητεύειν τινά (§ 38. 1):—but also

b. That, in general, certain classes of verbal notions which we consider either entirely or partially intransitive appeared to the Greeks as transitive. Under this head come

(*a*) The verbs which denote *emotions* (Jelf 549 sq.): ἐλεεῖν, Mt. ix. 27, Mk. v. 19, Ph. ii. 27, al. (Plat. *Symp.* 173 c, Æl. 13. 31); οἰκτείρειν, Rom. ix. 15, from the LXX (Soph. *El.* 1403, Xen. *Cyr.* 5. 4. 32, Lucian, *Abd.* 6, *Tim.* 99); ἐπαισχύνεσθαί τινα and τι, Mk. viii. 38, H. xi. 16, Rom. i. 16 (Plat. *Soph.* 247 c,—compare αἰσχύνεσθαι Soph. *Œd. R.* 1079, Eurip. *Ion* 1074), once ἐπαισχ. ἐπί, Rom. vi. 21 (compare Isocr. *Permut.* 778). On the other hand, σπλαγχνίζεσθαι takes ἐπί as a rule, only once governing the genitive, Mt. xviii. 27 (see § 33). Ἐντρέπεσθαί τινα, *to be afraid of any one* (Mt. xxi. 37, L. xviii. 2, H. xii. 9), is a later construction, not found before Plutarch: in earlier writers we find ἐντρέπεσθαί τινι.[1]

(β) The verbs of *treating well* or *ill* (harming, benefiting), *speaking well* or *ill of any one* (Jelf 583): ἀδικεῖν, βλάπτειν, ὠφελεῖν, λυμαίνεσθαί, ὑβρίζειν τινά (Xen. *Hell.* 2. 4. 17, Lucian, *Pisc.* 6); ἐπηρεάζειν τινά (with dative of the person, Xen. *Mem.*

---

[1] [A mere misprint for τινός (ed. 5), see Jelf 510.]

1. 2. 31); λοιδορεῖν τινά, Jo. ix. 28 (Matth. 384. Rem. 2, Jelf 566. 2); βλασφημεῖν τινά, Mt. xxvii. 39, A. xix. 37, Rev. xiii. 6, al., but also βλασφημεῖν εἴς τινα L. xii. 10 (compare Demosth. *Cor. Nav.* p. 715 c, Diod. S. 2. 18, and in the LXX, *Hist. Drac.* 9,—so in Greek writers ὀνειδίζειν εἴς τινα, ὑβρίζειν εἴς τινα Lucian, *Tim.* 31), and βλασφημεῖν ἔν τινι 2 P. ii. 12 (in Greek writers also βλ. περί τινος, Isocr. *Permut.* 736); ὀνειδίζειν τινά, Mt. v. 11 (and in the LXX, compare Rom. xv. 3),[1] for which earlier writers used ὀνειδίζειν τινί or εἴς τινα;[2] κακῶς ἐρεῖν τινά, A. xxiii. 5 (Plat. *Euthyd.* 284 e, Diod. S. *Vat.* p. 66); also καταρᾶσθαί τινα, Mt. v. 44,[3] Ja. iii. 9 (Wisd. xii. 11, Ecclus. iv. 5, al.,—καταρᾶσθαί τινι Xen. *An.* 7. 7. 48). All these constructions ultimately rest on the simple λέγειν or εἰπεῖν τινά, Jo. i. 15, viii. 27, Ph. iii. 18, al., Jud. vii. 4; compare Herm. Soph. *Œd. C.* 1404, Matth. 416. We find however καλῶς ποιεῖν with the dative of the person, L. vi. 27,[4] and similarly εὖ ποιεῖν, Mk. xiv. 7 : here the accusative is always preferred in Greek prose;[5] compare however *Odyss.* 14. 289, ὃς δὴ πολλὰ κάκ᾽ ἀνθρώποισιν ἑώργει. Ποιεῖν τινά τι, *to do something to some one*, also occurs in the N. T., Mt. xxvii. 22, Mk. xv. 12 :[6] compare Aristoph. *Nub.* 258 sq.

(γ) Ὀμνύειν τινά, Ja. v. 12 (οὐρανόν), *to swear by*; compare Hos. iv. 15, Xen. *Cyr.* 5. 4. 31, Herod. 2. 10. 3 (Jelf 566. 2).

The N. T. writers however do not uniformly adopt these concise constructions. As in ordinary Greek, several verbs vary between a transitive and a neuter meaning : κλαίειν τινά Mt. ii. 18 (from the LXX[7]), but ἐπί τινα L. xix. 41, xxiii. 28 ; πενθεῖν τινά 2 C. xii. 21, but ἐπί τινι Rev. xviii. 11 ;[8] κόπτεσθαί τινα L. viii. 52 (Eur. *Troad.* 628, 1 Macc. ii. 70), and ἐπί τινα Rev.

---

[1] Schæf. *Plutarch* V. 347.
[2] [And also ὀνειδίζειν τινά, see examples in Liddell and Scott s. v. (but *Il.* 1. 211 is very doubtful).]
[3] [The clause is omitted in the best MSS. : this verb has an accusative in Mk. xi. 21, and probably in L. vi. 28, where *Rec.* has the dative. Wisd. xii. 11 is not an example in point.]
[4] A. xvi. 28, μηδὲν πράξῃς σεαυτῷ κακόν, is of a different kind : we often meet with this and similar examples in Greek writers, as Lys. *Accus. Agor.* 41, Xen. *Cyr.* 5. 4. 11, 5. 5. 14, 8. 7. 24.
[5] See *Biblioth. Brem. Nova* I. 277.
[6] [If we omit ἂν λέγετε : the received text leaves the construction doubtful.]
[7] [The citation is from Jer. xxxi. (xxxviii.) 15, but this clause is altogether different in the LXX text.]
[8] [The most probable reading is ἐπ᾽ αὐτήν.]

i. 7, xviii. 9; εὐδοκεῖν τινά H. x. 6, 8, from the LXX[1] (Lev. xxvi. 34, Ps. l. 18), but usually εὐδ. ἔν τινι. Ὀμνύειν is commonly treated as a neuter verb, and construed with κατά τινος H. vi. 13, 16 (Amos viii. 14, Zeph. i. 5, Is. xlv. 23[2]), or with ἔν τινι Mt. v. 34 sqq.,[3] Rev. x. 6 (Jer. v. 2, 7, Ps. lxii. 12). On the other hand, instead of εὐχαριστεῖν (τινὶ) ἐπί τινι, we find (with the passive verb) the construction εὐχαρ. (τινί) τι in 2 C. i. 11; and in 2 C. ix. 2, xi. 30, καυχᾶσθαι takes an accusative of the thing.

With Jude 15, τῶν ἔργων ἀσεβείας αὐτῶν ὧν (ἃ) ἠσέβησαν, compare Zeph. iii. 11, τῶν ἐπιτηδευμάτων σου ὧν ἠσέβησας εἰς ἐμέ: ἀσεβεῖν τι, Plat. Legg. 12. 941 a, is of a different kind (Matth. 413. 11).

Ἱερουργεῖν, ἐργάζεσθαι, and ἐμπορεύεσθαι are real transitives; and as the phrase ἱερουργεῖν θυσίαν was in use (Palæph. 5. 3, compare Acta Apocr. 113), Paul could figuratively say ἱερ. τὸ εὐαγγέλιον (Rom. xv. 16). The accusative after ἐμπορεύεσθαι does not always denote the merchandise; we find also ἐμπορ. τινα, Ez. xxvii. 21, 2 P. ii. 3, —in the latter passage with the meaning *trade in*, (wish to) *make a gain of a man*. With Rev. xviii. 17, ὅσοι τὴν θάλασσαν ἐργάζονται, comp. Appian, Pun. 2, Boisson. Philostr. p. 452: γῆν ἐργαζ., Paus. 6. 10. 1, is similar.

Εὐαγγελίζεσθαι (of Christian preaching) takes an accusative of the person in the N. T., as a transitive verb, L. iii. 18, A. viii. 25, xiv. 21; compare εὐαγγ. τινά τι A. xiii. 32. Yet εὐαγγ. τινι is also in use, see L. iv. 18, Rom. i. 15, G. iv. 13, 1 P. iv. 6.

An accusative is also found with βασκαίνειν *fascinare* in G. iii. 1. With the meaning *invidere* this verb takes the dative (Philostr. Epp. 13), see Lob. p. 463: the ancient grammarians themselves, however, are not agreed on the distinction between these two constructions, see Wetstein II. 221 sq.

Παραινεῖν, which in Greek writers usually takes the dative of the person (Æsch. Dial. 2. 13, Pol. 5. 4. 7), is followed by an accusative in A. xxvii. 22. *Vice versâ*, we find διδάσκειν τινί in Rev. ii. 14 v. l., as in some later writers.[4]

Φυλάσσεσθαι (*to beware of*) governs an accusative in A. xxi. 25, 2 Tim. iv. 15 (as frequently in Greek authors, Xen. Mem. 2. 2. 14, Lucian, Asin. 4, Diod. S. 20, 26), as if *to observe some one for oneself*. In L. xii. 15 it is joined with ἀπό; this construction also is not unknown in classical Greek (Xen. Cyr. 2. 3. 9). Similarly φοβεῖσθαι,

---

[1] [The LXX text (Ps. xxxix. 7) has not εὐδοκεῖν at all: H. x. 6, 8 are rather examples of εὐδοκεῖν τι, but we probably have εὐδ. τινά in Mt. xii. 18.]
[2] Schæf. Long. p. 353.
[3] [In ver. 35, ὀμνύειν εἰς.]
[4] See Schæf. Plutarch V. 22.

to be afraid in reference to something, to fear something (for one-self), is usually found with an accusative, but sometimes with ἀπό (sibi ab al. timere), as Mt. x. 28, μὴ φοβεῖσθε ἀπὸ τῶν ἀποκτενόντων [1] τὸ σῶμα . . . . φοβήθητε δὲ μᾶλλον τὸν δυνάμενον κ.τ.λ. The Greeks said φοβεῖσθαι ὑπό τινος or τινι (yet compare φόβος ἀπό τινος Xen. Cyr. 3. 3. 53, 6. 3. 27): φοβεῖσθαι ἀπό is an imitation of the Hebrew מִן (or מִפְּנֵי) יָרֵא, Jer. i. 8. The same analogy is followed by βλέπειν ἀπό (a pregnant expression) Mk. viii. 15, xii. 38, and by προσέχειν ἀπό Mt. xvi. 6.[2] But in Ph. iii. 2 βλέπετε τὴν κατατομήν is *look at, observe the concision*, and here *beware of* is only a derived meaning: the use of βλέπειν τι in such a sense (*beware of*) would receive no confirmation from φυλάσσεσθαί τι, since the middle voice is here essential.

Φεύγειν governs the accusative, 1 C. vi. 18, 2 Tim. ii. 22, in a figurative sense (to flee *i.e.* to shun a vice);[3] but is once followed by ἀπό, in 1 C. x. 14, φεύγετε ἀπὸ τῆς εἰδωλολατρείας. This latter construction is otherwise very common in the N. T. (as in the LXX), and φεύγειν ἀπό τινος means either *to flee away from some one*, in different senses (Jo. x. 5, Rev. ix. 6, Mk. xiv. 52, Ja. iv. 7), or—including the result of the fleeing—*to escape from some one* (Mt. xxiii. 33). In Greek writers φεύγειν ἀπό is only used in a strictly local sense, as Xen. Cyr. 7. 2. 4, Mem. 2. 6. 31, Plat. Phæd. 62 d, Pol. 26. 5. 2.

On χρῆσθαί τι see § 31. 1. *i.*[4]

The accusative of the place *to which* after verbs of motion was, after the full development of the prepositions, mostly confined to poetry: Matth. p. 747 [? § 409]. In the N. T. the general character of the language would lead us to expect that a preposition would be always used in such cases. A. xxvii. 2, μέλλοντι πλεῖν τοὺς κατὰ τὴν Ἀσίαν τόπους (where however some good MSS. prefix εἰς), is no exception: the words must be rendered, *to sail by the places along the coast of Asia*, and in this signification the best authors use πλεῖν as a pure verb transitive, with the accusative (sometimes the accus. of the coast-regions[5]). Compare Poppo on Thuc. 6. 36 (Jelf 559).

2. A neuter verb which expresses a feeling or an action is

---

[1] [On this form see above, p. 100.]
[2] [Compare also αἰσχύνεσθαι ἀπό, 1 Jo. ii. 28.]
[3] [And once in the sense of *escaping*, H. xi. 34. (A. Buttm. p. 146.)]
[4] ["The LXX once use ὑστερεῖν with the accusative, in the sense of the impersonal δεῖ (Ps. xxii. 1, οὐδέν με ὑστερήσει), and some of the oldest MSS. have the same construction in Mk. x. 21, ἕν σε ὑστερεῖ:" A. Buttm. p. 169.]
[5] Wahl's parallels (Xen. *Hell.* 4. 8. 6, Pol. 3. 4. 10) only support the construction πλεῖν τὴν θάλασσαν or τὰ πελάγη; of this, however, 1 Macc. xiii. 29 and Ecclus. xliii. 24 will serve as examples.

frequently followed by an accusative of its cognate noun (*nomen conjugatum*), or of the noun which is cognate to a verb of similar meaning; such nouns being in fact already included in the verb, since they merely express its notion in a substantival form. This combination, however, is only used when the notion of the verb is to be extended,[1]—either by an (objective [2]) genitive, as in 1 P. iii. 14, τὸν φόβον αὐτῶν μὴ φοβηθῆτε (Is. viii. 12), Col. ii. 19, αὔξει τὴν αὔξησιν τοῦ θεοῦ (Plat. *Legg.* 10. 910 d, ἀσεβεῖν ἀνδρῶν ἀσέβημα· 1 Macc. ii. 58, ζηλῶσαι ζῆλον νόμου· Judith ix. 4);—or by means of an adjective, Mt. ii. 10, ἐχάρησαν χαρὰν μεγάλην σφόδρα· Jo. vii. 24, τὴν δικαίαν κρίσιν κρίνετε· 1 Tim. i. 18, ἵνα στρατεύῃ τὴν καλὴν στρατείαν (Plut. *Pomp.* 41), Mk. iv. 41, ἐφοβήθησαν φόβον μέγαν· 1 Tim. vi. 12, 2 Tim. iv. 7, Rev. xvii. 6, 1 P. iii. 6 (Gen. xxvii. 33, Zach. i. 15, Jon. i. 10, iv. 1, 6, Wisd. ix. 3 [3]). This is very common in Greek writers; see especially Lob. *Paral.* p. 501 sqq.[4] Compare Plat. *Protag.* 360 b, αἰσχροὺς φόβους φοβοῦνται· Xen. *Mem.* 1. 5. 6, δουλεύειν δουλείαν οὐδεμιᾶς ἧττον αἰσχράν· Her. 5. 119, μάχην ἐμαχέσαντο ἰσχυρήν (magnam pugnavimus pugnam, Terent. *Adelph.* 5. 3. 57), Plat. *Apol.* 28 b, τοιοῦτον ἐπιτήδευμα ἐπιτηδεύσας· p. 36 c, εὐεργετεῖν τὴν μεγίστην εὐεργεσίαν· Alciphr. 2. 3, δεῖταί μου πάσας δεήσεις· Lysias, 1. *Theomnest.* 27, πολλοὺς δὲ καὶ ἄλλους κινδύνους μεθ᾽ ὑμῶν ἐκινδύνευσε (Plat. *Conv.* 208 c), Demosth. *Neær.* 517 b, *Ep.* p. 121 b, Aristot. *Polit.* 3. 10, *Rhet.* 2. 5. 4, Long. 4. 3, Æschin. *Ep.* 1. 121 b, Lucian, *Asin.* 11, Philostr. *Apoll.* 2. 32: see also Georgi, *Vind.* 199 sq., Wetst. II. 321 (Gesen. *Lg.* p. 810 [5]). This construction is found with a passive verb in Rev. xvi. 9, ἐκαυματίσθησαν οἱ ἄνθρωποι καῦμα μέγα (Plat. *Euthyd.* 275 e, ὠφελεῖται τὴν μεγίστην ὠφέλειαν· Plutarch, *Cæs.* 55, al.).

---

[1] Herm. Soph. *Phil.* 281, Eurip. *Androm.* 220 sq., Krüg. p. 19 sq. [Don. p. 501: for the different kinds of such accusatives see Jelf 548. 2. See also Riddell, Plat. *Apol.* p. 110 sq.]
[2] [This word objective is surely a misprint: at all events an objective genitive is of rare occurrence in this construction. See especially Lobeck, *Paral.* p. 513 sq.: "In proverbio ... Ταντάλου φόβον φοβοῦμαι minime significatur Tantalum timeo, sed timeo id quod Tantalus pertimescere dicitur sive Tantalico quodam timore angor."]
[3] [In this passage there is no qualifying adjective.]
[4] See Fischer, *Well.* III. i. 422 sq., Bernh. p. 106 sq., Ast, Plat. *Polit.* 316, Weber, *Dem.* p. 471, Matth. p. 744 sq. [?], § 408, 421. Rem. 3.
[5] [Gesen. *Heb. Gr.* p. 221 (Bagst.).]

So with a relative pronoun : Jo. xvii. 26, ἡ ἀγάπη ἣν ἠγάπησάς με· E. ii. 4, Mk. x. 38, τὸ βάπτισμα ὃ ἐγὼ βαπτίζομαι βαπτισθῆναι.

It is a different case when the cognate noun denotes the objective result of the action, and consequently a *concrete* notion ; as διαθήκην διατίθεσθαι (Jud. ii. 2), μαρτυρίαν μαρτυρεῖν, πλοῦτον πλουτεῖν (Dan. xi. 2), ψήφισμα ψηφίζεσθαι, ἁμαρτάνειν ἁμαρτίαν (1 Jo. v. 16), for *make a covenant, bear a testimony,* etc. (Ewald, *Gr.* 595). Here the nouns do not absolutely need to be supported by adjectives, etc. (as αἰσχρὰν ἁμαρτίαν ἁμαρτάνειν Soph. *Phil.* 1249, Plat. *Phæd.* 113 e, Lucian, *Tim.* 112, Dio Chr. 32, 361): compare E. iv. 8 (from the LXX), ἠχμαλώτευσεν αἰχμαλωσίαν· Jud. v. 12, 2 Chr. xxviii. 17, Demosth. *Steph.* 2. 621 b. Yet it is only in connexion with relative clauses that these expressions are usually found : Jo. v. 32, ἡ μαρτυρία, ἣν μαρτυρεῖ περὶ ἐμοῦ 1 Jo. v. 10, H. viii. 10, αὕτη ἡ διαθήκη, ἣν διαθήσομαι (x. 16,—but in viii. 9 διαθήκην ποιεῖν), A. iii. 25, L. i. 73, 1 Jo. ii. 25, Mk. iii. 28 : compare Isocr. *Ægin.* 936, Lucian, *Paras.* 5. It cannot however be denied that such combinations in Hebrew and Greek have greater fulness and vividness than our general expressions *make a covenant, bear testimony.*

Lastly, we must entirely exclude the cases in which the substantive denotes something objective and material which exists apart from the action of the verb, as φυλάσσειν φυλακάς (the watches) Xen. *An.* 2. 6. 10, φόρον φέρειν Aristoph. *Av.* 191, Aristot. *Pol.* 2. 8, Lucian, *Paras.* 43. In the N. T. compare L. ii. 8, φυλάσσοντες φυλακὰς τῆς νυκτός· viii. 5, τοῦ σπεῖραι τὸν σπόρον αὐτοῦ· Mt. xiii. 30, δήσατε δεσμὰς[1] πρὸς τὸ κατακαῦσαι, *bind bundles* ; Mt. vii. 24, ὅστις ᾠκοδόμησεν τὴν οἰκίαν αὐτοῦ· L. vi. 48 ; compare also 1 P. iv. 2 (ἀκοὴν ἀκούειν Obad. 1). In some of these instances no other form of expression was possible (compare also ἀποστόλους ἀποστέλλειν, legatos legare Cic. *Vatin.* 15, γράμματα γράφειν Dem. *Polycl.* 710 b), and the connexion of the noun with the verb is merely etymological and historical. On these constructions in general (which in Greek writers are much more diversified) see Wunder on Lobeck's edition of Soph. *Ajax* p. 37 sqq.

Akin to this construction are ὅρκον ὀμνύαι L. i. 73[2] (De-

---

[1] [The reading δήσατε εἰς δ. (*Rec.*, Tisch. ed. 8) is strongly supported.]
[2] [Noticed in the preceding paragraph.]

SECT. XXXII.] THE ACCUSATIVE. 283

mosth. *Apat.* 579 c), βιοῦν χρόνον 1 P. iv. 2 (ζῆν βίον, Diod. S. *Exc. Vat.* p. 49); δέρειν (πληγὰς) πολλάς, ὀλίγας, to which is further joined an accusative of the person (compare L. xii. 47) : see Wunder *l. c.* p. 86. L. ii. 44, ἦλθον ἡμέρας ὁδόν, *they went a day's journey,* and A. viii. 39, ἐπορεύετο τὴν ὁδὸν αὐτοῦ (compare ὁδὸν βαδίζειν Plut. *Coriol.* 9, and in the LXX 1 S. vi. 9, Num. xxi. 33, Ex. xiii. 17), scarcely need any remark ; yet see Wunder p. 41 sq. (Jelf 558).

The dative-construction is analogous : φωνεῖν φωνῇ μεγάλῃ A. xvi. 28, and βοᾶν or κράζειν φωνῇ μεγ. Mk. xv. 34, Mt. xxvii. 50, A. vii. 60, ὅρκῳ ὀμνύναι A. ii. 30, χαρᾷ χαίρειν 1 Th. iii. 9 [1] (ἀγαλλιᾶσθαι χαρᾷ ἀνεκλαλήτῳ 1 P. i. 8), κηρύσσειν φωνῇ μεγάλῃ Rev. v. 2 [*Rec.*] ; also ποίῳ θανάτῳ ἤμελλεν ἀποθνῄσκειν Jo. xii. 33, xviii. 32. Compare Aristot. *Pol.* 3. 9, Plut. *Coriol.* 3 (Jon. i. 16, *Act. Ap.* 4), Krüg. p. 18 (Bengel on Rev. xviii. 2) : compare § 54. 3.

3. It has been maintained that in several places, in accordance with the Hebrew idiom, a preposition, ἐν (בְּ), takes the place of the accusative of the object ; but when the passages are more closely examined, we soon find that the preposition was admissible in its proper meaning.

a. A. xv. 7, ὁ θεὸς ἐν ἡμῖν ἐξελέξατο διὰ τοῦ στόματός μου ἀκοῦσαι τὰ ἔθνη κ.τ.λ., must not be compared with בָּחַר בּ. The meaning is, *amongst us* (the apostles) ; for, in the first place, the singular μου is used by Peter immediately afterwards ; and, secondly, we must have regard to the mention of τὰ ἔθνη (as the apostolic sphere of operation) : " God has made the choice amongst us, that the Gentiles should be instructed through me." See also Olshausen *in loc.* On the Hebrew בָּחַר בּ, sometimes rendered in the LXX by ἐκλέγ. ἐν, 1 S. xvi. 9, 1 K. viii. 16, 1 Chr. xxviii. 4, Neh. ix. 7 (which however Gesenius did not even feel it necessary to explain), see Ewald, *Gr.* 605.[2]

b. Ὁμολογεῖν ἐν, Mt. x. 32, L. xii. 8, *to make a confession on some one,* i.e., with another turn of the phrase, *respecting*[3] *some one.* Bengel gives a different explanation. The Hebrew הוֹדָה עַל, Ps. xxxii. 5, has not quite the same meaning.

---

[1] [Here ἢ χαίρομεν may be for ἣν χ., by attraction : see Ellic. and Alf. *in loc.*]

[2] [Ewald compares this with the use of בּ after verbs of *clinging to, taking hold of,* the fundamental notion being that of " immediate proximity " (*Lehrb.* p. 556 sq.) : Gesenius's view (*Thes.* s. v. בּ) is substantially the same.]

[3] [The German preposition here used (*über*) means both *over* and *respecting.*—Bengel says " ἐν, *in :* i.e. quum de me quæritur." Similarly Fritzsche : " testimonium edere in aliquo, i.e. in alicujus causa." Meyer's explanation resembles Winer's : compare Cremer. But see Westcott, *Canon* p. 301 ; also Godet *in loc.*]

284   THE ACCUSATIVE.   [PART III.

4. *Double Accusative.*

a. Two accusatives, one of the person and the other of the thing (Matth. 417 sq., Jelf 582 sq., Don. p. 500), are found, as a rule, with verbs of *clothing* and *unclothing*, Jo. xix. 2, Mt. xxvii. 28,[1] 31, Mk. xv. 17, Rev. xvii. 4; of (*giving to eat* and) *giving to drink*, Mk. ix. 41, 1 C. iii. 2;[2] of *anointing*, Rev. iii. 18 (H. i. 9); of *loading*, L. xi. 46; of *adjuring* (by), A. xix. 13, 1 Th. v. 27; of *reminding of* (ἀναμιμνήσκειν), 1 C. iv. 17, Xen. *Cyr.* 3. 3. 37, Her. 6. 140 (but ἀναμν. τινά τινος Xen. *Cyr.* 6. 4. 13); of *teaching*, Jo. xiv. 26; of *asking* (either *requesting* or *inquiring*), Mt. vii. 9, Jo. xvi. 23, 1 P. iii. 15 (αἰτεῖν), Mt. xxi. 24 (Lob. *Paral.* p. 522), Mk. iv. 10 (ἐρωτᾶν). Εὐαγγελίζεσθαι is only once construed with a double accusative, in A. xiii. 32; compare Heliod. 2. 10, Alciphr. 3. 12, Euseb. *H. E.* 3. 4 *v. l.* For κρύπτειν τινά τι (Matth. 421) κρύπτειν τι ἀπό τινος is always used or at all events implied; see Col. i. 26, L. xviii. 34, xix. 42. After διδάσκειν the person taught is in one passage (Rev. ii. 14) expressed by ἔν τινι (as if, *to give instruction on some one*[3]), but this reading is not well attested: other and better MSS. have ἐδίδασκε τῷ Βαλάκ, comp. Thilo, *Apocr.* I. 656 (לְ לִמֵּד, Job xxi. 22). Besides αἰτεῖν τινά τι we meet with αἰτεῖν τι παρά or ἀπό τινος, A. iii. 2, ix. 2, Mt. xx. 20 (Xen. *An.* 1. 3. 16). Χρίειν τινά is joined with a dative of the material in A. x. 38, as ἀλείφειν uniformly is (Mk. vi. 13, Jo. xi. 2, al.). We also find ὑπομιμνήσκειν τινὰ περί τινος, 2 P. i. 12; περιβάλλεσθαι ἐν,[4] Rev. iii. 5, iv. 4 [*Rec.*]; ἠμφιεσμένος ἐν, Mt. xi. 8, L. vii. 25 (with the dative in Plat. *Protag.* 321 a). For ἀφαιρεῖσθαί τινά τι we find ἀφαιρ. τι ἀπό τινος L. xvi. 3.

We may perhaps explain H. ii. 17, ἱλάσκεσθαι τὰς ἁμαρτίας (compare Ecclus. xxviii. 5, Dan. ix. 24 Theodot.), *expiare peccata*, on

---

[1] [Mt. xxvii. 28 is very doubtful: in Rev. xvii. 4 *Rec.* has the dative, but apparently without any authority.]

[2] To this class belongs also ψωμίζειν, Num. xi. 4, Dt. viii. 16, Wis. xvi. 20; for this we find ψωμίζειν τινά τινι Jambl. *Pyth.* 13. But in 1 C. xiii. 3 ψωμίζειν πάντα τὰ ὑπάρχοντα is *to convert into food (use as food) all my goods*.

[3] 2 Chr. xvii. 9 לִמֵּד בִּיהוּדָה is not a certain example of this construction in Hebrew, as the meaning probably is *teach in Judah*.—In A. vii. 22, ἐπαιδεύθη πάσῃ σοφίᾳ does not stand for πᾶσαν σοφίαν (compare Diod. S. 1. 91); the dative points out the *means* of the education, whilst ἐπαιδ. πᾶσαν σοφίαν would be *edoctus est* (institutus ad) *sapientiam*. The true reading however is probably ἐν π. σοφίᾳ: compare Plat. *Crito* 50 d.

[4] [To this should probably be added περιβάλλειν τινί τι, L. xix. 43 (*Rec.*, Treg., Westcott): A. Buttmann p. 149.]

SECT. XXXII.] THE ACCUSATIVE. 285

the supposition that the expression ἱλάσκεσθαι τὸν θεὸν τὰς ἁμαρτίας had come into use: the verb is then used altogether in a passive sense, in 1 S. iii. 14, ἐξιλασθήσεται ἀδικία οἴκου Ἠλί.

The accusative neuter of pronouns (τί, τὸ αὐτό, πάντα) and of adjectives (μέγα, etc.), which is joined to many verbs along with an accus. or genitive of the person (as βλάπτειν L. iv. 35, ὠφελεῖν G. v. 2, comp. Lucian, *Tim.* 119, ἀδικεῖν A. xxv. 10, G. iv. 12, Phil. 18, μνησθῆναι 1 C. xi. 2), must be referred essentially to the same principle;[1] only the construction with the double accusative has stopped short, so to speak, at the first stage.[2] I should thus explain Mt. xxvii. 44. It is scarcely necessary to adduce examples of intransitive verbs which are joined with such an accusative (of the thing), and thus become to a limited extent transitives. See however 1 C. ix. 25 πάντα ἐγκρατεύεται, xi. 2,[3] Ph. i. 6,[4] ii. 18, 2 C. vii. 14 (but compare above, no. 1), Mt. ix. 14, Rev. v. 4, al. Fritzsche thus explains Rom. vi. 10, ὃ ἀπέθανεν· and G. ii. 20, ὃ νῦν ζῶ ἐν σαρκί: see above § 24. Rem. 3.

b. An accusative of subject and predicate (Matth. 420, Don. p. 500, Jelf 375. 5): Jo. vi. 15 [*Rec.*], ἵνα ποιήσωσιν αὐτὸν βασιλέα· L. xix. 46, ὑμεῖς αὐτὸν (οἶκον) ἐποιήσατε σπήλαιον λῃστῶν· H. i. 2, ὃν ἔθηκε κληρονόμον (i. 13), Ja. v. 10, ὑπόδειγμα λάβετε τῆς κακοπαθείας . . . . τοὺς προφήτας· H. xii. 9, τοὺς τῆς σαρκὸς πατέρας εἴχομεν παιδευτάς· Ph. iii. 7, ταῦτα (κέρδη) ἥγημαι ζημίαν· 2 P. iii. 15, τὴν τοῦ κυρίου ἡμῶν μακροθυμίαν σωτηρίαν ἡγεῖσθε· L. i. 59, ἐκάλουν αὐτὸ . . . . Ζαχαρίαν· ver. 53 (Pol. 15. 2. 4). This double accusative is especially found after verbs of *making, naming* (nominating), *setting up, regarding as*, etc.: Mt. iv. 19, xxii. 43, Jo. v. 11, x. 33, xix. 7, A. v. 31, vii. 10, xx. 28, L. xii. 14, xix. 46, Rom. iii. 25, vi. 11, viii. 29, 1 C. iv. 9, ix. 5, 2 C. iii. 6, E. ii. 14, Ph. ii. 29, Tit. ii. 7, H. vii. 28, xi. 26, Ja. ii. 5, Rev. xxi. 5, 2 S. ii. 5, 13, iii. 15.

The accusative of the predicate (of destination) is however sometimes annexed by means of the preposition εἰς: as A. xiii. 22, ἤγειρεν αὐτοῖς τὸν Δαυὶδ εἰς βασιλέα· vii. 21, ἀνεθρέψατο

---

[1] Matt. 415. Rem. 3, 421. Rem. 2, Rost pp. 492, 498 (Jelf 578. Obs. 2, 579. 6).
[2] We also say *jem. etwas, viel*, etc., *fragen*, but not *jem. eine Nachricht fragen.*
[3] [1 C. xi. 2 is quoted above, and is evidently retained here (from ed. 5) by accident.]
[4] ["The accus. αὐτὸ τοῦτο is not governed by πεποιθώς, but is *appended* to it as specially marking the 'content and compass of the action' (Madvig, *Synt.* § 27. a.), or, more exactly, 'the object in reference to which the action extends' (Krüg. § 46. 4. 1 sq.):" Ellicott *in loc.*—On the "quantitative accus." see Riddell, Plat. *Apol.* p. 112 sq., Ellic. on Ph. iv. 13 (Jelf 578. Obs. 2).]

αὐτὸν ἑαυτῇ εἰς υἱόν *for her son*,[1] xiii. 47 (compare also the passive λογίζεσθαι εἴς τι A. xix. 27, Rom. ii. 26, ix. 8, § 29. 3. Rem.): or by means of ὡς, 2 Th. iii. 15, καὶ μὴ ὡς ἐχθρὸν (τοῦτον, ver. 14) ἡγεῖσθε (בְּ תַּשְׁחֵת). This is a Hebraistic construction (Ewald, *Gr.* 603), and is often used by the LXX in imitation of the Hebrew: Is. xlix. 6, 2 K. iv. 1, Judith iii. 8, v. 11, Gen. xii. 2, xliii. 17, 1 S. xv. 11, Esth. ii. 7, iv. 4.[2] What has been quoted from the older Greek writers as parallel with the construction with εἰς is of a different kind; as for instance the εἰς of destination, Her. 1. 34, πάντες τοῖσι χρέονται ἐς πόλεμον· also Eurip. *Troad.* 1201, οὐ γὰρ εἰς κάλλος τύχας δαίμων δίδωσι· Alciphr. 3. 28. In later writers, however, we find real parallels: e.g. Niceph. Constant. p. 51 (ed. Bonn), ὁ τῆς πόλεως ἅπας δῆμος . . . . ἀναγορεύουσιν εἰς βασιλέα Ἀρτέμιον· p. 18, εἰς γυναῖκα δίδωμί σοι αὐτήν· Geo. Pachym. I. 349, τὴν ἐκείνου ἔκγονον λαβὼν εἰς γυναῖκα· Theophan. contin. p. 223, κεχρισμένος εἰς βασιλέα: see, in general, the indices to Pachymeres, Leo Grammaticus, and Theophanes, in the Bonn edition; also *Acta Apocr.* p. 71.

To the same mode of expression might be referred H. xi. 8, λαμβάνειν εἰς κληρονομίαν· and perhaps A. vii. 53, ἐλάβετε τὸν νόμον εἰς διαταγὰς ἀγγέλων, *ye received the law for* (i. e. *as*) *ordinances of angels*, see Bengel *in loc.*; but it is easier to give εἰς the meaning which it bears in Mt. xii. 41. In Ph. iv. 16, the construction εἰς τὴν χρείαν μοι ἐπέμψατε is evidently different from τὴν χρείαν μοι ἐπ., and hence has no place here.

L. ix. 14, κατακλίνατε αὐτοὺς κλισίας ἀνὰ πεντήκοντα (in rows by fifties), and Mk. vi. 39, ἐπέταξεν αὐτοῖς ἀνακλῖναι πάντας συμπόσια συμπόσια (in separate table-companies), are substantially of the same kind as the above examples. These accusatives are most easily understood as predicative; see § 59.

5. Verbs which in the active voice govern an accusative of both person and thing, retain the latter in the passive: 2 Th. ii. 15, παραδόσεις ἃς ἐδιδάχθητε· L. xvi. 19, ἐνεδιδύσκετο πορφύραν· H. vi. 9. Compare Ph. iii. 8; also 1 C. xii. 13, omitting [the second] εἰς. So also in the constructions noticed above, no. 2:

---

[1] Compare Xen. *An.* 4. 5. 24, πώλους εἰς δασμὸν βασιλεῖ τρεφομένους; whereas Arrian (*Al.* 1. 26. 5) has, τοὺς ἵππους, οὓς δασμὸν βασιλεῖ ἔτρεφεν, see Ellendt *in loc.*

[2] [There is some mistake in the last reference.—All these passages illustrate the construction with εἰς: the pleonastic use of ὡς with these verbs need not be considered Hebraistic, see § 65. 1.]

L. xii. 48, δαρήσεται ὀλίγας (compare δέρειν τινὰ πληγάς) Mk. x. 38, τὸ βάπτισμα, ὃ ἐγὼ βαπτίζομαι, βαπτισθῆναι· Rev. xvi. 9 (compare Lucian, *Tox.* 61, Dion. Hal. IV. 2162. 8). The accusative of the predicate passes into a nominative in H. v. 10, προςαγορευθεὶς . . . . ἀρχιερεύς· Mt. v. 9, αὐτοὶ υἱοὶ θεοῦ κληθήσονται· Ja. iv. 4, ἐχθρὸς θεοῦ καθίσταται.

Those verbs also which in the active voice govern a dative of the person with an accusative of the thing, retain the latter in the passive, being treated in the passive voice exactly like causative verbs: G. ii. 7, πεπίστευμαι τὸ εὐαγγέλιον (from πιστεύω τινί τι; in the passive, πιστεύομαί τι), 1 C. ix. 17, Rom. iii. 2, 1 Tim. i. 11,[1] see Fischer, *Well.* III. I. 437, Matth. 424. 2. Περίκειμαι follows the same analogy: A. xxviii. 20, τὴν ἅλυσιν ταύτην περίκειμαι (from ἅλυσις περίκειταί μοι), H. v. 2; see D'Orville, *Charit.* p. 240, Matth. *l. c.*

In this way the accusative came to be used with passive verbs, in general, to indicate the more remote object, and especially the *part* of the subject which is in the state or condition indicated by the verb: 1 Tim. vi. 5, διεφθαρμένοι τὸν νοῦν (as if from διαφθείρειν τινὶ τὸν νοῦν), 2 Tim. iii. 8, Jo. xi. 44, δεδεμένος τοὺς πόδας καὶ τὰς χεῖρας· Ph. i. 11, πεπληρωμένοι καρπὸν δικαιοσύνης·[2] 2 C. iii. 18, τὴν αὐτὴν εἰκόνα μεταμορφούμεθα·[3] H. x. 22 sq. On this compare Valcken. *ad Herod.* 7. 39, Hartung, *Casus* 61 (Don. p. 500, Jelf 584).

Whether Mt. xi. 5, πτωχοὶ εὐαγγελίζονται, and H. iv. 2, ἐσμὲν εὐηγγελισμένοι (ver. 6)—compare 2 S. xviii. 31, Joel ii. 32—fall under the above rule,[4] or whether they should be derived from εὐαγγελίζεσθαί τινά τι, remains doubtful: see however § 39. 1.

6. The accusative employed to denote a material object *mediately* was gradually extended more and more, and thus there arose certain concise constructions of various kinds, which

---

[1] On the other hand, see e. g. 1 C. xiv. 34, οὐκ ἐπιτρέπεται αὐταῖς λαλεῖν· A. xxvi. 1.

[2] [See Ellic. *in loc.* and on Col. i. 9. This construction of πληροῦσθαι is followed by γέμω in Rev. xvii. 3, 4, γέμον τὰ ὀνόματα, τὰ ἀκάθαρτα. In modern Greek words of fulness may take an accus., see Mullach p. 331. For 2 C. vi. 13 see below, § 66. 1. *b.*—It will be observed that πληροῦσθαι, like μεριμνᾶν, is found in the N. T. with all three cases.]

[3] ["Μεταμορφοῦν, though often construed with εἰς, yet, as a verb of *developing into a certain form*, has a right to take a simple accusative" (i. e. of the state *into which*): "this accus. (of the thing) remains unchanged when the verb is passive:" Meyer *in loc.* "The compounds of μετὰ which denote *change* generally take an accus. of the new state or position:" Jelf 636. *Obs.*]

[4] [That is, the rule that πιστεύω τινί τι may pass into πιστεύεταί τι.]

we are compelled to resolve by prepositions, etc.: in these the N. T. participates to a moderate extent only. First of all, in definitions of time and space we ourselves can still apprehend the accusative as the case of the object : L. xxii. 41, ἀπεσπάσθη ἀπ' αὐτῶν ὡσεὶ λίθου βολήν, *he withdrew a stone's cast* (as if it were, by his withdrawing he accomplished the distance of a stone's cast); Jo. vi. 19, ἐλαληκότες ὡς σταδίους εἴκοσι πέντε (Matth. 425. 1), 1 P. iv. 2, τὸν ἐπίλοιπον ἐν σαρκὶ βιῶσαι χρόνον· Jo. ii. 12, ἐκεῖ ἔμειναν οὐ πολλὰς ἡμέρας· L. i. 75, ii. 41, xv. 29, xx. 9, Jo. i. 40, v. 5,[1] xi. 6, Mt. ix. 20, A. xiii. 21, H. xi. 23, iii. 17. (Madv. 29 sq.) Thus in the N. T., as elsewhere, the accusative is the ordinary designation of *duration* of time (in Jo. v. 5, however, ἔτη belongs to ἔχων, see Meyer). Sometimes it denotes the (approximate) *point* of time, as in Jo. iv. 52, ἐχθὲς ὥραν ἑβδόμην ἀφῆκεν αὐτὸν ὁ πυρετός· A. x. 3, Rev. iii. 3 ; but in this case περί with the accus. is more frequently used. See Krüg. p. 17 (Don. p. 498, Jelf 577 sq.).

When the accusative, either a single word or a phrase, is annexed to other words to define them more exactly, as regards kind, number, degree, or sphere, the construction most nearly resembles the use of the accusative with passive verbs noticed above (no. 5) :[2] Jo. vi. 10, ἀνέπεσαν οἱ ἄνδρες τὸν ἀριθμὸν ὡσεὶ πεντακισχίλιοι (*as regards number*),—compare Isocr. *Big.* 842, Aristot. *Pol.* 2. 8, Ptol. 4. 6. 34 (many other examples are given by Lobeck, *Phryn.* p. 364 sq., *Paral.* p. 528) ; Jude 7, τὸν ὅμοιον τούτοις τρόπον ἐκπορνεύσασαι· Mt. xxiii. 37, ὃν τρόπον ὄρνις ἐπισυνάγει· 2 Tim. iii. 8 (Plat. *Rep.* 7. 517 c, Plut. *Educ.* 4. 4, 9. 18), A. xviii. 3, σκηνοποιὸς τὴν τέχνην (Lucian, *Asin.* 43, Agath. 2. 46, *Acta Apocr.* p. 61). This accusative however is very rare in the N. T.: even in A. xviii. 3 the best MSS. have τῇ τέχνῃ, compare § 31. On the other hand, we meet with a number of purely adverbial adjectives, which possibly were in very common use in the colloquial language : as μακράν *to a distance, far,* μάτην *in cassum,* ἀκμήν (the moment) *now,* τὴν ἀρχήν (Jo. viii. 25), δωρεάν, τὸ τέλος (1 P. iii. 8), comp. § 54. 1. See on the whole Herm. *Vig.* p. 882 sq. To

---

[1] [Jo. v. 5 is wrongly quoted here : the true construction is given in the next sentence to this.]

[2] As to Hebrew, comp. Ewald p. 591 sq. [Gesen. *Gr.* p. 193 (Bagst.), Kalisch, *Gr.* I. 248 sq.]

the same category belong also certain parenthetical phrases, as in Rom. xii. 18, εἰ δυνατόν, τὸ ἐξ ὑμῶν, μετὰ πάντων ἀνθρ. εἰρηνεύοντες· ix. 5 (i. 15¹), H. ii. 17, v. 1, Rom. xv. 17 (Matth. 283, Madv. 31, Jelf 579, Don. p. 502).

How the accusative of quality coincides with the dative has been already noticed. Thus τῷ ἀριθμῷ is sometimes found instead of τὸν ἀριθμόν. Where in the N. T. the dative is used, we commonly find the accusative in Greek writers: as τὸ γένος (*natione*) Xen. *Cyr.* 4. 6. 2, Herod. 1. 8. 2, Diod. S. 1. 4, Arr. *Al.* 1. 27. 8, and τῷ γένει Mk. vii. 26, A. iv. 36 (Palæph. 6. 2, 11. 2); ἐκλύεσθαι τῇ ψυχῇ H. xii. 3, and τὴν ψυχήν Diod S. 20. 1; βραδεῖς τῇ καρδίᾳ L. xxiv. 25, but βραδὺς τὸν νοῦν Dion. H. *De Lys.* p. 243 (Lips.). See Krüg. p. 18, Lob. *Paral.* p. 528 (Wetstein, *N. T.* I. 826). In Demosth. *Ep.* 4. p. 118 b, θρασὺς τῷ βίῳ stands by the side of μὴ πολίτης τὴν φύσιν. For τοῦτον τὸν τρόπον even Greek prose writers more frequently use κατὰ τ. τ. τρόπον.

We have a very singular expression in Mt. iv. 15, ὁδὸν θαλάσσης (from Isaiah), usually rendered *by the way*. Such passages as 1 S. vi. 9, εἰ ὁδὸν ὁρίων αὐτῆς πορεύσεται,² Num. xxi. 33, Ex. xiii. 17 (compare L. ii. 44) do not justify this use of an accusative side by side with vocatives in an address, without any government (by a verb): this would lie altogether beyond the limits of a prose style (Bernh. p. 114 sq.). Thiersch's remarks (p. 145 sq.) do not decide the point. Can it be that we ought to read οἱ ὁδὸν θαλ. (οἰκοῦντες), according to the LXX?³ Meyer supplies εἶδε (from ver. 16) as the governing verb, but this is harsh.⁴ The topographical difficulties of the ordinary translation are not insuperable;

---

¹ [This passage is taken differently below, § 34. 2. If it comes in here, τὸ κατ᾽ ἐμέ is parenthetical, "as far as I am concerned, there is readiness" (Meyer, ed. 3). In § 34 Winer joins τό with πρόθυμον, taking κατ᾽ ἐμέ as an attributive: so Fritzsche (propensio ad me attinens), Meyer (ed. 4), al. Bengel and others take τὸ κατ᾽ ἐμέ as the subject, πρόθ. as the predicate ("my part is ready," Vaughan): that the phrase τὸ κατ᾽ ἐμέ is elsewhere used adverbially (Fritzsche) is no sufficient objection to this.]

² Wunder on Lobeck, *Ajax* 41 sq.

³ [It is hardly correct to speak of reading οἱ ὁδ. θαλ. "according to the LXX." The *Vat.* and *Sin.* MSS. agree in . . . . Νεφθ. καὶ οἱ λοιποὶ οἱ τὴν παράλιον (*Vat.* -λίαν) καὶ πέραν τ. Ἰορδ. κ. τ. λ. After Νεφθ., *Alex.* inserts ὁδὸν θαλάσσης; and after παράλιον, κατοικοῦντες: in both these additions it has the support of one of the correctors of *Sin.*,—the one whom Tisch. indicates by Cᵃ (about the 7th century). In no reading therefore does ὁδὸν θαλ. occur in connection with οἱ.]

⁴ [Meyer took this view in his 1st and 2nd editions, but in edd. 3, 4, 5, he regards ὁδόν as an adverbial accus., "sea-wards:" similarly De W., Bleek, A. Buttm., Grimm. In the LXX see especially 1 K. viii. 48, 2 Chr. vi. 38, Dt. xi. 30 (quoted by Meyer and Thiersch), where ὁδόν is not under the government of a verb, but answers to the Hebrew דֶּרֶךְ, used absolutely in the sense of *versus*. Meyer and Bleek take πέραν τ. Ἰ. as an independent clause indicating a new region, *Peræa*.]

only πέραν τ. Ἰορδ. must not be regarded (as in Isaiah) as an independent member, for with such a clause Matthew has here no direct concern.

7. It has been maintained that in certain passages the accusative is altogether absolute; but a closer examination will show the grammatical reason for this case in the structure of the sentence. Thus Rom. viii. 3, τὸ ἀδύνατον τοῦ νόμου .... ὁ θεὸς τὸν ἑαυτοῦ υἱὸν πέμψας .... κατέκρινε τὴν ἁμαρτίαν, is really equivalent to τὸ ἀδύνατον τοῦ νόμου ἐποίησεν ὁ θεός, πέμψας .... καὶ κατακρίνων κ.τ.λ. (and here ἀδύνατον need not be taken in a passive sense). Τὸ ἀδύνατον may however be a nominative placed at the head of the sentence (compare Wis. xvi. 17).[1] In A. xxvi. 3 the accusative γνώστην ὄντα is certainly to be explained as an anacoluthon; such instances are of frequent occurrence when a participle is annexed, see § 63. I. 2. a.[2] In L. xxiv. 46 sq., ἔδει παθεῖν τὸν Χριστὸν ... καὶ κηρυχθῆναι ἐπὶ τῷ ὀνόματι αὐτοῦ μετάνοιαν .... ἀρξάμενον[3] ἀπὸ Ἱερουσαλήμ, the accusative in itself (in the construction of the accusative with the infinitive) is grammatically clear: there is merely some looseness in the reference of ἀρξάμενον, *beginning* (i.e., *the* κηρύσσων *beginning*),—or it may be taken impersonally, in the sense of *a beginning being made* (compare Her. 3. 91): see also Kypke I. 344 sq. In Rev. i. 20 the accusatives depend on γράψον (ver. 19), as has long been admitted. Lastly, in Rev. xxi. 17, ἐμέτρησε τὸ τεῖχος τῆς πόλεως ἑκατόν τεσσαρ. πηχῶν, μέτρον ἀνθρώπου κ.τ.λ., the last words are a loose apposition to the sentence ἐμέτρησε τὸ τεῖχος κ.τ.λ.: compare Matth. 410 (Jelf 580, Don. p. 502).[4] On an accusative in apposition to a whole sentence, as in Rom. xii. 1, see § 59. 9.

---

[1] [See § 63. 2. *d*; and on L. xxiv. 47, § 66. 3.]
[2] Schwarz (*De Solœc.* p. 94 sq.) has not adduced any example that is exactly of the same kind.
[3] [Tregelles, Alford, Tischendorf, Westcott and Hort, read ἀρξάμενοι: see § 63. 2. *a.*]
[4] Compare further Matthiæ, Eur. *Med.* p. 501, Hartung p. 54, Wannowski, *Syntax. Anom.* p. 128 sqq.

Section XXXIII.

Verbs (neuter) connected by means of a preposition with a dependent noun.

A considerable number of verbs, especially such as denote an emotion or a tendency of the mind, are joined to their predicate by means of a preposition. In this point N. T. usage sometimes agrees with that of classic writers, sometimes rather betrays a Hebrew-Oriental colouring.

a. Verbs of *rejoicing* or *grieving*, which often take a simple dative in Greek authors (Fritz. *Rom.* III. 78 sq.), are in the N. T. usually followed by ἐπί with the dative:[1] as χαίρειν, Mt. xviii. 13, L. i. 14, A. xv. 31, 1 C. xiii. 6, Rev. xi. 10 (compare Xen. *Cyr.* 8. 4. 12, Diod. S. 19. 55, Isocr. *Permut.* 738, Arrian, *Ind.* 35. 8); εὐφραίνεσθαι, Rev. xviii. 20 (Ecclus. xvi. 1, 1 Macc. xi. 44, Xen. *Conv.* 7. 5); συλλυπεῖσθαι, Mk. iii. 5 (Xen. *Mem.* 3. 9. 8, compare χαλεπῶς φέρειν ἐπί τινι Xen. *Hell.* 7. 4. 21). Sometimes however these verbs take ἐν (λυπεῖν ἐν, Jacobs, *Achill. Tat.* p. 814): as χαίρειν, L. x. 20, Ph. i. 18 (Col. i. 24, compare Soph. *Trach.* 1119); εὐφραίνεσθαι, A. vii. 41; ἀγαλλιᾶσθαι, 1 P. i. 6 (but ἀγάλλεσθαι ἐπί Xen. *Mem.* 2. 6. 35, 3. 5. 16).

Of the verbs which signify *to be angry*, ἀγανακτεῖν is construed with περί (to be angry *on account of* some one), Mt. xx. 24, Mk. x. 41; but ὀργίζεσθαι (like ἀγανακτεῖν ἐπί Lucian, *Abdic.* 9, Aphthon. *Progymn.* c. 9, p. 267) with ἐπί τινι, Rev. xii. 17, compare Joseph. *Bell. Jud.* 3. 9. 8. In the LXX we even find ὀργίζεσθαι ἔν τινι, Jud. ii. 14, and in later Greek ὀργίζεσθαι κατά τινος, as Malal. pp. 43, 102, 165, al. The opposite, εὐδοκεῖν, like the Hebrew חָפֵץ בְּ and after the example of the LXX, is construed with ἐν (*to have pleasure in*), whether the reference is to persons (Mt. iii. 17, L. iii. 22, 1 C. x. 5), or to things, 2 C. xii. 10, 2 Th. ii. 12 (θέλειν ἐν Col. ii. 18, compare 1 S. xviii. 22?[2]): Greek writers would be content with the simple dative.

---
[1] Compare Wurm, *Dinarch.* p. 40 sq.
[2] [The objections to this interpretation are, (1) that this harsh Hebraism is not found elsewhere in the N. T.; (2) that in the O. T. this construction occurs only in connexion with a personal object (Ellicott, Meyer, A. Buttm. p. 376): the latter objection is overstated, see Ps. cxi. 1, cxlvi. 10. On the other explanations see Ellicott and Alford *in loc.* The former supplies καταβρα βεύειν after θέλων (so Meyer, A. Buttm.): by Alford, Wordsworth, and others, θέλων is

'Αρκεῖσθαι, which usually takes a dative (L. iii. 14, H. xiii. 5), is once construed with ἐπί (3 Jo. 10).

b. Verbs signifying *to wonder, be amazed*, are followed by ἐπί with the dative, as they very frequently are in Greek writers: θαυμάζειν, Mk. xii. 17, L. xx. 26 ; ἐκπλήσσεσθαι, Mt. xxii. 33, Mk. i. 22, xi. 18, L. iv. 32, A. xiii. 12. We find also θαυμάζειν περί τινος, L. ii. 18 (Isæus 3. 28 [1]), and θαυμάζ. διά τι *to wonder on account of something*, Mk. vi. 6, as in Æl. 12. 6, 14. 36, θαυμάζειν τινὰ διά τι. In L. i. 21, however, θαυμ. ἐν τῷ χρονίζειν may mean *while he delayed*; yet compare Ecclus. xi. 21. On ξενίζεσθαί τινι see above, § 31. 1. *f.*

c. Of verbs signifying *to pity*, σπλαγχνίζεσθαι is usually followed by ἐπί, either with the accusative (Mt. xv. 32, Mk. vi. 34, viii. 2, ix. 22), or with the dative, L. vii. 13, Mt. xiv. 14 ; once only by περί, Mt. ix. 36. 'Ελεεῖσθαι [ἐλεεῖν] is treated as a transitive verb; see § 32. 1.

d. Verbs of *relying on, trusting, hoping, boasting*, are construed with ἐπί, ἐν, and εἰς. Πέποιθα ἐπί τινι, Mk. x. 24, L. xi. 22, 2 C. i. 9 (Agath. 209. 5, 306. 20); ἐπί τι or τινα, Mt. xxvii. 43, 2 Th. iii. 4; ἔν τινι, Ph. iii. 3.[2] Πιστεύειν ἐπί τινι, Rom. ix. 33, 1 P. ii. 6, from the LXX: on πιστεύειν εἰς or ἐπί τινα *believe on some one*, see above, § 31. 5. 'Ελπίζειν ἐπί with dative, Rom. xv. 12, Ph. iv. 10 [3] (Pol. 1. 82. 6), and with accusative 1 Tim. v. 5, 1 Macc. ii. 61 ; εἰς, Jo. v. 45, 2 C. i. 10, 1 P. iii. 5, Ecclus. ii. 9 (Herod. 7. 10. 1, Joseph. *Bell. Jud.* 6. 2. 1, ἡ εἰς τινα ἐλπίς Plut. *Galba* c. 19); ἐν, 1 C. xv. 19 (Xen. *Cyr.* 1. 4. 25, *Mem.* 4. 2. 28, Pol. 1. 59. 2 ἐλπίδα ἔχειν ἔν τ.).[4] Καυχᾶσθαι ἐπί τινι, Rom. v. 2 (Ps. xlviii. 7, Ecclus. xxx. 2, Diod. S. 16. 70, like σεμνύνεσθαι Diog. L. 2. 71, Isocr. *Big.* p. 840, and φυσιοῦσθαι Diog. L. 6. 24); more frequently ἔν τινι, Rom. ii. 17, 23, v. 3, 1 C. iii. 21, G. vi. 13 (Ps. cxlix. 5, Jer. ix. 23): but

---

connected closely with καταβραβευέτω ("of purpose," Alford : "by the exercise of his mere will," Wordsworth). Lightfoot, whose explanation agrees with Winer's, quotes *Test. xii. Patr.* Asher 1, ἐὰν ἡ ψυχὴ θέλῃ ἐν καλῷ.]

[1] Compare Schoemann, *Isæus* p. 244.
[2] [A Buttmann (p. 175) adds πιστ. εἰς, G. v. 10, considering εἰς ὑμᾶς as expressing the *object* of the trust : so Meyer, De Wette, Lünemann. Others, "with regard to you :" see Ellicott *in loc.* There is the same uncertainty in 2 Th. iii. 4.]
[3] [This should be 1 Tim. iv. 10.]
[4] [On the constructions of ἐλπίζω in the N. T. see Ellicott on 1 Tim. iv. 10. See also § 31. 1. *c.* note.]

not κατά in 2 C. xi. 18 (see Meyer *in loc.*), or ὑπέρ in 2 C. vii. 14,—comp. ix. 2.

e. Of verbs which signify *to sin*, ἁμαρτάνειν is connected by εἰς with the object sinned against, Mt. xviii. 21, L. xvii. 4, 1 C. vi. 18, al.; compare Soph. *Œd. C.* 972, Her. 1. 138, Isocr. *Panath.* p. 644, *Permut.* p. 750, *Ægin.* pp. 920, 934, Marc. Anton. 7. 26, Wetstein I. 443 : this verb is also followed by πρός τινα Joseph. *Antt.* 14. 15. 2, περί τινα Isocr. *Permut.* 754 (ἁμαρτ. τινί 1 S. xiv. 33, 1 K. viii. 31, 33, Jud. x. 10).

f. The verbs ἀρέσκειν *please* and φανῆναι *appear* do not take the dative of the person to whom something gives pleasure or appears in a certain light, but are followed by the Hellenistic preposition ἐνώπιον : A. vi. 5, ἤρεσεν ὁ λόγος ἐνώπιον παντὸς τοῦ πλήθους (Dt. i. 23), L. xxiv. 11, ἐφάνησαν ἐνώπιον αὐτῶν ὡςεὶ λῆρος τὰ ῥήματα. In the LXX ἀρέσκειν is also joined with ἐναντίον τινός, Num. xxxvi. 6, Gen. xxxiv. 18, 1 Macc. vi. 60.[1]

g. Of verbs of *seeing*, βλέπειν is often followed by εἰς (*intueri*), Jo. xiii. 22, A. iii. 4,—a construction which is not unknown to Greek writers, see Wahl.

The use of the preposition μετά or σύν with verbs of *following* (compare *comitari cum aliquo* in Latin inscriptions), as in Rev. vi. 8, xiv. 13,[2] is, strictly speaking, an instance of pleonasm. Ἀκολουθεῖν ὀπίσω τινός (אַחֲרֵי), Mt. x. 38 (Is. xlv. 14), is Hebraistic.

Substantives derived from such verbs as the above are in like manner joined with their object by means of a preposition: as πίστις ἐν Χριστῷ, G. iii. 26, E. i. 15, al.; παρουσία πρὸς ὑμᾶς, Ph. i. 26 ; θλίψεις ὑπὲρ ὑμῶν, E. iii. 13 ; ζῆλος ὑπὲρ ἐμοῦ, 2 C. vii. 7 : see Fritz. *Rom.* I. 195, 365 sq.

SECTION XXXIV.

ADJECTIVES.

1. Though the two classes of nouns, substantives and adjectives, differ in the notions which they express, yet the latter (including participles) are also found within the circle of substantives. In this usage—which is much more varied in Greek than, for in-

---

[1] [Also in Dt. i. 23 (quoted above), according to *Vat.*]
[2] See Wetstein, *N. T.* I. 717, Lob. p. 354, Schæf. *Demosth.* V. 590, Herm. *Lucian* p. 178, Krüg. p. 74. (Jelf 593. *Obs.* 2.)

stance, in Latin—the adjective may appear either with or without the article, and may have any gender, the latter being determined sometimes by an original ellipsis, sometimes by the power of the masculine and neuter genders to denote men and things (Krüg. p. 2 sq., Jelf 436, Don. p. 388). Thus we find ἡ ἔρημος (γῆ), τῇ ἐπιούσῃ (ἡμέρᾳ), διοπετές (ἄγαλμα) A. xix. 35, τὸ σηρικόν (ὕφασμα ?) Rev. xviii. 12, ὁ σοφός, ὁ κλέπτων E. iv. 28, βασιλικός, ὁ ἄρχων, ἀλλότριοι *strangers*, κακοποιοί *evildoers*, τὸ ἀγαθόν (τὸ πνευματικόν, ψυχικόν, 1 C. xv. 46 ?).

On the adjectives which are made substantives through ellipsis see § 64. In the class of personal designations (as σοφός, οἱ σοφοί) the following belong characteristically to the N. T. : ὁ πιστός *the believer*, πιστοί *believers*, ἅγιοι, ἐκλεκτοί, ἁμαρτωλοί Rom. xv. 31, xvi. 2, 1 C. vi. 2, 2 C. vi. 15, 1 Tim. i. 15, v. 10, 2 Tim. ii. 10, H. xii. 3, Mt. xxiv. 22. So even with an adjective as an attributive, Rom. i. 7, 1 C. i. 2, κλητοῖς ἁγίοις ; or with a genitive, as in Rom. viii. 33 ἐκλεκτοὶ θεοῦ. In all these instances the adjective indicates persons (men) to whom the particular quality is attached, though there is no necessity for supplying ἄνθρωποι (or ἀδελφοί). So also where ὁ ἀληθινός is used for *God* (1 Jo. v. 20), or ὁ ἅγιος τοῦ θεοῦ for *Christ* (L. iv. 34), or ὁ πονηρός for *the devil*, there is no ellipsis of these substantives : the notion is grammatically complete, *the True One, the Holy One of God*, and we must look elsewhere to learn what Persons are especially so named in the language of the Bible.

2. Especially frequent and diversified are the substantivised neuters (Krüg. p. 4); indeed many of these regularly fill the place of a substantive derivable from the same root, though not always actually existent. These refer not merely to material notions, as μέσον, ἔσχατον, μικρόν, βραχύ, ὀλίγον, φανερόν, κρυπτόν, ἔλαττον, ἄρσεν, κ.τ.λ. (particularly with prepositions, as εἰς τὸ μέσον Mk. iii. 3, Jo. xx. 19, μετὰ μικρόν Mt. xxvi. 73, ἐν ὀλίγῳ A. xxvi. 29, ἐν τῷ φανερῷ Mt. vi. 4 [*Rec.*], εἰς φανερόν Mk. iv. 22);—but also to the non-material and abstract, especially with an appended genitive, as Rom. ii. 4 τὸ χρηστὸν τοῦ θεοῦ (ἡ χρηστότης)· H. vi. 17 τὸ ἀμετάθετον τῆς βουλῆς· Rom. viii. 3, ix. 22, 1 C. i. 25, 2 C. iv. 17, Ph. iii. 8 τὸ ὑπερέχον τῆς γνώσεως· iv. 5, τὸ ἐπιεικὲς ὑμῶν. We find another construction in the place of the genitive in Rom. i. 15, τὸ κατ' ἐμὲ πρόθυμον (τὸ πρόθυμον, *the purpose*, Eur. *Iph. Taur.* 983 [989]). The plurals of adjectives are as a rule concretes, and denote whole classes of things (or persons): τὰ ὁρατὰ καὶ ἀόρατα Col. i. 16, ἐπουράνια and ἐπίγεια Jo. iii. 12, Ph. ii. 10, τὰ βα-

θέα Rev. ii. 24, ἀρχαῖα 2 C. v. 17. These are sometimes more exactly defined by the context : thus in Jo. iii. 12 ἐπουράνια means heavenly *truths ;* in Ph. ii. 10, heavenly *beings ;* in E. ii. 6 and iii. 10, heavenly *places* (= οὐρανοί, compare the variant in E. i. 20), etc. In Rom. i. 20, τὰ ἀόρατα τοῦ θεοῦ, the plural has reference to the two attributes specified in the following words, viz. ἥ τε ἀΐδιος δύναμις καὶ θειότης ; and Philippi has explained the word more correctly than Fritzsche. (On E. vi. 12, πνευματικὰ τῆς πονηρίας, see Rem. 3.)

We must not bring in here 1 P. i. 7, τὸ δοκίμιον τῆς πίστεως, for δοκίμιον is a substantive proper (there is no adjective δοκίμιος).[1] In Rom. i. 19 also τὸ γνωστὸν τοῦ θεοῦ is not simply equivalent to ἡ γνῶσις τ. θ. ; if it were so, it would be hard to see why Paul did not use an expression so familiar to him as ἡ γνῶσις. The meaning is either *what is known* (to man) *of God,* or *what may be known of* (or *in*) *God.*[2] I prefer the former as the more simple : Paul is speaking of the *objective* knowledge, of the sum of what is known of God (from what source, see ver. 20). This objective γνωστόν becomes subjective, inasmuch as it φανερόν ἐστιν ἐν αὐτοῖς. Hence it is evident why Paul did not write ἡ γνῶσις.

This mode of expression, which arises quite simply out of the nature of the neuter, is not unknown to Greek writers : the later prose authors in particular have adopted it from the technical language of philosophy. At the same time, the examples collected by Georgi (*Hierocr.* I. 39) need very much sifting. As real parallels may be quoted Demosth. *Phil.* 1. p. 20 a, τὸ τῶν θεῶν εὐμενές· *Fals. Leg.* p. 213 a, τὸ ἀσφαλὲς αὐτῆς· Thuc. 1. 68, τὸ πιστὸν τῆς πολιτείας· 2. 71, τὸ ἀσθενὲς τῆς γνώμης· Galen, *Protrept.* 2, τὸ τῆς τέχνης ἄστατον, and τὸ τῆς βάσεως εὐμετακύλιστον· Heliod. 2. 15. 83, τὸ ὑπερβάλλον τῆς λύπης· Plat. *Phædr.* 240 a, Strabo 3. 168, Philostr. *Ap.* 7. 12, Diod. S. 19. 55, Diog. L. 9. 63. With the participle this construction is especially common in Thucydides (and the Byzantines).[3] An abstract noun and a neuter adjective are combined in Plutarch, *Agis* 20, ἡ πολλὴ εὐλάβεια καὶ τὸ πρᾷον καὶ φιλάνθρωπον.

3. On the other hand, the notion which should be expressed by an attributive[4] adjective is sometimes, by a change of con-

---

[1] On this passage, and on Ja. i. 3, see Fritz. *Prälim.* p. 44.
[2] For the latter meaning of γνωστός, called in question by Tholuck, see Soph. *Œd. R.* 362 (Herm.), Plat. *Rep.* 7. 517 b, Arrian, *Epict.* 2. 20. 4, and comp. Schulthess, *Theol. Annal.* 1829, p. 976.
[3] Comp. Ellendt, Arr. *Al.* I. 253, Niebuhr, *Index* to Dexippus, Eunapius, and Malchus.
[4] On the substitution of a substantive for a *predicative* adjective, on rhetorical grounds (as in 2 C. iii. 9, εἰ ἡ διακονία τῆς κατακρίσεως δόξα), see § 58.

struction, expressed by a substantive. Yet the N. T. is by no means poor in adjectives. It even contains no inconsiderable number which were unknown to the (earlier) Greeks,—some of these coined by the Apostles themselves: as ἐπιούσιος, σαρκικός, πνευματικός, παρείσακτος, πύρινος, ἀκατάκριτος, ἀκρογωνιαῖος, ἀνεπαίσχυντος, αὐτοκατάκριτος, ἀχειροποίητος, βρώσιμος, ἐπιπόθητος, εὐπερίστατος, ἰσάγγελος, κατείδωλος, κυριακός, ταπεινόφρων,[1] etc.

In this case—

a. Sometimes the principal substantive stands in the genitive: 1 Tim. vi. 17, μὴ ἠλπικέναι ἐπὶ πλούτου ἀδηλότητι, *not to trust on uncertainty of riches*, i. e., on riches which are uncertain; Rom. vi. 4, ἵνα ἡμεῖς ἐν καινότητι ζωῆς περιπατήσωμεν· vii. 6. This mode of expression, however, is not arbitrary, but is chosen for the purpose of giving more prominence to the main idea, which, if expressed by means of an adjective, would be thrown more into the background. Hence it belongs to rhetoric, not to grammar. Compare Zumpt, *Lat. Gr.* § 672; and for examples from Greek authors see Held, Plut. *Timol.* p. 368.

Strictly speaking, those passages only should be brought in here in which a substantive governing a genitive is connected with a verb which, from the nature of the case, suits the genitive rather than the governing noun, and consequently points out the genitive as the principal word; as in "ingemuit corvi *stupor*," or 1 Tim. *l. c.*, ἐλπίζειν ἐπὶ πλούτου ἀδηλότητι. Such passages as Col. ii. 5, βλέπων τὸ στερέωμα τῆς πίστεως· 2 C. iv. 7, ἵνα ἡ ὑπερβολὴ τῆς δυνάμεως ᾖ τοῦ θεοῦ· G. ii. 14, ὀρθοποδεῖν πρὸς τὴν ἀλήθειαν τοῦ εὐαγγελίου· ii. 5, also 2 Th. ii. 11, πέμπει ἐνέργειαν πλάνης, must decidedly be excluded from this class.[2] In H. ix. 2, ἡ πρόθεσις τῶν ἄρτων means

---

[1] [On σαρκικός see above, p. 122. Of the remaining words, βρώσιμος (Lev. xix. 23) occurs in Æsch. *Prom.* 479; πύρινος (Ez. xxviii. 14, 16, Ecclus. xlviii. 9) and πνευματικός are used by Aristotle; παρείσακτος (Prol. Sir. παρ. πρόλογος) by Strabo (17. p. 794); ἀνεπαίσχυντος by Josephus (*Antt.* 18. 7. 1); ταπεινόφρων (Pr. xxix. 23) by Plutarch (*Mor.* p. 336. e); ἀκρογωνιαῖος occurs in Is. xxviii. 16.]

[2] Fritzsche (*Rom.* I. 367 sq.) has raised objections against this distinction; he seems however to have misunderstood it. In the passages which belong to the second class the language is merely logical; in those of the first class, rhetorical. When we say *to live according to the truth of the Gospel*, we use the proper and natural expression,—the *truth* of the Gospel is the rule of the life. But when we say *corvi stupor ingemuit*, the language is figurative, just as in *His blood called for vengeance*. Cic. *Nat. D.* 2. 50. 127 [" multæ etiam (bestiæ) insectantes odoris intolerabili fœditate depellunt "] belongs to the second class, and *fœdo odore* would be a less accurate expression.

SECT. XXXIV.]   ADJECTIVES.   297

the laying out of the loaves; and in 1 P. i. 2, as a glance at the context will show, ἁγιασμὸς πνεύματος is not synonymous with πνεῦμα ἅγιον. The phrase λαμβάνειν τὴν ἐπαγγελίαν τοῦ πνεύματος, A. ii. 33, G. iii. 14, signifies *to receive, attain, the promise of the Spirit;* this takes place when we receive the promised blessing itself (κομίζεσθαι τὴν ἐπαγγελίαν), when promise passes into fulfilment.

b. Much more frequently, that substantive which expresses the notion of a (mostly non-material) quality stands in the genitive: L. iv. 22, λόγοι τῆς χάριτος· xvi. 8, οἰκονόμος τῆς ἀδικίας· xviii. 6, κριτὴς τῆς ἀδικίας· Col. i. 13, υἱὸς τῆς ἀγάπης·[1] Rev. xiii. 3, ἡ πληγὴ τοῦ θανάτου *mortal wound,* Rom. i. 26, πάθη ἀτιμίας· 2 P. ii. 10, Ja. i. 25, H. i. 3.[2] Such expressions in prose follow the Hebrew idiom (which employs this construction not merely through poverty in adjectives,[3] but also through the vividness of phraseology which belongs to oriental languages); in the more elevated style, however, there are examples in Greek authors.[4] In later writers phrases of this kind find their way into plain prose (Eustath. *Gramm.* p. 478).

If the genitive of a personal pronoun is annexed, it is joined in translation with the notion expressed by the combination of the two substantives: H. i. 3 τῷ ῥήματι τῆς δυνάμεως αὐτοῦ, *through His powerful word,* Col. i. 13, Rev. iii. 10, xiii. 3. It is usual to go farther still, and maintain[5] that, when two substantives are so combined as to form a single principal notion, the *demonstrative* pronoun, in accordance with the Hebrew idiom (?), agrees grammatically with the governed noun.[6] Thus in A. v. 20, τὰ ῥήματα τῆς

---

[1] [It may perhaps be doubted whether this passage (with most of those in which the genitive has some qualifying word,—"the expression thus losing its *general* character," A. Buttm.) should come in here: see Ellicott *in loc.* On H. i. 3 see Alford.]

[2] But in 2 Th. i. 7, ἄγγελοι δυνάμεως αὐτοῦ means *angels of His power,* i.e., angels who serve His power.

[3] Ewald p. 572. [*Lehrb.* p. 533.]

[4] See Erfurdt, Soph. *Œd. R.* 826, compare Pfochen, *Diatr.* p. 29; but the examples cited by Georgi (*Vind.* p. 214 sqq.) are almost all useless.—The genitive of the *material* does not come in here: λίθου κριός, for example, was to the Greeks exactly equivalent to our *ram of stone,* and the opinion that an adjective should have been used rests merely on a comparison of the Latin idiom. Likewise ὀσμὴ εὐωδίας, Ph. iv. 18 (compare Aristot. *Rhet.* 1. 11. 9), is probably *odour of fragrance,* and is not really put for ὀσμὴ εὐώδης. That 1 C. x. 16, τὸ ποτήριον τῆς εὐλογίας, and Rom. i. 4, πνεῦμα ἁγιωσύνης, are not to be explained by the above rule, is now admitted by the best commentators. Still more unsatisfactory examples are given by Glass, I. 26 sq. [The genitive in ὀσμὴ εὐωδίας is taken below (§ 65. 2) as a genitive of quality, not of material.]

[5] See e.g. Vorst, *Hebraism.* p. 570 sq., Storr, *Observ.* p. 234 sq.

[6] In proof that this is a Hebraism, Ezr. ix. 14, בְּעַמֵּי הַתּוֹעֵבוֹת הָאֵלֶּה, is quoted: but here it is not at all necessary to connect אֵלֶּה with the second substantive.

ζωῆς ταύτης, ταύτης would stand for ταῦτα, *these words of life;* xiii. 26, ὁ λόγος τῆς σωτηρίας ταύτης, *this doctrine of salvation;* Rom. vii. 24, ἐκ τοῦ σώματος τοῦ θανάτου τούτου, compare the Peshito ܡܢ ܦܓܪܐ ܗܢܐ ܕܡܘܬܐ

But this canon (which even Bengel follows) is purely imaginary. In Rom. vii. 24, Paul himself may have joined τούτου with σώματος, but if the pronoun is connected with θανάτου it is not without meaning: the apostle had already spoken repeatedly of θάνατος (ver. 10 sqq.), and therefore could refer back to it: see De Wette *in loc.* In A. xiii. 26 also, as the σωτὴρ Ἰησοῦς had been mentioned in ver. 23, ὁ λόγος τῆς σωτηρίας ταύτης is *the word of this salvation* (effected through Christ). In A. v. 20 the pronoun refers to the salvation which the apostles were at that very time proclaiming. Even the Hebrew combination, as אֱלִילֵי כַסְפּוֹ Is. ii. 20, or שֵׁם קָדְשׁוֹ Ps. lxxxix. 21—which is required by rule, but which is also much more natural, since the two words are really one—is not thus literally rendered by the LXX (compare Is. *l. c.* τὰ βδελύγματα αὐτοῦ τὰ ἀργυρᾶ· Dt. i. 41, τὰ σκεύη τὰ πολεμικὰ αὐτοῦ· Ps. lxxxix. *l. c.*, ἐν ἐλαίῳ ἁγίῳ); and one really cannot see what could lead such writers as Luke and Paul to use so abnormal a construction in sentences so simple.[1]

Rem. 1. Some have found in L. xi. 33, εἰς κρυπτὴν τίθησι, an imitation of the Hebrew use [2] of the feminine adjective to express the neuter. Absurd! Κρυπτή was already in use as a substantive, with the meaning *covered place* or *way, subterranean receptacle, vault* (Athen. 5. 205), and suits this passage well. On the other hand, Mt. xxi. 42 (Mk. xii. 11), παρὰ κυρίου ἐγένετο αὕτη (τοῦτο), καὶ ἐστὶ θαυμαστὴ (θαυμαστόν), is a quotation from Ps. cxvii. 23: yet even the LXX may have used the feminine here in reference to κεφαλὴ γωνίας (Wolf, *Cur. ad h. l.*).

Rem. 2. We have also to mention another Hebraistic [3] usage,—a periphrasis (as it is said) for certain concrete adjectives when used as substantives, formed by means of υἱός or τέκνον followed by a genitive of the abstract noun: υἱοὶ ἀπειθείας E. ii. 2, i.e. *disobedient ones*, υἱοὶ φωτός L. xvi. 8, Jo. xii. 36, τέκνα φωτός E. v. 8, τέκνα ὀργῆς E. ii. 3, τέκνα ὑπακοῆς 1 P. i. 14, τέκνα κατάρας 2 P. ii. 14, ὁ υἱὸς τῆς ἀπωλείας 2 Th. ii. 3. Every one must feel that these combinations are not mere idle periphrases, but that they express the idea with more vividness and therefore with more force. This mode of expression is to be traced to the more lively imagi-

---

[1] The examples quoted from Greek authors by Georgi (*Vind.* p. 204 sqq.) and Munthe (*Obs. Act. v.* 20) lose all plausibility when more closely examined (Fritz. *Mark*, Exc. 1. p. 771 sq.).
[2] Gesen. *Lehrgeb.* p. 661, Vorst, *Hebraism.* p. 282 sq. [Gesen. *Heb. Gr.* p. 180 (Bagst.), Kalisch, *Heb. Gr.* I. 244.]
[3] Vorst, *Hebraism.* p. 467 sqq. [Kalisch I. 262.]

nation of the orientals, by which the most intimate connexion (derivation from and dependence on)—even when the reference is to what is not material—is viewed under the image of the relation of son or child to parent (Ecclus. iv. 11). Hence *children of disobedience* are those who belong to ἀπείθεια as a child to his mother, disobedience having become their nature, their predominant disposition: compare in Hebrew Dt. iii. 18, xxv. 2, 2 S. xii. 5, Ps. lxxxix. 23.

(The expressions παῖδες ἰατρῶν, δυστήνων [1]—used especially by Lucian—grammatically rather resemble υἱοὶ τῶν ἀνθρώπων; neither Schwarz nor Georgi has been able to find in Greek prose an example of παῖς or τέκνον combined with an *abstract* noun, as in the above quotations. From ecclesiastical writers compare Epiphan. *Opp.* I. 380 b, οἱ υἱοὶ τῆς ἀληθινῆς πίστεως. In German [or English] we cannot really expect to find parallels, for such a phrase as "child of death" is derived from Bible language; in the more elevated style, however, we sometimes meet with similar phrases, as for instance, "every man is a child of his age." [2] Of a different kind is 2 Th. ii. 3, ὁ ἄνθρωπος τῆς ἁμαρτίας,—not equivalent to ὁ ἁμαρτωλός—*the man of sin*, i.e., the man who pre-eminently belongs to sin, the representative of sin, in whom sin is personified.)

Rem. 3. E. vi. 12, τὰ πνευματικὰ τῆς πονηρίας, is peculiar. The Greek idiom with which this is compared by the commentators,[3] παρθενικοί for παρθένοι (Lobeck, *Paral.* p. 305 sq.), was in the better ages merely poetical, and besides is not entirely analogous. In the Byzantines, however, we find e.g. ἡ ἱππική for ἡ ἵππος (Ducas p. 18). Τὰ δαιμόνια also, which was originally an adjective, and which is used as a substantive in later Greek by the side of δαίμονες, presents on the whole a true analogy; a genitive in combination with this word, as τὰ δαιμόνια τοῦ ἀέρος, would present no difficulty. In this passage the abstract would be used designedly, in antithesis to πρὸς αἷμα καὶ σάρκα,—"not against material, but against spiritual opposing powers, ye have to maintain your struggle." If however πνευματικά be not taken as equivalent to πνεύματα, the only alternative will be to regard it as a collective plural,—similar in kind to τὰ λῃστρικά Polyæn. 5. 14 (*robber-hordes*, from τὸ λῃστρικόν *robbery*, Lob. *Phryn.* p. 242), and to translate, *the spiritual communities of wickedness*, the evil spirit-powers. See Meyer *in loc.*

---

[1] Schæf. *Dion.* 313.
[2] See on the whole Steiger on 1 P. i. 14, Gurlitt in *Stud. u. Krit.* 1829, p. 728 sq.
[3] See Koppe *in loc.*, Fischer, *Weller* III. i. 295.

Section XXXV.

THE COMPARATIVE DEGREE.[1]

1. The comparative degree is usually expressed in the N. T. in exactly the same manner as in classical Greek, viz. by what is known as the comparative form of the adjective,—the thing with which the comparison is made being placed in the genitive, or (especially where it is a complete sentence) preceded by the connective ἤ.[2] See Jo. iv. 12, μὴ σὺ μείζων εἶ τοῦ πατρὸς ἡμῶν; i. 51, xiii. 16, Mk. xii. 31, 1 C. i. 25, 1 Tim. v. 8, H. xi. 26; Jo. iv. 1, πλείονας μαθητὰς ποιεῖ ἢ Ἰωάννης· 1 C. xiv. 5, 1 Jo. iv. 4; Rom. xiii. 11, ἐγγύτερον ἡμῶν ἡ σωτηρία ἢ ὅτε ἐπιστεύσαμεν· 2 P. ii. 21, 1 C. ix. 15 (Klotz, Devar. p. 583). After πλείων and ἐλάττων, ἤ is often omitted when a numeral follows (Matth. 455. Rem. 4, Jelf 780, Don. p. 393): A. xxiv. 11, οὐ πλείους εἰσί μοι ἡμέραι δεκαδύο· iv. 22, xxiii. 13, xxv. 6[3] (compare Ter. Ad. 2. 1. 46, plus quingentos colaphos infregit mihi).[4] In L. ix. 13 ἤ is inserted.

It is sometimes doubtful whether a genitive that follows a comparative contains the second member of the comparison, or is independent of the comparison. In H. iii. 3, πλείονα τιμὴν ἔχει τοῦ οἴκου κ.τ.λ., we must probably consider οἴκου as dependent on πλείονα; but in 1 C. xiii. 13, μείζων τούτων ἡ ἀγάπη may mean *greater (the greatest) of (among) these*, see no. 3. Compare also 1 C. xii. 23, L. vii. 42 (Lucian, *Fug.* 6).

The comparative is sometimes strengthened by μᾶλλον,[5] as in 2 C. vii. 13, περισσοτέρως μᾶλλον (Plat. *Legg.* 6. 781 a), Ph. i. 23, πολλῷ μᾶλλον κρεῖσσον (*very far better*),—so in reference to another comparative, Mk. vii. 36, ὅσον αὐτοῖς διεστέλλετο, αὐτοὶ μᾶλλον περισσότερον ἐκήρυσσον (see Fritz. *in loc.*[6]): also by ἔτι, H. vii. 15,

---

[1] Compare, in general, G. W. Nitzsch, *De comparativis Græcæ linguæ modis*, in his edition of Plato's *Ion* (Lips. 1822).

[2] In such cases the LXX even use the genitive of the infinitive (Gen. iv. 13).

[3] [Compare p. 744 sq. In most of the N. T. examples the comparative is followed by an indeclinable word: A. Buttmann quotes Mt. xxvi. 53, where we should probably read πλείω δώδεκα λεγιῶνας. Compare p. 313 (ἐπάνω).]

[4] See Lob. p. 410 sq., Held, Plut. *Æm. P.* p. 261.

[5] Μᾶλλον is not joined to the superlative. In 2 C. xii. 9, ἥδιστα οὖν μᾶλλον καυχήσομαι ἐν ταῖς ἀσθενείαις μου, this word belongs to the whole clause ἥδιστα καυχ. κ.τ.λ., *rather therefore will I very gladly glory*, i.e., rather than, repining at the ἀσθένειαι (ver. 8 sq.), beseech God that I may be freed from them: ἥδιστα indicates the degree of the καυχᾶσθαι, μᾶλλον marks the antithesis to what has gone before.

[6] [Fritzsche renders this, *quantum autem ipse iis imperabat* (scil. ne portenti

SECT. XXXV.] THE COMPARATIVE DEGREE. 301

περισσότερον ἔτι κατάδηλον (*still more manifest*), Ph. i. 9 ; and lastly by πολύ, 2 C. viii. 22, πολὺ σπουδαιότερον. All this is very common in Greek writers (Krüg. p. 91 sq.). On μᾶλλον see Wyttenb. *Plut.* I. 238, Ast, Plat. *Phædr.* p. 395, *Legg.* p. 44, Boisson. *Aristæn.* p. 430 sqq. (in Latin compare Cic. *Pis.* 14, mihi .... quavis fuga *potius* quam ulla provincia esset optatior) ; as to ἔτι, compare Plat. *Pol.* 298 e, Xen. *Mem.* 1. 5. 6, *Cyr.* 5. 4. 20, *An.* 1. 9. 10 ; as to πολύ, Xen. *Mem.* 2. 10. 2, Lucian, *Tim.* 50 : sometimes ἔτι and πολύ are combined, Xen. *Mem.* 2. 1. 27, *Cyr.* 1. 6. 17, *An.* 7. 5. 15. (Don. p. 392, Jelf 784, 2.)

So also when the comparative is followed by prepositions which denote excess—as in L. xvi. 8, φρονιμώτερον ὑπὲρ τοὺς υἱοὺς τοῦ φωτός· H. iv. 12, Jud. xi. 25, xv. 2, xviii. 26 : H. ix. 23, κρείττοσι θυσίαις παρὰ ταύτας· i. 4, iii. 3, xi. 4, xii. 24, L. iii. 13—the design is to obtain greater expressiveness. For παρά compare Thuc. 1. 23, πυκνότερον παρὰ τὰ ἐκ τοῦ πρὶν χρόνου μνημονευόμενα· Dio C. 38. 97.[1] See Herm. *Vig.* p. 862 (Don. p. 393, Jelf 637).

2. Instead of the comparative form the positive is occasionally used :—

a. With μᾶλλον,—sometimes because the comparative form appeared unpleasing, sometimes from the wish to write more expressively (Krüg. p. 91) : A. xx. 35, μακάριόν ἐστι μᾶλλον διδόναι ἢ λαμβάνειν· 1 C. xii. 22, G. iv. 27.[2]

b. Followed by a preposition which conveys the notion of excess, as in Philostr. *Ap.* 3. 19, παρὰ πάντας Ἀχαίους μέγας. So in L. xiii. 2, ἁμαρτωλοὶ παρὰ πάντας τοὺς Γαλιλαίους (though it is true ἁμαρτωλός has no comparative), H. iii. 3.[3] In the LXX παρά and ὑπέρ are frequently thus used : Ex. xviii. 11, Num. xii. 3, Hag. ii. 9, Eccl. iv. 9, ix. 4, 1 S. i. 8.

c. Followed by ἤ : Aristot. *Probl.* 29. 6, παρακαταθήκην αἰσχρὸν ἀποστερῆσαι μικρὸν ἢ πολὺ δανεισάμενον (Held, Plut. *Timol.* 317 sq.). This is rare on the whole, but the kindred expression βούλομαι or θέλω ἤ (*malle*) had become a common formula ; see Her. 3. 40, Polyb. 13. 5. 3, Plut. *Alex.* 7, *Sulla* 3.

---

famam disseminarent), *magis impensius prædicabant*, hoc est, *magis impensius rem divulgabant, ad quem modum valde iis imperabat.*]

[1] [This use of παρά is common in modern Greek (Mullach, *Vulg.* p. 333, J. Donalds. *Gr.* p. 34).—As to the meaning of the preposition, compare Riddell, Plat. *Ap.* p. 181.]

[2] [Meyer, Ellicott, and Alford take πολλὰ μᾶλλον as "not simply equivalent to πλείονα ἤ, but implying that both should have *many*, but the desolate one *more* than the other" (Ellicott *in loc.*). In the other examples also μᾶλλον is rather connected with the sentence than directly with the adjective.]

[3] [In H. iii. 3 παρά follows a *comparative*, not a positive.]

The simplest explanation of this is, that (from its use with comparatives) ἤ had come to be regarded as a particle of proportion, which presupposed or in some measure brought with it a comparison:[1] compare Plaut. *Rud.* 4. 4. 70, tacita bona est mulier semper quam loquens, and Tac. *Ann.* 3. 17.

In the N. T. we find—not only θέλω ἤ (1 C. xiv. 19) and λυσιτελεῖ ἤ, *satius est quam* (L. xvii. 2, Tob. iii. 6), but also— an extension of this construction on other sides (as in Greek writers, see Lys. *Affect. Tyr.* 1): L. xv. 7, χαρὰ ἔσται ἐπὶ ἑνὶ ἁμαρτωλῷ μετανοοῦντι ἢ ἐπὶ ἐνενηκονταεννέα δικαίοις, *greater joy than* etc. Compare Num. xii. 6, ἰσχύει οὗτος ἢ ἡμεῖς. With an adjective there is only one example of this kind, but in both records: Mt. xviii. 8, καλόν σοί ἐστιν εἰϛελθεῖν εἰς τὴν ζωὴν χωλὸν ἢ κυλλόν, ἢ δύο χεῖρας . . . ἔχοντα βληθῆναι κ.τ.λ., Mk. ix. 43. 45. The LXX use this construction frequently, as Gen. xlix. 12, Hos. ii. 7, Jon. iv. 3, 8, Lam. iv. 9, Tob. xii. 8, Ecclus. xxii. 15; it was naturally suggested to them by the Hebrew, in which the comparison is made to follow the adjective by means of the preposition מִן.

From Greek writers, compare with L. xvii. 2, ζῆν ἀταράχως συμφέρει ἢ τὸ τρυφᾶν κ.τ.λ. Æsop. 121 (ed. De Furia), Tob. vi. 13; and as regards adjective and adverb, Thuc. 6. 21, αἰσχρὸν βιασθέντας ἀπελθεῖν ἢ ὕστερον ἐπιμεταπέμπεσθαι· Plut. *Pelop.* 4 τούτους ἂν ὀρθῶς καὶ δικαίως προσαγορεύσεις συνάρχοντας ἢ ἐκείνους· Æsop. 134 (De Fur.).[2] (Don. p. 392, Jelf 779. *Obs.* 3.)

In L. xviii. 14, with the reading κατέβη οὗτος δεδικαιωμένος . . . . ἢ ἐκεῖνος, there would, in view of the above usage, be no difficulty whatever (compare Gen. xxxviii. 26, δεδικαίωται Θάμαρ ἢ ἐγώ), except that a comparison is not very suitable here: all the better MSS. however have ἢ γάρ,[3] which is without example. Yet the sentence might perhaps be thus resolved, on Hermann's theory (followed by Bornemann *in loc.*): *this man went justified . . . . or was it then the other* (who went etc.)? The γάρ would be added, as it is added to other interrogative words (and also to ἤ, as Xen. *Cyr.*

---

[1] The explanation given by Hermann (*Vig.* p. 884) and Schæfer (*Ind. Æsop.* p. 138) is more artificial, compare Held, Plut. *Tim.* p. 317: the older grammarians supplied μᾶλλον with the positive. [Hermann, taking *an forte* as the proper meaning of ἤ, thus renders Hom. *Il.* 1. 117, βούλομ' ἐγὼ λαὸν σόον ἔμμεναι, ἢ ἀπολίσθαι, *volo populum salvum esse : an perire volo?*]

[2] See D'Orville, *Charit.* p. 538, Boissonade, Marin. *Procl.* p. 78, Kypke I. 89, II. 228, and Nitzsch *l. c.* p. 71. [Riddell, Plat. *Apol.* p. 183.]

[3] See also Matthæi (small edition) *in loc.*

8. 3. 40, Soph. *Electr.* 1212 sq.), to strengthen the question. Some MSS. have ἤπερ (which in Jo. xii. 43 is not different from ἤ); but it is more probable that this was an emendation of ἢ γάρ, than that ἢ γάρ was derived from it, as the original reading. Lachmann, Tischend. (ed. 1), and Meyer read παρ' ἐκεῖνον,[1] which would present no difficulty of any kind (*justified past—passing over—the other*).

3. The comparative contrasts an object with but one standard of comparison, whether this standard be a single individual, or a united whole: Jo. xiii. 16, οὐκ ἔστι δοῦλος μείζων τοῦ κυρίου· v. 20, μείζονα τούτων δείξει αὐτῷ ἔργα· x. 29. If the appended genitive denotes *all* things of the same class (Mk. iv. 31, μικρότερος πάντων τῶν σπερμάτων· ver. 32, L. xxi. 3, 1 C. xv. 19, E. iii. 8), we must naturally take it as not including the object compared, *less than all* (other) *seeds*. In such a case the comparative may also be rendered by a superlative, *the least of all seeds*. This mode of expression is also found in Greek writers: Demosth. *Fals. Leg.* 246 b, πάντων τῶν ἄλλων χείρω πολίτην· Athen. 3. 247, πάντων καρπῶν ὠφελιμώτερα· Dio Chr. 3. 39, ἁπάντων πιθανώτερος. See Jacobs, *Anthol.* III. 247.

In 1 C. xiii. 13, μείζων τούτων ἡ ἀγάπη, the comparative is not put for the superlative. We must render, *greater of* (among) *these is love;* the comparative being chosen because love is contrasted with faith and hope as *one* category.

4. The comparative is not unfrequently used without any express mention of the standard of comparison [2] (Matth. 457 d, Krüg. p. 90). In most cases this may easily be perceived from the context, as in Jo. xix. 11, A. xviii. 20, 1 C. vii. 38 (compare ver. 36 sq.), xii. 31, H. ii. 1, vi. 16, ix. 11, Ja. iii. 1, 1 P. iii. 7; or the phrase is one in familiar use, as οἱ πλείονες *the majority* (in an assemblage), A. xix. 32, xxvii. 12, 1 C. ix. 19, al. Sometimes, however, the attentive reader finds the meaning of the comparative less obvious, and here earlier exegesis considered the comparative to be used for the positive [3] or the superlative:

---

[1] [This reading, supported by the authority of ℵ, B, D, L, is accepted by Bleek, Tregelles, Westcott and Hort, and others.]

[2] Reiz, *De Accent. Inclin.* p. 54, Ast, Plat. *Polit.* pp. 418, 538, Stallb. *Phileb.* p. 120, *Rep.* 1. 238. [Don. p. 392, Jelf 784, Webster, *Syntax* p. 58, Green, *Gr.* p. 110.]

[3] In Greek authors also the comparative is not used for the positive in such sentences as Lucian, *Epp. Sat.* 3. 32, τὸ ἥδιστον καὶ συμποτικώτερον καὶ ἰσοτιμία κ.τ.λ., or *Bis Accus.* 11, ὃς ἂν μεγαλοφωνότερος αὐτῶν ἦν καὶ θρασύτερος· Her. 2. 46, al. (Heusing. Plut. *Educ.* p. 3). Compare also Heinichen, Euseb. *Hist. Ec.* I. 210 sq., Herm. Luc. *Conscrib. Hist.* p. 284.

2 Tim. i. 18, *βέλτιον σὺ γινώσκεις*, thou knowest it better, i.e. better than I (Lucian, *Pisc.* 20, *ἄμεινον σὺ οἶσθα ταῦτα*) ; A. xxv. 10, *ὡς καὶ σὺ κάλλιον ἐπιγινώσκεις*, better than thou wishest to appear to know (according to the supposition of ver. 9, that he is guilty); 2 C. viii. 17, *τὴν μὲν παράκλησιν ἐδέξατο, σπουδαιότερος δὲ ὑπάρχων*, more zealous, i.e. than to have required an exhortation ; vii. 7, *ὥςτε με μᾶλλον χαρῆναι* more than for the (mere) arrival of Titus (ver. 6), compare ver. 13 ; A. xxvii. 13, *ἆσσον παρελέγοντο τὴν Κρήτην*, nearer than had before been possible (ver. 8); Ph. ii. 28, *σπουδαιοτέρως ἔπεμψα αὐτόν*, i.e. than I should have done, if you had not been made uneasy by the news of his illness (ver. 26) ; i. 12, *τὰ κατ' ἐμὲ μᾶλλον εἰς προκοπὴν τοῦ εὐαγγελίου ἐλήλυθεν*, more (rather) to the furtherance than, as was to be feared, to the hindrance ; Jo. xiii. 27, *ὃ ποιεῖς ποίησον τάχιον*, more quickly than thou appearest to intend to do, hasten the execution of the design, see Lücke *in loc.* Compare Senec. *Agam.* 965, *citius* interea mihi edissere, ubi sit gnatus ; also *ocius*, Virg. *Æn.* 8. 554. In 1 Tim. iii. 14, *ἐλπίζων ἐλθεῖν πρός σε τάχιον*, most render *τάχιον* as a positive (Lachmann's reading, *ἐν τάχει*, is a correction); some as if it were *ὡς τάχιστα*. The words mean : *this I write to thee, hoping* (although I hope) *to come to thee more quickly, sooner,* than thou wilt need these instructions. The reason why he writes, notwithstanding this hope, is given by the words *ἐὰν δὲ βραδύνω κ.τ.λ.*; compare ver. 15. H. xiii. 19 is, *that I may be restored to you sooner* (than I should be without your prayers [1]) ; xiii. 23, *if he come sooner* (than the date of my departure); Rom. xv. 15, *τολμηρότερον ἔγραψα ὑμῖν*, more boldly (more freely), i.e. than was necessary considering your Christian excellence (ver. 14). On Mk. ix. 42 see Fritz. *in loc :* [2] A. xviii. 26 does not require explanation. In 1 C. vii. 38, the relation between the positive *καλῶς ποιεῖ* and the comparative *κρεῖσσον ποιεῖ* is clear from ver. 36 sq. *Περισσοτέρως* also, so common in Paul, is never used without a comparison. In 2 C. i. 12, ii. 4, vii. 13, xi. 23, Ph. i. 14, G. i. 14, H. ii. 1, vi. 17, this comparison is ob-

---

[1] Böhme, who in his translation gives correctly the meaning of this passage, yet maintains in his commentary : *non est comparat. stricte intelligendus.*

[2] [Καλόν ἐστιν αὐτῷ μᾶλλον : "scil. *quam si viveret et discipulos suos corrumperet.*" (Fritzsche.)]

vious at once. In 1 Th. ii. 17, περισσοτέρως ἐσπουδάσαμεν τὸ πρόςωπον ὑμῶν ἰδεῖν κ.τ.λ., the explanation of the *more abundantly*[1] is probably given by the preceding words ἀπορφανισθέντες ἀφ' ὑμῶν πρὸς καιρὸν ὥρας. The loss of their personal intercourse for a time (which Paul calls a state of *orphanhood*) had made his longing greater than it would have been if he had never been thus united with them. In 2 P. i. 19 the meaning of βεβαιότερον is a question for hermeneutics to determine: the fluctuation of opinion in even the most recent commentaries shows how obscure the reference is. In 2 P. ii. 11, however, it can scarcely be doubted that after μείζονες we must supply "than those τολμηταὶ αὐθαδεῖς." On E. iv. 9 see Meyer.[2]

A. xvii. 21, λέγειν τι καὶ ἀκούειν καινότερον, is peculiarly characteristic. The comparative indicates that they wish to hear something *newer* (than that which was just passing current as *new*), and might seem to portray vividly the voracious appetite which the Athenians in particular had for news. The comparative however (usually νεώτερον) was regularly used by the Greeks in the question *what news?* They did not speak of what was "new" simply and absolutely (the positive), but contrasted it with what had been new up to the time of asking. See Her. 1. 27, Eurip. *Orest.* 1327, Aristoph. *Av.* 254, Theophr. *Ch.* 8. 1, Lucian, *Asin.* 41, Diod. S. *Exc. Vat.* p. 24, Plat. *Protag.* 310 b, and *Euthyphr.* c. 1 (see Stallbaum *in loc.*).

In Mt. xviii. 1 (Mk. ix. 34, L. ix. 46, xxii. 24), τῶν ἄλλων at once suggests itself as the complement: μέγιστος would have implied three or four degrees of rank amongst the Twelve.[3] So probably in Mt. xi. 11, ὁ δὲ μικρότερος ἐν τῇ βασιλείᾳ τ. οὐρ., the meaning is, ὁ μικρ. (τῶν) ἄλλων,—the comparative being chosen, it would seem, as corresponding to the preceding μείζων: compare Diog. L. 6. 5, ἐρωτηθεὶς τί μακαριώτερον ἐν ἀνθρώποις, ἔφη, εὐτυχοῦντα ἀποθανεῖν.[4] Others supply Ἰωάννου τοῦ βαπτιστοῦ after μικρότερος: see on the whole Meyer *in loc.* Likewise in A. xvii. 22, κατὰ πάντα ὡς δεισιδαιμονεστέρους ὑμᾶς θεωρῶ, it does not appear that we can join ὡς to the comparative as an intensive particle; we must translate, *In all respects* ("at every step," as it were) *I look on you as more religious men* (than others are, scil. ἄλλων). This was, as is well known, the character of the Athenians: see the commentators. The word θεωρεῖν was designedly chosen, compare ver.

---

[1] ["Because the time of separation was so short," Lünemann, Alford: because "the separation was προσώπῳ οὐ καρδίᾳ," Ellicott, al.]
[2] [Winer's view of this passage is given in § 59. 8. *a.*]
[3] Ramshorn, *Lat. Gr.* p. 316.
[4] Bauer, *Glossar. Theodoret.* 455, Boisson. *Philostr.* 491.

23; and θεωρεῖν ὡς, though not a common expression, can hardly be considered strange.

Rem. 1. It has been maintained that, when πρῶτος is used where two objects only are spoken of (as in Rev. xxi. 1, εἶδον οὐρανὸν καινὸν ..... ὁ γὰρ πρῶτος οὐρανός κ.τ.λ., *prius* cælum, H. x. 9, ἀναιρεῖ τὸ πρῶτον, ἵνα τὸ δεύτερον στήσῃ· Mt. xxi. 36, ἀπέστειλεν ἄλλους δούλους πλείονας τῶν πρώτων· A. i. 1, 1 C. xiv. 30), it stands for the comparative πρότερος. But this is only true from the standpoint of Latin usage; for in Greek it is quite common to find πρῶτος, δεύτερος, not πρότερος, ὕστερος, even where there is a distinct reference to two, and two only;[1] as indeed in German [and English] *former* and *latter* belong rather to the written than to the spoken language. Even πρῶτος with a genitive—as in Jo. i. 15, 30, πρῶτός μου (compare Ælian, *Anim.* 8. 12), and (the adverb) xv. 18, πρῶτον ὑμῶν—is, strictly speaking, not the same as *prior me, prius vobis*. The superlative simply includes the comparative, in accordance with Hermann's remark,[2] "Græcos ibi superlativum pro comparativo dicere, ubi hæc duo simul indicare volunt, et maius quid esse alio et omnino maximum."[3] Compare also Fritz. *Rom.* II. 421, note.

In L. ii. 2,[4] αὕτη ἡ ἀπογραφὴ πρώτη ἐγένετο ἡγεμονεύοντος τῆς Συρίας Κυρηνίου, even recent commentators, taking πρώτη for προτέρα, have maintained that the genitives ἡγεμονεύοντος κ.τ.λ. are dependent on this comparative, *it took place earlier than* (before) *Quirinius was governor*. But this is quite erroneous. If such were Luke's meaning, his language would be not only ambiguous (for the closest and most natural rendering is, *it took place as the first under the government of Quirinius*), but also awkward, if not ungrammatical. Huschke[5] has not succeeded in finding an example which is really parallel: he merely illustrates the very familiar construction of πρῶτος with the genitive of a noun. Tholuck's mistake[6] in regarding Jer. xxix. 2 (LXX) as parallel is exposed by Fritzsche *l. c.*

Rem. 2. Such examples as the following, in which two comparatives stand in mutual relation, need no comment: Rom. ix. 12, ὁ μείζων δουλεύσει τῷ ἐλάσσονι (from the LXX), compare 1 C. xii. 22, 2 C. xii. 15, Ph. i. 23 sq.; or with a word expressing proportion, H. i. 4, τοσούτῳ κρείττων γενόμενος ὅσῳ διαφορώτερον κεκληρονόμηκεν ὄνομα, (x. 25). Compare Xen. *Cyr.* 7. 5. 7, *Mem.* 1. 4. 10, Plat. *Apol.* 39 d. Of two comparatives connected by ἤ (Krüg. p. 90, Don. p. 390, Jelf 782) there is no example in the N. T.; but we find positives

---

[1] Compare Jacobs on Ælian, *Anim.* II. 38.
[2] On Eurip. *Med.* p. 343 (ed. Elmsley).
[3] [Meyer's view, "first in comparison with me," is simpler, and suits Jo. xv. 18 better.]
[4] [The true reading is probably αὕτη ἀπογραφή (without ἡ).]
[5] *Ueber den zur Zeit der Geburt J. Chr. gehaltenen Census* (Bresl. 1840).
[6] *Glaubwürdigk. der evang. Geschichte* p. 184.

with μᾶλλον similarly joined in 2 Tim. iii. 4, φιλήδονοι μᾶλλον ἢ φιλόθεοι.

5. In comparative sentences we sometimes find a part compared, not with the corresponding part, but with the whole (Bernh. p. 432, Jelf 781 *d*): Jo. v. 36, μαρτυρίαν μείζω τοῦ Ἰωάννου, *a testimony greater than John*, i.e. than that of John ; as in Her. 2. 134, πυραμίδα καὶ οὗτος ἀπελείπετο πολλὸν ἐλάσσω τοῦ πατρός, i. e. *than that of his father*, or in Lucian, *Salt*. 78, τὰ δι' ὀμμάτων φαινόμενα πιστότερα εἶναι τῶν ὤτων δοκεῖ. There is here no proper ellipsis, as the older grammarians thought; for if the sentence had been conceived by the Greek as it is by us, he would have said τῆς τοῦ Ἰωάννου, τῆς τοῦ πατρός.¹ We must rather recognise here a condensation of expression which was very familiar to the genius of the Greek language, and which is not only very common in connexion with comparatives proper,² but is also met with in other sentences of comparison :³ see § 66. In Latin, compare Juven. 3. 74, sermo promptus et *Isæo torrentior ;* Cic. *ad Brut.* 1. 12, *Orat.* 1. 44 : in Hebrew, Is. lvi. 5 (1 Esd. iii. 5). Mt. v. 20, also, ἐὰν μὴ περισσεύσῃ ὑμῶν ἡ δικαιοσύνη πλεῖον τῶν γραμματέων κ.τ.λ., is very naturally explained in the same way. Jesus could speak of a δικαιοσύνη γραμματέων, since their conduct assumed for itself this honourable title, and was by the people regarded and honoured as צדקה. On the other hand, 1 C. i. 25, τὸ μωρὸν τοῦ θεοῦ σοφώτερον τῶν ἀνθρώπων, means (without the usual—but forced—resolution⁴), *the foolishness of God is wiser than men* (are) ; i.e., what appears foolishness in God's arrangements is not only wisdom, but is even wiser than men,—outshines men in wisdom.

---

¹ Only when several parallel sentences of this kind follow one another the article is omitted in the last : Plat. *Gorg.* 455 e, ἡ τῶν λιμένων κατασκευὴ ἐκ τῆς Θεμιστοκλέους ξυμβουλῆς γέγονε, τὰ δ' ἐκ τῆς Περικλέους, ἀλλ' οὐκ ἐκ τῶν δημιουργῶν. Compare Siebelis, *Pausan.* IV. 291.
² Herm. *Vig.* p. 717, Schæf. *Melet.* 127, Matth. 453.
³ Franke, *Demosth.* p. 90, Weber, *Dem.* p. 399, Fritz. *Conjectan.* I. 1 sqq., and *Mark* p. 147.
⁴ Pott, Heydenreich, Flatt *in loc*.

Section XXXVI.

THE SUPERLATIVE.

1. We meet with one instance (in elevated style) in which the positive, followed by a substantive denoting a class, takes the place of the superlative: L. i. 42, εὐλογημένη σὺ ἐν γυναιξίν, *blessed* (art) *thou among women*. This is in the first instance a Hebrew construction,[1] which properly means: among women it is thou (alone) whom we can call *blessed*,—the blessing which others receive cannot come into any account when placed beside thine: hence, with rhetorical emphasis, *highly blessed*. Similar instances are found in the Greek poets:[2] e.g. Eurip. *Alcest.* 473, ὦ φίλα γυναικῶν (ὦ φιλτάτα), see Monk *in loc.*, Aristoph. *Ran.* 1081, ὦ σχέτλι' ἀνδρῶν, and still more Pind. *Nem.* 3. 80 (140), αἰετὸς ὠκὺς ἐν πετανοῖς. Compare also Himer. *Orat.* 15. 4, οἱ γενναῖοι τῶν πόνων, and Jacobs, *Æl. Anim.* II. 400.

The case is different in Mt. xxii. 36, ποία ἐντολὴ μεγάλη ἐν τῷ νόμῳ, *which kind of command is great in the law?* so that others appear insignificant in comparison,—hence not exactly *the greatest:* see Baumg.-Crusius *in loc.* In L. x. 42 also the positive is not put for the superlative; τὴν ἀγαθὴν μερίδα ἐξελέξατο means, "she has chosen the *good* part," in reference to the kingdom of heaven,—that which alone really deserves the name of *the good part:* Fritzsche is wrong (*Conject.* I. 19). Mt. v. 19, ὃς δ' ἂν ποιήσῃ . . . . οὗτος μέγας κληθήσεται, means *shall be called great*, a great one,—not exactly *the greatest* (as opposed to the ἐλάχιστος which precedes). Compare Herm. *Æschyl.* p. 214.

2. Of the well-known Hebrew mode of expressing the superlative, קֹדֶשׁ קָדָשִׁים, עֶבֶד עֲבָדִים, we find only the following examples in the N. T.: H. ix. 3, ἡ (λεγομένη) ἅγια ἁγίων,[3] *the most holy place* (which however hardly comes in here, since it had already assumed the nature of a standing appellation); Rev.

---

[1] Gesen. *Lehrg.* p. 692. [Kalisch, *Hebr. Gr.* I. 268.]
[2] But the parallels quoted by Kühnöl are not satisfactory.
[3] [In ed. 5 Winer writes ἁγία, as feminine (compare § 27. 3, where he speaks doubtfully): here, whilst joining this word with the feminine ἡ, he writes ἅγια, as neuter plural.—The explanation of Soph. *El.* 849 given below seems very doubtful (see Jebb *in loc.*): on the other examples from Sophocles see Campbell, *Soph.* I. 75.]

xix. 16, βασιλεὺς βασιλέων, κύριος κυρίων, *the highest King, Lord;* 1 Tim. vi. 15. But none of these expressions are pure Hebraisms : we find a similar repetition of the adjective (used substantivally) in the Greek poets, as Soph. *Electr.* 849, δειλαία δειλαίων· *Œd. R.* 466, ἄρρητ᾽ ἀρρήτων· *Phil.* 65, *Œd. C.* 1238, κακὰ κακῶν. See Bernhardy p. 154, Wex, *Antig.* I. 316 (Jelf 534. *Obs.* 2). Such a phrase as βασιλεὺς βασιλέων, however, is perfectly simple, and is more emphatic than ὁ μέγιστος βασιλεύς; compare Æschyl. *Suppl.* 524, ἄναξ ἀνάκτων, and even as a technical expression, Theophan. contin. 127, 387, ὁ ἄρχων τῶν ἀρχόντων.[1] For the similar phrase οἱ αἰῶνες τῶν αἰώνων see the passages in the Concordance.

3. What were formerly adduced as Hebraistic periphrases for the superlative [2] are for the most part either

(*a*) Figurative expressions, which are found in all languages, — and the illustration of which here belongs to N. T. rhetoric: or

(*b*) Constructions which have nothing to do with the superlative.

Examples of (*a*) are H. iv. 12, ὁ λόγος τοῦ θεοῦ τομώτερος ὑπὲρ πᾶσαν μάχαιραν δίστομον· Mt. xvii. 20, ἐὰν ἔχητε πίστιν ὡς κόκκον σινάπεως, *the least* faith ; iv. 16, καθημένοις ἐν χώρᾳ καὶ σκιᾷ θανάτου, in *the darkest* shadow. Compare Mt. xxviii. 3, Rev. i. 14, xviii. 5.

(*b*) In Col. ii. 19, αὔξησις τοῦ θεοῦ is not *glorious,* extraordinary increase, but *God's increase,* i. e., not merely "increase which is pleasing to God," but "increase produced by God" (compare 1 C. iii. 6). In 2 C. i. 12, ἐν ἁπλότητι καὶ εἰλικρινείᾳ θεοῦ, the meaning is not "*perfect* sincerity," but "sincerity which God effects, produces." In Ja. v. 11, τέλος κυρίου is not "*glorious* issue," but issue which the Lord has granted" (to Job). So

---

[1] See also Herm. *Æschyl.* p. 230, Georgi, *Vind.* 327, and *Nova Biblioth. Lubec.* II. 111 sq.

[2] See especially Pasor, *Gram.* p. 298 sq. The Hebrew idiom גָּדוֹל גְּדֹל is also found in later Greek poets ; see Boisson. *Nic. Eugen.* pp. 134, 383. Compare in the LXX σφόδρα σφόδρα Ex. i. 12, Judith iv. 2 : μέγας καὶ μέγας occurs on the Rosetta Inscription, line 19. Not essentially different is the phrase (μικρὸν) ὅσον ὅσον, H. x. 37, *a very very little* (Herm. *Vig.* p. 726), properly, *little how very, how very!* It is found in Greek authors with a substantive annexed, as in Aristoph. *Vesp.* 213, ὅσον ὅσον στίλην, *as big* (i. e. as small) *as a drop,* and hence it came to be used as = *quantillum:* we also find the simple ὅσον with a defining genitive, Arrian, *Indic.* 29. 15, σπείρουσιν ὅσον τῆς χώρης. The parallels adduced by Wetstein and Lösner do not support the phrase ὅσον ὅσον, but the simple μικρὸν ὅσον. Compare however Is. xxvi. 20.

also in Rev. xxi. 11, πόλις ἔχουσα τὴν δόξαν τοῦ θεοῦ, not *"great glory,"* but strictly " the glory (glorious brightness) of God," see Ewald *in loc ;* 1 Th. iv. 16, σάλπιγξ θεοῦ, not " *great* or *far-sounding* trumpet " (σάλπιγξ φωνῆς μεγάλης, Mt. xxiv. 31), but " God's trumpet," i. e., *trumpet sounding at God's command,*—or, more generally (since the word has not the article), such a trumpet as is used in the service of God (in heaven); Rev. xv. 2, κιθάραι τοῦ θεοῦ, *harps of God,* such as sound in heaven (*to the praise of God*), compare 1 Ch. xvi. 42.

The commentators have long been agreed that in Rom. i. 16, δύναμις θεοῦ signifies *God's power* (power in which God works); and there is no ground for charging Bengel with having regarded this as a Hebraistic periphrasis because he adds the explanation " magna et gloriosa." He merely brings into relief, in his usual manner, two qualities which a "virtus Dei" will possess, adding a reference to 2 C. x. 4.

Lastly, ἀστεῖος τῷ θεῷ, used of Moses in A. vii. 20, is rather an expression of intensity than a substitute for the superlative degree: it must strictly be rendered *beautiful for* (before) *God,* in the judgment of God, which is indeed equivalent to *admodum formosus* (compare 2 C. x. 4[1]). Exactly in the same manner are לֵאלֹהִים and לִפְנֵי יְהֹוָה used in Hebrew,[2]—compare Gen. x. 9, Jon. iii. 3 (LXX, πόλις μεγάλη τῷ θεῷ);[3] only this use of the *dative* is not in itself a Hebraism.[4]

Haab (p. 162) most erroneously maintains that even the word Χριστός is sometimes joined to a substantive merely to intensify its ordinary meaning: e.g. in Rom. ix. 1, 2 C. xi. 10, ἀλήθεια Χριστοῦ, ἐν Χριστῷ, *the most unquestionable truth.* Some have interpreted θρησκεία τῶν ἀγγέλων, Col. ii. 18, on the same principle, as meaning *cultus perfectissimus :* compare 2 S. xiv. 20, σοφία ἀγγέλου.

Rem. Of the superlative strengthened by πάντων[5] we find only one example in the N. T., viz. Mk. xii. 28, πρώτη πάντων. Compare Aristoph. *Av.* 473.

---

[1] Compare also Sturz, *Zonarœ glossœ sacrœ*, P. II. p. 12 sqq. (Grimmæ 1820).
[2] Gesen. *Lehrg.* p. 695. [Kalisch, *Hebr. Gr.* I. 199.]
[3] See Fischer, *Proluss.* 231 sqq., Wolle, *De usu et abusu αὐξήσεως nominum divinor. sacrœ*, in his *Comment. de Parenthesi sacra*, p. 143 sqq.
[4] Compare Heind. Plat. *Soph.* 336, Ast, Plat. *Legg.* p. 479 a.
[5] Weber, *Demosth.* p. 548.

Section XXXVII.

THE NUMERALS.

1. In expressing the day of the week εἷς is regularly used in the place of the ordinal πρῶτος:[1] Mt. xxviii. 1, εἰς μίαν σαββάτων Mk. xvi. 2, πρωΐ τῆς μιᾶς σαββάτων L. xxiv. 1, Jo. xx. 1, 19, A. xx. 7, 1 C. xvi. 2. The examples which have been cited from Greek authors as analogous to this merely prove that εἷς is used to denote the *first* member in partitions and enumerations,[2] some such word as δεύτερος or ἄλλος following, e. g. Her. 4. 161, Thuc. 4. 115, Herod. 6. 5. 2 sqq.[3] Here εἷς no more stands for πρῶτος than in Latin *unus* stands for *primus*, when it is followed by *alter, tertius*, etc. (Compare also Rev. ix. 12 with xi. 14, and G. iv. 24.) In Her. 7. 11. 8, however, εἷς retains its proper meaning *unus*; probably also in Paus. 7. 20. 1, where Sylburg renders it by *una*.[4] This use of εἷς for πρῶτος is Hebraistic[5] (as to the Talmud see Wetstein I. 544; in the LXX compare Ex. xl. 2, Num. i. 1, 18, Ezr. x. 16 sq., 2 Macc. xv. 36): classical Greek affords a parallel in combinations of numbers, as εἷς καὶ τριηκοστός Her. 5. 89, *one and thirtieth*. But we use the cardinal in a similar way (for brevity, in the first instance) in expressing the year or the page, *in the year eighteen, page forty*, etc.[6]

For the cardinal *one* the singular noun is sometimes used alone, as in A. xviii. 11 ἐκάθισεν ἐνιαυτὸν καὶ μῆνας ἕξ (Joseph. *Antt.* 15. 2. 3), Rev. xii. 14 τρέφεται ἐκεῖ καιρόν (contrast Ja. iv. 13). But there is no ellipsis in such cases (compare § 26. 1), since the singular itself expresses unity. A similar usage is found in all languages.

---

[1] [In Mk. xvi. 9 we have πρώτῃ σαββάτου.]
[2] Weber, *Demosth.* p. 161.
[3] Georgi, *Vind.* 54 sqq. Foertsch also (*Observ. in Lysiam*, p. 37) has only been able to adduce passages of this kind. On Diog. L. 8. 20 see Lobeck, *Aglaopham.* p. 429.
[4] In Chishull, *Antiq. Asiat.* p. 159, μιᾷ τῆς βουλῆς is rendered *die concilii prima*.
[5] Ewald, *Krit. Gr.* 496. [Gesen. *Hebr. Gr.* p. 196 (Bagst.), Kalisch, *Hebr. Gr.* I. 276.]
[6] [On τεσσαρισκαιδέκατος A. xxvii. 27, 33 (for the more usual τεσσαρακαιδ.), see Lob. p. 409, where Dion. H. VII. 12. 1338, Plut. *Vit. Cat.* III. 46, al., are quoted: compare also the Ionic τεσσερισκαιδέκατος, Her. 1. 84.—It may be mentioned here that the termination -πλάσιος does not occur in the N. T.: the later -πλασίων (Lob. p. 411) is found Mk. x. 30, L. viii. 8, xviii. 30. See also A. Buttmann, p. 30.]

2. We meet with an abbreviated use of the ordinal in 2 P. ii. 5, ὄγδοον Νῶε... ἐφύλαξε, *Noah as the eighth*, i. e., Noah with seven others. So in Plat. *Legg.* 3. 695 c, λαβὼν τὴν ἀρχὴν ἕβδομος· Plutarch, *Pelop.* c. 13, εἰς οἰκίαν δωδέκατος κατελθών· Appian, *Pun.* p. 12 (2 Macc. v. 27).[1] Greek authors usually add αὐτός; see Kypke II. 442, Matth. 469. 9 (Jelf 656. 3, Don. p. 462).

3. When the cardinals are repeated, they stand for distributives, as in Mk. vi. 7, δύο δύο ἤρξατο ἀποστέλλειν, *binos misit*, *two and two*. For this Greek writers use κατά or ἀνὰ δύο (Krüg. p. 80, Jelf 161, Don. p. 514): the latter of these occurs *e.g.* in L. x. 1,[2] and in Mk. vi. 7 (cited above) D has the same as a correction of δύο δύο.[3] This repetition of the cardinal is properly Hebraistic,[4] and is the simplest mode of expressing the distributive numeral: compare Lob. *Pathol.* p. 184. Yet isolated instances of a similar kind occur in Greek (poetry), e. g., Æschyl. *Pers.* 981, μυρία μυρία, that is, κατὰ μυριάδας; and there is an analogous combination in Mk. vi. 39, 40, ἐπέταξεν αὐτοῖς ἀνακλῖναι πάντας συμπόσια συμπόσια... ἀνέπεσον πρασιαὶ πρασιαί.

The following combinations are peculiar: ἀνὰ εἷς ἕκαστος, Rev. xxi. 21, and εἷς καθ᾽ εἷς (or καθεῖς), Mk. xiv. 19, Jo. viii. 9 (like ἓν καθ᾽ ἕν); also ὁ καθ᾽ εἷς, Rom. xii. 5 (3 Macc. v. 34). Greek writers use καθ᾽ ἕνα (1 C. xiv. 31, E. v. 33), giving to the preposition its proper government. Compare however ἀνὰ τέσσαρες Plut. *Æm.* 32 (but see Held), εἷς καθεῖς (Bekker writes καθείς) Cedren. II. 698, 723, εἷς παρ᾽ εἷς Leo, *Tact.* 7. 83, and the simple καθεῖς Theophan. contin. p. 39 and 101: other examples are cited from later writers by Wetstein (I. 627), see also Interp. ad Lucian. *Solœc.* 9. In these phrases the preposition simply plays the part of an adverb (Herm. *De Partic.* ἄν, p. 5 sq.): Döderlein's view[5] is different.

---

[1] Compare also Schæf. *Plutarch* V. 57, *Demosth.* I. 812.
[2] For this ἀνά the Syriac version always repeats the cardinal; e. g. Mk. vi. 40, ἀνὰ ἑκατόν, ܐܠܦ ܐܠܦ, ܚܡܫܝܢ ܚܡܫܝܢ [Cowper, *Syr. Gr.* p. 102.] In *Acta Apocr.* 92 we find ἀνὰ δύο δύο.
[3] [Κατὰ δύο also occurs: 1 C. xiv. 27.]
[4] See Gesen. *Lehrg.* p. 703: compare Gen. vii. 3, 9, and Leo Gramm. p. 11 (a quotation from Gen. *l. c.*). [Gesen. *Hebr. Gr.* p. 196 (Bagster), Kalisch I. 276. This usage is found in modern Greek: see Mullach, *Vulg.* p. 331, Sophocles, *Gr.* p. 142.]
[5] *Pr. de Brachylogia Serm. Gr. et Lat.* p. 10 (Erlang. 1831).

4. The well-known rule that in combinations of numbers καί is commonly inserted when the smaller number precedes, and not otherwise¹ (compare 1 C. x. 8, Jo. vi. 19, A. i. 15, vii. 14, xxvii. 37, Rev. iv. 4, xix. 4 ²), must not be too rigidly pressed,—at all events as regards the latter part of it.³ Exceptions are met with everywhere: in the N. T., at any rate, there are some which admit of no doubt, as Jo. ii. 20, τεσσαράκοντα καὶ ἓξ ἔτεσιν (without any variant), v. 5, τριάκοντα καὶ ὀκτὼ ἔτη (on preponderant authority), G. iii. 17, L. xiii. 11,⁴ 16, A. xiii. 20, Rev. xi. 2. Similar examples occur occasionally in Greek writers, as Her. 8. 1, εἴκοσι καὶ ἑπτά· Thuc. 1. 29, ἑβδομήκοντα καὶ πέντε· Dion. Hal. IV. 2090, ὀγδοήκοντα καὶ τρεῖς. In the LXX compare 1 K. ix. 28, xv. 10, 33, xvi. 23, 28, Gen. xi. 13: in Jud. x. 4 Tischendorf has τριάκοντα καὶ δύο υἱοί and τριάκοντα δύο πώλους in the same verse.⁵

5. If ἐπάνω is joined to a cardinal to express *above, more than*, the cardinal is not governed in the genitive, but is placed in the case required by the verb of the sentence: Mk. xiv. 5, πραθῆναι ἐπάνω τριακοσίων δηναρίων· 1 C. xv. 6, ὤφθη ἐπάνω πεντακοσίοις ἀδελφοῖς. Greek writers use the following words in a precisely similar manner, that is, without any influence on case: ἔλαττον, Plat. *Legg.* 9. 856 d, μὴ ἔλαττον δέκα ἔτη γεγονότας· Thuc. 6. 95; πλέον, Pausan. 8. 21. 1; περί, Zosim. 2. 30; εἰς or ἐς, Appian, *Civil.* 2. 96;⁶ μέχρι, Æschin. *Fals. Leg.* 37 (ed. Bremi); ὑπέρ, Plut. *Virt. Mul.* 208 (ed. Lips.), Joseph. *Antt.* 18. 1. 5.⁷ In Latin such constructions as "occisis *ad*

---

¹ Matth. 140; compare the Inscriptions in Chishull, *Antiq. Asiat.* p. 69 sq. (Don. p. 142.)
² Three numerals are sometimes thus combined: Rev. vii. 4, ἑκατὸν τεσσαράκοντα τέσσαρες· xiv. 3, xxi. 17, Jo. xxi. 11 ἑκατὸν πεντήκοντα τρεῖς.
³ Schoem. *Isæus* 332, Krüg. p. 78 (Jelf 165).
⁴ [In this verse καί is probably not genuine.]
⁵ [On δικαπέντε, G. i. 18, Lightfoot remarks: "This and the analogous forms of numerals occur frequently in the MSS. of Greek authors of the post-classical age, but in many cases are doubtless due to the transcribers writing out the words at length, where they had only the numeral letters before them. The frequent occurrence of these forms however in the *Tabulæ Heracleenses* is a decisive testimony to their use, at least in some dialects, much before the Christian era. They are found often in the LXX." This is the regular form in modern Greek for the numbers from 13 to 19 (Mullach p. 179).]
⁶ But compare Sturz, *Lex. Xen.* II. 68.
⁷ See Lob. p. 410 sq., Gieseler in Rosenmüller, *Repert.* II. 139 sqq., Sommer in the *Allg. Schulzeit.* 1831, p. 963.

hominum millibus quattuor" (Cæs. *Bell. Gall.* 2. 33), in the historians, are sufficiently familiar. (Jelf 780. *Obs.*)

Rem. 1. That the neuters δεύτερον, τρίτον, sometimes signify *for the second time, third time*, it is unnecessary to observe. These are occasionally combined with τοῦτο, as in 2 C. xiii. 1, τρίτον τοῦτο ἔρχομαι, *this is the third time that I come*, or *I am now coming for the third time;* compare Her. 5. 76 τέταρτον τοῦτο.

Rem. 2. The numeral adverb ἑπτάκις is once replaced by the cardinal, in the phrase ἕως ἑβδομηκοντάκις ἑπτά, Mt. xviii. 22, *seventy times seven* (times); compare Gen. iv. 24 (LXX) and שְׁבַע in Ps. cxix. 164 (instead of שֶׁבַע פְּעָמִים), and see Ewald p. 498. The strict meaning of this phrase would be *seventy times* (and) *seven*, i.e. seventy-seven times, which would not suit the passage. That we must not construe ἕως with ἑπτά but with ἑβδομηκ. is shown by the preceding ἕως ἑπτάκις.[1]

How variously the LXX express the numeral adverbs, the following passages will show: Ex. xxxiv. 23, Dt. xvi. 16, 2 K. vi. 10, Neh. vi. 4,[2] 2 S. xix. 43.

CHAPTER FOURTH.

THE VERB.

Section XXXVIII.

THE ACTIVE AND MIDDLE VOICES.

1. As transitive verbs in the active voice not unfrequently assume an intransitive (apparently a reflexive) meaning, so, conversely, we find transitive (causative) verbs formed from intransitives;—sometimes as a result of composition (*e.g.* διαβαίνειν H. xi. 29, παρέρχεσθαι L. xi. 42), sometimes by simple transference, as μαθητεύειν τινά[3] Mt. xxviii. 19 (θριαμβεύειν τινά 2 C. ii. 14 ?), βασιλεύειν τινά 1 S. viii. 22, 1 K. i. 43, Is. vii. 6,

---

[1] [This is against Fritzsche, whose explanation is "as far as 7 repeated 70 times." Meyer defends the other rendering, 77 *times*, on the ground that ἑβδομηκοντάκις ἑπτά occurs Gen. iv. 24 (LXX) as a rendering of שִׁבְעִים וְשִׁבְעָה, which can only mean "77 times:" this certainly seems a more weighty argument than the mere probability that a very high number would be used. On the same side are Origen, (Augustine,) Bengel, and Ewald: in favour of "seventy times seven" see De Wette *in loc.*, Bleek, *Syn. Erkl.* II. 93.]

[2] [In this passage the numeral is *omitted* by the LXX.]

[3] Compare also προστάττειν τινά *to commission some one*, *Act. Apocr.* p. 172.

1 Macc. viii. 13 (Lob. *Ajax* 385) : see § 32. 1.¹ The transitive verbs which are often or mainly used intransitively belong in meaning to certain classes of ideas, which may easily be learned from the following examples : ἄγειν (ἄγωμεν *let us go*), παράγειν Mt. xx. 30, 1 C. vii. 31, περιάγειν A. xiii. 11, βάλλειν A. xxvii. 14 (*to throw oneself, to rush*), ἐπιβάλλειν Mk. iv. 37 (*to beat in*), ἀπορρίπτειν A. xxvii. 43 (*to throw oneself off*), κλίνειν L. ix. 12 (*to decline*), ἐκκλίνειν Rom. xvi. 17, ἀνατέλλειν, βλαστάνειν, αὐξάνειν (Lob. *Ajax* p. 89 sq., 382 sqq.); στρέφειν A. vii. 42, ἀναστρέφειν A. v. 22 (*to return*), and especially ἐπιστρέφειν ; ἐκτρέπειν,² παραδιδόναι Mk. iv. 29, 1 P. ii. 23 (*to offer* or *give up oneself*), ἀπέχειν *to be distant*, ἐπέχειν A. xix. 22 (*to detain oneself,* i. e. *remain*), ὑπερέχειν, σπεύδειν. In the N. T. ἀνακάμπτειν and προκόπτειν are always intransitive.³ In these examples (mainly of verbs denoting *motion*), as conceived by a Greek, there was no ellipsis of any word (not even of ἑαυτόν); the verb denotes the action absolutely, *he plunges into the sea, he turns round,* but as there is no object named, the reader can only refer the action back to the subject.⁴

We must not bring in here Jo. xiii. 2, τοῦ διαβόλου βεβληκότος εἰς τὴν καρδίαν, whether we follow the received text, or the reading adopted by Lachmann and Tischendorf. In any case βάλλειν has an active meaning ; see Kypke.

Several verbs have a transitive (causative) meaning in some of their tenses, an intransitive in others. To this number belongs ἵστημι with its compounds (Buttm. II. 207), of which verb we need only say that the 1 aor. passive σταθῆναι (Mk. iii. 24) and the 1 fut. σταθήσομαι (Mt. xii. 25, 46) share in the intransitive meaning *stand*, and that in A. xxvii. 28 the 1 aor. διαστήσαντες signifies *having gone back*⁵ (compare στήσας, Malal. 2. p. 35, for στάς). Of

---

¹ [See also § 2. 1. *b.*]
² [ʼΕκτρέπειν is inserted by mistake: the active does not occur in the N. T., nor does it seem to be ever used intransitively. On παραδιδόναι see § 64. 4.]
³ [Others of these verbs (e.g. ἐκκλίνειν) are "always intransitive in the N. T." —A. Buttmann (p. 144) adds to the list ὑπάγω, ἐπανάγω, προάγω, ἔχω, ἐνισχύω, ἀναλύω, καταλύω, ἐγείρω (imper. ἔγειρε) ; and remarks that some of these verbs, when their meaning has been thus modified, take a new object—as περιῆγε τὰς κώμας Mk. vi. 6 (Mt. ii. 9, Ph. iv. 7).]
⁴ See on the whole Bos, *Ellips.* p. 127 sqq., Matth. 495, Bernh. p. 339 sq., Krüg. p. 154 sq., Poppo, *Thuc.* I. 186, Fritz. *Mark* p. 138 [Jelf 359, Don. p. 425 sqq., Green, *Gr.* p. 185 ; and see below § 64. 5]. On διδόναι and its compounds in particular see Jacobs, *Philostr.* p. 363 ; on παρέχειν, Ast, Plat. *Polit.* p. 470, Wyttenb. Plut. *Mor.* I. 405.
⁵ [Should we not rather refer this to § 64. 5, supplying τὴν ναῦν? See

φύω even the present tense is used intransitively in H. xii. 15, from the LXX (Il. 6. 149).¹—In 1 P. ii. 6, περιέχει ἐν τῇ γραφῇ, *is contained in the Scripture*, the verb is rather passive than intransitive: compare Joseph. *Antt.* 11. 4. 7, Malal. 9. 216, 18. 449, and see Krebs, *Observ.* 198.²

On the impersonal use of (the 3 pers. sing. of) certain verbs, as βροντᾷ, λέγει, φησί, see § 58. 9.

2. The middle voice (of transitive verbs³) refers back the action to the agent (Don. p. 433 sqq., Jelf 362),—either

a. Simply, as the direct object, as λούομαι *I wash myself*, κρύπτομαι *I conceal myself* (Jo. viii. 59), ἀπάγχομαι *I hang myself* (Mt. xxvii. 5), παρασκευάζομαι (1 C. xiv. 8):⁴ or

---

A. Buttm. p. 47. In modern Greek ἐστάθην is in regular use as an intransitive aorist: perhaps a faint passive force may be observed in most of the instances in which it occurs in the N. T.]

¹ [On Mt. xxiv. 32, Mk. xiii. 28, see § 15, s. v. φύω.]

² [With Lachmann's reading περιέχει ἡ γραφή, compare ἡ ἐπιστολὴ περιεῖχεν οὕτως 2 Macc. xi. 22, ὁ νόμος ὑμῶν περιέχει Ev. Nicod. c. 4, ὡς ἡ παράδοσις περιέχει Eus. H. E. 3. 1 (quoted with others by Grimm, *Wilkii Clavis* s. v.). A. Buttmann refers to his examination of this passage in *Stud. u. Krit.* 1858, p. 509. This use of περιέχω is not noticed by Rost and Palm or by Liddell and Scott.]

³ See L. Küster, *De vero usu verborum mediorum apud Græcos*, and J. Clerici *Diss. de verbis Græcorum mediis*, both reprinted in the work of Dresig mentioned below: for a more rational treatment see Herm. *Emend. Rat.* p. 178, Bernh. p. 342 sqq., Rost p. 573 sqq., Krüg. p. 162 sqq. See especially Poppo, *Progr. de Græcorum verbis mediis, passivis, deponentibus rite discernendis* (Frankf. on Oder, 1827), and Mehlhorn's corrections in his review of the work in Jahn's *Jahrb.* 1831, I. 14 sqq.; Sommer in Jahn's *Jahrb.* 1831, II. 36 sqq.; J. H. Kistemaker, *De origine ac vi verborum deponentium et mediorum Græcæ linguæ*, in the *Classical Journal*, No. 44 (Dec. 1820), No. 45 (March 1821). A monograph for the N. T. is, S. F. Dresigii *Commentarius de verbis mediis N. T. nunc primum editus cura J. F. Fischeri*: Lips. (1755) 1762.—On the whole, however, scholars have hitherto assumed too many verbs to be middle; very many we are justified in regarding as passive because of the *constant* use of the passive aorist,—for in Greek, as in Latin, the passive may be used for the reflexive. Thus κινέομαι, ἐγείρομαι, διακονεῖσθαι, ἁγνίζεσθαι, μεθύσκεσθαι, δογματίζεσθαι (Col. ii. 20), ἀτιμάζεσθαι (Fritz. *Rom.* I. 72), συσχηματίζεσθαι, were certainly conceived as passive, not middle verbs, like the Latin *moveri*, etc. Still more should ὀρέγεσθαι (*appetitu ferri*), βόσκεσθαι (*pasci*), etc.,—also αἰσχύνεσθαι,—be brought in here. Compare, in general, Rost's *Vorrede* to the 3d edition of his *Griech. Wörterb.* p. 9 sqq., and his *Gramm.* p. 270 [?573], Sommer *loc. cit.* [The aor. middle of ὀρέγεσθαι is in frequent use, and in some others of these verbs this tense sometimes occurs (see Veitch, *Greek V.* s. vv.). The aor. middle (imperative) of ἐγείρω occurs several times in the received text, but not in the texts of Tischendorf and Tregelles.]

⁴ What verbs regularly express this reflexive meaning by the middle voice, must be learnt from observation. In many—indeed in most (see Rost p. 574)—this meaning is always expressed, not by the middle, but by the addition of the reflexive pronoun, ἑαυτόν, κ.τ.λ.; see Buttm. 122. 2 (Jelf 363. 4, Don. p. 433). Thus for *show oneself* we find δεικνύειν ἑαυτόν (Mt. viii. 4, compare Her. 3. 119), for *kill oneself* always ἀποκτείνειν ἑαυτόν (Jo. viii. 22): compare also Jo. xxi. 18, 1 C. iii. 18, 2 Th. ii. 4, 1 Jo. i. 8 (in antithesis to a passive, Mt. xxiii. 12, 1 C.

b. *Mediately*, the action being performed *on* or in some way *for* the subject: ἐξαγοράζομαι *I buy for myself*, προέχομαι *I hold before myself* (Fritz. *Rom.* I. 171), νίπτομαι τὰς χεῖρας *I wash the hands for myself, I wash my hands* (Mk. vii. 3), σπάομαι τὴν μάχαιραν (Mk. xiv. 47), εἰςκαλοῦμαι *I call in to me* (A. x. 23), ἀπωθέομαι *I thrust away for myself* (from myself). Compare also περιποιεῖσθαι, κομίζεσθαι, καταρτίζεσθαι, ἐπικαλεῖσθαι (θεόν), Fritz. *Rom.* II. 403; and the following passages, Mt. vi. 17, L. vi. 7, x. 11, A. v. 2 sq., ix. 39, xviii. 18, xix. 24, xxv. 11, G. iv. 10, 1 P. v. 5, 2 Th. iii. 14, H. x. 5.

Sometimes the physical and the metaphysical significations of a verb are divided between the active and the middle: καταλαμβάνειν *seize*, καταλαμβάνεσθαι *comprehend* (understand), ἀνατιθέναι *set up*, ἀνατίθεσθαι *set forth, relate*,—probably also διαβεβαιοῦσθαι,[1] 1 Tim. i. 7, Tit. iii. 8 (compare Aristot. *Rhet.* 2. 13). On προβλέπεσθαι see below, no. 6.

In other instances a new meaning arises out of the middle voice: πείθομαι *I persuade myself*, i.e. *I obey*, ἀπολύομαι *solvo me*, i.e. *discedo*, παύομαι *I cease*, φυλάσσομαι *I observe some one for myself*, i.e. *I am on my guard against him*.[2] Entirely transitive are παραιτοῦμαί τι (I deprecate something *for myself*) *I decline* something, αἱροῦμαι *I take for myself, I choose*, ἀπειπάμην τι *I lay aside* (2 C. iv. 2), ἐκτρέπομαί τι (1 Tim. vi. 20), ἀποδίδομαί τι (I deliver over something *from myself*) *I sell* something, ἀποκρίνομαι (I give a decision *from myself*) *I answer*, ἐπικαλοῦμαι καίσαρα (A. xxv. 11) I call on the emperor *for myself, I appeal to the emperor*. So also λυτρόω properly means, *I set free*, acting as master; but

---

xi. 31, or an active, L. ix. 25, xxiii. 35); see Küster, *De verb. med.* p. 56. Lexicographers should no longer defer a more accurate investigation of the subject. See also Poppo *l. c.* p. 2, note, and Krüger p. 168.

[1] [Καταλαμβάνειν: in classical Greek it is the *active* that is used of the mental powers (Jo. i. 5?); in the N. T. the middle is always used with this reference. The active of ἀνατίθεσθαι does not occur in the N. T., and in classical Greek it is not always used in a physical sense. The active of διαβεβαιοῦσθαι seems not to occur in any author.]

[2] Φυλάσσεσθαι as a middle verb has also the meaning *sibi (aliquid) custodire*, see Heind. Plat. *Gorg.* p. 323 [Shilleto, Dem. *F. L.* p. 151]; and we find it used as early as Hesiod (*Op.* 263, 561) in reference to something which a man keeps in his mind. In the sense of (*legem*) *sibi observare*—as, in several MSS., L. xviii. 21, ταῦτα πάντα ἐφυλαξάμην ἐκ νιότητος·—it seems not to occur in classical Greek, but is common in the LXX. In this passage, however, ἐφύλαξα is the better reading. [Tisch., Treg., and others read ἐφυλαξάμην in Mk. x. 20.]

λυτροῦμαι, *I set free for myself* the slave of another (L. xxiv. 21). (Don. p. 436, Jelf 363. 6.)

When such a middle verb is joined with an accusative of a thing or quality belonging to the subject, the N. T. writers sometimes add the pronoun to the substantive: Mt. xv. 2, οὐ νίπτονται τὰς χεῖρας αὐτῶν· Rom. ix. 17, ὅπως ἐνδείξωμαι ἐν σοὶ τὴν δύναμίν μου.¹ A. vii. 58, ἀπέθεντο τὰ ἱμάτια αὐτῶν (where Tischendorf leaves out the pronoun without sufficient reason), H. vi. 17,² E. ii. 7, 1 P. iv. 19. In such cases the pronoun is redundant, and it is as a rule omitted by Greek writers, as indeed it frequently is in the N. T. (A. ix. 39, Mk. vii. 3, xiv. 47).

From the usage (*b*) we must also explain 2 C. iii. 18, ἡμεῖς πάντες . . . . τὴν δόξαν κυρίου κατοπτριζόμενοι: as it were, "*sibi* intueri," *to behold* (for ourselves) *the glory of the Lord* (as in a mirror); see Philo II. 107. In Rom. iii. 25 also, ὃν προέθετο ὁ θεὸς κ.τ.λ., recent commentators have noticed the use of the middle voice; but Philippi seems to come nearer to the true explanation than Fritzsche.³

3. *c.* Lastly, the middle voice not unfrequently denotes an action which takes place at the command or by the permission of the subject,—where a German would use the auxiliary (*sich*) *lassen,* and where in Latin we should commonly find *curare :*⁴ e.g. ἀδικεῖσθαι *to let oneself* be wronged, ἀποστερεῖσθαι *to let oneself* be defrauded (both in 1 C. vi. 7), ἀπογράφεσθαι *to have oneself* enrolled (L. ii. 1): compare also βαπτίζεσθαι, γαμεῖσθαι, and many others. Examples of middle verbs which in this case too receive a new and independent transitive meaning, are δανείζομαι, pecuniam mutuo dandam sibi curare, i.e. *mutuam sumere* (Mt. v. 42), μισθοῦμαι to get something let on hire to oneself, i.e. *to hire, engage,* Mt. xx. 1. (Don. pp. 435, 439, Jelf 362. 6, 363. 7.)

Some middle verbs combine with the reflexive meaning the reciprocal (Krüg. p. 165, Don. 440, Jelf 364): βουλεύεσθαι *to consult with one another* (Jo. xii. 10), συντίθεσθαι *to settle among themselves, agree* (Jo. ix. 22), κρίνεσθαι *to dispute,* go to law (1 C. vi. 1 : should we add the O. T. quotation Rom. iii. 4 ?).⁵

---

¹ Ἐπιδείκνυμαι is frequently thus used by Greek writers : see Engelhardt, Plat. *Lach.* p. 9, Schoem. Plutarch, *Agis* p. 144 (Don. p. 447).
² [H. vi. 17 is inserted by mistake : A alone (of the uncial MSS.) has the middle voice. In A. vii. 58 Tisch. restored αὐτῶν in ed. 8.]
³ [Philippi renders "set forth ;" Fritzsche, "esse voluit (destinavit)."]
⁴ Compare Sommer in Seebode, *Krit. Biblioth.* 1828, II. 733. [See Riddell, Plat. *Apol.* p. 150 sq.]
⁵ [The name "dynamic" (Krüg. p. 162) has been given to the middle when it

4. Although the middle voice possesses an accurately defined and characteristic meaning, yet in usage its forms are often mixed up with those of the passive voice, even in the best Greek writers.

(*a*) Not only are those tenses for which the middle voice has no special form (the present, imperfect, perfect, pluperfect[1]) borrowed from the passive, and the 1 aorist passive of several verbs (as φοβεῖσθαι, κοιμᾶσθαι, πορεύεσθαι, ἁγνίζεσθαι A. xxi. 24, 26,[2]—compare also § 39. 2) used also as 1 aorist middle :—but also

(*b*) A passive meaning is assumed by some of the middle tenses proper, particularly the future :[3] such a use of the aorist is far less common, and is indeed almost doubtful, especially in prose.[4] It has been supposed that the N. T. contains examples of this transfer of meaning: G. v. 12, ὄφελον καὶ ἀποκόψονται οἱ ἀναστατοῦντες ὑμᾶς,—yet here the middle yields a very suitable sense (see my *Comment. in loc.*) :[5] 1 C. x. 2, καὶ πάντες ἐβαπτίσαντο, which however may very fitly be rendered (see Meyer) *they all allowed themselves to be baptised;* ἐβαπτίσθησαν, the reading of very good MSS., is probably a correction. 1 C. vi. 11, ἀπελούσασθε, is similar. In A. xv. 22,

---

indicates an action not simply and absolutely, but as calling forth and exercising the powers of the agent: see Ellicott on E. ii. 7, G. v. 6, Col. i. 6, and Webster, *Syntax* p. 98. Compare Don. p. 438 : " The appropriative middle often exhibits a signification which might be called *intensive*, but which really implies an immediate reference to some result in which the agent is interested. One of the most common of the cases . . . . is that of the aorist ἰδεῖν and ἰδέσθαι, of which the former means simply ' to see,' the latter ' to behold, to look with interest or with a view to some contemplated and desired effect' . . . . For this reason ἰδοῦ is more frequently used than ἴδε in calling attention to something worth seeing . . . . In this particular use of the middle . . . . it will generally be found that the middle implies a certain special diligence and earnestness in the action."]

[1] See Buttm. I. 368 (Jelf 367. 2).
[2] [Above (page 316, note [3]) Winer calls ἁγνίζεσθαι a passive.]
[3] Monk, Eurip. *Hippol.* p. 169 (Lips.), Boisson. *Eunap.* p. 336, Poppo, *Thuc.* I. i. 192, Stallb. Plat. *Crit.* 16, and *Rep.* II. 230, Isocrat. *Areopag.* p. 229 (ed. Benseler), Weber, *Demosth.* p. 353 (Jelf 364. 7). According to Sommer *l. c.* the future middle itself was perhaps originally passive, and afterwards was preferred to the future passive on account of its more convenient form. Compare Rost p. 578.
[4] D'Orville, *Charit.* p. 358, Abresch. *Aristæn.* p. 178, Matth. 496. 5, and on Eur. *Hel.* 42 ; but compare Schæf. *Gnom.* 166, Lob. p. 320 (Jelf *l. c.*).
[5] [Winer's explanation agrees with that given by Alford, Lightfoot, al. : the force of the middle, however, is equally preserved in Ellicott's translation, " cut themselves off (from communion with you)."]

ἐκλεξαμένους—even if we were to connect it with ἄνδρας— would not be equivalent to ἐκλεχθέντας (see Kühnöl *in loc.*, Schwarz, *Comm.* p. 499), but would retain the middle signification, *who have allowed themselves to be chosen,* have undertaken the mission (with their own consent): ἐκλεχθέντας would be *who have been chosen,* whether willingly or against their will.[1] It is more probable however that ἐκλεξαμένους refers to ἀπόστολοι and πρεσβύτεροι, so that we must render, *after they had chosen men from among themselves;* see Elsner, *Observ.* I. 429, and compare § 63. I. 1.

5. We sometimes find the active voice used by Greek writers where the middle might have been expected.[2] 2 C. xi. 20, εἴ τις ὑμᾶς καταδουλοῖ, is wrongly brought in here by some, who render, *if any one enslaves you to himself, sibi* (G. ii. 4, where the middle is a *v. l.*). The apostle intends his language to be altogether general, *if any one enslaves you,* makes you slaves: the point is their becoming slaves,—*to whom* and *how* the context must show. In L. xii. 20 also the active is used correctly; ἀπαιτοῦσιν ἀπὸ σοῦ is *they require from thee*—the words are designed to express merely the removal of the ψυχή. On the other hand, the active ποιεῖν is sometimes found (at least in the received text) where Greek writers[3] would have used ποιεῖσθαι,[4] e.g. συνωμοσίαν ποιεῖν A. xxiii. 13 (Polyb. 1. 70. 6, Herod. 7. 4. 7), μονὴν ποιεῖν Jo. xiv. 23 (Thuc. 1. 131, and Poppo *in loc.*), πρόθεσιν ποιεῖν E. iii. 11[5] (but in the first two pas-

---

[1] So perhaps Plutarch, *Orator. Vit.* 7 (V. 149: Lips.), πιστευσάμενος τὴν διοίκησιν τῶν χρημάτων.
[2] Poppo, *Thuc.* I. i. 185, Locella, *Xen. Eph.* p. 233, Buttm. Soph. *Phil.* p. 161, Siebelis, *Pausan.* I. 5, Weber, *Demosth.* 252 sq.
[3] Küster p. 37 sqq., 67 sqq., Dresig p. 401 sqq., Krüg. p. 163.
[4] Ὁδὸν ποιεῖν Mk. ii. 23 (where however the MSS. vary), is probably not put for ὁδὸν ποιεῖσθαι Her. 7. 42 (like πορείαν ποιεῖσθαι L. xiii. 22), since there is here something unsuitable in the meaning *make a journey*: we may adopt the strict rendering, *plucking ears they made a way (a path) in the field.* Lachmann, in accordance with his principle, receives ὁδοποιεῖν, the reading of B. [Meyer agrees with Winer. On the other side see Alford *in loc.*, who urges that this phrase occurs Jud. xvii. 8 in the sense "make a journey," but does not notice Meyer's objection that, on this view of the passage, the *principal* action would be expressed by the *participle* (see below § 45. 6).]
[5] The middle of ποιεῖν is but seldom found in the N. T.—being used by scarcely any writer except Paul and Luke (in the Acts)—but wherever it occurs we may easily recognise the middle signification. As the lexicons do not usually present the active and the middle separately, a list of the phrases formed with the middle of this verb is here subjoined: A. i. 1, τὸν πρῶτον λόγον ἐποιησάμην· viii. 2, ἐποιήσαντο κοπετόν· xxv. 17, ἀναβολὴν ποιεῖσθαι· xxvii. 18, ἐκ-

sages the middle is restored by Lachmann): εὑρίσκειν also is used with the meaning *consequi*, instead of εὑρίσκεσθαι (see Fritz. *Matt.* p. 390).¹ Here and there the middle and the active are interchanged: ² L. xv. 6, συγκαλεῖ τοὺς φίλους· ver. 9, συγκαλεῖται τὰς φίλας κ.τ.λ., according to Lachmann's reading (Tisch. has the active in both verses).³ Here it was for the writer (Franke, *Demosth.* p. 95) to decide whether he would say *he called together to himself*, or generally, *he called together*; the latter was perfectly intelligible. Compare also Ja. iv. 2 sq., α ἰ τ ε ῖ τ ε καὶ οὐ λαμβάνετε, διότι κακῶς α ἰ τ ε ῖ σ θ ε· 1 Jo. iii. 22, compare v. 14 sq.:⁴ see Matth. 492 c (Foertsch, *Lys.* p. 39).⁵ In 1 C. ix. 5 περιάγεσθαι would be more appro-

---

βολὴν ποιεῖσθαι· Rom. i. 9, E. i. 16, 1 Th. i. 2, Phil. 4, μνείαν τινὸς ποιεῖσθαι· 2 P. i. 15, μνήμην τινὸς ποιεῖσθαι· i. 10, ἐκλογὴν ποιεῖσθαι βεβαίαν· Jude 3, σπουδὴν ποιεῖσθαι· Ph. i. 4, 1 Tim. ii. 1, δέησιν ποιεῖσθαι· Rom. xv. 26, κοινωνίαν ποιεῖσθαι· E. iv. 16, τὸ σῶμα τὴν αὔξησιν ποιεῖται· H. i. 3, δι' ἑαυτοῦ καθαρισμὸν ποιησάμενος τῶν ἁμαρτιῶν. In illustration of Greek usage much is collected by Dresig, p. 422 sqq.; see also V. Fritzsche, *Aristoph.* I. 538 sq. The distinction between the active and the middle is thus defined by Blume (*ad Lycurg.* p. 55): Est ποιεῖν, quotiescunque accusativus substantivi abstracti accedit, *aliquid efficere, parare, faciendum curare, produce, bring about, prepare,* ποιεῖσθαι *ipsum facere* cum substantivis junctum periphrasin facit verbi, quod aut notatione aut certe notione nomini apposito conveniat. (On λόγον ποιεῖν and ποιεῖσθαι see Weber, *Demosth.* p. 295.) [The above list of phrases formed with ποιεῖσθαι is not quite complete. We find δεήσεις π. L. v. 33, πρόνοιαν π. Rom. xiii. 14, οὐδενὸς λόγου ποιοῦμαι τὴν ψυχὴν τιμίαν ἐμαυτῷ A. xx. 24 (Tisch., Treg.); πορείαν μονήν, and συνωμοσίαν ποιεῖσθαι (L. xiii. 22, Jo. xiv. 23, A. xxiii. 13) are mentioned in the text. On this use of ποιεῖσθαι see Jelf 363. 6, Shilleto, Dem. *F. L.* p. 59. In A. viii. 2 (quoted above) the best MSS. have ἐποίησαν; for other examples of the active so used see L. x. 37 (xvi. 9), xviii. 7, Mk. xv. 1 (Schirlitz, *Grundz.* p. 274). In 1 Tim. ii. 1 ποιεῖσθαι is usually taken as passive (Vulgate, Ellicott); Bengel and Alford consider it middle: see Alford's note.]

¹ In Jo. v. 4, ἦν ἄνθρωπος ... τριάκ. καὶ ὀκτὼ ἔτη ἔχων ἐν τῇ ἀσθενείᾳ, we cannot say that ἔχων stands for ἐχόμενος; rather would ἔχειν ἐν ἀσθενείᾳ be equivalent to ἔχειν ἀσθενῶς (κακῶς). The following verse however shows that ἔχων is to be connected as a transitive with ἔτη.

² For an example in which the distinction between the active and the middle is distinctly marked, see Dion. H. IV. 2088, τόν τε ἀετὸν ἀνεσωσάμην, καὶ τὸν στρατοπεδάρχην ἔσωσα.

³ Thus along with καταλαμβάνεσθαι πόλιν, κ.τ.λ. (take, occupy), καταλαμβάνειν πόλιν is also in use; compare Schweighäuser, *Lexic. Polyb.* p. 330.

⁴ In Mk. xiv. 47 we find σπασάμενος τὴν μάχαιραν; but in Mt. xxvi. 51, ἀπέσπασε τὴν μάχαιρ. αὐτοῦ. [Both σπάω and σπάομαι are thus used in classical Greek; see Mullach, *Vulg.* p. 336. With the examples in the text compare ἀπειλεῖν 1 P. ii. 23, ἀπειλεῖσθαι A. iv. 17, 21. On Ja. iv. 2 see Green, *Notes* p. 189.]

⁵ We might bring in here those actives combined with the reflexive pronoun for which the middle was actually in use in a reflexive sense; as ταπεινοῦν ἑαυτόν Ph. ii. 8, Mt. xviii. 4, compare ταπεινοῦσθαι Ja. iv. 10 (Wetst. II. 271), δουλοῦν ἑαυτόν 1 C. ix. 19, ζωννύειν ἑαυτόν Jo. xxi. 18, γυμνάζειν ἑαυτόν 1 Tim. iv. 7, al. But in all these passages the reflexive pronoun stands in an

priate : περιάγειν τινά means *to lead some one about* for exhibition or for guidance (2 Macc. vi. 10, Pol. 12. 4. 14), but *to lead about with oneself* (in one's company) is περιάγεσθαι : perhaps however the active is so used in Xen. *Cyr.* 2. 2. 28. It would not be at all surprising if foreigners, who had not a native's instinctive insight into the language, should occasionally fail to notice the shades of meaning conveyed by the middle voice, delicate as these sometimes are : even in classical Greek the use of this voice seems to have often depended on the culture and tact of the individual writers. The use of the active καθάπτω (A. xxviii. 3, though not without variant) in the place of the middle καθάπτομαι belongs to later Greek; see Passow s.v.

For διέρρηξε τὰ ἱμάτια αὐτοῦ Mt. xxvi. 65, A. xiv. 4, we might have had διερρήξατο τὰ ἱμάτια (see above) ; but the active is also in use in such cases (Bernh. p. 348). The distinction between παρέχειν and παρέχεσθαι[1] is not uniformly observed by the Greeks themselves ; but in A. xix. 24, Col. iv. 1, Tit. ii. 7, the appropriateness of the middle voice will be easily recognised. In A. xvi. 16, ἐργασίαν πολλὴν παρεῖχε τοῖς κυρίοις αὐτῆς μαντευομένη, the active is more suitable than the middle would be, since it was only in actual fact, and not by design, that this gain was procured by the damsel.

6. Conversely, we find the middle joined with ἑαυτῷ in Jo. xix. 24, διεμερίσαντο ἑαυτοῖς (in Mt. xxvii. 35 simply διεμερίσαντο), compare Xen. *Cyr.* 1. 4. 13, 2. 1. 30, Lycurg. 11. 8, 17. 3 ; also with ἑαυτόν, in the place of the active with ἑαυτόν (Plat. *Protag.* p. 349 a, Blume, *Lycurg.* p. 90), in Tit. ii. 7 σεαυτὸν παρεχόμενος τύπον,—but the middle had so fully established itself in the sense *show oneself* (in this or that mental or moral quality) that the writer used this voice even where he had (on account of τύπον) expressed the reflexive by a separate word. Compare Xen. *Cyr.* 8. 1. 39, παράδειγμα . . . τοιόνδε ἑαυτὸν παρείχετο.[2] In Tit. i. 5, if with *Rec.* we read ἐπιδιορ-

---

antithesis (Krüg. p. 168), and in Jo. xxi., for instance, the middle would even be incorrect. Thus κείρειν ἑαυτόν would mean "to shave *oneself*," κείρισθαι "to *shave* oneself." Moreover, where ambiguity might arise from the identity of the passive and the middle form, it would be natural to use the active with ἑαυτόν.

[1] Rost p. 575, Krüg. p. 163 ; compare Küster, no. 49. [Don. p. 437, Green, *Gr.* p. 185, Ellicott on Col. iv. 1, Tit. ii. 7.]

[2] For other examples of the middle with ἑαυτῷ, ἑαυτόν, see Schæf. *Dion. Hal.* p. 88, Bornem. Xen. *An.* 76 sq., Bernh. p. 347, Mehlhorn *l. c.* 36, Poppo, *Thuc.* I. i. 189 ; compare also Epiphan. I. 380, ὁπλισάμενος ἑαυτόν. [Don. p. 435, Jelf 363. 2.]

θώσῃ (but better MSS. have ἐπιδιορθώσῃς), the middle voice is really used for the active.[1] As little can we recognise a middle meaning in ἀπεκδύεσθαι Col. ii. 15, ἀμύνεσθαι A. vii. 24 (compare Dion. H. I. 548), ἁρμόζεσθαι 2 C. xi. 2.[2] Perhaps also προέχεσθαι, Rom. iii. 9, stands for the active. Similar examples are met with in Greek writers, especially those of a later date.[3] To this head have been referred E. v. 13, πᾶν τὸ φανερούμενον φῶς ἐστί· and i. 23, τοῦ τὰ πάντα ἐν πᾶσι πληρουμένου. In the first passage, however, φανεροῦσθαι has just occurred as a passive, and to this the apostle immediately proceeds to add φανερούμενον, which must therefore be taken in the same sense (so Harless and Meyer): *everything if it is reproved is by the light made manifest, for everything that is made manifest is light.* In E. i. 23 πληρουμένου might be considered passive (so Holzhausen), but then there would be a difficulty in τὰ πάντα ἐν πᾶσι, as is well shown by Harless. For this reason I consider πληρουμένου middle (Xen. *Hell.* 5. 4. 56, 6. 2. 14, Demosth. *Polycl.* 707 b), *the fulness of Him who filleth all* ; the middle signification is not entirely lost,—"*from Himself, through Himself, He filleth all.*" In H. xi. 40 also the middle προβλέπεσθαι is correctly used: προβλέπειν would denote a mere perception, *seeing beforehand, foreseeing,* the middle expresses the mental act of *choosing beforehand, providing:* προορᾶσθαι and προϊδέσθαι are similarly used by Greek writers.

In the verb ἐνεργεῖν we find a distinction in usage between the active and the middle, the active being used by Paul of *personal* (1 C. xii. 6, G. ii. 8, E. i. 11, al.), the middle of *non-personal* activity (Rom. vii. 5, Col. i. 29, 2 Th. ii. 7, al.) ; hence in 1 Th. ii. 13 ὅς must be referred, not to θεός, but to λόγος.

7. From middle verbs must carefully be distinguished the deponents. These verbs, with a passive (middle) form, have a

---

[1] [The middle is received by Tisch., Westcott and Hort ; also by Ellicott and Alford, who consider this an instance of the "dynamic" middle (see above, p. 318). In Col. ii. 15, we must surely give to ἀπεκδύεσθαι its strict middle meaning (compare Col. iii. 9) : see the notes of Ellicott, Alford, and Lightfoot. On ἠμύνατο, A. vii. 24, see A. Buttm. p. 194.]

[2] Lösner, *Observ.* p. 320 sq. ["Medium active dici doceri nequit, sed eo respicitur ad eum, cui cura despondendi commissa est :" Wilke, *Clavis* s. v. (ed. Grimm).]

[3] Schæf. *Plutarch.* V. 101 ; Meineke, *Index ad Cinnam.* 244. In the passages quoted by Schweighäuser (*Lexic. Herod.* II. 185) the middle signification may for the most part be recognised.

transitive or a neuter meaning: their active form either does not occur at all (in prose), or is used in precisely the same signification (Rost p. 263, Don. pp. 265, 440, Jelf 368).[1] Such are δύνασθαι, δωρεῖσθαι, γίγνεσθαι, βιάζεσθαι, ἐντέλλεσθαι, εὔχεσθαι, ἐνθυμεῖσθαι, ἐργάζεσθαι, εὐλαβεῖσθαι, μάχεσθαι, μέμφεσθαι, φείδεσθαι, ἀσπάζεσθαι, ἔρχεσθαι, ἡγεῖσθαι, ἰᾶσθαι, λογίζεσθαι, προαιτιᾶσθαι,[2] with many others. On these it must be remarked that

a. Although most deponents have their aorist of the middle form (*middle deponents*, as αἰτιᾶσθαι, ἀσπάζεσθαι, ἐργάζεσθαι, φείδεσθαι), yet not a few have in its place the aorist passive (*passive deponents*): as βούλεσθαι, δύνασθαι, ἐπιμελεῖσθαι, εὐλαβεῖσθαι, σπλαγχνίζεσθαι, μωμᾶσθαι,[3] etc. (Don. p. 268).

b. Others have both forms of the aorist; though in this case one or other form predominates (in prose). To this class belongs ἀρνεῖσθαι, on which (against Buttmann[4]) see Poppo, *Thuc.* III. iv. 209: the N. T. writers always use the middle aorist ἠρνησάμην, which in Greek prose is the rarer form. On the other hand, διαλέγεσθαι has always a passive aorist in Biblical Greek (Don. p. 269 sq.).

c. Some middle deponents which possess an aorist (or perfect) middle with an active meaning have also an aorist or perfect passive with a passive meaning: e. g. ἐθεάθην Mt. vi. 1, Mk. xvi. 11 (Thuc. 3. 38),[5] ἐθεασάμην *I saw;* ἰάθην Mt. viii. 13, L. vi. 17 (Is. liii. 5, Plat. *Legg.* 6. 758 d), ἴαμαι Mk. v. 29, but ἰασάμην active; ἐλογίσθην frequently (compare Xen. *Cyr.* 3. 1. 33); ἀπεδέχθησαν[6] A. xv. 4 (comp. 2 Macc. iii. 9), aor. middle in

---

[1] The active of λυμαίνεσθαι, for instance, is found in later writers only; see Passow. On the other hand, the active of δωρεῖσθαι occurs as early as Pindar, *Olymp.* 6. 131. In the N. T. we find even εὐαγγελίζω, as frequently in the LXX.

[2] [The actives βιάζω, ἐντέλλω, occur, but not in Attic prose: see Veitch, *Gr. Verbs* s. vv.]

[3] [Μωμᾶσθαι does not belong to this class, but should come in under *c*: it is a *middle* deponent (2 C. viii. 20,—Æsch. *Ag.* 277), with a rare aorist passive (2 C. vi. 3) in a *passive* sense.—The aor. mid. of ἐπιμελεῖσθαι occurs, but only in late Greek.]

[4] ["In Epic poetry and Ionic prose the aorist middle alone is used; in classic Attic, with the exception of one instance in Euripides, two in Æschines, and one in Hyperides, the aorist passive. Buttmann and Matthiæ wrongly confine the aorist middle to poetry." Veitch s. v.]

[5] Compare Poppo, *Thuc.* III. i. 594 sq.

[6] [The best reading is παρεδέχθησαν.]

L. viii. 40, A. xviii. 27; παρητημένος L. xiv. 19, aor. middle H. xii. 19, 25; ἐρρύσθην 2 Tim. iv. 17, aor. middle Col. i. 13, 2 P. ii. 7, al.; ἐχαρίσθην 1 C. ii. 12, Ph. i. 29 (pluperf. Her. 8. 5), aor. middle often in the N. T. See on the whole Rost p. 577 (Don. p. 274).

d. The future passive of λογίζομαι, with *passive* meaning, occurs Rom. ii. 26; similarly ἰαθήσεται Mt. viii. 8, and ἀπαρνηθήσομαι L. xii. 9.[1] Of λογίζομαι even the present tense is used in a passive sense in Rom. iv. 5, comp. Ecclus. xl. 19 (not in 2 C. x. 2); so also of βιάζεσθαι Mt. xi. 12: compare Poppo, *Thuc.* I. 184, III. i. 31 (Don. p. 275, Jelf 368. 3. *c.*).

e. The perfect passive εἴργασμαι is sometimes active in meaning (2 Jo. 8,[2] Demosth. *Conon* 728 a, Xen. *Mem.* 2. 6. 6, Lucian, *Fugit.* 2), sometimes passive, as in Jo. iii. 21, Xen. *Mem.* 3. 10. 9, Plat. *Rep.* 8. 566 a (Rost *l. c.*, Don. *l. c.*). On the other hand, ἤρνημαι 1 Tim. v. 8, ἐντέταλμαι A. xiii. 47 (Herod. 1. 9. 23, Pol. 17. 2. 1, 1 S. xxi. 2, Tob. v. 1, al.) and δέδεγμαι A. viii. 14, have an active meaning only. See on the whole Buttm. II. 51, Bernh. p. 341; but especially Poppo in the above-cited *Progr.*, and Rost, *Gramm.* p. 264 sqq.

That amongst the verbs usually called deponent there are very many which should rather be considered middle verbs, is remarked by Rost (p. 263) and Mehlhorn (*l. c.* p. 39). This is already admitted in regard to πολιτεύεσθαι. But κτάομαι *to acquire for oneself*, ἀγωνίζομαι (Rost p. 575), βιάζεσθαι, μεγαλαυχεῖσθαι,[3] and perhaps δέχομαι, ἀσπάζομαι (a middle deponent, according to Passow), should also be regarded as middle, as in all of them the reflexive meaning is more or less apparent.[4] Meyer calls πληροῦσθαι in E. i. 23 a deponent, but improperly.[5] In the N. T. ὑστερεῖσθαι is always used in the same sense as the active ὑστερεῖν. Lastly, ἡττάομαι and μαίνομαι must be considered passives, according to the Greek conception of these verbs: see Sommer *l. c.* 36.

---

[1] [Add χαρισθήσομαι Phil. 22. Compare also ἐμνήσθην A. x. 31, Rev. xvi. 19 (Ez. xviii. 24), ἐπιλελησμένον ἐστίν L. xii. 6 (Is. xxiii. 16): A. Buttm. p. 52.]

[2] [In 2 Jo. 8 we have the 1 aor., not the perfect, of ἐργάζομαι: it is singular that this slip is found in five editions of the German (3rd to 7th). The perfect occurs twice only in the N. T., here and in 1 P. iv. 3.

[3] [In the N. T. we find the active only, in Ja. iii. 5 *Rec.* Here however the true reading is μεγάλα αὐχεῖ.]

[4] [Compare Don. p. 440 sq. Considering *all* deponents to be properly middle, Donaldson classifies them "according to the usages of the middle in which they respectively originated."]

[5] [In ed. 3, 4, Meyer calls attention to the use of the middle voice, and renders *qui sibi implet.*]

Section XXXIX.

THE PASSIVE VOICE.

1. When a verb which governs the dative or the genitive of the person (as πιστεύειν τινί, κατηγορεῖν τινός) is used in the passive, the Greeks are accustomed to make the noun which denotes the person the subject of the passive verb (Krüg. p. 159, Jelf 364. 5, Don. p. 432).

a. Dative: G. ii. 7, πεπίστευμαι τὸ εὐαγγέλιον, i. e. πεπιστευμένον ἔχω τὸ εὐαγγέλιον (active, πιστεύειν τινί τι); Rom. iii. 2, ἐπιστεύθησαν (the Jews, ver. 1) τὰ λόγια τοῦ θεοῦ· 1 C. ix. 17, οἰκονομίαν πεπίστευμαι: compare Diog. L. 7. 34, πιστευθέντες τὴν ἐν Περγάμῳ βιβλιοθήκην· Pol. 3. 69. 1, πεπιστευμένος τὴν πόλιν παρὰ Ῥωμαίων· 31. 26. 7, Herod. 7. 9. 7, Demosth. *Theocr.* 507 c, Appian, *Civ.* 2. 136, Strabo 4. 197, 17. 197, etc., etc. So also when this verb is used in the sense of *believing some one* (πιστεύειν τινί) we find the passive πιστεύομαι *I am believed:*[1] e.g. Xen. *An.* 7. 6. 33, Isocr. *Trapez.* p. 874, Demosth. *Callip.* 720 a; βασιλεύομαι, Aristot. *Nic.* 8. 11.—The case is different in 1 Tim. iii. 16, ἐπιστεύθη (Χριστὸς) ἐν κόσμῳ: this cannot be referred to πιστεύειν Χριστῷ, but presupposes the phrase πιστεύειν Χριστόν; just as ἐπιστεύθη τὸ μαρτύριον ἡμῶν, 2 Th. i. 10, is founded on πιστεύειν τι (1 Jo. iv. 16).

Other examples of the same construction are A. xxi. 3, ἀναφανέντες[2] τὴν Κύπρον, *when Cyprus became visible to them,* i.e. ἀναφανεῖσαν ἔχοντες τὴν Κ.; H. xi. 2, ἐν ταύτῃ ἐμαρτυρήθησαν οἱ πρεσβύτεροι (μαρτυρεῖν τινί), A. xvi. 2, al.; H. xiii. 16, εὐαρεστεῖται ὁ θεός (Bleek *in loc.*); further, H. viii. 5 καθὼς κεχρημάτισται Μωϋσῆς (Mt. ii. 12, 22, Joseph. *Antt.* 3. 8. 8), and Mt. xi. 5 (L. vii. 22) πτωχοὶ εὐαγγελίζονται· H. iv. 2. The passages last cited come in here because εὐαγγελίζεσθαι (see Fritz. *Matt.* p. 395) and χρηματίζειν (Joseph. *Antt.* 10. 1. 3, 11. 8. 4) are *usually* followed by the dative of the person. We should probably add Col. ii. 20, τί ὡς ζῶντες ἐν κόσμῳ δογματίζεσθε (δογματίζειν τινί 2 Macc. x. 8); see Meyer. In 3 Jo. 12 the passive μαρτυρεῖσθαι has a dative of the person, like the active.

b. Genitive. Of verbs governing a genitive κατηγοροῦμαι

---

[1] The reverse ἀπιστοῦμαι, Wis. vii. 17.
[2] [Tischendorf and Westcott and Hort read ἀναφάναντες, with *Rec.*]

alone is thus used: Mt. xxvii. 12, ἐν τῷ κατηγορεῖσθαι αὐτὸν ὑπὸ τῶν ἀρχιερέων· A. xxii. 30, τὸ τί κατηγορεῖται ὑπὸ (παρὰ) τῶν Ἰουδαίων· 2 Macc. x. 13.¹—(I can find no sufficient reason for supposing, with Meyer, that κεχάρισμαι is passive in 2 C. ii. 10.²)

In Rom. vi. 17, ὑπηκούσατε .... εἰς ὃν παρεδόθητε τύπον διδαχῆς, we have perhaps this construction in combination with attraction (for ὑπηκ. εἰς τύπον διδ., ὃν παρεδόθητε, i. e. παραδοθέντα ἔχετε); yet see above § 24. 2.

In H. vii. 11, ὁ λαὸς ἐπ᾽ αὐτῆς (ἱερωσύνης) νενομοθέτηται, the construction may very well be founded on νομοθετεῖν τινί, *the people has received the law* (based, resting) *on the priesthood;* compare viii. 6. The parallels for νομοθετεῖν τινά (τι) quoted from the LXX cannot be brought in here, since in this construction the verb always means *to lead some one according to the law:* as Ps. cxviii. 33, νομοθέτησόν με τὴν ὁδὸν τῶν δικαιωμάτων σου· xxiv. 8, νομοθετήσει ἁμαρτάνοντας ἐν ὁδῷ. In the Byzantines, however, we find νομοθετεῖν τινά (in reference to a country or a people), as Malal. pp. 72, 194. The regular construction of the passive occurs in Dt. xvii. 10, ὅσα ἂν νομοθετηθῇ σοι.

2. In many verbs which in ancient Greek have regularly the 1 aor. middle, in the middle sense, the N. T. writers use instead the 1 aor. passive (comp. § 38. 4). Thus we usually find ἀπεκρίθη,³ especially in the participle ἀποκριθείς:⁴ the aor. middle ἀπεκρίνατο occurs Mk. xiv. 61, L. iii. 16, xxiii. 9, Jo. v. 19, xii. 23, A. iii. 12, and more frequently as a variant, e.g. in Jo. i. 26, xii. 34, xviii. 34.⁵ Similarly διεκρίθη, Mt. xxi. 21, Mk. xi. 23, Rom. iv. 20; but ἐκρίθη is passive in A. xxvii. 1.⁶ In other examples of aor. passive for aor. middle which have been quoted from the N. T., προςεκλίθη A. v. 36, ἐνεδυναμώθη Rom. iv. 20, παρεδόθητε vi. 17, ταπεινώθητε 1 P. v. 6, Ja. iv. 10, the aorist is from the Greek (and also the N. T.) point of

---

¹ [Add κατεγνωσμένος ἦν, G. ii. 11 (A. Buttm. p. 188).]
² [Meyer gave this up in his 4th ed. (1862).]
³ Yet we find ἀπεκρίθη in MSS. as early as Xen. *An.* 2. 1. 22: on Plat. *Alc.* 2. p. 149 b, see Lob. p. 108. In the writers after Alexander it is not at all uncommon. [See Veitch, *Gr. Verbs* s. v.]
⁴ From this tense we find the fut. ἀποκριθήσομαι, Mt. xxv. 37, 45, and LXX.
⁵ Compare Sturz, *Dial. Alex.* p. 148 sq., Lobeck, *Phryn.* p. 108, Schoem. *Isœus* p. 305.
⁶ [For other examples see A. Buttm. p. 51 sq.—The aor. passive of θαυμάζω occurs Rev. xiii. 3 (Lach.) in an active sense; so also θαυμασθήσομαι Rev. xvii. 8 (Lach., Tisch. ed. 7): see Veitch p. 271, A. Buttm. p. 59.]

view really passive; just as in Latin *servari, delectari*, are used instead of *servare se, delectare se*, which agree with our idiom: compare Rost p. 573.[1] We must say the same of the 2 aor. καταλλαγήτω 1 C. vii. 11, 2 C. v. 20 (compare Rom. v. 10), and of the future (πρὸς) κολληθήσεται Mt. xix. 5 (E. v. 31).

Ἐκληρώθημεν E. i. 11 (see Harless *in loc.*), and προςεκληρώθησαν A. xvii. 4, are evidently passive.

3. That the perfect (Matth. 493) and the pluperfect passive have also a middle signification has been generally admitted since the so-called perfect and pluperfect middle disappeared from our grammars (Buttm. I. 362, Jelf 365. 3). In the N. T. compare A. xiii. 2 (εἰς) ὃ προςκέκλημαι αὐτούς, *to which I have called them for myself;* xvi. 10, προσκέκληται ἡμᾶς ὁ κύριος εὐαγγελίσασθαι αὐτούς, *the Lord has called us for Himself* etc. (compare Ex. iii. 18, v. 3); xxv. 12, καίσαρα ἐπικέκλησαι, *thou hast called for thyself to the emperor* (appealed to him); Rom. iv. 21, ὃ ἐπήγγελται δυνατός ἐστι καὶ ποιῆσαι (ὁ θεός), H. xii. 26; Jo. ix. 22, συνετέθειντο οἱ Ἰουδαῖοι· 1 P. iv. 3, πεπορευμένους ἐν ἀσελγείαις (1 S. xiv. 17, 2 K. v. 25, Job xxx. 28, Zeph. iii. 15, Demosth. *Nicostr.* 723 c, al.). On the perfect passive of deponents see § 38. 7.

On the other hand, 1 P. iv. 1 πέπαυται ἁμαρτίας (commonly rendered *peccare desiit*, compare Xen. *Cyr.* 3. 1. 18) may be taken as passive, *he has rest from sin, is secured against sin*, see Kypke *in loc.*: Ph. iii. 12, however, can in no case come in here.—Πολιτεύομαι (A. xxiii. 1) might according to Poppo's theory (since the active is in actual use as an intransitive verb) be regarded as a deponent; but see above, page 325. In Rom. xiv. 23 there can be no doubt that the apostle used κατακέκριται in a passive sense.

The perfect passive is said to stand for the perfect *active* in A. xx. 13, οὕτω γὰρ ἦν (ὁ Παῦλος) διατεταγμένος· and in 2 P. i. 3, τῆς θείας δυνάμεως . . . . τὰ πρὸς ζωὴν δεδωρημένης.[2] But in the first passage διατ. is middle (as in Polyæn. 6. 1. 5, Jos. *Antt.* 4. 2. 3, al.), *so had he arranged it;* and in 2 P. i. 3 δεδωρ. is from the deponent δωρέομαι.[3] Compare further Poppo, *Thuc.* I. i. 179 sqq.

---

[1] The use of the aor. middle of such verbs is commonly restricted to the cases in which an accusative follows, in the reflexive sense mentioned above, § 38. 2. Thus ἐσώθην is *me servavi* (servatus sum), but ἐσωσάμην τὸ σῶμα is used for *corpus meum* (mihi) *servavi*.

[2] Compare Jensii *Lectt. Lucian.* p. 247.

[3] Markland (*Explicatt. vett. aliquot locorum*, in the Leipsic reprint of his edition of Eurip. *Supplic.* p. 324 sq.) brings in here A. xiii. 48, so famous in the

Rem. 1. The future passive is used in a very peculiar manner in A. xxvi. 16, εἰς τοῦτο ὤφθην σοι, προχειρίσασθαί σε ὑπηρέτην καὶ μάρτυρα, ὧν τε εἶδες, ὧν τε ὀφθήσομαί σοι. Following the parallelism, we might render this *what thou hast seen and what I will cause thee to see*, ὀφθήσομαι being taken in a causative sense.[1] The other explanation (which in the main is adopted by Schott, Kühnöl, Heinrichs, Meyer, and De Wette), *de quibus*—in reference to which—or *quorum caussa tibi porro apparebo*, would on the whole suit the context better, and is probably the simpler of the two. On ὧν for ἅ, by attraction, see § 24. 2.[2]

Rem. 2. Since several verbs which in classic Greek are neuter are used as transitives in Hellenistic Greek (see above, § 38. 1), commentators occasionally take the passive (in accordance with this causal signification of the active) as equivalent to the Hebrew Hophal. Of such a usage, however, there is no certain or even probable example. In G. iv. 9, γνόντες θεόν, μᾶλλον δὲ γνωσθέντες ὑπ' αὐτοῦ, the antithesis of itself requires us to translate, *knowing God, rather however known* (recognised) *by God*; see my note *in loc.* 1 C. viii. 3, εἴ τις ἀγαπᾷ τὸν θεόν, οὗτος ἔγνωσται ὑπ' αὐτοῦ, must not be rendered,[3] *is veram intelligentiam consecutus est.* The meaning is, *whoever imagines that he knows anything* (in whom therefore there exists a γνῶσις φυσιοῦσα), *such a one has not yet known, as a man ought to know; if however a man loves God* (compare the preceding words ἡ ἀγάπη οἰκοδομεῖ), *he*—has not only known as a man ought to know, but—*is known by Him* (God), is himself the object of the highest and truest knowledge, the Divine. In 1 C. xiii. 12, ἄρτι γινώσκω ἐκ μέρους, τότε δὲ ἐπιγνώσομαι καθὼς καὶ ἐπεγνώσθην, the last word certainly refers to God's knowledge, and the true meaning of the words was given by Nösselt: " then shall we know all perfectly (not ἐκ μέρους, not as ἐν αἰνίγματι), as perfectly as God knows us."[4] That γινώσκειν signifies *cognoscere facere, edocere* has not yet been proved from Biblical Greek, and Pott cannot have understood what he was doing when he quoted Jo. v. 42, Rom. ii. 18. On the other hand, this meaning does certainly meet us in Demosth. *Cor.* p. 345 c (already cited by Stephanus in his *Thesaurus*), ὡμολόγηκε νῦν γ' ὑμᾶς ὑπάρχειν ἐγνω-

---

Predestination controversy, punctuating the verse thus, καὶ ἐπίστευσαν, ὅσοι ἦσαν τεταγμένοι, εἰς ζωὴν αἰώνιον, and translating, "et fidem professi sunt, quotquot (tempus, diem) constituerant, in vitam æternam." This exposition is likely to find as little favour with an unbiassed exegete as most of the expositions given by English philologers, though certainly more attention is given to the N. T. by these than by the philologers of Germany.

[1] See Döderlein, Soph. *Œd. C.* p. 492, Bornem. in Rosenm. *Rep.* II. 289.
[2] [Meyer compares Soph. *Œd. Rex* 788, ὧν μὲν ἱκόμην = τούτων δι' ἅ. There is good authority for με after εἶδες (Westcott and Hort); with this reading the two relatives agree in construction.]
[3] As it is by Erasmus, Beza, Nösselt, Pott, Heydenreich, al.
[4] Ph. iii. 12 sq. is similar, as regards the combination of the active and the passive verb. Compare Arrian, *Epict.* 3. 23. 8, δύναταί τις ὠφελῆσαι καὶ ἄλλους μὴ αὐτὸς ὠφελημένος; Liban. *Ep.* 2.

σμένους ἐμὲ μὲν λέγειν ὑπὲρ τῆς πατρίδος, αὐτὸν δ᾽ ὑπὲρ Φιλίππου: though it is true this disappears if we follow Dissen in reading ἡμᾶς (with one MS.),[1] *nos esse cognitos* (h. e. de nobis constare), *me quidem verba facere pro patria* etc.

Rem. 3. Here and there it has appeared doubtful whether a verb is middle or passive. The decision is grammatical only so far as it may be shown that the verb in question either was never used in the passive or in the middle, or that the middle had an active meaning. Hence we are justified in regarding ἀτιμάζεσθαι, Rom. i. 24, as a passive; so also οἰκοδομεῖσθαι 1 C. viii. 10, παύεσθαι 1 P. iv. 1,[2] ἀνανεοῦσθαι E. iv. 23: on the other hand, in 1 C. i. 2, οἱ ἐπικαλούμενοι τὸ ὄνομα τοῦ κυρίου, the verb can only be middle. In other cases the context must decide,—e.g. in 2 C. ii. 10, where κεχάρισμαι must be considered middle (against Meyer), and in Rom. iii. 9, where προέχεσθαι cannot be passive;—or else the known view of the writer, gathered from other passages, e.g. E. vi. 10 ἐνδυναμοῦσθε.

Section XL.

THE TENSES.

1. The N. T. grammarians and commentators[3] have been chargeable with the grossest mistakes in regard to the tenses of the verb.[4] In general, these[5] are used in the N. T. exactly as in Greek writers.[6] The aorist refers to the past simply (the

---

[1] [On the frequent interchange of ἡμεῖς and ὑμεῖς in MSS. see Scrivener, *Introd.* p. 11: for examples in Demosthenes see *e.g.* Shilleto, *Fals. Leg.* p. 58, Weber, *Dem.* pp. 11, 12, 16, comp. p. 18. Liddell and Scott retain ὑμᾶς, and render "are determined;" so also Rost and Palm.]

[2] [It is not easy to see how these principles apply to πέπαυται 1 P. iv. 1, see above, p. 328: of ἐπικαλέω both passive and middle are found in the N. T., but when the passive is combined with ὄνομα it is in a different construction from that found in 1 C. i. 2. On E. iv. 23, vi. 10, see Ellicott: on 2 C. ii. 10 (Meyer) see p. 327.]

[3] Compare Bertholdt, *Einleit.* VI. 3151: "it is well known that in the use of the tenses the N. T. writers were very little bound by the laws of grammar."

[4] Occasioned in part by the parallel passages, which, it was thought, must be considered exactly alike, even in point of grammar. The abuse of parallelism in exegesis deserves a special investigation.

[5] The Greeks regarded the present, the perfect, and the future, as the three principal tenses: Plut. *Isid.* c. 9, ἐγώ εἰμι τὸ γεγονὸς καὶ ὂν καὶ ἐσόμενον. Compare *Odyss.* 16. 437.

[6] Besides the well known grammatical works—especially Herm. *Emend. Rat.* p. 180 sqq., Schneider, *Vorles. über griech. Grammat.* I. 239 sqq., Krüg. p. 170 sqq.—compare L. G. Dissen, *De temporibus et modis verbi Græci* (Gött. 1808), H. Schmidt, *Doctrinæ tempor. verbi Gr. et Lat. expositio histor.* (Hal. 1836–1842, four parts).—An earlier treatise by G. W. Oeder, *Chronol. Grammat.* (Gött. 1743,—included in Pott's *Sylloge*, VII. 133 sqq.), is less serviceable. The *enallage temporum* had been already combated by A. zum Felde in his *De*

simple occurrence of an event at some past time, considered as a momentary act), and is the ordinary tense of narration; the imperfect and the pluperfect always have reference to subordinate events which stood related, in respect of time, with the principal event (as relative tenses); and lastly, the perfect brings the past into connexion with the present time, and represents an action as a completed one, in relation to the present time. Strictly and properly speaking, no one of these tenses can ever stand for another, as the commentators have in so many ways maintained:[1] where such an interchange seems to exist,[2] either it exists in appearance only, there being in point of fact some assignable reason (especially of a rhetorical kind) why this tense is used and no other; or else it must be ascribed to a certain inexactness belonging to the popular language, through which the relation of time was not conceived and expressed with perfect precision (Krüg. p. 182 sq.). The latter case is chiefly exemplified in the interchange (or combination) of tenses which express the same main relation of time, e.g. the past tenses.

2. Hence the present tense—which expresses present time in all its relations (and especially in rules, maxims, and dogmas of permanent validity, compare Jo. vii. 52)—

a. Is used for the future in appearance only, when an action still future is to be represented as being as good as already present, either because it is already firmly resolved on, or because it must ensue in virtue of some unalterable law (exactly as in Latin, German, etc.):[3] Mt. xxvi. 2, οἴδατε, ὅτι μετὰ δύο ἡμέρας τὸ πάσχα γίνεται (that the Passover *is*) καὶ ὁ υἱὸς τοῦ

---

enall. præs. temp. in S. S. usu (Kil. 1711), and by Woken in the work mentioned above (p. 7, note 1): compare also the opinion of Aristides in Georgi, *Vind.* p. 252. [Don. p. 404 sqq.; Jelf 394 sqq.; Clyde, *Gr. Syntax* pp. 71–85; Goodwin, *Moods and Tenses* pp. 1–64; Farrar, *Gr. Synt.* pp. 110–127, Green, *Gr.* p. 127 sqq., Webster, *Syntax* p. 80 sqq.]

[1] The arbitrary interchange of tenses (enallage temporum) is reckoned amongst the Hebraisms, on the supposition that in Hebrew the preterite is used for the future and the future for the preterite *promiscue.* How incorrect this representation is, has been already shown by Gesenius (*Lehrgeb.* p. 760 sqq.), and still more thoroughly by Ewald (*Krit. Gr.* p. 523 sqq.).

[2] Compare Georgi, *Vind.* p. 252 sqq., *Hierocrit.* I. 58 sq.

[3] [Don. p. 405, Jelf 397, Green p. 131 sq., Ellicott on G. iii. 8. A. Buttmann (p. 204) divides the examples of present for future into two classes, those in which the signification of the verb includes a future idea (as ἔρχομαι—compare the Attic use of εἶμι, not found in the N. T.,—ὑπάγω, πορεύομαι, γίνομαι); and those in which the future sense follows from the context. Several of his examples however (especially of the former kind) seem doubtful.]

ἀνθρ. παραδίδοται εἰς τὸ σταυρωθῆναι (*is delivered*,—this, as a Divine decree, is firmly fixed); Jo. xiv. 3, ἐὰν πορευθῶ... πάλιν ἔρχομαι καὶ παραλήψομαι (xxi. 23); Mt. xvii. 11, Ἠλίας μὲν ἔρχεται (this was a point of the Jewish Christology) καὶ ἀποκαταστήσει πάντα, compare Jo. vii. 42; L. xii. 54, ὅταν ἴδητε τὴν νεφέλην ἀνατέλλουσαν ἀπὸ δυσμῶν, εὐθέως λέγετε· ὄμβρος ἔρχεται (a law of the weather, taught by experience); Col. iii. 6, δι' ἃ ἔρχεται ἡ ὀργὴ τοῦ θεοῦ ἐπὶ τοὺς υἱοὺς τῆς ἀπειθείας (in accordance with a law of God's moral government of the world); H. iv. 3, 1 C. iii. 13, xv. 2, E. v. 5: hence the phrase ἔρχεται ὥρα ὅτε in the mouth of Jesus, Jo. iv. 21, xvi. 2; hence too the Jewish designation of the Messiah, ὁ ἐρχόμενος (הַבָּא). We may also bring in here the formula (peculiar to John) ὅπου εἰμὶ ἐγώ, followed by a future (Jo. xii. 26, xiv. 3, xvii. 24), unless we prefer the rendering *where I am*, where I have my home. It would be a mistake to change the more select present tense into the future, in translating these passages.[1] Elsewhere we find the present tense used of that which is just about to take place; which some one is on the point of doing, is already preparing to do:[2] Jo. x. 32, διὰ ποῖον αὐτῶν ἔργον λιθάζετέ με (they had already seized the stones); Jo. xiii. 6, κύριε, σύ μου νίπτεις τοὺς πόδας (he had already assumed the attitude of one who washes); xiii. 27,[3] xvi. 17 (ὑπάγω), xvii. 11, xxi. 3, 1 C. xii. 31, 2 C. xiii. 1, Rom. xv. 25.[4]

Many other passages have been brought under this head with much less plausibility. In Jo. iii. 36 the thought is weakened if ἔχει is taken for ἕξει. The notion of ζωή, as used by John, not only permits but almost requires the present tense; apart from this, however, ἔχειν ζωὴν αἰώνιον might very well be said of one who, though not as yet in the actual enjoyment of the eternal life, yet in his certain hope already *has* it as a possession belonging to him.[5] The same applies to Jo. v. 26. Mt. v. 46 is rightly ex-

---

[1] Compare Poppo, *Thuc.* I. i. 153, Krüg. p. 171; as to Latin, Ramshorn p. 401.
[2] Herm. *Vig.* p. 746, and on Soph. *Œd. C.* 91, Bekker, *Specim. Philostr.* p. 73 sq., Schoemann, *Isœus*, p. 202.
[3] Ὁ ποιεῖς, ποίησον τάχιον, quod (jam) facis, quo jam occupatus es, id (fac) perfice ocius. Comp. Arrian, *Epict.* 4. 9. 18, ποίει ἃ ποιεῖς· 3. 23. 1, and Senec. *Benef.* 2. 5, fac, si quid facis: see Wetstein I. 931. What is here commanded, recommended, lies not in the verb, but in the adverb annexed.
[4] See on the whole Held, Plut. *Timol.* p. 335 sq.
[5] In the words which immediately follow, οὐκ ὄψεται ζωήν, the apostle very accurately distinguishes the future from the present.

SECT. XL.]   THE TENSES.   333

plained by Fritzsche;¹ but I cannot agree with him in regarding Mt. iii. 10 as a general maxim, *every tree which does not bear good fruit is hewn down* (it is customary to hew down such trees). These words are connected by οὖν with ἡ ἀξίνη πρὸς τὴν ῥίζαν τῶν δένδρων κεῖται, and they require a special explanation which shall have reference to the δένδρα before mentioned, *the axe is already lying at the root of the trees, accordingly every tree . . . is* (will be) *without fail hewn down:* that is, from the fact that the axe is already laid we may infer what fate awaits the worthless trees. In 1 C. xv. 35, πῶς ἐ γ ε ί ρ ο ν τ α ι οἱ νεκροί, the resurrection is not spoken of as an event (of future time), but as a dogma: *how does the resurrection of the dead take place* (according to thy teaching)? compare ver. 42. In the same way we can say, Christ *is* the Judge, the punishments of the lost *are* eternal, etc. Similarly in Mt. ii. 4, ποῦ ὁ Χριστὸς γεννᾶται (as if, where is the birthplace of the Messiah?), and Jo. vii. 52.—In 2 C. v. 1, οἴδαμεν ὅτι, ἐὰν ἡ ἐπίγειος ἡμῶν οἰκία τοῦ σκήνους καταλυθῇ, οἰκοδομὴν ἐκ θεοῦ ἔ χ ο μ ε ν, the future ἕξομεν would be less precise: the words are designed to indicate the instantaneous acquisition of a new habitation, as soon as the καταλύεσθαι has taken place. In Mt. vii. 8, the present (of that which regularly occurs, Krüg. p. 170) is combined with the future in a maxim of general application: compare Rom. vi. 16, G. ii. 16. On the other hand, in Mt. iii. 11 the present and the future (of one who is to come) are purposely distinguished; the former relates to the personality proclaimed, which is permanent (and even now existing), the future βαπτίσει to a particular function which he will discharge. Of two parallel passages in the Synoptic Gospels, one has the present ὁ εἷς παραλαμβάνεται (Mt. xxiv. 40), the other the future εἷς παραληφθήσεται (L. xvii. 34) : in the former, the fact which has been introduced by a future (ἔσονται) is vividly conceived as present (see below); in the latter, it is described in all its parts as future. Compare also Jo. xvi. 14, 15, H. i. 11.

b. The present is used for the aorist, as an historical tense, only when the narrator wishes to bring a past event vividly before us, as if it were taking place at the present moment (Longin. c. 25 ²): Jo. i. 29, τῇ ἐπαύριον βλέπει . . . καὶ λέγει (in ver. 32, καὶ ἐμαρτύρησεν); i. 44, εὑρίσκει Φίλιππον καὶ λέγει (above, ἠθέλησεν), compare ver. 46, xiii. 4 sq.; Mt. xxvi. 40, ἔρχεται πρὸς τοὺς μαθητὰς καὶ εὑρίσκει αὐτοὺς καθεύδοντας. Such a present is often introduced suddenly in the midst of aorists (Jo. ix. 13, xviii. 28, xix. 9, A. x. 11, Mk. v. 15), or the present and aorist are combined in a single verse, as in Mk. vi. 1, ix. 2, xi.

---

¹ [Fritzsche's note on ἔχετι is, (what reward have ye) "entered in God's book of account?"]
² Matth. 504: comp. Zumpt, *Lat. Gr.* § 501 (Don. p. 405, Jelf 395. 2).

15, Jo. xx. 6, 19. In the Synoptic Gospels we find the present used by one narrator, the aorist by another; compare Mt. xxi. 13 with Mk. xi. 27 sq.,[1] Mt. xxii. 23 with Mk. xii. 18. This present also occurs in the apocalyptic vision, as Rev. xi. 9, xii. 2. As to the LXX, where this usage is very rare, see Thiersch p. 187.[2] Suddenness, in a series of past events, is very characteristically expressed by the present in Mt. ii. 13, ἀναχωρησάντων αὐτῶν ἰδοὺ ἄγγελος κυρίου φαίνεται κατ' ὄναρ κ.τ.λ.

For similar examples see Xen. *Hell.* 2. 1. 15, *Cyr.* 4. 6. 4, 10, 5. 4. 3, *Ages.* 2. 19, 20, Thuc. 1. 48, 2. 68, Paus. 1. 17. 4, 9. 6. 1, Arrian, *Al.* 7. 17. 5, Dion. H. IV. 2113, Achill. Tat. 4. 4, p. 85.[3]

c. Sometimes the present tense includes a preterite (Madv. 110. Rem. 1, Jelf 396. 2), viz., when the verb indicates a state which commenced at an earlier period but still continues,—a state in its continuance: Jo. xv. 27, ἀπ' ἀρχῆς μετ' ἐμοῦ ἐστέ· viii. 58, πρὶν Ἀβραὰμ γενέσθαι ἐγὼ εἰμί (compare Jer. i. 5, πρὸ τοῦ με πλάσαί σε ἐν κοιλίᾳ, ἐπίσταμαί σε· Ps. lxxxix. 2), 2 P. iii. 4, 1 Jo. iii. 8. We might bring in here A. xxv. 11, εἰ μὲν ἀδικῶ καὶ ἄξιον θανάτου πέπραχά τι (compare Xen. *Cyr.* 5. 2. 24); but ἀσικῶ denotes the quality presented to the cognisance of the judge, ἄδικός εἰμι; see Bernh. p. 370, Matt. 504. 2 [Madv. 110. Rem. 2]. In Jo. viii. 14 we find first an aorist, then a present: οἶδα πόθεν ἦλθον . . . ὑμεῖς δὲ οὐκ οἴδατε, πόθεν ἔρχομαι.

In 1 Jo. iii. 5 the sinlessness of Jesus is regarded as being in faith still present (see Lücke). In A. xxvi. 31, οὐδὲν θανάτου ἄξιον ἢ δεσμῶν πράσσει, the reference is not to Paul's previous life, but to his conduct generally, *this man* (as if, so simple an enthusiast) *does nothing bad.* See Bengel *in loc.:* Kühnöl is wrong. Compare Jo. vii. 51.—In H. ii. 16 the more recent commentators have perceived that ἐπιλαμβάνεται is not to be taken as a preterite:[4] in ix. 6 also εἰσίασιν is a pure present. Bengel rightly renders κοιμῶνται in 1 C. xi. 30 by *obdormiunt:* all recent commentators have either rendered

---

[1] [Mt. xxi. 13 should be xxi. 23: in Mk. xi. 28 the best reading is ἴλεγον.]
[2] [Thiersch remarks that the historic present is scarcely ever used by the LXX (who found nothing in the Hebrew that exactly answered to it), except in the two verbs ὁρᾷ and λέγει, but that in these verbs *it is very common* (Gen. xxxvii. 29, Ex. xiv. 10, xxxii. 17, 18, 19, al.). See also Gen. xxxiii. 17 (ἀπαίρει), and xxxix. 16 (καταλιμπάνει).]
[3] Jacobs, *Xen. Ephes.* 5. 12. p. 113 ; compare Abresch, *Aristæn.* p. 11 sq., Ast, Plat. *Phædr.* p. 335, Ellendt, Arr. *Al.* II. 68.
[4] Georgi, *Vind.* 25, Palairet 479.

it by a preterite or passed it without remark; but even in the Byzantine writers κοιμᾶσθαι means only *to fall asleep, die,* not *to be dead*.¹ On παράγεται, 1 Jo. ii. 8, see Lücke.² That ἐστί is used for ἦν in Jo. v. 2, no intelligent expositor will allow to be even possible: on the other hand, however, the present tense is not necessarily an evidence that at the time when John wrote the locality still remained as here described.³

In *dependent* sentences the present might seem to stand for the imperfect, as in Jo. ii. 9, οὐκ ᾔδει, πόθεν ἐ σ τ ί ν· iv. 1, ἤκουσαν οἱ φαρισαῖοι, ὅτι Ἰησοῦς . . . π ο ι ε ῖ καὶ β α π τ ί ζ ε ι· Mk. v. 14, ἐξῆλθον ἰδεῖν, τί ἐ σ τ ι τὸ γεγονός· xii. 41, xv. 47, Jo. i. 40, v. 13, 15, vi. 5, 24, 64, L. vii. 37, xix. 3, A. iv. 13, ix. 26, x. 18, xii. 3, H. xi. 8, 13 : the preterite which in most instances we find in a greater or smaller number of MSS. is evidently a correction.⁴ This however is a regular Greek construction (see Vig. p. 214 sq. and compare below, § 41. b. 5), which really results from a mingling of the *oratio recta* and the *oratio obliqua;*⁵ compare Pol. 5. 26. 6, 8. 22. 2, 4, Æl. 2. 13 *ext.,* Long. *Past.* 1. 10. 13. The imperfect or aorist in these passages might have indicated that the circumstance asked after or heard of was past at the time of inquiring or hearing: compare Jo. ix. 8, οἱ θεωροῦντες αὐτὸν τὸ πρότερον, ὅτι τυφλὸς ἦν· L. viii. 53, Mt. xxvii. 18, A. iv. 13. (Jelf 886.)

3. The imperfect tense is used, as in Greek prose (Bernh. p. 372 sq., Krüg. p. 172 sqq., Don. p. 409, Jelf 398),

a. When a past action is to be indicated in relation to another simultaneous action, as continuing at the time when the latter took place:⁶ Jo. iv. 31, ἐν τῷ μεταξὺ ἠρώτων αὐτόν (viii. 6, 8); L. xiv. 7, ἔλεγε . . . ἐπέχων, πῶς τὰς πρωτοκλισίας ἐξελέγοντο, *how they* (at that time) *were choosing out;* xxiv. 32, ἡ καρδία ἡμῶν καιομένη ἦν ἐν ἡμῖν, ὡς ἐλάλει ἡμῖν ἐν τῇ ὁδῷ· A. viii. 36, ὡς ἐπορεύοντο κατὰ τὴν ὁδόν, ἦλθον ἐπί τι ὕδωρ· x. 17, xvi. 4, xxii. 11, L. vi. 19, Jo. v. 16, xii. 6.

b. To indicate a past action of somewhat long duration, or continuously repeated:⁷ Jo. iii. 22, ἐκεῖ διέτριβε μετ' αὐτῶν καὶ

---

¹ [Compare however τῶν κοιμωμένων 1 Th. iv. 13, and the epitaph quoted by Alford *in loc., ἱερὸν ὕπνον κοιμᾶται κ. τ. λ.*]
² ["John is thinking much more of the diffusion of the holy light of life from Christ, than of its origination in Christ."]
³ Compare Schoem. Plut. *Agis* p. 135 sqq.
⁴ [In very few of *these* passages is a preterite given as a variant by Tisch. or by Griesbach. The perfect is the best reading in Mk. xv. 47.]
⁵ Porson, Eurip. *Orest.* p. 36 (Lips.). On the still more extended use of the present for a preterite in parenthetical sentences see Buttm. *Gr.* § 124. Rem. 6, and *ad Philoct.* p. 129.
⁶ Bremi, *Demosth.* p. 19.
⁷ Matth. 497 b, 502; Schoem. Plut. *Agis* p. 137, Held, Plut. *Æm. P.* p. 267.

ἐβάπτιζεν· Rom. xv. 22, ἐνεκοπτόμην τὰ πολλὰ τοῦ ἐλθεῖν· 1 C. X 4, ἔπινον γὰρ ἐκ πνευματ. ἀκολουθούσης πέτρας, where ἔπιον denotes simply the past and now completed action, ἔπινον its continuance during the journey through the wilderness ; xiii. 11, ὅτε ἤμην νήπιος, ὡς νήπιος ἐλάλουν· A. xiii. 11, περιάγων ἐζήτει χειραγωγούς· Mt. xiii. 34, χωρὶς παραβολῆς οὐκ ἐλάλει (throughout the time of His ministry). Compare L. v. 15, vi. 23, viii. 41,52,xvii. 28,xxiv. 14,27,[1] Mt.iii. 5, xxvii. 39, Mk. i. 7, 31, Jo. v. 18, vii. 1, xi. 5, xiii. 22 sq., xii. 2, xxi. 18, A. vi. 1, 7 (Thuc.1.29), ix. 20, xi. 20, xviii.25, xxvi. 1, 11,xxviii. 6, Rev. i. 9,[2] 1 P. iii. 5, 2 P. ii. 8, H. xii. 10, Col. iii. 7, al. ; Xen. An. 1. 2. 18, 4. 5. 18, 5. 4. 24, 6. 3. 3, Mem. 1. 1. 5, Apol. Socr. 14. Hence the imperfect is used to express a custom or practice, as in Mk. xv. 6, κατὰ ἑορτὴν ἀπέλυεν αὐτοῖς ἕνα δέσμιον· xiv. 12 (Demosth. Phil. 2. 27 b); compare Herm. Vig. p. 746.

c. To denote an action commenced in past time but not actually accomplished :[3] L. i. 59, ἐκάλουν αὐτὸ ... Ζαχαρίαν (his mother objected, and he is called John), Mt. iii. 14, ὁ δὲ Ἰωάννης διεκώλυεν αὐτόν (compare ver. 15), A. vii. 26, συνήλλασσεν αὐτοὺς εἰς εἰρήνην [4] (Moses), compare ver. 27. Similarly in Eurip. Iph. T. 360, Herc. F. 437, Her. 1. 68, Thuc. 2. 5, Demosth. Mid. 396 b, Xenoph. An. 4. 5. 19, Mem. 1. 2. 29, Paus. 4. 9. 4.[5]—H. xi. 17 (προςέφερεν) has no place here. G. i. 13, however, would be an example if πορθεῖν were rendered *destroy ;* but see my note *in loc.*[6]

d. The imperfect sometimes seems to take the place of the aorist in narration, when events are described at which the narrator was present : L. x. 18, ἐθεώρουν τὸν σατανᾶν ὡς ἀστραπὴν ἐκ τοῦ οὐρανοῦ πεσόντα.[7] By this means the narration is made

---

[1] [The aorist is best attested here.]
[2] [There is no imperfect in Rev. i. 9.]
[3] Herm. Soph. *Aj.* 1106 : in eo, quod quis voluit facere, nec tamen perfecit, quod aptius adhiberi tempus potest, quam quod ab ea ipsa ratione nomen habet, imperfectum ? Compare Madv. 113. See also Schæf. *Demosth.* I. 337, *Plutarch* IV. 398, Poppo, *Thuc.* III. i. 646, Engelhardt, Plat. *Menex.* p. 282, Maetzner, *Antiph.* p. 220, Schoem. *Isæus* p. 178.
[4] This is the reading of good MSS., see Fritz. *De Crit. Conformat.* p. 31. [So Lachm. and Tregelles read, also Westcott and Hort.]
[5] Compare Held, Plut. *Timol.* p. 337, note.
[6] [Winer prefers to render πορθῶν by *vastare :* in favour of the simple rendering " was destroying," see Meyer, Ellicott, Alford *in loc.*]
[7] [Meyer explains this imperfect as used with reference to the time of sending the disciples forth.]

more graphic and animated than it would have been if the writer had used the aorist, which simply relates, condensing each action into a single point. Compare also A. xvi. 22, ἐκέλευον ῥαβδίζειν,[1] *they gave orders* (whilst I was present) etc.: see Matth. 497 a. Hence this case reduces itself to the first[2] (Jelf 401. 3).

In no passage is it necessary to take this tense as used for the pluperfect.[3] In A. iv. 13 the words ἐθαύμαζον ἐπεγίνωσκόν τε αὐτούς, ὅτι σὺν τῷ Ἰησοῦ ἦσαν· must be closely joined: *they wondered and* (excited by this very wonder to more careful observation) *recognised that they* etc. Kühnöl's explanation (after Raphel, *Annot.* II. 37) is incorrect.

In many passages the readings vary between aorist and imperfect— e.g. Mk. vi. 12, xiv. 70 (see Fritz. *in loc.*[4]), A. vii. 31, viii. 17 [? vii. 17],—as indeed in MSS. of classical authors the forms of these two tenses are frequently interchanged,[5] and the tenses sometimes differ but little in meaning.[6] It is often left to the writer's choice whether he shall regard the action as transient (momentary) or as lasting, as a point or as an extension in time: Kühner II. 74 [II. 144, ed. 2]. Thus compare Mt. xxvi. 59, ἐζήτουν ψευδομαρτυρίαν . . . . καὶ οὐχ εὗρον, with Mk. xiv. 55, καὶ οὐχ εὕρισκον; also Mt. xix. 13 with Mk. x. 13. Hence, especially in the case of the verbs *say, go, send*, the (later) Greeks not unfrequently use the imperfect where the aorist seems to be required:[7] compare Mk. ii. 27, iv. 10, v. 18, vii. 17, x. 17, L. iii. 7, vii. 36, viii. 9, 41, x. 2, A. iii. 3, ix. 21.

For examples of the combination of imperfects and aorists, each tense preserving its distinct meaning, see L. viii. 23, κατέβη λαῖλαψ . . . . καὶ συνεπληροῦντο καὶ ἐκινδύνευον· xv. 28, Mk. vii. 35, xi. 18, Ja. ii. 22, Mt. xxi. 8 sq., Jo. vii. 14, xii. 13, 17, xx. 3, A. xi. 6 sq., xxi. 3 (Jon. i. 5), Phil. 13, 14, 1 C. xi. 23 (in 1 C. xiii. 11 the aorist and perfect are similarly combined): compare Thuc. 7. 20, 44, Xen. *An.* 3. 4. 31, 5. 4. 24, Plutarch, *Agis* 19, Arrian, *Al.* 2. 20. 3.[8]

---

[1] Compare Jacobs, *Achill. Tat.* p. 620.
[2] Compare Herm. Soph. *Œd. C.* p. 76, and Soph. *Aj.* p. 139, Poppo, *Thuc.* I. i. 155, Ellendt, Arr. *Al.* I. 225, Schoem. Plut. *Agis* pp. 84, 142, Matth. 505, Bernh. p. 373. [Matthiæ and Bernhardy mention κελεύω as a verb whose imperfect is often used where we should expect an aorist. So also Krüger, p. 172.]
[3] On the other hand, see Poppo *l. c.*, Bornem. Xen. *An.* p. 5, Krüger, *Dion. H.* p. 304.
[4] [Fritzsche receives ἠρνήσατο (on slender authority), but explains ἠρνεῖτο, *negabat*,—quum ancilla argueret. Westcott, with greater probability, takes the word as implying "a repeated denial" (*St. John*, p. 266).]
[5] Compare Boisson. *Eunap.* p. 431, and on Philostr. *Her.* p. 530.
[6] Schæf. *Plutarch* IV. 346, Siebelis, *Pausan.* IV. 290.
[7] Poppo, *Thuc.* III. i. 570 sq., Held, Plut. *Tim.* p. 484 sq.
[8] Specially instructive is Diod. S. *Exc. Vat.* p. 25. 9 sqq., ὁ Κροῖσος μετεπέμπετο ἐκ τῆς Ἑλλάδος τοὺς ἐπὶ σοφίᾳ πρωτεύοντας . . . μετεπέμψατο δὲ καὶ Σόλωνα κ.τ.λ. Compare also Plat. *Parmen.* 126 c., ταῦτα εἰπόντες

The imperfect might seem to stand for the present[1] in Col. iii. 18, ὑποτάσσεσθε τοῖς ἀνδράσιν, ὡς ἀνῆκεν, ἐν κυρίῳ, ut par est, and E. v. 4 v. l. (μὴ ὀνομαζέσθω ἐν ὑμῖν) αἰσχρότης ἢ μωρολογία ἢ εὐτραπελία, ἃ οὐκ ἀνῆκεν (καθὼς πρέπει immediately preceding). In Col. iii., however, we must render *ut oportebat, ut par erat, as was fit* (in the past as well as now [2]), as indeed every such admonition really presupposes that up to this time the duty enjoined remained unperformed [3] (Krüg. p. 173). On this passage and on E. v. 4 see § 41. *a*. 2. In Mt. xxvii. 54 ἦν is used with reference to one now dead, *He was God's son*.

4. The perfect tense is used in full accordance with its meaning when the past is set in relation to the present, i.e., when something past is to be indicated as now (in the present) absolutely completed (*I have commanded*, my command is in regard to the present a command that was once given [4]): here the result of the action is usually, but not necessarily (Krüg. p. 174), conceived as *enduring*. The following examples are specially instructive: L. xiii. 2, δοκεῖτε, ὅτι οἱ Γαλιλαῖοι οὗτοι ἁμαρτωλοὶ παρὰ πάντας . . . . ἐγένοντο, ὅτι τοιαῦτα πεπόνθασιν, *that these Galileans became sinners, because they have suffered*, etc.,— not simply, *they suffered* once or at some past time (this would be the aorist), but—they stand recorded in history as men who were cut off by (a violent) death; L. iv. 6, ὅτι ἐμοὶ παραδέδοται (ἡ ἐξουσία), i.e., I am in possession of it, it having been delivered to me, *commissam habeo potestatem,*—the aorist would mean *it was delivered to me*, and it would remain uncertain

---

ἐβαδίζομεν καὶ κατελάβομεν τὸν Ἀντιφῶντα κ.τ.λ.; and from the LXX, Num. xxxiii. 38 sq., ἀνέβη Ἀαρὼν καὶ ἀπέθανεν . . . . Ἀαρὼν ἦν τριῶν καὶ εἴκοσι καὶ ἑκατὸν ἐτῶν, ὅτε ἀπέθνησκεν.—See Reisig, Soph. *Œd. C.* p. 254 sq., Stallb. Plat. *Phæd.* p. 29, Ellendt, Arr. *Al.* II. 67 sq.

[1] See however Mehlhorn, *Anacr*. p. 235 sq.; compare Fuhr, *Dicæarch*. p. 156 sq.

[2] See Matth. 505. Rem., Bornem. *Schol.* p. 181 (Don. p. 411, Jelf 398. 4).

[3] To take ἀνῆκεν (with Huther) as a perfect with present meaning is as unnecessary as it is grammatically inadmissible. Are καθήκειν and προσήκειν perfects also? Are we then to suppose that the rare perfect ἧκα maintained itself just in these particular formulas, even in Attic Greek? No example can be found in which we are compelled to give these words a present signification, provided we have attained the power of realising the Greek conception, and keeping that of our own language in the background.

[4] Herm. *Emend. Rat.* p. 186: γέγραφα tempus significat præteritum terminatum præsenti tempore ita, ut res, quæ perfecto exprimitur, nunc peracta dicatur, illudque jam, peractam rem esse, præsens sit. Poppo in his *Progr. Emendanda et supplenda ad Matthiæi Gramm. Gr.* (Frankf. on Oder, 1832), p. 6, thus defines the nature of the perfect: actionem plane præteritam, quæ aut nunc ipsum seu modo finita est aut per effectus suos durat, notat. [Don. p. 408, Jelf 399, Green, *Gr.* p. 138, Webster, *Synt.* p. 85.]

whether the possession of it was still retained or not; L. v. 32, οὐκ ἐλήλυθα καλέσαι δικαίους, *I am not here* (on earth) *in order to* etc. (Mt. ix. 13 simply narrates, οὐκ ἦλθον *I came not, I was not sent*), compare vii. 20, 50; Rom. vii. 2, ἡ ὕπανδρος γυνὴ τῷ ζῶντι ἀνδρὶ δέδεται νόμῳ, *is bound to* (and hence belongs to); G. ii. 7, πεπίστευμαι τὸ εὐαγγέλιον, *concreditum mihi habeo* etc. (his apostolic vocation still continues, he is now in the exercise of it), and similarly 1 Th. ii. 4, καθὼς δεδοκιμάσμεθα ὑπὸ τοῦ θεοῦ πιστευθῆναι τὸ εὐαγγέλιον; 1 C. xi. 15, ἡ κόμη ἀντὶ περιβολαίου δέδοται (γυναικί), *she has* (by a permanent arrangement of nature) *her hair instead of* etc.; H. x. 14, μιᾷ προςφορᾷ τετελείωκεν εἰς τὸ διηνεκὲς τοὺς ἁγιαζομένους (where the antithesis in μιᾷ . . . . τετελείωκεν must not be overlooked); Jo. xix. 22, ὃ γέγραφα, γέγραφα· Mk. x. 40, xi. 21, xvi. 4, L. xiii. 12, Jo. vii. 19, 22, viii. 33, xiii. 12,[1] xv. 24, xix. 30, xx. 21, A. viii. 14, Rom. iii. 21, v. 2, ix. 6, 1 C. ii. 11, iv. 4, vii. 14 sq., x. 13, 2 C. iii. 10, vi. 11, Col. ii. 14, iii. 3, H. i. 4, iii. 3, vii. 6, 14, viii. 6, 13, ix. 18, 26, xii. 2, 1 Jo. v. 9 sq., 3 Jo. 12, 1 P. iv. 1, Rev. iii. 17. Hence in citations from O. T. prophecies we find γέγραπται very frequently, also κεχρημάτισται (H. viii. 5), or εἴρηκε, H. i. 13, iv. 4, etc.[2]

The perfect and aorist are combined (compare Weber, *Dem.* p. 480) in L. iv. 18, ἔχρισέ με εὐαγγελίσασθαι, ἀπέσταλκέ με κηρῦξαι, *He anointed me . . . . and has sent me* (the former is regarded as an event which once occurred, the latter as continuing to operate); Mk. xv. 44, Πιλᾶτος ἐθαύμασεν εἰ ἤδη τέθνηκε· καὶ . . . . ἐπηρώτησεν αὐτόν, εἰ πάλαι ἀπέθανε (the latter referring to the occurrence of death, the act of dying, the former to the effect, the state of *being dead*); H. ii. 14, ἐπεὶ τὰ παιδία κεκοινώνηκε σαρκὸς καὶ αἵματος, καὶ αὐτὸς μετέσχε (at his incarnation) τῶν αὐτῶν· 1 C. xv. 4, ὅτι ἐτάφη (an event that once took place, long since past) καὶ ὅτι ἐγήγερται τῇ τρίτῃ ἡμέρᾳ (it continues in its effects in the new life of Jesus); 2 C.

---

[1] Γινώσκετε, τί πεποίηκα ὑμῖν; where the completed action (ἔνιψα) is represented as extending its influence into the present, in its symbolic meaning. Compare xv. 18.

[2] So also in 2 C. xii. 9, εἴρηκέ μοι· ἀρκεῖ σοι ἡ χάρις μου, this perfect is used of a communication (from the Lord) which is to be represented, not simply as then received, but as continuing in force: *He has told me*, and with this I must rest satisfied. What Rückert could find strange here I cannot see. Meyer now takes the right view.

i. 19, ix. 2, A. xxi. 28, Jo. viii. 40, iv. 38, xiii. 3 [*Rec.*], 1 Jo. i. 1.[1] Other characteristic examples are Col. i. 16, ὅτι ἐν αὐτῷ ἐκτίσθη τὰ πάντα (the fact of creation) .... τὰ πάντα δι' αὐτοῦ καὶ εἰς αὐτὸν ἔκτισται (dogmatic view of the completed and now existent creation), Jo. xvii. 14, xx. 23 (Meyer[2]), 1 C. xv. 27, Col. iii. 3. The perfect is used altogether for the narrative aorist in Rev. v. 7 ἦλθε καὶ εἴληφε (τὸ βιβλίον), where there is no variant, and in Rev. viii. 5. This purely aoristic sense of the perfect is found especially in later writers (particularly the Scholiasts, Poppo, *Thuc.* III. ii. 763), see Bernh. p. 379.[3] Less singular are 2 C. xi. 25, ... ἔλαβον, ἐρραβδίσθην .... ἐλιθάσθην .... ἐναυάγησα, νυχθήμερον ἐν τῷ βυθῷ πεποίηκα· H. xi. 28, πίστει πεποίηκε τὸ πάσχα καὶ τὴν πρόσχυσιν τοῦ αἵματος (preceded and followed by simple aorists); compare also ver. 17. In such enumerations of particular facts it was of no consequence whether the aorist or the perfect was used; both are equally suitable,—I was stoned, I suffered shipwreck, I have spent a day, etc. In Mk. iii. 26 no one will suppose that μεμέρισται after ἀνέστη is used as an aorist because the aorist μερισθῇ occurs in ver. 25.

The perfect is used

a. For the present, only in so far as the perfect denotes an action or a state the commencement and establishment of which belong, as completed events, to past time (Herm. *Vig.* p. 748, Jelf 399. 3): Jo. xx. 29, ὅτι ἑώρακάς με, πεπίστευκας, where

---

[1] Compare Lucian, *Dial. D.* 19. 1, ἀφώπλισας αὐτὸν καὶ νενίκηκας.
[2] ["Ἀφίενται, become remitted (by God); κεκράτηνται, are retained (by God): here the *perfect* is used, because the word indicates no *new act* on the part of God." Similarly Bengel: "illud præsens, hoc præteritum. Mundus *est* sub peccato." The true reading, however, is probably ἀφίενται.]
[3] Schæf. *Demosth.* I. 468, Wyttenbach, Plut. *Mor.* I. 321 sq. (Lips.), Lehrs, *Quæstion. Epic.* p. 274, Index to Petr. Patric. in the Bonn edition, p. 647. [A. Buttmann (pp. 196-7) remarks that the use of the present in historical narration was the foundation of this usage: he suggests that the influence of the Latin perfect may perhaps be traced here. The most plausible examples of the use of a perfect in the sense of the aorist (besides those given in the text) are Rev. vii. 14, 2 C. ii. 13, i. 9: A. Buttmann (who does not mention these) quotes 2 C. xi. 25, L. iv. 18, H. xi. 17, Ja. i. 24. As however it is admitted by all that the N. T. writers ordinarily use this tense with complete accuracy, the proper meaning cannot be given up in any passage without the clearest necessity; and we may doubt whether there is any passage (except *perhaps* those quoted from the Apocalypse) in which this necessity has been shown to exist. On the perfects in H. vii., xi., see Green, *Gr.* p. 142. The perfect γέγονα is frequently (but wrongly) assumed to have an aoristic meaning: see Alford on 1 C. xiii. 11, 1 Th. ii. 1, 1 Tim. ii. 14.]

the words point to the *commencement* of the (still existing) faith, iii. 18, xi. 27 ; v. 45, Μωϋσῆς, εἰς ὃν ἠλπίκατε, on whom you have hoped (placed your hope) and still hope, *in quo repositam habetis spem vestram:* similarly in 2 C. i. 10, εἰς ὃν ἠλπίκαμεν· 1 Tim. vi. 17, Jude 6. On ἑώρακα Jo. ix. 37, al., see below. 2 Tim. iv. 8, ἠγαπηκότες τὴν ἐπιφάνειαν αὐτοῦ, is strictly *who have fixed their love on,* and therefore now love. The pluperfect of such verbs naturally has the signification of an imperfect (L. xvi. 20). Jo. i. 34, κἀγὼ ἑώρακα καὶ μεμαρτύρηκα, certainly does not come in here : the latter perfect seems to represent the testimony borne by John to Christ at his baptism as a completed act of enduring validity, *I have seen it and have testified it.* The explanation of the perfects in H. vii. 6 (9) must be substantially the same; it is manifest that more is intended than the mere narration of the fact.

b. In reference to a *future* action, after sentences which express a supposition (εἰ or ἐάν with future or aorist, rarely a participle). Here, the condition being fulfilled, the action is conceived (to follow immediately and) to be entirely settled :[1] Eurip. *El.* 686, εἰ παλαισθεὶς πτῶμα θανάσιμον πεσεῖ, τέθνηκα ἐγώ· Soph. *Philoct.* 75, and Livy 21. 43, si eundem animum habueritis, *vicimus*[2] (Krüg. p. 175, Don. p. 409, Jelf 399. 4). In the N. T. see Rom. xiv. 23, ὁ διακρινόμενος, ἐὰν φάγῃ, κατακέκριται· *he is condemned,* the sentence of condemnation is pronounced (in the same moment) and remains pronounced over him, he lies under condemnation; iv. 14, 1 C. xiii. 1, 2 P. ii. 19, 20 ; and with a participle, Jo. iii. 18, ὁ μὴ πιστεύων ἤδη κέκριται· Rom. xiii. 8. But the perfect does not stand for the future in Jo. v. 24, μεταβέβηκεν ἐκ τοῦ θανάτου εἰς τὴν ζωήν; here there is no reference whatever to a future event, but to something that has already taken place (ἔχει ζωὴν αἰώνιον); compare 1 Jo. iii. 14, Lücke, *Comment.* II. 52. In Jo. xvii. 10, δεδόξασμαι, Christ speaks proleptically, in reference to the dis-

---

[1] We do not find in the N. T. any clear example of the Hebrew prophetic preterite (Gesen. *Lehrg.* p. 764), which the LXX usually render by a future. We have something analogous in Greek, when the soothsayers begin with the future but continue in the aorist, *Iliad* 4. 158 sqq., Pind. *Pyth.* 4. 56, *Isthm.* 5. 51 ; see Böckh, *Not. Crit.* p. 462.

[2] Comp. Poppo, *Thuc.* I. i. 156, Ast, Plat. *Polit.* p. 470, Herm. Aristoph. *Nub.* p. 175 sq., Matthiæ, Eurip. *Med.* p. 512, and *Gr.* 500.

ciples who already believed on him, compare xvi. 11 : in xiv. 7, however, καὶ ἀπ' ἄρτι γινώσκετε αὐτὸν καὶ ἑωράκατε αὐτόν must be rendered, *from this time ye know him and have seen him* (not, as Kühnöl, *eum mox accuratius cognoscetis et quasi oculis videbitis*); compare Demosth. *Lacrit.* 597 a, ἀνθρώπῳ, ὃν ἡμεῖς οὔτε γινώσκομεν οὔθ' ἑωράκαμεν πώποτε: see further Lücke *in loc.*

In Ja. v. 2, ὁ πλοῦτος ὑμῶν σέσηπε, καὶ τὰ ἱμάτια ὑμῶν σητόβρωτα γέγονεν, the perfect does not stand for a present or future, but the case indicated by the apostle in ταλαιπωρίαις ὑμῶν ταῖς ἐπερχομέναις is viewed as already present, and consequently the σήπειν of the riches as already completed In Jo. xvii. 22 δέδωκα is not *tribuam;* Christ looks on his life as closed, the disciples have already taken his place. In L. x. 19 δέδωκα and δίδωμι are equally appropriate: Tischendorf rightly decides for the former.

In proof that the perfect is also used for the pluperfect—which is not impossible—Haab (p. 95) wrongly adduces Jo. xii. 7, εἰς τὴν ἡμέραν τοῦ ἐνταφιασμοῦ τετήρηκεν αὐτό. Here τετήρ. must be taken as a real perfect (*she has reserved it*, and therefore uses it now); Jesus wishes figuratively to represent *this* anointing as that which prepares him for the tomb. But the reading is uncertain.

That the perfects (and aorists) of a number of verbs have in themselves and in accordance with established usage the signification of a present, is well known, and is a natural consequence of the (inchoative) primary meaning of these verbs.[1] Such are κέκτημαι *I possess*,[2] from κτάομαι *I acquire;* κεκοίμημαι (I have fallen asleep) *I sleep*, from κοιμάομαι *I fall asleep;* οἶδα *I know*, from εἴδω *I see;* ἕστηκα *I stand*, from ἵστημι *I place*, properly *I have placed myself*, —hence also 2 Th. ii. 2, ἐνέστηκεν ἡ ἡμέρα τοῦ Χρ. (compare Palairet *in loc.*), Rom. ix. 19 τίς ἀνθέστηκε, *who resists him?* compare xiii. 2, 2 Tim. iv. 6 ἐφέστηκε: also ἔοικα Ja. i. 6, 23. The pluperfect of such verbs naturally takes the place of an imperfect, as εἱστήκεισαν Mt. xii. 46, ᾔδειν Jo. ii. 9, xx. 9, al. Κέκραγα also (Jo. i. 15), from κράζω, has a present meaning[3] (Buttm. II. 57, Bernh. p. 279, Jelf *l. c.*), and ἑώρακα sometimes signifies *I* (have obtained a view of and) *see*, Jo. ix. 37, 1 Jo. iv. 20. In Ph. iii. 7, however, ἥγη-

---

[1] Fritz. *Rom.* I. 254, Bengel on Rom. iii. 23 (Don. p. 273 sq., Jelf 399).

[2] This meaning has been wrongly given to other tenses of this verb in some passages of the N. T. L. xviii. 12 is, *of all that I acquire*, quæ mihi redeunt : L. xxi. 19, *through endurance acquire for yourselves*, or *ye will acquire, your souls*,—they will then, and not till then, become your real, inalienable property. Schott is now right. On 1 Th. iv. 4 see De Wette, [or Ellicott and Alford]. Yet κτῶμαι seems to stand for *possideo* in Æsop. 142. 2. On κοιμῶνται 1 C. xi. 30, which is commonly taken for κεκοίμηνται, see above, 2 (c).

[3] [In classical writers, who very rarely use the present κράζω. In Jo. i. 15, *hath cried* seems the more probable meaning.]

μαι (Matth. 505) must be taken as a true preterite, in antithesis to ἡγοῦμαι, ver. 8.—Conversely, the present ἥκω denotes *I am come, I am here* (Matth. 504. 2), Jo. ii. 4, iv. 47, 1 Jo. v. 20. So also ἀκούω may sometimes be used in the sense of *audisse*, as in 1 C. xi. 18 (Xen. *An.* 5. 5. 8, *Mem.* 3. 5. 9, Plat. *Gorg.* 503 c, Philostr. *Apoll.* 2. 8, see Lucian, *Fug.* 7 [1]), but only when the hearing continues (in its efficacy),—as we also say *I hear* that you are sick; compare 2 Th. iii. 11 and Schoem. Plut. *Cleom.* p. 246 : [2] to express an act of hearing completed in past time, a Greek must say ἀκήκοα. In like manner ἀπέχω may be translated by *accepisse* in Mt. vi. 2, 5, 16, Ph. iv. 18; this word however is properly like the German *weghaben* (to have in full, to have already received [3]).

5. The aorist.[4]

a. In narration the aorist is used for the pluperfect [5]

α. In temporal subordinate sentences: A. v. 24, ὡς ἤκουσαν τοὺς λόγους .... διηπόρουν· L. vii. 1, ἐπειδὴ ἐπλήρωσεν τὰ ῥήματα .... εἰςῆλθεν· ii. 39, xxii. 66, Jo. vi. 16, ix. 18, xiii. 12, xxi. 9, A. xxi. 26 ; compare Thuc. 1. 102, οἱ Ἀθηναῖοι .... ἐπειδὴ ἀνεχώρησαν .... ξύμμαχοι ἐγένοντο· Æsch. *Ep.* 1. p. 121 c: Madv. 114 (Jelf 404).

β. In relative sentences: A. i. 2, ἐντειλάμενος τοῖς ἀποστόλοις οὓς ἐξελέξατο· ix. 35,[6] Jo. xi. 30, iv. 45, 46, L. xix. 15,[7] xxiv. 1 : Madv. 114 (Jelf *l. c.*). The aorists in a sentence with ὅτι, Jo. vi. 22, are probably to be taken in the same way : see the commentators. The explanation of this idiom is, that the Greeks—who in such cases scarcely ever use the pluperfect (Bernh. p. 380)—viewed the occurrence simply as a past event, not in its relation to another event also past. The same use of the aorist is found in independent sentences if they contain some supplementary notice (Mt. xiv. 3 sq.): whether Jo. xviii. 24 is an instance of this kind is not a question which grammar can decide. In Mt. xxvi. 48 ἔδωκεν is probably not to be taken as

---

[1] Ast, Plat. *Legg.* p. 9 sq., Franke, *Demosth.* p. 62.
[2] Exactly in the same way πυνθάνομαι *I learn*, Dem. *Callipp.* p. 719 c, al.
[3] Wyttenbach, Plut. *Mor.* II. 124, Palair. p. 25.
[4] E. A. Fritsch, *De Aoristi vi ac potest.* (Frankf. 1837), H. Schmidt, *Der griech. Aorist in s. Verhältnissen zu d. übrigen Zeitformen* (Halle, 1845). [For the N. T. see Green, *Gr.* p. 133, Webster, *Synt.* p. 89.]
[5] Poppo, *Thuc.* I. i. 157, Jacob, Luc. *Toxar.* p. 98, and Luc. *Alex.* p. 106, Kühner, *Gr.* II. 79 [II. 145, ed. 2].
[6] [That is, if the meaning is "who had turned to the Lord." Meyer and Alford take this clause as expressing the *consequence* of the miracle, "who turned etc." Lünemann adds Mt. ii. 9, xxvii. 55.]
[7] [Here διδώκει is now received by most editors.]

a pluperfect (as by Fritz.), see Baumg.-Crusius and Meyer *in loc.* In such sentences, however, the pluperfect is regularly used in the N. T., as in classical Greek: Jo. xi. 19, 57, viii. 20, A. ix. 21, Mk. xiv. 44, Mt. vii. 25.

Haab,[1] in a most uncritical manner, has referred to this head many other passages, in some of which the aorist has its own original meaning, whilst the rest are simply examples of differences between the accounts given by the evangelists, which accounts we have no right arbitrarily to force into harmony. Of the latter kind is Jo. xviii. 12, συνέλαβον τὸν Ἰησοῦν. According to the other evangelists (Mt. xxvi. 50 sq., Mk. xiv. 46), Jesus was seized and bound [2] before Peter struck with his sword; but John may intend so to represent the occurrence as if Peter struck in with the sword at the moment when the watch laid hands on Jesus. On Mt. xxvii. 37, καὶ ἐπέθηκαν ἐπάνω τῆς κεφαλῆς αὐτοῦ τὴν αἰτίαν αὐτοῦ γεγραμμένην, De Wette very well remarks: "As regards the *fact*, this must certainly be taken as a pluperfect (though we cannot deny the possibility that the present narrator, not being an eye-witness, may have believed that this inscription was not set up until this time), but as regards the words it is a simple preterite: *the narrator does not here take into account the order of time.* That his narration is not exact is clear even from the fact that, after saying that the soldiers sat down to watch Jesus, he then brings in (ver. 38) the crucifixion of the two thieves, τότε σταυροῦνται κ.τ.λ. Are we to take this also as a pluperfect?"[3]— In Mk. iii. 16, ἐπέθηκε τῷ Σίμωνι ὄνομα Πέτρον is not *imposuerat*, for the circumstance had not been previously mentioned by Mark, and we cannot take John's account (i. 43) and import it into Mark's narrative. In A. vii. 5 also ἔδωκεν does not stand for a pluperfect, as the antithesis itself shows, *He did not give . . . . but he promised:* equally needless is such a supposition in A. iv. 4, viii. 2, xx. 12.[4] On Mk. xvi. 1, as compared with L. xxiii. 56, see Fritz. *in loc.*[5]

There is no passage in which it can be certainly proved that the aorist stands for the perfect. L. i. 1, ἐπειδήπερ πολλοὶ ἐπεχείρησαν . . . . ἔδοξε κἀμοί· is simple narration, *since many undertook, I too thought* etc.: similarly in ii. 48, τέκνον, τί ἐποίησας . . . . ἐζητοῦμέν σε. More specious examples of this interchange would

---

[1] *Gr.* p. 95: compare also Pasor p. 235.
[2] [The act of *binding* is mentioned by St. John only.]
[3] [There is no difficulty whatever in supposing (with Meyer) that the thieves were crucified by *another band* of soldiers after Jesus had been nailed to the cross. On ver. 37 see Alford's note.]
[4] Mt. xxviii. 17, οἱ δὲ ἐδίστασαν, is wrongly brought in here by Markland (*Explicatt. vett. aliquot locorum,* in the Leipsic reprint of his edition of Eurip. *Suppl.,* p. 326): on this passage see Valcken. *Annot. Crit.* p. 350. [See above, § 17. 2.]
[5] [See Ellic. *Hist. L.* pp. 377-8, Ebrard, *Gospel Hist.* p. 445, Greswell, *Dissert.* III. 265 sq.]

perhaps be L. xiv. 18, ἀγρὸν ἠγόρασα· xiv. 19, ζεύγη βοῶν ἠγόρασα κ.τ.λ.· Ph. iii. 12, οὐχ ὅτι ἤδη ἔλαβον ἢ ἤδη τετελείωμαι· Jo. xvii. 4, ἐγώ σε ἐδόξασα ἐπὶ τῆς γῆς, τὸ ἔργον ἐτελείωσα κ.τ.λ. But in all these instances the action is merely represented as having occurred, as filling a point of past time, as simply and absolutely past (in L. xiv. in antithesis to a present act),—I *bought* a field, a yoke of oxen, etc. : in Ph. iii. the ἔλαβον seems merely to indicate reaching the goal as an illustrious fact, whilst τετελείωμαι denotes the consequence of this. So also in Rom. xiv. 9, Rev. ii. 8, the aorists simply narrate, and here it was not even possible to use the perfect in reference to the death of Christ. In Mk. xi. 17 the perfect now stands in the text, but the aorist would also have been in place : see Fritz. *in loc.* As to classical usage comp. Böckh, *Pind.* III. 185, Schæf. Eurip. *Phœn.* p. 15, Matth. 497. Rem. (Jelf 404). It is often left entirely to the writer's choice which of these two tenses he will use, since the distinction between them is in itself sometimes but small : compare Xen. *Mem.* 1. 6. 14, Dion. H. IV. 2320, Alciphr. 3. 46.[1] Here and there the MSS. of the N. T. (as also those of Greek authors, see for instance Jacobs, *Achill. Tat.* pp. 434, 566) vary between the aorist and the perfect :[2] e. g. in Jo. vi. 32, 1 C. ix. 15.[3]

b. It is only in appearance that the aorist stands for the future (Herm. *Vig.* p. 747, compare above, 4. *b*)[4] in Jo. xv. 6, ἐὰν μή τις μείνῃ ἐν ἐμοί, ἐβλήθη ἔξω ὡς τὸ κλῆμα : in such a case (supposing this to have occurred) *he was cast out*, not *he becomes cast out;* the "not-remaining" has this as its instanta-

---

[1] ["The relation of time expressed by the perfect is as it were compounded of the relations denoted by the present and the aorist, since the action has its commencement in the past but extends into the present, either in itself or in its effects. We must not suppose that the aorist in the cases we are considering is designed to express *both* these aspects of the perfect, but that the writer drops for the moment all connexion with the present, and takes the narrator's point of view. This point of view is more familiar to a writer than any other, and hence there results as a natural consequence, if not a distaste for the perfect tense, yet a preference for the aorist:" A. Buttm. p. 171 (197). Compare Clyde, *Synt.* p. 80.—See further Green p. 134, Ellicott on Col. i. 21 ; and on the necessity of rendering the aorist in some cases by the *English* perfect, see Ellicott on 1 Th. ii. 16 (*Trans.*).]

[2] [Especially between ἔδωκα and δίδωκα (A. Buttmann p. 199). Of this one variation there are nearly thirty examples in St. John's Gospel alone.]

[3] In Mt. xxi. 20, if we take πῶς as an exclamation *quam*, we should expect ἐξήρανται (as Mk. xi. 21, in good MSS.) instead of ἐξηράνθη : the latter passage however is not entirely parallel, and Mt. xxi. 20 should probably be rendered *how did the fig-tree suddenly wither?* They wish to have it explained how the withering, which (according to this Evangelist) took place before their eyes, had been brought about : hence they allude to the fact of ξηραίνεσθαι, not the result.

[4] In 1 C. xv. 49 the aor. ἐφορέσαμεν might seem to stand for the futurum exactum ; but Paul places himself at the παρουσία as his point of view, and speaks as a narrator of the past life on earth. [Meyer explains ἐβλήθη, Jo. xv. 6, in a similar way ; so Alford.]

neous consequence ; he who has severed himself from Christ is like a branch that has been broken off and thrown away : with this βληθῆναι are connected the presents συνάγουσιν, etc. On this passage compare Herm. *De Emend.* p. 192 sq., and *Vig. l. c.* Rev. x. 7, ὅταν μέλλῃ σαλπίζειν, καὶ ἐτελέσθη τὸ μυστήριον, in the mouth of the angel relating to the future, is, *Then is completed the mystery* (1 C. vii. 28). Compare Eur. *Med.* 78, ἀπωλόμεσθ' ἄρ', εἰ κακὸν προςοίσομεν νέον παλαιῷ· Plat. *Gorg.* 484 a. The aorist is never used in this manner where there is no antecedent sentence.—In Jo. xvii. 18, ἀπέστειλα is *I sent them:* this took place when the apostles were chosen. In Jo. xiii. 31, Jesus says νῦν ἐδοξάσθη ὁ υἱὸς τοῦ ἀνθρώπου, the traitor Judas having departed and having as it were already completed his deeds. Ἐξέστη in Mk. iii. 21 has a present sense, *insanit ;* compare ver. 22. Jude 14 is a literal quotation from the (Greek) Book of Enoch, and the aorist brings the coming of Christ before our view, as having already taken place. In Rom. viii. 30, ἐδόξασε is used because he in regard to whom God has accomplished the δικαιοῦν has already obtained from Him the δοξάζεσθαι also, though the reception of the δόξα as an actual possession belongs to the future.

1. In no passage of the N. T. does the aorist express an habitual act (Madv. 111 a,[1] Don. p. 412, Jelf 402). In L. i. 51 the μεγαλεῖα of God (ver. 49) are represented as deeds already performed, only the several parallel members must not be taken in too strictly historical a sense. Jo. viii. 29, οὐκ ἀφῆκέ με μόνον ὁ πατήρ, is, *the Father left me not alone* (on the earth) ; i. e., besides sending me (πέμψας) he also granted me (up to this time) his constant help. Equally unnecessary is it to take ἐδίδαξεν, 1 Jo. ii. 27, in this sense : Lücke explains it correctly in his 2nd edition. On Rom. viii. 30 see above. Heb. x. 5, 6, is a literal quotation from Ps. xl., referred back to the event of Christ's εἰςέρχεσθαι εἰς τὸν κόσμον. In H. i. 9 (from the LXX), ἠγάπησας δικαιοσύνην κ.τ.λ. assigns the motive for that which follows, διὰ τοῦτο ἔχρισέ σε ὁ θεός, and the former is as true an aorist as the latter. With more reason might Ja. i. 11, ἀνέτειλεν ὁ ἥλιος σὺν τῷ καύσωνι καὶ ἐξήρανε τὸν χόρτον κ.τ.λ, be considered an example of this use of the aorist (compare 1 P. i. 24), as it was taken by Piscator : these aorists however simply narrate (as describing an actual event), and all taken together they mark the rapid succession of the events, *the sun rose, and*

---

[1] Schæf. *Demosth.* I. 247, Wex, *Antig.* I. 326.

(immediately) *withered*, etc.,[1]—scarcely had the sun risen when the flower withered.—Such passages as E. v. 29 exhibit the transition to this use of the aorist [to express an habitual act], which easily follows from the primary meaning of the tense (Herm. *De Emend. Rat.* p. 187).[2]—In Ja. i. 24, κατενόησεν ἑαυτὸν καὶ ἀπελήλυθε καὶ εὐθέως ἐπελάθετο ὁποῖος ἦν, neither aorist nor perfect is used for the present, but the case mentioned in ver. 23 by way of example is taken as actual fact, and the apostle falls into the tone of narration.

2. In 1 C. ix. 20, ἐγενόμην τοῖς Ἰουδαίοις ὡς Ἰουδαῖος, Pott quite needlessly takes the aor. for a *present:* the apostle is relating how he has acted hitherto. The same mistake is made by Heumann in 1 C. iv. 18, and by several commentators in Ja. ii. 6 ἠτιμάσατε (which even Gebser renders by a present). The aor. ἐδοξάσθη, Jo. xv. 8, is now explained by Tholuck more correctly than before : it is the proleptic aorist, as in E. ii. 6, Rom. viii. 30.—In Mt. iii. 17 (xii. 18, xvii. 5, 2 P. i. 17), from the LXX, the aor. εὐδόκησα may be explained very simply, My delight fell on him, he became the object of my love; see Meyer.—Hermann, *Vig.* p. 746 (no. 209), treats merely of poetic usage : his observations have been more closely defined by Moller in an acute essay in the *Zeitschrift f. Alterth.-Wiss.* 1846, no. 134–136.

The aorist ἔγραψα is used in letters instead of the present γράφω, in reference to the very letter which is now being written, exactly as *scripsi* in Latin. In the same way a writer uses ἔπεμψα *misi*, looking at the fact that for the receiver of the letter the πέμπω has changed itself into an ἔπεμψα. For examples of the latter in the N. T., see A. xxiii. 30, Ph. ii. 28 (ἔπεμψα), Phil. 11 (ἀνέπεμψα), and probably also συνεπέμψαμεν 2 C. viii. 18 (Demosth. *Ep.* 3, Alciphr. 3. 30, 41) : similarly ἠβουλήθην 2 Jo. 12. For ἔγραψα, however, we cannot even quote 1 C. v. 11 : this aorist refers in every case either to an earlier letter (1 C. v. 9, 2 C. ii. 3, 4, 9, vii. 12, 3 Jo. 9), or to a whole epistle now concluded (Rom. xv. 15, Phil. 19, G. vi. 11, 1 P. v. 12), or to a group of verses just completed (1 C. ix. 15, 1 Jo. ii. 21, 26,

---

[1] Bornem. Xen. *Apol.* p. 53.
[2] [Compare the following observations from A. Buttm. p. 175 (202). "Winer's assertion that in the N. T. the aor. never expresses what is habitual, is so far true that the word 'habitual' but imperfectly indicates the peculiar character of this aorist ; but it cannot be denied that the *gnomic* aorist occurs in the N. T. The objection that the use of this idiom would imply too nice an observance of the laws of classical Greek, and greater acquaintance with it than can be assumed in the case of the N. T. writers, may be decisive in regard to some of these, but not all. Rather is the use of the aorist, as the most usual historical tense, perfectly in harmony with the character of the *popular* mode of expression, which so readily breaks loose from the form of abstract representation, and involuntarily falls into the tone of narration." He quotes Ja. i. 11, 24, 1 P. i. 24, as the clearest instances.—Krüger also and Curtius (p. 278, Transl.) prefer the name *gnomic* aorist : Jelf, *iterative* aorist.]

v. 13).¹ The present γράφω is commonly used when reference is made to a letter now being written, see 1 Jo. ii. 12, 13, 1 C. iv. 14, xiv. 37, 2 C. xiii. 10, al.: on 1 Jo. ii. 13 sq. see Lücke.² The Greeks themselves did not strictly observe this use of the aorist (or perfect) for the present; compare Diog. L. 7. 9.³

3. Lastly, the aorist is not used *de conatu*⁴ (Kühnöl) in Mk. ix. 17, ἤνεγκα τὸν υἱόν μου; the words mean, *I brought my son* to thee (and here place him before thee). That there is no need to take ἐξῆλθε, Jo. xi. 44, in this sense, is perceived by Kühnöl himself; and Tholuck acts rightly in not even mentioning this interpretation. On Mt. xxv. 1 see Meyer.

6. The future tense⁵ does not always indicate pure actual futurity, but sometimes possibility (as indeed the future and the possible are closely allied), and expresses what *can* or *should* or *must* take place (ethical possibility); see Herm. *Vig.* p. 747, Jacob, Luc. *Tox.* p. 134, Krüg. p. 179 (Don. p. 407, Jelf 406). This is particularly the case in questions. (Some passages, it is true, are not to be fully depended upon, through the great similarity between the forms of the future and the aorist conjunctive, and the variation in the readings of the MSS.) L. xxii. 49, κύριε, εἰ πατάξομεν ἐν μαχαίρᾳ, *are we to strike* etc. ?—properly, *shall we* (with thy permission) *strike*, wilt thou permit us to strike ? Compare Eur. *Ion* 771, εἴπωμεν ἢ σιγῶμεν; ἢ τί δράσομεν; Rom. x. 14, πῶς οὖν ἐπικαλέσονται,⁶ εἰς ὃν οὐκ ἐπίστευσαν; *how can they call* etc. ? Rom. iii. 6, ἐπεὶ πῶς κρινεῖ ὁ θεὸς τὸν κόσμον; Jo. vi. 68, Mt. xii. 26, 1 Tim. iii. 5, 1 C. xiv. 16 (Plat. *Lys.* 213 c, τί οὖν δὴ χρησόμεθα; Lucian, *Tox.*

---

¹ [Bp. Ellicott maintains the same view, in his notes on G. vi. 11, Phil. 19. On the other side see Bp. Lightfoot's note on the former passage, where ἔγραψα is held to mark "the point at which St. Paul takes the pen into his own hand."]

² ["Lücke, after Rickli, with much ingenuity tries to fix ἔγραψα on the preceding portion of the epistle, keeping γράφω for the following . . . Lücke subsequently gave up this view: see note in Bertheau's edition of Lücke p. 265." Alford *in loc.* By De Wette and others γράφω is understood to refer rather to the whole epistle, and ἔγραψα to what has preceded this point: Beza and Düsterd. refer both γράφω and ἔγραψα to the whole epistle. The latter view is taken by Alford and Haupt; also by A. Buttmann (p. 198).]

³ See Wyttenbach, Plut. *Moral.* I. 231 sq. (Lips.).

⁴ Schæfer (*Plutarch* IV. 398) declares himself against Herm. Soph. *Aj.* 1105: compare however Herm. *Iphig. Taur.* p. 109. (Jelf 403. *Obs.* 3.)

⁵ The 3 future passive κεκράξομαι, which occurs once (L. xix. 40) in not a few MSS., stands for the 1 fut., which in this verb is not in use, and has not the meaning which elsewhere belongs to this form, on which see Matth. 498, Madv. 115 b, Janson, *De Græci serm. paulo post futuro* (Rastenburg, 1844).

⁶ [More probably ἐπικαλέσωνται.]

47, πῶς οὖν .... χρησόμεθα τοῖς παροῦσι ;). In Mt. vii. 24, however, ὁμοιώσω retains the simple signification of the future, as also does τολμήσω in Rom. xv. 18. In Rom. v. 7 something is spoken of which *will* hardly occur at any time : 1 C. viii. 8 is similar.—In Rom. vi. 1, 15, the conjunctive is the better reading, and also in L. iii. 10, Jo. vi. 5 : in Rom. vi. 2, however, ζήσομεν has most support, and the future here forms a good antithesis to the aorist ἀπεθάνομεν. In Mk. iv. 13 and 1 C. xiv. 7 we have true futures. In Mt. vii. 16 ἐπιγνώσεσθε does not contain an injunction (ye *shall*, ye *must*), but simply points to that which the future will itself bring: by their fruits (by observing these, in the course of your observation) ye *will* know them. In Rom. vi. 14 the future expresses an assurance, and is essentially connected with the apostle's reasoning. 1 C. xv. 29, ἐπεὶ τί ποιήσουσιν οἱ βαπτιζόμενοι ὑπὲρ τῶν νεκρῶν is probably to be rendered, *else* (if Christ has not risen) *what will they do* (have recourse to) *who have themselves baptised over the dead* (and consequently are in this case deceived) ? The present ποιοῦσιν is a correction. Τί οὖν ἐροῦμεν, wherever it occurs, is *quid dicemus*, not *quid dicamus?* 1 C. xiv. 15, προςεύξομαι τῷ πνεύματι, προςεύξομαι δὲ καὶ τῷ νοΐ, is not the expression of a resolve (προςεύξωμαι is probably only a correction), but a Christian maxim which the believer intends to follow ; and the future has a more decided tone than the conjunctive. In 2 C. iii. 8 ἔσται refers to the future δόξα. (As to such phrases as θέλεις ἑτοιμάσομεν, and τί αἱρήσομαι οὐ γνωρίζω, where the conjunctive might have been used, see § 41. *a*, and *b*. 4.)

The future is used of a case that is merely *conceivable* in the formula ἐρεῖ τις, *dicat* aliquis, 1 C. xv. 35, Ja. ii. 18. Here however the Greek speaks more positively than the Roman: *some one will say,*—I foresee this, it is just what I expect. So also ἐρεῖς οὖν *dices igitur*, Rom. ix. 19, xi. 19. The future meaning must certainly be retained in H. xi. 32, ἐπιλείψει με διηγούμενον ὁ χρόνος, *time* (I foresee) *will fail me, deficiet me tempus*: compare Philostr. *Her.* p. 686, ἐπιλείψει με ἡ φωνή· also " longum *est* narrare," for the Germanised-Latin, " longum *esset* narrare."[1] In L. xi. 5 also, τίς ἐξ ὑμῶν ἕξει φίλον καὶ

---

[1] It is a different case when the thought is expressed by the optative with ἄν, as in Dion. H. 10. 2086, ἐπιλείποι ἄν με ὁ τῆς ἡμέρας χρόνος.

πορεύσεται πρὸς αὐτὸν μεσονυκτίου, the future is quite in place: take away the interrogation and we have the ordinary future, "No one of you will go to his friend at midnight,"—such an instance of importunity will never occur. Lastly, in Mt. v. 39, 41, xxiii. 12, the notion of possibility attaches itself rather to ὅςτις than to the future: in Ja. ii. 10 the better MSS. have the conjunctive.—To take the future as expressing simply a *wish* in Rom. xvi. 20, Ph. iii. 15, iv. 7, 9, 19, Mt. xvi. 22, would be a great blunder.

On the use of the future for the imperative see § 43. 5.

Some have most perversely taken the future as used for the preterite in Rev. iv. 9, ὅταν δώσουσι τὰ ζῶα δόξαν . . . . τῷ καθημένῳ ἐπὶ τοῦ θρόνου . . . . πεσοῦνται οἱ εἴκοσι τέσσαρες πρεσβύτεροι κ.τ.λ.: the true rendering is, *When* (as often as) *the beasts shall give glory* . . . . *shall fall down.*—On the other hand, the future does sometimes border on the present tense in general maxims, as G. ii. 16, ἐξ ἔργων νόμου οὐ δικαιωθήσεται πᾶσα σάρξ (Rom. iii. 20): this however is the expression of a law which (from the time when Christianity first appeared) *will continue in force* in the world. We have substantially the same case in Rom. iii. 30, ἐπείπερ εἷς ὁ θεός, ὃς δικαιώσει περιτομὴν ἐκ πίστεως κ.τ.λ., where δικαιοῦν is viewed as an act of God which will continue to be thus performed throughout the Christian dispensation. In L. i. 37 we find the future ἀδυνατήσει, in an O. T. reminiscence, of that which belongs to no particular time, but will always be true (Theocr. 27. 9, see Herm. *Emend. Rat.* p. 197); compare Rom. vii. 3. But in Mt. iv. 4 ζήσεται rather denotes (after Dt. viii. 3) a rule established by God, *shall live.*

Rem. 1. The combination of different tenses by means of καί,[1] of which occasional examples have already been given, arises in some cases from the fact that, when not writing with rigorous precision, we may at times really use different tenses without any difference of sense: in other cases, as H. ii. 14, 1 C. x. 4, xv. 4, Ja. i. 24, Jo. iii. 16, Ph. iii. 7 sq., 1 P. iv. 6, al., it is the result of design. In the Apocalypse we probably have examples of the former kind, as iii. 3, xi. 10, xii. 4, xvi. 21, al. In none of these passages are the tenses incorrect, and those who looked on such a combination of tenses as something altogether extraordinary[2] only displayed their own imperfect knowledge of Greek: see my *Exeget. Studien*, I. 147 sq.

Rem. 2. The above statement of the significations of the different tenses mainly applies to the indicative mood (and the parti-

---

[1] Poppo, *Thuc.* I. i. 274 sq., Reisig, *Œd. Col.* 419, Jacobs, *Achill. Tat.* p. 700, Stallb. Plat. *Euthyphr.* p. 59 a.

[2] As for instance Eichhorn, *Einl. ins N. T.* II. 378.

ciple) alone: see Herm. *Emend.* p. 189. In the other moods, especially the conjunctive, optative, and imperative, the aorist is but seldom used in reference to past time (1 P. iv. 6 ?[1]); for the most part it retains, as contrasted with the present tense, no more of its own meaning than the reference to the rapid passing of the action or its completion at once (Herm. *Vig.* p. 748)—compare present and aorist in Jo. iii. 16—without relation to any particular time: Rost p. 594, Madv. 111 (Don. p. 413 sqq., Jelf 405).

SECTION XLI.

THE INDICATIVE, CONJUNCTIVE, AND OPTATIVE MOODS.[2]

1. The distinction between these moods is thus defined by Hermann. The indicative denotes the *actual*, the conjunctive and optative that which is merely *possible;* the conjunctive being used for that which is *objectively* possible (the realisation of which depends on circumstances),[3] the optative for what is *subjectively* possible (that which is simply conceived in the mind,—a wish is of this nature).[4] See Herm. *Emend. Rat.* I. 205 sqq., *Vig.* p. 901 sq., and more at large in *De Particula ἄν* p. 76 sq.;[5] compare also Schneider, *Vorles.* I. 230 sqq.[6] With Klotz (*ad Devarium*), we have throughout followed this

---

[1] [So De Wette renders, *may have been judged:* similarly Huther. Compare Aristoph. *Ran.* 1405 ἵν' ἔλέης (Buttm. *Gr. Gr.* p. 409).]
[2] Compare K. H. A. Lipsius, *Comm. de modorum usu in N. T.:* P. I. (Lips. 1827).
[3] "In conjunctivo sumitur res experientia comprobanda . . . . ; conjunctivus est debere quid fieri intelligentis ac propterea expectantis quid eveniat:" Herm. *Partic.* ἄν p. 77.
[4] Klotz, *Devar.* II. 104: Optativus modus per se non tam optationis vim in se continet, quam cogitationis omnino, unde proficiscitur etiam omnis optatio. Herm. *Partic.* ἄν p. 77: Optativus est cogitantis quid fieri, neque an fiat neque an possit fieri quærentis.
[5] p. 77: Apertum est, in indicativo veritatem facti ut exploratam respici, in conjunctivo rem sumi experientia comprobandam, in optativo veritas rationem haberi nullum, sed cogitationem tantummodo indicari. How Kühner has combined this distinction between the conj. and the optat. with a *temporal* meaning originally possessed by these moods (*Griech. Gr.* II. 87 sq.), cannot be further explained here. [See Kühner II. 179 sqq. (ed. 2); also Don. p. 546 sq., *New Crat.* p. 621 sqq.]
[6] Different views from the above are maintained by W. Scheuerlein, (Progr.) *Ueber den Charakter des Modus in der gr. Sprache* (Halle 1842); W. Bäumlein, *Ueber die gr. Modi und die Partikeln κιν und ἄν* (Heilbronn 1846),—see Jahn, *Jahrb.* vol. 47, p. 353 sq., and *Zeitschr. f. Alterthumswiss.* 1848, pp. 104–106, 1849, pp. 30–33; Aken, *Grundzüge der Lehre von Tempus u. Modus im Griech.* (Güstrow 1850). Compare also Döderlein, *Ueber Modi u. Conjunctionen,* in his *Reden u. Aufsätze* (Erlangen 1843, no. 9). [Lünemann adds another work by Aken, *Die Grundzüge der Lehre vom Tempus und Modus im Griech. hist. und vergleichend aufgestellt.* (Rost. 1861.)]

theory, as it does not appear that anything *decidedly* better has yet been proposed,—least of all by Madvig. The N. T. use of these moods is in the main points perfectly regular,[1] except that we observe the optative (as in the later Greek writers who did not strive after ancient refinement) already retreating more into the background (even more than in Josephus[2]), and replaced in some constructions by the conjunctive.[3]

a. IN INDEPENDENT SENTENCES.

2. The use of the indicative in independent sentences is very simple in Greek, and in reference to N. T. usage we have only two points to notice:—

a. The imperfect indicative is sometimes found (as in Latin[4]) where in German the conjunctive would be used: 2 C. xii. 11, ἐγὼ ὤφειλον ὑφ' ὑμῶν συνίστασθαι, *debebam commendari, I ought to have been recommended*; Mt. xxv. 27, ἔδει σε βαλεῖν, *thou oughtest to have* etc. (2 C. ii. 3, A. xxiv. 19, xxvii. 21); Mt. xxvi. 9, ἠδύνατο τοῦτο πραθῆναι κ.τ.λ.; xxvi. 24, καλὸν ἦν αὐτῷ εἰ οὐκ ἐγεννήθη, *it would be* (would have been) *good for him*, *satius erat*; 2 P. ii. 21, κρεῖττον ἦν αὐτοῖς μὴ ἐπεγνωκέναι τὴν ὁδὸν τῆς δικαιοσύνης (Aristoph. *Nub.* 1215, Xen. *An.* 7. 7. 40, Philostr. *Apoll.* 7. 30, Lucian, *Dial. Mort.* 27. 9, Diog. L. 1. 64); A. xxii. 22, οὐ γὰρ καθῆκεν αὐτὸν ζῆν, *he ought not to have lived*, i.e. he ought to have been put to death long ago, *non debebat* or *debuerat vivere*.[5] Here the Greeks and Romans simply indicate that, apart from any condition, something *was good*, that *it was necessary* that something should happen (or not happen); and the reader, by comparing this assertion with the actual fact, may infer the disapproval of the latter. In German we set out from the present state of things, and by using

---

[1] This against Hwiid, whom Kühnöl (*ad Acta* p. 777) quotes with approval.
[2] [Compare Green, *Gr.* p. 153: "In Josephus the use of the optative mood is affected and over-acted."]
[3] In modern Greek, as is well known, the optative has entirely disappeared; and it is still a question how far the use of this mood extended in the ancient popular language. We not unfrequently find that forms and expressions on which certain niceties of a written language are based, are persistently avoided by the common people.
[4] Zumpt § 519 sq. [Madvig § 348 e].
[5] Compare Matth. 505. 2. Rem., Stallb. Plat. *Symp.* p. 74. [Don. pp. 411, 541, Jelf 398. 3, 858. 3, Jebb, Soph. *Ajax* p. 183.]

the conjunctive express our disapproval of this in its origin. Hence both moods are correctly conceived. We must not suppose that in the examples quoted above there is an ellipsis of ἄν; for, in the mind of the Greek, all such sentences shut out any thought of a condition under which " something would have been good," " must have taken place." [1] A somewhat different explanation must be given of ἐβουλόμην etc. (without ἄν) in the sense of *vellem*, as in A. xxv. 22, ἐβουλόμην καὶ αὐτὸς τοῦ ἀνθρώπου ἀκοῦσαι, *I should wish* (being made curious by your statement) *also to hear the man*; Aristoph. *Ran.* 866, Æschin. *Ctesiph.* 274 b, Arrian, *Epict.* 1. 19. 18, Lucian, *Dial. Mort.* 20. 4, *Abdic.* 1, *Char.* 6, al. Here the speaker does not refer merely to a wish that was previously excited—at the same time with some other action (*volebam*), but to a wish now felt: the wish however is not expressed directly (*volo*), because this is admissible only when the accomplishment is viewed as dependent entirely on the will (1 Tim. ii. 8, 1 C. xvi. 7, Rom. xvi. 19, al.),— or by ἐβουλόμην ἄν, because this involves the antithesis *but I do not wish* (Herm. *Partic.* ἄν p. 66 sq.),—or by the far weaker βουλοίμην ἄν (Xen. *Œc.* 6. 12, Krüg. p. 186) *velim*, I might wish;—but definitely, *I wished*, i.e. if the thing were possible, if you would permit it (and therefore *I do wish it*, on this supposition): see Bernh. p. 374, Kühner II. 68.[2] In such expressions therefore a conditional clause is implied.[3] So also in Rom. ix. 3, ηὐχόμην γὰρ αὐτὸς ἐγὼ ἀνάθεμα εἶναι ἀπὸ τοῦ Χριστοῦ ὑπὲρ τῶν ἀδελφῶν μου (*optarem ego* etc.), and in G. iv. 20, where see my note.[4] The case is different in 2 C. i. 15, Phil. 13, 14, where the aorists simply narrate, and also in 2 Jo. 12, ἠβουλήθην.

In Jo. iv. 4, al., ἔδει is a real imperfect indicative, denoting an

---

[1] See Herm. *Partic.* ἄν § 12.
[2] [Both these grammarians point out the appropriate use of the *imperfect* tense in these expressions, to denote "an action which is not completed (*sine effectu*), though under certain conditions it would be completed" (Kühner *l. c.*). See also Ellic. on G. iv. 20, Alford on Rom. ix. 3.]
[3] Schoemann's explanation is different (*Isœus* p. 435): "Addita particula ἄν voluntatem significamus a conditione suspensam, *vellem, si liceret*; omissa autem particula etiam conditionis notio nulla subintelligitur, sed hoc potius indicatur, vere nos illud voluisse, etiamsi omittenda fuerit voluntas, scilicet quod frustra nos velle cognovimus." This subtle distinction, however, would hardly apply in all passages.
[4] ["*Vellem autem adesse*, quod nunc quidem fieri non potest:" Winer *l. c.*]

actual fact. On the other hand, in H. ix. 26, ἐπεὶ ἔ δ ε ι αὐτὸν πολλάκις παθεῖν, we should have expected ἄν, as the writer is speaking of something which *on a certain supposition* would necessarily have taken place : the MSS. however do not supply the particle, and it was as allowable to omit it as it is for us to say, *for* (otherwise,—if this were the design) *it was necessary*[1] that he should often suffer; compare Herm. Eur. *Bacch.* p. 152, Bernh. p. 390, and see § 42. 2. It has also been usual in Rom. xi. 6, 1 C. vii. 14, v. 10, to render the indicative present after ἐπεί (*otherwise, alioquin*) by the conjunctive. The first two passages however simply mean, *for* (in the case supposed, if ἐξ ἔργων) *grace is no longer grace,* —*for* (supposing that the husband is not sanctified in the wife) *your children are unclean.* In 1 C. v. 10 almost all the better MSS. read ὠφείλετε.[2]

In 1 C. vii. 7, θ έ λ ω πάντας ἀνθρώπους εἶναι ὡς καὶ ἐμαυτόν, we must not (with Pott) take θέλω for θέλοιμι or ἤθελον. Paul actually has this wish, fixing his eye merely on the advantage which would thus accrue to men (Christians), not on the obstacles: had he referred to these, he must have said *I could wish, velim* or *vellem.* The passage was correctly explained by Baumgarten. The same remark applies to 1 C. vii. 28, where Pott takes φείδομαι for φειδοίμην ἄν. 2 C. xii. 9, ἀρκεῖ σοι ἡ χάρις μου, inaccurately rendered by Luther *be content with my grace,* is correctly explained by all recent commentators. In 1 C. v. 7, καθώς ἐστε ἄζυμοι, some have given a different point to this mood, rendering ἐστε by *esse debetis ;* this is erroneous, see Meyer.

3. *b.* The present indicative is sometimes found in direct questions, where in Latin the conjunctive would be used, in German the auxiliary *sollen :*[3] e. g., Jo. xi. 47, τί ποιοῦμεν ; ὅτι οὗτος ὁ ἄνθρωπος πολλὰ σημεῖα ποιεῖ, *quid faciamus ? what must we do ?* (Lucian, *Pisc.* 10, *Asin.* 25). In strictness, however, the indicative here intimates that there is no doubt that something must (at once) be done, as we also say, *what do we ?* a stronger and more decided expression than *what shall we do ?* Τί ποιῶμεν is said by one who invites deliberation (compare A. iv. 16 [4]); he who says τί ποιοῦμεν presupposes on the part of those concerned, not merely a general resolution to do something, but a resolution to do some particular thing, and wishes only to lead to the actual declaration what this is.[5] On this

---

[1] [That is, to say *it was necessary,* for *it would have been.* Winer's words are *musste er öfters leiden.*]
[2] See also Ast, Plat. *Legg.* p. 162 sq., Stallb. Plat. *Euthyphr.* p. 57.
[3] [Corresponding to our *must, should, ought.*]
[4] [Where ποιήσωμεν is well supported.]
[5] [A. Buttmann (p. 208 sq.) maintains that this explanation is artificial, and considers ποιοῦμεν here to be an example of present used for future (§ 40. 2, 6).]

SECT. XLI.] THE INDICATIVE, CONJUNCTIVE, OPTATIVE MOODS. 355

(rhetorical) use of the present indicative, which occurs mainly in colloquial language, see Heind. Plat. *Gorg.* p. 109, and *Theæt.* p. 449, Stallb. Plat. *Rep.* I. 141, Bernh. p. 396 (Jelf 397. *a*). The Greeks go farther still, even saying πίνομεν *we drink*, i. e. *we will drink*, when they are about immediately to proceed to drink, when they are already raising the cup.¹ We can however scarcely regard G. vi. 10, ἐργαζόμεθα τὸ ἀγαθόν (the reading of some good MSS., especially A and B, received by Lachmann ²), as an example of this kind: see Meyer *in loc.* As to Jo. xxi. 3 compare § 40. 2.

1 C. x. 22 ἢ παραζηλοῦμεν τὸν κύριον; (still rendered as a conjunctive by Schott) probably means, *or are we provoking God?* is this the meaning of our conduct, that we are stirring up the wrath of God? Παραζηλοῦμεν does not express what is yet to take place (as is maintained by Rückert, al.), but what is actually taking place already. Rom. viii. 24 ὃ βλέπει τις, τί καὶ ἐλπίζει; is not *quare insuper speret?* (Schott)—for if we remove the interrogation the sentence will not be, *this he may not still hope for*, but *this he does not still hope for*. On the future indicative for the conjunctive see § 40. 6.

The indicatives in Ja. v. 13, κακοπαθεῖ τις ἐν ὑμῖν, ... ἀσθενεῖ τις ἐν ὑμῖν, of a case which is regarded as *actually present*, offer no difficulty,—*some one is afflicted among you, some one is weak among you*, etc.: compare Demosth. *Cor.* 351 c, where it is not necessary to place a note of interrogation (as Krüger does, p. 184). Even the preterite is thus used by Greek writers, see Matth. 510. (Jelf 860. 8 sq.) [See § 60. 4.]

4. The conjunctive is found in independent sentences

a. To express a challenge or invitation, or a resolve, *conjunctivus adhortativus* (Matth. 516. 1, Jelf 416, Don. p. 548): Jo. xiv. 31, ἐγείρεσθε, ἄγωμεν ἐντεῦθεν· xix. 24, 1 C. xv. 32, φάγωμεν καὶ πίωμεν, αὔριον γὰρ ἀποθνήσκομεν Phil. iii. 15, ὅσοι οὖν τέλειοι, τοῦτο φρονῶμεν· 1 Th. v. 6, γρηγορῶμεν καὶ νήφωμεν· L. viii. 22. Occasionally the MSS. are divided between the conjunctive and the future, e. g. in H. vi. 3, 1 C. xiv.

---

¹ Jacobs, *Achill. Tat.* p. 559.
² [This reading was adopted by Lachmann in his *smaller* edition: in the larger he substituted the subjunctive, which is now generally received. B, quoted above for the indic., has the subj. *prima manu*. On the meaning which ἐργαζόμεθα would probably have in this passage, see Meyer *in loc.* ("*we do good*, this is our maxim"); also Winer *in loc.*, who takes it as an exhortation. A. Buttmann (p. 210) agrees with Meyer; but favours Rückert's explanation of παραζηλοῦμεν, quoted below.]

356   THE INDICATIVE, CONJUNCTIVE, OPTATIVE MOODS.   [PART III.

15, Ja. iv. 13 : in the first two passages, however, the conjunctive is best attested.¹

   b. In questions of doubt or uncertainty, *conjunctivus deliberativus* (Matth. 516. 2, Bernh. p. 396, Kühner II. 102 sq., Jelf 417, Don. *l. c.*): Mk. xii. 14, δῶμεν ἢ μὴ δῶμεν; *should we give or not give ?* Rom. vi. 1, ἐπιμένωμεν τῇ ἁμαρτίᾳ ; 1 C. xi. 22. So also in the 2nd and 3rd persons : L. xxiii. 31, εἰ ἐν τῷ ὑγρῷ ξύλῳ ταῦτα ποιοῦσιν, ἐν τῷ ξηρῷ τί γένηται ; Mt. xxvi. 54, πῶς πληρωθῶσιν αἱ γραφαί ; *how are the Scriptures to be fulfilled ?* xxiii. 33, πῶς φύγητε (Jo. v. 47 *v. l.*). Under this head comes also the conjunctive as used in such formulas as L. ix. 54, θέλεις εἴπωμεν πῦρ καταβῆναι ἀπὸ τοῦ οὐρανοῦ ; ² *is it thy will, should we say ?*   Mt. xiii. 28, xxvi. 17, Mk. xiv. 12, L. xxii. 9. Compare Eurip. *Phœn.* 722, βούλει τράπωμαι δῆθ᾽ ὁδοὺς ἄλλας τινάς ; Xen. *Mem.* 2. 1. 1, βούλει σκοπῶμεν ; Æsch. *Ctesiph.* 297 c, Lucian, *Dial. M.* 20. 3.   See also Mt. vii. 4, ἄφες ³ ἐκβάλω τὸ κάρφος κ.τ.λ., 1 C. iv. 21.⁴ It is wrong to supply ἵνα or ὅπως in such cases ; ⁵ no word is left out, any more than in such a sentence as *it appears they are coming*. In certain passages some MSS. have the future (from the LXX, see H. viii. 5), a tense which is sometimes (Luc. *Navig.* 26), though rarely, used by Greek writers in such expressions ; see Lob. *Phryn.* p. 734, Fritz. *Matt.* pp. 465, 761: compare *e. g.* Ex. xxv. 40, ὅρα ποιήσεις κατὰ τὸν τύπον κ.τ.λ.⁶

   In questions, the 3rd person of the deliberative conjunctive is less common in the N. T. than the future, according to the testimony of the MSS. (see above § 40. 6), and this tense must be retained in Rom. x. 14 sq.: ⁷ in Greek writers, however, the conjunctive is not

---

¹ [In H. vi. 3 Tisch. and others read ποιήσομεν with ℵBKL : 1 C. xiv. 15 is quoted above (§ 40. 6) with the *future,* and the conj. is pronounced a correction.]
² Herm. *De Ellips.* p. 183 (Jelf 417).
³ [It is interesting to notice that in modern Greek ἄς (a shortened form of ἄφες) with the subj. is *regularly* used to express the 1 and 3 persons of the imperative, as ἄς γράψωμεν *let us write* (Mullach, *Vulg.* pp. 223, 360, J. Donaldson, *Mod. Greek Gr.* p. 22). L. vi. 42, and perhaps Mt. xxvii. 49 (ἄφες ἴδωμεν), Mk. xv. 36 (ἄφιτε ἴδωμεν), are the remaining N. T. examples of this expression : Grimm (Wilkii *Clavis* s. v.) quotes ἄφες ἴδω, ἄ. δείξωμεν from Epictet. *Diss.* 3. 12, 1. 9. See A. Buttm. p. 210, Jelf 416.]
⁴ [This is a different case, as θέλετε is entirely separated from ἔλθω.]
⁵ Lehmann, *Lucian*, III. 466. [Madvig 123. 5, Jebb, Soph. *Elect.* p. 11.]
⁶ [This is the passage quoted in H. viii. 5, just mentioned.]
⁷ [Lachm., Treg., Alford, Westcott and Hort have the subjunctive in each case ; Tischendorf has the future once (ἀκούσονται).]

at all uncommon in this person,[1] as Soph. *Aj.* 403, ποῖ τις φύγῃ; *Œd. Col.* 170, ποῖ τις φροντίδος ἔλθῃ (1 person in ver. 311), Plat. *Soph.* 225 a, Arrian, *Epict.* 3. 22. 96. In L. xi. 5 the future indicative and the conjunctive are combined, τίς ἐξ ὑμῶν ἕξει φίλον καὶ πορεύσεται πρὸς αὐτὸν . . . . καὶ εἴπῃ αὐτῷ; see Matth. 516. 3, Herm. *De Partic.* ἄν p. 87.[2]

On Ja. iv. 15, ἐὰν ὁ κύριος θελήσῃ καὶ ζήσωμεν (ζήσομεν) καὶ ποιήσωμεν (ποιήσομεν) τοῦτο ἢ ἐκεῖνο, a learned controversy has been carried on between Fritzsche[3] and Bornemann.[4] The former reads ποιήσομεν, the latter ποιήσωμεν: according to Fritzsche the consequent clause begins with καὶ ποιήσομεν, according to Bornemann with καὶ ζήσωμεν. The former renders the verse, *if the Lord will and we live, then will we also do this or that;* the latter, *if it please God, let us seek our sustenance, let us do this or that.* Every one must feel that there is something awkward in, *If God will, we will live;* and Bornemann has himself felt this, as he translates ζήσ. *we will use our life.* But this explanation lacks simplicity, and is not supported by Biblical usage. The occurrence of καί at the commencement of the apodosis cannot in itself excite question (2 C. xi. 12). On this point therefore I must agree with Fritzsche. On the other hand, he was wrong in maintaining that ποιήσομεν is supported by much more testimony than ζήσομεν. The critical authorities are nearly equal; only ποιήσομεν—though not ζήσομεν—is still quoted (by Dermout) from the Codex Meermannianus.[5] Considering how easily a mistake in transcription might occur, we should probably select as the most suitable reading, ἐὰν ὁ κύριος θελήσῃ καὶ ζήσωμεν, καὶ ποιήσωμεν κ.τ.λ. (ver. 13).[6]

5. The optative mood is found in independent sentences where a wish is expressed: A. viii. 20, τὸ ἀργύριόν σου σὺν σοὶ εἴη εἰς ἀπώλειαν· Rom. xv. 5, Phil. 20, ἐγώ σου ὀναίμην· 1 P. i. 2,

---

[1] Stallbaum, Plat. *Men.* p. 103, Krüg. p. 185 (Jelf 417).
[2] Stallb. Plat. *Phileb.* p. 26, and *Phæd.* p. 202, Bornem. *Luc.* p. 147, Bäumlein p. 182.
[3] *Leipz. Literatur-Zeit.* 1824, p. 2316, and *N. krit. Journ.* V. p. 3 sqq.
[4] *N. krit. Journ.* VI. p. 130 sqq.
[5] [A cursive MS. of the 12th century (quoted in the Gospels as 122, in the Catholic Epistles as 177); it was collated by Dermout (*Collect. Crit.* I. p. 14); Scrivener, *Introd.* p. 183.]
[6] [So Griesbach; De W. also reads ζήσωμεν (on exegetical grounds) and inclines towards ποιήσωμεν, making the apodosis begin at καὶ ποιήσωμεν. Tregelles, Tisch., Lachm., Huther, A. Buttmann (p. 362), Wordsworth, Alford, Westcott and Hort, read the future in both clauses. Of these, Tregelles and Tischendorf divide the verse thus, ἐὰν ὁ κ. θελ. καὶ ζήσομεν, καὶ π. τ. ἢ ἐκ., mainly influenced perhaps by the authority of ancient versions; e.g. the Vulgate has *si dominus voluerit et si* (Cod. Amiat. omits *si*) *vixerimus, faciemus,* etc.: on ἐάν with the future indicative, see below § 41. *b.* 2. The rest commence the apodosis with καὶ ζήσομεν. The ancient testimony is the same in the case of both futures: that of the best known cursives is given by Alford *in loc.*]

2 P. i. 2, 1 Th. iii. 11 sq., v. 23, 2 Th. iii. 5. (In 2 C. ix. 10, 2 Tim. ii. 7, we must read the future, and in A. i. 20 the imperative λαβέτω.) As to the LXX see some remarks in Thiersch, *Pent.* p. 101. Compare 1 K. viii. 57, Ps. xl. 3, Tob. v. 14, x. 12, xi. 16.

In Hebrew a question is frequently used for the optative to express a wish, as in 2 S. xv. 4 τίς με καταστήσει κριτήν, *utinam quis me constituat!* This idiom however occurs in Greek poets (Fritz. *Rom.* II. 70). Rom. vii. 24 τίς με ῥύσεται κ.τ.λ. has been thus explained, but without sufficient reason: the question of perplexity, of conscious helplessness, is, as such, peculiarly appropriate here, and there is no need to suppose a μετάβασις εἰς ἄλλο γένος.

b. IN DEPENDENT SENTENCES.

1. Since every purpose has reference to the future, consequently to something yet to be carried into effect, the two particles of design ἵνα and ὅπως (both primarily signifying *quo modo, ut*,—as to μή see § 56) are naturally construed with the conjunctive and optative, these moods being distinguished as above. The future is the only tense of the indicative that can be used with these particles, so long as the writer's conception is correct.[1]

a. In the N. T. ἵνα and ὅπως are commonly followed by the conjunctive,—not only

(a) After a present tense, as in Mt. vi. 2, ποιοῦσιν . . . . ὅπως δοξασθῶσιν ὑπὸ τῶν ἀνθρώπων· 2 Tim. ii. 4, οὐδεὶς στρατευόμενος ἐμπλέκεται ταῖς τοῦ βίου πραγματείαις, ἵνα τῷ στρατολογήσαντι ἀρέσῃ· ii. 10, πάντα ὑπομένω διὰ τοὺς ἐκλεκτούς, ἵνα καὶ αὐτοὶ σωτηρίας τύχωσι· Mk. iv. 21, L. viii. 12, Rom. xi. 25, 1 Jo. i. 3, H. ix. 15, 1 C. vii. 29, G. vi. 13 (the conjunctive here denoting[2] that which was viewed as a *consequence which must actually follow*, that which was actually and immediately designed, and hence that was objectively possible);—and after an imperative or a future, as in 1 Tim. iv. 15, ἐν τούτοις ἴσθι, ἵνα σου ἡ προκοπὴ φανερὰ ᾖ· Mt. ii. 8, ἀπαγγείλατέ μοι, ὅπως κἀγὼ ἐλθὼν προϛκυνήσω αὐτῷ· v. 16, xiv. 15, A. viii. 19, xxiii. 15, 1 C. iii. 18, 1 Jo. ii. 28, Jo. v. 20, μείζονα τούτων δείξει αὐ-

---

[1] See in general Franke in the *Darmstädter Schulzeit.* 1839, p. 1236 sqq., and Klotz, *Devar.* II. 615 sqq. [Don. p. 597 sqq., Jelf 805 sqq., Green p. 168 sqq., Webster p. 128 sqq.]
[2] Herm. *Vig.* p. 850.

τῷ ἔργα, ἵνα ὑμεῖς θαυμάζητε· Ph. i. 26;—also after the *conjunctivus adhortativus* or *deliberativus* (Rom. iii. 8, L. xx. 14, Jo. vi. 5, al.);—all this is in accordance with the rules laid down above, and is perfectly regular:[1]—but also

(β) After a past tense, even where used in reference to what is really[2] past.[3] Sometimes we may find a reason for the use of this mood in preference to the optative (Herm. *Vig.* p. 791, Krüg. p. 191).[4] Thus in the following passages the conjunctive might indicate an action which still continues, either in itself or at all events in its consequences, or which is frequently repeated:[5] 1 Tim. i. 16, ἠλεήθην ἵνα ἐν ἐμοὶ πρώτῳ ἐνδείξηται Ἰ. Χριστὸς τὴν πᾶσαν μακροθυμίαν· i. 20, οὓς παρέδωκα τῷ σατανᾷ, ἵνα παιδευθῶσι μὴ βλασφημεῖν· Tit. i. 5, κατέλιπόν σε ἐν Κρήτῃ, ἵνα τὰ λείποντα ἐπιδιορθώσῃ· ii. 14, ὃς ἔδωκεν ἑαυτὸν περὶ ἡμῶν, ἵνα λυτρώσηται ἡμᾶς· Rom. vi. 4, συνετάφημεν αὐτῷ, ἵνα . . . . καὶ ἡμεῖς ἐν καινότητι ζωῆς περιπατήσωμεν· 1 Jo. iii. 5, ἐφανερώθη, ἵνα τὰς ἁμαρτίας ἡμῶν ἄρῃ· iii. 8, ἐφανερώθη, ἵνα λύσῃ τὰ ἔργα τοῦ διαβόλου· v. 13, ταῦτα ἔγραψα ὑμῖν, ἵνα εἰδῆτε· compare L. i. 4 (Plat. *Crit.* 43 b, *Rep.* 9. 472 c, *Legg.* 2. 653 d, Xen. *Mem.* 1. 1. 8, Ælian 12. 30). In other passages (e.g., A. v. 26, ἤγαγεν αὐτούς, ἵνα μὴ λιθασθῶσιν· A. ix. 21, εἰς τοῦτο ἐληλύθει, ἵνα . . . . ἀγάγῃ) the conjunctive may denote an intended result *of the occurrence of which the speaker entertained no doubt whatever;* compare Mk. viii. 6, ἐδίδου τοῖς μαθηταῖς αὐτοῦ, ἵνα παραθῶσι (*that they should* etc.—a thing which they certainly could not refuse to do), xii. 2, A. xxv. 26, προήγαγον αὐτὸν ἐφ᾽ ὑμῶν, ὅπως τῆς ἀνακρίσεως γενομένης σχῶ τί γράψω. The optative would express a purpose the issue of which was uncertain (Matth. 518. 4, 5, Jelf 809). Lastly, Mt. xix. 13, προσηνέχθη αὐτῷ τὰ παιδία, ἵνα τὰς χεῖρας ἐπιθῇ αὐτοῖς, and Mk. x. 13, προσέφερον

---

[1] Herm. *Vig.* p. 850.
[2] For where a perfect is used in the sense of a present the connexion of ἵνα or ὅπως with the conjunctive can excite no surprise; see Jo. vi. 38, L. xvi. 26, A. ix. 17, 1 Jo. v. 20 [*Rec.*].
[3] Compare Gayler, *De partic. Gr. sermon. negat.* p. 176 sq.
[4] Wex, in his *Epist. crit. ad Gesenium* p. 22 sqq. (Lips. 1831), distinguishes several other cases. But the question is whether such fine distinctions are in harmony with the character of a living language.
[5] Herm. *Vig.* p. 850 and on Eur. *Hec.* p. 7, Heind. Plat. *Protag.* § 29, Stallb. Plat. *Crit.* p. 103, Ast, Plat. *Legg.* p. 93, Klotz, *Devar.* II. 618. [See Jelf 806: compare Shilleto, Dem. *F. L.* p. 34, Riddell, Plat. *Apol.* p. 152 sq.]

αὐτῷ παιδία, ἵνα ἅψηται αὐτῶν, are perhaps to be explained on the principle that the Greeks sometimes express the thoughts of another person in the direct form, or as if the person were still present, and hence use the moods which he would have used:[1] so here, *that he may lay,* for *that he might lay* (the optative). By this means the scene described is more vividly brought before the reader's view (Klotz *l.c.* p. 618 sq., 682). Compare Jo. xviii. 28, Mt. xii. 14.

As however in all the multitude of examples which the N. T. furnishes of ἵνα after a past tense we do not find a single one in which the optative is used,[2] this nice distinction can by no means be attributed to the sacred writers. It would rather seem that the optative—a mood which in later Greek fell more and more into disuse, and which in the language of ordinary intercourse may perhaps never have been subject to the laws of written Attic Greek—was unconsciously avoided by them, even where a more refined grammatical instinct would certainly have preferred it (e.g., in Jo. iv. 8, vii. 32, L. vi. 7, xix. 4, 2 C. viii. 6, H. ii. 14, xi. 35, Ph. ii. 27, al.). Even Plutarch commonly uses the conjunctive in this case;[3] and in Hellenistic Greek it is throughout the predominant mood, as may be seen from any page of the LXX, the Apocrypha, the Pseudepigraphic writers, etc. (Thilo, *Acta Thom.* p. 47).

b. The future indicative (after the present and the perfect, compare Herm. *Vig.* p. 851): Rev. xxii. 14 [*Rec.*], μακάριοι οἱ

---

[1] Heind. Plat. *Protag.* pp. 502, 504, Poppo, Xen. *Cyr.* p. 189 sq., Thuc. I. i. 141 sq. (Jelf 806).

[2] [Unless indeed we suppose that the verbs in Mk. xiv. 10 ἀπῆλθε . . . . ἵνα παραδοῖ, Mk. ix. 30 οὐκ ἤθελεν ἵνα τις γνοῖ (see also Mk. v. 43, L. xix. 15, Jo. xiii. 2), are in the optative mood: this is the opinion of Tischendorf,—at all events so far as γνοῖ is concerned (*Proleg.* p. 57, ed. 7). There are however strong reasons for regarding these forms as subjunctives, formed after the model of verbs in ωω:

(1) ἵνα is certainly not followed by the optative of *any other verbs* (on E. i. 17, iii. 16, see below);
(2) δίδωμι borrows several forms from verbs in ωω (see above, p. 95);
(3) the same form is found after ὅταν (compare Jelf 843) and in connexion with a present tense in Mark iv. 29; compare 1 C. xv. 24 (Lachm., Tisch., Treg.). See also 1 Th. v. 15 (Tisch.), ὁρᾶτε μή τις ἀποδοῖ; Mk. viii. 37, τί γὰρ δοῖ.

This view is taken by A. Buttm. (pp. 46, 233) and by Meyer (on 1 C. xv. 24).]

[3] Even in the older writers the conjunctive with particles of design after a past tense is more common than grammarians were formerly willing to admit. See Bremi, *Lys.* Exc. 1, p. 435 sqq.

SECT. XLI.] THE INDICATIVE, CONJUNCTIVE, OPTATIVE MOODS. 361

ποιοῦντες τὰς ἐντολὰς αὐτοῦ, ἵνα ἔσται ἡ ἐξουσία αὐτῶν κ.τ.λ. (immediately followed by the conjunctive), iii. 9, vi. 4, 11, xiv. 13 *v. l.*, Jo. xvii. 2 ἔδωκας αὐτῷ ἐξουσίαν ... ἵνα ... δώσει αὐτοῖς (al. δώσῃ), 1 P. iii. 1, 1 C. xiii. 3 *v. l.*, G. ii. 4 *v. l.*: compare also the variants in Rev. viii. 3, ix. 20, xiii. 16.[1] In E. vi. 3 however (a quotation from the O. T.)[2] there is at ἔσῃ a change to the direct construction, and this future is not to be considered dependent on ἵνα: in the same way might be explained the variants ἐξαναστήσει and καθίσεσθε in Mk. xii. 19, L. xxii. 30. Ὅπως is not found with the future in the N. T. (for in Mk. v. 23 ὅπως .... ζήσεται is but weakly supported),[3] though in Greek writers this construction is not uncommon (Xen. *An.* 3. 1. 18, Theophr. *Char.* 22, Isocr. *Perm.* 746, Dem. *Mid.* 398 b, Soph. *Philoct.* 55 [4]): the future then usually denotes a *lasting state*,[5] whilst the aorist conjunctive is used of something which rapidly passes. Elmsley (Eurip. *Bacch.* p. 164) does not hesitate to admit this construction with ἵνα, as well as with ὅπως. Against this see Herm. Soph. *Œd. Col.* 155, *De Partic.* ἄν p. 134, Klotz, *Devar.* II. 630: in all the passages quoted for ἵνα with a future, ἵνα may be very well rendered *ubi* or *in which case*. Real examples however are found in the later writers (Cedren. II. 136), the Fathers (Epiphan. II. 332 b), and the Apocryphal writers (*Evang. Apocr.* p. 437, Thilo, *Apocr.* 682. Comp. Schæfer, *Dem.* IV. 273). This construction is tolerably well supported in the N. T., as the above examples will show, though the forms of the indicative and conjunctive might easily be interchanged by itacism.

c. Very peculiar is the connexion of ἵνα with a *present* in-

---

[1] [There can be little doubt that we must read the future in Rev. xxii. 14, iii. 9, viii. 3, ix. 20, xiv. 13, 1 P. iii. 1, G. ii. 4 (L. xxii. 30 is doubtful); and the subjunctive in Rev. xiii. 16, Mk. xii. 19. In Jo. xvii. 2, Treg., Meyer, Tisch. read δώσῃ, Alford, Scrivener, Westcott and Hort, δώσει: see Scriv. *Introd.* p. 548. In 1 C. xiii. 3 we must read either ἵνα καυχήσωμαι or ἵνα καυθήσομαι (p. 89), and in 1 C. ix. 21 either ἵνα κερδάνω or ἵνα κερδανῶ (p. 107). The future is received by recent editors in Mk. xv. 20, L. xiv. 10, xx. 10, Jo. vii. 3, A. xxi. 24, 1 C. ix. (15) 18, Ph. ii. 11, Rev. vi. 4, xiii. 12; but here and there it is uncertain whether the future is dependent on ἵνα or not.]

[2] [Ἔσῃ is not found in Ex. xx. 12, Dt. v. 16, but may have been brought into E. vi. 3 from Dt. xxii. 7 *Al.*: see Ellic. *in loc.*, who (with Meyer, Alford, al.) takes ἔσῃ as dependent on ἵνα.]

[3] [Lachm., Tisch., and Treg. have this construction in Mt. xxvi. 59: in Rom. iii. 4, we should probably read νικήσεις.]

[4] Compare Bornem. Xen. *An.* p. 498, Klotz *l. c.* p. 683 sq., Gayler, *De Part. Neg.* p. 211, 321, Rost p. 656 (Jelf 811).

[5] [Or perhaps a *more certain sequence*: see Alford and Ellicott on G. ii. 4.]

dicative,[1]—of which we have two examples (almost without any variant), 1 C. iv. 6 ἵνα μάθητε . . . ἵνα μὴ φυσιοῦσθε· G. iv. 17 ζηλοῦσιν ὑμᾶς . . . ἵνα αὐτοὺς ζηλοῦτε,—for the present indicative after a particle of design is clearly illogical. Hence it was maintained by Fritzsche (*Matt.* p. 836 sq.) that in both these instances ἵνα is not the conjunction but the adverb *ubi;* and this view (after Fritzsche himself had given it up as regards 1 C. iv. 6 [2]) has been taken up again by Meyer, who translates, *in which case ye then are not puffed up,*—*where* (in which state of things) *ye are zealous in regard to them.* But apart from the fact that ἵνα does not once occur in the whole Greek Bible as an adverb of place, the use of the present tense would be singular in both passages: in 1 C. iv. 6 moreover we might have expected οὐ rather than μή. Besides, as Meyer himself allows, the ἵνα of purpose would in each case much better suit the apostle's meaning. I think therefore that we must regard this use of the conj. ἵνα with the present indicative as a faulty construction of later Greek.[3] We cannot indeed regard *Acta Ignat.* p. 538 (ed. Ittig) as a certain example of this construction, as we might if necessary take ἀπολοῦνται to be the Attic future; and in *Geopon.* 10. 48. 3, Himer. 15. 3, the indicative may easily have been a mistake of transcription for the conjunctive. This construction, however, occurs too frequently in later writers for us to assume a clerical error in every case. See Malal. 10. p. 264, ἐπιτρέψας ἵνα πάντες . . . βαστάζουσιν 12. p. 300, ἐποίησε κέλευσιν ἵνα . . . χρηματίζουσι· *Acta Pauli et Petri* 7, προάγει, ἵνα μία πόλις ἀπόλλυται· 20, ἐδίδαξα ἵνα τῇ τιμῇ ἀλλήλους προηγοῦνται· *Acta Pauli et Theclæ* p. 45, ἵνα γάμοι μὴ γίνονται ἀλλὰ οὕτως μένουσιν· *Evang. Apocr.* p. 447.[4] And in the N. T. itself this construction has found its way into

---

[1] Valckenaer's note on 1 Cor. mixes up the preterite, future, and present indicative, and is consequently rendered useless.

[2] Fritzschior. *Opusc.* p. 186 sqq.: here he alters the text, reading (for ἵνα μὴ . . . φυσιοῦσθε) ἵνα μὴ . . . . φυσιοῦσθαι. Against this see Meyer *in loc.*

[3] In modern Greek (e.g. in the *Confess. Orthod.*) it is quite common to find νά or διὰ νά with the present indicative. [The standing rule in modern Greek is that νά or διὰ νά expressing a *purpose* is followed by the subjunctive or (as in classical Greek) by a past tense of the indicative. See Mullach, *Vulg.* p. 364 sq.]

[4] In Xen. *Athen.* 1. 11, ἵνα λαμβάνων μὲν πράττει (which even Sturz quotes in his *Lexic. Xenoph.*) was long ago changed into λαμβάνωμεν πράττει: see Schneider *in loc.* [Meyer mentions an earlier example than those quoted in the text, Barnab. *Ep.* 7. 11, ἵνα . . . δι' αὐτὸν παθεῖν; but Hilgenfeld and Müller, with Cod. Sin. and the Latin *Interp.* (quia), read ὅτι for ἵνα. See also Tisch. *Proleg.* p. 58 (ed. 7), where Ign. *ad Eph.* 4, Basilic. T. VII. p. 147 B, are quoted.]

SECT. XLI.] THE INDICATIVE, CONJUNCTIVE, OPTATIVE MOODS. 363

another passage, Jo. xvii. 3, where good MSS. read ἵνα . . . . γινώσκουσι. Either then Paul actually wrote thus (see however Bengel on 1 C. iv. 6 [1]), or else mistakes of transcription established themselves in these passages at an early period: in any case it is worthy of remark that both instances of this construction are found in verbs in οω.[2]

Where ἵνα is joined with the optative (after a present), as in E. iii. 16, κάμπτω τὰ γόνατά μου πρὸς τὸν πατέρα τοῦ κυρίου ἵνα δώῃ ὑμῖν κ.τ.λ. (where however very good MSS. have δῷ), E. i. 17, ἵνα is not, strictly speaking, a particle of design: the sentence which ἵνα commences expresses the object of the wish and prayer (*that* [3] *he may give*), and the optative is used as being the *modus optandi*: see Harless on E. i. 17. Yet even with the meaning *in order that* ἵνα and ὅπως are found with the optative when they are dependent on a clause which contains a wish, Soph. *Phil.* 325, *Ajax* 1200: see Herm. on the latter passage, and Wex, *Epist. Crit.* p. 33 (Jelf 807. δ). —It is unnecessary to read δώῃ in Eph. *ll. cc.*, with Lachmann and Fritzsche (*Rom.* III. 230): there is no sufficient warrant for introducing this Ionic conjunctive into the N. T.

2. In hypothetical sentences we find a fourfold construction[4] (Herm. *Vig.* pp. 834, 902,[5] Don. p. 537 sqq., Jelf 850 sqq.):—

---

[1] [Bengel says, "Subjunctivus; . . . . singularis ratio contractionis." Similarly Green, *Gr.* p. 171: "In two places the Indicative of the Present appears, which may still be no more than an anomalous form of the Subjunctive in verbs of that termination." Alford (on 1 C. iv. 6) inclines towards the same view: compare also Ellicott on G. iv. 17. A. Buttmann (pp. 38, 235) thinks that familiarity with the Attic future insensibly led the N. T. writers to use the present for the future in contracted verbs more freely than in other verbs.—For a curious illustration see Ex. i. 16, ὅταν μαιοῦσθε . . . . καὶ ὦσι.]

[2] [This construction was received by Tisch. (ed. 7) in 1 Jo. v. 20, Tit. ii. 4, Jo. xvii. 3, G. vi. 12, Jo. iv. 15, 1 Th. iv. 13, Rev. xiii. 17; but in ed. 8 he has returned to the subjunctive in all these passages except the first four. The indicative is strongly supported in 1 Jo. v. 20 (Treg., Alf., Westcott and Hort): it is also received by Tregelles in Tit. ii. 4, Jo. xvii. 3, iv. 15. See A. Buttm. p. 235. In 2 P. i. 10 Lachm. reads ἵνα ποιῆσθε, but on slender authority.]

[3] [Not *in order that*, but the simple objective *that*. In E. iii. 16 the best MSS. and texts have δῷ: ἵνα δοθείη, E. vi. 19 *Rec.*, has very little support. In Jo. xv. 16, Tisch. reads δῷ in ed. 8, for δώῃ (ed. 7). On δώῃ and δῴη see p. 94.]

[4] [The theory of hypothetical sentences given (after Hermann) in the text is in the main adopted by most grammarians (including Kühner, ed. 2). Its correctness (especially as regards the second and third classes, *b* and *c*) is impugned by Professor Goodwin. See his articles in the *Proceedings of the American Academy*, vol. vi, *Journal of Philology*, v. 186-205, viii. 18-38; also *Moods and Tenses* pp. 87 sqq., *Elem. Greek Grammar*, pp. 263 sqq.]

[5] See also *ad* Soph. *Antig.* 706, *ad* Soph. *Œd. C.* 1445, *ad* Eurip. *Bacch.* 200, Klossmann, *De ratione et usu enuntiatorum hypothet. linguæ Gr.* (Vratisl. 1830); Kiesling, 2 *Programm. de enunciatis hypothet. in lingua Gr. et Lat.* (Cizæ, 1835, 1845); Recknagel, *Zur Lehre von den hypothetischen Sätzen mit Rücksicht auf die Grundformen derselben in der griech. Sprache* (Nürnberg, 1843 etc., III.).—We may easily conceive that in many sentences εἰ and ἐάν

a. Condition purely and simply: *if your friend comes, salute him,*—the case being put as an actual fact. Here we find the indicative with εἰ, " quæ particula per se nihil significat præter conditionem : " Klotz, *Devar.* p. 455, compare p. 487.

b. Condition with assumption of *objective* possibility, where experience will decide whether the thing is really so or not: *if your friend should come* (I do not know whether he will come or not, but the event will show). Here we have ἐάν (εἰ ἄν, see Hermann, *Partic.* ἄν p. 95 sqq.) with the conjunctive.

c. Condition with assumption of *subjective* possibility, a condition merely supposed in thought: *if your friend were to come* (the case is conceivable and credible), *I should like to greet him.* Here we have εἰ with the optative.

d. Condition with the belief that the thing is not really so : *if there were a God, he would govern* (which implies, *but there is not*); *if God had existed from eternity, he would have prevented evil* (implying, *but he has not so existed*). Here we find εἰ with the indicative,—the imperfect indicative in the former case, and in the latter the aorist or (much more rarely) the pluperfect (Krüg. p. 195): in the apodosis also one of these two tenses is employed. Why a *preterite* is used in this case is explained by Hermann (*Vig.* p. 821): compare with this Stallbaum on Plat. *Euthyphr.* p. 51 sq. On the whole subject see Klotz, *Devar.* p. 450 sqq.

For ἐάν we sometimes find ἄν in good MSS. (especially B), as in Jo. xii. 32, xvi. 33,[1] xx. 23, L. iv. 7 (where however Tisch. makes no remark): on this see Herm. *Vig.* pp. 812, 822 (Jelf 851. *Obs.*). It is not uncommon in Greek writers, even the Attic; though these prefer the form ἤν, which does not occur in the N. T.

These rules are regularly used in the N. T., as the following examples will show :—

a. (*a*) Mt. xix. 10, εἰ οὕτως ἐστὶν ἡ αἰτία τοῦ ἀνθρώπου . . . οὐ συμφέρει γαμῆσαι· 1 C. vi. 2, ix. 17, Rom. viii. 25, Col. ii. 5,—present followed by present. Mt. xix. 17, εἰ θέλεις εἰσελθεῖν εἰς τὴν ζωήν, τήρει τὰς ἐντολάς· viii. 31, xxvii. 40, Jo. vii.

---

might be used with equal propriety, so that the choice would be left entirely to the writer; also that the later writers do not carefully observe the distinction between them. It may be worthy of remark that in mathematical hypotheses (the correctness or incorrectness of which is not left for future experience to decide) Euclid almost invariably uses ἐάν with the conjunctive.

[1] [Read xvi. 23 : recent editors receive ἄν here and in Jo. xiii. 20, xx. 23.]

4, 1 C. vii. 9,—present followed by imperative. Rom. viii. 11, εἰ τὸ πνεῦμα τοῦ ἐγείραντος Ἰησοῦν ... οἰκεῖ ἐν ὑμῖν, ὁ ἐγείρας ... ζωοποιήσει καὶ τὰ θνητὰ σώματα ὑμῶν· Mt. xvii. 4, A. xix. 39, Jo. v. 47,—present followed by future. 1 C. xv. 16, εἰ νεκροὶ οὐκ ἐγείρονται, οὐδὲ Χριστὸς ἐγήγερται, *if the dead do not rise* (I assume this case), *then Christ also has not risen*, xiii. 1,[1] 2 P. ii. 20 (Rom. iv. 14),—present followed by perfect: compare Demosth. *Ep.* 3. p. 114 b. Mt. xii. 26, εἰ ὁ σατανᾶς τὸν σατανᾶν ἐκβάλλει, ἐφ' ἑαυτὸν ἐμερίσθη, compare ver. 28, L. xi. 20,—present followed by aorist: compare Origen, *De die Domin.* p. 3 (Jani), εἰ δὲ τοῦ ἔργου ἀπέχεις, εἰς τὴν ἐκκλησίαν δὲ οὐκ εἰσέρχῃ, οὐδὲν ἐκέρδανας.

(β) A. xvi. 15, εἰ κεκρίκατέ με πιστὴν τῷ κυρίῳ εἶναι, εἰσελθόντες ... μείνατε,—perfect followed by imperative. 2 C. v. 16, εἰ καὶ ἐγνώκαμεν κατὰ σάρκα Χριστόν, ἀλλὰ νῦν οὐκέτι γινώσκομεν,—perfect followed by present: compare Demosth. *c. Bœot.* p. 639 a. Jo. xi. 12, εἰ κεκοίμηται, σωθήσεται· Rom. vi. 5, —perfect followed by future. 2 C. ii. 5, εἴ τις λελύπηκεν, οὐκ ἐμὲ λελύπηκεν,—perfect followed by perfect. 2 C. vii. 14, εἴ τι αὐτῷ ὑπὲρ ὑμῶν κεκαύχημαι, οὐ κατῃσχύνθην,—perfect followed by aorist.

(γ) Rom. xv. 27, εἰ τοῖς πνευματικοῖς αὐτῶν ἐκοινώνησαν τὰ ἔθνη, ὀφείλουσι κ.τ.λ., 1 Jo. iv. 11,—aorist followed by present. Jo. xviii. 23, εἰ κακῶς ἐλάλησα, μαρτύρησον περὶ τοῦ κακοῦ· Rom. xi. 17, 18, Col. iii. 1, Phil. 18,—aorist followed by imperative. Jo. xiii. 32, εἰ ὁ θεὸς ἐδοξάσθη ἐν αὐτῷ, καὶ ὁ θεὸς δοξάσει αὐτὸν ἐν ἑαυτῷ· xv. 20,[2]—aorist followed by future.

---

[1] [This does not come in here, as the protasis has ἐάν.]
[2] The only correct rendering of εἰ ἐμὲ ἐδίωξαν, καὶ ὑμᾶς διώξουσι· εἰ τὸν λόγον μου ἐτήρησαν, καὶ τὸν ὑμέτερον τηρήσουσι, is, *if they persecuted me they will also persecute you*, etc. I consider the words to be merely a special amplification of the thought which precedes, οὐκ ἔστι δοῦλος μείζων τοῦ κυρίου αὐτοῦ : your lot will be what mine has been, and persecution and acceptance are the only possible issues. The words themselves leave it for the moment undetermined which of these Jesus himself had experienced : what *follows* shows how he wished his words to be understood. It must not be overlooked that Jesus is looking at the conduct of the Jews *as a whole* and *in the gross*, without any reference to individual exceptions. In a new exposition of the passage by Rector Lehmann (in the *Progr. Lucubrationum sacrar. et profan.*, Part I. : Lübben, 1828), a *vis proportionalis* is attributed to εἰ : quemadmodum me persecuti sunt, ita et vos persequentur ; quemadmodum (prout) meam doctrinam amplexi observarunt, ita et vestram, etc. But this signification of the particle should have been established by decisive examples : in Jo. xiii. 14, 32, it clearly has *not* this meaning. The writer seems to have confounded the simply comparative *ut* ... *ita* (coordinating two propositions between which there is

(δ) Mt. xxvi. 33, εἰ πάντες σκανδαλισθήσονται ἐν σοί, ἐγὼ οὐδέποτε σκανδαλισθήσομαι,—future followed by future (as in Isocr. *Archid.* p. 280, Porphyr. *Abstin.* 1. 24): in Ja. ii. 11, however, where in *Rec.* the perfect follows the future, the verbs in the conditional clause should probably be read in the present tense. When the future is thus used, we have the nearest approach to the construction with ἐάν (Krüg. p. 196); but *if all shall be offended in thee*, is a more decided expression than *if all should be offended*. In the latter case there is, in general, uncertainty whether all will be offended; in the former, this is assumed as an impending fact (Christ had distinctly assured his disciples of this): compare Herm. *Vig.* p. 900. (Jelf. 854. *Obs.* 7.)

b. Ἐάν,—where *objective* possibility with the prospect of decision is to be expressed; here there is necessarily a reference to something future in every instance (Herm. *Vig.* p. 834): Jo. vii. 17, ἐάν τις θέλῃ τὸ θέλημα αὐτοῦ ποιεῖν, γνώσεται κ.τ.λ., Mt. xxviii. 14, ἐὰν ἀκουσθῇ τοῦτο ἐπὶ τοῦ ἡγεμόνος, ἡμεῖς πείσομεν αὐτόν. Hence the consequent clause commonly contains a future (Mt. v. 13, Rom. ii. 26, 1 C. viii. 10, 1 Tim. ii. 15) or—what is tantamount—an aorist with οὐ μή (A. xiii. 41, Jo. viii. 51 sq.), or an imperative (Jo. vii. 37, Mt. x. 13, xviii. 17, Rom. xii. 20, xiii. 4). More rarely the verb in the consequent clause is in the present tense, used either in a future sense (Xen. *An.* 3. 2. 20), or of something enduring (Mt. xviii. 13, 2 C. v. 1),[1] or in a general maxim (Mk. iii. 27, 1 C. ix. 16, Jo. viii. 16, 54, A. xv. 1, Diog. L. 6. 44, 10. 152). Perfects in the apodosis have the meaning of a present, Rom. ii. 25, vii. 2, Jo. xx. 23: on Rom. xiv. 23 and Jo. xv. 6 see § 40. 4 *b*, 5 *b*. We find an aorist in the apodosis in 1 C. vii. 28, ἐὰν δὲ καὶ γήμῃς, οὐχ ἥμαρτες, *thou hast not sinned*, thou art not in this case a sinner. Compare Matth. 523. 2, Klotz, *Devar.* II. 451 sq. The conjunctive after ἐάν may be either present or aorist: the latter, which on the

---

a necessary reciprocal action) with the proportional *prout, in so far as.* These two are quite distinct; the former may in a free translation be used to represent *ei*, but the latter expresses an idea which lies beyond the limits of both *ei* and *si*. It is easy to see that Lehmann really gives two meanings to *ei* in this passage, first that of *ut*, and then that of *prout*. See further Lücke *in loc.*

[1] [The present in 2 C. v. 1 is differently explained in § 40. 2. *a.*]

whole is more common, is usually rendered in Latin by the *futurum exactum*.

That in 1 C. vii. 11 ἐάν refers to a case which (possibly) has already occurred (as Rückert maintains) is incorrect; compare Meyer *in loc.* In 2 C. x. 8 Rückert takes ἐάν in a concessive sense; this also is corrected by Meyer.

c. Εἰ with the optative, of *subjective* possibility (Herm. *Partic.* ἄν p. 97):—

a. Where a condition is conceived as frequently recurring (Klotz p. 492, Krüg. p. 197, Don. p. 539, Jelf 855): 1 P. iii. 14,[1] εἰ καὶ πάσχοιτε διὰ δικαιοσύνην, μακάριοι, *even if ye should suffer.* Here the πάσχειν is not represented as something which will occur in the future, but is simply conceived in the mind as something which may very possibly take place, without any reference to determinate time (and as often as it may take place). Elsewhere only in parenthetical clauses, but with the same reference: 1 C. xv. 37, σπείρεις ... γυμνὸν κόκκον, εἰ τύχοι (*if possibly it should so happen*) σίτου,—Dem. *Aristocr.* 436 c, Lucian, *Navig.* 44, *Amor.* 42, *Toxar.* 4;[2] 1 P. iii. 17, κρεῖττον ἀγαθοποιοῦντας, εἰ θέλοι τὸ θέλημα τοῦ θεοῦ, πάσχειν· compare Isocr. *Nicocl.* p. 52.

β. After a preterite, where the condition is represented as the subjective view of the agent: A. xxvii. 39, κόλπον τινὰ κατενόουν ἔχοντα αἰγιαλὸν εἰς ὃν ἐβουλεύοντο, εἰ δύναιντο, ἐξῶσαι τὸ πλοῖον· also A. xxiv. 19, οὓς ἔδει ἐπὶ σοῦ παρεῖναι καὶ κατηγορεῖν, εἴ τι ἔχοιεν πρός με, *if they had anything against me* (in their own belief). See Krüg. p. 196 (Jelf 885). In A. xx. 16 we might in like manner expect the optative,[3] yet even Greek writers sometimes (and not merely in an established formula as here, εἰ δυνατόν ἐστι) use the indicative in the *oratio obliqua*; e. g., Æl. 12. 40, ἐκηρύχθη τῷ στρατοπέδῳ, εἴ τις ἔχει ὕδωρ ἐκ τοῦ Χοάσπου, ἵνα δῷ βασιλεῖ πιεῖν (comp. Engelhardt, *Plat. Apol.* p. 156). See also no. 5, below. (After ἐάν in the

---

[1] [Compare Green p. 162, where this passage and ver. 17 are quoted as instances which "illustrate the preference given to this construction when the hypothetical circumstance is of an unwelcome sort: as in the expression εἰ δέ τι πάθοι. Xen. *Anab.* V. iii. 6."]

[2] See Jacob on this passage and Wetstein on 1 C. xv. 37.

[3] [The optative εἴη is received by Lachm., Treg., Alford, Westcott and Hort, on very good authority. In A. xxvii. 39 the more probable rendering appears to be, *they took counsel whether they could,* etc.]

oratio obliqua no one will expect to find the optative in the N. T. ; see A. ix. 2, Jo. ix. 22, xi. 57, Buttm. § 126. 8. Compare, however, Herm. *Vig.* p. 822.)

For examples of (*d*) see § 42.

The N. T. text presents very few exceptions to these rules, and these are for the most part confined to particular MSS.

(*a*) Εἰ is joined with the conjunctive[1] in 1 C. ix. 11 εἰ ἡμεῖς ὑμῶν τὰ σαρκικὰ θερίσωμεν (the reading of good MSS.), xiv. 5, ἐκτὸς εἰ μὴ διερμηνεύῃ (al. διερμηνεύει), *except the case if he interpret it, except he interpret it;* Rev. xi. 5 *v. l.*[2] (Ecclus. xxii. 26). This construction was for a long time banished from editions of the Attic writers, but it is now admitted to occur even in prose.[3] The distinction between εἰ and ἐάν or ἤν with the conjunctive is thus defined by Hermann :[4] εἰ puts the condition simply, but in combination with the conjunctive it puts it as depending on the event ; so also does ἐάν, but less decisively, inasmuch as the ἄν represents the condition as depending on accidental circumstances, *if possibly* or *perhaps*. This would suit the two passages quoted above : ἐκτὸς εἰ μὴ διερμηνεύῃ, *nisi si interpretetur*, a point which the event will decide,—refertur ad certam spem atque opinionem, futurum id esse (vel non esse) : whilst ἐάν would make the matter doubtful, *if perhaps* (a thing which might possibly happen) *he should interpret*. The latter would clearly be unsuitable, as a gift of interpretation did exist, and was frequently exercised (ver. 26 sq.). In the later prose writers this conjunctive becomes more and more common,[5] especially in the Byzantines (Index to Malalas and Theophanes), also in the Hellenistic writers (Thilo, *Acta Thom.* p. 23), and almost regularly in the *Canon. Apost.* and the *Basilica :* from the LXX compare Gen. xliii. 3, 4. In these writers it is impossible to lay down any distinction between εἰ with the conjunctive and with the indicative (many question the existence of any such distinction even in Attic

---

[1] L. ix. 13 probably means *unless perhaps we must buy,* and the mood is independent of εἰ, as in the classical formula ὥσπερ ἂν εἰ, Matth. 523. 3 (Jelf 432). Plat. *Crat.* 425 d, εἰ μὴ ἄρα δὴ . . . καὶ ἡμεῖς . . . ἀπαλλαγῶμεν, would be a similar instance, but others read ἀπαλλαγεῖμεν. [Meyer and Green (p. 159) take the conjunctive as depending on εἰ, expressing a pure hypothesis.]

[2] In 1 Th. v. 10 the received text, with all the better MSS., has ἵνα, εἴτε γρηγορῶμεν εἴτε καθεύδωμεν, ἅμα σὺν αὐτῷ ζήσωμεν,—where (after a preterite in the principal sentence) a more exact writer would have used the optative in both cases : compare Xen. *An.* 2. 1. 14. Here however ἵνα takes the conjunctive in accordance with *b.* 1 (ἵνα . . . ζήσωμεν), and in conformity with this the verbs in the dependent clauses with εἴτε are also put in the conjunctive.

[3] See Herm. Soph. *Aj.* 491, *De Partic.* ἄν p. 96, Poppo, *Cyrop.* p. 209, and *Emendanda ad Matth. Gramm.* (Frankf. on O. 1832), p. 17, Schoem. *Isæus* p. 463, Klotz, *Devar.* II. 500 sqq. [Green, *Gr.* p. 158 sq. ; Jelf 854.]

[4] *De Partic.* ἄν p. 97, and on Soph. *Œd. R.* p. 52 sq. ; compare Klotz *l. c.* p. 501.

[5] Jacobs, *Achill. Tat.* p. 681, and *Athen.* p. 146, Locella, *Xen. Ephes.* p. 185; Jacob, Luc. *Tox.* p. 53, Jacobitz, *Index* p. 473, Schæf. *Ind. ad Æsop.* p. 131.

Greek¹), and hence it remains doubtful whether this nicety was present to Paul's mind.

(b) Ἐάν is joined with the indicative (Klotz p. 468),—not merely

(α) With the present indicative (Lev. i. 14, *Acta Apocr.* 259), as in Rom. xiv. 8 (in good MSS.), ἐὰν ἀποθνήσκομεν, τῷ κυρίῳ ἀποθνήσκομεν,—a general maxim, *cum morimur* (without reference to the fact that the event will decide whether we die or not),—and in 1 Th. iii. 8 (in G. i. 8 the indicative has not much support²); or the future, as Jo. viii. 36, ἐὰν ὁ υἱὸς ὑμᾶς ἐλευθερώσει· A. viii. 31, where however the conjunctive is better supported, L. xi. 12, ἐὰν αἰτήσει ᾠόν (according to many uncial MSS.,—*cum petet*, not *petierit*), and vi. 34,³ see Klotz pp. 470, 472 sq.: this is of frequent occurrence,⁴ see Ex. viii. 21 (Lev. iv. 3), Malalas 5. p. 136, Cantacuz. 1. 6. p. 30, 1. 54. p. 273 (*Basilic.* I. 175, Thilo, *Act. Thom.* p. 23, Schæf. *Ind. ad Æsop.* p. 131), though in these passages the forms differ so little as hardly to allow a positive decision :—but also

(β) With a preterite indicative, in 1 Jo. v. 15 ἐὰν οἴδαμεν (without variant), compare Ephraemius 6298. So even when the tense is in meaning a true preterite, as Job xxii. 3, Theodoret III. 267, Malalas 4. p. 71, ἐὰν κἀκείνη ἠβούλετο· Nili *Ep.* 3. 56, ἐὰν εἶδες· Ephraem. 5251.⁵

Sometimes we find ἐάν and εἰ in two parallel clauses : as A. v. 38 sq., ἐὰν ᾖ ἐξ ἀνθρώπων ἡ βουλὴ αὕτη ἢ τὸ ἔργον τοῦτο, καταλυθήσεται (*if it should be of men*, a point which the result will decide), εἰ δὲ ἐκ θεοῦ ἐστίν, οὐ δύνασθε καταλῦσαι αὐτό (*if it is from God*, a case which I put); L. xiii. 9, κἂν μὲν ποιήσῃ καρπόν· εἰ δὲ μήγε . . . . ἐκκόψεις· si fructus *tulerit ;* . . . . sin minus (si non *fert*) etc., Plat. *Rep.* 7. 540 d ; G. i. 8 sq.⁶ Compare Her. 3. 36, Xen. *Cyr.* 4. 1. 15, Plat. *Phæd.* 93 b, Isocr. *Evag.* p. 462, Lucian, *Dial. M.* 6. 3, Dio Chr. 69. 621. In most passages of this kind εἰ or ἐάν might just as well have been used twice, though the choice of the one

---

¹ Rost p. 637 ; compare Matth. p. 525 b.
² In all these passages, it is true, the form might easily be introduced through an error of transcription (Fritz. *Rom.* III. 179) ; but Klotz (p. 471 sqq.) has adduced examples from good writers to which this would not apply.
³ [This should have been quoted above : Tisch. (in ed. 7) and Treg. receive the *present*, but quote no MS. as containing the future. The indicative is received by Tisch. and Treg. in A. viii. 31, Mt. xviii. 19, L. xix. 40 (future), and 1 Th. iii. 8 (present) : Westcott and Hort retain the subjunctive in Mt. xviii. 19, but read the indicative in the three other passages. In L. xi. 12 ἐάν should probably be omitted.]
⁴ Compare Fabric. *Pseudepigr.* I. 678, 687.
⁵ See Jacobs, *Act. Monac.* I. 147 ; compare Hase, *Leo Diac.* p. 143, Schæf. *ad Bastii Ep. Crit.* p. 26, Poppo, *Thuc.* III. i. 313, III. ii. 172. When such examples occur in early writers, it has been usual to correct the text (see also Bernhardy, *Dionys.* p. 851), sometimes without any MS. authority (Arist. *Anim.* 7. 4. p. 210, Sylb.). In Dinarch. *c. Philocl.* 2, however, Bekker retains ἐὰν . . . . εἴληφε, which after Klotz's remarks must be left unaltered.
⁶ See Herm. *Vig.* p. 834, Jacob, Luc. *Tox.* p. 143, Weher, *Dem.* p. 473.

conjunction or the other manifestly proceeds from a different conception of the relation; see Fritz. *Conject.* I. 25. Εἰ and ἐάν are used distinctively in two mutually subordinate clauses in Jo. xiii. 17, εἰ ταῦτα οἴδατε, μακάριοί ἐστε, ἐὰν ποιῆτε αὐτά (*if ye know . . . in case ye do them*), and 1 C. vii. 36, εἴ τις ἀσχημονεῖν ἐπὶ τὴν παρθένον αὐτοῦ νομίζει, ἐὰν ᾖ ὑπέρακμος κ.τ.λ., Rev. ii. 5. Compare Krüg. p. 197 (Jelf 860. 10).

3. Particles of time (Krüg. p. 201, Don. p. 578 sqq., Jelf 840 sqq.):—

1. Those which in narration denote a definite past event (*as, when*, etc.) are naturally construed with the preterite or the historical present of the indicative: ὅτε Mt. vii. 28, ix. 25, Mk. xi. 1, xiv. 12, L. iv. 25, 1 C. xiii. 11; ὡς Mt. xxviii. 9, L. i. 23, vii. 12, Jo. iv. 40, A. xvi. 4, al.; ὁπότε L. vi. 3; ἡνίκα 2 C. iii. 15 (Lachm.,[1] Tisch.): compare Klotz p. 613. So also ἕως and ἕως οὗ,[2] Mt. i. 25, ii. 9, Jo. ix. 18, A. xxi. 26, al. (Matth. 522. 1).

2. Those which express a future event (*when, as soon as, until*)

a. Are joined with the indicative (future) when they refer to a fact which is quite definitely conceived; as in Jo. iv. 21, ἔρχεται ὥρα, ὅτε . . . . προσκυνήσετε τῷ πατρί· L. xvii. 22, ἐλεύσονται ἡμέραι, ὅτε ἐπιθυμήσετε· xiii. 35, Jo. v. 25, xvi. 25. See Herm. *Vig.* p. 915. With ἕως we sometimes find the present indicative instead of the future[3] (§ 40. 2), as in Jo. xxi. 22, 1 Tim. iv. 13, ἕως ἔρχομαι, like ἕως ἐπάνεισιν Plut. *Lycurg.* c. 29.[4] The

---

[1] [Lachmann (in both editions) has ἡνίκα ἂν ἀναγινώσκηται. In L. vi. 3 we should probably read ὅτε: ὁπότε does not occur elsewhere in the N. T.]

[2] This formula, the German *bis dass* [the English *until that*, Jud. v. 7], is mainly but (without ἄν) not entirely confined to the later prose writers. As early as Her. 2. 143 we find ἕως οὗ ἀπιδέξαν, and μέχρις οὗ in Xen. *An.* 1. 7. 6, 5. 4. 16, al.: the same in Plutarch frequently,—more fully μέχρι τούτου, ἕως οὗ, Palæph. 4. 2. [In one of the passages quoted above, Jo. ix. 18, we have ἕως ὅτου, not ἕως οὗ; the N. T. writers also use μέχρις οὗ, ἄχρις οὗ, and ἄχρι ἧς ἡμέρας in the sense *until*; see A. Buttm. p. 230 sq. Besides ἕως, ἕως ὅτου (Mt. v. 25) and ἄχρις οὗ (H. iii. 13) are used with the meaning *as long as*; see the note below. Similar combinations are ἐν ᾧ *whilst* (Mk. ii. 19, al.,—used in L. xix. 13 with ἔρχομαι in the same sense as ἕως ἔρχομαι 1 Tim. iv. 13), and ἀφ' οὗ *since* (Rev. xvi. 18, al.). Ἄν is very seldom found in the N. T. with any of these compound conjunctions: perhaps the only examples in the best texts are ἄχρι οὗ ἄν Rev. ii. 25, ἀφ' οὗ ἄν L. xiii. 25. There is not much authority for ἄν in Mt. xxvi. 36, 1 C. xi. 26, xv. 25.]

[3] [There are only two examples of the future indicative with a particle signifying *until*, viz. L. xiii. 35 (but see below, p. 372, note [2]), and Rev. xvii. 17, ἄχρι τελεσθήσονται.]

[4] Ἕως naturally takes the indicative when used in the sense *as long as*, of

use of the present indicative with ὅτε is of a different kind. This construction we find in sentences and maxims of altogether general application, as in Jo. ix. 4, ἔρχεται νὺξ ὅτε (i. e. ἐν ᾗ) οὐδεὶς δύναται ἐργάζεσθαι· H. ix. 17, ἐπεὶ μήποτε ἰσχύει (διαθήκη), ὅτε ζῇ ὁ διαθέμενος; see Herm. *l. c.* p. 915.

b. If however the future event is only (objectively) *possible,* and yet is regarded as one which under certain circumstances must actually take place, the conjunctive is commonly used with the particles compounded with ἄν (ὅταν, ἐπάν, ἡνίκα ἄν): see § 42. Similarly when the particle of time expresses duration or repetition in the future (ὅταν, ὁσάκις ἄν), or a point of time *until* which something is to take place (ἕως ἄν); see Matth. 522. 1 (Don. p. 581, Jelf 841). In the latter case, however, we also find the conjunctive alone with ἕως, ἕως οὗ, ἄχρι, πρίν, etc., as often in Greek writers, especially the later:[1] Mk. xiv. 32, καθίσατε ὧδε, ἕως προςεύξωμαι, *until I shall have prayed;* 2 P. i. 19, καλῶς ποιεῖτε προσέχοντες .... ἕως οὗ ἡμέρα διαυγάσῃ· L. xiii. 8, ἄφες αὐτὴν καὶ τοῦτο τὸ ἔτος, ἕως ὅτου σκάψω περὶ αὐτήν· xii. 50, xv. 4, xxi. 24, xxii. 16, xxiv. 49 (H. x. 13), 2 Th. ii. 7, 1 C. xi. 26, xv. 25, G. iii. 19, E. iv. 13 ; L. ii. 26, μὴ ἰδεῖν θάνατον, πρὶν ἢ ἴδῃ τὸν Χριστόν.[2] See Plutarch, *Cat. Min.* 59, ἄχρις οὗ τὴν ἐσχάτην τύχην τῆς πατρίδος ἐξελέγξωμεν· *Cœs.* 7, μέχρις οὗ καταπολεμηθῇ Κατιλίνας· Plat. *Eryx.* 392 c, Æsch. *Dial.* 2. 1, Lob. *Phryn.* p. 14 sq.[3] The very clear distinction which Hermann makes between the two constructions (*De Partic.* ἄν p. 109, adding however a limitation immediately

---

something actually existing, as in Jo. ix. 4, Jo. xii. 35, *v. l.* (Plat. *Phœd.* 89 c, Xen. *Cyr.* 1. 6. 9, 7. 2. 22, Plut. *Educ.* 9. 27, al.,—Klotz, *Devar.* II. 565). The same mood follows an imperative in Mt. v. 25, ἴσθι εὐνοῶν τῷ ἀντιδίκῳ σου ταχύ, ἕως ὅτου εἶ ἐν τῇ ὁδῷ μετ' αὐτοῦ, where, as a merely possible case is indicated, we should have expected the conjunctive : these words, however, contain a general maxim, in which the case is represented as one actually existing. On the other hand, in L. xvii. 8, διακόνει μοι, ἕως φάγω καὶ πίω (the better MSS. omit ἄν), the conjunctive is used of an uncertain limit in the future.

[1] [A. Buttm. (p. 230) suggests that in this construction ἕως, etc., follow the analogy of the final particles ἵνα, ὅπως, to which they are allied in meaning. Compare Green, *Gr.* (1st ed.) p. 64.]

[2] [This is the only example in the N. T. of πρίν or πρὶν ἤ with the subjunctive (the true reading is perhaps πρὶν ἂν ἴδῃ), as A. xxv. 16 is the only example of the optative construction. A. Buttm. remarks that in both passages a negative has preceded, according to the usual rule (Don. p. 583, Jelf 848). On the correctness of this rule see Shilleto, Dem. *F. L.* p. 127.]

[3] Stallb. Plat. *Phileb.* p. 61 sq., Held, Plut. *Timol.* p. 369 sq., Jacobs, *Achill. Tat.* p. 568.

afterwards, p. 111 ¹) may appear to be supported by the above passages, but disappears again, so far as the N. T. is concerned, when we compare the passages in which ἕως ἄν is used (§ 42. 5). In Rev. xx. 5 [*Rec.*], οἱ λοιποὶ .... οὐκ ἔζησαν, ἕως τελεσθῇ τὰ χίλια ἔτη, does not mean *until* .... *were completed* (in narrative style), but is a concise expression for *they remained* (*and remain*) *dead until* .... *shall be completed*.

3. The optative (without ἄν) occurs once only in the N. T. after a particle of time, in the *oratio obliqua*: A. xxv. 16, οὐκ ἔστιν ἔθος Ῥωμαίοις χαρίζεσθαί τινα ἄνθρωπον εἰς ἀπώλειαν, πρὶν ἢ ὁ κατηγορούμενος κατὰ πρόσωπον ἔχοι τοὺς κατηγόρους, τόπον τε ἀπολογίας λάβοι κ.τ.λ.: see Klotz p. 727 (Don. p.583 sq.,Jelf 848). Elsewhere,where we might expect this mood, we find the conjunctive, Mt. xiv. 22, A. xxiii. 12, 14, 21, Mk. ix. 9, L. ii. 26, Rev. vi. 11. This may in part be explained as a mixture of the *oratio recta* and the *oratio obliqua*: see below, no. 5. With Mt. xiv. 22 compare Thuc. 1. 137, τὴν ἀσφάλειαν εἶναι μηδένα ἐκβῆναι ἐκ τῆς νεώς, μέχρι πλοῦς γένηται· Alciphr. 3. 64 (Poppo, *Thuc.* I. i. 142, Krüg. p. 202, Jelf 887). In one instance of this kind, Mk. vi. 45 (left by Fritzsche entirely without notice), even the indicative is well supported: this must be explained in the same way, see Meyer *in loc.*

Ὅτε also is joined with the conjunctive in L. xiii. 35, ἕως ἥξει, ὅτε εἴπητε:² this construction can hardly be found in Attic prose (Klotz p. 688 ³), but—as used *de eventu*—it is not incorrect, *quando dixeritis*. The future indicative would be more suitable in the mouth of Christ, and would correspond better to ἥξει; compare Diod. Sic. *Exc. Vatic.*

---

¹ Compare Klotz, *Devar.* p. 568. ["Ita jam moribundus quis diceret adstantibus amicis μίμνετε ἕως θάνω, non item ἕως ἄν θάνω, quod potius ei conveniret qui non ita propinquam sibi putaret mortem esse."—Herm. *l. c.*]

² [There is great difference of opinion as to the reading. Lachmann reads ἕως ἄν ἥξει, ὅτε εἴπητε: Meyer, Tisch. (ed. 8), Treg., Alford, Westcott and Hort omit ἄν; Treg. and Alford bracket the words ἥξει ὅτε, which Westcott and Hort omit. A. Buttm. (p. 231 sq.) takes the subjunctive as depending in signification upon the notion of aim or end implied by ἕως. As to ἄν with future indicative see Klotz p. 117 sqq., Jelf 424.]

³ [Klotz's words are: "Si res non ad cogitationem refertur et eventus tantum modo spectatur, dubitare non potest quin etiam conjunctivus ad ὅτι particulam adjungi possit: ejus rei satis certum exemplum e scriptis Atticorum notatum non habeo." After quoting *Iliad* 21. 322 sq., and referring to the construction of εὖτε with the conjunctive in Æsch. *Theb.* 338 sq., he adds: "satis usum testatur id, quod in ceteris particulis relativis etiam Attici haud raro conjunctivum sine ἄν particula usurpant."]

103. 31 (Lips.). See further on ὅτε with conjunctive Jacobs, *Anthol. Pal.* III. 100, and in *Act. Monac.* I. ii. 147 (Jelf 842).

4. With interrogative words in indirect questions we find

a. The indicative, where the question relates to some actual matter of fact, i.e., to the existence of something (*is it ? is it not ?*), or to the quality of its existence (*how ? where ? wherefore ?* etc.), whether the verb in the principal sentence is in the present or in the preterite (Plut. *Arist.* 7, Xen. *An.* 2. 6. 4, Plat. *Phil.* 22 a, *Rep.* 1. 330 e, *Conv.* 194 e, Diog. L. 2. 69, Klotz, *Devar.* p. 508): Mk. xv. 44, ἐπηρώτησεν αὐτόν, εἰ πάλαι ἀπέθανεν· Mt. xxvi. 63, Jo. i. 40, εἶδον ποῦ μένει· Mk. v. 16, διηγήσαντο αὐτοῖς, πῶς ἐγένετο τῷ δαιμονιζομένῳ· A. xx. 18, ἐπίστασθε . . . . πῶς μεθ' ὑμῶν ἐγενόμην (he had actually been with them), 1 Th. i. 9, ἀπαγγέλλουσιν, ὁποίαν εἴςοδον ἔσχομεν πρὸς ὑμᾶς· Jo. ix. 21, πῶς νῦν βλέπει, οὐκ οἴδαμεν· ix. 15, x. 6, οὐκ ἔγνωσαν τίνα ἦν ἃ ἐλάλει, *what it was* (signified), iii. 8, vii. 27, xx. 13, A. v. 8, xii. 18, xv. 36, xix. 2, L. xxiii. 6, Col. iv. 6, E. i. 18, 1 C. i. 16, iii. 10, 2 Th. iii. 7, 1 Tim. iii. 15 ; also Jo. ix. 25 (where the ἁμαρτωλὸν εἶναι had been asserted), " whether he *is* a sinner ? " The Latin language uses the conjunctive in such cases, taking a different view of the relation.[1] The tense of the direct question is introduced into the indirect, A. x. 18, ἐπυνθάνετο, εἰ Σίμων ἐνθάδε ξενίζεται· H. xi. 8 : compare Plat. *Apol.* 21 b, ἠπόρουν, τί ποτε λέγει· Plutarch, *Opp.* II. 208 b, 220 f., 221 c, 230 f., 231 c, al., Polyb. 1. 60. 6, 4. 69. 3, Diog. L. 6. 42, 2. 69. This is done very frequently, indeed almost regularly, by Greek writers. (Jelf 886. 2. *d.*)

b. The conjunctive, to express something objectively possible, something which may or should take place (Klotz, *Dev.* p. 511, Jelf 417, 879): Mt. viii. 20, ὁ υἱὸς τοῦ ἀνθρώπου οὐκ ἔχει, ποῦ τὴν κεφαλὴν κλίνῃ, *where he might lay*, ubi reponat (Krüg. p. 190), Rom. viii. 26, τί προςευξώμεθα καθὸ δεῖ, οὐκ οἴδαμεν, *what we are to pray* (on the variant προςευξόμεθα see Fritz. *in loc.*), Mt. vi. 25, x. 19, Mk. xiii. 11, L. xii. 5, 11, H. viii. 3, 1 P. v. 8.[2] Compare Stallb. Plat. *Phæd.* p. 202, and *Rep.*

---

[1] In Greek that which is objective is expressed in the objective mood ; in Latin the objective proposition is made to depend on the act of asking and inquiring, and is for this very reason put as a mere conception, *interrogo quid sit.* Compare *Jen. L.Z.* 1812, No. 194.

[2] [The best texts have καταπαύῃ.]

I. 72, Xen. *Mem.* 2. 1. 21, *Cyr.* 1. 4. 13, *Anab.* 1. 7. 7, 2. 4. 19, Isocr. *Paneg.* c. 41, Plat. *Rep.* 368 b. So also after a preterite, A. iv. 21, μηδὲν εὑρίσκοντες τὸ πῶς κολάσωνται αὐτούς· L. xix. 48, xxii. 2, Mk. iii. 6, συμβούλιον ἐποίουν ... ὅπως αὐτὸν ἀπολέσωσι· xi. 18, xiv. 1, 40 : here the optative might have been used (Lucian, *Dial. D.* 17. 1, 25. 1, al., Kühner II. 103, Herm. *Vig.* p. 741), but the conjunctive is found instead because there is a reference to the direct question which they proposed to themselves, πῶς αὐτὸν ἀπολέσωμεν ;—the deliberative conjunctive, compare Thuc. 2. 52.[1]

The future indicative may take the place of the conjunctive in such cases (owing to the affinity of the two forms[2]): Ph. i. 22, τί αἱρήσομαι (without variant), οὐ γνωρίζω, *what I should choose*, Mk. ix. 6 : see Demosth. *Funebr.* 152 b, Thuc. 7. 14, Herod. 5. 4. 16, Jacob, Luc. *Toxar.* 151. On the other hand, in 1 C. vii. 32, 33, 34, ἀρέσῃ is the reading of the best MSS. In Mk. iii. 2, παρετήρουν αὐτόν, εἰ .... θεραπεύσει,[3] the meaning is, *whether he will* (would) *heal*, and the future tense was necessary, as in 1 C. vii. 16.[4]

c. The optative is used of subjective possibility, of something simply conceived in the mind; and hence this mood is found in narration after a preterite, when some one is introduced with a question which has reference to his own conceptions alone : L. xxii. 23, ἤρξαντο συζητεῖν πρὸς ἑαυτούς, τὸ τίς ἄρα εἴη ἐξ αὐτῶν, *who he may be*, i.e., *whom they should suppose it to be* ; i. 29, iii. 15, viii. 9, xv. 26, xviii. 36 (2 Macc. iii. 37), A. xvii. 11, ἐδέξαντο τὸν λόγον .... ἀνακρίνοντες τὰς γραφάς, εἰ ἔχοι ταῦτα οὕτως, *whether it was so*, xxv. 20 ; compare Her. 1. 46, 3. 28, 64, Xen. *An.* 1. 8. 15, 2. 1. 15, *Cyr.* 1. 4. 6, and Hermann *l. c.*, p. 742. See also A. xvii. 27, ἐποίησε ... πᾶν

---

[1] [Under this head come εἰ καταλάβω Ph. iii. 12, εἴ πως καταντήσω Ph. iii. 11 (Rom. xi. 14), εἴ πως εὐοδωθήσομαι Rom. i. 10. Of the dubitative μή one example (L. iii. 15 μήποτε εἴη) is quoted in the text : 2 Tim. ii. 25, μήποτε δῴη (δῴη Lachm., see § 14. 1) is somewhat irregular ; on this optative see Ellic. *in loc.*, Jelf 814. *c.* In this example, as in several quoted above, the indirect question depends on a verb implied, not expressed. L. xi. 35, σκόπει μὴ τὸ φῶς .... ἐστίν, seems to come in here most naturally (A. Buttm. p. 243, Meyer *in loc.*), not in connexion with verbs of fearing (§ 56. 2), though indeed their construction is very possibly an application of the indirect question (Don. p. 560 sq., Rost and Palm s. v. μή). On G. ii. 2 and 1 Th. iii. 5 see below § 56. 2. See A. Buttm. p. 256, and compare Green, *Gr.* p. 174 sq.]

[2] Hermann, Eurip. *Ion* p. 155 : ubique in conjunctivo inest futuri notatio, cujus ille cumque temporis sit ; compare Bäumlein 106 sq.

[3] [Tisch. now (ed. 8) reads θεραπεύει, which is probably the true reading in L. vi. 7.]

[4] See Stallbaum, Plat. *Gorg.* p. 249.

ἔθνος . . . ζητεῖν τὸν θεόν, εἰ ἄραγε ψηλαφήσειαν, *whether they might possibly feel* etc., A. xxvii. 12 (Thuc. 2. 77): see Matth. 526, Klotz p. 509.[1] (Jelf 877. *Obs.* 5.)

The distinction between the moods in dependent sentences after τίς, etc., is very well illustrated by A. xxi. 33, ἐπυνθάνετο, τίς ἂν εἴη καὶ τί ἐστι πεποιηκώς.[2] That the prisoner had committed some crime was *certain*, or was assumed by the centurion as certain, and τί ἐστι πεπ. inquires after the matter of fact of the πεποιηκέναι; but the centurion has as yet no conception *who* he is, and wishes to form one. Compare Xen. Ephes. 5. 12, ἐτεθαυμάκει, τίνες τε ἦσαν καὶ τί βούλοιντο· Stallb. Plat. *Euthyphr.* p. 107, Jacob, Luc. *Tox.* 139: see also Dio Chr. 35. 429, 41. 499, Heliod. 1. 25, 46, 2. 15. 81.

In the formula οὐδείς ἐστιν ὅς or τίς ἐστιν ὅς (in the same sense), even when followed by a future, the indicative is always used, and quite correctly: Mt. x. 26, οὐδέν ἐστι κεκαλυμμένον, ὃ οὐκ ἀποκαλυφθήσεται, *there is nothing which shall not be revealed* (though the Romans would say, *nihil est, quod non manifestum futurum sit*), xxiv. 2, 1 C. vi. 5, Ph. ii. 20, A. xix. 35, H. xii. 7 (Judith viii. 28, Tob. xiii. 2); compare Vig. p. 196 sq., Bernh. p. 390. Once only do we find the conjunctive, and then in combination with the indicative: L. viii. 17, οὐ γάρ ἐστι κρυπτόν, ὃ οὐ φανερὸν γενήσεται, οὐδὲ ἀπόκρυφον, ὃ οὐ γνωσθήσεται καὶ εἰς φανερὸν ἔλθῃ (where B and L have ὃ οὐ μὴ γνωσθῇ καὶ εἰς φ. ἔλθῃ[3]): see below, § 42. 3. *b.* In the example quoted by Lobeck (*Phryn.* p. 736) from Josephus, *Antt.* 13. 6, there is similar uncertainty. On the meaning of this conjunctive see below, § 42. 3. *b.*

In Jo. vii. 35 the future indicative is quite in order, ποῦ οὗτος μέλλει πορεύεσθαι (λέγων), ὅτι ἡμεῖς οὐχ εὑρήσομεν αὐτόν; *whither will he go, since we* (according to his assertion, ver. 34) *shall not find him?*[4] In οὐχ εὑρήσομεν the words spoken by Jesus (ver. 34) are repeated in the tense and mood which he had actually used. Nor is there any inaccuracy in A. vii. 40 (from the LXX), ποίησον ἡμῖν θεούς, οἳ προπορεύσονται ἡμῶν, *qui antecedant* (see Matth. 507. I. 1), Ph. ii. 20, 1 C. ii. 16; compare Demosth. *Polycl.* 711 b, Plat. *Gorg.* 513 a, Xen. *Hell.* 2. 3. 2, Aristot. *Nic.* 9. 11.

The use of the future indicative with εἰ or εἰ ἄρα in such cases as

---

[1] [On such forms as παραδοῖ (sometimes found in an indirect question, e.g. Mk. xiv. 11) see above, p. 360.]

[2] [Recent editors omit ἄν, following the oldest MSS.]

[3] [Lachm., Treg., Tisch., Westcott and Hort, adopt this reading, with ℵBLΞ, 33.]

[4] [Two explanations seem intermingled here. In ed. 5 Winer supplied λέγων, but took ὅτι in the sense of *that:* "whither will he go (saying) that we etc." In this edition he gives to ὅτι its causal meaning (with Meyer), but still retains λέγων. Probably this word is found here by accidental transference from the former edition.]

the following is also worthy of notice : A. viii. 22, δεήθητι τοῦ θεοῦ, εἰ ἄρα ἀφεθήσεταί σοι ἡ ἐπίνοια τῆς καρδίας σου· Mk. xi. 13, ἦλθεν εἰ ἄρα εὑρήσει τι ἐν αὐτῇ, *he went to it, if haply he should find*, etc. (in Latin, *si forte .... inveniret*). The words are here expressed in the mood which would be actually used by the speaker : I will go to it and see whether haply I shall find etc. Of a different kind is the future indicative after εἴπως in Rom. i. 10, but this too is well established.

In E. v. 15 the conjunctive or the future indicative must have been used if the meaning were, *take heed how ye should (will) live strictly :* with the present indicative the inquiry has reference to the *mode* (the *How*) of the ἀκριβῶς περιπατεῖν, actually existent as a Christian duty : look to it *in what way* you carry into effect the ἀκριβῶς περιπατεῖν, how ye set about the work of living exactly. Compare Fritzschior. *Opusc.* p. 209. 1 C. iii. 10, ἕκαστος βλεπέτω πῶς ἐποικοδομεῖ, is not exactly parallel with this passage, inasmuch as, after the preceding ἄλλος ἐποικοδομεῖ, there can be no doubt at all that an actual act of building is spoken of.

5. In the *oratio obliqua* (Herm. Soph. *Trach.* p. 18) we but seldom find the optative : A. xxv. 16, πρὸς οὓς ἀπεκρίθην ὅτι οὐκ ἔστιν ἔθος ʽΡωμαίοις χαρίζεσθαί τινα ἄνθρωπον, πρὶν ἢ ὁ κατηγορούμενος κατὰ πρόσωπον ἔχοι τοὺς κατηγόρους τόπον τε ἀπολογίας λάβοι κ.τ.λ.: indeed the instances in which the words of another are quoted indirectly are rare in the N. T. In the few examples which do occur the indicative is commonly used, either because the interposed sentence, where the optative might have been expected, is expressed in the words of the narrator [1] (L. viii. 47, Mt. xviii. 25, Mk. ix. 9, A. xxii. 24), or because, through a mixture of two constructions, the mood of the *oratio recta* is substituted for that of the *oratio obliqua*,—a change which would be very natural in the language of conversation. See A. xv. 5, ἐξανέστησάν τινες τῶν . . . Φαρισαίων, λέγοντες ὅτι δεῖ περιτέμνειν κ.τ.λ., L. xviii. 9, εἶπε καὶ πρός τινας τοὺς πεποιθότας ἐφ᾽ ἑαυτοῖς, ὅτι εἰσὶ δίκαιοι (contrast Matth. 529. 2 [2]), A. xii. 18, ἦν τάραχος οὐκ ὀλίγος . . . τί ἄρα ὁ Πέτρος ἐγένετο· ix. 27, xxiii. 20, 1 C. i. 15. We find similar examples in Attic writers, though usually in sentences of greater length : see Isocr. *Trapez.* 860, Demosth. *Phorm.* 586, *Polycl.* 710, 711, Lys. *Cœd. Eratosth.* 19, Xen. *Cyr.* 2. 4. 3, 3. 2. 27,

---

[1] Bäumlein, *Gr. Modi*, p. 270.
[2] [That is, contrast the examples given by Matthiæ, *l. c.*, which, though of the same kind as the above N. T. examples, contain the *optative.*]

SECT. XLI.] THE INDICATIVE, CONJUNCTIVE, OPTATIVE MOODS. 377

4. 5. 36, *Hell.* 2. 1. 24 ; and of later writers, Ælian 11. 9, Diog. L. 2. 32, 74, Pausan. 6. 9. 1. See Heindorf, Plat. *Soph.* p. 439 sq., Matth. 529. 5, Bernh. p. 389.[1]

Rem. 1. The consecutive particle ὥστε is commonly joined with the infinitive, as indeed the simple infinitive may be appended in a consecutive sense : compare § 44. Yet the finite verb is also used,—not merely where ὥστε begins a new sentence (in the sense of *quare, itaque*), either in the indicative (Mt. xii. 12, xix. 6, xxiii. 31, Rom. vii. 4, xiii. 2, 1 C. xi. 27, xiv. 22, 2 C. iv. 12, v. 16, G. iii. 9, iv. 7, 1 Th. iv. 18,[2] 1 P. iv. 19, al.),[3] or in the *conjunctivus exhortativus* (1 C. v. 8), or the imperative (1 C. iii. 21, x. 12, Ph. ii. 12, iv. 1, Ja. i. 19, al., Soph. *El.* 1163, Plutarch, *Them.* c. 27) ;—but also where the sentence with ὥστε is a necessary complement of what precedes, as in Jo. iii. 16, οὕτως ἠγάπησεν ὁ θεὸς τὸν κόσμον, ὥστε . . . ἔδωκεν· G. ii. 13 (but in A. xiv. 1 οὕτως ὥστε is followed by the infinitive). The same is very common in Greek writers. Thus we find ὥστε with a finite verb after οὕτω in Isocr. *Areopag.* pp. 343, 354, *De Big.* p. 838, *Ægin.* p. 922, *Evag.* 476, Lysias, *Pro Mantith.* 2, and *Pro Mil.* 17, Xen. *Cyr.* 1. 4. 15, 2. 2. 10, Diog. L. 9. 68 ; after εἰς τοσοῦτον, Isocr. *De Big.* p. 836, Soph. *Œd. R.* 533.[4] In the better writers indeed the distinction may be, that ὥστε with the indicative joins the facts together merely objectively as facts, as *præcedens* and *consequens*, whilst ὥστε with the infinitive brings them into closer connexion and represents one as proceeding out of the other.[5]

Rem. 2. In the N. T., as in later Greek, ὄφελον (ὤφελον) is treated entirely as a particle, and joined with the indicative ; either with the preterite indicative, as in 1 C. iv. 8 ὄφελον ἐβασιλεύσατε, *would that ye had become kings,*—imperfect, 2 C. xi. 1 ὄφελον ἀνείχεσθέ μου μικρόν, *O that you would have patience with me a little ;*— or with the future, as in G. v. 12. With the former construction of ὄφελον compare Arrian, *Epictet.* 2. 18. 15, ὄφελόν τις μετὰ ταύτης ἐκοιμήθη· Gregor. *Orat.* 28 (Ex. xvi. 3, Num. xiv. 2, xx. 3[6]). When once it had become customary to regard ὄφελον as a particle, it was as logical to join the imperfect or aorist indicative with it as with εἴθε, see Matth. 513. Rem. 2, Klotz, *Devar.* p. 516 (aor. de re, de qua, quum non facta sit olim, nunc nobis gratum fore significamus, si facta esset illo tempore) : the future fills the place of the optative. In Rev. iii. 15 some MSS. have ὄφελον ψυχρὸς εἴης,

---

[1] [See Jelf 885 sq., Don. p. 587, and compare Mullach, *Vulg.* p. 372.]
[2] [In this passage and the next ὥστε is joined with the *imperative*, not the indicative : on ὥστε with imperative see Ellic. on Ph. ii. 12.]
[3] Gayler, *De Partic. Negat.* p. 218 sq.
[4] See Gayler *l. c.* p. 221 sq. : compare Schæf. *Plutarch* V. 248.
[5] Klotz, p. 772, compare Bäumlein *l. c.* p. 88. [Jelf 863, Don. p. 593 sq., Shilleto, Dem. *Fals. Leg.* p. 202 sq., Ellicott on G. ii. 13.]
[6] [Job xiv. 13 is singular : εἰ γὰρ ὄφελον . . . ἐφύλαξας.]

others ἧς :[1] both readings give equally good sense. (Jelf 856. *Obs.* 2, Don. p. 549.)

Section XLII.

THE CONJUNCTION ἄν WITH THE THREE MOODS.[2]

1. The particle ἄν gives to the expression in which it stands a general impress of dependence upon circumstances (a fortuita quadam conditione), and consequently represents the matter as conditioned and contingent,[3]—*forte, si res ita ferat, perhaps, possibly* (if it should so happen).[4] It may be joined with any of the three moods, either in an independent or in a dependent sentence. In the N. T. however, as in later Greek generally, it is used with far less freedom and variety than in (Attic) Greek writers ;[5] in particular, it never occurs in combination with participles.

In an independent and simple sentence, ἄν is used by the N. T. writers

a. with the aorist indicative, to indicate that, on a certain condition, something *would* have taken place (a hypothetical sentence being implied in the context) ;[6] as in L. xix. 23, διὰ τί οὐκ ἔδω-

---

[1] [Recent editors read ἧς : the optative has not much support.]
[2] On the use of this particle see the following monographs : Poppo, *Pr. de usu partic. ἄν apud Græcos* (Frankf. on Oder 1816), also included in Seebode's *Miscell. Crit.* I. 1 ; Reisig, *De vi et usu ἄν particulæ*, in his edition of Aristoph. *Nubes* (Leipz. 1820), pp. 97–140. I have in the main followed Hermann's theory, from which Buttmann diverges to some extent, and Thiersch (*Acta Monac.* II. 101 sqq.) still more. This theory is most fully developed in the *Libb.* 4 *de Partic.* ἄν, incorporated in the London edition of Steph. *Thesaurus*, and in Hermann's *Opuscul.* Tom. IV., and also published separately (Lips. 1831). In all the main points Klotz (*Devar.* II. 99) agrees with Hermann : Hartung's treatment (*Partik.* II. 218 sq.) differs considerably. B. Matthiä (*Lexic. Eurip.* I. 189 sqq.) entirely reverses the view hitherto held respecting the meaning of ἄν : he maintains that it is a particle of confirmation and assertion, and gives us to understand that his exposition is a "divina et qua nihil unquam verius exstitit descriptio."—Compare further Bäumlein, *Ueber die gr. Modi* (referred to above, § 41. 1), and Moller in Schneidewin, *Philolog.* VI. 719 sqq. [Donalds. *New Cr.* p. 349 sqq., *Gr.* p. 537 etc., Jelf 424 etc.]
[3] Herm. *Vig.* pp. 903, 820, *De Partic.* ἄν p. 10 sq. (Jelf 424.)
[4] We may perhaps also compare the South-German *halt.*
[5] Ἄν is not found more rarely in the LXX than in the N. T. (Bretschneider, *Lexic.* p. 22, says "multo rarius") : in particular, we always find it in hypothetical sentences where it *is required*. It is sometimes joined to the optative (Gen. xix. 8, xxxiii. 10, xliv. 8), and to the participle (2 Macc. i. 11, 3 Macc. iv. 1). Indeed we find it on almost every page. On ἄν in the Apocrypha see Wahl, *Clav. Apocr.* p. 34 sqq.
[6] Matth. 509, Rost p. 611 sqq. (Jelf 424, Don. p. 539 sqq.)

SECT. XLII.] THE CONJUNCTION ἄν WITH THE THREE MOODS. 379

κας τὸ ἀργύριόν μου ἐπὶ τὴν τράπεζαν; καὶ ἐγὼ ἐλθὼν σὺν τόκῳ ἂν ἔπραξα αὐτό, *I should* (if this διδόναι τὸ ἀργύριον ἐπὶ τὴν τράπεζαν had taken place) *have exacted it with interest.* Here the omitted antecedent clause is easily supplied from the interrogation διὰ τί . . . : τράπεζαν. Similarly in the parallel passage, Mt. xxv. 27, ἔδει σε βαλεῖν τὸ ἀργύριόν μου τοῖς τραπεζίταις, καὶ ἐλθὼν ἐγὼ ἐκομισάμην ἂν τὸ ἐμὸν σὺν τόκῳ· and also in H. x. 2, ἐπεὶ οὐκ ἂν ἐπαύσαντο προςφερόμεναι, where we may supply from ver. 1, *had these sacrifices for ever perfected—completely cleared from sin—those who offered them.* Compare Xen. *An.* 4. 2. 10, Thuc. 1. 11, Plat. *Symp.* 175 d, *Rep.* 8, 554 b, Aristot. *Rhet.* 2. 2. 11, Diog. L. 2. 75. In the LXX, see Gen. xxvi. 10, Job iii. 10, 13, and (with the pluperfect) 2 S. xviii. 11.

b. With the optative, where subjective possibility is connected with a condition (opinio de eo, quod ex aliqua conditione pendet, Herm. *Partic. ἄν* p. 164 sqq.[1]); A. xxvi. 29, εὐξαίμην ἂν τῷ θεῷ, *I should pray to God* (if I were simply to follow my thoughts, i.e. the wish of my heart). We find the same formula (parallel with βουλοίμην ἄν) in Dio C. 36. 10, also εὔξαιτ' ἄν τις Xen. *Hipparch.* 8. 6, ὡς ἂν ἐγὼ εὐξαίμην Diog. L. 2. 76: similarly ἀξιώσαιμ' ἄν, Liban. *Oratt.* p. 200 b.

So in a direct question: A. ii. 12, λέγοντες τί ἂν θέλοι[2] τοῦτο εἶναι; *what may this intend to signify* (I assume that it is to signify something); A. xvii. 18, τί ἂν θέλοι ὁ σπερμολόγος οὗτος λέγειν; it being presupposed that his words have a meaning. See also L. vi. 11,[3] Gen. xxiii. 15, Dt. xxviii. 67, Job xix. 23, xxv. 4, xxix. 2, xxxi. 31, Ecclus. xxv. 3. Compare *Odyss.* 21. 259, Xen. *Cyr.* 1. 4. 12, Diog. L. 2. 5, Krüg. p. 186 sq. (Don. p. 542, Jelf 425.)

We have what amounts to a hypothetical construction in A. viii. 31, πῶς ἂν δυναίμην, ἐὰν μή τις ὁδηγήσῃ με; for without an interrogation it would run, οὐκ ἂν δυναίμην. Compare Xen. *Apol.* 6, ἢν αἰσθάνωμαι χείρων γιγνόμενος . . . πῶς ἄν . . . ἐγὼ ἔτι ἂν ἡδέως βιοτεύοιμι;

---

[1] Klotz p. 104 : Adjecta ad optativum ista particula hoc dicitur : nos rem ita animo cogitare, si quando fiat, h. e. rem, si fiat, ita fieri oportere ex cogitatione quidem nostra. Compare Madvig 136.
[2] [Recent editors read τί θέλει.]
[3] [This passage comes in below, no. 4.]

In one passage ἄν stands without any mood (Herm. *Partic.* ἄν p. 187), according to most MSS.: 1 C. vii. 5, μὴ ἀποστερεῖτε ἀλλήλους, εἰ μή τι ἂν ἐκ συμφώνου, *unless perhaps* (unless if perhaps this can be done) with mutual consent.¹

2. After conditional clauses with εἰ we find ἄν in the apodosis with the indicative, to denote hypothetical reality (Rost p. 635, Matth. 508, Don. p. 539 sqq., Jelf 856):—

a. With the imperfect indicative (the most common case), when the writer wishes to express *I should do it*. The antecedent clause may contain either an imperfect or an aorist.

(α) Imperfect: L. vii. 39, οὗτος εἰ ἦν προφήτης, ἐγίνωσκεν ἄν κ.τ.λ., *if he were a prophet, he would perceive*, xvii. 6,² Mt. xxiii. 30 (see Fritzsche), Jo. v. 46 (viii. 19), viii. 42, ix. 41, xv. 19, xviii. 36, G. i. 10, H. viii. 4, 7, 1 C. xi. 31, A. xviii. 14. Compare 2 Macc. iv. 47, Valckenaer on L. xvii. 6.³

(β) Aorist: H. iv. 8, εἰ γὰρ αὐτοὺς Ἰησοῦς κατέπαυσεν, οὐκ ἂν περὶ ἄλλης ἐλάλει, *if Joshua had given them rest, he would not speak* etc. (in the words previously cited, ver. 5). Compare the present ὁρίζει in ver. 7. See also G. iii. 21, and compare Jer. xxiii. 22, Bar. iii. 13.

b. With the aorist, to express *I should have done it* (Herm. *Vig.* p. 813): Mt. xi. 21, εἰ ἐγένοντο . . . πάλαι ἂν μετενόησαν, *if . . . had been done, they would long ago have repented*, 1 C. ii. 8, Rom. ix. 29 (from the LXX), Gen. xxx. 27, xxxi. 27, 42,⁴

---

¹ [Compare κἄν (Mk. vi. 56, al.), ὡς ἄν 2 C. x. 9, and Green p. 230: "In the later Greek the particle ἄν is sometimes combined with καί and ὡς, so as simply to produce a strengthened term, without being in any way material to the syntax." See also Jelf 430. Compare A. Buttm. p. 219: "If we supply an optative, such as γένοιτο, which may combine with ἄν (the principle on which some similar cases in the Greek poets must be explained), we depart entirely from Paul's *usus loquendi*. Hence we must supply either the indicative (2 C. xiii. 5) or the conjunctive (L. ix. 13), and combine ἄν with the restrictive particle εἰ μήτι, so as to form one whole. There is another possible assumption, in which there is nothing opposed to the character of N. T. ellipses or of Paul's style, viz. that ἄν here stands for ἐάν, the predicate being ἀποστερῆτε or γένηται, implied in the previous words. The only objection to this view is the extremely rare occurrence of ἄν for ἐάν in the N. T." (See above, § 41. 2,—also Jelf 860. 7, 861. *Obs.* 4.)]

² [Here ἔχετε is probably the true reading: see below. Mt. xxiii. 30 is thus explained by Fritzsche: si in (impia) majorum ætate viveremus, quam nos aliter, ac patres, in prophetas consuleremus, nos, qui vel mortuorum nunc pie revereamur sepulcra !]

³ [Both A. xviii. 14 and 2 Macc. iv. 47 have an aorist in the apodosis, an imperfect in the protasis.]

⁴ [In Gen. xxxi. 42, Jud. xiii. 23, an imperfect stands in the conditional clause.]

xliii. 9, Jud. xiii. 23, xiv. 18, Is. i. 9, xlviii. 18, Ps. l. 18, liv. 13, Judith xi. 2, al.,—where the conditional clause also contains an aorist: Jo. xiv. 28, εἰ ἠγαπᾶτέ με, ἐχάρητε ἄν, *if ye loved me ye would have rejoiced*, xviii. 30, A. xviii. 14,—an imperfect in the conditional clause (Bar. iii. 13[1]): Mt. xii. 7, εἰ ἐγνώκειτε . . . . οὐκ ἂν κατεδικάσατε *if ye had known, ye would not have condemned*, Jud. viii. 19, Job iv. 12,—a pluperfect in the conditional clause (compare Demosth. *Pantœn.* p. 624 b, Liban. *Oratt.* p. 117 c). In this case the pluperfect sometimes takes the place of the aorist with ἄν, as in 1 Jo. ii. 19, εἰ ἦσαν ἐξ ἡμῶν, μεμενήκεισαν ἂν μεθ' ἡμῶν, *mansissent* (atque adeo manerent), Jo. xi. 21 (in ver. 32 the aorist[2]), xiv. 7. See Soph. *Œd. R.* 984, Æsch. *Ctes.* 310 a, Demosth. *Cor.* 324 a, Plat. *Phœd.* 106 c, Diog. L. 3. 39, Æsop 31. 1, Lucian, *Fugit.* 1; and compare Herm. *Partic.* ἄν p. 50.

On the whole subject see Hermann, *Partic.* ἄν, I. cap. 10. This distinction between the tenses seems not to have been understood by some of the translators of the N. T.; by others it has been neglected.[3]

The apodosis with ἄν is absorbed by an interrogative clause in 1 C. xii. 19, εἰ ἦν τὰ πάντα ἓν μέλος, ποῦ τὸ σῶμα; also in H. vii. 11, εἰ τελείωσις διὰ τῆς . . . . ἱερωσύνης ἦν, τίς ἔτι χρεία κ.τ.λ., for οὐκέτι ἂν ἦν χρεία κ.τ.λ. For an example of ἄν in an interrogative apodosis see Wisd. xi. 26, πῶς ἔμεινεν ἄν τι, εἰ μὴ σὺ ἠθέλησας; On A. viii. 31 see above.

---

[1] [This passage is out of place here; it is rightly quoted above under a. (β).]
[2] [The best critical texts have the aorist in both verses.]
[3] [This can hardly be meant to imply that the rules given above are *never* violated in the N. T.,—that we never find the imperfect where the aorist might have been expected,—for Winer refers below to a modification of the rule, thus expressed by Madvig *l. c.*: "Sometimes, either in both clauses or in only one of them, the imperfect is used instead of the aorist, of relations belonging to the past; mostly (yet not always, especially in the poets) to denote an abiding state or a continued series of actions" (p. 95 of Transl.). Similarly Krüger p. 195, Buttmann, *Gr. Gramm.* p. 425, Kühner on Xen. *Mem.* 1. 1. 5, Curtius, *Gr. Gramm.* p. 296 (Transl.): compare also Kühner, *Gr.* II. 175, 971 sq. (ed. 2), Jelf 856. *Obs.* 1, Bleek on H. vii. 11, xi. 15. Such exceptional instances, however, are probably very few in the N. T.: there seems no sufficient reason for reckoning 1 C. xi. 31 or G. iii. 21 amongst them. When ἦν occurs in the protasis, it must occasionally be rendered *had been*, see Jo. xi. 21, 32, 1 Jo. ii. 19, (A. xviii. 14); compare Alford on H. viii. 7. In Jo. viii. 19, Rom. vii. 7 (quoted in the text) the word used is ᾔδειν, which can scarcely be reckoned with pluperfects.]

In Mk. xiii. 20, εἰ μὴ κύριος ἐκολόβωσε . . . . οὐκ ἂν ἐσώθη πᾶσα σάρξ, the two aorists do not stand for imperfects; the meaning is, *if the Lord had not* (in his decree) *shortened the days, all flesh would have perished* (might even now be looked upon as already destroyed). In H. xi. 15, εἰ μὲν ἐκείνης ἐμνημόνευον . . . . εἶχον ἂν καιρὸν ἀνακάμψαι, it is probable that the writer used the imperfect in the principal clause because he is speaking of a *continued* action (of past time),[1] just as the imperfect is used in Latin (*haberent*) :[2] *if they thought that . . . . they had* (during their life) *time to return,* and consequently would not have made this declaration (ver. 13) at the end of their life: the aorist would have represented the ἔχειν καιρόν as something which occurred once and quickly passed. Another view of the imperfect in hypothetical clauses (Franke, *Demosth.* pp. 59, 74) is foreign to the context.

We sometimes find ἄν omitted in the apodosis, especially in connexion with the imperfect tense.[3] This omission becomes more and more frequent in later Greek, and is found in cases where there is no aim after the emphasis—the idea of decision —originally conveyed by this construction (Kühner II. 556).[4] The examples may be thus arranged:—

a. Imperfect in both clauses: Jo. ix. 33, εἰ μὴ ἦν οὗτος παρὰ θεοῦ, οὐκ ἠδύνατο ποιεῖν οὐδέν, *were he not from God, he would be able to do nothing;* Diog. L. 2. 24, Lycurg. *Orat.* 8. 4, Plat. *Sympos.* 198 c, *Gorg.* 514 c. In Jo. viii. 39 the MSS. are almost equally divided as to the omission or insertion of ἄν: if it originally stood in the text it may have been absorbed by the νῦν which immediately follows.[5]

b. Aorist in the apodosis, with an ellipsis of ἦν in the protasis: G. iv. 15, εἰ δυνατὸν τοὺς ὀφθαλμοὺς ὑμῶν ἐξορύξαντες ἐδώκατέ μοι, where ἄν has not much support.

c. Aorist in protasis, imperfect in apodosis: Jo. xv. 22, εἰ μὴ ἦλθον . . . . ἁμαρτίαν οὐκ εἶχον, *if I had not come, they would not have sin;* compare Diog. L. 2. 21.

---

[1] Matth. 508. b, Madvig. 117. *a.* Rem. 1.
[2] Zumpt, *Gramm.* 525 [Madvig 347. b. *Obs.* 2].
[3] Herm. Eur. *Hec.* 1087, Soph. *Elect.* p. 132, *Partic.* ἄν p. 70 sqq. Bremi, *Exc.* 4 *ad Lys.* p. 439 sq., Matth. 508. Rem. 5. [Don. p. 540, Jelf 858, Ellicott on G. iv. 15. In modern Greek ἄν is omitted in this case: see Mullach, *Vulg.* p. 359.]
[4] Similar to these examples are such Latin sentences as the following: Flor. 4. 2. 19, *peractum erat* bellum sine sanguine, si Pompeium opprimere (Cæsar) potuisset; Horat. *Od.* 2. 17. 27, Liv. 34. 29, Cic. *Fam.* 12. 24. 2, Tac. *Annal.* 3. 14, Sen. *Consol. ad Marc.* I. See Zumpt, *Gr.* 519. b. [Madvig 348, Don. p. 396.]
[5] [Tischendorf and Tregelles read εἰ . . . . ἐστι . . . . ἐποιεῖτε (without ἄν): see below. Westcott and Hort read ἐστι, but in the next clause ποιεῖτε.]

d. Pluperfect in the conditional clause (Jud. viii. 19), imperfect in the principal clause: Jo. xix. 11, οὐκ εἶχες ἐξουσίαν οὐδεμίαν κατ' ἐμοῦ, εἰ μὴ ἦν σοι δεδομένον ἄνωθεν, *thou wouldst not have . . . . if it were not* (had not been) *given to thee,* A. xxvi. 32; Rom. vii. 7, *non cognoram . . . . nisi diceret,*—so also in the words which immediately precede, τὴν ἁμαρτίαν κ.τ.λ., where with εἰ μὴ διὰ νόμου we must repeat ἔγνων. This omission of ἄν is particularly common with καλὸν ἦν, ἔδει, ἐχρῆν, κ.τ.λ.;[1] compare Mt. xxvi. 24, καλὸν ἦν αὐτῷ, εἰ οὐκ ἐγεννήθη κ.τ.λ. See above § 41. *a.* 2.[2]

2 C. xi. 4, εἰ ὁ ἐρχόμενος ἄλλον Ἰησοῦν κηρύσσει . . . . καλῶς ἀνείχεσθε (ἀνέχεσθε, found in B alone, is received by Lachmann[3]), is rendered, *if . . . preached, ye would bear with* etc. Here we should certainly expect to find ἐκήρυσσεν; but, as several words intervene, the writer might easily fall into such an anacoluthon (*if . . . . preaches another Jesus . . . . ye would bear with it*), using ἀνείχεσθε as if he had written ἐκήρυσσεν, instead of following up the κηρύσσει with ἀνέχεσθε. Or we may suppose that he changes the expression designedly, that he may not give pain to the Corinthians, altering the harsh ἀνέχεσθε into the hypothetical and therefore milder ἀνείχεσθε: in this case, however, ἄν was the more to be expected as in the antecedent clause there is no aim at a hypothetical period: compare also Klotz, *Devar.* p. 487 sq.[4] We have a similar example in Diog. L. 2. 69, εἰ τοῦτο φαῦλόν ἐστιν, οὐκ ἂν ἐν ταῖς τῶν θεῶν ἑορταῖς ἐγίνετο:[5] Demosth. *Nexr.* 815 a is of a different kind.

---

[1] Madvig 118, Bäumlein p. 140 sq. (Don. p. 541, Jelf 858. 3).
[2] [In the place referred to Winer maintains that there is no real ellipsis of ἄν in such examples.]
[3] [Alford and Westcott and Hort follow Lachmann in this reading. A. Buttmann (*Gr.* p. 226, *Stud. u. Kr.* 1858, *vid. infr.*) maintains that this is an example of the first class of conditional sentences, not the fourth. He takes the same view of Jo. xix. 11, where however he would *prefer* to read ἔχεις.]
[4] [Klotz's words will make the meaning clearer: "Si ratione rem consideramus, in ejus modi locis " (*i. e.* ubi apodosis aliam orationis formam habet) "condicionis et apodosis propria conjunctio nulla est, veram postquam simpliciter posita est hypothetica enuntiatio, alio quodam modo concipitur cogitatione apodosis, ut non exaequata sit totius enuntiationis ratio, sed condicio illa nihil adferat ad apodosin nisi externam rationem sententiarum."]
[5] [In this passage we have in the protasis the present indicative, and in the apodosis a past tense of the indicative with ἄν. L. xvii. 6, εἰ ἔχετε . . . . ἐλέγετε ἄν, is precisely similar to this, as also is Jo. viii. 39 with the reading εἰ . . . . ἐστε . . . . ἐποιεῖτε ἄν (the reading, however, is doubtful, see p. 382, note [5]). These passages—with some others in which the present tense is less strongly supported, viz. Jo. xiv. 28, H. xi. 15 (where however μνημονεύουσιν has now the support of ℵ)—are carefully examined by A. Buttmann in an interesting paper in the *Studien und Kritiken*, 1858 (p. 474 sqq.). His view is, that the writer uses this form when he does not wish to imply an *absolute* denial of the truth of the hypothesis, whilst at the same time he does deny that the hypothesis is true *in the sense required by the apodosis.* Hence, in strictness, we

That in Rom. iv. 2, ἔχει καύχημα does not stand for εἶχεν ἄν κ., as was maintained by Rückert, will be easily perceived by any one who attends to Paul's reasoning: of recent commentators, Köllner has rightly opposed this view.

3. In relative clauses, after ὅς, ὅςτις, ὅσος, ὅπου, etc., ἄν is found

a. With the indicative, when some actual fact, and therefore something certain, is spoken of, " sed cujus vel pars aliqua, vel ratio et modus dubitationem admittunt " (Herm. *Vig.* p. 819):[1] Mk. vi. 56, ὅπου ἂν εἰςεπορεύετο, *where perchance he entered*, ubicunque intrabat (this might occur in different places and repeatedly) ὅσοι ἂν ἥπτοντο[2] αὐτοῦ, *so many of them as (at any time) touched him*: καθότι ἄν, A. ii. 45, iv. 35; ὡς ἄν, 1 C. xii. 2. In all these instances we have a (relative) preterite, as in Gen. ii. 19, xxx. 42, Is. lv. 11, 2 S. xiv. 26, Ez. i. 20, x. 11, Esth. viii. 17, 1 Macc. xiii. 20,—and also in Greek writers, as Lucian, *Dial. M.* 9. 2, *Demon.* 10, Demosth. I. *Steph.* p. 610 b (Agath. 32. 12, 117. 12, 287. 13, Malal. 14. 36). The *present* indicative—which Klotz (p. 109 sqq.), in opposition to Hermann, maintains to be inadmissible—is not even externally supported in L. viii. 18, x. 8, Jo. v. 19: in Mk. xi. 24 Lachmann has rightly restored from the MSS. the indicative without ἄν.[3] The present occurs frequently in the LXX, see Ps. ci. 3, Pr. i. 22, Lev. xxv. 16.

In Mt. xiv. 36 we have ὅσοι ἥψαντο, διεσώθησαν· in the place of ὅσοι ἂν ἥπτοντο, ἐσώζοντο· of the parallel passage, Mk. vi. 56. Both expressions are correct, according as the writer conceived the fact as in every respect definite or not. The former must be

---

have a condensation of two sentences into one, the hypothesis to which the apodosis really corresponds being suppressed. Thus in Jo. viii. 39: "if ye are, as ye say, Abraham's children (and in a natural sense ye certainly are), ye would (if ye were his children in the true sense of the word) do Abraham's works:" contrast with this ver. 42, where the truth of the hypothesis is at once denied. He quotes Aristoph. *Av.* 792 sqq. (compare 785) as another parallel instance. For a different example of the same combination of tenses see Jud. xiii. 23 *Al.*]

[1] Klotz p. 145: In his locis quum res ipsa, quæ facta esse dicatur, certa sit, pertinet illud, quod habet in se particula ἄν incerti, magis ad notionem relativam, sive pronomen, sive particula est. [Compare Jelf 827. c, 424. 3. β, Green, *Gr.* p. 164.]

[2] [The best texts now have ἥψαντο: in some of the passages of the LXX quoted in the next sentence, we have the aorist, not the imperfect.]

[3] [In Rev. xiv. 4 we should probably read ὅπου ἂν ὑπάγει. The reading of Pr. i. 22 is uncertain; Lev. xxv. 16 is inserted by mistake.]

SECT. XLII.] THE CONJUNCTION ἄν WITH THE THREE MOODS. 385

rendered, *all who* (as many as) *touched him*, of the persons who were surrounding him at that time (ver. 35). Mark's narration does not refer to any particular place (as is shown by ὅπου ἂν εἰσεπορεύετο); he says generally, *all who at any time touched him*. Compare Hermann, *Partic. ἄν* p. 26.

b. With the conjunctive, when the matter referred to is objectively possible, i.e., when something whose occurrence is regarded as only conditional is spoken of.

(*a*) The aorist conjunctive (the tense which occurs most frequently) is used of that which may possibly happen in the future, and corresponds to the Latin *futurum exactum*: Mt. x. 11, εἰς ἣν δ' ἂν πόλιν ἢ κώμην εἰϲέλθητε, *into what city ye may possibly have entered, in quamcunque urbem, si quam in urbem*; xxi. 22, ὅσα ἂν αἰτήσητε, *quæcunque petieritis*; xii. 32, Mk. ix. 18, xiv. 9, L. x. 35, A. ii. 39, iii. 22, 23, viii. 19, Rom. x. 13, xvi. 2,[1] Ja. iv. 4, 1 Jo. iv. 15, Rev. xiii. 15, al. For examples from Greek writers see Bornem. *Luc.* p. 65 (Jelf 829). From the LXX, compare Gen. xxi. 6, 12, xxii. 2, xxiv. 14, xxvi. 2, xxviii. 15, xliv. 9 sq., Ex. i. 22, ix. 19, x. 28, Lev. v. 3, 15, 17, xi. 32, xx. 6, 9, 15, 17 sq., Num. v. 10, vi. 2, Dt. xvii. 9, Is. xi. 11. In the place of the conjunctive we find the future indicative[2] in Dt. v. 27, Jer. xlix. 4, Jud. x. 18, xi. 24,—Malch. *Hist.* p. 238, Cinnam. I. 6 (Bonn ed.): see Matth. 528. Rem. 3 (Jelf 827 *a*).

(β) The present conjunctive is used of that which possibly might now occur, or which usually occurs, or which is to be represented as something continued: G. v. 17, ἵνα μή, ἃ ἂν θέλητε, ταῦτα ποιῆτε· (*what you may possibly desire*), Col. iii. 17, πᾶν ὅ τι ἂν ποιῆτε 1 Th. ii. 7,[3] ὡς ἂν τροφὸς θάλπῃ κ.τ.λ., L. ix. 57, Jo. ii. 5, v. 19, 1 C. xvi. 2, Ja. iii. 4,[4] Col. iii. 23. On the whole see Hermann, *Partic. ἄν* p. 113 sqq., *Vig.* p. 819. From the LXX, compare Gen. vi. 17, xi. 6, 1 S. xiv. 7, Lev. xv. 19, Ex. xxii. 9; this tense however is much less common than the aorist.

In 2 C. viii. 12 we find a combination of two constructions, εἰ ἡ προθυμία πρόκειται, καθὸ ἐὰν ἔχῃ, εὐπρόσδεκτος, οὐ καθὸ οὐκ ἔχει. The distinction is clear: the positive ἔχειν might be variously con-

---

[1] [In Rom. xvi. 2 the tense is the *present*.]
[2] [We have this construction in Mk. viii. 35, A. vii. 7, in the best texts.]
[3] [In the better reading, ὡς ἐὰν τρ. θάλπῃ, it seems probable that ἐάν is the conjunction (Vulg. *tamquam si foveat*).—The best attested reading in Mk. iv. 26, ὡς ἂ. βάλῃ. is very irregular.]
[4] [We should here read ὅπου βούλεται. In Gen. xi. 6, quoted below, we find the aorist, not the present.]

ceived in regard to degree (καθό), *according to what he may happen to have;* the negative οὐκ ἔχειν is single and altogether definite. Compare Lev. xxiv. 20, xxv. 16, xxvii. 12 ; xi. 34, πᾶν βρῶμα, ὃ ἔσθεται, εἰς ὃ ἂν ἐπέλθῃ ὕδωρ.

In Attic prose relatives joined with the conjunctive mood are usually accompanied by ἄν; there are however well-attested examples of the omission of this particle (Rost p. 669 sq.), and Hermann (*Partic.* ἄν p. 113) has pointed out the case in which this omission was necessary.[1] As regards the N. T., the reading of good MSS. in L. viii. 17 is οὐ γάρ ἐστι . . . . ἀπόκρυφον, ὃ οὐ γνωσθῇ (al. γνωσθήσεται) καὶ εἰς φανερὸν ἔλθῃ ;[2] this must be rendered *which may not become known and come to light.* The relative here refers to something which is conceived with perfect definiteness, not to *anything whatever, quodcunque.* On the other hand, in Ja. ii. 10, ὅστις ὅλον τὸν νόμον τηρήσῃ, πταίσῃ δὲ ἐν ἑνί, we might have expected ἄν; but it is not really required, as in the writer's conception the case is altogether definite, *qui (si quis) . . . . custodiverit.* So also in Mt. x. 33. In Mt. xviii. 4 Lachm. has restored the future.[3]

4. In indirect questions ἄν is joined with the optative (after a preterite or an historic present): L. i. 62, ἐνένευον τῷ πατρί, τὸ τί ἂν θέλοι καλεῖσθαι αὐτόν, *how he would perhaps wish to have him named* (it being supposed that he has a wish in this case,—τί θέλοι κ.τ.λ. would be, *how he wished to have him named*), A. v. 24, x. 17, xxi. 33 (see above, § 41. *b.* 4), L. vi. 11, διελάλουν πρὸς ἀλλήλους, τί ἂν ποιήσειαν τῷ Ἰησοῦ, *what they might possibly do with Jesus, quid forte faciendum videretur* (discussing the various possibilities in a doubting mood), ix. 46.

---

[1] Compare Schæf. *Demosth.* I. 657, Poppo, *Observ.* p. 143 sqq., *Jen. Lit.-Zeit.* 1816, April, No. 69, and *ad Cyrop.* pp. 129, 209 ; on the other side, Bäumlein p. 212 sqq. [See also Green, *Gr.* p. 163 sq. A. Buttmann holds that, as the N. T. writers omit ἄν only after the compound relatives (including πᾶς ὅς), not after the simple ὅς, the particle was omitted because it seemed superfluous with pronouns whose meaning was already general.—But there are very few (if any) well-attested examples of the omission, besides Ja. ii. 10, Mt. x. 33.]

[2] [When this passage was quoted in § 41. 4, two readings were mentioned, οὐ γνωσθήσεται (Griesb., Meyer, De W., Tisch. ed. 7) and οὐ μὴ γνωσθῇ (Lachm., Treg., Tisch. ed. 8, Alford, Westcott and Hort). It does not appear that any editor reads οὐ γνωσθῇ, or indeed that any MS. has this reading, except L,—in which however μή is written over the line. If we read γνωσθήσεται, the above explanation will apply to ἔλθῃ ; with the other reading we have the ordinary construction of οὐ μή.]

[3] [The use of relative sentences to express *purpose* or *destination* must not be left unnoticed. In this sense the relative is usually followed by the future indicative in Greek prose (Madvig 115 a, Krüg. p. 180) ; in Epic poetry we find the subjunctive, which also occurs occasionally in prose (Thuc. 7. 25. 1), see Jelf 836. 4. In the N. T. see A. xxi. 16, H. viii. 3 (subj.), Mt. xxi. 41, L. vii. 4 (future). See A. Buttm. p. 229, Green p. 177.]

SECT. XLII.] THE CONJUNCTION ἄν WITH THE THREE MOODS. 387

Similarly Jo. xiii. 24, with the reading νεύει τούτῳ Σίμων Π. πυθέσθαι τίς ἂν εἴη περὶ οὗ λέγει (*who he might be,* whom they should possibly suppose him to be); but the better reading is νεύει .... καὶ λέγει αὐτῷ· εἰπὲ τίς ἐστιν περὶ οὗ λέγει. See Klotz p. 509: compare Esth. iii. 13. (Jelf 425, 879.)

5. The particles of time are followed by the conjunctive with ἄν (Matth. 521), when the reference is to an (objectively possible) action, a case which may or will occur, but in regard to which there is no certainty *when* (how often) it will occur (Hermann, *Partic.* ἄν p. 95 sqq., Don. p. 581, Jelf 842).

a. ὅταν (i.e., ὅτ' ἄν): Mt. xv. 2, νίπτονται τὰς χεῖρας, ὅταν ἄρτον ἐσθίωσιν, *when* (i.e., *as often as*) *they eat,* Jo. viii. 44, 1 C. iii. 4, L. xi. 36; xvii. 10, ὅταν ποιήσητε πάντα, λέγετε, *when ye shall have done,* Mt. xxi. 40, ὅταν ἔλθῃ ὁ κύριος .... τί ποιήσει, *quando venerit.* So usually with the aorist conjunctive for the Latin *futurum exactum,* Mk. viii. 38, Jo. iv. 25, xvi. 13, Rom. xi. 27, A. xxiii. 35, 1 C. xv. 27,[1] xvi. 3, 1 Jo. ii. 28; and also H. i. 6 (as was pointed out by Böhme and Wahl). The present conjunctive, on the other hand, usually indicates an action of frequent recurrence, not limited to any particular time (Matth. 521), or else represents something which in itself is future simply as an event (1 C. xv. 24,[2] where it stands by the side of the aorist conjunctive).

Similar to this are ἡνίκα ἄν, 2 C. iii. 16 (*when it shall have turned*); ὁσάκις ἄν (*as often as*), 1 C. xi. 25, 26 (with the present); ὡς ἄν, *as soon as,* Rom. xv. 24, 1 C. xi. 34, Ph. ii. 23.[3]

b. The conjunctions which answer to *until*: ἕως ἄν,[4] Mt. x. 11, ἐκεῖ μείνατε, ἕως ἂν ἐξέλθητε· Ja. v. 7, L. ix. 27; ἄχρις οὗ ἄν, Rev. ii. 25 (Gen. xxiv. 14, 19, Jos. ii. 16, xx. 6, 9, Ex.

---

[1] [On this passage ("When God shall have declared that all things have been subjected to him") see Alford's note. In 1 Jo. ii. 28 we must read ἐάν.]
[2] [The received text has the aorist, but there is no doubt that we must read παραδιδῷ or -διδοῖ (on the latter form, found with ὅταν in Mk. iv. 29 also, see above, p. 360, note²): ὅταν indicates "the uncertainty of the time when" (Alford *in loc.*).]
[3] [In this purely temporal sense ὡς ἄν is at least very rare in Attic prose; see Klotz, *Devar.* p. 759, A. Buttm. p. 232, Ellicott on Ph. 2. 23. To the conjunctions mentioned above add ἀφ' οὗ ἄν L. xiii. 25, and ἐπάν Mt. ii. 8, L. xi. 22, 34.]
[4] In Ex. xv. 16, Jer. xxiii. 20, according to the usual text, we find ἕως ἄν and ἕως with the conjunctive in parallel clauses. [In Ja. v. 7, quoted in the next line, ἄν is probably not genuine.]

xv. 16, Is. vi. 11, xxvi. 20, xxx. 17, Tob. vii. 11, and often). Compare Soph. *Œd. R.* 834, Xen. *Cyr.* 3. 3. 18, 46, *An.* 5. 1. 11, Plat. *Phœd.* 59 e, al.; this is the usual construction in Attic prose (Rost p. 623, Don. p. 581 sq., Jelf 846). Compare also § 41. *b.* 3. 2. (*b*).—Πρὶν ἄν does not occur in the N. T.[1]

In Rev. iv. 9, ὅταν δώσουσι τὰ ζῷα δόξαν . . . . πεσοῦνται οἱ εἴκοσι τέσσαρες κ.τ.λ. (the correct reading), ὅταν is joined with the future instead of the conjunctive, *quando dederint*,—as in *Iliad.* 20. 335, ἀλλ᾽ ἀναχωρῆσαι, ὅτε κεν ξυμβλήσεαι αὐτῷ: other MSS. have δῶσι or δώσωσι.[2] In L. xi. 2, xiii. 28, Mt. x. 19, there is preponderant authority for the conjunctive. The use of the indic. *present* with ὅταν in Rom. ii. 14, ὅταν ποιεῖ (which should rather be regarded as a mistake of transcription for ποιῇ) is very doubtful: we should read ποιῶσιν with Lachm. and Tischendorf. In Mk. xi. 25, however, ὅταν στήκετε is supported by good MSS., and—as the words are designed to express merely an external definition of time,[3] *cum statis precantes*—the indicative (according to Klotz, *Devar.* p. 475 sq.) is just as admissible as in Lycurg. 28. 3 it is well attested by MS. authority.[4] In this case the present and future indicative are sometimes found with ὅταν even in earlier writers (see Klotz *l. c.*, and p. 477 sq., 690 [5]), where it was formerly considered inadmissible:[6] in later writers it occurs more frequently,[7] compare e.g., Ex. i. 16, *Act. Apocr.* 126.

More singular is the construction of ὅταν in narration with an indicative preterite (imperfect): Mk. iii. 11, τὰ πνεύματα . . . . ὅταν αὐτὸν ἐθεώρει, προσέπιπτεν (without any variant), *when at any time* (quandocunque) *they saw him.* Here Greek writers would probably have used (ὅτε or ὁπόταν with) the optative, see Herm. *Vig.* p. 792;[8] but it is as easy to explain the indic. here as in ὅσοι ἄν ἥπτοντο (see above, 3. *a*). Compare Gen. xxxviii. 9, Ex. xvii.

---

[1] [Πρὶν ἄν ἴδῃ is received by Treg., Westcott (and Tisch. *Syn. Ev.*) in L. ii. 26: here it follows a negative clause, as usual (Don. p. 583, Jelf 848. 4). In ed. 8 Tisch. reads πρὶν ἢ ἄν ἴδῃ. See above, p. 371.]

[2] [On 1 Tim. v. 11, where Tisch. (ed. 7) and Alford read the future with ὅταν, see Ellicott's note. He remarks that "the only correct principle of explaining these usages of ἐάν and ὅταν with the indicative" is "the restriction of the whole conditional force to the particle, and the absence of necessary internal connexion between the verb in the protasis and that in the apodosis."]

[3] [Not an *internal* relation of cause or condition.]

[4] Bekker conjectures ὦσι, others read ὅτ᾽ ἂν, and Blume even says, "indicativus per grammaticas leges h. l. ferri nequit." [The reading in question is ὅταν . . . εἰσί.—In ed. 7 Tisch. received ὅταν with the present indicative in Mk. xi. 25, xiii. 4, 7, L. xi. 2; but in all these passages, except the first, he now reads the subjunctive.]

[5] Most of the examples quoted by Gayler, *De Partic. Negat.* p. 193 sq., are probably doubtful.

[6] Jacobs, *Anthol. Palat.* III. 61, *Achill. Tat.* 452, Matth. 521. note.

[7] Jacobs in *Act. Monac.* I. 146, Schæf. *Ind. Æsop.* 149.

[8] Fritzsche (*Mark* p. 801) prefers to write ὅτ᾽ ἄν, in order to show that in this case ἄν belongs to the verb, in the sense of *at any time:* compare Schæf.

SECT. XLII.] THE CONJUNCTION ἄν WITH THE THREE MOODS. 389

11, Num. xi. 9, 1 Sam. xvii. 34, Ps. cxix. 7, Thiersch, *Pent.* p. 100 (so with ἡνίκα ἄν Gen. xxx. 42, Ex. xxxiii. 8, xxxiv. 34, xl. 36, ὁπότε ἐάν Tob. vii. 11, ἐάν Jud. vi. 3,—where also a frequently repeated action of past time is referred to); also Polyb. 4. 32. 5, 13. 7. 10 (see Schweigh. on the latter passage), Aristid. *Lept.* § 3. 6 : compare Poppo, *Thuc.* III. i. 313.[1] In the Byzantine writers ὅταν is joined with the aorist indicative even when it signifies *when* (in reference to a single event of past time), Ephraem. 7119, 5386, 5732, Theophan. pp. 499, 503. Compare also Tischendorf in the *Verhandel.* p. 142.[2]

When the final particle ὅπως is joined with ἄν, it indicates a purpose the possibility of attaining which is still doubtful, or the attainment of which is viewed as depending upon circumstances, *ut sit, si sit*,[3]—*ut, si fieri possit, ut forte.*[4] See Isocr. *Ep.* 8. p. 1016, Xen. *Cyr.* 5. 2. 21, Plat. *Gorg.* 481 a, *Conv.* 187 e, *Legg.* 5. 738 d, al., Demosth. *Halon.* 32 c; also Stallbaum, Plat. *Lach.* p. 24, Krüg. p. 192.[5] In the N. T. we have only two examples of this construction (for A. xv. 17 and Rom. iii. 4 are quotations from the O. T., and in Mt. vi. 5 ἄν has been removed from the text in accordance with many authorities), but the explanation just given is applicable to these : A. iii. 19, ὅπως ἂν ἔλθωσιν καιροὶ ἀναψύξεως, *ut forte* (si meæ admonitioni μετανοήσατε καὶ ἐπιτρέψατε parueritis) *veniant tempora* etc.; L. ii. 35. So also in the two quotations from the LXX, especially in A. xv. 17, the meaning is clear. Compare further Gen. xii. 13, xviii. 19, 1. 20, Ex. xx. 20, 26, xxxiii. 13, Num. xv. 40, xvi. 40, xxvii. 20, Dt. viii. 2, xvii. 20, 2 S. xvii. 14, Ps. lix. 7, Hos. ii. 3, Jer. xlii. 7, Dan. ii. 18, 1 Macc. x. 32.

In the N. T. ἄν is never found with the optative after conjunctions and relatives; in the LXX however see Gen. xix. 8

Dem. III. 192. See however Klotz, *Devar.* p. 688 sq. [Compare Jelf 424. 3. β, 841. *Obs.* 2.]

[1] The LXX use even ὡς ἄν with a preterite indicative, when speaking of a single definite past action; e. g., Gen. vi. 4, xxvii. 30, ὡς ἂν ἐξῆλθεν Ἰακώβ κ.τ.λ.

[2] [There are in the N. T. two well-attested examples of ὅταν with the aorist indicative : Mk. xi. 19, ὅταν ὀψὲ ἐγίνετο (probably meaning, *whenever evening came*), Rev. viii. 1, ὅταν ἤνοιξε. In modern Greek ὅταν is freely used with the indicative, see Mullach, *Vulg.* p. 368.]

[3] See Herm. Eur. *Bacch.* 593, 1232, *Partic.* ἄν p. 120 sq.

[4] Compare Bengel on A. iii. 19, Rom. iii. 4.

[5] [So Don. p. 600 : "When the final sentence expresses an *eventual* conclusion, i. e. one in which an additional hypothesis is virtually contained, we may subjoin ἄν to ὡς or ὅπως; thus Soph. *Electr.* 1495 sq., 'in order that you may, *as by going there you will*, etc.'" Compare Jelf 810, Green p. 169.]

(but compare xvi. 6), xxxiii. 10, 2 Macc. xv. 21. With the infinitive it occurs once, in 2 C. x. 9, ἵνα μὴ δόξω ὡ ς ἂ ν ἐ κ φ ο β ε ῖ ν ὑμᾶς, *that I may not appear perchance to terrify you.* In the *oratio recta* (Hermann, *Partic.* ἄν p. 179, Krüg. p. 348, Jelf 429) this would be ὡς ἂν ἐκφοβοῖμι ὑμᾶς, tamquam qui velim vos terrere.[1]

After relatives we frequently find ἐάν in the place of ἄν in the N. T. text (as in the LXX and Apocrypha,[2] and occasionally in the Byzantine writers, e. g., Malalas 5. pp. 94, 144), according to the best and most numerous authorities: see Mt. v. 19 (not vii. 9), viii. 19, x. 42, xi. 27, Jo. xv. 7, L. xvii. 33, 1 C. vi. 18, xvi. 3, G. vi. 7, E. vi. 8, al.[3] This is not uncommon in the MSS. of Greek writers, even the Attic: recent philologers,[4] however, uniformly substitute ἄν.[5] This the N. T. editors have not yet ventured to do, and the use of ἐάν for ἄν may have been really a peculiarity of the later (if not indeed of the earlier) popular language.[6] Compare L. x. 8.

SECTION XLIII.

THE IMPERATIVE MOOD.

1. The imperative mood regularly expresses a summons or command, sometimes however merely a permission (*imperativus permissivus*), a consent or acquiescence[7] (Krüg. p. 188, Jelf 420): 1 C. vii. 15, εἰ ὁ ἄπιστος χωρίζεται, χωριζέσθω, *he may separate himself* (there can and should be no hindrance on the part of the Christian spouse); xiv. 38 [*Rec.*], εἴ τις ἀγνοεῖ, ἀγνοείτω (the hope of further successful instruction is renounced). Whether this or the ordinary meaning should be assigned to the imperative in any particular passage, must be decided not by grammatical but

---

[1] [It seems much simpler to suppose that ὡς and ἄν here coalesce, with the meaning *quasi*: so Meyer, Alford, Green (see the note quoted above, p. 380), A. Buttmann (p. 219). Green quotes Polyb. *Hist.* I. 46, Philo, *Mundi Opif.* I. 13: ὡσάν is thus used in modern Greek. On the classical ὡσπεραυεί see Jelf 430. 1; and on κἄν, as used in Mk. vi. 56, al., § 64. I. 1.]

[2] See Wahl, *Clav. Apocryph.* p. 137 sq., Thilo, *Act. Thom.* p. 8.

[3] [The reading is rather doubtful in some of these examples. See Alford vol. I. *Proleg.* p. 98 (ed. 6), Ellic. on E. vi. 8, A. Buttm. p. 63, Green p. 164 (Jelf 423).]

[4] In opposition to Schneider, Xen. *Mem.* 3. 10. 12.

[5] See Schæfer, *Julian,* p. v, Herm. *Vig.* p. 835, Bremi, *Lys.* p. 126, Boissonade, *Æn. Gaz.* p. 269, Stallb. Plat. *Lach.* p. 57. A more moderate opinion is expressed by Jacobs, *Athen.* p. 88; yet see his note in *Lection. Stob.* p. 45, and *Achill. Tat.* p. 831 sq. Compare also Valckenaer on 1 C. vi. 18.

[6] Almost like our *etwan* in relative sentences, *was etwan geschehen sollte* (wann etwas geschieht, was es sein sollte).

[7] According to Moller (Schneidewin, *Philolog.* VI. 124 sqq.) the *present* imperative only should be used. We have the present, it is true, in the N. T. passages which are quoted above, but we cannot regard this as settling the question for the N. T.

SECT. XLIII.] THE IMPERATIVE MOOD. 391

by hermeneutical considerations ; and these will not allow us to make the imperative permissive either in Mt. viii. 32 (on the ground that *sufferance* is expressed in the parallel passage, L. viii. 32), or in Jo. xiii. 27, 1 C. xi. 6. On Jo. xiii. 27 see Baumgarten-Crusius : [1] in 1 C. xi. 6, κειράσθω as well as κατακαλυπτέσθω must be taken as implying logical necessity,—one thing necessarily supposes the other. On the other hand, in Mt. xxvi. 45, καθεύδετε τὸ λοιπὸν καὶ ἀναπαύεσθε, Jesus,—his spirit peaceful, mild, and resigned, through the influence of his prayer, —probably speaks permissively, *sleep on then further and rest.* Irony at this moment of solemn feeling is not to be thought of. In Mt. xxiii. 32, however, there probably is irony in the words : if they are taken as permissive, the tone of the discourse loses in force. In Rev. xxii. 11 the whole is a challenge : let every man, by continuing in the course which he has followed hitherto, ripen against the approaching judgment of Christ: the fate of all is as if already determined.

2. When two imperatives are connected by καί, the first sometimes contains the condition (supposition) upon which the action indicated by the second will take place, or the second expresses a result which will certainly ensue (Matth. 511. 5. c) :[2] e. g., Bar. ii. 21, κλίνατε τὸν ὦμον ὑμῶν ἐργάσασθαι τῷ βασιλεῖ ... καὶ καθίσατε ἐπὶ τὴν γῆν· Epiphan. II. 368, ἔχε τοὺς τοῦ θεοῦ λόγους κατὰ ψυχήν σου καὶ χρείαν μὴ ἔχε Ἐπιφανίου. In the N. T. this explanation has been applied to E. iv. 26 (from Ps. iv. 5), ὀργίζεσθε καὶ μὴ ἁμαρτάνετε, *be angry and sin not,* i. e., if ye are angry, do not sin, do not fall into sin (Rückert) ; and to Jo. vii. 52, ἐρεύνησον καὶ ἴδε, *search and thou wilt see* (Kühnöl) : compare *divide et impera.* This is certainly very common in Hebrew; see Ewald, *Krit. Gr.* p. 653. But in Jo. vii.

---

[1] [See Alford *in loc.* ; and on Mt. xxvi. 45, Ellicott, *Hist. L.* p. 330.]
[2] The examples which Bornemann (on L. xxiv. 39) quotes from Greek authors are of a different kind. Still this mode of expression cannot be regarded as a real Hebraism, see Gesen. *Lehrg.* p. 776,—where however some passages are quoted which are doubtful (as Ps. xxxvii. 27), or which should at all events have been separated from the rest (Gen. xlii. 18, Is. viii. 9). These passages have no analogy to E. iv. 26 (see below) ; for Paul's words, if interpreted by them, could only mean, *if ye are angry, ye do not sin,* or even, *if ye would not sin, then be angry.* It is surprising therefore that, notwithstanding this, Zyro (*Stud. u. Krit.* 1841, 3. Heft, p. 685) has again had recourse to this so-called Hebraism. [On the Hebrew idiom see Gesen. *Hebr. Gr.* p. 212 (Bagster) Kalisch, *Hebr. Gr.* I. 300.]

the expression is more forcible than καὶ ὄψει (Lucian, *Indoct.* 29) would have been: the result of the search is so certain, that a challenge to *search* is at the same time a challenge to *see*. In L. x. 28 we have the regular construction. In E. iv. 26, Paul's meaning undoubtedly is, that when we are angry we must not fall into sin,—compare ver. 27 (see Bengel and Baumg.-Crus. *in loc.*); and ver. 31 cannot be urged against this. It is only the grammatical estimate of the expression that is doubtful. Either we have a single logical sentence, ὀργιζόμενοι μὴ ἁμαρτάνετε, split up into two grammatical sentences, or else ὀργίζεσθε must be taken as permissive (compare the similar passage Jer. x. 24). For Meyer's assertion that, when two imperatives are closely connected, we cannot take one as permissive and the other as jussive, is incorrect: we have no difficulty in saying, *Now go* (I give you leave), *but do not stay out above an hour!* [1]

In 1 Tim. vi. 12 the words ἀγωνίζου τὸν καλὸν ἀγῶνα τῆς πίστεως, ἐπιλαβοῦ τῆς αἰωνίου ζωῆς (where the asyndeton is not without force) must be simply translated, *strive the good strife of faith, lay hold* (in and through the strife) *of eternal life:* compare Mk. iv. 39 and Fritzsche *in loc.* Here the ἐπιλαμβ. τῆς ζωῆς is not represented (as it might have been) as the result of the contest, but as itself the substance of the striving; and ἐπιλαμβ. does not signify *attain, receive*. In 1 C. xv. 34, ἐκνήψατε δικαίως καὶ μὴ ἁμαρτάνετε, we obviously have a twofold summons; that expressed by the aorist is to be carried into effect at once without delay, the other (expressed by the present) requires continued effort.

Such constructions as Jo. ii. 19, λύσατε τὸν ναὸν τοῦτον, καὶ ἐν τρισὶν ἡμέραις ἐγερῶ αὐτόν· Ja. iv. 7, ἀντίστητε τῷ διαβόλῳ, καὶ φεύξεται ἀφ' ὑμῶν (ver. 8), E. v. 14 (from the LXX [2]), ἀνάστα ἐκ τῶν νεκρῶν, καὶ ἐπιφαύσει σοι ὁ Χριστός· may certainly be resolved in the same way as two imperatives connected by καί,—*if ye resist the devil, he will* etc. This however needs no remark from the grammarian, as the imperative is here used altogether in its usual sense (as a summons); and the conformation of these sentences may

---

[1] [Meyer makes this assertion in reference to two imperatives which are *connected by καί*: in Winer's example and in Jer. x. 24 the conjunction is *but* not *and*. "The following interpretation seems the most simple: both imperatives are *jussive*; as however the second imperative is used with μή, its jussive force is thereby enhanced, while the affirmative command is by juxta-position so much obscured, as to be *in effect* little more than a participial member, though its intrinsic jussive force is not to be denied:" Ellicott *in loc.* Similarly Meyer, Alford, Eadie.]

[2] ["From the LXX" is out of place here, as the *words* do not occur in the LXX, and in Is. lx. 1 the construction is different. On this use of the imperative as the protasis to a future see Don. p. 549, Jelf 420. *Obs.* 2.]

—nay *must*, as being incomparably more forcible,—be retained in our own language. Comp. Lucian, *Indoct.* 29, τοὺς κουρέας τούτους ἐπίσκεψαι καὶ ὄψει· *Dial. D.* 2. 2, εὔρυθμα βαῖνε καὶ ὄψει· Plat. *Theæt.* 149 b, *Rep.* 5. 467 c, and see Fritzsche, *Matt.* p. 187. To consider the imperatives in Jo. ii. 19 and xx. 22 simple substitutes for the future, as even recent commentators have done (appealing to the Hebrew of such passages as Gen. xx. 7, xlv. 18), is preposterous.[1] Inasmuch as every command belongs to future time, the future tense, as the general expression of futurity, may sometimes take the place of the imperative (see below, no. 5); but the special form of the imperative cannot be used *vice versâ* in the place of the more general (the future). This would throw language into confusion; indeed the above canon, like so many others, had its origin in the study of the scholar, not in observation of language as actually used by men. Olshausen has rightly declared himself against Tholuck (and Kühnöl) on Jo. xx. 22, and Tholuck has now corrected his error. In L. xxi. 19 the future is the better reading, see Meyer *in loc.*[2]

3. The distinction between the aorist and present imperative[3] is in general observed by the N. T. writers, as may easily be perceived. For

a. The aorist imperative (compare § 40. Rem. 2) is used in reference either to an action which rapidly passes and should take place at once,[4] or at any rate to an action which is to be undertaken once only: Mk. i. 44, σεαυτὸν δεῖξον τῷ ἱερεῖ· iii. 5, ἔκτεινον τὴν χεῖρά σου· vi. 11, ἐκτινάξατε τὸν χοῦν· Jo. ii. 7, γεμίσατε τὰς ὑδρίας ὕδατος κ.τ.λ., xi. 44, λύσατε αὐτὸν (Λάζαρον) καὶ ἄφετε αὐτὸν ὑπάγειν· 1 C. v. 13, ἐξάρατε τὸν πονηρὸν ἐξ ὑμῶν αὐτῶν· A. xxiii. 23, ἑτοιμάσατε στρατιώτας διακοσίους, *have immediately . . . . in readiness to march.* See also Mk. ix. 22, 43, x. 21, xiii. 28, xiv. 15, 44, xv. 30, L. xx. 24, Jo. ii. 8, iv. 35, vi. 10, xi. 39, xiii. 29, xviii. 11, xxi. 6, A. iii. 4, vii. 33, ix. 11, xvi. 9, xxi. 39, xxii. 13, 1 C. xvi. 1, E. vi. 13, 17, Col. iii. 5, Tit. iii. 13, Phil. 17, Ja. iii. 13, iv. 8, 9, 1 P. iv. 1, 2 P. i. 5, 10. Where the reference is to something which is to be carried out at once, νῦν or νυνί is sometimes joined to the aorist imperative,

---

[1] Glass. *Philol. Sacr.* I. 286.
[2] [Tisch. has now (ed. 8) returned to κτήσασθε, following ℵ.]
[3] Hermann, *Emend. Rat.* p. 219, *Vig.* p. 748 : comp. H. Schmidt, *De Imperativi temporibus in lingua Græca* (Wittenberg 1833), and especially Bäumlein, *Gr. Modi* p. 169 sqq. In reference to the latter, see Moller in Schneidewin, *Philologus* VI. 115 sqq. (Don. p. 413, Jelf 405. 1).
[4] Ast, Plat. *Polit.* p. 518, Schæf. *Demosth.* IV. 488.

as in A. x. 5, xxiii. 15, 2 C. viii. 11. Also where the injunction is strengthened by δή the aorist imperative is employed; see A. xiii. 2, 1 C. vi. 20, Judith v. 3, vii. 9, Bar. iii. 4 (Xen. *Cyr.* 1. 3. 9, Soph. *El.* 524, Klotz, *Devar.* p. 395).

b. The present imperative is used in reference to an action which is already commenced and is to be continued,[1] or which is lasting and frequently repeated. Hence it is commonly employed in the measured and unimpassioned language of laws and moral precepts: e.g., Rom. xi. 20, μὴ ὑψηλοφρόνει (a thing which thou art now doing), xii. 20, ἐὰν πεινᾷ ὁ ἐχθρός σου, ψώμιζε αὐτόν (do this always in such a case), xiii. 3, θέλεις μὴ φοβεῖσθαι τὴν ἐξουσίαν; τὸ ἀγαθὸν ποίει· Ja. ii. 12, οὕτω λαλεῖτε καὶ οὕτω ποιεῖτε, ὡς διὰ νόμου ἐλευθερίας κ.τ.λ., 1 Tim. iv. 7, τοὺς βεβήλους καὶ γραώδεις μύθους παραιτοῦ. Compare Ja. iv. 11, v. 12, 1 Tim. iv. 11, 13, v. 7, 19, vi. 11, 2 Tim. ii. 1, 8, 14, Tit. i. 13, iii. 1, 1 C. ix. 24, x. 14, 25, xvi. 13, Ph. ii. 12, iv. 3, 9, E. ii. 11, iv. 25, 26, 28, vi. 4, Jo. i. 44, xxi. 16, Mk. viii. 15, ix. 7, 39, xiii. 11, xiv. 38. Hence the present imperative is in ordinary conversation a milder and less confident form, and frequently expresses no more than advice (Moller *l. c.* p. 123 sq.).

The present and aorist imperative are sometimes found in combination, each preserving its own meaning: e.g., Jo. ii. 16, ἄρατε ταῦτα ἐντεῦθεν, μὴ ποιεῖτε τὸν οἶκον τοῦ πατρός μου οἶκον ἐμπορίου· 1 C. xv. 34, ἐκνήψατε δικαίως καὶ μὴ ἁμαρτάνετε· A. xii. 8, περιβαλοῦ τὸ ἱμάτιόν σου καὶ ἀκολούθει μοι· Rom. vi. 13, μηδὲ παριστάνετε τὰ μέλη ὑμῶν ὅπλα ἀδικίας τῇ ἁμαρτίᾳ, ἀλλὰ παραστήσατε ἑαυτοὺς τῷ θεῷ ὡς ἐκ νεκρῶν ζῶντας· Mk. ii. 9, Jo. v. 8, 11, ii. 8. Compare Plat. *Rep.* 9. 572 d, θὲς τοίνυν πάλιν .... νέον υἱὸν ἐν τοῖς τούτου αὖ ἤθεσι τεθραμμένον. Τίθημι. Τίθει τοίνυν καὶ τὰ αὐτὰ ἐκεῖνα περὶ αὐτὸν γιγνόμενα (Matth. 501); Xen. *Cyr.* 4. 5. 41, Demosth. *Aphob.* 2. p. 557 c, 588 a, Eurip. *Hippol.* 475 sq., *Heracl.* 635.

4. Here and there this distinction may seem to be disregarded (1 P. ii. 17[2]), and in particular the *aorist* imperative may seem to be used where in strictness the *present* was required

---

[1] Poppo, *Thuc.* III. ii. 742.
[2] ["Give honour to all men,—to each man according as the case which requires it arises; q. d., in every case render promptly every man's due:" Alford *in loc.*]

SECT. XLIII.]   THE IMPERATIVE MOOD.   395

(Bernh. p. 393, Jelf 405). We must remember, however, that in many cases it depends entirely on the writer's preference whether or not he shall represent the action as falling in a single point of time and momentary,—whether simply as commencing, or also as continuing. Nor must we overlook the fact that, in general, the aorist imperative is considered more forcible and urgent than the present (see no. 3), and that the strengthening of expressions is to a great extent of a subjective nature.[1] The following passages must be estimated according to these principles: μείνατε ἐν ἐμοί Jo. xv. 4, al. (compare μένετε L. ix. 4, 1 Jo. ii. 28, μένε 2 Tim. iii. 14, μενέτω 1 C. vii. 24, al.); 1 Jo. v. 21, φυλάξατε ἑαυτοὺς ἀπὸ τῶν εἰδώλων (similarly in 1 Tim. vi. 20, 2 Tim. i. 14,—contrast 2 P. iii. 17, 2 Tim. iv. 15); H. iii. 1, κατανοήσατε τὸν ἀπόστολον καὶ ἀρχιερέα τῆς ὁμολογίας ἡμῶν· Mk. xvi. 15, πορευθέντες εἰς τὸν κόσμον ἅπαντα κηρύξατε τὸ εὐαγγέλιον· Jo. xiv. 15, τὰς ἐντολὰς τὰς ἐμὰς τηρήσατε· Ja. v. 7, μακροθυμήσατε ἕως τῆς παρουσίας τοῦ κυρίου.   Compare Mt. xxviii. 19, 2 Tim. i. 8, ii. 3, iv. 2, 1 P. i. 13, ii. 2, v. 2. In all these instances it will be found that the aorist imperative is quite in place. In Rom. xv. 11 (from the LXX) and Jo. vii. 24 we even find the present and aorist imperative of the same verb thus combined.[2] In several places the reading is uncertain (A. xvi. 15, Rom. xvi. 17), as indeed in the MSS. of Greek authors these two forms are often interchanged (Elmsley, Eurip. *Med.* 99, 222), especially where they differ by a single letter only. Lastly, there are cases in which one of the two imperatives has gone out of use (thus we always find λάβε, never λάμβανε), or else one of the two forms predominates, as in the N. T. φέρε as compared with ἔνεγκε. See Bäumlein, *Modi* p. 172.

On the (present) imperative after μή see § 56. 1.

The perfect imperative is used when an action, completed in itself, is to endure in its effects; e.g., Mk. iv. 39, in Christ's address to the

---

[1] Compare Schoem. *Isæus* p. 235. In opposition to Schæf. *Demosth.* III. 185, Schoemann remarks: tenuissimum discrimen esse apparet, ut sæpenumero pro lubitu aut affectu loquentis variari oratio possit. Nam quid mirum, qui modo lenius jusserat: σκοπεῖτε (Demosth. *Lept.* 483), eundem statim cum majore quadam vi et quasi intentius flagitantem addere: λογίσασθε. Et plerumque, si non semper, apud pedestres quidem scriptores, in tali diversorum temporum conjunctione, præs. imperativus antecedit, sequitur aoristus. [The last remark is not always applicable to the N. T. (Ellicott on 1 Tim. vi. 12).]

[2] [This is the case in Rom. vi. 13, quoted above. The reading in Jo. vii. 24 (and also in Jo. xiv. 15, quoted above) is uncertain.]

troubled sea, πεφίμωσο, *be* (and remain) *stilled.* Compare also ἔρ-ρωσο, ἔρρωσθε, A. xxiii. 30 [*Rec.*], xv. 29. See Herm. *Emend. Rat.* p. 218, Matth. 500, Bäuml. p. 174 (Jelf 420. 2). Compare Xen. *Mem.* 4. 2. 19, Thuc. 1. 71, Plat. *Euthyd.* 278 d, *Rep.* 8. 553 a.

5. There are other modes of expression which sometimes fill the place of the imperative :—

a. The originally elliptical phrase, (*I command*) *that*—or (*see*) *that—you linger not!* expressed in Greek by ὅπως with the future indicative (see Madvig 123, Don. p. 602, Jelf 812. 2), as ὅπως ἐπέξει τῷ μιαρῷ Dem. *Mid.* 414 c, Eurip. *Cycl.* 595, Aristoph. *Nub.* 823,—more rarely with the conjunctive (Xen. *Cyr.* 1. 3. 18, Lucian, *Dial. D.* 20. 2). In the N. T. the (weakened—see § 44. 8) ἵνα with the conjunctive is thus used in Mk. v. 23, ἵνα ἐλθὼν ἐπιθῇς τὰς χεῖρας αὐτῇ· 2 C. viii. 7 (but not 1 C. v. 2, 1 Tim. i. 3); and in the 3rd person, E. v. 33, ἡ γυνὴ ἵνα φοβῆται τὸν ἄνδρα (an imperative precedes). In the Greek poets, however, we find ἵνα itself in this construction : see Soph. *Œd. C.* 155.[1] At a later period it appears in prose, as Epict. 23, ἂν πτωχὸν ὑποκρίνεσθαί σε θέλῃ (ὁ διδάσκαλος), ἵνα καὶ τοῦτον ἐκφυῶν ὑποκρίνῃ· Arrian, *Epict.* 4. 1. 41; in the Byzantine writers, indeed, it is even found with the present indicative (Malal. 13. p. 334, 16. p. 404). In Latin, compare Cic. *Fam.* 14. 20, ibi ut sint omnia parata.

b. A negative question with the future (Herm. *Vig.* p. 740, Rost. p. 690), *will you not come at once?* Aristoph. *Nub.* 1296, οὐκ ἀποδιώξεις σεαυτὸν ἀπὸ τῆς οἰκίας; Xen. *Cyr.* 2. 3. 22. Compare A. xiii. 10, οὐ παύσῃ διαστρέφων τὰς ὁδοὺς κυρίου; 4 Macc. v. 10, οὐκ ἐξυπνώσεις; This construction however is for the most part harsher than the imperative. (Don. p. 550, Jelf 413. 2.)

c. The future, in categorical sentences (especially in the negative form[2]), *thou wilt not touch it!* Mt. vi. 5, οὐκ ἔσῃ ὡς οἱ ὑποκριταί· v. 48 (Lev. xi. 44). In Greek this mode of ex-

---

[1] [If this is an example of this construction, it is a solitary example of classical Greek. The Schol. takes ἵνα μή as imperatival: so also Hartung, *Part.* II. 140. On the other hand Schneidewin, Reisig, Ellendt (*Lex. Soph.* s. v. ἵνα), Wunder, al., give the usual meaning *lest,* connecting the clause with one of the following verbs (φύλαξαι, μιτάσταθ'): the best lexicons and grammars exclude the imperatival ἵνα μή from classical Greek.]

[2] [As in Hebrew a prohibition is *always* expressed by the future : Kalisch, *Heb. Gr.* I. 284, Gesen. *Heb. Gr.* p. 208 (Bagst.).]

pression was considered milder than the imperative.¹ In Hebrew, however, it has established itself in the decisive language of legislation,² and hence we find it in the O. T. citations, Mt. v. 21, 27, 33, οὐ φονεύσεις, οὐ μοιχεύσεις· L. iv. 12, A. xxiii. 5, Rom. vii. 7, xiii. 9, 1 C. ix. 9 (H. xii. 20 from the LXX). In the fourth commandment only, τίμα τὸν πατέρα κ.τ.λ., is the imperative used, Mt. xv. 4, xix. 19, E. vi. 2, al., as in the LXX. In Rom. vi. 14, however, the future expresses simple expectation. This form of expression may in itself be either harsh or mild, according to the tone in which the words are uttered.

d. The infinitive, as in German *fortgehen!* Not to speak of the ancient and epic language, this construction is found in the Greek prose writers, not merely where a command is given in excitement or with imperious brevity,³ but also in requests, wishes, and prayers.⁴ Compare the ancient form of greeting, χαίρειν, A. xv. 23, Ja. i. 1. In the N. T. this construction has often been extended beyond its true limits;⁵ thus 1 Th. iii. 11, 2 Th. ii. 17, iii. 5, have been most erroneously quoted as examples, for, as the accentuation shows, the verbs are in the optative mood. In other instances a change of structure in sentences of some length has been overlooked. In L. ix. 3, for example, we find μήτε ῥάβδον . . . ἔχειν, as if μηδὲν αἴρειν had preceded: εἶπεν πρὸς αὐτούς might be followed by either construction, and the writer certainly used ἔχειν as an infinitive dependent on εἶπεν. In the parallel passage, Mk. vi. 8 sq., there is again a change of construction, of a different kind. Compare Arrian, *Al.* 4. 20. 5, σὺ νῦν φύλαξον τὴν ἀρχήν· εἰ δὲ . . . σὺ δὲ . . . παραδοῦναι. Similarly in Rom. xii. 15, see § 63.⁶ In other

---

¹ Matth. 498 d, Bernh. p. 378, Sintenis, Plut. *Themist.* 175 sqq., Stallb. Plat. *Rep.* II. 295, Weber, *Demosth.* p. 369 sq. (Don. p. 407, Jelf 413. 1). As to the Latin see Ramshorn p. 421.
² Ewald, *Krit. Gr.* p. 531.
³ Herm. Soph. *Œd. R.* 1057, Schæf. *Demosth.* III. 530, Poppo, *Thuc.* I. i. 146, Bernh. p. 358 (Don. p. 552, Jelf 671 *a*). Thus in laws and rules of life, in Hesiod, *Opp. et dd.*, Theognis, Hippocrates, Marcus Antoninus. See Gayler, *Partic. Neg.* p. 80 sq.
⁴ Bremi, *Demosth.* p. 230, Stallb. Plat. *Rep.* I. 388, Fritz. *Rom.* III. 86, Madv. 141. Rem. 2. (Don. *l. c.*, Jelf 671 *b*.)
⁵ Georgi, *Hierocr.* I. i. 28.
⁶ [This passage is not directly noticed in § 63, but in an earlier edition of this work (ed. 5, p. 383) Winer explained the infinitives χαίρειν, κλαίειν, as arising out of a *variatio structuræ* (§ 63. II. 1). Fritzsche, Alford, Vaughan, take the infinitive as used for the imperative. Ellicott says of Ph. iii. 16: "This is perhaps the only certain instance of a pure imperatival infinitive in the N. T. ;

instances the regular grammatical connexion has been misunderstood: in Rev. x. 9 δοῦναι certainly belongs to λέγων, and in Col. iv. 6 εἰδέναι is an explanatory infinitive appended to the preceding predicates of the λόγος. In one passage only, Ph. iii. 16, πλὴν . . . . τῷ αὐτῷ στοιχεῖν, it seems simplest to regard the infinitive as used for the imperative: here it marks well the unchangeable law for the development of the Christian life. Compare Stallbaum, Plat. *Gorg.* 447 b.

With the imperatival use of ἵνα (5. *a*) Gieseler[1] connects a construction employed by John and others, e.g., Jo. i. 8, οὐκ ἦν ἐκεῖνος τὸ φῶς, ἀλλ᾽ ἵνα μαρτυρήσῃ, rendering this *but he was to bear witness* (ix. 3, xiii. 18). But the words cannot have this meaning unless ἵνα signifies *in order that*, and then an ellipsis—at all events one of a general kind, such as γέγονε τοῦτο [2]—lies at the root of the phrase; though John himself, through his familiarity with the idiom, has nothing more than '*but in order that*' actually present to his mind in the several passages: compare Fritzsche, *Matt.* p. 840 sq. The commentator, on the other hand, can in every instance easily supply some special word from the context, and this he must do if he would fulfil his duty. Thus in Jo. i. 8, *he himself was not the light of the world, but* he appeared (ἦλθεν, ver. 7) *that he might bear witness.* In ix. 3, *neither has this man sinned nor his parents, but* he was born blind *that . . . . might become manifest* (compare 1 Jo. ii. 19). In Jo. xiii. 18 there is probably an aposiopesis, easily explained psychologically, *I speak not of you all, I know those whom I have chosen, but* (I have made this choice) *in order that . . . . may be fulfilled* etc. (see Baumg.-Crus. *in loc.*); unless we prefer to suppose that Jesus, instead of expressing the mournful truth in his own words, continues in the words of the Psalmist (compare 1 C. ii. 9). In Jo. xv. 25 the words ἐμίσησάν με δωρεάν in the quotation show that μεμισήκασιν is to be repeated before ἵνα. In Mk. xiv. 49 it is the coming out of the Jews against Jesus in the manner described in ver. 48, that is declared to have been predicted.[3] Lastly, in Rev.

---

other instances, e.g., Rom. xii. 15, pass into declarations of duty and of what *ought to be* done." A. Buttmann (p. 271) doubts whether there is any real example of this (mainly poetical) usage in the N. T. He would supply some such word as λέγω (the ellipsis of which before the formula χαίρειν is shown by the dative which precedes, Ja. i. 1, al.) in L. ix. 3, Rom. xii. 15, Ph. iii. 16.— The pure imperatival infinitive stands for the *second* person only (Jelf 671 *a*, Ellic. *l. c.*).]

[1] In Rosenm. *Repert.* II. 145.

[2] It is not sufficient to say (as De Wette does) that there is nothing to be supplied: it is necessary in any case to show how and by what means ἵνα comes to have this meaning.

[3] [That is, ἵνα depends on ὡς ἐπὶ λῃστὴν ἐξήλθατε: this would be clearer if (with Fritz., Tisch., Alf.) we removed the note of interrogation at the end of ver. 48.]

xiv. 13 we may supply before ἵνα ἀναπ. κ.τ.λ. the verb ἀποθνήσκουσι, from the preceding ἀποθνήσκοντες.[1]

Rem. Here and there in the N. T. text it is doubtful whether a verbal form should be taken as imperative or as (the 2nd pers. of the) indicative: e.g., H. xii. 17, ἴστε, ὅτι καὶ μετέπειτα θέλων κληρονομῆσαι τὴν εὐλογίαν ἀπεδοκιμάσθη· 1 C. vi. 4, βιωτικὰ μὲν οὖν κριτήρια ἐὰν ἔχητε, τοὺς ἐξουθενημένους ἐν τῇ ἐκκλησίᾳ, τούτους καθίζετε· i. 26, xi. 26, Rom. xiii. 6, E. ii. 22, Ph. ii. 15, 22, Jo. xiv. 1, 1 P. i. 6, ii. 5.[2] In all such cases the question must be decided by the context, and the matter belongs to the province of hermeneutics, not of grammar.

Section XLIV.

THE INFINITIVE.[3]

1. The infinitive, inasmuch as it expresses the notion of the verb absolutely, that is, without reference to any subject, is of all the verbal forms least capable of taking a place in the grammatical sentence as a part of speech. It appears in this character :—

(a) When it is used to express a *brief, hurried command* (§ 43. 5. d);

(b) When it is introduced adverbially into a sentence;

(c) When it is attached (annexed) to a sentence absolutely.

The only example of (b) is the phrase ὡς ἔπος εἰπεῖν, H. vii. 9 (Krüg. p. 204). With (c) we might compare (Krüg. p. 205, Jelf 679) Ph. iv. 10, ἀνεθάλετε τὸ ὑπὲρ ἐμοῦ φρονεῖν, *in respect of . . . . being disposed*, though here another explanation is possible.[4]

Relating to this, (c), or essentially one with it, is the infinitive which is added to a sentence as a *complement* (*infinitivus epexegeticus*), usually to express *design* (Rost p. 697, Don. p. 598, Jelf 669): Mt. ii. 2, ἤλθομεν προςκυνῆσαι αὐτῷ (*in order*) *to worship him*. So after ἔρχομαι, Mt. xi. 7, xx. 28, H. ix. 24,

---

[1] [Others regard ἵνα as depending on μακάριοι (Düsterdieck, Alford, A. Buttmann).]

[2] [Lünemann adds H. xiii. 23. The list might of course be greatly enlarged: e.g., see Mt. xxiv. 33, xxvii. 65, Jo. v. 39, viii. 38, xv. 18, E. v. 5, H. vii. 4, Ja. ii. 1, 1 Jo. ii. 27.]

[3] K. E. A. Schmidt, *Ueber den Infinitiv* (Prenzlau, 1823), M. Schmidt, *Ueber Infinit.* (Ratisbon, 1826), Eichhoff, *Ueber den Infin.* (Crefeld, 1833). Comp. Mehlhorn in the *Allgem. Lit. Z.* 1833: Ergzbl. No. 110.

[4] [Below (3. c) Winer takes τὸ φρονεῖν as an object-infinitive, perhaps regarding ἀνεθάλετε as a *transitive* verb (De W., Lightfoot, al.),—though as taken above the infinitive is a kind of object (see Ellicott *in loc.*). Meyer and Alford take τὸ ὑπὲρ ἐμοῦ as the object of φρονεῖν, this infinitive being dependent on ἀνεθάλετε.]

Rev. xxii. 12, Jo. iv. 15, L. i. 17; after πέμπω or ἀποστέλλω, Mk. iii. 14, 1 C. i. 17, xvi. 3; and after other verbs, A. v. 31, Rom. x. 7, 1 C. x. 7. See also 2 C. xi. 2, ἡρμοσάμην ὑμᾶς ἑνὶ ἀνδρὶ παρθένον ἁγνὴν παραστῆσαι τῷ Χριστῷ· Col. i. 22, 2 C. ix. 5, x. 13, 16, Jo. xiii. 24 [*Rec.*], νεύει τούτῳ πυθέσθαι (compare Diod. S. 20. 69), Rev. xvi. 9, οὐ μετενόησαν δοῦναι αὐτῷ δόξαν· 2 P. iii. 2 (1 S. xvi. 1), Ph. iv. 12. Elsewhere it expresses the consequence (as in the ancient language design and consequence were not yet severed [1]): Col. iv. 6, ὁ λόγος ὑμῶν . . . . ἅλατι ἠρτυμένος . . . εἰδέναι πῶς κ.τ.λ., *seasoned with salt, to know* (so that you may know), H. v. 5; [2]—or the mode of performance, A. xv. 10, τί πειράζετε τὸν θεὸν ἐπιθεῖναι ζυγὸν ἐπὶ τὸν τράχηλον τῶν μαθητῶν, *imponendo jugum*, H. v. 5 (1 P. iv. 3). Lastly, in E. iii. 6 the infinitival clause expresses the content of the μυστήριον (ver. 4); compare also E. iv. 22. In Greek authors this lax use of the infinitive is carried much farther.[3] The infinitive of design, in particular, is frequently used, see Soph. *Œd. C.* 12, Thuc. 1. 50, 4. 8, Her. 7. 208, Plut. *Cim.* 5, Arrian, *Al.* 1. 16. 10, 4. 16. 4 (Matth. 532, Krüg. p. 213); though after verbs of *going, sending,* the participle is even more common in Greek writers (compare A. viii. 27, xxiv. 11).

Such relations are sometimes indicated with greater clearness by prefixing ὥστε to the infinitive; e.g., L. ix. 52,[4] Mt. xxvii. 1. With the latter passage, Fritzsche's explanation of which is very forced,[5] compare Strab. 6. 324, Schæf. on Bos, *Ellips.* p. 784, and on Soph. *Œd. Col.* p. 525, Matth. 531. Rem. 2. In the Byzantine writers the use of ὥστε with the infinitive instead of the simple infinitive is peculiarly common; see *e.g.* Malal. p. 385, ἐβουλεύσατο ὥστε ἐκβληθῆναι τὴν πενθεράν· p. 434.[6] We find a parallel to L. ix. 52 in Euseb. *H. E.* 3. 28. 3, εἰσελθεῖν ποτὲ ἐν βαλανείῳ ὥστε λούσασθαι. And it would be better even to admit that the N. T. contains ex-

---

[1] Bäumlein, *Modi* p. 339. [On this infinitive see Don. p. 595, Jelf 669.]
[2] [This passage is quoted again in the next sentence: in ed. 5 it is associated (as here) with Col. iv. 6, and so it is usually explained.]
[3] Schæf. *Soph.* II. 324; Jacob, Luc. *Tox.* 116; Held, Plut. *Æm. P.* 185 sq.
[4] [In L. ix. 52 the reading of א and B is ὡς ἑτοιμάσαι: on this construction see below.]
[5] ["In talibus locis aut verbum de conatu explicandum (*ita, ut supplicio afficere eum conarentur*), aut, quod hic prætulerim, rei conditio mente adjicienda est: *consilium inierunt* . . . . *ita, ut eum interficerent*, nempe, *si possent:*" Fritzsche *in loc.* Meyer: "in their intention the result of their consultation would be *that they would put him to death.*" See also Jelf 863. 2 *b* ("the result or effect" sometimes "includes the notion of an aim or purpose"), Madvig 166 b, Don. p. 597. Other passages of the same kind are L. iv. 29, xx. 20.]
[6] Compare also Heinichen, *Ind. ad Euseb.* III. 545.

SECT. XLIV.]   THE INFINITIVE.   401

amples of the extended application of ὥστε which is thus exhibited in later Greek, than to resort to forced interpretations.

We find only one example of ὡς with the infinitive, viz. A. xx. 24, οὐδενὸς λόγον ποιοῦμαι, οὐδὲ ἔχω τὴν ψυχήν μου τιμίαν ἐμαυτῷ, ὡς τελειῶσαι τὸν δρόμον μου μετὰ χαρᾶς, *in order to complete my course*, etc. See Bornem. *Schol.* p. 174 sq.[1]

Other forms of the epexegetical infinitive attach themselves more easily to a sentence or a member of a sentence, and assume the form of a word under grammatical government, for which indeed they were in some cases taken by the older grammarians :[2]—

(*a*) Mk. vii. 4, πολλὰ ἃ παρέλαβον κρατεῖν (*observanda acceperunt*), Mt. xxvii. 34, ἔδωκαν αὐτῷ πιεῖν ὄξος· E. iii. 16, Thuc. 2. 27, 4. 36, Lucian, *Asin.* 43, Diog. L. 2. 51.

(*b*) 1 C. ix. 5, ἔχομεν ἐξουσίαν γυναῖκα περιάγειν· ix. 4, L. viii. 8, ὁ ἔχων ὦτα ἀκούειν ἀκουέτω· ii. 1, A. xiv. 5, E. iii. 8, H. xi. 15, καιρὸς ἀνακάμψαι· iv. 1 (Plat. *Tim.* 38 b, Æsch. *Dial.* 3. 2); see Matth. 532. d, e (Jelf 669). Here the infinitive may even have a subject joined with it, as in Rom. xiii. 11.[3] The infinitive is also attached to an adjective : 2 Tim. i. 12, δυνατὸς τὴν παραθήκην μου φυλάξαι (Thuc. 1. 139), H. xi. 6, vi. 10, οὐκ ἄδικος ὁ θεὸς ἐπιλαθέσθαι κ.τ.λ., 1 P. iv. 3, 1 C. vii. 39, Mk. i. 7, 2 C. iii. 5, L. xv. 19, A. xiii. 25, H. v. 11, 2 Tim. ii. 2, L. xxii. 33.[4]

2. But the infinitive may also appear in a sentence as an integral member of it, and then its nature as a noun may be perceived with more or less clearness: in such cases it takes the place sometimes of the subject, sometimes of the object. It appears as the subject (Matth. 534 a, Jelf 663) in such sentences as the following: Mt. xii. 10, εἰ ἔξεστι τοῖς σάββασι θεραπεύειν, *is it allowed to heal on the Sabbath* (is healing . . . . allowed) ? xv. 26, οὐκ ἔστι καλὸν λαβεῖν τὸν ἄρτον τῶν τέκνων· 1 Th. iv. 3,

---

[1] [On ὡς with infinitive expressing *purpose*, see Don. p. 597, Krüg. p. 289, Rost p. 666, Madv. 166. Rem. 2.]

[2] As by those who, in the example quoted under (*b*), ἔχομεν ἐξουσίαν περιάγειν, held that τοῦ was omitted before the infinitive (Haitinger in *Act. Monac.* III. 301). The infinitive has τοῦ when it is definitely conceived as a genitive (noun) ; without τοῦ it is the epexegetic infinitive. The two constructions are somewhat differently conceived (Matth. 532. e). So in Latin : Cic. *Tusc.* 1. 41, tempus est *abire* (compare Ramshorn p. 423), elsewhere *abeundi*. On the whole see Stallbaum, Plat. *Phil.* p. 213, *Euthyphr.* p. 107. (As in L. i. 9 we find ἔλαχε τοῦ θυμιᾶσαι, so in Demosth. *Neær.* 517 c. λαγχάνει βουλεύειν.)

[3] Compare Schoem. Plut. *Cleom.* 187.

[4] Compare Ast, Plat. *Legg.* p. 117, Stallb. Plat. *Euthyd.* 204, Weber, *Demosth.* 261, Bernh. p. 361.

26

τοῦτό ἐστι θέλημα τοῦ θεοῦ .... ἀπέχεσθαι .... ἀπὸ τῆς πορνείας (preceded by ὁ ἁγιασμὸς ὑμῶν, which might also have been expressed by an infinitive), A. xx. 16, ὅπως μὴ γένηται αὐτῷ χρονοτριβῆσαι (Weber, *Dem.* 213), Mt. xix. 10, E. v. 12, Ph. i. 7, G. vi. 14, Ja. i. 27, Rom. xiii. 5, 1 C. xi. 20 [see p. 403], H. vi. 6, ix. 27, 1 P. ii. 15, Rev. xiii. 7. If in such a case the infinitive itself has a subject expressed, whether a substantive, an adjective, or a participle, this subject usually stands in the accusative case, in close grammatical union with the infinitive: Mt. xvii. 4, καλόν ἐστιν ἡμᾶς ὧδε εἶναι· Mt. xix. 24, Jo. xviii. 14, 1 C. xi. 13, 1 P. ii. 15, A. xxv. 27, L. ix. 33, xviii. 25.[1] If this subject is brought into the principal clause (as in Ph. i. 7, δίκαιον ἐμοὶ τοῦτο φρονεῖν κ.τ.λ.), the attributives which are construed with the infinitive stand either in the accusative (Mt. xviii. 8, καλόν σοί ἐστιν εἰςελθεῖν εἰς τὴν ζωὴν χωλὸν ἢ κυλλόν), or, by an attraction very common in Greek writers, in the case of the subject. For the latter construction, see 2 P. ii. 21, κρεῖττον ἦν αὐτοῖς, μὴ ἐπεγνωκέναι τὴν ὁδὸν τῆς δικαιοσύνης ἢ ἐπιγνοῦσιν ἐπιστρέψαι· A. xv. 25 *v.l.*;[2] and compare Thuc. 2. 87, Demosth. *Funebr.* 153 a, 156 a, Xen. *Hier.* 10. 2 (Bernh. p. 359, Krüg. p. 206, Jelf 672).[3] In H. ii. 10 the two constructions are combined, ἔπρεπεν αὐτῷ ... ἀγαγόντα ... τελειῶσαι·[4] compare Mk. ix. 27,[5] Mt. xviii. 8 (Plut. *Coriol.* 14).

Remark further :—

a. The infinitive, when used as subject, sometimes takes the article, —namely where it expresses directly the notion of the verb in a substantival form. This is the case not merely in such sentences as Rom. vii. 18, τὸ θέλειν παράκειταί μοι, τὸ δὲ κατεργάζεσθαι τὸ καλὸν οὔ· 2 C. vii. 11, αὐτὸ τοῦτο τὸ κατὰ θεὸν λυπηθῆναι πόσην κατειργάσατο ὑμῖν

---

[1] Compare Matthiæ, Eur. *Med.* p. 526, Schwarz, *De Solœc. Discip. Chr.* p. 88 sq. (Jelf 675).
[2] [Other examples of this kind are A. xxvii. 3 (with the reading πορευθέντι), xvi. 21. With H. ii. 10 compare L. i. 74, A. xxv. 27 : in A. xi. 12, xxvi. 20, Mt. xviii. 8, the transition from dative to accusative is less remarkable, since the participle stands *after* the infinitive. See A. Buttm. p. 305 sq., Alford on H. ii. 10.]
[3] Zumpt 600. [Madvig, *Lat. Gr.* 393.]
[4] [A. Buttmann remarks that πρέπει (πρέπον ἐστί) has four constructions in the N. T. : (1) with dative and infinitive, Mt. iii. 15 ; (2) with dative, followed by the accusative and infinitive, H. ii. 10 ; (3) with accusative and infinitive, 1 C. xi. 13 ; (4) it is also used personally (H. vii. 26). Ἔξεστι, which usually has the first of these constructions, is occasionally followed by the accusative and infinitive, viz. in L. vi. 4, xx. 22, Mk. ii. 26. With δεῖ we find the accusative and infinitive, or the infinitive alone : χρή occurs once only (Ja. iii. 10), with accusative and infinitive. See A. Buttm. pp. 278, 147, Jelf 674.]
[5] [This should be ix. 47 : here however there is good authority for οἵ.]

σπουδήν· Ph. i. 21,—in which the finite verb with its adjuncts forms a complete predicate; but also in connexion with the impersonal formulas, καλόν, αἰσχρόν ἐστι, etc. (Rost p. 692), if the idea expressed by the infinitive is to be brought out with greater force, as in 1 C. vii. 26, καλὸν ἀνθρώπῳ τὸ οὕτως εἶναι· G. iv. 18, καλὸν τὸ ζηλοῦσθαι ἐν καλῷ πάντοτε· Rom. xiv. 21, 1 C. xi. 6. In the passages first quoted the article could not well have been left out; in 1 C. vii. 26 the expression would have lost in force had there been no article, καλὸν ἀνθρώπῳ οὕτως εἶναι, *it is good for man to be so* (compare 1 C. vii. 1, xiv. 35).[1] Ph. i. 29 also may be referred to the second category: in 1 Th. iv. 6 we find an infinitive of this kind with the article annexed to another without it,—compare Plat. *Gorg.* 467 d, Xen. *Cyr.* 7. 5. 76: in Rom. iv. 13, however, the infinitival clause τὸ κληρονόμον εἶναι is a kind of apposition to ἡ ἐπαγγελία. With the above examples compare Plat. *Phæd.* 62 d, *Gorg.* 475 b, Xen. *Mem.* 1. 2. 1, Diod. S. 1. 93.

b. In the place of the infinitive, principally where its subject is to be specially indicated, we sometimes find a complete sentence formed with ἐάν, εἰ, or ἵνα, according to the sense: Mk. xiv. 21, καλὸν ἦν αὐτῷ, εἰ οὐκ ἐγεννήθη· 1 C. vii. 8, καλὸν αὐτοῖς ἐστίν, ἐὰν μείνωσιν ὡς κἀγώ· Jo. xvi. 7, συμφέρει ὑμῖν, ἵνα ἐγὼ ἀπέλθω. (On ἵνα see below, no. 8.) This is to be referred in part to the general character of the (later) popular language, which has a preference for circumstantiality, in part to the Hellenistic colouring of the N. T. language. Yet we find similar instances in Greek authors (Isocr. *Nicocl.* pp. 40, 46).

The infinitive is the subject when it is joined with ἐστί in the sense *it is lawful*, or *it is possible*, etc., as in H. ix. 5.[2] 1 C. xi. 20, however, may also (against Wahl and Meyer) be rendered, *if ye come together, it is not a celebration of the Lord's Supper:* the genitive absolute can be taken up thus without the aid of τοῦτο.

3. The infinitive denotes the object (predicate) wherever it appears as a necessary complement of a verbal notion; not merely after θέλειν, δύνασθαι, τολμᾶν, ἐπιχειρεῖν, σπουδάζειν, ζητεῖν,[3] etc., but also after the verbs of *believing, hoping* (I hope to come, etc.), *saying, maintaining* (I maintain that I was present). It is not necessary to quote from the N. T. examples of the regular construction: we need only remark

---

[1] We certainly cannot assume any distinction in *meaning* between the infinitive with, and the infinitive without the article. In German also we say, *Das Beten ist segensreich*, and *beten ist segensreich*, without any difference in the sense. But the infinitive has more weight in the sentence when made substantival by the article. [See Ellicott on 1 Th. iii. 3, Jelf 670.—In G. iv. 18, quoted above, τό is very doubtful.]

[2] Ast, *Lexic. Plat.* I. 622 a.

[3] Against Bornemann, *Schol.* p. 40, see Fritzsche, *Rom.* II. 376, and compare Blume, *Lycurg.* p. 151. [The point proved by Fritzsche is the frequent use of the infinitive with ζητεῖν in classical Greek: see also Liddell and Scott, s. v.]

a. If in such a case the infinitive has a subject of its own, different from that of the principal verb, this with all its adjuncts is put in the accusative (*accus. cum infin.*): 1 Tim. ii. 8, βούλομαι προςεύχεσθαι τοὺς ἄνδρας· 2 C. xiii. 7, H. vi. 11, ἐπιθυμοῦμεν ἕκαστον ὑμῶν τὴν αὐτὴν ἐνδείκνυσθαι σπουδὴν κ.τ.λ., 2 P. i. 15, 1 C. vii. 10, A. xiv. 19, νομίσαντες αὐτὸν τεθνάναι· 2 C. xi. 16, μή τίς με δόξῃ ἄφρονα εἶναι·[1] Rom. xv. 5, ὁ θεὸς δῴη ὑμῖν τὸ αὐτὸ φρονεῖν· 2 Tim. i. 18. More commonly however we find a complete sentence with ἵνα after verbs of *intreating, commanding*, etc. (see no. 8), and a sentence with ὅτι after verbs of *saying, believing* (Mt. xx. 10, A. xix. 26, xxi. 29, Rom. iv. 9, viii. 18, G. v. 10). Ἐλπίζω always has this construction in the N. T.[2]

If on the other hand the subject of the infinitive is the same as that of the finite verb, any attributives which it may have are put in the nominative: Rom. xv. 24, ἐλπίζω διαπορευόμενος θεάσασθαι ὑμᾶς· 2 C. x. 2, δέομαι τὸ μὴ παρὼν θαρρῆσαι (Philostr. *Apoll.* 2. 23), Rom. i. 22, Ph. iv. 11, 2 P. iii. 14, Jude 3 (L. i. 9 ?).[3] This is a kind of attraction; compare Krüger, *Gramm. Untersuch.* III. 328 sqq. (Jelf 672). The subject itself is not repeated: see Ja. ii. 14, 1 C. vii. 36. Even in this construction, however, we sometimes (though rarely) find the accusative (with infinitive): in this case the subject is always repeated in the form of a pronoun.[4] See Rom. ii. 19, πέποιθας σεαυτὸν ὁδηγὸν εἶναι τυφλῶν· Ph. iii. 13, ἐγὼ ἐμαυτὸν οὐ λογίζομαι κατειληφέναι· L. xx. 20, ὑποκρινομένους, ἑαυτοὺς δικαίους εἶναι· A. xxvi. 2, Rev. ii. 2, 9;[5] probably also E. iv. 22, where I regard ἀποθέσθαι ὑμᾶς as dependent on ἐδιδάχθητε. Compare Her. 2.

---

[1] If the substantive to which the infinitive refers is governed by the principal verb in the dative, the noun annexed to the infinitive may also be put in this case, as in A. xxvii. 3 . . . . τῷ Παύλῳ χρησάμενος ἐπέτρεψεν πρὸς τοὺς φίλους πορευθέντι ἐπιμελείας τυχεῖν, unless the dative here is a correction; see Bornem. *in loc.* On the other hand, in L. i. 74 sq. we have τοῦ δοῦναι ἡμῖν ἀφόβως ἐκ χειρὸς ἐχθρῶν ῥυσθέντας λατρεύειν αὐτῷ κ.τ.λ. [See the last paragraph.]

[2] [This is likely to mislead. Ἐλπίζω is frequently followed by the infinitive in the N. T., but not by the *accusative and* infinitive, though the example quoted in the next sentence, Rom. xv. 24, is the same in principle : ἐλπίζω ὅτι (L. xxiv. 21, al.) is a late construction.]

[3] In 1 Tim. i. 3 also, πορευόμενος belongs to παρεκάλεσα: standing so near προςμεῖναι, it would necessarily be in the accusative if it belonged to this infinitive. [On L. i. 9 see § 45. 6.]

[4] Herm. *Vig.* p. 743 (Jelf 673. 1).

[5] [A. Buttmann (p. 274) adds L. xxiii. 2, A. v. 36, viii. 9 (xxv. 4), Rev. iii. 9, A. xxv. 21, 2 C. vii. 11.—A. xxvi. 2 need not come in here.]

SECT. XLIV.]   THE INFINITIVE.   405

2, Xen. *Cyr.* 5. 1. 21, νομίζοιμι γὰρ ἐμαυτὸν ἐοικέναι κ.τ.λ., 1. 4. 4 (where see Poppo), *An.* 7. 1. 30, *Mem.* 2. 6. 35, Diod. S. 1. 50, *Exc. Vat.* p. 57, Philostr. *Apoll.* 1. 12 : see Krüger *l. c.* p. 390. In the passages first quoted it is probable that this construction was chosen for the sake of antithesis (see Plat. *Symp.* c. 3 and Stallb. *in loc.*, compare Krüg. *l. c.* p. 386 sq.) or of clearness : *I do not suppose that I myself have already* etc. For the same reason, as it seems to me, was ὑμᾶς joined to the infinitive in E. iv. 22, as in ver. 21 another subject, Jesus, had intervened. Later writers however use this construction where there is no antithesis.[1]

b. After verbs of *saying (maintaining), thinking* the infinitive sometimes expresses—not what according to the speaker's assertion *is,* but—what *ought to be,* inasmuch as these verbs contain rather the notion of advising, requiring, or commanding.[2] See A. xxi. 21, λέγων, μὴ περιτέμνειν αὐτοὺς τὰ τέκνα, *he said they ought not to* (must not) *circumcise their children,*—he commanded them not to circumcise, etc.; xv. 24 (?),[3] Tit. ii. 2, A. xxi. 4, τῷ Παύλῳ ἔλεγον μὴ ἀναβαίνειν εἰς Ἱεροσόλυμα, *they said to Paul he should not go up,* they advised him not to go up. Compare Eurip. *Troad.* 724. In all these instances, if the sentence were resolved into the direct construction, we should have the imperative, μὴ περιτέμνετε τὰ τέκνα ὑμῶν. On this infinitive—which even modern scholars explain by an ellipsis of δεῖν (against this see Herm. *Vig.* p. 745)—see Lob. *Phryn.* p. 753 sqq., Bernh. p. 371.[4] Too many N. T. passages, however, have been thus explained. In Rom. xiv. 2, ὃς μὲν πιστεύει φαγεῖν πάντα means *the one has confidence to eat,* and the notion of *lawfulness* is contained in πιστεύειν. In Rom. xv. 9, δοξάσαι expresses not what the Gentiles ought to do, but what they actually do; see Fritz. *in loc.* In Rom. ii. 21 sq. and E. iv. 22 sq. (see above) the verbs *preach* and *be taught,* on which the infinitives depend, may from their nature denote either that which *is* (and must be

---

[1] Compare Heinichen, Euseb. *H.E.* 1. 118.
[2] See also Elmsley, Soph. *Œd. T.* p. 80, Matth. 531.
[3] [The clause is omitted by recent editors.]
[4] Buttm. Demosth. *Mid.* p. 131, Engelhardt, Plat. *Lach.* p. 81, *Jen. Lit.-Zeit.* 1816, No. 231. [Against supposing an ellipsis see Jelf 884. 4, Riddell, Plat. *Apol.* p. 148, Krüg. 212, Madvig 146. The last two grammarians explain this usage by reference to the meaning of the governing verb, as implying a command or requirement : compare Liddell and Scott, s. v. λέγω.]

believed), or that which *should be* (should be done); and we say in like manner, *they preached not to steal, ye have been taught to put off.* In A. x. 22 the verb is χρηματίζεσθαι, which is used almost regularly of a directing oracle, a divine injunction. Lastly, if the infinitive must be translated by " may " after verbs of *requesting*, this meaning is already contained in the signification of the governing verb itself in the particular context; as in 2 C. x. 2, δέομαι τὸ μὴ παρὼν θαρρῆσαι τῇ πεποιθήσει, as if, *I beg of you my not being bold*, i.e., I beseech you to take care that I may not be bold.[1]

c. The article stands before an object-infinitive to make it a substantive, and thus give it greater prominence (Rost p. 693, Jelf 670), Rom. xiii. 8, xiv. 13 (L. vii. 21 *v. l.*), 1 C. iv. 6 [*Rec.*], 2 C. ii. 1, viii. 10, Ph. iv. 10 (compare above, no. 1);[2] especially at the commencement of a sentence (Thuc. 2. 53, Xen. *Mem.* 4. 3. 1), as in 1 C. xiv. 39, τὸ λαλεῖν γλώσσαις μὴ κωλύετε (compare Soph. *Phil.* 1241, ὅς σε κωλύσει τὸ δρᾶν). In Phil. ii. 6, οὐχ ἁρπαγμὸν ἡγήσατο τὸ εἶναι ἴσα θεῷ, the infinitive with the article forms the direct object of ἡγήσατο, and ἁρπαγμόν is the predicate; compare Thuc. 2. 87, οὐχὶ δικαίαν ἔχει τέκμαρσιν τὸ ἐκφοβῆσαι, and Bernh. p. 316 [p. 356].

Deserving of special mention is the accusative with infinitive after ἐγένετο,[3]—a construction particularly common in Luke's writings. See Mk. ii. 23, ἐγένετο παραπορεύεσθαι αὐτόν, *accidit, ut transiret;* A. xvi. 16, ἐγένετο παιδίσκην τινὰ .... ἀπαντῆσαι ἡμῖν· xix. 1, ἐγένετο Παῦλον διελθόντα .... ἐλθεῖν εἰς Ἔφεσον· iv. 5, ix. 3, 32, 37, 43, xi. 26, xiv. 1, xxi. 1, 5, xxii. 6, xxvii. 44, xxviii. 8, 17, L. iii. 21 sq., vi. 1, 6, xvi. 22, al.[4] Here the infinitive clause is to be regarded as the (enlarged) subject of ἐγένετο, just as after συνέβη (see below), and in Latin after *æquum est, apertum est,* etc.,[5]—*there came to pass Jesus's*

---

[1] In 2 C. ii. 7, also, the infinitives ὥστε .... χαρίσασθαι καὶ παρακαλέσαι denote not what *is* but what *should be.* We must not however supply δεῖν. The influence of the clause with ἱκανόν extends, as it were, to these infinitives: *the censure is sufficient* .... *in order now on the contrary to forgive him,* etc.
[2] Herm. Soph. *Aj.* 114.
[3] [On the various constructions found in the N. T. after καὶ ἐγένετο or ἐγένετο δέ, see below, § 65. 4. *e.*]
[4] We have the same construction in A. xxii. 17, ἐγένετό μοι ὑποστρέψαντι εἰς Ἱερουσαλήμ .... γενέσθαι με ἐν ἐκστάσει; where the infinitive might have been directly annexed to ἐγένετό μοι ὑποστρέψαντι (accidit mihi), and perhaps would have been so annexed if the writer had not been led away from the construction with which he had begun by the intervening genitive absolute, καὶ προςευχομένου μου ἐν τῷ ἱερῷ (Jelf 674. *Obs.* 3). [In A. xi. 26, quoted above, we should read αὐτοῖς, not αὐτούς: compare xxii. 6.]
[5] Zumpt, *Gr.* 600. [Madvig, *Lat. Gr.* 398 a.]

passing by, etc. Hence the construction is correctly conceived in Greek, though the frequent use of ἐγένετο with the infinitive in the place of the historic tense of the main verb is in the first instance due to an imitation of the Hebrew וַיְהִי. Grammatically parallel with this is the use of συνέβη by Greek writers; e. g., συνέβη τὴν πόλιν . . . . εἶναι κυριεύουσαν Diod. S. 1. 50, 3. 22, 39, Plat. *Legg.* 1. 635 a, Demosth. *Polycl.* 709 c, Dion. H. IV. 2089, and frequently, especially in Polybius: this also occurs in 2 Macc. iii. 2, and once in the N. T., A. xxi. 35. We find an approach towards the construction in question (ἐγένετο with infinitive) in Theogn. 639, πολλάκι . . . . γίγνεται εὑρεῖν ἔργ' ἀνδρῶν,—with which Mt. xviii. 13 is most nearly allied. It appears in full [?] in Plat. *Phædr.* 242 b, τὸ δαιμόνιόν τε καὶ τὸ εἰωθὸς σημεῖόν μοι γίγνεσθαι ἐγένετο; and is particularly common in the later writers, e. g., Codin. p. 138, ἐγένετο τὸν βασιλέα ἀθυμεῖν· Epiphan. Monach. (ed. Dressel) p. 16, ἐγένετο αὐτοὺς ἀναβῆναι εἰς Ἱερουσαλήμ. (Jelf 669. 1.)

The use of the accusative with the infinitive in other cases is, as has already been remarked, proportionally rare in the N. T. We more commonly find a sentence with ὅτι in its place, exactly after the manner of the later (popular) language, which resolves the more condensed constructions, and loves the circumstantial and explicit. Hence in Latin, for example, the use of *ut* where the older language used the accusative with infinitive; hence in particular the use of *quod* after *verba dicendi et sentiendi*, which became more and more frequent in the age of declining Latinity, especially in the non-Italian provinces.[1] There is another point which must not be overlooked—that the N. T. writers prefer after *verba dicendi* to let the words spoken follow in the direct form, in accordance with the vividness of oriental phraseology.

4. The infinitive, when by means of the article it has received a decidedly substantival character, is also employed in the oblique cases. In the N. T., the case most commonly met with is the genitive, which occurs here far more frequently than in Greek authors.

a. Sometimes this genitive is dependent on nouns and verbs that regularly govern this case: 1 C. ix. 6, οὐκ ἔχομεν ἐξουσίαν τοῦ μὴ ἐργάζεσθαι;[2] 1 P. iv. 17, ὁ καιρὸς τοῦ ἄρξασθαι τὸ κρίμα κ.τ.λ., A. xiv. 9, πίστιν ἔχει τοῦ σωθῆναι· xx. 3, ἐγένετο γνώμη τοῦ ὑποστρέφειν· L. xxiv. 25, βραδεῖς τῇ καρδίᾳ τοῦ πιστεύειν· A. xxiii. 15, ἕτοιμοι τοῦ ἀνελεῖν (Ez. xxi. 11,

---

[1] In German, the more condensed construction "er sagte, ich sei zu spät gekommen" is in the popular language resolved into "er sagte, *dass* ich zu spät gekommen wäre."
[2] [The best MSS. omit τοῦ in this verse.]

1 Macc. v. 39), L. i. 9, ἔλαχε τοῦ θυμιᾶσαι (1 S. xiv. 47), 2 C. i. 8, ὥστε ἐξαπορηθῆναι ἡμᾶς καὶ τοῦ ζῆν· 1 C. xvi. 4, ἐὰν ᾖ ἄξιον τοῦ κἀμὲ πορεύεσθαι, *if it is worthy of* (worth) *the journeying* etc. Compare also 1 C. x. 13, 2 C. viii. 11, L. xxii. 6, Ph. iii. 21, Rom. vii. 3,[1] xv. 23, H. v. 12, Rev. ix. 10[2] (Gen. xix. 20, Ruth ii. 10, Neh. x. 29, Judith ix. 14, al.). Sometimes the MSS. vary between the infinitive with and without τοῦ, e. g., in Rev. xiv. 15: elsewhere we find the two forms in parallel sentences (H. v. 12, 1 Th. iv. 9). For examples from Greek authors see Georgi, *Vind.* p. 325 sq., Matth. 540 (Jelf 678. 3). In these it is common to find several words inserted between the article and the infinitive, see Demosth. *Funebr.* 153 a, 154 c, *Aristocr.* 431 a: this is not the case in the simple language of the N. T.

Under this head come also L. i. 57, ἐπλήσθη ὁ χρόνος τοῦ τεκεῖν αὐτήν· and ii. 21 (compare Gen. xxv. 24, xlvii. 29), the genitive being, in the mind of the Greek writer, immediately dependent on χρόνος. In the Hebrew the case is somewhat different, the infinitive with לְ being used: see Ewald p. 621.

b. Elsewhere the genitive of the infinitive stands in relation to whole sentences as an expression of *design*.[3] Here earlier scholars supplied ἕνεκα (compare Dem. *Fun.* 156 b) or χάριν. See L. xxiv. 29, εἰσῆλθεν τοῦ μεῖναι σὺν αὐτοῖς· Mt. xxiv. 45, ὃν κατέστησεν ὁ κύριος ἐπὶ τῆς οἰκετείας αὐτοῦ τοῦ δοῦναι αὐτοῖς τὴν τροφήν· iii. 13, παραγίνεται ἐπὶ τὸν Ἰορδάνην τοῦ βαπτισθῆναι· xiii. 3, L. ii. 27, v. 7, xxi. 22, xxii. 31, A. iii. 2, xxvi. 18, 1 C. x. 13, H. x. 7, G. iii. 10; with a negative, A. xxi. 12, παρεκαλοῦμεν .... τοῦ μὴ ἀναβαίνειν αὐτὸν εἰς Ἱερουσαλήμ· Ja. v. 17, H. xi. 5. This construction is principally used by Luke (and Paul). We find parallel examples however in Greek prose, especially from the time of Demosthenes; and this use of the genitive arises so certainly out of the fundamental notion of this case (Bernh. p. 174 sq.[4]) that there is no ground for assuming

---

[1] ["Free from the law, from being, etc.:" Fritzsche takes the same view. (On the negative μή see § 65. 2 β.) But both here and in 1 C. x. 13 the clause is usually taken as expressing purpose (Meyer).]
[2] [Scholz inserts τοῦ before ἀδικῆσαι on insufficient authority.]
[3] See Valcken. Eurip. *Hippol.* 48, Ast, Plat. *Legg.* p. 56, Schæf. *Demosth.* II. 161, V. 368, Ellendt, Arr. *Al.* I. 338, Matth. 540. [Don. pp. 480, 598, Jelf 492, 678. 2. *b*, Madv. 170 c. Rem., Ellicott on G. iii. 10, A. Buttm. p. 266 sqq.]
[4] [Bernh. connects this usage with the genitive which follows words denoting

the existence of either ellipsis or Hebraism. Compare Xen. *Cyr.* 1. 6. 40, τοῦ δὲ μηδ᾽ ἐντεῦθεν διαφεύγειν, σκοποὺς τοῦ γιγνομένου καθίστης· Plat. *Gorg.* 457 e, φοβοῦμαι οὖν διελέγχειν σε, μή με ὑπολάβῃς οὐ πρὸς τὸ πρᾶγμα φιλονεικοῦντα λέγειν, τοῦ καταφανὲς γενέσθαι κ.τ.λ., Strabo 15. 717, Demosth. *Phorm.* 603 b, Isocr. *Ægin.* 932, Thuc. 1. 23, 2. 22, Heliod. 2. 8. 88, 1. 24. 46, Dion. H. IV. 2109, Arrian, *Al.* 2. 21. 13, 3. 25. 4, 3. 28. 12. In L. ii. 22, 24, we find the infinitive with and without τοῦ in the same principal sentence. If the infinitive in this construction is accompanied by a subject, this stands in the accusative (L. v. 7).

In Ph. iii. 10 also this infinite expresses design; τοῦ γνῶναι is connected with ver. 8, and is a resumption of the thought there expressed.

In the LXX this infinitive occurs on every page. Compare Gen. i. 14, xxiv. 21, xxxviii. 9, xliii. 17, Jud. v. 16, ix. 15, 52, x. 1, xi. 12, xv. 12, xvi. 5, xix. 3, xx. 4, Ruth i. 1, 7, ii. 15, iv. 10, Neh. i. 6, 1 S. ix. 13, 14, xv. 27, 2 S. vi. 2, xix. 11, Jon. i. 3, Joel iii. 12, Judith xv. 8, 1 Macc. iii. 20, 39, 52, v. 9, 20, 48, vi. 15, 26.

Different from this, and more closely connected with the notion of the genitive,—and therefore to be brought under the head of 4. *a*, —is the use of the infinitive with τοῦ after verbs which express *distance, detention,* or *prevention from;* for these verbs have of themselves the power of directly governing the genitive, and are regularly followed by the genitive of nouns: Rom. xv. 22, ἐνεκοπτόμην . . . τοῦ ἐλθεῖν· L. iv. 42, καὶ κατεῖχον αὐτὸν τοῦ μὴ πορεύεσθαι (compare Isocr. *Ep.* 7. 1012, ἀπέχειν τοῦ τινὰς ἀποκτείνειν· Xen. *Mem.* 2. 1. 16, *An.* 3. 5. 11). With pleonastic negative (§ 65): A. xiv. 18, μόλις κατέπαυσαν τοὺς ὄχλους τοῦ μὴ θύειν αὐτοῖς (compare παύειν τινά τινος, and παύεσθαι followed by the infinitive with τοῦ in Diod. S. 3. 33, Phalar. *Ep.* 35, also ἡσυχάζειν τοῦ ποιεῖν Malalas 17. p. 417), A. xx. 27, οὐχ ὑπεστειλάμην τοῦ μὴ ἀναγγεῖλαι ὑμῖν πᾶσαν τὴν βουλὴν τοῦ θεοῦ (compare ver. 20), 1 P. iii. 10, παυσάτω τὴν γλῶσσαν αὐτοῦ ἀπὸ κακοῦ καὶ χείλη αὐτοῦ τοῦ μὴ λαλῆσαι δόλον· L. xxiv. 16, οἱ ὀφθαλμοὶ ἐκρατοῦντο τοῦ μὴ ἐπιγνῶναι αὐτόν (Xen. *Laced.* 4. 6), Rom. vi. 6,[1] A. x. 47, Sus. 9, 3 (1) Esdr. ii. 24, v. 69, 70, Gen. xvi. 2, *Act. Thom.* § 19, *Protev. Jac.* 2, al. Perhaps also φεύγειν and ἐκφεύγειν τοῦ ποιῆσαι should in strictness be thus explained (as the Greeks said φεύγειν τινός), Xen. *An.* 1. 3. 2. Compare Bernh. p. 356, Buttmann, Demosth. *Mid.* Exc. 2. p. 143.

---

aiming at, striving after (Jelf 510). By Donaldson and Jelf it is directly connected with the *causal* genitive: "When the genitive after these verbs appears in the form of an infinitive with the article, the cause generally assumes the character of a motive of action." (Don. p. 480.)]

[1] [Is not this a clause of *purpose?*]

In Rom. i. 24, παρέδωκεν αὐτοὺς ὁ θεὸς . . . εἰς ἀκαθαρσίαν τοῦ ἀτιμάζεσθαι τὰ σώματα αὐτῶν ἐν ἑαυτοῖς, the infinitive depends immediately on the noun ἀκαθαρσ., and there is nothing strange in the omission of τήν before this noun (Rom. xv. 23, 1 C. ix. 6): the genitive points out in what the ἀκαθαρσία consisted, *commisit impuritati, quæ cernebatur in*, etc. Fritzsche is more circumstantial: "virgula post ἀκαθαρσ. collocata ante τοῦ mente repete ἀκαθαρσίαν." What need there can be for this I cannot see, since ἀκαθαρσίαν and ἀτιμάζεσθαι stand close together, and the genitive can so well be understood as indicating the sphere of the ἀκαθαρσία. Similarly in Rom. viii. 12 the infinitive τοῦ κατὰ σάρκα ζῆν must be considered dependent on ὀφειλέτην, in accordance with the regular phrase ὀφειλέτην εἶναί τινος: see Fritz. *Matt.* p. 844. In L. i. 74 also τοῦ δοῦναι is most simply taken in connection with ὅρκον; compare Jer. xi. 5.

It soon became usual, however, to employ this construction in a looser sense,—not only

a. After verbs which contain in themselves the notion of (*requesting*),[1] *commanding*,[2] *resolving*, and which therefore mediately express *design*: e. g., A. xv. 20, κρίνω . . . ἐπιστεῖλαι αὐτοῖς τοῦ ἀπέχεσθαι, *to send them an injunction to abstain*; L. iv. 10 (from the LXX), τοῖς ἀγγέλοις αὐτοῦ ἐντελεῖται περὶ σοῦ τοῦ διαφυλάξαι· A. xxvii. 1 (where τοῦ ἀποπλεῖν cannot be connected with the following παρεδίδουν without forcing the words); compare Ruth ii. 9, 1 K. i. 35, 1 Macc. i. 62, iii. 31, v. 2, ix. 69, Malal. *Chron.* 18. 458, Ducas pp. 201, 217, 339, al., Fabric. *Pseudepigr.* I. 707, *Vit. Epiph.* p. 346 :—but also

b. for epexegesis, where the simple infinitive with or without ὥστε might have been used, and where the meaning of the genitive has been lost in the mixture of consequence and purpose. This is very common in the LXX, ʔ with the infinitive denoting both design and consequence:—as to εἰς τό with the infinitive see below. In the N. T. compare A. vii. 19, οὗτος κατασοφισάμενος . . . ἐκάκωσε τοὺς πατέρας ἡμῶν τοῦ ποιεῖν ἔκθετα τὰ βρέφη κ.τ.λ., *so that they exposed* (compare Thuc. 2. 42, and Poppo *in loc.*), and—a still harsher instance—A. iii. 12, ὡς πεποιηκόσι τοῦ περιπατεῖν αὐτόν (1 K. xvi. 19). In both these passages Fritzsche's explanation (*Matt.* p. 846) must certainly be rejected:

---

[1] Comp. Malalas 14. 357, ᾐτήσατο ἡ Αὔγουστα τὸν βασιλέα, τοῦ κατελθεῖν εἰς τοὺς ἁγίους τόπους· 17. 422, πυκνῶς ἔγραφε τοῖς αὐτοῖς πατρικίοις τοῦ φροντισθῆναι τὴν πόλιν· 18. 440, κιλεύσας τοῦ δοθῆναι αὐταῖς χάριν προικὸς ἀνὰ χρυσίου λιτρῶν εἴκοσι κ.τ.λ., 18. 461.
[2] A construction parallel to κελεύειν ἵνα.

SECT. XLIV.]   THE INFINITIVE.   411

if his principles were followed, many passages of the LXX could not be explained at all, or only in a very forced manner. Compare especially Jos. xxii. 26, εἴπαμεν ποιῆσαι οὕτω τοῦ οἰκοδομῆσαι· 1 K. xiii. 16, οὐ μὴ δύνωμαι τοῦ ἐπιστρέψαι (1 Macc. vi. 27), xvi. 19, ὑπὲρ τῶν ἁμαρτιῶν αὐτοῦ, ὧν ἐποίησε τοῦ ποιῆσαι τὸ πονηρόν κ.τ.λ., Judith xiii. 20, ποιῆσαι σοι αὐτὰ ὁ θεὸς εἰς ὕψος αἰώνιον τοῦ ἐπισκέψασθαί σε ἐν ἀγαθοῖς· 1 Macc. vi. 59, στήσωμεν αὐτοῖς τοῦ πορεύεσθαι τοῖς νομίμοις· Joel ii. 21, ἐμεγάλυνε κύριος τοῦ ποιῆσαι.

How diversified the use of the infinitive with τοῦ is in the LXX will appear from the following examples,—which might be easily classified, and in which a genitival relation may be more or less clearly perceived: Gen. xxxi. 20, xxxiv. 17, xxxvii. 18, xxxix. 10, Ex. ii. 18, vii. 14, viii. 29, ix. 17, xiv. 5, Jos. xxiii. 13, Jud. ii. 17, 21, 22, viii. 1, ix. 24, 37, xii. 6, xvi. 6, xviii. 9, xxi. 3, 7, 1 S. vii. 8, xii. 23, xiv. 34, xv. 26, 1 K. ii. 3, iii. 11, xii. 24, xv. 21, xvi. 7, 31, Ps. xxxix. 14, Jon. i. 4, iii. 4, Mal. ii. 10, 3 (1) Esdr. i. 33, iv. 41, v. 67, Judith ii. 13, v. 4, vii. 13, Ruth i. 12, 16, 18, iii. 3, iv. 4, 7, 15.[1] See also Thilo, *Act. Thom.* p. 20, Tischend. in the *Verhandeling.* p. 141: compare *Acta Apocr.* pp. 68, 85, 124, 127, al. This infinitive is by no means rare in the Byzantine writers: e. g., see Malal. 18. 452, 18. 491, and compare the index to Ducas p. 639, where we find even εἰ βούλεται τ ο ῦ εἶναι φίλος (p. 320, compare p. 189), δύναται τοῦ ἀνταποκριθῆναι (p. 203).

We must recognise in this usage an exaggeration of declining (Hellenistic) Greek, unless we prefer to resort to unnatural interpretations. It would seem that the infinitive with τοῦ had come to be regarded by the Hellenists as the representative of the Hebrew infinitive with לְ in its manifold relations; and, as usually happens in the case of established formulas, the proper signification of the genitive was no longer thought of.[2] An analogous case is the Byzantine use of ὥστε with the infinitive after such verbs as βουλεύεσθαι, δοκεῖν, etc.; see the index to Malalas in the Bonn edition.[3] Compare above, no. 3.

In Rev. xii. 7, ἐγένετο πόλεμος ἐν τῷ οὐρανῷ, ὁ Μιχαὴλ καὶ οἱ ἄγγελοι αὐτοῦ τοῦ πολεμῆσαι (where the *Rec.* has the correction ἐπολέμησαν), we have a construction which I am not able to explain (and Lücke says the same in regard to himself[4]),—unless it be admissible to

---

[1] [As to the LXX see Thiersch, *Pent.* pp. 173-175.]
[2] In Æsop. 172 (De Fur.) we find ἔμελλεν αὐτὸς τοῦ καταδῦσαι ταύτην: here Schæfer, having before his mind only that use of τοῦ with the infinitive which is referred to above, no. 4. *b*, would reject the τοῦ.
[3] The Greeks themselves might conceive this infinitive as a genitive, even when it follows such verbs as δύναμαι, θέλω, etc., inasmuch as the action expressed by the infinitive is always dependent on the principal verb, as a part on the whole.
[4] *Einleit. in die Offenbar. Joh.* (2 ed.), p. 454 sq.

regard ὁ Μιχ. καὶ οἱ ἄγγ. αὐτοῦ as a parenthesis (awkwardly introduced, it is true), which made it necessary for the writer to take up again the ἐγένετο πόλεμος by means of τοῦ πολεμῆσαι. Fritzsche's explanation [1] (*Matt.* p. 844) I consider artificial. Still less possible would it be to regard τοῦ πολεμῆσαι as an imitation of the (later) Hebrew idiom לְהִלָּחֶם בָּם, *pugnandum iis erat*,[2] as is done by Ewald and also by Züllig: in no instance do even the LXX render the Hebrew construction in this strange fashion. If we had merely ἐγένετο τοῦ πολεμῆσαι, A. x. 25 (see below) would be a parallel instance, and the construction might possibly be explained. Perhaps however an ancient gloss has found its way into the text, or else something has fallen out at an early period before τοῦ πολεμῆσαι. Bornemann's proposal [3] to read ἐγένετο πόλεμος ἐν τῷ οὐρανῷ ὁ Μιχαήλ κ.τ.λ. is not even plausible; and to supply (with Hengstenberg) *made war* before τοῦ πολεμῆσαι would make John chargeable with strange verbosity.

In A. x. 25, ἐγένετο τοῦ εἰσελθεῖν τὸν Πέτρον—where τοῦ is critically established—cannot be compared with the idiom mentioned in Gesen. *Lehrg.* p. 786 sq.,[4] for this would require ἐγένετο ὁ Πέτρος τοῦ εἰσελθεῖν. It is an extension of the infinitive with τοῦ beyond its proper limits,[5] which it is certainly surprising to meet with in Luke. Bornemann maintains that the whole clause is spurious: for his view of the true text of the passage the reader is referred to his own essay.

In L. xvii. 1, ἀνένδεκτόν ἐστι τ ο ῦ μὴ ἐλθεῖν τὰ σκάνδαλα, some MSS. omit τοῦ: if it is genuine (and Lachm. and Tisch. have retained it), the genitive is probably to be accounted for by the notion of distance or exclusion which is implied in ἀνένδεκτον; compare above, no. 4. *b*. Meyer's view is different.[6]

5. The dative of the infinitive expresses the *cause*,—a notion which regularly belongs to the dative case (see § 31. 6. c): [7]

---

[1] [That "Michael and his angels" is parenthetical (the subject of ἐπολέμησαν mentally supplied), so that τοῦ πολεμῆσαι depends on ὁ πόλεμος understood.]

[2] [Gesen. *Heb. Gr.* p. 216, Kalisch, *Heb. Gr.* I. 298.]

[3] *Jen. L.Z.* 1845, No. 183. [Düsterdieck agrees with Winer in considering the text corrupt.—A. Buttmann (p. 268) takes τοῦ πολ. as depending upon ἐγένετο κ.τ.λ., the subject of this infinitive being ὁ Μιχ. καὶ οἱ ἄγγ. αὐ.: the use of the nominative for the accusative he regards as a *constructio ad synesin*, the infinitival clause being equivalent to a subordinate sentence with a finite verb. A more probable explanation is suggested by Dr. Hort; that Μιχαὴλ . . . τοῦ πολεμῆσαι κ.τ.λ. is explanatory of πόλεμος, some *participle* (e. g., *going*, στρατευόμενοι) being supplied in the mind before τοῦ πολεμῆσαι.]

[4] [The use of לְ הָיָה in the sense *in eo erat ut* (Gen. xv. 12): see note [2].]

[5] Comp. *Acta Apocr.* p. 66, ὡς ἐγένετο τοῦ τελέσαι αὐτοὺς διδάσκοντας κ.τ.λ. A. ii. 1 would be an example of the same kind, if we were to read [with D] καὶ ἐγένετο ἐν ταῖς ἡμέραις ἐκείναις τοῦ συμπληροῦσθαι.

[6] [Meyer takes ἀνένδεκτον substantivally, "impossibility of the not-coming exists."—No uncial MS. omits τοῦ.]

[7] Matth. 541, Schæf. *Demosth.* II. 163, Stallb. Plat. *Tim.* p. 203. [Jelf 678. 3. *c*, Madv. 155.]

2 C. ii. 13, οὐκ ἔσχηκα ἄνεσιν τῷ πνεύματί μου τῷ μὴ εὑρεῖν Τίτον, *because I found not.* Compare Xen. *Cyr.* 4. 5. 9, Demosth. *Pac.* 21 c, *Funebr.* 156 b, *Ep.* 4. p. 119 b, Achill. Tat. 5. 24, Lucian, *Abdic.* 5, Diog. L. 10. 27, Liban. *Ep.* 8, Athen. 9. 375, Joseph. *Antt.* 14. 10. 1, Simplic. *in Epict. Enchir.* c. 38. p. 385, Schweigh. *Agath.* 5. 16. This infinitive has been taken as an expression of *design* in 1 Th. iii. 3, τῷ μηδένα σαίνεσθαι ἐν ταῖς θλίψεσι, *that no one may be shaken,* as if, for the not-being-shaken (Schott *in loc.*): the clause is thus subordinate to εἰς τὸ στηρίξαι, and is therefore expressed in a different form. No such dative infinitive however is found in Greek writers, and we must read with good MSS. τὸ μηδένα σαίνεσθαι, which indeed now stands in the text: see above, no. 1, Rem.[1]

6. An oblique case of the infinitive is frequently—almost more frequently in the N. T. than in Greek writers—combined with a preposition, especially in historical narration; in this case the article is never omitted (Herm. *Vig.* p. 702, Krüg. p. 110, Jelf 678),[2] though several words may be inserted between the article and the infinitive (A. viii. 11, H. xi. 3, 1 P. iv. 2).[3] Mt. xiii. 25, ἐν τῷ καθεύδειν τοὺς ἀνθρώπους, *during the sleeping of men (whilst men slept)*; G. iv. 18, L. i. 8, A. viii. 6 (Xen. *Cyr.* 1. 4. 5, *Hiero* 1. 6): A. iii. 26, εὐλογοῦντα ὑμᾶς ἐν τῷ ἀποστρέφειν κ.τ.λ., *through turning away* (H. iii. 12). Ph. i. 23, ἐπιθυμίαν ἔχων εἰς τὸ ἀναλῦσαι, *desire after dissolution;* Ja. i. 19, βραδὺς εἰς τὸ λαλῆσαι, *slow for speaking;* 1 C. x. 6, εἰς τὸ μὴ εἶναι ὑμᾶς ἐπιθυμητὰς κακῶν, *in order that ye may not be;* ix. 18, 2 C. iv. 4, vii. 3, Mt. xxvi. 2, L. iv. 29, A. vii. 19 (Xen. *Cyr.* 1. 4. 5, *An.* 7. 8. 20), Rom. iv. 18 (see Philippi *in loc.*); 1 Th. ii. 16,

---

[1] [This reference is carried on from ed. 5, but the notice to which it refers is omitted from the 6th edition. After observing that the N. T. presents but few examples of the loosely appended infinitives which are common in classical Greek, Winer says: "If in 1 Th. iii. 3 we read τὸ μ. σ., with the better MSS., the infinitive probably depends on παρακαλέσαι, and is explanatory of περὶ τῆς πίστεως" (p. 375 : ed. 5). Similarly De W., Hofmann, A. Buttm. (p. 263), Ellicott. For other explanations see the notes of Ellicott and Alford *in loc.* See also Green, *Crit. Notes* p. 170.]

[2] On the other hand, compare Theodoret III. 424, ἀπὸ κυβεύειν τὸ ὄνομα· IV. 851, παρὰ συγκλώθεσθαι· Psalt. Sal. 4. 9. Some examples of this kind are found in the Greek prose writers (Bernh. p. 354, Kühner II. 352, Jelf *l.c.*), but they are not free from doubt.

[3] Yet not so many words as we often find in Greek writers, who frequently interpose entire clauses (Xen. *Œc.* 13. 6, *Cyr.* 4. 5. 9, 7. 5. 42, al.): in the N. T., too, the adjuncts *follow* the infin., as a rule. We have no instance of ἄχρι or μέχρι with the infinitive, only one of ἕνεκα.

2 C. viii. 6, εἰς τὸ παρακαλέσαι ἡμᾶς Τίτον, *so that we besought Titus* (literally, up to the point of beseeching, etc.),[1] Rom. vii. 5, H. xi. 3. H. ii. 15, διὰ παντὸς τοῦ ζῆν, *through the whole life;* Ph. i. 7, διὰ τὸ ἔχειν με ἐν τῇ καρδίᾳ ὑμᾶς, *because I have you* etc.;[2] A. viii. 11, xviii. 2, H. vii. 23, x. 2, L. ii. 4, Mk. v. 4 (Xen. *Cyr.* 1. 4. 5, *Mem.* 2. 1. 15, Aristot. *Rhet.* 2. 13, Pol. 2. 5. 2). Ja. iv. 15, ἀντὶ τοῦ λέγειν ὑμᾶς, *instead of your saying* (Xen. *Apol.* 8, Plat. *Rep.* 1. 343 a). Mt. vi. 8, πρὸ τοῦ ὑμᾶς αἰτῆσαι, *before you ask;* L. ii. 21, xxii. 15, A. xxiii. 15 (Zeph. ii. 2, Plat. *Crit.* 48 d). Mt. vi. 1, πρὸς τὸ θεαθῆναι αὐτοῖς, *in order to be seen by them;* 2 C. iii. 13, 1 Th. ii. 9 :[3] L. xviii. 1, ἔλεγεν παραβολὴν πρὸς τὸ δεῖν πάντοτε προσεύχεσθαι, *in reference to the duty,* etc. Mt. xxvi. 32, μετὰ τὸ ἐγερθῆναί με, *after my rising* (resurrection), *when I shall have risen;* L. xii. 5, Mk. i. 14, A. vii. 4, xv. 13 (Herod. 2. 9. 6, 3. 5. 10). 2 C. vii. 12, εἵνεκεν τοῦ φανερωθῆναι τὴν σπουδὴν ὑμῶν (Demosth. *Fun.* 516 a, b, Plat. *Sis.* 390 b, Diod. S. *Exc. Vat.* p. 39; also *Inscript. Rosett.* 11).[4]

The use of the infinitive with εἰς or πρός to express purpose is particularly common in Paul's writings. The author of the Epistle to the Hebrews prefers a derivative noun in such cases; see Schulz, *Hebräerbr.* p. 146 sqq.[5] Compare however 1 C. vii. 35.

---

[1] No objection can be raised against resolving the infinitive with εἰς τό by *so that,* as this preposition when joined with nouns expresses either aim or result : compare Eurip. *Bacch.* 1161. [Fritzsche agrees with Winer in admitting this meaning (*Rom.* I. 63, 242): Meyer (see notes on Rom. i. 20, 2 C. viii. 6) maintains that the combination always denotes *purpose.* Ellicott remarks (on 1 Th. ii. 12) that it is "commonly used by St. Paul simply to denote the *purpose,* and probably in no instance is simply indicative of *result* (ecbatic);" but adds, "still there appear to be several passages in which the purpose is so far blended with the subject of the prayer, entreaty, etc., or the issues of the action, that it may not be improper to recognise a secondary and weakened force in reference to purpose, analogous to that in the parallel use of ἵνα." Alford distinctly admits the eventual sense in his note on H. xi. 3, but speaks somewhat inconsistently in his notes on Rom. i. 20, iv. 18. A. Buttm. (p. 264 sq.) divides the examples into 4 classes, as εἰς τό with infinitive denotes *purpose,*—or a *designed result,*—or follows such verbs as δεῖσθαι, ἐρωτᾶν, whose meaning relates to the future (1 Th. ii. 12, al.),—or replaces the epexegetical infinitive (1 Th. iv. 9). See Jelf 625. 3, 803. *Obs.* 1.]

[2] Against the other interpretation, in which ὑμᾶς is taken as the subject, see Van Hengel *in loc.* Even where the subject is placed after the infinitive, the correct view is always decided by the context: e.g., Simplic. *Enchir.* 13. p. 90, διὰ τὸ πολεμίους μιμεῖσθαι τοὺς συγγυμναστάς. Compare Jo. i. 49.

[3] [On πρὸς τό with infinitive, as signifying (never mere result, but) always the subjective purpose, see Alford's note (from Meyer) on 2 C. iii. 13.]

[4] [Add ἕως τοῦ ἐλθεῖν αὐτόν, A. viii. 40 (1 K. xxii. 27); ἐκ τοῦ ἔχειν, 2 C. viii. 11.]

[5] [There are certainly many verbal nouns in this Epistle (Davidson, *Intr.* III.

SECT. XLIV.] THE INFINITIVE. 415

If in this construction the infinitive has a subject expressed, this is put in the accusative, even when it is identical with the subject of the principal sentence: H. vii. 24, ὁ δὲ διὰ τὸ μένειν αὐτὸν εἰς τὸν αἰῶνα . . . . ἔχει· L. ii. 4. The predicates also stand in the accusative, L. xi. 8, δώσει αὐτῷ διὰ τὸ εἶναι αὐτοῦ φίλον: with this contrast Xen. *Cyr.* 1. 4. 3, διὰ τὸ φιλομαθὴς εἶναι . . . . αὐτὸς ἀνηρώτα (Matth. 536, Jelf 672. 4). The attraction, however, by which the use of the nominative is really to be explained, is neglected by Greek writers both in this and in other cases.

The infinitive (without the article) joined with πρίν or πρὶν ἤ[1] may also be regarded as an *infinitivus nominascens*, for κατάβηθι πρὶν ἀποθανεῖν τὸ παιδίον μου (Jo. iv. 49) is equivalent to κατ. πρὸ τοῦ ἀποθανεῖν κ.τ.λ. The infinitive with this particle is used, not merely with a future or an imperative in relation to an event still future (Matth. 522. 2. *c*), as in Mt. xxvi. 34 (A. ii. 20), but also in relation to events of the past (Xen. *Cyr.* 3. 3. 60, *An.* 1. 4. 13, Herod. 1. 10. 15) in combination with preterites; see Mt. i. 18, A. vii. 2, Jo. viii. 58. As to πρὶν ἤ compare Her. 2. 2, 4. 167.

7. The well known distinction between the present and the aorist infinitive, and also that between the aorist and the future infinitive (Herm. *Vig.* p. 773),[2] are for the most part very clearly observed in the N. T.

The aorist infinitive is used

a. In narration, in reference to a preterite on which it is dependent (in accordance with the parity of tenses which Greek writers particularly observe [3]): Mk. ii. 4, μὴ δυνάμενοι προςεγγίσαι αὐτῷ . . . . ἀπεστέγασαν· xii. 12, ἐζήτουν αὐτὸν κρατῆσαι· v. 3, οὐδεὶς ἠδύνατο αὐτὸν δῆσαι· L. xviii. 13, οὐκ ἤθελεν οὐδὲ τοὺς ὀφθαλμοὺς εἰς τὸν οὐρανὸν ἐπᾶραι· Jo. vi. 21, vii. 44, Mt. i. 19, viii. 29, xiv. 23, xviii. 23, xxiii. 37, xxvi. 40, xxvii. 34, Mk. vi. 19, 48, L. vi. 48, x. 24, xv. 28, xix. 27, A. x. 10, xvii. 3, xxv. 7, Col. i. 27, G. iv. 20, Phil. 14, Jude 3. This is quite in order, and requires no illustration from Greek writers (Madv. 172 b).—(Sometimes however the present infinitive is used, as in

---

247), but Stuart shows that εἰς τό with infinitive is not at all uncommon; see his *Comm.* p. 175 (London 1834).]
[1] Reitz, *Lucian* IV. 501: ed. Lehm. (Jelf 848. 6, Don. p. 584).
[2] Stallb. Plat. *Euthyd.* p. 140: Aoristus (infin.) quia nullam facit significationem perpetuitatis et continuationis, prouti vel initium vel progressus vel finis actionis verbo expressæ spectatur, ita solet usurpari, ut dicatur vel de eo, quod statim et e vestigio fit ideoque etiam certo futurum est, vel de re semel tantum eveniente, quæ diuturnitatis et perpetuitatis cogitationem aut non fert aut certe non requirit, vel denique de re brevi et uno veluti temporis ictu peracta. (Don. p. 415, Jelf 405. 4.)
[3] See Schæfer, *Demosth.* III. 432, Stallb. *Phileb.* p. 86, *Phæd.* p. 32.

Jo. xvi. 19, A. xix. 33, L. vi. 19 : in Mt. xxiii. 37 also we find the present,[1] but in the parallel passage, L. xiii. 34, the aorist infinitive.) The aorist imperative also is regularly followed by the aorist infinitive : Mt. viii. 22, ἄφες τοὺς νεκροὺς θάψαι τοὺς ἑαυτῶν νεκρούς· xiv. 28, Mk. vii. 27.

b. After any tense whatever, when the reference is to an action which rapidly passes, is completed all at once, or is to commence immediately (Herm. *Vig. l. c.*) : Mk. xiv. 31, ἐάν με δέῃ συναποθανεῖν σοι· xv. 31, ἑαυτὸν οὐ δύναται σῶσαι· Mt. xix. 3, εἰ ἔξεστιν ἀνθρώπῳ ἀπολῦσαι τὴν γυναῖκα· 1 C. xv. 53, δεῖ τὸ φθαρτὸν τοῦτο ἐνδύσασθαι ἀφθαρσίαν. Compare Jo. iii. 4, v. 10, ix. 27, xii. 21, A. iv. 16,[2] Rev. ii. 21, 2 C. x. 12, xii. 4, 1 Th. ii. 8, E. iii. 18. Under this head comes also Jo. v. 44,—where πιστεύειν means *to put faith in, become a believer in.*

c. After verbs of *hoping, promising, commanding, wishing,* and many others, the Greeks not unfrequently use the aorist infinitive,[3]—viz., where they wish to represent the action in itself, simply and absolutely (" ab omni temporis definiti conditione libera et immunis," Stallb. Plat. *Euthyd.* p. 140, Weber, *Dem.* p. 343).[4] Here the present infinitive would have respect to the duration of the action, or represent it as occurring at this present time; and the future infinitive (after verbs of *hoping* and *promising*) is used of that which will not occur until some uncertain time in the future.[5] Of these three tenses the aorist is the only one used with ἐλπίζω in the N. T.,[6] and there is no example which presents any difficulty, especially as the particular mode of regarding the subject frequently depends entirely on the writer's preference : L. vi. 34 παρ' ὧν ἐλπίζετε ἀπολαβεῖν· Ph. ii. 23

---

[1] [Not present, but second aorist.]
[2] [Here the best MSS. have the present.]
[3] Lob. *Phryn.* p. 751 sq., Poppo, Xen. *Cyr.* p. 153, Ast, Theophr. *Char.* p. 50 sq., Jacobs, *Achill. Tat.* pp. 525, 719, Weber, *Dem.* p. 343, and especially Schlosser, *Vindic. N. T. locor. adv. Marcland.* (Hamb. 1742), p. 20 sqq. [Jelf 405. 7, Riddell, Plat. *Apol.* p. 147.]
[4] It is less probable that the aorist infinitive is used here to indicate that the action is one which quickly passes by (Herm. Soph. *Aj.* p. 160, Krüg. *Dion. H.* p. 101, and others) : this point hardly comes into consideration in the expression of a hope or command.
[5] Held, Plut. *Timol.* p. 215 sq. ; compare Stallb. Plat. *Crit.* p. 138, Pflugk Eur. *Heracl.* p. 54 sq.
[6] [Lünemann remarks that the future is a variant once, A. xxvi. 7 (in B).]

SECT. XLIV.]   THE INFINITIVE.   417

τοῦτον ἐλπίζω πέμψαι, ὡς ἂν ἀπίδω κ.τ.λ., ii. 19, 2 Jo. 12, ἐλπίζω γενέσθαι πρὸς ὑμᾶς· 3 Jo. 14, A. xxvi. 7, Rom. xv. 24, 1 Tim. iii. 14, 1 C. xvi. 7, 2 C. x. 15.¹ Ἐπαγγέλλεσθαι also is commonly joined with the aorist infinitive, as in Mk. xiv. 11, ἐπηγγείλατο αὐτῷ δοῦναι· A. iii. 18, vii. 5; similarly ὄμνυμι, A. ii. 30, ὅρκῳ ὤμοσεν αὐτῷ ὁ θεὸς ἐκ καρποῦ τῆς ὀσφύος αὐτοῦ καθίσαι ἐπὶ τοῦ θρόνου,—but with future infinitive in H. iii. 18 (Weber, *Demosth.* p. 330). After κελεύειν the aorist infinitive is more common than the present, the latter being used for the most part of a lasting action; e.g., A. xvi. 22, ἐκέλευον ῥαβδίζειν· xxiii. 35, ἐκέλευσεν αὐτὸν ἐν τῷ πραιτωρίῳ φυλάσσεσθαι· xxiii. 3, xxv. 21, al.² Παρακαλεῖν is followed by the aorist infinitive in Rom. xii. 1, xv. 30, 2 C. ii. 8, E. iv. 1, al.; but by the present in Rom. xvi. 17, 1 Th. iv. 10, 1 Tim. ii. 1.

This will explain the use of the aorist infinitive after ἕτοιμος and ἐν ἑτοίμῳ ἔχειν (in reference to the future), 2 C. x. 6, xii. 14, 1 P. i. 5, A. xxi. 13. Here the present infinitive is less common in the N. T.: in Greek writers the aorist is on the whole rare, yet compare Dion. H. III. 1536 (Joseph. *Antt.* 12. 4. 2, 6. 9. 2). Πρίν also is in the N. T. uniformly joined with the aorist infinitive, and, where πρίν refers to future time, this tense has the signification of the *futurum exactum*: see Herm. Eurip. *Med.* p. 343 (Don. p. 584, Jelf 848. *Obs.* 6).

Whether in any other cases than that noticed in 7. *a* the aorist infinitive has in the N. T. the signification of a preterite, is a disputed point. Rom. xv. 9, τὰ ἔθνη ὑπὲρ ἐλέους δοξάσαι τὸν θεόν, might in the first instance be taken as an example of this, as the infinitive is dependent on λέγω, ver. 8 (Madvig 172 a), and is parallel with a perfect γεγενῆσθαι, while Paul would certainly have used a present to denote a continued act of praise. Probably, however, he merely wished to express the action of praising absolutely, without any reference to time. In 2 C. vi. 1 also it is not necessary to give δέξασθαι the sense of a preterite, as is done by Meyer and others; though the connexion which Fritzsche³ suggests between vi. 1 and v. 20 is somewhat far-fetched.—In the later language the perfect infinitive, as a more expressive form, takes the place of the aorist infinitive in such cases: see below, p. 420.

---

¹ The perfect infinitive follows ἐλπίζω in 2 C. v. 11, ἐλπίζω καὶ ἐν ταῖς συνειδήσεσιν ὑμῶν πεφανερῶσθαι, *that I have been made manifest*: here ἐλπίζω does not stand for νομίζω, but indicates an opinion which still waits for confirmation. The perfect infinitive, after the preceding πεφανερώμεθα, needs no explanation: compare *Iliad* 15. 110, ἤδη νῦν ἔλπομ' Ἄρηΐ γε πῆμα τετύχθαι, appositely cited by Meyer. See also below, p. 420.
² [On this verb see below, 8. *a*. note.]
³ *Rom.* III. 241. [Meyer now renders "ne recipiatis."]

27

The present infinitive is the general expression for an action which is now taking place, or which continues (either in itself or in its results), or which is frequently repeated : Jo. ix. 4, ἐμὲ δεῖ ἐργάζεσθαι τὰ ἔργα τοῦ πέμψαντός με· vii. 17, ἐάν τις θέλῃ τὸ θέλημα αὐτοῦ ποιεῖν· xvi. 12, οὐ δύνασθε βαστάζειν ἄρτι· iii. 30, A. xvi. 21, xix. 33, G. vi. 13, 1 C. xv. 25, 1 Tim. ii. 8, Tit. i. 11, Ph. i. 12. Hence it is used in general maxims : L. xvi. 13, οὐδεὶς οἰκέτης δύναται δυσὶ κυρίοις δουλεύειν· Mk. ii. 19, A. v. 29, Mt. xii. 2, 10, Ja. iii. 10, al. Verbs of *thinking, believing,* are joined with the present infinitive when the reference is to something which already exists, or at least has already commenced,[1] as in 1 C. vii. 36, Ph. i. 17 (16). As to κελεύειν with the present infinitive, see above.

If this distinction is not invariably observed where it might have been expected, this is explained by the fact that in many cases it depends entirely on the writer whether an action shall be represented as enduring, or as rapidly passing and filling but a single point of past time (compare L. xix. 5, Mt. xxii. 17); and also that it is not every writer who is sufficiently careful in such points. Hence we sometimes find the two tenses used in parallel passages, though the reference is the same in both cases ; compare Mt. xxiv. 24 and Mk. xiii. 22, Mt. xiii. 3 and L. viii. 5, —also Jude 3. Instances of the same kind are met with even in the better Greek authors: e.g., Xen. *Cyr.* 1. 4. 1, εἴ τι τοῦ βασιλέως δέοιντο, τοὺς παῖδας ἐκέλευον τοῦ Κύρου δεῖσθαι διαπράξασθαί σφισι· ὁ δὲ Κῦρος, εἰ δέοιτο αὐτοῦ οἱ παῖδες, περὶ παντὸς ἐποιεῖτο διαπράττεσθαι; 6. 1. 45, ἢν ἐμὲ ἐάσῃς πέμψαι, and in 46, ἐκέλευσε πέμπειν; 2. 4. 10, οὓς ἄν τις βούληται ἀγαθοὺς συνεργοὺς ποιεῖσθαι . . . . οὓς δὲ δὴ τῶν εἰς τὸν πόλεμον ἔργων ποιήσασθαί τις βούλοιτο συνεργοὺς προθύμους;[2] Demosth. *Timocr.* 466 a, μὴ ἐξεῖναι λῦσαι μηδένα (νόμον), ἐὰν μὴ ἐν νομοθέταις, τότε δ᾿ ἐξεῖναι τῷ βουλομένῳ . . . . λύειν. Compare also Arrian, *Al.* 5. 2. 6. Sometimes however there is a perceptible distinction between the two tenses in parallel sentences, e.g., Xen. *Cyr.* 5. 1. 2, 3, *Mem.* 1. 1. 14. Her. 6. 117, al.: see Matth. 501, Weber, *Dem.* pp. 195, 492. In the N. T. compare Mt. xiv. 22, ἠνάγκασε τοὺς μαθητὰς

---

[1] Herm. Soph. *Œd. C.* 91.—See Ast, Plat. *Legg.* p. 204.
[2] Compare Poppo *in loc.*

ἐμβῆναι εἰς τὸ πλοῖον (an action which rapidly passes) καὶ προάγειν (a continued action) αὐτόν κ.τ.λ., L. xiv. 30, Ph. i. 21. On the whole see Maetzner, *Antiphon.* p. 153 sq.

Where it is a matter of indifference which of the two tenses shall be used, the aorist infinitive (as being less precise in its meaning) is on the whole more common than the present, especially after ἔχω *possum*,[1] δύναμαι, δυνατός εἰμι, θέλω, etc. The present and aorist infinitive are not unfrequently interchanged in MSS. of Greek authors; see Xen. *Cyr.* 2. 2. 13, Arrian, *Al.* 4. 6. 1, Elmsley, Eur. *Med.* 904, 941, al. So also in the N. T. : compare Jo. x. 21, A. xvi. 7, 1 C. xiv. 35, 1 Th. ii. 12.

What is said above will also explain the use of the aorist infinitive after a hypothetical clause in Jo. xxi. 25, ἅτινα, ἐὰν γράφηται καθ᾽ ἕν, οὐδὲ αὐτὸν οἶμαι τὸν κόσμον χωρῆσαι, *non comprehensurum esse*, where some would unnecessarily introduce ἄν. Compare Isocr. *Trapez.* 862, Demosth. *Timoth.* 702 a, Thuc. 7. 28, Plat. *Protag.* 316 c,—in some of which passages, however, εἰ with the optative has preceded.[2] The omission of ἄν gives greater confidence to the expression; see Stallb. Plat. *Protag.* p. 43, and compare Lösner, *Obs.* p. 162 sq. The use of the future infinitive (also without ἄν, compare Herm. *Partic.* ἄν, p. 187) is not singular in such a connexion; see Isocr. *Ep.* 3. p. 984.

As regards the construction of μέλλειν with the infinitive, this verb is in Greek writers most frequently followed by the future infinitive.[3] More rarely is it joined with the present infinitive (compare Dion. H. IV. 2226. 8, Arrian, *Al.* 1. 20. 13, 5. 21. 1, and Krüg. *Dion.* p. 498), though there is nothing very strange in this combination, as the notion of futurity is already contained in μέλλειν itself, and an analogy is presented by the construction of ἐλπίζειν. Still more rarely do we find μέλλειν with an aorist infinitive (Plat. *Apol.* 30 b, Isocr. *Callim.* p. 908, Thuc. 5. 98, Paus. 8. 28. 3, Æl. 3. 27), and indeed this construction is pronounced by some ancient grammarians (e.g., Phrynich. p. 336) to be un-Greek, or at all events un-Attic; it has however been sufficiently vindicated by a fair number of well-attested examples.[4] In the N. T., μέλλειν is followed (*a*) most frequently, in the Gospels *always*, by the present infinitive :—(*b*) occasionally by the aorist, usually in reference to actions which rapidly pass by, as in Rev. iii. 2, μέλλει ἀποθανεῖν· iii. 16, μ. ἐμέσαι· xii. 4, μ. τεκεῖν· G. iii. 23, τὴν μέλλουσαν πίστιν ἀποκαλυφθῆναι· compare Rom. viii. 18 (but contrast 1 P. v. 1) ;—(*c*) more rarely by the

---

[1] Herm. Eur. *Suppl.* p. 12. *Praef.*
[2] [Tregelles, Westcott and Hort, read χωρήσειν, with the most ancient of our MSS. See Jelf 405. 7.]
[3] Compare also Ellendt, Arr. *Al.* II. 206 sq.
[4] See Böckh, Pind. *Olymp.* 8. 32, Elmsley, Eur. *Heracl.* p. 117, Bremi, *Lys.* p. 745 sqq. : compare also Herm. Soph. *Aj.* p. 149 (Jelf 408).

future,¹ in A. xi. 28, λιμὸν μέγαν μέλλειν ἔσεσθαι· xxiv. 15, ἀνάστασιν μέλλειν ἔσεσθαι νεκρῶν· xxvii. 10 (xxiv. 25).

The perfect infinitive is frequently used, especially in narration, to denote some event altogether past in its relation to present time : A. xvi. 27, ἔμελλεν ἑαυτὸν ἀναιρεῖν, νομίζων ἐκπεφευγέναι τοὺς δεσμίους, *that they had fled*, and hence *were away*; xxvii. 13, δόξαντες τῆς προθέσεως κεκρατηκέναι, *that they had* (already) *accomplished their purpose*, and hence were now in possession of its advantages. See also A. viii. 11, xxvii. 9, xxvi. 32, H. xi. 3, Rom. iv. 1, xv. 8, 19, Mk. v. 4, Jo. xii. 18, 29, 2 Tim. ii. 18 (1 P. iv. 3), 2 P. ii. 21. In several of these passages, after verbs of *saying* and *thinking*, a Greek writer would perhaps have been contented with the aorist infinitive (Madv. 172). On 2 C. v. 11 see p. 417, note;¹ on 1 Tim. vi. 17, § 40. 4.

8. That the N. T. writers sometimes (see p. 421, note ¹) use ἵνα in cases where, according to the rules of (written) Greek prose, we should have expected the simple infinitive (present or aorist, not perfect), was rightly admitted by the earlier Biblical philologers, but is positively denied by Fritzsche :² up to this time, however, Fritzsche has hardly had any follower, with the exception of Meyer.³ It might indeed be possible in such phrases as

---

¹ [It is singular that ἔσεσθαι is the only future infinitive joined with μέλλω.]
² Exc. 1 *ad Matth.*: see however *Rom.* III. 230. [In *Rom. l. c.* Fritz. says: ut interdum ἵνα cum conjunctivo post verba rogandi et precandi *rem*, quam preceris, designet (3 Esdr. iv. 46, cf. θέλω ἵνα Jo. xvii. 24, et similia), tamen multo frequentius in N. T. post illa verba ἵνα *precantis consilium* declarat.]
³ On the other hand, Tittmann (*Synon*. II. 46 sqq.), Wahl (also in his *Clav. Apocr.* p. 272), and Bretschneider agree with me in the view maintained above. Compare also Robinson, *A Greek and English Lexicon of the N. T.* (New York, 1850) p. 352 sq. (Edinburgh, 1857 : p. 374 sq.). [Meyer still maintains that ἵνα always expresses purpose. He takes the same view of εἰς τό and τοῦ with infinitive: indeed these three constructions should certainly be considered together, see Jelf 803. *Obs.* 1. In Bp. Ellicott's note on E. i. 17, he states that the uses of ἵνα in the N. T. are three, *final, subfinal* ("especially after verbs of entreaty, *not* of command"), *eventual* ("apparently in a few cases") : compare his note on Col. iv. 16, which seems to go beyond this statement. See also Alford on 1 C. xiv. 13. A. Buttmann's classification is nearly the same as in the case of εἰς τό (see above, p. 414, note¹): (1) ἵνα of *purpose*; (2) ἵνα after verbs whose meaning is akin to *purpose* (*wish, request, command*); (3) ἵνα after such verbs as *make, persuade, permit,* etc., to indicate an *effect* as designed by the subject (here ἵνα is essentially equivalent to ὥστε with infinitive) ; (4) the cases in which the notion of purpose has disappeared, and in which ἵνα merely indicates a reference to something still *future*, the dependent sentence frequently completing the incomplete notion of the verb : here ἵνα represents the infinitive (with or without ὥστε), especially the future infinitive, so seldom used

Mt. iv. 3, εἰπέ, ἵνα οἱ λίθοι οὗτοι ἄρτοι γένωνται· xvi. 20, διεστείλατο τοῖς μαθηταῖς, ἵνα μηδενὶ εἴπωσιν κ.τ.λ., and especially Mk. v. 10, παρεκάλει αὐτὸν πολλά, ἵνα μὴ αὐτοὺς ἀποστείλῃ κ.τ.λ., to retain the original meaning of ἵνα, and translate, *speak* (a word of power) *in order that these stones may become bread,—he gave the disciples a charge, in order that they might tell no man,—he besought him earnestly, in order that he might not send them.* But, on the other hand, it is still very singular that in a multitude of instances, when we are expecting that the *object* of the request or command will be mentioned, the writer should prefer to specify the *purpose*, which in such combinations is usually absorbed by the object; and on the other hand, the very possibility of such an explanation shows how nearly akin are purpose and object in such a case, and consequently how easily ἵνα might come into use as an expression of the latter. Hence it is far simpler to suppose that the later language, in accordance with its general character, resolved the more condensed infinitive construction into a sentence proper, and to some extent weakened the signification of ἵνα,[1] on the same principle as the Romans used *ut* after *impero, persuadeo, rogo,*—the object of the command or request being always something to be effected, and therefore something which is *designed* by the person commanding or beseeching.[2] We already meet with traces of this application of ἵνα in writers of the κοινή.

a. After verbs of *desiring* and *requesting*, ἵνα begins in these writers to pass into "that" of the objective sentence;[3] as in Dion. H. I. 215, δεήσεσθαι τῆς θυγατρὸς τῆς σῆς ἔμελλον, ἵνα με πρὸς αὐτὴν ἀγάγοι· II. 666 sq., κραυγὴ . . . . ἐγένετο καὶ

---

in the N. T. (*Gram.* pp. 235–239). See also Lightfoot on G. v. 17, Ph. i. 9, Col. i. 9, iv. 16, Green p. 171 sq., Webster p. 130 sq.]

[1] *Weakened*, because originally ἵνα was used only to express a direct purpose, —*I come that I may help thee.* Even *sufficiently worthy to be preserved* was expressed in early writers, not by ἵνα (Mt. viii. 8, Jo. i. 27, vi. 7, al.), but by the infinitive, perhaps with ὥστε (Matth. 531, Jelf 666). But it does not follow that the weakened ἵνα is generally equivalent to ὥστε : this use of ἵνα is rather, as we can still perceive in most cases, an extension of *eo consilio ut*. Hence if on the one side we maintain the above principles, and on the other deny that ἵνα stands for ὥστε (§ 53. 10), we are not inconsistent.

[2] Those who oppose this view should at least confess that the use of ἵνα in the cases considered is not in accordance with the (earlier) prose usage of the Greeks. This is the least requirement of grammatical fairness.

[3] An isolated instance in earlier Greek is ἀξιοῦν ἵνα, Demosth. *Cor.* 335 b.

δεήσεις .... ἵνα μένῃ κ.τ.λ.· Charit. 3. 1, παρεκάλει Καλιρρόην ἵνα αὐτῷ προςέλθῃ· Arrian, *Epict.* 3. 23. 27 (see Schæf. Melet. p. 121). In Hellenistic writers, however, this usage is quite common: see 2 Macc. ii. 8, Ecclus. xxxvii. 15, xxxviii. 14, 3 (1) Esdr. iv. 46, Joseph. *Antt.* 12. 3. 2, 14. 9. 4, Ignat. *Philad.* p. 379,*Cod. Pseudepigr.* I. 543, 671, 673, 730, II. 705. *Act. Thom.* 10, 24, 26, *Acta apoc.* p. 36.[1] On ἵνα after verbs of *commanding* and *directing*,[2] see Herm. *Orph.* p. 814, and compare Leo Philos. in *Epigr. Gr. Libb.* 7 (Frankf. 1600) p. 3, εἰπὲ κασιγνήτῃ κρατεροὺς ἵνα θῆρας ἐγείρῃ· Malal. 3. p. 64, *Basilic.* I. 147; κελεύειν and θεσπίζειν ἵνα, 3 (1) Esdr. vi. 31, Malal. 10. p. 264; ἐπιτρέπειν ἵνα, Malal. 10. p. 264; διδάσκειν ἵνα, *Acta Petri et Pauli* 7.[3] So also in the N. T. we may translate such passages as the following without rigorously pressing ἵνα, by *command her that, I implored the Lord that, she besought him that,* like the Latin *præcipe, rogavit, imploravit ut*, etc.: L. x. 40, εἰπὸν αὐτῇ ἵνα μοι συναντιλάβηται (iv. 3, Mk. iii. 9, Jo. xi. 57, xiii. 34, xv. 17), 2 C. xii. 8, τὸν κύριον παρεκάλεσα ἵνα ἀποστῇ ἀπ' ἐμοῦ (Mk. v. 18, viii. 22, L. viii. 31, 1 C. i. 10, xvi. 12, 2 C. ix. 5), Mk. vii. 26, ἠρώτα αὐτὸν ἵνα τὸ δαιμόνιον ἐκβάλῃ (Jo. iv. 47, xvii. 15, L. vii. 36), L. ix. 40, ἐδεήθην τῶν μαθητῶν σου ἵνα ἐκβάλωσιν (xxii. 32), Ph. i. 9, προσεύχομαι ἵνα ἡ ἀγάπη ὑμῶν .... περισσεύῃ.

b. Moreover θέλειν ἵνα will also simply stand for our *wish that.*[4] Compare Arrian, *Ep.* 1. 18. 14, Macar. *Hom.* 32. 11, *Cod.*

---

[1] In the Acts Luke never uses this construction, but always joins ἐρωτᾶν and παρακαλεῖν with the infinitive, see viii. 31, xi. 23, xvi. 39, xix. 31, xxvii. 33: in his Gospel, too, ἐρωτᾶν is once followed by the infinitive (v. 3), a construction which also occurs in Jo. iv. 40, 1 Th. v. 12. In Matthew, παρακαλεῖν is commonly followed by the direct words of the suppliant. [These statements require qualification. In the Acts we also find ἐρωτᾶν ὅπως, παρακαλεῖν ὅπως (xxiii. 20, xxv. 2): in ix. 38 παρακαλεῖν is followed by the *oratio directa*, in xxi. 12 by the infinitive with τοῦ. Παρακαλεῖν is followed by λέγων and the *oratio directa* three times in Matthew, and twice by ἵνα or ὅπως.—Ἐρωτᾶν with the infinitive occurs also in L. viii. 37.]

[2] Κελεύειν is never construed with ἵνα in the N. T. [A. Buttmann (p. 275) notices "the unclassical use of this verb with the *passive* infinitive and accusative" (Mt. xviii. 25, and often), and sees in this the influence of the Latin *jubere* (Roby II. 142). This construction is found in the N. T. with some similar words (Mk. vi. 27, al.). The tense of the infinitive is usually the aorist.]

[3] Analogous to this is the use of the infinitive with τοῦ after verbs of *intreating, exhorting, commanding*: Malal. 17. 422, πυκνῶς ἔγραφε τοῖς αὐτοῖς πατρικίοις τοῦ Φροντισθῆναι τὴν πόλιν· 18. 440, κελεύσας τοῦ δοθῆναι αὐταῖς χάριν προικὸς ἀνὰ χρυσίου λιτρῶν εἴκοσι κ.τ.λ.; 461, ᾔτησε πᾶς ὁ δῆμος τοῦ ἀχθῆναι πάνδημον· p. 172. See the index to Ducas, p. 639 sq. (Bonn ed.).

[4] Hence was derived the periphrasis for the infinitive in modern Greek, θέλω

Pseudepigr. I. 704, Thilo, *Apocr.* I. 546, 684, 706, Tischend. in the *Verhandel.* p. 141. If in Mt. vii. 12 ὅσα ἂν θέλητε ἵνα ποιῶσιν ὑμῖν means *wish with the design that they may do it,* one cannot see why θέλειν ἵνα should not have become an ordinary construction in the language, for θέλειν may always be taken in this way. And are we to render Mk. vi. 25, θέλω ἵνα μοι δῷς τὴν κεφαλὴν Ἰωάννου, by *I wish, in order that thou mayest give me?* What then is the proper object of the wish? Is it not the obtaining of John's head? Then why this roundabout mode of expressing it? In Mk. ix. 30 also, if οὐκ ἤθελεν ἵνα τις γνῷ meant, *he wished not, in order that any one should know of it,* how affected a sentence would this be! That no one should know of it was the very object of his wish. Compare also A. xxvii. 42, βουλὴ ἐγένετο, ἵνα τοὺς δεσμώτας ἀποκτείνωσι· Jo. ix. 22, συνετέθειντο οἱ Ἰουδαῖοι ἵνα . . . . ἀποσυνάγωγος γένηται· xii. 10 (Ecclus. xliv. 18); and, as a single early instance of this construction in Greek writers, Teles in Stob. *Serm.* 95, p. 524. 40, ἵνα Ζεὺς γένηται ἐπιθυμήσει. To this head belongs also ποιεῖν ἵνα, Jo. xi. 37, Col. iv. 16, Rev. iii. 9 (analogous to ποιεῖν τοῦ with the infinitive,—see above, no. 4), also διδόναι ἵνα, Mk. x. 37 (see Krebs *in loc.*).

c. Lastly, in Mt. x. 25, ἀρκετὸν τῷ μαθητῇ, ἵνα γένηται ὡς ὁ διδάσκαλος αὐτοῦ, is *satis sit discipulo non superare magistrum, ut ei possit par esse redditus,* an easy or a satisfactory rendering? Compare Jo. i. 27, vi. 7, Mt. viii. 8: the infinitive is used in Mt. iii. 11, 1 C. xv. 9, L. xv. 19, al. In Jo. iv. 34, ἐμὸν βρῶμά ἐστιν, ἵνα ποιῶ τὸ θέλημα τοῦ πέμψαντός με, is the use of ἵνα completely justified by the rendering, *meus victus hoc continetur studio, ut Dei satisfaciam voluntati?* In that case σπουδάζειν ἵνα would be the ordinary and the simplest construction. That in Jo. xv. 8 the clause beginning with ἵνα cannot denote the design with which God glorifies himself (Meyer),

---

νὰ γράφω or γράψω, for γράφειν, γράψαι. To what an extent the use of the particle νά—which is found as early as the Byzantine writers, e. g. in Cananus (compare also Boissonade, *Anecd.* IV. 367)—is carried in modern Greek, may be shown by a few examples from the *Confessio Orthod.*: p. 20 (ed. Normann), πρέπει νὰ πιστεύωμεν (pp. 24, 30); p. 36, λέγεται νὰ κατοικᾷ· p. 43, ἐφοβεῖτο νὰ δουλεύῃ (*he hesitated*, compare Mt. i. 20), p. 113, ἠμπορεῖ νὰ δεχθῇ· p. 211, θέλει, ἐπιθυμᾷ νὰ ἀποκτήσῃ· p. 235, ἔχουσι χρέος νὰ νουθετοῦσι· p. 244, εἵμισθαν χρεωφειλέται νὰ ὑπογένωμεν. Hence in almost all the passages noticed above the modern Greek translator has retained ἵνα in the form νά.

has been already shown by Lücke: compare also xvii. 3. I very much fear also that the resolution of Mt. xviii. 6, συμφέρει αὐτῷ, ἵνα κρεμασθῇ μύλος ὀνικός .... καὶ καταποντισθῇ κ.τ.λ., into συμφέρει αὐτῷ κρεμασθῆναι μύλον ὀνικὸν .... ἵνα καταποντισθῇ κ.τ.λ. (by an attraction), will generally be considered harsh: Meyer's expedient here is too manifest a shift. See further L. xvii. 2, xi. 50,[1] Jo. xvi. 7, 1 C. iv. 2, 3, Ph. ii. 2; also L. i. 43, πόθεν μοι τοῦτο, ἵνα ἔλθῃ ἡ μήτηρ τοῦ κυρίου κ.τ.λ.,[2]—on which passage Hermann remarks (*Partic. ἄν* p. 135), "fuit hæc labantis linguæ quædam incuria, ut pro infinitivo ista constructione uteretur." In fact, to an unprejudiced reader all these sentences with ἵνα will convey exactly what a Greek writer would have expressed by the simple infinitive (Matth. 532 e); and the change is the same in principle as the use of *æquum est ut, mos est ut, expedit ut,* in Latin (especially of the silver age), where the simple infinitive (in the place of the subject) would have been sufficient.[3] Sometimes we find this mode of expression and the infinitive construction combined,—as in 1 C. ix. 15, καλὸν γάρ μοι μᾶλλον ἀποθανεῖν, ἢ τὸ καύχημά μου ἵνα τις κενώσῃ, where it is not difficult to see what led the apostle to change the construction: in this passage, however, it is not certain that ἵνα is genuine.[4]—Hence that which in the examples quoted under (*a*), and even under (*b*), still called to mind the old function of the particle of design, disappeared entirely at a later period in the examples last illustrated; and now it is easy to explain how modern Greek, extending this usage more and more, now expresses *every* infinitive by means of νά.[5] But how low the popular language had sunk even in the second century, is shown here and there by Phrynichus, especially p. 15 sq. (ed. Lobeck).

The examples quoted by Wyttenbach[6] from Greek writers, in support of this lax use of ἵνα for ὥστε, are not all to the point. In

---

[1] [No doubt this should be Jo. xi. 50.]
[2] Analogous to this is Arrian, *Epictet.* 1. 10. 8, πρῶτόν ἐστιν, ἵνα ἐγὼ κοιμηθῶ. Compare further *Acta Apocr.* pp. 8, 15, 29.
[3] See Zumpt 623.
[4] [There is strong evidence for οὐδεὶς κενώσει.]
[5] [In all ordinary cases this periphrasis is used, see Mullach, *Vulg.* pp. 221, 373, J. Donalds. *Gr.* p. 32, Sophocles, *Gr.* p. 173. It is held by some that certain forms used with the auxiliary verbs are infinitives (J. Donalds. p. 23, Soph. p. 91): against this see Mullach p. 241 sqq., where it is maintained that these also are conjunctive forms.]
[6] Plutarch, *Mor.* I. 409 (ed. Lips.), p. 517 (ed. Oxon.).

πείθειν ἵνα, Plut. *Apophth.* 183 a, the clause with ἵνα is not a complement of the verb, *to effect by persuasion that*, etc. ; πείθειν is used absolutely, *to speak persuasively to some one in order that*. Plut. *Fort. Alex.* p. 333 a, τί μοι τοιοῦτο συνέγνως, ἵνα τοιαύταις με κολακεύσῃς ἡδοναῖς, means *what of this kind have you perceived in me, in order to flatter?* i. e., in brief, what could induce you to flatter me? In *Adv. Colol.* p. 1115 a (240, ed. Tauchnitz), ποῦ τῆς ἀοικήτου τὸ βιβλίον ἔγραφεν, ἵνα . . . μὴ τοῖς ἐκείνου συντάγμασιν ἐντύχῃς, that which in strictness was merely a *consequence* is attributed to the writer of the book as a *purpose;* just as we also say, In what desert then did he write his book, that you might not meet with it? Liban. *Decl.* 17. p. 472, οὐδείς ἐστιν οἰκέτης πονηρός, ἵνα κριθῇ τῆς Μακεδόνων δουλείας ἄξιος, means *no slave is bad in order to be condemned;* here ἵνα does not stand for ὡς after an intensive word (*so bad that*), but expresses the purpose which might bring into existence the πονηρία of the slaves : see § 53. 10. These passages are not strictly parallel to the N. T. examples quoted above, but we see in them the gradual transition to the construction of which we are speaking.—The construction ὅρα ὅπως has no connexion whatever with this subject; and the use of ὅπως after verbs of *requesting, commanding*, etc. (Mt. viii. 34, ix. 38, L. vii. 3, x. 2, xi. 37, A. xxv. 3, Phil. 6, al.), which is not uncommon in Greek writers,[1] is usually explained otherwise :[2] see however Tittmann, *Syn.* II. 59.

John's use of this particle[3] deserves still further notice, and particularly the case in which ἵνα appears as the complement of a demonstrative pronoun. These instances are of two kinds :—

a. 1 Jo. iii. 11, αὕτη ἐστὶν ἡ ἀγγελία, ἵνα ἀγαπῶμεν, *that we should love*, iii. 23 ; compare Jo. vi. 40. Here the notion of *purpose* which belongs to ἵνα is still perceptible (in the manner explained above, p. 420 sq.) ; as it also is in Jo. iv. 34, ἐμὸν βρῶμά ἐστιν ἵνα ποιῶ τὸ θέλημα τοῦ πέμψαντος, *that I should do* (should strive to do), vi. 29. No one will maintain that here ἵνα is equivalent to ὅτι.

b. In Jo. xv. 8, however, ἐν τούτῳ ἐδοξάσθη ὁ πατήρ μου, ἵνα καρπὸν πολὺν φέρητε, the clause with ἵνα certainly stands for an infinitive, ἐν τῷ καρπὸν πολὺν φέρειν ὑμᾶς. Similar to this are Jo. xvii. 3, αὕτη ἐστὶν ἡ αἰώνιος ζωή, ἵνα γινώσκωσιν κ.τ.λ.,[4] xv. 13, 1 Jo. iv. 17, 3 Jo. 4 ; also L. i. 43, πόθεν μοι τοῦτο, ἵνα ἔλθῃ, for τὸ ἐλθεῖν τὴν μήτερα (see above). The same may be said of the phrase χρείαν ἔχειν ἵνα,

---

[1] Schæf. *Demosth.* III. 416, Held, Plut. *Timol.* p. 439, Holwerda, *Emendatt. Flav.* p. 96 sq.
[2] Matth. 531. Rem. 2, Rost p. 662. [Viz., by reference to the original meaning of ὅπως, *in what way*. Rost's words however do not seem to be intended to apply to these particular verbs. Compare Jelf 664. *Obs.* 3.]
[3] Compare Lücke I. 603, II. 632 sq., 667 sq. [See especially Westcott, *Introd. to Gospels* p. 270, and *St. John* p. lii. ; also his notes on Jo. vi. 29, xvii. 3.]
[4] Arrian, *Epict.* 2. 1. 1 is wrongly adduced by Schweighäuser (*Lexic. Epictet.* p. 356) as an example of this particular construction.

Jo. ii. 25, xvi. 30, 1 Jo. ii. 27 (*Ev. Apocr.* p. 111), and also of Jo. xviii. 39. But in Jo. viii. 56, ἠγαλλιάσατο ἵνα ἴδῃ, the meaning is not *he rejoiced in order that he might see*, and still less *he rejoiced that* (ὅτι) *he saw*, but *he rejoiced that he should see:*[1] this meaning, however, could hardly have been expressed by a Greek author by means of the simple ἵνα, though the notion of destination (design) is contained in the particle. In Jo. xi. 15 ἵνα is simply a particle of design. Lastly, the phrases ἔρχεται or ἐλήλυθεν ἡ ὥρα, ἵνα δοξασθῇ (xii. 23, xiii. 1, xvi. 2, 32) mean, *the time is come in order that*, etc., i. e., the time appointed for the purpose that, etc. A Greek writer, it is true, would have expressed this meaning by the infinitive, ἐλήλυθεν ἡ ὥρα (τοῦ) δοξασθῆναι, or perhaps by ὥστε δοξασθῆναι.[2] Compare *Ev. Apocr.* p. 127.

On Rom. ix. 6, οὐχ οἷον δὲ ὅτι ἐκπέπτωκεν ὁ λόγος τοῦ θεοῦ, where the infinitive seems to be replaced by a clause with ὅτι, see § 64. I. 6.

Rem. 1. It might seem that the infinitive active is sometimes used in the place of the infinitive passive (D'Orville, *Charit.* p. 526) : e. g., compare 1 Th. iv. 9, περὶ τῆς φιλαδελφίας οὐ χρείαν ἔχετε γράφειν ὑμῖν (H. v. 12[3]), with 1 Th. v. 1, οὐ χρείαν ἔχετε ὑμῖν γράφεσθαι (also with H. vi. 6). Both expressions, however, are equally correct; that with the active infinitive meaning *ye have no need for writing to you*, i. e., *that any one*, or *that I, should write to you*,—q. d., ye do not need the writing. Indeed the active infinitive is probably the form more commonly used by Greek authors in such combinations.[4] Compare especially Theodoret II. 1528, IV. 566.

Rem. 2. Ὅτι is joined with the infinitive in A. xxvii. 10, θεωρῶ ὅτι μετὰ πολλῆς ζημίας οὐ μόνον τοῦ φορτίου καὶ τοῦ πλοίου, ἀλλὰ καὶ τῶν ψυχῶν ἡμῶν μέλλειν ἔσεσθαι τὸν πλοῦν. Compare Xen. *Hell.* 2. 2. 2, εἰδώς, ὅτι, ὅσῳ ἂν πλείους συλλεγῶσιν ἐς τὸ ἄστυ, θᾶττον τῶν ἐπιτηδείων ἔνδειαν ἔσεσθαι; *Cyr.* 1. 6. 18, 2. 4. 15, *An.* 3. 1. 9, Plat. *Phæd.* 63 c, Thuc. 4. 37. This is a mixture of two constructions (Herm. *Vig.* p. 500, Jelf 804. 7), μέλλειν ἔσεσθαι τὸν πλοῦν, and ὅτι μέλλει ἔσεσθαι ὁ πλοῦς, and is found especially after *verba sentiendi* and *dicendi*.[5] It occurs so frequently in the best writers (even in short sentences, Arrian, *Al.* 6. 26. 10), that the construction had

---

[1] [It is hard to believe that this meaning (which is equivalent to *rejoiced because he knew that he should see*) can be conveyed by ἠγαλλ. ἵνα. The most natural paraphrase appears to be *he rejoiced in desire that he might see*. Comp. Westcott *in loc.*]

[2] The conjunctive will not allow us to take ἵνα as *where* in these cases (Hoogev. *Particul.* I. 525 sq.) ; we should then have to regard the conjunctive aorist as the simple equivalent of the future (Lob. *Phryn.* p. 723). See however Tittmann, *Synon.* II. 49 sq.

[3] [That is, if we read τίνα, not τινά.]

[4] See Elmsley, Eurip. *Heracl.* p. 151 (Lips.), Jacobs, Philostr. *Imagg.* 620 ; and, in regard to χρή and δεῖ in particular, Weber, *Demosth.* p. 306. [Madvig 148 b, 150, Jelf 667. *Obs.* 5.]

[5] Schæf. ad Bast. *Ep. Cr.* p. 36, Ast, Plat. *Legg.* p. 479, Wyttenb. Plut. *Mor.* I. 54, Boisson. *Philostr.* 284, *Æn. Gaz.* p. 230, Fritz. *Quæst. Luc.* p. 172 sq.

almost ceased to be felt by the Greek as an anacoluthon: we can only ascribe to the ὅτι a *vis monstrandi*, as when it stands before the oratio directa. Compare Klotz, *Devar.* p. 692.—Similarly ἵνα is joined with an infinitive in 3 (1) Esdr. vi. 31.

Rem. 3. We find an echo of the Hebrew infinitive absolute in a quotation from the LXX, Mt. xv. 4, θανάτῳ τελευτάτω (Ex. xix. 12, Num. xxvi. 65); and in the language of the N. T. itself, Rev. ii. 23, ἀποκτενῶ ἐν θανάτῳ (compare מוֹת יָמוּת), and L. xxii. 15, ἐπιθυμίᾳ ἐπεθύμησα κ.τ.λ. The LXX frequently express the infinitive absolute by means of this construction,—which is not discordant with Greek idiom (§ 54. 3),—joining to the verb the ablative of a cognate noun; see Gen. xl. 15, xliii. 2, 1. 24, Ex. iii. 16, xi. 1, xviii. 18, xxi. 20, xxii. 16, xxiii. 24, Lev. xix. 20, Num. xxii. 30, Dt. xxiv. 15, Zeph. i. 2, Ruth ii. 11, Judith vi. 4 (*Test. Patr.* p. 634) : on this see Thiersch, *Pent.* p. 169 sq. Another mode in which the infinitive absolute is translated by the LXX is noticed below, § 45. 8.

Rem. 4. There is nothing singular in the accumulation in one sentence of several infinitives, one depending on another; e. g., 2 P. i. 15, σπουδάσω ἑκάστοτε ἔχειν ὑμᾶς ... τὴν τούτων μνήμην ποιεῖσθαι. In Greek writers it is not uncommon to find three such infinitives in close proximity (Weber, *Demosth.* p. 351).

Section XLV.

THE PARTICIPLE.

1. The participle shows its verbal nature in two ways:—

(1) It governs the case of its verb as directly as the verb itself: L. ix. 16, λαβὼν τοὺς ἄρτους· 1 C. xv. 57, τῷ διδόντι ἡμῖν τὸ νῖκος· L. viii. 3, ἐκ τῶν ὑπαρχόντων αὐταῖς· 2 C. i. 23, φειδόμενος ὑμῶν οὐκ ἦλθον· 1 C. vii. 31, H. ii. 3, L. xxi. 4, ix. 32, al.

(2) It regularly retains the power of expressing the relation of *time*; and the participle can indicate this relation more completely in Greek, a language rich in participial forms, than in Latin or German. The temporal meaning of the participles corresponds with what has been said above (§ 40) respecting the various tenses. The following examples will illustrate the simple and ordinary usage:—

a. Present: A. xx. 23, τὸ πνεῦμα διαμαρτύρεταί μοι λέγον κ.τ.λ., Rom. viii. 24, ἐλπὶς βλεπομένη οὐκ ἔστιν ἐλπίς· 1 Th. ii. 4, θεῷ τῷ δοκιμάζοντι τὰς καρδίας· 1 P. i. 7, χρυσίου τοῦ ἀπολλυμένου· H. vii. 8 ;—denoting something which is actually present, or which regularly happens in all time.[1]

b. Aorist: Col. ii. 12, τοῦ θεοῦ τοῦ ἐγείραντος Χριστὸν ἐκ τῶν νεκρῶν· Rom. v. 16, δι' ἑνὸς ἁμαρτήσαντος (a thing which happened once), A. ix. 21.

c. Perfect: A. xxii. 3, ἀνὴρ γεγεννημένος ἐν Ταρσῷ, ἀνατεθραμμένος δὲ ἐν τῇ πόλει ταύτῃ (qualities whose operation extends onwards out of the past), Jo. xix. 35, ὁ ἑωρακὼς μεμαρτύρηκεν· Mt. xxvii. 37, ἐπέθηκαν . . . τὴν αἰτίαν αὐτοῦ γεγραμμένην· A. xxiii. 3, 1 P. i. 23, 2 P. ii. 6, Jo. v. 10, vii. 15, E. iii. 18.

d. Future (rare in the N. T.[2]): 1 C. xv. 37, οὐ τὸ σῶμα τὸ γενησόμενον σπείρεις ; and, from a stand-point in past time, H. iii. 5, Μωυσῆς πιστὸς . . . ὡς θεράπων εἰς μαρτύριον τῶν λαληθησομένων, *of that which was to be spoken* (revealed). Compare A. viii. 27, xxiv. 11, L. xxii. 49.

The present participle

a. Sometimes, when combined with a preterite, represents the imperfect tense : A. xxv. 3, παρεκάλουν αὐτὸν αἰτούμενοι χάριν· Rev. xv. 1, εἶδον ἀγγέλους ἑπτὰ ἔχοντας πληγάς· H. xi. 21, Ἰακὼβ ἀποθνήσκων . . . ηὐλόγησεν· A. vii. 26, ὤφθη αὐτοῖς μαχομένοις· xviii. 5, xx. 9, xxi. 16, 2 P. ii. 23,[3] 2 C. iii. 7 ;[4] also in reference to a lasting state, A. xix. 24, 1 P. iii. 5 (Jelf 705. *a*).

b. Sometimes denotes that which will happen immediately, or is certain to take place : Mt. xxvi. 28, τὸ αἷμα τὸ περὶ πολλῶν ἐκχυννόμενον· vi. 30, τὸν χόρτον αὔριον εἰς κλίβανον βαλλόμενον· 1 C. xv. 57, Ja. v. 1. Thus we find ὁ ἐρχόμενος as a designation of the Messiah, הַבָּא, not *venturus*, but *the coming one ;* there is a steadfast and firm belief that he is coming (Mt. xi. 3, L. vii. 19, al.).

The participle ὤν also, in combination with a preterite, or qualified by an adverb of time, is not unfrequently an imperfect participle : see Jo. i. 49, v. 13, xi. 31, 49, xxi. 11, A. vii. 2, xi. 1, xviii. 24,

---

[1] Schoem. Plut. *Agis* p. 153, Schæf. *Plut.* V. 211 sq.
[2] [A. Buttmann (p. 296) remarks that the use of this participle in the sense of the *final* sentence—so common in classical Greek (Don. p. 599, Jelf 811. 3)—is in the N. T. confined to the book of Acts.]
[3] [Evidently a mistake for 1 P. ii. 23.]
[4] Bornem. Xen. *Cyr.* p. 264.

2 C. i. 23,¹ viii. 9 ; E. ii. 13, νυνὶ ἐν Χριστῷ Ἰησοῦ ὑμεῖς οἵ ποτε ὄντες κ.τ.λ., Col. i. 21 ; 1 Tim. i. 13, μὲ τὸ πρότερον ὄντα βλάσφημον. Compare Aristot. *Rhet.* 2. 10. 13, πρὸς τοὺς μυριοστὸν ὄντας· Lucian, *Dial. Mar.* 13. 2, ὀψέ ζηλοτυπεῖς ὑπερόπτης πρότερον ὤν. In Jo. iii. 13, however, ὤν ² signifies *who* (essentially) *is in heaven, who appertains to heaven ;* ³ so also in i. 18. In Jo. ix. 25, ὅτι τυφλὸς ὢν ἄρτι βλέπω probably means *whereas I am a blind man* (from infancy), *as a blind man ;* only, inasmuch as ἄρτι implies a reference to a *previous state*, the words might perhaps be rendered *whereas I was blind*. This participle is decidedly present in 1 C. ix. 19, ἐλεύθερος ὢν ἐκ πάντων πᾶσιν ἐμαυτὸν ἐδούλωσα, *whereas* (although) *I am free, I made myself servant ;* the apostle's ἐλευθερία was something permanent. On the other hand, in Rev. vii. 2, εἶδον . . . . ἄγγελον ἀναβαίνοντα (which Eichhorn strangely enough declared a solecism), *I saw him ascend* (whilst he was ascending), an imperfect participle is quite in place, since the reference is to something which is not completed in a moment. But ἀποθνήσκοντες, Rev. xiv. 13, can only be a present participle.

The present participle has been too often taken for a future, in cases where the present-signification is for the most part quite sufficient :—

a. In combination with a present tense or an imperative mood : Rom. xv. 25, πορεύομαι διακονῶν τοῖς ἁγίοις (the διακονεῖν commences with the journey), 1 P. i. 9, ἀγαλλιᾶσθε . . . . κομιζόμενοι, *as receivers* (such they already are in the certainty of their faith), Ja. ii. 9. On 2 P. ii. 9 see Huther.⁴

b. Joined with an aorist : ⁵ 2 P. ii. 4, παρέδωκεν εἰς κρίσιν τηρουμένους, *as those who are reserved* (from the stand-point of the present time), A. xxi. 2, εὑρόντες πλοῖον διαπερῶν εἰς Φοινίκην, *which sailed, was on her passage* (Xen. *Eph.* 3. 6. *init.*), L. ii. 45, ὑπέστρεψαν εἰς Ἰερουσαλὴμ ἀναζητοῦντες αὐτόν, *seeking him* (the seeking began on their journey back), Mk. viii. 11, x. 2. Compare A. xxiv. 17, xxv. 13, where the future participle is used of actions which are only intended.

c. Joined with a perfect : A. xv. 27, ἀπεστάλκαμεν Ἰούδαν καὶ Σίλαν . . . . ἀπαγγέλλοντας τὰ αὐτά, *as announcers, with the announcement*

---

¹ [Inserted by mistake.]
² See Lücke and Baumgarten-Crusius *in loc.*
³ Ὁ ὢν ἐν τῷ οὐρανῷ, with the meaning "qui erat in cælo," would almost coincide in sense with ὁ ἐκ τοῦ οὐρανοῦ καταβάς : evidently, however, it is intended to express something special and more emphatic, and the climax in these predicates is not to be mistaken. Still ὁ ὤν does not form a third predicate, co-ordinate with the two others, but is, as Lücke rightly remarks, an exposition of the predicate ὁ υἱὸς τοῦ ἀνθρώπου.
⁴ ["Κολαζομένους must be taken as a true present : the reference is to the punishment which they suffer before the last judgment, for which (ver. 4) they are reserved." Huther *in loc.*]
⁵ Lobeck, Soph. *Aj.* p. 234.

(as soon as they set out they appeared in the character of announcers), 1 C. ii. 1, Demosth. *Dionys.* 739 c, Pol. 28. 10. 7.—In 2 P. iii. 11, τούτων πάντων λυομένων means *since all this is dissolved,* i. e., is in its nature destined to dissolution,—the lot of dissolution is, as it were, already inherent in these things : λυθησομένων would merely have expressed the simple future, *since dissolution will at some time take place.* The apostolic (Pauline) terms οἱ ἀπολλύμενοι, οἱ σωζόμενοι (used as substantives), denote *those who are lost* (not merely will be lost at some future time, but are already lost, inasmuch as they have turned away from the faith and thus incurred eternal death), *those who are saved.* On A. xxi. 3 see below, no. 5.

d. Joined with the *conjunctivus exhortativus:* H. xiii. 13, ἐξερχώμεθα .... τὸν ὀνειδισμὸν αὐτοῦ φέροντες, where the participial clause (*bearing,* etc.) is in immediate connexion with ἐξερχώμεθα; the future participle would have removed the action into some indefinite future time. Compare also 1 C. iv. 14.

Still less can the present participle stand for the aorist. In 2 C. x. 14, οὐ γὰρ ὡς μὴ ἐφικνούμενοι εἰς ὑμᾶς ὑπερεκτείνομεν ἑαυτούς means, *as if we reached not to you* (in reality we do reach to you). In 2 P. ii. 18 the present participle ἀποφεύγοντας, received into the text by Lachmann, shows that those referred to had only just begun to flee : such persons are most accessible to seduction. On E. ii. 21 and iv. 22, see Meyer.[1]

The aorist participle in the course of a narration sometimes expresses a simultaneous action (Krüg. p. 178, Jelf 405. 5), as in A. i. 24, προςευξάμενοι εἶπον, *praying they said* (the prayer follows), Rom. iv. 20, E. ii. 8,[2] Col. ii. 13, Ph. ii. 7, 2 P. ii. 5 ; sometimes an action which had previously taken place (where we look for the pluperfect), as in Mt. xxii. 25, ὁ πρῶτος γαμήσας ἐτελεύτησε· A. v. 10, xiii. 51, 2 P. ii. 4, E. i. 4 sq., ii. 16. If the principal verb relates to something future, the aorist participle corresponds to the Latin *futurum exactum:* 1 P. ii. 12, ἵνα ... ἐκ τῶν καλῶν ἔργων ἐποπτεύσαντες[3] δοξάσωσιν τὸν θεόν· iii. 2, E. iv. 25, ἀποθέμενοι τὸ ψεῦδος λαλεῖτε ἀλήθειαν· Mk. xiii. 13, A. xxiv. 25, Rom. xv. 28, H. iv. 3,'Herm. *Vig.* p. 774 (Jelf 705*b*). —The perfect participle also sometimes has in a narration the meaning of the pluperfect: Jo. ii. 9, οἱ διάκονοι ᾔδεισαν οἱ ἠντληκότες· A. xviii. 2, εὑρὼν Ἰουδαῖον .... προςφάτως ἐληλυθότα ἀπὸ τῆς Ἰταλίας· H. ii. 9, Rev. ix. 1.

---

[1] [In each of these passages Meyer takes the present participle as denoting an action in progress, a process now going on.]
[2] [A mistake : perhaps for E. iv. 8.—E. i. 4 sq., below, should probably be E. i. 3, 5.]
[3] [The best texts have ἐποπτεύοντες.]

SECT. XLV.]   THE PARTICIPLE.   431

The aorist participle never stands for the future participle. Not in Jo. xi. 2 (the event which had happened long before presents itself to the writer's mind as a past event, though it is not narrated by him until ch. xii.), or in H. ii. 10, where ἀγαγόντα refers to Christ living in the flesh, who in this personal manifestation itself led many to glory (this work began with his very advent).¹ On H. ix. 12 see below.² It is an abuse of parallelism to render Mk. xvi. 2, ἀνατείλαντος τοῦ ἡλίου, *as the sun rose* (so Ebrard still), on the ground that in Jo. xx. 1 (compare L. xxiv. 1) we find σκοτίας ἔτι οὔσης. Such small differences between the accounts of the Evangelists need not trouble us.³ On Jo. vi. 33, 50, ἄρτος ὁ καταβαίνων ἐκ τοῦ οὐρανοῦ, as contrasted with the ἄρτος ὁ καταβὰς ἐκ τ. οὐρ. of ver. 41 and 51, see Lücke.⁴—Nor does the aorist participle stand for the perfect in 1 P. i. 13.

The perfect participle κατεγνωσμένος,* G. ii. 11, has been wrongly rendered *reprehendendus,* for both grammar and context give the meaning *blamed:* see Meyer. So also in Rev. xxi. 8 ἐβδελυγμένος is *abominated.* On the other hand, the present participle ψηλαφώμενον, H. xii. 18, means *which could be felt;* for to that which *is felt* belongs, as a property, the capability of being felt, just as τὰ βλεπόμενα may denote *that which is visible.* Compare Kritz, *Sallust.* II. 401 sq.

The participles of the aorist and the perfect are combined, and the proper distinction of meaning maintained, in 2 C. xii. 21, τῶν προημαρτηκότων καὶ μὴ μετανοησάντων· 1 P. ii. 10, οἱ οὐκ ἠλεημένοι νῦν δὲ ἐλεηθέντες (from the LXX⁵),—the former denoting a state, the latter

---

¹ [Winer here refers the participle to τὸν ἀρχηγόν: in § 42. 2, however, he connects it with the subject indicated in αὐτῷ. The latter is the view of most recent commentators: see especially Alford's note.]

² [Winer barely mentions this passage in no. 6: from the connexion in which it is there introduced he seems to have taken εὑράμενος as expressing an *antecedent* act (Kurtz, Lünemann), rather than one that was *contemporaneous* with εἰσῆλθεν (Bleek, Delitzsch, Alford).]

³ [It is in great measure from the fact that *St. Mark himself* gives a different note of time (λίαν πρωΐ, ver. 2) that others have been led to conclude that " ἀνατείλαντος τοῦ ἡλίου is not to be referred to the actual phenomenon, but to be regarded only as a general definition of time:" Ellicott, *Hist. L.* p. 377. Bp. Ellicott refers to Robinson (*Biblioth. Sacra* II. 168), as giving examples from the LXX "which dilute the objection arising from the use of the aorist." In none of these examples, however (Jud. ix. 33, Ps. ciii. 22, 2 K. iii. 22, 2 S. xxiii. 4), does the aorist *participle* occur.]

⁴ ["When John makes the descent of the bread of God from heaven the essential, inherent predicate of the idea expressed, he uses the present; when the descent from heaven is regarded as a definite fact in the manifestation of Christ, the aorist." Lücke *in loc.*]

* Κατεγνωσμένος ἦν is strictly the pluperfect middle,—had condemned himself, stood *self-condemned.* Paul merely pointed out the flagrant inconsistency of Peter, by contrasting Peter's present with his previous proceedings and expressed views. *E. M.*

⁵ [In the LXX (*Alex.*) this is ἐλεήσω τὴν οὐκ ἠλεημένην.]

an event. On 1 Jo. v. 18 see Lücke: comp. Ellendt, Arr. *Al.* I. 129. The combination of the present and the aorist participle in one sentence (Jo. xxi. 24, H. vi. 7, 10), or of the perfect and the present participle (Col. ii. 7), hardly requires mention.

2. As regards the grammatical construction of the participle, either

a. It belongs to the principal sentence as a complement, e. g., Mt. xix. 22, ἀπῆλθεν λυπούμενος (Rost p. 711):—or

b. It is employed, for the sake of periodic compactness, to form subordinate sentences; and in this case it may be resolved by means of relatives or conjunctions (Rost p. 711, Matth. 565 sq.[1]). See Jo. xv. 2, πᾶν κλῆμα μὴ φέρον καρπόν, *which does not bear fruit*; Rom. xvi. 1, συνίστημι Φοίβην, οὖσαν διάκονον· L. xvi. 14, al. Rom. ii. 27, ἡ ἀκροβυστία τὸν νόμον τελοῦσα, *if it fulfils* (through fulfilling); A. v. 4, οὐχὶ μένον σοὶ ἔμενε; *if it remained* (unsold), *did it not remain to thee?* Rom. vii. 3, 2 P. i. 4, 1 Tim. iv. 4 (Xen. *Mem.* 1. 4. 14, 2. 3. 9, Plat. *Symp.* 208 d, Schæf. *Melet.* p. 57, Matth. 566. 4). A. iv. 21, ἀπέλυσαν αὐτοὺς μηδὲν εὑρίσκοντες κ.τ.λ., *because they found nothing;* 1 C. xi. 29, H. vi. 6 (Jude 5, Ja. ii. 25), Xen. *Mem.* 1. 2. 22, Lucian, *Dial. M.* 27. 8. Rom. i. 32, οἵτινες τὸ δικαίωμα τοῦ θεοῦ ἐπιγνόντες οὐ μόνον κ.τ.λ., *although they knew* (had perceived); 1 C. ix. 19, 1 Th. ii. 6, Ja. iii. 4, al.; compare Xen. *Mem.* 3. 10. 13, Philostr. *Apoll.* 2. 25, Lucian, *Dial. M.* 26. 1. The most common case in narration is the resolution of participles by particles of time: 2 P. ii. 5, ὄγδουν Νῶε ... ἐφύλαξεν, κατακλυσμὸν κόσμῳ ἐπάξας, *when he brought on the world;* L. ii. 45, μὴ εὑρόντες ὑπέστρεψαν, *after they had failed*[2] *in their search;* Ph. ii. 19, A. iv. 18, καλέσαντες αὐτοὺς παρήγγειλαν· Mt. ii. 3; A. xxi. 28, ἐπέβαλον ἐπ' αὐτὸν τὰς χεῖρας κράζοντες, *whilst they cried,* etc.; Rom. iv. 20, ἐνεδυναμώθη τῇ πίστει δοὺς δόξαν τῷ θεῷ κ.τ.λ. (Don. p. 579, Jelf 696).

When participles are used limitatively (*although*), this meaning is often indicated by a prefixed καίτοι or καίπερ, as in Ph. iii. 4, H. iv. 3, v. 8, vii. 5, 2 P. i. 12;[3] compare Xen. *Cyr.* 4. 5. 32, Plat.

---

[1] [Jelf 695 sqq., Don. p. 578 sqq., Webster, *Syntax* p. 113 sq.]
[2] [It will be seen that the English participle often furnishes a simple rendering (*not having found, crying,* etc.): the above renderings follow the German, which resolves the participles into sentences.]
[3] [Similarly καὶ ταῦτα with a participle, H. xi. 12: Don. p. 608, Jelf 697. *d.*]

SECT. XLV.]   THE PARTICIPLE.   433

Protag. 318 b, Diod. S. 3. 7, 17. 39. This meaning is sometimes brought into prominence by an antithetical ὅμως (Krüg. p. 231): 1 C. xiv. 7, ὅμως τὰ ἄψυχα φωνὴν διδόντα . . . . ἐὰν διαστολὴν μὴ δῷ, πῶς γνωσθήσεται τὸ αὐλούμενον κ.τ.λ., *a thing* (an instrument) *without life, although giving a sound, is notwithstanding not understood, unless,* etc. (Don. p. 607, Jelf 697. *d.*)

3. Two or more participles, in different relations (either co-ordinate with or subordinate to one another), and unconnected by καί, are frequently joined to one principal verb, especially in the historical style:—not merely

a. When one participle precedes and the other follows the finite verb, as in L. iv. 35, ῥῖψαν αὐτὸν τὸ δαιμόνιον εἰς μέσον ἐξῆλθεν ἀπ' αὐτοῦ, μηδὲν βλάψαν αὐτόν, *throwing him down* (after having thrown him down) *the spirit went out from him, doing him no harm,*—without injuring him at all; x. 30, A. xiv. 19, xv. 24, xvi. 23, Mk. vi. 2, 2 C. vii. 1, Tit. ii. 12 sq., H. vi. 6, x. 12 sq., 2 P. ii. 19 (Lucian, *Philops.* 24, *Peregr.* 25):—but also, and more frequently,

b. When the participles, without any copula, all precede or all follow the verb: Mt. xxviii. 2, ἄγγελος κυρίου καταβὰς ἐξ οὐρανοῦ, προςελθὼν ἀπεκύλισε τὸν λίθον κ.τ.λ., A. v. 5, ἀκούων Ἀνανίας τοὺς λόγους τούτους, πεσὼν ἐξέψυξε· L. ix. 16, λαβὼν τοὺς πέντε ἄρτους . . . . ἀναβλέψας εἰς τὸν οὐρανὸν εὐλόγησεν· 1 C. xi. 4, πᾶς ἀνὴρ προσευχόμενος ἢ προφητεύων κατὰ κεφαλῆς ἔχων καταισχύνει κ.τ.λ., *every man who prays or prophesies, in praying* etc.; L. vii. 37 sq., xvi. 23, xxiii. 48, A. xiv. 14, xxi. 2, xxv. 6, Mk. i. 41, v. 25–27,[1] viii. 6 ; Col. i. 3 sq. εὐχαριστοῦμεν . . . . προςευχόμενοι . . . . ἀκούσαντες, *praying . . . . after having heard;* 1 Th. i. 2 sq., H. i. 3, xi. 7, xii. 1, 1 C. xv. 58, Jo. xiii. 1 sq., Col. ii. 13, Ph. ii. 7, Phil. 4, Jude 20, al. In Greek writers nothing is more common. Compare Xen. *Hell.* 1. 6. 8, *Cyr.* 4. 6. 4, Plat. *Rep.* 2. 366 a, *Gorg.* 471 b, Strabo 3. 165, Lucian, *Asin.* 18, *Alex.* 19, Xen. Ephes. 3. 5, Alciphr. 3. 43 *init.*, Arrian, *Al.* 3. 30. 7 (Jelf 706).[2]—(In several N. T. passages there is more or less MS. evidence in favour of the copula καί; e. g. in A. ix. 40, Mk. xiv. 22, al.)

---

[1] [In verses 25, 26, the participles are joined by conjunctions. In Mt. xxviii. 2 also, quoted above, we should probably read καὶ προςελθών.]
[2] See Heindorf, Plat. *Protag.* p. 562, Herm. Eurip. *Ion* p. 842, Stallb. Plat. *Phileb.* § 32, and Plat. *Euthyphr.* p. 27, *Apol.* p. 46 sq., Boisson. *Aristænet.* p. 257, Jacob *ad* Lucian. *Tox.* p. 43, Ellendt, Arr. *Al.* 11. 322, al.

The mutual relation of the participles is of a different kind in L. ii. 12, εὑρήσετε βρέφος ἐσπαργανωμένον κείμενον ἐν φάτνῃ,[1] *ye shall find a swaddled child lying in a manger:* here the former participle occupies the place of an adjective.

4. The participle, where it is merely used as a complement or predicatively, sometimes discharges the function which in Latin and German* is discharged by the infinitive (Rost p. 704 sqq.[2]), —viz. in the following well-known combinations:—

(*a*) A. v. 42, οὐκ ἐπαύοντο διδάσκοντες· xiii. 10, H. x. 2, Rev. iv. 8 ; A. xii. 16, ἐπέμενε κρούων· L. vii. 45, 2 Macc. v. 27 ; 2 P. i. 19, ᾧ καλῶς ποιεῖτε προςέχοντες· A. x. 33, xv. 29, Ph. iv. 14, 3 Jo. 6 (Plat. *Symp.* 174 e, *Phæd.* 60 c, Her. 5. 24, 26), 2 P. ii. 10, 2 Th. iii. 13.

(*b*) Mk. xvi. 5, εἶδον νεανίσκον καθήμενον· A. ii. 11, ἀκούομεν λαλούντων αὐτῶν· vii. 12, Mk. xiv. 58.

On rational[3] principles, however, the participle is at least as appropriate as the infinitive in these cases ; the preference given to the former by the Greeks rests on a nice distinction, not felt by other nations. The meaning of οὐκ ἐπαύοντο διδάσκοντες is *teaching* (or *as teachers*) *they did not cease ;*[4] of εἶδον καθήμενον, *they saw him* (*as one*) *sitting.* The participle expresses an action or a state which already exists, not one which is first occasioned or produced by the principal verb. See on the whole Matth. 530. 2, Krüg. p. 221 sqq.[5]

The following instances are of a less common kind:—

Under (*a*): 1 C. xiv. 18 (*Rec.*), εὐχαριστῶ τῷ θεῷ πάντων ὑμῶν μᾶλλον γλώσσαις λαλῶν,[6] *that I speak* (as one speaking),—

---

[1] [Probably we should read καὶ κείμενον.]
* Junior readers are reminded that, in copiousness of participial phraseology, the English comes much nearer the Greek than either the Latin or the German. The Greek idiom, when it differs from the Latin or German as above, often agrees entirely with the English, *e.g.—they ceased teaching, he continued knocking.*—E. M.
[2] [Don. p. 588, Jelf 681 sqq., Webster p. 110 sqq.]
[3] [See Introduction, § 4, p. 8, note².]
[4] It would make no essential difference if, with G. T. A. Krüger (*Untersuch. aus dem Gebiete der lat. Sprachl.* III. 356 sqq., 404 sqq.), we were to regard this use of the nominative participle as an instance of attraction. See further Herm. *Emend. Rat.* p. 146 sq.
[5] For more precise distinctions, in regard to Greek usage, see Weller, *Bemerkungen zur gr. Syntax* (Meiningen 1845).
[6] Lachmann and Tischendorf read λαλῶ with many uncial MSS. With this reading we have two unconnected sentences side by side,—*I thank God, I speak more than you all* (for *that I speak*, etc.) ; compare Bornem. Xen. *Conv.* p. 71. In A we find neither λαλῶν nor λαλῶ.

compare Her. 9. 79; A. xvi. 34, ἠγαλλιάσατο πεπιστευκὼς τῷ θεῷ (Eurip. *Hipp.* 8, Soph. *Phil.* 882, Lucian, *Paras.* 3, *Fug.* 12, Dion. H. IV. 2238). Rom. vii. 13 does not come under this head; see Rückert *in loc.*[1]

Under (*b*): L. viii. 46, ἐγὼ ἔγνων δύναμιν ἐξεληλυθυῖαν (Thuc. 1. 25, γνόντες ... οὐδεμίαν σφίσιν ἀπὸ Κερκύρας τιμωρίαν οὖσαν· Xen. *Cyr.* 1. 4. 7,—see Monk, Eurip. *Hipp.* 304, and *Alcest.* 152);[2] H. xiii. 23, γινώσκετε τὸν ἀδελφὸν Τιμόθεον ἀπολελυμένον, *ye know that ... is set at liberty*; A. xxiv. 10, ἐκ πολλῶν ἐτῶν ὄντα σε κριτὴν τῷ ἔθνει τούτῳ ἐπιστάμενος· compare Demosth. *Ep.* 4. p. 123 a (but in L. iv. 41, ᾔδεισαν τὸν Χριστὸν αὐτὸν εἶναι,—where a Greek prose writer would probably have used the participle[3]); 2 Jo. 7, οἱ μὴ ὁμολογοῦντες Ἰησοῦν Χριστὸν ἐρχόμενον ἐν σαρκί· 1 Jo. iv. 2, πνεῦμα ὃ ὁμολογεῖ Ἰησοῦν Χριστὸν ἐν σαρκὶ ἐληλυθότα.[4] On the use of the participle with *verba dicendi* see Matth. 555. Rem. 4, Jacobs, *Æl. Anim.* II. 109. The verb αἰσχύνεσθαι, in particular, has this construction in Greek prose; e. g. Xen. *Cyr.* 3. 2. 16, αἰσχυνοίμεθ' ἄν σοι μὴ ἀποδιδόντες· 5. 1. 21, αἰσχύνομαι λέγων· *Mem.* 2. 6. 39, Diog. L. 6. 8, Liban. *Oratt.* p. 525 b. And in this example we may see how correct was the choice of the participle in the cases just mentioned; for with this verb Greek writers join an infinitive as well as a participle, making however an essential distinction between the two constructions.[5] The participle is used only when some one is already doing (or has already done) a thing of which—at the moment of doing it—he is ashamed: the infinitive denotes shame at some action yet to be done (not yet actually performed): compare *e. g.* Isocr. *ad Philipp.* p. 224, *Big.* p. 842, Xen. *Mem.* 3. 7. 5. This distinction is correctly observed

---
[1] Compare Heusing. Plut. *Pœdag.* p. 19.
[2] Several commentators bring in here E. iii. 19, γνῶναι τὴν ὑπερβάλλουσαν τῆς γνώσεως ἀγάπην τοῦ Χριστοῦ: this cannot be, since the participle is too clearly marked as an attributive by its position between the article and the noun. For another reason we cannot regard Ph. ii. 28, ἵνα ἰδόντες αὐτὸν πάλιν χαρῆτε, as an example of this construction; for the meaning is *in order that ye, seeing him, may again rejoice.*
[3] Compare Mehlhorn in *Allg. L. Z.* 1833, no. 110: but see Elmsley, Eur. *Med.* 580.
[4] The passage from Isocrates (*Paneg.* c. 8) usually quoted as a parallel (still so quoted by Matth. 555. Rem. 4) was corrected by Hier. Wolf: compare Baiter *in loc.* [See however Sandys, *Isocr.* p. 61.] Other examples are examined by Weber, *Dem.* p. 278.
[5] See Poppo, Xen. *Cyr.* p. 286 sq. In the case of πυνθάνομαι the two constructions coincide: see Ellendt, Arr. *Al.* I. 145.

in L. xvi. 3, ἐπαιτεῖν αἰσχύνομαι, *I am ashamed to beg* (Ecclus. iv. 26, Sus. 11): had the speaker already become a beggar, he must have said ἐπαιτῶν αἰσχύνομαι. Ἄρχομαι is always followed by the infinitive in the N. T., as it usually is in Greek authors: *he began speaking* is indeed a less suitable expression than *he continued speaking*. See however Rost p. 708.

Ἀκούειν¹ also is sometimes construed with a predicative participle, —not merely where direct personal hearing is signified (Rev. v. 13, A. ii. 11), but also with the meaning *learn, be informed* (through others), L. iv. 23, A. vii. 12, 2 Th. iii. 11, ἀκούομέν τινας περιπατοῦντας· and 3 Jo. 4 (Xen. *Cyr.* 2. 4. 12).² In the latter sense it is more frequently followed by ὅτι, once³ by the accusative and infinitive, 1 C. xi. 18, ἀκούω σχίσματα ἐν ὑμῖν ὑπάρχειν (ὑπάρχοντα); compare Xen. *Cyr.* 1. 3. 1, 4. 16. The construction is different in E. iv. 22, if ἀποθέσθαι ὑμᾶς .... τὸν παλαιὸν ἄνθρωπον is dependent on ἠκούσατε or ἐδιδάχθητε in ver. 21 (*that ye should lay aside*): see § 44. 3.

The participial construction here discussed is used by Greek authors (in prose as well as poetry) with much more variety than by the N. T. writers:⁴ indeed the use of παύεσθαι with the infinitive is even condemned by ancient grammarians, though wrongly.⁵

In 1 Tim. v. 13, ἅμα δὲ καὶ ἀργαὶ μανθάνουσι περιερχόμεναι, almost all recent commentators regard the participle as used for the infinitive, *they learn* (accustom themselves) *to go about idle*, and this gives a suitable sense. But whenever the participle joined with μανθάνειν has reference to the subject, this verb means *to perceive, understand, notice, remark*, something which is already existing; see Her. 3. 1, διαβεβλημένος ὑπὸ Ἀμάσιος οὐ μανθάνεις (see Valcken. *in loc.*), Soph. *Ant.* 532, Æsch. *Prom.* 62, Thuc. 6. 39, Plut. *Pæd.* 8. 12, Dion. H. IV. 2238, Lucian, *Dial. D.* 16. 2.⁶ In the sense of

---

¹ [On this verb see A. Buttm. p. 301 sqq. He maintains that, when ἀκούω denotes *direct* hearing, it may be followed by the genitive and participle (A. ii. 11, al.), but not by the accusative and participle; so that when we seem to have this latter construction (as in A. ix. 4, xxvi. 14, Rev. v. 13) the participle is really in apposition to the object. This is the classical usage, see Liddell and Scott s. v.—Mk. v. 36, with a passive verb, is an exception.]

² Compare Rost in *Griech. Wörterb.* I. 143.

³ [*Twice:* 1 C. xi. 18, Jo. xii. 18. Other verbs which have this construction in Greek authors (e. g., γινώσκειν, εἰδέναι, ἀπαγγέλλειν, al.) are in the N. T. seldom or never so used, but are followed by ὅτι or by the accusative with infinitive. Once (A. xxvi. 22) λαλέω is followed by a participle. (A. Buttm. pp. 301, 305.)]

⁴ See Jacobs, *Anthol.* III. 235, and *Achill. Tat.* p. 828, Ast, Plat. *Polit.* p. 500, Schæf. Eurip. *Hec.* p. 31.

⁵ See Schæf. *Apoll. Rhod.* II. 223, Ast, Theophr. *Char.* p. 223 sq. (Jelf 688. *Obs.* 1).

⁶ In Xen. *Cyr.* 6. 2. 29, ἕως ἂν μάθωμεν ὑδροπόται γενόμενοι (a passage which however would not be quite decisive), λάθωμεν has long stood in the text.

learning μανθάνω is followed by the infinitive, as in Ph. iv. 11, and also 1 Tim. v. 4 [1] (Matth. 530. 2, Jelf 683). Hence we should have to regard this example as an incorrect extension of the construction beyond its rational limits. Perhaps however we should connect μανθάνουσι with ἀργαί, and take περιερχόμεναι as a participle proper (*they learn idleness, going about in the houses*); this would be an abbreviated mode of expression, such as we sometimes find elsewhere with an adjective (Plat. *Euthyd.* 276 b, οἱ ἀμαθεῖς ἄρα σοφοὶ μανθάνουσιν,[2] and frequently διδάσκειν τινὰ σοφόν), which does not, like the participle, include the notion of time and mood.[3] This explanation—which is adopted by Beza, Piscator, al., and has recently been approved by Huther—is supported by the fact that ἀργαί is taken up again in the following clause as the principal word, and the strengthened epithets φλύαροι καὶ περίεργοι are in like manner accompanied by a participle, λαλοῦσαι τὰ μὴ δέοντα.

The combination of a verb belonging to class (*a*) with an adjective[4] can excite no surprise: the only N. T. example is A. xxvii. 33, τεσσαρεσκαιδεκάτην σήμερον ἡμέραν προσδοκῶντες, ἄσιτοι (ὄντες) δια‑τελεῖτε. Compare Xen. *Cyr.* 1. 5. 10, ἀναγώνιστος διατελεῖ· *Hell.* 2. 3. 25 (Jelf 682. 3).

Some have wrongly supposed that the participle stands for the infinitive in 1 Tim. i. 12, πιστόν με ἡγήσατο θέμενος εἰς διακονίαν. The meaning is, *He counted me faithful, in that he appointed me for the ministry:* by this very act he gave the proof that he considered me faithful. In another sense, indeed, the writer might have said θέσθαι εἰς διακονίαν.

5. The present participle is frequently found (in the historical style) in combination with the verb εἶναι, especially with ἦν or ἦσαν, though also with the future. Sometimes this combination appears to be a simple substitute for the corresponding person of the finite verb (Aristot. *Metaph.* 4. 7, Bernh. p. 334,[5] Jelf 375): e.g., in Mk. xiii. 25, οἱ ἀστέρες τοῦ οὐρανοῦ ἔσονται πίπτοντες (where there immediately follows, as a parallel

---

[1] Matthies has passed over in silence the grammatical difficulty. Leo—after Casaubon, *ad Athen.* p. 452—would render μανθάνουσι by *solent:* he has not noticed that this meaning belongs to the preterite only.

[2] [The reading of this passage is doubtful: Bekker omits σοφοί.—Ellicott and Alford receive Winer's explanation of 1 Tim. v. 13. A. Buttmann strongly opposes it (p. 303 sq.), adopting Bengel's view that μανθάνουσι is to be taken absolutely: similarly Wordsworth, Grimm (*Clavis* s. v.), Green (*Crit. Notes* p. 173).]

[3] Under this head comes also Dio Chr. 55. 558, ὁ Σωκράτης ὅτι μὲν παῖς ὢν ἐμάνθανε λιθοξόος τὴν τοῦ πατρὸς τέχνην, ἀκηκόαμεν (*S. learned as a stone-cutter*, etc.).

[4] [So with a verb of class (*b*) in Mk. vi. 20: see A. Buttm. p. 304.]

[5] In some tenses (as the perfect and pluperfect passive and plural) this became, as every one knows, the usual mode of expression, and so figures in the paradigm of the verb.

member, καὶ αἱ δυνάμεις αἱ ἐν τοῖς οὐρανοῖς σαλευθήσονται,— Matthew has πεσοῦνται), Ja. i. 17, πᾶν δώρημα τέλειον ἄνωθέν ἐστι καταβαῖνον κ.τ.λ., L. v. 1, A. ii. 2. More frequently, however, it is used to express that which is *lasting* (rather a state than an action),[1]—a meaning which can also be expressed, though less distinctly in relation to what is past, by the form of the imperfect tense [2] (compare Beza on Mt. vii. 29): Mk. xv. 43, ἦν προςδεχόμενος τὴν βασιλείαν τοῦ θεοῦ (L. xxiii. 51), A. viii. 28, ἦν τε ὑποστρέφων καὶ καθήμενος ἐπὶ τοῦ ἅρματος αὐτοῦ (an imperfect immediately follows), A. i. 10, ii. 42, viii. 13, x. 24, Mt. vii. 29, Mk. ix. 4, xiv. 54, L. iv. 31, v. 10, vi. 12, xxiv. 13. Hence this combination is especially found where an event is spoken of in relation to some other event, as in L. xxiv. 32, ἡ καρδία ἡμῶν καιομένη ἦν ἐν ἡμῖν· ὡς ἐλάλει κ.τ.λ.; or where a *custom* is mentioned, as in Mk. ii. 18, ἦσαν οἱ μαθηταὶ Ἰωάννου . . . νηστεύοντες, *they used to fast,*—an explanation to which Meyer objects without reason. In L. xxi. 24 also, Ἰερουσαλὴμ ἔσται πατουμένη ὑπὸ ἐθνῶν, the words seem intended to express an enduring state, whereas the two futures which precede, πεσοῦνται and αἰχμαλωτισθήσονται, denote transient events: compare Mt. xxiv. 9. In some other passages εἶναι is not the mere auxiliary: Mk. x. 32, ἦσαν ἐν τῇ ὁδῷ ἀναβαίνοντες εἰς Ἰεροσόλυμα, *they were on the road* (compare ver. 17) *travelling to Jerusalem* (Lucian, *Dial. Mar.* 6. 2), Mk. v. 5, 11,[3] ii. 6, L. ii. 8, xxiv. 53; Mk. xiv. 4, ἦσάν τινες ἀγανακτοῦντες, *there were some* (present) *who were angry:* or else the participle has rather assumed the nature of an adjective, as in Mt. xix. 22, ἦν ἔχων κτήματα, *he was wealthy,* ix. 36, L. i. 20.[4] Perhaps also in some cases the verb was thus resolved into participle and substantive verb in order that the verbal notion, appearing in the form of a noun, might receive more attention (Madv. 180 d): e. g., 2 C. v. 19 (see Meyer *in loc.*), 1 C. xiv. 9, Col. ii. 23. In L. vii. 8, ἐγὼ ἄνθρωπός εἰμι ὑπὸ ἐξουσίαν τασσόμενος, the participle does not directly depend on εἰμι, but is an epithet belonging to a sub-

---

[1] What Stallbaum (Plat. *Rep.* II. 34) says about the distinction between this construction and the finite verb, amounts to the same thing.
[2] It belongs to the character of the popular language to resolve more concise forms of speech, for the sake of attaining greater clearness or expressiveness: see p. 407.
[3] Herm. Soph. *Philoct.* p. 219.
[4] Compare Stallb. Plat. *Rep.* II. 34.

SECT. XLV.] THE PARTICIPLE. 439

stantive. In Jo. i. 9, ἦν and ἐρχόμενον must not be joined together: the latter is an attributive belonging to ἄνθρωπον (see Meyer).

This use of the participle is by no means foreign to Greek writers; in these indeed, especially in Herodotus, we find not merely the present but also the other participles thus used.[1] Compare Eurip. *Herc. F.* 312 sq., εἰ μὲν σθενόντων τῶν ἐμῶν βραχιόνων ἦν τις σ' ὑβρίζων· Her. 3. 99, ἀπαρνεόμενός ἐστιν· Xen. *An.* 2. 2. 13, ἦν ἡ στρατηγία οὐδὲν ἄλλο δυναμένη· Herod. 1. 3. 12, κρατήσας ἦν τοῖς ὅπλοις (where προςηγάγετο has preceded), Lucian, *Eunuch.* 2, δικασταὶ ψηφοροῦντες ἦσαν οἱ ἄριστοι.[2] In late writers (e. g., Agath. 126. 7, 135. 5, 175. 14, 279. 7, al., Ephraemius—see *Index* s. v. εἶναι) and in the LXX this construction is much more common, though in the case of the LXX it was but seldom suggested by the Hebrew. In Aramaic however, as is well known, the use of the participle and verb substantive as a periphrasis for the finite verb had become established, and thus in Palestinian writers there may have existed a national preference for this mode of expression.

A. xxi. 3, ἐκεῖσε ἦν τὸ πλοῖον ἀποφορτιζόμενον τὸν γόμον, cannot be rendered (as by Grotius, Valcken., al.) *eo navis merces expositura erat:* it means, *thither the ship unloaded her cargo,* i. e., if expressed in detail, was going thither in order to unload. (It is not necessary to take ἐκεῖσε for ἐκεῖ.[3]) The use of this construction ἦν ἀποφορτιζόμενον in reference to that which was actually in course of performance, must not be overlooked.

In L. iii. 23 ἦν and ἀρχόμενος are not to be taken together: ἦν ἐτῶν τριάκοντα forms the main predicate, and ἀρχόμενος is added as a closer definition. The idiom mentioned by Viger (p. 355)[4] is not similar; and we cannot say of one who is entering on his thirtieth year that he is *beginning thirty years;* he is rather on the point of completing thirty years.—In Ja. iii. 15, οὐκ ἔστιν αὕτη ἡ σοφία ἄνωθεν κατερχομένη ἀλλ' ἐπίγειος, ψυχική κ.τ.λ., the participle rather assumes

---

[1] [In L. xxiii. 19 we must read ἦν . . . βληθείς.—This periphrasis is very common in St. Luke: see Davidson, *Introd. to N. T.* I. 195. On Jo. i. 9 see Westcott's note.]
[2] See Reiz, *Lucian* VI. 537 (ed. Lehm.), Couriers on Lucian, *Asin.* p. 219, Jacob, *Quæst. Lucian.* p. 12, Ast, Plat. *Polit.* p. 597, Boisson. *Philostr.* 660, and *Nicet.* p. 81, Matth. 560. [For the N. T. see also A. Buttm. pp. 308-313, Green p. 180, Webster p. 115.]
[3] Compare Bornem. *Schol.* p. 176.
[4] [The use of ἀρχόμενος in the sense of ἐν ἀρχῇ (Jelf 696. Obs. 1).—The position of ἀρχόμενος in this verse varies in different MSS.: recent editors place it after Ἰησοῦς. Most however are now agreed in the rendering, *when he began* (his public ministry): see Ellicott, *Hist. Lect.* p. 104, Green, *Crit. Notes* p. 50.]

the character of an adjective, and ἔστιν belongs to the following adjectives also.[1]

A. viii. 16, μόνον βεβαπτισμένοι ὑπῆρχον εἰς τὸ ὄνομα τοῦ κυρίου Ἰησοῦ, is not an example of ὑπάρχω with a participle as a mere periphrasis for the finite verb (Matth. 560), for βεβαπτισμένοι ἦσαν would be the regular expression, there being no other form for this tense and person. In Ja. ii. 15, to γυμνοὶ ὑπάρχωσιν is added λειπόμενοι as a predicate.[2] L. xxiii. 12, however, may be a partial example of this construction: for προϋπῆρχον ἐν ἔχθρᾳ ὄντες Luke might have said πρότερον ἐν ἔχθρᾳ ἦσαν. On this combination of ὑπάρχειν with the participle ὤν see Bornem. *Schol.* p. 143.

We have no example in the N. T. of the use of γίνομαι (in the sense of εἶναι) with a participle [3] to form a periphrasis of this kind: H. v. 12, γεγόνατε χρείαν ἔχοντες, means *ye have become persons needing*, etc.; Mk. ix. 3, τὰ ἱμάτια αὐτοῦ ἐγένοντο στίλβοντα, *became shining*; L. xxiv. 37,[4] 2 C. vi. 14, Rev. xvi. 10 are similar to these. In Mk. i. 4, however, the words ἐγένετο Ἰωάννης must be taken by themselves (exstitit Joannes), and the participles which follow are attributive. So also in Jo. i. 6.

Most certainly we have no periphrasis for the finite verb in such expressions as θεός ἐστιν ὁ ἐνεργῶν ἐν ὑμῖν κ.τ.λ. Ph. ii. 13, 1 C. iv. 4, al. (the copula is usually omitted, as in Rom. viii. 33, H. iii. 4, al.), *God is the worker* (it is God that works). Compare Fritz. *Rom.* II. 212 sq., Krüg. p. 218.

6. To omit the verb substantive in this construction, and thus make the participle a simple substitute for a finite verb, is a liberty which Greek prose writers allow themselves but seldom,[5] and then only in simple tense and mood forms.[6] Commentators have frequently and without hesitation assumed this usage to exist in the N. T., taking no notice of the corrections which are found in the notes and observations of classical scholars.[7] But in almost all these N. T. passages we either find amongst the

---

[1] Compare Franke, *Demosth.* p. 42.
[2] [Winer follows the reading of the best texts, which omit ὦσι.]
[3] Heind. Plat. *Soph.* 273 sq., Lob. Soph. *Ajax* v. 588.
[4] [Are we then to join γινόμενοι with πτοηθέντες?]
[5] Compare Fritz. *Rom.* I. 282. As to the Byzantine writers, who do use the participle simply for the finite verb, see the index to Malalas in the Bonn edition, p. 797. (We are not here speaking of the poets: see *e.g.* Hermann's review of Müller's *Eumenides*, p. 23.)
[6] See Herm. *Vig.* p. 776, Matth. 560. Rem., Siebelis, *Pausan.* III. 106, Wannowski, *Synt. Anom.* 202 sq. The restriction under which Mehlhorn (*Allg. Lit. Z.* 1833, No. 78) allows this ellipsis probably can neither be fully justified on rational grounds, nor be established from the usage of Greek writers, especially the later.
[7] Herm. *Vig.* pp. 770, 776 sq., Bremi in the *Philol. Beitr. aus der Schweiz*, I. 172 sqq., Bornem. Xen. *Conv.* p. 146, and *Schol. in Luc.* p. 183, Döderlein on Soph. *Œd. Col.* p. 593 sq., Bernh. p. 470.

preceding or following words a finite verb to which the participle is annexed (and in this case we must not allow the ordinary punctuation of the text to embarrass us), or else we have an example of anacoluthon, the writer having lost sight of the construction with which he commenced the sentence.[1] Several passages have already been correctly explained by Ostermann, in Crenii *Exercitatt.* II. 522 sq.

a. In 2 C. iv. 13 ἔχοντες must be connected with the following πιστεύομεν, *since we have . . . . we also believe.* In 2 P. ii. 1, both ἀρνούμενοι and ἐπάγοντες are attached to παρεισάξουσιν; these participles however are not co-ordinate, but ἐπάγοντες is annexed to the sentence οἵτινες .... ἀρνούμενοι. In Rom. v. 11, ἀλλὰ καὶ καυχώμενοι does not stand in such parallelism with σωθησόμεθα that we should necessarily look for καυχώμεθα (v. l.): the meaning appears to be, *but not merely shall we be saved* (simply and actually), *but glorying,*—so saved that we glory (the joyful consciousness of those who are saved). In 2 C. viii. 20 στελλόμενοι is connected in sense with συνεπέμψαμεν, ver. 18. In H. vi. 8, ἐκφέρουσα does not stand for ἐκφέρει, but this participle is parallel to πιοῦσα and τίκτουσα in ver. 7, and by δέ is placed in antithesis to these two words: with ἀδόκιμος and κατάρας ἐγγύς, however, we must supply ἐστί. In 2 P. iii. 5 συνεστῶσα is a true participle (epithet), and the preceding ἦσαν belongs to ἡ γῆ also. In H. vii. 2 ἑρμηνευόμενος must be joined with Μελχισεδέκ in ver. 1; since ὁ συναντήσας and ᾧ ἐμέρισεν are parenthetical clauses, and the main verb of the sentence comes in after all the predicates in ver. 3, μένει ἱερεύς κ.τ.λ.[2] In E. v. 21 ὑποτασσόμενοι is certainly attached to the principal verb πληροῦσθε ἐν πνεύματι, like the other participles in verses 19, 20, and must not be taken (as by Koppe, Flatt, al.) for an imperative: the following words αἱ γυναῖκες κ.τ.λ. (ver. 22) are then annexed without any verb of their own —for ὑποτάσσεσθε is certainly a gloss—as a further exposition of this ὑποτασσόμενοι. In 1 P. v. 7 also the participle must be

---

[1] Poppo, *Thuc.* III. iii. 138.
[2] [The construction of this period depends mainly on the reading adopted in ver. 1, ὁ συναντήσας or ὃς συναντήσας (Lachm., Alf.): the latter reading rests on strong MS. authority. Bleek thinks that, if this reading is adopted, it is most in accordance with the style of this Epistle to assume an ellipsis of ἐστί, taking συναντήσας .... ἐμέρισεν Ἀβραάμ as grammatically parenthetical; Alford assumes an anacoluthon.]

joined with the preceding imperative, ver. 6. 1 P. iii. 1 refers back to ii. 18, where the participle is connected with the imperatives of ver. 17; just as in 2 Th. iii. 8 ἐργαζόμενοι is parallel with ἐν κόπῳ καὶ μόχθῳ, and this with δωρεάν, as an adjunct to the verb ἄρτον ἐφάγομεν. In H. x. 8 λέγων belongs to the following verb εἴρηκεν, ver. 9 : in x. 16 διδούς may very well be joined with διαθήσομαι. Rom. vii. 13 was long ago explained correctly. 1 P. iv. 8 is clear in itself.

b. In A. xxiv. 5 the sentence begins with the participle εὑρόντες τὸν ἄνδρα, and should have been continued in ver. 6 by ἐκρατήσαμεν αὐτόν κ.τ.λ.; but the writer annexes this principal verb to the interposed relative clause ὃς καὶ . . . . ἐπείρασε. In 2 P. i. 17, λαβὼν γὰρ παρὰ θεοῦ κ.τ.λ., the construction is interrupted by the parenthetical clause φωνῆς . . . . εὐδόκησα; and the apostle continues in ver. 18 with καὶ ταύτην τὴν φωνὴν ἡμεῖς ἠκούσαμεν, not, as he had intended, with ἡμᾶς εἶχε ταύτην τὴν φωνὴν ἀκούσαντας, or the like.[1] Θαρροῦντες, 2 C. v. 6, is taken up again after several interposed clauses in θαρροῦμεν δέ, ver. 8. In 2 C. vii. 5, οὐδεμίαν ἔσχηκεν ἄνεσιν ἡ σὰρξ ἡμῶν, ἀλλ' ἐν παντὶ θλιβόμενοι, ἔξωθεν μάχαι κ.τ.λ., we may supply ἤμεθα (from ἡ σὰρξ ἡμῶν);[2] but it is also allowable to suppose an anacoluthon (Fritz. *Diss.* II. p. 49), as if Paul had written in the former part of the sentence οὐδεμίαν ἄνεσιν ἐσχήκαμεν τῇ σαρκὶ ἡμῶν. In 2 C. v. 12 ἀφορμὴν διδόντες is to be regarded as a true participle, but we must take the previous clause as if the words ran οὐ γὰρ γράφομεν ταῦτα πάλιν ἑαυτοὺς συνιστάνοντες; or—what comes to the same thing—we must supply from συνιστάνομεν the more general word λέγομεν or γράφομεν. See Meyer *in loc.* In 1 P. ii. 11 ἀπέχεσθε is now restored to the text,[3] and with this ἔχοντες (ver. 12) is regularly connected: in A. xxvi. 20 ἀπήγγελλον was long ago substituted for ἀπαγγέλλων. On Rom. xii. 6 sqq., H. viii. 10, and 1 P. iii. 1, 7, see § 63. (In Rev. x. 2 ἔχων is added, in an independent construction, and here ἐστί may be supplied.)

---

[1] Fritz. *Diss. in* 2 *Cor.* II. 44. Yet we might also suppose that the writer had intended to say, *receiving from God honour and glory* . . . . *he was declared to be the beloved Son of God*, and that the construction was interrupted by the *direct* quotation of the words spoken by the voice from heaven.
[2] Herm. *Vig.* p. 770.
[3] [Tisch. read ἀπέχισθι in 1849, but in his 7th and 8th editions ἀπέχισθαι. Recent editors agree in receiving the infinitive. See § 63. 2.]

Nor can the participle stand for the finite verb in Rom. iii. 23, πάντες . . . . ὑστεροῦνται τῆς δόξης τοῦ θεοῦ, δικαιούμενοι δωρεάν κ.τ.λ.,—though even Ostermann gives the explanation ὑστεροῦνται καὶ δικαιοῦνται. The connexion is thus conceived by the apostle, as his words show,—*and fall short of praise with God, being* (since they are) *freely justified,* etc. : the latter is a proof of the former.

1 C. iii. 19, ὁ δρασσόμενος τοὺς σοφοὺς ἐν τῇ πανουργίᾳ αὐτῶν, is a quotation from the O. T. : it is not a complete sentence, the apostle taking those words only which were suitable to his purpose ; compare H. i. 7. What the apostle quotes incompletely, we must not seek to complete by supplying ἐστί.—On 1 P. i. 14 see Fritz. *Conject.* I. 41 sq. We may either take the participle μὴ συσχηματιζόμενοι as depending upon ἐλπίσατε, or, regarding this participial clause as parallel with κατὰ τὸν καλέσαντα κ.τ.λ., join it with γενήθητε (ver. 15): I prefer the latter course.—As little reason is there for changing the participle into a finite verb in such proverbial expressions as 2 P. ii. 22, κύων ἐπιστρέψας ἐπὶ τὸ ἴδιον ἐξέραμα, and ὗς λουσαμένη κ.τ.λ. The words run, *a dog who turns to his own vomit :* they are spoken δεικτικῶς, as it were, with reference to a case actually observed,—just as when we say, *a black sheep!* when we notice a bad man amongst good.

In a different way the participle has been taken for the finite verb in cases where it appeared to denote an action which followed that indicated by the finite verb.[1] In the N. T., however, we have not a single certain example of this kind. L. iv. 15, ἐδίδασκεν . . . . δοξαζόμενος ὑπὸ πάντων, means, *He taught . . . . being* (whilst he was teaching) *praised by all ;* Ja. ii. 9, εἰ δὲ προςωποληπτεῖτε, ἁμαρτίαν ἐργάζεσθε ἐλεγχόμενοι ὑπὸ τοῦ νόμου κ.τ.λ., is, *Ye commit sin, being* (since ye are) *convicted* (as προςωπολημπτοῦντες ye are convicted, etc.): Gebser's explanation is wrong. H. xi. 35, ἐτυμπανίσθησαν οὐ προςδεξάμενοι τὴν ἀπολύτρωσιν, *since they did not accept the* (offered) *deliverance :* προςδεξάμενοι denotes what preceded the τυμπανίζεσθαι, rather than what followed it. Compare H. ix. 12. A. xix. 29 is not an example of that use of the aorist participle in narration which is treated of by Herm. *ad Vig.* p. 774 :[2] ὥρμησάν τε ὁμοθυμαδὸν εἰς τὸ θέατρον, συναρπάσαντες Γάϊον καὶ Ἀρίσταρχον, means either *having carried off Gaius,* etc. (from their dwelling) *with them,* or *carrying off . . . . with them.* In L. i. 9, ἔλαχεν τοῦ θυμιᾶσαι εἰσελθὼν εἰς τὸν ναὸν τοῦ κυρίου, the participle probably belongs to the infinitive (as it is taken in the Vulgate),—*to burn incense, entering into the temple ;* Meyer's explanation is artificial. On Rom. iii. 23 see above : Rom. ii. 4 is clear in itself.

Another peculiarity which is occasionally met with in Greek writers, the use of the participle to express the principal notion, the

---

[1] Bähr in Creuzer, *Melet.* III. 50 sq.
[2] [According to which συναρπάσαντες would be equivalent to καὶ συνήρπασαν.]

secondary being conveyed by the finite verb,[1] has been without reason intruded on the N. T. by some, who have entirely forgotten that this usage cannot be assumed to exist in the absence of any limitation arising out of the nature of the notions expressed. The assumption that in 2 C. v. 2 στενάζομεν . . . . ἐπιποθοῦντες stands for ἐπιποθοῦμεν στενάζοντες, is particularly unfortunate: the participle must be taken as annexed to the verb, and explained as an expression of *cause*, as in ver. 4 στενάζομεν βαρούμενοι.

7. The present participle (with the article) is not unfrequently used substantivally, and then, having become a noun, excludes all indication of time. In E. iv. 28, ὁ κλέπτων μηκέτι κλεπτέτω, the present does not stand for the aorist ὁ κλέψας, which is found in some MSS., but the words mean, *let the stealer* (i. e., *the thief*) *steal no more ;* H. xi. 28. So also when the participle is followed by an object-accusative or by other adjuncts: G. i. 23, ὁ διώκων ἡμᾶς ποτέ, *our former persecutor ;* Mt. xxvii. 40, ὁ καταλύων τὸν ναόν, *the destroyer of the temple* (in his own imagination); Rev. xv. 2, οἱ νικῶντες ἐκ τοῦ θηρίου·[2] xx. 10, G. ii. 2 (οἱ δοκοῦντες, see Kypke II. 274,—compare also Pachym. I. 117, 138, al.), 1 Th. i. 10, v. 24, 1 P. i. 17, Rom. v. 17, Jo. xii. 20 (xiii. 11). Compare Soph. *Antig.* 239, οὔτ᾽ εἶδον ὅςτις ἦν ὁ δρῶν· Paus. 9. 25. 5, ὁποῖά ἐστιν αὐτοῖς καὶ τῇ μητρὶ τὰ δρώμενα· Diog. L. 1. 87, βραδέως ἐγχειρεῖ τοῖς πραττομένοις (*faciendis*), Soph. *Electr.* 200, ὁ ταῦτα πράσσων· Plat. *Cratyl.* 416 b, ὁ τὰ ὀνόματα τιθείς· Demosth. *Theocrin.* 508 b, and frequently in the orators ὁ τὸν νόμον τιθείς (Bremi, *Dem.* p. 72) (*legislator*), ὁ γράφων τὴν μαρτυρίαν. Strabo 15. 713, Arrian, *Al.* 5. 7. 12.[3] In A. iii. 2, also, οἱ εἰσπορευόμενοι is substantival, *the enterers, those entering ;* and we cannot say with Kühnöl (*Matt.* p. 324) that this present participle is used for the future, on the ground that in ver. 3 we find μέλλοντας εἰσιέναι. In ver. 3 the more exact expression was quite in place, since the man who addressed the two apostles detained them a short time during their εἰσιέναι.—In other places, where there is a

---

[1] Matth. 557. 1, Herm. Soph. *Aj.* 172, Stallb. Plat. *Gorg.* p. 136 (Jelf 705. 3).
[2] Quoted by Eichhorn (*Einleit. N. T.* II. 378) as a strange use of the present participle.
[3] Poppo, *Thuc.* I. i. 152, Schæf. Eurip. *Orest.* p. 70, Demosth. V. 120, 127, *Poet. Gnom.* 228 sq., and *Plutarch* V. 211 sq., Weber, *Demosth.* p. 180, Bornem. *Schol.* p. 10, Jacob, Luc. *Alex.* p. 22, Maetzner, *Antiphon* p. 182.

distinct reference to past time, we find the aorist participle used as a substantive: e. g., Jo. v. 29, A. ix. 21, 2 C. vii. 12, al. Compare ὁ ἐκείνου τεκών, Eurip. *Electr.* 335; οἱ τῶν ἰόντων τεκόντες, Æschyl. *Pers.* 245 (Aristoph. *Eccl.* 1126 ἡ ἐμὴ κεκτημένη· Lucian, *Tim.* 56).

Such present participles with the article appear entirely in the character of substantives where they are joined with a genitive, as in 1 C. vii. 35, πρὸς τὸ ὑμῶν αὐτῶν συμφέρον[1] (Demosth. *Cor.* 316 c, τὰ μικρὰ συμφέροντα τῆς πόλεως).[2]

8. In quotations from the O. T. we sometimes find a participle joined with a person of *the same verb*, the participle standing first. See A. vii. 34, ἰδὼν εἶδον, from Ex. iii. 7 (compare Lucian, *Dial. Mar.* 4. 3), H. vi. 14, εὐλογῶν εὐλογήσω σε καὶ πληθύνων πληθυνῶ σε (from Gen. xxii. 17), Mt. xiii. 14, βλέποντες βλέψετε (from Is. vi. 9). This combination is extraordinarily common in the LXX—see Jud. i. 28, iv. 9, vii. 19, xi. 25, xv. 16, Gen. xxvi. 28, xxxvii. 8, 10, xliii. 6, Ex. iii. 7, 1 S. i. 10, iii. 21, xiv. 28, 1 K. xi. 11, Job vi. 2, Ruth ii. 16, 1 Macc. v. 40, Judith ii. 13,[3]—and is an imitation in Greek of the Hebrew absolute infinitive;[4] though the LXX, once accustomed to the construction, sometimes use it where in the Hebrew there is no absolute infinitive (e. g., Ex. xxiii. 26). This mode of expression was however well chosen, though, with the exception of the isolated example in Lucian (ἰδὼν εἶδον), no completely parallel instance can be found in Greek prose. Georgi (*Vind.* p. 196 sq.) has mingled together expressions of different kinds.[5] In the examples which are apparently parallel the participle has a special relation of its own; as in Her. 5. 95, φεύγων ἐκφεύγει, *fuga evadit* (Diod. S. 17. 83), and still more clearly in Xen. *Cyr.* 8. 4. 9, ὑπακούων σχολῇ ὑπήκουσα.[6] Lucian, *Parasit.* 43, φεύγων ἐκεῖθεν .... εἰς τὴν Ταυρέου πα-

---

[1] [The reading of the best texts is σύμφορον.]
[2] See Lob. Soph. *Aj.* 238 sq., Held, Plut. *Æm.* p. 252.
[3] See Thiersch, *Pent. Al.* p. 164 sqq.
[4] Ewald, *Krit. Gr.* 560 sqq. [Gesen. *Heb. Gr.* p. 213 (Bagst.), Kalisch, *Heb. Gr.* I. 294.]
[5] Some passages are cited according to false readings. Plat. *Tim.* 30 c runs thus: τίνι τῶν ζώων αὐτὸν εἰς ὁμοιότητα ὁ ξυνιστὰς ξυνίστησι. Plat. *Lach.* 185 d, σκοπούμενοι σκοποῦμεν, has been questioned by recent critics: Matth. (§ 559) proposes to read σκοποῦμεν ἃ σκοποῦμεν. Here however the strangeness lies rather in the combination of active and middle.
[6] It is scarcely necessary to say that the phrase ἰδὼν οἶδα (scio me vidisse) Athen. 6. 226, Arrian, *Ind.* 4. 15, cannot be brought in here: compare also ἀκούσας οἶδα, Lucian, *Dial. Mort.* 28. 1.

λαίστραν κατέφυγε; see Gataker, *De Stylo* c. 9,[1] Lob. *Paral.* p. 522 [532]. The imitations of this construction appear in the later writers, e. g., Anna, *Alex.* 3. 80, Euseb. *H. E.* 6. 45. Originally the participle thus used carried emphasis, though indeed at a later period it may have lost its force. This emphasis may be perceived in the three passages quoted above: we mark it either by the voice and the arrangement of the words, or by corresponding adverbs etc.,—*I have indeed seen, I will certainly (richly ?) bless thee, with your own eyes shall ye see,* etc. A. xiii. 45, οἱ Ἰουδαῖοι ἀντέλεγον τοῖς ὑπὸ τοῦ Παύλου λεγομένοις, ἀντιλέγοντες καὶ[2] βλασφημοῦντες, is an example of a somewhat different kind: ἀντέλεγον is taken up again in the participle and strengthened by βλασφημοῦντες (Jelf 705. 4).

E. v. 5, τοῦτο ἴστε γινώσκοντες, does not come in here: ἴστε refers to what has been said in verses 3 and 4, and γινώσκοντες is construed with ὅτι,—*this however ye are aware of, knowing* (considering) *that,* etc. That 1 P. i. 10, 12 [11 ?], A. v. 4, do not fall under this rule is obvious to every one. How Kühnöl could cite H. x. 37 ὁ ἐρχόμενος ἥξει (he leaves out the article, it is true) as an example of this usage, must remain a mystery.

Rem. 1. On the absolute use of the participle see §§ 59 and 66. Such a participle is τυχόν, 1 C. xvi. 6, introduced into the sentence like an adverb: see Xen. *An.* 6. 1. 20, Plat. *Alcib.* 2. 140 a. (Jelf 700. 2. *a.*)

Rem. 2. Sometimes two finite verbs are so closely connected by καί, that, logically, the first must be taken as a participle; e. g., Mt. xviii. 21, ποσάκις ἁμαρτήσει εἰς ἐμὲ ὁ ἀδελφός μου καὶ ἀφήσω αὐτῷ, that is, ἁμαρτήσαντι τῷ ἀδελφῷ. This separation of one (logical) sentence into two grammatical sentences is a peculiarity of the oriental languages, and is of frequent occurrence: see § 66. 7. (Jelf 752.)

Rem. 3. Luke and Paul—but still more the author of the Epistle to the Hebrews—are peculiarly fond of the participial construction, and Paul accumulates participles on participles: compare 1 Th. ii. 15 sq., Tit. ii. 12, 13, 2 C. iv. 8, 9, 10. In historical narration, however, the use of participles in the N. T. is, in general, less frequent and less varied than in the Greek historians. The historical style of the N. T. runs rather in simple sentences (mainly connected by

---

[1] Gataker rightly set aside Æschyl. *Prom.* 447, but was finally constrained to admit Lucian, *Dial. Mar. l. c.* as a true example. This example, looked at from a *linguistic* point of view, approaches the Hebrew mode of expression: Thiersch doubts this without reason.

[2] [Lachmann, Tregelles, Westcott and Hort omit the words ἀντιλέγοντες καί.]

the oft-recurring καί), and disregards the periodic structure, used by the Greeks with so much skill. Compare however Bornem. Xen. *Cyr.* p. 465. [§ 60. 8 sq.]

CHAPTER FIFTH.
THE PARTICLES.

SECTION XLVI.

THE PARTICLES IN GENERAL.

1. Though the inflexions of the noun and verb, which have been syntactically examined in the preceding sections, enable us to construct sentences, either simple or complex (the former chiefly by means of the cases, so widely used in Greek, the latter by means of the infinitive, participle, etc.), yet these inflexions are not sufficient by themselves to express the great variety of relations out of which sentences grow. Hence the language has a large store of so-called *particles*, which render possible the formation of all conceivable sentences, in any conceivable connexion with one another. These particles are divided into prepositions, adverbs, and conjunctions (Rost p. 725); though grammarians have not yet been able to agree amongst themselves on the lines of demarcation which separate these classes. See especially Hermann, *Emend. Rat.* p. 149 sqq.

Interjections are not words but *sounds*, and lie beyond the borders of syntax and of grammar generally.

2. Without attempting to settle the dispute of the grammarians on the definition of these three classes of particles, we may assume so much as this:—

(1) That the distinction must be made according to *meaning*, not according to *words*: as it was long ago perceived that *e. g.* prepositions frequently assume the nature of adverbs and *vice versa* (Herm. *l. c.*, p. 161), and indeed that prepositions were originally adverbs.

(2) That all particles either have for their proper office the completion of a simple sentence, and hence are confined within its limits, or are designed to link sentence to sentence. Particles of the latter kind are rightly called conjunctions; and if in grammar we consider rather speech (thinking in words) than (pure) thought, we may reckon with these the particle of com-

parison ὡς (ὥσπερ), the particles of time (ἐπεί, ὅτε, ὁπότε, etc.), the negative particle of design μή, etc.,—these words having also a connective power. Hence these particles belong, according to their nature, to two classes, adverbs and conjunctions. Within the boundaries of the simple sentence, and serving to complete its structure, we find the adverbs and the prepositions; the latter of these denoting merely *relations* (of substantives), the former *inherent attributes* of words which denote a quality or a state, i. e., of adjectives and verbs, since verbs are really compounded of the copula and a word denoting quality or state. See especially Herm. *l. c.*, p. 152 sqq.

An entirely satisfactory classification of the particles will perhaps never be effected, for here the empirical principles of language do not altogether run parallel with the rational principles of pure thought. On the relation of particles to the structure of sentences many good remarks will be found in Grotefend, *Grundzüge einer neuen Satztheorie* (Hannover, 1827), Krüger, *Erörterung der grammat. Eintheilung u. grammat. Verhältn. der Sätze* (Frankf. on M. 1826). Compare also Werner in the *Neu. Jahrb. für Philol.* 1834, p. 85 sqq.

3. The N. T. language has but partially appropriated the wealth of Greek particles, as it is displayed in the refined language of the Attic writers. Not merely was the (later) popular language of the Greeks in general more sparing in the use of particles, but the N. T. writers, transferring the Jewish colouring to their Greek style, felt under no obligation to give the nicer shades to the relations between their sentences. From the nature of the case, however, they could least easily dispense with the *prepositions*, and most easily with the *conjunctions* in all their manifold variety. N. T. Grammar, if it would not encroach on the province of Lexicography, must not take each individual particle and lay open the whole mass of its significations, but must distinctly classify and carefully examine all the directions of thought in the indication of which the particles are employed, showing at every point *to what extent* the N. T. writers in expressing these have made use of the store of Greek particles. Besides this, however, in the present state of N. T. lexicography and exegesis, it is necessary to exhibit in outline the organism of the meanings of the principal particles, and to protest most emphatically against the arbitrary doctrine of a (so-called) *enallage particularum*.

[SECT. XLVII.] THE PREPOSITIONS IN GENERAL.

Up to the most recent period the Greek particles in general had not received any examination even of an empirical kind (particularly with regard to the different periods of the language), still less any rational examination, which could be considered at all exhaustive. The works of Matt. Devarius [1] and H. Hoogeveen [2] are no longer found satisfactory, especially as they entirely exclude the prepositions. On the other hand, J. A. Hartung's treatise (*Lehre von den Partikeln der griechischen Sprache*: Erlangen, 1832–33) deserves acknowledgment; and still more useful are the acute researches with which R. Klotz has enriched his edition of Devarius (Lips. 1835, 1842). Schraut's work [3] is too fanciful. E. A. Fritzsch has pursued the comparative method in his *Vergleichende Bearbeitung der griechischen und lateinischen Partikeln* (Giessen, 1856). As regards Biblical Greek, a *Lexicon particularum* for the LXX and the Apocrypha is still a desideratum, as in the concordances and even in Schleusner's *Thesaurus Philologico-criticus* these words are entirely passed over. In Bruder's N. T. concordance the particles are carefully inserted. Tittmann's treatment of the N. T. particles [4] is not altogether satisfactory: the work, moreover, was broken off by the death of the writer — an acute scholar, but one who had not given sufficient attention to the actual usage of the language.

SECTION XLVII.

THE PREPOSITIONS IN GENERAL,[5] AND THOSE WHICH GOVERN THE GENITIVE IN PARTICULAR.

1. The prepositions run parallel with the cases of the language, and hence each, according to its significations, is combined with some particular case, that case namely, whose fundamental meaning agrees with the fundamental meaning of the preposition. The prepositions are employed where the cases are insufficient to express a relation (for these relations are in the highest degree diversified),—occasionally also where the simple case might have sufficed, but did not appear to the speaker

---

[1] Edited by Reusmann (Lips. 1793).
[2] Amsterdam 1769.—An epitome by Schütz (Lips. 1806).
[3] *Die griech. Partik. im Zusammenhange mit den ältesten Stämmen der Sprache* (Neuss, 1848).
[4] *De usu particularum N. T.* Cap. 1, 2 (Lips. 1831): also in his *Synonyma N. T.* II. 42 sqq.
[5] Compare Herm. *De Emend. Rat.* p. 161 sqq.; B. G. Weiske, *De præposition. Gr. Comment.* (Gorlic. 1809–10); K. G. Schmidt, *Quæstion. grammat. de præposition. Gr.* (Berlin 1829); Döderlein, *Reden u. Aufs.* II. No. 3; Bernh. p. 195 sqq.; Schneider, *Vorles.* p. 181 sqq. [Donalds. *Gr.* p. 503 sqq., *New Crat.* p. 312 sqq.; Jelf 472, 614 sqq.; Clyde, *Synt.* pp. 41, 121, 184–202; Farrar, *Synt.* p. 86 sqq.; A. Buttm. pp. 321–344; Webster, *Synt.* pp. 149–185; Green, *Gr.* p. 203 sqq. Compare Curtius, *Elucidations* c. xix.]

sufficiently marked for his purpose, on account of the great variety in its uses. Prepositions are proportionally used with greater frequency in the N. T. than in Greek prose, because the apostles had not that inherent sensitiveness to the force of the cases in their extended applications which was possessed by educated native Greeks; and because the Oriental loves vividness of expression,—as indeed the Hebrew-Aramaic language uses prepositions to express almost all the relations which were in Greek indicated by the case alone.

2. In examining a preposition, it is important, in the first place, to obtain a clear and distinct conception of its true primary meaning, from which all its significations proceed, as rays from a centre; and to trace back to this all its varieties of meaning,— i. e., to see clearly how the transition to any given application was effected in the mind of the speaker or writer: and, secondly, to apprehend the necessity of the choice of this or that particular case to accompany the preposition (either generally, or for a certain cycle of its meanings),[1] and to use the knowledge we thus obtain for the purpose of marking the boundary lines which separate the meanings of the various prepositions. The former investigation, viz. the discovery of the primary meaning—which presents itself to view sometimes in the construction with the genitive, sometimes in that with the dative or with the accusative —will show in its true light the interchange of the prepositions amongst themselves, which has been supposed to exist in the N.T. to an unlimited extent. The latter must be pursued without seeking for subtleties; and we must bear in mind throughout that in expressing one and the same relation (especially if it be metaphysical) a preposition may be joined with different cases, according to the conception which the particular writer has formed of this relation, and the degree of clearness with which the relation is conceived: compare Hermann, *Emend. Rat.* p. 163.

In dealing with the N. T. language, it is only necessary further

1. To consider how far the later Greek, particularly the popular spoken language, enlarged the use of the prepositions, obliterated the nicer distinctions, or even fell into a misuse of these particles.

---

[1] Bernhardi, *Allg. Sprachl.* I. 164 sq. (Don. p. 503 sq., Jelf 472, 617.)

SECT. XLVII.]   THE PREPOSITIONS IN GENERAL.   451

2. To have constant regard to the Hebrew-Aramaic language, which delights in the use of prepositions, and which differs from Greek in the aspect under which it views a number of relations (compare *e. g.* ὀμόσαι ἔν τινι, ἀποκτείνειν ἐν ῥομφαίᾳ).
3. Lastly, not to neglect the peculiarly Christian mode of thought which lies at the root of the use of several prepositions (as ἐν Χριστῷ, ἐν κυρίῳ).[1]

Until a recent period the abuse of the prepositions by the N. T. philologers in lexicons and commentaries (see *e. g.* Koppe's N. T.) was truly horrible:[2] it had however at once its model and its support in the purely empirical treatment of the Hebrew prepositions which prevailed until the time of Ewald; see my *Exeget. Studien* I. 27 sqq. Wahl was the first to take a better course, and now almost all have begun to be ashamed of such wild license.

In considering the relation between the Greek and the Hebrew-Aramaic elements in the use of prepositions, we must not fail to notice—(1) That to many turns of expression which the mother-tongue had rendered familiar to the N. T. writers parallels may be found in Greek poetry and later prose, so varied are the applications of the Greek prepositions :—(2) That, if in the more Hebraistic portions of the N. T. (in the Apocalypse especially) an explanation may naturally be sought for in Hebrew usage, it does not follow that in all books without distinction the Greek prepositions, with which the apostles had received the power of expressing a multitude of special relations, are to be referred back to the Hebrew prepositions; for careful observation shows that the apostles had already become accustomed to conceive prepositional relations in the Greek manner: —(3) That, especially in Paul (and John), the use of several prepositions (e. g., ἐν) in a mode unknown to Greek writers stood in a close relation to the language of *dogma*, and belongs to the apostolic (Christian) colouring of the N. T. diction.

3. First of all, the proper and the derived meanings of each preposition must be accurately distinguished. The former always have immediate reference to *local* relations (Bernhardi I. 290); if these are contemplated in great variety by any nation, there will also arise a great variety of prepositions in the language of that nation. There are only two simple local relations, —that of *rest* and that of *motion* (including *direction*, which is regarded more or less as motion). Motion is either motion

---

[1] [Compare Ellicott, *Aids to Faith* p. 465 sq., Green, *Gr.* p. 226 sq.]
[2] Tittmann, *De Scriptor. N. T. diligentia gramm.* p. 12 (*Synon.* I. 207): nulla est, ne repugnans quidem significatio, quin quæcunque præpositio eam in N. T. habere dicatur.

towards or motion *from*. The dative corresponds to the notion of rest, the accusative to that of motion *towards*, the genitive to that of motion *from*. (Don. p. 503, Jelf 614 sqq.)

Local designations having particular prepositions corresponding to them are the following :—

(*a*) Of rest : *in*, ἐν ; *by*, παρά ; *on*, ἐπί ; *over*, ὑπέρ ; *under* (ὑπό) ; *between* (*with*), μετά ; *before*, πρό ; *behind*, μετά ; *upon* (*up*), ἀνά ; *around*, (ἀμφί) περί ; *opposite*, ἀντί.

(*b*) Of (direction or) motion *towards* a point : *into*, εἰς ; *towards*, κατά ; *to*, πρός ; *upon*, ἐπί ; *along, by*, παρά ; *under*, ὑπό.

(*c*) Of (direction or) motion *from* : *out of*, ἐκ ; *from*, ἀπό ; *from under*, ὑπό ; *down from*, κατά ; *from beside*, παρά. With the last cycle is connected the local *through* (διά),[1] for which the Hebrews use מִן, and which we sometimes express by *out of* (e.g., to go *out of* the door).

4. The type of local relations is first applied to notions of *time* : hence most prepositions have had temporal meanings assigned to them. Then follows the transference to non-material, purely metaphysical relations, which are conceived by every nation under a more or less material form, and hence are very differently expressed in different languages. Thus the Greek says λέγειν περί τινος, the Roman *dicere de aliqua re*, the Hebrew דִּבֶּר בְּ, the German frequently *über etwas sprechen*. By the first the object is viewed as the centre which the speaker as it were *encompasses* (to speak *about* something) ; the Roman views it as a whole from which the speaker imparts something (to the hearer),—*de*, as if "*from the subject* to say something";[2] the Hebrew, as the basis of the speaking (to discourse *on* something) ; the German, as a surface lying before the speaker, *over* which the speaking spreads (for in this combination *über* is followed by the accusative).

The notion of *origin* and consequently of *cause* is most simply comprised in the prepositions *from, out of* (ἀπό, ὑπό, παρά, ἐκ) ; that of *occasion* and therefore also of *motive* in πρός, εἰς,[3] ἐπί with the dative, and διά with the accusative (*on account of*) : in this case the idea suggested by ἐπί is that of the *basis* on

---

[1] Compare Winer, *Progr. de verborum cum præpositionibus compositorum in N. T. usu* V. p. 3.
[2] On the primary meaning of the Latin *de*, see Heidtmann in the *Zeitschr. f. Alterth.-Wiss.* 1846, No. 109 sq.
[3] As in German *auf das Gerücht*.

which something rests, just as we for the same reason use *ground* for *ratio*. *Design* and *aim* are expressed by the prepositions *to, for,*—ἐπί with the dative, εἰς and πρός with the accusative: *condition* by ἐπί with the dative, as we also say with the same transference of meaning *auf Lohn Recht sprechen,*[1] and the like. The object forming the basis on which an emotion rests is indicated by ἐπί with the genitive;[2] as we also say *to rejoice over, pride oneself on,* etc. Speaking *in reference to* an object is designated as λέγειν περί τινος (see above). The *norma* or *rule* is indicated either by *towards* (πρός, κατά), or by *out of* (ἐκ). In the former construction the rule is viewed as that *towards which* something should direct itself; in the latter, that which is regulated is viewed as proceeding *out of,* being derived *from,* that which regulates. Lastly, the *means* is very simply expressed by διά with the genitive, sometimes by ἐν.

5. One preposition certainly may stand for another in certain cases. Amongst these, however, we must not reckon the cases in which a metaphysical relation is expressed equally well by several prepositions;[3] as in *loqui de re* and *super re,* ζῆν ἔκ and ἀπό τινος, ὠφελεῖσθαι ἀπό and ἔκ τινος (Xen. *Cyr.* 5. 4. 34, *Mem.* 2. 4. 1),—also ὠφελεῖσθαι ἐπί τινι, ἀποκτείνεσθαι ἀπό and ἔκ τινος (Rev. ix. 18), ἀποθνήσκειν ἔκ τινος (Rev. viii. 11) and ὑπό τινος, ἀποθνήσκειν ὑπέρ and περὶ τῶν ἁμαρτιῶν, ἀγωνίζεσθαι περί and ὑπέρ τινος, ἐκλέγεσθαι ἀπό and ἐκ τῶν μαθητῶν.[4] This cannot be called an *enallage* of prepositions. On the other hand, especially in expressing local relations, the *wider* preposition may be used for the *narrower* (compare L. xxiv. 2, ἀπο-

---

[1] [So in English, *serve on hire, on these terms.*]
[2] [Evidently this should be "ἐπί with the *dative.*"]
[3] Thus Paul sometimes uses two different prepositions in parallel clauses, for the sake of variety: e. g., Rom. iii. 30, ὅς δικαιώσει περιτομὴν ἐκ πίστεως καὶ ἀκροβυστίαν διὰ τῆς πίστεως· E. iii. 8 sq. [? ii. 8 sq.]
[4] Different languages sometimes express the same relation by means of directly opposite prepositions, because the relation was looked at differently. Thus we say "*zur* Rechten" ["*to* the right"]; the Romans, Greeks, and Hebrews, "*a* dextra," etc. Even the same language may express a relation, especially if of a metaphysical kind, by opposite prepositions. We say "*auf* die Bedingung" and "*unter* der Bedingung" [to which our own "*on*" and "*under* the condition" nearly correspond]. In South Germany they speak of a relative or friend *to* (zu) some one; in Saxony, of a relative or friend *of* (von) some one. How ridiculous would it be to maintain in such cases that *of* (von) is sometimes equivalent to *to* (zu),—*on* (auf) to *under* (unter) !

κυλίειν τὸν λίθον ἀπὸ τοῦ μνημείου· with Mk. xvi. 3, ἐκ τῆς θύρας τοῦ μνημείου, which corresponds more fully with the circumstances of the case, *out of* the door—hewn in the rock), for it is not always necessary to speak with exact precision, and inadvertence on the writer's part may lead to the use of the less definite expression in the place of the more definite. It is only in appearance that an interchange of prepositions takes place when a preposition is used in a pregnant sense, i. e., when it includes a second relation, the antecedent or the consequent of that which it properly denotes (e. g., κατοικεῖν εἰς τὴν πόλιν, εἶναι ὑπὸ νόμον), or when attraction takes place, as in αἴρειν τὰ ἐκ τῆς οἰκίας (Mt. xxiv. 17), ἀποτάξασθαι τοῖς εἰς τὸν οἶκον (L. ix. 61).

An arbitrary interchange of prepositions (of which the older N. T. commentaries are full, and which was in part supported by a misuse of parallel passages, especially in the Gospels) would never have been dreamed of, had it been customary to regard languages as living organs of communication for the different nations. It is truly absurd to suppose that any one could have said " he is travelling *into* Egypt " instead of " he is travelling *in* Egypt " (εἰς for ἐν), or " all things are *for* him " in the place of " all things are *from* him." We cannot even regard it as entirely a matter of indifference whether, e. g., *through* is expressed by διά or by ἐν, especially in the case of διὰ Ἰησοῦ Χριστοῦ, and ἐν Ἰησοῦ Χριστῷ. The Latin language also usually makes a distinction between *per* (before names of persons) and the ablative (of things). Exact observation shows generally how correctly even prepositions which are closely allied are discriminated by the N. T. writers (e. g., in Rom. xiii. 1, οὐκ ἔστιν ἐξουσία εἰ μὴ ἀπὸ[1] θεοῦ, αἱ δὲ οὖσαι ὑπὸ τοῦ θεοῦ τεταγμέναι εἰσίν),[2] and we should seek to do honour both to them and to ourselves by uniformly acknowledging their carefulness.

Where a relation may be expressed equally well by either of two prepositions, the choice of the one in the N. T. in preference to the other may perhaps belong to the colouring of Hellenistic Greek: at any rate the grammarian must take this into consideration as a possible case. Planck is mistaken, however, when he supposes[3] that ἀγαθὸς πρός τι (E. iv. 29) is less correct Greek than ἀγαθὸς εἴς τι: the former frequently occurs, e. g., Theophr. *Hist. Plant.* 4. 3. 1, 7, 9. 13. 3, Xen. *Mem.* 4. 6. 10, al.[4]

---

[1] [The best texts now have ὑπό.]
[2] Hence I cannot from my own observation understand what Lücke (*Apokal.* II. 458) says of an irregular and inconsistent use of prepositions in the N. T.
[3] *Articuli nonnulli Lex. nov. in N. T.* p. 14 (Goett. 1824).
[4] See Schneider, Plat. *Civ.* II. 278.

With the prepositions which are construed with different cases in different senses it is sometimes possible to join either of two cases with equal correctness, where a *metaphysical* relation is to be expressed (e.g., we may have ἐπί with either genitive or accusative) : indeed the MSS. are sometimes divided between the two cases, see Rom. viii. 11. In the N. T. this principle has often been wrongly applied to διά: see below, § 47. i. Rem. d, and compare § 49. c. Purely external notions, however, admit of no such interchange in careful writers : only very late authors, especially the Byzantines, take this license,—confounding for example μετά with genitive and μετά with accusative ; see the index to Malalas s. v. (Bonn edition).[1] Indeed the later writers have so completely lost all sensitiveness to the force of the cases, that they even begin to join prepositions with cases entirely different in nature, e.g., ἀπό with the accusative and dative, κατά with the dative, σύν with the genitive : see the index to Leo Grammaticus and to Theophanes.[2] The opinion recently revived, that confusion of this kind exists in the N. T. in consequence of the absence of cases in Hebrew, is sufficiently refuted by the fact that the N. T. writers, except in a very few doubtful instances, show clearly that they correctly felt the distinctions between the cases.

The position of prepositions is a simpler matter in the N. T. than in Greek writers (Matth. 595, Jelf 651). As a rule, they are placed immediately before the noun. Only those conjunctions which can never stand first in a clause are admitted between the preposition and the noun : as δέ, Mt. xi. 12, xxii. 31, xxiv. 22, 36, A. v. 12 ; γάρ, Jo. iv. 37, v. 46, A. viii. 23, Rom. iii. 20 ; τε, A. x. 39, xxv. 24 ; γε, L. xi. 8, xviii. 5 ; μέν and μὲν γάρ, Rom. xi. 22, A. xxviii. 22, 2 Tim. iv. 4.

PREPOSITIONS WITH THE GENITIVE.

a. Ἀντί,—the Latin *ante*—has the local meaning (*straight*) *before, against* (*over against*). Figuratively used, it denotes barter and exchange (Plat. *Conv.* 218 e), in which one thing is placed *against* another, is given *for* it ("tooth *for* tooth," Mt. v. 38), and consequently takes its place. Ἀντί governs the genitive because this is the case of (procession from and) exchange ; see above, p. 258. Examples of this meaning are 1 C. xi. 15, ἡ κόμη ἀντὶ περιβολαίου δέδοται (τῇ γυναικί), *her hair .... for, in the place of, a covering* (to serve her as a covering,

---

[1] Compare Schæf. *Ind. ad Æsop.* p. 136, Boisson. *Anecd.* IV. 487, V. 84. In *Acta Apocr.* p. 257 we find μετά with the accusative close by μετά with the genitive, the preposition meaning *with* in both places.

[2] The examples of ἐν with the accusative are of a different kind : see Schæf. Dion. *Comp.* p. 305, Ross, *Inscriptt. Gr.* I. 37 (Don. p. 510, Jelf 625).

—compare Lucian, *Philops.* 22, Liban. *Ep.* 350), H. xii. 16, ὃς ἀντὶ βρώσεως μιᾶς ἀπέδοτο τὰ πρωτοτόκια αὐτοῦ· xii. 2, ἀντὶ τῆς προκειμένης αὐτῷ χαρᾶς ὑπέμεινε σταυρόν (*for* the joy ordained for him,—setting the death of the cross *over against* this), Mt. xx. 28, δοῦναι τὴν ψυχὴν αὐτοῦ λύτρον ἀντὶ πολλῶν· xvii. 27, ἐκεῖνον (στατῆρα) λαβὼν δὸς αὐτοῖς ἀντὶ ἐμοῦ καὶ σοῦ· ii. 22, Ἀρχέλαος βασιλεύει ἀντὶ Ἡρώδου, *for Herod, in Herod's place,*—compare Her. 1. 108, Xen. *An.* 1. 1. 4, 1 K. xi. 44. Hence ἀντί is chiefly the preposition which denotes the *price, for* which merchandise is given or received (H. xii. 16); then the retribution (Lev. xxiv. 20) and the recompense (here bordering on a causal sense, like the German *ob*). Thus ἀνθ᾽ ὧν means (as a recompense) *for the fact (that)*, i. e., *because*, L. i. 20, xix. 44, Plat. *Menex.* 244, Xen. *An.* 5. 5. 14, 1 K. xi. 11, Joel iii. 5,—or *wherefore* (therefore) L. xii. 3 ; ἀντὶ τούτου E. v. 31 (from the LXX[1]), *therefore (for this)*, compare Pausan. 10. 38. 5. In one passage ἀντί is used with a peculiar application, but one which points to the primary meaning of the preposition: Jo. i. 16, ἐλάβομεν . . . . χάριν ἀντὶ χάριτος, *grace upon grace* (Theognis, *Sent.* 344, ἀντ᾽ ἀνιῶν ἀνίας), properly *grace over against grace, grace for grace,*—in the place of grace (new) grace; hence, unintermitting grace, grace continually renewed.[2] (Don. p. 504, Jelf 618.)

b. Ἀπό, ἐκ, παρά, and ὑπό, collectively express that which the genitive indicates in the most general way, the idea of *procession from;* they differ in regard to the relation in which the objects previously stood to one another. Ἐκ unquestionably points to the most intimate connexion, ὑπό to one less intimate; a still more remote association is expressed by παρά (de chez moi, מֵעִם), and especially by ἀπό.[3] Hence, if we arrange these prepositions according to the closeness of the connexion implied by them, beginning with that which indicates the closest con-

---

[1] [In Gen. ii. 24 ἀντί is not found.]
[2] [The most interesting parallel is given by Wetstein from Philo: διὸ τὰς πρώτας ἀεὶ χάριτας, πρὶν κορεσθέντας ἐξυβρίσαι τοὺς λαχόντας, ἐπισχὼν καὶ ταμιευσάμενος, εἰσαῦθις ἑτέρας ἀντὶ ἐκείνων, καὶ τρίτας ἀντὶ τῶν δευτέρων, καὶ ἀεὶ νέας ἀντὶ παλαιοτέρων . . . . ἐπιδίδωσι (*De Post. Caini* i. 254).]
[3] The distinction between ἀπό and ἐκ is perceptible in L. ii. 4 (comp. also A. xxiii. 34), but the two prepositions are used synonymously in Jo. xi. 1 (see Lücke *in loc.*), Rev. ix. 18. Compare also L. xxi. 18 with A. xxvii. 34. In Mk. xvi. 3, L. xxiv. 2, ἀπό and ἐκ are parallel to each other: one is the more precise (and suitable), " *out of* the door; " the other the looser, " (*away*) *from* the grave." See p. 454.

nexion, their order will be, ἐκ, ὑπό, παρά, ἀπό. Further, if we are thinking simply of procession from an object, we use ἀπό; if definitely of procession from a personal object, παρά or ὑπό. If the personal object is merely indicated generally as the starting point, we use παρά; if as the true efficient producing principle, ὑπό; hence ὑπό is the preposition which regularly follows passive verbs. Lastly, ἀπό has attached to it the signification of *distance* and *separation,* and both ἀπό and ἐκ express the notion of *dividing, severing,* which is not directly conveyed by either παρά or ὑπό.

Παρά is properly used in relation to objects which come from the *neighbourhood* of a person,—come out of his *sphere*: thus it is opposed to πρός with the accusative in Lucian, *Tim.* 53. Thus in Mk. xiv. 43, παραγίνεται ὄχλος πολὺς . . . παρὰ τῶν ἀρχιερέων, *from the chief priests* (men whom the chief priests had about them, with them, as their servants,—compare Lucian, *Philops.* 5, Demosth. *Polycl.* 710 b); Mk. xii. 2, ἵνα παρὰ τῶν γεωργῶν λάβῃ ἀπὸ τοῦ καρποῦ, a part of the produce, which was *in the hands of the vine-dressers;* Jo. xvi. 27, ὅτι ἐγὼ παρὰ τοῦ θεοῦ ἐξῆλθον (compare i. 1, ὁ λόγος ἦν πρὸς τὸν θεόν); Jo. v. 41 (Plat. *Rep.* 10. 612 d), xv. 26, E. vi. 8, L. ii. 1, 2 P. i. 17. Hence παρά is joined with verbs of *inquiring* and *requesting,* Mt. ii. 4, 16, Mk. viii. 11, Jo. iv. 9; of *learning,* 2 Tim. iii. 14, A. xxiv. 8 (Xen. *Cyr.* 2. 2. 6, Plat. *Euth.* 12 e); the matter to be learned etc. being regarded as existing in some one's (intellectual) possession. (This relation is more loosely expressed by ἀπό in Mk. xv. 45, G. iii. 2: by ἔκ τινος, Xen. *Œc.* 13. 6, it is defined more sharply.) It is only in later writers that παρά with passive verbs has exactly the force of ὑπό.[1] In A. xxii. 30, τί κατηγορεῖται παρὰ τῶν Ἰουδαίων, Luke could not well have said ὑπὸ τῶν Ἰουδαίων, for as yet they had presented no accusation,—had not taken action in the way of impeachment: the meaning is, *with what he is charged on the part of the Jews.*[2] In Mt. xxi. 42, παρὰ κυρίου ἐγένετο αὕτη (from the LXX) means *from God—divinitus,* through means which exist in the power of God—*this came to pass.* In Jo. i. 6, ἐγένετο ἄνθρωπος ἀπεσταλμένος παρὰ θεοῦ·

---

[1] Bast, *Ep. Crit.* pp. 156, 235, Ellendt, Arr. *Alex.* II. 172.
[2] [The best texts now have ὑπό.]

the meaning is, *he appeared, sent from God;* compare ver. 1, ἦν πρὸς τὸν θεόν. (Don. pp. 431, 521, Jelf 637.)

There is not a single passage in the N. T. in which παρά with the genitive stands for παρά with the dative, as it is sometimes supposed to do in Greek writers.¹ In 2 Tim. i. 18 εὑρίσκειν conveys the idea of *obtaining* (it is otherwise in L. i. 30, εὗρες χάριν παρὰ τῷ θεῷ, *with God*). Mk. v. 26 is an example of attraction. In Mk. iii. 21, οἱ παρ' αὐτοῦ probably means *his kindred;*² see Fritz. *in loc.*, and compare Susanna 33. On the use of παρά as a periphrasis for the genitive see § 30. 3, Rem. 5. Any one may see that τὰ παρ' ὑμῶν, Ph. iv. 18, τὰ παρ' αὐτῶν, L. x. 7, are not simply equivalent to τὰ ὑμῶν (ὑμέτερα), τὰ αὐτῶν: in both passages the phrase is joined with a verb of receiving, —receiving that which comes from you, i. e., your gifts,—eating what is offered, what is set before you, from (by) them.

Ἐκ originally denotes *procession out of the interior*—the compass, the limits—of anything, and is the antithesis of εἰς (L. x. 7, xvii. 24, Herod. 4. 15. 10. Æsch. *Dial.* 3. 11). L. vi. 42, ἔκβαλε τὴν δοκὸν ἐκ τοῦ ὀφθαλμοῦ (it was ἐν τῷ ὀφθαλμῷ); Mt. viii. 28, ἐκ τῶν μνημείων ἐξερχόμενοι· A. ix. 3, περιήστραψεν αὐτὸν φῶς ἐκ τοῦ οὐρανοῦ· Mt. i. 16, ἐξ ἧς (Μαρίας) ἐγεννήθη Ἰησοῦς· i. 3, 1 P. i. 23. L. v. 3, ἐδίδασκεν ἐκ τοῦ πλοίου, is concisely expressed,—*taught out of the ship* (speaking from on board); compare ii. 35. Akin to this is the use of ἐκ to indicate the *material*, Mt. xxvii. 29, Rom. ix. 21, compare Herod. 8. 4. 27;³ then the *mass* or *store* out of which something comes, from which it is derived, as Jo. vi. 50, φαγεῖν ἐξ ἄρτου· L. viii. 3, 1 Jo. iv. 13, ἐκ τοῦ πνεύματος αὐτοῦ δέδωκεν ἡμῖν, *from his spirit he has given to us;* further, the *class* from which some one is, to which he belongs, as Jo. vii. 48, μή τις ἐκ τῶν ἀρχόντων ἐπίστευσεν; Jo. iii. 1, ἄνθρωπος ἐκ τῶν φαρισαίων· xvi. 17, εἶπον ἐκ τῶν μαθητῶν (τινές), 2 Tim. iii. 6, 2 Jo. 4, Rev. ii. 10,—a man's *native country*, *out of* which he comes, A. xxiii. 34,—the progenitor from whom he is descended, as Ἑβραῖος ἐξ Ἑβραίων (Plat. *Phædr.* 246 a),⁴ compare H. ii. 11; and lastly, the *condition*

---

¹ Schæf. Dion. *Comp.* p. 118 sq., Held, Plut. *Timol.* p. 427 (Jelf 637. *Obs.* 1).
² [In the original there follows the parenthesis ("those descended *from him*, his family"). The words are probably inserted by mistake, as they are inapplicable to the present case, and as Fritzsche—to whom Winer refers—expressly rejects this meaning (which belongs to the phrase in 1 Macc. xiii. 52).]
³ Ellendt, Arr. *Alex.* I. 150.
⁴ Compare δουλίκδουλος, Diod. S. *Exc. Vat.* p. 31.

SECT. XLVII.] PREPOSITIONS WITH THE GENITIVE. 459

from which any one comes out, Rev. ix. 20,—or (by brachylogy) out of which he undertakes something, as 2 C. ii. 4 ἐκ πολλῆς θλίψεως . . . ἔγραψα ὑμῖν. Sometimes we find ἐκ used in a local sense like the Latin *ex* for *de* (*down from*), as in A. xxviii. 4, κρεμάμενον τὸ θηρίον ἐκ τῆς χειρός (Judith viii. 24, xiv. 11, *Odyss.* 8. 67, Her. 4. 10, Xen. *Mem.* 3. 10. 13), A. xxvii. 29 ; or less definitely,[1] H. xiii. 10, φαγεῖν ἐκ τοῦ θυσιαστηρίου, *from the altar* (that which was offered *on* the altar) ;[2] and even of simple direction *from*, as in Mt. xx. 21, ἵνα καθίσωσιν . . . εἷς ἐκ δεξιῶν κ.τ.λ., H. i. 13 (Bleek *in loc.*). The German phrase is *to the right*, but the Roman also says *a dextra*, and the Hebrew מִן. In such designations indeed it is of no consequence whether we suppose the motion to take place from the object whose position we are fixing (towards ourselves), or from ourselves towards the object: the former conception is chosen by the Greeks (ἐκ δεξιᾶς), the latter by the Germans. Compare Goeller on Thuc. 8. 33; and for analogous examples see Thuc. 1. 64, 3. 51, and Her. 3. 101, οἰκέουσι πρὸς νότον ἀνέμου.

When used of *time*, ἐκ denotes the starting-point of a temporal series, the period *since which* something has been in existence : A. xxiv. 10, ἐκ πολλῶν ἐτῶν ὄντα σε κριτήν κ.τ.λ., Jo. vi. 66, ix. 1, A. ix. 33, G. i. 15 ; ἐξ ἱκανοῦ L. xxiii. 8, like ἐκ πολλοῦ.[3] The Greek use of the preposition *out of* results from his more vivid conception of the relation. He does not look on the period, as we do, as a point *from which* a reckoning is made,

---

[1] Mk. xvi. 3 does not come in here ; see above, no. 5 (p. 454).—We must not forget that sometimes the same relation is viewed somewhat differently in two different languages, and yet correctly in both : e. g., Rom. xiii. 11, ἐγερθῆναι ἐξ ὕπνου, "aufstehen *vom* Schlafe" [i. e., "arise *from* sleep"]. In Rev. vi. 14 ἐκ is probably used designedly, as the mountains are fixed *in* the earth. This is certainly the case in Jo. xx. 1.

[2] Mt. xvii. 9, καταβαίνειν ἐκ τοῦ ὄρους, stands by itself in the N. T. (Ex. xix. 14, xxxii. 1) : elsewhere we find καταβαίνειν ἀπὸ τοῦ ὄρους, Mt. viii. 1, Mk. ix. 9, L. ix. 37.

[3] The N. T. passages formerly quoted to show that ἐκ has also the meaning *statim post*, fail to prove this. L. xi. 6 means come in *from a journey ;* L. xii. 36, return *from the wedding ;* Jo. iv. 6, wearied *from his journey ;* 2 C. iv. 6, *out of* darkness light, etc. In several of these passages the rendering *immediately after* would be altogether unsuitable ; in others it would drag in a note of time where nothing was directly present to the writer's mind but *from, out of,* specifying state or condition. Least of all can H. xi. 35 be an example of this meaning. [In L. xxiii. 8, quoted above in the text, ἐξ ἱκανῶν χρόνων is no doubt the true reading.]

but as a surface *out of which* something extends (as in ἐξ ἡμέρας, ἐξ ἔτους, etc.).

In a figurative sense, this preposition denotes any kind of *source* and *cause* from which something proceeds or results (hence ἐκ and διά are allied [1]), whether this source (cause) be material or personal: A. xix. 25, Rom. x. 17, 2 C. ii. 2, iii. 5. The following examples of this use of ἐκ deserve special notice: Rev. viii. 11, ἀποθνήσκειν ἐκ τῶν ὑδάτων (xix. 18,[2] Dio C. p. 239. 27, compare *Iliad* 18. 107); Rev. xv. 2, νικᾶν ἔκ τινος [3] (victoriam ferre *ex* aliquo, Liv. 8. 8 *extr.*); 1 C. ix. 14, ἐκ τοῦ εὐαγγελίου ζῆν (L. xii. 15,— compare ζῆν ἀπό, Aristot. *Pol.* 3. 3,[4] and *ex* rapto vivere, Ovid, *Met.* 1. 144); L. xvi. 9, ποιήσατε ἑαυτοῖς φίλους ἐκ τοῦ μαμωνᾶ τῆς ἀδικίας; Rom. i. 4, ὁρισθέντος υἱοῦ θεοῦ ἐξ ἀναστάσεως νεκρῶν (the source of proof and conviction, —compare Ja. ii. 18). The reference to persons [5] is especially frequent and varied: compare further Jo. iii. 25, ἐγένετο ζήτησις ἐκ τῶν μαθητῶν Ἰωάννου (Plat. *Theæt.* 171 a), Mt. i. 18, ἐν γαστρὶ ἔχουσα ἐκ πνεύματος ἁγίου· Jo. vii. 22, οὐκ ἐκ τοῦ Μωϋσέως ἐστὶν (ἡ περιτομή), Rom. xiii. 3, ἕξεις ἔπαινον ἐξ αὐτῆς (ἐξουσίας), Jo. x. 32, πολλὰ καλὰ ἔργα ἔδειξα ὑμῖν ἐκ τοῦ πατρός μου· vi. 65 (Her. 8. 114), xviii. 3, 1 C. vii. 7, 2 C. ii. 2, Rom. v. 16 (where Fritzsche's rendering *per* is inexact). Ἐκ is especially so used in reference to rulers, magistrates, judges; see Xen. *An.* 1. 1. 6, *Cyr.* 8. 6. 9, Her. 1. 69, 121, 2. 151, Polyb. 15. 4, 7. In a special application this preposition denotes the *state of mind*, the *feeling*, out of which something springs, as in 1 Tim. i. 5 (Rom. vi. 17), Mk. xii. 30, Ph. i. 16,[6] 1 Th. ii. 3 (Plato, *Phil.* 22 b,

---

[1] Franke, *Dem.* p. 8, Held, Plut. *Tim.* 331; compare Fritz. *Rom.* I. 332.
[2] [Read ix. 18, as in ed. 5.]
[3] [A. Buttmann regards this as a Latinism (p. 147). In Grimm's edition of Wilke's *Clavis* it is explained as an example of brachylogy, "vincendo se liberare e potestate belluæ." Alford cites Thuc. 1. 120, ἀδικουμένους ἐκ μὲν εἰρήνης πολεμεῖν κ.τ.λ. (see Jelf 621. 2); but surely this is entirely different from νικᾶν ἐκ τοῦ θηρίου.]
[4] Demosth. *Eubul.* 540 b, ζῆν ἐκ τοῦ δικαίου, cited by Wahl in his *Clavis*, does not come under this head.
[5] This usage is carried very far, especially in Herodotus: see Schweighaeus. *Lex. Herod.* p. 192. See further *e.g.* Diog. L. 1. 54, Philostr. *Soph.* 2. 12, al., and Sturz, *Lexic.* Xen. II. 88. (Don. p. 430, Jelf 621. 3. *b.*)
[6] [Here Winer takes οἱ μὲν as the subject of the sentence, and joins ἐξ ἀγάπης with κηρύσσουσι understood: this construction is followed by the ancient versions, our own Auth. Ver., Alford, Lightfoot, al. A little lower down Ph. i. 17 is quoted for εἶναι ἐξ, which implies that οἱ ἐξ ἐριθείας (ὄντες) is the subject:

Xen. *An.* 7. 7. 43, ἐκ τῆς ψυχῆς φίλος ἦν· Arrian, *Ep.* 3. 22. 18, Aristoph. *Nub.* 86); then the *occasion*, as in Rev. xvi. 21, ἐβλασφήμησαν τὸν θεὸν ἐκ τῆς πληγῆς (but not, as Meyer maintains,[1] in 1 C. x. 17), and the *reason* (ratio), Rev. viii. 13,—for both occasion and reason are the source out of which the result flows (Lucian, *Asin.* 46, Demosth. *Con.* 727 b [2]); the *substratum* of a judgment (that out of which a judgment is derived), Mt. xii. (33) 37,[3] Rev. xx. 12, Xen. *Cyr.* 2. 2. 21, 2. 3. 6, Æsop. 93. 4 (we use a different figure, *decide by* or *according to* something,— compare ἐν, 1 Jo. iii. 19, v. 2),—and consequently the *standard*, 2 C. viii. 11. Occasionally *price* is expressed by means of ἐκ, as in Mt. xxvii. 7, ἠγόρασαν ἐξ αὐτῶν (ἀργυρίων) ἀγρόν (Palæph. 46. 3), since for us the possession proceeds out of the money paid for it: compare Mt. xx. 2, where the language is abbreviated. On ἐξ ἔργων εἶναι and the like, G. iii. 10, Rom. iii. 26, iv. 14, 16, Ph. i. 17, Tit. i. 10, see my note on the first of these passages.[4] In general, the phrase εἶναι ἔκ τινος shares in all the preposition's variety of meaning: compare further, for instance, 1 C. xii. 15, ὅτι οὐκ εἰμὶ χείρ, οὐκ εἰμὶ ἐκ τοῦ σώματος. Our expression is the reverse of this; we say *to belong to* the body.[5]

That ἐκ never stands for ἐν (as it is supposed sometimes to do in Greek writers, see Poppo on Thuc. 2. 7, 8. 62) is quite certain. As to attraction, e. g., Mt. xxiv. 17, αἴρειν τὰ ἐκ τῆς οἰκίας, see § 66. 6; and compare Poppo, *Thuc.* III. ii. 493.

Ὑπό signifies *from under, away from under* (מִתַּחַת): Hesiod, *Theog.* 669, Ζεὺς . . . . ὑπὸ χθονὸς ἧκε κ.τ.λ., Plat. *Phædr.* 230 b. Next it commonly accompanies passive verbs,[6] to in-

---

this is the view taken (in both verses) by Meyer, De W., Ellicott, and others. The construction must be the same in both verses.]
[1] [Not now: he renders "for from the one bread we all receive a portion."]
[2] Other passages quoted (e. g., by Bretschneider) for the signification *on account of* must be set aside. Rom. v. 16 reduces itself very simply to the idea of *source*. A. xxviii. 3 may be rendered *gliding out of the heat;* but recent editors read ἀπό.
[3] See Kypke *in loc.*
[4] [There Winer merely says "εἶναι ἐκ, ut alibi, significat, *pendere aliquem ab aliqua re*, stare ab aliqua parte." See Ellicott *in loc.*, and § 51. 1.]
[5] [On this preposition see Don. p. 506 sq., Jelf 621, Green p. 204, Webster, p. 154 sq.]
[6] The transition would be exemplified by 2 P. ii. 7, ὑπὸ τῆς τῶν ἀθέσμων ἀναστροφῆς ἐρρύσατο, if we were thus to group the words (out of the power of the evil conduct, *under* the influence of which Lot had fallen): compare *Iliad* 9. 248, ἐρύεσθαι ὑπὸ Τρώων ὀρυμαγδοῦ· 23. 86. On the whole see Herm. Eurip. *Hec.* p. 11. In this passage, however, the ordinary arrangement of the words,

dicate the subject *from* whom the action proceeds, *in whose power* it was, therefore, to do it or to leave it undone. It is also joined with neuter verbs the meaning of which can receive a passive turn ; 1 C. x. 9, ὑπὸ τῶν ὄφεων ἀπώλοντο· Mt. xvii. 12, 1 Th. ii. 14, 2 C. xi. 24: compare Demosth. *Olynth.* 3. p. 10 c, Lucian, *Peregr.* 19, Xen. *Cyr.* 1. 6. 45, *An.* 7. 2. 22, Lysias, *in Theomnest.* 4, Pausan. 9. 7. 2, Plat. *Apol.* 17 a, *Conv.* 222 e, Philostr. *Apoll.* 1. 28, Polyæn. 5. 2. 15 (Porson, Eur. *Med.* p. 97, Ellendt, *Lex. Soph.* II. 880). The power which has produced death, destruction, etc., is here looked upon as *actively efficient*, and the expressions are equivalent to *be killed by, be destroyed by*, etc.: had ἀπό been used (compare παθεῖν ἀπό Mt. xvi. 21), this power would merely be represented as that from which a result proceeded. In the former case the writer might have substituted the active construction, *the serpents destroyed*, etc., without any change of meaning; in the latter such an expression would be inaccurate. Compare βλάπτεσθαι ἀπό τινος, as differing from βλάπτεσθαι ὑπό τινος, Xen. *Cyr.* 5. 3. 30, Æschin. *Dial.* 2. 11.[1]—Ὑπό is not restricted to persons or to animate beings, but is also used of inanimate agencies; see 1 C. vi. 12, Col. ii. 18, Ja. i. 14, al. (Don. p. 526, Jelf 639).

2 P. i. 17, φωνῆς ἐνεχθείσης αὐτῷ τοιᾶσδε ὑπὸ τῆς μεγαλοπρεποῦς δόξης, simply means *when this voice was borne to him by the sublime majesty:* all other explanations are arbitrary.

Ἀπό as used of place is *from*, in the widest sense,—whether that which comes *from* an object had previously been *on, at, with, by*, or even *in* the object; hence this preposition is mainly the antithesis of ἐπί with the accusative (Diog. L. 1. 24). See for example, L. xxiv. 2, εὗρον τὸν λίθον ἀποκεκυλισμένον ἀπὸ τοῦ μνημείου; Mt. xiv. 29, καταβὰς ἀπὸ τοῦ πλοίου, coming down *from* the ship (he had been *on* the ship); iii. 16, ἀνέβη ἀπὸ τοῦ ὕδατος, up *from* the water (not, *out of* the water); xv. 27, τῶν

---

connecting ὑπὸ τῆς κ.τ.λ. with καταπονούμενον, is to be preferred.—L. viii. 14 also must be recognised as an example of ὑπό with a passive (the active verb is used in Mt. xiii. 22, Mk. iv. 19). Bornemann (combines and) explains the words differently, but not satisfactorily: he is followed however by Meyer. [Bornemann and Meyer join ὑπό with πορευόμενοι: Bornemann's rendering is "inter curas . . . . vitam degunt" (Jelf 639. 2. c).]

[1] On the whole see Engelhardt, Plat. *Apol.* p. 174 sq., Lehmann, *Lucian* VIII. 450, II. 23, Schulz, *Abendmahl* p. 218.

ψιχίων τῶν πιπτόντων ἀπὸ τῆς τραπέζης (they were *on* the table); A. xxv. 1, ἀνέβη εἰς Ἱεροσόλυμα ἀπὸ Καισαρείας, *from* (not *out of*) Cæsarea.

In its further development ἀπό becomes, both for physical and for metaphysical relations, the preposition

a. Of *separating* and *desisting from*, as in Mt. vii. 23, ἀποχωρεῖτε ἀπ' ἐμοῦ· L. xxiv. 31, ἄφαντος ἐγένετο ἀπ' αὐτῶν· H. iv. 4, κατέπαυσεν ἀπὸ πάντων τῶν ἔργων· Rev. xviii. 14 (compare also ἀποκρύπτειν, παρακαλύπτειν ἀπό, Mt. xi. 25, L. ix. 45, and the pregnant phrases in Col. ii. 20, Rom. ix. 3, 2 Th. ii. 2, A. viii. 22, 2 C. xi. 3, and the like): consequently of *remoteness from*, Jo. xxi. 8 (Rev. xii. 14,—compare Xen. *An.* 3. 3. 9, Soph. *Œd. Col.* 900).

b. Much more frequently of *procession from*, in any manner and under any aspect. It is specially used in a temporal sense to indicate the starting point or the commencement of a period (*from, since*), as Mt. ix. 22, xxv. 34, 2 Tim. iii. 15, A. iii. 24,—or the starting point of a series, Mt. ii. 16, L. xxiv. 27, Jude 14 (ἀπὸ ... ἕως Mt. i. 17, xi. 12, A. viii. 10, ἀπὸ ... εἰς 2 C. iii. 18). Hence ἀπό indicates the *source, material, mass,* or *body* from which anything comes; as in Mt. iii. 4 (Lucian, *Dial. Deor.* 7. 4, Her. 7. 65), A. ii. 17, ἐκχεῶ ἀπὸ τοῦ πνεύματός μου (from the LXX), L. vi. 13, xv. 16, Jo. xxi. 10, Mt. vii. 16. Further ἀπό denotes, with great variety of application, the *origin* (Jude 23), *extraction* (from a people or country), hence *place of abode, sect*, Mt. xxi. 11, xxvii. 57, Jo. xi. 1, xii. 21, A. ii. 5, xv. 5, H. vii. 13 (Polyb. 5. 70. 8, Plut. *Brut.* c. 2, Her. 8. 114); and is especially used concretely to express the *personal* origin of an action—regarded simply as *origin*, not as a power consciously self-acting, in which sense παρά is used with neuter verbs (Schulz, *Abendm.* p. 215 sqq.[1]) and ὑπό with pas-

---

[1] When ἀπό follows verbs of *receiving, borrowing*, etc., it is simply a general indication of *whence*. Thus in Mt. xvii. 25, ἀπὸ τίνων λαμβάνουσι τέλη; it is *kings* who are the λαμβάνοντες: παρά would express *immediate* procession from, and would be used here if the *tax-gatherers* were the λαμβάνοντες. In λαμβάνειν παρά τινος the τις is always viewed as *acting* (as giving and offering), in λαμβάνειν ἀπό τινος simply as *possessing*. In 3 Jo. 7 we should have had μηδὲν λαμβάνοντες παρὰ τῶν ἐθνῶν if the writer had wished to say that the ἔθνη had *proffered* an acknowledgment. Col. iii. 24, ἀπὸ κυρίου ἀπολήψεσθε τὴν ἀνταπόδοσιν, means, *it shall proceed from the Lord*: παρὰ κυρίου, which Paul might here have used instead, would represent the Lord as the (direct) *giver*. On the other hand, παρά is strictly in place in Christ's words in Jo. x. 18, ταύτην

sive,[1] both in Greek writers and in the N. T. :[2] A. xxiii. 21, τὴν ἀπὸ σοῦ ἐπαγγελίαν (see above, § 30. 3. Rem. 5), Rom. xiii. 1 [*Rec.*], οὐ γάρ ἐστιν ἐξουσία εἰ μὴ ἀπὸ θεοῦ (followed immediately by αἱ δὲ οὖσαι ὑπὸ τοῦ θεοῦ τεταγμέναι εἰσίν), Mt. xvi. 21, παθεῖν ἀπὸ τῶν πρεσβυτέρων (Lucian, *Dial. Deor.* 6. 5, Plat. *Phæd.* 83 b), Mk. xv. 45, γνοὺς ἀπὸ τοῦ κεντυρίωνος· Mt. xii. 38, θέ-

---

τὴν ἐντολὴν ἔλαβον παρὰ τοῦ πατρός. Thus Paul writes in 1 C. xi. 23, παρέλαβον ἀπὸ τοῦ κυρίου, *of the Lord have I received;* not, the Lord himself has (directly, personally, as in an ἀποκάλυψις) communicated it to me. Some uncial MSS. here have παρά, but this is certainly a correction; see Schulz *l. c.* p. 215 sqq., and comp. *N. Theol. Annal.* 1818, II. 820 sqq. [See also Ellicott on G. i. 12. Lightfoot (on G. i. 12) maintains that this distinction between παρά and ἀπό after λαμβάνειν cannot be insisted on. "It is true, that while ἀπό contemplates only the giver, παρά in a manner connects the giver with the receiver, denoting the *passage* from the one to the other, but the links of the chain between the two may be numerous, and in all cases where the idea of transmission is prominent παρά will be used in preference to ἀπό, be the communication direct or indirect; so Ph. iv. 18, δεξάμενος παρὰ 'Επαφροδίτου τὰ παρ' ὑμῶν: comp. Plat. *Symp.* 202 E."]

[1] Here and there the MSS. are divided between ἀπό and ὑπό (Mk. viii. 31, Rom. xiii. 1): this is frequently the case in Greek authors, see Schæf. *Melet.* pp. 22, 83 sq., Schweighaeuser, *Lex. Polyb.* p. 69, al. The use of ἀπό with passive verbs in the place of ὑπό becomes more and more common in later writers, especially the Byzantines; see *e. g.* the index to Malalas in the Bonn edition. In earlier Greek it is on the whole rare: see however Poppo, *Thuc.* III. i. 158, Bernh. p. 224. [In modern Greek ἀπό is the preposition commonly used with passive verbs; see Mullach, *Vulg.* p. 385, Sophocles, *Gr.* p. 153.]

[2] Ja. i. 13, ἀπὸ θεοῦ πειράζομαι, simply means *from God I am tempted*, and is a more general expression than ὑπὸ θεοῦ πειράζομαι, which would be identical with θεὸς πειράζει με. The following words, πειράζει δὲ αὐτὸς οὐδένα, merely show that the apostle has *also* in his mind the conception of a direct temptation by God (compare Herm. Soph. *Œd. Col.* 1531, Schoemann, Plut. *Cleom.* p. 237): ἀπὸ θεοῦ is very frequently a kind of adverb, *divinitus.* In L. vi. 18, by πνευμάτων ἀκαθάρτων is intended the affliction or disease itself, and no one would find any difficulty in such a phrase as ὀχλούμενοι ἀπὸ νόσων. In L. ix. 22, xvii. 25, ἀποδοκιμάζεσθαι ἀπό is merely *to be rejected on the part of* the elders. It is easy to see that in A. xii. 20, διὰ τὸ τρέφεσθαι αὐτῶν τὴν χώραν ἀπὸ τῆς βασιλικῆς (Arist. *Pol.* 4. 6) this preposition does not stand for ὑπό: Schneckenburger (*ad* Ja. i. 13) maintains this, but he is not sufficiently careful in his distinctions. As to Mt. xi. 19, see Fritz. *in loc.*, and Lehmann, *Lucian* VI. 544. 2 C. vii. 13 certainly does not come in here; ἀπό is *from*. In A. x. 17 *Rec.*, οἱ ἀπεσταλμένοι ἀπὸ τοῦ Κορνηλίου (Arrian, *Epict.* 3. 22, 23) means simply *those sent from him;* ἀπεστ. ὑπό (a correction found in some MSS.) would be more definite, *whom he had* (directly) *sent:* compare 1 Th. iii. 6, ἐλθόντος Τιμοθέου πρὸς ἡμᾶς ἀφ' ὑμῶν—they had not *sent* him. In 1 C. i. 30, ὃς ἐγενήθη σοφία ἡμῖν ἀπὸ θεοῦ, *who became wisdom unto us from God*, ὑπό is certainly not required; compare Her. 5. 125, see also Stallb. Plat. *Rep.* I. 103. Lastly, in Ja. v. 4, ὁ μισθὸς ὁ ἀπεστερημένος ἀφ' ὑμῶν, this preposition is probably used designedly,— *on your part*, not (or not merely) that which has been held back directly by you.—The two prepositions occur together in manifestly different senses in L. v. 15 (in some MSS.) and in Rom. xiii. 1: compare Euseb. *H. E.* 2. 6. p. 115 (Heinichen). [In L. vi. 18 ἀπό may very well be joined with ἐθεραπεύοντο (Meyer): in Mt. xi. 19 the best texts have ἔργων for τέκνων. In Ja. v. 4 some join ἀφ' ὑμῶν with κράζει (Huther, Alford).]

SECT. XLVII.]   PREPOSITIONS WITH THE GENITIVE.   465

λομεν ἀπὸ σοῦ σημεῖον ἰδεῖν· A. ix. 13, G. i. 1, 1 C. iv. 5, 2 C. vii. 13, 1 Jo. ii. 20, iv. 21, Col. iii. 24, 2 Th. i. 9. Also in an abstract sense, the *efficient force* itself (so that we may render the preposition by *through*), A. xx. 9, κατενεχθεὶς ἀπὸ τοῦ ὕπνου· Rev. ix. 18 ; the *occasion* (A. xi. 19),[1] and the *motive*, Mt. xiv. 26, ἀπὸ τοῦ φόβου ἔκραξαν, *for fear*, xiii. 44, L. xxi. 26, xxii. 45, xxiv. 41, A. xii. 14 (Plutarch, *Lysand.* 23, Vig. p. 581); the objective *cause, propter*, Mt. xviii. 7, and according to some H. v. 7 (see Bleek),—or *præ* (in negative combinations), A. xxii. 11, οὐκ ἐνέβλεπον ἀπὸ τῆς δόξης τοῦ φωτός, *on account of* (for) *the brightness*,—their not seeing arose from the brightness, L. xix. 3, Jo. xxi. 6 (see Kypke), A. xxviii. 3 *v.l.*[2] Compare Held, Plut. *Tim.* 314 (Judith ii. 20, Gen. xxxvi. 7, al., Her. 2. 64). The preposition is used in a pregnant sense in A. xvi. 33, ἔλουσεν ἀπὸ τῶν πληγῶν, *he washed* and cleansed them *from the stripes*, i. e., from the blood with which they were besprinkled in consequence of the stripes. Mt. vii. 16 is easily explained : *from the fruits* (objectively) the knowledge will be *derived* (Arrian, *Epict.* 4. 8. 10). The case is different in L. xxi. 30, ἀφ᾽ ἑαυτῶν γινώσκετε· and 2 C. x. 7,[3] where ἀπό indicates the *subjective* power from which the knowledge proceeds, as indeed ἀφ᾽ ἑαυτοῦ often means *sponte*.[4]

According to Schleusner and Kühnöl ἀπό also denotes (1) *in :* A. xv. 38, τὸν ἀποστάντα ἀπ᾽ αὐτῶν ἀπὸ Παμφυλίας, *who had deserted them in Pamphylia*. But it is easy to see that the meaning is, *who had deserted them* (going off) *out of Pamphylia :* this is very different from ἐν II., which might signify that Mark remained in Pamphylia, though no longer connected with Paul : compare xiii. 13.—(2) *de :* A. xvii. 2, διελέγετο αὐτοῖς ἀπὸ τῶν γραφῶν. But this means, starting (in his discourses) *from the Scriptures*, or drawing *from them* his proofs (compare Epiphan. *Opp.* II. 340 d) : compare A. xxviii. 23. Nor is the meaning *de* sustained by Her. 4. 53, 195. Schweigh. *Lex. Her.* I. 77.—(3) *per :* A. xi. 19, διασπαρέντες ἀπὸ τῆς θλίψεως; but this is *on occasion of the persecution*.—(4) *modo, instar :* 2 Tim. i. 3, ἀπὸ προγόνων (see also Flatt *in loc.*) : the meaning is *from my forefathers* (Polyb. 5. 55. 9), with the feelings inherited from them. —On such passages as Jo. xi. 18, Rev. xiv. 20, see § 61. 5.

---

[1] Poppo, *Thuc.* III. i. 128, 598, Stallb. Plat. *Rep.* II. 180.
[2] [Most now read ἀπό here : this is not a " negative combination."]
[3] [Here some of the best MSS. read ἰφ᾽ ἑαυτοῦ, *by himself* (Vulg. *apud se*). See Meyer *in loc.*, Liddell and Scott s. v. ἐπί, A. I. 1. *d*, Jelf 633. I. 3. *e*.]
[4] [Don. p. 506, Jelf 620, Webster p. 152, Green p. 215.]

30

c. Ἀμφί does not occur in the N. T.

d. Πρό *before* (with a more general meaning than ἀντί) is used of *place* in A. v. 23 [*Rec.*], Ja. v. 9, also in A. xiv. 13 (compare Heliod. 1. 11. 30, Boeckh, *Corp. Inscript.* II. 605). More commonly of *time*,—either with nouns of time, as 2 Tim. iv. 21, πρὸ χειμῶνος· Jo. xiii. 1, 2 C. xii. 2, Mt. viii. 29, and the infinitive of verbs. (Mt. vi. 8, Jo. i. 49); or with personal words, as in Jo. v. 7 πρὸ ἐμοῦ· x. 8, Rom. xvi. 7. It is applied figuratively in Ja. v. 12, πρὸ πάντων, *ante omnia*, 1 P. iv. 8 (Xen. *Mem.* 2. 5. 3, Herod. 5. 4. 2). As to the original use of this preposition, by which its construction with a genitive is explained, see Bernh. p. 231.[1] (Don. p. 505, Jelf 619.)

e. Περί. The primary meaning of this preposition is clearly seen when it is joined with the dative case. It then expresses the notion of *encircling, inclosing* on several or on all sides, and is most nearly allied with ἀμφί, which denotes inclosing on *both* sides: hence περί differs from παρά, which merely indicates that one object is near (by the side of) another. When joined with a genitive, this preposition is almost invariably used by prose writers in a figurative sense (compare however *Odyss.* 5. 68),[2] to denote the object which is the *centre* of an action, around which, so to speak, the action moves,—e.g., *to fight, draw lots, care about* something (Mt. vi. 28, Mk. xiii. 32,[3] Jo. x. 13, xix. 24[4]); and then, very commonly, *decide, know, hear, speak of* or *concerning* something (de, super): see above, p. 452. In other places we render περί by *for* (e. g., intercede *for* some

---

[1] [Bernhardy considers *forwards from* (Jelf 619. 1. c), as in the Homeric Ἰλιόθι πρό, to be the original meaning. Compare however Curtius, *Elucidations*, p. 200 sq. "As adverbs the prepositions could primarily take the genitive, as the case of connexion. The genitive depends on ἀντί in precisely the same manner as in the German *Angesicht, Laut, Kraft*. With πρό, also, . . . the case is no doubt the same . . . . The most decisive confirmation of this view is found in the fact that all the improper prepositions, i. e., the prepositions which still continue to have more of the nature of adverbs, take the genitive."]

[2] That the local meaning *around, about*, is not without example in (later) prose is shown by Locella, *Xen. Ephes.* p. 269; compare Schæf. Dion. *Comp.* 351. Thus in A. xxv. 18 περὶ οὗ might be joined with σταθέντες (Meyer): compare ver. 7, περιέστησαν οἱ ἀπὸ Ἱεροσολύμων καταβεβηκότες Ἰουδαῖοι.

[3] [This example belongs to the next line: the verb is *know*.]

[4] Verbs of *caring*, etc., are also construed with ὑπέρ; see p. 478. The distinction is thus explained by Weber, *Dem.* p. 130: περί solam mentis circumspectionem vel respectum rei, ὑπέρ simul animi propensionem . . . . significat. This twofold construction is also found with verbs of *contending* (about or *for* something), and hence περί and ὑπέρ are sometimes found contrasted in the same passage; see Franke, *Dem.* p. 6 sq., [who quotes Æschin. 3. 10, Dem. 19. 214.]

one), as in Jo. xvi. 26, A. viii. 15, H. xiii. 18, L. xix. 37, 1 Th. i. 2 ; *on account of, on behalf of,* Jo. xv. 22, A. xv. 2, xxv. 15, 1 P. iii. 18,—though here our *um* [*about*] comes in in various ways; or *as regards, concerning,* Mt. iv. 6, Rom. xv. 14, 1 C. xii. 1, Jo. vii. 17, Demosth. *Ol.* 1. § 11. In this last sense we find περί with its substantive placed at the head of a complete sentence, as an absolute phrase,—an *exponendum ;* [1] e.g., 1 C. xvi. 1 περὶ τῆς λογίας κ.τ.λ., *quod ad pecunias attinet,* though these words are grammatically in direct connexion with ὥσπερ διέταξα. A still clearer example is 1 C. xvi. 12, περὶ Ἀπολλώ, πολλὰ παρεκάλεσα αὐτόν, ἵνα ἔλθῃ πρὸς ὑμᾶς κ.τ.λ. (compare *Papyri Taur.* 1. 6. 31): we find a similar use of *de,* e. g., Cic. *Fam.* 3. 12. Sometimes περί appears to signify *above,* and hence *præ,* as in the Homeric περὶ πάντων ἔμμεναι ἄλλων (Bernh. p. 260).[2] Some (as Beza) have taken it in this sense in 3 Jo. 2, περὶ πάντων εὔχομαί σε κ.τ.λ., *before all things*(Schott): Lücke supports this rendering by a passage from Dion. H. II. 1142 (where however περὶ ἁπάντων means *in regard to, in relation to,* etc.). It does not appear to me, however, that the impossibility of connecting περὶ πάντων with the following infinitives (Bengel and Baumg.-Crusius *in loc.*) has yet been clearly proved.[3] (Don. p. 515, Jelf 632.)

f. Πρός. The meaning which agrees with the primary force of the genitive, viz., *from* something, is shown by the local use of this preposition (Herm. *Vig.* p. 863), and is also clear in such examples as τὸ ποιεύμενον πρὸς τῶν Λακεδαιμονίων(Her.7.209), πάσχομεν πρὸς αὐτῆς (Alciphr. 1. 20, see Bernh. p. 264), εἶναι πρός τινος, *to be on the side of some one.* Compare *ad Herennium* 2. 27, *ab reo facere.* Hence also πρὸς ἐμοῦ, like *e re nostra, to my advantage, in accordance with my interests* (Lob. p. 10, Ellendt, *Arrian* I. 265). In the N. T. πρός in this sense has given way to ἀπό and ἐκ: it occurs once only, in A. xxvii. 34, τοῦτο(taking nourishment) πρὸς τῆς ὑμετέρας σωτηρίας ὑπάρχει,

---

[1] Stallb. Plat. *Rep.* II. 157, and *Tim.* p. 97.
[2] Even here however the preposition certainly retains the meaning *around, about,* as the relation was originally viewed. He is "excellent around all," who by his excellence keeps all in, as it were, so that no one can come forth out of the mass. "Before all" marks the relation on one side only, περί on all sides. [Compare Donalds. *New Crat.* p. 334 sqq.]
[3] [In his second edition Lücke takes the same view as Winer : so also Huther, De W., and Alford.]

conduces to your deliverance,—properly, *stands,* so to speak, *on the side of* your deliverance. Another example of a similar kind is Thuc. 3. 59, οὐ πρὸς τῆς ὑμετέρας δόξης, *non cedet vobis in gloriam.* (Don. p. 524, Jelf 638.)

g. *Ἐπί.* The primary meaning which might justify the construction with the genitive has here for the most part disappeared; unless we choose to render *e. g.* L. iv. 29, ὄρους, ἐφ' οὗ ἡ πόλις αὐτῶν ᾠκοδόμητο, *up from which* (on which upwards) *it was built* (Diod. S. 3. 47, Polyb. 10. 10. 5). *Ἐπί* usually denotes being *upon, over* a place (a point or a surface), whether the object is regarded as at rest or as moving to and fro.[1] So in Mt. x. 27, κηρύξατε ἐπὶ τῶν δωμάτων· xxiv. 30, ἐρχόμενον ἐπὶ τῶν νεφελῶν· ix. 2, 6, A. v. 15, viii. 28, Rev. xiii. 1, 1 C. xi. 10, L. xxii. 21; and especially ἐπὶ τῆς γῆς (opposed to ἐν τῷ οὐρανῷ), compare Xen. *An.* 3. 2. 19, Arrian, *Al.* 1. 18. 15. When applied to waters it denotes not merely the surface, as in Rev. v. 13 ἐπὶ τῆς θαλάσσης,[2] but also the bank or shore (compare Arrian, *Al.* 1. 18. 10), as Jo. xxi. 1, ἐπὶ τῆς θαλάσσης, *by the sea* (Polyb. 1. 44. 4, Xen. *An.* 4. 3. 28, 2 K. ii. 7,—compare the Hebrew על). Next it is applied to raised, elevated objects *on* which something is set up, e. g., *on the cross,* A. v. 30, Jo. xix. 19. The N. T. Lexicons give also the local meaning *by, near, beside,*[3] but of this there is no sufficient evidence. In L. xxii. 40, τόπος is to be understood of a mountain (though we also say *on* the spot); in Mt. xxi. 19, ἐπὶ τῆς ὁδοῦ means *on the road*;[4] A. xx. 9,

---

[1] Wittmann, *De natura et potest. præp.* ἐπί (Schweinf. 1846). In most cases the Latin language uses *in ;* but our own *auf* [*upon*] answers to ἐπί in many of its applications, and is used not merely of heights, but also of level surfaces. Ἐπ' ἐρημίας (Mk. viii. 4) is in its conception exactly like our "*auf* dem Felde" [literally, *on the field,*—compare *on the farm, on the estate*], though we do not use *auf* in this particular phrase. Comp. Mt. iv. 1, ἀνήχθη εἰς τὴν ἔρημον.

[2] We must also bring in here Jo. vi. 19, περιπατεῖν ἐπὶ τῆς θαλάσσης, *walk on the sea* (in Mt. xiv. 25, ἐπὶ τὴν θάλασσαν seems to be the true reading); compare Lucian, *Philops.* 13, βαδίζειν ἐφ' ὕδατος· *Vera Hist.* 2. 4, ἐπὶ τοῦ πελάγους διαθέοντες (Job ix. 8). *In itself* indeed ἐπὶ τῆς θαλάσσης might also be rendered *by the sea:* this Fritzsche (*Matt.* p. 502) certainly did not intend to deny.

[3] Even in the case of objects which are on the same level the Greeks spoke of an *upper part,* in accordance with a conventional or ethical view which in most instances we are able to follow. Thus a man may be said to stand *above the door* (Her. 5. 92) if he stands by the door *inside the room,* whilst a man who stands outside by the door may be said to stand *under* the door. Compare Bernh. p. 243, on the kindred preposition ὑπέρ. Languages differ very greatly in the view which is taken of the relation.

[4] [Alford renders *by the road-side,* quoting Meyer. Meyer now translates *over the road,* adding that we may either suppose that the tree simply projected

ἐπὶ τῆς θυρίδος, *upon* the window. In Jo. vi. 21, τὸ πλοῖον ἐγένετο ἐπὶ τῆς γῆς is said of a vessel coming to land, and ἐπί relates to the ascending beach : see however what is said above.

The figurative uses of ἐπί are very clear. It is applied to

(*a*) *Rule* or *superintendence over :* Mt. ii. 22, βασιλεύειν ἐπὶ[1] Ἰουδαίας· Rev. xi. 6, A. viii. 27, εἶναι ἐπὶ πάσης τῆς γάζης· vi. 3, xii. 20, Rom. ix. 5, εἶναι ἐπὶ πάντων E. iv. 6 ; compare Polyb. 1. 34. 1, 2. 65. 9, Arrian, *Al.* 3. 5. 4.[2]

(*b*) *The object of an action,—its substratum,* as it were : e. g., Jo. vi. 2, σημεῖα ἃ ἐποίει ἐπὶ τῶν ἀσθενούντων, *which he did on the sick* (compare Matth. 584. a. e). So especially in reference to *speaking*, as in G. iii. 16 οὐ λέγει . . . ὡς ἐπὶ πολλῶν, *as speaking upon many* (speaking of many) ; compare *scribere, disserere super re,* and Sext. Emp. *adv. Math.* 2. 24, 6. 25, Epict. *Ench.* 3.[3]

(*c*) *Presence before* (coram),—especially of appearing before judges, authorities, etc. (where we say *bring up before*) : Mt. xxviii. 14,[4] A. xxiii. 30, xxiv. 20, xxv. 9, 1 C. vi. 1, 1 Tim. vi. 13 (compare Æl. 8. 2, Lucian, *Catapl.* 16, Dio C. p. 825, Schoem. *Isæus* 293). Then in a general sense, 1 Tim. v. 19, ἐπὶ μαρτύρων, *before witnesses* (Xen. *Hell.* 6. 5. 38, *Vectig.* 3. 14, Lucian, *Philops.* 22, Mätzner, *Antiph.* p. 165),[5]—and also 2 C. vii. 14, *before,* i. e., *to* Titus.[6]

(*d*) In a kindred sense, with names of persons ἐπί denotes the time of a prince's reign, as A. xi. 28, ἐπὶ Κλαυδίου, *under Claudius,* Mk. ii. 26 (Raphel and Fritz. *in loc.*), L. iii. 2 (Her. 1. 15, Æschin. *Dial.* 3. 4, Xen. *Cyr.* 8. 4. 5, al.[7]) ; also simply the life-time of some one (ἐπ' ἐμοῦ, *in my time*), especially of influen-

---

over the road or that it was planted on an elevation by the road-side, or that the road here passed through a ravine. Ἐπὶ τῶν θυρῶν, A. v. 23, must apparently be taken as an exception to Winer's remark, unless we can give the preposition its figurative meaning *over* (oversight over,—see above).]

[1] [Here ἐπί is probably not genuine : in Rev. v. 10 we have βασιλεύειν ἐπὶ τῆς γῆς.]

[2] Reitz, *Lucian* VI. 448 (Bip.), Schæf. *Demosth.* II. 172, Held, Plut. *Timol.* 388.

[3] Heind. Plat. *Charm.* 62, Ast, Plat. *Legg.* p. 114, Schoem. Plut. *Agis* p. 76, Ellendt, *Arrian* I. 436.

[4] [Lünemann adds Mk. xiii. 9.]

[5] In Mt. xviii. 16, 2 C. xiii. 1, this formula is enlarged, ἐπὶ στόματος δύο μαρτύρων (after the Hebrew עַל־פִּי). Even here ἐπί is really nothing more than *by,—with (on) the testimony of . . . witnesses.*

[6] See Wetst. I. 443, 562, Schæf. *Melet.* p. 105.

[7] Bremi *Dem.* p. 165, Schweigh. *Lex. Her.* I. 243, Sturz, *Lex. Dion. C.* p. 148.

tial persons, as L. iv. 27, ἐπὶ 'Ελισσαίου (Xen. *Cyr.* 1. 6. 31, Plat. *Rep.* 10. 599 e, *Crit.* 112 a, Alciphr. 1. 5, ἐπὶ τῶν προγόνων· Arrian, *Epict.* 3. 23, 27). Then we find ἐπί thus used with nouns denoting a state or event (Xen. *Cyr.* 8. 7. 1, Herod. 2. 9. 7), Mt. i. 11, ἐπὶ τῆς μετοικεσίας Βαβυλῶνος, *at the time of the exile.* Lastly, it becomes a simple indication of time, as in H. i. 1, ἐπ' ἐσχάτου τῶν ἡμερῶν τούτων, *in the last of the days,* 1 P. i. 20, 2 P. iii. 3 (compare Num. xxiv. 14, Gen. xlix. 1; ἐπὶ τῶν ἀρχαίων χρόνων, Aristot. *Polit.* 3. 10, Polyb. 1. 15. 12, Isocr. *Paneg.* c. 44); and generally of that to which something else attaches itself, as in Rom. i. 10, ἐπὶ τῶν προςευχῶν μου, *with* (in) *my prayers,* 1 Th. i. 2, E. i. 16. Somewhat different is Mk. xii. 26, ἐπὶ τοῦ βάτου, *at the bush,*—a concise expression for "at the passage in which the bush is spoken of."

Sometimes we find ἐπί with the genitive, in a local sense, joined with verbs expressing direction, and even motion (Bernh. p. 246) *towards, to, upon.* See Mt. xxvi. 12, βαλοῦσα τὸ μύρον ἐπὶ τοῦ σώματος, *over the body*; A. x. 11, σκεῦός τι . . . καθιέμενον ἐπὶ τῆς γῆς, *descending to the earth,* Mk. xiv. 35, ἔπιπτεν ἐπὶ τῆς γῆς, *on the earth*; H. vi. 7. This is very common in Greek writers; see Her. 1. 164, 2. 73, 75, 119, 4. 14, 5. 33, Xen. *Cyr.* 7. 2. 1, *Hell.* 1. 6. 20, 3. 4. 12, 5. 3. 6, 7. 1. 28, al.[1] In this usage the preposition originally included the sense of remaining *at* or *on,* see Rost p. 560: Krüger's explanation (p. 339) is somewhat different.[2] In such examples as Rev. x. 2, L. viii. 16, Jo. xix. 19, A. v. 15 (τιθέναι ἐπὶ τοῦ κ.τ.λ.), like *ponere in loco,* the relation is viewed differently. (Don. p. 517, Jelf 633.)

h. Μετά properly signifies *between, amidst* (μέσος),[3] as in L. xxiv. 5, τί ζητεῖτε τὸν ζῶντα μετὰ τῶν νεκρῶν· Mk. i. 13: hence it denotes *with* (together with), L. v. 30, μετὰ τῶν τελωνῶν ἐσθίετε· Jo. xx. 7. It is thus applied to personal association (Jo. iii. 22, xviii. 22,[4] A. ix. 39, Mt. xii. 42, H. xi. 9 [5]), and

---

[1] Sturz, *Lex. Xen.* II. 258, Ellendt, Arr. *Al.* I. 339. Wittmann *u. s.* (see p. 458).
[2] The distinction was already felt by Bengel (on H. vi. 7).
[3] [See however Curtius, *Gr. Etym.* I. 258 (Transl.).]
[4] [A mistake, probably for xviii. 2, or 18.]
[5] Under this head comes also the Hebraistic phrase πληρώσεις με εὐφροσύνης μετὰ τοῦ προςώπου σου, A. ii. 28, from the LXX (אֶת־פָּנֶיךָ),—which cannot be taken in a merely local sense.

mutual action, as Jo. iv. 27, λαλεῖν μετά τινος· vi. 43, γογγύζειν μετ' ἀλλήλων· Mt. xviii. 23, συναίρειν λόγον μετά τινος: compare Rev. ii. 16,[1] 22, L. xii. 13. So especially in the expression of metaphysical (particularly of ethical) relations, as Mt. xx. 2, συμφωνεῖν μετά τινος· ii. 3, L. xxiii. 12, A. vii. 9, Rom. xii. 15, 1 Jo. i. 6 (εἶναι μετά τινος, Mt. xii. 30, compare Xen. *Cyr.* 2. 4. 7). Sometimes we find μετά used where we say *on* or *towards* (erga), as in L. x. 37, ὁ ποιήσας τὸ ἔλεος μετ' αὐτοῦ· i. 72[2] (עִם,—probably not in A. xiv. 27), the person affected being regarded by us, not as associated in the action, but as its object. But μετά is also applied to things, as in L. xiii. 1, ὧν τὸ αἷμα ἔμιξεν μετὰ τῶν θυσιῶν αὐτῶν· Mt. xxvii. 34,—usually to express that with which one is furnished, accompanied, surrounded, as L. xxii. 52, ἐξεληλύθατε μετὰ μαχαιρῶν· Jo. xviii. 3, Mt. xxiv. 31 (Dem. *Pantæn.* p. 628 c, Herod. 5. 6. 19). It is then used of attendant actions and circumstances, especially states of mind (Bernh. p. 255), as H. xii. 17, μετὰ δακρύων ἐκζητήσας (Herod. 1. 16. 10), 1 Tim. iv. 14, Mt. xiv. 7, Mk. x. 30, A. v. 26, xvii. 11, ἐδέξαντο τὸν λόγον μετὰ πάσης προθυμίας· Mt. xiii. 20, xxviii. 8, 2 C. vii. 15 (Eurip. *Hipp.* 205, Soph. *Œd. Col.* 1636, Alciphr. 3. 38, Aristot. *Magn. Mor.* 2. 6, Herod. 1. 5. 19); and, lastly, of the inner union of non-material things, as E. vi. 23, ἀγάπη μετὰ πίστεως.

The *instrument,* as such (Kypke I. 143 [3]), is never expressed by μετά in good prose. In 1 Tim. iv. 14, μετὰ ἐπιθέσεως τῶν χειρῶν is *with, amid imposition of hands* (conjointly with the act of imposition); and in Mt. xiv. 7, μεθ' ὅρκου is *interposito jurejurando* (H. vii. 21). Yet it borders on this meaning in L. xvii. 15, μετὰ φωνῆς μεγάλης δοξάζων (substantially equivalent to

---

[1] [The force of μετά is clear in πολεμεῖν μετά τινος (Rev. xii. 7, xiii. 4, xvii. 14,—נִלְחַם עִם, 1 S. xvii. 33, al.), but it must be remembered that in Greek writers this phrase has a very different meaning: see Wilke, *Clavis* s.v. μετά (ed. Grimm), Jelf 636. I. *b.*]

[2] [Add L. i. 58. "This language must be traced to the Septuagint; which also exhibits in the same connexion the simple Dative (Jos. ii. 12), as well as εἰς and ἐπί with the Accus. (Jos. ii. 14, 2 S. ii. 5). The expression ὅσα ὁ Θεὸς ἐποίησε μετ' αὐτῶν (A. xv. 4) is, however, quite distinct, and correctly expresses the conspiring agency of God with his servants by his miraculous interpositions." Green p. 218.]

[3] Μετὰ λύχνου, Fabric. *Pseudepigr.* II. 143, means *with a light,* i. e., furnished with it, carrying it with him,—*cum lumine,* not *lumine.* On the other hand, compare Leo Gramm. p. 260, μαχαίριον ἐπιφέρεται βουλόμενος ἀνελεῖν σε μετ' αὐτοῦ· p. 275, al. [Similarly in modern Greek; see Mullach p. 382.]

φωνῇ μεγάλῃ or ἐν φωνῇ μεγάλῃ), and perhaps in A. xiii. 17 :[1] compare Polyb. 1. 49. 9, ἤθροιζε μετὰ κηρύγματος· Lucian, *Philops.* 8, βοηθεῖν τινι μετὰ τῆς τέχνης, and the similar use of σύν,—at all events in the poets (Bernh. p. 214). As to Mt. xxvii. 66, see Fritzsche *in loc.*[2]

Μετά with the genitive never has the meaning *after:*[3] in Mk. x. 30, μετὰ διωγμῶν is *amid persecutions,* as μετὰ κινδύνων is *amidst dangers* (Thuc. 1. 18, al.). In Mt. xii. 41 μετά with the genitive is wrongly rendered *contra* by Kühnöl and Baumg.-Crusius. The words run thus : the Ninevites will at the last judgment appear *with* this generation,—i. e., when the men of this generation appear before the judgment-seat, the Ninevites will appear with them ; for what purpose (*against*), is first expressed by the following words.

The use of the genitive with this preposition is explained by the fact, that whatever accompanies or surrounds a person is in a certain sense dependent on him. (Don. p. 520, Jelf 636.)

i. Διά. The primary meaning is *through,* 1 C. xiii. 12 (Plat. *Phæd.* 109 c) : the idea of *going through* however, in a local sense, always has attached to it that of coming *forth* or *out.* (In Hebrew and Arabic indeed מן is the only preposition for the local *through;* compare also Fabric. *Pseudepigr.* I. 191, ἐκφεύγειν δι' αἰῶνος· Mt. iv. 4, ἐκπορεύεσθαι διά, from Dt. viii. 3, and διεξέρχεσθαι, Plat. *Rep.* 10. 621 a.[4]) For this reason διά governs the genitive. It occurs in a local sense in simple combinations : as L. iv. 30, αὐτὸς διελθὼν διὰ μέσου αὐτῶν ἐπορεύετο (Herod. 2. 1. 3) ; 1 C. iii. 15, σωθήσεται . . . ὡς διὰ πυρός· Rom. xv. 28, ἀπελεύσομαι δι' ὑμῶν εἰς Σπανίαν, i. e., *through your city* (Thuc. 5. 4, Plut. *Virt. Mul.* p. 192 Lips.) ; A. xiii. 49, διεφέρετο ὁ λόγος δι' ὅλης τῆς χώρας, *from one end to the other* (*throughout,*[5] Odyss. 12. 335, Plat. *Symp.* p. 220 b) ; 2 C. viii.

---

[1] Yet here we should probably take μετά as expressing accompaniment,—*with upraised arm,* holding up his arm over them (for protection).

[2] [Fritzsche considers this an example of brachylogy, the full expression being ἠσφαλίσαντο τὸν τάφον, σφραγίσαντις τὸν λίθον μετὰ τοῦ προσθεῖναι τὴν κουστωδίαν, = *firmarunt monumentum et obsignato lapide et custodibus appositis :* our Auth. Vers. agrees with this. Meyer joins μετά with ἠσφαλ. ; Bleek, al., with σφραγίσαντις. See Green p. 218.]

[3] In Fabric. *Pseudep.* II. 593 μετὰ τοῦ ἐλθεῖν is certainly a mistake of transcription for μετὰ τὸ ἐλθεῖν. The passages collected by Raphel (on Mk. *l. c.*) prove nothing.

[4] Compare Kühner II. 281 [II. 416, in ed. 2], and my 5th *Progr. de Verbis composit.* p. 3. (Jelf 627. I. *a.*)

[5] [Jelf 627. I. *b,* Riddell, Plat. *Apol.* p. 161.]

18, οὗ ὁ ἔπαινος . . . διὰ πασῶν τῶν ἐκκλησιῶν. In Greek, as in all languages, there is an easy transition from this local *through* to the (animate or inanimate) *instrument*, as that *through* which the result effected passes, as it were (compare especially 1 P. i. 7),—that which lies between the will and the act: e. g., 3 Jo. 13, οὐ θέλω διὰ μέλανος καὶ καλάμου γράφειν· 2 Jo. 12 (Plut. *Vit. Solon.* p. 87 e), 2 C. vi. 7, 1 C. xiv. 9, 2 Th. ii. 2 διὰ λόγου, δι' ἐπιστολῆς, *orally, by letter,* H. xiii. 22 διὰ βραχέων ἐπέστειλα ὑμῖν, *paucis scripsi vobis* (see § 64). Thence it is applied to non-material objects, as 1 C. vi. 14, ἡμᾶς ἐξεγερεῖ διὰ τῆς δυνάμεως αὐτοῦ· Rom. iii. 25, ὃν προέθετο ἱλαστήριον διὰ τῆς πίστεως· Rom. ii. 12, Ja. ii. 12, κρίνεσθαι διὰ νόμου. It is applied to persons, as in A. iii. 16, ἡ πίστις ἡ δι' αὐτοῦ· 1 C. iii. 5, διάκονοι, δι' ὧν ἐπιστεύσατε· H. iii. 16, οἱ ἐξελθόντες ἐξ Αἰγύπτου διὰ Μωϋσέως : so especially διὰ Ἰησοῦ Χριστοῦ of the mediatorial work of Christ in all its parts, Rom. ii. 16, v. 1, 2 C. i. 5, G. i. 1, E. i. 5, Ph. i. 11, Tit. iii. 6, al. ;[1] also διὰ πνεύματος (ἁγίου), Rom. v. 5, 1 C. xii. 8, E. iii. 16. Under this (instrumental) meaning must also be ranged 2 Tim. ii. 2, διὰ πολλῶν μαρτύρων (*intervenientibus multis testibus, by the mediation of*, i.e., here, *in the presence of* many witnesses); and H. vii. 9, διὰ Ἀβραὰμ καὶ Λευὶ δεδεκάτωται, *through Abraham,* i. e., in the person of Abraham as representative of the whole Israelitish people,—through Abraham's being tithed, Levi is also tithed. Διά is sometimes, but only seldom, used in reference to the *causa principalis*[2] (as in 1 C. i. 9, G. iv. 7 *v. l.*), and might appear

---

[1] This phrase has essentially the same meaning when it is combined with words of *praising, thanking,* etc., as in Rom. i. 8, vii. 25, xvi. 27, Col. iii. 17. Not only are the benefits for which we give thanks procured through Christ, but also the thanksgiving itself is offered (in a mode pleasing to God) through Christ, living with God, and continuing the work of mediation for his people. The Christian thanks God, not in his own person, but through Christ, whom he regards as the medium of his prayer, as He is the medium of his salvation. Philippi's remarks on Rom. i. 8 are inadequate : Bengel is better.

[2] On the Latin *per* for *a* see Hand, *Tursell.* IV. 436 sq. "The wrong done *through* me" and "the wrong done *by* me" may in the end express exactly the same thing, but the wrong-doer is viewed under different aspects in the two expressions. Διά is probably used designedly in Mt. xxvi. 24, τῷ ἀνθρώπῳ δι' οὗ ὁ υἱὸς τοῦ ἀνθρώπου παραδίδοται (the traitor was merely an instrument, compare Rom. viii. 32) : also in A. ii. 43, πολλά τε τέρατα καὶ σημεῖα διὰ τῶν ἀποστόλων ἐγίνετο, for the true Worker was God (A. ii. 22, xv. 12) ; compare διὰ χειρῶν, A. v. 12, xiv. 3. The fact that this more exact mode of expression is not adhered to in all passages and by all writers, proves nothing against this explanation.

here to be synonymous with ὑπό or παρά. Even in such cases however διά does not indicate the author as such, i. e., as the source *from* which something proceeds, but in strictness only as the person *through* whose labour, favour, etc., something is received (compare G. i. 1); the question whether this comes from him directly or indirectly is not touched.[1] We may also add with Fritzsche (*Rom.* I. p. 15): " est autem hic usus ibi tantum admissus, ubi nullam sententiæ ambiguitatem crearet." Thus in G. i. 1, after Paul has used ἀπό and διά distinctively, he sums up with διά alone—also standing in reference to God. Very many passages have been wrongly referred to this category. In Jo. i. 3, 17, the *per* of mediate agency is justified by the doctrine of the Logos; compare Origen *in loc.* (Tom. I. 108, Lommatzsch). Δι' οὗ in Rom. i. 5 is explained by xv. 15; in Rom. xi. 36, the presence of ἐκ and εἰς of itself renders this explanation of διά necessary; on G. iii. 19 see my note *in loc.* As to Rom. v. 2, no one will allow himself to be misled by Fritzsche's remark. In H. ii. 3, Christ is regarded as commissioned by God to proclaim salvation: on 1 P. ii. 14 [2] see Steiger.[3]

To the idea of *medium* we may also refer the use of διά to denote the *mental state* in which one does something; e. g., δι' ὑπομονῆς ἀπεκδέχεσθαι, τρέχειν, Rom. viii. 25, H. xii. 1, Plut. *Educ.* 5. 3,[4]—probably also 2 C. v. 7, διὰ πίστεως περιπατοῦμεν. Hence διά serves as a periphrasis for an adjective, as in 2 C. iii. 11, εἰ τὸ καταργούμενον (ἐστι) διὰ δόξης, i. e., ἔνδοξον (Matth. 580. 1. e). More loosely used, this preposition denotes that with

---

[1] Bremi (on Corn. Nep. 10. 1. 4) takes almost exactly the same view. Even if it were conceded that διά is perfectly identical with ὑπό, it would not follow that in G. iii. 19, (νόμος) διαταγεὶς δι' ἀγγίλων, the angels are indicated as the *authors* of the Mosaic Law (as Schulthess persistently maintained). If we are to depart from the simple explanation *ordained through angels*, reasons altogether different from those which Schulthess gives, and of a more positive kind, must be brought forward to justify the change.

[2] [Steiger refers αὐτοῦ to the *king:* similarly Alford and others.—On the use of διά in such passages as G. i. 1 see Ellicott and Lightfoot *in loc.* In G. iv. 7, referred to in the text, διὰ θεοῦ is certainly the most probable reading.]

[3] In 1 Th. iv. 2, τίνας παραγγελίας ἐδώκαμεν ὑμῖν διὰ τοῦ κυρίου Ἰησοῦ, the expression at first sight appears strange. But as the Apostle was not acting in his own person, but as moved through Christ, his charges were really given through Christ.

[4] Xen. *Cyr.* 4. 6. 6 is of a different kind. In 2 C. ii. 4, also, ἔγραψα ὑμῖν διὰ πολλῶν δακρύων is properly *through many tears:* " amid many tears " expresses something similar,—see above, s. v. μετά.

which some one is furnished, the circumstances and relations amid which he does something: 1 Jo. v. 6, ἐλθὼν δι' ὕδατος καὶ αἵματος, *came by means of water and blood;* H. ix. 12,—but see Bleek *in loc.;*[1] Rom. ii. 27, σὲ τὸν διὰ γράμματος καὶ περιτομῆς παραβάτην ὄντα, *with letter and circumcision,* i. e., although thou wast in possession of a written law, etc.; iv. 11; xiv. 20, ὁ διὰ προςκόμματος ἐσθίων, *who eateth with* (amid) *offence*—giving offence.[2]

When applied to time, διά signifies

(*a*) *During* (i. e., within the space of time), as in H. ii. 15, διὰ παντὸς τοῦ ζῆν (Xen. *Cyr.* 2. 1. 19, *Mem.* 1. 2. 61, Plat. *Conv.* 203 d); even if in the course of this period the action takes place but once or occasionally, as A. v. 19, xvi. 9, al. Of this laxer use of the preposition there are probably no examples in Greek writers.[3]

(*b*) *After:*[4] e. g., δι' ἐτῶν πλειόνων, A. xxiv. 17,—properly *interjectis pluribus annis, many years being passed through,*[5] i. e., after the lapse of many years;[6] also G. ii. 1. Compare Her. 6. 118, Plat. *Legg.* 8. 834 e, Arist. *Anim.* 8. 15, Polyb. 22. 26. 22, *Geopon.* 14. 26. 2, Plut. *Agis* 10, Lucian, *Icar.* 24, and in the

---

[1] ["The preposition διά may here be taken as denoting the means: it was Christ's own blood which opened to him, as it were, the entrance into the heavenly sanctuary:" Bleek *in loc.* Similarly Alford.]

[2] Markland, *Lys.* V. 329 (Reiske).

[3] Fritzsche in Fritzschior. *Opusc.* p. 164 sq. [In all the passages (A. v. 19, xvi. 9, xvii. 10, xxiii. 31) Meyer defends the meaning *through, throughout* (see his notes *ll. cc.* and on G. ii. 1). On the other side see Ellicott on G. ii. 1: ".... A. v. 19, where both the tense and the occurrence preclude the possibility of its being 'throughout the night;' so also A. xvi. 9; A. xvii. 10 is perhaps doubtful."]

[4] This signification of διά cannot be denied by any one who is not trying to find in G. ii. 1 his own foregone conclusion respecting the chronology of Paul's travels. That the preposition *may* mean "after" can be clearly shown; whether we derive this meaning (with Matth. 580. 1. a) from the idea of interval which is expressed by διά in its local sense, or from that of passing through a series of points of time (which are thus indicated as gone over, as *passed*): see Herm. *Vig.* p. 856. The assertion that it is only to a period of time after which something occurs *as its result* that διά can be thus applied, is a subtlety which has no foundation in the usage of the language, and which wrongly takes the notion of *means,* which is but a *derived* sense of διά, to explain one of the temporal applications of the preposition, though these are always most closely attached to the primary local meaning. Even were this conceded, however, it would be quite admissible to understand διὰ δεκατεσσάρων ἐτῶν in G. ii. 1 of a journey the necessity of which forced itself on Paul *in consequence of* 14 years of labour. At all events κατὰ ἀποκάλυψιν (ver. 2) could not be urged as a decisive argument on the other side.

[5] Her. 3. 157, διαλιπὼν ἡμέρας δέκα· Isocr. *Perm.* p. 746.

[6] See Perizon. *Ælian* p. 921 (ed. Gronov.), Blomfield, Æsch. *Pers.* 1006, Wetst. I. 525, 558. [Ellicott on G. ii. 1, Jelf 627. I. 2. *b*, Don. p. 511.]

LXX Dt. ix. 11. So, lastly, in Mk. ii. 1, δι' ἡμερῶν, *after some days* (Theophr. *Plant.* 4. 4, δι' ἡμερῶν τινων): compare διὰ χρόνου, Plat. *Euthyd.* 273 b, Xen. *Cyr.* 1. 4. 28 (Raphel, Kypke, and Fritz. *in loc.*).[1]   (Don. p. 510, Jelf 627.)

The following significations have been wrongly attributed to διά:—
(*a*) *Into:* 1 C. xiii. 12, βλέπομεν δι' ἐσόπτρου, is said according to the popular conception,—a man looks *through* a mirror, inasmuch as he imagines that the form he sees is behind the mirror.

(*b*) *Cum:* 1 C. xvi. 3, δι' ἐπιστολῶν τούτους πέμψω ἀπενεγκεῖν κ.τ.λ., must be rendered *by means of letters*, recommending them by letters (Syr.). It is true the apostle also intends that they shall take these letters *with them*, but the meaning of the preposition is nevertheless strictly retained.

(*c*) *Ad:* 2 P. i. 3, καλέσαντος ἡμᾶς διὰ δόξης καὶ ἀρετῆς is not *ad religionem christianam adduxit eo consilio, ut consequeremini felicitatem* etc., but, *called by means of glory and power*,—so that the power and majesty of God were manifested in this call (ver. 4, compare 1 P. ii. 9). Some MSS. read δόξῃ καὶ ἀρετῇ.[2]

(*d*) *On account of*, for διά with the accusative: this interchange is found in very late writers only, e. g., *Acta Apocr.* p. 252. In 2 C. ix. 13 διά rather expresses the occasion through which the δοξάζειν is brought about; the following words, ἐπὶ τῇ ὑποταγῇ, express *over*, i. e., *on account of* the obedience. 1 C. i. 21, οὐκ ἔγνω ὁ κόσμος διὰ τῆς σοφίας τὸν θεόν, may very well mean, *by means of their* (vaunted, see ver. 20) *wisdom*,—the wisdom did not enable them to attain this object; though the explanation given by others " for (very) wisdom " may be grammatically admissible, if we take this rendering as derived from " having wisdom with them " (see above). The words which immediately follow, διὰ τῆς μωρίας, are however decisive for the former view. Rom. vii. 4, ἐθανατώθητε τῷ νόμῳ διὰ τοῦ σώματος Χριστοῦ, is explained by ver. 1-3: *ye were slain to the law through the body of Christ*,—with the slaying of Christ's body (which slaying had reference to the law) ye have been slain to the law. In 1 C. xi. 12 it is the less possible to take διὰ τῆς γυναικός as used for διὰ τὴν γυναῖκα (which here would bring in an extraneous thought), since these words were clearly intended to be parallel to ἐκ τοῦ ἀνδρός: the distinction between the prepositions ἐκ and διά is obvious at once. In 2 C. viii. 8 (Schott), διὰ τῆς ἑτέρων σπουδῆς belongs to δοκιμάζων, as was seen by Bengel. In H. xi. 39, (Schott) πάντες μαρτυρηθέντες διὰ τῆς πίστεως means *praised through faith*, who through faith have obtained praise.

---

[1] [Fritzsche, Alford, and others thus explain Mt. xxvi. 61, Mk. xiv. 58, διὰ τριῶν ἡμιρῶν. Meyer renders *during three days:* see also Winer on G. ii. 1.]
[2] [This reading is adopted by Lachm., Tisch., Treg., Alford: Westcott and Hort retain the received text.]

Nor is there any foundation for the rendering *per* (Schott) in exhortations and adjurations (*by*), Rom. xii. 1, xv. 30, 1 C. i. 10, 2 C. x. 1, 2 Th. iii. 12.[1] To *exhort* or *conjure through* the mercy of God, *through* the name of Christ, means, to exhort etc. referring to, reminding of . . . . : διά indicates the motive which the writer presents to add strength to his exhortation.

k. Κατά has for its primary meaning *down* (down upon, down from), *de*,—compare κάτω (Xen. *An.* 4. 2. 17, ἁλλόμενοι κατὰ τῆς πέτρας· 1. 5. 8, τρέχειν κατὰ πρανοῦς γηλόφου· Her. 8. 53): Mt. viii. 32, ὥρμησε πᾶσα ἡ ἀγέλη κατὰ τοῦ κρημνοῦ (Galen, *Protrept.* 2, κατὰ κρημνῶν· Dio Chr. 7. 99, Porphyr. *Abstin.* 4. 15, Ælian 7. 14, Pausan. 10. 2. 2); 1 C. xi. 4, ἀνὴρ κατὰ κεφαλῆς ἔχων, *having* (a veil hanging) *down from the head;* compare also the figurative usage in 2 C. viii. 2, ἡ κατὰ βάθους πτωχεία, *poverty reaching down into the depth.*[2] It is next applied to the surface *over* (*through*) which something extends, and hence differs essentially from the local ἐν (with which it is frequently interchanged by later writers,—compare Ellendt, Arr. *Al.* I. 355): L. iv. 14, ἐξῆλθεν καθ' ὅλης τῆς περιχώρου· A. ix. 31, 42, x. 37;[3] compare Arrian, *Al.* 5. 7. 1, *Indic.* 13. 6. In its figurative use κατά denotes *hostile* direction *against* something, Mt. x. 35, xxvii. 1, A. vi. 13, 1 C. iv. 6, xv. 15,[4] Rom. viii. 33 : it is the antithesis of ὑπέρ, see Rom. xi. 2 compared with viii. 34, and 2 C. xiii. 8. Κατά is the preposition usually employed to express this relation: it seems however, like our *gegen*, strictly to imply no more than motion *on* or *to*, whereas ἀντί, like *contra*, has the notion of hostility included even in its local meaning. In *oaths* and *adjurations* (Mt. xxvi.

---

[1] [Here we should probably read, ἐν κυρίῳ Ἰησοῦ Χριστῷ.]

[2] To this head belongs A. xxvii. 14, ἔβαλε κατ' αὐτῆς ἄνεμος τυφωνικός : the tempestuous wind rushed (from above) down *upon* the island. In Mk. xiv. 3, κατέχειν αὐτοῦ κατὰ τῆς κεφαλῆς (holding the box of ointment over his head), good MSS. leave out the preposition. For καταχέειν κατά τινος see Plat. *Rep.* 3. 398 a, Apollod. 2. 7. 6. [In A. xxvii. 14 the rendering *down from Crete* (Overbeck, Alford, and others) seems best to suit the circumstances of the case. See Alford's note, Conybeare and Howson, *St. Paul* II. p. 401, Smith, *Dict. of Bible*, II. 757. In ed. 6 Winer's rendering was "down upon the *ship*." In Mk. xiv. 3 κατά is omitted in the best texts.]

[3] [L. xxiii. 5 is the only other example in the N. T., so that this usage is peculiar to St. Luke : it is singular that in each case the phrase is καθ' ὅλης τῆς . . . . Other examples given in the Lexicons are Polyb. 1. 17. 10, ἐσκιδασμένοι κατὰ τῆς χώρας· 3. 19. 7 : *Odyss.* 6. 102 also is quoted by Rost and Palm, but Nitzsch (II. 102), Ameis, and others with more reason retain the meaning *down from*.]

[4] [Here many give κατά its other meaning, *in regard to* (Jelf 628. I. 3. c).]

63, H. vi. 13, 16) κατὰ θεοῦ¹ probably means *down from God,*—God being called down, as it were, as witness or avenger (Krüg. p. 330). Kühner (II. 284²) takes a different view. (Don. p. 511, Jelf 628.)

1. Ὑπέρ has the local meaning of being *on the upper part of* (over) a place,—properly, without immediate contact, see Xen. *Mem.* 3. 8. 9, ὁ ἥλιος τοῦ θέρους ὑπὲρ ἡμῶν καὶ τῶν στεγῶν πορευόμενος (Herod. 2. 6. 19). Hence it is used in geographical language for *situation over* something, *imminere urbi*: Xen. *An.* 1. 10. 12, Thuc. 1. 137 (Dissen, *Pind.* p. 431). In the N. T. its meaning is always figurative.³

(1) The nearest approach to its local signification is in 1 C. iv. 6, ἵνα μὴ εἷς ὑπὲρ τοῦ ἑνὸς φυσιοῦσθε, if we render this, *that one may not be puffed up over the other* (so as to imagine himself elevated above the other).

(2) Still in connexion with the local sense, ὑπέρ denotes *for the benefit of, for* (the antithesis of κατά, Mk. ix. 40, Rom. viii. 31), e. g., to die, suffer, pray, care, exert oneself, *for* some one;⁴ as Jo. x. 15, xi. 50, Rom. v. 6, ix. 3 (compare Xen. *An.* 7. 4. 9, Diod. S. 17. 15, Strabo 3. 165, Eurip. *Alc.* 700, 711), L. xxii. 19, 2 C. v. 21, Ph. iv. 10, H. v. 1, vii. 25, xiii. 17, Col. i. 7, 24, probably also 1 C. xv. 29; the original idea being that of bending *over* some one, as it were, protecting and warding off (compare μάχεσθαι ὑπέρ τινος, Xen. *Cyr.* 2. 1. 21, Isocr. *Paneg.* 14).⁵

---

¹ Schæf. *Long.* p. 353 sq., Bernh. p. 238.
² [Jelf 628. 3. *d* (Don. p. 512). Bernhardy regards this usage as an incorrect extension of the classical ὀμόσαι κατά with genitive of *thing*. Whereas formerly this phrase was used in swearing *by a thing* ("because one holds the hand *over* it, or calls *down* the vengeance of the gods *upon* it:" Lidd. and Scott), it is applied in later Greek to swearing by a *deity*. Similarly Bleek (on H. vi. 13).]
³ Unless we render 1 C. xv. 29, βαπτίζεσθαι ὑπὲρ τῶν νεκρῶν *have themselves baptised over the dead.* The passage only admits of an archæological explanation. But it is strange that Meyer should pronounce the above rendering grammatically inadmissible because ὑπέρ does not occur elsewhere in the N. T. in the local sense. Might not then the preposition be used with this most simple local meaning in one single passage only? Van Hengel's remark (*Cor.* p. 136) deserves attention, though even this contains an arbitrary limitation. [See Alford and Stanley *in loc.*, and Smith, *Dict. of Bible* s. v. Baptism.]
⁴ See Benseler, Isocr. *Areopag.* p. 164 sq.
⁵ Hence in strictness ὑπέρ differs from περί, which merely signifies *on account of some one,* he being viewed as the object, the cause of the dying, praying, etc.: see Schæf. *Demosth.* I. 189 sq., and compare Reitz, *Lucian* VI. 642, VII. 403 sq. (ed. Lehm.), Schoem. *Isæus* p. 234, Franke, *Dem.* p. 6 sq. The two prepositions are, however, frequently interchanged in the MSS. of the

So also εἶναι ὑπέρ τινος, *to be for some one,* Mk. ix. 40, Rom. viii. 31, x. 1 [1] (Blume, *Lycurg.* p. 151). In most cases he who acts in behalf of another appears for him (1 Tim. ii. 6, 2 C. v. 15), and hence ὑπέρ sometimes borders on ἀντί, *instead of, loco* (see especially Eurip. *Alc.* 700), Phil. 13, Thuc. 1. 141, Polyb. 3. 67. 7.[2]

(3) Ὑπέρ denotes the subject *on* (about) which one speaks, writes, judges, etc.: e. g., Rom. ix. 27, Ph. i. 7, 2 C. viii. 23, Joel i. 3, Plutarch, *Brut.* 1, *Mar.* 3, Plat. *Apol.* 39 e, *Legg.* 6. 776, Demosth. 1. *Phil.* p. 20 a, Arrian, *Al.* 3. 3. 11, 6. 2. 6, Arrian, *Epict.* 1. 19. 26, Polyb. 1.14.1, Dion. H.V. 625, Æschin. *Dial.* 1. 8, Ælian, *Anim.* 11. 20, and frequently. Also that *over* (*for*) which one gives thanks or praise, as E. i. 16, v. 20, Rom. xv. 9; or *on* which one prides oneself, *of* which one boasts, as 2 C. vii. 4, ix. 2, xii. 5, 2 Th. i. 4: compare in Latin *super,* in Hebrew עַל,—" *de aliqua re loqui*" also is akin to this, see under περί.[3] Hence, generally, *in regard to* a thing, as in 2 C. i. 6, 8, 2 Th. ii. 1, ἐρωτῶμεν ὑμᾶς ὑπὲρ τῆς παρουσίας τοῦ κυρίου; compare Xen. *Cyr.* 7. 1. 17, ὑπέρ τινος θαρρεῖν, *to have no fear in regard to some one.* Akin to this is the causal meaning *on account of, for the sake of,* 2 C. xii. 8,—Hebr. עַל, yet compare the Latin *gratia* and Xen. *Cyr.* 2. 2. 11, and even the German *für* [*for*], which we can often make use of in such passages, and which presents a different combination of meanings: Rom. xv. 8, ὑπὲρ ἀληθείας θεοῦ (Philostr. *Apoll.* 1. 35, Xen. *An.* 1. 7. 3, al.). To this class belong Jo. xi. 4, ὑπὲρ τῆς δόξης τοῦ θεοῦ, *for the glory of God, gloriæ divinæ illustrandæ causa;* 2 C. xii. 19, ὑπὲρ τῆς ὑμῶν οἰκοδομῆς, *for your edification;* Rom. i. 5, 3 Jo. 7; also, with a difference of application, Ph. ii. 13, θεός ἐστιν ὁ ἐνεργῶν . . . . ὑπὲρ τῆς εὐδοκίας, *for the sake of his goodness,* in

---

N. T. (see G. i. 4, Rom. i. 8), as in those of Greek authors, and the writers themselves do not always observe the distinction. In 1 P. iii. 18 (E. vi. 18 sq.) ὑπέρ and περί are suitably combined: compare Thuc. 6. 78. [See Ellicott on G. i. 4, Ph. i. 7, E. vi. 19, and Lightfoot on G. i. 4.]

[1] [Winer renders (with Fritz., al.), ". . . is for them, for their salvation."]

[2] When, however, in dogmatic passages such phrases as ὑπὲρ ἡμῶν are used in speaking of the death of Christ (G. iii. 13, Rom. v. 6, 8, xiv. 15, 1 P. iii. 18, al.), we are not justified in directly translating ὑπέρ by *instead of,* on the ground of such parallel passages as Mt. xx. 28 (Fritz. *Rom.* I. 267). *Instead of* is the more definite preposition; ὑπέρ merely signifies *for* men, for their salvation, and leaves it undetermined in what sense Christ died *for* them. [See Ellicott on G. iii. 13, Phil. 13.]

[3] So with αἰσχύνεσθαι, ἀγανακτεῖν, etc., Stallb. Plat. *Euthyd.* p. 119.

order to satisfy his goodness. In 2 C. v. 20, ὑπὲρ Χριστοῦ πρεσβεύομεν . . . . δεόμεθα ὑπὲρ Χριστοῦ, the preposition probably means both times *for Christ*,[1] i. e., in his name and behalf (consequently in his stead). Compare Xen. *Cyr.* 3. 3. 14, Plat. *Gorg.* 515 c, Polyb. 21. 14. 9, Marle, *Floril.* p. 169 sq., and see above, no. 2 (at the close). Others take the second ὑπέρ as in formulas of asseveration (Bernh. p. 244, whose explanation[2] however is certainly incorrect), *by Christ, per Christum.* We find πρεσβεύειν ὑπέρ used in reference to a thing, in E. vi. 20, *to act as ambassador for* the Gospel (in the cause of the Gospel): compare Dion. H. IV. 2044, Lucian, *Toxar.* 34. (Don. p. 513, Jelf 630.)

Section XLVIII.

PREPOSITIONS GOVERNING THE DATIVE.

a. Ἐν.[3]

(1) In its *local* sense,[4] this preposition refers to a space within the limits of which something is situated. Hence, according to the different views of this relation, ἐν denotes

a. In the first place, *in* or—when applied to surfaces, tracts, or heights—*on;* Mt. xxiv. 40 ἐν τῷ ἀγρῷ, xx. 3 ἐν τῇ ἀγορᾷ, L. xix. 36, Rev. iii. 21, Jo. iv. 20, 2 C. iii. 3. In many phrases of this kind it would be more exact to use ἐπί.

b. Next it denotes *amongst*, in reference to masses: Mt. xi. 11, A. ii. 29, iv. 34, xx. 25, Rom. i. 5, 1 C. v. 1, 1 P. v. 1 sq., ii. 12. Allied to this is the use of ἐν to denote accompaniment, as L. xiv. 31, ἐν δέκα χιλιάσιν ἀπαντῆσαι· Jude 14 (Neh. xiii. 2, 1 S. i. 24,[5] 1 Macc. i. 17); also clothing (and armour, compare E. vi. 16,

---

[1] See De Wette, against Meyer. [Meyer now renders the preposition (both times) in the same way as Winer.]

[2] ["Properly, *for the welfare of* the object named, ὑπὲρ τοκέων, but also ὑπὲρ Ζηνός, to implore *by parents, by Zeus.*" Bernh. *l.c.* Compare Liddell and Scott, s. v.,—who however are mistaken in the statement that in Homer this formula is only found in conjunction with λίσσομαι: see *Il.* 15. 665.]

[3] In H. xi. 26, ἐν is (apparently) joined with the genitive, according to the reading of A and other MSS., received into the text by Lachm., τῶν ἐν Αἰγύπτου θησαυρῶν. Such combinations, by no means rare in Greek authors, are of course elliptical,—ἐν γῇ Αἰγύπτου. Usually, however, only such words as ναός, ἑορτή, οἶκος, are thus left out; and in this passage the weight of MS. evidence is on the side of τῶν Αἰγύπτου θησαυρῶν. As to the most ancient use of this preposition (in Homer), see Giseke in Schneidewin's *Philolog.* VII. 77 sqq.

[4] See Spohn, *Niceph. Blemmid.* p. 29 sqq.

[5] [These two examples would come in better in the next sentence.]

Krebs, *Obs.* 26), Mt. vii. 15, Mk. xii. 38, Jo. xx. 12 (Ælian 9. 34, Her. 2. 159, Callim. *Dian.* 241, Matth. 577. 2). More generally, ἐν is applied to that with which any one is furnished, which he carries with him: H. ix. 25, εἰσέρχεται ἐν αἵματι· 1 C. iv. 21, v. 8, 2 C. x. 14, Rom. xv. 29 (Xen. *Cyr.* 2. 3. 14).

c. By a further extension of meaning, ἐν denotes *at, on,*—sometimes of immediate connexion, as in Jo. xv. 4, κλῆμα ἐὰν μὴ μείνῃ ἐν τῇ ἀμπέλῳ, sometimes of mere proximity (*by,* παρά), as καθίζειν (εἶναι) ἐν δεξιᾷ θεοῦ, *on the right hand,* H. i. 3, viii. 1, E. i. 20, Plutarch, *Lysand.* 436 b, Dio C. 216. 50. This usage is much more common in Greek authors: see Xen. *Cyr.* 7. 1. 45, Isocr. *Panath.* p. 646, *Philipp.* p. 216, Plat. *Charm.* 153 b, Diod. S. 4. 78, 17. 10; and compare the commentators on Lucian VI. 640 (Lehm.), Jacob, Luc. *Alex.* p. 123.[1] But in Jo. x. 23 and L. ii. 7 ἐν signifies *in;* as it probably does in Jo. viii. 20 (where γαζοφυλάκιον denotes the treasury as a locality [2]), and in L. xiii. 4, as it was usual to say *in Siloam* because the fountain was surrounded with buildings: perhaps also in Mt. xxvii. 5, see Meyer *in loc.* It is obvious that the rendering *in* must be retained in formulas of quotation, e. g., ἐν Δαυίδ, H. iv. 7, Rom. ix. 25 (*in,* Cic. *Or.* 71, Quint. 9. 4. 8), and even Rom. xi. 2, ἐν Ἠλίᾳ (see Van Marle and Fritz. *in loc.*,[3] and compare Diog. L. 6. 104).

d. *Before, apud, coram* (see Isocr. *Archid.* p. 276, Lysias, *Pro Mil.* 11, Arrian, *Epict.* 3. 22. 8, Ast, Plat. *Legg.* 285). This meaning is not needed in 1 Tim. iv. 15 (where however πᾶσιν—not ἐν πᾶσιν—is the true reading); but 1 C. ii. 6 (xiv. 11) must be referred to this head, see above § 31. 8; compare Dem. *Bœot.* p. 636 a, Polyb. 17. 6. 1, 5. 29. 6, Appian, *Civ.*

---

[1] To render ἐν ᾗ in H. ix. 4 by *juxta quam* is a mere archæological makeshift.—Where the local ἐν is joined with personal names (in the plural), it is not so much *with* as *amongst* (a number, company, etc.). In 1 P. v. 2, we might (with Pott) render τὸ ἐν ὑμῖν ποίμνιον *the flock which is in your lands* (compare διά, Rom. xv. 28). Grammatically, it would also be possible to join τὸ ἐν ὑμῖν to ποιμάνατε, *quantum in vobis est, according to your power;* or (though this is certainly remote) to render τὸ ἐν ὑμῖν ποίμνιον, *the church committed to you,* as εἶναι or κεῖσθαι ἔν τινι means *rely, depend on some one.*
[2] [Winer regards γαζοφυλάκιον as here denoting that part of the court in which the treasure-chests were placed. Meyer maintains that there is no authority for this meaning, and renders ἐν *by* or *near.* In Mt. xxvii. 5, Meyer's rendering (referred to in the text) is "in the temple-building, i. e., the holy place." See Trench, *Syn.* p. 11, Ellicott, *Hist. L.* p. 340. The true reading is, no doubt, εἰς τὸν ναόν.]
[3] ["In narratione de Elia, quo loco libri sacri de Elia exponunt." Fritzsche.]

2. 137.¹ So also in 1 C. vi. 2, ἐν ὑμῖν κρίνεται ὁ κόσμος (as the orators frequently use ἐν ὑμῖν for *apud vos, judices*²); and the phrase ἐν ὀφθαλμοῖς τινός, *before the eyes of* (*ante oculos*), see Palairet and Elsner on Mt. xxi. 42,—though in this passage (from the LXX) the phrase is used in a figurative sense.

(2) The transition to the expression of *temporal* relations is very simple. Here our rendering is sometimes *in*, sometimes *on* (e. g., of festivals), as Matt. xii. 2, Jo. ii. 23; sometimes *at* (with the name of an event), as Mt. xxii. 28, 1 P. i. 7,—also 1 C. xv. 52, ἐν τῇ ἐσχάτῃ σάλπιγγι, *at the last trumpet* (when it sounds), 1 Th. iv. 16, H. iii. 8, and with the infinitive of a verb, Mt. xiii. 25, L. ix. 36, xvii. 11. Where it denotes *within* (Wex, Soph. *Ant.* p. 167), as in Jo. ii. 19, our *in* is quite sufficient (Her. 2. 29): in this case ἐν manifestly differs from διά, for ἐν τρισὶν ἡμέραις (Plat. *Menex.* 240 b) does not indicate that the space of three days will be occupied with something, but merely that something is to take place within the limits of this period, consequently before the expiration of the three days. Compare further, ἐν ᾧ, *whilst*, Jo. v. 7, Mk. ii. 19, Thuc. 6. 55, Plat. *Theæt.* 190 e, Soph. *Trach.* 925 (ἐν τούτῳ, *interea*, Xen. *Cyr.* 1. 3. 17, 3. 2. 12), ἐν οἷς, *during which*, L. xii. 1. Most closely allied to the temporal ἐν is the ἐν of *existence* or *continuance*, as H. vi. 18, ἐν οἷς ἀδύνατον ψεύσασθαι θεόν, *with which*, there existing these two assurances etc., Rom. ii. 12, ἐν νόμῳ ἥμαρτον, *with the law* (existing,—in possession of the law);—of *state*, either physical (as L. viii. 43, γυνὴ οὖσα ἐν ῥύσει αἵματος· Rom. iv. 10, Ph. iv. 11 ³), or metaphysical (L. iv. 36, Tit. i. 6), and especially of *disposition, frame of mind*, 1 Tim. ii. 2, 2 C. ii. 1, viii. 2, L. i. 44, 75, E. i. 4 (H. xi. 2), 2 P. ii. 3;—and lastly of *occupation*, as 1 Tim. iv. 15, ἐν τούτοις ἴσθι· Col. iv. 2, compare E. vi. 20 (Meyer *in loc.*), and the neuter ἐν οἷς, A. xxvi. 12. Compare Xen. *Cyr.* 3. 1. 1, 5. 2. 17, Soph. *Œd. R.* 570, Plat. *Phæd.* 59 a and Stallb. *in loc.*

(3) The application of ἐν to express non-material relations, which has already been partially noticed, is very diversified, and exhibits both an extension in usage characteristic of later

---

¹ Rückert says that in 1 C. xiv. 11 ἐν ἐμοί stands for ἐμοί,—one of those superficial observations which one does not expect to find set down so nakedly by any scholar at the present day.
² See Kypke on 1 C. vi. 2 (Jelf 622. I. *c*).
³ See Elsner *in loc.*, Kühner II. 274 (Jelf 622. 3. *d*).

Greek, and also a Hebrew colouring. Not merely does ἐν indicate that *in which* something is (metaphysically) contained, in which it consists (consistit), or shows itself—as 1 P. iii. 4, E. iv. 3 (ii. 15), 2 Th. ii. 9 (1 C. xi. 25), Ph. i. 9,—but it also denotes, with great variety of application,

a. The substratum or the sphere (the range, personal or not personal) *on* which or *in* which a power acts. See 1 C. ix. 15, ἵνα οὕτω (ver. 13 sq.) γένηται ἐν ἐμοί, *that it should thus be done on me* ; iv. 2, 6, ἐν ἡμῖν μάθητε, *learn on us;* Jo. xiii. 35, ἐν τούτῳ γνώσονται· Xen. *Cyr.* 1. 6. 41 (L. xxiv. 35, 1 Jo. iii. 19), Rom. xiv. 22, ὁ μὴ κρίνων ἐν ᾧ (ἐν τούτῳ ὃ) δοκιμάζει· 1 Th. v. 12, κοπιῶντες ἐν ὑμῖν, *who labour on you* ; Rom. i. 9, λατρεύειν ἐν τῷ εὐαγγελίῳ (1 Th. iii. 2 *v. l.*, συνεργὸς ἐν τῷ εὐαγγελίῳ), 1 C. vii. 15. It is used ethically in 2 C. iv. 2, περιπατοῦντες ἐν πανουργίᾳ (E. ii. 3, 10, v. 2), Rom. vi. 2, ζῆν ἐν ἁμαρτίᾳ (Fritz. *in loc.*), Col. iii. 7 (Cic. *Fam.* 9. 26): compare 1 C. vi. 20, 2 Th. i. 10, 1 Jo. ii. 8. Ἐν further denotes the object *on* (at, about) which one rejoices, prides himself, etc., as χαίρειν ἐν, καυχᾶσθαι ἐν: see § 33.

b. The measure or law (Thuc. 1. 77, 8. 89) *in* or *according to* which something is done, as E. iv. 16 (H. iv. 11) : compare the Hebrew בְּ. Many thus explain the preposition in H. x. 10, ἐν ᾧ θελήματι ἡγιασμένοι ἐσμέν, *according to* (in conformity with) *which will* : here, however, ἐν is more precise than κατά,—our being sanctified through the sacrificial death of Christ has its foundation *in* God's will. In no other passage does ἐν signify *secundum*, though numerous examples of this meaning are given in even the most recent N. T. lexicons.[1] In 1 C. xiv. 11, ἐν ἐμοί, *according to my judgment*, is properly *with me* (in my conception [2]) : in Rom. i. 24, viii. 15, xi. 25 *v. l.*, Ph. ii. 7, ἐν denotes the state, condition. 1 Th. iv. 15 must be rendered, *this I say to you in a word of the Lord ;* [3] compare 1 C. ii. 7, xiv. 6. In such phrases as περιπατεῖν ἐν σοφίᾳ, σοφία is not represented as the law *according to which*, but as an ideal possession, or as the sphere *in which* one walks (see above). To explain ἐν Χριστῷ, ἐν κυρίῳ, as meaning *according to the will* or *example*

---

[1] [This language is now too strong, the latest N. T. lexicons—e. g., Schirlitz's *Wörterbuch* and Grimm's edition of Wilke's *Clavis*—not being chargeable with this. In the latter work the meaning *secundum* is not given at all.]
[2] Compare Wex, *Antig.* p. 187. [See above, 1. *d.*]
[3] [Compare Ellicott *in loc.*]

of Christ, is to deprive the apostle's conception of its force. Lastly, 1 Tim. i. 18, ἵνα στρατεύῃ ἐν αὐταῖς (ταῖς προφητείαις) τὴν καλὴν στρατείαν, must probably be rendered in accordance with the figure, *in the prophecies*,—equipped with them, as it were, as the soldier fights *in armour*.

c. The (external) occasion: A. vii. 29, ἔφυγεν ἐν τῷ λόγῳ τούτῳ, *on this word* (at this word), Xen. *Equestr.* 9. 11. Hence sometimes the ground, as in Mt. vi. 7, ἐν τῇ πολυλογίᾳ αὐτῶν εἰσακουσθήσονται, *on account of their much speaking* (properly, *with* or *at* their much speaking, compare Ælian, *Anim.* 11. 31, Dio. C. 25. 5); ἐν τούτῳ, *therefore*,[1] in Jo. xvi. 30 and probably in 1 C. iv. 4 (compare Plutarch, *Glor. Athen.* c. 7, ἐν τούτοις); ἐν ᾧ, for ἐν τούτῳ ὅτι, *because*, Rom. viii. 3 (see Fritz.). In several languages, however, expressions which denote that which takes place *with, by,* or *at* a thing are thus used in reference to the *ground* or *reason*. In Latin *propter* strictly means *near*; and the German *weil* [*because*] is properly a particle of time (*whilst*). Ἐν is never joined with names of persons in the sense of *propter* (see my note on G. i. 24,[2] and compare Ex. xiv. 4);[3] and in general this meaning of ἐν has been intro-

---

[1] In H. xi. 2 ἐν ταύτῃ (τῇ πίστει) does not express the ground or reason, but the (spiritual) possession, *in hac (constituti)*; compare 1 Tim. v. 10 (Jo. viii. 21). In H. ii. 18, ἐν ᾧ πέπονθεν κ.τ.λ. is certainly to be resolved into ἐν τούτῳ ὅ, *in eo quod*; see above, p. 198. Ἐν ᾧ has exactly the same meaning in 1 P. ii. 12. In H. vi. 17, ἐν ᾧ may be referred to the preceding ὅρκος; but the rendering *quapropter, quare* (in which sense ἐφ' ᾧ is sometimes used), would not be unsuitable. In Rom. ii. 1, ἐν ᾧ may be translated *dum*, or rather—with the Vulgate—*in quo* (in qua re) judicas, etc., which gives an appropriate sense; see Fritzsche. In L. x. 20, ἐν τούτῳ . . . . ὅτι means (rejoice) *in this, that* etc.; compare Ph. i. 18. I do not know of any clear example in Greek authors of the use of ἐν τούτῳ, ἐν ᾧ, with the meaning *therefore, because.* The examples cited by Sturz (*Lexic. Xenoph.* II. 162) admit of a different explanation; and in Xen. *An.* 1. 3. 1, which Kypke (II. 194) brings in here, the better editions have ἐπὶ τούτῳ. Plat. *Rep.* 5. 455 b also, where Ast renders ἐν ᾧ *propterea quod*, may be otherwise explained; see Stallb. *in loc.*

[2] ["Celebrant Deum, ut qui *in me* invenissent celebrationis materiem." Winer *l. c.*]

[3] In 2 C. xiii. 4, the words ἀσθενοῦμεν ἐν αὐτῷ—as frequently ἐν Χριστῷ (so variously explained by commentators)—must be understood of fellowship with Christ, the relation εἶναι ἐν Χριστῷ (see below, p. 486 sq.). The apostle is not ἀσθενής *for Christ's sake* (as if, from regard to the interest of Christ, lest the Corinthians might possibly fall away), but *in Christ*, i. e., *in* and in accordance with his (apostolic) fellowship with Christ (who was himself ἀσθενής in a certain sense,—see the previous part of the verse). These words concisely indicate a state of things which resulted from the εἶναι ἐν Χριστῷ, just as ζῆν and δυνατὸν εἶναι are referred to fellowship with Christ (σύν). As little reason is there for rendering ὁ δέσμιος ἐν κυρίῳ, E. iv. 1, *the prisoner*

duced into too many passages, e. g., E. iii. 13, Jo. viii. 21, Ja. i. 25, 2 C. vi. 12, H. iv. 11.

d. The instrument and means,—chiefly in the book of Revelation. In the better Greek prose writers [1] this usage is confined to cases where we could use *in* (or *on*): e. g., καίειν ἐν πυρί, Rev. xvii. 16 (1 C. iii. 13),—compare 1 Macc. v. 44, vi. 31 (δῆσαι ἐν πέδαις Xen. *An.* 4. 3. 8,—compare Jud. xv. 13, xvi. 7, Ecclus. xxviii. 19, Stallb. Plat. *Crit.* p. 104, καλύπτειν ἐν ἱματίῳ Æl. *Anim.* 11. 15); μετρεῖν ἐν μέτρῳ, Mt. vii. 2 ; ἁλίζειν ἐν ἅλατι, Mt. v. 13, Rev. vii. 14, Ja. iii. 9, H. ix. 22. Here, however, through the influence of the Hebrew בְּ, ἐν is thus used (especially in Revelation) where there is no such limitation, and where a Greek writer would have used the simple dative as the *casus instrumentalis*. See L. xxii. 49, πατάσσειν ἐν μαχαίρᾳ· Rev. vi. 8, ἀποκτεῖναι ἐν ῥομφαίᾳ· xiii. 10, xiv. 15, κράζειν ἐν μεγάλῃ φωνῇ (2 P. ii. 16), Mt. vii. 6, καταπατεῖν ἐν τοῖς ποσίν· L. i. 51, Mk. xiv. 1, Rom. xv. 6 ; and compare Jud. iv. 16, xv. 15, xx. 16, 48, 1 K. xii. 18, Jos. x. 35, Ex. xiv. 21, xvi. 3, xvii. 5, 13, xix. 13, Gen. xxxii. 20, xli. 36, xlviii. 22, Neh. i. 10, 1 Macc. iv. 15, Judith ii. 19, v. 9, vi. 4, 12, al.[2] Isolated examples of this kind are, however, found in Greek writers ; see Himer. *Eclog.* 4. 16, ἐν ξίφει· Hippocr. *Aphor.* 2. 36, ἐν φαρμακείῃσι καθαίρεσθαι· Malal. 2. p. 50.[3] Ἐν is thus

---

for Christ's sake. Ph. i. 8, ἐπιποθῶ πάντας ὑμᾶς ἐν σπλάγχνοις Χριστοῦ Ἰησοῦ, is somewhat more remote : see Bengel.

[1] See Buttm. *Philoct.* p. 69, Boeckh, *Pind.* III. 487, Poppo, Xen. *Cyr.* p. 195 ; and the uncritical collections in Schwarz, *Comment.* p. 476, Georgi, *Vind.* p. 153 sq. [See Ellicott on 1 Th. iv. 18, Jelf 622. 3. *a.*]

[2] It would be wrong to give ἐν an instrumental sense in E. ii. 15 (p. 275) and E. vi. 4 ; in the latter passage παιδεία καὶ νουθεσία κυρίου constitute the sphere *in* which the children are trained (comp. Polyb. 1. 65. 7). In the phrase ἀλλάσσειν τι ἔν τινι, Rom. i. 23, I cannot agree with Fritzsche in taking ἐν as *per*, nor do I believe that the Hebrew בְּ in הֵמִיר בְּ is to be thus explained. *To change something in gold* is either an example of brachylogy, or else the gold is regarded as that *in* which the exchange is accomplished. Akin to this is the ἐν of price ; see above, and p. 487.

[3] Many passages which might be quoted from Greek writers as examples of this usage are to be otherwise explained : e. g., ὁρᾶν ἐν ὀφθαλμοῖς, Lucian, *Phalar.* 1. 5 ; ἐν ὄμμασιν ὑποβλέπειν, Lucian, *Amor.* 29 (compare Wex, *Antig.* I. 270) ; Porphyr. *de Antro Nymphar.* p. 261, ἀμφορέων, ἐν οἷς . . . ἀρυόμεθα ; Lucian, *Asin.* 44, ὡς τεθνηκὼς ἐν ταῖς πληγαῖς (*in* or *amid* the blows) ; Plat. *Tim.* 81 c, τιθραμμένης ἐν γάλακτι, brought up on milk (compare Jacobs, *Athen.* p. 57). In Lucian, *Conser. Hist.* 12, ἐν ἀκοντίῳ φονεύειν, the recent editors read ἰνί for ἐν, on MS. authority. In Lucian, *Dial. Mort.* 23. 3, however, all MSS. but one have καθικόμενον ἐν τῇ ῥάβδῳ (not exactly so in Ælian 2. 6) ; yet even here Lehmann regards the preposition as suspicious (compare Lucian, *Lapith.* c. 26). See also Engelh., Plat. *Menex.* p. 261, Dissen, *Pind.* p. 487.

joined with personal names, as in Mt. ix. 34, ἐν τῷ ἄρχοντι τῶν δαιμονίων ἐκβάλλειν τὰ δαιμόνια· A. xvii. 31, κρίνειν ἐν ἀνδρί,[1] *in a man* (compare Thuc. 7. 8. 2, Matth. 577. 2) ; but not in Jo. xvii. 10, 2 Th. i. 10, and certainly not in A. xvii. 28.[2] The phrase ὀμόσαι ἔν τινι, Mt. v. 34 sqq., does not mean *jurare per* (see Fritz. *in loc.*), but, more simply, swear *by* (*near, on*) something. In other passages also ἐν is not properly *through*. In 1 C. vii. 14, ἡγίασται ὁ ἀνὴρ ὁ ἄπιστος ἐν τῇ γυναικί means *he is sanctified in the wife*,—the basis rather than the means of the sanctification being indicated. In Rom. xv. 16, ἐν πνεύματι ἁγίῳ (not διὰ πνεύματος ἁγίου) is used designedly, *in the Holy Ghost* —an inward principle. Akin to 1 C. vii. 14 are 1 C. xv. 22, ἐν τῷ Ἀδὰμ πάντες ἀποθνῄσκουσι· A. iv. 2, ἐν Ἰησοῦ τὴν ἀνάστασιν τὴν ἐκ νεκρῶν καταγγέλλειν. Least of all can ἐν Χριστῷ (κυρίῳ) ever be translated *per Christum* (Fritz. *Rom.* I. 397,—this is distinctly διὰ Ἰησοῦ Χριστοῦ) : Rom. vi. 11, ζῶντες τῷ θεῷ ἐν Χριστῷ Ἰησοῦ (the Christian lives not merely *through Christ*, beneficio Christi, but *in Christ*, in a spiritually powerful fellowship with Christ), vi. 23, 2 C. ii. 14. Indeed this phrase always refers (usually in a concise, condensed manner) to εἶναι ἐν Χριστῷ, 1 Th. ii. 14, Rom. viii. 1, xvi. 11, 2 C. v. 17, G. i. 22 ; and Luther's "barbarous" rendering (Fritz. *Rom.* II. 85) must be retained.[3] So also in 1 C. xii. 3, ἐν πνεύματι θεοῦ

---

[1] [These examples are not very clear. A. xvii. 31 may be simply rendered *in the person of* (Meyer, Alford) : on Mt. ix. 34 see Green, *Gr.* p. 208.]

[2] In δεδόξασμαι ἐν αὐτοῖς (Jo. xvii. 10), ἐν αὐτοῖς is certainly more than δι᾽ αὐτῶν. He would be glorified *through them*, if they but effected objectively something which conduced to the glory of Christ ; he is glorified *in them*, in so far as they glorify Christ *in themselves*, with their persons. So also "to live and be *in God*" seems to express man's existing (being rooted, so to speak) in the divine power, with more precision than could have been conveyed by διά. When ἐν and διά are found in one sentence, διά expresses the external means, whilst ἐν refers to that which was effected *in* or *on* the person of some one, and which cleaves to it, as it were : E. i. 7, ἐν ᾧ (Χριστῷ) ἔχομεν τὴν ἀπολύτρωσιν διὰ τοῦ αἵματος αὐτοῦ (where Meyer is wrong), iii. 6. Even when the reference is to things, not persons, we can perceive the difference between ἐν (of metaphysical condition or power) and διά (of the means) ; e. g., 1 P. i. 5, τοὺς ἐν δυνάμει θεοῦ φρουρουμένους διὰ πίστεως (see Steiger), i. 22 [*Rec.*], ἡγνικότες ἐν τῇ ὑπακοῇ τῆς ἀληθείας διὰ πνεύματος· H. x. 10. Lastly, passages in which ἐν and διά are used in one sentence of material objects, as Col. i. 16 [?], 2 C. vi. 4-8, 1 C. xiv. 19 [*Rec.*], only show that the two prepositions are *as regards sense* of the same kind. In Mt. iv. 4 also ἐν παντὶ ῥήματι does not seem to be in meaning perfectly parallel to ἐπ᾽ ἄρτῳ μόνῳ ; but as ἐπί indicates the basis, so ἐν indicates the (spiritual) element of the life : in any case *through* or *by means of* would here be an inexact rendering.

[3] As the Christian abides in a most living (most intimate, hence ἐν) fellowship with Christ (through faith), he will do everything in the consciousness of this fellowship, and by means of powers resulting from this fellowship,—i. e., *in*

λαλῶν has the strict meaning " speaking *in* the spirit of God," as the principle in which he lives (Rom. ix. 1, xiv. 17, Col. i. 8).

e. 'Εν is used (Hebraistically) of the *price,* in Rev. v. 9, ἀγοράζειν ἐν τῷ αἵματι (1 Chr. xxi. 24). The value of the thing purchased is contained in the price (to this answers the ἐκ of price). (Don. p. 508, Jelf 622.)

Even the most recent lexicographers have unduly multiplied the meanings of this preposition, or have wrongly applied its true meanings to N. T. passages. Especially Proteus-like have been the explanations of ἐν ὀνόματί τινος. Here however ἐν presents no difficulty, but simply signifies *in*. A thing comes to pass " in a person's name " when it is comprehended or inclosed *in* his name, is set to the account of his personal agency (compare A. iv. 7), and not to that of the man who is the nearest, the direct subject (compare Jo. v. 43). Only the various verbs which are defined by ἐν ὀνόματι demand attention from the commentator, that he may in all cases most simply trace back the varied senses to the literal meaning of the formula. This requirement has not yet been satisfactorily met,[1] even by Meyer. Ph. ii. 10 seems to need separate treatment. Here ὄνομα points back to ὄνομα in ver. 9, and ἐν ὀνόματι denotes the name *into* which those who bow the knee are united, united into which all (πᾶν γόνυ) offer worship : the name which Jesus has received unites them all to bow the knee. 'Εν does not indicate the *finis* or *consilium* in Tit. iii. 5 ; ἔργα τὰ ἐν δικαιοσύνῃ are works done in the spirit of a δίκαιος : on L. i. 17, 1 C. vii. 15, see below [§ 50. 5]. Nor do we need *erga* for Mk. ix. 50, εἰρηνεύετε ἐν ἀλλήλοις, for we also use *amongst* here. Still less tenable are the following interpretations :—

(*a*) *Ex:*[2] H. xiii. 9, ἐν οἷς οὐκ ὠφελήθησαν οἱ περιπατήσαντες, *unde* (Schott) *nihil commodi perceperunt* (compare ὠφελεῖσθαι ἀπό, Æschin. *Dial.* 2. 11). If we joined ἐν οἷς with ὠφελήθησαν the preposition would denote the advantage which would have been founded *in them,*

Christ, in the Lord: the renderings frequently given, *as a Christian, in a Christian spirit,* etc., express much less than the pregnant phrase *in Christ*. So in Rom. xvi. 12, *who labour in the Lord,* conscious of their fellowship with the Lord (no worldly κοπιᾶν is meant) ; 1 C. xv. 18, *who fell asleep in Christ,* in conscious, enduring fellowship with Christ (compare 1 Th. iv. 16, Rev. xiv. 13) ; Rom. ix. 1 (which even Bengel misunderstood), *speak truth in Christ* (as one living in Christ) ; xiv. 14, *persuaded in the Lord* (in reference to a truth of which in his living union with Christ he is convinced). On 1 C. iv. 15 see Meyer. Εὑρίσκεσθαι ἐν Χριστῷ, Ph. iii. 9, is evidently to be thus explained : see also Rom. xv. 17, xvi. 2, 22, 1 C. vii. 39, Ph. iv. 1 (E. vi. 1), 1 P. v. 10. Fritzsche (*Rom.* II. 82 sqq.) maintains substantially the right view, but not without misapprehensions and the introduction of unnecessary matter. See also Van Hengel, *Cor.* p. 81.

[1] Yet better by Harless (*Eph.* p. 484) than by Van Hengel (*Phil.* p. 161 sq.).

[2] Fischer (*Well.* p. 141) gives this meaning to ἐν in such phrases as πίνειν ἐν ἀργύρῳ, χρυσῷ (Isocr. *Paneg.* c. 30, Diog. L. 1. 104, *bibere in* ossibus Flor. 3. 4. 2). On this fashion we might say that our *auf* (*on*) means *von* (*from*) ; for we speak of eating *on* (*auf*) silver plates, which, according to the analogy of " drinking *out of* silver cups," is equivalent to *from* (*von*) silver plates.

or have clung *to them* (Xen. *Ath. Rep.* 1. 3, Dem. *Pantœn.* 631 a); but ἐν οἷς belongs to περιπατήσαντες. In Mt. i. 20, τὸ ἐν αὐτῇ γεννηθέν means *that which is begotten in her (in ejus utero).*

(*b*) *Pro, loco :* Rom. xi. 17 (Schott), ἐνεκεντρίσθης ἐν αὐτοῖς (κλάδοις), is, *grafted on the branches* (which had been in part cut off).

(*c*) *Together with :* in A. xx. 32 ἐν τοῖς ἡγιασμένοις means *amongst the sanctified.* A. vii. 14, μετεκαλέσατο τὸν πατέρα αὐτοῦ Ἰακὼβ . . . ἐ ν ψ υ χ α ῖ ς ἑ β δ ο μ ή κ ο ν τ α, means (*consisting*) *in 70 souls :* בְּ is thus used in Dt. x. 22, but I do not know any similar example in Greek. Fritzsche's explanation of the words (*Mark*, p. 604)[1] appears to me too artificial; Wahl also has rejected it. E. vi. 2, ἥτις ἐστὶν ἐντολὴ πρώτη ἐν ἐπαγγελίᾳ, certainly does not mean *annexa, addita promissione*, but, *which is the first in promise*, i. e., in point of promise ("not ἐν τάξει:" Chrysost.); so Meyer.

(*d*) *By* [of the *agent*] : E. iv. 21, εἴγε ἐν αὐτῷ ἐδιδάχθητε, *if ye have been taught in him,* is closely connected with the following ἀποθέσθαι κ.τ.λ., and hence the meaning is "conformably to fellowship with Christ," "as believers on Christ."—As to ἐν for εἰς see § 50. 4.

b. **Σύν**, *with*, as distinguished from μετά, points to a closer and stricter conjunction,[2] such as (among persons) association in calling, belief, lot, etc.: A. ii. 14, xiv. 4, 20, 1 C. xi. 32. Hence it is especially used of spiritual fellowship, as that of believers with Christ (Rom. vi. 8, Col. ii. 13, 20, iii. 3, 1 Th. iv. 17, v. 10), or that of believers with Abraham (G. iii. 9), σύν denoting in all these instances, not a mere resemblance, but a real association. Then, applied to things, it denotes powers which work *with* a person, uniting themselves with him : e. g., 1 C. v. 4, xv. 10. In 2 C. viii. 19 it would be used of a less close conjunction,—*with the collection ;* but ἐν seems the preferable reading. Compare however L. xxiv. 21, σὺν πᾶσι τούτοις τρίτην ταύτην ἡμέραν ἄγει σήμερον, *with all this,* i.e., *joined with all this there is the fact that* etc.; see Neh. v. 18, and compare Joseph. *Antt.* 17. 6. 5. (Don. p. 508, Jelf 623.)

c. **Ἐπί**. The primary meaning is *upon, over* (both of elevations and of level surfaces),[3] in the local sense : Mt. xiv. 11,

---

[1] ["Per septuaginta quinque homines Josephus patrem suum et universam familiam in Ægyptum arcessivit, h. e., Josephus eo, quod septuaginta quinque homines in Ægyptum arcesseret, patrem suum et cognatos suos omnes eo traduxit :" Fritz. *l. c.* Meyer follows this explanation.]

[2] Krüger (p. 322): "σύν τινι denotes rather coherence, μετά τινος rather coexistence." [See also Ellicott on G. iii. 9, E. vi. 23.]

[3] According to Krüger (p. 340), ἐπί with the genitive denotes a more accidental, free connexion; ἐπί with the dative denotes rather *belonging to.*

SECT. XLVIII.] PREPOSITIONS GOVERNING THE DATIVE. 489

ἠνέχθη ἡ κεφαλὴ ἐπὶ πίνακι· Mk. i. 45, ἐπ' ἐρήμοις τόποις (see above on ἐπί with the genitive, and compare ἀνάγειν εἰς τὴν ἔρημον Mt. iv. 1), Mk. vi. 39, L. xxi. 6, Rev. xix. 14; also Jo. iv. 6, ἐπὶ τῇ πηγῇ, *over* (on) *the well* (the margin of the well lying higher than the well itself), Rev. ix. 14, Xen. *An.* 1. 2. 8, 5. 3. 2, *Cyr.* 7. 5. 11, Isocr. *Paneg.* c. 40, Dio C. 177. 30 (see above, § 47. g).[1] Sometimes it signifies *at*, as in Jo. v. 2, ἐπὶ τῇ προβατικῇ, *at the sheep-gate*, A. iii. 10, 11, Mt. xxiv. 33, ἐπὶ θύραις (Xen. *Cyr.* 8. 1. 33, yet see note,[3] p. 468); and is thus applied to persons, A. v. 35, πράσσειν τι ἐπί τινι, to do something *on*[2] some one (compare δρᾶν τι ἐπί τινι, Her. 3. 14, Æl. *Anim.* 11. 11). Lastly, ἐπί is *with*—both of place (*apud*), as A. xxviii. 14, ἐπ' αὐτοῖς[3] ἐπιμεῖναι, and of time, as H. ix. 26, ἐπὶ συντελείᾳ τῶν αἰώνων, *sub finem mundi*; further, Ph. i. 3, εὐχαριστῶ τῷ θεῷ ἐπὶ πάσῃ τῇ μνείᾳ ὑμῶν, *with every mention*, Mk. vi. 52, οὐ συνῆκαν ἐπὶ τοῖς ἄρτοις·[4] 2 C. ix. 6, σπείρειν, θερίζειν ἐπ' εὐλογίαις, *with blessings*, so that blessings are associated therewith. So, with a different application, in H. ix. 15, τῶν ἐπὶ τῇ πρώτῃ διαθήκῃ παραβάσεων, *with* (under) *the first covenant*, during the continuance of the first covenant. It is thus applied to persons in H. x. 28 (from the LXX), ἐπὶ τρισὶ μάρτυσι, *with* (before) *three witnesses, adhibitis testibus.* Ἐπί is also used of that which (in point of time) is directly annexed to, which follows *upon*, as in Xen. *Cyr.* 2. 3. 7, ἀνέστη ἐπ' αὐτῷ Φεραύλας, *immediately after* (Appian, *Civ.* 5. 3, Pausan. 7. 25. 6, Dio C. 325. 89, 519. 99[5]). Some have thus explained A. xi. 19, ἀπὸ τῆς θλίψεως τῆς γενομένης ἐπὶ Στεφάνῳ (see Alberti *in loc.*), but

---

[1] The signification *upon* may also be traced in L. xii. 53, ἔσονται . . . πατὴρ ἐφ' υἱῷ καὶ υἱὸς ἐπὶ πατρί, *the father will be on him*, i. e., pressing on him, a load on him; as we say colloquially, *Vater und Sohn liegen sich auf dem Halse* [literally, *father and son lie on each other's neck*, i. e., plague each other]. Here however *against* correctly expresses the sense; but I cannot bring myself to give ἐπί this meaning in L. xxiii. 38, as Wahl does. Rom. x. 19 is of an entirely different kind.

[2] [Here the German and the English prepositions do not agree: we say *at the gate*, but *on* or *to the man*, though the German *an* is used in both cases. Similarly in the next sentence we should not use *with* in rendering H. ix. 26.]

[3] [We should probably read παρ' αὐτοῖς.]

[4] [That is, *at the* (miracle of the) *loaves they understood not*: so Fritz., De W., Bleek, Meyer. Alford takes ἐπί as expressing basis, foundation.]

[5] [Compare Wurm, *Dinarch.* p. 39 sq., Ellendt, Arr. *Al.* I. 30 (Don. p. 518, Jelf 634. 2. *b.*).

here ἐπί rather means *over* (on account of) or *against* (Matthäi *in loc.*).[1]

In a figurative sense, ἐπί denotes, in general, the basis on which an action or a state rests, as in Ph. iii. 9. So in Mt. iv. 4 (from the LXX), ζῆν ἐπ' ἄρτῳ (parallel with ἐν ῥήματι), after the Hebrew עַל חָיָה, Dt. viii. 3,—though the phrase is also found in Greek writers, see Plat. *Alcib.* 1. 105 c, Alciphr. 3. 7 (compare *sustentare vitam*). Under this head comes the phrase ἐπὶ τῷ ὀνόματί τινος (Lucian, *Pisc.* 15, compare Schoem. *Isæus* p. 463 sq.), to do something *on the name of* some one, i. e., to do it resting on, or having reference to, this name. In the N. T. we meet with ἐπὶ τῷ ὀνόματι Ἰησοῦ Χριστοῦ in different applications: e. g., *to teach on the name of Christ* (L. xxiv. 47, A. iv. 17, v. 28, 40), the teacher referring to Christ as the original Teacher, by whom he is delegated; *to cast out devils on the name of Christ* (L. ix. 49), making the power of exorcism to depend on his name (pronounced as a formula of exorcism); *to be baptised on the name of Christ*, the baptism being founded on the confession of his name (A. ii. 38); *to receive some one on the name of Christ* (Mt. xviii. 5), i. e., because he bears this name, confesses it, etc.—Ἐπί is then specially applied to denote

a. Over—of superintendence: L. xii. 44, ἐπὶ τοῖς ὑπάρχουσι καταστήσει αὐτόν,[2] compare Xen. *Cyr.* 6. 3. 28 (as elsewhere ἐπί with genitive, Lob. *Phryn.* p. 474 sq.).

b. Over and above, to,—of addition to something already existing. See L. iii. 20, προσέθηκε καὶ τοῦτο ἐπὶ πᾶσι· Mt. xxv. 20, ἄλλα πέντε τάλαντα ἐκέρδησα ἐπ' αὐτοῖς, *in addition to* those 5 talents (if ἐπ' αὐτοῖς is genuine [3]), L. xvi. 26, ἐπὶ πᾶσι τούτοις, *over and above* (besides) *all this*, Lucian, *Conscr. Hist.* 31, Aristoph. *Plut.* 628 (compare Wetstein and Kypke *in loc.*), Ph. ii. 17, Col. iii. 14, E. vi. 16 (compare Polyb. 6. 23. 12). Hence Jo. iv. 27, ἐπὶ τούτῳ ἦλθον οἱ μαθηταί, *on this,*—when Jesus was thus speaking with the Samaritan, the disciples came. The application is somewhat different in 2 C. vii. 13, ἐπὶ τῇ παρακλήσει περισσοτέρως μᾶλλον ἐχάρημεν, *in addition to*, i. e., *besides my comfort I rejoiced*, etc.

---

[1] Compare Schæfer, *Plutarch* V. 17, Maetzner, *Antiph.* p. 288.
[2] [This and Mt. xxiv. 47 seem the only N. T. examples (Jelf 634. II. 1. c.).]
[3] [All recent editors omit these words.]

c. *Over* (*at, about*),—indicating the object after verbs denoting an emotion, as θαυμάζειν, ἀγαλλιᾶν, πενθεῖν, λυπεῖσθαι, ὀργίζεσθαι, μετανοεῖν: see L. i. 47, xviii. 7, Mk. iii. 5, xii. 17, Mt. vii. 28, Rom. x. 19, 2 C. xii. 21,[1] Rev. xii. 17, xviii. 11 [2] (Plat. *Symp.* 217 a, 206 b, Isocr. *Paneg.* 22, Lucian, *Philops.* 14, Aristot. *Rhet.* 2. 10. 1, Palæph. 1. 8, Joseph. *Antt.* 5. 1. 26, al.). So with εὐχαριστεῖν, *to give thanks over* (for), 1 C. i. 4, 2 C. ix. 15, Ph. i. 3 sqq., Polyb. 18. 26. 4. Then with verbs of speaking, Rev. x. 11, προφητεῦσαι ἐπὶ λαοῖς (xxii. 16 *v. l.*), Jo. xii. 16, ταῦτα ἦν ἐπ' αὐτῷ γεγραμμένα (Her. 1. 66, Paus. 3. 13. 3): compare Schoemann, Plut. *Agis* p. 71.

d. *On*,—of supposition and condition (Xen. *Symp.* 1. 5, Diod. S. 2. 24, Lucian, *Conscr. Hist.* 38, Æsop. 21. 1): ἐπ' ἐλπίδι, *on hope*,[3] 1 C. ix. 10 (Plat. *Alcib.* 1. 105 b,—ἐπ' ἐλπίσι, Dio C. 1003. 21, Herod. 3. 12. 20), H. ix. 17, ἐπὶ νεκροῖς, *over dead persons*, i. e., not until there are dead persons, when death has taken place.[4] Also of the motive: L. v. 5, ἐπὶ τῷ ῥήματί σου χαλάσω τὸ δίκτυον, *on thy word*, induced by thy word; A. iii. 16, ἐπὶ τῇ πίστει, *on account of faith*; A. xxvi. 6, Mt. xix. 9 (1 C. viii. 11 *v. l.*[5]); compare Xen. *Mem.* 3. 14. 2, *Cyr.* 1. 3. 16, 1. 4. 24, 4. 5. 14, Her. 1. 137, Lucian, *Hermot.* 80, Isocr. *Areop.* 336, Dio Chr. 29. 293. Hence ἐφ' ᾧ, *wherefore*, Diod. S. 19. 98 (ἐφ' ᾧπερ, Dio C. 43. 95, al.), *and because*, 2 C. v. 4, Rom. v. 12, also probably Ph. iii. 12 [6] (*on account of the fact that* . . ., for ἐπὶ τούτῳ ὅτι, see Fritz. *Rom.* I. 299 sq.), *eo quod.*[7]

---

[1] [Winer connects ἐπὶ τῇ ἀκαθαρσίᾳ with μετανοησάντων (as in A. V.), not with πενθήσω (Meyer). There is no other example of μετανοεῖν ἐπί in the N. T.; in the LXX see Joel ii. 13, Jon. iii. 10, al. To the verbs given above, Lünemann adds μακροθυμεῖν.]

[2] [Here ἐπ' αὐτήν appears the true reading: there is no other example of πενθεῖν ἐπί τινι in the N. T.]

[3] [If "on hope" is not allowable in English, we must say *resting on hope, with hope.*]

[4] Several of these passages, however, may be referred to the most general meaning *with*, *by* (see above): so Fritz. *Rom.* 1. 315. [With H. ix. 17 compare Soph. *El.* 237, also Eurip. *Ion* 228.]

[5] Ἀπολεῖται ὁ ἀσθενῶν ἀδελφὸς ἐπὶ τῇ σῇ γνώσει (where however good authorities read ἐν) is properly, *he perishes over thy knowledge*, i. e., because thy knowledge asserts itself,—in brief, *through* thy knowledge. But it does not follow that ἐπί by itself can mean *through*, as Grotius (on Rom. v. 12) maintains.

[6] [The different meanings are examined by Bp. Ellicott: see also Bp. Lightfoot *in loc.*]

[7] Greek writers commonly use the plural ἐφ' οἷς (but ἐπὶ τῷδε, Ellendt, Arr. *Al.* I. 211).—Rothe (*Versuch über Rom.* v. 12 sqq., p. 17 sqq.) has recently maintained that in the N. T. ἐφ' ᾧ always means *on the supposition, under-*

e. To, for,—of aim and of result:[1] 1 Th. iv. 7, οὐκ ἐκάλεσεν ἡμᾶς ὁ θεὸς ἐπὶ ἀκαθαρσίᾳ, *to uncleanness,* G. v. 13 (like καλεῖν ἐπὶ ξενίᾳ, Xen. *An.* 7. 6. 3, and the like,—see Sintenis, Plut. *Them.* p. 147), 2 Tim. ii. 14, E. ii. 10. Compare Xen. *An.* 5. 7. 34, *Mem.* 2. 3. 19, Plat. *Rep.* 3. 389 b, Diod. S. 2. 24, Arrian, *Al.* 1. 26. 4, 2. 18. 9, Diog. L. 1. 7. 2, and the index to Dio C. p. 148 sq. (ed. Sturz). So also, according to some, ἐφ᾽ ᾧ in Ph. iii. 12, *to which (for which).*

f. According to,—of the norm or rule: L. i. 59, καλεῖν ἐπὶ τῷ ὀνόματι, *after the name* (Neh. vii. 63). Under this head probably comes Rom. v. 14, ἐπὶ τῷ ὁμοιώματι τῆς παραβάσεως Ἀδάμ, ad (Vulg. *in*) *similitudinem peccati Adami;* for other explanations see Meyer *in loc.* 2 C. ix. 6, however, cannot be taken thus (as by Philippi, *Röm. Br.* p. 172); see above, p. 489. (Don. p. 518, Jelf 634.)

When ἐπί with the dative, in the local sense, is joined with a verb of direction or motion (Mt. ix. 16, Jo. viii. 7,—but not Mt. xvi. 18, A. iii. 11), the notion of *remaining and resting at* is implied.

d. **Παρά,** *by* (i. e., properly, *beside, by the side of,* in a local sense), is found once only with a dative of the thing, in Jo. xix. 25 (Soph. *Œd. C.* 1160, Plat. *Ion* 535 b). Elsewhere it is always joined with the dative of the person (Krüg. p. 335), and

a. Sometimes denotes the external *by, beside* (L. ix. 47), or in some one's vicinity, circle, or care: 2 Tim. iv. 13, φελόνην ἀπέλιπον παρὰ Κάρπῳ· 1 C. xvi. 2 (Aristot. *Pol.* 1. 7), L. xix. 7 (where παρὰ ἁμαρτωλῷ belongs to καταλῦσαι), Col. iv. 16, Rev. ii. 13, A. x. 6, xviii. 3.

b. Sometimes, and more frequently, it refers to that which is *by* or *with* some one in a *metaphysical* sense, that which is in the possession, power, etc., of some one (*penes*). See Mt. xix. 26, παρὰ ἀνθρώποις τοῦτο ἀδύνατόν ἐστιν, παρὰ δὲ θεῷ πάντα δυνατά· Rom. ii. 11, οὐ γάρ ἐστι προςωποληψία παρὰ θεῷ· ix. 14, L. i. 37 (where παρὰ τοῦ θεοῦ is a mere error of transcription[2]), compare Demosth. *Cor.* 352 a, εἴ ἐστι παρ᾽ ἐμοί τις

---

standing, condition, that,—in so far as; but there is no passage which will admit this meaning without a forced interpretation; compare Rückert, *Comment. zu Röm.* I. 262 (2 Aufl.).

[1] [See Ellicott on 2 Tim. ii. 14.]
[2] [The genitive is now received into the best texts on strong MS. evidence. Meyer renders "on the part of God no word shall be powerless." Compare Shilleto, Dem. *F. L.* p. 37; also Riddell, Plat. *Apol.* p. 164 sq.]

ἐμπειρία; Ja. i. 17, 2 C. i. 17. It is especially used to signify *in the judgment of*, as A. xxvi. 8, τί ἄπιστον κρίνεται παρ' ὑμῖν κ.τ.λ. (*apud vos*); Rom. xii. 16, μὴ γίνεσθε φρόνιμοι παρ' ἑαυτοῖς (Pr. iii. 7), *with yourselves*, i. e. *in your own opinion*, 1 C. iii. 19, 2 P. iii. 8 (Her. 1. 32, Plat. *Theæt.* 170 d, Soph. *Trach.* 586, Eurip. *Bacch.* 399, *Electr.* 737, Bernh. p. 257). So also in 2 P. ii. 11, οὐ φέρουσι κατ' αὐτῶν παρὰ κυρίῳ (before him, as Judge) βλάσφημον κρίσιν, if the words παρὰ κυρίῳ were genuine;[1] and substantially in 1 C. vii. 24, ἕκαστος ἐν ᾧ ἐκλήθη, ἐν τούτῳ μενέτω παρὰ θεῷ, *with, before God*, from the point of view of God's judgment. That παρά with the dative can directly signify direction *towards*[2] is not proved (Wahl in *Clavis*) by L. ix. 47, and still less by L. xix. 7 (see above, p. 492). (Don. p. 521, Jelf 637.)

e. Πρός has the same primary meaning, but in the N. T. is used only in its local sense, *by, at, on, in the* (immediate) *neighbourhood of*; e. g., Jo. xviii. 16, πρὸς τῇ θύρᾳ· xx. 11, 12, Mk. v. 11. No illustration from Greek authors is needed here.[3] So also in Rev. i. 13, περιεζωσμένος πρὸς τοῖς μαστοῖς ζώνην, *girt at the breast with a girdle* (Xen. *Cyr.* 7. 1. 33). L. xix. 37, ἐγγίζοντος ἤδη πρὸς τῇ καταβάσει τοῦ ὄρους τῶν ἐλαιῶν, must be rendered, *when he was already near by* etc.[4]—Πρός with the dative occurs far more frequently in the LXX than in the N. T. (Don. p. 523, Jelf 638.)

f. Περί and ὑπό are not found with the dative in the N. T.

---

[1] [ℵ is now added to the authorities in favour of the words: Tregelles, Westcott and Hort, insert them within brackets.]

[2] If παρά with the dative were found joined to a verb of motion, we should have to consider it an example of attraction, as in the similar case with ἐν. In Xen. *An.* 2. 5. 27, however, which even Kühner cites as the only instance, later editors read παρὰ Τισσαφέρνην, on MS. authority. On the other hand see Plutarch, *Themist.* c. 5, and Sintenis *in loc.* Yet it is not to be denied that the notion of *whither* is originally contained in the dative itself (p. 268); compare Hartung, *Ueber die Casus*, p. 81. [Kühner now reads the accusative in Xen. *An.* 2. 5. 27.]

[3] For there is no truth in Münter's remark, *Symbolæ ad interpretationem evangelii Johannis*, p. 31.

[4] [Meyer says: "πρός does not denote motion towards (De Wette), but we have a pregnant combination of the direction (ἐγγίζοντος) with the 'where:' Kühner II. p. 316" (Jelf 645. 1. *d*). Compare A. Buttmann, *Gr.* p. 340.]

Section XLIX.

PREPOSITIONS WITH THE ACCUSATIVE.

a. *Εἰς*: the antithesis of ἐκ, Rom. i. 17, v. 16.

α. In a local sense, εἰς denotes not merely *into* and *in among* (L. x. 36, A. iv. 17, also Mk. xiii. 14, εἰς τὰ ὄρη, as we say *into the mountains*), or *to*, of countries and cities, as in Mt. xxviii. 16, A. x. 5, xii. 19, al.;—but also (of level surfaces) *on*, as Mk. xi. 8, ἔστρωσαν εἰς τὴν ὁδόν· A. xxvi. 14, Rev. ix. 3, and even simply *to* (*ad*), *towards* (of motion or direction), e. g., Mk. iii. 7 [1] (Polyb. 2. 23. 1), Mt. xxi. 1, Jo. xi. 38, ἔρχεται εἰς τὸ μνημεῖον, *he comes to the tomb* (compare ver. 41), Jo. iv. 5 (compare ver. 28), xx. 1 (compare ver. 11), A. ix. 2, L. vi. 20, ἐπάρας τοὺς ὀφθαλμοὺς εἰς τοὺς μαθητάς, *towards the disciples*, Rev. x. 5 (εἰς τὸν οὐρανόν), Xen. *Cyr.* 1. 4. 11, Æschin. *Dial.* 2. 2. Where εἰς is joined with names of persons, it does not often mean *to* (πρός, or ὡς, Madv. 28, Bernh. p. 215), but *amongst, inter*, as in A. xx. 29, xxii. 21, L. xi. 49, Rom. v. 12, xvi. 26, Plat. *Prot.* 349 a, *Gorg.* 526 b. In this case it sometimes borders on the dative, as in L. xxiv. 47 : see above, § 31. 5.[2] Once it signifies *into the house of*, in A. xvi. 40, εἰσῆλθον εἰς τὴν Λυδίαν (as several [3] MSS. read) : [4] compare Lys. *Orat.* 2 *in.*, Strabo 17. 796. The better MSS. however have πρός.

b. In a temporal sense, εἰς denotes sometimes a point of time *for* which, A. iv. 3 (Herod. 3. 5. 2), or *until* which, Jo. xiii. 1, 2 Tim. i. 12 ; [5] sometimes a period (*for, on*, like ἐπί), L. xii. 19, εἰς πολλὰ ἔτη (Xen. *Mem.* 3. 6. 13).

c. When transferred to metaphysical relations, εἰς is used to express a mark or aim of any kind ; e. g., A. xxviii. 6, μηδὲν

---

[1] [We should probably read πρός in Mk. iii. 7.]

[2] Likewise in 1 C. xiv. 36, 2 C. x. 14, εἰς is a more choice expression than πρός, since in all these passages it is a metaphysical reaching to some one (into the knowledge of him, or into intercourse with him) that is spoken of.

[3] [No uncial MS. : Tischendorf says that *Rec.* has εἰς " cum minusculis ut videtur paucis."]

[4] See Valcken. *in loc.* : compare Fischer, *Well.* III. ii. p. 150, Schoem. *Isæus* 363, and on Plut. *Agis.* p. 124 (Jelf 625. 1. *a*).

[5] In this sense the more expressive ἕως (or μέχρι) is more commonly used ; and several passages quoted by the lexicographers for the meaning *usque ad* are not purely temporal, but contain the εἰς of destination or aim, as G. iii. 17 [with the reading εἰς Χριστόν], iii. 23, E. iv. 30.

SECT. XLIX.]   PREPOSITIONS WITH THE ACCUSATIVE.   495

ἄτοπον εἰς αὐτὸν γινόμενον, *towards* (on) *him;* compare Plut. *Moral.* p. 786 c.   Hence εἰς denotes

(*a*) The measure (Bernh. p. 218) to which something comes up : 2 C. x. 13, εἰς τὰ ἄμετρα καυχᾶσθαι· iv. 17 [1] (Lucian, *Dial. Mort.* 27. 7).   Compare also the familiar phrases εἰς μάλιστα and εἰς τρίς.

(β) The state into which something passes : A. ii. 20, Rev. xi. 6, H. vi. 6.   Compare also E. ii. 21 sq.

(γ) The result : Rom. x. 10 (xiii. 14), 1 C. xi. 17, εἰς τὸ κρεῖττον συνέρχεσθε.

(δ) The direction of the mind, feeling, or conduct *towards* (*erga* and *contra*): 1 P. iv. 9, φιλόξενοι εἰς ἀλλήλους· Rom. viii. 7 (Her. 6. 65), xii. 16, Mt. xxvi. 10, 3 Jo. 5, Col. iii. 9, 2 C. viii. 24, x. 1, L. xii. 10.   Col. i. 20 also, ἀποκαταλλάττειν τι εἰς αὐτόν, reduces itself to this ; compare διαλλάττειν πρός τινα, Demosth. *Ep.* 3. p. 114, Thuc. 4. 59, al.[2]   Εἰς is further applied to the direction of the thought, as A. ii. 25, Δαυὶδ λέγει εἰς αὐτόν, *aiming at him* (dicere *in* aliquem, compare Kypke *in loc.*), E. i. 10, v. 32, H. vii. 14, compare A. xxvi. 6,[3]—of the desire (*after* something), Ph. i. 23,—and of the will generally. Then to the occasion, Mt. xii. 41, εἰς τὸ κήρυγμα Ἰωνᾶ, *at the preaching;* and to the destination and purpose (Bernh. p. 219), as L. v. 4, χαλάσατε τὰ δίκτυα ὑμῶν εἰς ἄγραν, *for* the *draught;* 2 C. ii. 12, ἐλθὼν εἰς τὴν Τρωάδα εἰς τὸ εὐαγγέλιον, *for the Gospel,* i. e., in order to preach the Gospel; A. ii. 38, vii. 5, Rom. v. 21, vi. 20,[4] viii. 15, ix. 21, xiii. 14,[5] xvi. 19, H. x. 24, xii. 7,[6] 1 P. iv. 7, 2 P. ii. 12, 2 C. ii. 16, vii. 9, G. ii. 8, Ph. i. 25 ; εἰς ὅ, *for which,* Col. i. 29, 2 Th. i. 11 (compare 1 P. ii. 8) ; εἴς τι, Mt. xxvi. 8. By this are explained the phrases ἐλπίζειν, πιστεύειν εἴς τινα ; also the passages in which εἰς, joined with personal words, signifies *for,* as Rom. x. 12, πλουτῶν εἰς πάντας· L. xii. 21, 1 C. xvi. 1,

---

[1] [Corrected (for iv. 14) from ed. 5.]
[2] It is not necessary to regard this (with Fritz. *Rom.* I. 278) as a pregnant expression. It is obvious that this phrase and that which Greek writers preferred, διαλλάττειν πρός τινα, are founded on the same conception. [Compare Ellicott on Col. *l. c.*]
[3] Likewise ὁμόσαι εἰς Ἱεροσόλυμα, Mt. v. 35, must substantially be referred to this head : see Fritz. *in loc.*
[4] [Probably vi. 19.]
[5] [This is quoted by Winer for both *result* and *purpose:* see below.]
[6] [With the reading εἰς παιδείαν, found in all the uncial MSS. See Alford *in loc.*, but correct the assertion that Tischendorf had returned to εἰ παιδείαν : this is true of 1849, but in his 7th and 8th editions Tischendorf reads εἰς.]

al. (and hence borders on the dative, see above) ; and, lastly, the looser combinations in which εἰς is rendered *in reference to, as regards, with respect to* (Bernh. p. 220, Bornem. Xen. *Cyr.* p. 484), as A. xxv. 20, 2 P. i. 8, Rom. iv. 20, xv. 2 (of things, Xen. *Mem.* 3. 5. 1, Philostr. *Apoll.* 1. 16), and 2 C. xi. 10, E. iii. 16,[1] iv. 15, Rom. xvi. 5 (of persons). Objective and subjective destination, result and purpose, are sometimes not to be separated, e. g., in H. iv. 16, L. ii. 34, Rom. xiv. 1, Jude 21. Our own *zu* (*for*) also includes both.[2]—See further § 29. 3. Rem. (Don. p. 509, Jelf 625).

Εἰς does *not* bear the following meanings.—*Sub:* Rom. xi. 32 (compare G. iii. 22) ; here εἰς retains the meaning *into*, for we can just as well say *shut up into* (*in*) something.—*With* (of the instrument) : in A. xix. 3, εἰς τὸ Ἰωάννου βάπτισμα (ἐβαπτίσθημεν) is a direct answer to the question, εἰς τί οὖν ἐβαπτίσθητε; The strict answer would have been, *unto that unto which John baptised :* hence the expression is abbreviated, or rather inexact.—Nor does this preposition properly mean *before, coram*, in A. xxii. 30 (see Kühnöl) :[3] ἔστησεν (αὐτὸν) εἰς αὐτούς means *he placed him amongst them*, in the midst of them (εἰς μέσον). 2 C. xi. 6, ἐν παντὶ φανερωθέντες εἰς ὑμᾶς, is strictly *towards you* (erga), in the same sense as πρός elsewhere. That εἰς is ever equivalent to διά with the genitive is a mere fiction : εἰς διαταγὰς ἀγγέλων, A. vii. 53, most simply means *on* or *at injunctions of angels* (which indeed *in sense* amounts to *in consequence of* such injunctions), unless the explanation mentioned in § 32. 4. *b* be preferred.—As to εἰς for ἐν see § 50.

b. Ἀνά, denoting (motion) *on, up* [4] (Bernh. p. 233 sq.) occurs in the N. T.,

(1) In the phrase ἀνὰ μέσον, joined with the genitive of a place, *in the midst of, in between*, Mk. vii. 31, Mt. xiii. 25 ; and, in a figurative sense, with the genitive of a person, in 1 C. vi. 5, διακρῖναι ἀνὰ μέσον τοῦ ἀδελφοῦ.

(2) With numerals, in a distributive sense : Jo. ii. 6, ὑδρίαι

---

[1] [Compare however Ellicott *in loc.*, and on iv. 15. On πιστεύειν εἰς see p. 267, and Ellicott on G. ii. 16, 1 Tim. i. 16. On βαπτίζειν εἰς (below) see Ellicott on G. iii. 27.]

[2] In Jo. iv. 14, however, ἁλλομένου εἰς ζωὴν αἰώνιον is probably (against Baumg.-Crusius) to be rendered *into*.

[3] Compare Heind. *Protag.* 471, Stallb. Plat. *Symp.* p. 43 sq.

[4] Herm. *De Partic.* ἄν p. 5 : Primum ac proprium usum habet in iis, quæ in al. rei superficie ab imo ad summum eundo conspiciuntur : motus enim significationem ei adhærere quum ex eo intelligitur, quod non est apta visa quæ cum verbo εἶναι componeretur, tum docet usus ejus adverbialis, ut ἀλλ᾽ ἄνα ἐξ ἱδράνων. Compare also Spitzner, *De vi et usu præpositionum ἀνά et κατά* (Viteb. 1831).

χωροῦσαι ἀνὰ μετρητὰς δύο ἢ τρεῖς, *containing two or three μετρηταί apiece*, L. ix. 3, x. 1, Mk. vi. 40 (where Lachmann reads κατά, with B¹). This usage is common in Greek writers, and the preposition thus gradually assumes the nature of an adverb (Bernh. p. 234). The distributive meaning probably grew out of such phrases as ἀνὰ πᾶν ἔτος, *on every year, year by year.* (Don. p. 514, Jelf 624.)

Hug maintains (*Freiburg. Zeitschr.* vi. 41 sq.) that Jo. ii. 6 must be rendered *containing towards, about, two or three* μετρηταί; but he has not succeeded in proving that ἀνά was used in this sense. In Polyb. 2. 10. 3, Dio Cass. 59. 2, ἀνά manifestly has its distributive meaning: in Polyb. 1. 16. 2 no one will believe that the writer intends merely to state the strength of the Roman legion indefinitely, as *towards* 4,000 foot and 300 horse. In Her. 7. 184, ἀνὰ διηκοσίους ἄνδρας λογιζομένοισι ἐν ἑκάστῃ νηί is a pleonastic expression, such as we meet with frequently: we ourselves could say without any difficulty, *200 apiece .... in every ship:* Rev. iv. 8, ἓν καθ' ἓν αὐτῶν ἔχον ἀνὰ πτέρυγας ἕξ, is a similar example. To express *towards, about, amounting to* a number, the Greeks use ἐπί with the accusative.

c. Διά with the accusative is the preposition which denotes the *ground* (ratio), not the *purpose* (not even in 1 C. vii. 2).² It answers to *on account of* (so in Jo. vii. 43, x. 19, xv. 3, al.); or, where the motive of an action is intended, to *from*, as Mt. xxvii. 18, διὰ φθόνον, *from envy*, E. ii. 4, διὰ τὴν πολλὴν ἀγάπην (Diod. S. 19. 54, διὰ τὴν πρὸς τοὺς ἠτυχηκότας ἔλεον· Aristot. *Rhet.* 2. 13, Demosth. *Conon* 730 c). Rom. iii. 25, which even Reiche has misunderstood, was correctly explained by Bengel.³ In H. v. 12, διὰ τὸν χρόνον means *on account of the time*, considering the time (during which you have enjoyed Christian instruction),⁴—not, as Schulz renders, *after so long*

---

¹ [Tisch., Westcott and Hort, read κατά. In L. ix. 3 ἀνά is doubtful. Lünemann adds Mt. xx. 9.]

² It is only *per consequens* that the notion of purpose is implied in διὰ τὰς πορνείας, *on account of the fornications let every man have his own wife:* the fornications are the ground of this injunction, inasmuch as the design is that they may be prevented. In Greek writers also *purpose* is sometimes thus linked with διά; see the commentators on Thuc. 4. 40, 102. [Winer's view that διά does not *directly* denote purpose seems to be held by most grammarians. On the other side see Jelf 627. 3. *a*, Liddell and Scott s. v., Arnold and Poppo on Thuc. 4. 40, Poppo on Thuc. 2. 89, Shilleto, Demosth. *Fals. Leg.* pp. 3, 153.]

³ [Bengel's rendering is *propter prætermissionem peccatorum:* see Trench, *Syn.* § xxxiii., Alford *in loc.*]

⁴ The phrase occurs with substantially the same meaning in Polyb. 2. 21. 2, and frequently: see Bleek *in loc.*—Schulz would introduce the temporal meaning of διά into H. ii. 9; but διὰ τὸ πάθημα τοῦ θανάτου means *on account of*

a time. Sometimes διά with the accusative appears to indicate the means, as indeed the ground or motive and the means are in themselves very nearly akin (comp. Demosth. *Cor.* 354 a, Xen. *Mem.* 3. 3. 15, Liv. 8. 53), and the poets sometimes join the accusative with διά even when it is used in a local sense, see Bernh. p. 236. See *e.g.* Jo. vi. 57, κἀγὼ ζῶ διὰ τὸν πατέρα καὶ ὁ τρώγων με ζήσεται δι' ἐμέ; which exactly resembles Long. *Pastor.* 2. p. 62 (Schæf.) διὰ τὰς νύμφας ἔζησε· Plut. *Alex.* 668 e. Here, however, the proper meaning is, *I live by reason of the Father*, i. e., because the Father lives. Compare Plat. *Conv.* 283 e; and see Fritz. *Rom.* I. 197, who quotes as parallel Cic. *Rosc. Am.* 22. 63, ut, *propter quos* hanc suavissimam lucem adspexerit, eos indignissime luce privarit. More or less similar are Demosth. *Zenoth.* 576 a, Aristoph. *Plut.* 470, Æschin. *Dial.* 1. 2, Dion. H. III. 1579.[1] H. v. 14 and vi. 7, however, certainly have no place here. The same may be said (against Ewald and De Wette) of Rev. xii. 11, ἐνίκησαν διὰ τὸ αἷμα: compare vii. 14, and the words which immediately follow, καὶ οὐκ ἠγάπησαν τὴν ψυχήν κ.τ.λ. As to Rom. viii. 11 (where it is true the reading is uncertain), see Fritzsche;[2] and as to Jo. xv. 3, Meyer *in loc.* In 2 Cor. iv. 5, H. ii. 9, 2 P. ii. 2 (where Schott still renders διά by *per*, which even gives a false sense,—see on the other hand Bengel *in loc.*), and in Rev. iv. 11, *on account of* is altogether suitable. The same may be said of Rom. viii. 20 (where Schott still has *per*):[3] in Rom. xv. 15, διὰ τὴν χάριν τὴν δοθεῖσάν μοι, it will not be supposed that διά denotes the means because we find in xii. 3 διὰ τῆς χάριτος τῆς δοθείσης μοι; both expressions are appropriate. 1 Jo. ii. 12 is rightly translated by Lücke. 2 P. ii. 2 is clear of itself. In 2 P. iii. 12, δι' ἥν may be referred to ἡ τοῦ θεοῦ ἡμέρα, and rendered *on account of*; but is not without meaning if joined (as by Bengel) with παρουσία.

---

the *suffering of death,* and is explained by the well-known connexion which the apostolic writers assume between the sufferings and the exaltation of Christ.

[1] Compare Wyttenbach, Plut. *Mor.* II. p. 2 (Lips.), Sintenis, Plut. *Themist.* 121, Poppo, *Thuc.* III. ii. 517.

[2] ["*Propter ejus qui in vobis habitat spiritum*, i. q. quoniam ejus spiritus domicilium in vobis collocavit." Fritzsche.—א is now added to the authorities for the genitive, which is received by Tischendorf and Westcott and Hort.]

[3] Here διὰ τὸν ὑποτάξαντα forms an antithesis to οὐχ ἑκοῦσα, *not voluntarily, but by reason of him who subjected,*—at the will and command of God. Probably Paul designedly avoided saying διὰ τοῦ ὑποτάξαντος, as if ὁ θεὸς ὑπέταξεν αὐτήν. The proper and immediate cause of the ματαιότης was Adam's sin.

Lastly, in G. iv. 13 δι' ἀσθένειαν τῆς σαρκός is probably not to be understood (Schott) as expressing state, condition (δι' ἀσθενείας) but means *on account of, by occasion of* an infirmity: see Meyer *in loc.* (Don. p. 510, Jelf 627.)

d. Κατά in its local primary sense denotes

a. Motion *down upon* (compare Æschin. *Dial.* 3. 19), or *in, through, over* (Xen. *Cyr.* 6. 2. 22): L. viii. 39, ἀπῆλθε καθ' ὅλην τὴν πόλιν κηρύσσων· xv. 14, λιμὸς κατὰ τὴν χώραν, *through the land,* over the whole land; A. viii. 1 (2 Macc. iii. 14, Strabo 3. 163); A. v. 15, ἐκφέρειν κατὰ[1] τὰς πλατείας, *through the streets,* along the streets; A. viii. 36 (Xen. *An.* 4. 6. 11), L. ix. 6, xiii. 22, A. xi. 1, xxvii. 2 (Xen. *Cyr.* 8. 1. 6, Raphel on Acts *l. c.*).[2] In all cases it is applied to levels and extended surfaces. So also in A. xxvi. 3, τὰ κατὰ τοὺς Ἰουδαίους ἔθη καὶ ζητήματα, *the customs ... which extend through* (are usual amongst) *the Jews.*[3]

b. Motion *upon* or *towards,* as Ph. iii. 14 (κατὰ σκοπόν, *towards the mark*), A. viii. 26, xvi. 7, L. x. 32 (Æsop 88. 4, Xen. *Cyr.* 8. 5. 17); also mere direction towards (geographical situation, *versus*), A. ii. 10, τῆς Λιβύης τῆς κατὰ Κυρήνην· xxvii. 12, λιμένα βλέποντα κατὰ λίβα[4] (Xen. *An.* 7. 2. 1). Thus κατὰ πρόςωπόν τινος means *towards the face of,* i.e., *before the eyes of,* L. ii. 31, A. iii. 13; similarly κατ' ὀφθαλμούς, G. iii. 1, Xen. *Hiero* 1. 14, like κατ' ὄμμα, Eurip. *Androm.* 1064, and κατ' ὄμματα, Soph. *Ant.* 756. In Rom. viii. 27, also, κατὰ θεὸν ἐντυγχάνειν does not mean *apud Deum* (in a local sense), but strictly *towards God, before God.*[5] Akin to this is the use of

---

[1] [Lachm., Tisch., Treg., Westcott and Hort, read καὶ εἰς for κατά.]
[2] Κατά in its local sense is not really synonymous with ἐν (as is maintained by Kühnöl on A. xi. 1): κατὰ τὴν πόλιν means *throughout the city,* καθ' ὁδόν *along the road,* on the road (as a line). Even κατ' οἶκον, where the primary meaning of κατά is most concealed, differs in its conception from ἐν οἴκῳ (as *at the house* differs from *in the house*).—In several phrases in which ἐν might have been employed κατά has established itself by usage.
[3] Hence arises the meaning *with,* as in οἱ καθ' ὑμᾶς ποιηταί, A. xvii. 28 (compare xiii. 1), and other phrases; see above, p. 241 [and 193]. Κατά with a personal pronoun thus forms, mainly in later writers, a mere periphrasis for the possessive pronoun: see Hase, *Leo Diac.* p. 230.
[4] [See Alford *in loc.,* Conyb. and Howson, *St. Paul* II. 400, Smith, *Dict. of Bible* II. 830.]
[5] Against this explanation (which has been adopted by Fritz., Krehl, al.) various objections have recently been raised, especially by Meyer and Philippi. The least important of these is, that in this case we should have had κατ' αὐτόν:

the preposition in regard to time: either as in A. xvi. 25, κατὰ τὸ μεσονύκτιον, *towards midnight;* or as in Mt. xxvii. 15, καθ' ἑορτήν, *during the feast*,[1] Mt. i. 20, κατ' ὄναρ, *during the dream,* secundum quietem (Herod. 2. 7. 6, κατὰ φῶς by day Xen. *Cyr.* 3. 3. 25, κατὰ βίον Plat. *Gorg.* 488 a), H. ix. 9,[2]—also H. iii. 8 (from the LXX), κατὰ τὴν ἡμέραν τοῦ πειρασμοῦ, *at the day,* etc., and κατὰ τὸ αὐτό, *at the same time,* A. xiv. 1. Next it is used of both place and time in a distributive sense;—in the first instance with plural nouns, as κατὰ φυλάς, *by tribes,* Matt. xxiv. 7, κατὰ τόπους (A. xxii. 19), κατὰ δύο, *by two,* 1 C. xiv. 27 (Plat. *Ep.* 6. 323 c), Mk. vi. 40 *v. l.;* then very frequently with a singular noun, as A. xv. 21, κατὰ πόλιν, *from city to city* (Diod. S. 19. 77, Plut. *Cleom.* 25, Dio Chr. 16. 461, Palæph. 52. 7), κατ' ἐνιαυτόν, *year by year,* H. ix. 25 (Plat. *Pol.* 298 e, Xen. *Cyr.* 8. 6. 16 ; κατὰ μῆνα, Xen. *An.* 1. 9. 17, Dio C. 750. 74), καθ' ἡμέραν, *daily,* A. ii. 46, 1 C. xvi. 2 (Herm. *Vig.* p. 860).[3]

In its figurative use, κατά is the preposition of relation and reference to something. Sometimes in a general sense, as in E. vi. 21, τὰ κατ' ἐμέ, quæ ad me pertinent, A. xxv. 14 ; or to define a general expression more exactly (Her. 1. 49, Soph. *Trach.* 102, 379), E. vi. 5, οἱ κατὰ σάρκα κύριοι, *in respect of the flesh, as regards the flesh;* Rom. ix. 5, ἐξ ὧν (Ἰουδαίων) ὁ Χριστὸς τὸ κατὰ σάρκα (1 P. iv. 14), A. iii. 22, Rom. vii. 22,—also Rom. xi. 28 and xvi. 25. Sometimes in a special sense, to denote

(a) The standard, rule, law,—*according to* or *in conformity with:* E. iv. 7, Mt. xxv. 15, Jo. ii. 6, L. ii. 22, κατὰ νόμον, H. ix. 19 (Xen. *Cyr.* 5. 5. 6), A. xxvi. 5, Rom. xi. 21, κατὰ φύσιν· Mt. ix. 29, κατὰ τὴν πίστιν ὑμῶν, *suitably to your*

---

it is not difficult to feel the emphasis which lies in the substantive, and such an emphasis is also visibly marked by the position of κατὰ θεόν, though ὑπὲρ ἁγίων contains the principal moment of thought. The rendering *according to God* introduces an entirely superfluous thought into the passage, for certainly from the πνεῦμα no intercession different from this could be expected.

[1] [This is taken distributively by Fritzsche and Grimm.—Κατ' ὄναρ Meyer regards as simply adverbial, *in the way of a dream, dream-wise* (§ 51. 2. g).]

[2] [Winer in all probability refers here to the reading καθ' ὅν (Rec., Tischendorf ed. 2) : recent editors (including Tischendorf) read καθ' ἥν.]

[3] Καθ' ἑαυτόν, *by oneself,* is commonly referred to this usage (see *e. g.* Passow), but wrongly, for the formula is not distributive. Καθ' ἑαυτόν properly means *in reference to oneself,* and thus confines something to a single subject; hence the meaning *by oneself,* adv. *seorsum.* On ἔχειν καθ' ἑαυτόν see Fritz. *Rom.* III. 212.

SECT. XLIX.] PREPOSITIONS WITH THE ACCUSATIVE. 501

faith, as it deserves; 2 C. iv. 13, Rom. ii. 2, κατὰ ἀλήθειαν·
Mt. ii. 16, κατὰ [τὸν] χρόνον, *according to the time.* Hence it
denotes similarity, kind (pattern): H. viii. 8 sq., συντελέσω . . .
διαθήκην καινήν, οὐ κατὰ τὴν διαθήκην, ἣν ἐποίησα κ.τ.λ. (1 K.
xi. 10), A. xviii. 14. When joined with names of persons κατά
commonly denotes *according to some one's mind*, Col. ii. 8
(E. ii. 2), 2 C. xi. 17,—and *will*, Rom. xv. 5, 1 C. xii. 8,[1]—or
according to the model and *example* of some one, as G. iv. 28,
κατὰ Ἰσαάκ, *after the manner of Isaac, ad exemplum Isaaci,*
1 P. i. 15, E. iv. 23[2] (Plat. *Parm.* 126 c, Lucian, *Pisc.* 6. 12,
Eunuch. 13, Dio C. 376. 59[3]). It is also used of authors: τὸ
κατὰ Ματθαῖον εὐαγγέλιον is *the Gospel* (the Gospel history) *as
written down by Matthew* (as apprehended and exhibited by
Matthew). On εἶναι κατὰ σάρκα, κατὰ πνεῦμα, Rom. viii. 5,
see the commentators. Of a more general kind is the (Pauline)
formula κατ' ἄνθρωπον, *after the fashion of man, in the ordinary
manner of men*[4] (in various contexts), Rom. iii. 5, G. i. 11, iii.
15, 1 C. ix. 8, 1 P. iv. 6 (see Wiesinger *in loc.*): see Fritz.
Rom. I. 159 sq.[5] Compare, in the same direction, Rom. iv. 4,
κατὰ χάριν, *in the way of grace;* 1 C. ii. 1, καθ' ὑπεροχὴν λόγου·
Ph. iii. 6, E. vi. 6, Rom. xiv. 15, A. xxv. 23, ἀνδράσι τοῖς κατ'
ἐξοχὴν τῆς πόλεως.

(*b*) The occasion[6] (and the motive)—a meaning very nearly
related to the preceding (hence in Rom. iv. 4 κατὰ χάριν may
also be *from grace*): Mt. xix. 3, ἀπολῦσαι τὴν γυναῖκα κατὰ
πᾶσαν αἰτίαν, *on any ground* (Kypke *in loc.*, compare Pausan. 5.
10. 2, 6. 18, 2. 7), Rom. ii. 5, A. iii. 17, κατὰ ἄγνοιαν ἐπράξατε,
in consequence of ignorance (Raphel *in loc.*), Ph. iv. 11, οὐχ ὅτι

---

[1] Compare Stallb. Plat. *Gorg.* p. 91.
[2] [This should be either iv. 22 or iv. 24.]
[3] Compare Kypke and Wetstein on G. iv. 28, Marle, *Floril.* p. 64 sq.
[4] [See Ellicott on G. i. 11, Lightfoot on G. iii. 15.]
[5] In 2 C. vii. 9, 10, λυπεῖσθαι κατὰ θεόν and λύπη κατὰ θεόν do not mean *sorrow produced by God* (Kypke *in loc.*), but, as Bengel strikingly says, "animi Deum spectantis et sequentis,"—*sorrow according to God*, i. e., according to God's mind and will. In the next sentence, Paul might have written in the same way ἡ κατὰ τὸν κόσμον λύπη. But ἡ τοῦ κόσμου λύπη has a somewhat different meaning, *sorrow of the world*, i. e., such as the world (those who belong to the world) has and feels (naturally, respecting things of the κόσμος). This difference in the expressions was also rightly estimated by Bengel. In 1 P. iv. 6 κατὰ ἀνθρώπους means *after the manner of men*, and is defined more exactly by the annexed σαρκί, as κατὰ θεόν means *after the manner of God*, and is more exactly defined by πνεύματι (for God is πνεῦμα).
[6] [Ellicott on Tit. iii. 5, Jelf 629. 3. *e.*]

καθ' ὑστέρησιν λέγω, *from want* (in consequence of my suffering want), Tit. iii. 5, 1 P. i. 3, κατὰ τὸ αὐτοῦ ἔλεος·[1] E. i. 5, Her. 9. 17 (κατὰ τὸ ἔχθος), al. Compare Diog. L. 6. 10, Arrian, *Al.* 1. 17. 13. Also H. xi. 7, ἡ κατὰ πίστιν δικαιοσύνη, *the righteousness which is in consequence of faith*.

(c) Destination *for* or *to* (Jo. ii. 6), 2 Tim. i. 1,[2] Tit. i. 1 (compare Rom. i. 5, εἰς); and (necessary) result, 2 C. xi. 21, κατ' ἀτιμίαν λέγω, *for dishonour* (Her. 2. 152, Thuc. 5. 7, 6. 31). The meaning *cum* must be given up, though κατά may sometimes be rendered *with*. In Rom. x. 2, ζῆλος θεοῦ ἀλλ' οὐ κατ' ἐπίγνωσιν is *zeal of*[3] *God, but not according to* (in accordance with) *knowledge*, i. e., such as manifests itself in consequence of knowledge (compare above κατ' ἄγνοιαν), 1 P. iii. 7. In H. xi. 13, κατὰ πίστιν ἀπέθανον κ.τ.λ. means, *they died in conformity with faith, without having received*, etc.: it was in conformity with faith (with the nature of πίστις) that they died as those who had only seen from afar the fulfilment of the promises, for the thought which belongs to κατὰ πίστιν is contained in the second participial clause. (Don. p. 511, Jelf 629.)

e. Ὑπέρ denotes motion *over* and *beyond* (Her. 4. 188, Plat. *Crit.* 108 e, Plut. *Virt. Mul.* p. 231 Lips.). In the N. T. κατά never has this *local* meaning, but is always used figuratively, to denote *beyond, above,* in number, rank, or quality. See A. xxvi. 13, φῶς περιλάμψαν . . . ὑπὲρ τὴν λαμπρότητα τοῦ ἡλίου· Mt. x. 24, οὐκ ἔστι μαθητὴς ὑπὲρ τὸν διδάσκαλον· Phil. 16, Mt. x. 37, ὁ φιλῶν πατέρα ὑπὲρ ἐμέ (Æsch. *Dial.* 3. 6), 2 C. i. 8 (Epict. 31, 37), G. i. 14; also 2 C. xii. 13, τί γάρ ἐστιν ὃ ἡττήθητε ὑπὲρ τὰς λοιπὰς ἐκκλησίας, *small beyond the other churches* (gradation downwards). As to ὑπέρ after comparatives, see § 35. 1. (Don. p. 513, Jelf 630.)

f. Μετά denotes motion *in amongst* (*Iliad* 2. 376); then motion *behind, after* something. In prose however it is more

---

[1] Accordingly κατά is sometimes found in parallelism with the (instrumental) dative, as in Arrian, *Al.* 5. 21. 4, κατ' ἔχθος τὸ Πώρου μᾶλλον ἢ φιλίᾳ τῇ 'Αλεξάνδρου. See Fritz. *Rom.* I. 99.

[2] Matthies gives an artificial explanation, remarking that it cannot be lexically shown that κατά denotes the *aim*. But this meaning is very simply contained in the nature of this preposition. See further Matth. 581. b. α, ς. [See Ellicott on Tit. i. 1, 2 Tim. i. 1, Jelf 629. 3. *d.*]

[3] [Winer here renders the genitive literally: in § 30. 1 he gives the explanation " zeal *for* God."]

SECT. XLIX.]   PREPOSITIONS WITH THE ACCUSATIVE.   503

frequently used for (rest) *behind,—post :* H. ix. 3, μετὰ τὸ δεύτερον καταπέτασμα (Paus. 3. 1. 1). In all other passages of the
N. T. μετά is the temporal *after* (as the antithesis of πρό).
This is its meaning in Mt. xxvii. 63, where the popular expression can present no difficulty (see Krebs, *Obs.* p. 87 sq.); and
in 1 C. xi. 25, μετὰ τὸ δειπνῆσαι, which we have no right to
render *whilst they were eating* on account of Mt. xxvi. 26
(ἐσθιόντων αὐτῶν),—compare on the other side L. xxii. 20.
Indeed even the familiar μεθ' ἡμέραν, *interdiu*,[1] properly means
post lucem, after daybreak. (Don. p. 520, Jelf 636.)

g. Παρά in its primary sense denotes motion *beside, by*, in
reference to a line or extended surface : Mt. iv. 18, περιπατῶν
παρὰ τὴν θάλασσαν . . . εἶδε κ.τ.λ., *walking along the seaside*
(Xen. *Cyr.* 5. 4. 41, *An.* 4. 6. 4, 6. 2. 1, Plat. *Gorg.* 511 e),
Mt. xiii. 4, ἔπεσε παρὰ τὴν ὁδόν, *fell by the side of* (along) *the
road.* It is then applied to a point in space, which belongs
however to an extended object, as ἔρχεσθαι παρὰ τὴν θάλασσαν
to the sea, Mt. xv. 29, A. xvi. 13 ; ῥίπτειν or τιθέναι παρὰ τοὺς
πόδας τινός, *by the feet*, Mt. xv. 30, A. iv. 35.[2] But παρά is also
thus used with verbs of rest,[3] e. g., to *sit, stand, lie*, παρὰ τὴν
θάλασσαν or τὴν λίμνην or παρὰ τὴν ὁδόν (*propter* mare,
viam), Mt. xx. 30, L. v. 1 sq., xviii. 35, H. xi. 12, A. x. 6, ᾧ
ἐστὶν οἰκία παρὰ θάλασσαν (ver. 32); compare Xen. *An.* 3.
5. 1, 7. 2. 11, Paus. 1. 38. 9, Æsop. 44. 1.[4]

Further παρά indicates that something has not hit the mark,
but has fallen *beside* the mark; and hence, according to the
nature of the words with which it is connected, it sometimes
signifies *beyond* (as Rom. xii. 3, with which Fritzsche compares
Plutarch, *Mor.* 83 sq., θαυμασταὶ παρ' ὃ δεῖ), sometimes *below*,
as in 2 C. xi. 24, πεντάκις τεσσαράκοντα παρὰ μίαν, *forty passing
over one, forty save one* (Joseph. *Antt.* 4. 8. 1,—compare H. ii.
7, from the LXX). See Bernhardy, p. 258.

In the former sense παρά is used figuratively,

(*a*) In comparisons : L. xiii. 2, ἁμαρτωλοὶ παρὰ πάντας, *beyond all* (more than all,—see ὑπέρ, and compare § 35. 2),

---

[1] Ellendt, Arr. *Alex.* 4. 13. 10 (Jelf 636. 2).
[2] Compare Held, Plut. *Timol.* 356.
[3] The transition to this usage is found in such expressions as Polyb. 1. 55. 7, ἐν τῇ παρὰ τὴν Ἰταλίαν κειμένῃ πλευρᾷ τῆς Σικελίας, *lying* (extending) *by* (towards) *Italy.*
[4] Hartung, *Die Casus* p. 83.

iii. 13, H. i. 9 (from the LXX), iii. 3 (Dio Cass. 152. 16). Analogous to this is ἄλλος παρά, 1 C. iii. 11, *other than*, just as ἄλλος ἤ is used elsewhere.[1] Rom. xiv. 5, κρίνειν ἡμέραν παρ' ἡμέραν, *to judge* (esteem) *day before day*, i. e., prefer one day to another.

(*b*) With the meaning *against, contrary to*: A. xviii. 13, παρὰ νόμον (Xen. *Mem.* 1. 1. 18, Lucian, *Demon.* 49); Rom. i. 26, παρὰ φύσιν, *præter* naturam (Plat. *Rep.* 5. 466 d, Plut. *Educ.* 4. 9); Rom. iv. 18, παρ' ἐλπίδα, *præter* spem (Plat. *Pol.* 295 d); Rom. xvi. 17, H. xi. 11 (Thuc. 3. 54, Xen. *An.* 2. 5. 41, 5. 8. 17, 6. 4. 28, Philostr. *Apoll.* 1. 38): we also speak of *overstepping, transgressing*, the law. The opposite would be κατὰ φύσιν κ.τ.λ.; compare Xen. *Mem. l. c.*, Plut. *Educ.* 4. 9.

(*c*) Rom. i. 25, παρὰ τὸν κτίσαντα, *passing over the Creator*: consequently, *instead of the Creator*.

Once παρά indicates the ground or reason: in 1 C. xii. 15, παρὰ τοῦτο, *on this account*,—properly, *by the side of this*, since this is so [2] (Plut. *Camill.* 28, Dio C. 171. 96, Lucian, *Paras.* 12, and often). In Latin *propter*, from *prope* (compare *propter flumen*), has become the ordinary causal preposition.[3] (Don. p. 521, Jelf 637.)

h. Πρός, *to, towards*, with verbs of motion or of mere direction: see A. iv. 24, E. iii. 14, 1 C. xiii. 12, πρόςωπον πρὸς πρόςωπον, *face* turned *towards face*. Sometimes the import of the accusative is apparently lost, πρός signifying *with*,—particularly in connexion with names of persons, Mt. xiii. 56, Jo. i. 1,[4] 1 C. xvi. 6 (Demosth. *Apat.* 579 a); but here πρός indicates (ideal) *annexation*. The appropriateness of this case is still discernible in Mk. iv. 1, ὁ ὄχλος πρὸς τὴν θάλασσαν ἐπὶ τῆς γῆς ἦν, *towards the sea* (by the sea) *on the land*, Mk. ii. 2, and still more so in A. v. 10, xiii. 31, Ph. iv. 6: see Fritz. *Mark*, p. 201 sq., and compare Schoem. *Isæus*, p. 244. The Latin *ad* unites both meanings.

---

[1] Compare Stallb. Plat. *Phileb.* p. 51 (Jelf. 503. *Obs.* 2).
[2] Weber, *Demosth.* p. 521 (Don. p. 522, Jelf 637. 3. *d*).
[3] Vig. p. 862, V., Fritzsche, *Quæst. Lucian.* p. 124 sq., Mätzner, *Antiph.* p. 182.
[4] [Compare Huther on 1 Jo. i. 2: "In the N. T. πρός with the accusative has frequently the meaning *with*, but differs from πρός with the dative in that it indicates *being with* as not merely a *being near* or *beside*, but as a living union,"—implying rather the active notion of intercourse, than a mere passive idea. Similarly Luthardt, *Das Johann.-Evang.* I. 290, Meyer and Westcott on Jo. i. 1.]

The temporal applications of πρός justify themselves at the first glance: πρὸς καιρόν *for a time,* L. viii. 13, Jo. v. 35, H. xii. 10 sq., and πρὸς ἑσπέραν *towards evening,* L. xxiv. 29 (Wetstein I. 826). Compare above,[1] s. v. ἐπί.

In its figurative use πρός indicates the point towards which something is directed. Hence the result and issue, as 2 P. iii. 16, ἃ . . . στρεβλοῦσιν . . . πρὸς τὴν ἰδίαν αὐτῶν ἀπώλειαν· H. v. 14, ix. 13, 1 Tim. iv. 7 (Simplicius *in Epict.* 13. p. 146), Jo. xi. 4. This preposition, however, particularly indicates the direction of the mind towards something; e. g., H. i. 7, πρὸς τοὺς ἀγγέλους λέγει, *in reference to* (pointing to them in what he says), L. xx. 19, Rom. x. 21 (but not H. xi. 18), like *dicere in aliquem.* Compare Plutarch, *De εἰ ap. Delph.* c. 21, Xen. *Mem.* 4. 2. 15. Specially, πρός denotes

(*a*) The state of feeling *towards* some one, *erga* and *contra*:[2] L. xxiii. 12, 1 Th. v. 14, 2 C. iv. 2, vii. 12, A. vi. 1, H. xii. 4, Col. iv. 5, Rev. xiii. 6.

(*b*) Design (direction of the will), and aim (purpose): 1 C. x. 11, xii. 7, Mt. vi. 1, H. vi. 11, A. xxvii. 12, 2 C. xi. 8, 1 P. iv. 12. Hence πρὸς τί, *for what purpose* (quo consilio), Jo. xiii. 28; compare Soph. *Aj.* 40.

(*c*) Consideration of, regard to something: Mt. xix. 8, Μωσῆς πρὸς τὴν σκληροκαρδίαν ὑμῶν ἐπέτρεψεν κ.τ.λ., having regard to, *on account of* your stubbornness (Polyb. 5. 27. 4, 38. 3. 10).

(*d*) The rule or law *according to* which one guides himself, *in conformity with:* L. xii. 47, G. ii. 14, 2 C. v. 10, Lucian, *Conscr. Hist.* 38, Plat. *Apol.* 40 e, Æschin. *Dial.* 3. 17. Hence also the standard *according to* which a comparison is made: Rom. viii. 18, οὐκ ἄξια τὰ παθήματα τοῦ νῦν καιροῦ πρὸς τὴν μέλλουσαν δόξαν ἀποκαλυφθῆναι, *compared with*,—as if, held *to,* or *by,* Bar. iii. 36 (Thuc. 6. 31, Plat. *Gorg.* 471 e, *Hipp. Maj.* 281 d, Isocr. *Big.* p. 842, Aristot. *Pol.* 2. 9. 1, Demosth. *Ep.* 4. 119 a.[3] (Don. p. 523, Jelf 638.)

---

[1] [Probably "below,"—referring to what is said of ἐπί with *accusative.*]
[2] This meaning (*against*) is but rarely found with verbs which do not themselves contain the notion of hostility, as Sext. Empir. 3. 2 (Dio C. 250. 92). This is added in qualification of what is said in my *Observationes in epist. Jac.* p. 16. [Winer *loc. cit.* had denied that πρός *itself* ever has the meaning *contra.* Compare Lightfoot, *Colossians,* p. 272 sq.]
[3] Compare Wolf, *Leptin.* p. 251, Jacobs, Æl. *Anim.* II. 340.

That in such phrases as διατίθεσθαι διαθήκην πρός τινα, διακρίνεσθαι πρός τινα, εἰρήνην ἔχειν πρός τινα (Rom. v. 1), κοινωνία πρός τι, 2 C. vi. 14 (comp. Philo, *ad Caj.* 1007, Himer. *Eclog.* 18. 3), etc.,[1] πρός does not signify *cum*,[2] but has the simple meaning "towards," has been already admitted by Bretschneider and by Wahl. In H. iv. 13 also, πρὸς ὃν ἡμῖν ὁ λόγος, the preposition expresses direction, and Kühnöl might have spared his remark "πρός significat *cum*" (compare Elsner *in loc.*).—Schleusner's explanation of the phrase εὔχεσθαι πρὸς θεόν, *precari a deo*, only deserves notice as a striking example of unlimited empiricism.

i. **Περί**, *about* (*round about*), is used in the first instance of place: as A. xxii. 6, περιαστράψαι φῶς περὶ ἐμέ, *to shine round about me*, to encircle me with light, L. xiii. 8 ; also with verbs of rest, Mk. iii. 34, οἱ περὶ αὐτὸν καθήμενοι· Mt. iii. 4, εἶχε ζώνην περὶ τὴν ὀσφύν, *about the loins* (encircling them). Then of time: Mk. vi. 48 περὶ τετάρτην φυλακήν, *about the fourth nightwatch* (*circa* in Latin), Mt. xx. 3 (Æschin. *Ep.* 1. 121 b), A. xxii. 6. Lastly, of the object around which an action or a state moves, so to speak: A. xix. 25, οἱ περὶ τὰ τοιαῦτα ἐργάται (Xen. *Vectig.* 4. 28), L. x. 40 (Lucian, *Indoct.* 6), 1 Tim. vi. 4, νοσῶν περὶ ζητήσεις (Plat. *Phædr.* 228 e). Hence it is sometimes equivalent to *in regard to*,[3] as Tit. ii. 7, 1 Tim. i. 19, 2 Tim. iii. 8, Xen. *Mem.* 4. 3. 2, Isocr. *Evag.* 4 ; compare *errorem circa literas habuit*, and the like, in Quintilian and Suetonius. See above, § 30. 3. Rem. 5, and Ast, Plat. *Legg.* p. 37, but especially *Glossar. Theodoret.* p. 317 sqq.

The phrase οἱ περὶ τὸν Παῦλον, *Paul and his companions*, A. xiii. 13,[4] is worthy of note: compare οἱ περὶ Ξενοφῶντα, Xen. *An.* 7. 4. 16, οἱ περὶ Κέκροπα, Xen. *Mem.* 3. 5. 10. In later writers this formula is also used to denote the principal person alone (Herm. *Vig.* p. 700); and it is probable that Jo. xi. 19, αἱ περὶ Μάρθαν καὶ Μαρίαν, should be thus understood, for

---

[1] See Alberti, *Observ.* p. 303, Fritz. *Rom.* I. 252.
[2] The Greeks also use μετά in such phrases, but apparently it was rather in the later language that this became common : Malal. 2. 52, ἐπολέμησαν μετ' ἀλλήλων· 13. p. 317, 337, 18. p. 457. [See above, s. v. μετά (with genitive).]
[3] [Ellicott on 1 Tim. i. 19.]
[4] Greek writers, as is well known, form a similar periphrasis with ἀμφί, but in plain prose περί is much more common. The fact that οἱ περὶ τὸν Παῦλον denotes, not merely those surrounding Paul (companions, etc.), but together with these the principal person himself, probably arises from the graphic power of the preposition : περί indicates that which *incloses*, and hence the phrase means *the Paul-company*, so to speak. Somewhat analogous is the German *Müllers* (genitive), in the sense of *Müller and his household*: in Franconia they say instead *die Müllerschen*,—still including the head of the family.

the following αὐταῖς can only refer to the two sisters.[1] Examples, not however clearly distinguished, may be found in Wetstein I. 915 sq., Schwarz, *Commentar.* p. 1074, Schweigh. *Lexic. Polyb.* p. 463. See also Bernh. p. 263. (Don. p. 516, Jelf 632.)

k. Ὑπό primarily denotes local motion *under:* Mt. viii. 8, ἵνα μου ὑπὸ τὴν στέγην εἰσέλθῃς· L. xiii. 34, ἐπισυνάξαι τὴν νοσσιὰν ὑπὸ τὰς πτέρυγας (Xen. *Cyr.* 5. 4. 43, Plutarch, *Thes.* 3). It is also used of rest, i.e., of being (extending) *under* a surface, as in A. ii. 5, οἱ ὑπὸ τὸν οὐρανόν· L. xvii. 24 (Plat. *Ep.* 7. 326 c), 1 C. x. 1 (Her. 2. 127, Plut. *Themist.* 26, Æsop. 36. 3);[2] also Rom. iii. 13 (from the LXX), ἰὸς ἀσπίδων ὑπὸ τὰ χείλη αὐτῶν, *under* (behind) *their lips,*—compare Her. 1. 12, κατακρύπτειν ὑπὸ τὴν θύρην. Thence in a figurative sense:[3] Rom. vii. 14, πεπραμένος ὑπὸ τὴν ἁμαρτίαν, *sold under sin*—into the power of sin; Mt. viii. 9, ἔχων ὑπ' ἐμαυτὸν στρατιώτας (Xen. *Cyr.* 8. 8. 5), *under me*, i.e., subjected to me (to my power); 1 P. v. 6; and frequently εἶναι or γίνεσθαι ὑπό τι, *to be placed in subjection to*, Mt. viii. 9, Rom. iii. 9, 1 Tim. vi. 1, G. iii. 10, iv. 2, 21 (Lucian, *Abdic.* 23). It is used of time in A. v. 21, ὑπὸ τὸν ὄρθρον (Lucian, *Amor.* 1), *close upon, towards* (like the local ὑπὸ τὸ τεῖχος): in this sense ὑπό is frequently used in Greek, e. g., ὑπὸ νύκτα, ὑπὸ τὴν ἕω, etc.,[4] and *sub* in Latin. (Don. p. 525, Jelf 639.)

l. Ἐπί. 1. Of place. Motion *over* (over a surface): Mt. xxvii. 45, σκότος ἐγένετο ἐπὶ πᾶσαν τὴν γῆν· xiv. 19, ἀνακλιθῆναι ἐπὶ τοὺς χόρτους·[5] A. vii. 11 (xvii. 26). Motion *upon* or *to*, either from above or from below; hence, down *upon*, as Mt. x. 29, ἐπὶ γῆν, A. iv. 33; up *on*, A. x. 9, ἀνέβη ἐπὶ τὸ δῶμα· Mt. xxiv. 16, 1 P. ii. 24 (Xen. *Cyr.* 3. 1. 4); also *on* (motion on), Jo. xiii. 25, ἐπιπίπτειν ἐπὶ τὸ στῆθος, *on* the breast (Jo. xxi. 20): *up before* (a high tribunal), Mt. x. 18, L. xii. 11. Ἐπί

---

[1] [Lachm., Treg., Westcott and Hort, read τὴν M. for τὰς περὶ M.—Meyer argues against the opinion that the sisters alone are meant: see also Alford *in loc.*]

[2] Thus in Eur. *Alc.* 907, λῦπαί τε φίλων τῶν ὑπὸ γαῖαν (changed by Monk into ὑπὸ γαίας) would be admissible. Compare Matthiæ, Eur. *Hec.* 144. The phrase certainly does not belong to later Greek merely (Palæph. 10. 1).

[3] Bernh. p. 267, Boissonade, *Nic.* p. 56.

[4] See Alberti, *Observ.* p. 224, Ellendt, Arr. *Al.* I. 146, Schweigh. *Lexic. Polyb.* p. 633.

[5] [Here, and also A. xvii. 26, recent editors receive the genitive.]

also denotes generally the mark or aim *towards, on, to* which (one goes, strives, comes, etc.): L. xv. 4, xxii. 52, A. viii. 36, Ph. iii. 14 *v. l.*, Xen. *Cyr.* 1. 6. 39, *An.* 6. 2. 2 (Kypke *in loc.*). It is seldom merely *to* (of persons), Mk. v. 21, A. i. 21.[1] From the primary meaning may easily be explained A. x. 10, ἔπεσεν ἐπ' αὐτὸν ἔκστασις (v. 5), A. i. 26, ἔπεσεν ὁ κλῆρος ἐπὶ Ματθίαν· v. 28, ἐπαγαγεῖν ἐπί τινα τὸ αἷμα ἀνθρώπου τινός· Jo. i. 33, al. Our *auf* (*upon*), which is almost always applicable as a rendering for ἐπί, represents the same view: only in Mt. xxvii. 29, ἐπέθηκαν κάλαμον ἐπὶ τὴν δεξιάν, we should say *into*, not *upon*; here however better MSS. have ἐν τῇ δεξιᾷ, and the common reading is not justified by Rev. xx. 1. It is only in appearance that ἐπί is joined with verbs of rest: Mt. xiii. 2, ὁ ὄχλος ἐπὶ τὸν αἰγιαλὸν εἰστήκει, *stood* (had placed itself) *over the shore;* compare *Odyss.* 11. 577, Diod. S. 20. 7. Mt. xix. 28, καθίσεσθε ἐπὶ δώδεκα θρόνους (Paus. 1. 35. 2), 2 C. iii. 15, κάλυμμα ἐπὶ τὴν καρδίαν κεῖται· A. x. 17, xi. 11, must be judged of in the same way as the similar examples of εἰς. See § 50. 4, Ellendt, Arr. *Alex.* II. 91.[2]

2. When applied to time, ἐπί denotes the period *over* which something extends, as in L. iv. 25 ἐπὶ ἔτη τρία, *over, during,*

---

[1] We must not class with such passages L. x. 9, ἤγγικεν ἐφ' ὑμᾶς ἡ βασιλεία τοῦ θεοῦ. Here a gift from heaven is spoken of, which comes *down* on men. Compare A. i. 8.

[2] Ja. v. 14, προσευξάσθωσαν ἐπ' αὐτόν, may mean, *let them pray over him* (pray, folding their hands over him,—compare A. xix. 13), or *pray down upon, towards, him;* but it may also signify *pray over,* or *above him* [expressing a relation of *rest*, not of *motion*], for we very often find ἐπί with the accusative where we might have expected ἐπί with the genitive or dative. A recent commentator should not have dismissed this explanation so lightly. In L. v. 25, ἐφ' ὃ κατέκειτο (the reading of the best MSS.) may either be explained in accordance with the above remark, or be rendered *on which he lay stretched* (the reference is to a *surface*). What has been said will entirely justify ἔστη ἐπὶ τὸν αἰγιαλόν, which is received in Jo. xxi. 4 by Lachm. [and Tisch. in ed. 8] on good authority; compare Xen. *Cyr.* 3. 3. 68, and see above in the text. Matthäi is wrong in calling this a *semigræcam correctionem.* Certainly the difference between ἐπί with the accusative and ἐπί with the genitive and dative is sometimes but small. If however it is supposed that the accusative *stands for* the genitive or dative in Mk. xv. 24 (we also say *über die Kleidung loosen*, cast lots *over* the clothing), Ph. ii. 27 (receive sorrow *upon* sorrow, one sorrow coming upon that which already exists), a closer examination of the passages will soon show that this view is incorrect. On the other hand, the dative might certainly have been used in L. xxiii. 28, Rev. xviii. 11,—compare L. xix. 41, Rev. xviii. 20; and in Rev. v. 1 the accusative [?] would even have been more correct. But the two constructions [ἐπί τινι and ἐπί τι with e. g. κλαίω] express conceptions somewhat different, as indeed we also say *sich über eine Sache freuen*. [In L. xix. 41 recent editors receive αὐτήν. On Rev. v. 1 see Alford.]

three years, A. xiii. 31, xix. 10, H. xi. 30 (compare Her. 3. 59, 6. 101, Thuc. 2. 25, Xen. *Cyr.* 6. 2. 34, Plat. *Legg.* 12. 945 b, Strabo 9. 401): hence ἐφ' ὅσον, Mt. ix. 15, 2 P. i. 13 (Polyæn. 6. 22), *as long as*. More rarely ἐπί indicates the point of time *towards* or *about* which something happens, as in A. iii. 1 (see Alberti *in loc.*).

3. In a figurative sense, ἐπί denotes

(*a*) The number and the degree up to which something comes: Rev. xxi. 16, ἐπὶ σταδίους δώδεκα χιλιάδων¹ (Her. 4. 198, Xen. *Cyr.* 7. 5. 8, Polyb. 4. 39. 4), Rom. xi. 13, ἐφ' ὅσον, *in quantum*, i. e., *quatenus*.

(*b*) Superintendence and power *over*: Rev. xiii. 7, ἐδόθη αὐτῷ ἐξουσία ἐπὶ πᾶσαν φυλήν· H. iii. 6, x. 21 (Xen. *Cyr.* 4. 5. 58). Compare L. ii. 8, xii. 14, βασιλεύειν ἐπί τινα, L. i. 33, Rom. v. 14, also Malal. 5. p. 143.

(*c*) The direction of the mind (feeling),—hence *towards*,² *erga* and *contra*: Mt. x. 21, L. vi. 35, 2 C. x. 2, Rom. ix. 23 (but not 1 P. iii. 12), Sturz, *Ind. to Dio Cass.* p. 151. Hence with verbs of *trusting, setting hope upon*, Mt. xxvii. 43, 2 C. ii. 3, 1 Tim. v. 5, 1 P. i. 13; also σπλαγχνίζεσθαι ἐπί τινα, *to have compassion upon* (towards), Mt. xv. 32, Mk. viii. 2.

(*d*) The direction of thought and of discourse, as Mk. ix. 12, H. vii. 13 (Rom. iv. 9 ³). Direction of will: hence we find ἐπί where design and aim are expressed, L. xxiii. 48 (Plat. *Crito* 52 b), Mt. iii. 7 (Xen. *Mem.* 2. 3. 13, *Cyr.* 7. 2. 14, Fischer, *Ind. ad Palæph.* s. v. ἐπί), Mt. xxvi. 50, ἐφ' ὅ (Plat. *Gorg.* 447 b); and also where aim and result coincide, as H. xii. 10. Lastly, the preposition assumes an entirely general sense, *in regard to*, as Mt. xxv. 40, 45: for Rom. xi. 13, see above, (*a*). As to πιστὸς ἐπί τι, Mt. xxv. 21, see Fritz. *in loc.*⁴

---

¹ Here we also say *an*, *auf*.
² Franke, *Demosth.* 127.
³ [That is, if λέγεται be supplied (§ 64. 2, Fritz., Alford).]
⁴ [" Rarior est constructio πιστὸν εἶναι ἐπί τι. Noli autem putare, arctissime cohærere ἐπί cum voce πιστός, sed significat *fidelem esse ratione rei habita*." Fritz. *l. c.*]

Section L.

INTERCHANGE, ACCUMULATION, AND REPETITION OF PREPOSITIONS.

1. The same preposition may be found in the same sentence, or in parallel passages (especially of the synoptical Gospels), joined with different cases and expressing different relations: H. ii. 10, δι' ὃν τὰ πάντα καὶ δι' οὗ τὰ πάντα· Rev. v. 1, xi. 10, xiv. 6; compare 1 C. xi. 9, 12, οὐκ ἀνὴρ διὰ τὴν γυναῖκα, ... ἀνὴρ διὰ τῆς γυναικός. Compare Demosth. *Philipp.* 2. p. 25 c. A more remote example of this kind is H. xi. 29, διέβησαν τὴν ἐρυθρὰν θάλασσαν ὡς διὰ ξηρᾶς; where the compound διαβαίνειν is followed by the accusative, and then διά itself by the genitive. Compare Jos. xxiv. 17, οὓς παρήλθομεν δι' αὐτῶν; Wis. x. 18.

A nice distinction between the meanings of a preposition when thus joined to different cases sometimes almost entirely disappears in usage: Mt. xix. 28, ὅταν καθίσῃ ... ἐπὶ θρόνου δόξης αὐτοῦ, καθίσεσθε καὶ ὑμεῖς ἐπὶ δώδεκα θρόνους; xxiv. 2, οὐ μὴ ἀφεθῇ λίθος ἐπὶ λίθον· and Mk. xiii. 2,[1] οὐ μὴ ἀφεθῇ λίθος ἐπὶ λίθῳ. Compare Jos. v. 15, where we find in one sentence ἐφ' ᾧ νῦν ἕστηκας ἐπ' αὐτοῦ; Gen. xxxix. 5, xlix. 26, Ex. viii. 3, xii. 7, Jon. iv. 10. See also Rev. v. 1, 13, vi. 2, 16, vii. 1, xiii. 16. Thus the Greeks use with equal frequency ἀναβαίνειν ἐπὶ τοὺς ἵππους and ἐπὶ τῶν ἵππων:[2] in the LXX we even find ἀναβαίνειν ἐπὶ ταῖς οἰκίαις, Joel ii. 9. In Rev. xiv. 9 we have λαμβάνει τὸ χάραγμα ἐπὶ τοῦ μετώπου αὐτοῦ ἢ ἐπὶ τὴν χεῖρα αὐτοῦ: see also xiii. 1. Compare further Diog. L. 2. 77, ... ἐπὶ τί ἥκου; ἔφη ἐπὶ τῷ μεταδώσειν κ.τ.λ.; Pol. 6. 7. 2, τραφέντας ὑπὸ τοιούτοις· but in 10. 25. 1, τραφεὶς καὶ παιδευθεὶς ὑπὸ Κλέανδρον; and on the whole matter see Jacobs, *Anthol.* III. 194, 286, Bernh. p. 200 sq. (Jelf 648). It is in connexion with ἐπί that we most frequently meet with this apparent indifference as to case.[3] Compare ἐλπίζειν ἐπί τινι and τινα, 1 Tim. iv. 10, v. 5; πεποιθέναι ἐπί τινι and τινα, 2 C. i. 9, ii. 3; καταστῆσαι ἐπί τινος and τινι, L. xii. 42, 44 (κόπτεσθαι ἐπί τινα in Rev. i. 7, and ἐπί τινι in xviii. 9 *v. l.*); ὁ ἐπὶ τοῦ κοιτῶνος, A. xii. 20, and ὁ ἐπὶ ταῖς ἄρκυσι,

---

[1] [Better L. xxi. 6: in Mk. *l. c.* the most probable reading is λίθον.]
[2] Bornem. Xen. *Conv.* p. 272.
[3] Schneider, Plat. *Civ.* I. 74.

Xen. *Cyr.* 2. 4. 25 : see Lob. *Phryn.* p. 474 sq. Moreover, on ἐπί expressing *aim* with the genitive see Bremi, *Æsch.* p. 412, with the dative and accusative, Stallb. Plat. *Gorg.* p. 59 ; on ἐφ' ἑαυτοῦ and ἐφ' ἑαυτῷ, Schoem. *Isœus* p. 349 ; on παρά with the genitive instead of the dative, Schæf. *Dion.* p. 118 sq. Hence in particular cases in which Greek writers do not happen to furnish exact parallels (as L. i. 59, καλεῖν ἐπί τινι· compare Ezr. ii. 61, Neh. vii. 63, al.) we should not be justified in pronouncing the construction un-Greek, particularly if something analogous is met with (Matth. 586. η), or if the case employed can very well be *conceived* in combination with the preposition. On the other hand, the N. T. writers never write ἐπὶ Κλαυδίῳ or Κλαύδιον in the place of ἐπὶ Κλαυδίου ; nor do they ever join ἐπί expressing *condition* with the genitive or accusative. It was not until a later period that the interchange of cases joined in different senses to a preposition (e. g., the use of μετά with genitive and accusative without alteration of meaning), began to appear in the written language : see above, p. 455.

That in one and the same sentence the same preposition with the same case should be used to express different relations and meanings, cannot be considered strange in Greek any more than in other languages. See, for example, L. xi. 50, ἵνα ἐκζητηθῇ τὸ αἷμα πάντων τῶν προφητῶν . . . . ἀπὸ τῆς γενεᾶς ταύτης ἀπὸ τοῦ αἵματος Ἅβελ κ.τ.λ.; Rom. xv. 13, εἰς τὸ περισσεύειν ὑμᾶς ἐν τῇ ἐλπίδι ἐν δυνάμει πνεύματος ἁγίου ; Jo. ii. 23, ἦν ἐν τοῖς Ἱεροσολύμοις ἐν τῷ πάσχα ἐν τῇ ἑορτῇ ; 2 C. vii. 16, χαίρω ὅτι ἐν παντὶ θαρρῶ ἐν ὑμῖν ; xii. 12, 1 C. iii. 18, Rom. i. 9, E. i. 3, 14, ii. 3, 7, iv. 22, vi. 18, Ph. i. 26, ii. 16, 1 Th. ii. 14, 2 Th. i. 4, Col. i. 29, ii. 2, iv. 2, H. v. 3, ix. 11 sq., Jo. iv. 45 (xvii. 15[1]), A. xvii. 31, 2 P. i. 4 (Philostr. *Her.* 4. 1, Arrian, *Epict.* 4. 13. 1).

2. The two *different* prepositions in the same sentence in Phil. 5, ἀκούων σου τὴν ἀγάπην καὶ τὴν πίστιν, ἣν ἔχεις πρὸς τὸν κύριον Ἰησοῦν καὶ εἰς πάντας τοὺς ἁγίους, are usually explained by referring the words πρὸς τὸν κύριον, as regards the sense, to πίστιν, and εἰς πάντας τοὺς ἁγίους to ἀγάπην. Such a *chiasmus*[2] would not be at all strange in itself ; compare Plat. *Legg.* 9. 868 b (see Ast, *Animadv.* p. 16), Horat. *Serm.* 1. 3. 51, and the commentators *in loc.* It is simpler however to take πίστις

---

[1] [Placed within brackets probably because of the two explanations of τοῦ πονηροῦ, *the evil one* (Meyer, Luthardt, al.), *the evil* (Olshausen, al.).]
[2] [Jelf 904. 3.—See Ellicott *in loc.* ; also on E. iv. 12.]

in the sense of *fidelity*, and to consider both prepositional clauses, πρὸς τὸν κύριον καὶ εἰς πάντας τοὺς ἁγίους, as equally dependent on πίστις, making no distinction between the prepositions; see Meyer. Some MSS. have εἰς in the place of πρός, but this is a mere correction, occasioned by the tendency towards making the phraseology uniform, and by observation of the fact that elsewhere faith in Christ is always πίστις ἡ εἰς Χριστόν : the expression πίστιν ἔχειν πρός τινα, however, presents no difficulty whatever, and it occurs at least in Epiphan. *Opp.* II. 335 d. As to L. v. 15,[1] Jo. vii. 42, 2 C. x. 3, 1 Th. ii. 3, Rom. iv. 18, x. 17, E. iv. 12, 1 Jo. iii. 24, 1 Th. iv. 7, 1 P. ii. 12, no remark is required: on 1 C. iv. 10, 2 C. iv. 17, iii. 5, xiii. 3, 1 C. xii. 8, see the more recent commentators. On the other hand, in 1 Th. ii. 6, οὔτε ζητοῦντες ἐξ ἀνθρώπων δόξαν οὔτε ἀφ' ὑμῶν οὔτε ἀπ' ἄλλων, the two prepositions are entirely synonymous, as also in Jo. xi. 1, A. xix. 23.[2] In Rom. iii. 30 Paul certainly intended no distinction in sense, for from a dogmatic point of view πίστις may with equal propriety be conceived of either as the source or as the means of blessedness (G. iii. 8, E. ii. 8). From Greek writers compare Paus. 7. 7. 1, αἱ ἐκ πολέμων καὶ ἀπὸ τῆς νόσου συμφοραί ; Isocr. *Permut.* 738, Arrian, *Al.* 2. 18. 9, Diod. S. 5. 30.[3] There is just as little distinction between the prepositions in 2 Jo. 2, τὴν ἀλήθειαν τὴν μένουσαν ἐν ἡμῖν καὶ μεθ' ἡμῶν ἔσται ; and in Ex. vi. 4, ἐν ᾗ (γῇ) καὶ παρῴκησαν ἐπ' αὐτῆς ; Jon. iv. 10. Lastly, the distinction which Billroth makes between διὰ δόξης and ἐν δόξῃ in 2 C. iii. 11 can hardly stand when confronted with actual usage: see above, p. 482, and on διά expressing *state*, p. 474. On the other hand, the difference in meaning between κατά and ἐπί in 1 C. xi. 4, 10, and between ἐκ and διά in 1 P. i. 23, is obvious.

3. Prepositions of kindred meaning are interchanged in parallel passages of the Gospels and elsewhere. Thus in Mt. xxvi. 28 (Mk. xiv. 24 [4]) we find αἷμα τὸ περὶ πολλῶν ἐκχυνόμενον, but in L. xxii. 20, τὸ ὑπὲρ πολλῶν ἐκχ.; Mt. vii. 16, μή τι συλλέγουσιν ἀπὸ ἀκανθῶν σταφυλήν, but L. vi. 44, οὐκ ἐξ ἀκανθῶν συλλέ-

---

[1] [Recent editors omit ὑπ' αὐτοῦ.]
[2] [A mistaken reference : perhaps A. xxiii. 34.]
[3] Schæf. *Gnom.* p. 203, and *Soph.* I. 248, Bornem. Xen. *Mem.* p. 45.
[4] [Here recent editors read ὑπέρ.]

γουσι σῦκα; Mt. xxiv. 16, φευγέτωσαν ἐπὶ τὰ ὄρη (upon the mountains,—compare Palæph. 1.10), but Mk. xiii. 14, φευγέτωσαν εἰς τὰ ὄρη (into the mountains); Jo. x. 32, διὰ ποῖον αὐτῶν ἔργον λιθάζετέ με; but in ver. 33, περὶ καλοῦ ἔργου οὐ λιθάζομέν σε; H. vii. 2, ᾧ καὶ δεκάτην ἀπὸ πάντων ἐμέρισεν Ἀβραάμ, but ver. 4, ᾧ καὶ δεκάτην Ἀβραὰμ ἔδωκεν ἐκ τῶν ἀκροθινίων; Rom. iii. 25, εἰς ἔνδειξιν τῆς δικαιοσύνης αὐτοῦ, but ver. 26, πρὸς τὴν ἔνδειξιν τῆς δικαιοσύνης αὐτοῦ. Compare Xen. Cyr. 5. 4. 43, πρὸς αὐτὸ τὸ τεῖχος προσήγαγον . . . οὐκ ἐθέλω ὑπ' αὐτὰ τὰ τείχη ἄγειν. To this head belong also H. xi. 2, ἐν ταύτῃ (τῇ πίστει) ἐμαρτυρήθησαν οἱ πρεσβύτεροι, but ver. 39, πάντες μαρτυρηθέντες διὰ τῆς πίστεως ("*in* faith,"[1] meaning *ut instructi fide*); the phrases εὔχεσθαι, προσεύχεσθαι, εὐχαριστεῖν, δέησις, περί or ὑπέρ τινος (Rom. x. 1, 2 C. i. 11, E. vi. 18, Col. i. 3, 9, 1 C. i. 4, E. i. 16, compare *Acta Apocr.* p. 53); and the expressions *suffer* or *die* περὶ or ὑπὲρ ἁμαρτιῶν (the former *on account of*, the latter *for sins*), 1 C. xv. 3, 1 P. iii. 18. Sometimes even good MSS. are divided between ὑπέρ and περί (G. i. 4), as indeed these prepositions were often interchanged by the transcribers: compare Weber, *Dem.* p. 129. In Eurip. *Alc.* 180, where οὗ θνήσκειν πέρι occurs instead of the more usual ὑπέρ, some recent editors have proposed to correct the text (see Monk *in loc.*), but certainly without sufficient reason.

Sometimes we find a preposition used in one of two parallel phrases and omitted in the other: e. g., 1 P. iv. 1, παθόντος ὑπὲρ ἡμῶν σ α ρ κ ί, immediately followed by ὁ παθὼν ἐ ν σ α ρ κ ί;[2] in L. iii. 16, A. i. 5, and xi. 16, βαπτίζειν ὕ δ α τ ι, but βαπτίζειν ἐ ν ὕ δ α τ ι in Mt. iii. 11, Jo. i. 26, 33.[3] This difference does not affect the sense, but the two phrases were in the first instance differently conceived. Πάσχειν ἐν σαρκί means *to suffer in the flesh* (body), but πάσχειν σαρκί *to suffer according to* (§ 31. 6) *the flesh;* βαπτίζειν ἐν ὕδατι, *to baptise* (by immersing) *in water*, but βαπτίζειν ὕδατι, *to baptise with water*. Here and in most other passages it is obvious that the expressions are equivalent in sense,[4] but it is not to be supposed that one is used for the other. Compare further E. ii. 1, νεκροὶ τοῖς παραπτώμασι,

---

[1] [See above, p. 484: Delitzsch connects ἐν ταύτῃ closely with the verb.]
[2] [Recent editors omit ἐν, on strong MS. authority.]
[3] But always βαπτίζειν ἐν πνεύματι, never βαπτίζειν πνεύματι. [The latter is received by Westcott and Hort in Mk. i. 8.]
[4] So in Aristot. *Anim.* 4. 10. p. 111 (Sylb.) λαμβάνεσθαι τριόδοντι is *to be caught with a trident* (like τῇ χειρί *with the hand*), but ληφθῆναι ἐν τῷ τριόδοντι, which immediately follows, is *to have been caught on the trident*. Schneider and Bekker however read ἄν for ἐν after ληφθῆναι.

but Col. ii. 13, νεκροὶ ἐν τοῖς παραπτώμασι ; 2 C. iv. 7, ἵνα ἡ ὑπερβολὴ τῆς δυνάμεως ᾖ τοῦ θεοῦ καὶ μὴ ἐξ ἡμῶν; Mt. vii. 2, compared with L. vi. 38, 1 Jo. iii. 18.

4. It was at one time supposed that, in the N. T.,[1] the prepositions ἐν and εἰς in particular [2] are directly and without distinction used for each other. It was maintained that, in virtue of the Hebrew idiom, ἐν with verbs of motion or direction is equivalent to *in* with the accusative : e. g., Mt. x. 16, ἐγὼ ἀποστέλλω ὑμᾶς ὡς πρόβατα ἐν μέσῳ λύκων· Jo. v. 4, ἄγγελος κατέβαινεν ἐν τῇ κολυμβήθρᾳ· L. vii. 17, ἐξῆλθεν ὁ λόγος ἐν ὅλῃ τῇ Ἰουδαίᾳ· Mk. v. 30, ἐπιστραφεὶς ἐν τῷ ὄχλῳ· Rom. v. 5, ἡ ἀγάπη τοῦ θεοῦ ἐκκέχυται ἐν ταῖς καρδίαις ἡμῶν· L. v. 16, Jo. viii. 37, 1 C. xi. 18, al. (In Rev. xi. 11 the reading is very doubtful; and Mk. i. 16 and 1 Tim. iii. 16 certainly have no place here.) It was also held that εἰς in combination with verbs of rest is *in* with the ablative : e. g., A. vii. 4, (ἡ γῆ) εἰς ἣν ὑμεῖς νῦν κατοικεῖτε· Mk. ii. 1, εἰς οἶκόν [3] ἐστι· Jo. i. 18, ὁ ὢν εἰς τὸν κόλπον τοῦ πατρός· ix. 7, νίψαι εἰς τὴν κολυμβήθραν, and elsewhere.[4]

a. To begin with ἐν: Greek writers—in the first place Homer—are accustomed sometimes to join this preposition with verbs of motion in order to indicate at the same time the result of the motion, that is, *rest*.[5] This usage (the result of a love of conciseness peculiar to the Greek nation) is not found in the earlier prose writers ; for in Thuc. 4. 42, 7. 17, Xen. *Hell.* 7. 5. 10, the readings are now corrected on MS. authority [6] (Matth. 577).

---

[1] Glassii *Philol. S.* I. 412 sq. (ed. Dathe).
[2] See also Sturz, *Lexic. Xen.* II. 68, 166.
[3] [Ἐν οἴκῳ, Lachm., Treg., Tisch. (ed. 8), Westcott and Hort.]
[4] To these two cases the above observation must here be limited ; for where either ἐν or εἰς might equally well be used, according to the view taken of the relation, it cannot be said that one stands for the other : e. g., τοῦτο ἐγίνετό μοι and τοῦτο ἐγίνετο εἰς ἐμέ.
[5] The same may be said of the Hebrew ב, when it occurs in conjunction with verbs of motion : see my *Exeget. Studien* I. 49 sqq., [Ewald, *Lehrb.* p. 556]. Compare further Krebs, *Obs.* 78 sq.—Ἥκω ἐν does not come under this head (Lucian, *Paras.* 34, compare Poppo, *Thuc.* III. ii. 891). Nor can perfects or pluperfects with ἐν, as καταπεφυγέναι ἐν τόπῳ, Plat. *Soph.* 260 c, Thuc. 4. 14, etc., be considered parallel to the examples given above. They show however the origin of this usage (compare Bernh. p. 208), and in good writers the usage is in general confined to such cases (Krüg. p. 321). Lastly, the (not uncommon) combination ἔρχεσθαι ἐν, L. ix. 46, xxiii. 42, Rev. xi. 11, al., is perhaps also to be excepted, when it means *to arise in*. [In Rev. xi. 11 Lachm., Tisch., and Düsterd. read ἐν αὐτοῖς : ℵ has εἰς αὐτούς.]
[6] [There is still some difference of opinion on this point. In Thuc. 4. 42 the

SECT. L.] REPETITION OF PREPOSITIONS. 515

In later writers see *e. g.* Ælian 4. 18, κατῆλθε Πλάτων ἐν Σικελίᾳ, i. e., *he came (and remained) in Sicily* ; Paus. 6. 20. 4, αὐτοὶ κομίσαι φασὶ τῆς Ἱπποδαμείας τὰ ὀστᾶ ἐν Ὀλυμπίᾳ· 7. 4. 3, al., Alciphr. 2. 3. p. 227 (Wagn.), Xen. Eph. 2. 12, Arrian, *Epict.* 1. 11. 32, Æsop 16, 127, 343 (De Fur.), Dio Cass. 1288. 23.[1] This may be applied to Mt. x. 16,[2] Rev. xi. 11.[3] Perhaps also (with Baumg.-Crusius) to Jo. v. 4, especially if these words are a later addition ; for the other explanation, *he went down in the pool* (into its depths, in order to produce the ταραχή, see Lücke), has this against it, that in so circumstantial a narrative the angel's descent from heaven must have been mentioned before anything else.   In all the other passages it is only in appearance that ἐν stands for εἰς : L. vii. 17 means *went forth* (spread abroad) *in all Judæa* ; Mk. v. 30, *he turned round in the crowd* ; L. v. 16, *he was in the deserts, withdrawing himself.* In Mt. xiv. 3, ἔθετο ἐν φυλακῇ, if the word[4] is genuine, is conceived exactly in the same way as the Latin *ponere in loco* (for which we in German say *put into*, taking a different but still a correct view of the relation) : a similar case is Jo. iii. 35, πάντα δέδωκεν ἐν τῇ χειρὶ αὐτοῦ· 2 C. viii. 16 (*Iliad* 1. 441, 5. 574,—compare also Ellendt, *Lexic. Soph.* I. 598).   So also in Mt. xxvi. 23, ὁ ἐμβάψας ἐν τῷ τρυβλίῳ, *who dips in the dish,* just as accurate an expression as our *dip into the dish* (compare Æsop 124. 1) : 1 C. xi. 18, συνέρχεσθαι ἐν ἐκκλησίᾳ means *come together in an assembly* (as we speak of meeting *in the market, in society*) ; Ph. iv. 16, ὅτι καὶ ἐν Θεσσαλονίκῃ . . . εἰς τὴν χρείαν μου ἐπέμψατε, is an instance of brachylogy,—*ye sent to me in Thessalonica,* i. e., to me when I was in Thessalonica (compare Thuc. 4. 27, and Poppo *in loc.*).   In Jo. viii. 37 we

---

reading ἐν Λευκαδίᾳ ἀπῄεσαν is retained by Poppo,—also by Kühner (*Gr.* II. 469 : ed. 2) and Jelf (645. 1. *a*). Poppo says : Bekkerus invitis omnibus membranis ἀπῄεσαν ; sed ἀπῄεσαν ἐν videntur valere posse ἀπῆλθον καὶ ἀπῇσαν ἐν (ed. min. II. ii. p. 68).]

[1] Compare Heind. Plat. *Soph.* p. 427 sq., Poppo, *Thuc.* I. i. 178 sq., Schæf. *Demosth.* III. p. 505.

[2] [Meyer closely connects together πρόβατα ἐν μέσῳ λύκων : "ye as my messengers will be in the situation of sheep who are in the midst of wolves."]

[3] The fact that εἰσέρχεσθαι ἐν appears to be an imitation of בּוֹא בְ does not affect the question, for the Hebrew phrase is undoubtedly to be explained in the same way.

[4] [That is, the verb ἔθετο. In ed. 2 Tisch. omitted καὶ ἔθετο : in ed. 8 he reads καὶ ἐν φυλακῇ ἀπέθετο (Westcott and Hort,—also Lachm. and Treg., with addition of τῇ).]

may be in doubt how to take ἐν ὑμῖν (see Lücke), but there is no doubt that ἐν does not stand for εἰς. On Ja. v. 5 see De Wette.[1] In Mt. xxvii. 5, ἐν τῷ ναῷ is *in the temple*. In Rom. v. 5 the use of the perfect tense might of itself have led to the true explanation : compare Poppo on Thuc. 4. 14.[2]

b. The passages quoted as examples of the use of εἰς for ἐν are more singular. In Greek authors, however, εἰς is not unfrequently joined to verbs of rest. Such combinations originally included the additional idea of the (preceding or accompanying) *motion*, in accordance with the principle of breviloquence referred to above.[3] See *e. g.* Xen. *Cyr.* 1. 2. 4, νόμῳ εἰς τὰς ἑαυτῶν χώρας ἕκαστοι τούτων πάρεισιν· Ælian 7. 8, Ἡφαιστίων εἰς Ἐκβάτανα ἀπέθανε· Isæus 5. 46 (compare A. xxi. 13),[4] Diod. S. 5. 84, διατρίβων εἰς τὰς νήσους· Paus. 7. 4. 3. (The combination of εἰς with such verbs as ἵζειν, καθέζεσθαι—καθῆσθαι —Mk. xiii. 3, compare Eurip. *Iph. T.* 620, is of a somewhat different kind.[5]) By this may be explained : Mk. ii. 1, where we also say *er ist ins Haus* [*he is into the house* [6]], i. e., he has gone into the house, and is there now (Her. 1. 21, Arrian, *Al.* 4. 22. 3, Paus. 8. 10. 4 and Siebelis *in loc.*, Liv. 37. 18 ?, Curt. 3. 5. 10, Vechner, *Hellenol.* p. 258 sq.),—compare Mk. xiii. 16, L. xi. 7 ; A. viii. 40, Φίλιππος εὑρέθη εἰς Ἄζωτον, *Philip was found* carried away *to Azotus* (compare ver. 39, πνεῦμα κυρίου ἥρπασε τὸν Φίλιππον) [7]—compare Esth. i. 5, *Evang. Apocr.* p.

---

[1] [This passage is explained below, no. 5. In Mt. xxvii. 5 we should probably read εἰς τὸν ναόν.]

[2] Passages of Greek authors in which ἐν has been wrongly supposed to stand for εἰς are more correctly explained by Ellendt, Arr. *Al.* I. 247. On εἰς for ἐν see *ib.* II. 91. On Latin phrases in which *in* with the ablative has appeared to stand for *in* with the accusative, see Kritz, *Sallust.* II. 31 sq.

[3] Heind. Plat. *Protag.* p. 467, *Acta Monac.* I. 64 sq., II. 47, Schæf. *Demosth.* I. 194 sq., Schoem. Plut. *Agis.* 162 sq., Herm. Soph. *Aj.* 80, Jacobs, Æl. *Anim.* p. 406 (Jelf 646). As to Latin see Hartung, *Ueber die Casus*, p. 68 sqq.

[4] Εἰς χωρίον τῆς Ἀρκαδίας θνήσκει, Steph. Byz. p. 495 (Mein.), is different.

[5] See Buttm. Demosth. *Mid.* p. 175, Schweigh. *Lexic. Herod.* I. 282, Valcken. *Herod.* 8. 71, al., Poppo, *Thuc.* III. i. p. 659, Fritz. *Mark*, p. 558. [Fritzsche renders Mk. xiii. 3, *quum in montem olivarum consedisset;* adding "nam καθῆσθαι est *sedere*, consequens verbi *considere* καθίζειν (ἑαυτόν)."]

[6] [Compare the English provincial expression *to home*, for *at home*. The use of *to* for *at* with names of places is very common in Devonshire and Cornwall ; see Stoddart, *Philos. of Language*, p. 173, Farrar, *Gr. Synt.* p. 98, Halliwell, *Arch. Dict.* s. v. "to." Comp. Jamieson, *Dict.* s. v. "intill."—In Mk. ii. 1 we must read ἐν οἴκῳ.]

[7] Wesseling, *Diod. Sic.* II. 581.

SECT. L.] REPETITION OF PREPOSITIONS. 517

447; A. vii. 4, εἰς ἣν ὑμεῖς νῦν κατοικεῖτε (Xen. An. 1. 2. 24, Xen. Eph. 2. 12, Theodoret, Opp. I. 594); Mk. x. 10, where the arrangement of the words must be remarked; also probably A. xviii. 21, δεῖ με τὴν ἑορτὴν τὴν ἐρχομένην ποιῆσαι εἰς Ἱεροσόλυμα, —but the genuineness of these words has been suspected, and they are rejected by the recent editors; Jo. xx. 7, ἐντετυλιγμένον εἰς ἕνα τόπον, *wrapped together* (and put) *into one place*. In A. xii. 19, however, εἰς Καισάρειαν belongs grammatically to κατελθών: in A. xx. 14, εἰς is *to*. In A. xix. 22, ἐπέσχε χρόνον εἰς τὴν Ἀσίαν is probably not simply local, *he remained behind in Asia*, but, *he remained behind for Asia*, in order to labour there still. In A. iv. 5, συναχθῆναι αὐτῶν τοὺς ἄρχοντας ... εἰς Ἱεροσόλυμα, Beza's is the only admissible explanation:[1] here however the good MSS. have ἐν. In A. ii. 39, οἱ εἰς μακράν are those who dwell *far away in the distance*.[2] Jo. i. 18, ὁ ὢν εἰς τὸν κόλπον (although here said in reference to God), must probably be traced back to the originally local meaning of the phrase,— "who rests placed on or against the bosom."[3] In Jo. ix. 7, εἰς τὴν κολυμβήθραν belongs, as regards the sense, to ὕπαγε as well as to νίψαι (compare ver. 11), *go down and wash into the pool* (compare L. xxi. 37), see Lücke; though in itself νίπτεσθαι εἰς ὕδωρ is as correct an expression as *in aquam macerare* (Cato, R. rust. 156. 5) or our *sich in ein Becken waschen* (Arrian, Epict. 3. 22. 71).[4] Still easier is Mk. i. 9, ἐβαπτίσθη εἰς τὸν Ἰορδάνην. In L. viii. 34, ἀπήγγειλαν εἰς τὴν πόλιν κ.τ.λ. means *they carried word of it into the city*: Mt. viii. 33 is more circumstantial, ἀπελθόντες εἰς τὴν πόλιν ἀπήγγειλαν πάντα κ.τ.λ. Not unlike this is Mk. i. 39; compare Jo. viii. 26. In Mk. xiii. 9, καὶ εἰς συναγωγὰς δαρήσεσθε,—where the weakly supported ἐν is ob-

---

[1] ["Arcessitis videlicet qui urbe aberant, ut sollennis esset hic conventus."]
[2] [The German can imitate the accusative case, die *ins Weite hin* Wohnenden, —*into the distance*.]
[3] Compare as analogous expressions *in aurem, oculum dormire*, Terent. *Heaut.* 2. 2. 101, Plin. *Epp.* 4. 29, Plaut. *Pseud.* 1. 1. 121. De Wette rejects the above explanation "as being altogether unsuitable here." But why should not figurative expressions of this kind, transferred from human relations to God, be taken in the sense which was originally inherent in them, in which they took their rise? The phrase already exists; and when we apply it to what is not material, we take it just as it is, without thinking of the physical relation which was its starting point. [See Westcott's note on Jo. i. 18.]
[4] Jer. xli. (xlviii.) 7, וַיִּשְׁחָטֵם אֶל־תּוֹךְ הַבּוֹר, ἔσφαξεν αὐτοὺς εἰς τὸ φρέαρ, *he slew* (and cast) *them into the well*. Comp. 1 Macc. vii. 19.

viously a correction,—the words εἰς συναγωγάς cannot well be joined with the preceding παραδώσουσι (Meyer) without entirely destroying the parallelism. The simplest rendering, *ye shall be scourged into the synagogues*, presents no archæological difficulty, but we should rather have expected to read of scourging *in the synagogues*: the pregnant construction, (taken) *into the synagogues ye shall be scourged*, would still be harsh for Mark. L. iv. 23, ὅσα ἠκούσαμεν γενόμενα εἰς **Καπερναούμ**, may very well mean, *done (towards) on Capernaum*,—compare A. xxviii. 6 ; and ἐν, which is the reading of some good MSS., is certainly a correction.[1] See on the whole Beyer, *De Præpositionum ἐν et εἰς in N. T. permutatione*[2] (Lips. 1824).[3]

5. Let us now turn to some passages of the N. T. Epistles, in which it is said that these prepositions are interchanged, and especially that ἐν is used for εἰς, in the expression of *metaphysical relations*.[4] No one will find any difficulty in 2 Tim. iii. 16, H. iii. 12, 2 P. ii. 13, or in E. i. 17, vi. 15. Ph. i. 9, ἵνα ἡ ἀγάπη

---

[1] Soph. *Aj.* 80, ἐμοὶ ἀρκεῖ τοῦτον ἐς δόμους μένειν, can no longer be quoted as a parallel, for Lobeck has shown that the true reading is ἐν δόμοις ; see also Wunder, *Ueber Lobecks Ausg.* p. 92 sq. As to Xen. *Cyr.* 2. 1. 9, however, see Bornem. in *Index*, s. v. εἰς. So also Lycurg. 20. 3, διακαρτερεῖν εἰς τὴν πατρίδα, is not "they held out *in* their country."

[2] 'Εν and ἐς (εἰς) may have originally been the same preposition, as indeed Pindar, following the Æolic dialect, uses ἐν with the accusative for εἰς : see Pindar (ed. Böckh) 1. pp. 294, 378, al. (Don. p. 509, Jelf 625.) But we can no more found on this an argument for the interchange of the two prepositions in the Greek written language when more fully developed and fixed in its forms, than we can now arbitrarily interchange *vor* und *für* in German, on the ground that in the earlier language they were really the same word.

[3] [See also Green p. 209, Webster p. 161, and especially A. Buttmann p. 332 sqq. A. Buttmann divides the examples in which εἰς has been supposed to stand for ἐν into four classes, as follows :—(1) There is in the clause a verb of motion, to which εἰς belongs in part, so that this is a case of attraction (a σχῆμα ἀπὸ κοινοῦ): almost all the examples of this classical usage are found in St. Luke's writings, see L. xxi. 37, A. ii. 39 (ἐπαγγελία), vii. 4, xii. 19, Mt. ii. 23, al. (2) The verb of rest is one which includes the idea of previous motion (Mk. xiii. 3, A. xx. 14, Mk. xiv. 60, al.). (3) The verb with εἰς is εἶναι or γίνεσθαι : these verbs, expressing notions which are perfectly general and therefore easily definable, receive through their union with εἰς the meaning of equally general verbs of motion, e.g., *come*, *go*: compare Her. 1. 21, 5. 38, Thuc. 6. 62, al. (L. xi. 7, Jo. i. 18, Mk. ii. 1 *Rec.*, L. i. 44, al.). (4) In the remaining instances, he says, " we are compelled either to *supply* the missing idea of motion, or to admit a *more negligent use of* εἰς, recognising in these examples the first steps towards the ultimate confusion of the two prepositions:" the latter he regards as the more probable alternative in most cases. Under the last head he quotes A. viii. 40, xix. 22, xxi. 13, xxv. 4, Mk. i. 9, 39, al. It is noteworthy that in most of these passages εἰς is joined with a proper name of place.]

[4] Compare also Rückert on G. i. 6.

.... περισσεύῃ ἐν ἐπιγνώσει, is *in knowledge,*—the end is not expressed until ver. 10, εἰς τὸ δοκιμάζειν. So also in Phil. 6, ὅπως ἡ κοινωνία τῆς πίστεώς σου ἐνεργὴς γένηται ἐν ἐπιγνώσει. In Ja. v. 5, ἐν ἡμέρᾳ σφαγῆς, the parallelism with ἐθησαυρίσατε ἐν ἐσχάταις ἡμέραις (ver. 3) of itself requires the rendering *on the day of slaughter;* and this yields a good sense,—see Theile *in loc.*[1] In E. ii. 16, ἐν ἑνὶ σώματι points to εἰς ἕνα καινὸν ἄνθρωπον (ver. 15): the κτισθέντας εἰς ἕνα ἄνθρωπον he accordingly reconciles ἐν ἑνὶ σώματι with God. In Rom. i. 24, εἰς ἀκαθαρσίαν belongs directly to παρέδωκεν, and ἐν ταῖς ἐπιθυμίαις is *in their lusts;* compare ver. 27, ἐν τῇ ὀρέξει αὐτῶν. In 1 C. i. 8, ἐν τῇ ἡμέρᾳ must be construed with ἀνεγκλήτους, and this in apposition to ὑμᾶς; so also in 1 Th. iii. 13, ἐν τῇ παρουσίᾳ, parallel with ἔμπροσθεν τοῦ θεοῦ, is directly dependent upon ἀμέμπτους. 2 Th. ii. 13, εἵλατο ὑμᾶς ὁ θεὸς ... εἰς σωτηρίαν ἐν ἁγιασμῷ πνεύματος κ.τ.λ., means, *chosen to salvation in holiness of the Spirit:*[2] the ἁγιασμὸς πνεύματος is the spiritual state in which the "being chosen to salvation" is realised. 1 Jo. iv. 9 is simply *therein manifested itself the love of God on us.*[3] In Rom. ii. 5, however, θησαυρίζεις σεαυτῷ ὀργὴν ἐν ἡμέρᾳ ὀργῆς is an example of brachylogy,—*thou art treasuring up for thyself wrath* (which will break forth) *on the day of wrath:* 1 Th. iv. 7, οὐκ ἐκάλεσεν ἡμᾶς ὁ θεὸς ἐπὶ ἀκαθαρσίᾳ ἀλλὰ ἐν ἁγιασμῷ,—for ὥςτε εἶναι (ἡμᾶς) ἐν ἁγιασμῷ.[4] In the same way might 1 C. vii. 15 and E. iv. 4 be explained: others however understand ἐν as specifying the ethical character of the κλῆσις,—see especially Harless on the latter passage. In 1 C. *l. c.* the perfect tense must not be overlooked. Διδόναι ἐν ταῖς καρδίαις (2 C. i. 22), and the like (Rom. v. 5), need no remark after what has been said above, p. 515. Lastly, εἰς does not stand for ἐν in Rom. vi. 22, ἔχετε τὸν καρπὸν ὑμῶν εἰς ἁγιασμόν; here εἰς obviously indicates the ethical end. Rom. xiii. 14 is a similar case. In

---

[1] ["Similes sunt pecudibus quæ ipso adeo mactationis die se pascunt saginantque lætæ ac securæ." Theile *in loc.* De W., referred to in § 50. 4. *a*, takes the same view.]
[2] [Winer's words may mean either *of the Spirit* or *of the spirit.*]
[3] [Winer seems intentionally to leave it an open question whether ἐν ἡμῖν shall be connected with ἡ ἀγάπη (Huther, Ewald), or with ἐφανερώθη (Düsterdieck, Brückner, Alford). In ed. 5 Winer expressly rejected the former view of the connexion.]
[4] [See below, § 66. 3.]

E. iii. 16, κραταιοῦσθαι εἰς τὸν ἔσω ἄνθρωπον is *to become strong for* (in reference to) *the inner man.*

It is in itself improbable that the apostles, in expressing clearly conceived dogmatic relations, would use ἐν for εἰς or εἰς for ἐν, to the perplexity of their readers. At all events it would have been as easy for them to write εἰς as it is for the commentators who wish to smuggle in this preposition.

The canon of an arbitrary interchange of these prepositions is not sustained by an appeal to Suidas and the Fathers:[1] or by the fact that ἐν and εἰς sometimes alternate in parallel passages,—e. g., Mt. xxi. 8, ἔστρωσαν τὰ ἱμάτια ἐν τῇ ὁδῷ, but Mk. xi. 8, εἰς τὴν ὁδόν; Mt. xxiv. 18, ὁ ἐν τῷ ἀγρῷ μὴ ἐπιστρεψάτω, Mk. xiii. 16, ὁ εἰς τὸν ἀγρόν κ.τ.λ.; Mk. i. 16, ἀμφιβάλλοντας ἀμφίβληστρον ἐν τῇ θαλάσσῃ, Mt. iv. 18, βάλλοντας ἀμφίβληστρον εἰς τὴν θάλασσαν,—the former, *they cast about* (turned about) *the net in the sea*, the latter *they cast it into the sea*, different points of time and different acts in their occupation being indicated. In Rom. v. 21, ἐβασίλευσεν ἡ ἁμαρτία ἐν τῷ θανάτῳ is *in death*—which is actually existent, but ἵνα ἡ χάρις βασιλεύσῃ διὰ δικαιοσύνης εἰς ζωὴν αἰώνιον, *to life*—as the end to be attained: εἰς ζωὴν αἰώνιον however probably depends directly on δικαιοσύνης (see Fritzsche). Compare also 2 C. xiii. 3.

It cannot however be denied that the principle according to which εἰς is joined with verbs of rest, as *vice versa* ἐν with verbs of motion, was overlooked by the writers of later times, particularly the Scholiasts[2] and the Byzantine writers. By these εἰς and ἐν are used promiscuously, and in fact ἐν begins to predominate with verbs of motion: see Leo Diac. p. xii. (ed. Hase), Blume, *Lycurg.* p. 56, Niebuhr's index to Agathias, also the indices to Theophanes and to Menandri *Hist.* in the Bonn edition.[3] In modern Greek, indeed, one only of the two prepositions is retained.[4] Compare further *Argum. ad* Demosth. *Androt.* § 17, Theodoret, *Opp.* II. 466, 804, III. 869, Epiphan. *Hær.* 46. 5, *Pseudepiph. Vit. Proph.* p. 241, 248, 332, 334, 340, 341, *Basilic.* I. 150, III. 496. The same may be noticed in the LXX, the Apocrypha, and the *Libri Pseudepigraphi*,[5] in many passages. In the N. T., however, there is at all events no example

---

[1] 2 C. xii. 2, ἁρπαγέντα ἕως τρίτου οὐρανοῦ, is thus quoted by Clem. Alex. (*Pædag.* I. p. 44, ed. Sylb.), ἐν τρίτῳ ἁρπασθεὶς οὐρανῷ. On the other hand, Pr. xvii. 3, δοκιμάζεται ἐν καμίνῳ ἄργυρος κ.τ.λ., runs thus in *Strom.* II. p. 172, δοκιμ. . . . εἰς κάμινον.

[2] Compare Hermann on Böckh's *Behandl. d. Inschrift.*, p. 181 sq.

[3] Niceph. Const. p. 48, τυφλώσας ἐν τῇ Ῥώμῃ ἐξέπεμψε· Theophan. p. 105, Γρηγόριος παρρησιαστικώτερον ἐδίδασκεν . . . . εἰς τὸ εὐκτήριον τῆς ἁγίας ἀναστάσεως· pp. 62, 65, 68, Malal. 18. 467.

[4] ["Ἐν is very seldom used, though it is becoming more common. It occurs regularly in several phrases, as ἐν τοσούτῳ, ἐν τῇ Ἑλλάδι, etc." J. Donalds. *Mod. Greek Gr.* p. 32. See also Mullach, *Vulg.* p. 380.]

[5] Compare Wahl, *Clav. Apocr.* p. 165, 195, Fabric. *Pseudepigr.* I. 598, 629,

more singular than those which are found in the earlier writers of the κοινή.

6. It is an especial peculiarity of Paul's style to use different prepositions in reference to one noun, that by means of these prepositions collectively the idea may be defined on every side. See *e.g.* G. i. 1, Παῦλος ἀπόστολος οὐκ ἀπ' ἀνθρώπων οὐδὲ δι' ἀνθρώπου, ἀλλὰ διὰ Ἰησοῦ Χριστοῦ καὶ θεοῦ πατρός κ.τ.λ.; i.e., in no respect an apostle who comes forward under human authority (not *from men* as the ultimate authority, nor *through a man* as medium or mediator). Rom. iii. 22, (πεφανέρωται) δικαιοσύνη θεοῦ διὰ πίστεως Ἰησοῦ Χριστοῦ εἰς πάντας καὶ ἐπὶ πάντας;[1] i.e., it is most completely bestowed on all believers (it reveals itself *into* all and *over* all),—Syr. ܟܠܗܘܢ ܥܠ ܘܥܠ ܟܠܗܘܢ : Bengel *in loc.* is arbitrary, following the ancient expositors,—Rückert is in perplexity. Rom. xi. 36, ἐξ αὐτοῦ (θεοῦ) καὶ δι' αὐτοῦ καὶ εἰς αὐτὸν τὰ πάντα: i. e., the world stands in connexion with God in all relations. It is *out of him*, inasmuch as he has created it (the ultimate cause); *through him*, inasmuch as he (continually) operates upon it; *to him*, inasmuch as he is the end and aim to which everything in the world has reference."[2] Col. i. 16, ἐν αὐτῷ (Χριστῷ) ἐκτίσθη τὰ πάντα . . . . τὰ πάντα δι' αὐτοῦ καὶ εἰς αὐτὸν ἔκτισται: i.e., the universe stands in a necessary and all-sided relation to Christ. First, of the past (by the aorist): *in him* was the world created, inasmuch as he, the Divine λόγος, was the personal ground of the Divine creative act (just as "*in* Christ" God redeemed the world). Then of the existing world (the perfect): all is created *through him*, as the personal medium, and *to* (for) *him*, as κύριος πάντων in the most comprehensive sense. In ver. 17, πρὸ πάντων points back to δι' αὐτοῦ, and ἐν αὐτῷ συνέστηκεν is explanatory of εἰς αὐτόν. E. iv. 6, εἷς θεὸς καὶ πατὴρ πάντων ὁ ἐπὶ πάντων καὶ διὰ πάντων καὶ ἐν πᾶσιν ἡμῖν:[3] i. e., God is the God and Father of all in every conceivable respect,—ruling *over all*,

---

Bretschneider, *Lexic. Man.* p. 139, *Acta Apocr.* pp. 5, 13, 38, 65, 66, 68, 71, 88, 91, 93, 94, 263, and almost on every page.
[1] [The last three words are omitted by recent editors.]
[2] Theodoret thus explains the passage: αὐτὸς τὰ πάντα πεποίηκεν, αὐτὸς τὰ γεγονότα διατελεῖ κυβερνῶν . . . . εἰς αὐτὸν ἀφορᾶν ἅπαντας προσήκει ὑπὲρ μὲν τῶν ὑπαρξάντων χάριν ὁμολογοῦντας, αἰτοῦντας δὲ τὴν ἔπειτα προμήθειαν, αὐτῷ δὲ χρὴ καὶ τὴν προσήκουσαν ἀναπέμπειν δοξολογίαν.
[3] [So Scholz: *Rec.* ὑμῖν. The pronoun is omitted in the best texts.]

working *through all*, dwelling *in all* (filling them with his Spirit). 2 P. iii. 5, γῆ ἐξ ὕδατος καὶ δι' ὕδατος συνεστῶσα τῷ θεοῦ λόγῳ: *out of* water (as the matter in which it lay inclosed) and *through water*,—i. e., through the agency of the water, which partly retired into the lower parts, and partly formed the clouds in the sky. In 1 C. xii. 8 sq. the prepositions διά, κατά, ἐν, in parallel members, refer the Spirit's gifts to the πνεῦμα from whom they are all derived: διά indicates the Spirit as the medium, κατά as the disposer (ver. 11), ἐν as the *continens*. It is easy to understand the antithesis of ἐκ (or ἀπό) and εἰς—starting point and goal, Rom. i. 17, 2 C. iii. 18 (compare in a *local* sense Mt. xxiii. 34).

In 1 C. viii. 6, where the parallel prepositions are referred to different subjects, θεὸς ἐξ οὗ, and κύριος Ἰησοῦς Χριστὸς δι' οὗ, there cannot be a moment's doubt respecting the choice of the prepositions and their meaning.

The following parallels may be quoted from Greek writers: Marc. Anton. 4. 23, ἐκ σοῦ (ὦ φύσις) πάντα, ἐν σοὶ πάντα, εἰς σὲ πάντα· Heliod. 2. 25, πρὸ πάντων καὶ ἐπὶ πᾶσιν· Philostr. *Apoll*. 3. 25, τοὺς ἐπὶ θαλάττῃ τε καὶ ἐν θαλάττῃ· Isocr. *Big.* p. 846, τὰ μὲν ὑφ' ὑμῶν, τὰ δὲ μεθ' ὑμῶν, τὰ δὲ δι' ὑμᾶς, τὰ δ' ὑπὲρ ὑμῶν· *Acta Ignat.* p. 368, δι' οὗ καὶ μεθ' οὗ τῷ πατρὶ ἡ δόξα. Other passages may be found in Wetstein II. 77, and Fritz. *Rom.* II. 556.

7. If two or more nouns depending on the same preposition are directly joined together by a copula, the preposition is most naturally *repeated* when these nouns denote objects which are to be taken by themselves, as independent,[1] and *not repeated* when these reduce themselves to a single main idea, or (if they are proper names) to one common class;

a.[2] L. xxiv. 27, ἀρξάμενος ἀπὸ Μωσέως καὶ ἀπὸ πάντων τῶν προφητῶν (A. xv. 4), 1 Th. i. 5, ἐν δυνάμει καὶ ἐν πνεύματι ἁγίῳ καὶ ἐν πληροφορίᾳ πολλῇ· Jo. xx. 2,[3] 2 Tim. iii. 11, A. xxviii. 2, Mk. vi. 4, x. 29, xii. 33, Rev. vi. 9. Hence the preposition is almost always repeated when two nouns are connected

---

[1] Weber, *Demosth.* p. 189 (Jelf 650): as to Latin see Kritz, *Sallust*, I. 226, Zumpt, *Gr.* 745. [Madvig, *Lat. Gr.* 470.]

[2] [There are some mistakes in the examples quoted in this paragraph. A. xv. 4 and xxv. 23 are instances of the *non-repetition* of the preposition; in 2 Tim. iii. 11 there is no copula; A. xvii. 9 does not contain καί . . . καί,—in ed. 5 it is quoted under (*b*), with A. xvii. 15.]

[3] On this passage Bengel remarks: Ex præpositione repetita colligi potest, non una fuisse utrumque discipulum.

SECT. L.] REPETITION OF PREPOSITIONS. 523

by καί .... καί¹ or τε καί: A. xxvi. 29, καὶ ἐν ὀλίγῳ καὶ ἐν πολλῷ (two circumstances which cannot coexist), L. xxii. 33, 1 C. ii. 3, Phil. 16, A. xvii. 9 (compare Xen. *Hier.* 1. 5, but contrast Soph. *Trach.* 379); Ph. i. 7, ἔν τε τοῖς δεσμοῖς μου καὶ ἐν τῇ ἀπολογίᾳ· A. xxv. 23, al. Compare Xen. *Cyr.* 1. 6. 16, Thuc. 8. 97, Diod. S. 19. 86, 20. 15, Paus. 4. 8. 2.²

b. Jo. iv. 23, ἐν πνεύματι καὶ ἀληθείᾳ (two sides of one main idea),—see Lücke ; L. xxi. 26, ἀπὸ φόβου καὶ προςδοκίας τῶν ἐπερχομένων (essentially *one* state of mind), E. i. 21, 1 Th. i. 8,³ A. xvi. 2, xvii. 15 (compare Xen. *Cyr.* 1. 2. 7, Aristot. *Eth. Nic.* 7. 11 *init.*, Thuc. 3. 72, 2. 83, Paus. 10. 20. 2). Also with τε .... καί, A. xxviii. 23, ἀπό τε τοῦ νόμου Μωσέως καὶ τῶν προφητῶν· i. 8, xxvi. 20 (Franke, *Demosth.* p. 65), Paus. 10. 37. 2, 25. 23, Xen. *Hell.* 1. 1. 3, Herod. 6. 3. 2. For examples with proper names see A. vi. 9, τῶν ἀπὸ Κιλικίας καὶ Ἀσίας· xiv. 21, ὑπέστρεψαν εἰς τὴν Λύστραν καὶ Ἰκόνιον καὶ Ἀντιόχειαν·⁴ xvi. 2, ix. 31, Mt. iv. 25.

If the connexion is *disjunctive* the preposition is usually repeated; if *antithetical*, invariably. See Col. iii. 17, ὅ τι ἐὰν ποιῆτε ἐν λόγῳ ἢ ἐν ἔργῳ· ii. 16, Mt. vii. 16, xvii. 25,⁵ L. xx. 4, Jo. vii. 48, A. iv. 7, viii. 34, Rom. iv. 9, 1 C. iv. 3, 21, xiv. 6, Rev. xiii. 16,—compare Paus. 7. 10. 1 (on the other hand, only H. x. 28, ἐπὶ δυσὶν ἢ τρισὶ μάρτυσιν· 1 Tim. v. 19 ⁶); Rom. iv. 10, οὐκ ἐν περιτομῇ, ἀλλ' ἐν ἀκροβυστίᾳ· vi. 15, viii. 4, ix. 24, 1 C. ii. 5, xi. 17, 2 C. i. 12, iii. 3, E. i. 21, vi. 12, Jo. vii. 22, xvii. 9, al. (Alciphr. 1. 31).⁷ Lastly, in comparative combinations the preposition is always repeated: A. xi. 15, Rom. v. 19, 1 C. xv. 22, 2 Th. ii. 2, H. iv. 10.⁸ In general, the tendency towards the repetition of the preposition is stronger in the N. T. than in

---

¹ Bremi, *Lys.* p. 3 sq.
² As to the different cases in which Greek prose writers repeat the preposition after τε καί, see Sommer in *Jahrb. f. Philol.* 1831, p. 408 sq. ; compare Stallb. *Phileb.* p. 156, Weber, *Dem.* p. 189.
³ [Lachm. and Tischendorf repeat ἐν. In A. i. 8, quoted below, the reading is uncertain.]
⁴ [Here recent editors repeat εἰς.]
⁵ [Corrected for vii. 16, 25 : also below, A. xi. 15 for xi. 18.]
⁶ [Add Mk. xiii. 32 (where the best texts have ἤ), 1 Tim. ii. 9,—and with an adjective, 1 P. i. 11. (A. Buttm. p. 342.)]
⁷ The preposition is not repeated with an adjective in an antithesis of this kind: 1 P. i. 23, οὐκ ἐκ σπορᾶς φθαρτῆς ἀλλὰ ἀφθάρτου.
⁸ As to the usage of Greek writers see Schæf. *Julian*, p. 19 sq., Held, Plut. *Æm.* 124, Krüg. p. 319 (Jelf 650. 6).

Greek prose writers (Bernh. p. 201, Krüg. p. 319 sq., Schoem. Plut. *Cleom.* p. 229), who either frequently or usually neglect to repeat the preposition not merely in the case of substantives which are simply connected,[1] but also after ἀλλά or ἤ,[2] before words in apposition,[3] and in answers.[4] In the N. T., on the other hand, the omission of the preposition is even singular in A. xxvi. 18, ἐπιστρέψαι ἀπὸ σκότους εἰς φῶς καὶ τῆς ἐξουσίας τοῦ σατανᾶ ἐπὶ τὸν θεόν· vii. 38, 1 C. x. 28, H. vii. 27 ; but compare Aristot. *Eth. Nicom.* 10. 9. 1, περί τε τούτων καὶ τῶν ἀρετῶν, ἔτι δὲ καὶ φιλίας κ.τ.λ.,[5] Lysias, 1. *in Theomnest.* 7, Dion. H. IV. 2223. 1, Diog. L. *Procem.* 6, Strabo 16. 778, Diod. S. 5. 31, Plutarch, *Sol.* c. 3.

In Jude 1 we must not repeat ἐν from the preceding clause before Ἰησοῦ Χριστῷ,—this would be harsh : the dative is a *dativus commodi, kept for Christ.* The preposition is not, as a rule, repeated before a noun in apposition, L. xxiii. 51, Rom. ix. 3, E. i. 19, 1 P. ii. 4 ; it is only in the case of epexegetic apposition that the repetition can take place, as in Rom. ii. 28, ἡ ἐν τῷ φανερῷ ἐν σαρκὶ περιτομή· Jo. xi. 54 (in 1 Jo. v. 20 there is no apposition). We find the same in Greek writers, but the repetition is not usual unless the word in apposition is separated from the principal word.[6]

The repetition of the preposition before each of a series of nouns which follow one another without any conjunction—as in E. vi. 12, ἀλλὰ πρὸς τὰς ἀρχάς, πρὸς τὰς ἐξουσίας, πρὸς τοὺς κοσμοκράτορας . . . . πρὸς τὰ πνευματικὰ κ.τ.λ., Jo. xvi. 8 (compare Aristot. *Rhet.* 2. 10. 2)—is of a rhetorical nature, or serves to give greater prominence to the several notions. See Dissen, *Pind.* p. 519.

Greek writers do not, as a rule, repeat before the relative the preposition by which its antecedent is governed : Plat. *Legg.* 10. 909 d, ἀπὸ τῆς ἡμέρας, ἧς ἂν ὁ πατὴρ αὐτῶν ὀφλῇ τὴν δίκην· 12. 955 b, ἐν ἱεροῖς . . . . οἷς ἂν ἐθέλῃ· 2. 659 b, ἐκ ταὐτοῦ στόματος, οὗπερ τοὺς θεοὺς ἐπεκαλέσατο κ.τ.λ., Plat. *Phæd.* 21, *Gorg.* 453 e, *Lach.* 192 b, Thuc. 1. 28, Xen. *Conv.* 4. 1, *An.* 5. 7. 17, *Hiero* 1. 11, Aristot. *Probl.* 26. 4, 16, Paus. 9. 39. 4 (Bernh. p. 203 sq.,[7] Don. p. 363, Jelf 650. 3). So also in the N. T., in A. xiii. 39, ἀπὸ πάντων, ὧν οὐκ ἠδυνήθητε . . . . δικαιωθῆναι, δικαιοῦται· xiii. 2,

---

[1] Bornem. Xen. *Conv.* 159.
[2] Schæf. *Demosth.* V. 569, 760, *Plutarch* IV. 291, Poppo, *Thuc.* III. iv. 493, Weber, *Dem.* p. 389, Franke, *Dem.* 6.
[3] Stallb. Plat. *Gorg.* p. 112, 247 ; compare Bornem. *Schol.* p. 173.
[4] Stallb. Plat. *Sympos.* p. 104 sq., *Gorg.* p. 38, *Rep.* I. 237.
[5] See Zell, Aristot. *Eth.* p. 442.
[6] Fritzsche, *Quæst. Lucian.* p. 127, Matth. 594 d.
[7] Compare Bremi, *Lys.* p. 201, Schæf. *Soph.* III. 317, Dion. *Comp.* p. 325, *Meletem.* p. 124, *Demosth.* II. 200, Heller, Soph. *Œd. C.* p. 420, Ast, Plat. *Legg.* p. 108, Wurm, *Dinarch.* p. 93, Stallb. Plat. *Rep.* II. 291.

ἀφορίσατε . . . εἰς τὸ ἔργον, ὃ προςκέκλημαι αὐτούς· L. i. 25, xii. 46, Mt. xxiv. 50, Rev. ii. 13 [1] (not 1 C. vii. 20) ; but not in Jo. iv. 53, ἐν ἐκείνῃ τῇ ὥρᾳ, ἐν ᾗ εἶπεν· A. vii. 4, xx. 18 (Jon. iv. 10). With the latter examples compare Demosth. *Timoth.* 705 b, ἐν τοῖς χρόνοις, ἐν οἷς γέγραπται τὴν τιμὴν τῶν φιαλῶν ὀφείλων· Aristot. *Anim.* 5. 30, Plat. *Soph.* 257 d, Xen. *Cyr.* 1. 2. 4, Diog. L. 8. 68, Heinich. *Euseb.* II. 252. As to Latin, see Ramshorn p. 378.[2] If antecedent and relative are separated by several words, the Greek writers also prefer to repeat the preposition : Her. 1. 47, Xen. *Vectig.* 4. 13, Lucian, *Necyom.* 9, Dio Chr. 17. 247.

In Greek writers, and especially the poets, a preposition which belongs to two successive nouns is sometimes expressed before the second only ; see Herm. *Vig.* p. 854, Lob. *Soph. Aj.* v. 397 sq., the commentators on Anacr. 9. 22, Kühner II. 320 [477 : ed. 2] al. (Jelf 650. 2.) It was supposed that an example of this kind had been discovered in the N. T. (Heinich. *Euseb.* II. 252) : Ph. ii. 22, ὅτι, ὡς πατρὶ τέκνον, σὺν ἐμοὶ ἐδούλευσεν κ.τ.λ. Here however there is rather a *variatio structuræ:* Paul says σὺν ἐμοί recollecting that he could not well write ἐμοὶ ἐδούλευσεν,—"he has, like a son serving his father, served *with me* etc." See on the whole the counter-remarks of Bernhardy (p. 202), but compare Franke, *Demosth.* p. 30. [§ 63. II. 1.]

Rem. 1. It is an especial peculiarity of later Greek to combine prepositions with adverbs, particularly adverbs of place and time (Krüg. p. 300 sq., Jelf 644),—either so as to modify the meaning of the adverb by means of the preposition, as ἀπὸ πρωΐ A. xxviii. 23, ἀπὸ πέρυσι 2 C. viii. 10, ix. 2, ἀπ' ἄρτι Mt. xxvi. 29, ἀπὸ τότε Mt. iv. 17, xxvi. 16,[3] ἔκπαλαι 2 P. ii. 3, ὑπερλίαν 2 C. xi. 5, xii. 11 (compare ὑπέρευ, Xen. *Hiero* 6. 9) ; or so that the preposition, because it appeared weakened by diversified use, was blended with an expressive adverb,[4] as ὑποκάτω, ὑπεράνω, κατέναντι. Sometimes also the adverb is strengthened by the preposition, as παραυτίκα. To the former class belong also numeral adverbs, such as ἐφάπαξ Rom. vi. 10, al. (Dio Cass. 1091. 91, 1156. 13, analogous to ἐςάπαξ Franke, *Demosth.* p. 30, πρὸς ἅπαξ Malal. 7. p. 178), ἐπὶ τρίς A. x. 16, xi. 10 ; the examples cited by Kypke (Vol. II. p. 48) have the similar εἰς τρίς, which occurs as early as Her. 1. 86, Xen. *Cyr.* 7. 1. 4,—compare Herm. *Vig.* p. 857. Many of these compounds are only to be found in writers later than Alexander,[5] some only in the Scholiasts ;[6] others, as ἀπὸ πέρυσι (for which was used προπέρυσι or

---

[1] [Here the reading is doubtful.—In Jo. iv. 53, quoted immediately below, the *first* ἐν is doubtful.]
[2] Beier, Cic. *Offic.* I. 123. [Madvig, *Lat. Gr.* 322, *Obs.* 1, Zumpt 778.]
[3] [Lünemann adds Mt. xvi. 21, L. xvi. 16.]
[4] Compare in German, *oben auf dem Dache.*
[5] Yet ἐς ἀεί, ἐς ἔπειτα, ἐς ὀψέ, and the like, occur in Thucydides (1. 129, 130, 4. 63, 8. 23). On ἀπὸ μακρόθεν and similar expressions see § 65. 2.
[6] Lob. *Phryn.* p. 46 sqq. : compare however Kühner II. 315 [468 : ed. 2].

ἐκπέρυσι) are not to be met with even there. Compare also in the LXX ἀπὸ ὄπισθεν (מֵאַחֲרֵי), 1 S. xii. 20, and Thilo, *Act. Thom.* p. 25.—In the orthography of these compounds, whether connected (Krüg. p. 300) or separate, even the most recent N. T. editors observe no consistency.[1]

Rem. 2. The ancient use of (the simple) prepositions without case for *adverbs* maintained itself, with certain restrictions, in the prose of all periods (Bernh. p. 196, Jelf. 640). In the N. T. we find but one example of this : 2 C. xi. 23, διάκονοι Χριστοῦ εἰσίν; —ὑ π ὲ ρ ἐγώ, *I more.* The examples adduced by Kypke *in loc.* are not all of the same kind. In prose, the preposition when thus used is commonly supported by δέ or γε (Bernh. p. 198, Jelf 640) : μετὰ δέ is particularly common. The example just quoted (2 Cor. xi.) may perhaps be best compared with the use of πρός for *besides*, e. g., Demosth. 1. *Aphob.* 556 a, Franke, *Demosth.* p. 94.[2] The form ἔνι with accent thrown back, for ἐνί (ἐν), including the verb substantive, occurs sometimes in the N. T. ; see p. 96. Bornemann[3] wished to introduce ἄπο, *far from* (Buttm. II. 378), into Mt. xxiv. 1, but on insufficient grounds.

SECTION LI.

USE OF PREPOSITIONS TO FORM PERIPHRASES.

1. When prepositions in combination with nouns serve as periphrases for adverbs or (mostly with the aid of the article) for adjectives, the admissibility of this usage must be shown from the fundamental meanings of the preposition,[4] lest a merely empirical procedure should lead to errors. We notice therefore :—

a. 'Ἀπό : as ἀπὸ μέρους, Rom. xi. 25, 2 C. i. 14, *in part*, —(looked at) *from the part;* ἀπὸ μιᾶς (γνώμης), L. xiv. 18,[5] *unanimously* (proceeding *from* one opinion).

b. Διά with the genitive usually denotes a state of mind,

---

[1] [See Lipsius, *Gramm. Untersuch.* p. 125 sqq., and above, § 5. 2.—Krüger is in favour of writing the words separately.]

[2] ["We find in Greek authors no certain example of this use of ὑπέρ, except Soph. *Ant.* 514." Meyer on 2 C. *l. c.* In ed. 5 Winer added : Bengel takes ὑπέρ adverbially in E. iii. 20, but the arrangement of the words would then be too artificial for Paul, and the sentence would after all be tautological.]

[3] *Stud. u. Krit.* 1843, p. 108 sq.

[4] This is not altogether free from difficulty, especially as different views of a relation prevail in different languages : e. g., ἀπὸ μέρους, *in* part ; ἐκ δεξιῶν, *on the right* ; *ab* oriente, *towards* the East. At the root of several such phrases there lies some contraction or condensation of expression.

[5] [See below, § 64. 5.]

viewed as a medium or means. Thus δι' ὑπομονῆς, H. xii. 1, may be rendered *perseveringly, assidue* (similarly, Rom. viii. 25, δι' ὑπομονῆς ἀπεκδεχόμεθα κ.τ.λ.,—compare δι' ἀφροσύνης, *imprudenter*, Xen. *Cyr.* 3. 1. 18, and δι' εὐλαβείας, *timide*, Dion. H. III. 1360 [1]); compare also *e.g.* δι' ἀσφαλείας, Thuc. 1. 17. Of a different nature is H. xiii. 22, διὰ βραχέων ἐπέστειλα ὑμῖν, *breviter*,—strictly, *by means of few* (words), *paucis;* compare διὰ βραχυτάτων, Dem. *Pant.* 624 c, and see below, § 64. 5. In 2 C. iii. 11, εἰ τὸ καταργούμενον διὰ δόξης κ.τ.λ. (see above, p. 474), διὰ δόξης is adjectival, and denotes a quality with which something is invested.

c. Eἰς denotes a degree *up to* which something comes: L. xiii. 11, εἰς τὸ παντελές, *up to completeness, most completely* (Ælian 7. 2, εἰς κάλλιστον Plat. *Euthyd.* 275 b, ἐς τὸ ἀκριβές Thuc. 6. 82). This however can hardly be called a periphrasis for the adverb.

d. Ἐκ: e. g., ἐκ μέρους, 1 C. xii. 27, *ex parte*,—looked at *from the part*. Ἐκ is then used principally of the *standard* (*secundum*); as in ἐκ τῶν νόμων, *secundum leges, legibus convenienter* (as if, receiving its direction *from*). Hence ἐξ ἰσότητος, *according to equality, equally,* 2 C. viii. 13; ἐκ μέτρου, *according to measure, moderately,* Jo. iii. 34. Compare ἐξ ἀδίκου, *injuste*, Xen. *Cyr.* 8. 8. 18; ἐξ ἴσου, Her. 7. 135, Plat. *Rep.* 8. 561 b; ἐκ προσηκόντων, Thuc. 3. 67; and see Ast, Plat. *Legg.* p. 267, Bernh. p. 230 (Jelf 621. 3. *e*). It also expresses the *source;* as ἐξ ἀνάγκης, H. vii. 12, compare Thuc. 3. 40, 7. 27, Dio C. 853. 93,—(proceeding) *out of necessity*, i. e., *necessarily;* similarly ἐκ συμφώνου, 1 C. vii. 5, *ex composito*, which however, differently turned (*according* to an agreement), approaches the previous class. In the phrases οἱ ἐκ πίστεως (G. iii. 7), οἱ ἐκ περιτομῆς (A. x. 45), ὁ ἐξ ἐναντίας (Tit. ii. 8), οἱ ἐξ ἐριθείας (Rom. ii. 8), and the like, ἐκ denotes *party* (dependence), and consequently *belonging to,—those of faith,* those who belong to faith, who stand (as it were) on the side of faith. Compare Polyb. 10. 16. 6, Thuc. 8. 92. The relation is purely material in Mk. xi. 20, ἐκ ῥιζῶν, *out from the roots, radicitus.* The temporal ἐκ τρίτου, Mt. xxvi. 44 (1 Macc. ix. 1, Babr. 95. 97, 107.

---

[1] See Pflugk, Eur. *Hel.* p. 41.

16, *Evang. Apocr.* p. 439, compare ἐξ ὑστέρου Her. 1. 108), and similar expressions—for which we, on the contrary, say *zum Dritten* [*to* instead of *from*]—are probably explained most simply as " (beginning) *from* or *out of* the third time." In later writers we find likewise ἐκ πρώτης (Babr. 71. 2), ἐκ δευτέρης (114. 5).

e. Ἐν. The cases in which ἐν with a substantive may be taken adverbially—as ἐν ἀληθείᾳ, ἐν ἐκτενείᾳ, ἐν δικαιοσύνῃ, Mt. xxii. 16, Mk. xiv. 1, Col. iv. 5, A. xvii. 31 (ἐν δίκῃ, Plat. *Crat.* p. 419 d, ἐν τάχει, Thuc. 1. 90) [1]—the less require explanation, as we ourselves in every case can use *in* with the corresponding substantive: the substantives denote for the most part abstract notions, especially qualities or dispositions in which one does something. Equally intelligible is the use of this preposition with a substantive in an adjectival sense; as ἔργα τὰ ἐν δικαιοσύνῃ, τὸ μένον ἐν δόξῃ (ἐστί), 2 C. iii. 11, and the like.

2. *f*. Ἐπί with the genitive is frequently found with abstract nouns which denote a quality *with which* one acts in a certain way, as ἐπ' ἀδείας, *with fearlessness;* or an objective notion with the subsistence of which something harmonises, as Mk. xii. 32, ἐπ' ἀληθείας, *with subsistence* or *existence of truth, truly* (Dio C. 699. 65, 727. 82). With the dative, this preposition expresses the basis on which something rests, so to speak: A. ii. 26, ἡ σάρξ μου κατασκηνώσει ἐπ' ἐλπίδι, *with, in confidence* (in God),—therefore *securely, tranquilly*. The phrases ἐπὶ τὸ αὐτό, ἐφ' ὅσον, ἐπὶ πολύ, have no difficulty.

g. Κατά. The phrase ἡ κατὰ βάθους πτωχεία, 2 C. viii. 2, is probably to be explained as *the poverty reaching down into the depth*, the deepest poverty (compare Strabo 9. 419); Xen. *Cyr.* 4. 6. 5 is no parallel, for ὁ κατὰ γῆς means *terra conditus*. The adverbial καθ' ὅλου probably means, in strictness, *throughout the whole* (in universum), since κατά with the genitive has sometimes this meaning. The instances in which κατά with the accusative of a substantive forms a periphrasis for an adverb (as κατ' ἐξουσίαν, κατ' ἐξοχήν, κατὰ γνῶσιν) require no explanation:[2]

---

[1] But in Jo. iv. 23 the words ἐν πνεύματι καὶ ἀληθείᾳ, depending on προςκυνήσουσιν, are not to be resolved or diluted into the adverbs πνευματικῶς καὶ ἀληθῶς: ἐν denotes the sphere in which the προςκυνεῖν moves.

[2] See Schæf. *Long.* p. 330.

SECT. LII.]   VERBS COMPOUNDED WITH PREPOSITIONS.   529

compare κατὰ τάχος, Dio C. 84. 40, 310. 93 ; κατὰ τὸ ἰσχυρόν, Her. 1. 76; καθ᾽ ὁρμήν, Soph. *Philoct.* 562; κατὰ τὸ ἀνεπιστῆμον, Æschin. *Dial.* 3. 16; κατὰ τὸ ὀρθόν, Her. 7.143. See Bernhardy p. 241 (Jelf 629. II. 3). As to ἡ κατ᾽ ἐκλογὴν πρόθεσις, Rom. ix. 11, οἱ κατὰ φύσιν κλάδοι, Rom. xi. 21, see § 30. 3. Rem. 5.

h. Πρός with accusative: e. g., Ja. iv. 5, πρὸς φθόνον, *invidiose,* — compare πρὸς ὀργήν, Soph. *El.* 369 (properly *according to envy, according to anger*); also πρὸς ἀκρίβειαν, Sext. Emp. *Hypot.* 1. 126, for ἀκριβῶς.

On the periphrases for certain cases (especially the genitive) formed by prepositions, as ἐκ, κατά, see § 30. 3. Rem. 5.

SECTION LII.

CONSTRUCTION OF VERBS COMPOUNDED WITH PREPOSITIONS.

1. In this section we shall naturally leave out of consideration those compound verbs in which the meaning of the preposition is either obscured (e. g., ἀποδέχεσθαι, ἀποκρίνεσθαι, ἀποθνήσκειν), or blended with the meaning of the verb into one common idea (μεταδιδόναι, *impart,* προάγειν τινά, *præire aliquem, to precede some one,* ἀποδεκατοῦν τι, *to tithe something,* συγκλείειν τι, *to inclose something*) ; or in which the preposition, approaching the nature of an adverb, intensifies the verb (ἐπιζητεῖν, διατελεῖν, διακαθαρίζειν, συντελεῖν, *perpugnare*). Our attention will be confined to verbs in which the preposition continually maintains its independent action as a preposition ; so that the verb is attended, not merely by the object which properly belongs to it, (if it is a transitive verb), but also by another noun, which depends upon this preposition: as ἐκβάλλειν *to cast out of,* ἀναφέρειν *to bring something up to,*[1] etc.

What is the full significance of the compound verbs of the N. T., and how far they can stand for the simple verbs, are questions which have not yet been examined exhaustively and on rational principles. Compare however C. F. Fritzsche, *Fischers und Paulus Bemerkungen über das Bedeutungsvolle der griechischen Präpositionen in den damit zusammengesetzten Verbis* etc. (Leipz. 1809) ; Tittmann, *De vi præpositionum in verbis compositis in N. T. recte dijudicanda* (Lips. 1814) ;[2] J. van Voorst, *De usu verborum cum præpositionibus compositorum in*

---

[1] Our *herauswerfen aus, hinaufbringen auf.*
[2] Included in his *Synonyma N. T.* (I. 217 sqq.).

530   VERBS COMPOUNDED WITH PREPOSITIONS.   [PART III.

N. T. (Leid. 1818, 2 Spec.), *Theol. Annal.* 1809, II. 474 sqq.[1] Until very lately translators and expositors of the N. T. appeared to vie with one another in diluting[2] the compound verbs.[3] In order to restrict this arbitrariness, I have opened a new inquiry into the subject : *De verborum cum præpositionibus compositorum in N. T. usu* (Lips. 1834–1843 : 5 Commentationes).[4] As to Greek in general compare Cattier, *Gazophylacium* sect. 10, p. 60 sqq. (ed. Abresch), C. F. Hachenberg, *De significatione præpositionum Græcarum in compositis* (Traj. ad Rh. 1771).

2. In this case we find a threefold construction of compound verbs.

a. The preposition with which the verb is compounded is repeated before the noun; as Mt. vii. 23, ἀποχωρεῖτε ἀπ' ἐμοῦ· H. iii. 16, οἱ ἐξελθόντες ἐξ Αἰγύπτου.[5]

b. The noun is governed by a different preposition substantially the same in meaning; as Mt. xiv. 19, ἀναβλέψας εἰς τὸν οὐρανόν· Mk. xv. 46, προςεκύλισε λίθον ἐπὶ τὴν θύραν.

c. Without the intervention of a second preposition, the verb takes that case which in signification suits the notion of the verb, and which therefore is usually the case governed by the preposition contained in the verb; as Mk. iii. 10, ἐπιπίπτειν αὐτῷ, L. xv. 2, συνεσθίει αὐτοῖς, etc. Thus the genitive follows compounds of ἀπό, κατά (*against*), πρό; the accusative, compounds of περί (Mt. iv. 23, περιάγειν τὴν Γαλιλαίαν,[6] A. ix. 3).

3. Which of these constructions is the regular one, must be learned from observation of the actual usage. Sometimes two of them or all three are in use together: compare ἐπιβάλλειν,— also parallel passages such as Mt. xxvii. 60 and Mk. xv. 46, Jo. ix. 6 and 11, A. xv. 20 [*Rec.*] and 29.[7] We must not however overlook the fact that in this case a distinction is often made by

---

[1] Brunck, Aristoph. *Nub.* 987, Zell, Aristotel. *Ethic.* p. 383, Stallb. Plat. *Gorg.* p. 154.
[2] [Literally, *flattening* (Verflachung).]
[3] Compare *e.g.* Seyffarth, *De indole ep. ad Hebr.* p. 92.
[4] [Unfortunately, these five parts are all that Winer published. Parts 1 and 2 deal with general questions (the alleged redundancy of the preposition in compound verbs,—how far compound verbs can stand for simple) : in the remaining three parts Winer examines the compounds of ἀνά, ἀντί, ἀπό, διά, occurring in the N. T.]
[5] See Bornem. Xen. *Conv.* p. 219, Winer, 2. *Progr. de verb. compp.* p. 7 sqq.
[6] [The probable reading here is ἐν τῇ Γ. : Mt. ix. 35 may be substituted.]
[7] Thus we find ἀποστῆναι, *deficere*, with ἀπό in Xen. *Cyr.* 5. 4. 1, and with the simple genitive in 4. 5. 11.

usage between the various constructions. No one will think it a matter of indifference whether the compounds with εἰς are joined with the noun by means of the preposition εἰς (or πρός), or are followed by the simple case.[1] Ἐκπίπτειν in its literal meaning is followed by ἐκ, whilst in a figurative sense (like *spe excidere*) it takes a genitive, as in G. v. 4, 2 P. iii. 17, Philostr. *Apoll.* 1. 36 (see however Diod. S. 17. 47).[2] We find προςφέρειν τινί used of persons, *offerre alicui (aliquid)*, but προςφέρειν ἐπὶ τὰς συναγωγάς, *to bring before the (authorities of the) synagogues*, L. xii. 11 [*Rec.*].[3] Compare also προςέρχεσθαί τινι, *adire aliquem*, and προςέρχεσθαι πρὸς τὸν Χριστόν, 1 P. ii. 4; ἐφιστάναι τινί (of a person), A. iv. 1, and ἐφιστάναι ἐπὶ τὴν οἰκίαν, A. xi. 11. See in general my 2. *Progr. de verb. compp.* p. 10 sq.

4. The details of the N. T. usage are as follows:—

1. Ἀπό. The verbs compounded with ἀπό

(a) Usually repeat the preposition.[4] Thus we find ἀπό after ἀπέρχεσθαι (where a personal noun follows[5]), Mk. i. 42, L. i. 38, ii. 15, Rev. xviii. 14 (Lucian, *Salt.* 81); after ἀποπίπτειν, A. ix. 18 (in a material sense, compare Her. 3. 130 and Polyb. 11. 21. 3,—in a figurative sense the verb does not occur in the N. T.); ἀφιστάναι *desistere a*, or *to withdraw oneself from some one*, A. v. 38, L. ii. 37,[6] xiii. 27, 2 C. xii. 8, 1 Tim. vi. 5 [*Rec.*], al. (Polyb. 1. 16. 3),—but not in 1 Tim. iv. 1, see below; ἀπορφανίζεσθαι, 1 Th. ii. 17; ἀποσπᾶσθαι, L. xxii. 41, A. xxi. 1 (Polyb. 1. 84. 1, Dion. H. *Judic. Thuc.* 28. 5); ἀφορίζειν, Mt. xxv. 32; ἀποβαίνειν, L. v. 2 (Polyb. 23. 11. 4, al.); ἀποχωρεῖν, Mt. vii. 23, L. ix. 39; ἀφαιρεῖσθαι, L. x. 42, xvi. 3 (Lucian, *Tim.* 45); ἀπαίρεσθαι, Mt. ix. 15; ἀπαλλάττεσθαι, L. xii. 58,

---

[1] Εἰσιέναι, εἰσέρχεσθαι, are in prose usually joined with εἰς in a local sense (e. g., εἰς τὴν οἰκίαν); with τινά or τινί, like *incessere aliquem*, when the verbs are used of desires, thoughts, etc. (Demosth. *Aristocr.* 446 b, Herod. 8. 8. 4, al.): yet see Valcken. Eurip. *Phœn.* 1099. On εἰσέρχεσθαι, in particular, see my 2. *Progr. de verb. compp.* p. 11 sq.

[2] So also ἀπέχεσθαι *abstinere* usually takes a genitive in Greek authors: in the N. T. it is sometimes followed by ἀπό, A. xv. 20 [*Rec.*], 1 Th. iv. 3, v. 22.

[3] Compare πρὸς τοῖς ἱστοῖς τριχιλίαι προςήρτηντο, Polyb. 8. 6. 5, 3. 46. 8, but (figuratively) 9. 20. 5, προςαρτᾶν πολλά τινα τῇ στρατηγίᾳ.

[4] Compare in general Erfurdt, Soph. *Œd. R.* p. 225.

[5] [But see also Mk. v. 17, A. xvi. 39.]

[6] [In this passage and in L. x. 42 (quoted below) ἀπό should probably be omitted. These passages will therefore come under (c).]

A. xix. 12 ; ἀποκρύπτειν, Mt. xi. 25 ;[1] ἀποστρέφειν, Rom. xi. 26 (from the LXX); also once, Col. ii. 20, after the figurative ἀποθνήσκειν (compare Porphyr. *Abstin.* 1. 41),—which elsewhere, viewed as expressing one single notion (*to die off*), is followed by the dative: see below, (*d*).

(*b*) Ἀπολαμβάνειν is followed by παρά (with a personal noun[2]) in L. vi. 34 [*Rec.*]; compare Diod. S. 13. 31, Lucian, *Pisc.* 7. (By ἀπό, in the sense of *taking away* forcibly, Polyb. 22. 26. 8.)

(*c*) The genitive follows ἀποφεύγειν, 2 P. i. 4 (but not in 2 P. ii. 20); ἀπαλλοτριοῦν, E. ii. 12, iv. 18 (Polyb. 3. 77. 7); ἀφιστάναι, *deficere a*, 1 Tim. iv. 1 (Polyb. 2. 39. 7, 14. 12. 3); ἀποστερεῖσθαι (figurative), 1 Tim. vi. 5.

(*d*) The dative is joined with ἀποθνήσκειν, *to die to a thing*, G. ii. 19, Rom. vi. 2 : in Rom. vi. 10 the dative is to be explained differently. Similarly, ἀπογίνεσθαι ταῖς ἁμαρτίαις, 1 P. ii. 24.[3]

2. Ἀνά. Verbs compounded with ἀνά, in which the preposition expresses the local *up* (to), are construed

(*a*) With εἰς, when the place is indicated towards which the action is directed: ἀναβαίνειν, *travel up to*, L. xix. 28, Mk. x. 32 (Her. 9. 113), or *go up* (*upon* a mountain, *into* heaven, etc.), Mt. v. 1, xiv. 23, Mk. iii. 13 (Herod. 1. 12. 16, Plat. *Alcib.* 1. 117 b, Dio C. 89. 97); ἀναβλέπειν, Mt. xiv. 19 (Mk. vii. 34, L. ix. 16), A. xxii. 13 ; ἀνάγειν, Mt. iv. 1, L. ii. 22, A. xx. 3 (Herod. 7. 10. 15); ἀναλαμβάνεσθαι, Mk. xvi. 19 ; ἀναπίπτειν, L. xiv. 10 ; ἀναφέρειν, Mt. xvii. 1, L. xxiv. 51 ; ἀναχωρεῖν, Mt. ii. 14, iv. 12, al.; ἀνέρχεσθαι, Jo. vi. 3, G. i. 18.[4]

(*b*) With πρός,—chiefly when the motion is directed towards a person : as ἀναβαίνειν πρὸς τὸν πατέρα, Jo. xx. 17 ; ἀνακάμπτειν,[5] Mt. ii. 12 ; ἀναπέμπειν, L. xxiii. 7 (ἀναβλέπειν πρός τινα, Plat. *Phæd.* 116 d, Arrian, *Epict.* 2. 16. 41). Yet in

---

[1] [The probable reading here is ἔκρυψας. We may substitute L. x. 21.]
[2] [Also by ἀπό, Col. iii. 24. Compare Mk. vii. 33.]
[3] [To the list of verbs followed by ἀπό in the N. T. should be added ἀπαιτεῖν, ἀπελαύνειν, ἀπέχειν (Mt. xv. 8, al.), ἀποκυλίειν, ἀπολύεσθαι, ἀποπλανᾶσθαι, ἀποστέλλεσθαι (A. xi. 11, 1 P. i. 12,—with ἐκ in Jo. i. 24 if οἱ be omitted), ἀποτινάσσειν, ἀποφέρεσθαι, ἀποχωρίζεσθαι. Under (*b*) come ἀπάγειν ἐκ (A. xxiv. 7 *Rec.*), ἀποκυλίειν ἐκ (Mk. xvi. 3) ; compare ἀπέρχεσθαι ἔξω τοῦ συνεδρίου, A. iv. 15. Ἀπέχεσθαι takes a genitive (1 Tim. iv. 3, 1 P. ii. 11), also ἀπό (1 Th. iv. 3, al.) : see above. Ἀπολύεσθαι probably governs a genitive in L. xiii. 12.]
[4] [Also ἀνασπᾶσθαι εἰς, A. xi. 10. Compare ἀναστὰς εἰς, Mk. xiv. 60.]
[5] [This is hardly one of the verbs in which ἀνά "expresses the local *up*."—With ἀναπέμπειν τινί compare ἀνάγειν τινί, A. xii. 4. See also A. xxi. 31.]

this case we also find ἐπί τινα, L. x. 6 (ἀνακάμπτειν, compare Diod. S. 3. 17), or the dative, L. xxiii. 11, ἀναπέμπειν τινί.

(c) With ἐπί, when the object to which the action is directed is to be definitely marked as an elevation or as a surface on which the motion terminates: see Polyb. 8. 31. 1, ἀναφέρειν ἐπὶ τὴν ἀγοράν, *up to the market*, and the reverse ἀναβαίνειν ἐπὶ τὴν οἰκίαν, after the Latin *ascendere*, Polyb. 10. 4. 6 ; ἀναβαίνειν ἐπὶ δικαστήριον is common in Greek writers. Thus ἀναβιβάζειν ἐπὶ τὸν αἰγιαλόν, Mt. xiii. 48 (Xen. *Cyr.* 4. 2. 28, Polyb. 7. 17. 9), ἐπὶ τὸ κτῆνος, L. x. 34[1] (Palæph. 1. 9, Xen. *Cyr.* 4. 5. 16, compare 7. 1. 38); ἀνακλίνεσθαι ἐπὶ τοὺς χόρτους, Mt. xiv. 19; ἀναπίπτειν ἐπὶ τὴν γῆν, Mt. xv. 35, or ἐπὶ τῆς γῆς, Mk. viii. 6; ἀναβαίνειν ἐπὶ τὸ δῶμα, L. v. 19, and ἐπὶ συκομορέαν, L. xix. 4 (compare Xen. *Cyr.* 4. 1. 7, 6. 4. 4, Her. 4. 22, Plut. *Educ.* 7. 13, Arrian, *Epict.* 3. 24, 33, Lys. 1. *Alcib.* 10, Paus. 6. 4. 6); ἀναφέρειν ἐπὶ τὸ ξύλον, *up on the tree* (cross), 1 P. ii. 24;[2] ἀνακάμπτειν ἐπί, L. x. 6 (Plut. *Educ.* 17. 13).

3. Ἀντί. The verbs compounded with ἀντί (*against*) are regularly followed by the dative: as Mt. vii. 2 [*Rec.*], L. xiii. 17, Jo. xix. 12, Rom. xiii. 2, al. See however H. xii. 4, ἀνταγωνίζεσθαι πρός τι (compare ver. 3, ἡ εἰς αὐτὸν ἀντιλογία). Similarly ἀντικεῖσθαι πρός, Polyb. 2. 66. 3, Dio C. p. 204 and 777.[3]

4. Ἐκ. Verbs compounded with ἐκ are followed sometimes by ἐκ (when an actual "out of" is to be expressed), sometimes by ἀπό or παρά, where merely *direction from* or *from the vicinity of* is indicated. Thus we have ἐκβάλλειν ἐκ, Mt. xiii. 52, Jo. ii. 15, 3 Jo. 10, al. (Plat. *Gorg.* 468 d), and ἀπό, Mt. vii. 4,[4] ἐκκλίνειν ἀπό, 1 P. iii. 11, Rom. xvi. 17 ; ἐκκόπτειν ἐκ, Rom. xi. 24 (Diod. S. 16. 24); ἐκπίπτειν ἐκ, A. xii. 7 (Arrian, *Ind.* 30. 3); ἐκλέγεσθαι ἐκ, Jo. xv. 19 (Plat. *Legg.* 7. p. 811 a);[5] ἐκπορεύεσθαι ἐκ, Mt. xv. 11, 18, Rev. ix. 18 (Polyb. 6. 58. 4), and ἀπό,

---

[1] [A mistake: the verb here is ἐπιβιβάζειν. In the next passage ἐπὶ τοῦ χόρτου is probably the true reading. In Mk. vi. 39 ἀνακλίνειν is followed by ἐπί with the *dative*. We have ἀνατέλλειν ἐπί in Mt. v. 45.]
[2] We find ἀναβαίνειν with the simple accusative (ἀναβαίνειν ἵππον) in Dion. H. 2252. 7, Pausan. 10. 19. 6.
[3] [Compare L. xiv. 6 (omitting αὐτῷ) ; also, more remotely, L. xxiv. 17.]
[4] [Here we must read ἐκ ; for ἀπό see (Mk. xvi. 9 *Rec.*) A. xiii. 50; for παρά, Mk. xvi. 9. Ἐκβάλλειν ἔξω with genitive, L. iv. 29, al.]
[5] [Ἐκλέγεσθαι ἀπό, L. vi. 13.]

Mk. vii. 15 (*v. l.*,[1] not Mt. xxiv. 1), or παρά, Jo. xv. 26 ; ἐκφεύγειν ἐκ, A. xix. 16 ; ἐξαίρειν and ἐξαιρεῖν ἐκ, 1 C. v. 2,[2] A. xxvi. 17 ; ἐξέρχεσθαι ἐκ, Mt. ii. 6, A. vii. 3, al. (Her. 9. 12), or παρά, L. ii. 1. The simple genitive but rarely occurs with these verbs; in a local sense only with ἐξέρχεσθαι, Mt. x. 14 (and even here the reading is not quite certain, see the variants,[3]—but compare ἐκβαίνειν τινός, Jacobs, *Philostr.* p. 718). In a figurative sense, however, ἐκπίπτειν regularly takes a genitive (as *spe excidere*), G. v. 4, 2 P. iii. 17, Plat. *Rep.* 6. 496 c, Lucian, *Contempl.* 14 (but is found with ἐκ, Her. 3. 14, Dio C. p. 1054. 57); so also ἐκκρέμασθαι, L. xix. 48. Lastly, ἐκφεύγειν even in the physical sense is followed by the accusative (of the power escaped from), as 2 C. xi. 33, ἐκφεύγειν τὰς χεῖράς τινος (Sus. 22),—so Her. 6. 40 [? 104], and frequently: ἐκ is used only to define the place, A. xix. 16, ἐκφυγεῖν ἐκ τοῦ οἴκου (compare Ecclus. xxvii. 20).[4]

5. Ἐν. Verbs compounded with ἐν have a very simple construction. When they denote direction *into* (to) something, they are followed by εἰς; when rest *in* or *on* a place, by ἐν. Thus we have ἐμβαίνειν εἰς, Mt. viii. 23, xiv. 22, Jo. vi. 17 (Her. 2. 29, Plat. *Crat.* 397 a) ; ἐμβάλλειν εἰς, L. xii. 5 (Dio C. p. 288. 79, Plat. *Tim.* 91 c, Lucian, *Tim.* 21); ἐμβάπτειν εἰς, Mk. xiv. 20 (but ἐμβάπτειν ἐν, *dip in the dish*, Mt. xxvi. 23); ἐμβλέπειν εἰς, Mt. vi. 26, A. i. 11 ;[5] ἐμπίπτειν εἰς, L. x. 36 (Her. 7. 43, Plat. *Tim.* 84 c, Lucian, *Hermot.* 59), 1 Tim. iii. 6; ἐμπτύειν εἰς, Mt. xxvi. 67, xxvii. 30. Ἐνδημεῖν ἐν, 2 C. v. 6; ἐνοικεῖν ἐν, 2 C. vi. 16, Col. iii. 16 (with accusative, Her. 2. 178); ἐνεργεῖν ἐν, Ph. ii. 13, E. i. 20, al.; ἐγγράφειν ἐν, 2 C. iii. 2 (like ἐγγλύφειν ἐν, Her. 2. 4); ἐμμένειν ἐν (τῇ διαθήκῃ), H. viii. 9. At the same time,

---

[1] [Here recent editors read ἐκ for ἀπό (Mt. xx. 29). In Mt. xxiv. 1 we have the simple verb πορεύεσθαι, and (according to almost all MSS. and editors) with ἀπό. We find ἔξω in Mk. xi. 19.]

[2] [In this verse ἀρθῇ is the best reading : we may substitute ver. 13.]

[3] [Ἔξω τῆς οἰκίας is probably the true reading : there is another example in Rec., A. xvi. 39, but it is not well supported. Ἐξέρχεσθαι ἀπό (L. ix. 5, al.) is not mentioned in the text. Ἐκφέρειν ἔξω is probably the true reading in Mk. viii. 23.]

[4] [Ἐκ is also found in the N. T. after ἐξάγειν, ἐξαγοράζειν, ἐξαλείφειν, ἐξολεθρεύειν, ἐκτινάσσειν (Mt. x. 14, Lachm., Tisch.). Ἀπό follows ἐκβαίνειν, ἐκζητεῖν, ἐκκαθαίρειν, ἐκπλεῖν, ἐξηχεῖσθαι, ἐξωθεῖν. (The derivative verbs ἐκδικεῖν and ἐκδημεῖν are found with both ἀπό and ἐκ: L. xviii. 3, Rev. xix. 2, 2 C. v. 6, 8.)]

[5] [Here we must probably read βλέποντες. In Mk. viii. 25 ἐμβλέπειν takes an accusative.]

the construction with the dative in both significations is not altogether rare; compare ἐμβλέπειν τινί (dative of *person*), Mk. x. 21, 27, L. xxii. 61, Jo. i. 36, 43 (Plat. *Rep.* 10. 609 d, Polyb. 15. 28. 3); ἐμπτύειν τινί, Mk. x. 34, xiv. 65, xv. 19; ἐμμένειν τινί (πίστει), A. xiv. 22 (Xen. *Mem.* 4. 4. 4, Lycurg. 19. 4, Lucian, *Tim.* 102). Ἐντρυφᾶν, *to revel in something*, is followed by the simple dative in Greek writers (e.g., Diod. S. 19. 71), but in 2 P. ii. 13 ἐν is repeated: ἐγκεντρίζειν, Rom. xi. 24, has two constructions—being first followed by εἰς and then by the simple dative.[1]

6. *Εἰς.* Still more simple is the construction of verbs compounded with εἰς, as εἰσάγειν, εἰςπορεύεσθαι, εἰσφέρειν, εἰσέρχεσθαι:[2] in every instance εἰς is repeated. Compare Poppo, *Thuc.* III. i. 210; see however Herm. Eurip. *Ion* p. 98, and my 2. *Progr. de verbis compp.* p. 13.

7. *Ἐπί.* The verbs compounded with ἐπί are divided between the construction with ἐπί repeated (more rarely εἰς), and that with the simple dative: many however have both constructions. Ἐπιβάλλειν εἰς τι (*into* something) or ἐπί τι (*upon, on* something, Plat. *Prot.* 334 b), Mk. iv. 37, L. v. 36, ix. 62 [ἐπί τινι, Mt. ix. 16],—also with a dative of the person, 1 C. vii. 35, Mk. xi. 7, A. iv. 3 (Polyb. 3. 2. 8, 3. 5. 5);[3] ἐπιβαίνειν ἐπί or εἰς, A. xxi. 6 [*Rec.*], xx. 18 (Mt. xxi. 5),—also with a dative of the place, A. xxvii. 2 (Polyb. 1. 5. 2, Diod. S. 16. 66); ἐπιβλέπειν ἐπί, L. i. 48, Ja. ii. 3, Plut. *Educ.* 4. 9 (with εἰς, Plat. *Phœdr.* 63 a); ἐπικεῖσθαι ἐπί τινι, Jo. xi. 38,—also with a dative of the person, 1 C. ix. 16; ἐπιπίπτειν ἐπί τι, L. i. 12, A. x. 10 [*Rec.*], or ἐπί τινι A. viii. 16, or with a dative of the

---

[1] [Εἰς is also found in the N. T. after ἐγκαταλείπειν, ἐγκρύπτειν, ἐμβιβάζειν, ἐμπτύειν, ἐνδύειν, ἐντυλίσσειν. Ἐν follows ἐγκατοικεῖν, ἐγκαυχᾶσθαι, ἐνάρχεσθαι, ἐνδοξάζεσθαι, ἐνειλεῖν, ἐνευλογεῖσθαι, ἐνδυναμοῦσθαι (ἐγκακεῖν). The simple dative is found with ἐμμαίνεσθαι, ἐμπαίζειν, ἐμπλέκεσθαι, ἐντρίφεσθαι, ἐντυλίσσειν, ἐντυπούσθαι, ἐντυγχάνειν, ἐμβριμᾶσθαι, ἐνέχειν, ἐγκαλεῖν, ἐννεύειν (ἐντέλλεσθαι, ἐλλογᾶν, ἐμφανίζειν). Ἐνδείκνυσθαι has all three constructions (2 C. viii. 24, 1 Tim. i. 16, 2 Tim. iv. 14).]

[2] [This verb is also followed by ἐν in L. ix. 46, and perhaps in Rev. xi. 11 (see § 50. 4); by ὑπό τι, Mt. viii. 8; by ἐπί τινα, A. i. 21 (see § 66. 3,—so also εἰσφέρειν ἐπί τι, L. xii. 11): in Rev. xi. 11 some MSS. have εἰσῆλθεν αὐτοῖς. Εἰσέρχεσθαι, εἰσπορεύεσθαι, εἰσιέναι, are also followed by πρός τινα, in the sense of *visiting, going into the house of* some one.]

[3] As to ἐπιβάλλειν τὴν χεῖρα ἐπί τινα and τινι (Lucian, *Tim.* 10), in particular, see Fritz. *Mark*, p. 637.—We find, in a material sense, Polyæn. 5. 2. 12, ποίᾳ πόλει βούλοιτο ἐπιπλεῦσαι.

person, Mk. iii. 10, A. xx. 10 (Polyb. 1. 24. 4); ἐπιρρίπτειν ἐπί τι, 1 P. v. 7; ἐπιτιθέναι ἐπί τι, Mk. iv. 21,¹ Mt. xxiii. 4, A. ix. 17, al.,—or with a dative, usually of the person (L. xxiii. 26, Mk. vii. 32, A. ix. 12, 1 Tim. v. 22, al.), rarely of the thing, Jo. xix. 2 (Lucian, *Tim.* 41, 122); ἐπέρχεσθαι ἐπί τι, L. i. 35, A. viii. 24, xiii. 40 [*Rec.*], or with the dative of the thing, L. xxi. 26; ἐπαίρειν ἐπί or εἴς τι, Jo. xiii. 18,² L. xviii. 13; ἐποικοδομεῖν ἐπί τι, 1 C. iii. 12, or ἐπί τινι, E. ii. 20,—but also with ἐν, Col. ii. 7; ἐπιδεῖν ἐπί τι, A. iv. 29; ἐπιφέρειν with a dative of the thing, Ph. i. 17;³ ἐφικνεῖσθαι εἴς τινα, 2 C. x. 14;⁴ ἐφάλλεσθαι ἐπί τινα, A. xix. 16 (1 S. x. 6, xi. 6). On the other hand, ἐπιγράφειν is followed by ἐν in 2 C. iii. 2,⁵—compare Plut. *De Lucri Cupid.* p. 229, al., Palæph. 47. 5 (not so in Num. xvii. 2, Pr. vii. 3). The following verbs take the dative only: ἐπεκτείνεσθαι, Ph. iii. 14 (*to stretch out towards*); ἐπιφαίνειν and ἐπιφαύειν [? ἐπιφαύσκειν], when these verbs are joined with names of persons, E. v. 14, L. i. 79,—compare Gen. xxxv. 7 [*Alex.*]; also ἐπιφέρειν in the sense of *adding* one thing *to* another, Ph. i. 17. Ἐπισκιάζειν sometimes takes a dative of the person, A. v. 15 and probably Mk. ix. 7 (*provide a sheltering shade for some one,* compare Ps. xc. 4); sometimes an accusative, Mt. xvii. 5, L. ix. 34 (*to overshadow, envelop,* as a transitive verb). In the LXX we also find ἐπισκιάζειν ἐπί τινα, Ex. xl. 32,⁶ Ps. cxxxix. 8.⁷

---

¹ [Here the best reading is τεθῇ. Ἐπιτιθέναι is also followed by ἐπί τινος, ἔν τινι (Mt. xxvii. 29, in the best texts), ἐπάνω τινός (Mt. xxvii. 37).]

² [Ἐπαίρεσθαι κατά τινος, 2 C. x. 5: in A. xxvii. 40 a dative follows, but this may be a *dativus commodi.*—Ἐποικοδομεῖν τινί, Jude 20.]

³ [Here ἐγείρειν is now generally received: there is no other example of ἐπιφέρειν τινί in the N. T. This example is given a second time below.]

⁴ [In the previous verse ἐφικέσθαι ἄχρι ὑμῶν.]

⁵ [This is a mistake: the verb here is ἐγγράφειν (see above, s. v. ἐν). The construction ἐπιγράφειν ἐν occurs A. xvii. 23: this verb is also followed by ἐπί τινος (H. viii. 10, probably, see Bleek or Alford *in loc.*), and by ἐπί τι in H. x. 16, according to the best reading.]

⁶ [A mistake for xl. 29 (35).]

⁷ [Several other verbs of this class are followed by ἐπί in the N. T. We find ἐπί τι or τινα after ἐπιβιβάζειν, ἐπικαλεῖσθαι, ἐπιρράπτειν, ἐπισκηνοῦν, ἐπιχρίειν (in most texts), ἐπάγειν (also ἐπάγειν τινί), ἐπανίστασθαι, ἐπαναπαύεσθαι (also with τινί, Rom. ii. 17), ἐπεισέρχεσθαι, ἐπεγείρειν (also κατά τινος, A. xiv. 2): ἐπί τινι after ἐπαισχύνεσθαι (Rom. vi. 21,—elsewhere this verb is either absolute or a simple transitive), and ἐπιδύειν: similarly ἐπικαθίζειν ἐπάνω τινός, Mt. xxi. 7. Εἰς follows ἐπανάγειν (L. v. 4), and ἐπιφώσκειν (Mt. xxviii. 1): on ἐπέχειν εἰς, A. xix. 22, see § 50. 4. Ἐπιπορεύεσθαι is followed by πρός; ἐπισυνάγειν by πρός and by ὑπό (with accusative). It is not easy to say how many examples of the construction with the simple dative should come in here: we may mention ἐπαγωνίζεσθαι,

8. *Διά*. Of the compounds of διά but few repeat the preposition. In the N. T. compare διαπορεύεσθαι διὰ σπορίμων L. vi. 1, compare Diod. S. *Exc. Vat.* p. 30 (but also—though with a different meaning, *obire*—διαπορεύεσθαι πόλεις, A. xvi. 4); διέρχεσθαι διά, Mt. xii. 43, 2 C. i. 16, *to go through* (and consequently, *out of*) *something*[1] (compare Strabo 8. 332); and the pregnant phrase διασώζειν δι' ὕδατος, 1 P. iii. 20. Most of these verbs are, as transitives, followed by the accusative: as διαπλεῖν, *sail through*, A. xxvii. 5 ; also διέρχεσθαι, when it means *to go throughout*, L. xix. 1, A. xv. 3 ; διαβαίνειν, H. xi. 29, etc.

9. *Κατά*. Those compounds of κατά which denote an action tending down to some point of space are followed by ἀπό or ἐκ, when the *terminus a quo* is to be expressed; as καταβαίνειν ἀπὸ τοῦ οὐρανοῦ, L. ix. 54, 1 Th. iv. 16, καταβαίνειν ἐκ τοῦ οὐρανοῦ, Jo. iii. 13, vi. 41. Where the *terminus ad quem* is to be indicated (Dio C. 108. 23, 741. 96), they take ἐπί, εἰς, or πρός,[2] according to the nature of the mark aimed at (L. xxii. 44, Mk. xiii. 15 [*Rec.*], A. xiv. 11); perhaps also in A. xx. 9 the simple dative, καταφέρεσθαι ὕπνῳ.[3] On the other hand, καθῆσθαι, καθίζειν, κατατιθέναι ἔν τινι, are *to set down in a place*, etc. Κατηγορεῖν, *to accuse*, is usually construed with the genitive of the person, the signification of the κατά being present to the mind: once we find κατηγορεῖν τι κατά τινος, L. xxiii. 14 ; similarly ἐγκαλεῖν κατά τινος, Rom. viii. 33, compare Soph. *Philoct.* 328. Analogous to the former construction is κατακαυχᾶσθαί τινος, *to boast against some one*, Rom. xi. 18 (compare Ja. ii. 13), and καταμαρτυρεῖν τινός, Mt. xxvi. 62, xxvii. 13 ; but κατακαυχᾶσθαι κατά τινος, Ja. iii. 14.[4]

ἐπέχειν, ἐπιπλήσσειν, ἐπιφωνεῖν (ἐπαρκεῖν, ἐπακολουθεῖν, ἐπιστέλλειν, ἐπιτάσσειν, ἐπιτιμᾶν, ἐπιτρίπειν). 'Επιμένειν is followed by τινι, ἔν τινι, πρός τινα (ἐπί or rather παρά τινι, A. xxviii. 14) ; ἐπιστρέφειν by ἐπί and πρός with accusative, and by εἰς (ἐν, L. i. 17, see § 50. 4) ; ἐφιστάναι by τινι, ἐπί τι (or τινα), and ἐπάνω τινός.]

[1] [Similarly διαφέρειν διὰ τοῦ ἱεροῦ, Mk. xi. 16. These verbs are not unfrequently followed by the distributive κατά (e. g., L. viii. 1). In several passages compounds of διά are joined with other prepositions in a pregnant sense. See Winer, 5. *Progr. de verb. compp.* p. 9 ; and below, § 66. 2.]

[2] [Also ἕως, Mt. xi. 23, L. x. 15.]

[3] As we find elsewhere καταφέρεσθαι εἰς ὕπνον or ἐφ' ὕπνῳ, see Kühnöl *in loc.* : ὕπνῳ might also be taken as an ablative. [On Mt. xx. 18 see above, p. 263.]

[4] [The simple genitive is also found after καταγελᾶν, καταγινώσκειν, καταδυναστεύειν, κατισχύειν, κατακυριεύειν, καταλαλεῖν, καταναρκᾶν, καραστρηνιάζειν, καταφρονεῖν, κατεξουσιάζειν (καθάπτειν, A. xxviii. 3) : on κατέχειν with genitive of infinitive see above, p. 409. In Mk. xiv. 3 the best reading appears to be κατέχειν

10. Μετά. Verbs compounded with μετά, in which this preposition signifies *trans*—as μεταβαίνειν, μεταμορφοῦν, μετασχηματίζειν, μετανοεῖν, μετοικίζειν,[1] al.—naturally take εἰς to express passing over *into*. Compare Vig. p. 639.

11. Παρά. Verbs compounded with παρά are followed by ἀπό or παρά (but compare § 47, p. 457 sqq.), when the place *whence* is to be indicated. See A. i. 25, ἀφ' ἧς (ἀποστολῆς) παρέβη, as in Dt. xvii. 20, Jos. xi. 15, al.; ἐξ ἧς in Dt. ix. 12, 16.[2] Παραλαμβάνειν ἀπό τινος, 1 C. xi. 23, and παρά τινος, 1 Th. iv. 1, 2 Th. iii. 6; παραφέρειν ἀπό τινος, Mk. xiv. 36, L. xxii. 42; παρέρχεσθαι ἀπό τινος, Mt. v. 18, Mk. xiv. 35.[3]

12. Περί. The compounds with περί have for the most part become pure transitives, and accordingly govern the accusative; as περιέρχεσθαι, 1 Tim. v. 13 (*obire*), περιζωννύναι, E. vi. 14, περιϊστάναι, A. xxv. 7. We find in a material sense, with περί repeated, περιαστράπτειν (once only, A. xxii. 6,—in the parallel passage, A. ix. 3, the verb is transitive), περιζώννυσθαι, Rev. xv. 6 (περὶ τὰ στήθη), περικεῖσθαι, Mk. ix. 42, L. xvii. 2 (περισπᾶσθαι, L. x. 40). The dative follows περιπίπτειν (λῃσταῖς, πειρασμοῖς) in L. x. 30, Ja. i. 2 (Thuc. 2. 54, Polyb. 3. 53. 6, Lycurg. 19. 1), and περικεῖσθαι in H. xii. 1.[4]

13. Πρό. Of the verbs compounded with πρό only προπορεύεσθαι repeats the preposition: L. i. 76, προπορεύσῃ πρὰ προςώπου[5] κυρίου (Dt. ix. 3). In the LXX this verb is also

αὐτοῦ τῆς κεφαλῆς: for the omission of κατά before the second genitive see Plat. *Legg.* 7. 814 d, Her. 4. 62 (Meyer *in loc.*). On the constructions of κατηγορεῖν see p. 254.]

[1] [Μεταμορφοῦν is used absolutely in the N. T. except in 2 C. iii. 18, where the passive is followed by an accusative (see p. 287): the following εἰς δόξαν is correlative with ἀπὸ δόξης (p. 463). Μετανοεῖν is not found in the N. T. with εἰς in this sense; on Mt. xii. 41, L. xi. 32, see p. 495. In Ph. iii. 21 μετασχηματίζειν is followed by a proleptic adjective (§ 66. 3).]

[2] [In ver. 16 we find ἀπό, not ἐξ.]

[3] [Compounds in which παρά means *beside*, *near*, govern a dative (see Ellicott on Ph. i. 25): παρεῖναι, παραγίνεσθαι, παριστάναι (also ἐνώπιον, κατενώπιόν τινος), παρατιθέναι (also εἰς), παραμένειν (also πρός τινα, see p. 504), παρέχειν, παραδιδόναι, παρακεῖσθαι, παρακολουθεῖν (παρεμβάλλειν, L. xix. 43, Tisch.): compare παραδρεύειν τινί, 1 C. ix. 13. We find also παραχειμάζειν ἐν; παραλαμβάνειν πρός (also μεθ' ἑαυτοῦ), παρακαθίζεσθαι πρός (with accusative); παραβάλλειν and παραδιδόναι εἰς. Παρεῖναι is followed by εἰς and πρός τινα, also ἐπί τινος; παραγίνεσθαι by εἰς, πρός and ἐπί (with accusative); παράγειν by παρά. Some of these examples (also παροικεῖν εἰς, H. xi. 9) really come under § 66. 2. d.]

[4] [Also περιτιθέναι, and probably περιβάλλειν in L. xix. 43 (περιβεβλημένος ἐπὶ γυμνοῦ, Mk. xiv. 51). Περιπίπτειν εἰς, A. xxvii. 41.]

[5] [Westcott and Hort read ἐνώπιον. Πρό is repeated with three verbs in which its force is temporal: προκηρύσσειν (A. xiii. 24), προορίζειν (1 C. ii. 7), προγινώσκειν (1 P. i. 20). With L. i. 17 compare προσῆσθαι ἐνώπιον, A. ii. 25. Προάγειν ἐπί

followed by ἐνώπιον (Ps. lxxxiv. 14 [*Alex.*], xcvi. 3 [1]) and ἔμπροσθεν (Gen. xxxii. 16, Is. lviii. 8). So in L. i. 17, προελεύσεται ἐνώπιον αὐτοῦ; but in xxii. 47, προήρχετο αὐτούς. See further no. 2.[2]

14. *Πρός*. Verbs compounded with πρός repeat this preposition when the local *to* is to be expressed. See *e. g.* προϛπίπτειν πρὸς τοὺς πόδας τινός, Mk. vii. 25, and compare Dio C. 932. 82, 1275. 53,—but προϛπίπτειν τοῖς γόνασι, Diod. S. 17. 13 [and L. v. 8]; προϛτίθεσθαι πρὸς τοὺς πατέρας, A. xiii. 36; also προϛκολλᾶσθαι πρὸς τὴν γυναῖκα, *to cleave to*, Mk. x. 7, E. v. 31.[3] They are also followed by ἐπί: as προϛτιθέναι ἐπὶ τὴν ἡλικίαν, Mt. vi. 27. More rarely we find the dative thus used: προϛέρχεσθαι ὄρει, H. xii. 22; προϛπίπτειν οἰκίᾳ, Mt. vii. 25 (Xen. *Eq.* 7. 6, Philostr. *Ap.* 5. 21); and, of direction, προϛφωνεῖν τινί, *to call to*, Mt. xi. 16, A. xxii. 2, compare Diod. S. 4. 48 (but προϛφωνεῖν τινά, *to call some one to oneself*, L. vi. 13). On the other hand, the dative is almost invariably used when the object approached is a person, as προϛπίπτειν τινί (*to fall down before some one*), Mk. iii. 11, v. 33, A. xvi. 29, προϛφέρειν τινί (Philostr. *Ap.* 5. 22), προϛέρχεσθαί τινι, *to accost some one;* or when the *approach* itself is to be taken in a *figurative* sense, as προϛάγειν τῷ θεῷ, *to bring to God*, 1 P. iii. 18 (προϛάγειν τῷ κυρίῳ frequently occurs in the LXX), προϛκλίνεσθαί τινι, *to adhere to*, A. v. 36. Compare προϛέχειν τινί, H. vii. 13, A. xvi. 14; προϛεύχεσθαί τινι, Mt. vi. 6, 1 C. xi. 13; προϛτιθέναι λόγον τινί, H. xii. 19; προϛτίθεσθαι τῇ ἐκκλησίᾳ, A. ii. 41.[4] If the verb implies the notion of rest, (πρός τινι), it is either construed thus with the dative,—as προϛμένειν τινί (A. xi. 23, 1 Tim. v. 5), προϛεδρεύειν (1 C. ix. 13 [*Rec.*], Polyb. 8. 9. 11, 38. 5. 9), προϛκαρτερεῖν (Mk. iii. 9, Col.

τινός (A. xxv. 26), and προγράφειν κατ᾽ ὀφθαλμούς (G. iii. 1) should perhaps be mentioned.]

[1] [Here the word is ἐναντίον, and so in Ps. lxxxiv. 14 *Vat.*]

[2] [The genitive follows προϊστάναι (1 Tim. iii. 4, 5, al.), προνοεῖν (1 Tim. v. 8), προπορεύεσθαι (A. vii. 40).]

[3] [This quotation from Gen. ii. 24 (where *Alex.* has the simple dative after the verb) occurs three times in the N. T., and in every case the reading is doubtful. In E. v. 31 πρὸς τὴν γυναῖκα is more generally received, though the dative has considerable support; in Mt. xix. 5 the best editors read the simple verb. In Mk. x. 7 Tisch., Westcott and Hort, omit the clause; Tregelles reads πρός.]

[4] [Τῇ ἐκκλησίᾳ is not found in A. ii. 41: the phrase occurs in the received text of A. ii. 47 (the best MSS. omit τῇ ἐκκλησίᾳ), and in no other passage. In A. xi. 24 (v. 14) we find προϛτίθεσθαι τῷ Κυρίῳ.]

iv. 2, Rom. xii. 12, compare Polyb. 1. 55. 4, 1. 59. 12, Diod. S. 20. 48, and frequently) ; or, in expressing purely local relations, followed by ἐν, as προςμένειν ἐν Ἐφέσῳ, 1 Tim. i. 3.[1]

15. *Σύν.* The compounds of σύν but seldom repeat this preposition, as in Col. ii. 13 (συζωοποιεῖν), or take μετά instead (Weber, *Dem.* p. 210), as in Mt. xxv. 19 (συναίρειν), 2 C. viii. 18 (συμπέμπειν), Mt. xx. 2 (συμφωνεῖν), xvii. 3 (συλλαλεῖν), Mk. xiv. 54.[2] Most frequently they are followed by the simple dative. The examples of this construction (amongst which are 1 C. xiii. 6, Ja. ii. 22, but not Rom. vii. 22[3]) are to be found on almost every page of the N. T.: in Greek authors, also, these verbs are almost invariably so construed. A. i. 26, συγκατεψηφίσθη μετὰ τῶν ἕνδεκα ἀποστόλων is a pregnant expression.

16. *Ὑπό.* None of the verbs compounded with ὑπό repeat the preposition.[4] When they express direction *towards* (ὑπάγειν, ὑποστρέφειν, al.) they are followed by εἰς or πρός; when ὑπό signifies *under*, as in ὑποπλεῖν, they are treated as transitives.

17. *Ὑπέρ.* The verbs compounded with ὑπέρ are for the most part used absolutely. Only ὑπερεντυγχάνειν repeats ὑπέρ, Rom. viii. 26 *v. l.* (compare Judith v. 21, Ecclus. xxxvi. 27); and in Rom. xii. 3 ὑπερφρονεῖν is joined with παρά. Ὑπερβαίνειν in 1 Th. iv. 6 and ὑπεριδεῖν in A. xvii. 30 are used transitively in a figurative sense.[5]

Rem. In Greek authors it is not uncommon for the preposition of a compound verb to continue in force for a second verb[6] (Franke, *Demosth.* p. 30). Of this usage the N. T. contains no clear example.

---

[1] [Πρός also occurs after προςέρχεσθαι (1 P. ii. 4), προςκόπτειν (Mt. iv. 6,—with ἐν in Rom. xiv. 21) : in H. v. 7 πρός κ.τ.λ. probably belongs to the *nouns*, not to προςενέγκας (see Delitzsch *in loc.*). Ἐπί τι follows προςκυλίειν and προςφέρειν (L. xii. 11 *Rec.*, Mt. v. 23) : ἐν follows προςκαρτερεῖν in A. ii. 46. The simple dative is joined with προςαναλίσκειν, προςανατίθεσθαι, προςκληροῦσθαι, προςλαλεῖν, προςκυνεῖν (ἐνώπιόν τινος in L. iv. 7, al.), προςοχθίζειν, προςπορεύεσθαι, προςτάσσειν, προςκόπτειν, προςηλοῦν, προςκυλίειν (Mt. xxvii. 60), προςηγνύναι, προςψαύειν.]

[2] [Σύν is repeated with συσταυροῦν Mt. xxvii. 44 (συνάγειν 1 C. v. 4), συνέρχεσθαι A. xxi. 16. Μετά follows συνάγειν in Mt. xxviii. 12 ; συνακολουθεῖν in Mk. v. 37; συνεσθίειν in G. ii. 13. (Πρός is found after συζητεῖν, συλλογίζεσθαι, συμβάλλειν, συλλαλεῖν.)]

[3] [In favour of the rendering, *I rejoice with the law*, see Meyer and Vaughan *in loc.*]

[4] [Except in ὑπέταξεν ὑπὸ τοὺς πόδας, E. i. 22, 1 C. xv. 27, probably quoted from Ps. viii. 7 (ὑπέταξεν ὑποκάτω τῶν ποδῶν,—so in H. ii. 8).—The dative is found after ὑπακούειν, ὑποτάσσειν (1 C. xv. 27, al.).]

[5] [In 2 Th. ii. 4 we find ὑπεραίρεσθαι ἐπί. The genitive follows ὑπερβάλλειν (E. iii. 19), and ὑπερέχειν (Ph. ii. 3).]

[6] [As συμπονεῖν καὶ φέρειν for συμφέρειν (Krüg. p. 345). Compare Jelf 650. *Obs.* 4.]

SECTION LIII.

THE CONJUNCTIONS.

1. Conjunctions—whose office it is to join together words or clauses—are divided into classes according to the kind of connexion expressed. These classes are the same in every cultivated language, and are eight in number [1] (Krüg. p. 345).[2] The primitive conjunctions are monosyllabic, καί, τοί,[3] τε, δέ, μέν, οὖν; many are evidently derived from pronouns or adjectives, as ὅτε, ὅτι, ὡς, τοι, ἀλλά, etc.; others are compound, as ἐάν (εἰ ἄν), ἐπεί, ὥστε, γάρ (γε ἄρα), τοίνυν, etc. Some, in accordance with their signification, govern a particular mood; as εἰ, ἐάν, ἵνα, ὅπως, ὅτε, al. See in general Hermann, *Emend.* p. 164 sqq. The chief conjunctions of each class which are current in Greek prose generally are also found in the N. T., and with their legitimate meanings:[4] only τοι, μήν are not used (by themselves), and many compounds which express nicer shades of meaning (e. g., γοῦν) were not required in the N. T. style.

It should further be remarked that the causal conjunctions, for the most part, originally expressed that which is objectively or temporally present (e. g., ὅτι, ἐπεί, ἐπειδή). This connexion of thought may also be observed in the prepositions (p. 451 sq.), and likewise in Latin and German; e. g., *quod, quoniam, quando, quandoquidem, weil*.[5]

2. The simplest and most general connexion of words and clauses, the simple coupling together of words and clauses which stand side by side, is formed by the conjunctions καί and τε (*et* and *que*). The latter of these occurs most frequently in Luke's writings (especially in the Acts), and next to these in the Epistle to the Hebrews. Mt. ii. 13, παράλαβε τὸ παιδίον καὶ τὴν μητέρα αὐτοῦ καὶ φεῦγε εἰς Αἴγυπτον· A. x. 22, ἀνὴρ

---

[1] [Krüger now has *nine* classes,—copulative, disjunctive, adversative, comparative, hypothetical, temporal, final, consecutive, and causal conjunctions.]

[2] Compare O. Jahn, *Grammaticor. Gr. de conjunctionibus doctrina* (Gryph. 1847).

[3] [Mentioned again in the next line. Τοι is regarded as derived either from τῷ or from τοί = σοί; see Kühner II. 703 (ed. 2), Liddell and Scott s. v.]

[4] Schleiermacher, *Hermen.* p. 66, goes too far; what he says on p. 130 is more correct. It is only in regard to the position of certain conjunctions that the N. T. language differs from the earlier prose.

[5] [Literally *while*. Compare in English, *seeing that, being* (Abbott, *Shaksp. Gr.* p. 277), in the sense of *since*.]

φοβούμενος τὸν θεόν, μαρτυρούμενός τε ὑπὸ ὅλου τοῦ ἔθνους· iv. 13, θεωροῦντες . . . ἐθαύμαζον, ἐπεγίνωσκόν τε αὐτούς κ.τ.λ. The distinction between καί and τε is, that καί simply *connects* (notions of the same kind), τε *annexes* (something added). Hermann says " καί conjungit, τε adjungit :" compare with this Klotz, *Devar.* II. 744.[1] Hence τε rather denotes an internal (logical), καί rather an external relation.

In the N. T., as well as in classical Greek, τε[2] thus indicates an addition, complement, explanation,—something which flows out of what has preceded, or is some detail belonging to it[3] (Rost p. 728); see Jo. vi. 18, A. ii. 33, 37, iv. 33, v. 42, vi. 7, viii. 13, 28, 31, x. 28, 48, xi. 21, xii. 6, xv. 4, 39, xix. 12, xx. 7, xxi. 18, Rom. xvi. 26. Hence, as a rule, τε denotes something of inferior importance (Jo. iv. 42, A. xvi. 34). Sometimes however τε may even be used to give prominence. In H. ix. 1, εἶχε καὶ ἡ πρώτη (διαθήκη) δικαιώματα λατρείας τό τε ἅγιον κοσμικόν, the last object, as a detail, and as presupposed in δικαιώματα λατρείας,[4] is annexed by means of τε : as however the writer (ver. 2 sqq.) goes into particulars respecting the sanctuary, it is clear that τὸ ἅγιον was for him the principal notion in ver. 1. There is nothing strange in such a use of τε, for that which is not homogeneous with what has preceded (καί), but is added to it, may be either the more or the less important of the two, according to circumstances : compare also H. xii. 2. It is indeed by the subjective view of the writer that the choice of τε is in many cases determined ; see Klotz *l. c.* In the N. T. τε and δέ have often been interchanged by the early transcribers : e. g., A. vii. 26, viii. 6, ix. 23, xi. 13, xii. 8, 12, xiii. 44, xxvi. 20,[5] al. (Don. p. 573, Jelf 754).

3. In the N. T. style, as in that of the Bible generally, the simple connexion by καί[6] is frequently chosen where in the

---

[1] On καί and τε (derived from τοι, Herm. Soph. *Trach.* 1015) compare the different views of philologers ; Herm. *Vig.* p. 835, *ad* Eurip. *Med.* p. 331, Hand, *De Partic.* τε (Jen. 1832, 2 Progr.), Bernh. p. 482 sq., Sommer in the *N. Jahrb. f. Philol.* 1831, III. 400 sq., Hartung, *Part.* I. 58 sqq. [On τε see Curtius, *Grundz.* pp. 133, 444.]

[2] On the Latin *que*, see Zumpt, *Gr.* § 333, Hand, *Tursellin.* II. 467 sq. Compare Bauermeister, *Ueber die Copulativpartikeln im Latein.* (Luckau, 1853).

[3] ["Like 'que,' τε appends to the foregoing clause (which is to be conceived as having a separate and independent existence, Jelf, *Gr.* § 754. 6) an additional, and very frequently a new thought ;—a thought which, though not necessary to (Herm. *Viger,* No. 315), is yet often supplemental to, and a further development of, the subject of the first clause ; compare Acts ii. 33, Heb. i. 3." Ellicott on E. iii. 19.]

[4] [Against this see Delitzsch *in loc.*]

[5] [Probably xxvi. 10.]

[6] Of "and" uniting separate sentences, it is only necessary to mention specially one case, which is often overlooked,—that in which a writer joins one O. T. quotation to another : e. g. A. i. 20, γενηθήτω ἡ ἔπαυλις . . . ἐν αὐτῇ (Ps. lxviii.), καὶ τὴν ἐπισκοπὴν . . . ἕτερος (Ps. cviii.), H. i. 9 sq. (see Bleek), Rom. ix. 33.

more reflective languages a conjunction of more special meaning would have been used. This peculiarity led astray the earlier Biblical philology into the assumption that καί in the N. T., as ן in Hebrew, was the conjunction-general, uniting in itself all meanings of the conjunctions, and indeed those of many adverbs.[1] But—as in Greek authors (Klotz, *Dev.* II. 635), so also in the N. T.—καί has only two meanings, *and, also*.[2] These however admit of various shades, which we should ourselves express by special words: thus *also* rises into *even, vel, adeo* (Fritz. *Rom.* I. 270, Jacob, Luc. *Alex.* p. 50). But in many passages there is not even such a modification as this, but καί, as the simple copula, was chosen by the writer either in accordance with the simplicity of Biblico-oriental thought, or designedly—on rhetorical grounds: sometimes both these causes coincide. The translator, however, has no right to destroy the colouring of the original by introducing special conjunctions.

In the narrative syle, especially of the synoptic Gospels, the several facts are in great measure strung together by καί, as simply following one another; though δέ and οὖν, μετὰ τοῦτο, εἶτα, etc., would have given more variety to the language, and the use of the participial and relative constructions would have more clearly distinguished between principal and subordinate sentences. E. g.: Mt. i. 24 sq., παρέλαβεν τὴν γυναῖκα αὐτοῦ καὶ οὐκ ἐγίνωσκεν αὐτὴν ἕως οὗ ἔτεκεν υἱόν, καὶ ἐκάλεσεν τὸ ὄνομα αὐτοῦ Ἰησοῦν· iv. 24 sq., vii. 25, 27, L. v. 17; see § 60. 3. One case deserves special mention,—that in which a writer gives a note of time, and then annexes the fact by means of καί; as in Mk. xv. 25, ἦν ὥρα τρίτη καὶ ἐσταύρωσαν αὐτόν (a supplementary remark, as it were, to ver. 24), *it was the third hour and (when) they crucified him:* here the correction ὅτε was early introduced. From this must be distinguished L. xxiii. 44, ἦν ὡσεὶ ὥρα ἕκτη καὶ σκότος ἐγένετο. Here, if ὅτε had been used, the time would have stood out as the principal matter, and the fact would be regarded as subordinate: the two were to be indicated as co-ordinate, and hence καί. This structure is also found in Greek writers (Matth. 620. 1. a, Madv. 185, Jelf 752); Plat. *Symp.* 220 c, ἤδη ἦν μεσημβρία καὶ ἄνθρωποι ᾐσθάνοντο· Arrian, *Al.* 6.

[This last example is quite different. St. Paul quotes Is. xxviii. 16, *introducing into* the verse certain words from Is. viii. 14: the καί belongs to the passage itself.]

[1] See still Schleusner, *Lexic.* s. v.

[2] Klotz, *l. c.*: In omnibus locis, ubicunque habetur καί particula, aut simpliciter copulat duas res, aut ita ponitur ut præter alias res, quæ aut re vera positæ sunt aut facile cogitatione suppleri possunt, hanc vel illam rem esse aut fieri significet, et in priore caussa "*und*" reddi solet, in posteriore *etiam, quoque, vel,* sicuti res ac ratio in singulis locis requirit.

9. 8, ἤδη πρὸς τῇ ἐπάλξει ἦν καὶ . . . ὤθει· Thuc. 1. 50, Xen. An. 1. 1. 8. The case is still less similar when, in a prophetic announcement, the note of time is placed first, and a sentence annexed by means of καί,—an arrangement which gives more solemnity to the language : see L. xix. 43, H. viii. 8, 1 C. xv. 52. So also in such exhortations as αἰτεῖτε καὶ δοθήσεται ὑμῖν· L. x. 28, τοῦτο ποίει καὶ ζήσῃ, there is more force in the parallelism of the two verbs than in some such construction as τοῦτο ποιῶν ζήσῃ (Franke, Demosth. p. 61). Compare Demosth. Olynth. 3. 11 c, ὁρᾶτε ταῦθ᾽ οὕτως ὅπως . . . καὶ δυνήσεσθε ἐξιέναι καὶ μισθὸν ἕξετε.

In such cases as 1 C. v. 2, ". . . and ye are puffed up," Mt. iii. 14, "I had need to be baptised of thee, and thou comest to me," Jo. vi. 70, "Have not I chosen you . . . ? and of you one is a traitor," Jo. xi. 8, xiv. 30, H. iii. 9, astonishment or sorrow is more eloquently expressed by the simple and, than it would be by the more full-sounding however, nevertheless, notwithstanding. In the mere juxtaposition the contrast speaks as it were of itself. On the other hand, in Mt. xxvi. 53, ἢ δοκεῖς, ὅτι οὐ δύναμαι ἄρτι παρακαλέσαι τὸν πατέρα μου καὶ παραστήσει μοι πλείω δώδεκα λεγεῶνας ἀγγέλων; H. xii. 9, οὐ πολὺ μᾶλλον ὑποταγησόμεθα τῷ πατρὶ τῶν πνευμάτων καὶ ζήσομεν; Ja. v. 18, Rev. xi. 3, that which was the object or purpose of the first action, and might have been expressed as such (ἵνα . . .), is by means of the καί consecutivum presented independently as a consequence, because it was the writer's point to give the second member all possible emphasis. A Greek writer, aiming at the same object, would probably have laid out his sentence thus: οὐ πολὺ μᾶλλον ὑποταγέντες τῷ πατρὶ . . . ζήσομεν; See also Rom. xi. 35, Mk. i. 27, Mt. v. 15, and compare Ewald p. 653: in the LXX see Ruth i. 11, Jon. i. 11. From later Greek may be quoted Malal. 2. p. 39, ἐκέλευσε καὶ ἐκαύθη ἡ μυσερὰ κεφαλὴ τῆς Γοργόνος.

In regard to the other uses of καί, as they may be simply traced back to the two meanings " and," " also," we have only to remark [1]—

---

[1] ["The use of καί in the N. T., as the Aramaic o would have led us à priori to suppose, is somewhat varied. Though all are really included in the two broad distinctions et and etiam (see especially Klotz, Devar. vol. II. p. 635), we may perhaps conveniently enumerate the following subdivisions. Under the first (et) καί appears as, (α) simply copulative; (β) adjunctive, i.e. either when the special is annexed to the general as here," that is, in Ph. iv. 12, 1st καί—" Mark i. 5, Eph. vi. 19, al., or conversely the general to the special, Matth. xxvi. 59 ; (γ) consecutive, nearly 'and so,' Ph. iv. 9, Matth. xxiii. 32, 1 Thess. iv. 1, compare James ii. 23, al. Under the second (etiam) καί appears as, (δ) ascensive, 'even,' a very common and varied usage (compare notes on Eph. i. 11), or conversely, descensive, Gal. iii. 4, Eph. v. 12, where see notes ; (ε) explanatory, approaching nearly to 'namely,' 'that is to say,' John i. 16, Gal. ii. 20, vi. 16, where see notes ; (ζ) comparative, especially in double-membered clauses, see notes on Eph. v. 23 ; to all which we may perhaps add a not uncommon use of καί, which may be termed (η) its contrasting force, as here (2nd καί), and more strongly, Mark xii. 12, 1 Thess. ii. 18 ; compare 1 Cor. ix. 5, 6

SECT. LIII.] THE CONJUNCTIONS. 545

(a) The καί before interrogatives comes back to the meaning "and :" Mk. x. 26, καὶ τίς δύναται σωθῆναι; L. x. 29, Jo. ix. 36, 1 P. iii. 13, 2 C. ii. 2. This usage is familiar enough in Greek writers, see Plat. *Theæt.* 188 d, Xen. *Cyr.* 5. 4. 13, 6. 3. 22, Lucian, *Herm.* 84, Diog. L. 6. 93, Diod. S. *Exc. Vat.* p. 30 ; in Latin also *et* is thus used. We ourselves so use *and* (" And what did he do ? "), when we stop a speaker with an abrupt, urgent question. There is however no example in the N. T. of the use of καί before an imperative, to give urgency to it.[1] All the passages formerly quoted as examples of this usage are of a different kind. In Mt. xxiii. 32 the καί is consecutive ; *ye declare yourselves to be sons . . . then fill up*, etc. In L. xii. 29 καί means *also* or *and* (consequently) ; in Mk. xi. 29 καί is *and ;* in 1 C. xi. 6, *also*. The intensive καί *after* interrogatives—as in Rom. viii. 24 [*Rec.*], ὃ γὰρ βλέπει τις, τί καὶ ἐλπίζει; *why doth he yet hope for it ?*—points to the meaning *also*. (Jelf 759, 760.)

(b) Καί is never really adversative. First of all, those passages must be set aside in which καὶ οὐ, καὶ μή (Fritz. *Mark*, p. 31), καὶ οὐδείς, etc., occur ; as Mt. xi. 17, xii. 39, xxvi. 60, Mk. i. 22, vii. 24, ix. 18, Jo. iii. 11, 32, vii. 30 (contrast ver. 44), x. 25, xiv. 30, A. xii. 19, Col. ii. 8, al. Here the opposition lies in the negation, and is neither increased by δέ nor diminished by the simple καί (Schæf. *Dem.* I. 645). But also in such sentences as Mk. xii. 12, ἐζήτουν αὐτὸν κρατῆσαι καὶ ἐφοβήθησαν τὸν ὄχλον· 1 Th. ii. 18, ἠθελήσαμεν ἐλθεῖν πρὸς ὑμᾶς . . . καὶ ἐνέκοψεν ἡμᾶς ὁ σατανᾶς· Jo. vii. 28, 1 Jo. v. 19, the author probably had in his thought two clauses in simple juxtaposition, whereas we are more inclined to bring the *opposition* into prominence. In A. x. 28, Mt. xx. 10 (*the first thought that they would receive more, and received also each a denarius*), we ourselves use *and* to bring out the startling result : see above. No one then will think it strange that in 1 C. xii. 4, 5, 6, δέ and καί should alternate. Lastly, in 1 C. xvi. 9 Paul connects together two circumstances (one favourable, the other unfavourable) which detain him in Ephesus; and hence καί is the simple copula.[2] (Jelf 759. 3.)

(c) The epexegetic καί—the καί of more exact definition, *namely*[3] —is in strictness merely *and* (*and indeed*) : Jo. i. 16, *out of his*

(2nd καί). In such a case the particle is not adversative, as often asserted, but copulative and contrasting ; the opposition arises merely from the juxtaposition of clauses involving opposing or dissimilar sentiments. These seven heads apparently include all the more common uses of καί in the N. T. ; for further examples see the well arranged list in Bruder, *Concord.* s. v. καί." Ellicott on Ph. iv. 12.—See also Webster, *Syntax*, p. 132.]

[1] Hoogeveen, *Doctr. Partic.* I. 538 sqq., Hartung I. 148 (Jelf 759. 4.)
[2] Even in Hoogeveen's time it was seen that *but* is not really a meaning of καί : sciant non ex se sed ex oppositorum membrorum natura hanc (notionem) nactam esse καί particulam (Hoogeveen, *Doctr. Partic.* I. 533).
[3] Herm. *Philoct.* 1408, Bremi, *Demosth.* p. 179. Compare Volcm. Fritzsche, *Quæst. Lucian.* p. 9, Jacob, Luc. *Alex.* p. 33 sq., Weber, *Demosth.* p. 438. [On Jo. i. 16 see Westcott's note.]

fulness have all we received, namely grace for grace; 1. C. iii. 5, xv. 38, E. vi. 18, G. vi. 16, H. xi. 17, A. xxiii. 6. But this meaning has been introduced into too many passages. In Mt. xiii. 41, xvii. 2, xxi. 5, καί is *and;* in Mk. xi. 28 the correct reading is probably ἤ. In Mt. iii. 5, καὶ ἡ περίχωρος τοῦ Ἰορδάνου, if rendered "that is to say, the Jordan-country," would be an incorrect adjunct to ἡ Ἰουδαία; for neither do the two geographical notions absolutely coincide, nor is the former included in the latter. It is such a combination as, *all Hesse and the Rhine-country, all Baden and the Breisgau:* compare Krüg. p. 357. In the phrase θεὸς καὶ πατήρ, καί is simply *and* (at the same time), not *namely, that is.*

(*d*) The signification *especially* may be questioned altogether (Bornem. *Luc.* p. 78, Fritz. *Mark,* p. 11) in those cases in which to a *general* there is added a *special* designation, which was really included in the former. Thus in Mk. i. 5, ἐξεπορεύετο πᾶσα ἡ Ἰουδαία χώρα καὶ οἱ Ἱεροσολυμῖται πάντες (xvi. 7), the special statement is made prominent by its very position, but καί is simply *and.* Compare H. vi. 10. Sometimes, on the other hand, the special terms come first, and καί is placed immediately before the general word under which these are included: e. g., Mt. xxvi. 59, οἱ ἀρχιερεῖς καὶ οἱ πρεσβύτεροι κ α ὶ τ ὸ σ υ ν έ δ ρ ι ο ν ὅ λ ο ν, *and* (in one word) *the whole Sanhedrin.*[1] In H. iii. 19 καί stands at the close of an entire exposition (before the final result): so also in 1 C. v. 13 in some MSS.

(*e*) When καί signifies *also* (which is not the case in E. v. 2, for instance),[2] it may sometimes be rendered by *indeed, just.*[3] See H. vii. 26, τοιοῦτος γὰρ ἡμῖν καὶ ἔπρεπεν ἀρχιερεύς, ὅσιος κ.τ.λ., *for such a high priest was just suitable for us;* H. vi. 7, 1 P. ii. 8 (Jo. viii. 25), Col. iii. 15, 2 C. iii. 6, 2 Tim. i. 12. Elsewhere it might be rendered *vicissim* (as in 1 C. i. 8, Ph. ii. 9), but " also " is perfectly sufficient.

(*f*) When καί appears in the apodosis after a particle of time (ὅτε, ὡς),—as in L. ii. 21, ὅτε ἐπλήσθησαν ἡμέραι ὀκτὼ τοῦ περιτεμεῖν αὐτόν, κ α ὶ ἐκλήθη τὸ ὄνομα αὐτοῦ Ἰησοῦς· or in L. vii. 12, ὡς ἤγγισε τῇ πύλῃ τῆς πόλεως, κ α ὶ ἰδοὺ ἐξεκομίζετο τεθνηκώς· A. i. 10, x. 17 [*Rec.*],—the construction really designed was,[4] ἐπλή-

---

[1] See Fritz. *Matt.* p. 786, *Mark,* p. 652. Compare Volc. Fritzsche, *Quæst. Lucian.* p. 67, Stallb. Plat. *Gorg.* p. 83 and *Rep.* II. 212.

[2] On καί *also* after relatives (H. i. 2, 1 C. xi. 23, al.) see Klotz, *Devar.* II. 636; and on the whole subject see Krüg. p. 359. The correct explanation of this " also " must in every case be obtained from the context. In 1 C. xv. 1 sq. we find καί several times repeated, forming a climax.

[3] Herm. *Vig.* p. 837, Poppo, *Thuc.* III. ii. 419. [See also Ellicott on E. i. 11, Alford on 2 C. iii. 6, Riddell, Plat. *Apol.* p. 168 sq., Liddell and Scott s. v. καί B. II. 1. With relatives, this καί answers to the Latin *qui idem:* see Klotz II. 636.—The καί in κἀγώ, Rom. iii. 7, is thus explained by some: see Meyer, Grimm s. v.—In several of the passages cited above for this use of καί some of the best commentators with reason prefer the simple *also,* seeking the explanation in the context: see *e. g.* Bleek and Delitzsch on H. vii. 26, Meyer and Ellicott on Col. iii. 15.]

[4] [That is, there is a mixture of two constructions: see § 65. 3.]

σθησαν δὲ ἡμέραι ... καὶ ἐκλήθη, ἤγγισε τῇ πύλῃ ... καὶ ἐξεκομίζετο.¹ In Jo. i. 19, however, we must not (with Baumg.-Crusius) thus connect ὅτε ἀπέστειλαν ... with καὶ ὡμολόγησε ; the clause ὅτε ἀπέστειλαν κ.τ.λ. attaches itself to αὕτη ἐστὶν ἡ μαρτυρία κ.τ.λ. : see Lücke *in loc.* As to καί commencing a parenthesis, as in Rom. i. 13 (Fritz. *in loc.*), see § 62. 1.

On καὶ γάρ see no. 8 ; on καὶ δέ, no. 7. Καί γε, *et quidem*, occurs in L. xix. 42,² A. ii. 18,—in both places without any intervening word, contrary to the usage of the earlier written language : as to later writers see Klotz, *Devar.* II. 318.

4. This connexion assumes the form of correlation when two words or clauses are, by means of καί ... καί (τε ... τε, A. xxvi. 16) or τε ... καί, joined together as corresponding to each other.³ Καί ... καί (or τε ... τε) is used when the members are presented to the writer's mind from the first as coordinate, *et ... et, both ... and, as well ... as:* τε ... καί, when to the first member he annexes a second, *et ... que, not only ... but also* (Klotz, *Devar.* II. 740). See Mt. x. 28, ὁ δυνάμενος καὶ ψυχὴν καὶ σῶμα ἀπολέσαι· 1 C. x. 32, ἀπρόσκοποι καὶ Ἰουδαίοις καὶ Ἕλλησιν καὶ τῇ ἐκκλησίᾳ· Ph. iii. 10, iv. 3 ; A. xxi. 12, παρεκαλοῦμεν ἡμεῖς τε καὶ οἱ ἐντόπιοι· L. ii. 16, ἀνεῦρον τήν τε Μαριὰμ καὶ τὸν Ἰωσὴφ καὶ τὸ βρέφος κ.τ.λ. (Krüg. p. 367). In the former case the members must be regarded as combined into one whole (one completed group) ; in the latter the second member is added to the first. The latter combination, however, does not in itself convey any expression

---

¹ [Similarly in Rev. x. 7 (§ 40. 5. *b*),—possibly A. xiii. 19,—and frequently after καὶ ἐγένετο (§ 65. 4. e).—Winer only incidentally refers to other cases in which καί commences the apodosis (§ 41. *a*. 4). It stands thus after εἰ or ἐάν in 2 C. ii. 2, Ja. iv. 15, Rev. iii. 20 Tisch. (καὶ εἰςελ.), Rev. xiv. 10, and perhaps in Ph. i. 22 : in Ja. ii. 4 καί is very doubtful. Compare 2 C. xi. 12. See Ellicott and Alford on Ph. i. 22 for an explanation of the true force of καί (*also*) in this case : see also Hartung, *Partik.* I. 130, Lightfoot on Ph. *l. c.*, A. Buttm. p. 362 (Jelf 759. *Obs.* 3). Compare no. 7 (*b*) on the similar use of δέ (Jelf 770).]

² [Καί γε here is doubtful, but is probably the true reading in A. xxvii. 27 : compare καὶ ὄφελόν γε, 1 C. iv. 8.—"There is a difference between this case" (καί ... γε) "and that in which καί and γε stand together, so that γε affects" not an intervening word, but "καί itself. Lucian has some examples of this combination, in which καί γε denotes *and indeed, and truly* (*Imag.* 11, *Tragop.* 251). It is said not to occur in older and better writers, though in Hippocr. p. 258. 11 we read καί γε in the sense *and even*, and Lysias (*in Theomn.* 2. § 7) uses καί γε in the sense of καί τοι : Hesychius may have had this latter passage in mind when he gave καί τοι as the explanation of καί γε." Rost u. Palm, *Lex.* I. 541. See also Klotz, *Dev.* II. 319, Bornem. *Luc.* p. 122 (Jelf 735).]

³ Such cases as Mk. ii. 26, καὶ ἔδωκεν καὶ τοῖς σὺν αὐτῷ οὖσιν· Jo. v. 27 [*Rec.*], where καί ... καί are not parallel to each other (the second καί signifying *also*), do not come under this head. Compare Soph. *Philoct.* 274.

of the relative value of the two members (Rost p. 728 sq.¹):
compare A. iv. 27, v. 24, Rom. i. 14, H. xi. 32, al. In the
course of lengthened enumerations, groups (pairs) are thus
formed by means of τε ... καί (... καί): H. xi. 32 [*Rec.*],
Βαράκ τε καὶ Σαμψὼν καὶ Ἰεφθάε, Δαυῒδ τε καὶ Σαμουὴλ
καὶ τῶν προφητῶν· 1 C. i. 30, H. vi. 2, A. ii. 9, 10, Ph. i. 7.

By καί ... καί are connected not only similar but also contrasted
clauses: Jo. vi. 36, καὶ ἑωράκατέ με καὶ οὐ πιστεύετε,—both seeing
and not-believing exist. So also in Jo. xv. 24, and probably in
xvii. 25 (Jelf 757. 2). In 1 Cor. vii. 38 the parallelism of the
contraria is disturbed by the pre-eminence given to the second
member. On τε and δέ in correspondence,—the latter particle com-
bining opposition ("lenis oppositio," Klotz II. 741) with connexion,
as in A. xxii. 28 [*Rec.*], *and the chiliarch answered ... Paul on the
other hand said*, and in A. xix. 3,—see Stallb. Plat. *Phileb.* p. 36,
Rep. II. 350, Herm. Eur. *Med.* p. 362 sq., Klotz *l. c.* (Jelf 754. 5).

Τε and καί are either placed together, between the two words which
they connect into one group (as in L. xxi. 11, φόβητρά τε καὶ σημεῖα·
A. ix. 18²), or are separated by one or two of these words, as L. xxiii.
12, ὅτε Πιλᾶτος καὶ ὁ Ἡρώδης· Jo. ii. 15, A. ii. 43, πολλά τε τέρατα
καὶ σημεῖα· x. 39, ἔν τε τῇ χώρᾳ τῶν Ἰουδαίων καὶ Ἱερουσαλήμ· Rom. i.
20, A. xxviii. 23, al. : here the article, preposition, or adjective in the
first member, serves for the second also. It is otherwise in Ph. i. 7,
ἔν τε τοῖς δεσμοῖς μου καὶ ἐν τῇ ἀπολογίᾳ κ.τ.λ.

In A. xix. 27 and xxi. 28 we find τε καί in one and the same clause,
in the sense of *que etiam:* ³ this is unusual in Greek writers, if indeed
it is not inadmissible.

5. Correlation appears in its sharpest form as *comparison:*
ὡς (ὥςπερ, καθώς⁴) ... οὕτως. The force of οὕτως is not unfrequently enhanced by καί, as in Ja. ii. 26, ὥςπερ τὸ σῶμα
χωρὶς πνεύματος νεκρόν ἐστι, οὕτως καὶ ἡ πίστις χωρὶς τῶν
ἔργων νεκρά ἐστιν· Jo. v. 21, Rom. v. 18, 21, 1 C. xv. 22, 2 C.
i. 7, E. v. 24, H. v. 3, 2 P. ii. 12⁵ (Jelf 760. 3). Sometimes

---

¹ [Here Rost maintains that the second member is usually the more important (Don. p. 573, Jelf 758). See Ellicott on 1 Tim. iv. 10.]
² [These passages illustrate an ambiguity of which we have a few examples in
the N. T. (see L. xii. 45, A. xiii. 1), for τε may here be independent of καί, and
may simply annex the clause (*and*): see A. ix. 29, xv. 32, xix. 6. Compare
Xen. *Anab.* 7. 6. 3, and Kühner II. 787.]
³ [" Here τε belongs to the sentence, καί to the particular word : in the converse case, A. xxvi. 10, καὶ πολλούς τε κ.τ.λ., καί belongs to the sentence, τε to
the word." A. Buttm. p. 360 sq.]
⁴ [Καθά, Mt. xxvii. 10 ; καθάπερ, 1 Th. ii. 11, al. ; καθώςπερ, H. v. 4 ; καθό,
Rom. viii. 26, al. ; καθότι, A. ii. 45, al. See Ellicott on G. iii. 6, 1 Th. ii. 11, E.
i. 4. On ὡς see Grimm, *Clavis* s. v.]
⁵ [Here οὕτως is not expressed.]

indeed καί even takes the place of the particle of comparison [1] in the second member: Mt. vi. 10, γενηθήτω τὸ θέλημά σου ὡς ἐν οὐρανῷ καὶ ἐπὶ γῆς· Jo. vi. 57, x. 15, xiii. 33, xvii. 18, A. vii. 51. See Bornemann, *Luc.* p. 71.

The popular language is fond of introducing καί into comparisons in other cases besides these, though the "also" is already contained in the particle of comparison; as 1 C. vii. 7, θέλω πάντας ἀνθρώπους εἶναι ὡς καὶ ἐμαυτόν· L. xi. 1, A. vii. 51, xv. 8, xxvi. 29. Thus we find καί in both members: [2] Rom. i. 13, ἵνα τινὰ καρπὸν σχῶ καὶ ἐν ὑμῖν καθὼς καὶ ἐν τοῖς λοιποῖς ἔθνεσιν· Mt. xviii. 33, Col. iii. 13, Rom. xi. 30 *v. l.* See Stallb. Plat. *Rep.* I. 372, Klotz, *Devar.* II. 635, Fritz. *Rom.* I. 37, II. 538 sq.

6. Next in order comes *disjunction*. Simple disjunction is effected by ἤ,—which, especially in impassioned language, is often repeated several times (Rom. viii. 35): ἢ καί, *or also, or even,* Mt. vii. 10, L. xviii. 11, Rom. ii. 15, xiv. 10, 1 C. xvi. 6 (compare Fritzsche, *Rom.* I. 122 [3]). Correlative disjunction is expressed by ἤ . . . ἤ, εἴτε . . . εἴτε, *sive . . . sive,* whether single words or entire clauses are opposed to one another: Mt. vi. 24, 1 C. xiv. 6 (ἤτοι [4] . . . ἤ, Rom. vi. 16), Rom. xii. 6, 1 C. xii. 13, 1 P. iv. 15,[5] al. (Don. p. 573, Jelf 777.)

Ἤ never stands for καί in the N. T., as καί never stands for ἤ (Marle, *Floril.* 124, 195,—compare Schæfer, *Demosth.* IV. 33); [6] but

---

[1] ["It is more correct to say that οὕτως is omitted before the καί, and that καί, retaining its proper meaning (*also*), takes on itself in addition the relation which οὕτως would have expressed." A. Buttm. p. 362.]

[2] ["In sentences thus composed of correlative members, when the enunciation assumes its most complete form, καί appears in *both* members, e. g., Rom. i. 13; compare Kühner, Xen. *Mem.* I. 1. 6. Frequently it appears only in the *demonstrative*, or only in the *relative* member; see Hartung, *Partik.* Vol. I. p. 126. In all these cases however the particle καί preserves its proper force. In the former case, 'per aliquam cogitandi celeritatem,' a double and reciprocal comparison is instituted between the two words to each of which καί is annexed; see Fritz. *Rom.* vol. I. p. 37: in the two latter cases a single comparison only is enunciated between the word qualified by καί and some other, whether expressed or understood." Ellicott on E. v. 23.]

[3] According to the nature of the ideas, the second, annexed by ἢ καί, may either be a supplementary addition (Bengel on Rom. ii. 15), inferior in weight to the first, or may have its force enhanced by the καί (as in 1 C. xvi. 6). See Klotz, *Devar.* II. 592.

[4] [By Klotz (II. 609), Rost u. Palm, Fritzsche, Meyer (on Rom. *l. c.*), ἤτοι (*aut sane*) is regarded as giving special emphasis to the former alternative: compare Don. p. 573, Jelf 777. 5. Hartung (II. 356) assigns it an *exclusive* force, "either *only* . . . . or:" so De Wette, Alford.]

[5] [An example of *simple* disjunction. On the comparative ἤ, which really belongs to this class (Don. p. 575, Jelf 779), see § 35. In one passage, Jo. xii. 43, the negative force of ἤ is increased by περ (ἤπερ): see Jelf 779. *Obs.* 5.]

[6] On *aut* for *et* see Hand, *Tursellin.* I. 540. On the other hand, disjunction

there are cases in which either particle might be used with equal correctness, each in its proper meaning (Poppo, *Thuc.* III. ii. 146); e. g., 1 C. xiii. 1, 2 C. xiii. 1 (compare Mt. xviii. 16), and also the passage from Heraclides quoted by Marle.¹ Where *dissimilia* are connected by καί (Col. iii. 11), they are merely joined to one another as distinct objects, not expressly indicated as different or opposed. In Mt. vii. 10 καὶ ἐάν brings in a second case, to which the speaker proceeds (*further*); but the best reading is probably ἢ καί. In L. xii. 2 the true completion of the sentence is καὶ οὐδὲν κρυπτόν. In Mt. xii. 27 Schott rightly renders καί by *porro*. Arranged as the clauses are in Mt. xii. 37, ἤ would be altogether out of place: the same may be said of Rom. xiv. 7.

It has been urged on polemic grounds, on the Protestant side, that ἤ is used for καί in 1 C. xi. 27, ὃς ἂν ἐσθίῃ τὸν ἄρτον τοῦτον ἢ πίνῃ τὸ ποτήριον τοῦ κυρίου. But—not to mention that here some good MSS. have καί (as in ver. 26, 28, 29)—ἤ may be very easily explained from the primitive mode of celebrating the Lord's Supper,² without lending any support to the Romish dogma of the *communio sub una:* see Bengel and Baumgarten *in loc.*³ If however we were disposed to refer ἤ to a real distinction in the administration of the sacrament, more indeed would follow from this passage (grammatically considered) than the Romish expositors can wish to deduce,—namely, the possibility of communicating by means of *the cup* alone! In A. i. 7 (x. 14⁴), xi. 8, xvii. 29, xxiv. 12, Rom. iv. 13, ix. 11, E. v. 3, ἤ stands in a *negative* sentence (Thuc. 1. 122, Ælian, *Anim.* 16. 39, Sext. Empir. *Hypot.* 1. 69⁵), where the Romans also use *aut* for *et* (Cic. *Tusc.* 5. 17, *Catil.* 1. 6. 15, Tac. *Annal.* 3. 54, al.⁶). In οὐχ ὑμῶν ἐστὶν γνῶναι χρόνους ἢ καιρούς, both γνῶναι χρόνους and γνῶναι καιρούς (we may think of *either* one *or* the other) are equally denied; so that in sense this sentence exactly coincides with γνῶναι χρόνους καὶ καιρούς. Lastly, when καί and ἤ occur in parallel passages (Mt. xxi. 23, L. xx. 2), the relation is differently conceived by the different writers; and it would be a manifest abuse of parallelism to infer that the two particles are synonymous.

Ἤ and καί have not unfrequently been interchanged by transcribers

---

by ἤ may to a certain extent include connexion by καί. If we say, "He who murders father *or* mother deserves the severest punishment," we naturally mean at the same time that he who murders both parents is not less liable to punishment. The *minus* includes the *majus*.

¹ On καὶ . . . καί, vel . . . vel, see Schoem. *Isœus* p. 307 (Jelf 757. *Obs.* 2).
² [Since "the bread was partaken of in the course of the meal, the wine at its close." Meyer.]
³ Even in our mode of communicating it is conceivable that one might receive the bread devoutly, but the cup in a state of sensuous (perhaps even sinful) distraction. Hence we also could say, "He who receives the bread *or* the cup unworthily."
⁴ [Here the best texts have καί.]
⁵ Fritz. *Rom.* III. 191 sq., Jacobs, Philostr. *Imag.* p. 374, and Ælian, *Anim.* p. 457.
⁶ Hand, *Tursell.* I. 534, [Madvig, *Lat. Gr.* 458. c.]

SECT. LIII.] THE CONJUNCTIONS. 551

(Jo. viii. 14, A. x. 14, 1 C. xiii. 1, al., Mätzner, *Antiph.* p. 97). Compare also Fritzsche, *Mark,* p. 275 sq., Jacob, Luc. *Alex.* p. 11. Tholuck, *Bergpred.* p. 132 sq., obtains no very clear result.[1]

7. *Opposition* finds its expression partly in the simple adversative form (δέ, ἀλλά), partly in the concessive sentence (μέντοι, ὅμως, ἀλλά γε). Μέν . . . δέ originally expressed a mutual relation between the opposed members, and therefore a grouping of contrasted clauses (1 P. iii. 18, iv. 6). This relation, however, has become weakened into simple correspondence (Rom. viii. 17, 1 C. i. 23), and has, logically, even sunk down below parallelism by means of καί . . . καί (Hartung II. 403 sqq.).[2]

The distinction between ἀλλά and δέ is, in general, the same as that between the Latin *sed* and *autem* (*vero* [3]). The former (the neuter plural of ἄλλος with altered accent, Klotz, *Dev.* II. 1 sq.) —which may frequently be rendered *notwithstanding, nevertheless, imo*—expresses proper and sharp opposition, annulling something which has gone before, or indicating that no attention is to be paid to it. Δέ, a weakened form of δή (Klotz *l. c.* p. 355), connects whilst it opposes, i. e., it adds something different, distinct, from that which precedes (Schneider, *Vorles.* I. 220). After a negative ἀλλά is used (οὐκ . . . ἀλλά, *not . . . but*); but we also find οὐ (μή) . . . δέ, *not . . . however* (*not . . . rather*), as in A. xii. 9, 14, H. iv. 13, vi. 12, Ja. v. 12, Rom. iii. 4,—οὔπω . . . δέ, H. ii. 8 (Thuc. 4. 86, Xen. *Cyr.* 4. 3. 13[4]). More particularly,

(a) Ἀλλά is used when a train of thought is broken off or interrupted (Jelf 774); either by an objection, as Rom. x. 19, 1 C. xv. 35, Jo. vii. 27 (see Klotz, *Devar.* II. 11, and compare Xen. *Mem.* 1. 2. 9, 4. 2. 16, *Cyr.* 1. 6. 9),—or by a correction, Mk. xiv. 36, 2 C. xi. 1,—or by a question, H. iii. 16 (compare Xen. *Cyr.* 1. 3. 11, Klotz II. 13),—or by a command, encouragement, or entreaty, A. x. 20, xxvi. 16, Mt. ix. 18, Mk. ix. 22, L. vii. 7, Jo. xii. 27 (compare Xen. *Cyr.* 1. 5. 13, 2. 2. 4, 5. 5. 24, Arrian, *Al.* 5. 26. 3 [5]). In all these cases that which has preceded is opposed (and annulled) by

---

[1] [1 C. ix. 15, καλὸν γάρ μοι μᾶλλον ἀποθανεῖν, ἢ τὸ καύχημά μου οὐδεὶς κενώσει (as the oldest MSS. read), is variously explained. Meyer takes ἤ as *alioquin* (Jelf 777. *Obs.* 3); but it is much more probable that there is an aposiopesis after ἤ. See Alford and Stanley *in loc.* Prof. Evans (*Speak. Comm.* III. 303) holds that the change of reading does not essentially alter the construction : "After ἤ supply ἵνα . . . After μᾶλλον ἤ the negative in οὐδείς logically vanishes, and οὐδείς is equivalent to τις." Such a construction (even if possible) seems much less easy and natural than the aposiopesis.]

[2] [Don. p. 575 sqq., Jelf 764-774. See also Webster, *Syntax*, p. 133, 119.]

[3] See Hand, *Tursell.* I. 559,—compare 425. [Madvig, *Lat. Gr.* 437, Zumpt 348, Donalds. *Lat. Gr.* p. 196, Ellicott on G. iii. 22.]

[4] Compare Hartung, *Partik.* I. 171, Klotz, *Devar.* II. 360 [". . . ut in particula quidem δέ non respici videatur praecedens negatio, sed per simplicem adfirmationem illud ponatur, quod est contrarium rei praecedenti." Klotz p. 361. See also Ellicott on E. iv. 15, Ph. iii. 12.]

[5] See Palairet p. 298, Krebs p. 208, Klotz, *Devar.* II. 5 (Jelf 774).

something else. Compare also Jo. viii. 26, and Lücke *in loc.* When ἀλλά stands in the apodosis, after conditional particles, it brings out the clause antithetically and therefore with greater force, like the Latin *at.* See 1 C. iv. 15, ἐὰν μυρίους παιδαγωγοὺς ἔχητε ἐν Χριστῷ, ἀλλ' οὐ πολλοὺς πατέρας (*yet not, on the other hand*), 2 C. iv. 16, xi. 6, xiii. 4 [*Rec.*], Col. ii. 5; and compare Her. 4. 120, Xen. *Cyr.* 8. 6. 18, Lucian, *Pisc.* 24, Ælian, *Anim.* 11. 31.[1]—The case is different in Rom. vi. 5, εἰ σύμφυτοι γεγόναμεν τῷ ὁμοιώματι τοῦ θανάτου αὐτοῦ, ἀλλὰ καὶ τῆς ἀναστάσεως ἐσόμεθα, *so shall we however* etc.: see Fritzsche *in loc.*[2]

The absorption by ἀλλά of the negative "no," after a negative question—as in Mt. xi. 8, τί ἐξήλθατε θεάσασθαι; κάλαμον ὑπὸ ἀνέμου σαλευόμενον; ἀλλὰ τί ἐξήλθατε ἰδεῖν; and in 1 C. vi. 6, x. 20, Jo. vii. 48 sq.—needs no comment.[3] Ἀλλὰ μὲν οὖν, Ph. iii. 8, is *at sane quidem:* ἀλλά opposes the present ἡγοῦμαι to the perfect ἥγημαι, as a correction.[4] In Rom. v. 14, 15, ἀλλά occurs twice, with a different reference in each case: in 1 C. vi. 11 it is repeated several times emphatically, with the same reference.[5]

(*b*) Δέ is often used when the writer merely subjoins something new, different and distinct from what precedes, but on that account not sharply opposed to it (Herm. *Vig.* p. 845): in 2 C. vi. 14 sqq., 1 C. iv. 7, xv. 35, we find it in a succession of questions (Hartung I. 169, Klotz, *Devar.* II. 356). Hence in the Synoptic Gospels καί and

---

[1] See Kypke II. 197, Niebuhr, *Ind. ad Agath.* p. 409, Klotz, *Devar.* II. 93 (Jelf *l. c. Obs.* 1).

[2] ["Male cum h. l. 1 Cor. iv. 15 . . . . contendas. Ibi enim ἀλλά post enuntiationes hypotheticas, quibus aliquid conceditur, in apodosi gravem ad præcedentem aut vocem aut sententiam oppositionem infert, *at.*" Fritzsche *l. c.* See especially Ellicott on Ph. i. 18, who remarks on such examples as this: "the primary force of ἀλλά is so far obscured that it does practically little more than impart a briskness and emphasis to the declaration."]

[3] See Schweigh. Arr. *Epict.* II. ii. 839, Raphel *ad* 1 C. *l. c.*

[4] Ἀλλ' ἤ, after a direct or indirect negation, occurs (occasionally in the LXX, e. g., Job vi. 5, and) three times in the N. T., in L. xii. 51, 2 C. i. 13, 1 C. iii. 5; in the last passage, however, it is probably not genuine. After Klotz's careful investigation (*Devar.* II. 31 sqq.)—in which he followed Krüger (*De formulæ* ἀλλ' ἤ *et affinium particularum post negationes vel negativas sententias usurpatarum natura et usu,* Brunsvic. 1834)—ἀλλ' ἤ must certainly be referred to ἄλλο, not to ἀλλά. Thus L. xii. 51 will be, *I have not come to bring on earth . . . . aught but division.* The fact that in 2 C. i. 13 ἀλλά itself precedes, does not invalidate this explanation: compare Plat. *Phæd.* 81 b, and see Klotz p. 36. [Compare Riddell, Plat. *Apol.* p. 175, Sandys, Isocr. *Paneg.* p. 46 sq., Jelf 773. 5.]

[5] [Πλήν occurs in the N. T. (1) as a preposition with the genitive, *except,* Mk. xii. 32, al. (in A. xv. 28, πλέον . . . . πλήν). (2) With ὅτι, A. xx. 23, Ph. i. 18 (in the best texts). (3) In all other passages πλήν approaches more or less nearly to ἀλλά. Its exceptive force is most visible in Rev. ii. 25, where ἄλλος precedes; see Jelf 779. *Obs.* 2. It introduces a correction in Mt. xxvi. 39, L. xxii. 42 (being parallel with ἀλλά in Mk. xiv. 36, quoted above): it follows a negative in L. xii. 31, xxiii. 28. In L. xix. 27 it is used to "break off and pass to another subject" (Liddell and Scott, s. v.). In L. xxii. 22 it follows μίν. In most passages it may be rendered by *notwithstanding, nevertheless,* or (better still) by the old-fashioned *howbeit.* See Don. p. 572, 576, Jelf 773. *Obs.* 4, Webster, *Syntax,* p. 145, Ellicott on Ph. i. 18, Lightfoot on Ph. iii. 16.]

δέ are sometimes parallel : in 2 C. vi. just quoted, ἤ is inserted in the midst of several repetitions of δέ.[1] Like the German *aber*, δέ is used in particular when an explanation is annexed,—whether as an integral part of a sentence (1 C. ii. 6, σοφίαν λαλοῦμεν ἐν τοῖς τελείοις, σοφίαν δὲ οὐ τοῦ αἰῶνος τούτου· iii. 15, Rom. iii. 22, ix. 30, Ph. ii. 8), or as itself an independent sentence, as in Jo. vi. 10, ix. 14, xi. 5, xxi. 1, G. ii. 2, E. v. 32, Ja. i. 6 :[2] also when, after a parenthesis or digression, the interrupted train of thought is taken up again (Herm. *Vig.* p. 846 sq., Klotz II. 376, Poppo, Xen. *Cyr.* p. 141 sq.), as in 2 C. x. 2,[3] ii. 12, v. 8, E. ii. 4, compare Plat. *Phæd.* p. 80 d, Xen. *An.* 7. 2. 18, Paus. 3. 14. 1 (*autem*, Cic. *Off.* 1. 43, Liv. 6. 1. 10). In an explanation which is at the same time a correction (e. g., 1 C. i. 16), the adversative signification of the particle is still perceptible. Sometimes δέ introduces a climax (H. xii. 6), or marks the steps in a regular progression of clauses (2 P. i. 5–7). On δέ in the apodosis see Weber, *Demosth.* p. 387, and (especially for the case in which δέ follows participles which stand in the place of a protasis, as Col. i. 21[4]) Jacobs, Æl. *Anim.* I. 26 *Præf.* When in a didactic passage δέ is frequently repeated (as in 1 P. iii. 14 sq.[5]), we must seek the explanation of the particle in the relations of the several clauses. In narrative we often find a number of sentences simply connected by δέ: see Acts viii. 1–3, 7–9.

Καὶ . . . δέ, in one and the same clause (as often in the best authors, Weber, *Dem.* p. 220), signifies *et . . . vero, atque etiam, and also*,—καί being *also* and δέ *and*, according to Krüger (p. 358), whilst Hartung (I. 187 sq.) maintains the reverse. See Mt. xvi. 18, H. ix. 21, Jo. vi. 51, xv. 27, 1 Jo. i. 3, A. xxii. 29, 2 P. i. 5.[6] In the reverse order, δὲ καί (2 P. ii. 1), the particles mean *but also*.

The N. T. use of μέν (a weakened form of μήν [7]) requires no special remark, for μέν . . . δέ . . . δέ Jude 8 (not 2 C. viii. 17) is easily explained. When μέν is answered by ἀλλά, as in Rom. xiv. 20, al. (compare *Iliad* 1. 22 sqq., Xen. *Cyr.* 7. 1. 16), the second member is made to stand out with greater prominence (Klotz, *Devar.* II. 3).

---

[1] Greek authors also, as all readers know, use δέ very frequently in narration. [In 2 C. *l. c.* the true reading is, no doubt, ἤ . . . δέ . . . ἤ . . . δέ.]

[2] [Jelf 767. 3 (Don. p. 576), Ellicott on G. ii. 2.]

[3] ["After the relative sentence the παρακαλῶ is taken up again by δέομαι δέ, the particle δέ standing in adversative relation to the contents of the relative sentence:" Meyer *in loc.* See also Ellicott on E. ii. 4, Jelf 767. 4.]

[4] Klotz, *Devar.* II. 374. [See Jelf 770. *Obs.* 2, Ellicott and Lightfoot on Col. i. 21. In A. xi. 17 *Rec.* and 1 P. iv. 18 (possibly) δέ is found in the apodosis after εἰ. See below, p. 749, and A. Buttm. p. 364.]

[5] See Wiesinger. Here, however, the third δέ is rejected by Lachmann [and other modern editors].

[6] Schæf. *Long.* p. 349 sq., Poppo, *Thuc.* III. ii. 154, Ellendt, Arr. *Alex.* I. 137. [See also Ellicott's full note on 1 Tim. iii. 10 (Jelf 769).]

[7] This occurs in the N. T. in H. vi. 14 only (and even there not without variant), in the genuine Greek combination ἤ μήν, to express an oath: see Hartung II. 376, 388 (Don. p. 569, Jelf 728. *a*). [The editors are divided between ἤ μήν and εἰ μήν, the latter having the support of the oldest MSS. : see § 55. 9. On the etymology of μέν (of which Donaldson considers the "emphatic and affirmative" μήν to be a lengthened form) see *New Crat.* p. 281 sq.]

Where μέν and καί are found in correspondence (A. xxvii. 21 sq.), we have an unmistakeable anacoluthon : see Herm. *Vig.* p. 841, Mätzner, *Antiph.* 257. On μέν not followed by δέ see § 63. I. 2. e. Against the lawfulness of supplying μέν before δέ (Wahl, *Clav.* p. 307) see Fritz. *Rom.* II. 423 : compare Rost p. 736 sq. (Don. p. 575-578, Jelf 765 sqq.)

The opposition conveyed by *yet, however,* is very rarely expressed in the N. T. Μέντοι is used most frequently by John, where another writer would have used a simple δέ :[1] once (Jo. xii. 42) he strengthens μέντοι by prefixing ὅμως. The latter particle only occurs twice besides, in Paul's Epistles (1 C. xiv. 7, G. iii. 15). Καίτοιγε however occurs in A. xiv. 17, in reference to something which has preceded, and with the meaning *although, quamquam.*[2] There is nothing peculiar in the N. T. use of ἀλλά γε, *yet on the other hand,* L. xxiv. 21, 1 C. ix. 2, al.[3] (Klotz, *Dev.* II. 24 sq.), except that γε immediately follows ἀλλά—a collocation of which there is probably no example in good writers (Klotz *l. c.* p. 15). The correlation *though . . . yet* is expressed by εἰ καί . . . ἀλλά in Col. ii. 5, εἰ γὰρ καὶ τῇ σαρκὶ ἄπειμι, ἀλλὰ τῷ πνεύματι σὺν ὑμῖν εἰμί; by εἰ καί . . . γε in L. xviii. 4 sq.[4] In general, εἰ καί signifies *although, si etiam, quamquam* (indicating something as an actual fact[5]), whilst καὶ εἰ is *even if, etiam*

---

[1] [Μέντοι occurs five times in St. John's Gospel, and also in 2 Tim. ii. 19, Ja. ii. 8, Jude 8. In all these instances—probably not excepting Ja. ii. 8, see De W., Brückner, Alford, Wordsw. (*Vulg.* "tamen")—it has this adversative force. See Ellicott on 2 Tim. *l. c.*, Jelf 730. *a,* 736. 3.]

[2] [Καίτοι itself occurs in H. iv. 3, with a participle (§ 45. 2), and with a finite verb in A. xiv. 17 (in the best texts). Strengthened by γε, placed immediately after it ("ut ipsa particularum notio eo modo acuatur, quasi Latine dicas *quamquam quidem :*" Klotz II. 654), it occurs in Jo. iv. 2, and in the received text of A. xiv. 17. In A. xvii. 27 the best reading is καί γε. (Don. p. 607, Jelf 772. *Obs.* 2.)]

[3] [These are the *only* examples of ἀλλά γε; but we have ἀλλὰ μὲν οὖν γε in Ph. iii. 8. The rendering given by Bornemann in L. xxiv. 21 (*Schol.* p. 160), "at sane," "at nimirum," seems more suitable than that given above (compare however § 61. 5) : it expresses better the mixture of opposition and affirmation which belongs to this combination. ("Hinc factum est, ut particulæ unam fere notionem . . . . exprimere videantur, qua cum aliqua adfirmatione vel potius exceptione aliquid opponatur antecedentibus :" Klotz II. 25.) Similarly in 1 C. ix. 2, *yet certainly, yet at all events.* See Meyer *ll. cc.*]

[4] [Also in L. xi. 8. On this use of γε (*at any rate, at all events*) in the apodosis see Liddell and Scott, *Lex.* s. v. II. 3. *a,* Hartung I. 380. On the position of γε in the sentence, see § 61. 5.—Γε very rarely occurs in the N. T., except in connexion with other particles (καί, καίτοι, ἀλλά, ἄρα, ἄρα, εἰ, εἰ δὲ μή, μὲν οὖν, μήτι) : probably the only examples besides those just quoted are 1 C. iv. 8 (where γε strengthens ὄφελον) and Rom. viii. 32, ὅς γε,—see no. 8. (Εἴ γε, L. xix. 17.) See Don. p. 568, Jelf 735, Webster p. 122.]

[5] [Practically this includes two cases, which in English require different renderings. (1) Where that which the sentence expresses is (in the writer's belief) an actual fact : here εἰ καί is *though* (L. xviii. 4, 2 C. xii. 11). (2) Where the writer concedes or assumes that the supposition is correct (1 C. iv. 7, 2 C. iv. 3). Here we are not always able to express καί in translation. Sometimes however its "ascensive" force (placing in relief either the whole clause or some

si (merely putting something as a supposed case[1]): compare Herm. *Vig.* p. 832, Klotz, *Devar.* II. 519 sq. (Jelf 861. 2.)

8. The *temporal* relation of sentences is expressed by ὡς, ὅτε (ὅταν), ἐπεί,—also by ἕως, μέχρι, πρίν; see § 41. *b.* 3, § 60. 4. A *consequence* is indicated by οὖν, τοίνυν, ὥςτε (μενοῦν); and more sharply and distinctly by ἄρα, διό (ὅθεν), τοιγαροῦν (οὐκοῦν in Jo. xviii. 37 only). The *causal* relation is expressed by means of ὅτι, γάρ (διότι, ἐπεί);[2] whilst ὡς, καθώς, καθότι (subjoining a clause), introduce rather an explanation than a reason. Lastly, a *condition* is indicated by εἰ (εἴγε, εἴπερ), ἐάν; § 41. *b.* 2.

(*a*) Of the particles which express a consequence, οὖν[3] is the most common; it is also the proper syllogistic particle.[4] Its reference in any particular instance may be gathered more or less easily from the context: e. g., Mt. iii. 8, 10, xii. 12, 1 C. xiv. 11 (see Meyer *in loc.*), Mt. xxvii. 22, A. i. 21, Rom. vi. 4. It is also very frequently used, like the German *nun*, simply to mark the progress of a narration (where it is only in virtue of a connexion in *time* that the second of two events can be said to rest on the first as its basis); see Jo. iv. 5, 28, xiii. 6, and compare Schæf. *Plutarch*, IV. 425. Like the German *also* or *nun*, οὖν is used especially after a parenthetical clause to take up the train of thought[5] (1 C. viii. 4, xi. 20),

---

single word) is very easily recognised—see 1 C. vii. 21, *if thou art even able*, etc., 1 P. iii. 14, Ph. ii. 17; compare *εἰ οὐδέ*, L. xii. 26. Perhaps "even if," though apparently inexact, is the most idiomatic translation in some passages, as this combination is used with considerable latitude in English. In some examples καί belongs to the following word in the sense of *also* (L. xi. 18, 2 C. xi. 15). Εἰ καί is found once with the optative (1 P. iii. 14), in every other instance with the indicative: Ph. iii. 12 is a different case, see p. 374. See Ellicott on Ph. ii. 17, Alford on this passage and on 2 C. v. 16.]

[1] [This combination is very rare in the N. T., for in almost all the examples of καὶ εἰ the καί is simply copulative (Mt. xi. 14, al.). The only instances seem to be 1 P. iii. 1, 1 C. viii. 5 (καὶ γὰρ εἴπερ): in Mk. xiv. 29 we must read εἰ καί, and in 2 C. xiii. 4 εἰ is not genuine. Meyer and Alford, however, are hardly justified in asserting that in this last passage καὶ γὰρ εἰ could only mean "even if," "even putting the case that." Καὶ εἰ would naturally have this meaning, and in the examples quoted by Hartung (I. 141) καὶ γὰρ εἰ is *for even if*. Still, as the double force of καὶ γάρ is acknowledged (see below p. 560), it is surely possible that εἰ, if genuine, might here stand out of connexion with the καί, this particle being merely copulative. Krüger (§ 69. 32. 21) expressly admits this meaning of καὶ γὰρ εἰ.]

[2] [Also by ὅς γε, Rom. viii. 32, *seeing that he*. (Don. p. 606, Jelf 735. 9.)]

[3] [Lünemann here refers to a work by V. C. F. Rost, *Ueber Ableitung, Bedeutung und Gebrauch der Partikel οὖν* (Gött. 1859).]

[4] [Compare Don. p. 596: "The particle οὖν is indicative rather of continuation and retrospect than of inference: and, in general, it should be rendered rather 'accordingly,' 'as was said,' 'to proceed,' than 'therefore,' which is properly expressed by ἄρα and its compounds." See also Don. p. 571, Ellicott on G. iii. 5, 21, Ph. ii. 1, Webster p. 144.]

[5] Heind. Plat. *Lys.* p. 52, Bornem. Xen. *Mem.* p. 285, Jacob, Luc. *Alex.*

or when the writer proceeds to explain or illustrate (by examples or otherwise), as in Rom. xii. 20 [*Rec.*].[1] (Jelf 737. 3. 5.)

Ἄρα: *accordingly, quæ cum ita sint, rebus ita comparatis*. The primary office of ἄρα may certainly have been to introduce " *leviorem conclusionem*,"[2] as indeed it occurs mainly in dialogue and in the language of common life (Klotz, *Devar.* II. 167, 717); but in later Greek the usage of the particle became extended, and particular writers, at all events, use it to express rigorous logical inference. *Ἄρα* inclines towards its original meaning when it stands in the apodosis (after conditional clauses), as in Mt. xii. 28, 2 C. v. 15 [*Rec.*], G. iii. 29, H. xii. 8 (compare Xen. *Cyr.* 1. 3. 2, 8. 4. 7),—or draws an inference either from the assertion (compare 1 C. v. 10, xv. 15, where it may be rendered *really, in fact, indeed*[3]) or from the conduct of another person (L. xi. 48). Of the N. T. writers Paul uses ἄρα most frequently, and that particularly when he analyses the contents of an O. T. quotation (Rom. x. 17, G. iii. 17,—compare H. iv. 9), or gives a résumé of a discussion (Rom. viii. 1, G. iv. 31 v. l.); though in these cases he as frequently uses οὖν. In questions, ἄρα refers either to some words or fact previously related (Mt. xix. 25, L. viii. 25, xxii. 23, A. xii. 18, 2 C. i. 17), or to some thought which exists in the mind of the speaker (Mt. xviii. 1), and which is more or less clearly shown to the reader. It then means *under these circumstances, rebus ita comparatis,* and sometimes *naturally, as may be conceived* (Klotz II. 176). Εἰ ἄρα, *si forte* (Mk. xi. 13, A. viii. 22), and ἐπεὶ ἄρα (1 C. vii. 14), also resolve themselves into this signification (Klotz II. 178).

The combination ἄρα οὖν, placed at the beginning of a sentence (see against this Hermann, *Vig.* p. 823), *accordingly then, hinc ergo*

---

p. 42, Dissen, Demosth. *Cor.* p. 413, Poppo, *Thuc.* III. iv. 738. [In both these cases we use our English *then* (so then, so now, accordingly, etc.).]

[1] [Μὲν οὖν. The examples of μὲν οὖν are of two different kinds. (1) Μέν is in correspondence with δέ,—so that here we have merely a combination of οὖν with the distributive formula μέν . . . δέ: see Mk. xvi. 19, Ph. ii. 23, al. (In several examples which appear to belong to this class, the δέ which follows has no connexion with the μέν: see A. Buttm. p. 370.) Sometimes however—as in the cases of the simple μέν—the second member is not expressed in strict form: see § 63. 2. e, where Winer thus explains Rom. xi. 13, H. ix. 1. (2) Οὖν in its proper sense is combined with the confirmative μέν (Jelf 729 sq., Ellicott on Ph. iii. 8) : many examples of this kind are found in the Acts, οὖν usually signifying " continuation and retrospect" (Don. p. 596). As in classical Greek, the emphatic addition may pass into a *correction* (Don. p. 577, Jelf *l.c.*, Herm., *Vig.* p. 845), *nay rather,*—see L. xi. 28 (1 C. vi. 4, 7). In this last sense the N. T. writers, perhaps more frequently, use μενοῦνγε: see Rom. ix. 20, x. 18, L. xi. 28 *Rec.*, Ph. iii. 8 (Tisch., Westcott).]

[2] [Quoted from Klotz *l. c.* Compare Don. p. 567, 597, Jelf 788 sq., Ellicott on G. v. 11, Webster p. 121 sq. Ἄρα is strengthened by γε in Mt. vii. 20, xvii. 26, A. xi. 18 *Rec.* ("itaque ergo," see Fritz. *Matt.* p. 563) : ἄρα γε also follows εἰ, A. xvii. 27. In classical Greek we find γε joined with ἄρα (A. viii. 30), but not with ἄρα.]

[3] Klotz p. 169 : compare Stallb. Plat. *Rep.* I. 92, Hoogeveen, *Doctrina Particul.* I. 109 sq.

(ἄρα expressing conclusion, οὖν continuation[1]), is a favourite formula with Paul: see Rom. v. 18, vii. 3, viii. 12, ix. 16, al. I do not know of an example of ἄρ' οὖν in any Greek author: in Plat. *Rep.* 5. p. 462 a the more recent texts have ἆρ' οὖν[2] (in a question); compare Schneider *in loc.*, Klotz, *Devar.* II. 180.

Διό (δι' ὅ) is used most frequently by Paul and Luke:[3] τοίνυν, *in truth then, indeed now,* and τοιγαροῦν (the strengthened τοιγάρ, Klotz II. 738), *wherefore then,* are rare.—On ὥστε and its constructions see p. 377.

(*b*) Ὅτι points in general to some existing fact, something which lies before us, and hence answers to *that* as well as to *because, quod:* in the latter case it is sometimes brought out more prominently by prefixing διὰ τοῦτο (*propterea quod*). In some instances it is used elliptically. See L. xi. 18, *if Satan also is at variance with himself, how will his kingdom stand?* (I ask this) *because ye say* "*Through Beelzebub,* etc.;" L. i. 25, Mk. iii. 30 (*Act. Apocr.* p. 57), Bornem. *Luc.* p. 5 sq. (Jelf 849. *Obs.* 1). So also in Jo. ii. 18, where the case is not altered if we render ὅτι *in regard to the fact that*[4] (Fritz. *Matt.* p. 248 sq.). In Mt. v. 45, however, ὅτι is simply *because.* In some passages it has been doubted whether ὅτι means *because* or *that:* this question must be decided on hermeneutical grounds.

The compound διότι (chiefly found in later Greek), *for this reason that,* and then *because* (Fritz. *Rom.* I. 57 sq.[5]), is used most frequently by Paul and Luke.

---

[1] Compare Hoogeveen, *Doctr. Part.* I. 129 sq., II. 1002. [Ellicott on G. vi. 10.]

[2] [I have ventured to write ἆρ' οὖν (ed. 5) for ἄρ' οὖν (editions 6, 7): the latter is surely a misprint. Klotz, *l. c.,* says we must certainly write ἆρ' here; and Schneider, also quoted by Winer, corrects ἄρ' into ἆρ'.—Compare A. Buttm. p. 371.]

[3] [On διό, *on which account,* see Ellicott on G. iv. 31, Klotz II. 173 ("οὖν est fere Latinum *quod quum ita sit;* . . . . διό est *quam ob rem,* ut etiam hoc aptius duas res conjungat"), A. Buttm. p. 233: διότι has been taken in this sense in 1 Th. ii. 18 (1 P. ii. 6), but even here probably has its ordinary meaning. The strengthened form διόπερ, *for which very reason,* occurs 1 C. viii. 13, x. 14, xiv. 13 *Rec.* Ὅθεν, *whence it follows that, wherefore,* occurs in this sense five or six times in the Ep. to the Hebrews, also Mt. xiv. 7, A. xxvi. 19. On τοίνυν (L. xx. 25, 1 C. ix. 26, H. xiii. 13, Ja. ii. 24 *Rec.*) see Jelf 790, Shilleto, Dem. *Fals. L.* p. 12, Alford on 1 C. ix. 26. Τοιγαροῦν occurs in 1 Th. iv. 8, H. xii. 1: "τοιγάρ proprie significat *hac de caussa igitur* . . . . saepenumero ad τοιγάρ particulas accedit οὖν particula, quod si fit, syllogistica sententiae ratio magis exstat:" Klotz *l. c.* See also Ellicott on 1 Th. *l. c.* (Webster p. 146.)]

[4] [Taking ὅτι as = εἰς ἐκεῖνο, ὅτι, "hence in meaning equivalent to *quatenus:*" Meyer *in loc.,*—who adopts this meaning in several passages (e.g., Jo. ix. 17, xvi. 9, Mk. xvi. 14, 2 C. i. 18). On ὅτι *because* and the antecedent it implies see Jelf 849. 3; on certain cases in which its meaning seems to lie between "because" and "that," see Ellicott on 2 Th. iii. 7; on 1 Tim. vi. 7 (δῆλον being omitted), see Alford *in loc.*]

[5] [Fritzsche here maintains that διότι is sometimes simply "nam," *for,* in the N. T.: this is denied by Meyer (on Rom. i. 19) and Ellicott (on 1 Th. ii. 8, G.

The most common causal particle in cultivated prose is γάρ, which corresponds to the German *denn* (*for*). In accordance with its etymology, however, this particle (a compound of γε and ἄρα, ἄρ) expresses generally an affirmation or assent (γε) which stands in relation to what precedes (ἄρα !),[1]—*sane igitur, certe igitur, sane pro rebus comparatis* (*enim*, in its first signification). It is from this primary meaning of the particle that its power to express a *reason* is derived. In conformity with this primary meaning, γάρ (to pass over familiar details) is used

(*a*) First, and very naturally, to introduce explanatory clauses: whether these appear as supplementary additions (or, in some instances, parentheses), as Mk. v. 42, xvi. 4, 1 C. xvi. 5, Rom. vii. 1; or whether they fall into the regular course of the writing, as in 2 C. iv. 11, Rom. vii. 2, Ja. i. 24, ii. 2, H. ix. 2, G. ii. 12. Here γάρ is to be rendered by *in fact, indeed, that is* (Klotz, p. 234 sq.). Explanation in the wider sense, however, includes every argument or demonstration (even H. ii. 8), which we introduce with "for" (*denn*); the German *ja*, however, comes nearer to the primary signification of γάρ (Hartung I. 463 sqq.).[2] This is especially illustrated by those passages in which it was at one time supposed that something must be supplied[3] before γάρ, *for:* Mt. ii. 2, *Where is the king of the Jews that has been born? the fact is, we have seen his star:* Mt. xxii. 28, 1 C. iv. 9, 2 C. xi. 5, Ph. iii. 20, 1 P. iv. 15, 2 P. iii. 5. Klotz's words (p. 240) are here in point : " Nihil supplendum est ante enuntiationem eam, quæ infertur per particulam γάρ, sed ut omnis constet oratio, *postea demum* aliquid tacita cogitatione adsumendum erit, sed nihil tamen alieni, verum id ipsum, quod ea

---

ii. 16). In modern Greek γάρ has disappeared, διότι (and ἐπειδή) having taken its place : Mullach, *Vulg.* p. 395.]

[1] See Hartung I. 457 sqq., Schneider, *Vorles.* I. 219, Klotz, *Devar.* II. 232 sq. "Si sequimur originem ipsam ac naturam particulæ γάρ, hoc dicitur conjunctis istis particulis: *Sane pro rebus comparatis*, ac primum adfirmatur res pro potestate particulæ γι, deinde refertur eadem ad antecedentia per vim particulæ ἄρα." (Klotz p. 232.) [Compare Don. p. 605 : "The particle γι = 'verily' combined with ἄρα = 'therefore' or 'further,' is written γάρ. This combination does not differ very much in signification from γοῦν = γι οὖν. Γάρ signifies 'the fact is,' 'in fact,' 'as the case stands ;' it may often be rendered 'for,' but this English particle is much less extensive in its applications." (Jelf 786, Webster p. 123.) On the explicative γάρ see Ellicott on G. ii. 6, 1 Th. ii. 20 ; and on the particular case in which it follows a parenthesis (G. ii. 6, according to Ellicott and Lightfoot) see Shilleto, Dem. *Fals. Leg.* p. 60 sq. It will be seen that our "for" may be used in many of the examples quoted below, for which another rendering is suggested.]

[2] As in Mt. ii. 20, Gehe ins Land Israel, es sind ja gestorben (*Go into the land of Israel; they are in fact dead*, etc.).

[3] This practice has been carried even to a pedantic extent; e. g., in Mt. iv. 18, xxvi. 11, Mk. iv. 25, v. 42, 2 C. ix. 7. In the sentence "He makes clothes, for he is a tailor," if we were to supply between the clauses, "One cannot wonder at this," it would appear ridiculous to every body. As to the Latin *nam* see Hand, *Tursell.* IV. 12 sqq.

sententia quæ præcedit γάρ particulæ enuntiavit;" the fact is, we have seen his star,—therefore he must have been born somewhere (Mt. ii. 2).

(*b*) In answers and rejoinders (Klotz p. 240 sq.). Here the same primary meaning displays itself; for in Jo. ix. 30, ἐν γὰρ τούτῳ θαυμαστόν ἐστιν κ.τ.λ., the answerer first of all makes reference to the words of the Pharisees related in ver. 29 (ἄρα), and then adds an asseveration (γε): sane quidem mirum est etc., *in this then it is certainly, truly, indeed wonderful.* So also in 1 C. viii. 11, ix. 9, 10, xiv. 9, 1 Th. ii. 20: in none of these passages is there anything to be supplied before γάρ.¹ Equally unnecessary are such supplements in the case of *admonitions* (Klotz p. 242), e. g., Ja. i. 7, *Let not then that man indeed think* etc.; ἄρα here points back to ὁ γὰρ διακρινόμενος and γε joins a corroboration with the inference.

(*c*) In questions. Here γάρ seems to have wandered farthest from its primary meaning. Indeed the origin of this usage may have been afterwards lost sight of, and γάρ merely regarded as the sign of an urgent question,—urgent, because justified by the connexion in which it stands ² (Klotz p. 247). In many passages, however, the essentially inferential force of γάρ (ἄρα !), *igitur rebus ita comparatis, adeo,* may still be perceived. In Mt. xxvii. 23 Pilate's question, τί γὰρ κακὸν ἐποίησεν, refers back to the demand of the Jews in ver. 22, σταυρωθήτω. From this Pilate deduces what in his question he expresses as the opinion of the Jews: *quid igitur* (since ye demand his crucifixion) *putatis eum mali fecisse?* So also in Jo. vii. 41: *does then the Messiah come out of Galilee? num igitur putatis, Messiam,* etc. When γάρ is thus used, the reference to what precedes is clear in every case,—not excepting A. xix. 35, viii. 31. Here also the usual practice has been to supply something before the question, were it but a *nescio* or a *miror*:³ against this see Klotz p. 234, 247.

Lastly, Klotz (p. 236, 238) appears to be right in denying the truth of the common assertion, that even prose writers (as Hero-

---

¹ A. xvi. 37, Παῦλος ἔφη· δείραντες ἡμᾶς δημοσίᾳ ἀκατακρίτους, ἀνθρώπους Ῥωμαίους ὑπάρχοντας ἔβαλον εἰς φυλακήν, καὶ νῦν λάθρᾳ ἡμᾶς ἐκβάλλουσιν; He immediately answers the question himself: οὐ γάρ, ἀλλὰ ... αὐτοὶ ἡμᾶς ἐξαγαγέτωσαν, *non sane pro rebus comparatis.* In the ἄρα element γάρ looks back to the circumstances described in the preceding words, and by the γε adds a corroboration based on this,—"continet" (as Klotz says, p. 242) "cum adfirmatione conclusionem, quæ ex rebus ita comparatis facienda sit."

² The peculiar force of such questions with γάρ results from their being suggested by the very words of the other person, or by the circumstances: hence there exists a right to require an answer. See *e. g.* 1 C. xi. 22. [On τί γάρ; Ph. i. 18 (Rom. iii. 3), see Ellicott's full note on the former passage (Don. p. 605, 385).]

³ Herm. *Vig.* p. 829, and *ad* Aristoph. *Nub.* 192, Wahl, *Clav.* 79 sq. [Compare also Alford on H. xii. 3. Donaldson's explanation ("With the interrogative γάρ expresses the effect of something observed:" p. 605) is substantially the same as that given by Klotz.]

dotus [1]) not unfrequently, in the liveliness of their thought, place the causal clause with γάρ *before* the sentence which it confirms.[2] In the N. T.[3] there is certainly no need of this canon. Of Jo. iv. 44, Meyer's explanation [4] is no doubt correct. In H. ii. 8, the clause ἐν γὰρ τῷ ὑποτάξαι τὰ πάντα gives the proof that there is nothing which was not made subject to him by God's decree; and hence, indirectly, that (ver. 5) the world to come also has been made subject to him. The words νῦν δὲ οὔπω κ.τ.λ. show that already the subjection has at least commenced. We must distinguish the promise of Scripture from the actual fulfilment, which however has already begun. 2 C. ix. 1 stands in obvious connexion with viii. 24. 1 C. iv. 4, οὐδὲ ἐμαυτὸν ἀνακρίνω· οὐδὲν γὰρ ἐμαυτῷ σύνοιδα ἀλλ᾽ οὐκ ἐν τούτῳ δεδικαίωμαι, is to be rendered, *I am indeed conscious of nothing, but* etc.

(*d*) Γάρ is repeated several times, changing its reference: see Rom. ii. 11–14, iv. 13–15, v. 6, 7, viii. 5 sq., x. 2–5, xvi. 18 sq., Ja. i. 6, 7, ii. 10, iv. 14, 1 C. iii. 35 [iii. 3 sq.?], ix. 16 sq., H. vii. 12–14 (Lycurg. 24. 1, 32. 3).[5] In such passages γάρ is often used to establish a series of thoughts subordinated to one another (Ja. i. 6, 1 C. xi. 8, Rom. viii. 5 sqq.): see Fritz. *Rom.* II. 111.[6] In some instances, however, we find the same words repeated with γάρ, that some further statement may be annexed: e. g., in Rom. xv. 27 (but not 2 C. v. 4).

Καὶ γάρ is either *etenim* (simply connecting) or *nam etiam* (giving prominence): see Klotz, *Devar.* II. 642 sq. This latter meaning (which has frequently been passed over by the commentators, those on the N. T. included [7]) is found in Jo. iv. 23, A. xix. 40, Rom.

---

[1] See Kühner II. 453 (Jelf 786. *Obs.* 3).
[2] See Matthiæ, Eurip. *Phœn.* p. 371, Stallb. Plat. *Phæd.* p. 207, Rost, *Gr.* p. 744. Hermann, Eurip. *Iph. Taur.* 70: sæpe in ratione reddenda invertunt Græci ordinem sententiarum, caussam præmittentes: quo genere loquendi sæpissime usus est Herodotus. Compare also Hoogeveen I. 252. [Klotz, *l. c.*, attacks the notion that there is a transposition of clauses: this stands or falls with the rendering of γάρ. If γάρ be rendered "the fact is," or "profecto" (Donaldson, Klotz *l. c.*), there is no transposition.]
[3] Fritzsche, 2. *Diss. in 2 Cor.* p. 18 sq., Tholuck on Jo. iv. 44 and H. ii. 8.
[4] [Namely, that Jesus did not hesitate to return into Galilee, because a prophet has no honour in his own country, but must acquire his honour abroad, and this Jesus had done. Brückner's objection to this seems very just,—that it supposes the Evangelist to have left out that part of the statement which was really essential. See Ellicott, *Hist. Lect.* p. 133, Alford *in loc.* There is much to be said for Origen's view, that by τῇ ἰδ. π. is meant *Judæa*: see especially Westcott *in loc.*]
[5] See Engelhardt, Plat. *Apol.* p. 225, Fritzsche, *Quæst. Luc.* 183 sq.
[6] [Whether successive clauses beginning with (the argumentative) γάρ are ever (in the N. T.) *co-ordinate*, assigning reasons for the same statement, is a disputed point. The affirmation is usually maintained: see Grimm, *Wilkii Clavis* s. v., Fritzsche and Alford on Mt. vi. 32. Meyer (on Mt. *l. c.*, Rom. viii. 6, xvi. 19) rejects this usage for the N. T., maintaining that in the passages which appear to exemplify it the second γάρ is explicative.]
[7] Weber, *Demosth.* p. 271, Fritzsche, *Rom.* II. p. 433. [On καὶ γάρ see Ellicott on Ph. ii. 27, 2 Th. iii. 10. Once (Jo. iv. 45) καὶ and γάρ are separated.]

xi. 1, xv. 3, xvi. 2, 1 C. v. 7, 2 C. ii. 10, al. : in several of these passages even Wahl renders καὶ γάρ by *etenim*.

Τε γάρ, Rom. vii. 7, is *for also* or *for indeed:*[1] in H. ii. 11 (Rom. i. 26 [2]), however, τε and καί correspond, and in 2 C. x. 8 there is probably an anacoluthon (Klotz II. 749).

Ἐπεί, from a particle of time, has become a causal particle, like our *weil* and the Latin *quando*.[3] Ἐπειδή entirely answers to the Latin *quoniam*, formed from *quom* (quum) and *jam*. Ἐπείπερ *since indeed* (Herm. *Vig.* p. 786) occurs once only, Rom. iii. 30 (and here not without variant [4]); see Fritzsche *in loc.* (Jelf 849, Don. p. 605.)

Καθώς and ὡς in appended clauses furnish illustration rather than strict proof, and are to be considered equivalent to the Latin (*quoniam*) *quippe, siquidem*, and our obsolete *sintemal*. On ὡς—which in 2 Tim. i. 3, G. vi. 10, Mt. vi. 12, signifies *as*—compare Ast, Plat. *Polit*. p. 336, Stallb. Plat. *Symp*. p. 135, Lehmann, *Lucian* I. 457, III. 425, al. As to ἐφ' ᾧ, *because*,[5] see p. 491.

(c) Εἰ has the compounds εἴγε, " if, that is,"[6] *quandoquidem* (when no doubt exists), and εἴπερ *if only, provided that* (implying no decision),

---

[1] Herm. Soph. *Trach*. p. 176, Schæf. *Dem*. II. 579, Plutarch IV. 324, Klotz, *Devar*. II. 749 sqq. [Shilleto, Dem. *Fals. Leg*. p. 96.]
[2] [Here τε γάρ is answered by τε (Rom. xiv. 8, 2 C. v. 13), unless we ought to read δέ for τε in ver. 27.—On μὲν γάρ see § 63. I. 2. e : in this combination γάρ retains its ordinary force.]
[3] [Also our *since*. Neither ἐπεί nor ἐπειδή is used *of time* in the N. T., except in L. vii. 1, where recent editors read ἐπειδή (*Rec*. ἐπεὶ δέ). On ἐπειδή see Ellicott on Ph. ii. 26.—A relative adverb *of place* is sometimes used *of time, manner*, etc. Compare οὗ, Rom. v. 20 ; ὅπου, 1 C. iii. 3, also 2 P. ii. 11.]
[4] [The weight of MS. evidence is in favour of εἴπερ (Lachmann, Westcott and Hort, Alford). On ἐπείπερ Fritzsche remarks : " infert ἐπείπερ rem certam nullique dubitationi obnoxiam."—'Ἐπειδήπερ, L. i. 1, "*quoniam quidem*: this word does not occur elsewhere in the N. T., or in the LXX and Apocrypha, but is often used by classical authors." Meyer *in loc.* Lünemann quotes Arist. *Phys*. 8. 5, Dion. Hal. 2. 72, Philo, *ad Caj*. § 25, and Hartung, *Partik*. I. 342 sq. On the force of περ see Don. p. 572, *New Cr*. p. 388, Jelf 734.]
[5] [Οὗ εἵνεκεν, L. iv. 18 (Is. lxi. 1), is often taken in this sense (compare οὕνεκα), in conformity with the Hebrew : see Meyer. The more natural rendering, however, is *wherefore* (Vulg., Syr.).]
[6] [Winer's German rendering *wenn nämlich* (in ed. 6, *wann nämlich*) does not very well agree with *quandoquidem*. His note on G. iii. 4, εἴγε καὶ εἰκῇ, will show the view which he took of this particle : " *quandoquidem, siquidem etiam frustra,*—i. e. puto equidem, ista omnia vobis frustra contigisse."— It is not easy to decide on the distinction between these two particles in the N. T. Hermann's canon (*Vig. l. c.*), that a writer introduces by εἴγε an assumption which he believes to be correct and true, seems at all events inapplicable to N. T. usage. See Meyer and Ellicott on G. iii. 4, E. iii. 2 (who maintain that in all cases it is the context and not the particle that suggests this meaning) ; Lightfoot on G. iii. 4 ("εἴπερ is, if anything, more directly affirmative than εἴγε" in the N. T.) ; Green, *Crit. Notes*, p. 119 sq. (who holds that the difference between the particles in N. T. usage is simply that εἴγε " is the more pointed of the two "). Accepting Klotz's estimate of the proper force of εἴγε (as indicating that if the assumption be correct the conclusion *must*

—see Herm. *Vig.* p. 834, and compare Klotz, *Devar.* II. 308, 528: these compounds are almost confined to Paul's Epistles. The distinction just named shows itself in most passages. On E. iii. 2 see Meyer: the use of εἴπερ in 1 P. ii. 3, and probably in 2 Th. i. 6, appears to be of a rhetorical nature. On these passages and on Rom. viii. 9, Col. i. 23, see Fritz. *Prälimin.* p. 67 sq.[1]

Εἰ itself retains the meaning "if" even in those passages in which, as regards the sense, it stands for ἐπεί, *since* (A. iv. 9, Rom. xi. 21, 1 Jo. iv. 11, 2 P. ii. 4, al.). So far as the expression is concerned, the sentence is conditional (*if*, as is actually the case), and the categorical sense does not for the moment come into consideration. Sometimes this usage rests on rhetorical grounds.[2] The same may be said of the expressions in which εἰ may be rendered *that:* see § 60. 6. The use of εἰ to express a wish, *if only, O that* (in which case Greek writers commonly use εἴθε or εἰ γάρ, Klotz, *Devar.* II. 516), is found, according to recent commentators, in L. xii. 49; the verse being punctuated thus, καὶ τί θέλω; εἰ ἤδη ἀνήφθη, *And what do I wish?* (answer) *O that it were already kindled!* See Meyer[3] *in loc.:* as to the aorist see Klotz, *l. c.,* "si de aliqua re sermo est, de qua, quum non facta sit olim, nunc nobis gratum fore significamus, si facta esset illo tempore." There is however something artificial in such a question in the mouth of Jesus. Of the objections which Meyer raises against the ordinary explanation—*How* (how earnestly) *do I wish that it were already kindled!*—the second is of less weight than (in point of usage) the first. (Don. p. 549, Jelf 856. *Obs.* 2.)

---

certainly follow), we have no English expression which will of itself convey the full meaning of the particle: "if, that is," "if at least," will suit the passages of the N. T. in which it occurs, viz., 2 C. v. 3, G. iii. 4, E. iii. 2, iv. 21, Col. i. 23 (Rom. v. 6, Westcott and Hort). Εἴπως may be translated "if only," "if really," "provided that:" Rom. iii. 30, viii. 9, 17, 1 C. viii. 5, xv. 15 (2 C. v. 3, Lachmann), 2 Th. i. 6, 1 P. ii. 3 *Rec.* We must however remember that this particle, like εἰ, is sometimes used rhetorically where there is no real doubt: see Ellicott on 2 Th. i. 6. Ἐάνπερ (H. iii. 6 *Rec.,* iii. 14, vi. 3) is similar to εἴπερ.]

[1] [The compound εἴπως, *if (whether) by any means* or *possibly,* occurs A. xxvii. 12, Rom. i. 10, xi. 14, Ph. iii. 11. Similarly μήπως (§ 56. 2).]

[2] Dissen, Demosth. *Cor.* p. 195; Bornemann, Xen. *Conv.* p. 101.

[3] [In his fifth edition Meyer has given up this view (which is defended by Grotius, Stier, Alford, al.), and now—with De W., Bleek, Grimm, al.—renders the passage as Winer does below (*How earnestly do I wish that* etc.). Meyer's "first objection" had been that τί cannot = ὡς: he now quotes as parallel Mt. vii. 14 (reading τί with Lachmann, Tregelles, Bleek, al.,—see however Tisch. ed. 8, Green, *Dev. Crit.* p. 13), 2 S. vi. 20, Cant. vii. 6. (In modern Greek τί is used in this sense, e.g., τί καλὸς ἄνθρωπος! See Mullach, *Vulg.* p. 210, 321.) The second objection had reference to the use of εἰ instead of ὅτι, though preceded neither by such a verb as θαυμάζω, nor by a verb which implies *attempt* (Jelf 804. 9, 877. *Obs.* 5): on this point he refers to Ecclus. xxiii. 14, Her. 9. 14. 6. 52. It seems however very doubtful whether any sufficient reason has yet been assigned for forsaking the usual meaning of εἰ, and the interpretation adopted in our A. V. See Green, *Crit. Notes,* p. 57.]

9. Final clauses are expressed by means of the conjunctions ἵνα, ὅπως (ὡς). Objective clauses[1]—which, as they express the *object* of the principal sentence in the form of a perception or judgment, are merely exponents of its predicate, and hence strictly take the place of the objective case in the simple sentence[2] (*I see that this is good, I say that he is rich*)—are introduced by ὅτι or ὡς. Yet for clauses of both kinds conjunctions are less indispensable, as the infinitive presents a convenient means of expression (§ 44).

Ὅτι is the proper objective particle, like *quod* and *that*. It is used in this sense when *e. g.* it follows forms of asseveration, as in 2 C. xi. 10, ἔστιν ἀλήθεια Χριστοῦ ἐν ἐμοί· G. i. 20,[3] ἰδοὺ ἐνώπιον τοῦ θεοῦ· 2 C. i. 18, πιστὸς ὁ θεός· Rom. xiv. 11,—for in all these forms there is implied "I declare." Compare Fritzsche, *Rom.* II. 242 sq. When ὅτι introduces the *oratio recta*, it is to be taken in exactly the same way; see Madvig 192, and compare Weber, *Demosth.* p. 346. [See Jelf 802. *Obs.* 8; and below, p. 683.]

Ὡς, the adverb of the pronoun ὅς (Klotz, *Devar.* II. 757), retains the meaning *how, ut*, when it follows verbs of *knowing, saying*, etc. (Klotz p. 765): A. x. 28, ἐπίστασθε ὡς ἀθέμιτόν ἐστιν ἀνδρὶ Ἰουδαίῳ, *ye know how it is not lawful for a Jew*.[4] Thus ὅτι and ὡς, when used in an objective clause, proceed from different conceptions on the part of the speaker, but agree in sense.

Ὅπως, like *ut* (quo), is properly an adverb, *how*, πῶς (Klotz, *Devar.* II. 681,—compare L. xxiv. 20), but has also come into use as a conjunction. Ἵνα was originally a relative adverb, *where, whither* (Klotz *l. c.* p. 616): from local direction it was transferred to direction of will (design), and thus may be compared with the Latin *quo* (Don. p. 570).—Ὡς denoting *design* (Klotz p. 760) does not occur in the N. T., except in the well-known phrase ὡς ἔπος εἰπεῖν, H. vii. 9; compare Matth. 545. Recent grammarians are inclined to give a different explanation of this formula; see Klotz II. 765,[5] Madvig 151.—On the N. T. use of ἵνα for the infinitive, see p. 420 sqq.

10. The use of all these conjunctions, devised for the expression

---

[1] Weller, *Ueber Subjects- und Objectssätze etc.* (Meiningen, 1845).

[2] Thiersch, *Gr. Grammat.* p. 605 (Lon. p. 584, Jelf 800).

[3] [Lightfoot (comparing ἴδε ὅτι, Ps. cxviii. 159, Lam. i. 20) inclines towards taking ἰδού here as a *verb* (ἰδοῦ).]

[4] [It may be questioned whether in such passages as this ὡς does not mean *how* in the stricter sense, qualifying some particular word, "*how unlawful*, etc." (Meyer). See Ellicott on Ph. i. 8, Meyer on Rom. i. 9, A. Buttm. p. 245.]

[5] [Klotz considers the clause rather consecutive than final: similarly Jelf 864. 1, Kühner II. 1008 (ed. 2). Compare however Donaldson, p. 599, Roby *Lat. Gr.* II. 282. On ὡς with infinitive see above, p. 400 sq.]

of the various relations of sentences, would be set aside again in its regularity, if it were really the practice of the N. T. writers —according to the doctrine long assumed as true by the exegetes (following indeed the scholiasts [1] and the earlier philologers), and taught in hermeneutics (Keil, *Hermen.* p. 67)—to use one conjunction for another, so as frequently to make δέ equivalent to γάρ, γάρ to οὖν, ἵνα to ὥστε, etc.[2] But in every case such confusion of conjunctions exists in appearance only. The appearance of interchange sometimes arises from the possibility of conceiving the general relation of two sentences to each other in various ways,[3] so that the precise logical connexion in any particular passage is the result of some mode of thought characteristic of the writer (or of his nation—see below, s. v. ἵνα), and therefore not familiar to the reader; in other instances it is to be explained by a conciseness of expression which is foreign to the genius of our own language.

Wherever the apostles write δέ, they had in some way or other "but" in their thought; and it is the duty of the commentator to reproduce in his own mind this very connexion of thought, and not, for the sake of convenience, to dream of an

---

[1] Fischer *ad Palæph.*, p. 6.—This principle is assumed by Pott, Heinrichs, Flatt, Kühnöl, Schott, and even by D. Schulz.

[2] Even better expositors are not free from this arbitrariness: thus Beza takes ἀλλά for *itaque* in 2 C. viii. 7. In opposition to such procedure see my *Progr. Conjunctionum in N. T. accuratius explicandarum caussæ et exempla* (Erlangen, 1826). It is strange indeed to see how the commentators (up to a recent period) take the apostles to task again and again, and almost always supply them with a different conjunction from that which actually stands in the text. If a calculation were made, we should certainly find that in Paul's Epistles, for instance, there are not more than six or eight passages in which the apostle has hit upon the right particle, and does not need the commentator to help him out. This has introduced great arbitrariness into N. T. exegesis. Are we to suppose that Paul and Luke knew Greek no better than many of their censors? The Hebrew usage cannot be appealed to here by any who do not take a wholly irrational view of the Hebrew language: indeed such an arbitrary use of *quid pro quo* is not possible in any human speech. The arbitrariness of the N. T. interpreters was rendered the more obvious by the fact that different commentators often assigned entirely different meanings to a conjunction in the same passage. Thus in 2 C. viii. 7 ἀλλά is used for γάρ according to some, according to others for οὖν, etc.: in H. v. 11 some take καί as used for ἀλλά, whilst others give it the meaning *licet:* in H. iii. 10 Kühnöl leaves it to our choice whether we will take δέ as standing for καί, or as used in the sense of *nam.* Thus the mere subjective judgment had the most unmeasured scope.— The translators of the N. T. books (not excepting even the excellent Schulz in the Epistle to the Hebrews) are also deserving of censure, since they render the conjunctions in the most arbitrary manner.

[3] On such a case compare Klotz II. p. 5, and what is remarked below (after the paragraph on οὖν).

interchange of conjunctions, perhaps directly opposite in meaning. For how absurd would it be to think that the apostles could actually write " for " where they intended " but," or " but" where they should have written " for." Any child can distinguish such relations as these. How imbecile then must they have been if they wrote " for " when they intended the very opposite—" therefore." Those interpreters only who have never accustomed themselves to think of the language of the N. T. as a *living* language, or who shun the labour of following with exactness a writer's thought, could imagine anything of the kind; and it is no honour to Biblical exegesis that such principles should have long remained in favour. In the mind of man, like always joins itself to like. If then a conjunction is apparently used in a strange signification, we must first of all labour to show how in his thought the writer was *led* from the primary to the unusual meaning of the word. This however was never thought of: had it been seriously considered, the chimera would at once have vanished into air.

As purely fictitious as this canon of " unlimited interchange" is the doctrine of the " weakening " of conjunctions, which teaches that even particles with a sharply defined meaning, such as *for, but*, are in many cases altogether redundant, or are mere particles of transition. (See *e. g.* no. 3, below.) The more recent commentators indeed have abandoned this arbitrary but convenient canon; and hence we shall merely pick out some peculiarly specious examples, in which the true meaning of a conjunction long remained unrecognised, or in which the better commentators are not agreed as to the connexion of thought.

1. Ἀλλά never stands

(a) For οὖν. In 2 C. viii. 7 ἀλλά means simply *but* (*at*). From Titus, to whom he had given a commission, Paul turns to the readers of the Epistle, calling upon them on their side to do that which he desires; for the clause with ἵνα is to be taken in an imperatival sense. —E. v. 24 is not an inference from ver. 23. The proposition of ver. 22, that wives ought to be subject to their husbands ὡς τῷ κυρίῳ, is proved in the 23rd and 24th verses,—first from the *position* held by Christ and by the husband (both are κεφαλαί), *but* secondly (and this is the main point) from the *claim* (on obedience) which—as for Christ, so also for the husband—results from this relative position. The 24th verse, far from merely repeating the contents of ver. 22, is that which gives the conclusion of the argument, and explains the words ὑποτασσ. τοῖς ἀνδράσιν ὡς τῷ κυρίῳ. The significant apposition αὐτὸς σωτὴρ τοῦ σώματος does not interrupt the progress of the sentence ; whereas Meyer's explanation, in which these words are taken as forming an independent sentence, introduces a thought which arrests the argument.[1] On A. x. 20 (Elsner *in loc.*) see above, no. 7, p. 551.

(*b*) For εἰ μή. Mk. ix. 8 [*Rec.*], οὐκέτι οὐδένα εἶδον, ἀλλὰ τὸν Ἰησοῦν μόνον, means : They *no longer* saw any one (of those whom they had previously seen, ver. 4), *but* (they saw) Jesus alone. In Mt. xx. 23 (Raphel and Alberti *in loc.*) we must after ἀλλά repeat δοθήσεται from the preceding δοῦναι, and render the conjunction *but*.[2]

(*c*) For *sane, profecto.* Ἀλλά has not this meaning either in Jo. viii. 26 (see above, no. 7, p. 552), or in Jo. xvi. 2, where it means *imo* or *at*, as in A. xix. 2, 1 C. vi. 6. Rom. vi. 5, where ἀλλά (καί) occurs in the apodosis, has certainly no place here.

2. Δέ never means

(*a*) *Therefore, then.* In 1 C. xi. 28 δέ means *but*, in contrast to the ἀναξίως ἐσθίειν of ver. 27 : *But let a man examine himself* (that he may not bring upon himself such guilt). 1 C. viii. 9 adds to the general principle of ver. 8 a restriction for actual practice, in the form of an exhortation : *But take heed that this liberty* etc. In Rom. viii. 8, if Paul had wished to regard the proposition θεῷ ἀρέσαι οὐ δύνανται as a consequence of what precedes, he might have continued with *therefore* (which meaning Rückert here assigns to δέ) ; he passes however from the ἔχθρα εἰς θεόν to the other side of the same truth, θεῷ ἀρέσαι οὐ δύνανται. Had not a clause been introduced between these two sentences, no one would have found any difficulty here. In Ja. ii. 15 δέ (if genuine) means *jam vero, atqui*.

(*b*) *For.*[3] In Mk. xvi. 8 [*Rec.*] εἶχε δέ is a mere illustration, the *cause* of this τρόμος and ἔκστασις being assigned in the words ἐφοβοῦντο

---

[1] [Meyer's view is defended by Ellicott and Alford : see their notes.]
[2] [Even in Mk. iv. 22 ἀλλά is simply *but* (but rather), not *save, except*. It has frequently been maintained that we have in the N. T. instances of the converse practice, the use of εἰ μή (ἐὰν μή) in the sense of ἀλλά (G. i. 7, ii. 16, Rom. xiv. 14, 1 C. vii. 17, Rev. xxi. 27, Mt. xii. 4, L. iv. 26, 27) : see Jelf 860. 5. *b*, Green, *Gr.* p. 230 sq. There is no sufficient reason for believing that this interchange exists in the N. T. See Meyer *ll. cc.* ; Fritz. *Rom.* III. 195, *Matt.* p. 421 ; Winer, Ellicott, Lightfoot, Eadie, on G. i. 7. On G. i. 19 Lightfoot remarks : "The question is not whether εἰ μή retains its exceptive force or not, for this it seems always to do (see note on i. 7), but whether the exception refers to the whole clause or to the verb alone." Similarly Winer (on G. ii. 16) : "Sunt duae sententiae invicem conflatae : non consequitur quisquam δικαιο-σύνην ex operibus legis, et : non consequitur quisquam δικαιοσ. nisi per fidem."]
[3] Poppo, *Thuc.* II. 291, *Ind. ad Xen. Cyr.* s. v., Bornem. *Ind. ad Xen. Anab.* s. v. On the other side see Herm. *Vig.* p. 846, Schaef. *Demosth.* II. 128 sq., V. 541, Lehm. *Lucian* I. 197, Wex, *Antig.* I. 300 sq. In the signification *to wit, that is,* the two conjunctions coincide : δέ annexes a new proposition which is to be added to what precedes ; the clause introduced by γάρ appears as an

SECT. LIII.]   THE CONJUNCTIONS.   567

γάρ : some good MSS., however (which Lachmann follows), have γάρ in the place of δέ. Similarly in Jo. vi. 10 the words ἦν δὲ χόρτος κ.τ.λ. are a supplementary explanation : see above. In 1 Th. ii. 16 ἔφθασε δέ κ.τ.λ. presents a contrast to the purpose of the Jews expressed in εἰς τὸ ἀναπληρῶσαι αὐτῶν τὰς ἁμαρτίας, *But* (as, by their actions, they would have it so) *the punishment has come upon them for this*. In Mt. xxiii. 5 the words πλατύνουσι δέ κ.τ.λ. contain the details of the general statement which precedes, πάντα τὰ ἔργα αὐτῶν ποιοῦσι πρὸς τὸ θεαθῆναι : the γάρ which recent editors have received was probably introduced by some who stumbled at δέ. In 1 Tim. iii. 5 εἰ δέ τις κ.τ.λ. signifies, *But if any one* etc. : if ver. 6 be taken into consideration, these words form a parenthetical clause, contrasted with τοῦ ἰδίου οἴκου προϊστάμενον. 1 C. iv. 7 is, *who separates thee* (declares thee pre-eminent) ? *But what hast thou which thou didst not receive ?*—that is, " *But* if thou appealest to the pre-eminence which thou possessest, I ask thee, Hast thou not received it ? " In 1 C. vii. 7 (Flatt, Schott) δέ signifies *potius*. In 1 C. x. 11 the words ἐγράφη δέ form an antithesis to what precedes, as is shown by the very position of the verb, at the head of its clause : *all this happened . . ., but it was recorded* etc. In 1 C. xv. 13 δέ is really adversative. If Christ is risen, then the resurrection of the dead is a reality ; *but* if the resurrection of the dead is not a reality, then (reasoning backwards) Christ also is not risen. Ver. 14 contains a further inference, *But if Christ is not risen, then* etc. The one proposition of necessity establishes or annuls the other. In 2 P. i. 13 δέ introduces a sentence antithetical to καίπερ εἰδότας (ver. 12). On Ph. iv. 18 see Meyer.

(*c*) Nor is δέ ever a mere copula [1] or particle of transition. Mt. xxi. 3 (Schott) is, *Say, The Lord hath need of them, but immediately he will let them go :* i.e., these words will not remain without effect, *rather* will he immediately, etc. In A. xxiv. 17 the narration proceeds by means of δέ to another event. In 1 C. xiv. 1 δέ is *but : but* the διώκειν τὴν ἀγάπην must not hinder you from ζηλοῦν τὰ πνευματικά. Meyer's view of 2 C. ii. 12 is more correct than De Wette's : Paul goes back to ver. 4. In 1 C. xi. 2 it would be a mistake to consider δέ (as Rückert does) a mere indication that the writer proceeds to a new subject (thus Luther has left the word untranslated, Schott renders it by *quidem*): the words attach themselves without any break to the exhortation which immediately precedes, μιμηταί μου γίνεσθε, —*yet* (in this exhortation I intend no blame) *I praise you* etc. In Rom. iv. 3, also, Luther and many others have in translation omitted δέ (at the commencement of a quotation, in which the LXX have καί) ; but neither here by Paul, nor by James in ch. ii. 23, is the

---

explanation confirming what precedes. In the main the two modes of expression often amount to the same thing, see Herm. *Vig.* p. 845. (Jelf 768. 3.)

[1] [And yet must frequently be rendered *and*, as our *but* is often far too strong. In Mt. xxi. 3 it is easy to trace the amount of opposition implied by the connective δέ without resorting to Winer's somewhat forced explanation.]

adversative particle inserted arbitrarily or without thought: it brings out the ἐπίστευσε more forcibly, and as it were antithetically.

3. Γάρ has been wrongly taken for

(a) The adversative *but*.[1] 2 C. xii. 20 means, *All this I say for your edification, for I fear* etc.: this is the very reason of my saying what I have said. In Rom. iv. 13 the clause with γάρ gives the proof of the last words of ver. 12, τῆς ἐν ἀκροβυστίᾳ πίστεως τοῦ πατρός κ.τ.λ. In Rom. v. 6 sq. the first γάρ simply points to the fact in which the love of God (ver. 5) manifested itself, the death of Christ for ungodly men; the second γάρ explains *a contrario* how the death (of the innocent) for an unrighteous man is a display of surpassing love; the third γάρ justifies the assertion μόλις ὑπὲρ δικαίου κ.τ.λ. 1 C. v. 3: "And *you* have not felt compelled to exclude the man? *For I* (on my part), *absent in body*, . . . *have already determined* etc. That you, therefore, who have the man before your eyes, would inflict the (milder) punishment of exclusion, might surely have been expected." Pott here takes γάρ for *alias!* On 1 C. iv. 9 see above, p. 558. 2 C. xii. 6: *Of myself I will not boast, for if I should wish to boast I shall not be a fool* (and hence I *could* boast). In Ph. iii. 20 ἡμῶν γάρ κ.τ.λ. stands in most direct relation to οἱ τὰ ἐπίγεια φρονοῦντες, *those whose mind is on earthly things!* (a summary of ver. 19), *For our conversation is in heaven*, —it is for this reason that I warn you against them (ver. 18 sq.). In Rom. viii. 6 the clause with γάρ states the reason why οἱ κατὰ πνεῦμα (ver. 4) τὰ τοῦ πνεύματος φρονοῦσιν, viz., because the φρόνημα τῆς σαρκός leads to death, but the φρόνημα τοῦ πνεύματος to life: ver. 5 contains the proof of ver. 4. The true explanation of Col. ii. 1 was pointed out by Bengel.[2] H. vii. 12 (Kühnöl, "autem") contains the reason of ver. 11: *for* the alteration of the priestly succession and the abolition of the law are necessarily connected; see Bleek *in loc.* In 2 P. iii. 5 (Pott) it is explained how such men can come forward with such frivolous assertions (ver. 3, 4). H. xii. 3 supports the preceding resolve (τρέχωμεν κ.τ.λ.) by a reference to the example of Christ.

(b) *Therefore, then.* In L. xii. 58 all difficulty is removed by Bengel's remark: "γάρ saepe ponitur, ubi propositionem excipit tractatio." 1 C. xi. 26 explains εἰς τὴν ἐμὴν ἀνάμνησιν (ver. 25). In Rom. ii. 28 the connexion is this: an uncircumcised man who acts according to the law may pass judgment on thee, who, though circumcised, transgressest the law, *for* it is not what is external (as circumcision) that *makes the true Jew*. On H. ii. 8 see above, p. 560.

---

[1] Markland, Eur. *Suppl.* v. 8, Elmsley, Eur. *Med.* 121. See on the other side Herm. *Vig.* p. 846, Bremi in the *N. krit. Journ.* IX. 533.

[2] ["Declarat, cur verbo *certans* usus sit (i. 29), nam sequitur mox, *certamen.*" Bengel.]

(c) *Although*: Jo. iv. 44 (see Kühnöl). In this verse γάρ is simply *for;* πατρίς can only mean *Galilee* (ver. 43). [See above, p. 560.]

(d) *On the contrary:* 2 P. i. 9 (Augusti). Δέ might have been used if the meaning intended had been, *But (on the contrary) he who lacketh these* (virtues) etc. With γάρ, the sentence confirms (illustrates) *a contrario* (μή) the words which precede, οὐκ ἀργοὺς ... Χριστοῦ ἐπίγνωσιν,—*for he who lacketh these is blind:* by this means a more forcible reason is supplied to the exhortation which follows (ver. 10).

(e) *Notwithstanding* (ἀλλ' ὅμως): 2 C. xii. 1 [1] (here there certainly is great fluctuation in the reading, but the common reading δή is not so decidedly false as Meyer maintains it to be), *It is in truth of no advantage to me to boast myself* (xi. 22 sq.); *for I will now come* (I will, that is, now come,—Klotz, *Devar.* II. 235) *to visions and revelations of the Lord.* Paul places in contrast (compare ver. 5) *boasting of himself* (of his own merits) and boasting of the marks of distinction accorded him by God. Of the latter he will boast (ver. 5); hence the meaning is, *Yet boasting* (of myself) *is of no advantage, for now I will come to a subject of boasting which excludes and renders superfluous all boasting of self.*

(f) The mere copula. In Rom. iii. 2 πρῶτον μὲν γάρ commences the *proof* of the assertion πολὺ κατὰ πάντα τρόπον. A. ix. 11: *Inquire in the house of Judas for Saul of Tarsus, for he is praying* (thou wilt therefore find him there), *and he saw a vision* (which prepared him for thee): compare Bengel *in loc.* A. xvii. 28, τοῦ γὰρ καὶ γένος ἐσμέν, is a verse quoted verbatim from Aratus: γάρ may also be taken as giving a reason for ἐν αὐτῷ ζῶμεν καὶ κινούμεθα καὶ ἐσμέν. In A. iv. 12 the clause οὐδὲ γὰρ ὄνομά ἐστιν κ.τ.λ. develops more precisely and consequently proves the statement ἐν ἄλλῳ οὐδενὶ ἡ σωτηρία: an attentive reader perceives at once what the second sentence contains beyond the first. In A. xiii. 27 we may, with Bengel, Meyer, al., explain the connexion thus: *To you, ye* (foreign) *Jews . . . is this word of salvation sent, for those who dwell in Jerusalem have spurned this Saviour.* Yet it is more probable that Paul intended to continue thus: *"for* he is proved to be the Messiah foretold to our fathers;" compare ver. 29, 32 sqq. The reasoning loses in external compactness through the narration of the events in which the prophecies had received their fulfilment. In any case γάρ is no mere particle of transition, as Kühnöl maintains. In 2 C. iii. 9 the words εἰ γὰρ ἡ διακονία κ.τ.λ. appear to me so far to contain a confirmation of the thought of the passage, as that διακονία τῆς δικαιοσύνης expresses something more definite than διακονία τοῦ πνεύματος: *if* (although) *the ministration of death was glorious . . . . how should not the ministration of the Spirit be much more glorious?* [2] Fritzsche's explanation (*Diss. Corinth.* I.

---

[1] [Meyer defends γάρ (as the more difficult reading); but Lachmann, Tischendorf, Tregelles, Westcott and Hort, agree in adopting, καυχᾶσθαι δεῖ, οὐ συμφέρον μέν, ἐλεύσομαι δέ.]

[2] [It is perhaps by accident that ver. 9 itself is not translated. In ed. 5 there

p. 18 sq.) I consider artificial. In Mt. i. 18 (Schott), after the words τοῦ Ἰησοῦ Χριστοῦ ἡ γένεσις οὕτως ἦν the detailed account begins (as is frequently the case) with γάρ, *namely, that is.*

4. Οὖν has been incorrectly explained, as equivalent to

(*a*) *But.* In A. ii. 30 (Kühnöl) προφήτης οὖν ὑπάρχων is simply annexed as an inference to the preceding sentence. David is dead and buried: *therefore* those words which he appears to utter of himself were spoken by him in the character of a prophet, in reference to the resurrection of Christ. A. xxvi. 22 is not an antithesis to ver. 21: Paul, reviewing his apostolic life up to the period of this imprisonment, comes to this conclusion,—*I continue then, by God's help, up to this day* etc. Even Kühnöl in his *Comment.* (p. 805) correctly renders οὖν *igitur,* but in the *Index* gives it the meaning *sed, tamen!* Mt. xxvii. 22, τί οὖν ποιήσω Ἰησοῦν, is, *What am I then* (since you have decided for Barabbas) *to do with Jesus?*

(*b*) *For.* In Mt. x. 32 πᾶς οὖν ὅστις does not assign a reason for the statement πολλῶν στρουθίων διαφέρετε ὑμεῖς, but is a resumption and continuation of the main thought (ver. 27), κηρύξατε . . . . καὶ μὴ φοβεῖσθε: Fritzsche takes a different view.[1] In the parallel passage, L. xii. 8 λέγω δὲ ὑμῖν· πᾶς ὃς ἂν ὁμολογήσῃ κ.τ.λ., the δέ is not essentially different, but it gives more prominence to the sentence. In 1 C. iii. 5 τίς οὖν ἐστιν Ἀπολλώς; *Who then* (in accordance with this partisanship) *is Apollos?* In 1 C. vii. 26 οὖν introduces the γνώμη which the apostle has just said (ver. 25) that he will give.

(*c*) A mere copula, or as being altogether redundant. Rom. xv. 17 (Köllner) becomes plain at once by a reference to ver. 15, 16 (διὰ τὴν χάριν κ.τ.λ.). In Mt. v. 23 even Schott passes over οὖν entirely; but without doubt it introduces a practical inference (a warning) from ver. 22, which speaks of the guilt of anger, etc. In Mt. vii. 12 it is more difficult to define the connexion, and even the more recent commentators are widely apart: Tholuck has probably pointed out the right view,[2] but his survey of the different expositions is far from being complete. In Jo. viii. 38, καὶ ὑμεῖς οὖν ἃ ἠκούσατε παρὰ τοῦ πατρὸς ποιεῖτε, the οὖν is most certainly not redundant; by this particle the conduct of the Jews (*accordingly ye also*) is, with keenest irony, set over against the conduct of Jesus, as following from the same rule.

Of these four conjunctions δέ and οὖν are those which most readily approximate in meaning; and hence there are passages in

---

follows: *For the ministration of justification is* (the ministration of justification is, that is to say) *more glorious than the ministration of condemnation.*]

[1] [Fritzsche connects this verse with ver. 23.—Meyer takes οὖν as conclusive, and as referring to the previous context generally, from ver. 16.]

[2] [Tholuck considers οὖν to refer to the preceding part of ch. vii. Compare Alford's note.]

SECT. LIII.]   THE CONJUNCTIONS.   571

which either might be used with equal propriety (e.g., Mt. xviii. 31), though even when used as mere continuatives (in narration) they are not really identical. Instead of saying "Jesus found two fishermen, who .... Moreover he said to them, etc.," I may also say "Jesus found .... He said therefore to them, etc." The sense is but little affected by the change, but the two sentences are differently conceived. In the former case, after mentioning the *coming* and *finding*, I add the *speaking* as a new and distinct fact. In the latter case the thought is, *He said therefore* (taking advantage of this circumstance) *to them*. But we have no right to say that a narrator who uses δέ here should have used οὖν, or *vice versa.*—Sometimes also γάρ and δέ would be equally correct; see above, 10. 2. *b* (p. 566 sq.). In Jo. vi. 10 the evangelist writes: "Jesus said, Make the men sit down: *now* there was much grass in the place." He might have written, "*For* there was much grass etc." In the latter case, the circumstance would have been represented as the occasion of the direction given, whereas in the former the clause is simply explanatory: see Klotz II. 362, and compare Herm. *Vig.* p. 845 sq. Hence the two forms differ in their conception. For this reason no one has a right to adduce passages from the Synoptic Gospels,—e. g. L. xiii. 35 as compared with Mt. xxiii. 39—to prove the complete identity of δέ and γάρ. But even if δέ and οὖν, δέ and γάρ, are in such cases *nearly* equivalent, still it does not follow that they can be interchanged in all their meanings, even those which are most sharply defined. As for γάρ and ἀλλά, these particles are far too strongly marked to be interchangeable at will, or to be used as expletives.

There is considerable variation of reading even in the oldest MSS. (and versions[1]) in respect of these conjunctions. For δέ and γάρ see Mt. xxiii. 5, Mk. v. 42, xii. 2,[2] xiv. 2, L. x. 42, xii. 30, xx. 40, Jo. ix. 11, xi. 30, al., Rom. iv. 15 (Fritz. *Rom.* II. 476). For δέ and οὖν, L. x. 37, xiii. 18, xv. 28, Jo. vi. 3, ix. 26, x. 20, xii. 44, xix. 16, A. xxviii. 9, al. For οὖν and γάρ, A. xxv. 11, Rom. iii. 28.

5. Ὅτι is never equivalent to

(*a*) Διό, *wherefore*, in which sense the Hebrew כִּי is sometimes taken, but incorrectly.[3] In L. vii. 47 nothing but a blind opposition

---

[1] Hence, when a conjunction is in question, the versions should not without great caution be cited as authorities in the critical apparatus. Yet in nothing have the earlier critics shown such negligence as in dealing with the ancient versions: even those which are more familiar, and which are most easily accessible, are cited incorrectly ten times to one,—cited, that is, in cases where, either from the character of the language or from the principles of the translator, they cannot give, and did not intend to give, any evidence respecting a variant. It is to be regretted that this critical apparatus remains unsifted, even in the most recent editions of the Greek Testament.

[2] [This should no doubt be L. xii. 2. Jo. ix. 11 is out of place: it illustrates the interchange of δέ and οὖν.]

[3] See Winer, *Simonis* s. v. : see however Passow s. v. ὅτι. [In the latest works founded on Passow, as the Lexicons of Rost u. Palm, Liddell and Scott (ed. 5),

to Romanists (see Grotius and Calovius *in loc.*) could misinterpret ὅτι: see Meyer *in loc.*[1] On 2 C. xi. 10 see above, no. 9 (p. 563). —Nor does this particle stand for the direct interrogative διὰ τί[2] in Mk. ix. 11, as De Wette and others maintain. De Wette adduces in support of his view the passages cited by Krebs from Josephus; not considering that in these passages ὅ τι (ὅ,τι, as Lachmann writes) appears as a pronoun in an indirect question, —a usage which does not need the authority of Josephus (Kypke I. 178). On this passage however see above, p. 208. Fritzsche, on very slight authority, reads τί οὖν (from Matthew); but this is undoubtedly a correction. In Mk. ix. 28 the better MSS. (even A) have διὰ τί,[3] as in Mt. xvii. 19. In Mk. ii. 16, also, D at least has διὰ τί: Lachmann reads τί ὅτι. If however ὅτι be received, it will not of necessity be an interrogative. On Jo. viii. 25 (Lücke) see § 54. 1.

(*b*) *Quanquam.* Kühnöl renders L. xi. 48, *though they killed them, but ye* etc.: this verse was correctly explained long ago by Beza. Kühnöl himself has (in ed. 4) given up this signification as regards Mt. xi. 25: Jo. viii. 45 also is correctly explained by him in his 3rd edition.

(*c*) Ὅτε. On 1 Jo. iii. 14 see Baumg.-Crusius. In 1 C. iii. 13 (Pott) it is evident that ὅτι specifies more exactly why ἡ ἡμέρα δηλώσει κ.τ.λ. Everyone knows that the *transcribers* have often confounded ὅτι and ὅτε[4] (compare Jo. xii. 41, 1 C. xii. 2, 1 P. iii. 20, al.); and hence in those passages of the LXX in which ὅτι appears to mean *when* (1 K. viii. 37 included), we must without hesitation read ὅτε. In all the passages cited by Pott (on 1 C. iii. 13) the editions of the LXX actually have ὅτε, on good MS. authority.

(*d*) *Profecto.* In Mt. xxvi. 74 ὅτι is recitative: in 2 C. xi. 10 it signifies *that* (as after formulas of swearing),—see above, no. 9. In Rom. xiv. 11, cited from Is. xlv. 23, the meaning is, *By my life I swear, that* etc.

It has been maintained that ὅτι is sometimes—e.g., in Mt. v. 45 —equivalent to ὅς; against this see Fritzsche on Mt. *l.c.* This verse explains and proves from the treatment of πονηροί by the heavenly Father, that by ἀγαπᾶν τοὺς ἐχθρούς κ.τ.λ. they become children of this Father.

6. Ἵνα, *in order that* (sometimes preceded by a preparatory διὰ τοῦτο, Jo. xviii. 37, A. ix. 21, Rom. xiv. 9, al.), is said to be fre-

---

the meaning *therefore* does not occur. In ed. 4 of Liddell and Scott's *Lexicon* this signification is received for *Il.* 16. 35, al.]

[1] [Who agrees with Bengel: "Remissio peccatorum *probatur a fructu.*"]

[2] Palairet, *Observ.* 125, Alberti *Observ.* 151, Krebs, *Observ.* 50, Griesbach, *Commentar. Crit.* II. 138, Schweigh. *Lexic. Herod.* II. 161.

[3] [The only uncials quoted for this reading are ADKΠ: all recent editors read ὅτι (ὅ τι).—On these passages see p. 208 sq.]

[4] See Schæf. *Greg. Cor.* p. 491, Schneider, *Plat. Rep.* I. 393, Siebelis, *Ind. Pausan.* p. 259.

quently used in the N. T. ἐκβατικῶς, denoting the actual consequence (Glass. I. 539 sqq.) ; in Greek writers also this force has sometimes been assigned to the particle.[1] Even if we should grant the general possibility of such a use of ἵνα, as the Latin *ut* denotes both purpose and consequence,—though the weakening of ἵνα in later Greek (see § 44. 8) could prove nothing on this side,—yet no one will deny that commentators have made most unlimited use of this canon, and are chargeable with great exaggeration.[2] The whole theory (of which Devarius, for instance, knows nothing) was denied by Lehmann (*Lucian*, I. 71), and afterwards by Fritzsche (Exc. 1 *ad Matth.*), and by Beyer (*N. krit. Journ.* IV. 418 sqq.) ; compare also Lücke, *Comment. zu Joh.* II. 371 sq., Meyer on Mt. i. 22. Beyer's view was combated by Steudel in Bengel's *N. Archiv.* IV. 504 sq. ; Tittmann also (*Synon.* II. 35 sqq.) declared himself in favour of ἵνα ἐκβατικόν.[3] Others—as Olshausen (*Bibl. Comment.* II. 250) and Bleek (*Hebr.* II. i. 283)—would have the ecbatic meaning admitted for certain passages at all events.

First and especially, most commentators hitherto have overlooked the fact that ἵνα must frequently be judged of in accordance with the Hebrew teleology, in which the actual issues of events are spoken of interchangeably with the Divine purposes and decrees, or rather in which every (important, and especially every surprising) event is represented as disposed and designed by God (see *e. g.* Ex. xi. 9, Is.

---

[1] See Hoogeveen, *Doctr. Particul.* I. 524 sq., the commentators on Lucian, *Nigr.* 30, Weiske, Xen. *Anab.* 7. 3. 28. Compare also Ewald, *Apocal.* p. 233.

[2] If indeed, with Kühnöl (*Hebr.* p. 204), we lay it down as a principle that ἵνα only "*sæpius*" denotes "consilium," we shall easily reach the conclusion that the conjunction may be taken ἐκβατικῶς.

[3] Tittmann thinks he has discovered examples of ἵνα ἐκβατικόν even in the Attic poets. This meaning, however, ἵνα clearly has *not* in Aristoph. *Nub.* 58, δεῦρ' ἔλθ' ἵνα κλάῃς, and the remark on the next page will remove all difficulty from Aristoph. *Vesp.* 313. In Marc. Anton. 7. 25, also, ἵνα is certainly telic. What short and easy work Tittmann makes with the N. T., in order to carry through his canon, is shown by the mode in which he deals with Jo. i. 7 (p. 45), where really no unbiassed expositor will take the second ἵνα as ecbatic. Even Kühnöl has not done this. [There is still controversy upon this subject, but the field of disputed passages is now greatly narrowed. In most of the examples noticed below, few perhaps will hesitate to accept Winer's exposition ; but fewer still will attempt to press the full telic meaning in every case. With Winer agree Grimm (*Clavis*, s. v.), Beelen (*Gramm. N. T.* p. 479 sq.), Schirlitz (*Grundz.* p. 351 sq.),—also Ellicott, Alford (see notes on 1 C. xiv. 13, 1 Th. v. 4), and Eadie. Ellicott distinctly recognises the "eventual" use of ἵνα ("apparently in a few cases, and due perhaps more to what is called Hebrew teleology than grammatical depravation") ; and in such examples as 1 Th. v. 4 (see also Ph. i. 9, Col. iv. 16) modifies the final sense. More favour is shown to the ecbatic meaning by Lightfoot (on G. i. 17) and A. Buttmann (p. 239), Green (*Gr.* p. 172 sq.), and Jowett (on 1 Th. v. 4). If however we are at liberty to render ἵνα ὑμεῖς θαυμάζητε in Jo. v. 20 "so that ye will wonder" (A. Buttmann *l. c.*), and in G. v. 17 take ἵνα as denoting simply the *result*, it is hard to see how the final meaning can be maintained in a multitude of other passages. Surely, whilst allowing that the particle has lost *some part of* its strict force in some examples cited above (though *not* in Jo. v. 20, G. v. 17), we must hold that the final meaning is "never to be given up except on the most distinct counter-arguments" (Ellicott). See Westcott, *Introd. to Gospels*, p. 270 : also Winer's remarks on ἵνα in § 44 (pp. 420–426).]

vi. 10 and Knobel *in loc.*, and compare Rom. xi. 11 [1]); and that for this reason ἵνα may often be used in Bible language where we, in accordance with our view of the Divine government of the world, should have used ὥστε. In other passages a more accurate examination would have shown that, even according to ordinary modes of thought, ἵνα is perfectly correct. In other cases, again, it has escaped observation that we sometimes use a conjunction of purpose on rhetorical grounds, by a kind of hyperbole: e. g., "I must needs then go there that I might catch an illness!" compare Is. xxxvi. 12, Ps. li. (l.) 6, Liv. 3. 10, Plin. *Paneg.* 6. 4 ;—" I have built the house then in order to see it burnt down!" Lastly, it has not been noticed that ἵνα simply expresses what (in the established course of nature and life) is the *necessary* result,—the result therefore which is, so to speak, unconsciously designed by the person who does the act: [2] see below, on Jo. ix. 2.

Passing over those examples which to any attentive reader are self-explanatory (e.g., 1 P. i. 7, where Pott—from mere force of habit, as it were—takes ἵνα for ὥστε), we select some in which ἵνα has been explained *de eventu* by expositors of the better class. In L. ix. 45 ἵνα indicates (the Divine) purpose, compare Mt. xi. 25: it was intended that they should not as yet understand it,—otherwise they would have been perplexed with regard to Jesus. In L. xiv. 10 ἵνα is parallel with the μήποτε of ver. 8, and most obviously expresses design (not without reference to the application of the parable),— " be humble, in order that thou mayest be accounted worthy of his heavenly kingdom :" it is in the following clause, τότε ἔσται κ.τ.λ., that the *result* is expressed. On Mk. iv. 12 (Schott) see Fritzsche and Olshausen; also below, p. 577. Compare also L. xi. 50, Mt. xxiii. 34 sq. Jo. iv. 36 means : this is so ordered, *to the end that* etc. In Jo. vii. 23 (Steudel) the words ἵνα μὴ λυθῇ ὁ νόμος Μωϋσέως express the purpose which lies at the root of the custom περιτομὴν λαμβάνει ἄνθρωπος ἐν σαββάτῳ. Jo. ix. 2 is to be explained from the Jewish teleology, which, in its national exaggeration, the disciples accepted. Severe, mysterious bodily afflictions *must* be divinely ordained punishments of sin : Who then has by his sin moved the penal justice of God to cause this man to be born blind ? The *necessary*, though not intentional, consequence of the ἁμαρτάνειν is meant : see Lücke *in loc.* In Jo. xi. 15 ἵνα πιστεύσητε is added to δι' ὑμᾶς by

---

[1] See Baumg.-Crusius, *Bibl. Theol.* p. 272, Tholuck, *Ausleg. d. Br. a. d. Röm.* p. 395 sqq. (3 Aufl.).—It is going too far to say that the Israelites confounded *throughout* the ideas of design and result (Unger, *De Parabol.* p. 173). It was only in their *religious* view of life (in the language of devotion, Baumg.-Crus. *Joh.* I. 198) that the interchange took place. Where this influence did not operate, the clear distinction between *in order that* and *so that* would of necessity force itself on the Israelites; and it is well known that in their language they have provided for the expression of "*so that*" a form which shows how correctly the distinction was felt.

[2] Compare Lücke, *Joh.* I. 603, Fritzsche on Rom. viii. 17. [Alford on L. xiv. 10.]

way of explanation: *I rejoice on your account* (that I was not there), *in order that ye may believe*,—i. e., now ye cannot help believing. In Jo. xix. 28 ἵνα means *in order that*,—whether we connect ἵνα τελειωθῇ ἡ γραφή with πάντα ἤδη τετέλεσται (Luther, so also Meyer), or with the following λέγει (Lücke, De Wette): in the latter case ἵνα denotes a purpose ascribed to Jesus by the evangelist. On Jo. xvi. 24 see Lücke.[1] In Rom. xi. 31 ἵνα does not express the design of the ἀπειθοῦντες, but the counsel of God which connected itself with this unbelief (compare ver. 32), to accord them salvation out of compassion (not as merited by them). In the connexion of the Divine plan their unbelief has as its aim, that etc.: compare also ver. 11. The same explanation applies to Rom. v. 20 sq., and probably to 2 C. i. 9. The same teleological view is clearly implied in Jo. xii. 40, a quotation from the O. T. Rom. ix. 11 is plain to any attentive reader, and we may fairly wonder that ἵνα can still be taken by Reiche as ecbatic. In 2 C. v. 4 also the meaning is clear: it is incomprehensible how even Schott could render ἵνα by *ita ut*. In 1 C. v. 5 the words εἰς ὄλεθρον τῆς σαρκός show that with the apostolic παραδοῦναι τῷ Σατανᾷ there is combined a purpose of doing good to the πνεῦμα; and hence ἵνα is unquestionably *in order that*. In 1 C. vii. 29 the words ἵνα καὶ οἱ ἔχοντες κ.τ.λ. express the (Divine) purpose for which ὁ καιρὸς συνεσταλμένος ἐστί. E. ii. 9 is to be similarly explained. In E. iii. 10 ἵνα γνωρισθῇ κ.τ.λ. is probably grammatically dependent on ἀποκεκρυμμένου, ver. 9: see Meyer *in loc.* In E. iv. 14 ἵνα μηκέτι κ.τ.λ. expresses the negative purpose of that which has been spoken of in ver. 11–13.

As to G. v. 17 (Usteri, Baumg.-Crusius) see Meyer *in loc.*[2] In 1 C. xiv. 13, ὁ λαλῶν γλώσσῃ προσευχέσθω, ἵνα διερμηνεύῃ· means, *Let him pray*—not in order to display his χάρισμα τῶν γλωσσῶν, but —*with the intention, design, of interpreting* (the prayer). 1 Jo. iii. 1: *Behold! how great love the Father shewed us,* (with the design) *that we might be called children of God.* See Lücke *in loc.*; Baumg.-Crusius wavers. In Rev. viii. 12 ἵνα indicates the object contemplated in the πλήττεσθαι of the sun, etc.; for πλήττεσθαι does not denote, as many suppose, the darkening of the heavenly bodies in itself, but is the O. T. הִכָּה, used of the offended Deity: see Ewald *in loc.* In Rev. ix. 20 ἵνα μή expresses the design of the μετανοεῖν; "they did not amend, *in order that* they might no longer serve the demons etc." The perception that they were serving mere demons and wooden idols should have brought them to repentance, in order that they might escape from so degrading a service. In 1 Th. v. 4 (Schott, Baumg.-Crusius) ἵνα denotes a purpose of God:

---

[1] ["Henceforth would they ask in his name and receive, and so theirs would be a completed joy. "Ἵνα indicates the objective aim of αἰτεῖτε καὶ λήψεσθε." Lücke *l. c.*]

[2] [Who takes ἵνα as expressing the purpose of the "powers contending with one another in the conflict." Similarly Ellicott.]

see Lünemann *in loc.* So also in the formula ἐλήλυθεν ἡ ὥρα ἵνα, peculiar to John, ἵνα has its final meaning. Thus Jo. xii. 23: *The hour has* (according to the Divine decree) *come*—and therefore is here—*in order that I* etc.: compare xiii. 1, xvi. 2, 32. Inaccurate interpreters have taken ἵνα in these passages (as also in 1 C. iv. 3, vii. 29) as used for ὅτε or ὅταν. 2 C. vii. 9 (Rückert, Schott): *ye were brought into sorrow, in order that* (God's purpose) *ye might be spared a more severe punishment.* 1 C. v. 2: *Ye did not rather mourn, in order that . . . might be put away?* Here indeed ὥστε might have been used, if the αἴρεσθαι had been regarded as the natural consequence of the πενθῆσαι: Paul however regards it as the object in view,—"Ye should rather have mourned, in order to put him away." In 2 C. xiii. 7 the double ἵνα indicates, first negatively, then positively, Paul's design in praying thus. The true explanation of Rom. iii. 19 may probably now be considered settled [1] (see also Philippi): only Baumg.-Crusius still wavers. On Rom. viii. 17 see p. 574. In 2 C. i. 17 ἵνα retains its proper meaning, whether we render the verse, *What I resolve, do I resolve according to the flesh, that* (with the design that) *with me yea may be* (unalterably) *yea, and nay nay* (i.e., merely to show myself consistent)?—or thus . . . *in order that with me there may be the Yea yea and the Nay nay* (that both should be found with me at the same time,—that what I had affirmed I should deny again)? In 2 C. iv. 7, ἵνα ἡ ὑπερβολή κ.τ.λ. points to God's purpose in the fact that ἔχομεν τὸν θησαυρὸν τοῦτον ἐν ὀστρακίνοις σκεύεσιν. In H. xi. 35 the words ἵνα κρείττονος ἀναστάσεως τύχωσιν declare the purpose for which these persons refused the ἀπολύτρωσις. On H. xii. 27 see Bleek and De Wette.[2] In Rev. xiv. 13 (Schott) we should probably supply ἀποθνήσκουσι, from the preceding ἀποθνήσκοντες, before ἵνα ἀναπαύσωνται. A different view is taken by Ewald and De Wette; compare above, § 43. 5.

In the formula ἵνα, ὅπως, πληρωθῇ τὸ ῥηθέν (Matthew), or ἡ γραφή, ὁ λόγος (John), it was for a long time customary to dilute ἵνα into *ita ut*. There can however be no doubt that, in the mouth, as of the Jewish teachers, so also of Jesus and the apostles, this formula (used in reference to an event *which has already taken place*) has the stricter sense, *that it might be fulfilled.* Compare also Olshausen and Meyer on Mt. i. 22. The words were not indeed intended to signify that God had caused an event to take place, or had *irresistibly impelled* men to act in a certain way, in order that the prophecies might be fulfilled (Tittm. *Synon.* II. 44): the formula is far from expressing anything fatalistic (Lücke, *Joh.* II. 536).[3] To

---

[1] [It is given very clearly in Alford's note.]
[2] [Who regard ἵνα as dependent on τῶν σαλευομένων τὴν μετάθεσιν.]
[3] On Mt. i. 22 Bengel says—in the dogmatic language of his age, but on the whole correctly: "ubicunque hæc locutio occurrit, gravitatem evangelistarum *tueri debemus* et, quamvis hebeti visu nostro, credere ab illis notari eventum

this formula we must also refer Mk. iv. 12, *All comes to them in parables, in order that they may see and yet not perceive*, etc.,—instead of "in order that the declaration, *They will see and yet not perceive* (Is. vi. 10), may be accomplished." We ourselves are accustomed to interweave such quotations with our own language, when we can presume that they are well known. Jesus cannot have intended to assert a *general impossibility* of understanding such parables (for then indeed it would have been strange that he should speak in parables); but to every one who did not understand parables so clear applied the prophet's words, *he sees and does not understand*, and that there would be such men is just what had been predicted.[1]

In the faulty language of the Apocalypse ἵνα is apparently once (Rev. xiii. 13) used for ὥστε, ὡς, after an adjective which includes the notion of intensity: *magna miracula* (i. e., tam magna) *ut*. This would be at all events as admissible as the use of ὅτι after an intensive word; compare Ducas p. 34, 28, p. 182, Theophan. Cont. p. 663, Cedren. II. 47, Canan. p. 465, Theod. *H. E.* 2. 6, p. 847 (ed. Hal.), and my *Erlang. Pfingstprogr.* 1830, p. 11. See however p. 424 sq. The case is different in 1 Jo. i. 9 (a passage which even De Wette and Schott misinterpret): *He is faithful and just in order to forgive us* (for the purpose of forgiving). Compare our own expression, *he is a sagacious man to perceive* . . . : to say *he is a sagacious man, so that he perceives*, would in the main give the same sense, but the conception would be somewhat different. Of a similar kind to this are the passages which Tittmann quotes (*Synon.* II. 39) from Marc. Anton. 11. 3, Justin M. p. 504. When Bengel says (on Rev. *l. c.*) "ἵνα frequens Joanni particula; in omnibus suis libris non nisi semel, Jo. iii. 16, ὥστε posuit," the remark is indeed correct, but must not be understood to mean that John used ἵνα for ὥστε without distinction. The cause of the rare occurrence of ὥστε in John's writings is to be found partly in their dogmatic character, partly in the fact that he indicates consequence by other turns of expression.

Ἵνα has been taken as used for ὅτι in Mk. ix. 12, γέγραπται ἐπὶ τὸν υἱὸν τοῦ ἀνθρώπου, ἵνα πολλὰ πάθῃ καὶ ἐξουδενωθῇ. But these words probably mean, *in order that he may suffer;* and they are to be taken as the answer to the question,[2] ἔρχεται or ἐλεύσεται being supplied before ἵνα. No one will be led astray by the example which Palairet (*Obs.* 127) quotes from Soph. *Aj.* 385, οὐχ ὁρᾷς, ἵν' εἶ κακοῦ; where ἵνα is an adverb. (Ὅπως has been taken as used for ὅτι, ὡς, in Xen. *Cyr.* 3. 3. 20, 8. 7. 20: see Poppo *ll. cc.*)

---

non modo talem, qui formulæ cuipiam veteri respondeat, sed plane talem, qui *propter veritatem divinam non potuerit non subsequi* ineunte N. T."

[1] [See Alford *in loc.*, and on Mt. xiii. 12.]

[2] [Winer evidently intends to follow Lachmann's punctuation of the verse, in which a note of interrogation is placed at ἀνθρώπου. So Meyer, Tisch. (ed. 8), but not Tregelles, Westcott and Hort, or De Wette, Ewald, Bleek. With the other punctuation this verse resembles some of the examples quoted in § 44. 8, p. 425 sq., the notion of design being really present in γέγραπται. Compare Bengel: "quia scriptum erat, ideo pati debuit."]

In the same way ὅπως, *in order that*, has been erroneously taken by many as used for *ita ut*.[1] In L. ii. 35 (Baumg.-Crusius ?) we hardly need to have recourse to the Hebrew teleology in order to understand the conjunction. A. iii. 19 is plain, if, as ver. 21 requires, we understand ὅπως ἀποστείλῃ τὸν Χριστόν (ver. 20) of the opening of the heavenly kingdom. What has been said above in reference to ἵνα (p. 574 sq.) will make Mt. xxiii. 35 clear. Phil. 6 is connected with ver. 4, *I make mention of thee in my prayers, in order that*, etc.: Meyer's objections to this view are groundless. H. ii. 9 (Kühnöl) receives so much light from ver. 10, that hardly any other commentator will now explain ὅπως by *ita ut*. On ὅπως πληρωθῇ see above.

In the N. T., as elsewhere, ὡς as a particle of comparison always means *as*, never *so* (for οὕτως); this Pott (1 P. iii. 6) might have learned from Bengel. Nor is there any reason for writing ὥς anywhere in the N. T.: indeed this form is very rare in prose writers, with the exception of the Ionic.[2] In H. iii. 11, iv. 3 (from the LXX), ὡς may be rendered *that (so that)*, in which signification it is sometimes found with the indicative in good Greek writers (Her. 1. 163, 2. 135 [3]). On Mk. xiii. 34 and similar passages see Fritzsche:[4] to assume an anacoluthon (in Mk. *l. c.*), as Meyer does, is altogether unnecessary.[5]

---

[1] Kühnöl, *Act.* 129, Tittm. *Synon.* II. 55, 58.

[2] Heindorf and Stallbaum on Plat. *Protag.* c. 15.

[3] [These examples from Herodotus differ from the passage in question in one important point,—in each case there is οὕτω in the previous clause: see also Xen. *Conv.* 4. 37. It is very doubtful whether ὡς with the indicative, not preceded by οὕτως, is ever used in classical Greek with the meaning *so that*. In Ps. xcv. (xciv.) 11, from which the quotation is taken, the Hebrew אֲשֶׁר may bear this meaning (Delitzsch, Hupfeld, Perowne); but in the example usually quoted as parallel, Gen. xi. 7, it seems clear that the conjunction signifies *in order that* (Winer, Gesenius, Kalisch, al.). In Ps. xcv. 11 Ewald's rendering is "where:" compare ver. 9. Most probably, therefore, we should (with Bleek, Lünemann, Alford) keep to the simple meaning "as," "according as" (*Vulg.:* "sicut"), in H. iii, iv.]

[4] [Fritzsche's rendering is: *quo modo* (i. e. *si paullo latius dicas res ita habet, ut.* . . .) *homo, qui* . . . *etiam* servo atriensi præcepit ut vigilaret. Meyer (who also takes καί as *etiam*) supplies a suppressed apodosis (§ 63. 1, 64. I. 7), *so I also command you*, Watch. Compare Mt. xxv. 14, and see Green, *Cr. Notes*, p. 41.]

[5] [A few particles of various kinds, not noticed elsewhere, may be conveniently brought together here.—Δή (Curtius, *Grundz.* p. 581, Don. *New Crat.* p. 376 sq.) is rare in the N. T. In most instances it is joined to an imperative or *conjunctivus adhortativus*, adding urgency to the command, etc. (Jelf 720. 2). Once, in Mt. xiii. 23, it is found with ὅς, and gives exactness to the relative (Jelf 721. 2, Klotz, *Devar.* II. 404), "and this now is the man who etc. :" see Meyer *in loc.*, who quotes from Erasmus, "ut intelligas ceteros omnes infrugiferos, *hunc demum* reddere fructum." In 2 C. xii. 1 the received text has δή (*sane, profecto*), but the true reading is δεῖ. On δήπου, H. ii. 16, *surely, I suppose, of course*, see Klotz p. 427 sq. and Alford's note *in loc.* (compare Jebb, Soph. *Aj.* p. 85). Δήποτε (*cunque*, Klotz p. 425, Jelf 160. *b*) is joined to ὅς in Jo. v. 4 *Rec.:* Lachmann reads οἱῳδηποτοῦν. — Πού is almost always the indefinite adverb of place: once, Rom. iv. 19, it is used with a numeral adjective, *about*. (Ὅς and ὡσεί are similarly used with numerals: see L. viii. 42, ix. 14, al.) In A. xxvii. 29 the true reading is μή που (μήπου, Tischendorf):

Section LIV.

THE ADVERBS.

1. The more indispensable adverbs are for the exact expression of circumstantial relations, the more easily can we understand how the N. T. writers, though inferior to Greek prose authors in the use of the conjunctions, should have in great measure appropriated to themselves the large store of Greek adverbs, throughout its whole extent. It is only in respect of *intension*, i. e., in regard to those finer shades of meaning which are expressed by many of the simple adverbs (e. g., ἄν) or by adverbial combinations, that their use of these words betrays the foreigner, who could not feel the need of these niceties of language.

The derivative (adjectival) adverbs are the more numerous in the N. T., because in the case of not a few adjectives later Greek had provided special adverbial forms;[1] and other adverbs, which at an earlier period were confined to poetry, had now found their way into ordinary prose. Thus compare ἀκαίρως (Ecclus. xxxii. 4), ἀναξίως (2 Macc. xiv. 42), ἀνόμως (2 Macc. viii. 17), ἀποτόμως (from Polybius onwards), ἐκτενῶς (the same, Lob. *Phryn.* p. 311), ἀπερισπάστως (the same, Lob. p. 415), ἑτοίμως (for which, at all events in Attic Greek, ἐξ ἑτοίμου was used), εὐθύμως (from Polybius onwards), ἐσχάτως (compare Lob. p. 389), εὐαρέστως (Arrian, *Epict.* 1. 12. 21), κενῶς Arrian, *Epict.* 2. 17. 6. (εἰς

---

on δήπου see above.—Ποτέ is always temporal, except, perhaps, in G. ii. 6, ὁποῖοί ποτε (*qualescunque, of what kind soever*). In the compounds πώποτε, οὐδέποτε, μηδέποτε, the particle has its temporal force (compare also ἤδη ποτέ, Ph. iv. 10, *tandem aliquando*), but in μήποτε it is almost always possibly, haply. In οὔπω, οὐδέπω and μηδέπω, πώ is always *yet*.—The temporal adverbs νῦν, νυνί (used in the N. T. without the distinction observed in Attic Greek,—see Fritz. *Rom.* I. 182), are frequently argumentative, "then," "things being so:" see Ellicott on 1 Th. iii. 8, 2 Th. ii. 6 (Jelf 719, Grimm, *Clavis* s. vv.). There is a similar change of application in the case of ἤδη (1 C. vi. 7, Meyer), ἔτι (Rom. iii. 7, al.), οὐκέτι (G. iii. 18, Rom. vii. 17).—The particle of asseveration νή, common in Attic Greek, occurs once in the N. T., in 1 C. xv. 31 (Don. p. 570, Jelf 733): on the (elliptical) accusative see Jelf 566. 2. Akin to νή is ναί (Shilleto, Dem. *F. L.* p. 205-7), which occurs not unfrequently in the N. T. as a particle of affirmation and confirmation: see Ellicott on Ph. iv. 3, Don. p. 570, Jelf 733. The N. T. word ἀμήν is somewhat similar. Of the interjections in the N. T. the most noticeable are ἴα, οὐά, οὐαί, on which see Schirlitz, *Grundz.* p. 373 sq., Grimm s. vv.]

[1] [Instead of using the neuter adjective, etc. (p. 580).]

κενόν), προςφάτως, τελείως, πολυτρόπως and πολυμερῶς, ῥητῶς, ἐθνικῶς in the Biblical sense.¹ Amongst the other adverbs also there are some which belong to later Greek, and are censured by the grammarians: e. g., ὑπερέκεινα (see Thom. M. p. 336), οὐρανόθεν,² παιδιόθεν, μακρόθεν (Lob. p. 93 sq.).

The expression of an adverbial notion by means of a neuter adjective or participle,³ a usage which becomes more and more common in later writers, does not in the N. T. overpass the limits maintained in earlier prose. Compare πρῶτον, ὕστερον, πρότερον and τὸ πρότερον, πλησίον, τυχόν, ἔλαττον, πολύ, τὸ νῦν ἔχον, A. xxiv. 25, *for the present* (Vig. p. 9, compare Herm. p. 888), τοὐναντίον, λοιπόν and τὸ λοιπόν (Herm. *Vig.* p. 706), ταχύ, πυκνά, ἴσα, μακρά, πολλά (both *often* and *σφόδρα*), and τὰ πολλά (*for the most part*). For most of these no adverbial forms exist. In general, the N. T. diction presents no peculiarity in regard to the use of adjectives, with or without a preposition (elliptically or not), in the place of adverbs: compare *e.g.* τοῦ λοιποῦ,⁴ πεζῇ, πάντῃ, καταμόνας, κατ' ἰδίαν, ἰδίᾳ, καθόλου, εἰς κενόν, and see the lexicons s. vv. Instead of κατὰ ἑκούσιον Phil. 14 (Num. xv. 3) Greek writers more commonly use ἑκουσίως, ἑκουσίᾳ,⁵ or ἐξ ἑκουσίας. Of genuine Greek combinations, such as παραχρῆμα, it is not necessary to speak. On the other hand, the use of abstract substantives with prepositions in the

---

¹ [These adverbs do not all fully answer to the description by which they are introduced. Ἀκαίρως occurs in Plat. *Timæus* 33 a, *Rep.* 606 b; ἀναξίως, Plat. *Rep.* 388 d; ἀνόμως, Thuc. 4. 92; ἀποτόμως, Dem. 1402. 16, Isocr. *Archid.* p. 126 b; ἑτοίμως, Æsch. *Suppl.* 75, Xen. *An.* 2. 5. 2, Thuc. 1. 80; εὐθύμως (Plat. *Axioch.* 365 b), Æsch. *Ag.* 1592 (1570); τελείως, Isocr. c. *Soph.* p. 294 e, Arist. *Metaph.* 4. 16, 9. 4. Ἐκτινῶς is used by Macho (ap. Athen. 579 e): if εὐαρίστως is not found in early authors, εὐαρεστοτέρως occurs in Xen. *Mem.* 3. 5. 5. Lobeck's note (*Phryn.* p. 389) does not relate to ἐσχάτως, which is used by Xenophon (*An.* 2. 6. 1), but to the phrase ἐσχάτως ἔχειν.]
² [This word is used by Homer and Hesiod, but not by the earlier *prose* writers.]
³ Yet what Hermann (Eur. *Hel.* p. 30 sq.) has said in illustration of this use of the neuter deserves consideration. [Hermann's observation is to the effect that the adjective does not here stand for an adverb, but has its proper force (e. g., ἄκραντα ὁρμᾶν = ἄκραντα πράττειν ὁρμῶντα), the verb on which the accusative depends always denoting some action.]
⁴ Herm. *Vig.* p. 706, Van Marle, *Florileg.* p. 232 sq. [See also Ellicott on G. vi. 17.—" In *affirmative* prepositions τὸ λοιπόν is usual: in *negative* τοῦ λοιποῦ." Shilleto, Dem. *F. L.* p. 84.]
⁵ [Ἑκουσίᾳ is perhaps doubtful: see Buttmann, Dem. *Mid.* § 12 c. The nearest parallel (in any early writer) to κατὰ ἑκούσιον seems to be καθ' ἑκουσίαν Thuc. 8. 27. See Lightfoot on Phil. 14.]

place of actually existing adverbs is more common in the N. T. than in Greek writers, in accordance with the national colouring of the Hebrew-Aramæan language. Thus we have ἐν ἀληθείᾳ, Mt. xxii. 16; ἐπ' ἀληθείας, L. xxii. 59 (for ἀληθῶς); ἐν δικαιοσύνῃ, A. xvii. 31 (for δικαίως). See above, § 51.

The phrase ἡμέρᾳ καὶ ἡμέρᾳ, 2 C. iv. 16, would be altogether without example for the N. T., if it were intended as a periphrasis for the adverb *daily*, which is usually expressed in the N. T., as elsewhere, by καθ' ἡμέραν or τὸ καθ' ἡμέραν: compare יוֹם יוֹם.[1] Probably however Paul used this expression (*day by day*) designedly, in order to indicate the progressive nature of the ἀνακαινοῦσθαι; whereas καθ' (ἑκάστην) ἡμέραν ἀνακαινοῦται might have been taken in a different sense. Analogous to this (but in a local sense) are Mk. vi. 39, ἐπέταξεν ἀνακλῖναι πάντας συμπόσια συμπόσια, *catervatim* (compare Ex. viii. 14), ver. 40, ἀνέπεσον πρασιαὶ πρασιαί, *areolatim*: see § 37. 3. These are, strictly speaking, instances of apposition: compare L. ix. 14. The examples which Georgi has collected (*Vindic.* p. 340) are of a different kind.

The use of the simple accusative of a noun (substantive) in an adverbial sense is really the result of contraction in the structure of the sentence (Herm. *Vig.* p. 883 [2]). Under this head come, besides the familiar example χάριν,—

(a) Τὴν ἀρχήν, *throughout, altogether* (Herm. *Vig.* p. 723). In this sense τὴν ἀρχήν is probably to be taken in Jo. viii. 25 (see Lücke's careful examination of the passage); *altogether what I also say unto you*,—(I am) altogether that which in my words I represent myself as being.[3] Not the slightest occasion is presented by the context for

---

[1] See Vorst, *Hebr.* 307 sq., Ewald, *Kr. Gr.* p. 638. Compare ἡμέρᾳ τῇ ἡμέρᾳ, Georg. Phrantz. 4. 4, p. 356. [For the Hebrew idiom see Gesen. *Gr.* p. 183, Kalisch I. 97. Meyer takes ἡμέρᾳ καὶ ἡμέρᾳ as a "pure Hebraism,—which is not even found in the LXX."]

[2] ["Τὸν δὲ σκότος ὅσσ' ἐκάλυψεν: quod compositum est ex his, τὸν δὲ σκότος ἐκάλυψεν, et τοῦ δὲ ὅσσε σκότος ἐκάλυψεν. Sæpe his frequens usus fecit, ut nomina pene adverbiorum vim nanciscerentur, ut ὁ ὄχλος ἀκμὴν διέβαινε, *quum maxime*,—ἀρχὴν δὲ θηρᾶν οὐ πρέπει τἀμήχανα, *omnino*. Nempe hæc proprie sic mente concipiebantur, ὁ ὄχλος ἀκμὴν εἶχε διαβαίνων, οὐ πρέπει οὐδὲ ἀρχὴν ποιεῖν θηρῶντα τὰ ἀμήχανα." Hermann, p. 882.]

[3] [The great objection to this view is, that ἀρχήν seems never to have the meaning *omnino* unless the sentence in which it occurs is either formally or virtually *negative*. Lücke (*Joh.* II. 304 sq.) passes in review a number of examples adduced by Lennep (Phalar. *Ep.* p. 82 sqq., p. 251 sq.), and arrives at the conclusion that there are a few—though very few—exceptional instances to which this canon will not apply. The exceptions he specifies are examined and (I think) satisfactorily set aside by Brückner, in his edition of De Wette's

making the sentence interrogative instead of categorical. Meyer's explanation seems to me the least satisfactory, on account of its complicated character.

(b) Ἀκμήν, used in later Greek for ἔτι (Mt. xv. 16). See Lob. *Phryn.* p. 123 sq.

Adverbs may be joined not only to verbs but also to nouns: as in 1 C. xii. 31, καθ' ὑπερβολὴν ὁδὸν ὑμῖν δείκνυμι (see no. 2), and 1 C. vii. 35, πρὸς τὸ εὐπάρεδρον τῷ κυρίῳ ἀπερισπάστως.

2. The adverbial notion is sometimes conceived concretely as *adjectival,* and joined to a substantive (Matth. 446, Kühner II. 382),—not only in cases where a predicate really belongs (logically) to the substantive and not to the verb (though in our own language we use an adverb),[1] but also where such direct

---

Handbuch on John (ed. 5 : 1863). Brückner sums up thus : "The rule therefore is as follows. Τὴν ἀρχήν or ἀρχήν (the article being either inserted or omitted as in the case of τέλος) *without* a negative invariably means *from the beginning, from the very first:* for τὴν ἀρχήν in this sense see Plat. *Symp.* p. 190 b, *Eryx.* 398 b, Arrian, *An.* III. 11. 1, Lucian I. 669 (ed. Reitz),—for ἀρχήν, Her. 1. 9. In negative sentences also it *may* have this meaning, see Xen. *Cyr.* I. 2. 3. When however the word means *omnino,* there is always a negative present, or the thought of the sentence is negative." If this conclusion be accepted—unless we venture to suppose, *without any evidence* (see Green, *Crit. Notes,* p. 74), that the word was at a later period used in the sense "altogether" in all sentences without distinction (in which case no objection can be urged against Winer's rendering of the verse)—we must either give up this meaning here, or (following high ancient authorities, as Chrysostom, Cyril, al.) give the sentence a negative cast by reading it as a question (Lücke, Lachmann, Tisch. in ed. 7, Westcott and Hort in their text, A. Buttmann, p. 253) or as an exclamation (Ewald) : see Westcott *in loc.* The possible renderings, on the evidence which we possess, seem to be the following. (1) *Why do I even speak to you at all?* On ὅ, τι or ὅτι see above, p. 208 : on καί see Herm. *Vig.* p. 837, and above, p. 546. (2) *That I am even speaking to you at all!* (3) *From the beginning—from the very first—*(I am) *that which I also speak to you.* This is De Wette's rendering as modified by Brückner. (De Wette himself added to his rendering of τὴν ἀρχήν the more than doubtful gloss "before all things.") The chief objections to this translation are the position of τὴν ἀρχήν—which would more naturally be joined to λαλῶ—the use of λαλῶ (not λέγω), and the καί. Of these three renderings the third seems the least probable.—Meyer's interpretation referred to in the text is probably that of his second edition (1852), adhered to in his later editions, *What I from the beginning am also speaking to you* (do ye ask)? i.e., "Who I am, is that which from the commencement constitutes the substance of my words ; and can ye then still ask respecting this ?" His earlier view of the passage was given in a note appended to the first edition of his commentary on Acts.(1835) : here he arranges the words as *two* questions, the first being τὴν ἀρχήν; ("*The chief point* do ye ask ?") Other explanations will be found in his elaborate note, see vol. II. 24-29 (Transl.) : compare also the notes of Tholuck and Alford, and Stier, *Words of the Lord Jesus,* V. 337 sqq. (Transl.).]

[1] As in Jo. iv. 18, τοῦτο ἀληθὲς εἴρηκας, *this hast thou said as* (something) *true,* hoc verum dixisti : τοῦτο ἀληθῶς εἴρηκας (which, according to Kühnöl, would have been the correct expression here) is ambiguous. Compare Xen. *Vectig.* 1. 2, ὅπως δὲ γνωσθῇ, ὅτι ἀληθὲς τοῦτο λέγω· Demosth. *Halon.* 34 b, τοῦτό γε ἀληθὲς λέγουσιν.

reference of the predicate to the substantive seemed to give clearness to the sentence.[1] A. xiv. 10, ἀνάστηθι ἐπὶ τοὺς πόδας σου ὀρθός; Mk. iv. 28, αὐτομάτη ἡ γῆ καρποφορεῖ, A. xii. 10 (Iliad 5. 749); Rom. x. 19, πρῶτος Μωϋσῆς λέγει (as the first), 1 Tim. ii. 13, Jo. xx. 4, al.; [2] L. xxi. 34, μήποτε ἐπιστῇ ἐφ' ὑμᾶς αἰφνίδιος ἡ ἡμέρα ἐκείνη (v. l. αἰφνιδίως); A. xxviii. 13, δευτεραῖοι ἤλθομεν εἰς Ποτιόλους; 1 C. ix. 17, εἰ γὰρ ἑκὼν τοῦτο πράσσω . . . . εἰ δὲ ἄκων κ.τ.λ. Compare also L. v. 21, 1 C. ix. 6, al.[3]

These particular adjectives are frequently, indeed almost regularly, so used in Greek authors. For αὐτόματος, see Her. 2. 66, Lucian, Necyom. 1, Xen. An. 5. 7. 3, 4. 3. 8, Cyr. 1. 4. 13, Hell. 5. 1. 14, Dion. H. I. 139, Wetst. I. 569; for πρῶτος, Xen. An. 2. 3. 19, Cyr. 1. 4. 2, Paus. 6. 4. 2, Charit. 2. 2; for δευτεραῖος, Her. 6. 106, Xen. Cyr. 5. 2. 2, Arrian, Al. 5. 22. 4, Wetst. II. 654; for αἰφνίδιος, Thuc. 6. 49, 8. 28,—" subitus irrupit," Tac. Hist. 3. 47. In the case of other adjectives, however, this usage is not uncommon. See Xen. Cyr. 5. 3. 55, αὐτὸς παρελαύνων τὸν ἵππον . . . . ἥσυχος κατεθεᾶτο κ.τ.λ.; 6. 1. 45, εὖ οἶδ', ὅτι ἄσμενος ἂν πρὸς ἄνδρα . . . . ἀπαλλαγήσεται· Demosth. Zenoth. 576 b, 2 Macc. x. 33, Pflugk, Eurip. Hel. p. 48 (contrast A. xxi. 17); Xen. Cyr. 7. 5. 49 v. l., εἰ ταῦτα πρόθυμός σοι συλλάβοιμι; 4. 2. 11, ἐθελούσιοι ἐξιόντες; Dio Chr. 40. 495, πυκνοὶ βαδίζοντες; Isocr. Ep.

---

[1] Compare especially Bremi, Exc. 2. ad Lys. p. 449 sq., Mehlhorn, De adjectivorum pro adverbio positorum ratione et usu (Glogav. 1828): see also Vechner, Hellenol. 215 sqq., Zumpt, Lat. Gr. § 682, 686, Kritz, Sall. I. 125, II. 131, 216. This usage is more prevalent in Latin than in Greek. Eichhorn misapplies the rule when he maintains (Einleitung ins N. T. II. 261) that in Jo. xiii. 34 ἐντολὴν καινὴν δίδωμι may mean, I will give you the commandment anew (καινῶς): in this case John must at all events have written (ταύτην) τὴν ἐντολὴν καινὴν δίδωμι. In Jo. v. 44, the order of the words is by itself sufficient to show that μόνου is not adverbial, see Lücke in loc.: [see also above, p. 163, note[2].]

[2] The ordinal adjectives cannot take the place of ordinal adverbs unless the first, second, etc., are used of the person—i.e., unless the words indicate something which this person did before all other persons (was the first to do). When a first action is ascribed to a person, in contradistinction to other subsequent actions of the same person, the adverb only must be used. Compare also Kritz, Sallust II. 174. [Hence, if (with Tisch., Meyer, al.) we read πρῶτος in Jo. i. 41 (42), the meaning must be, either that Andrew was the first to find Simon, whom both disciples had sought for (Bengel, Lücke, al.), or that each disciple had sought his own brother, and that Andrew was the first to succeed in his quest (Meyer).]

[3] [See also Mk. xii. 22 Rec. (ἔσχατος), Mt. xiv. 13 Tisch. (πεζός), and Ellicott's note on Col. ii. 3 (ἀπόκρυφοι).]

8, τελευτῶν (at last) ὑπεσχόμην. Compare Palairet 214, Valcken. on Her. 8. 130, Ellendt, Arr. *Al.* I. 156, Krüg. p. 240 sq. (Don. p. 458 sqq., Jelf 714).

How far it is correct to teach that adjectives stand for adverbs, will be obvious from what has been said. But it is also a mistake to suppose that adverbs are used in the place of adjectives (Ast, Plat. *Polit.* p. 271[1]) : e. g., in Mt. i. 18, ἡ γένεσις οὕτως ἦν· xix. 10, εἰ οὕτως ἐστὶν ἡ αἰτία τοῦ ἀνθρώπου (Rom. iv. 18, from the LXX), 1 P. ii. 15 ; 1 Th. ii. 10, ὡς ὁσίως καὶ δικαίως καὶ ἀμέμπτως ὑμῖν ἐγενήθημεν· ver. 13 ; Rom. ix. 20, τί με ἐποίησας οὕτως. In the passages first quoted εἶναι is not the mere copula (as in αὕτη or τοιοῦτό ἐστι), but expresses *existence, state,* or *nature (comparatum esse).*[2] In Rom. ix. 20 οὕτως expresses the mode of ποιεῖν, the consequence of which is that he is this particular person.[3] So also in 1 C. vii. 7, ἕκαστος ἴδιον ἔχει χάρισμα, ὃς μὲν οὕτως, ὃς δὲ οὕτως, the adverbs are quite in place : *Each has his own* (special) *gift of grace, one in this manner, the other in that.* (Don. p. 454 sq., Jelf 375.)

Certain adverbs approach more nearly to adjectives :—

(*a*) Some adverbs of place, as ἐγγὺς εἶναι, χωρίς τινος εἶναι (E. ii. 12), πόρρω εἶναι (L. xiv. 32) : Krüg. p. 275.

(*b*) Those adverbs of degree which are joined to substantives (ὤν being understood) ; as μάλα στρατηγός, Xen. *Hell.* 6. 2. 39. See Bernh. p. 338 (Jelf 456). These adverbs are usually placed before the noun, but sometimes follow it. 1 C. xii. 31 is thus understood even by early expositors : καὶ ἔτι καθ᾽ ὑπερβολὴν ὁδὸν ὑμῖν δείκνυμι, *a surpassing way.* The adverbial adjunct follows the noun in 1 C. viii. 7, τῇ συνειδήσει ἕως ἄρτι τοῦ εἰδώλου· Ph. i. 26, 2 P. ii. 23 ;[4] probably also in 2 C. xi. 23, see Meyer *in loc.*

3. The adverbial notion of *intenseness* is not unfrequently expressed by joining to the verb a participle of the same verb (see § 45. 8), or the dative (ablative) of a cognate noun. Thus : L. xxii. 15, ἐπιθυμίᾳ ἐπεθύμησα, *I have earnestly desired ;* Jo. iii. 29, χαρᾷ χαίρει, *impense lœtatur ;* A. iv. 17, ἀπειλῇ ἀπειλησώμεθα, *let us positively forbid ;* A. v. 28, παραγγελίᾳ παρηγγείλαμεν ὑμῖν ; A. xxiii. 14, ἀναθέματι ἀνεθεματίσαμεν, *we have most solemnly vowed,* Ja. v. 17 ; and from the LXX, Mt. xiii. 14

---

[1] His article in the *Landshuter Zeitschrift für Wissenschaft und Kunst,* III. ii. 133 sqq., I have not been able to examine.

[2] In Jo. vi. 55 there is a difference of reading. Recent editors prefer ἀληθής : see Lücke, who however well refutes the opinion that ἀληθῶς is synonymous with ἀληθής.

[3] Compare Bremi, Æsch. *Ctesiph.* p. 278, Bernh. p. 337 sq., Herm. Soph. *Ant.* 633, Wex, *Antig.* I. 206, Mehlhorn in the *Allg. Lit.-Zeit.* 1833 (Ergzbl. No. 108), Lob. *Paral.* p. 151. As to Latin, see Kritz, Sall. *Cat.* p. 306 sq.

[4] [Obviously a mistake,—perhaps for 2 P. ii. 3, in which verse De Wette joins ἔκπαλαι with τὸ κρίμα. Another example is G. i. 13.]

(Is. vi. 9), Mt. xv. 4, θανάτῳ τελευτάτω (Ex. xxi. 15). The latter mode of expression is of frequent occurrence in the LXX and Apocrypha, and is there an imitation of the Hebrew absolute infinitive: compare Is. xxx. 19, lxvi. 10, Dt. vii. 26, Ex. xxi. 20, Jos. xxiv. 10, 1 S. xii. 25, xiv. 39, Ecclus. xlviii. 11, Judith vi. 4 (Vorst, *Hebr.* p. 624 sq.). It is however occasionally found in Greek authors:[1] e. g., Plat. *Symp.* 195 b, φεύγων φυγῇ τὸ γῆρας.[2] *Phædr.* 265 d, ἐμοὶ φαίνεται τὰ μὲν ἄλλα παιδιᾷ πεπαῖσθαι· Photius, cod. 80. 113, σπουδῇ σπουδάζειν· Soph. *Œd. R.* 65, ὕπνῳ εὕδοντα· Æl. 8. 15, νίκῃ ἐνίκησε.

Of a different nature are those passages in which the dative of the noun is accompanied by an adjective (or other adjunct), as in ταῖς μεγίσταις τιμαῖς ἐτίμησαν, ζημιούτω τῇ νομιζομένῃ ζημίᾳ (Schwarz, *Comm.* p. 49): this coincides with the idiom illustrated in § 32. 2. Compare Xen. *An.* 4. 5. 33, Plut. *Coriol.* 3, Aristoph. *Plut.* 592, Æschyl. *Prom.* 392, Hom. *Hymn. in Merc.* 572: from the N. T. see 1 P. i. 8, ἀγαλλιᾶσθε χαρᾷ ἀνεκλαλήτῳ κ.τ.λ. Nor has Demosth. *Bœot.* 1. 639 a, γάμῳ γεγαμηκώς, any connexion with this construction; the phrase means *having espoused by marriage,* i.e., living in lawful wedlock,—for γαμεῖσθαι by itself is also used of concubinage. I should even except Xen. *An.* 4. 6. 25, οἱ πελτασταὶ δρόμῳ ἔθεον, as δρόμος denotes a particular kind of running,—racing, trotting. On Soph. *Œd. Col.* 1625 (1621) see Herm. *in loc.*[3]

4. Certain adverbial notions the Greeks had become accustomed to conceive as *verbal.* In such cases the principal verb of the sentence is that which represents the adverb, the verb to be qualified being placed in dependence on this, in the form of an infinitive or a participle; see Matth. 552 sqq., and compare Kritz, *Sallust* I. 89 (Don. p. 580, Jelf 693). Thus: H. xiii. 2, ἔλαθόν τινες ξενίσαντες, they were not apparent (to themselves) as entertaining, *they entertained unconsciously;* see Wetstein *in loc.,* and compare Josephus, *Bell. Jud.* 3. 7. 3, Tob. xii. 13.[4] A. xii. 16, ἐπέμενε κρούων, he knocked persistently

---

[1] Schæf. *Soph.* II. 313, Ast, Plat. *Epin.* 586, Lob. *Paral.* p. 524.
[2] Lobeck *l. c.* shows that this phrase was used by Greek writers only in a figurative and not in a physical sense, as in Jer. (xxvi.) xlvi. 5.—An analogous construction in Latin is the well-known *occidione occidere.*
[3] [Hermann joins φόβῳ with στῆσαι, not with δείσαντας.]
[4] We find however instances of the other construction, which answers to our own usage: as Æl. 1. 7, οὗτοι, ὅταν αὐτοὺς λαθόντες ὑοσκυάμου φάγωσι. The infinitive instead of the participle follows λανθάνειν in Leo, *Chronogr.* p. 19.

(Jo. viii. 7): compare Lösner, *Obs.* 203. Mk. xiv. 8, προέλαβε μυρίσαι, *antevertit ungere, she anointed beforehand* (see Kypke *in loc.*): φθάνω also is sometimes joined with the infinitive,[1]—compare *rapere occupat* in Hor. *Od.* 2. 12. 28. Mt. vi. 5, φιλοῦσι προςεύχεσθαι, *they gladly pray, they love to pray* (compare Æl. 14. 37, φιλῶ τὰ ἀγάλματα ... ὁρᾶν); see Wetstein and Fritzsche *in loc.* On L. xxiii. 12 see Bornemann.[2]

Whether θέλω,[3] as a finite verb (for that the participle has this adverbial sense is well known,—compare Meyer on Col. ii. 18),[4] is ever used to express the adverbial notion *gladly, willingly, voluntarily* (*sponte*), has recently been questioned. And indeed in Jo. viii. 44, τὰς ἐπιθυμίας τοῦ πατρὸς ὑμῶν θέλετε ποιεῖν must be rendered, *the lusts of your father it is your will, ye are resolved and inclined, to do* (carry into effect),—either in a general sense (your hearts impel you to follow the desires of Satan), or with the meaning in "seeking to kill me" (ver. 40). The plural, in which De Wette finds a difficulty, has already been explained by Lücke.[5] So also in Jo. vi. 21 the explanation given by Kühnöl and others is unnecessary; unless we are attempting, with nothing before us to authorise such an attempt, to harmonise the narrative of this evangelist with that given by Matthew and Mark. At the same time we must admit so much as this, that ἤθελον ποιῆσαι, *they purposed, were inclined to do* (Aristot. *Polit.* 6. 8), may in a definite context (when it is clear

---

[1] See Wyttenbach, Juliani *Orat.* p. 181.

[2] [Bornemann quotes two examples of the construction ὑπάρχω ὤν, viz., Herod. ὑπῆρξε ἰόντα ταῦτα· Dem. *Mid.* 526, ὑπῆρχεν ὤν; and compares Dem. *De Cor.* 305. 22, καὶ τὰ μὲν τῆς πόλεως οὕτως ὑπῆρχεν ἔχοντα. See also Kühner II. 36.]

[3] 'Εθίλω? Herm. Soph. *Philoct.* p. 238. [In Soph. *Phil.* 1327 Buttmann writes συγχώρει 'θέλων (for θέλων), maintaining that in the signification "voluntarius," "sponte," the form ἐθέλω was *always* used: Hermann *in loc.* positively denies the truth of this assertion. In his *Gramm.* (§ 150. 36, see also A. Buttmann p. 375) Buttmann says that ἐθέλω is always used *in the idiom of which Winer is here speaking.*]

[4] In 2 P. iii. 5, λανθάνει τοῦτο θέλοντας, I prefer the explanation *latet eos hoc* (that which follows) *volentes,* i. e., *volentes ignorant,* to the other, *latet eos* (that which follows), *hoc* (that which precedes) *volentes,* i. e., *contendentes*: the former brings out more clearly what was criminal in the conduct of the scoffers. In Col. ii. 18 θέλων must not be taken adverbially. [On the interpretations of θέλων here see above, p. 291 sq.]

[5] [Lücke's remarks are to the effect that our Lord's language here is *general,* descriptive of the character of the Jews, θέλετε being a "timeless" present: in being children of the devil there is involved having the will and desires of the devil.]

that the reference is not to a mere act of will)[1] signify *they did it purposely, willingly, gladly.* See *e. g.* Isocr. *Callim.* 914, οἳ δυστυχησάσης τῆς πόλεως προκινδυνεύειν ὑμῶν ἠθέλησαν, *who were inclined to rush into danger for you* (and have by their act given evidence of this inclination), *who willingly rushed into danger for you* (Xen. *Cyr.* 1. 1. 3). The formula ἐθέλουσι ποιεῖν, where not used to indicate a mere act of will, means, according to the nature of the case, either *they are glad to do it,* as in Demosth. *Ol.* 2. p. 6 a, ὅταν μὲν ὑπ' εὐνοίας τὰ πράγματα συστῇ καὶ πᾶσι ταὐτὰ συμφέρει . . . . καὶ συμπονεῖν καὶ φέρειν τὰς συμφορὰς καὶ μένειν ἐθέλουσιν οἱ ἄνθρωποι; or *they do it of their own accord,* as in Xen. *Hier.* 7. 9, ὅταν ἄνθρωποι ἄνδρα ἡγησάμενοι . . . ἱκανὸν . . . στεφανῶσι . . . καὶ δωρεῖσθαι ἐθέλωσι.[2] Compare further Stallb. Plat. *Symp.* p. 56, and *Gorg.* p. 36, Ast, Plat. *Legg.* p. 28. Accordingly, in Mk. xii. 38, L. xx. 46, τῶν θελόντων περιπατεῖν ἐν στολαῖς, *who are disposed to walk about*—i. e., who love to walk about, is not incorrect Greek (though a Greek author would have preferred to say τῶν φιλούντων περιπατεῖν); but this phrase should perhaps be directly referred to the Hebraistic θέλειν τι *delectari re,* as indeed in Mk. *l. c.* the accusative ἀσπασμούς is immediately added as the object of θέλειν.

5. This transformation of an adverbial into a verbal notion is carried still farther in Hebrew.[3] In this language we not only find the verb which represents the adverb joined in grammatical construction with the verb proper (an arrangement which clearly shows that the two are essentially connected),—as in וַיֹּסֶף לִשְׁלֹחַ, i. e., *he sent again,*—but also the two verbs in a finite form connected by *and,* as, *he does much and weeps* (Ewald p. 631).[4] The latter mode of expression (a kind of ἓν διὰ δυοῖν

---

[1] Here (Jo. vi. 21), according to the account given in *this* Gospel, there seems to have been the will only. [On the other side, see Westcott and Alford *in loc.*, Trench, *Miracles* p. 304, Luthardt, *Das. Joh.-Ev.* I. 489 (ed. 2).]

[2] Compare also Origen, *c. Marcion.* p. 35 (Wetst.), τὰ δικαίως ἐν ταῖς γραφαῖς εἰρημένα βούλει ἀδίκως νοεῖν, *thou art disposed to understand,*—thou purposely understandest.

[3] [Gesen. *Gr.* p. 225 sq., Kalisch I. 310.]

[4] It is only in particular instances that the LXX render these Hebrew phrases literally. See *e.g.* Jud. xiii. 10, ἐτάχυνεν ἡ γυνὴ καὶ ἔδραμε· 1 S. xxv. 42, Ps. cv. 13, Dan. x. 18, Hos. i. 6; and on the other hand, Gen. xxvi. 18, xxx. 31, Job xix. 3, Ps. xxxii. 3. The formula וַיֹּסֶף is sometimes rendered in the LXX by a participle: see Gen. xxxviii. 5, προσθεῖσα ἔτι ἔτεκεν υἱόν· xxv. 1, προσθέμενος Ἀβραὰμ ἔλαβε γυναῖκα· Job xxix. 1, xxxvi. 1. One example of this

in verbs) was retained in certain phrases in all periods of the language; but in other cases it perceptibly passes into the former construction, which thus becomes predominant. The former idiom is imitated in L. xx. 11 sq., προςέθετο πέμψαι (contrast Mk. xii. 4, καὶ πάλιν ἀπέστειλεν), A. xii. 3, προςέθετο συλλαβεῖν καὶ Πέτρον, *he further apprehended Peter also*, Mk. xiv. 25 *v. l.* In the LXX προςτιθέναι and the middle προςτίθεσθαι are often thus used, e.g., Gen. iv. 2, xi. 6,[1] Ex. x. 28, xiv. 13, Dt. iii. 26, xviii. 16, Jos. vii. 12, al.; also with a passive infinitive, Jud. xiii. 21. Of the ~~former~~ [latter] more simple construction also the N. T. has been supposed to furnish examples:[2] e. g., Rom. x. 20, ἀποτολμᾷ καὶ λέγει, *he speaks out freely*; L. vi. 48, ἔσκαψε καὶ ἐβάθυνε, *he dug deep* (Schott); Col. ii. 5, χαίρων καὶ βλέπων, *seeing with delight* (Bengel and Schott). But in many of the passages which have been brought in here this mode of explanation is altogether inadmissible; as in 2 C. ix. 9, ἐσκόρπισεν, ἔδωκε τοῖς πένησιν, which must be rendered, *he dispersed abroad, he gave to the poor* (Ps. cxi. 9). In others it is not required; e. g., L. vi. 48, *he dug and deepened* ("crescit oratio," Beza). Jo. viii. 59, ἐκρύβη καὶ ἐξῆλθεν ἐκ τοῦ ἱεροῦ (Baumg.-Crusius), means *he concealed himself and went away*; i.e., either he withdrew from their sight—made himself invisible (in which case a miraculous ἀφανισμός of Christ is here recorded), or he concealed himself and (soon after) went away (Lücke, Meyer). The narrator might very well from this point of view thus combine together and connect by καί two events which, though not strictly simultaneous, followed each other in quick succession. We ought perhaps, with Bengel, to give the preference to the former explanation, as more in accordance with the character of John's Gospel: if the words διελθὼν διὰ μέσου αὐτῶν are genuine, this view is certainly correct. The word ἀναστρέψω in A. xv. 16 is not found in the LXX version of Am. ix. 11, which the apostle is quoting, nor is there any corresponding word in

---

kind is found in the N. T., in L. xix. 11. Compare further Thiersch, *De Pentat. Alex.* p. 177.

[1] [This reference is incorrect. Perhaps we should read Ex. xi. 6, which is a similar example (both in Hebrew and in Greek), except that the dependent infinitive is understood, not expressed.]

[2] The examples which Kühnöl (on L. vi. 48) has adduced as analogous, collected out of Xenophon, Plautus, and Persius, every one who has learnt to make distinctions in language will perceive to be of a different kind.

SECT. LIV.]   THE ADVERBS.   589

the Hebrew text. The sense intended by the apostle probably is, *I will turn again* to him. In many O. T. passages שׁוּב must thus be taken independently; see *e. g.* Jer. xii. 15, אָשׁוּב וְרִחַמְתִּים, *I will turn back*—to them, in antithesis to Jehovah's turning away from them,—*and have compassion on them* : in the LXX, ἀναστρέψω καὶ ἐλεήσω αὐτούς. In A. xv. 16 the *iterum* is already contained in the compounds ἀνοικοδομήσω, ἀνορθώσω. Similarly in Mt. xviii. 3, ἐὰν μὴ στραφῆτε καὶ γένησθε κ.τ.λ., and A. vii. 42, ἔστρεψεν ὁ Θεὸς καὶ παρέδωκε, the verb στρέφω is independent, *turn oneself* ; i. e., in these particular passages, *turn round* or *back* (turn away from). That in L. i. 68 ἐπεσκέψατο (פָּקַד) must be taken separately, is self-evident. Rom. x. 20, quoted above, rather corresponds to the Latin *audet dicere*, in which phrase we do not look on the first verb as expressing an accessory idea. We must render the words, *he emboldens himself and says* : ἀποτολμᾷ indicates his taking courage, and λέγει the result of this, the outward expression of the courage in bold words. In Col. ii. 5 Paul probably intends to say two things :[1] " In spirit I am present among you, *rejoicing* (about you, σὺν ὑμῖν) *and beholding your order* etc." To the general statement is added a special instance. It is also possible that in the words βλέπων κ.τ.λ. the object rejoiced over is subjoined, and that καί should be rendered *that is, to wit*. In no case, however, since *rejoicing* denotes something which does not exist until produced by βλέπειν, could the adverbial notion, thus expressed by the finite verb in an independent form, *precede* the principal notion :[2] indeed, even Hebrew usage, if examined more accurately, would not countenance such an arrangement.[3] In Ja. iv. 2, φονεύετε καὶ ζηλοῦτε does not mean, *Ye*

---

[1] In Joseph. *Bell. Jud.* 3. 10. 2, quoted by Wetstein, the MSS. have χαίρω καὶ βλέπων, or simply βλέπων.

[2] Where the adverbial notion is promoted grammatically to an independence which does not logically belong to it, it can only maintain this independence when following the principal verb. Compare Plutarch, *Cleom.* 18, εἰσελθὼν καὶ βιασάμενος, which is equivalent to βίᾳ εἰσελθών.

[3] The Hebrew verbs which, when standing before another finite verb, are taken in an adverbial sense, express either a notion which is conceived independently (as in Job xix. 3, *Ye are not ashamed and ye stun me*), or a general notion which is defined with greater precision by a more special notion contained in the following verb, as *He hastened and ran to meet the Philistines, he turned back and digged*, etc. Similarly in 1 S. ii. 3 ; though this poetical passage cannot be adduced in explanation of the prose of the N. T.

are jealous even unto death (Schott), *indulge deadly jealousy* ;[1] but, as Stolz translates, *ye murder and are jealous.* See Kern *in loc.* In Rev. iii. 19 each of the two verbal notions may very well be taken by itself. Züllig and others assume a ὕστερον πρότερον ; the right view is taken by Hengstenberg.[2]

Against rendering Mk. x. 21, ἠγάπησεν αὐτὸν καὶ εἶπεν αὐτῷ, by *blande eum compellavit* (Schott, al.), see Meyer *in loc.*[3]

6. As prepositions are sometimes used without a case, as adverbs (see § 50. Rem. 2, p. 526), so conversely, and still more frequently, adverbs—especially adverbs of place and time—are joined with cases (Don. p. 526, Jelf 526 sqq.). Ἅμα, which is thus used as early as Her. 6. 118, ἅμα τῷ στρατῷ, has in later Greek almost become a preposition; see Mt. xiii. 29, ἅμα αὐτοῖς, = σὺν αὐτοῖς, and compare Lucian, *Asin.* 41, 45, Polyb. 4. 48. 6, al. (Klotz, *Devar.* II. 97 sq.). Ἕως is thus used of time and place[4] (compare ἕως τούτου): here the Greeks used ἄχρι, μέχρι, or in a local sense ἕως εἰς, ἕως ἐπί (yet compare Diod. S. 1. 27, ἕως ὠκεανοῦ). Also with names of persons, *as far as;* see L. iv. 42, A. ix. 38, Lam. iii. 39. Χωρίς in Jo. xv. 5 means *separated from* (μὴ μένοντες ἐν ἐμοί, ver. 4), compare Xen. *Cyr.* 6. 1. 7, Polyb. 3. 103. 8 ; then very frequently *without, besides.* Πλησίον in Jo. iv. 5 takes a genitive, as in the LXX ; compare Xen. *Mem.* 1. 4. 6, Æschin. *Dial.* 3. 3: in Greek authors it also takes a dative. Παραπλήσιον, on the other hand, is followed by a dative in Ph. ii. 27, with very slight variation in the

---

[1] Gebser gains nothing by referring to Ja. i. 11 and iii. 14 in support of this explanation. In the former passage, ἀνέτειλεν ὁ ἥλιος . . . καὶ ἐξήρανε expresses the rapid scorching of the herbage more strikingly than ἀνατείλας ἐξήρανε: compare *veni vidi vici*, not *veniens vidi*, or *veni vidensque vici*. The rising and the scorching are spoken of as one ; not, *when it has risen it is wont to scorch.* It is by the use of finite verbs to express the several moments of thought that the rapid succession is more vividly portrayed. The second passage, Ja. iii. 14, μὴ κατακαυχᾶσθε καὶ ψεύδεσθε κατὰ τῆς ἀληθείας, I render (and Wiesinger now agrees with me), *do not boast and lie against the truth*: κατὰ τῆς ἀληθείας properly belongs to κατακαυχᾶσθαι (Rom. xi. 18). In order however to explain κατακαυχᾶσθε the apostle introduces immediately after it a stronger expression. By resolving the words into μὴ κατακαυχώμενοι ψεύδεσθε κατὰ τῆς ἀληθείας, we gain nothing but the tautology κατὰ τῆς ἀληθείας ψεύδεσθαι, whilst the κατά in κατακαυχᾶσθε is entirely lost.

[2] [*Revel.* Vol. I. p. 192 (Clark) : Hengstenberg's view may also be seen in Alford's note.]

[3] ["This interpretation of ἀγαπᾶν rests entirely on *Odyss.* 23. 214, where however the verb simply means *love*, as here." Meyer.]

[4] Klotz, *Devar.* II. 564.

MSS. Ἐγγύς governs the genitive in Jo. iii. 23, vi. 19, xi. 18, al., and the dative in A. ix. 38, xxvii. 8 : ὀψέ the genitive, Mt. xxviii. 1. The genitive is also found with ἔμπροσθεν, ὀπίσω (in Hellenistic Greek only), ὄπισθεν, ὑπερέκεινα, ἔλαττον, and with ἔσω and ἔξω. Several of these words are so frequently joined with a case that they may be taken as true prepositions ; indeed in ἕως, χωρίς, ἄχρι and μέχρι the adverbial meaning is perceptibly thrown into the shade, and in ἄνευ is (in the N. T.) entirely lost.[1]

Under this head comes also μέσον γενεᾶς σκολιᾶς, the reading of Ph. ii. 15 which Lachmann and Tischendorf have rightly received into the text (compare Theophan. p. 530). But in Mt. xiv. 24, τὸ πλοῖον ἤδη μέσον τῆς θαλάσσης ἦν, μέσον is an adjective,—*navis jam media maris erat:* see Krebs *in loc.*—The general usage of the N. T. in regard to the combination of adverbs with the genitive will appear very simple if compared with the far bolder constructions of the same kind which are found in the Greek of all periods. See Bernh. p. 157 sq.

Such combinations as ἕως ἄρτι, ἕως πότε, ἕως ὅτου, ἕως πρωΐ, ἕως ἔξω, ἕως κάτω, etc., are indeed especially common in later Greek prose (from the LXX compare ἕως τότε Neh. ii. 16, ἕως τίνος [Ex. xvi. 28], ἕως οὗ Gen. xxvi. 13), but are in particular instances confirmed by the authority of earlier writers. See Bernh. p. 196, Krüg. p. 300 sq. (Jelf 644).

As to adverbs with the article in the place of nouns, see § 18. 3.

7. The adverbs of place are sometimes interchanged in good prose, originally in consequence of attraction ; see Herm. *Vig.* p. 790 [2] (Jelf 646). The chief instance of this interchange (which is not confined to relative clauses, § 23. 2) is the combination of adverbs of rest with verbs denoting motion, where the writer intends at the same time to express the idea of continuance in the place (Herm. *l. c.*, Bernh. p. 350,—see also § 50. 4, on ἐν): compare Mt. ii. 22, ἐφοβήθη ἐκεῖ ἀπελθεῖν· xvii. 20, xxviii. 16. In later Greek, however, ἐκεῖ is used as a direct equi-

---

[1] [The following adverbs, besides those mentioned in the text, are found with a genitive in the N. T. : ἄτερ, ἄντικρυς, ἀντίπερα, ἐκτός, ἐντός, ἐναντίον, ἕνεκα, ἔξωθεν, ἐπάνω, ἐπέκεινα, μεταξύ, πέραν, πλήν, ὑποκάτω, χάριν,—ἀπέναντι, ὑπεράνω,—παρεκτός, ἔναντι, ἐνώπιον, κατενώπιον, κατέναντι, ὑπερεκπερισσοῦ. The last five words appear to be confined to the language of the LXX, Apocrypha, and N. T. (though the adjective ἐνώπιος is of earlier date) : παρεκτός belongs to very late Greek : ἀπέναντι and ὑπεράνω are found in writers of the κοινή.]

[2] Herm. Soph. *Antig.* 517, Wex, *Antig.* I. 107, Weber, *Demosth.* p. 446, Krüger, *Grammatische Untersuchungen*, III. 306 sqq.

valent for ἐκεῖσε, ποῦ and ὅπου stand for ποῖ and ὅποι, οὗ for *whither*. They are thus used in the LXX and even in the N. T., where *e. g.* ὅποι does not once occur. See Jo. xviii. 3, ὁ Ἰούδας . . . ἔρχεται ἐκεῖ μετὰ φανῶν καὶ λαμπάδων (Arrian, *Epict.* 24. 113),[1] Rom. xv. 24, ὑφ' ὑμῶν προπεμφθῆναι ἐκεῖ (*to Spain*), Jo. vii. 35, iii. 8 (πόθεν ἔρχεται καὶ ποῦ ὑπάγει), viii. 14, xi. 8, L. xxiv. 28, Ja. iii. 4, Rev. xiv. 4, al. This is a misuse of the words, which is easily accounted for in colloquial language (in the case of ὧδε and ἐνθάδε, ἐνταυθοῖ, the meanings *hic* and *huc* coalesced at a still earlier period,—see Krüg. p. 302 [2]), and which ought not to be disowned for the written Greek of the N.T.[3] (Jelf 605. *Obs.* 5). With respect to other adverbs of place, we not only find ἔσω used to denote *rest within* (ἔνδον not occurring at all in the N. T.), Jo. xx. 26, A. v. 23 (Ez. ix. 6, Lev. x. 18), but also ἐκεῖσε in the sense of ἐκεῖ, A. xxii. 5, ἄξων καὶ τοὺς ἐκεῖσε ὄντας :[4] see Wetstein on A. xxii. 5, and compare especially οἱ ἐκεῖσε οἰκέοντες, Hippocr. *Vict. San.* 2. 2. p. 35, and the index to Agathias, to Menander, and to Malalas, in the Bonn edition. On the other hand, A. xiv. 26, ὅθεν ἦσαν παραδεδομένοι τῇ χάριτι, is—as was seen by Luther—altogether according to rule (compare Meyer *in loc.*); and Hemsterhuis's emendation ᾔεσαν is in any case inadmissible. In A. xxi. 3 ἐκεῖσε retains its proper meaning, as does ποῦ in L. xii. 17. The adverbs ἔξωθεν, ἔσωθεν, κάτω, as is well known, represent in prose usage both relations, *from without* and *without*, motion and rest *beneath*, etc. That the usage of the later prose writers keeps pace with

---

[1] In Her. 1. 121 ἐλθὼν ἐκεῖ plainly signifies *being arrived there* (compare the preceding words ᾔει χαίρων ἐς Πέρσας); and ἔρχεσθαι might, if necessary, be thus rendered in Jo. xviii. 3. In H. vi. 20, ὅπου πρόδρομος εἰσῆλθε may mean *where . . . entered* [as distinguished from *whither . . . entered*]: see Böhme, whom Bleek has not understood.

[2] [If the reference to Krüger includes all these words, there is some change in the later edition (4th: 1862): in this Krüger mentions neither ἐνταυθοῖ nor ὧδε. On ἐνταυθοῖ see Shilleto, Dem. *F. L.* p. 183 ; on ὧδε, Liddell and Scott s. v., Hayman, *Odyss.* Vol. I. Append. p. 24. See Jelf 605. *Obs.* 5.]

[3] Several passages indeed which are really of a different nature have been referred to this head, e. g., Mt. xxvi. 36, L. xii. 17, 18 : here ἐκεῖ and οὗ [ποῦ?] certainly mean *there, where*. Not so in L. x. 1, where Hölemann's rendering *ubi iter facere in animo erat* is incorrect, since ἔρχεσθαι does not mean *iter facere*. Compare Herm. Soph. *Antig.* p. 106.

[4] [Unless Meyer's view be preferred,—that this example belongs to the class examined in § 50. 4. *b*, the sense being *who had come to Damascus and were then at Damascus*. See Alford *in loc.*]

that of the N. T. may be seen from the examples collected by Lobeck (*Phryn.* p. 43 sq., 128) and Thilo (*Act. Thom.* p. 9).¹

The (relative) adverbs of place are, as it is well known, also used in reference to persons; compare Rev. ii. 13, παρ' ὑμῖν, ὅπου ὁ σατανᾶς κατοικεῖ (Vechner, *Hellenol.* p. 234). Occasionally these adverbs are used with some looseness in their reference. See Jo. xx. 19, τῶν θυρῶν κεκλεισμένων ὅπου ἦσαν οἱ μαθηταί, *the doors there* (the doors of the chamber), *where;* Mk. ii. 4. Compare Mt. ii. 9 (Krüg. p. 302).

SECTION LV.

THE NEGATIVE PARTICLES.

1. The Greek language has, as is well known, two series of negative words, viz., οὐ, οὔτε, οὐκέτι (οὐδείς), κ.τ.λ., and μή, μήτε, μηκέτι (μηδείς), κ.τ.λ. The distinction between the two series has been most completely developed by Hermann (*Vig.* p. 804 sqq.): compare Matth. 608 sq., Madvig 200 sqq. (Don. p. 552 sqq., Jelf 738 sqq.). *Οὐ* stands where something is to be directly denied (as matter of fact); *μή*, where something is to be denied as mere matter of thought (in conception and conditionally): the former is the *objective*, the latter the *subjective* negative.² That this distinction is substantially observed in

---

[1] Compare further Buttm. *Philoct.* p. 107, Stallb. Plat. *Euthyphr.* p. 95 sqq., Schoem. Plut. *Cleom.* p. 186, Hartung, *Casus* p. 85 sqq. ; also Kypke and Elsner on Mt. ii. 22.—We must not, it is true, overlook the fact that such forms as ποῦ, ποῖ, and ἐκεῖ, ἐκεῖσε, might easily be interchanged by the *transcribers*, and indeed are often confounded in the MSS. of Greek authors (Schæf. Eurip. *Hec.* 1062). In the N. T., however, the variations of this kind which have been noted are extremely few. It is also very unusual to meet with corrections (such as ἐκεῖ in A. xxii. 5): the readers were already too much accustomed to this use of the adverbs to take offence at it. It may be added that the early (Homeric) Greek agrees with later prose usage in the interchange of local adverbs, whilst in Attic prose the forms are kept more distinct.

[2] Compare further L. Richter, *De usu et discrimine particularum οὐ et μή* (Crossen, 1831-34, 3 Commentt.) ; F. Franke, *De particulis negantibus linguæ Gr.* (Rintel. 1832-33, 2 Commentt.), reviewed by Benfey in *N. Jahrb. f. Philol.* XII. 147 sqq. ; Bäumlein in the *Zeitschr. f. Alterthumswiss.* 1847, No. 97-99, [and his *Untersuchungen über griech. Partikeln* (Stuttgart, 1861), p. 256-315.] See also the observations (relating directly to particular usages of the two negatives, but also very instructive in regard to their general character) which are found in Herm. Soph. *Œd. R.* 568, *Aj.* 76, *Philoct.* 706, Eurip. *Androm.* 379, Elmsley, Eurip. *Med.* p. 155 (Lips.), Schæf. *Demosth.* I. 225, 465, 587, 591, II. 266, 327, 481, 492, 568, III. 288, 299, IV. 258, V. 730, Stallb. Plat. *Phæd.* p. 43, 144.— Hermann's theory has been controverted by Hartung (*Lehre von den griech. Partikeln*, II. 73 sqq.), who takes Thiersch's principles as his basis; and he has been

the N. T.¹ will become evident if, before proceeding further, we notice—

a. Certain passages in which both forms of negation occur together.

Jo. iii. 18, ὁ πιστεύων εἰς αὐτὸν οὐ κρίνεται, ὁ δὲ μὴ πιστεύων ἤδη κέκριται, ὅτι μὴ πεπίστευκεν κ.τ.λ. (compare Herm. *Vig.* p. 805). Here κρίνεσθαι is denied as a matter of fact by οὐ; i. e., it is declared that a judgment does not in fact exist. The second πιστεύων is by means of μή negatived in conception merely, for ὁ μὴ πιστεύων means *whoever does not believe, if any one does not believe;* ὁ οὐ πιστεύων would indicate some particular man who does not believe. Hence also we have ὅτι μὴ

---

followed by Rost (*Gramm.* p. 743). In the main, however, Hartung ultimately agrees with Hermann, and the doubt through which he was led to the views which he has adopted has been resolved by Klotz (*Devar.* II. 666). G. F. Gayler's treatise, *Particularum Græci sermonis negantium accurata disputatio* (Tubing. 1836), is an industrious collection of examples, but lacks clearness of judgment.—On the distinction between *non* and *haud* in Latin, see Franke I. 7 sq., the Review in *Hall. L.Z.* 1834, No. 145, and Hand, *Tursell.* III. 16 sqq. (who explains οὐ as the qualitative, μή as the modal negative). The comparison between the Hebrew אַל and μή (Ewald p. 530) is less capable of being carried through: it is precisely in the nicer usages of μή that the Hebrew particle ceases to correspond with it. [The above reference to (an older edition of) Rost's *Gr.* is left as it stands in Winer's text: in his 7th edition Rost substantially agrees with Hermann.—Thiersch's words, as quoted by Hartung (p. 105), are as follows: "μή denies not independently and directly, but in relation to something else,—as when a case is supposed, a condition or design stated, or when a wish, will, command, or a fear, apprehension, or care is expressed." Hartung lays great stress on such examples as Hom. *Il.* 15. 41 (10. 330, Aristoph. *Av.* 194, al.), where μή is used in an oath, though the sentence is grammatically independent: see Kühner II. 743 (ed. 2), Bäumlein p. 286 (Jelf 741. *e*).]

¹ The almost invariable observance by the N. T. writers of this (in itself nice) distinction is due, not to their theoretical acquaintance with it, but to the instinct acquired through much intercourse with those who spoke Greek. In exactly the same manner we learn the (sometimes conventional) distinctions *e.g.* of the synonyms of our own language. In particular instances, however, a foreigner might well go wrong; as indeed even Plutarch (see Schæf. *Demosth.* III. 289, *Plutarch* V. 6, 142, 475), Lucian (Schæf. *Demosth.* I. 529, Schoemann, Plut. *Agis* p. 93, Fritzsche, *Quæst. Lucian.* p. 44), Pausanias (Franke I. 14), Ælian (Jacobs, *Æl. Anim.* p. 187)—compare Madvig 207. Rem., Matth. 608. Rem.—are said to have sometimes confounded the two negatives. Compare also Ellendt, *Præf. ad Arrian.* I. 24 sq., on ὅτι μή for ὅτι οὐ. Yet I would not affirm that in these passages grammatical acuteness could not occasionally discover the reason why οὐ or μή is used. We must indeed constantly bear in mind that there is sometimes no stringent reason in favour of one or the other, but either negative may be used with equal correctness, according to the mode in which the writer conceives the matter (Herm. *Vig.* p. 806). [On the use of the negatives in the N. T. see A. Buttm. *Gr.* p. 344-356, Green, *Gr.* p. 186-202, Webster, *Syntax*, p. 138-144, Jelf 746. *Obs.* The first number of the *American Journal of Philology* contains an interesting paper (by the editor, Professor Gildersleeve) on "The encroachments of μή on οὐ in later Greek."]

πεπίστευκεν, because the words merely suppose a case (*quod non crediderit*). This is not at variance with 1 Jo. v. 10, ὁ μὴ πιστεύων τῷ θεῷ ψεύστην πεποίηκεν αὐτόν, ὅτι ο ὐ πεπίστευκεν εἰς τὴν μαρτυρίαν κ.τ.λ. Here the apostle in the last clause passes suddenly from mere conception (ὁ μὴ πιστεύων) to actual fact; the μὴ πιστεύειν had already commenced, and John now represents to himself an actual unbeliever.

Mk. xii. 14, ἔξεστι κῆνσον .... δοῦναι ἢ ο ὐ; δῶμεν, ἢ μὴ δῶμεν; In the first instance inquiry is made as to the objective basis of the payment of tribute; in the second, a subjective principle is expressed,—*should we give*, etc. Compare Herm. *Vig.* p. 806, and on Aristoph. *Thesmoph.* 19, Stallb. Plat. *Rep.* II. 270.

E. v. 15, βλέπετε πῶς ἀκριβῶς περιπατεῖτε, μ ὴ ὡς ἄσοφοι ἀλλ' ὡς σοφοί. Here μὴ ὡς ἄσοφοι κ.τ.λ. is a direct explanation of πῶς, and, like it, is dependent on βλέπετε; hence the subjective negation.

2 C. x. 14, ο ὐ γάρ, ὡς μ ὴ ἐφικνούμενοι εἰς ὑμᾶς, ὑπερεκτείνομεν ἑαυτούς: *we do not overstretch ourselves* (an objective denial), *as if we had not reached to you*,—a mere conception, in reality it is otherwise. With this contrast 1 C. ix. 26.

Rom. xi. 21, εἰ γὰρ ὁ θεὸς τῶν κατὰ φύσιν κλάδων ο ὐ κ ἐφείσατο, μήπως οὐδὲ σοῦ φείσεται: *if .... has not spared* (a statement of fact,—he has in reality not spared them), *so (it is to be feared) that he will not spare thee also*. Here the apostle might have expressed the sentence categorically, *so will he not spare thee also;*[1] but he prefers to give it a milder turn by means of μήπως,—*lest possibly the* οὐδὲ σοῦ φείσεται *be realised*, and every apprehension is subjective (Rev. ix. 4 [2]). Compare Plat. *Phæd.* 76 b, φοβοῦμαι, μ ὴ αὔριον τηνικάδε οὐκέτι ᾖ ἀνθρώπων οὐδεὶς ἀξίως οἷός τε τοῦτο ποιῆσαι· p. 84 b, οὐδὲν δεινόν, μὴ φοβηθῇ, ὅπως μὴ .... οὐδὲν ἔτι οὐδαμοῦ ᾖ· Thuc. 2. 76. See Gayler p. 427, 430.

1 Jo. v. 16, ἐάν τις ἴδῃ τὸν ἀδελφὸν αὐτοῦ ἁμαρτάνοντα ἁμαρτίαν μ ὴ πρὸς θάνατον ... πᾶσα ἀδικία ἁμαρτία ἐστὶ καὶ ἔστιν ἁμαρτία ο ὐ πρὸς θάνατον. In the first instance, as sub-

---

[1] [Μήπως is not found in ℵ, A, B, C; and is now rejected by most of the editors.—It will be observed that E. v. 15 does not contain both negatives.]

[2] [A comparison of earlier editions seems to show that this passage is only quoted here as another example of a verse containing both negatives.]

jective observation is spoken of, μή is used, depending on ἐὰν ἴδῃ; in the latter οὐ, since a principle of objective validity is stated,—a dogmatically real idea established.

John vi. 64, εἰσὶν ἐξ ὑμῶν τινές, οἳ ὀ ὐ πιστεύουσιν· ᾔδει γὰρ .... ὁ Ἰησοῦς, τίνες εἰσὶν οἱ μ ὴ πιστεύοντες. Here οὐ οὐ πιστεύουσιν declares a matter of fact; οἱ μὴ πιστεύοντες a conception,—*those, whoever they might be, who believed not (qui essent, qui non crederent).*—Compare also [1] Rom. v. 13, Jo. v. 23, xiv. 24, xv. 24, A. iv. 20, x. 14, xxv. 17 sq., 1 Jo. iv. 8, v. 12, 3 Jo. 10, 2 Th. iii. 10, G. iv. 8, 2 C. ii. 13, H. iv. 2, 15.[2]

b. But the same result which these passages give is also obtained from those in which μή occurs alone:—

Mt. xxii. 25, μ ὴ ἔχων σπέρμα ἀφῆκε τὴν γυναῖκα αὐτοῦ τῷ ἀδελφῷ αὐτοῦ. Here μὴ ἔχων is said with reference to the law which made this provision (ἐάν τις ἀποθάνῃ μὴ ἔχων κ.τ.λ., ver. 24): *not having ... he left behind,* as a non-possessor in the sense of the law he left, etc.; οὐκ ἔχων would exhibit the not-having as if narrating a pure matter of fact. In Mk. xii. 20 it stands in the narrative form, οὐκ ἀφῆκε σπέρμα.

Col. i. 23, εἴγε ἐπιμένετε τῇ πίστει .... καὶ μ ὴ μετακινούμενοι ἀπὸ τῆς ἐλπίδος: here the *not being shaken* (in a sentence beginning with εἴγε) is put as a condition, consequently as a mere conception.

2 Th. i. 8, διδόντος ἐκδίκησιν τοῖς μ ὴ εἰδόσι θεὸν καὶ τοῖς μ ὴ ὑπακούουσι τῷ εὐαγγελίῳ. Here the expression is general, denoting *such as know not God,* whoever they are, wherever such are found (hence a *conception*). Compare ii. 12.

---

[1] [It will not be supposed that in all these examples of μή a *classical* writer would have chosen the subjective negation: this point is examined below.]

[2] In the following passages from Greek authors οὐ and μή appear together in the same sentence, the distinction between them being more or less clearly marked: Sext. Emp. *adv. Math.* 1. 3. 68, ταῦτα ο ὐ κ ἀπολογουμένου ἦν, ἀλλὰ κακοῖς ἐπισπληροῦντος κακὰ καὶ μηκέτι μετρίως, ἀλλὰ ἄρδην ἐπισπωμένου τὰς ἀπορίας· 2. 60, λεκτέον, ὡς εἰ μηδέν ἐστι ῥητορικῆς τέλος, οὐδέν ἐστι ῥητορική· (2. 107); 2. 110; *Hypotyp.* 3. 1. 2; Lucian, *Catapl.* 15, ἐγὼ ἅτε μηδὲν ἔχων ἐνέχυρον ἐν τῷ βίῳ, ο ὐ κ ἀγρόν, ο ὐ συνοικίαν, ο ὐ χρυσόν, κ.τ.λ.: Soph. *Antig.* 686, ο ὔ τ' ἂν δυναίμην, μ ή τ' ἐπισταίμην λέγειν· *Philoct.* 1048; Demosth. *Callicl.* 736 b, *Pac.* 23 a, *Phorm.* 604 a; Xen. *Cyr.* 2. 4. 27; Aristot. *Polit.* 6. 8, *Rhet.* 1. 11, 31, 2. 2, 15; Lucian, *Dial. Mort.* 16. 2, *Adv. indoct.* 5; Strabo 3. 138, 15. 712; Himer. *Oratt.* 23. 18; Plutarch, *Pompej.* 23, *Apophth.* p. 183 sq.; Ælian, *Anim.* 5. 28; Joseph. *Antt.* 16. 9. 3. Compare further Gayler p. 291. From the Fathers, compare Origen, *c. Marc.* p. 26 (Wetst.); from the Apocryphal writers, *Acta Apocr.* p. 107. Particularly noteworthy is Agath. 2. 23, ἐφ' ὅτῳ ἂν σώματι μ ὴ θᾶττον καταπταῖεν οἱ ὄρνεις ἢ οἱ κύνες ο ὐ κ αὐτίκα ἐπιφοιτῶντες διασπαράξαιεν κ.τ.λ.

Rom. xiv. 21, καλὸν τὸ μὴ φαγεῖν κρέα. The not eating is presented as a conception, *if any one eats not;* τὸ οὐ φαγεῖν would represent the not eating as something objective, possibly an actually existing practice.

Rom. xv. 1, ὀφείλομεν δὲ ἡμεῖς . . . . καὶ μὴ ἑαυτοῖς ἀρέσκειν: in verse 3, where a fact is narrated, καὶ γὰρ ὁ Χριστὸς οὐχ ἑαυτῷ ἤρεσεν.

Hence we naturally find μή with the optative, when this mood expresses a pure wish (Franke I. 27): Mk. xi. 14, μηκέτι ἐκ σοῦ εἰς τὸν αἰῶνα μηδεὶς καρπὸν φάγοι (where however some MSS. read φάγῃ), and 2 Tim. iv. 16. Similarly in imperatival clauses, as Rom. xiv. 1, τὸν ἀσθενοῦντα τῇ πίστει προςλαμβάνεσθε, μὴ εἰς διακρίσεις διαλογισμῶν (xii. 11), Ph. ii. 12—where some wrongly join μὴ ὡς ἐν τῇ παρουσίᾳ κ.τ.λ. with ὑπηκούσατε, in which case οὐ must certainly have been used, not μή.

According to the distinction defined above, μή will as a rule express the weaker (compare also Herm. *Philoct.* 706), and οὐ, as categorical, the stronger negation. Occasionally, however, μή is more forcible than οὐ (Herm. Soph. *Antig.* 691[1]); for the denial of the (very) conception of a thing expresses more than the denial of its (empirical) actual existence. See below, no. 5. In a similar manner, the Latin *haud* is sometimes the stronger, sometimes the weaker negative; see Franke I. 7, and compare Hand. *Tursellinus* III. 20.

Where οὐ belongs to a single word (verb), the meaning of which is directly opposite to that of some other word existing in the language, the negative and verb coalesce to express this contrary idea: e.g., οὐκ ἐᾶν, *to prevent* (A. xvi. 7), οὐ θέλειν, *nolle* (1 C. x. 1).[2] See Franke I. 9 sq., and compare below no. 6 [5?]. When οὐ combines with nouns to express one idea, it annuls their meaning altogether. See Rom. x. 19, παραζηλώσω ὑμᾶς ἐπ' οὐκ ἔθνει, *about a no-nation;* ix. 25, καλέσω τὸν οὐ λαόν μου λαόν μου καὶ τὴν οὐκ ἠγαπημένην ἠγαπημένην· 1 P. ii. 10: all these are quotations from the O. T. Compare Thuc. 1. 137, ἡ οὐ διάλυσις, *the not-breaking down* (the bridge had not been broken down), 5. 50, ἡ οὐκ ἐξουσία· Eurip. *Hippol.* 196, οὐκ

---

[1] [On Hermann's view of this passage see Jelf 746. *Obs.* See also Donalds. *Antig.* p. 190.]

[2] [It has often been supposed that οὐ γὰρ ἔκρινα, 1 C. ii. 2, is an example of this kind (see *e. g.* Stanley *in loc.*), but this may well be doubted: see Meyer and Alford.]

ἀπόδειξις.¹ As to the difference between this combination and that of μή with the substantive (ἡ μὴ διάλυσις), see Franke *l. c.* I. 9: many examples of both are given by Gayler p. 16 sqq. (Don. p. 558, Jelf 738, 745).

The simple accentuated οὔ, *no* (Mt. v. 37, Ja. v. 12, 2 C. i. 17 sq.), occurs in answer to a question only in Mt. xiii. 29 and Jo. i. 21:² for passages from Greek authors see Gayler p. 161. The fuller expression οὐκ ἔγωγε would have been more in accordance with usage.

2. We proceed to the consideration of the cases of most frequent recurrence in which the negation is effected by μή.

Μή is used

(*a*) In (wishes) commands, resolutions, and encouragements, —not merely in conjunction with the verb of the sentence, i.e., with the imperative or conjunctive employed, as in Mt. vii. 1, μὴ κρίνετε· G. v. 26, μὴ γινώμεθα κενόδοξοι· 2 Th. iii. 10 (on this see § 56. 1):—but also with words which are considered as integral parts of the command, etc., as in 1 P. v. 2, ποιμάνατε ... μὴ ἀναγκαστῶς· 1 P. i. 13 sq., 1 Tim. v. 9, L. vi. 35, 1 C. v. 8, Rom. xiii. 13, Ph. ii. 4, 12, H. x. 25, A. x. 20.

(*b*) In final sentences. With ἵνα, Mt. vii. 1, xvi. 20, Rom. xi. 25, E. ii. 9, H. xii. 3, Mk. v. 43, 2 C. v. 15, vii. 9, E. iv. 14; with ὅπως, L. xvi. 26, 1 C. i. 29, Mt. vi. 18, A. viii. 24, xx. 16. So also with particular words of the final sentence: Rom. viii. 4, E. ii. 12,³ Ph. i. 27 sq., iii. 9, 2 Th. ii. 12, H. xii. 27.

(*c*) In conditional sentences (Herm. *Vig.* p. 805). With εἰ, Jo. xv. 22, εἰ μὴ ἦλθον, ἁμαρτίαν οὐκ εἴχοσαν· xviii. 30, εἰ μὴ ἦν οὗτος κακὸν ποιῶν, οὐκ ἄν σοι παρεδώκαμεν· Mt. xxiv. 22, A. xxvi. 32, Rom. vii. 7, Jo. ix. 33; with ἐάν, Mt. v. 20, xii. 29, Rom. x. 15, 2 Tim. ii. 5. Here the negative has not always reference to the whole sentence, but is also found with particular words which are conceived as conditional: see 1 Tim. v. 21, Tit. i. 6, εἴ τις ἐστὶν ἀνέγκλητος ... μὴ ἐν κατηγορίᾳ ἀσωτίας· ii. 8, Ja. i. 4, 26.

In all these cases the necessity of the subjective negation is

---

[1] See Monk *in loc.*, Sturz, *Ind. ad Dion. Cass.* p. 245, Fritz. *Rom.* II. 424.

[2] [It also occurs in Jo. xxi. 5, and Jo. vii. 12 is a similar instance: compare οὐ γάρ A. xvi. 37, οὐ πάντως Rom. iii. 9 (§ 61. 4). In such cases, especially if ἀλλά follows, we more frequently find the strengthened form οὐχί (Jo. ix. 9, L. xiii. 3, al.). This form is, however, most common in interrogations (Mt. v. 46, al.): in ordinary negation it is rare.]

[3] [Inserted by mistake: the sentence is not one of *purpose*.]

obvious; for every condition, design, intention, or command belongs to the sphere of the mere conception.

In conditional sentences we not unfrequently—in the N. T. indeed pretty frequently—meet with οὐ, and not μή. The older writers restrict this usage, with logical necessity, to the case in which some particular word only of the conditional sentence (not the *verb* of the sentence merely, see Krüg. p. 306) is negatived, the negative coalescing with this word to express a single idea.[1] Thus in Soph. *Aj.* 1131, εἰ τοὺς θανόντας οὐκ ἐᾷς θάπτειν, *if thou preventest* (*Iliad* 4. 55); Lys. *Agor.* 62, εἰ μὲν οὐ πολλοὶ (i.e., ὀλίγοι) ἦσαν· Thuc. 3.55, εἰ ἀποστῆναι Ἀθηναίων οὐκ ἠθελήσαμεν· Her. 6. 9. Compare Gayler p. 99 sqq., Matth. 608 b, Krüg. p. 306 (Don. p. 555, Jelf 744. 1).[2] Accordingly there is nothing strange in Mt. xxvi. 42, L. xvi. 31, Jo. v. 47, Rom. viii. 9, 1 C. vii. 9, 2 Th. iii. 10, 14, 1 Tim. iii. 5, v. 8, Rev. xx. 15, al.; and as little in 2 C. xii. 11, εἰ καὶ οὐδέν εἰμι.[3]

On the other hand, Lipsius[4] has quoted a number of other passages, which, either in reality or in appearance, are at variance with the canon laid down above; as indeed the N. T. writers, in general, more frequently express *if not* by εἰ οὐ than

---

[1] Herm. *Vig.* p. 833, Eurip. *Med.* p. 344, Soph. *Œd. C.* 596, Schæf. *Plut.* IV. 396, Mehlhorn, *Anacr.* p. 139, Bremi, *Lys.* p. 111, Schoem. *Isæus* p. 324 sq. Schæfer says (*Dem.* III. 288): οὐ poni licet, quando negatio refertur ad sequentem vocem cum eaque sic coalescit, unam ut ambæ notionem efficiant; μή ponitur, quando negatio pertinet ad particulam conditionalem. Comp. Rost p. 751 sq.

[2] On the analogous ὅπως οὐ see Held, Plut. *Timol.* 357.

[3] [The difficulty of exactly classifying the N. T. examples of εἰ οὐ is illustrated by the fact that some passages (Jo. v. 47, iii. 12) are quoted by Winer twice, under different heads. He has perhaps brought too many passages under the principle stated above: A. Buttmann goes to the other extreme. A. Buttmann's classification (*Gr.* p. 344–348) is faulty in containing nothing which directly answers to Winer's class (*a*); though in the corresponding section of the *Griech. Gr.* the same usage is allowed for classical Greek. He explains most examples of εἰ οὐ as arising out of antithesis—(1) to a positive notion preceding (Mk. xi. 26, Jo. v. 47, A. xxv. 11, Rom. viii. 9, 1 C. vii. 9, Ja. iii. 2), or following (1 C. ix. 2, Jo. x. 37, L. xi. 8, xviii. 4, 1 C. xi. 6,—Ja. ii. 11, 2 P. ii. 4, 5); or (2) to an apodosis which is either formally or virtually negative (1 C. xv. 13–17, Rom. xi. 21, L. xvi. 31, 2 Th. iii. 10, H. xii. 25; L. xvi. 11 sq., Jo. iii. 12, 1 Tim. iii. 5, 1 C. xv. 29, 32). In L. xiv. 26, 2 Jo. 10, 1 C. xvi. 22, 2 Th. iii. 14, 1 Tim. v. 8, Rev. xx. 15, he ascribes οὐ to the somewhat lax usage of the N. T., "in which conditional sentences of the 1st class are in general negatived by οὐ." See further Green, *Gr.* p. 195, Webster, *Synt.* p. 139; also Prof. Evans's notes on 1 C. vii. 9, xvi. 22.—In modern Greek the negative which corresponds to οὐ (δέν, a truncated form of οὐδέν) regularly appears in the protasis of a conditional sentence (Mullach, *Vulg.* p. 390, Sophocles, *Gramm.* p. 184 sq.).]

[4] *De modorum in N. T. usu,* p. 26 sqq.

by εἰ μή, which most commonly signifies *unless*.[1] We divide these passages into four classes.

   a. L. xii. 26, εἰ οὐδὲ ἐλάχιστον δύνασθε, τί περὶ τῶν λοιπῶν μεριμνᾶτε; cannot be taken into account at all, since here εἰ is conditional in appearance only, and in reality is equivalent to ἐπεί (Krüg. p. 306). Translate: *If*—as is clear from what has been adduced—i. e., *since ye cannot do even the least*, etc. (For the same reason we always find θαυμάζω εἰ οὐ;[2] comp. Kühner II. 406.) So also Rom. xi. 21, Jo. iii. 12, v. 47, x. 35, H. xii. 25, 2 P. ii. 4. Compare Soph. *Œd. Col.* 596, εἰ θέλοντάς γ' οὐδὲ σοὶ φεύγειν καλόν, *si, quum te volunt recipere, ne tibi quidem decorum est exsulem esse;* Æschin. *Ep.* 8, εἰ δὲ οὐδὲ σὺν ἐκείνῳ διέγνωκας ἐξιέναι κ.τ.λ.; Sext. Empir. *Math.* 7. 434, εἰ οὐδ' αὐτὸ τοῦτο ᾔδει κ.τ.λ.; Xen. *An.* 7. 1. 29, Æsop 23. 2. See Bernh. p. 386, Franke, *Demosth.* p. 202, Gayl. p. 118, Herm. *Æschyl.* II. 148 (Jelf 744).

   b. Other passages, if more accurately examined, are in accordance with the above canon. Of this kind are, not only 1 C. xi. 6, εἰ γὰρ οὐ κατακαλύπτεται γυνή, καὶ κειράσθω, *if a woman is unveiled, she should also be shorn*, 2 Th. iii. 10;—but also Jo. x. 37, εἰ οὐ ποιῶ τὰ ἔργα τοῦ πατρός μου, μὴ πιστεύετέ μοι· εἰ δὲ ποιῶ, κἂν ἐμοὶ μὴ πιστεύητε, τοῖς ἔργοις πιστεύσατε, *if I leave undone the works of my Father* (and thus *withhold from you the proofs of my divine mission*) etc., *but if I do them*, etc.; Jo. iii. 12, Rom. viii. 9, Rev. xx. 15. Compare Lys. *Accus. Agor.* 76, ἐὰν μὲν οὖν φάσκῃ Φρύνιχον ἀποκτεῖναι, τούτων μέμνησθε . . . . ἐὰν δ' οὐ φάσκῃ, ἔρεσθε αὐτόν κ.τ.λ., *but if he deny it;* Sext. Emp. *Math.* 2. 111, εἰ μὲν λήμματά τινα ἔχει . . . . εἰ δὲ οὐκ ἔχει κ.τ.λ., *but if he is destitute of them;* 9. 176, εἰ μὲν οὐκ ἔχει, φαυλόν ἐστι τὸ θεῖον . . . . εἰ δὲ ἔχει, ἔσται τι τοῦ θεοῦ κρεῖττον· *Hypotyp.* 2. 5, 160, 175, Lucian, *Paras.* 12, Galen, *Temper.* 1. 3, Marc. Anton. 11. 18, p. 193 (Mor.). Compare also Euseb. *De die domin.* p. 9 (Jani). Nor can any ob-

---

[1] Εἰ οὐ and εἰ μή are well distinguished in one sentence in *Acta Thom.* p. 57 (ed. Thilo).

[2] [This assertion is too strong, as is shown by Thuc. 4. 85 (Plat. *Phœd.* 62 a). These passages are quoted, with others, by Buttmann (*Griech. Gr.* § 148. 2. b. note), who says that θαυμάζω εἰ requires μή, unless there is some special reason for οὐ. See also Sandys, Isocr. *Demon.* p. 34. Kühner himself in his second edition (II. 749) quotes examples of θαυμάζειν εἰ μή.]

SECT. LV.]   THE NEGATIVE PARTICLES.   601

jection be raised against 1 C. xv. 13, εἰ ἀνάστασις νεκρῶν οὐκ ἔστι, *if resurrection of the dead is a nonentity*: compare the preceding words, πῶς λέγουσί τινες ὅτι ἀνάστασις νεκρῶν ο ὐ κ ἔστιν ; With verse 16 compare Philostr. *Apoll.* 4. 16, p. 154.

 c. Where the sentence with εἰ οὐ merely negatives the notion expressed affirmatively by a corresponding sentence, though οὐ does not coalesce with the negatived word to express one antithetical idea. See 1 C. ix. 2, εἰ ἄλλοις οὐκ εἰμὶ ἀπόστολος, ἀλλάγε ὑμῖν εἰμί, si aliis non *sum* apostolus, vobis certe *sum ;* also L. xi. 8 ; compare xviii. 4. In antitheses of this kind also εἰ οὐ is used by later writers : e. g., Sext. Empir. *Math.* 11. 5, εἰ μὲν ἀγαθόν ἐστιν, ἓν τῶν τριῶν γενήσεται, εἰ δὲ ο ὐ κ ἔ σ τ ι ν ἀγαθόν, ἤτοι κακόν ἐστιν, ἢ οὔτε κακόν ἐστιν οὔτε ἀγαθόν ἐστιν· Diog. L. 2. 36, εἰ μὲν γάρ τι τῶν προσόντων λέξειαν, διορθώσονται, εἰ δ᾽ ο ὔ, οὐδὲν πρὸς ἡμᾶς,—where the sense is not, " if however they *conceal* it," but, " if however they do *not* say what is serviceable." [1] Compare Jud. ix. 20, Judith v. 21, Demosth. *Epp.* p. 125 a, *Basilic.* II. 525, and Poppo, Xen. *Anab.* p. 358.

 d. Where οὐ denies antithetically, as in the last case, but no directly affirmative sentence is actually expressed. Examples of this kind are Ja. ii. 11, εἰ οὐ μοιχεύσεις (referring to the preceding μὴ μοιχεύσῃς), φονεύσεις δέ, γέγονας παραβάτης νόμου, *if thou dost not commit adultery, but dost murder,*[2] i. 23, iii. 2 ; 1 C. xvi. 22, εἴ τις οὐ φιλεῖ τὸν κύριον, ἤτω ἀνάθεμα (where the rendering *if any one hates the Lord* would probably not represent the apostle's meaning) ; 2 Jo. 10, εἴ τις ἔρχεται πρὸς ὑμᾶς καὶ ταύτην τὴν διδαχὴν οὐ φέρει· L. xiv. 26.

 For the later prose writers, therefore (who use εἰ οὐ—as stronger and more emphatic than εἰ μή—much more frequently than the earlier writers, who employ it somewhat sparingly) we may lay down the following rule :[3] Where an emphasis rests on the negative of a conditional sentence,[4] εἰ οὐ is used (as *si*

---

[1] Macar. *Homil.* 1. 10.   Compare also ἐὰν οὐ in Diog. L. 1. 105, ἐὰν νἱος ὢν τὸν οἶνον ο ὐ φ έ ρ ῃ ς, γέρων γενόμενος ὕδωρ ο ἴ σ ε ι ς.
[2] Equivalent to εἰ οὐ μοιχεύων ἔσῃ, φονεύων δὲ : compare Arrian, *Epict.* 1. 29. 35, 2. 11. 22.   Contrast Thuc. 1. 32, εἰ μὴ μετὰ κακίας, δόξης δὲ μᾶλλον ἁμαρτίᾳ . . . . ἐναντία τολμῶμεν.
[3] Compare also Anton, *Prog. de discrimine particularum* οὐ *et* μή, p. 9 (Gorlic. 1823).
[4] Mehlhorn *l. c.* gives the rule thus : ubi simpliciter negatio affirmationi ita opponatur, ut negandi particula voce sit acuenda, semper οὐ poni, ubi contra

non in Latin); where however the negative is not emphatic, *if not* is expressed by εἰ μή, as in Latin by *nisi*. Hence the use of εἰ οὐ to express "If thou dost *not* commit adultery" (with a reference to μὴ μοιχεύσῃς), "If any one does *not* love the Lord" (as he ought to do), "If I am *not* an apostle to others," "If thou art *not* the Christ" (Jo. i. 25, compare ver. 20). The emphasis is occasioned by an antithesis, either open (1 C. ix. 2)[1] or concealed (1 C. xvi. 22). It lies however in the nature of the case that here also οὐ negatives a *part* only of the conditional sentence, and not the conditional sentence itself.[2]

Ὥστε (Krüg. p. 307), even when it merely expresses an actual result, is in the N. T. always followed by μή and the infinitive;[3] see Mt. viii. 28, Mk. i. 45, ii. 2, iii. 20, 1 C. i. 7, 1 Th. i. 8. Only in 2 C. iii. 7 a logical reason for μή is supplied by the conditional sentence (Engelhardt, Plat. *Apol.* p. 219).

Ὅτι and ἐπεί, *because* (in the *oratio recta*), are regularly followed by οὐ, see Jo. viii. 20, 37, Rom. xi. 6, L. i. 34 (Bäumlein p. 773): we find ὅτι μή in Jo. iii. 18, in a sentence of a conditional character. Yet in H. ix. 17, though in the *oratio recta*, we have διαθήκη ἐπὶ νεκροῖς βεβαία, ἐπεὶ μήποτε ἰσχύει, ὅτε ζῇ ὁ διαθέμενος. Böhme's explanation is: μήποτε appears to be here used to deny the very conception of ἰσχύειν, and thus to express a stronger negation than οὔποτε would have conveyed. But Böhme's translation of μήποτε by *nondum* is incorrect; it signifies *never* (Heliod. 2. 19). Perhaps also the writer's preference of μήποτε to οὔποτε is rather to be ascribed to the fact that he is speaking generally, not of any particular testament. Yet later writers often connect the subjective negative with ἐπεί (ὅτι) *quandoquidem*, not only where something is clearly indicated as a subjective reason (as is perceptibly the case even in Ælian 12. 63, —compare also Philostr. *Apoll.* 7. 16, Lucian, *Hermot.* 47), but also where an objectively valid reason is assigned by the clause,[4] inasmuch as the reason comes back ultimately to a conception. Others (Bengel,

---

verbum voce inprimis notandum μή esse debere. Compare also Poppo on Xen. *Anab. l. c.*

[1] Compare also e. g. Æsop 7. 4, εἰ οὐ σοὶ τοῦτο προσέφερεν, οὐκ ἂν ἡμῖν αὐτὸ συνεβούλευες, if it were not useful to *thee*, thou wouldst not counsel it to *us*.

[2] [The preference for οὐ when there is an antithesis, or where a single word is negatived, is well illustrated by the occasional occurrence of οὐ in imperatival and final sentences: 1 P. iii. 3, 1 C. v. 10 (Meyer), Rev. ix. 4, 2 Tim. ii. 14 (οὐδέν). These passages are quoted by A. Buttmann (p. 352).]

[3] [That is, we find in the N. T. no examples of ὥστε with the indicative when a *negative* consequence is expressed. Of course, where ὥστε has the meaning *itaque, quare* (p. 377) it may be followed by either οὐ or μή, according to the nature of the sentence. On ὥστε with οὐ and the infinitive see Shilleto, Dem. *F. L.* p. 202 sqq., Don. p. 594.]

[4] Gayler p. 183 sqq., Madvig 207. Rem. 2. On Lucian and Arrian in particular see Ellendt, Arr. *Al.* I. *Præf.* p. 23 sqq. Compare also Ptol. *Geogr.* 8. 1. 3.

SECT. LV.]   THE NEGATIVE PARTICLES.   603

Lachmann¹) take μήποτε in H. ix. 17 as an interrogative word, as indeed ἐπεί frequently introduces a question, see Rom. iii. 6, 1 C. xiv. 16, xv. 29 (Klotz, *Devar.* II. 543): in this passage, however, such an explanation seems to me too rhetorical for the style.

3. *Μή* is further used—

(*d*) In relative sentences with ἄν (ἐάν): L. viii. 18, ὃς ἂν μὴ ἔχῃ· A. iii. 23 (from the LXX), πᾶσα ψυχή, ἥτις ἐὰν μὴ ἀκούσῃ· Rev. xiii. 15, ὅσοι ἂν μὴ προςκυνήσωσιν· L. ix. 5. In none of these cases is there a denial of matter of fact in regard to definite subjects; the language is conditional and relates to a conception,—*whoever has not, whoever may not have*. Relative sentences without ἄν regularly have οὐ (Jo. iv. 22, προςκυνεῖτε ὃ οὐκ οἴδατε· L. xiv. 27, ὅστις οὐ βαστάζει· Rom. x. 14, 1 C. v. 1, 2 C. viii. 10, 1 Jo. iv. 6, al.), in so far as they deny something as a matter of fact. Sometimes however we find μή in such sentences, where the negation merely relates to a conception (a supposition, condition): e. g., 2 P. i. 9, ᾧ μὴ πάρεστι ταῦτα, τυφλός ἐστιν, *whosoever, if any one*, etc. See Hermann, *Vig.* p. 805, Krüg. p. 306. In 1 Tim. v. 13, Tit. i. 11, τὰ μὴ δέοντα and ἃ μὴ δεῖ (compare Rom. i. 28, Soph. *Phil.* 583) express a mere ethical conception, *quæ, si quæ non sunt honesta*: ἃ οὐ δεῖ would denote directly *inhonesta*, indicating the objectively existent genus of the unseemly.² In Col. ii. 18 μή before ἑώρακεν³ has been expunged by recent critics: Tischendorf however has in his 2nd Leipsic edition restored it to the text, and certainly it has the greater weight of external authority in its favour. (Meyer states the evidence imperfectly.) If the negative is genuine⁴ (some authorities have οὐ), μή is used because,

---

¹ [So Tischendorf (ed. 7), Delitzsch, Westcott and Hort, Lünemann (somewhat doubtfully): this is the explanation given by Œcumenius and Theophylact. Bleek, Kurtz, Alford, and Tischendorf (ed. 8) agree with Winer: see also Green, *Gr.* p. 202.]
² Compare Gayler p. 240 sq. [Ellicott on Tit. i. 11, Green p. 196, Don. p. 555 sq., Jelf 743.]
³ Compare Philostr. *Apoll.* 7. 27, διελέγετο ἂν μὴ ἐκείνῳ προὔβαινε, quæ illi haud prodessent. From the LXX may be quoted Ex. ix. 21, ὃς μὴ προςέσχε τῇ διανοίᾳ εἰς τὸ ῥῆμα κυρίου, which is opposed to ὁ φοβούμενος τὸ ῥῆμα κυρίου, ver. 20: here therefore the use of ὃς μή is exactly like that of εἰ δὲ μή in antithesis. For an example of οὐ and μή after relatives in parallel clauses see Arrian, *Epict.* 2. 2. 4.
⁴ [The negative is omitted by Ewald, Meyer, Tischendorf (ed. 8), Alford, Tregelles: see Tregelles, *Printed Text*, p. 204, and Green, *Dev. Crit.* p. 154. The negative is absent from the texts of Lightfoot and Westcott and Hort

as the sentence was conceived by the writer, this relative clause has a subjective character, like μηδεὶς ὑμᾶς καταβραβευέτω.[1]

In many of the instances in which ὅς is followed by οὐ it has been supposed (Lipsius, *Mod.* p. 14) that μή would be more correct, since the words appear to express a mere conception : e. g., Mt. xxiv. 2, οὐ μὴ ἀφεθῇ ὧδε λίθος ἐπὶ λίθον, ὃ s ο ὐ καταλυθήσεται. Here however μή is not required, inasmuch as the words deny something as a matter of fact. In some cases the conjunctive would have been used in Latin, and therefore μή might have been expected : Mt. x. 26, οὐδέν ἐστι κεκαλυμμένον, ὃ ο ὐ κ ἀποκαλυφθήσεται· L. viii. 17, xii. 2, Mt. xxiv. 2 ; compare 1 K. viii. 46. From Greek authors (Herm. *Vig.* p. 709) see Eur. *Hel.* 509 sq., ἀνὴρ γὰρ οὐδεὶς ὧδε . . . ὃς . . . ο ὐ δ ώ σ ε ι βοράν· Lucian, *Sacrif.* 1, οὐκ οἶδα, εἴ τις οὕτω κατηφής ἐστι, ὅστις ο ὐ γελάσεται· Soph. *Œd. R.* 374, οὐδεὶς ὃς οὐχὶ τῶνδ᾽ ὀνειδιεῖ τάχα. In all these instances the relative sentence is conceived as a definite, objective predicate, as if the sentence ran, ἀνὴρ οὐδεὶς ὧδε οὐ δώσει βοράν. So even in the construction with the optative ; see Isocr. *Evagor.* p. 452, οὐκ ἔστιν, ὅστις ο ὐ κ ἂν Αἰακίδος προκρίνειεν· *ib.* p. 199, Plutarch, *Apophth.* p. 196 c. Closely allied to this construction is the formula τίς ἐστιν, ὃς οὐ, with the present indicative (A. xix. 35, H. xii. 7,—compare Dion. *Comp.* 11, p. 120 ed. Schæf.), equivalent in sense to οὐδείς ἐστιν, ὃς ο ὐ (for which Strabo, 6. 286, has οὐδὲν μέρος αὐτῆς ἐστίν, ὃ μ ὴ . . . τυγχάνει). More remote is οὐδείς ἐστιν, ὃς ο ὐ, with a past tense ; in this combination no one would expect to find μή. See Xen. *An.* 4. 5. 31, Thuc. 3. 81, Lucian, *Tox.* 22, *Asin.* 49, and compare Heindorf, Plat. *Phæd.* p. 233, Weber, *Demosth.* p. 356 sq. See further Gayler p. 257 sqq., where however the examples are not properly distinguished.

4. (*e*) With infinitives (Matth. 608 e, Krüg. p. 308) :—not only where they depend on *verba cogitandi, dicendi, imperandi, cupiendi* (naturally also in the construction of the accusative with the infinitive), as in Mt. ii. 12, v. 34, 39, L. ii. 26, v. 14, xx. 7, xxi. 14, A. iv. 17, 18, 20, v. 28, x. 28, xv. 19, 38, xix. 31, xxi. 4, xxiii. 8, xxvii. 21, Rom. ii. 21 sq., xii. 3, xiii. 3, 1 C. v. 9, 11, 2 C. ii. 1, x. 2, H. ix. 8, al. ; or where a purpose is expressed, as in 2 C. iv. 4, ἐτύφλωσε τὰ νοήματα . . . εἰς τὸ μὴ αὐγάσαι· 1 Th. ii. 9, ἐργαζόμενοι πρὸς τὸ μὴ ἐπιβαρῆσαι· A. xx. 27, οὐχ ὑπεστειλάμην τοῦ μὴ ἀναγγεῖλαι· 1 P. iv. 2 :—but also where

---

(*Appendix*, p. 127), but these editors consider the true reading of the passage to be lost. See a good paper by G. Findlay in the *Expositor*, vol. xi. p. 385.]

[1] The N. T. does not happen to furnish an example of the use of μή after particles of time (Gayler p. 185 sqq.). Οὐ sometimes occurs in a temporal sentence with the indicative mood, see Jo. ix. 4, xvi. 25, 2 Tim. iv. 3, A. xxii. 11 : this is quite according to rule.

the infinitive is the subject of a sentence (as in 2 P. ii. 21, κρεῖττον ἦν αὐτοῖς μὴ ἐπεγνωκέναι· L. xvii. 1¹), or where an infinitive under the government of a preposition would, if resolved, become a finite verb with οὐ, as in Ja. iv. 2, οὐκ ἔχετε διὰ τὸ μὴ αἰτεῖσθαι ὑμᾶς (= ὅτι οὐκ αἰτεῖσθε ὑμεῖς), L. viii. 6, A. xxviii. 18, H. x. 2. In the former of these two cases, however, ἐπεγνωκέναι (2 P. ii. 21) is still denied merely as a conception (in point of fact they had known it); and in the latter the cause is not stated objectively, but is presented in the first instance as a conception of the speaker. For examples from Greek authors in illustration of all these points, see Gayler p. 294 sqq. Compare Rost p. 757, Bäumlein no. 99, p. 788 sq. (Don. p. 590 sq., Jelf 745). The words which essentially belong to the infinitive clause are in like manner negatived by μή; see *e. g.* 2 C. x. 2.

The cases in which οὐ is used, and may or must be used, in the infinitive *construction*, are pointed out by Rost p. 754 sq., Krüger p. 308 sq., Bäumlein p. 778. In Jo. xxi. 25, ἐὰν γράφηται καθ' ἕν, οὐδ' αὐτὸν οἶμαι τὸν κόσμον χωρῆσαι τὰ γραφόμενα βιβλία, the negation belongs to οἶμαι: compare Xen. *Mem.* 2. 2. 10, ἐγὼ μὲν οἶμαι, εἰ τοιαύτην μὴ δύνασαι φέρειν μητέρα, ἀγαθά σε οὐ δύνασθαι φέρειν. In H. vii. 11, τίς ἔτι χρεία κατὰ τὴν τάξιν Μελχισεδὲκ ἕτερον ἀνίστασθαι ἱερέα καὶ οὐ κατὰ τὴν τάξιν Ἀαρὼν λέγεσθαι, the negation does not belong to the infinitive, but negatives the words κατὰ τὴν τάξιν Ἀαρών. We often find οὐ thus joined with some particular word of a dependent sentence: see Krüg. p. 306 (Jelf 745. *Obs.* 3).²

If after *verba intelligendi* or *dicendi* in the oratio recta, etc., that which is asserted, observed, etc., is expressed by a clause with ὅτι, the negative employed is οὐ: L. xiv. 24, λέγω ὑμῖν, ὅτι οὐδεὶς τῶν ἀνδρῶν . . . . γεύσεται τοῦ δείπνου· xviii. 29, Jo. v. 42, ἔγνωκα ὑμᾶς ὅτι τὴν ἀγάπην τοῦ θεοῦ οὐκ ἔχετε κ.τ.λ., viii. 55, A. ii. 31, al. The clause with ὅτι appears here as a pure objective sentence, just as in the indirect question (§ 41. *b.* 4); as if the words ran, οὐδεὶς . . . γεύσεται, τοῦτο ὑμῖν λέγω. The infinitive construction, on the other hand, brings the verb into immediate connexion with, and consequently dependence upon, λέγω, ὁρῶ, κ.τ.λ. Compare Krüg. p. 286, 305, Madvig 200 (Don. p. 590, Jelf 742. 1).

---

¹ [With the reading ἀνένδεκτόν ἐστι μὴ ἐλθεῖν: see above, p. 412.]
² [See also Rom. vii. 6, A. xix. 27, 2 Tim. ii. 14 (A. Buttmann p. 350 sq.): compare Green, *Gr.* p. 197 sq. On οὐ with infinitive see Don. p. 591 (Jelf 745).]

5. (*f*) **Μή** is found with participles[1] (Gayler p. 274 sqq., Krüg. p. 309), not only when they belong to a sentence which, as expressing command, purpose, condition, etc., requires the subjective negative (see no. 2), as in E. v. 27, Ph. i. 28, ii. 4, iii. 9, 2 Th. ii. 12, H. vi. 1, Ja. i. 5, Tit. ii. 9 sq., Rom. viii. 4, xiv. 3, Mt. xxii. 24, A. xv. 38, L. iii. 11, 2 C. xii. 21 (compare Soph. *Œd. Col.* 1155, 980, Plat. *Rep.* 2. 370 e, Xen. *Cyr.* 1. 4. 26, Krüg. p. 310) :—but also

(*a*) When they refer not to particular persons but to a *genus* conceived of in the mind. Thus in Mt. xii. 30, ὁ μὴ ὢν μετ' ἐμοῦ κατ' ἐμοῦ ἐστίν, the meaning is, *whoever is not with me;* i.e., whoever belongs to the number of those persons of whom I form a mental conception, *si quis non stet a meis partibus* (Herm. *Vig.* p. 805, Matth. 608 c, Krüg. p. 309): ὁ οὐκ ὢν μετ' ἐμοῦ would denote some particular individual who in point of fact was not with him. See also Mt. xxv. 29, L. vi. 49, Jo. x. 1, xii. 48, xx. 24 [xx. 29?], Rom. iv. 5, xiv. 22, Ja. ii. 13, iv. 17, 1 Jo. ii. 4, 1 C. vii. 37. Hence we find μή with πᾶς ; see Mt. xiii. 19, Jo. xv. 2. To this class belongs also 2 Jo. 7, πολλοὶ πλάνοι εἰσῆλθον εἰς τὸν κόσμον οἱ μὴ ὁμολογοῦντες Ἰησοῦν Χριστόν κ.τ.λ.: these words do not mean *many seducers, namely those men, who do not confess* (οἱ οὐχ ὁμολογοῦντες), but *many seducers, all those who do not confess, quicunque non profitentur.*

---

[1] [See Don. p. 554, Jelf 746, Clyde, *Synt.* p. 110, 113, Green, *Gr.* p. 201 sq., Webster, *Synt.* p. 114, 139, A. Buttm. p. 350 sqq. ; Ellicott on 1 Tim. vi. 4, 1 Th. ii. 15, G. iv. 8, and in *Aids to Faith* p. 467.—It is very easy to confound two different questions,—whether μή is in itself admissible, and whether a classical writer would have preferred it to οὐ. After what Winer has said on the former point, there will hardly be much doubt as to the abstract lawfulness of using μή, at all events in most of the examples quoted : as to the latter, it is certain that in many instances the participle would have been accompanied by οὐ in classical Greek.—It will be useful to compare with the observations in the text A. Buttmann's classification of examples "*a.* The participle with the article is regularly negatived by μή: the exceptions are all cases of antithesis (Rom. ix. 25 al.), unless τὰ οὐκ ἀνήκοντα be the true reading in E. v. 4.—*b.* The anarthrous participle takes μή when it represents a hypothetical sentence. When it expresses actual matter of fact, and would be resolved by means of the relative, or by *whereas, since, whilst, without,* etc., the negative is sometimes οὐ, sometimes, and more commonly (though the circumstances may be exactly similar), μή. When οὐ is used, it is often in consequence of antithesis (2 C. iv. 8, al.), or because the negative affects some particular word rather than the clause itself.— *c.* When the participle with εἶναι is a periphrasis for a finite verb, the negative employed is μή, if it is the participle that is negatived (and not the copula—and by consequence the whole sentence).—*d.* When the sentence to which the participle belongs requires μή, the participle takes this negative,—sometimes even where there is an antithesis."—In modern Greek the participle invariably takes μή : see Mullach, *Vulg.* p. 29, 389, Sophocles, *Gr.* p. 192.]

(β) When, though the reference is to particular persons, the attribute ascribed to them by the participle is ascribed only conditionally or in conception: L. xi. 24, ὅταν .... ἐξέλθῃ .... διέρχεται δι' ἀνύδρων τόπων ζητοῦν ἀνάπαυσιν, καὶ μὴ εὑρίσκον λέγει, *if he finds it not, in case he does not* etc.; Rom. ii. 14; G. vi. 9, θερίσομεν μὴ ἐκλυόμενοι· L. xii. 47, ἐκεῖνος ὁ δοῦλος (ver. 45 sq.) ὁ μὴ ἑτοιμάσας μηδὲ ποιήσας πρὸς τὸ θέλημα δαρήσεται (this was put as one of two possible cases); 1 C. x. 33, πάντα πᾶσιν ἀρέσκω, μὴ ζητῶν τὸ ἐμαυτοῦ συμφέρον, *I seek to please all* (a conception of the mind), *as one who,—inasmuch as I* etc.; 1 C. ix. 21, 2 C. vi. 3, Rom. xv. 23, 1 Th. iii. 1, 5 ;[1] Jo. vii. 15, πῶς οὗτος γράμματα οἶδε μὴ μεμαθηκώς; *whereas he has not learned* (whereas we know him to be one who has not learned,—compare Philostr. *Apoll.* 3. 22, ὃς καὶ γράφει μὴ μαθὼν γράμματα); L. vii. 33, ἐλήλυθεν Ἰωάννης μήτε ἐσθίων ἄρτον μήτε πίνων οἶνον, *without eating or drinking* (spoken from the stand-point of those who, remarking this, are in the next clause introduced as speaking),—οὔτε ἐσθίων οὔτε πίνων would express the predicates simply as matters of fact. In L. iv. 35, τὸ δαιμόνιον ἐξῆλθεν ἀπ' αὐτοῦ μηδὲν βλάψαν αὐτόν, Luke does not use the last words to relate a mere matter of fact (οὐδὲν βλάψαν αὐτόν, *without injuring him*): he only intends to exclude the supposition that the evil spirit may in some way have injured the demoniac,—*without having done* (as one might perhaps suppose he would have done) *harm to him.* Μή may frequently be explained on this principle: see A. v. 7, xx. 22, H. xi. 8, xiii. 27,[2] Mt. xxii. 12. Compare the words of Klotz (*Devar.* p. 666): quibus in locis omnibus propterea μή positum est, non οὐ, quod ille, qui loquitur, non rem ipsam spectat sed potius cogitationem rei, quam vult ex animo audientis amovere (Plut. *Pompej.* c. 64); Herm. *Vig.* p. 806. In Mt. xviii. 25, μὴ ἔχοντος αὐτοῦ ἀποδοῦναι ἐκέλευσεν αὐτὸν ὁ κύριος αὐτοῦ πραθῆναι κ.τ.λ., the first words certainly do express an actual fact (*since he had not*), but they are in this construction brought into close connexion with ἐκέλευσεν,—*he commanded because the man had not,* because he knew that the man had not, etc. So

---

[1] Against Rückert see Lünemann *in loc.* [Rückert asserts that μηκέτι is here incorrectly used for οὐκέτι: see Ellicott.]

[2] [Probably for H. xi. 8, 13, 27: H. xi. 13 is mentioned in ed. 5.]

also in A. xxi. 34, L. ii. 45, xxiv. 23, A. ix. 26, xiii. 28, xvii. 6, xxvii. 7, 20, 1 P. iv. 4, 2 P. iii. 9: compare Plut. *Pompej.* c. 23, *Alex.* 51, Polyb. 17. 7. 5, 5. 30. 5. As to Rom. ix. 11 see Fritzsche *in loc.*[1] In A. xx. 29, οἶδα ὅτι εἰϛελεύσονται ... λύκοι βαρεῖς εἰς ὑμᾶς, μὴ φειδόμενοι τοῦ ποιμνίου, the whole belongs to the region of conceptions, as is shown by the future tense. In H. ix. 9 also the words μὴ δυνάμεναι κατὰ συνείδησιν τελειῶσαι κ.τ.λ. express the writer's own view: οὐ δυνάμεναι would indicate a property actually inherent (*unable* etc.),—but such sacrifices Israelites would not have offered. 1 C. i. 28, ἐξελέξατο ὁ θεὸς τὰ μὴ ὄντα, ἵνα τὰ ὄντα καταργήσῃ: here τὰ οὐκ ὄντα would have signified (Herm. *Vig.* p. 889) *the non-existent* (as a single negative notion), whilst τὰ μὴ ὄντα is intended to signify *the things which were looked upon as—which passed as—things which did not exist;* the writer negatives ὄντα as a conception, and does not speak of that which in actual fact is *non-existent.*[2] In 2 C. iv. 18 (even in the latter part of the verse, which is categorical), contrasted with τὰ βλεπόμενα stands τὰ μὴ βλεπόμενα, not τὰ οὐ βλεπόμενα (H. xi. 1). The latter would denote that which in point of fact is not seen (τὰ ἀόρατα); τὰ μὴ βλεπόμενα, in combination with μὴ σκοπούντων ἡμῶν, expresses the *subjective* stand-point of believers: compare H. xi. 7. So also in 2 C. v. 21, τὸν μὴ γνόντα ἁμαρτίαν ὑπὲρ ἡμῶν ἁμαρτίαν ἐποίησε, the words μὴ γνόντα relate to the conception of him who makes Christ to be ἁμαρτία: τὸν οὐ γνόντα would be objective, equivalent to τὸν ἀγνοοῦντα[3] (Isæus 1. 11, and Schoemann *in loc.*). In 2 C. vi. 3 we do not find οὐδεμίαν ἐν οὐδενὶ διδόντες προςκοπήν, as this would merely represent a quality actually existent; but μηδεμίαν ἐν μηδενὶ κ.τ.λ., because the quality is regarded in connexion with παρακαλοῦμεν (ver. 1) as one that is subjectively maintained, continually striven after. Compare further L. vii. 30, Jo. vii. 49, 1 C. ix. 20 sq. Μή is thus used with ὡς in subjective language: 1 C. iv. 7, τί καυχᾶσαι ὡς μὴ λαβών; iv. 18, vii. 29,

---

[1] [" Οὕτω γεννηθέντων οὐδὲ πραξάντων κ.τ.λ. foret 'quum nondum nati essent neque fecissent:' μήπω γεν. μηδὲ πρ. valet 'etiamsi nondum nati essent neque fecissent,' i. q. ἐν τῷ μήπω γεγεννῆσθαι αὐτοὺς μηδὲ πρᾶξαι." Fritz. *l. c.*]
[2] In Xen. *An.* 4. 4. 15 μὴ ὄντα and οὐκ ὄντα are united.
[3] Rückert's purely empirical and incorrect statement (in his note *in loc.*), that between the article and the participle Greek writers never use οὐ but always μή, has already been duly refuted by Meyer. [This "empirical" remark is (for the N. T.) not far from the truth: see p. 606, note [1]. Compare Madvig 207.]

2 C. x. 14, 1 P. ii. 16 (Gayler p. 278 sq.); the case is different in 1 C. ix. 26, see below.

On the other hand, when οὐ is joined to participles (and adjectives)—a much less common case than the preceding—we have a direct denial of matter of fact (Gayler p. 287 sq., Matth. 608 d); and hence this construction is especially found when predicates are denied of persons who are definitely present to the mind,[1] Ph. iii. 3 [*Rec.*], ἡμεῖς ἐσμὲν ἡ περιτομή, οἱ πνεύματι θεῷ λατρεύοντες . . . . καὶ οὐκ ἐν σαρκὶ πεποιθότες: in regard to ἡμεῖς, since they are in fact πνεύματι θεῷ λατρεύοντες, the ἐν σαρκὶ πεποιθότες is directly denied. 1 P. ii. 10 (from the LXX), ὑμεῖς . . . . οἱ οὐκ ἠλεημένοι, νῦν δὲ ἐλεηθέντες; Rom. ix. 25 (from the LXX). H. xi. 35, ἔλαβον γυναῖκες . . . . ἄλλοι δὲ ἐτυμπανίσθησαν οὐ προςδεξάμενοι τὴν ἀπολύτρωσιν, *not accepting*, i. e., spurning. Col. ii. 19, εἰκῇ φυσιούμενος . . . . καὶ οὐ κρατῶν, although the sentence is imperatival (ver. 18, μηδεὶς ὑμᾶς καταβραβευέτω, and ἃ μὴ ἑώρακεν κ.τ.λ.), for in the words οὐ κρατῶν the apostle passes to an actually existing predicate: A. xvii. 27, L. vi. 42. 1 C. ix. 26, ἐγὼ οὕτω πυκτεύω, ὡς οὐκ ἀέρα δέρων: here οὐκ ἀέρα δέρων is a concrete predicate which Paul attributes to himself, and ὡς is qualitative, whereas ὡς μὴ ἀέρα δέρων would be, *as if I did not beat the air*. G. iv. 27 (from the LXX), εὐφράνθητι στεῖρα ἡ οὐ τίκτουσα κ.τ.λ., *not-bearing one!*—of an historical person. See further 1 C. iv. 14, 2 C. iv. 8 sq., A. xxvi. 22, xxviii. 17, H. xi. 1; and for adjectives with οὐ, Rom. viii. 20, H. ix. 11. Compare Xen. *Cyr.* 8. 8. 6, Her. 9. 83, Plat. *Phæd.* 80 e, Demosth. *Zenothem.* p. 576 b, Strabo 17. 796, 822, Diod. S. 19. 97, Philostr. *Apoll.* 7. 32, Ælian 10. 11, Lucian, *Philops.* 5, *Peregr.* 34.

In 1 P. i. 8 we meet with both negatives, ὃν οὐκ εἰδότες ἀγαπᾶτε, εἰς ὃν ἄρτι μὴ ὁρῶντες πιστεύοντες δὲ ἀγαλλιᾶσθε κ.τ.λ. Here οὐκ εἰδότες expresses the negative idea, (*personally*) *unacquainted with*,—a matter of fact; whilst μὴ ὁρῶντες signifies *although ye see not*,—referred to the conception of the persons addressed: " believing, ye rejoice in him, and the thought

---

[1] The difference between οὐ and μή with the participle is well illustrated by Plat. *Phæd.* 63 b, ἠδίκουν ἂν οὐκ ἀγανακτῶν, *injuste facerem ego, qui non indignor*, compared with ἠδίκουν ἂν μὴ ἀγανακτῶν (the reading of Olympiodorus), *injuste facerem si non indignarer*. Compare also Joseph. *Antt.* 16. 7. 5, ὁ δὲ Φερώρας εἰς μέσον ἀπείληπτο, μηδὲν εὔσχημον εἰς ἀπολογίαν ἔχων . . . . ἀκοῦσαι δ᾽ οὐ πιστευόμενος.

that ye do not see him does not keep you back from rejoicing." A similar instance of the use of both οὐ and μή with participles in the same sentence is found in Lucian, *Indoct.* 5, καὶ ὁ κυβερνᾶν οὐκ εἰδὼς καὶ ἱππεύειν μὴ μεμελετηκώς κ.τ.λ. : compare also Lycurg. 11. 9 and Blume *in loc.* In Rom. i. 28 we find παρέδωκεν αὐτοὺς ὁ θεὸς εἰς ἀδόκιμον νοῦν, ποιεῖν τὰ μὴ καθήκοντα ; but in E. v. 3 sq., πορνεία καὶ πᾶσα ἀκαθαρσία ... μηδὲ ὀνομαζέσθω ἐν ὑμῖν .... ἡ εὐτραπελία, τὰ οὐκ ἀνήκοντα. The latter, as an apposition, is to be resolved into, *which are the unseemly things* (which a Christian has to avoid),—which actions are not seemly : some MSS. indeed have ἃ οὐκ ἀνῆκεν. In G. iv. 8, τότε οὐκ εἰδότες θεὸν ἐδουλεύσατε κ.τ.λ., the words look back to an historic past, and οὐκ εἰδότες expresses a single notion, *ignorantes Deum*, ἄθεοι. Contrast with this 1 Th. iv. 5, τὰ ἔθνη τὰ μὴ εἰδότα τὸν θεόν, and 2 Th. i. 8, τοῖς μὴ εἰδόσι θεόν, in dependent construction.

Still there are some instances in which μή may appear to stand for οὐ. In Rom. iv. 19, however, καὶ μὴ ἀσθενήσας τῇ πίστει οὐ[1] κατενόησε τὸ ἑαυτοῦ σῶμα κ.τ.λ., the meaning is, *he considered not his body, quippe qui non esset imbecillis.* Κατενόησε is a fact, the *being weak in faith* only a conception, to be denied : οὐκ ἀσθενήσας would be *strong in faith.* With a different construction indeed the apostle might have written οὐκ ἠσθένησεν .... ὥστε κατανοῆσαι κ.τ.λ. ; compare Plut. *Reg. Apophth.* p. 81 (Tauchn.). On the other hand, H. vii. 6, ὁ δὲ μὴ γενεαλογούμενος ἐξ αὐτῶν δεδεκάτωκε τὸν Ἀβραάμ, may be explained on the principle that the Greeks (especially in antitheses, compare ver. 5), where they wish to express a very strong denial (and the emphasis rests on the negation), use μή, and thus deny the very conception. See above, p. 597, and Hermann on Soph. *Antig.* 691,—a passage which will be quoted immediately. In L. i. 20, ἔσῃ σιωπῶν καὶ μὴ δυνάμενος λαλῆσαι, the subjective negative is the more appropriate, as the words speak of an attribute in its announcement merely, consequently as a conception (ἔσῃ) : so also in A. xiii. 11.

Most remarkable of all is the union of the subjective and objective negatives in A. ix. 9, ἦν ἡμέρας τρεῖς μὴ βλέπων καὶ οὐκ ἔφαγεν οὐδὲ ἔπιεν : compare Epiphan. *Opp.* II. 368 a, ἦν δὲ ὁ βασιλεὺς μὴ δυνάμενος λαλῆσαι. Here however the not eating and not drinking are related as matters of fact, whilst the βλέπειν, which from verse 8 might have been supposed to be returning, is denied antithetically as a conception. Hermann's remark (Soph. *Antig.* 691) is applicable here : μή fortius est, quia ad oppositum refertur :

---

[1] [Οὐ is omitted in the best texts. In 1 P. i. 8 (quoted above) we must read ἰδόντες ; in E. v. 4, ἃ οὐκ ἀνῆκεν.]

nam οὐκ ἐᾶν simpliciter est *prohibere,* μὴ ἐᾶν autem dicitur, quum, quem credas siturum, non sinit. So in this verse οὐ βλέπων would have simply meant *blind;* μὴ βλέπων is *not seeing,*—said of one who had been, and might appear to be again, possessed of sight. Compare also Jo. vii. 49, ὁ ὄχλος οὗτος, ὁ μὴ γινώσκων τὸν νόμον. Here it is denied that the ὄχλος possesses a quality which it might and should have possessed; μὴ γινώσκων expresses blame, οὐ γινώσκων would be the simple predicate *unacquainted with the law.* See further L. xiii. 11, Mk. v. 26, A. ix. 7 (compare verse 3).

However true Schæfer's remark[1] may be—" In scriptis cadentis Græcitatis vix credas, quoties participialis constructio (the genitive absolute, in particular) non οὐ cet., ut oportebat, sed μή cet. adsciscat"—yet every passage, even in the writers of the κοινή, must be very carefully examined, before we assert that μή is used in it instead of οὐ (Fritz. *Rom.* II. 295). In particular, as has been already said, must we never overlook the fact that the choice of the negative, especially in combination with the participle, not unfrequently depends on the mode in which the writer prefers to view the subject before him (Herm. *Vig.* p. 804, 806, Matth. 608 *init.,* 608 c). On the general question compare further Jacobs, *Anthol. Pal.* III. 244, Bähr in Creuzer, *Melet.* III. 20, Schæf. Eurip. *Med.* 811 (ed. Porson).[2]

6. A continued negation is, as is well known, expressed by the compound negatives οὐδέ (μηδέ), οὔτε (μήτε).[3] The difference between these two words has been frequently discussed by modern philologers, but has not yet been decided with complete unanimity, or developed in all its relations. See especially Herm. Eurip. *Med.* 330 sqq. (also in his *Opusc.* III. 143 sqq.), and *ad Philoct.* p. 140; also Franke, *Comm.* II. 5 sqq., Wex, *Antig.* II. 156 sqq., Klotz, *Dev.* II. 706 sqq.[4] (Jelf 775 sq.)

---

[1] *Demosth.* III. 495. Compare also Schæfer, *Plutarch* V. 6; Thilo, *Acta Thom.* p. 28; and above, p. 594, note [1]. [Shilleto, Dem. *F. L.* p. 4.]

[2] On Ælian 3. 2, ὁ δὲ μηδὲν διαπαραχθεὶς εἶπεν· 14. 33, ὅς οὐδὲν διαταραχθεὶς εἶπεν, see Fritz. *Rom.* II. 295.—Οὐ has moreover been considered to stand for μή with a participle; sometimes in Plutarch, see Held on Plut. *Tim.* p. 457 sq.; also in Ælian, see Jacobs, *Æl. Anim.* II. 187. In *Basilic.* I. 150, παίδων οὐχ ὑπόντων, *si filii non exstant,* it appears to me that οὐ takes the place of μή: these words would properly mean, *since there are no children.* (Gayler, p. 591, quotes Polyb. 7. 9. 12, τῶν θεῶν οὐ δόντων ὑμῖν καὶ ἡμῖν; but this reading is merely a conjecture of Casaubon's.) In Lucian, *Saltat.* 75, however, the transition from μήτε to οὔτε is the result of anacoluthon. We have a different combination of οὐ and μή with participles in Ælian, *Anim.* 5. 28: see Jacobs *in loc.*

[3] Where οὐδέ does not point to a negation contained in the preceding words, it signifies *also not,* or *not even* (Klotz, *Devar.* p. 707). On the latter meaning see Franke II. 11. [On the former see Riddell, Plat. *Apol.* p. 172: οὐδέ is sometimes *but not* (Soph. *El.* 132, 1034).]

[4] Compare Hand, *De Partic.* τὶ *Dissert.* 2, p. 9 sqq.; Engelhardt, Plat. *Lach.*

That οὐδέ and οὔτε run parallel with the conjunctions δέ and τε, and must in the first instance be explained from the meaning of these particles, admits of no doubt. Accordingly, we may say with Hermann that οὔτε and μήτε are " adjunctivæ," οὐδέ and μηδέ " disjunctivæ " (as δέ is properly *but*, and denotes a contrast, Franke II. 5): that is, οὐδέ and μηδέ add negation to negation, whilst οὔτε and μήτε divide a single negation into parts (which, naturally, are mutually exclusive).[1] Thus: Mt. vii. 6, μὴ δῶτε τὸ ἅγιον τοῖς κυσί, μηδὲ βάλητε τοὺς μαργαρίτας κ.τ.λ., is, *give not* .... *and moreover cast not* (two different actions being equally negatived, i. e., forbidden); Mt. vi. 26, οὐ σπείρουσιν οὐδὲ θερίζουσιν οὐδὲ συνάγουσιν κ.τ.λ., *they sow not and they reap not and they gather not in*. With these contrast Mt. xii. 32, οὐκ ἀφεθήσεται αὐτῷ οὔτε ἐν τούτῳ τῷ αἰῶνι οὔτε ἐν τῷ μέλλοντι,—forgiveness will not be granted *either* in this world *or* in the world to come (the single negation οὐκ ἀφεθήσεται is divided into two parts, in regard to time); L. ix. 3, μηδὲν αἴρετε εἰς τὴν ὁδὸν μήτε ῥάβδον μήτε πήραν μήτε ἄρτον μήτε ἀργύριον.

When the particles are thus used, we commonly find in correspondence—

(*a*) Οὐ ... οὐδέ, Mt. vi. 28, vii. 18, L. vi. 44, Jo. xiii. 16, xiv. 17, A. ix. 9, Rom. ii. 28; μή ... μηδέ, Mt. vi. 25, x. 14, xxiii. 9 sq., Mk. xiii. 15, L. xvii. 23, Jo. iv. 15, A. iv. 18, Rom. vi. 12 sq., 2 C. iv. 2, 1 Tim. i. 3 sq.; οὐ ... οὐδέ ... οὐδέ, Mt. xii. 19, Jo. i. 13, 25;[2] μή ... μηδέ ... μηδέ, Rom. xiv. 21, Col. ii. 21, L. xiv. 12 (*not ... and not ... and not*).

(*b*) οὐ ... οὔτε ... οὔτε, Mt. xii. 32; μή ... μήτε ... μήτε, 1 Tim. i. 7; μή ... μήτε ... μήτε ... μήτε, Ja. v. 12 (μήτε three times), Mt. v. 34 sq. (μήτε four times), *not ... neither ... nor*, etc. Still more frequently, however, we meet with οὔτε (μήτε) not preceded by any simple negative: Jo. v. 37, ο ὔ τ ε

---

p. 69 sq.; Stallb. Plat. *Lach.* p. 65; also *Jen. Lit.-Zeit.* 1812, No. 194. p. 516, and Hartung, *Partik.* I. 191 sqq.

[1] Benfey in the *Neu. Jahrb. f. Philol.* XII. 155: "As τε ... τε can only connect notions or propositions which, being mutually supplementary, constitute a unity, so it is only in such cases that οὔτε ... οὔτε can be used. This higher unity is subdivided by the negatived parts which supplement each other; in these, neither the negation of one part nor that of the other is a whole, but each must first be supplemented."

[2] In Jud. i. 27 οὐ is followed by οὐδέ repeated fourteen times.

SECT. LV.] THE NEGATIVE PARTICLES. 613

φωνὴν αὐτοῦ ἀκηκόατε πώποτε οὔτε εἶδος αὐτοῦ ἑωράκατε· Mt. vi. 20, xxii. 30, L. xiv. 35, Jo. viii. 19, ix. 3, A. xv. 10, 1 Th. ii. 5 sq., Rom. viii. 38 (ten times); Mt. xi. 18, ἦλθε γὰρ Ἰωάννης μήτε ἐσθίων μήτε πίνων· A. xxvii. 20, H. vii. 3 [1] (*neither . . . nor*).

Accordingly, οὔτε and μήτε regularly [2] point to another οὔτε or μήτε (or to τε or καί), just as τε . . . τε (τε . . . καί) correspond to each other ; whereas οὐδέ and μηδέ attach themselves to a preceding οὐ or μή,—as indeed δέ always looks to something which has gone before. It may therefore be truly said,— it follows indeed from the meaning of τε and δέ,—that a closer connexion is expressed by the sequence οὔτε . . . οὔτε than by οὐ . . . οὐδέ (Klotz, *Devar.* p. 707 sq.[3]). In this correlation it is a matter of indifference whether the things denied are single words (conceptions) only or whole sentences, and whole sentences may as correctly be negatived by οὔτε . . . οὔτε (A. xxviii. 21, Plat. *Rep.* 10. 597 c, *Phædr.* 260 c), as single words by οὐ . . . οὐδέ ;[4] in the latter case the verb belongs to all the members negatived. See Mt. x. 9, μὴ κτήσησθε χρυσὸν μηδὲ ἄργυρον μηδὲ χαλκόν· 2 P. i. 8, οὐκ ἀργοὺς οὐδὲ ἀκάρπους καθίστησιν· Mt. xxii. 29, xxiv. 20, xxv. 13, 1 Jo. iii. 18. In Mt. x. 9 we might have had the other form of negation, had Matthew written μηδὲν κτήσησθε μήτε χρυσὸν μήτε ἄργυρον κ.τ.λ.: compare Franke II. 8. Mt. vi. 20, and Mt. x. 9 as compared with L. ix. 3, are peculiarly instructive for the perception of the distinction between οὐδέ and οὔτε.

The sequence οὔτε . . . . οὔτε . . . . καὶ οὐ, Jo. v. 37 sq. (as the clauses are combined in that explanation of the passage which has

---

[1] 1 C. vi. 9 sq., οὔτε . . . οὔτε . . . οὔτε . . . οὔτε . . . οὔτε . . . οὔτε . . . οὔτε . . . οὔτε [or more probably οὐ] . . . οὐ . . . οὐ, is remarkable only for the accumulation of negatives. There is nothing singular in the use of οὐ after οὔτε, though it cannot be supported by the passage which Gayler (p. 386) quotes, Soph. *Antig.* 4 sq.: compare (Dio C. 205. 6, 412. 59) Klotz, *Devar.* p. 711. See further below, no. 9.

[2] As to a single μήτε, the other being suppressed, see Herm. Soph. *Philoct.* p. 139 sq., and in general Franke II. 13 sq.

[3] "Cum οὔτε et ad priora respicere possit et ad sequentia, aptior connexio est singulorum membrorum per eas particulas, multo autem dissolutior et fortuita magis conjunctio membrorum per οὐδέ . . . οὐδέ particulas, quia prius οὐδέ nunquam respicit ad ea quæ sequuntur sed ad priora . . . alterum autem οὐδέ per aliquam oppositionis rationem, quam habet δέ particula, sequentia adjungit prioribus, non apte connexa, sed potius fortuito concursu accedentia." On this account, however, δέ is stronger than τε. Franke II. 6, 15.

[4] Hence Matthiæ (609. 1. a) does not express himself accurately.

recently been most commonly adopted), is as admissible grammatically as οὔτε . . . τε οὐ (Herm. Soph. *Antig.* 759, Poppo, *Thuc.* III. i. p. 68). As however the clause with καί . . . οὐ does not stand in precisely the same relation as would have been indicated by οὔτε, I consider it preferable not to include this clause (καί . . . οὐ) in the partition: see Meyer *in loc.*[1]

From this it further follows that

a. Οὐδέ . . . οὐδέ (μηδέ . . . μηδέ), in the sense of *neither . . . nor* (no simple negative having preceded), cannot be correlative;[2] but when to one negation another is annexed, and negation strung on negation, the first is expressed by οὐ or μή: it is this which gives the antithetical and disjunctive δέ the basis it requires.[3] Mk. viii. 26, λέγων, μηδὲ εἰς τὴν κώμην εἰσέλθῃς μηδὲ εἴπῃς τινί κ.τ.λ., cannot be rendered *neque . . . neque;* the first μηδέ is *ne . . . quidem,* the second *also . . . not:* see Meyer *in loc.*[4] Compare Eurip. *Hippol.* 1052 and Klotz, *Devar.* p. 708. The case is somewhat different when the first οὐδέ connects the sentence with what precedes, as for instance (with οὐδὲ γάρ) in G. i. 12, οὐδὲ γὰρ ἐγὼ παρὰ ἀνθρώπου παρέλαβον αὐτὸ οὐδὲ ἐδιδάχθην. On this passage, however, see below.

b. Since οὔτε and μήτε always co-ordinate one member of a partition with another, μήτε cannot be tolerated in Mk. iii. 20, ὥστε μὴ δύνασθαι μήτε ἄρτον φαγεῖν;[5] for here μὴ φαγεῖν is dependent on δύνασθαι. As the words now stand, they can only mean, *that they neither were able nor ate* (the first μή standing for μήτε). The meaning however obviously is, *that*

---

[1] [Meyer has changed his view, and now connects together οὔτε . . . οὔτε . . . καὶ οὐ (compare Jo. iv. 11, quoted below), observing that the change of expression gives more independence to the new moment of thought.]

[2] On Thuc. 1. 142 see Poppo *in loc.*; on Xen. *An.* 3. 1. 27, Poppo's index to the *Anab.* p. 535.

[3] On οὐδέ and μηδέ after an affirmative sentence, see Engelhardt, Plat. *Lach.* p. 64 sq., Franke p. 6, 8 sq.

[4] [The second clause is probably not genuine.]

[5] That μήτε should have remained unaltered even in the latest edition of Griesbach's N. T., may justly excite surprise. What is still more remarkable is, that neither Griesbach nor Schulz has even noticed the variant μηδέ, found in *approved* MSS. See on the other hand Scholz *in loc.* [Tisch. has now returned to μήτε in this passage (with ℵCD etc.), and in L. xx. 36 to οὔτε (with ℵQR etc.). In his note on L. xii. 26 (in ed. 7) he says, "Mihi non dubium videtur quin fatiscente Græcitate etiam οὔτε pro οὐδέ sit dictum; hinc videndum est ne emendationem paucorum testium sequamur:" compare also A. Buttmann p. 369. See also Rev. ix. 20 (Tisch.). In modern Greek—at all events in the language of common life (Lüdemann, *Lehrb.* p. 112)—μήτε is used in the sense *not even;* see Mullach, *Vulg.* p. 391.]

SECT. LV.] THE NEGATIVE PARTICLES. 615

they were not able even to eat; and hence we must read μηδέ, which is found in the better MSS. (see Fritzsche *in loc.*), and is received by Lachmann and Tischendorf, but not by Scholz. For the same reason it is necessary to read οὐδέ in Mk. v. 3, οὐδὲ ἁλύσει· L. xii. 26, οὐδὲ ἐλάχιστον δύνασθε· vii. 9, οὐδὲ ἐν τῷ Ἰσραήλ:[1] also in L. xx. 36, where οὐδὲ γὰρ ἀποθανεῖν ἔτι δύνανται (as good MSS. read) does not run parallel with the previous sentence οὔτε . . . οὔτε, but contains the proof of it, *neque enim*.[2] Compare further Mt. v. 36. In these passages also Scholz reproduced the old mistakes.

c. Since by οὔτε . . . οὔτε members of a partition are negatived, and these members rigorously exclude each other (Herm. *Med.* p. 332), the reading of some MSS. in Mk. xiv. 68, οὔτε οἶδα οὔτε ἐπίσταμαι (received by Lachmann and Tischendorf into the text), cannot stand: *neque novi neque scio* cannot well be said, since the two verbs are almost identical in meaning. Compare Franke II. 13, Schæf. *Demosth.* III. 449, Fritz. *in loc.* Griesbach received into the text οὐκ οἶδα οὐδὲ ἐπίσταμαι (compare Cicero, *Rosc. Am.* 43, *non*—not *neque*—*novi neque scio*), which, from the meaning of the two verbs, is very suitable.[3]

d. Οὐ may be followed by οὔτε, the former negative being taken (in regard to sense) as standing for οὔτε:[4] hence in Rev.

---

[1] Accordingly, we should read οὐδέ in *Act. Apocr.* p. 168. Döderlein, however (*Progr. de Brachylogia sermonis Græci*, p. 17), holds that οὔτε is correct in such cases; maintaining that, as τε (like καί) has the meaning *etiam*, οὔτε can also be used for *ne . . . quidem*. Against this see Franke II. 11. [Jelf (775. *Obs.* 6) asserts that in some passages οὔτε and μήτε are thus used, and quotes Xen. *Rep. Lac.* 10. 7 (al. μηδέ), Xen. *Memor.* I. 2. 47. The latter passage, however, is a clear example of οὔτε . . . τε : see Kühner's note.]

[2] Bornemann connects οὔτε with the following καί (see below, p. 619); but the sentence καὶ υἱοί κ.τ.λ. must be joined with ἰσάγγελοι γάρ.

[3] There is no doubt that with the reading οὔτε . . . οὔτε "the two notions are present to the mind under one common principal notion" (Meyer); but this takes for granted that there really are *two* notions, which in an affirmative sentence might be connected by *both . . . and.* [In this passage οὔτε . . . οὔτε is strongly supported, and now stands in the best texts.]

[4] See Hermann, *Med.* p. 333 sqq., 401, and Soph. *Antig.* p. 110; in opposition to Elmsley, Eurip. *Med.* 4, 5, and Soph. *Œd. T.* 817. Compare Franke II. 27 sq.; Mätzner, *Antiphon* p. 195 sq.; Ellendt, *Lex. Soph.* II. 444; Klotz, *Dev.* p. 709 sq. "In rare cases, and in virtue of a rhetorical figure, it is allowable to drop the supplemental particle of one *οὐ*, by which means the member in which it stands, being thus deprived of its supplemental symbol, apparently obtains greater independence, and consequently greater rhetorical force; just as, in the place of 'neither father nor mother,' we may more poetically say 'not

ix. 21 οὔτε¹ must not be altered (Matth. 609. 1. ζ, Jelf 775. 2), —though such a sequence is said to be confined to poetry (Franke II. 28). The same correlation is to be recognised in Rev. v. 4, οὐδεὶς ἄξιος εὑρέθη ἀνοῖξαι τὸ βιβλίον οὔτε βλέπειν αὐτό (the reading retained by Tischendorf),—compare Klotz, *Dev.* II. 709 sq., and the passage there quoted from Aristot. *Polit.* 1. 3: the author might indeed have written οὐδεὶς ἄξιος εὑρέθη οὔτε ἀνοῖξαι τὸ βιβλίον οὔτε βλέπειν. In E. iv. 27, however, μή ... μήτε cannot be tolerated; the best MSS. unanimously give μηδέ, which has already been received into the text by Lachmann. This construction² is a species of anacoluthon: when the writer begins with οὐ, he has not as yet the following parallel member in his thoughts. In some cases this arrangement may be adopted designedly, for the purpose of giving prominence to the first word. In Rev. xii. 8 also οὐδέ appears to me more correct, and it has been received by Knapp. On the other hand, in Jo. i. 25, εἰ σὺ οὐκ εἶ ὁ Χριστὸς οὔτε Ἠλίας οὔτε ὁ προφήτης, an alteration of the conjunctions into οὐδέ would grammatically be unnecessary (compare Herm. Soph. *Philoct.* p. 140); the better MSS. however have οὐδέ. In Rev. v. 3 also, οὐδεὶς ἠδύνατο ἐν τῷ οὐρανῷ οὐδὲ ἐπὶ τῆς γῆς, οὐδὲ ὑποκάτω τῆς γῆς ἀνοῖξαι τὸ βιβλίον οὐδὲ βλέπειν αὐτό, the relation of the negatives is correct: *no one ... also not on earth, also not ... to open, also not* (not even) *to look*.³

e. As to οὔτε (repeated) .... οὐδέ, A. xxiv. 12 sq., according to the reading adopted by Lachmann⁴ and Bornemann from B, see Herm. Soph. *Œd. Col.* 229, Franke II. 14 sqq., Klotz, *Devar.* II. 714. Here οὐδέ is not parallel with οὔτε, but begins a new sentence: "They *neither* found me in the temple .... *nor* in the synagogues .... *moreover* they *cannot* etc." Most MSS.,

---

father nor mother.'" Benfey *l.c.* p. 155. Compare Herm. *l.c.* p. 331, 401, and Franke II. 27 (who takes a different view); also Döderlein, *Progr. de Brachylogia*, p. 6. [Franke holds that there is an ellipsis of the first οὔτε.]
¹ Οὐ μετενόησαν ἐκ τῶν φόνων αὐτῶν, οὔτε ἐκ τῶν ... οὔτε ἐκ τῆς ... οὔτε ἐκ τῶν κ.τ.λ. (instead of the perfectly regular οὐ μετενόησαν οὔτε ἐκ τῶν φόνων οὔτε κ.τ.λ.) is just as allowable as *Odyss.* 9. 136 sqq., ἵν' οὐ χρεὼ πείσματός ἐστιν, οὔτ' εὐνὰς βαλέειν, οὔτε πρυμνήσι' ἀνάψαι· or *Odyss.* 4. 566: see Klotz, *Devar.* p. 710. In Rev. *l. c.* no variant is noted.
² [Viz., οὐ (μή) ... οὔτε (μήτε): the reference is not to Eph. iv. 27.]
³ [We must probably read οὔτε βλέπειν. Tisch. (ed. 8) reads οὔτε three times in the verse: this reading presents a double illustration of the text, οὐδείς ... οὔτε ... οὔτε ... γῆς, and (οὐδείς ...) ἀνοῖξαι ... οὔτε βλέπειν αὐτό.]
⁴ [Tischendorf and Westcott and Hort read οὐδέ; Tregelles, Alford, οὔτε.]

however, have οὔτε in ver. 13: with this reading, οὔτε .... εὗρόν με and οὔτε παραστῆσαι δύνανται are regular correlative sentences, and οὔτε ἐν ταῖς συναγωγαῖς and οὔτε κατὰ πόλιν belong to the first sentence as subordinate members. On L. xx. 36 see p. 615.

That in negative sentences the subordinate members are introduced by ἤ, has been already remarked (§ 53. 6). In A. xvii. 29, however, with the reading found in D (and received by Bornemann), οὐκ ὀφείλομεν νομίζειν οὔτε χρυσῷ ἢ ἀργύρῳ κ.τ.λ., ἤ would be coordinate with οὔτε,—a construction of which another example is hardly to be found (Matth. *Eurip.* VII. 178). Still, as we meet with the sequence τε . . . ἤ (Klotz, *Devar.* II. 742 sq.), οὔτε . . . ἤ may be admissible. But the other authorities omit οὔτε here.

It is more difficult to say whether μηδέ, οὐδέ, can be followed by μήτε, οὔτε. Almost all the more recent philologers decide in the negative (see Matth. 609. 1. β),[1] on the ground that, as the stronger οὐδέ (Matth. 609. 1. a, β) precedes, the weaker οὔτε cannot follow. Compare also Fritz. *Mark*, p. 158.[2] Yet in the editions of Greek authors we find not a few passages in which οὐδέ is followed by οὔτε,—e. g., Thuc. 3. 48 (see Poppo *in loc.*), Lucian, *Dial. Mort.* 26. 2, *Catapl.* 15, Plat. *Charm.* 171 b, Aristot. *Physiogn.* 6. p. 148 (Franz): it is usual however to correct such readings, commonly with more or less support from the MSS. That οὔτε and μήτε cannot be *parallel* to an οὐδέ or μηδέ may be taken as a rule (though the reason alleged for it does not appear to me decisive); but where these particles have nothing to do with οὐδέ or μηδέ as a *conjunction*, I consider the sequence correct. This condition is satisfied in the two following cases:[3]—

a. When οὐδέ signifies *ne . . . quidem* (Klotz, *Devar.* II. 711,—compare 2 Macc. v. 10), or *also not*, or connects the negative sentence[4] with a preceding sentence to which the δέ

---

[1] Engelhardt *l. c.* p. 70; Lehmann, *Lucian*, III. 615 sq.; Franke II. 18, al. [Liddell and Scott s. vv.: compare Jelf 776. *Obs.* 5.]
[2] Bornemann (Xen. *Anab.* p. 26) and Hand (*l. c.* p. 13) consider οὐδέ . . . οὔτε admissible.
[3] Compare also Döderlein in Passow's *WB.*, s. v. οὐδέ.
[4] [Winer's words are: "or connects with a preceding sentence the negative sentence to which the δέ points back." As this yields no sense, we must either make the correction which I have adopted in the text, or write τε for δέ in Winer's sentence. A comparison of earlier editions of the original work seems to show that the former correction of the misprint is the more probable.]

points.¹ In G. i. 12, οὐδὲ γὰρ ἐγώ . . . παρέλαβον αὐτὸ οὔτε ἐδιδάχθην, the common reading is to be retained, if the words are rendered, *for also I have not received it, nor have I learnt it*,—or *neque enim ego* (instead of οὐ γάρ) *accepi didicique* (*-ve*): compare Hoogeveen, *Doctr. Particul.* II. 980 sq. See Plat. *Charm.* 171 b, Hom. *in Cerer.* 22 (Herm. *Emend.* p. 39), Lysias, *Orat.* 19. p. 157 (Steph.). The οὐδέ which is found in some good MSS. in the place of οὔτε is probably a correction.

b. When οὔτε (μήτε) is not co-ordinate with, but subordinate to, the οὐδέ (μηδέ) which precedes: e. g., "I harbour no enmity, and I work not against the schemes of others, and not against their attempts." Xen. *Mem.* 2. 2. 11, μηδ᾽ ἕπεσθαι μηδὲ πείθεσθαι μήτε στρατηγῷ μήτε ἄλλῳ ἄρχοντι (the first two words, however, are of doubtful authority); *Cyr.* 8. 7. 22, μήποτ᾽ ἀσεβὲς μηδὲν μηδὲ ἀνόσιον μήτε ποιήσητε μήτε βουλεύσητε; Plat. *Legg.* 11. 916 e. Here the negation μηδέ is divided into two parts (μήτε . . . . μήτε): Dem. *Callipp.* 718 c, Judith viii. 18. Compare Held, Plut. *Timol.* p. 433 sq., Matth. 609. 1. b, Kühner II. 440 (Jelf 776. 3, 5). Accordingly, in A. xxiii. 8 the reading μὴ εἶναι ἀνάστασιν, μηδὲ ἄγγελον (μηδὲ εἶναι μήτε ἄγγελον) μήτε πνεῦμα would be admissible; and τὰ ἀμφότερα which immediately follows would give some support to it.² This reading is received by Tischendorf in his 2nd Leipsic edition. The sentence, it is true, would be simpler if we were to read μηδὲ πνεῦμα, or (with the better MSS., and with Lachmann and Bornemann) μήτε ἄγγελον μήτε πνεῦμα;—though indeed an unusual turn of expression might easily be changed by transcribers into one that was familiar.—In 1 Th. ii. 3, the nature of the notions combined leads me to consider οὐκ ἐκ πλάνης οὐδὲ ἐξ

---

¹ Hand *l.c.*: "intelligitur, nexum, quem nonnulli grammatici inter οὐδί et οὔτι intercedere dixerunt, nullum esse, nisi quod οὐ in voc. οὐδί cum οὔτι cohæreat. Nam si in aliquibus Hom. locis ista vocc. hoc quidem ordine nexa videntur exhiberi, in iis δί pertinet ad superiora conjungenda." Compare Hartung I. 201, Klotz p. 711.

² See Hoogeveen, *Doctr. Partic.* I. 751. Kühnöl would translate τὰ ἀμφότερα *tria ista*; but very unsuccessfully defends this rendering by *Odyss.* 15. 78, ἀμφότερον, κῦδός τε καὶ ἀγλαΐην καὶ ὄνειαρ, for here the first two words, connected by τε καί, are regarded as expressing one main idea. If in A. xxiii. 8 we read μηδί, still ἀμφότερα does not signify *tria*; but the writer combines together ἄγγελον and πνεῦμα, according to their logical import, as one principal conception. [א is now added to the authorities for μήτε, which now stands in the best texts. See A. Buttm. p. 367 sq., Fritz. *Mark*, p. 158.]

SECT. LV.] THE NEGATIVE PARTICLES. 619

ἀκαθαρσίας οὐδὲ ἐν δόλῳ the more appropriate reading: so the passage stands in the better MSS. and in Lachmann's text. In any such case as this I think accurate writers would, for the sake of clearness, use ἤ in preference to οὔτε: see § 53. 6.

In 1 C. iii. 2 οὔτε of the received text is a mere error of transcription; the best MSS. have ἀλλ' οὐδὲ ἔτι νῦν δύνασθε, *ne nunc quidem:* compare A. xix. 2, Lucian, *Hermot.* 7, *Conscr. Hist.* 33, and Fritz. *Mark,* p. 157. In 2 Th. ii. 2 also the best MSS. have εἰς τὸ μὴ ταχέως σαλευθῆναι . . . μηδὲ θροεῖσθαι μήτε διὰ πνεύματος κ.τ.λ. (Lachmann, Tischendorf). In 2 Th. iii. 8 οὐδέ is the only correct reading. In L. vii. 9, xii. 27, A. xvi. 21, οὐδέ was received by Griesbach, and rightly: in A. iv. 12 also οὐδέ is the true reading. In Ja. iii. 12, recent editions (including those of Lachmann and Tischendorf) have οὔτε ἁλυκὸν γλυκὺ ποιῆσαι ὕδωρ. This reading is only tenable on the assumption (a harsh assumption certainly) that James had in his mind as the antecedent clause οὔτε δύναται συκῆ ἐλαίας ποιῆσαι κ.τ.λ.: otherwise we must read οὐδέ, which is found in some MSS.[1]

In such passages as the following there is nothing strange: L. x. 4 [*Rec.*], μὴ βαστάζετε βαλλάντιον, μὴ πήραν μηδὲ ὑποδήματα (*not . . . not . . . also not*); Mt. x. 9, μὴ κτήσησθε χρυσὸν μηδὲ ἄργυρον μηδὲ χαλκὸν εἰς τὰς ζώνας ὑμῶν, μὴ πήραν εἰς ὁδόν, μηδὲ δύο χιτῶνας, μηδὲ ὑποδήματα κ.τ.λ.

We remark in passing that the distinction between οὐδέ (μηδέ) and καὶ οὐ (καὶ μή) which is brought out by Engelhardt, and still more strikingly by Franke[2] (καὶ οὐ, καὶ μή), after affirmative sentences,—*and not, yet not, et non, ac non*), appears to be founded in the nature of the case, and may also be recognised in the N. T. Compare καὶ οὐ, Jo. v. 43, vi. 17, vii. 36, A. xvi. 7, 2 C. xiii. 10; καὶ μή, Ja. i. 5, iv. 17, 1 P. ii. 16, iii. 6, H. xiii. 17.

For particularly instructive passages of Greek authors illustrating the distinction between οὐδέ and οὔτε, see Isocr. *Areop.* p. 345, οὐκ ἀνωμάλως οὐδὲ ἀτάκτως οὔτε ἐθεράπευον οὔτε ὠργίαζον κ.τ.λ.; *Permut.* p. 750, ὥστε μηδένα μοι πώποτε μηδ' ἐν ὀλιγαρχίᾳ μηδ' ἐν δημοκρατίᾳ μήτε ὕβριν μήτε ἀδικίαν ἐγκαλέσαι· Her. 6. 9, Isocr. *Ep.* 8. p. 1016, Xenoph. *Ages.* 1. 4, Demosth. *Timocr.* 481 b. Compare Matth. 609. 1. b.

7. In two parallel sentences we sometimes find οὔτε or μήτε followed, not by a second negative, but by a simple copulative (καί or τε): Jo. iv. 11, οὔτε ἄντλημα ἔχεις, κ α ὶ τὸ φρέαρ ἐστὶ βαθύ,—as in Latin *nec haustrum habes et puteus* etc. (Hand, *Tursell.* IV. 133 sqq.); 3 Jo. 10. Compare Arrian, *Al.* 4. 7. 6, ἐγὼ οὔτε τὴν ἄγαν ταύτην τιμωρίαν Βήσσου ἐπαινῶ.

---

[1] [א reads (οὔτως) οὐδὶ, but the best critical texts have οὔτι.]
[2] Engelhardt, Plat. *Lach.* p. 65, Franke II. 8 sq.

... καὶ ὑπαχθῆναι 'Αλέξανδρον ξύμφημι κ.τ.λ.; Paus. 1. 6. 5, Δημήτριος οὔτε παντάπασιν ἐξειστήκει Πτολεμαίῳ τῆς χώρας, καί τινας τῶν Αἰγυπτίων λοχήσας διέφθειρεν· Lucian, Dial. Mar. 14. 1, Stallb. Plat. Protag. p. 20. Here τε is more common.[1] See Hartung, Partik. I. 193, Klotz, Devar. p. 713, 740, Götting. Anzeig. 1831, p. 1188 (Jelf 775. 3).

On the other hand, in Ja. iii. 14 the second negation is omitted, or rather the effect of the negative is continued to the annexed sentence: μὴ κατακαυχᾶσθε καὶ ψεύδεσθε κατὰ τῆς ἀληθείας. So also in 2 C. xii. 21, Mt. xiii. 15, Mk. iv. 12, Jo. xii. 40, A. xxviii. 27: compare Sext. Emp. adv. Math. 2. 20, Diod. S. 2. 48, Æl. Anim. 5. 21.[2] Several commentators have found the converse of this in E. iv. 26, ὀργίζεσθε καὶ μὴ ἁμαρτάνετε, considering the words to stand for μὴ ὀργίζεσθε καὶ (μὴ) ἁμαρτάνετε. In Greek writers (even in prose) we do find many instances in which οὐδέ or οὔτε is expressed in the second member of a sentence only, and must be supplied in the first.[3] For the prose of the N. T., however, such a construction would be exceedingly harsh, and there is no need for introducing it in this passage (especially as we have not μήτε ἁμαρτάνετε): see § 43. 2.

In L. xviii. 7, according to the best attested reading, ὁ θεὸς οὐ μὴ ποιήσῃ τὴν ἐκδίκησιν τῶν ἐκλεκτῶν αὐτοῦ .... καὶ μακροθυμεῖ ἐπ' αὐτοῖς,—especially if μακροθυμεῖ means *delay* —the negative is dropped in the second clause, and the interrogative μή (*num*) is alone repeated.[4]

It is hardly necessary to mention οὐδέ .... δέ, H. ix. 12, as οὐ .... δέ is of so very frequent occurrence.

8. It has frequently been laid down as a rule, that sentences containing a simple negation which are followed by ἀλλά (δέ), or in which οὐ (μή) forms an antithesis to a preceding affirmative sentence (Mt. ix. 13, from the LXX, H. xiii. 9, L. x. 20), are not always [5] to be taken as simply and absolutely ne-

---

[1] Jacobitz, Luc. *Tox.* c. 25; Weber, *Demosth.* p. 402 sq. [Comp. A. xxvii. 20.]
[2] Gataker, *Advers. Miscell.* 2. 2, p. 268; Jacobs, *Æl. Anim.* II. 182; Boissonade, *Nicet.* p. 390.
[3] See Schæf. on Bos, *Ellips.* p. 777; Herm. Soph. *Aj.* 239, 616: Döderlein, *Brachylog.* p. 5 sq.; Poppo, *Thuc.* III. iv. 841 (Jelf 775. *Obs.* 3, 776. *Obs.* 4, Don. p. 610).
[4] Bornemann in the *Sächs. Bibl. Studien,* I. 69.
[5] As for instance in Mk. v. 39, τὸ παιδίον οὐκ ἀπέθανεν ἀλλὰ καθεύδει,—where

gative, but, "by a Hebraism, found also in Greek prose writers," must be rendered *not so much . . . as*,[1] or else, *not only . . . but also*[2] (non solum . . . sed etiam[3]). For example: A. v. 4, οὐκ ἐψεύσω ἀνθρώποις, ἀλλὰ τῷ θεῷ, *not so much to men* (the apostle Peter), *as rather to God*; 1 C. xv. 10 [*Rec.*], οὐκ ἐγὼ δὲ (ἐκοπίασα), ἀλλ' ἡ χάρις τοῦ θεοῦ ἡ σὺν ἐμοί,—rendered by Augustine, *non ego solus, sed gratia Dei mecum* (Jo. v. 30);[4] L. x. 20, μὴ χαίρετε ὅτι . . . χαίρετε δὲ ὅτι κ.τ.λ., nolite *tam* propterea lætari . . . *quam potius* etc.

On more accurate examination, however, all the N. T. passages to which this canon is applied are found to belong to one of the two following classes:—

(*a*) In some the *unconditional* negation is actually intended, as a careful consideration of the context proves. Mt. ix. 13, ἔλεον θέλω καὶ οὐ θυσίαν,—where *Christ*, using the words of the prophet (Hos. vi. 6), requires that mercy (the feeling) should *really* be put in the place of sacrifices (mere symbols); compare the words which follow, οὐ γὰρ ἦλθον καλέσαι δικαίους, ἀλλ' ἁμαρτωλούς. Jo. vii. 16, ἡ ἐμὴ διδαχὴ οὐκ ἔστιν ἐμή, ἀλλὰ τοῦ

---

certainly the latter idea does annul the former; Mt. ix. 12, x. 34, xv. 11, 2 C. xiii. 7.

[1] Non tam . . . quam, οὐ τοσοῦτον . . . ὅσον, Heliod. 10. 3, Xen. Eph. 5. 11; οὐχ οὕτως . . . ὡς, Dio Chr. 8. 130; οὐ μᾶλλον ἤ, Xen. *Hell*. 7. 1. 2.

[2] The former rendering (*non tam . . . quam*), as the following examples will show, has been by far the most common in the N. T. The fact that in N. T. Greek the relative negation *non solum . . . sed* is frequently, but *non tam . . . quam* never, actually expressed, might appear to justify this.

[3] Compare Blackwall, *Auct. Cl. Sacr.* p. 62, Glass I. 418 sqq., Wetstein and Kypke on Mt. ix. 13, Heumann on 1 C. x. 23 sq., Kuinoel, *Acta* p. 177, Haab, *Gr.* p. 145 sqq., Bos, *Ellips.* p. 772 sq., al.: Valcken. *Opusc.* II. 190, *Dion. H.* IV. 2121. 10, Jacobs, *Anth. Pal.* III. p. lxix.

[4] It is no wonder that exegetes should have been partial to such a weakening of these formulas, since even classical philologers have thought themselves obliged to soften a strong expression in passages of ancient writers, where there was not the slightest occasion for doing so. Thus Dion. H. IV. 2111, δόξῃ τὸ ἀνδρεῖον ἐπιτηδεύων οὐκ ἀληθείᾳ, is still rendered by Reiske, *te fortitudinis studiosum esse opinione magis quam re ipsa.* A similar inpropriety may be seen in Alberti, *Observ.* p. 71. On the error introduced by Palairet (*Obs.* p. 236) into Macrob. *Saturn.* 1. 22, see my *Grammat. Excurse* p. 155. The above observations will easily clear up Cic. *Off.* 2. 8. 27.—A reference to Glass *l. c.* p. 421 will show any one how the older Biblical interpreters allowed themselves to be influenced even by dogmatic motives in the explanation of this formula.—In 1 P. i. 12, the dilution of οὐ . . . δὲ into *non tam . . . quam* (see Schott, even in the latest edition) was the result of a misunderstanding of διακονεῖν. Even the simple οὐ Flatt would limit by a μόνον in 1 C. vii. 4! On 1 C. ix. 9 the passage cited from Philo by the commentators [see Alford *in loc.*] throws sufficient light.

πέμψαντός με, where Jesus is speaking of the *origin* of his teaching (verses 15, 17, 18); *My teaching* (that which ye regard as mine,—compare ver. 15) *does not appertain to me, but to God*, has not me as its author, but God. In calling it ἡ ἐμὴ διδαχή Jesus quotes the opinion of the Jews, who in the words πῶς οὗτος γράμματα οἶδε, μὴ μεμαθηκώς, regarded this teaching as a possession acquired by means of study.[1] Compare Jo. v. 30,[2] xii. 44. Jo. vi. 27, ἐργάζεσθε μὴ τὴν βρῶσιν τὴν ἀπολλυμένην, ἀλλὰ τὴν βρῶσιν τὴν μένουσαν εἰς ζωὴν αἰώνιον, ἣν ὁ υἱὸς τοῦ ἀνθρώπου ὑμῖν δώσει; here Jesus censures the conduct of the multitude who have come to him *as Messiah*, and the thought "*not so much* for ordinary food *as rather* for heavenly" (Kühnöl) would be meaningless. On ver. 26 see Lücke. In 1 C. vii. 10 Paul makes a distinction between *the Lord's* injunctions and *his own*: so *vice versa* in ver. 12, referring there to the words of Christ in Mt. v. 32. The recent commentators take the right view. As to 1 C. xiv. 22 (compare ver. 23) no doubt can exist: compare also 1 C. x. 24 (Schott) and Meyer *in loc.*, E. vi. 12, H. xiii. 9, 1 C. i. 17 and Meyer *in loc.* So also in 2 C. vii. 9, χαίρω οὐχ ὅτι ἐλυπήθητε ἀλλ' ὅτι ἐλυπήθητε εἰς μετάνοιαν; the λυπηθῆναι in itself (the idea so far as it is contained in λυπηθῆναι), taken absolutely, is denied in the first clause, but only that it may be taken up again in the second with the qualification εἰς μετάνοιαν. Similarly in the phrase *non bonus sed optimus* (see the note below), *non* cancels the "good" (in the positive degree)—"*good* he is not," in order that its place may be taken by the only correct word, *optimus*,— in which, to be sure, *bonus* is included.

(*b*) In other passages the writer prefers to use the absolute instead of the conditioned (relative) negation on *rhetorical* grounds,—not for the purpose of really (logically) annulling the

---

[1] Bengel: "*non est mea*, non ullo modo *discendi* labore parta."
[2] It would be a similar case if, for example, some one were to say of a commentator who quotes largely, *Thy learning is not thine but Wetstein's*. "Thy learning" is here set down only problematically: and if we were to infer from this that the speaker intended really to ascribe (that) learning *in some measure, in some respect*, to the person in question, the conclusion would not be logical but merely *grammatical*. On the phrase *non bonus sed optimus* (Fritz. *Diss.* 2. in 2 *Cor.* p. 162) a hint had already been given by Hermann (Eur. *Alcest.* p. 29). Of a similar kind are the passages cited by Heumann *l. c.*: Cic. *Arch.* 4. 8, se non interfuisse sed egisse; Vell. Pat. 2. 13, vir non sæculi sui sed omnis ævi optimus. Compare also 2 C. vii. 9.

first conception, but in order that he may direct undivided attention to the second, the first disappearing from view in the presence of the second (compare Meyer on A. v. 4): 1 Th. iv. 8 (Schott), *rejects not man, but God.*[1] He certainly does also reject the apostle, who declares the truth of God; but Paul here wishes the thought that it is really God, as the true author of this declaration, who is rejected, to come before the mind with all its force. The force of the thought is immediately impaired, if the words are rendered, *he rejects not so much man as God.* Such a translation is no better than, for instance, diluting an asyndeton (which also is rhetorical in its nature) by inserting the copula. I hold therefore that οὐκ ... ἀλλά, when used in cases where the logical meaning requires *non tam ... quam*, always belongs to the rhetorical colouring of the language, and hence must be retained in translation. This is done by all the better translators. The speaker has chosen this mode of negation designedly, and the formula is not to be estimated on the principles of mere grammar. The question whether any particular passage comes under this head, or not, must be decided, not by the feeling of the commentator, but by the context and by the nature of the ideas connected. The following passages must be dealt with on this principle: Mt. x. 20 (Schott), οὐχ ὑμεῖς ἐστὲ οἱ λαλοῦντες, ἀλλὰ τὸ πνεῦμα τοῦ πατρὸς ὑμῶν· Mk. ix. 37 (Schott), ὃς ἐὰν ἐμὲ δέξηται, οὐκ ἐμὲ δέχεται, ἀλλὰ τὸν ἀποστείλαντά με· 1 C. xv. 10 [*Rec.*], περισσότερον αὐτῶν πάντων ἐκοπίασα· οὐκ ἐγὼ δέ, ἀλλ' ἡ χάρις τοῦ θεοῦ ἡ σὺν ἐμοί· Jo. xii. 44, ὁ πιστεύων εἰς ἐμὲ οὐ πιστεύει εἰς ἐμέ, ἀλλ' εἰς τὸν πέμψαντά με· A. v. 4 (compare Plut. *Apophth. Lac.* 41, and see Duker on Thuc. 4. 92), L. x. 20 (where several MSS. insert μᾶλλον after δέ), 2 C. ii. 5 [2] (Schott). On L. xiv. 12 sq. see Bornemann and De Wette *in loc.*[3]

---

[1] Compare Demosth. *Euerg.* 684 b, ἡγησαμένη ὑβρίσθαι οὐκ ἐμέ (in point of fact, however, he had been outraged) ἀλλ' ἑαυτὴν (τὴν βουλὴν) καὶ τὸν δῆμον τὸν ψηφισάμενον κ.τ.λ.; Æsop 148. 2, οὐ σύ με λοιδορεῖς, ἀλλ' ὁ πύργος, ἐν ᾧ ἕστασαι. Klotz, *Devar.* p. 9: οὐκ ἐκινδύνευσεν ἀλλ' ἔπαθεν est: *non periclitatus sed passus est*, quibus verbis hoc significatur: non dico istum periclitatum esse sed passum, ita ut, cum ille dicatur passus esse, jam ne cogitetur quidem de eo, quod priori membro dictum est.

[2] [With the punctuation, οὐκ ἐμὲ λελύπηκεν ἀλλ' ἀπὸ μέρους (ἵνα μὴ ἐπιβαρῶ) πάντας ὑμᾶς.]

[3] This view—stated in the first edition of this work, in accordance with the observations of De Wette (*A. L.-Z.* 1816, No. 41, p. 321) and a reviewer in

Where (οὐ) μή ... ἀλλὰ καί are correlative, as in Ph. ii. 4, μὴ τὰ ἑαυτῶν ἕκαστος σκοποῦντες, ἀλλὰ καὶ τὰ ἑτέρων ἕκαστος, the sentence was originally planned for οὐ ... ἀλλά, and the καί was afterwards inserted because the writer, on coming to the second clause, wished to soften and limit the thought. Similar passages are not uncommon in Greek writers; see Fritz. *Mark,* Exc. 2, p. 788, and compare Poppo, *Thuc.* III. iii. 300. On the Latin *non* ... *sed etiam* or *quoque* see Ramshorn p. 535 sq., Kritz, *Vell. Pat.* p. 157 sq.

The converse of this is οὐ μόνον ... ἀλλά (without καί,—see Lehmann, *Lucian* II. 551): here the writer drops the μόνον, and instead of proceeding with an expression parallel to that which has gone before, brings in one of heightened meaning (which commonly includes the former).[1] A. xix. 26, ὅτι οὐ μόνον Ἐφέσου, ἀλλὰ σχεδὸν πάσης τῆς Ἀσίας ὁ Παῦλος οὗτος πείσας μετέστησεν ἱκανὸν ὄχλον, *that he not only at Ephesus but in all Asia* etc.,—where in strictness we should have had, *but also in other places.* Compare 1 Jo. v. 6, οὐκ ἐν τῷ ὕδατι μόνον, ἀλλ' ἐν τῷ ὕδατι καὶ τῷ αἵματι. On the Latin *non solum (modo)* ... *sed* see Hand, *Tursell.* IV. 282 sqq., Kritz, *Sall. Cat.* p. 80. In Ph. ii. 12 the second member is strengthened in a different manner.

1 Tim. v. 23, μηκέτι ὑδροπότει, ἀλλ' οἴνῳ ὀλίγῳ χρῶ, is to be rendered, *be no longer a water-drinker* (ὑδροποτεῖν, compare Her. 1. 71. Athen. 1. 168), *but use a little wine:* ὑδροποτεῖν is different from ὕδωρ πίνειν, and signifies *to be a water-drinker,* i.e., to make use of water as the ordinary and exclusive drink. He who "drinks *a little* wine" naturally ceases to be a water-drinker in this sense of the word; hence there is no need to supply μόνον. The note of Matthies *in loc.* is incorrect.

9. Two negatives occurring together in the same [2] principal sentence either [3]

(*a*) Coalesce to form an affirmation: A. iv. 20, οὐ δυνάμεθα

---

the *Theol. Annal.* of 1816 (p. 873)—was assailed by Fritzsche in his 2nd *Dissert. in 2 Cor.* p. 162 sq. His objections were examined by Beyer (*N. krit. Journ. d. Theol.*, vol. 3, part 1), and Fritzsche took up the subject again in the 2nd Exc. to his *Comm. in Marc.,* p. 773 sqq. The above was in the main already written before I received this Excursus, and substantially coincides with what I expressed in the 2nd edition of my *Grammar* (p. 177) and in my *Grammat. Excurse* (p. 155). Meyer and Baumgarten-Crusius decidedly agree with me in the various passages quoted above; but I am especially gratified by the remarks of my acute colleague Klotz (*Devar.* II. 9 sq.) in corroboration of my view. On *non* ... *sed* compare Kritz, *Sall. Jug.* p. 533, Hand, *Tursell.* IV. 271.

[1] See Stallb. *Plat. Symp.* p. 115, Fritz. *l. c.* p. 786 sqq., Klotz, *Devar.* p. 9 sq.

[2] Such a case as Rom. xv. 8 [probably xv. 18], in which the two negatives which are to be changed into an affirmation stand in two different clauses which are united by attraction, does not require special mention.

[3] Klotz, *Devar.* p. 695 sqq.; E. Lieberkühn, *De negationum Græc. cumulatione* (Jen. 1849). [Jelf 747; Shilleto, Dem. *Fals. L.* p. 50; Clyde, *Gr. Synt.* p. 96; Farrar, *Gr. Synt.* p. 181 sq.]

SECT. LV.] THE NEGATIVE PARTICLES. 625

ἡμεῖς ἃ εἴδομεν καὶ ἠκούσαμεν, μὴ λαλεῖν, *non possumus . . . non dicere*, i. e., *we must declare* (compare Aristoph. *Ran.* 42, οὗτοι μὰ τὴν Δήμητρα δύναμαι μὴ γελᾶν); 1 C. xii. 15, οὐ παρὰ τοῦτο οὐκ ἔστιν ἐκ τοῦ σώματος, therefore [1] *it still is of the body* (belongs to it). In the former passage the negative particles belong to different verbs,—first the δύνασθαι is negatived and then the λαλεῖν: in Syriac, ܠܐ ܡܫܟܚܝܢܢ ܕܠܐ ܢܡܠܠ. In the latter, οὐκ ἔστιν expresses a single idea, which is negatived by the first οὐ; the "not-belonging to the body" is denied.[2] For οὐκ εἶναι thus used in a negative sentence compare Demosth. *Androt.* 420 c, Ælian 12. 36. See further Mt. xxv. 9 *Rec.* Compare Poppo, *Thuc.* III. iv. 711, Matth. 609. 2. Or (and more frequently)—

(*b*) They are reducible to a single negation, and (originally) serve only to give more decisiveness to the principal negation, which would have been sufficient by itself, and to impress the negative character on the sentence in all its parts.[3] Jo. xv. 5, χωρὶς ἐμοῦ οὐ δύνασθε ποιεῖν οὐδέν, *non potestis facere quidquam*, i. e., *nihil potestis facere* (Dem. *Callipp.* 718 c); 2 C. xi. 8, παρών . . . οὐ κατενάρκησα οὐδενός· A. xxv. 24, ἐπιβοῶντες μὴ δεῖν αὐτὸν ζῆν μηκέτι· Mk. xi. 14, μηκέτι εἰς τὸν αἰῶνα ἐκ σοῦ μηδεὶς καρπὸν φάγῃ· 1 C. i. 7, ὥστε ὑμᾶς μὴ ὑστερεῖσθαι ἐν μηδενὶ χαρίσματι· Mt. xxii. 16, Mk. i. 44, v. 37, vii. 12, ix. 8, xii. 34, xv. 4 sq., Mt. xxiv. 21, L. iv. 2, viii. 43 (viii. 51 *v. l.*), x. 19, xx. 40, xxii. 16, Jo. iii. 27, v. 30, vi. 63, ix. 33, xvi. 23 sq., xix. 41, A. viii. 16, 39, Rom. xiii. 8, 1 C. viii. 2 *v. l.*, 2 C. vi. 3,

---

[1] ["Therefore" loses its meaning when the sentence is thus changed into an affirmative form. "It is not on this account not-of-the-body."]

[2] [The same view is taken by Lachmann, Tischendorf, Bengel, Stanley, Meyer (in his last edition), A. Buttm. (p. 354), Grimm (*Clavis* s. v. οὐ), Jelf (747. *Obs.* 2): so also in *Vulg.*, "non ideo non est de corpore." De Wette and some others prefer the rendering *num ideo non est corporis?* taking the negatives as strengthening each other. This meaning, however, would surely have been expressed by μή . . . . οὐκ (see p. 641): besides, the repetition of the simple negative in a short sentence of this character would be very strange. See Kühner II. 759. Compare Riddell, Plat. *Apol.* p. 221.]

[3] As in popular German. The accumulation of negatives is however a genuine German idiom; and it is only through the influence of the Latin, which so completely permeates our scientific culture, that it has disappeared from the diction of the educated. As to Latin usage, see Jani, *Ars poet. Lat.* p. 236 sq. [Farrar, *Syntax* p. 181 sq., Madvig, *Lat. Gr.* 460. *Obs.* 2, Roby II. 471-473.]

2 Th. ii. 3, 1 P. iii. 6, 1 Jo. i. 5, Rev. xviii. 4,¹ 11, 14, al.² So especially when the notions *every, at any time, always, everywhere,* are added to the negative sentence for the necessary or the rhetorical extension of its meaning (Böckh, *Nott. Pind.* p. 418 sq.);³ or when the negation is divided into parts, as in Mt. xii. 32, οὐκ ἀφεθήσεται αὐτῷ οὔτε ἐν τούτῳ τῷ αἰῶνι οὔτε ἐν τῷ μέλλοντι.⁴ In this way a sentence may contain a series of negations: L. xxiii. 53, οὗ οὐκ ἦν οὐδέπω οὐδεὶς κείμενος· Mk. v. 3. Compare Ælian, *Anim.* 11. 31, ὡς οὐδεπώποτε οὐδένα οὐδὲν ἀδικήσας· Plat. *Parmen.* 166 a, ὅτι τἆλλα τῶν μὴ ὄντων οὐδενὶ οὐδαμῇ οὐδαμῶς οὐδεμίαν κοινωνίαν ἔχει· *Phæd.* 78 d, Her. 2. 39, οὐδὲ ἄλλου οὐδενὸς ἐμψύχου κεφαλῆς γεύσεται Αἰγυπτίων οὐδείς; Lysias, *Pro Mantith.* 10, Xen. *Anab.* 2. 4. 23, Plat. *Phil.* 29 b, *Soph.* 249 b, Lucian, *Chronol.* [? *Cronos.*] 13, Dio. C. 635. 40, 402. 35, 422. 24.⁵ When οὐδέ is used in the sense of *ne . . . . quidem,* Greek writers usually join another negative to the verb:⁶ so in L. xviii. 13, οὐκ ἤθελεν οὐδὲ τοὺς ὀφθαλμοὺς εἰς τὸν οὐρανὸν ἐπᾶραι.

In 1 C. vi. 10, after several partitive clauses (οὔτε, οὔτε, οὐ, οὐ), the negative is again repeated with the predicate for the sake of clearness, βασιλείαν θεοῦ οὐ κληρονομήσουσι: the best MSS. however omit it, and it is not received by Lachmann. So also in Rev. xxi. 4, ὁ θάνατος οὐκ ἔσται ἔτι, οὔτε πένθος οὔτε κραυγὴ οὔτε πόνος οὐκ ἔσται ἔτι, the writer might without hesitation have omitted the second οὐκ. The nearest approach to this is Æschin. *Ctesiph.* 285 b, οὐδέ γε ὁ πονηρὸς οὐκ ἄν ποτε γένοιτο δημοσίᾳ χρηστός, see Bremi *in loc.* (c. 77): compare also Plat. *Rep.* 4. 426 b, and Herm. Soph. *Antig. l. c.* If inverted, οὐκ ἔσται ἔτι οὔτε πένθος κ.τ.λ., the sentence would be quite regular. In A. xxvi. 26 *Rec.* we find the

---

¹ [Rev. xviii. 4 is a mistake.]
² In the LXX compare Gen. xlv. 1, Num. xvi. 15, Ex. x. 23, Dt. xxxiv. 6, Jos. ii. 11, 1 S. xii. 4; and especially Hos. iv. 4, ὅπως μηδεὶς μήτε δικάζηται μήτε ἐλέγχῃ μηδείς. In such sentences the transcribers sometimes omit a negative: see Fritz. *Mark,* p. 107.
³ This mode of expression is not however always employed: compare A. x. 14, οὐδέποτε ἔφαγον πᾶν κοινὸν καὶ ἀκάθαρτον (without any variant), 1 Jo. iv. 12.
⁴ Klotz, *Devar.* II. 698: "in hac enuntiatione ita repetita est negatio, quod unumquodque orationis membrum, quia eo amplificabatur sententia, quasi per se stare videbatur."
⁵ See Wyttenb. Plat. *Phæd.* p. 199, Ast, Plat. *Polit.* p. 541, Boisson. Philostr. *Her.* p. 446, and *Nicet.* p. 243; and especially Herm. Soph. *Antig.* p. 13, Gayler p. 382 sq.
⁶ Comp. Stallb. Plat. *Rep.* I. 279, Poppo, *Thuc.* III. ii. 460.

combination λανθάνειν αὐτόν τι τούτων ο ὐ πείθομαι οὐδέν; but the better MSS. omit either οὐδέν or τι.[1]

On the pleonastic μή after verbs in which the idea of negation is already contained, see § 65. 2.

Rem. A peculiar mode of negation is constituted by the conjunction εἰ in formulas of swearing, in virtue of an aposiopesis of the apodosis: Mk. viii. 12, ἀμὴν λέγω ὑμῖν, εἰ δοθήσεται τῇ γενεᾷ ταύτῃ σημεῖον, i. e., *no sign shall be given;* H. iii. 11, iv. 3 (from the LXX), ὤμοσα, εἰ εἰςελεύσονται εἰς τὴν κατάπαυσίν μου. This is an imitation of the Hebrew אִם (compare Gen. xiv. 23, Dt. i. 35, 1 K. i. 51, ii. 8, 2 K. iii. 14, al.), and a formula of imprecation must in all cases be supplied as the apodosis. In the passage last quoted (H. iv. 3), supply, *then will I not live, will not be Jehovah;* in those passages in which men are the speakers, the suppressed clause is, *so shall God punish me* (compare 1 S. iii. 17, 2 S. iii. 35), *then will I not live,* etc.[2] Compare Aristoph. *Equit.* 698 sq., εἰ μή σ᾽ ἐκφάγω . . . οὐδέποτε βιώσομαι; Cic. *Fam.* 9. 15. 7, *moriar, si habeo.* Ἐάν also is thus used in the LXX: see Neh. xiii. 25, Cant. ii. 7, iii. 5. Of the opposite ἐὰν μή or εἰ μή (in an affirmative sense) there is no example in the N. T.: compare Ez. xvii. 19. Haab (p. 226) most inconsiderately refers to this head Mk. x. 30 and 2 Th. ii. 3.[3]

Section LVI.

CONSTRUCTION OF THE NEGATIVE PARTICLES.

1. The subjective negative μή, *ne,* together with its compounds, is used in *independent* sentences to express a negative wish or a warning:—

a. In the former case it is naturally joined with the (aorist) optative (Franke I. 27),—the mood which would have been used had there been no negation; e. g., in the frequently recurring formula μὴ γένοιτο, L. xx. 16, Rom. iii. 6, ix. 14, G. ii. 17

---

[1] [א has both τι and οὐθέν. Tregelles brackets the latter word: Meyer takes it in an adverbial sense, and suggests that it was the supposition that there were two accusatives of the object, τι and οὐδέν, which led to the omission of one of these words in several MSS.]

[2] Ewald, *Krit. Gr.* p. 661. [Gesen. *Hebr. Gr.* p. 246.]

[3] [The positive asseveration לֹא אִם is rendered in the LXX sometimes by ἦ μήν (Job i. 11, ii. 5, in the Roman text), sometimes by εἰ μή (1 K. xx. 23 *Vat., Al.,*—also for כִּי in Is. xlv. 23 *Vat., Sin.*). Either through a confusion between these two expressions, or by an orthographical corruption of ἦ (Fritzsche on Bar. ii. 29, —compare *Etym. Mag.* 416. 41), we frequently find εἰ μήν in exactly the same sense: see Ez. xxxiii. 27, xxxiv. 8, xxxv. 6, Bar. ii. 29 (Job i. 11 *Vat., Al., Sin.*). There is often considerable confusion between these forms in the leading MSS. In H. vi. 14 (from the LXX) εἰ μήν is very strongly supported: in Gen. xxii. 17 also, the source of the quotation, it is found in several of the best MSS. See Bleek *in loc.,* A. Buttm. p. 359, Grimm, *Clavis* s. v. εἰ.]

(Sturz, *Dial. Alex.* p. 204 sq.), and in μὴ αὐτοῖς λογισθείη, 2 Tim. iv. 16 (Plat. *Legg.* 11. 918 d). Similarly with μηκέτι in Mk. xi. 14 *Rec.*, μηκέτι ἐκ σοῦ εἰς τὸν αἰῶνα μηδεὶς καρπὸν φάγοι, *may no one ever again* etc. ! Yet the conjunctive φάγῃ would here be more appropriate in the mouth of Christ, if it had but stronger external evidence in its favour. See further Gayler p. 76 sqq., 82.

b. In the latter case μή is joined with

(*a*) The imperative present,—usually to denote something which one is already doing, and which also is not transient (Herm. *Vig.* p. 809): Mt. vi. 19, μὴ θησαυρίζετε ὑμῖν· vii. 1, μὴ κρίνετε· Jo. v. 14, μηκέτι ἁμάρτανε. Compare Mt. xxiv. 6,[1] 17 [*Rec.*], Jo. xiv. 1, xix. 21, Mk. xiii. 7, 11, Rom. xi. 18, E. iv. 28, 1 Tim. v. 23, 1 P. iv. 12.

(β) The conjunctive aorist,—to denote something transient which must not take place at all (Herm. *l. c.*). See L. vi. 29, ἀπὸ τοῦ αἴροντός σου τὸ ἱμάτιον καὶ τὸν χιτῶνα μὴ κωλύσῃς ; Mt. x. 34, μὴ νομίσητε (do not conceive the thought), ὅτι ἦλθον κ.τ.λ. ; Mt. vi. 13, L. xvii. 23, A. xvi. 28. So in legislative prohibitions (Mt. vi. 7, Mk. x. 19, Col. ii. 21), where not the recurrence or continuance of the action, but the action absolutely and in itself (even a single performance of it), is interdicted. The imperative aorist, which properly has this meaning, and which is not at all uncommon in later writers (Gayler p. 64),[2] does not occur in the N. T., and is doubtful in the LXX. On the other hand, we often find the present imperative used in reference to what should not be begun at all (Herm. *l. c.*, Franke I. 30): compare Mt. ix. 30, E. v. 6, 1 Tim. v. 22, 1 Jo. iii. 7. On the whole subject see Herm. *De præceptis Atticistar.* p. 4 sqq. (*Opusc.* I. 270 sqq.) ; and compare Herm. Soph. *Aj.* p. 163, Bernh. p. 393 sq., Franke I. 28 sqq.—In L. x. 4 the imperative and the conjunctive occur in the same sentence.[3] (Jelf 420. 3, Don. p. 413.)

---

[1] Here, as was rightly observed by H. Stephanus in the preface to his Greek Testament of 1576, ὁρᾶτε must be followed by a comma. If we directly connect ὁρᾶτε with μή, we must have θροῆσθε instead of θροεῖσθε. This has not been noticed by Tischendorf. [Tischendorf introduced the comma in ed. 7, but dropped it in ed. 8.]

[2] Compare Bremi, *Exc.* 12. *ad Lys.* p. 452 sqq.

[3] [Delitzsch and Grimm (*Clavis* s. v. μή) suppose that μὴ σκληρύνητε, H. iii. 15, is an example of the use of μή with the *present* conjunctive, instead of the aorist. But why must σκληρύνητε be *present*, as ἐσκλήρυνα was in actual use (Ex. x. 1)?]

In Rom. xiii. 8 also μή is joined with the present imperative, μηδενὶ μηδὲν ὀφείλετε; for the subjective negatives prevent our taking ὀφείλετε as indicative. Reiche's observations on the opposite side are a marvellous mixture of the obscure and the half true. If however he supposes that the subjective negatives are so used in some of the passages cited by Wetstein, he is very greatly mistaken; in these we have the infinitive or the participle,—moods which are regularly joined with μή.

On οὐ with the indicative future—partly in quotations of O. T. laws (as Mt. v. 21, οὐ φονεύσεις· xix. 18, A. xxiii. 5, Rom. xiii. 9), partly in the language of the N. T. itself (as Mt. vi. 5, οὐκ ἔσεσθε ὥσπερ οἱ ὑποκριταί), where μή with the conjunctive might have been expected—compare § 43. 5. Not unlike this is Xen. *Hell.* 2. 3. 34: see Locella, *Xen. Ephes.* p. 204, Franke I. 24.

On μή with the future indicative as a mild prohibition, see Weber, *Demosth.* p. 369.

Where μή in a prohibitive sense is joined with the *third* person (as is frequently the case in laws,—see Franke *l. c.* p. 32), the mood employed is (in the N. T. invariably) the imperative, not the conjunctive;[1] the present imperative being used if that which is forbidden is already in existence, the aorist if something which does not yet exist is to be avoided (for the future also). For the present, see Rom. vi. 12, μὴ οὖν βασιλευέτω ἡ ἁμαρτία ἐν τῷ θνητῷ ὑμῶν σώματι· xiv. 16, 1 C. vii. 12, 13, Col. ii. 16, 1 Tim. vi. 2, Ja. i. 7, 1 P. iv. 15, 2 P. iii. 8. For the aorist: Mt. vi. 3, μὴ γνώτω ἡ ἀριστερά σου κ.τ.λ., xxiv. 18, μὴ ἐπιστρεψάτω ὀπίσω· Mk. xiii. 15, μὴ καταβάτω εἰς τὴν οἰκίαν; also probably Mt. xxiv. 17 (according to good MSS.), where *Rec.* has καταβαινέτω. Compare Xen. *Cyr.* 7. 5. 73, 8. 7. 26, Æschin. *Ctes.* 282 c, Matth. 511. 3, Kühner II. 113. Hence no examples from the LXX are required here; otherwise, besides Dt. xxxiii. 6 and 1 S. xvii. 32, many might be quoted,—e.g., Jos. vii. 3, 1 S. xxv. 25, 2 S. i. 21, Jud. vi. 39. (Jelf 420. *Obs.* 5.)

If a dehortation is to be expressed in the first person (plural), μή stands with the conjunctive, either present or aorist according to the distinction mentioned above (Herm. Soph. *Aj.* p. 162). Thus in Jo. xix. 24, μὴ σχίσωμεν; but in 1 Jo. iii. 18, μὴ ἀγαπῶμεν λόγῳ (as some were doing), G. vi. 9, 1 Th. v. 6, Rom. xiv. 13, 1 C. x. 8. In G. v. 26 the MSS. are divided, some having μὴ γινώμεθα κενόδοξοι (*Rec.*), others γενώμεθα. The

---

[1] Herm. Soph. *Aj.* p. 163. [In Mt. xxi. 19 Tregelles reads μηκέτι γίνηται.]

better MSS. are in favour of the former reading, which is received by Lachmann and Tischendorf; and the apostle may certainly intend to censure a fault which was already in existence in the church: the previous context makes this probable. Meyer takes a different view. For examples of the 1 plural conjunctive in Greek writers see Gayler p. 72 sq.

2. In *dependent* sentences we find μή (μήπως, μήποτε, etc.):—

(*a*) With the meaning *in order that* ... *not*. In this sense however ἵνα μή is more commonly used. Here the conjunctive is used after the present tense and the imperative mood: 1 C. ix. 27, ὑπωπιάζω μου τὸ σῶμα ... μήπως ... ἀδόκιμος γένωμαι· 2 C. ii. 7, xii. 6, Mt. v. 25, xv. 32, L. xii. 58, and frequently. The optative follows past tenses: A. xxvii. 42, τῶν στρατιωτῶν βουλὴ ἐγένετο, ἵνα τοὺς δεσμώτας ἀποκτείνωσι, μή τις ἐκκολυμβήσας διαφύγοι. In the last passage good MSS. have διαφύγῃ,[1] which is received by Lachmann and Tischendorf (Bernh. p. 401, Krüg. p. 191, Jelf 805); but this may be a correction or an error in transcription. We also meet with the conjunctive in the O. T. quotation which occurs in Mt. xiii. 15, A. xxviii. 27: here however there is still less difficulty, as a *permanent* result is intended. The future indicative is found by the side of the conjunctive aorist in Mk. iv. 12 (from the LXX),[2] μήποτε ἐπιστρέψωσι καὶ ἀφεθήσεται (according to good

---

[1] [No uncial MS. has the optative here, and in no other passage of the N. T. is the optative found after the final μή.—In 2 C. ix. 4 the conjunctive follows the epistolary aorist.]

[2] [This certainly is a free quotation from Is. vi. 10, but ἀφεθήσεται (or ἀφεθῇ) is substituted for ἰάσομαι of the LXX. The same passage is quoted in Mt. xiii. 14 sq., A. xxviii. 26 sq. (with μήποτε), Jo. xii. 40 (with ἵνα μή): in all cases ἰάσομαι is the reading now received. In Mk. *l. c.* Fritzsche stands alone amongst recent editors in receiving the future into the text. He thus gives his reasons: "Nam primo ἀφιδῇ vulgare est, exquisitum ἀφεθήσεται, deinde illud ob conjunctivos præcedentes scripserunt librarii vel quod grammaticæ timerent, ignari, Futurum hic non modo justum esse, sed longe præstare Conjunctivo, quia *id, quod e re consequatur* enuntiandum fuit:—*ne quando resipiscant et veniam consecuturi sint*: cf. Hermann ad Soph. *El.* v. 992 et Heindorf ad Plat. *Cratyl.* p. 36." Hermann *l. c.* distinguishes between ὅρα μὴ κτησώμεθα (*cave ne contrahamus*) and ὅρα μὴ κτησόμεθα (*cave ne contracturæ simus*). This case however belongs to (*b*) below. In other cases the future indicative is very rarely found with the final μή in classical Greek (except in Homer); see Bernh. p. 402, Rost p. 661, Matthiæ 519. 7, Goodwin, *Syntax* p. 68. In the N. T., however, this construction is undoubted (as in the case of ἵνα, see p. 361): besides the examples just quoted see Mk. xiv. 2 (placed by Winer under the next head, p. 632), Mt. vii. 6 (where a conjunctive follows). See also Mt. v. 25, L. xii. 58: here a conjunctive is followed by a future, which may however be independent (compare ἰάσομαι in the passages cited above). In several other passages the future is a

MSS.), but it is not necessary to regard this tense as jointly dependent on μήποτε: even so taken, however, the future would be very appropriate, see Fritzsche *in loc.* The same may be said of ἰάσομαι, A. xxviii. 27 (Bornemann, ἰάσωμαι): compare L. xiv. 8 sq. In Mt. vii. 6 Lachmann and Tischendorf read μήποτε καταπατήσουσιν, where Griesbach and Scholz note no variant whatever.

(*b*) For *that not, lest haply*, after ὅρα, βλέπε, or φοβοῦμαι and the like (Herm. *Vig.* p. 797, Rost, *Gr.* p. 662 sq.).[1] In this combination we find

a. The indicative,—when at the same time a conjecture or apprehension is expressed that something does actually exist, will exist, or has existed.—Present indicative: L. xi. 35, σκόπει μὴ τὸ φῶς τὸ ἐν σοὶ σκότος ἐστίν. See Herm. Soph. *Aj*. 272, μὴ ἐστί verentis quidem est ne quid nunc sit, sed indicantis simul, putare se ita esse, ut veretur: compare Gayler p. 317 sq., *Protev. Jacobi* 14.[2]—Future indicative: Col. ii. 8, βλέπετε μή τις ἔσται ὑμᾶς ὁ συλαγωγῶν, *ne futurus sit, ne existat, qui*

---

variant,—and that not only where its form merely differs by a vowel from that of the conjunctive: see Mt. v. 25 (παραδώσει), L. xiv. 8, al., Mt. xxvii. 64, L. xiv. 12. See Green, *Gr.* p. 175. (On the combination of future and conjunctive see Paley on *Æsch. Pers.* 120.)]

[1] [There is great difference of opinion as to this construction. By many it is considered a variety of the indirect question: see Don. p. 560 sq., Jelf 814, Kühner II. 1037 (ed. 2), Rost u. Palm, *Lex.* s. v. μή, Rost, *Gr.* p. 664, Hartung, *Part.* II. 137, Riddell, Plat. *Apol.* p. 140, 171. Others connect the construction with that of the final sentence: see Liddell and Scott s. v. μή, Curtius, *Gr.* p. 292 (Trans.), Krüg. p. 193 (compare however p. 194), Buttm. *Griech. Gr.* p. 432, Green, *Gr.* p. 176 sq., and compare Goodwin, *Synt.* p. 66, 84. Compare further Klotz II. 667, Madvig 124 a. For the N. T. see A. Buttm. p. 242 sq., Green *l. c.*, Webster *Synt.* p. 141 sq. On the different tenses and moods used see especially Shilleto, Dem. *F. L.* p. 200 sq., Jebb, Soph. *El.* p. 59, Goodwin *l. c.* p. 80–85.—L. xi. 35 is a very simple instance of the indirect question. 2 Tim. ii. 25, . . . μήποτε δώῃ (or very possibly δῴη), *whether haply*, is somewhat elliptical, but is an example of the same principle: see Ellicott *in loc.*, and compare Jelf 877. *Obs.* 5, A. Buttm. p. 256.—Mk. xiv. 2, quoted below, seems naturally to belong to (*a*).]

[2] We cannot, with De Wette, pronounce this view inappropriate, on the ground that "an absolute, general warning is here expressed." This is the very question. A challenge to examination, with the apprehension that such may be the case, might certainly be given by Jesus to the Jews of that age, their prevalent religious character being such as is presupposed in other parts of the N. T.; and this challenge is in reality a general one. "Let every one see to it, lest possibly the second of the alternatives mentioned in ver. 34, in regard to the spiritual eye, may exist in his case." The apprehension that Jesus would thus be countenancing the doctrine of a total corruption of man's understanding, is groundless; and Niemeyer (*Hall. Pred.-Journ.* 1832. Nov.) should not have been induced by this to take the indicative as used for the conjunctive,—an interpretation which he supports by passages of a totally different nature.

etc.; H. iii. 12, Mk. xiv. 2, Her. 3. 36, Plat. *Cratyl.* 393 c, Achill. Tat. 6. 2 (p. 837: ed. Jac.), Xen. *Cyr.* 4. 1. 18, al. Compare Stallb. Plat. *Rep.* I. 336.—Preterite indicative, after a present: G. iv.11, φοβοῦμαι ὑμᾶς, μήπως εἰκῆ κεκοπίακα (*have laboured*).[1] Compare Thuc. 3. 53, Plat. *Lys.* 218 d, Diog. L. 6. 5, Lucian, *Pisc.* 15 (Job i. 5): see Gayler p. 317, 320.

β. The conjunctive (Gayler p. 323 sqq.); to express the object of a mere apprehension, which may perhaps not be confirmed. Present conjunctive: H. xii. 15 (from the LXX), ἐπισκοποῦντες . . . μή τις ῥίζα πικρίας . . . ἐνοχλῇ. See Herm. Soph. *Aj.* 272 : μὴ ᾖ verentis est, ne quid nunc sit, simulque nescire se utrum sit necne significantis. The aorist is the tense commonly used, in reference to something still future: Mt. xxiv. 4, βλέπετε, μή τις ὑμᾶς πλανήσῃ· 2 C. xi. 3, φοβοῦμαι, μήπως . . . φθαρῇ τὰ νοήματα ὑμῶν· xii. 20, L. xxi. 8, A. xiii. 40, 1 C. viii. 9, x. 12. The conjunctive mood is found in narration after past tenses; see A. xxiii. 10, εὐλαβηθεὶς μὴ διασπασθῇ . . . ἐκέλευσε· xxvii. 17, 29. The same usage occurs in the best Greek prose after verbs of *fearing*, in cases where the apprehension appears sufficiently well founded (Rost p. 662): e. g., Xen. *An.* 1. 8. 24, Κῦρος δείσας, μὴ ὄπισθεν γενόμενος κατακόψῃ τὸ Ἑλληνικόν· *Cyr.* 4. 5. 48, πολὺν φόβον ἡμῖν παρείχετε μή τι πάθητε· Lysias, *Cœd. Eratosth.* 44, ὃ ἐγὼ δεδιὼς μή τις πύθηται ἐπεθύμουν αὐτὸν ἀπολέσαι. Compare also Thuc. 2. 101, Plat. *Euthyd.* 288 b, Herod. 4. 1. 3, 6. 1. 11.[2] The future indicative and the conjunctive occur together in 2 C. xii. 20 sq., φοβοῦμαι, μήπως οὐχ οἵους θέλω εὕρω ὑμᾶς κἀγὼ εὑρεθῶ ὑμῖν . . . μὴ πάλιν ἐλθόντος μου ταπεινώσει με ὁ θεός κ.τ.λ.

The same principles must be applied to elliptical passages such as the following (Gayl. p. 327), Mt. xxv. 9 *Rec.*, μήποτε οὐκ ἀρκέσῃ ἡμῖν καὶ ὑμῖν, *lest haply there be insufficient*, i. e., it is to be feared *that there will not suffice.* Recent editors prefer μήποτε οὐ μὴ ἀρκέσῃ, a reading for which there is no preponderant authority: in this case μήποτε is taken by itself—*no, in no wise.*[3] Rom. xi. 21,

---

[1] Herm. Eur. *Med.* p. 356, Poppo, *Thuc.* I. i. 135, Stallb. Plat. *Meno* p. 98 sqq.

[2] See Matth. 520, Bornem. Xen. *Symp.* p. 70, Gayler p. 324 sq.

[3] [Tisch. in ed. 8 returns to οὐκ, in deference to א ; but the MS. evidence for οὐ μή is very strong (Winer estimates the evidence differently below, § 64. 7), and this reading is generally received. Meyer and Bleek agree with Winer's second explanation (taking μήποτε by itself), and refer to Bornemann in the *Stud. u. Krit.* 1843 (p. 110). Bornemann, however, quotes no example of μήποτε thus used, but contents himself with such passages as Mt. xxvi. 5. A. Buttmann

εἰ ὁ θεὸς τῶν κατὰ φύσιν κλάδων οὐκ ἐφείσατο, μήπως οὐδὲ σοῦ φείσεται (incomparably better supported than φείσηται), *if God has not spared,* (I fear and conjecture) *that possibly he will not spare thee also, ne tibi quoque non sit parciturus:* compare Gen. xxiv. 39.

In G. ii. 2, ἀνέβην . . . . ἀνεθέμην . . . . μήπως εἰς κενὸν τρέχω ἢ ἔδραμον, Fritzsche, in his *Conject.* (I. p. 50 note), considered the translation *ne operam meam luderem aut lusissem* faulty in two respects: first, because in this case the optative might have been expected instead of τρέχω (after a past tense); and secondly, because the indicative ἔδραμον would here indicate what the apostle cannot intend to say, viz., that he *has laboured* in vain. Hence he took the words as a direct question: *num frustra operam meam in evangelium insumo an insumsi?* Fritzsche himself, however, afterwards felt how artificial this interpretation was; and in the *Opuscul. Fritzschiorum* (p. 173 sq.) he has given a different rendering. The difficulty in respect of τρέχω, indeed, disappears entirely for the N. T.; nay, the present conjunctive [1] is quite in place, since Paul is speaking of apostolic activity which *still continues.* The preterite indicative ἔδραμον, however, would at once be justified by the assumption that Paul has given to the whole sentence that turn of expression which he would have used had the words been spoken directly,—*that I may not perchance run or have run* (for "should run or should have run"); compare above, p. 360. Simpler still, however, is Fritzsche's present view of the preterite, that it is used in a hypothetical sense:[2] "ne forte frustra *cucurrissem*,"—which might easily have been the case, if I had not communicated my teaching . . . in Jerusalem. We must not indeed refer the ἀνεθέμην (as Fritzsche does) to a purpose on the part of Paul to receive instruction (for the mere communication could not secure him from having *run in vain,* but only the assent of the apostles): rather must Paul have been convinced in his own mind that his view is the right one, and have merely purposed to obtain for himself the weighty declaration of the apostles, without which his apostolic labour would have been fruitless both for the present and for the past. See De Wette *in loc.*[3]

In 1 Th. iii. 5 μήπως is joined with both indicative and conjunctive: ἔπεμψα εἰς τὸ γνῶναι τὴν πίστιν ὑμῶν, μήπως ἐπείρασεν

(p. 353) considers οὐ μὴ ἀρκέσῃ dependent on μήποτε, and it is hard to see any valid objection to this. The elliptical use of μήποτε (Gen. xxiv. 5, xxvii. 12, l. 15, al.) is very common in later writers: the particle thus comes to mean little more than *perhaps, perchance.* See Sturz, *Dial. Alex.* p. 184, A. Buttm. p. 354.—On Rom. xi. 21 see § 55. 1.]

[1] Usteri and Schott conclude that τρέχω is indicative, from the fact that ἔδραμον follows; as if there were not instances in which the same particle, from a difference in the thought, may be—sometimes actually is—joined with different moods: see 1 Th. iii. 5, to be quoted immediately. [A. Buttm. (p. 353) and Meyer take τρέχω as indicative, pressing the analogy of ἔδραμον, but neglecting 1 Th. iii. 5.]

[2] Matth. 519. 7, *De Partic.* ἄν p. 54 (Don. p. 603, Jelf 813).

[3] [See especially Ellicott *in loc.;* also Green p. 176 sq.]

ὑμᾶς ὁ πειράζων καὶ εἰς κενὸν γένηται ὁ κόπος ἡμῶν, *I sent to learn your faith,* (fearing) *lest haply the tempter should have tempted you, and my labour should be fruitless.* The different moods here require no vindication. The temptation (the shaking of their faith) might have already taken place; but the question whether the apostle's labour was thereby rendered fruitless depended on the result of the temptation, which was as yet unknown to the apostle, and he might therefore speak of the object of his fear as something future. Fritzsche's rendering (*Opusc. Fritz.* p. 176), " ut . . . cognoscerem, *an forte* Satanas vos tentasset et *ne forte* labores mei irriti essent," seems to me harsh, since it requires us to take μήπως in two different senses. That on my view of the passage, however, the future γενήσεται must have been used, instead of γένηται, I cannot at all allow: the future construction is far too strongly marked to be used in expressing an apprehension which may not be confirmed, and the confirmation of which is at all events not relegated to a future period, more or less remote.[1] See also Herm. Soph. *Aj.* p. 48, and *Partic.* ἄν p. 126 sq., Matth. 519. 8.

Rem. Verbs of *fearing* are regularly followed by the simple μή, μήπως, etc., not by ἵνα μή. Hence in A. v. 26 ἵνα μὴ λιθασθῶσιν must not be connected with ἐφοβοῦντο τὸν λαόν, as it is by most commentators (Meyer included); it is rather dependent on ἤγαγεν αὐτοὺς οὐ μετὰ βίας, and the words ἐφοβοῦντο γὰρ τὸν λαόν must be regarded as a parenthesis.[2]

3. The intensive οὐ μή (of that which *in no wise* will or shall happen)[3] is sometimes, indeed most commonly, joined

---

[1] [" The future would have represented something to occur at some indefinite future time, the aorist subjunctive is properly used of a transient state occurring in particular cases; see Matth. *Gr.* § 519. 8, and compare Madvig, *Synt.* § 124. 1, who correctly observes that μή with future, after verbs of fearing, etc., always gives prominence to the notion of futurity." Ellicott *in loc.*]

[2] [Most of the leading MSS. omit ἵνα. Meyer, who retains ἵνα and connects ἵνα μή with ἐφοβοῦντο, quotes a parallel instance from Diod. S. 2. 329, and urges that ὅπως μή is sometimes used with verbs of *fearing* (Jelf 814. *Obs.* 5). A. Buttm. (p. 242) maintains that with neither reading would the clause depend on ἐφοβοῦντο.]

[3] Thus οὐ μή regularly refers to the future: Mt. xxiv. 21, οἵα οὐ γέγονεν . . . . οὐδ' οὐ μὴ γένηται.—That this formula is to be regarded as elliptical, οὐ μὴ ποιήσῃ standing for οὐ δέδοικα or οὐ φόβος (οὐ δέος) ἐστί (*there is no fear*) μὴ ποιήσῃ, is now the prevailing opinion of philologers: see Ast, *Plat. Polit.* p. 365, Matthiæ, Eurip. *Hippol.* p. 24. *Sprachl.* 517, Herm. Soph. *Œd. C.* 1028, Hartung II. 156. If this be so, we must assume that the Greeks had lost sight of the origin of the expression, for " there is no *fear* that " would be unsuitable in many passages; in the N. T. see Mt. v. 20, xviii. 3, L. xxii. 16, Jo. iv. 18 [probably iv. 48]. At an earlier period Hermann had explained the formula differently (Eurip. *Med.* p. 390 sq.); compare also the view still taken by Gayler (p. 402).—The connective οὐδὲ μή (καὶ οὐ μή) occurs in the N. T. once only, Rev. vii. 16 *v. l.*, but frequently in the LXX (e. g., Ex. xxii. 21, xxiii. 13, Jos. xxiii. 7); οὐδεὶς μή, Wis. i. 8.—Οὐ μή is of very frequent occurrence in the LXX, and its prevalence may probably be referred to that striving after great expressiveness which is characteristic of the later language: the examples

with the conjunctive aorist, sometimes with the conjunctive present (Stallb. Plat. *Rep.* I. 51,—see below), sometimes also[1] with the indicative future.[2] The distinction between the conjunctive aorist and the future indicative (which alone occur in the N. T.) is thus defined by Hermann (Soph. *Œd. Col.* v. 853): " *Conjunctivo aoristi* locus est aut in eo, quod jam actum est" (see however Ellendt, *Lex. Soph.* II. 411 sq.), " aut in re incerti temporis, sed semel vel brevi temporis momento agenda: *futuri* vero usus, quem ipsa verbi forma nonnisi in rebus futuris versari ostendit, ad ea pertinet, quæ aut diuturniora aliquando eventura indicare volumus aut non aliquo quocunque, sed remotiore aliquo tempore dicimus futura esse." The inquiry whether this distinction is well-founded for the N. T., is rendered difficult by the variations in the MSS., which in many passages are divided between the future and the aorist conjunctive. As far as our present apparatus criticus enables us to judge, we must certainly read the conjunctive in Mt. v. 18, 20, 26, x. 23, xviii. 3, xxiii. 39, Mk. xiii. 2, 19, 30, L. vi. 37, xii. 59, xiii. 35, xviii. 17, 30, xxi. 18, Jo. viii. 51, x. 28, xi. 26, 56, 1 Th. iv. 15, 1 C. viii. 13, 2 P. i. 10, Rev. ii. 11, iii. 3, 12, xviii. 7, 21 sq., xxi. 25, 27.[3] There is preponderant authority for the conjunctive in Mt. xvi. 28, xxvi. 35, Mk. ix. 41, xvi. 18, L. i. 17, ix. 27, xviii. 7, 30, xxii. 68, Jo. vi. 35, viii. 12, 52, xiii. 8, Rom. iv. 8, G. v. 16, 1 Th. v. 3.[4] The conjunctive is at least as well supported as the future in Mk. xiv. 31, L. xxi. 33, Mt. xv. 5, xxiv. 35, G. iv. 30,

---

are collected by Gayler (p. 441 sqq.). Hitzig (*Joh. Marc.* p. 106) incorrectly asserts that in the N. T. the Gospel of Mark and the Revelation show a special predilection for οὐ μή: a concordance will prove the contrary. [On the constructions of οὐ μή, and on the origin of the formula, see Don. *New Crat.* p. 622 sqq., *Gr.* p. 562 sq., Jelf 748, Farrar, *Gr. Synt.* p. 183 sq., Riddell, Plat. *Ap.* p. 177, Goodwin, *Synt.* p. 184 : for the N. T. see Ellicott on G. iv. 30, v. 16, also on 1 Th. iv. 15 *Transl.*, A. Buttm. p. 211 sqq., Green p. 190 sqq., Webster p. 140. The construction of οὐ μή with the 2 pers. future indicative taken interrogatively (Don. *l. c.*, Jelf *l. c.*) is not found in the N. T.]

[1] Bengel's note on Mt. v. 18 is incorrect. [Here Bengel asserts that the subjunctive is always used with οὐ μή.]
[2] See Ast, Plat. *Polit.* p. 365, Stallb. Plat. *Rep.* II. 36 sq., Ellendt, *Lex. Soph.* II. 409 sqq., Gayler p. 430 sqq.
[3] [I have changed L. xiii. 38 into xiii. 35. Rev. iii. 3 is doubtful.]
[4] [In Mt. xxvi. 35 the future is generally received. L. i. 17 is a mistake, perhaps for i. 15. L. xviii. 30 is in the first list. In Jo. vi. 35 the weight of evidence is decidedly in favour of πινάσῃ and διψήσει, which are received by recent editors : on the union of future and subjunctive, see Tisch. *in loc.* (ed. 7), and compare p. 630, note[2].]

H. x. 17, Rev. ix. 6 [1] (xviii. 14).[2] The future is decidedly favoured in L. x. 19, xxii. 34, Jo. iv. 4, x. 35 : [3] in Mt. xvi. 22 it stands without any variant, οὐ μὴ ἔσται σοι τοῦτο, (*absit*) *ne tibi accidat hoc.*

Hence the conjunctive is beyond dispute the ordinary form in the N. T. (compare Lob. *Phryn.* p. 722 sq.) : this is no less true in regard to Greek authors, see Hartung, *Partik.* II. 156 sq. Hermann's canon however, cited above, is on the whole inapplicable to the N. T.;[4] for though several passages might be explained in accordance with it, yet it is violated by others, and the aorist is used where we should necessarily have expected the future. See for example 1 Th. iv. 15, ὅτι ἡμεῖς οἱ ζῶντες οἱ περιλειπόμενοι εἰς τὴν παρουσίαν τοῦ κυρίου οὐ μὴ φθάσωμεν τοὺς κοιμηθέντας, where the point of time is perfectly definite, *on the day of Christ's second coming ;* H. viii. 11, where the words οὐ μὴ διδάξωσιν have reference to a particular time (the Messianic period, ver. 10), and also indicate something lasting ; compare Rev. xxi. 25. In fact, such a use of the conjunctive aorist in the sense of the future had become common in later Greek ; compare Lob. *l. c.* p. 723, Thilo, *Act. Thom.* p. 57. Madvig also (§ 124, Rem. 3) finds no sensible difference of meaning between the future and the aorist in this construction. (All the examples of οὐ μή in the LXX are collected by Gayler, p. 440 sqq.)

Dawes's canon, which leaves out of consideration any difference of meaning between the aorist and the future in this construction, but maintains in regard to the former that only the *second* aorist active (and middle) is to be admitted into the texts of Greek authors,

---

[1] [The conjunctive is certainly the true reading in Mt. xxiv. 35 : Rev. ix. 6 is doubtful. In all the other passages we should probably read the future.]

[2] We must also not overlook the possibility that the presence of the future in MSS. may sometimes have been occasioned by a future occurring in the words which precede or follow : e. g., Jo. viii. 12, οὐ μὴ περιπατήσει ἀλλ' ἕξει.

[3] [In L. xxii. 34 οὐ φωνήσει is best supported. For Jo. iv. 4, x. 35, we should probably read iv. 14, x. 5.]

[4] [It seems to be generally admitted that this canon cannot be applied to the N. T. Meyer however maintains that the two constructions are not perfectly identical in meaning, the future expressing more assurance and confidence than the conjunctive : see Mt. xxvi. 35, Jo. viii. 12 (Hartung II. 157). The only other question in regard to the meaning is, whether the formula is ever *imperatival* in the N. T. Ellicott, Meyer, and De Wette decide in the negative : see their notes on G. v. 16. The decision turns mainly on the interpretation of this passage (on which see also Green, *Cr. Notes* p. 153) and of Mt. xv. 5 (on which see below, § 64. II). The prohibitory sense is common in the LXX : see Thiersch, *De Pent. Alex.* p. 109, Green p. 193.]

SECT. LVI.] CONSTRUCTION OF THE NEGATIVE PARTICLES. 637

has met with almost general opposition.¹ Nor can it be applied to the N. T.: here the 1 aorist active is just as common as the 2 aorist, even in the case of verbs whose 2 aorist was much in use: see the variants in Rev. xviii. 14.

Occasionally οὐ μή is followed in a few MSS. by the *present* indicative; viz., in Jo. iv. 48, ἐὰν μὴ σημεῖα καὶ τέρατα ἴδητε, οὐ μὴ πιστεύετε· H. xiii. 5 (from the LXX), οὐ μή σε ἐγκαταλείπω.² In Rev. iii. 12, indeed, one MS. (cited by Griesbach) has the optative, οὐ μὴ ἐξέλθοι. The last instance is certainly a mistake of the transcriber, caused by not hearing correctly the word read; the conjunctive was long ago restored. (The case is different when the optative occurs in the *oratio obliqua*: see Soph. *Philoct.* 611 and Schæfer *in loc.*; compare also Schæfer, *Demosth.* II. 321.) In H. xiii. 5 also we must certainly read ἐγκαταλίπω. In Jo. iv. 48, however, πιστεύητε might perhaps be the true reading, for the *present* conjunctive is used by Greek writers after οὐ μή: e.g., Soph. *Œd. Col.* 1024, οὓς οὐ μή ποτε χώρας φυγόντες τῆσδ᾽ ἐπεύχωνται θεοῖς (according to Hermann and others), Xen. *Cyr.* 8. 1. 5, *An.* 2. 2. 12,³ *Hier.* 11. 15, ἐὰν τοὺς φίλους κρατῇς εὖ ποιῶν, οὐ μή σοι δύνωνται ἀντέχειν οἱ πολέμιοι (where, as in Jo. *l. c.*, a conditional clause with ἐάν precedes), and often in Demosthenes (Gayler p. 437). Still in this passage the weight of MS. authority is recorded in favour of πιστεύσητε, which is received by Lachmann and Tischendorf. What Hermann says (*Iphig. Taur.* p. 102) on the present indicative after οὐ μή will hardly protect the received reading. On L. xviii. 7 see § 57. 3, and p. 620.

This intensive οὐ μή is also found in dependent sentences; not merely in relative (Mt. xvi. 28, L. xviii. 30, A. xiii. 41), but also in objective sentences, after ὅτι, as L. xiii. 35 [*Rec.*], xxii. 16, Mt. xxiv. 34; Jo. xi. 56, τί δοκεῖ ὑμῖν, ὅτι οὐ μὴ ἔλθῃ εἰς τὴν ἑορτήν; *what think ye? that he will not come to the feast?* So also in the direct question, after τίς, in Rev. xv. 4, τίς οὐ μὴ φοβηθῇ; With Jo. xi. 56, etc., compare Xen. *Cyr.* 8. 1. 5, τοῦτο γὰρ εὖ εἰδέναι χρή, ὅτι οὐ μὴ δύνηται Κῦρος εὑρεῖν κ.τ.λ., and Thuc. 5. 69; with Rev. xv. 4, Neh. ii. 3, διὰ τί οὐ μὴ γένηται πονηρόν κ.τ.λ. On οὐ μή in a question without any interrogative pronoun, joined with the conjunctive or with the future (Ruth iii. 1), see § 57. 3.

Rem. *Not . . . except, no one . . . but, nothing but,* are com-

---

¹ See Matth. 517. Rem. 1, Stallb. Plat. *Rep.* II. 343, [Jelf 748. *Obs.* 3, A. Buttm. p. 213]: and on the other hand Bernh. p. 402 sq.
² [Tischendorf (ed. 8) and Alford adopt this reading, which has now the support of ℵ: the same form is found with οὐ μή in Dt. xxxi. 6, 8, 1 Chr. xxviii. 20, in *Alex.* If accepted, however, it would be the present *subjunctive* here.]
³ See Herm. on Elmsley, Eurip. *Med.* p. 390, Stallb. Plat. *Polit.* p. 51, Ast, Plat. *Polit.* p. 365.

monly expressed by οὐ . . , οὐδείς . . , οὐδέν . . εἰ μή; see Mt. xi. 27, xxi. 19, L. iv. 26, Jo. xvii. 12, al. (Klotz, *Devar.* II. 524). More rarely the negative is followed by πλήν, as in A. xx. 23, xxvii. 22. Ἤ occurs once only, in the received text of Jo. xiii. 10, ὁ λελουμένος οὐκ ἔχει χρείαν ἢ τοὺς πόδας νίψασθαι; and here most MSS. have εἰ μή, which Lachmann has received. This however might be a correction of the rarer ἤ, which does occasionally occur (Xen. *Cyr.* 7. 5. 41).

Section LVII.

THE INTERROGATIVE PARTICLES.

1. In the N. T.[1] those questions which do not commence with an interrogative pronoun or a special interrogative adverb (πῶς, ποῦ, etc.)

a. Are, if *direct*, usually expressed without any introductory particle (Jo. vii. 23, xiii. 6, xix. 10, A. xxi. 37, L. xiii. 2, 1 C. v. 2, Rom. ii. 21, G. iii. 21, etc., etc.).[2] Sometimes, however, contrary to the usage of the Greek written language (see below, no. 2), a question in which the inquirer merely expresses his uncertainty, without indicating any particular answer as expected by him, is introduced by εἰ.

b. If *indirect*, they are introduced by εἰ,—which in this case is still the conditional conjunction.[3]

In direct double questions πότερον . . . ἤ occurs once only, Jo. vii. 17.[4] Elsewhere the first question is not preceded by any particle (L. xx. 4, G. i. 10, iii. 2, Rom. ii. 3, al.); ἤ being placed before the second, if positive, and ἢ οὐ (Mt. xxii. 17, L. xx. 22) or ἢ μή (Mk. xii. 14)[5] if negative.[6] Ἤ is sometimes used in a question which stands related to a preceding categorical sentence (like *an* in Latin,—see Hand, *Tursell.* I. 349): 2 C. xi. 7, εἰ καὶ

---

[1] Compare Krüger p. 283 (Jelf 873).
[2] Hence there is sometimes a division of opinion amongst commentators whether a sentence is or is not to be taken as a question (e.g., Jo. xvi. 31, Rom. viii. 33, xiv. 22, 1 C. i. 13, 2 C. iii. 1, xii. 1, xii. 19, H. x. 2, Ja. ii. 4), or how many words are included in the question (e.g., Jo. vii. 19, Rom. iv. 1). On this, Grammar can as a rule offer no decision.
[3] As to how εἰ comes to have the meaning of an interrogative particle, see Hartung, *Partik.* II. 201 sqq. ; compare Klotz, *Dev.* II. 508.
[4] [This is an *indirect* double question.]
[5] Compare Bos, *Ellips.* p. 759, Klotz, *Devar.* II. 576 sq.
[6] [*Indirect* double questions: πότερον . . . ἤ, Jo. vii. 17 ; εἰ . . . ἤ, L. vi. 9 ; εἴτε . . . εἴτε, 2 C. xii. 2 sq. See A. Buttmann p. 249 sq. (Jelf 878). On the moods used in indirect questions see § 41. b. 4.]

ἰδιώτης τῷ λόγῳ, ἀλλ' οὐ τῇ γνώσει .... ἢ ἁμαρτίαν ἐποίησα ἐμαυτὸν ταπεινῶν; *or have I committed sin?* Rom. vi. 3 (Dio C. 282. 20), al.; compare Lehmann, *Lucian* II. 331 sq.

2. The following are examples of the singular use of εἰ in *direct* questions (a usage found mainly in Luke): A. i. 6, ἐπηρώτων αὐτὸν λέγοντες· κύριε, εἰ ... ἀποκαθιστάνεις τὴν βασιλείαν; L. xxii. 49, εἶπον· κύριε, εἰ πατάξομεν ἐν μαχαίρᾳ; Mt. xii. 10, xix. 3, L. xiii. 23, A. xix. 2, xxi. 37, xxii. 25, Mk. viii. 23. On Mt. xx. 15, see Meyer.[1] In the LXX, compare Gen. xvii. 17, xliii. 6, 1 S. x. 24, 2 S. ii. 1, xx. 17, 1 K. xiii. 14, xxii. 6, Jon. iv. 4, 9, Joel i. 2, Tob. v. 5, 2 Macc. vii. 7, Ruth i. 19. Originally this mode of expression may have involved an ellipsis, *I should like to know* (Meyer on Mt. xii. 10), as in German we sometimes use the indirect form, *ob das wahr ist?* But in that period of the language with which we are now concerned εἰ has come into all the rights of a directly interrogative particle,[2] like the Latin *an*, which late writers use in direct questions; and to press εἰ as the indirect *an* (Fritz. *Matt.* p. 425, *Mark*, p. 327), would be very forced. In a similar way *si*, by which the Vulgate render this εἰ, from an indirect (Liv. 39. 50) became a direct particle of interrogation.

That Greek writers also sometimes use εἰ in direct questions,[3] was maintained by Stallbaum (*Phileb.* p. 117), but was rightly denied, so far as Attic prose is concerned, by Bornemann (Xen. *Apol.* p. 39 sq.): Stallbaum afterwards retracted the admission he had made (Plat. *Alcib.* I. 231). Compare further Herm. on Lucian, *Conscr. Hist.* p. 221, Fritz. *Mark*, p. 328, Klotz, *Dev.* II. 511. In *Odyss.* 1. 158, quoted by Zeune (*ad Vig.* p. 506), ἦ was long ago substituted for εἰ; in Plat. *Rep.* 5. 478 d all good MSS. have ἐντός for εἰ; and in Aristoph. *Nub.* 483[4] εἰ does not mean *num*, but is the indirect interrogative *an*. So also in Demosth. *Callicl.* p. 735 b. Dio Chr. 30. 299, εἴ τι ἄλλο ὑμῖν προςέταξεν, ἐπέστειλεν ἢ διελέχθη; where follows the answer

---

[1] [Here Meyer retains the εἰ of *Rec.*, but takes it in its conditional sense: most editors read ἤ. In Mk. viii. 23 many read βλέπει, in which case the interrogation is not direct: Westcott and Hort have βλέπεις (βλέπει in the margin). In A. vii. 1 *Rec.* εἰ is accompanied by ἄρα.]

[2] Compare Schneider, Plat. *Civ.* I. 417.

[3] Hoogeveen, *Doctr. Partic.* I. 327.

[4] Palairet, *Observatt.* p. 60.

πολλὰ καὶ δαιμόνια, is perhaps corrupt (Reiske proposes ἢ τι ἄλλο); or else we must take it as an indirect question, *but* (one may ask, some one will perhaps ask) *whether he has enjoined anything else on you.* Even in Plat. *Civ.* 4. 440 e Schneider on MS. authority retains εἰ, changed by recent editors into (ἀλλ') ἢ; but explains this use of the particle, in a question apparently but not really direct, as arising out of an ellipsis. He removes the note of interrogation.

Ὅτι also has been taken as directly interrogative in the N. T., but on insufficient grounds: see § 53. 10. 5, [and § 24. 4].

The interrogative ἆρα was originally the paroxytone ἄρα. It is used in interrogative sentences—shown to be such by the inflexion of the voice—to express an inference from something which has preceded: the answer expected by the question may be either negative (in which case ἆρα is *num igitur*) or affirmative (*ergone*), see Klotz, *Devar.* II. 180 sqq.[1] The former is the more usual case in prose (Herm. *Vig.* p. 823), and is met with in the N. T.: L. xviii. 8, ἆρα εὑρήσει τὴν πίστιν ἐπὶ τῆς γῆς; *will he then find?* Similarly ἆράγε, A. viii. 30: compare Xen. *Mem.* 3. 8. 3, ἆράγε, ἔφη, ἐρωτᾶς με, εἴ τι οἶδα πυρετοῦ ἀγαθόν; οὐκ ἔγωγ', ἔφη. On the other hand, in G. ii. 17 ἆρα would stand for *ergone: Christ is then a minister of sin?*[2] Others read ἄρα without an interrogation: against this, however, is the fact that μὴ γένοιτο is never used by Paul except after a question. See Meyer *in loc.*[3] (Jelf 873. 2.)

To the interrogatives πῶς, πότε, ποῦ, κ.τ.λ., designed for direct questions, there correspond the relative forms ὅπως, ὁπότε, ὅπου, κ.τ.λ., for the indirect question (and construction): Buttm. II. 277. This distinction, however, is not always observed even by Attic writers,[4] and in later Greek it is frequently neglected. In the N. T. the direct interrogatives are the prevailing forms in the indirect construction: e. g., πόθεν Jo. vii. 27, ποῦ Mt. viii. 20, Jo. iii. 8. On πῶς see Wahl, *Clav.* p. 439. Ὅπου in the N. T. is used rather as a true relative.[5] (Jelf 877. *a.*)

---

[1] A different view is taken by Leidenroth, *De vera vocum origine ac vi per linguarum comparationem investiganda* (Lips. 1830), p. 59 sqq.—On ἆρα and ἄρα compare further Sheppard in the *Classical Museum*, No. 18.

[2] Compare Schæf. *Melet.* p. 89, Stallb. Plat. *Rep.* II. 223, Poppo, *Thuc.* III. i. 415.

[3] [On this passage see especially the notes of Ellicott and Lightfoot: see also A. Buttmann p. 247, who (with Wieseler) reads ἄρα, but retains the interrogation. On the force of γε in ἄράγε (giving more point to the question by *restricting* the attention to it) see Klotz, *Devar.* II. 192 sq.]

[4] See Kühner II. 583 [II. 1016: ed. 2], Herm. Soph. *Antig.* p. 80, Poppo, *Ind. ad Xenoph. Cyrop.*, s. vv. πῶς, ποῦ.

[5] [Ὅπως and ὅπου are the only particles of this kind which occur in the N. T.: ὁπότε in L. vi. 3 (*Rec.*, Tisch. ed. 8) is a simple conjunction. Ὅπως

SECT. LVII.] THE INTERROGATIVE PARTICLES. 641

3. In negative questions

(a) *Οὐ* is commonly used where an affirmative answer is expected,[1] for *nonne;* as in Mt. vii. 22, οὐ τῷ σῷ ὀνόματι προεφητεύσαμεν ; *have we not?* xiii. 27, L. xii. 6, xvii. 17, Ja. ii. 5, H. iii. 16, 1 C. ix. 1, xiv. 23. Sometimes also where the speaker himself regards the thing as denied, with an expression of indignation and reproach, as in A. xiii. 10, οὐ παύσῃ διαστρέφων τὰς ὁδοὺς κυρίου τὰς εὐθείας ; *wilt thou not cease?* The difference in the tendency of the question is indicated, as in German, by the difference of tone:[2] here *οὐ* negatives the verb,—*non desinere* =*pergere* (see Franke I. 15). Compare Plut. *Lucull.* c. 40, οὐ παύσῃ σὺ πλουτῶν μὲν ὡς Κράσσος, ζῶν δ' ὡς Λούκουλλος, λέγων δὲ ὡς Κάτων ; (Don. p. 561, Jelf 413). Similarly in L. xvii. 18, Mk. xiv. 60. Οὐκ ἄρα, A. xxi. 38, means *non igitur ; thou art not then* (according to my conjecture, which I now see to be denied) etc. : see Klotz, *Devar.* II. 186. *Nonne,* the rendering of the Vulgate, would probably, in combination with *yet,* be ἆρ' οὐ or οὔκουν : see Herm. *Vig.* p. 795, 824.

(b) *Μή* (μήτι [3]) is used where a negative answer is presupposed or expected, *surely not ?* (Franke *l. c.* p. 18).[4] Jo. vii. 31, μὴ πλείονα σημεῖα ποιήσει ; *he will surely not do more miracles?* (this is not conceivable) : Jo. xxi. 5, Rom. iii. 5 (where Philippi is incorrect), ix. 20, xi. 1, Mt. vii. 16, Mk. iv. 21, A. x. 47, al. The two negatives are found together in L. vi. 39, and the above-mentioned distinction is observed : μήτι δύναται τυφλὸς τυφλὸν ὁδηγεῖν ; οὐχὶ ἀμφότεροι εἰς βόθυνον πεσοῦνται ;

Hermann (*Vig.* p. 789) remarks that μή sometimes looks forward to an affirmative answer. The truth of this assertion is

---

occurs once only in an indirect question (L. xxiv. 20).—We find this substitution of direct for indirect interrogatives in modern Greek : see Mullach, *Vulg.* p. 321, Sophocles, *Gram.* p. 137, 178 sq.]

[1] Hartung, *Partik.* II. 88 (Don. p. 558 sq., Jelf 874).

[2] *Nicht* (wahr), *du willst aufhören?* (you will cease, will you not?) is *nonne desines?* but *nicht aufhören willst du* (will you not cease?) is *non desines?*

[3] [This combination of μή with the adverbial accusative τι (compare the Latin *numquid*) occurs frequently in the N. T., almost always in an interrogation. Properly signifying *in some respect, in any respect,* τι usually somewhat softens the question (*num fortasse*), sometimes apparently strengthens it (as it does the imperative,—e. g., in Æsch. *Sept. c. Th.* 686). We find εἰ μήτι in L. ix. 13, 1 C. vii. 5, 2 C. xiii. 5 (*Vulg.* : nisi forte): on μήτι γε see § 64. 6.—In the German renderings in this paragraph Winer is able to give the force of τι by the German *etwa* (*possibly, perchance*).]

[4] On the Latin *num* see Hand, *Tursell.* p. 320.

41

contested by Franke *l. c.* and others: in some passages of the N.T., however, this view has been taken,—see Lücke, *Joh.* I. 602, and compare Fritz. *Matt.* p. 432. But in every case the speaker frames his question for a negative reply, and would not be surprised if such were returned: Jo. iv. 33, *surely no one has brought him anything to eat?* (I cannot believe that, especially here in Samaria!): Jo. viii. 22, *he surely will not kill himself, will he?* (we cannot believe that of him). Compare Mt. xii. 23, Jo. iv. 29, vii. 26, 35. Here and there, indeed, there exists a disposition to believe that which is expressed in the question; but the speaker, in giving the question a negative cast, at all events assumes the appearance of desiring a negative reply.[1]—In Ja. iii. 14, also, εἰ ζῆλον πικρὸν ἔχετε . . . μὴ κατακαυχᾶσθε καὶ ψεύδεσθε κατὰ τῆς ἀληθείας, some have taken μή for *nonne,* but incorrectly: the sentence is categorical,—*do not boast* (of Christian wisdom, ver. 13) *against the truth.*

When μὴ οὐ appears in a question, οὐ belongs to the verb of the sentence, and μή alone expresses the interrogation: Rom. x. 18, μὴ οὐκ ἤκουσαν; *they have surely not been without hearing, have they?* Rom. x. 19, 1 C. ix. 4, 5, xi. 22 (Jud. vi. 13, xiv. 3, Jer. viii. 4, Xen. *Mem.* 4. 2. 12, Plat. *Meno* p. 89 c, *Lys.* 213 d, *Acta Apocr.* p. 79). On the other hand οὐ μή is merely a strengthened form of the simple negation, and is as admissible in a question as in any other sentence: Jo. xviii. 11, οὐ μὴ πίω αὐτό; *should I not drink it?* Arrian, *Epict.* 3. 22. 33. See § 56. 3.

In A. vii. 42 sq. (a quotation from Amos), μὴ σφάγια καὶ θυσίας προσηνέγκατέ μοι ἔτη τεσσαράκοντα ἐν τῇ ἐρήμῳ; *ye surely have not* (can ye have) *offered to me . . . . in the wilderness?* the speaker proceeds with καὶ ἀνελάβετε, because the meaning which the question conveys is, *Ye have offered to me no sacrifices during forty years, and have* (even) etc. A different explanation is given by Fritzsche (*Mark,* p. 66), for a refutation of which see Meyer *in loc.*

---

[1] [This observation, which accords with Jelf 873. 4. *Obs.* 2, Kühner II. 1024 (ed. 2), certainly seems to remove every difficulty. See also Don. p. 559, Rost p. 750, A. Buttm. p. 214, Meyer on Jo. iv. 29, Tholuck on Rom. iii. 5. In the last-mentioned passage Philippi is bold enough to propose the rendering "*Is not God unrighteous etc. ?*" but even those who speak of an affirmative answer as sometimes expected (Hermann, Krüger) venture on no other translation than that given above, *surely not?* Compare however Green p. 198 sqq.—On the alleged use of (the indirect interrogative) εἰ for εἰ μή in 1 C. vii. 16, see the notes of Meyer and Alford *in loc.*]

The original passage in Amos has not as yet been properly explained. Perhaps the prophet follows a tradition different from that contained in the Pentateuch.[1] On L. xviii. 7 see above, p. 620.

In Mt. vii. 9 [*Rec.*], τίς ἐστιν ἐξ ὑμῶν ἄνθρωπος, ὃν ἐὰν αἰτήσῃ ὁ υἱὸς αὐτοῦ ἄρτον, μὴ λίθον ἐπιδώσει αὐτῷ; there is a combination of two questions, *Who is there among you who . . . would give?* and *If any one were asked, he would surely not give?* (would he perchance give?) Compare L. xi. 11 and Bornemann *in loc.*[2]

Rem. As to Jo. xviii. 37 see especially Herm. *Vig.* p. 794. Οὔκουν is *non* (*nonne*) *ergo*, with or without an interrogation; οὐκοῦν is *ergo*, the negation being dropped. If then in this passage we were to read οὔκουν, interrogatively (οὔκουν βασιλεὺς εἶ σύ;), the meaning might be, *Art not thou then a king?* nonne ergo (Herm. *Vig.* p. 795) *rex es?* the speaker expecting an affirmative answer (in accordance with the words of Jesus ἡ βασιλεία ἡ ἐμή κ.τ.λ.): see no. 3. But οὐκοῦν, the reading received by the editors, is simpler,— οὐκοῦν βασιλεὺς εἶ σύ· *thou art then surely a king,* ergo rex es (perhaps with suppressed irony[3]), either without or with a question: Xen. *Cyr.* 2. 4. 15, 5. 2. 26, 29, Aristot. *Rhet.* 3. 18. 14, al. (This οὐκοῦν also was originally interrogative, *thou art a king, art thou not? is it not so?*[4] It is in this way that the particle obtained the meaning *then, consequently,* or *accordingly.*) In Jo. xviii. 37, as it seems to me, the words, in the mouth of the inquiring judge, are more suitably taken as a question; and they are thus explained by Lücke.[5] In any case, however, οὐκοῦν cannot be *non igitur,* as it is rendered by Kühnöl and Bretschneider: in this sense it would be necessary to write οὐκ οὖν.

---

[1] [On Amos v. 25 sq. and A. vii. 42 sq. see Pusey on Amos *l.c.,* Davidson, *Intr. to O. T.* III. 260, Smith, *Dict. of Bible* s. v. Remphan, Turpie, *The O. T. in the New,* p. 169 sqq.]

[2] [Bornemann remarks that Luke writes the latter part of the verse as if the protasis ἐὰν τὸν πατέρα αἰτήσῃ ὁ υἱὸς ἄρτον had preceded (compare ver. 12).]

[3] See Bremi, *Demosth.* p. 238.

[4] See Herm. *Vig.* p. 794 sq.; compare Ellendt, *Lexic. Soph.* II. 432 sq.— Rost (p. 747) and Gayler (p. 149) declare themselves against the plan of distinguishing by the accentuation.

[5] [Most are now agreed in writing οὐκοῦν βασιλεὺς εἶ σύ; Grimm (*Clavis* s. v.) prefers οὔκουν βασιλεὺς εἶ σύ; see Westcott's note.—Kühner has an excursus on this word in his edition of Xenoph. *Memor.* p. 513–523.]

B.

THE STRUCTURE OF SENTENCES, AND THE COMBINATION OF SENTENCES INTO PERIODS.

Section LVIII.

THE SENTENCE AND ITS ELEMENTS, IN GENERAL.

1. The essential elements of a simple sentence are the subject, the predicate, and the copula. As however the subject and the predicate may be completed and extended in a great variety of ways by means of adjuncts, so on the other hand we often find the predicate, sometimes the subject also, blended with the copula. The limits of the copula are never doubtful; but we are at times left in uncertainty what and how many words constitute the subject or the predicate (see Rom. i. 17, 2 C. i. 17, xi. 13, xiii. 7). Such a question as this belongs to hermeneutics, not to grammar.

The infinitive (by itself) where it stands for the imperative, as in Ph. iii. 16 (see § 43. 5), is an incomplete sentence; for here there is no grammatical indication of the subject, which in other cases is shown by the person of the verb.

2. As a rule, the subject and the predicate are nouns,—infinitives used as substantives being included under this name (Ph. i. 22, 29, 1 Th. iv. 3). Sometimes however they consist of an entire clause or sentence: L. xxii. 37, τὸ γεγραμμένον δεῖ τελεσθῆναι ἐν ἐμοί, τό· καὶ μετὰ ἀνόμων ἐλογίσθη· 1 Th. iv. 1, παρελάβετε παρ' ἡμῶν τὸ πῶς δεῖ ὑμᾶς περιπατεῖν· Mt. xv. 26, οὐκ ἔστιν καλὸν λαβεῖν τὸν ἄρτον τῶν τέκνων κ.τ.λ. The case of the subject is in independent sentences the nominative (in dependent, the accusative,—*accusativus cum infinitivo*); but by an ellipsis the partitive genitive may stand as the subject, as in A. xxi. 16 (§ 30. 8, Rem. 2). On the other hand, a use of ἐν as a *nota nominativi*, in imitation of the Hebrew בְּ *essentiæ*, is not to be thought of; the latter idiom is itself a grammatical figment (see § 29. Rem.).

The case in which the predicate consists of a participle with the article deserves special mention : Mt. x. 20, *οὐ γὰρ ὑμεῖς ἐστὲ οἱ λαλοῦντες·* Jo. v. 32, xiv. 28,[1] Ph. ii. 13, Rom. viii. 33, G. i. 7, al. This case must be carefully distinguished from that in which the participle is without the article (compare Matth. 270, Fritz. *Rom.* II. 212 sq.).

3. The copula regularly agrees in number, the predicate in both number and gender, with the subject. There is an exception to the latter rule when the predicate consists of a substantive ; for then the predicate may have a different gender and number from the subject. 2 C. i. 14, *καύχημα ὑμῶν ἐσμέν·* 1 Th. ii. 20, *ὑμεῖς ἐστὲ ἡ δόξα ἡμῶν καὶ ἡ χαρά·* Jo. xi. 25, *ἐγώ εἰμι ἡ ἀνάστασις καὶ ἡ ζωή·* viii. 12, 2 C. iii. 2, Rom. vii. 13, E. i. 23, *ἥτις (ἡ ἐκκλησία) ἐστὶ τὸ σῶμα αὐτοῦ* (see § 24. 3), 1 C. xi. 7, Col. iv. 11, L. xxii. 20.[2]

In regard to the copula also we meet with certain departures from the rule, even in prose, through the writer's allowing more influence to the *meaning* of the subject than to its grammatical *form*. This takes place in Greek more frequently than in Latin.

(*a*) A neuter plural is joined with a singular predicate (copula),—chiefly when the subjects are of a *material* nature, and consequently may be regarded as a mass :[3] Jo. x. 25, *τὰ ἔργα . . . μαρτυρεῖ περὶ ἐμοῦ·* 2 P. ii. 20, *γέγονεν αὐτοῖς τὰ ἔσχατα χείρονα τῶν πρώτων·* A. i. 18, xxvi. 24, Jo. ix. 3, x. 21, iii. 23, xix. 31, Rev. viii. 3.—But

(*a*) When the objects spoken of are intended to stand out prominently in their plurality and separateness (Weber, *Demosth.* p. 529), the predicate is in the plural : Jo. xix. 31, *ἵνα κατεαγῶσιν αὐτῶν* (of the three who were crucified) *τὰ σκέλη* (immediately preceded by *ἵνα μὴ μείνῃ τὰ σώματα*,—compare also Jo. vi. 13,[4] Rev. xxi. 12, xx. 7, Xen. *An.* 1. 7. 17). Other-

---

[1] [A mistake, probably for xiv. 21.]
[2] The case in which the neuter has a contemptuous force (as in 1 C. vi. 11, *ταῦτά τινες ἦτε*) must, grammatically considered, be brought in here. [On this passage see § 23. 5.]
[3] Bernh. p. 418, Matt. 300. [Don. p. 399, Jelf 384 sq., Farrar, *Gr. Synt.* p. 59 sq. : for the N. T., Green p. 187, Webster p. 50 sq., A. Buttm. p. 125 sq. In modern Greek neuter plurals regularly take a plural verb : see J. Donaldson, *Gr.* p. 33.]
[4] [Here Winer reads *ἐπερίσσευσαν* (see ed. 5, p. 419), with Tischendorf and others. In the passages next quoted, however, the singular is certainly the true reading : indeed in Rev. xxi. 12 there is no variant.]

wise the plural¹ is rare : 1 Tim. v. 25, τὰ ἄλλως ἔχοντα (ἔργα) κρυβῆναι οὐ δύνανται· Rev. i. 19, ἃ εἶδες καὶ ἃ εἰσίν (but immediately afterwards ἃ μέλλει γίνεσθαι), Rev. xvi. 20, L. xxiv. 11, —but not Rom. iii. 2 (see § 39. 1). Singular and plural stand side by side in 2 P. iii. 10.² This use of the plural verb is not uncommon in Greek writers (Rost p. 470, Kühner II. 50), especially where instead of the neuter noun some other substantive of the masculine or feminine gender may have been in the writer's mind ;³—though not in such cases only, compare Xen. *Cyr.* 2. 2. 2, *An.* 1. 4. 4, *Hipparch.* 8. 6, Thuc. 6. 62, Æl. *Anim.* 11. 37, Plat. *Rep.* 1. 353 c.

(β) When however the neuter noun denotes or implies *animate* objects, especially persons, the plural of the predicate is almost always used : Mt. x. 21, ἐπαναστήσονται τέκνα ἐπὶ γονεῖς καὶ θανατώσουσιν αὐτούς· Ja. ii. 19, τὰ δαιμόνια πιστεύουσιν καὶ φρίσσουσιν· Jo. x. 8, οὐκ ἤκουσαν αὐτῶν τὰ πρόβατα· Mk. iii. 11, v. 13, vii. 28, Mt. vi. 26, xii. 21, 2 Tim. iv. 17, Rev. iii. 2,⁴ 4, xi. 13, 18, xvi. 14, xix. 21 (Mt. xxvii. 52, πολλὰ σώματα τῶν κεκοιμημένων ἁγίων ἠγέρθησαν). In other passages the MSS. vary remarkably, and the singular has a preponderance of authority in Mk. iv. 4, L. iv. 41, viii. 38,⁵ xiii. 19, Jo. x. 12, 1 Jo. iv. 1, Rev. xviii. 3. In L. viii. 2, indeed, we find without any variant ἀφ' ἧς δαιμόνια ἑπτὰ ἐξεληλύθει· viii. 30, εἰςῆλθεν δαιμόνια πολλά· 1 Jo. iii. 10, φανερά ἐστιν τὰ τέκνα τοῦ θεοῦ καὶ τὰ τέκνα τοῦ διαβόλου. Compare further E. iv. 17, Rom. ix. 8. Singular and plural are combined in Jo. x. 4, τὰ πρόβατα αὐτῷ ἀκολουθεῖ, ὅτι οἴδασιν τὴν φωνὴν αὐτοῦ· x. 27, τὰ πρόβατα τῆς φωνῆς μου ἀκούει⁶ καὶ ἀκολουθοῦσίν μοι· Rev. xvi. 14 : compare 1 S. ix. 12. In Rev. xvii. 12, τὰ δέκα κέρατα δέκα βασιλεῖς εἰσίν, the noun of the predicate made the plural appear the more suitable number for the verb : compare 1 C. x. 11.

---

¹ [That is, when *material* objects are spoken of.]
² [The best texts have the singular twice.]
³ Herm. Soph. *El.* p. 67, Poppo, *Thuc.* I. i. 97 sq., *Cyrop.* p. 116 : see however Schneider, Plat. *Civ.* I. 93.
⁴ [Τὰ λοιπά being explained of *persons*. On this see Alford *in loc.*]
⁵ [In L. viii. 38, 1 Jo. iv. 1, there is no variation of reading. L. viii. 30 should come in here rather than below : the singular is the true reading, but the plural is a variant.]
⁶ [The plural is more probable here : in 1 C. x. 11, quoted in the following sentence, we should read συνέβαινεν.]

SECT. LVIII.] THE SENTENCE AND ITS ELEMENTS, IN GENERAL. 647

With Greek authors also the rule is to use the plural when animate objects are spoken of. Compare Xen. *Cyr.* 2. 3. 9, τὰ ζῶα ἐπίστανται· Plat. *Lach.* 180 e, τὰ μειράκια ἐπιμέμνηνται· Thuc. 1. 58, 4. 88, 7. 57, Eur. *Bacch.* 677 sq., Arrian, *Alex.* 3. 28. 11, 5. 17. 12: see Herm. *Vig.* p. 739.

The construction of neuters with a plural verb is found in Greek prose generally more frequently than is usually supposed, though certainly there is great variation in the MSS.[1] It is by later writers, however, that it is mainly used, and that without any discrimination of meaning: see Agath. 4. 5, 9. 15, 26. 9, 28. 1, 32. 6, 39. 10, 42. 6, al., Thilo, *Apocr.* I. 182, Boisson. *Psell.* p. 257 sq., Dressel, *Index* to Epiphan. Monach. p. 136. Jacobs's proposal[2] to correct all such passages, substituting the singular for the plural, he himself seems subsequently to have retracted;[3] where however MSS. have the singular, we should perhaps (with Boisson. *Eunap.* p. 420, 601) give it the preference in the better writers.

What has been said respecting the singular predicate after neuter nouns applies to the verbal form only. If the predicate consists of εἶναι or γίνεσθαι with an adjective, the latter stands in the plural, even though the verb may be singular: G. v. 19, φανερά ἐστιν τὰ ἔργα τῆς σαρκός· 1 C. xiv. 25, τὰ κρυπτὰ τῆς καρδίας αὐτοῦ φανερὰ γίνεται.

4. (*b*) Collectives which denote living beings have the predicate in the plural: Mt. xxi. 8, ὁ πλεῖστος ὄχλος ἔστρωσαν ἑαυτῶν τὰ ἱμάτια (Mk. ix. 15, L. vi. 19, xxiii. 1), 1 C. xvi. 15, οἴδατε τὴν οἰκίαν Στεφανᾶ, ὅτι . . . . εἰς διακονίαν τοῖς ἁγίοις ἔταξαν ἑαυτούς· Rev. xviii. 4, ἐξέλθετε ἐξ αὐτῆς, ὁ λαός μου (Hesiod, *Scut.* 327), also Rev. ix. 18, ἀπεκτάνθησαν τὸ τρίτον τῶν ἀνθρώπων· viii. 9 (contrast the singular in viii. 8 sq., 11), L. viii. 37,[4] A. xxv. 24. In other passages we find the plural and singular of the verb or predicate combined: Jo. vi. 2, ἠκολούθει αὐτῷ ὄχλος πολύς, ὅτι ἑώρων (xii. 9, 12 sq., 18), L. i. 21, ἦν ὁ λαὸς προσδοκῶν καὶ ἐθαύμαζον· A. xv. 12 (1 C. xvi. 15). We have the plural in relation to a collective in L. ix. 12, ἀπόλυσον τὸν ὄχλον, ἵνα ἀπελθόντες . . . καταλύσωσι κ.τ.λ. When the predicate consists of an adjective with εἶναι, this adjective not only stands in the plural, but also naturally receives

---

[1] Reitz, *Lucian* VII. 483 (Bip.), Ast, Plat. *Legg.* p. 46, Zell, Aristot. *Ethic. Nicom.* p. 4, 209, Bremi, *Lys.* exc. 10. p. 448 sq., Held, Plut. *Æm. P.* p. 280, Ellendt, *Præf. ad Arrian.* I. 21 sq., Bornem. Xen. *Cyrop.* p. 173.
[2] Jacobs, *Athen.* p. 228 : comp. also Heind. *Cratyl.* p. 137.
[3] Compare Jacobs, Philostr. *Imag.* p. 236.
[4] [The singular is supported by the best MSS. in this passage. In A. xxv. 24 the reading is not certain.]

the gender of the personal noun, as in Jo. vii. 49, ὁ ὄχλος οὗτος
... ἐπάρατοί εἰσιν. Attributives in this construction, however, may stand either in the plural or in the singular—the latter when they *precede* the substantive; Mk. ix. 15, πᾶς ὁ ὄχλος ἰδόντες ... ἐξεθαμβήθησαν (L. xix. 37, A. v. 16, xxi. 36, xxv. 24), L. xxiii. 1, ἀναστὰν ἅπαν τὸ πλῆθος ἤγαγον αὐτόν. Still the regular construction of collectives with a singular predicate is more commonly adopted by the N. T. writers.

In the LXX collectives are often joined with a plural predicate; see Jud. ii. 10, Ruth. iv. 11, 1 S. xii. 18 sq., 1 K. iii. 2, viii. 66, xii. 12, Is. li. 4, Judith vi. 18 : λαός almost always has a plural verb. In Greek authors, too, the usage is far from uncommon: see Her. 9. 23, ὥς σφι τὸ πλῆθος ἐπεβοήθησαν· Philostr. *Her.* p. 709, ὁ στρατὸς ἄθυμοι ἦσαν· Thuc. 1. 20, 4. 128, Xen. *Mem.* 4. 3. 10, Ælian, *Anim.* 5. 54, Plutarch, *Mar.* p. 418 c, Pausan. 7. 9. 3.[1] (Don. p. 399, Jelf 378.)

A substantially similar instance is 1 Tim. ii. 15, σωθήσεται δὲ (ἡ γυνὴ) διὰ τῆς τεκνογονίας, ἐὰν μείνωσιν (αἱ γυναῖκες) ἐν πίστει ; for the subject which we have to supply, ἡ γυνή, is to be understood of the whole race of women. But in Jo. xvi. 32, ἵνα σκορπισθῆτε ἕκαστος εἰς τὰ ἴδια, the plural verb is not directly the predicate of ἕκαστος, but ἕκαστος is an explanatory adjunct to the plural ; as in A. ii. 6, ἤκουον εἷς ἕκαστος τῇ ἰδίᾳ διαλέκτῳ· Rev. xx. 13 (v. 8), 1 P. iv. 10, A. xi. 29. See Hes. *Scut.* 283, Ælian, *Anim.* 15. 5, *Var. Hist.* 14. 46.[2] A. ii. 12 is similar, as also is 1 C. iv. 6, ἵνα μὴ εἷς ὑπὲρ τοῦ ἑνὸς φυσιοῦσθε κατὰ τοῦ ἑτέρου. On the other hand, in A. ii. 3 ἐφ' ἕνα ἕκαστον αὐτῶν indicates the singular subject of ἐκάθισεν,—for ἐκάθισαν is an obvious correction, to bring the verb into conformity with ὤφθησαν. Other examples of a transition from the plural to the singular of the verb are collected by Heindorf, Plat. *Protag.* p. 499, and Jacobs, Æl. *Anim.* II. 100.

The gender only of the predicate is affected by the collectives in L. x. 13, εἰ ἐν Τύρῳ καὶ Σιδῶνι ἐγενήθησαν αἱ δυνάμεις ... πάλαι ἂν ἐν σάκκῳ καθήμενοι (*the inhabitants*) μετενόησαν.

Rem. 1. L. ix. 28, ἐγένετο ... ὡςεὶ ἡμέραι ὀκτώ, has by some been considered an example of the *Schema Pindaricum*,[3] in which a singular verb is joined with a plural subject (masculine or feminine), the verb *preceding* the subject : here however ἐγένετο is to

---

[1] See Reitz, *Lucian*, VI. 533 (Lehm.), Jacobs, *Achill. Tat.* p. 446, Krüger, *Dion. H.* p. 234, Poppo, *Thuc.* III. i. 529 sq., Ellendt, Arr. *Alex.* I. 105.

[2] Wesseling, *Diod. Sic.* II. 105, Brunck, Aristoph. *Plut.* 784, Jacobs, *Achill. Tat.* p. 622 (Don. p. 372, Jelf 478).

[3] Matth. 303, Herm. Soph. *Trach.* p. 86 (Don. p. 399, Jelf 386. 1). [In Rev. ix. 12 we must now read ἔρχεται ἔτι δύο οὐαί. See A. Buttm. p. 126.]

be taken by itself, and the note of time ὡςεὶ ἡμέραι ὀκτώ is a structureless clause introduced parenthetically (see § 62. 2). *Vice versa*, in L. ix. 13 εἰσίν must not be taken with πλεῖον; the latter word is parenthetical and without construction (compare Xen. *An.* 1. 2. 11), and εἰσίν belongs to ἄρτοι.

That there is no disturbance of the construction when the imperative ἄγε, which is almost a mere interjection, is found in conjunction with a plural subject, is obvious : Ja. iv. 13, ἄγε νῦν οἱ λέγοντες· v. 1, ἄγε νῦν οἱ πλούσιοι. This usage is common in Greek prose e. g., Xen. *Cyr.* 4. 2. 47, 5. 3. 4, *Apol.* 14 :[1] the Latin *age* is similar (Hand, *Tursell.* I. 205). The same construction is found with φέρε (Himer. *Orat.* 17. 6).

Rem. 2. A word may here be said on the use of a plural verb or pronoun by a single speaker in reference to himself (Glass I. 320 sqq.). The communicative meaning is still manifest in Mk. iv. 30, πῶς ὁμοιώσωμεν τὴν βασιλείαν τοῦ θεοῦ ἢ ἐν τίνι αὐτὴν παραβολῇ θῶμεν; Jo. iii. 11. The plural occurs much more frequently in the Epistles (as among the Romans *scripsimus, misimus*), where the writer is speaking of himself as apostle : Rom. i. 5 (compare ver. 6),[2] Col. iv. 3 (immediately followed by δέδεμαι [3]), H. xiii. 18 (comp. ver. 19), G. i. 8. From such passages we must distinguish those in which the writer really includes others with himself, though it will be difficult in detail to determine when this is the case, and to what persons he is referring; in any case the question is not one which grammar can decide. In E. i. 3 sqq. and 1 C. iv. 9, however, we have without doubt true plurals. On Jo. xxi. 24 see Meyer.[4] (Jelf 390. 1.)

In 1 C. xv. 31, with the reading καθ᾽ ἡμέραν ἀποθνήσκω, νὴ τὴν ἡμετέραν καύχησιν, ἣν ἔχω, we should have singular and plural combined ; but ὑμετέραν is certainly the preferable reading.

5. We cannot say that there is any grammatical discordance between predicate and subject in such sentences as Mt. vi. 34, ἀρκετὸν τῇ ἡμέρᾳ ἡ κακία αὐτῆς· 2 C. ii. 6, ἱκανὸν τῷ τοιούτῳ ἡ ἐπιτιμία αὕτη. Here the neuter is used as a substantive, *a sufficiency for such a man as this;* like Virg. *Ecl.* 3. 80, triste lupus stabulis, *a sad thing for stalls.*[5] For examples in Greek writers see Her. 3. 36, σοφὸν ἡ προμηθίη· Xen. *Hier.* 6. 9, ὁ

---

[1] Compare Alberti, *Observ. on Ja.* iv. 13, Palairet, *Observ.* p. 502 sq., Wetstein II. 676, Bornem. Xen. *Apol.* p. 52 (Jelf 390. 2). [Compare ἴδε, νῦν ἠκούσατε, Mt. xxvi. 65 (A. Buttm. p. 70).]
[2] Van Hengel takes a different view, *Rom.* p. 52.
[3] [Does not this singular really tell the other way? See Meyer, Ellicott, Alford, Eadie, on this passage and on Col. i. 3. See also Delitzsch and Alford on H. xiii. 18 ; Lightfoot on G. i. 8, Col. iv. 3 ; Gifford on Rom. i. 5.]
[4] [See Westcott's note *in loc.*, and his *Introd.* p. xxxv.]
[5] Ast, Plat. *Polit.* p. 413, Herm. *Vig.* p. 699.

650 THE SENTENCE AND ITS ELEMENTS, IN GENERAL. [PART III.

πόλεμος φοβερόν· Diog. L. 1. 98, καλὸν ἡσυχία· Xen. Mem. 2. 3. 1, Plat. Legg. 4. 707 a, Plut. Pædagog. 4. 3, Lucian, Philops. 7, Isocr. Demon. p. 8, Plat. Conviv. p. 176 d, Aristot. Rhet. 2. 2. 46, Eth. Nic. 8. 1. 3, Lucian, Fug. 13, Plut. Mul. Virt. p. 225 (Tauchn.), Ælian, Anim. 2. 10, Dio Chr. 40. 494, Sext. Emp. Math. 11. 96. Compare Kühner, Gr. II. 45 [1] (Don. p. 398, Jelf 381). In Latin compare Ovid, Amor. 1. 9. 4, Cic. Off. 1. 4, Famil. 6. 21, Virg. Ecl. 3. 82, Æn. 4. 569, Stat. Theb. 2. 399, Vechner, Hellenol. p. 247 sqq.—On the rhetorical emphasis which occasionally attaches itself to this use of the neuter, see Dissen, Demosth. Cor. p. 396.

Of a different kind, but also deserving of notice, is 1 P. ii. 19, τοῦτο γὰρ χάρις. Compare τοῦτό ἐστιν ἀνάμνησις, Demosth., and Schæfer in loc. (Appar. V. 289), Hermann, Luc. Conscr. Hist. p. 305.

6. If the subject or the predicate [2] or both be complex (Matth. 299, Don. p. 400, Jelf 391 sqq.), the grammatical form of the predicate will be determined by the following rules:—

a. If the subject consist of words of the 1 and 3 person, the verb will stand in the 1 person plural: Jo. x. 30, ἐγὼ καὶ ὁ πατὴρ ἕν ἐσμεν· 1 C. ix. 6, ἢ μόνος ἐγὼ καὶ Βαρνάβας οὐκ ἔχομεν ἐξουσίαν κ.τ.λ. (1 C. xv. 11), Mt. ix. 14, L. ii. 48 (Eurip. Med. 1020). Only in G. i. 8 we find ἐὰν ἡμεῖς ἢ ἄγγελος ἐξ οὐρανοῦ εὐαγγελίζηται, the latter being regarded as the more exalted subject [3] (Isæus 11. 10). When to the 2 person there is joined a word of the 3 person, the former receives the preference as the more important, and the verb (placed *first*) stands in the 2 person: A. xvi. 31, σωθήσῃ σὺ καὶ ὁ οἶκός σου· xi. 14.

b. When the various singular subjects are of the 3 person, or are not names of persons,

(a) If the predicate *follows*, it regularly stands in the plural: A. iii. 1, Πέτρος καὶ Ἰωάννης ἀνέβαινον· iv. 19, xii. 25, xiii. 46, xiv. 14, xv. 35, xvi. 25, xxv. 13, 1 C. xv. 50, Ja. ii. 15.[4] If

---

[1] Compare Georgi, Hierocr. I. 51, Wetstein I. 337, Kypke, Obs. I. 40, Fischer, Well. III. a. p. 310 sq., Elmsley, Eur. Med. p. 237 (ed. Lips.), Held, Plut. Timol. p. 367 sq., Waitz, Aristot. Categ. p. 292.
[2] [It is hard to see why Winer adds "or the predicate," unless perhaps to include the case in which the copula agrees with the predicate instead of the subject (Don. p. 400, Jelf 389).]
[3] [Unless we ascribe the singular to the influence of ἤ (A. Buttm. p. 127).]
[4] [In this passage the plural follows two subjects connected by ἤ.]

one of the subjects is masculine, the predicate takes its gender from this subject (2 P. iii. 7). A common attributive is sometimes joined in construction with one subject only, either the first or the chief; see A. v. 29, ἀποκριθεὶς[1] Πέτρος καὶ οἱ ἀπόστολοι εἶπαν. Where this is not the case (as in A. iv. 19), if the nouns are of different genders, the attributive is masculine, e.g. A. xxv. 13, Ἀγρίππας καὶ Βερνίκη κατήντησαν . . . ἀσπασάμενοι τὸν Φῆστον· Ja. ii. 15. We also find a singular predicate when a number of subjects are connected by the disjunctive ἤ: Mt. v. 18, xii. 25, xviii. 8, E. v. 5.

(β) If the predicate *precedes*, it may stand either

1. In the plural, the writer having already before his mind a plurality of subjects; e. g., Mk. x. 35, προσπορεύονται αὐτῷ Ἰάκωβος καὶ Ἰωάννης· Jo. xxi. 2. Hence with καί . . . καί or τε . . . καί; L. xxiii. 12, ἐγένοντο φίλοι ὅ τε Πιλᾶτος καὶ ὁ Ἡρώδης (A. i. 13, iv. 27, v. 24, viii. 5 [2]), Tit. i. 15, μεμίανται[3] αὐτῶν καὶ ὁ νοῦς καὶ ἡ συνείδησις. Or,

2. In the singular, if the subjects are intended to be conceived singly, as in 1 Tim. vi. 4, ἐξ ὧν γίνεται φθόνος, ἔρις, βλασφημίαι, κ.τ.λ., Rev. ix. 17,[4] 1 C. xiv. 24, ἐὰν εἰσέλθῃ τις ἄπιστος ἢ ἰδιώτης (so usually when the disjunctive ἤ comes between the subjects, 1 C. vii. 15, 1 P. iv. 15 [5]), A. v. 38, xx. 4, 1 C. vii. 34,—or if the first subject only, usually as the principal subject, is in the first instance taken into consideration. For the latter case, Jo. ii. 2, ἐκλήθη (καὶ) ὁ Ἰησοῦς καὶ οἱ μαθηταὶ αὐτοῦ· iv. 53, viii. 52,[6] xviii. 15, xx. 3, A. xxvi. 30, L. xxii. 14, Mt. xii. 3, Phil. 23, Rev. i. 3, xii. 7, al.; Plat. *Theag.* 124 e, Paus. 9. 13. 3, 9. 36. 1, Diod. S. *Exc. Vat.* p. 25, Madvig 2. A participle or adjective belonging to the predicate stands in the plural: L. ii. 33, ἦν ὁ

---

[1] [Others explain this singular as referring to the fact that Peter was the only actual speaker: see Meyer and Alford *in loc.*, A. Buttm. p. 127.]

[2] [This should probably be xviii. 5.]

[3] [Winer takes this as plural, and A. Buttm. (p. 41) inclines to the same opinion: Krüger (p. 120) quotes κέκλινται from Xen. *De re eq.* 5. 2 (leg. 5. 5), κέκρινται from Demosth. *Androt.* 66, *Timocr.* 173; see also Paley on Æsch. *Pers.* 574, Jelf 224. 3. *Obs.* 3.—Ordinarily the word is taken as singular.]

[4] Thuc. 1. 47, Plat. *Gorg.* 503 e, 517 d, Lucian, *Dial. Mort.* 26. 1, Quint. *Inst.* 9. 4. 22.

[5] [This is not an example.]

[6] [In this passage, and in Jo. iv. 12, L. viii. 22 (quoted below as examples of αὐτὸς καί), the verb does not stand first, but comes between the first subject (which is in the singular number) and the rest. In L. xxii. 14, Mt. xii. 3, the first subject is not expressed, but is included in the person of the verb.]

πατὴρ αὐτοῦ καὶ ἡ μήτηρ θαυμάζοντες· Rev. viii. 7. On the whole subject compare Viger p. 194, D'Orville, *Charit.* 497, Schoemann, *Isæus* 462. When the subjects are connected by ἤ, Greek writers usually place the verb in the plural,[1] just as with ἄλλος ἄλλῳ and the like :[2] the distinction which Matthiæ[3] makes between the use of the two numbers (in connexion with ἤ) is not perceptible, at all events in the N. T.—In A. xxiii. 9, εἰ δὲ πνεῦμα ἐλάλησεν αὐτῷ ἢ ἄγγελος . . ., the singular is quite in order, as the words are arranged.

In the following examples one subject receives the most decided prominence among the rest : Jo. ii. 12, κατέβη εἰς Καφαρναοὺμ αὐτὸς καὶ οἱ μαθηταὶ αὐτοῦ· iv. 12, 53, L. vi. 3, viii. 22, A. vii. 15 ; here the singular predicate needs no justification. This mode of expression is of frequent occurrence in Hebrew (Gesen. *Lehrg.* p. 722), but even in the form αὐτός τε καί or καὶ αὐτὸς καί, Ruth i. 3, 6—is not uncommon in Greek writers.[4] Compare Demosth. *Euerg.* 688 a, εἰ διομεῖ ἐπὶ Παλλαδίῳ αὐτὸς καὶ ἡ γυνὴ καὶ τὰ παιδία κ.τ.λ. ; Alciphr. 1. 24, ὡς ἂν ἔχοιμι σώζεσθαι αὐτὸς καὶ ἡ γυνὴ καὶ τὰ παιδία.

7. When several subjects or predicates are combined in one sentence, and joined by a copulative particle, the simplest arrangement is when this particle is placed before the last only of the connected words. On the other hand, the disjunctive ἤ must be repeated before each of the words after the first: Mt. vi. 31, τί φάγωμεν ἢ τί πίωμεν ἢ τί περιβαλώμεθα ; L. xviii. 29, ὃς ἀφῆκεν οἰκίαν ἢ γυναῖκα ἢ ἀδελφοὺς ἢ γονεῖς ἢ τέκνα. The same repetition is also found sometimes with the copulative; e.g., Rom. ii. 7, τοῖς δόξαν καί τιμὴν καὶ ἀφθαρσίαν ζητοῦσι· xi. 33,[5] xii. 2 (Lucian, *Nigr.* 17). See Fritz. *Rom.* II. 553. Where such a series of words is introduced by ὡς, this word is brought in once only, at the beginning. In 1 P. iv. 15, however, by the repetition of ὡς before ἀλλοτριοεπίσκοπος this predicate is separated from those which precede, and stands out as distinct. It is not uncommon to find the copulative particle thus repeated before every word in a whole series (*polysyndeton*). Sometimes this is a mere reflexion of the Hebrew mode of expression (Ewald,

---

[1] Compare Porson, Eurip. *Hec.* p. 12 (Lips.), Schæf. *Melet.* p. 24, Schoem. *Isæus* p. 295.
[2] See Jacobs, *Philostr.* p. 377 (Jelf 478).
[3] Matthiæ, Eurip. *Hec.* 84, *Sprachl.* 304. Rem. 3. [Nearly the same view is taken by Jelf 393. 3. 8.]
[4] Matthiæ, Eur. *Iph. A.* 875, Weber, *Dem.* p. 261, Fritz. *Mark*, p. 70, 420.
[5] [The three genitives being taken as co-ordinate.—In Rom. xii. 2, al., the single article renders the repetition of καί necessary.]

SECT. LVIII.] THE SENTENCE AND ITS ELEMENTS, IN GENERAL. 653

Kr. Gr. p. 650); as in Mt. xxiii. 23, Rev. xvii. 15, xviii. 12, xxi. 8. Sometimes, however, the repetition seems intentionally adopted, securing to each particular notion its proper force. See Rom. vii. 12, ἡ ἐντολὴ ἁγία καὶ δικαία καὶ ἀγαθή· ix. 4, ὧν ἡ υἱοθεσία καὶ ἡ δόξα καὶ αἱ διαθῆκαι καὶ ἡ νομοθεσία καὶ ἡ λατρεία καὶ αἱ ἐπαγγελίαι· L. xiv. 21, τοὺς πτωχοὺς καὶ ἀναπήρους καὶ τυφλοὺς καὶ χωλοὺς εἰςάγαγε· 1 P. i. 4, iii. 8,[1] Jo. xvi. 8, A. xv. 20, 29, xxi. 25, Ph. iv. 12, Rev. ii. 19, v. 12, vii. 9, 12, viii. 5, Philostr. *Apoll.* 6. 24, Diod. S. *Exc. Vat.* p. 32. So especially with proper names: A. i. 26, xiii. 1, xx. 4, Mt. iv. 25, Jo. xxi. 2.

On the other hand, we sometimes find the copulative particle entirely omitted between the different parts of a sentence—*asyndeton* (Jelf 792, Don. p. 609):—

(*a*) In enumerations: 2 Tim. iii. 2, ἔσονται οἱ ἄνθρωποι φίλαυτοι, φιλάργυροι, ἀλάζονες, ὑπερήφανοι, βλάσφημοι, κ.τ.λ., 1 C. iii. 12, ἐποικοδομεῖ ἐπὶ τὸν θεμέλιον χρυσόν, ἄργυρον, λίθους τιμίους, ξύλα, χόρτον, καλάμην· 1 P. iv. 3, H. xi. 37, 1 Tim. i. 10, iv. 13, 15 (Cic. *Fam.* 2. 5, *Attic.* 13. 13), Rom. i. 29 sqq., ii. 19, Ph. iii. 5, Jo. v. 3, 1 C. xiii. 4–8, xiv. 26, [Tit.] ii. 4 sq., Ja. v. 6, 1 P. ii. 9, Mt. xv. 19. (Col. iii. 11 is peculiar.) Similarly in Demosth. *Phil.* 4. p. 54 a, *Pantæn.* p. 626 a, Plat. *Gorg.* p. 503 e, 517 d, *Rep.* 10. p. 598 c, Lycurg. 36. 2, Lucian, *Dial. Mort.* 26. 2, Heliod. 1. 5.

(*b*) In contrasts and antitheses, which thus obtain greater prominence: 2 Tim. iv. 2, ἐπίστηθι εὐκαίρως ἀκαίρως (like *nolens volens, honesta turpia, digni indigni,* ἄνω κάτω, Aristoph. *Ran.* 157, ἀνδρῶν γυναικῶν[2]), 1 C. iii. 2, γάλα ὑμᾶς ἐπότισα, οὐ βρῶμα· vii. 12, Jo. x. 16, Ja. i. 19. But the asyndeton is not necessary in such cases, see Col. ii. 8, 1 C. x. 20; compare Fritz. *Mark,* p. 31 sq., though, as it seems to me, too subtle a distinction is there drawn between the two modes of expression.[3]

Where plurals are found amongst the various subjects, the verb which follows is plural, A. v. 17, 29. This is not however necessarily the case; see Diod. S. 20. 72, δάκρυα καὶ δεήσεις καὶ θρῆνος ἐγένετο συμφορητός· Xen. *Rep. Ath.* 1. 2.

Rem. When several substantives, either in the subject or in

---

[1] [An example of *asyndeton*.—For A. i. 26 (line 10) read A. i. 13.]
[2] Beier, Cic. *Off.* I. 135, Kritz, *Sall.* I. 55, II. 323.
[3] [Defending καί in Mk. i. 22, Fritzsche says: Optime enim comparata est copula in tali loco, ubi exponitur de rebus *diversis* potius, quam *plane oppositis.*]

the predicate, are connected by καί, the first sometimes denotes an individual which is included in the second as its *genus*, e.g., Ζεὺς καὶ θεοί. Hence λοιποί has been supplied with the second word; but this mode of expression is adopted for the sake of giving prominence to one individual out of the whole mass, as the principal subject: A. v. 29, ὁ Πέτρος καὶ οἱ ἀπόστολοι (Theodoret III. 223, see Schæf. *Soph.* II. 314, 335), i. 14, Mk. xvi. 7, Mt. xvi. 14 (see however Meyer *in loc.*¹). Compare Mk. x. 41.

In Greek writers this Schema κατ' ἐξοχήν (Lob. *Soph. Ajax* p. 221) is an established usage. Compare Plat. *Protag.* p. 310 d, ὦ Ζεῦ καὶ θεοί (Plaut. *Capt.* 5. 1. 1, Jovi diisque ago gratias), *Iliad* 19. 63, Ἕκτορι καὶ Τρωσί· Æschin. *Timarch.* p. 171 c, Σόλων ἐκεῖνος, ὁ παλαιὸς νομοθέτης, καὶ ὁ Δράκων καὶ οἱ κατὰ τοὺς χρόνους ἐκείνους νομοθέται· Aristoph. *Nub.* 412 (Cic. *Tusc.* 4. 5. 9, Chrysippus et Stoici).² On Eurip. *Med.* 1141, considered by Elmsley an example of this idiom, see Herm. *Med.* p. 392 (ed. Lips.), and also Locella, *Xen. Ephes.* p. 208. (Of a different kind, and yet akin to this, is the Latin *exercitus equitatusque*, Cæs. *Bell. Gall.* 2. 11.)

8. If two predicate-verbs have a common object, this object is expressed once only if the two verbs govern the same case: L. xiv. 4, ἰάσατο αὐτὸν καὶ ἀπέλυσεν· Mt. iv. 11. In Greek authors the object is regularly expressed but once even when the verbs govern different cases (Krüg. p. 259): here the N. T. writers commonly repeat the object in the form of a pronoun, as in L. xvi. 2, φωνήσας αὐτὸν εἶπεν αὐτῷ. Compare, however, A. xiii. 3, ἐπιθέντες τὰς χεῖρας αὐτοῖς ἀπέλυσαν· E. v. 11, μὴ συγκοινωνεῖτε τοῖς ἔργοις τοῖς ἀκάρποις, μᾶλλον δὲ ἐλέγχετε· 2 Th. iii. 15, 1 Tim. vi. 2. See § 22. 1.

9. Of the three elements of the sentence the subject and the predicate are indispensable, whereas the simple copula is implied in the juxta-position of the subject and the predicate: thus ὁ θεὸς σοφός in Greek can only mean *God is wise*. So also where subject and predicate are enlarged, as in H. v. 13, πᾶς ὁ μετέχων γάλακτος ἄπειρος λόγου δικαιοσύνης· 2 C. i. 21, Rom. xi. 15 (see § 64. 2). But as the predicate usually blends with the copula, so may the subject be included in the copula, or in the copula blended with the predicate. This takes place—apart from any particular context—in the following cases:—

---

¹ [Meyer opposes Fritzsche's assertion that ἄλλον is to be supplied after ἵνα (τῶν προφητῶν): others had named particular prophets, this speaker says generally *one of the prophets.*—I have changed Mk. x. 14 into x. 41, from ed. 5 (p. 670): the reference is to οἱ δέκα (οἱ λοιποὶ δέκα in D).]

² See Ast, Theophr. *Char.* p. 120, Stallb. Plat. *Protag.* p. 25. [Bernh. p. 48 sq., Matth. 430. 8, Jelf 899. 5, Riddell, Plat. *Apol.* p. 215.]

(a) When the verb is of the 1 or 2 person, the subject is commonly left unexpressed (being thought of as present, Madvig 6 a): Jo. xix. 22, ὃ γέγραφα, γέγραφα· Rom. viii. 15, οὐκ ἐλάβετε πνεῦμα δουλείας. Indeed the pronouns ἐγώ, σύ, κ.τ.λ., are only inserted when emphasis is designed (§ 22. 6). If the name of the subject is appended to the pronoun of the 1 or 2 person, this is a case of apposition: G. v. 2, ἐγὼ Παῦλος λέγω ὑμῖν (E. iii. 1, Rom. xvi. 22, 2 C. x. 1, Phil. 19, Rev. i. 9, xxii. 8, al.), G. ii. 15,[1] ἡμεῖς φύσει Ἰουδαῖοι . . . εἰς Χριστὸν Ἰησοῦν ἐπιστεύσαμεν (2 C. iv. 11), L. xi. 39.

(b) In the 3 person (impersonally): viz.—

(a) The 3 plural active, where merely the general (acting) subjects are intended (Madvig 6 b). See Mt. vii. 16, μήτι συλλέγουσιν ἀπὸ ἀκανθῶν σταφυλήν; *surely they* (people) *do not gather? surely one does not gather?* Jo. xv. 6, xx. 2, Mk. x. 13, A. iii. 2, L. xvii. 23, Rev. xii. 6.[2]

(β) The 3 singular active, where there is before the mind no definite subject (Madv. 7 a) of which the verb is predicated, and where merely the existence of the action or state implied in the verb is indicated.[3] Thus ὕει, βροντᾷ (in Jo. xii. 29, βροντὴ γίνεται), *it rains*, etc. (like our *es läutet*); 1 C. xv. 52, σαλπίσει, *it will sound, one will sound the trumpet;* also 2 C. x. 10, αἱ ἐπιστολαί, φησί, βαρεῖαι, *it is said* (Wisd. xv. 12[4]). Yet in the concrete conception of the Greeks these expressions may have been elliptical in the first instance: ὕει, βροντᾷ Ζεύς (Xen. *Hell.* 4. 7. 4), σαλπίσει ὁ σαλπιγκτής, like the ἀναγνώσεται of the orators. See § 64. 3. On (the parenthetical) φησί, which is not uncommon in Greek authors, see Wolf, Demosth. *Lept.* p. 288, Wyttenbach, Plut. *Mor.* II. 105, Boisson. *Eunap.* p. 418: the use of *inquit* and *ait* in Latin is parallel.[5]

---

[1] [As in ver. 16 δέ is generally received, it is perhaps simplest to supply ἐσμέν in ver. 15 (Meyer, Hermann, Ellicott, Lightfoot).]

[2] See Fischer, *Well.* III. i. 347, Duker on Thuc. 7. 69, Bornem. *Luc.* p. 84.

[3] [On verbs used impersonally in the 3 pers. sing. see Don. p. 341, Jelf 373, Clyde, *Syntax* p. 114, Riddell, Plat. *Apol.* p. 155 sq., A. Buttm. p. 135. On ἀπέχει Mk. xiv. 41, περιέχει 1 P. ii. 6, see (A. Buttm. in) *Stud. u. Krit.* 1858, p. 506 sqq. In L. xxiv. 21 it seems probable that ἄγει is used impersonally, ἄγει (τὴν) ἡμέραν = ἡ ἡμέρα ἄγεται: see De W., Bleek, Wordsw. *in loc.*, A. Buttm. *Gr.* p. 134 sq. Meyer and Alford supply Ἰησοῦς as the subject; Bornemann and Grimm ὁ Ἰσραήλ.]

[4] [Here the variant φασίν (2 C. x. 10, Lachm.) is well supported.]

[5] See Heindorf, Horat. *Sat.* p. 146, Ramshorn, *Gramm.* p. 383.

(γ) More commonly, however, it is the 3 singular passive (Madv. 7 b) that is used in this impersonal sense : 1 C. xv. 42, σπείρεται ἐν φθορᾷ, ἐγείρεται ἐν ἀφθαρσίᾳ (see Van Hengel *in loc.*), 1 P. iv. 6, εἰς τοῦτο καὶ νεκροῖς εὐηγγελίσθη κ.τ.λ., Mt. vii. 2, 7, v. 21, al. We find this form in parallelism with the 3 plural active in L. xii. 48, ᾧ ἐδόθη πολύ, πολὺ ζητηθήσεται παρ' αὐτοῦ, καὶ ᾧ παρέθεντο πολύ, περισσότερον αἰτήσουσιν αὐτόν.[1]

The formulas of citation—λέγει, 2 C. vi. 2, G. iii. 16, E. iv. 8, al. ; φησί, 1 C. vi. 16, H. viii. 5 ; εἴρηκε, H. iv. 4 (compare the Rabbinical ואומר [2]) ; μαρτυρεῖ H. vii. 17 (εἶπε, 1 C. xv. 27)—are probably in no instance impersonal in the minds of the N. T. writers.[3] The subject (ὁ θεός) is usually contained in the context, either directly or indirectly : in 1 C. vi. 16 and Mt. xix. 5, φησί, there is an apostolic ellipsis (of ὁ θεός) ; in H. vii. 17 the best authorities have μαρτυρεῖται.

In the following passages there is nothing impersonal in the expression : Jo. xii. 40 (any one conversant with the Bible readily supplies ὁ θεός), 1 C. xv. 25 (θῇ, scil. Χριστός, supplied from αὐτόν) ; Rom. iv. 3, 22, ἐπίστευσεν Ἀβραὰμ τῷ θεῷ καὶ ἐλογίσθη αὐτῷ εἰς δικαιοσύνην, scil. τὸ πιστεῦσαι, supplied from ἐπίστευσεν ; Jo. vii. 51, where with ἐὰν μὴ ἀκούσῃ we must repeat ὁ νόμος, which is personified as a judge. In 1 Jo. v. 16, αἰτούμενος (θεός), supplied from αἰτήσει, will be more suitable [4] than αἰτῶν as a subject for δώσει. In H. x. 38, ἐὰν ὑποστείληται, it is probably simplest to regard the general term ἄνθρωπος, supplied from ὁ δίκαιος, as the subject of the verb.

The predicate is included in εἶναι when this verb signifies *existence* : Mt. xxiii. 30, εἰ ἤμεθα ἐν ταῖς ἡμέραις τῶν πατέρων κ.τ.λ., Jo. viii. 58, Rev. xxi. 1, ἡ θάλασσα οὐκ ἔστιν ἔτι. In this sense εἶναι may have adverbs annexed to it, for the sake of more exact definition : 1 C. vii. 26, καλὸν ἀνθρώπῳ τὸ οὕτως εἶναι.

---

[1] But this will not justify our saying that the 3 plural active is ever used—as in Chaldee, see my *Gramm.* § 49 [Gesen. *Hebr. Gr.* p. 221],—simply to express the passive ; for even in L. xii. 20 ἀπαιτοῦσιν may be conceived concretely, see Bornem. *in loc.*

[2] See Surenhusius, Βίβλος καταλλαγῆς, p. 11.

[3] [On the other side see Lightfoot on G. iii. 16 : compare Delitzsch on H. viii. 5.—In Mt. xix. 5 we have εἶπεν, not φησί.]

[4] So Lücke. [The same view is taken by Bengel, A. Buttmann (p. 133) and others : De Wette, Brückner, Düsterdieck, Huther, Alford supply ὁ αἰτῶν. In regard to H. x. 38, A. Buttm. (p. 134) agrees with Winer : in support of the more obvious interpretation, which takes ὁ δίκαιος as the subject of ὑποστείληται, see Bleek, Delitzsch, Lünemann, Kurtz, Alford *in loc.*—On the subject of this paragraph see further § 64. 3, 67. 1.]

Section LIX.

ENLARGEMENT OF THE SIMPLE SENTENCE IN THE SUBJECT AND PREDICATE: ATTRIBUTIVES: APPOSITION.

1. The subject and predicate of a sentence may be enlarged in a great variety of ways by adjuncts,—in the first place by attributive adjuncts, most commonly by adjectives (see no. 2). Personal nouns, in particular, denoting office, character, etc., receive with but slight extension of meaning the general personal attributes in the substantives ἄνθρωπος, ἀνήρ, γυνή, etc. (Matth. 430. 6, Jelf 439, Don. p. 368). See Mt. xviii. 23, ὡμοιώθη ... ἀνθρώπῳ βασιλεῖ· xiii. 45, xx. 1, xxi. 33 (*Iliad* 16. 263, ἄνθρωπος ὁδίτης· Xen. *Cyr.* 8. 7. 14, Plat. *Gorg.* 518 c), A. iii. 14, ᾐτήσασθε ἄνδρα φονέα χαρισθῆναι ὑμῖν· i. 16, L. xxiv. 19 (Plat. *Ion* p. 540 d, ἀνὴρ στρατηγός· Thuc. 1. 74, Palæph. 28. 2, ἀνὴρ ἁλιεύς· 38. 2, Plat. *Rep.* 10. 620 b, Xen. *Hi.* 11. 1 [1]). In 1 C. ix. 5, however, γυναῖκα is to be taken predicatively; nor must we bring in here passages in which the attributive is properly an adjective, as A. i. 11, xvii. 12, xxi. 9 (Nep. 25. 9), Jo. iv. 9. In the address ἄνδρες Ἰσραηλῖται (A. ii. 22), ἄνδρες Ἀθηναῖοι (xvii. 22, xix. 35), the emphasis rests on ἄνδρες; the address thus becomes expressive of respect (compare Xen. *An.* 3. 2. 2). Similar forms are of frequent occurrence in the Greek orators.

2. Adjectives (and participles) which are joined attributively as complements to substantives are, as a rule, placed *after* their nouns (Jelf 901), since the object itself is presented to the mind before its predicate; e. g., L. ix. 37, συνήντησεν αὐτῷ ὄχλος πολύς· Rev. xvi. 2, ἐγένετο ἕλκος κακὸν καὶ πονηρόν· Mt. iii. 4, Jo. ii. 6, 2 Tim. iv. 7 [*Rec.*], τὸν ἀγῶνα τὸν καλὸν ἠγώνισμαι· L. v. 36 sqq., Ph. iv. 1, Rev. vi. 12, 13. When, however, the attributive is to be brought into prominence in direct or indirect antithesis, it is placed before the substantive;[2] this is of especially

---

[1] See Fischer, *Ind. ad Palæph.* s. v. ἀνήρ, Vechner, *Hellenol.* p. 188. As to Hebrew, see my *Simonis* p. 54. [Gesen. *Hebr. Gr.* p. 188, Kalisch, *Hebr. Gr.* I. 265.]

[2] [These observations appear to require modification before they are applied to the case of an adjective joined to a noun *which has the article*. In ὁ καλὸς ἀγών the attributive stands out less prominently than in ὁ ἀγὼν ὁ καλός (p. 165), as in this latter arrangement of the words the mind is, so to speak, forced to receive separately the two moments of thought. Hence we should perhaps say that the adjective is—almost always (see Green p. 33)—emphatic when postfixed

42

frequent occurrence in the didactic style. Mt. xiii. 24, ὡμοιώθη ἡ βασιλεία τῶν οὐρανῶν ἀνθρώπῳ σπείραντι καλὸν σπέρμα (ver. 25, ἔσπειρεν ζιζάνια); L. viii. 15, τὸ (πεσὸν) ἐν τῇ καλῇ γῇ (ver. 12, 13, 14); Jo. ii. 10, πρῶτον τὸν καλὸν οἶνον τίθησιν, καὶ ὅταν μεθυσθῶσιν, τότε τὸν ἐλάσσω (Rom. i. 23, xiii. 3, Mk. i. 45, Mt. xii. 35); 1 C. v. 6, ὅτι μικρὰ ζύμη ὅλον τὸ φύραμα ζυμοῖ (Ja. iii. 5); 1 P. iv. 10, ἕκαστος καθὼς ἔλαβεν χάρισμα εἰς ἑαυτοὺς αὐτὸ διακονοῦντες ὡς καλοὶ οἰκονόμοι (the κακοὶ οἰκονόμοι do not so); H. x. 29 (compare ver. 28), viii. 6 ; Rom. vi. 12, μὴ βασιλευέτω ἡ ἁμαρτία ἐν τῷ θνητῷ ὑμῶν σώματι (because the σῶμα is θνητόν, for this reason it would be absurd to give oneself up to such dominion); 2 P. i. 4, Mk. xiv. 6, H. ix. 11, 12, 1 Tim. i. 19, 1 C. v. 7, 2 C. v. 1, 1 P. iv. 10, 19. Hence in apostolic language we find καινὴ κτίσις, καινὸς ἄνθρωπος, and usually ἡ καινὴ διαθήκη. But the postfixed adjective may also be emphatic, if rendered prominent by the article, as in Jo. iv. 11, πόθεν ἔχεις τὸ ὕδωρ τὸ ζῶν; x. 11, ἐγώ εἰμι ὁ ποιμὴν ὁ καλός,—or placed at the end of the sentence, as in Mk. ii. 21, οὐδείς ... ἐπιράπτει ἐπὶ ἱμάτιον παλαιόν· Jo. xix. 41, Mk. xvi. 17, γλώσσαις λαλήσουσι καιναῖς. We find both positions of the adjective in the same verse in Tit. iii. 9, μωρὰς ζητήσεις .... μάχας νομικάς. In general, it must be remembered that it often rests entirely with the writer whether he will emphasise the attributive, or not. Thus in Jo. xiii. 34, 1 Jo. ii. 7, 8, the apostle might have written καινὴν ἐντολήν, in distinct antithesis to the old commandments; but he writes ἐντολὴν καινήν, *a commandment, which is new*. In Rev. iii. 12 we have τῆς καινῆς Ἰερουσαλήμ, but in xxi. 2 Ἰερουσαλὴμ καινήν. In 2 P. iii. 13, καινοὺς οὐρανοὺς καὶ γῆν καινήν,[1] it was sufficient to make the adjective emphatic by position once only, where it is first used. As in A. vii. 36 and H. xi. 29 we have ἐρυθρὰ θάλασσα, so in the LXX we frequently find θάλασσα ἐρυθρά. [See further § 61.]

---

with the article (an arrangement which always gives some emphasis to the *substantive*), and *may* have emphasis when inserted between the article and the noun. Thus ἀγὼν καλός and ὁ καλὸς ἀγών will be the *natural* arrangements of the words without and with the article, apart from any special emphasis. See *e.g.* Jo. xvii. 2 sq., ... δώσει αὐτοῖς ζωὴν αἰώνιον· αὕτη δέ ἐστιν ἡ αἰώνιος ζωή κ.τ.λ.—When several adjectives are joined to a noun, there seems to have been a special preference for placing the noun first.]

[1] [This arrangement seems chosen for the sake of variety only: compare 1 C. xiii. 2. On the *Chiasmus* see Jelf 904. 3, Clyde, *Synt.* p. 171, Don. *Lat. Gr.* p. 252.]

SECT. LIX.] ATTRIBUTIVES : APPOSITION. 659

When two or more adjectives connected by καί are attached to the same substantive, they either precede or follow it, according to the above rule: 1 Tim. ii. 2, ἵνα ἤρεμον καὶ ἡσύχιον βίον διάγωμεν· Mt. xxv. 21, δοῦλε ἀγαθὲ καὶ πιστέ· L. xxiii. 50, ἀνὴρ ἀγαθὸς καὶ δίκαιος· A. xi. 24, Rev. iii. 14, xvi. 2. The explanation of such an arrangement of words as is found in Mt. xxiv. 45, ὁ πιστὸς δοῦλος καὶ φρόνιμος· H. x. 34,[1] is, that the second attributive is brought in afterwards by the writer as a supplement, or that he reserves it for the end of the sentence that it may have greater weight.

3. Two or more adjectives attached to nouns are, as a rule, connected by καί: 1 P. i. 4, εἰς κληρονομίαν ἄφθαρτον καὶ ἀμίαντον καὶ ἀμάραντον· i. 19, 2 P. ii. 14, al. Where the copula is absent, either the writer intends to give an enumeration of separate qualities, which are to be noted separately (§ 58. 6), as in 1 Tim. iii. 2 sqq., δεῖ τὸν ἐπίσκοπον ἀνεπίληπτον εἶναι, νηφάλιον, σώφρονα, κόσμιον, κ.τ.λ., Tit. i. 6, ii. 4 sq., Ph. ii. 2, Rev. v. 1, Job i. 8 (see § 58. 7),—perhaps rising into a climax, L. vi. 38 (Matth. 444, Don. p. 386, Jelf 792. m);—or one of the attributives stands in a closer relation to the substantive, forming with it (as it were) a single notion. To the latter class belong 1 P. i. 18, ἐκ τῆς ματαίας ὑμῶν ἀναστροφῆς πατροπαραδότου· Jo. xii. 3, μύρου νάρδου πιστικῆς πολυτίμου (where νάρδος πιστική indicates commercially, so to speak, a particular kind of nard, which is then declared to be πολύτιμος), Jo. xvii. 3, ἵνα γινώσκωσιν σὲ τὸν μόνον ἀληθινὸν θεόν· G. i. 4, 1 C. x. 4, Rev. i. 16, ii. 12, xii. 3, xv. 6, xx. 11 : this is sometimes shown by the very arrangement of the words, as in Jo. vii. 37, ἐν τῇ ἐσχάτῃ ἡμέρᾳ τῇ μεγάλῃ τῆς ἑορτῆς· H. ix. 11. Compare Her. 7. 23, σῖτος πολλὸς ἐφοίτα ἐκ τῆς Ἀσίας ἀληλεσμένος· Dion. H. IV. 2097, συναγαγόντες ἰδιωτικὸν συνέδριον πατρικόν: see Matth. 444 (Jelf 441).[2] Where the second predicate is a participle proper, no one will look for a connecting καί: A. xxvii. 6, εὑρὼν πλοῖον Ἀλεξανδρῖνον πλέον εἰς τὴν Ἰταλίαν· Mk. xiv. 14, Rev. x. 1.

When πολύς is added to a noun which already has an adjective, it is joined with it either according to the above rule (Jo. x. 32, πολλὰ καλὰ ἔργα ἔδειξα· 1 Tim. vi. 9), or as in A. xxv. 7, πολλά τε [3] καὶ βαρέα αἰτιώματα, where the word expressing the quality is

---

[1] [On these passages, and on 1 P. i. 18 (quoted below), see p. 166.]
[2] Dissen, *Pindar* p. 303 sq. (ed. Goth.), Herm. Eur. *Hec.* p. 54, Elmsley, Eur. *Med.* 807, Bornem. Xen. *Cyr.* p. 71. Compare Kritz on Sallust, *Jug.* 172.
[3] [There is no authority whatever for τε here.—For Mk. xiv. 14 (quoted above) read Mk. xiv. 15.]

brought into prominence, *many and* (indeed) *heavy* etc. Compare Her. 4. 167, 8. 61, Xen. *Mem.* 2. 9. 6, Lys. 26. 1 : see Matth. 444 (Don. p. 386, Jelf 759. *Obs.* 2). Under the same head come Jo. xx. 30, πολλὰ καὶ ἄλλα σημεῖα (contrast xxi. 25 ἄλλα πολλά), and L. iii. 18, πολλὰ καὶ ἕτερα (this combination also is not unknown to Greek writers, see Kypke on Jo. xx. 30), *many and other*,—for which we say *many other*.

4. From the natural rule, that the adjective must agree with its noun in gender and number, there are only occasional deviations,—where the writer has allowed the consideration of the meaning to prevail over that of the grammatical form.

(*a*) Masculine adjectives are joined to neuter or feminine substantives which signify persons (Herm. *Vig.* p. 715) : Rev. xix. 14, τὰ στρατεύματα ... ἠκολούθει αὐτῷ ... ἐνδεδυμένοι βύσσινον λευκὸν καθαρόν· Rev. v. 6, E. iv. 17, 18, 1 C. xii. 2, Mk. ix. 26. See Xen. *Mem.* 2. 2. 3, αἱ πόλεις ... ὡς παύσοντες· *Cyr.* 1. 2. 12, 7. 3. 8, Joseph. *Antt.* 6. 11. 6 (compare Liv. 7. 2) : a still bolder example is Aristid. I. 267 *extr.* (Jebb), ἅμιλλα καὶ σπονδὴ τῶν ἑκατέρωθεν μεγίστων πόλεων, καλούντων τι ὡς αὐτούς. See also Rev. xi. 15, ἐγένοντο φωναὶ μεγάλαι ... λέγοντες (v. 13); iv. 8, τὰ τέσσαρα ζῷα, ἓν καθ᾽ ἓν αὐτῶν ἔχων ἀνὰ πτέρυγας ἕξ, ... καὶ ἀνάπαυσιν οὐκ ἔχουσιν ἡμέρας καὶ νυκτὸς λέγοντες. (Don. p. 386, Jelf 378 sq.)

In E. iv. 18 ἐσκοτισμένοι does not belong to the subordinate sentence καθὼς καὶ τὰ ἔθνη, but to ὑμᾶς :[1] 2 Jo. 4, εὕρηκα ἐκ τῶν τέκνων σου περιπατοῦντας, only borders on this usage.

(*b*) Collectives in the singular (compare § 58. 4) are sometimes followed by a plural adjective : A. v. 16, συνήρχετο τὸ πλῆθος τῶν πέριξ πόλεων Ἰερουσαλὴμ φέροντες ἀσθενεῖς κ.τ.λ. (xxi. 36, L. xix. 37, compare Diod. S. 5. 43, Xen. Eph. 1. 3, Palairet, *Observ.* p. 201), A. iii. 11, συνέδραμεν πᾶς ὁ λαός ... ἔκθαμβοι· Jo. xii. 12, Rev. vii. 9, xix. 1 (Philostr. *Apoll.* 2. 12), L. ii. 13, πλῆθος στρατιᾶς οὐρανίου αἰνούντων τὸν θεόν κ.τ.λ. In Rev. iii. 9, however, τῶν λεγόντων is not an epithet of συναγωγῆς, but must be taken partitively. Singular and plural are combined in Mk. viii. 1, παμπόλλου ὄχλου ὄντος καὶ μὴ ἐχόντων, τί φάγωσι· A. xxi. 36.[2] Compare Diod. S. 14. 78, τοῦ πλήθους συντρέχοντος ... καὶ τοὺς μισθοὺς πρότερον ἀπαιτούντων· Virg. *Æn.* 2. 64,

---
[1] [This is surely impossible : the words which follow must have been for the moment overlooked.—On this *constructio ad sensum* see § 21.]
[2] [A. xxi. 36 is out of place here : it is very properly quoted above.]

undique visendi studio Trojana juventus circumfusa ruit certantque illudere capto.[1] (Matth. 434. 2, Jelf 378.)

The combination of two genders in Rev. xiv. 19 is singular: ἔβαλεν εἰς τὴν ληνὸν τοῦ θυμοῦ τοῦ θεοῦ τὸν μέγαν (as Tischendorf and others read). Ληνός is sometimes masculine in the LXX; see Gen. xxx. 38, 41 (*Vat.*).[2] But in A. xi. 28 Luke certainly wrote λιμὸν μεγάλην ... ἥτις: see Bornemann *in loc.* In Ph. ii. 1, for εἴ τις (σπλάγχνα) all recent editors read εἴ τινα.[3]

5. When an adjective belongs to two or more substantives which differ in gender or number (Jelf 391),

(*a*) The adjective is usually repeated with each substantive: Mk. xiii. 1, ἴδε ποταποὶ λίθοι καὶ ποταπαὶ οἰκοδομαί· Ja. i. 17, πᾶσα δόσις ἀγαθὴ καὶ πᾶν δώρημα τέλειον· Rev. xxi. 1, οὐρανὸν καινὸν καὶ γῆν καινήν· Jo. xi. 33, A. iv. 7, 1 C. xiii. 2, E. i. 21, 1 P. ii. 1, 2 P. iii. 13, 3 (1) Esdr. iii. 5. Compare Aristot. *Nicom.* 7. 9. 1, Demosth. *Pac.* 23 b.

(*b*) The adjective is expressed once only. If it precedes, it takes the gender and number of the first noun, as in L. x. 1, εἰς πᾶσαν πόλιν καὶ τόπον· 1 Th. v. 23, Rev. xiii. 7, vi. 14, vii. 9: compare Diod. S. 1. 4, μετὰ πολλῆς κακοπαθείας καὶ κινδύνων· Dem. *Con.* 728 a, Plutarch, *Mor.* 993 a. When the adjective stands last, it is sometimes plural, sometimes singular, and takes the gender of the nearest or of the principal substantive. See

---

[1] See further Poppo, *Thuc.* I. 102 sq., Bornem. Xen. *Apol.* p. 36, *Anab.* p. 354, Jacobs, *Anthol. Pal.* III. 811, Herm. Luc. *Conscr. Hist.* p. 301, Ast, Plat. *Legg.* p. 103 sq.

[2] Lücke (*Apokal.* II. 464) would either read, with a single MS. [no. 36, a cursive MS. of the 14th century], τοῦ μεγάλου, which is probably a correction, or assume a *constructio ad sensum*, the writer having only θυμὸς τοῦ θεοῦ before his mind when he wrote τὸν μέγαν. That the latter supposition involves considerable harshness, is admitted by Lücke himself. See also Matthäi's smaller edition, p. 63. [In his 2nd edition Lücke agreed with Winer. Peculiarities of this kind occur in Hebrew, see Gesen. *Hebr. Gr.* p. 187 sq., Kalisch II. 108. Düsterdieck (comparing Pr. xviii. 14) suggests that the writer first uses the ordinary feminine form τὴν ληνόν, but adds the epithet in the masculine because this form seemed more suitable to that which the image represents: see also Alford *in loc.*—In L. xix. 37 Lachmann and Tregelles read πάντων ὧν εἶδον δυνάμεων; but this reading is not strongly supported.]

[3] [Εἴ τις σπλάγχνα is received by Griesbach, Scholz, Lachmann (both editions), Tischendorf, Alford, Eadie, Lightfoot and others; and is supported by an overwhelming weight of evidence. Meyer and Ellicott read εἴ τινα on internal grounds: for this reading "no manuscript whatever has been cited" (Scrivener *Introd.* p. 549). Reiche and Scrivener prefer εἴ τι, which however is not found in any ancient MS., and is almost as difficult as εἴ τις in point of grammar. Of those who read εἴ τις, some defend it as an extreme example of *constructio ad sensum* (Eadie, Alford, A. Buttm. p. 81), others take it as a mistake on the part of the original scribe (see Lightfoot): other explanations (very unnatural) may be seen in Meyer's last edition, p. 71 sq. (Transl.). See further Green, *Gr.* p. 109.—In Mk. xiii. 14 we must read τὸ βδέλυγμα τῆς ἐρημώσεως ἑστηκότα, clearly a *constructio ad sensum*.]

H. ix. 9, δῶρά τε καὶ θυσίαι προσφέρονται μὴ δυνάμεναι κ.τ.λ., iii. 6 v.l., ἐὰν τὴν παρρησίαν καὶ τὸ καύχημα μέχρι τέλους βεβαίαν κατάσχωμεν· Rev. viii. 7. Compare *Iliad* 2. 136 sq., αἱ ἡμέτεραί τ' ἄλοχοι καὶ νήπια τέκνα εἴατ' ἐνὶ μεγάροις ποτιδέγμεναι· Thuc. 8. 63, πυθόμενος... καὶ τὸν Στρομβιχίδην καὶ τὰς ναῦς ἀπεληλυθότα· Xen. *Cyr.* 7. 5. 60. If the nouns are of the same gender, or if in the adjective the different genders cannot be indicated by different forms, the adjective is usually expressed once only, either with the first substantive—A. ii. 43, Mt. iv. 24, Mk. ii. 15, E. i. 21, 1 C. xi. 30 (2 P. i. 10), Rev. vi. 15,— or with the second (2 C. 1. 6).

In 1 P. i. 18, οὐ φθαρτοῖς ἀργυρίῳ ἢ χρυσίῳ ἐλυτρώθητε, it might seem that we have a plural adjective belonging to two [singular] nouns. Here however φθαρτοῖς must be regarded as a noun, ἀργυρίῳ and χρυσίῳ as words in apposition to it, added for more exact explanation: *not by means of perishable things, silver or gold.*

6. Of very frequent occurrence are *predicative* enlargements, which we should mark by *as* or *for*. See 1 Tim. ii. 7, εἰς ὃ ἐτέθην ἐγὼ κῆρυξ· 1 C. x. 6, ταῦτα τύποι ἡμῶν ἐγενήθησαν· x. 11 [*Rec.*], xv. 26, Mt. i. 18, Jo. iii. 2, xii. 46, 2 Tim. i. 11; 1 P. ii. 5, αὐτοὶ ὡς λίθοι ζῶντες οἰκοδομεῖσθε οἶκος πνευματικός· 1 C. ix. 5, ἀδελφὴν γυναῖκα περιάγειν· Rom. iii. 25, ὃν προέθετο ὁ θεὸς ἱλαστήριον; Ja. v. 10, ὑπόδειγμα λάβετε... τοὺς προφήτας· A. vii. 10, xix. 19, xx. 28, xxv. 14, xxvi. 5, L. xx. 43, 1 C. xv. 20, 23, 2 Cor. iii. 6, 1 Jo. iv. 10, 14 (2 Th. ii. 13, with the reading ἀπαρχήν), H. i. 2, xii. 9, 2 P. iii. 1, Rev. xiv. 4. Sometimes such a predicate is made prominent by the comparative particle ὡς, as in 2 C. x. 2, λογιζομένους ἡμᾶς ὡς κατὰ σάρκα περιπατοῦντας· 1 C. iv. 1,—compare 2 Th. iii. 15, 1 Tim. v. 1, 2; or the Hebraistic construction with εἰς is employed, as in A. xiii. 22, ἤγειρεν τὸν Δαυὶδ αὐτοῖς εἰς βασιλέα· xiii. 47, vii. 21 (see p. 285 sq.) The word to which the predicate refers is left out in 1 Tim. v. 1, παρακάλει (scil. αὐτόν, supplied from the preceding word πρεσβυτέρῳ) ὡς πατέρα. On the predicate placed first, see § 61. (Don. p. 500, 528, Jelf 375.)

The predicate is sometimes an adjective, as in H. vii. 24, ἀπαράβατον ἔχει τὴν ἱερωσύνην· Mk. viii. 17, H. v. 14, 1 C. xii. 12, Mt. xii. 13, ἀπεκατεστάθη (ἡ χεὶρ) ὑγιής· A. xiv. 10, xxvii. 43, xxviii. 13, Rom. x. 19, 1 C. iv. 9, ix. 17, Mk. iv. 28;—or a pronoun, Rom. ix. 24, οὓς (σκεύη ἐλέους) καὶ ἐκάλεσεν ἡμᾶς· Jo. iv. 23,[1] H.

---

[1] [With the rendering *for such the Father seeketh his worshippers to be*

x. 20. Conversely, a predicate is added to a pronoun in 1 P. iii. 21, ὁ (ὕδωρ) καὶ ὑμᾶς ἀντίτυπον νῦν σώζει. Such predicates are sometimes to be taken proleptically:[1] Mt. xii. 13, ἀπεκατεστάθη ὑγιής, i. e., ὥστε γενέσθαι ὑγιῆ (L. xiii. 35 v.l.), Ph. iii. 21, 1 C. i. 8, 1 Th. iii. 13. [§ 66. 3.]

7. There is especial variety in the *appositional* adjuncts,[2] which are appended without a conjunction (ἀσυνδέτως), mainly for the purpose of more exactly defining one nominal (or pronominal) notion by means of another. Apposition is

(a) *Synthetic*,—in the case of proper names, which are characterised by the word denoting the species to which they belong, or (if the names are common to several persons or things) are distinguished by means of a word expressive of quality : Mt. iii. 6, ἐν τῷ Ἰορδάνῃ ποταμῷ· H. xii. 22, προςεληλύθατε Σιὼν ὄρει· A. x. 32, οἰκία Σίμωνος βυρσέως· H. vii. 4, δεκάτην Ἀβραὰμ ἔδωκεν . . . . ὁ πατριάρχης· A. xxi. 39, Rev. ii. 24.

(b) *Partitive* (Rost p. 483 sq.): 1 C. vii. 7, ἕκαστος ἴδιον ἔχει χάρισμα, ὁ μὲν οὕτως, ὁ δὲ οὕτως· Mt. xxii. 5, A. xvii. 32, xxvii. 44. More simply in A. ii. 6, ἤκουον εἷς ἕκαστος τῇ ἰδίᾳ διαλέκτῳ κ.τ.λ., E. iv. 25.

(c) *Parathetic*,—where some quality of a person or thing is indicated: L. xxiii. 50, Ἰωσήφ, ἀνὴρ ἀγαθὸς καὶ δίκαιος· Jo. xiii. 14, εἰ ἐγὼ ἔνιψα ὑμῶν τοὺς πόδας, ὁ κύριος καὶ ὁ διδάσκαλος· viii. 40, H. ix. 24, A. xxii. 12, Ja. i. 8, Mt. xiv. 20, Rom. vii. 19. Compare 1 P. v. 1, al.

(d) *Epexegetic*,—when a word of less wide signification is added, and we should interpose *namely* : E. i. 7, ἐν ᾧ ἔχομεν (ver. 10) τὴν ἀπολύτρωσιν . . . . τὴν ἄφεσιν τῶν παραπτωμάτων· 1 P. v. 8, ὁ ἀντίδικος ὑμῶν, διάβολος· E. i. 13, ii. 15, iv. 13, Ph. iv. 18, 1 C. v. 7, 2 C. v. 1, vii. 6, Rom. viii. 23, Jo. vi. 27, vii. 2, Mk. xii. 44, A. viii. 38, 1 Jo. v. 20, Jude 4, Rev. xii. 1, al. So also after pronouns: Jo. ix. 13, ἄγουσιν αὐτὸν τόν ποτε τυφλόν· 1 Th. iv. 3, τοῦτό ἐστι θέλημα τοῦ θεοῦ, ὁ ἁγιασμὸς ὑμῶν (Xen. *Cyr.* 2. 2. 15, Plat. *Rep.* 9. 583 d, *Gorg.* 478 c), 2 C. ii. 1, ἔκρινα

(Alford, Meyer, Luthardt, al.) : others, *seeketh such as his worshippers*. In H. x. 20 the ordinary view is simpler, that ἥν (considered *predicative* by Winer) is the object of ἐνεκαίνισεν, and ὁδὸν πρόςφατον καὶ ζῶσαν predicative or descriptive.]

[1] Bornem. *Luc.* p. 39, Krüg. p. 240 (Don. p. 534 sq., Jelf 439. 2).
[2] Some well-weighed observations will be found in J. D. Weickert's *Progr. über die Apposition im Deutschen* (Lübben, 1829). Compare also Mehlhorn, *De appositione in Græca lingua*, Glog. 1838 (Sommer in the *Zeitschr. für Alterthumswiss.* 1839, No. 125 sq.), Rost p. 481 sqq. (Don. p. 368 sqq., Jelf 467.)

ἐμαυτῷ τοῦτο, τὸ μὴ .... ἐλθεῖν (Rost p. 481), E. i. 19, εἰς ἡμᾶς τοὺς πιστεύοντας· Rom. xiv. 13, 2 C. xiii. 9, Ph. iii. 3, Ja. i. 27, 1 P. i. 21, ii. 7 (2 P. iii. 2), 1 Jo. ii. 16, iii. 24,[1] al. (Bornem. *Luc.* p. 114 sq.): 1. C. xvi. 21, ὁ ἀσπασμὸς τῇ ἐμῇ χειρὶ Παύλου, i.e., τῇ χειρί μου Παύλου[2] (compare Cic. *Parad.* 4. 8, *Fam.* 5. 12, Liv. 4. 2, 7. 40). Even adverbs are followed by appositional adjuncts: L. iv. 23, ὧδε ἐν τῇ πατρίδι σου (Æschyl. *Choeph.* 654), Ja. iv. 1, πόθεν πόλεμοι καὶ μάχαι; οὐκ ἐντεῦθεν, ἐκ τῶν ἡδονῶν κ.τ.λ., Mk. viii. 4, 1 P. ii. 15.

Several appositional words may be joined to one subject (Rev. xii. 9, xiii. 16), and thus an apposition sometimes consists of several members (2 Th. ii. 3 sq.). In 2 P. ii. 18, however, we must not (with Lachmann and Tischendorf) take τοὺς ἐν πλάνῃ ἀναστρεφομένους as an apposition to τοὺς ὀλίγως ἀποφεύγοντας, but as an accusative governed by ἀποφεύγοντας.

We also have an example of apposition in Mk. viii. 8, ἦραν περισσεύματα κλασμάτων ἑπτὰ σπυρίδας, *they took up leavings, seven baskets.* In Mt. xvi. 13, with the reading τίνα με λέγουσιν οἱ ἄνθρωποι εἶναι, τὸν υἱὸν τοῦ ἀνθρώπου; the last words are in apposition: see Bornemann *Luc.* p. lii. To reject με—as Fritzsche, Lachmann, and others do—on the authority of Codex B[3] (for here the versions cannot count) seems to me hazardous. The word με may be cumbrous, but I cannot think it inappropriate: *Who say the people that I, the Son of man, am?* He had always designated himself Son of man, and now would hear what conception the people form of him as Son of man. On other passages in which the Dutch critics, in particular, have taken offence at such appositions, and rashly altered the text, see Bornemann's dissertation *de Glossematis N. T.* (*cap.* 5), prefixed to his *Scholia in Lucæ Evangelium*.

Under the head of apposition must be brought the well-known use of ἄλλος before a substantive—not found in Homer only, e. g., *Odyss.* 2. 412, μήτηρ δ' ἐμοὶ οὔτι πέπυσται οὐδ' ἄλλαι δμωαί, *nor others (namely) maids, Odyss.* 1. 132 (compare Thiersch, *Gr.* p. 588),—but also in prose writers. See *e. g.* Plat. *Gorg.* 473 c, εὐδαιμονιζόμενος ὑπὸ τῶν πολιτῶν καὶ τῶν ἄλλων ξένων, *and the others (namely) foreigners;* Xen. *An.* 5. 4. 25, οἱ πολέμιοι ὁμοῦ δὴ πάντες γενόμενοι ἐμάχοντο καὶ ἐξηκόντιζον τοῖς παλτοῖς· καὶ ἄλλα δόρατα ἔχοντες· 1. 5. 5.[4]

---

[1] An apposition is joined to the personal pronoun included in the verb: 1 P. v. 1, παρακαλῶ (ἐγὼ) ὁ συμπρεσβύτερος καὶ μάρτυς κ.τ.λ. Compare Lucian, *D. Deor.* 24. 2, Thuc. 1. 137, Xen. *Hell.* 2. 3. 42. To this head may also be referred 1 C. vi. 11, ταῦτά τινες ἦτε (ὑμεῖς, τινές, *ye*, that is, *some*). [Ταῦτά is no doubt a misprint for ταῦτά: see § 23. 5, 58. 3. note.]

[2] Lob. Soph. *Aj.* p. 74, Krüg. p. 133, Rost p. 483. [Don. p. 372, Jelf 467. 4: as to Latin, see Madvig 297 a, Don. p. 274.]

[3] [Now supported by ℵ. Μέ is rejected by Tischendorf, Tregelles (see his note), Alford, Westcott and Hort; bracketed by Lachmann; defended by Meyer and Bleek. But why cannot versions count here?]

[4] Compare Elmsley, Eurip. *Med.* p. 128 sq. (Lips.), Jacobs, *Athen.* p. 22 sq.,

SECT. LIX.] ATTRIBUTIVES: APPOSITION. 665

It is not likely that Jo. xiv. 16, καὶ ἄλλον παράκλητον δώσει ὑμῖν, is an example of this kind; but the analogous word ἕτερος is probably so used in L. xxiii. 32, ἤγοντο δὲ καὶ ἕτεροι δύο κακοῦργοι σὺν αὐτῷ ἀναιρεθῆναι, where the words have the appearance of giving the name κακοῦργος to Jesus. Compare L. x. 1, ἀνέδειξεν ὁ κύριος καὶ ἑτέρους ἑβδομήκοντα δύο. See Thuc. 4. 67, Antiph. 6. 24.

We have brevity of expression [p. 774] combined with apposition in 2 C. vi. 13, τὴν αὐτὴν ἀντιμισθίαν πλατύνθητε καὶ ὑμεῖς, (for τὸ αὐτό, ὅ ἐστιν ἀντιμισθία) : see Fritzsche, Dissert. in 2 Cor. II. 113 sqq.

An epexegetic apposition may be introduced by τοῦτ᾿ ἔστιν : Rom. vii. 18, ἐν ἐμοὶ τοῦτ᾿ ἔστιν ἐν τῇ σαρκί μου· A. xix. 4, Mk. vii. 2, H. ix. 11, xi. 16, xiii. 15, 1 P. iii. 20, Phil. 12. In E. v. 23 an apposition is annexed by means of αὐτός, and thus brought into prominence : ὡς καὶ ὁ Χριστὸς κεφαλὴ τῆς ἐκκλησίας, αὐτὸς σωτὴρ τοῦ σώματος.

The apposition is brought into the construction of a relative clause, in 1 Jo. ii. 25, αὕτη ἐστὶν ἡ ἐπαγγελία, ἣν αὐτὸς ἐπηγγείλατο ἡμῖν τὴν ζωὴν τὴν αἰώνιον; probably also in Ph. iii. 18 and 2 C. x. 13 (see Meyer in loc.). Compare Plat. Phæd. 66 c, τότε . . . ἡμῖν ἔσται οὗ ἐπιθυμοῦμεν . . . φρονήσεως· Hipp. maj. 281 c, οἱ παλαιοὶ ἐκεῖνοι, ὧν ὀνόματα μεγάλα λέγεται . . . Πιττακοῦ καὶ Βίαντος, . . . φαίνονται ἀπεχόμενοι· Rep. 3. 402 c, 7. 533 c, Apol. p. 41 a, Lucian, Eunuch. 4.[1]

8. That words in apposition, standing as they do on the same level with the nouns to which they are joined, agree with them in case, is a well-known rule : there is no such agreement in gender or number (Ramshorn p. 294). Thus a material (abstract) noun may stand in apposition to a personal noun, or a plural to a collective singular, or a singular to a plural. Ph. iv. 1, ἀδελφοί μου ἀγαπητοί . . . χαρὰ καὶ στέφανός μου· 1 C. iv. 13, xv. 20, Col. iii. 4, Ph. iv. 18, Rev. i. 6, xvi. 3; Soph. Œd. Col. 472, Eurip. Troad. 432; Plin. Epp. 9. 26, Demosthenes illa norma oratoris et regula; Liv. 1. 20. 3, virgines Vestæ, Alba, oriundum sacerdotium; Liv. 1. 27. 3, 8. 32. 5. 1 C. i. 2, τῇ ἐκκλησίᾳ τοῦ θεοῦ, ἡγιασμένοις ἐν Χριστῷ, τῇ οὔσῃ ἐν Κορίνθῳ· 1 Jo. v. 16, δώσει αὐτῷ ζωήν, τοῖς ἁμαρτάνουσιν μὴ πρὸς θάνατον :[2]

Krüger, Dion. p. 139, Poppo, Cyrop. p. 186, Volc. Fritzsche, Quæst. Lucian, p. 54 sq., Zell, Aristot. Ethic. p. 62. [Jelf 714. Obs. 2, Shilleto, Dem. F. L. p. 54, Paley, Eurip. I. 92, Sandys, Isocr. p. 40, Liddell and Scott s. v.]

[1] [Jelf 824. II. 4, Riddell, Plat. Apol. p. 192.]

[2] Bornemann's explanation (Bibl. Studien der sächs. Geistl. I. 71), which refers αὐτῷ to him who prays, and takes τοῖς ἁμαρτάνουσιν as a dativus commodi (he will give him life for those etc.), seems to me forced. Αὐτῷ cannot well be referred to the ἀδελφὸς ἁμαρτάνων ἁμαρτίαν μὴ πρὸς θάνατον, for here αἰτεῖν manifestly denotes intercession. [The last part of this note is not clear; for as

compare 1 K. xii. 10, Xen. *Mem.* 2. 3. 2, *Hi.* 3. 4. Compare Vig. p. 41. Still more heterogeneous is the apposition in Col. iii. 5, νεκρώσατε τὰ μέλη . . . πορνείαν, ἀκαθαρσίαν, κ.τ.λ., where the members and the vices of which they are the *media*—the instruments and the products—are placed side by side: see Matth. 433. Rem. 3.

There are, however,—apart from such instances as 1 C. xvi. 21, quoted above [τῇ ἐμῇ χειρὶ Παύλου],—exceptions to the rule that words in apposition agree in case:—

(*a*) An apposition is placed in dependence upon its noun, and joined to it in the genitive (Bengel on Jo. ii. 21): this is a very common grammatical arrangement. See 2 P. ii. 6, πόλεις Σοδόμων καὶ Γομόρρας (*Odyss.* 1. 2, Thuc. 4. 46,[1]—as in Latin *urbs Romæ, flumen Rheni*); L. xxii. 1, ἡ ἑορτὴ τῶν ἀζύμων (2 Macc. vi. 7, Διονυσίων ἑορτή), ii. 41, Jo. xiii. 1; 2 C. v. 5, τὸν ἀρραβῶνα τοῦ πνεύματος, *the pledge of* (consisting of) *the Spirit,* the Spirit as pledge (E. i. 14); Rom. iv. 11, σημεῖον ἔλαβε περιτομῆς (for which some authorities have the emendation περιτομήν); Jo. ii. 21, xi. 13, A. ii. 33, iv. 22, Rom. viii. 21, xv. 16, 1 C. v. 8, 2 C. v. 1, E. ii. 14, vi. 14, 16 sq., Col. iii. 24, H. vi. 1, xii. 11, Ja. i. 12, 1 P. iii. 3, al. Under this head will also come E. iv. 9, κατέβη εἰς τὰ κατώτερα (μέρη) τῆς γῆς (תַּחְתִּיּוֹת הָאָרֶץ), *to the lower parts,* namely, (to) *the earth,* or, to the lower parts which the earth constitutes.[2] A similar example is Is. xxxviii. 14, εἰς τὸ ὕψος τοῦ οὐρανοῦ; compare A. ii. 19, ἐν τῷ οὐρανῷ ἄνω . . . ἐπὶ τῆς γῆς κάτω. From ἀνέβη the apostle infers a κατέβη; now first of all and properly it was the earth to which Christ descended (and from which he ascended again): this, as contrasted with heaven—which is here called ὕψος,—is designated a depth or low region. Christ's descent into hell (of which we find these words explained in *Evang. Apocr.* p. 445), as a single event, cannot come into consideration here; and to

---

Winer considers αὐτῷ and τοῖς ἁμαρτάνουσιν as in apposition, he must himself refer αὐτῷ to the ἀδελφός κ.τ.λ.—Those who make ὁ αἰτῶν the subject of δώσει (see above, p. 656) naturally explain the datives as Winer does above. A. Buttm. takes αὐτῷ as the *dativus ethicus,* and τοῖς ἁμαρτάνουσιν as governed by δώσει, and ὁ θεός as the subject of this verb.]

[1] Krüg. p. 113 (Jelf 435. *d.*): compare also Hoffmann, *Gramm. Syr.* p. 298. [Cowper, *Syr. Gr.* p. 96.]

[2] [In support of this view—also taken by Meyer (ed. 2), Harless, De Wette,—see Eadie *in loc.*: on the other side see the notes of Meyer (ed. 3 and 4), Olshausen, Ellicott, Alford, and Wordsworth.]

refer αἰχμαλωτεύειν αἰχμαλωσίαν to this would be too limited a view.

The interpretation of ἀπαρχὴ τοῦ πνεύματος, Rom. viii. 23, to mean *the Spirit as first-fruits* (viz., of God's gifts of grace), has not yet been fully refuted, even by Meyer and Philippi. The main objection urged against it, that the genitive after ἀπαρχή is always (in Scripture language?—compare however Ex. xxvi. 21,[1] Dt. xii. 11, 17) a *partitive* genitive, would after all be a merely mechanical argument. In that case one could never say *my first-fruits, first-fruits of Pentecost*, etc.; but living languages do not allow themselves to be pent up within such narrow limits. Compare Fritz. *Rom.* II. 175. The Spirit is without question a gift of God, as truly so as the σωτηρία or the κληρονομία, and may very well be regarded as the first-fruits of the gifts of God; and this view is more nearly suggested by the phrase ἀρραβὼν τοῦ πνεύματος itself than Philippi is willing to admit. On the other hand, the use of πνεῦμα to denote the fulness of heavenly blessings, *those of the future world included,* is not found in the language of Scripture.[2]

The *genitivus appositionis* admits of easy explanation out of the nature of the genitive case,—*the sign of circumcision*, a genitive used for more exact definition of a general notion. Though not uncommon in Oriental usage,[3] in Greek it appears to be restricted to the geographical formula noticed above (and even this is on the whole of rare occurrence); for of the examples quoted by Bauer[4] from Thucydides there is not one which is altogether certain.[5] In Latin, however,—besides such examples as *verbum scribendi, vocabulum silentii*, which occur throughout the ancient

---

[1] [Perhaps Ex. xxv. 2.—Winer puts the objection in its extreme form. De Wette (ed. 4) says the genitive is *most naturally* partitive: Meyer (ed. 3), wherever in the LXX and Apocrypha ἀπαρχή is followed by a genitive *of the thing*, this genitive is partitive. See Alford.]

[2] In Col. ii. 17, ἅ ἐστι σκιὰ τῶν μελλόντων, τὸ δὲ σῶμα τοῦ Χριστοῦ, it would be a great mistake to consider τοῦ Χριστοῦ as a genitive of apposition. The words must undoubtedly be so explained as to make Χριστοῦ part of the predicate, in dependence on ἐστί : *but the body is Christ's, belongs to Christ*, is in Christ, with Christ.

[3] Gesen. *Lehrg.* p. 677, Ewald p. 579. [Gesen. *Hebr. Gr.* p. 189.]

[4] *Philologia Thucydideo-Paullina*, p. 31 sqq.

[5] Meyer on E. iv. 9 [ed. 2] cites Erfurdt on Soph. *Antig.* 355 and Schæfer on Apollon. Rhod. Schol. p. 235; but in neither place is anything said about the genitive of apposition. [The *genitivus definitivus* or *epexegeticus* (Matth. 343, Bernh. p. 143, Madvig 49 a, Riddell, Plat. *Apol.* p. 124) is nearly akin to this genitive. A. Buttm. (p. 78) strongly objects to our regarding these genitives as representing a relation of *apposition*, and certainly the name seems ill-chosen.]

languages, but which modern writers leave unnoticed,—compare Cic. *Off.* 2. 5, collectis ceteris causis, eluvionis, pestilentiæ, vastitatis, etc. (i.e., quæ consistunt in eluvione, pestilentia, etc.).[1]

(*b*) We sometimes find the nominative where from the structure of the sentence a different case might have been expected: Ja. iii. 8, τὴν γλῶσσαν οὐδεὶς δύναται δαμάσαι· ἀκατάστατον κακόν, μεστὴ ἰοῦ. The last words are to be regarded as a kind of exclamation, and are therefore appended in an independent construction: compare Mk. xii. 40, Ph. iii. 18 sq., Rev. i. 5, ἀπὸ Ἰησοῦ Χριστοῦ, ὁ μάρτυς ὁ πιστός, might be taken in the same way. In L. xx. 27, προςελθόντες τινὲς τῶν Σαδδουκαίων, οἱ ἀντιλέγοντες ἀνάστασιν μὴ εἶναι κ.τ.λ., τῶν ἀντιλεγόντων would have been more correct; nothing is gained by referring (as Meyer does [2]) to Bernhardy p. 68. Nor is the example quoted by Bornemann *in loc.*, Thuc. 1. 110, altogether analogous. We have however something similar in Corn. Nep. 2. 7, illorum urbem, ut propugnaculum *oppositum* esse barbaris,—where at all events the *gender* (as in L. xx. 27 the *case*) is conformed to that of a subordinate noun, and not to that of the main noun, to which it belongs in sense. A parallel N. T. example would be Mk. vii. 19, with the reading καθαρίζων [see p. 778]. On the other hand, there is an intentional anacoluthon in Demosth. *Aristocrat.* 458 a, ὁρᾷ ... τῆς πόλεως οἰκοδομήματα καὶ κατασκευάσματα τηλικαῦτα καὶ τοιαῦτα, ὥςτε ... προπύλαια ταῦτα, νεώςοικοι, στοαί, κ.τ.λ. And it is, in general, easy to understand how even a word in apposition, when designed to stand out independently, might be placed in the nominative, outside the construction of the sentence, —interposed as a pendent word, so to speak. (Jelf 477, 708.)

In 2 C. xi. 28 ἡ ἐπισύστασίς μου κ.τ.λ. is not an abnormal apposition to χωρὶς τῶν παρεκτός,—such a solecism as this cannot be ascribed to Paul,—but a subject-nominative, and as such emphatic.

The apposition joined to a vocative stands in the nominative in Rom. ii. 1, ὦ ἄνθρωπε πᾶς ὁ κρίνων· Rev. xi. 17, xvi. 7 (compare Bar. ii. 12, *Act. Apocr.* p. 51, 60), the epexegesis not being construed with the vocative, but introduced independently. Compare Bernh. p. 67. In Mt. vi. 9, the adjunct ἐν τοῖς οὐρανοῖς could not be joined to πάτερ by the copulative article in any other way, since the article has no vocative form.

9. An apposition may be joined, not to single words only,

---

[1] [Madvig, *Lat. Gr.* 286. *Obs.* 2, Zumpt 425, Mayor on Cic. *Phil.* 2. 78.]
[2] [Meyer now connects οἱ ἀντιλέγοντες with τινές.—Bernh. p. 68 refers to the subject noticed in Jelf 477. 2.]

but also to whole sentences (Krüg. p. 246,[1] Don. p. 373, 502, Jelf 580). In this case the nouns which constitute the apposition, standing either in the accusative or in the nominative according to the conformation of the sentence, may frequently be resolved into an independent sentence.[2]

(*a*) Substantives.—In the accusative :[3] Rom. xii. 1, παρακαλῶ ὑμᾶς, παραστῆσαι τὰ σώματα ὑμῶν θυσίαν ζῶσαν, ἁγίαν, εὐάρεστον τῷ θεῷ, τὴν λογικὴν λατρείαν,—that is, ἥτις ἐστὶ λογικὴ λατρεία, *qui est cultus* etc. ; 1 Tim. ii. 6, ὁ δοὺς ἑαυτὸν ἀντίλυτρον ὑπὲρ πάντων, τὸ μαρτύριον καιροῖς ἰδίοις. In the nominative : 2 Th. i. 4 sq., ὥστε ἡμᾶς αὐτοὺς ἐν ὑμῖν καυχᾶσθαι ἐν ταῖς ἐκκλησίαις τοῦ θεοῦ ὑπὲρ τῆς ὑπομονῆς ὑμῶν καὶ πίστεως ἐν πᾶσι τοῖς διωγμοῖς ὑμῶν καὶ ταῖς θλίψεσιν, αἷς ἀνέχεσθε, ἔνδειγμα τῆς δικαίας κρίσεως τοῦ θεοῦ κ.τ.λ. Compare Sueton. *Calig.* 16, decretum est, ut dies ... Parilia vocaretur, *velut argumentum* rursus conditæ urbis ; Curt. 4. 7. 13, repente obductæ cælo nubes condidere solem, *ingens* æstu fatigatis *auxilium* ; Cic. *Tusc.* 1. 43. 102, Hor. *Sat.* 1. 4. 110, Flor. 3. 21. See Eurip. *Orest.* 1105, *Herc. Fur.* 59, *Electr.* 231, Plat. *Gorg.* 507 d ; and as to Latin, Ramshorn p. 296. Bengel wrongly takes τὸ πλήρωμα in E. i. 23 as thus used ; this is a very simple instance of apposition (to σῶμα αὐτοῦ).[4]

(*b*) A neuter adjective or participle stands in relation to a whole sentence ; 2 Tim. ii. 14, διαμαρτυρόμενος ἐνώπιον τοῦ κυρίου μὴ λογομαχεῖν, εἰς οὐδὲν χρήσιμον· Mk. vii. 19 [*Rec.*], καὶ εἰς τὸν ἀφεδρῶνα ἐκπορεύεται, καθαρίζον πάντα τὰ βρώματα, *which* (namely the ἐκπορεύεσθαι εἰς τὸν ἀφεδρῶνα) *makes all meats clean,*—see however above, 8 (*b*), and compare § 63 [? 66. 3].— But we must not (with Meyer) take ἀνακαλυπτόμενον in 2 C. iii. 14 as an impersonal apposition of this kind ;[5] the word is an attributive to κάλυμμα.

In Rev. xxi. 17 μέτρον ἀνθρώπου is annexed as a loose apposition to ἐμέτρησε τὸ τεῖχος κ.τ.λ. Examples similar to this, though not exactly like it, are quoted by Madvig (§ 19).

10. A word in apposition will naturally follow the principal noun, though sometimes it is separated from it by several words,

---

[1] Erfurdt, Soph. *Œd. R.* 602, Monk, Eurip. *Alc.* 7, Matth. Eurip. *Phœn.* 223, *Sprachl.* 432. 5, Stallb. Plat. *Gorg.* p. 228.
[2] Wannowski, *Syntax. Anom.* p. 47 sqq., 197 sq.
[3] Compare also Lob. *Paralip.* p. 519. [Riddell, Plat. *Apol.* p. 114 sqq.]
[4] [See Meyrick's note, *Speak. Comm.* III. 548 sq.]
[5] [See Alford and Stanley : also Plumptre, *N. T. for Eng. Readers*, II. 373.]

for the sake of emphasis: 1 C. v. 7, τὸ πάσχα ἡμῶν ὑπὲρ ἡμῶν ἐτύθη, Χριστός· Rom. viii. 28, 2 C. vii. 6, H. vii. 4 (Stallb. Plat. *Euthyd.* p. 144, Weber, *Dem.* p. 152); Ja. i. 7 sq., μὴ οἰέσθω ὁ ἄνθρωπος ἐκεῖνος, ὅτι λήψεταί τι παρὰ τοῦ κυρίου, ἀνὴρ δίψυχος, ἀκατάστατος κ.τ.λ.,—where we should say, *he, a double-minded man* etc. Rom. vii. 21 does not come in here;[1] on 2 C. xi. 2 see Meyer (against Fritzsche). It is easy to see why the apposition *precedes* in 1 P. iii. 7, οἱ ἄνδρες συνοικοῦντες .... ὡς ἀσθενεστέρῳ σκεύει τῷ γυναικείῳ. But such a passage as Tit. i. 3, κατ᾽ ἐπιταγὴν τοῦ σωτῆρος ἡμῶν θεοῦ, is of a different kind. Here the predicate σωτὴρ ἡμῶν is the principal noun, which however is explained epexegetically (since in other passages Christ receives this name) by the apposition θεός. So also in Rom. iv. 12, 1 Tim. ii. 3, 2 Tim. i. 10, A. xxiv. 1, 1 P. iii. 15, v. 8, 2 P. i. 11, ii. 20 (iii. 7), Rev. ix. 11, Jo. vi. 27, L. ii. 1, Jude 4, H. ii. 9. Compare Æschin. *Ep.* 6. p. 124 b, Paus. 1. 10. 5, Alciphr. 3. 41, Diod. S. *Exc. Vat.* p. 60. Such examples are common in Latin: Cic. *Orat.* 1. 18, Liv. 1. 14, 10. 35, 27. 1, Cæs. *Bell. G.* 4. 1, 10, *Afr.* 98, Suet. *Tib.* 2, *Galb.* 4, *Otho* 1, Nep. 20. 1, 22. 3.

Under this head come also adjectives or substantives which stand at the head of a sentence, and—corresponding to the epexegetic apposition—announce the purport of the sentence (Krüg. p. 246 sq., Madv. 197, Jelf 580. 4): as H. viii. 1, κεφάλαιον ἐπὶ τοῖς λεγομένοις τοιοῦτον ἔχομεν ἀρχιερέα (Lycurg. *Orat.* 17. 6),—where there is no need to supply ἐστί. Compare Rom. viii. 3, 1 P. iii. 8.

11. In conclusion, we must notice summarily the inaccuracies (solecisms) in government and apposition which are found in the Apocalypse (especially in descriptions of visions), and which, from their number and character, give to the diction of this book the impress of considerable harshness.[2] In some instances these are the result of design; in others they are to be referred to negligence on the part of the writer. Considered from a Greek point of view, they may be explained as arising out of anacoluthon, the mixture of two constructions, *constructio ad*

---

[1] [Winer refers to Fritzsche, who takes τὸ καλόν as in apposition to τὸν νόμον. In 2 C. xi. 2 Fritzsche regards τῷ Χριστῷ as an apposition to ἑνὶ ἀνδρί.]

[2] On these—besides the well-known works of Stolberg and Schwarz (referred to above, p. 7)—see my *Exeget. Studien* p. 154 sqq. [Davidson, *Introd. to N. T.* III. 565 sqq., Green p. 237 sq.] What Hitzig (*Joh. Marcus:* Zürich, 1843, p. 65 sqq.) has collected on the language of the Apocalypse is in the service of a special critical purpose, and too much is set down to the account of Hebrew. Lücke passes a more moderate judgment (*Apokal.* II. 448 sqq.), but estimates too highly the merits of the learned Hitzig in this field.

SECT. LIX.] ATTRIBUTIVES: APPOSITION. 671

sensum, variatio structuræ, etc. In this light they should always have been considered, and not ascribed to the ignorance of the writer, or even regarded as Hebraisms: most of the examples indeed would be faulty in Hebrew, as in Greek, and to many Hebrew cannot have given more than indirect occasion. But with all the simplicity and the oriental tone of his language the author knows well and observes well the rules of Greek syntax; even in the imitation of Hebrew expressions he proceeds with caution (Lücke p. 447). Moreover to many of these roughnesses of language we find parallels in the LXX, and even in Greek writers, though not occurring in such rapid succession as in the Apocalypse. To come to details:[1]—

Rev. ii. 20 should probably be construed thus: ὅτι ἀφεῖς τὴν γυναῖκά σου Ἰεζάβελ· ἡ λέγουσα ἑαυτὴν προφῆτιν καὶ διδάσκει καὶ πλανᾷ κ.τ.λ., *who, giving herself out for a prophetess, teaches and seduces* etc. Rev. vii. 9, εἶδον, καὶ ἰδοὺ ὄχλος πολύς ... ἑστῶτες ἐνώπιον τοῦ θρόνου ... περιβεβλημένους, may be explained as containing a mixture of two constructions: in using the nominative the writer had ἰδού before his mind, but in using the accusative περιβεβλημένους the verb εἶδον, and thus he mixes together the two constructions. Compare iv. 4, xiv. 14, Judith x. 7, Stallb. Plat. *Euthyphr.* p. 32.[2] In Rev. ix. 14 ὁ ἔχων is probably used for a vocative prefixed to λῦσον. In Rev. v. 11 sq., ἤκουσα φωνὴν ἀγγέλων ... καὶ ἦν ὁ ἀριθμὸς αὐτῶν μυριάδες μυριάδων ... λέγοντες, the last word is not construed with μυριάδες, but (the words καὶ ἦν ... μυριάδων being taken as a parenthesis) with ἄγγελοι, as if the sentence had commenced with φωνὴν ἐπῆραν ἄγγελοι κ.τ.λ. Similar examples are Thuc. 7. 42, τοῖς Συρακουσίοις ... κατάπληξις οὐκ ὀλίγη ἐγένετο ... ὁρῶντες· Achill. Tat. 6. 13, πειρατήριον ταῦτα εἶναί σοι δοκεῖ, ... ἄνδρα τοιοῦτον λαβοῦσα· Plat. *Phæd.* p. 81 a, οὐκοῦν οὕτω μὲν ἔχουσα εἰς τὸ ὅμοιον αὐτῇ τὸ ἀειδὲς ἀπέρχεται τὸ θεῖόν τε ..., οἷ ἀφικομένῃ ὑπάρχει αὐτῇ εὐδαίμονι

---
[1] [In most of the examples in this paragraph the received reading is a manifest correction. Here and there the reading is somewhat doubtful (thus good MSS. have θρόνους in iv. 4, τὸν ὄφιν in xx. 2); but in almost every instance (not including ii. 20) the reading followed by Winer may be safely accepted.]

[2] In Rev. xiv. 14, εἶδον, καὶ ἰδοὺ νεφέλη λευκὴ καὶ ἐπὶ τὴν νεφέλην καθήμενον ὅμοιον υἱῷ ἀνθρώπου, ἔχων κ.τ.λ., it is probable that καθήμενον is not accusative masculine, but neuter, for "on the cloud something like a man etc." In the words which follow the construction immediately passes into the masculine. [It is singular that Winer afterwards inserted xiv. 14 in the text, as resembling iv. 4, still allowing this note to stand. Of Rev. ix. 14 also two different explanations are now given in this paragraph.]

εἶναι, πλάνης ... ἀπηλλαγμένῃ, ὥςπερ δὲ λέγεται κατὰ τῶν μεμνημένων, ὡς ἀληθῶς τὸν λοιπὸν χρόνον μετὰ θεῶν διάγουσα (for διαγούσῃ). Elsewhere λέγων or λέγοντες (iv. 1, vi. 9 sq., xi. 15) stands in connexion with φωνή, φωναί, etc., because the writer is thinking of the speakers themselves. We even find λέγων used quite absolutely in xi. 1,[1] xiv. 7, xix. 6,—as in the LXX, where it corresponds to the Hebrew לֵאמֹר, Gen. xv. 1, xxii. 20, xxxviii. 13, xlv. 16, xlviii. 2, Ex. v. 14, Jos. x. 17, Jud. xvi. 2, 1 Sam. xv. 12, 1 K. xii. 10: even in Rev. v. 12 it might be so taken. More singular is the irregular apposition (§ 59. 8.b) in Rev. iii. 12, τὸ ὄνομα τῆς πόλεως τοῦ θεοῦ μου, τῆς καινῆς Ἱερουσαλήμ, ἡ καταβαίνουσα ἐκ τοῦ οὐρανοῦ ... καὶ τὸ ὄνομά μου τὸ καινόν (where however ἡ καταβαίνουσα, since it cannot well be taken as a *nominativus tituli*, interrupts the structure of the sentence as a significant parenthesis,—as if for αὕτη ἐστὶν ἡ καταβαίνουσα); and also in Rev. xiv. 12, ὧδε ὑπομονὴ τῶν ἁγίων ἐστίν· οἱ τηροῦντες τὰς ἐντολάς κ.τ.λ. (i. 5), where there is a sudden transition to a new sentence, somewhat as in Ja. iii. 8, τὴν γλῶσσαν οὐδεὶς δύναται ἀνθρώπων δαμάσαι, ἀκατάσχετον κακόν, μεστὴ ἰοῦ θανατηφόρου. In Rev. viii. 9 also, ἀπέθανεν τὸ τρίτον τῶν κτισμάτων τῶν ἐν τῇ θαλάσσῃ, τὰ ἔχοντα ψυχάς, and in ix. 14, xvi. 3, it is probably by design that the apposition is interposed in an independent form: see also xx. 2. In Rev. xxi. 10 sqq., the structure changes repeatedly: first we find καταβαίνουσαν in regular agreement with τὴν πόλιν of ver. 10; then is inserted an independent sentence, ὁ φωστήρ κ.τ.λ.; ver. 12 comes back to πόλις, but the attributive commences a new sentence, ἔχουσα κ.τ.λ. Compare Cic. *Brut.* 35: Q. Catulus non antiquo more sed hoc nostro ... eruditus; multae literae, summa ... comitas etc. On the combination of two constructions, either of which is allowable (as in Rev. xviii. 12 sq., xix. 12), see § 63. II. 1: in xvii. 14 [? xvii. 4] there is less harshness. In i. 5 sq. τῷ ἀγαπῶντι κ.τ.λ. is connected with αὐτῷ ἡ δόξα κ.τ.λ.; but instead of writing καὶ ποιήσαντι κ.τ.λ., the writer interposes this thought in the form of an independent sentence. The combination of two different genders (as in xiv. 19) is noticed above, no. 4. *b*; still more singular are xi. 4, οὗτοί εἰσιν αἱ δύο ἐλαῖαι καὶ αἱ δύο λυχνίαι αἱ ἐνώπιον τοῦ κυρίου ἐστῶτες,—for ἐστῶσαι

---

[1] [Compare § 63. I. 1, A. Buttm. p. 384.—In xix. 6 recent editors read λεγόντων.]

is evidently a correction, v. 6 (iv. 8, xiv. 1, *v. l.*) : the attributives are construed *ad sensum*, the substantives denoting living beings of the male sex. On Rev. i. 4 see p. 79.

Inaccuracies of a different kind are noticed occasionally in the earlier pages of this work. By the side of διδάσκειν τινί (p. 284) may be placed αἰνεῖν τῷ θεῷ, Rev. xix. 5. The conjunction ἵνα is frequently found in good MSS. in combination with the indicative (p. 361 sq.) present : see xiii. 17, xx. 3.[1]

Section LX.

Connexion of sentences with one another: periods.[2]

1. In all continuous writing the connexion of sentences is the rule, the absence of connexion (*asyndeton*) the exception. There are two kinds of asyndeton,—the grammatical and the rhetorical.

a. Grammatically disconnected sentences are not merely such as begin a new division or section (of some length), the commencement of which is to be rendered conspicuous by this want of connexion; e.g., Rom. ix. 1, x. 1, xiii. 1, G. iii. 1, iv. 21, vi. 1, E. vi. 1, 5, 10, Ph. iv. 1, 4, 1 Tim. iii. 1, 14, v. 1, vi. 1, 3, 2 Tim. ii. 14, iv. 1, 1 P. v. 1, 2 P. iii. 1, 1 Jo. ii. 1, iv. 1 sq. They also occur where the language flows on without interruption,—sometimes in narration, where the mere order of succession may of itself serve as a connexion in regard to time; sometimes in the didactic style, especially in the expression of commands, maxims, etc., which, though still attached to a common thread, stand out more independently if thus isolated. Such examples in narration occur most frequently in John, and constitute one characteristic feature of his style: compare the oft-recurring λέγει or εἶπεν αὐτῷ, ἀπεκρίθη αὐτῷ,[3] i. 38, 40, 42, 44, 46 sq., 49, 52, ii. 4 sq., 7, 8, iii. 3, iv. 7, 11, 15, 17, 19, 21, 25, 26, 34, 50, i. 26, 49 sq., ii. 19, iii. 3, 5, 9, 10, [iv.] 13, 17. It cannot however be denied that by the asyndeton (compare Jo. xx. 26, xxi. 3), especially where it runs through several verses, the narration gains greatly in liveliness and impressiveness (as

---

[1] [Surely πλανᾷ may be taken as the subjunctive in xx. 3.]
[2] Schleiermacher, *Herm.* p. 116 sq.
[3] [In a few of the passages which follow, these expressions occur *without* asyndeton. For iii. 13, 17, we should evidently read iv. 13, 17.]

indeed we frequently find it in conjunction with the historic present),—see Jo. iii. 3–5, iv. 9–11, 15–17, v. 6–8, xx. 14–18 ; and the two kinds of asyndeton, the grammatical and the rhetorical, flow into each other.

The didactic asyndeton occurs in the Sermon on the Mount (Mt. v, vi, vii), and also in James, but most frequently in John, —in Christ's discourses and in the First Epistle. The writer is, so to speak, continually commencing anew, and a translator has no right to introduce a connective particle. Compare Jo. ii. 7, iii. 30–33, v. 43, 45, vii. 17, 18, x. 3, 4, 17 sq., xv. 2–24, 1 Jo. i. 6, 8–10, ii. 4, 6, 9 sq., 15, 18 sq., iii. 1 sq., 4–10, 18–20, iv. 4–10, 12, v. 1 sq., 5 sq., 9 sq., 12, 16–19, Ja. i. 16–18, iv. 7–10, v. 1–6, 8–10, Rom. xii. 9, 14, 16, 21, 1 Tim. iv. 11–16, v. 14, 22–24, Mt. x. 8.[1]

2. The rhetorical asyndeton—which was long ago treated of by Longinus,[2] Gregorius Corinthius, and Quintilian, and which is rightly reckoned amongst rhetorical figures[3]—is, by the very nature of the case, of more frequent occurrence in the Epistles of the N. T. than in the historical books : the commentators have not always regarded it from the right point of view. As the language receives from it terseness and swiftness of movement, it serves to render the style lively and forcible. On asyndeton within a sentence, see § 58. 7. Of rhetorical asyndeton between sentences we may distinguish the following cases (Bernh. p. 448, Kühner II. 459 sqq., Jelf 792) :—

The connecting particles are omitted

a. When in impassioned language several parallel clauses are annexed to one another, and especially in a climax ;[4] here the repetition of the copula would be clumsy. Mk. iv. 39, σιώπα, πεφίμωσο· 1 Cor. iv. 8, ἤδη κεκορεσμένοι ἐστέ· ἤδη ἐπλουτήσατε, χωρὶς ἡμῶν ἐβασιλεύσατε· xiii. 4–8, xiv. 26, 1 Th. v. 14, 1 P. ii.

---

[1] [Jo. ii. 7 is wrong,—probably 1 Jo. ii. 7. In 1 Jo. v. 5 the reading is doubtful : in Ja. iv. 7 δέ should be inserted.]
[2] Longinus 19, Gregorius Corinthius in Walz, *Rhet. Græci* VII. ii. 1211, Quintil. *Institut.* 9. 3. 50 sq.
[3] Glass, *Philol. Sacr.* I. 512 sq., Bauer, *Rhetor. Paull.* II. 591 sqq.; compare Hand, *Lat. Styl* p. 302. See Dissen, *Pindar,* Excurs. 2 (Gotha ed.), and Hermann's review in Jahns *Jahrbb.* I. 54 sqq.; also Nägelsbach, *Anmerk. zur Ilias,* p. 266 sqq. As to Latin, compare Ramshorn p. 514 sq. In Hebrew, many examples (which indeed require sifting) are given by Nolde, *Concordant. Particul.* p. 313 sqq.
[4] Reiz and Lehmann on Lucian, *Ver. Hist.* 2. § 35.

17, 1 Tim. iii. 16, 2 C. vii. 2, Ja. v. 6, 1 P. v. 10, al. Similarly in Demosth. *Phil.* 4. p. 54 a, *Pantæn.* 626 a, Xen. *Cyr.* 7. 1. 38 (Weber, *Demosth.* p. 363).

b. In antithesis: the force of the contrasted notions thus strikes the eye at once. 1 C. xv. 43 sq., σπείρεται ἐν ἀτιμίᾳ, ἐγείρεται ἐν δόξῃ, σπείρεται ἐν ἀσθενείᾳ, ἐγείρεται ἐν δυνάμει, σπείρεται σῶμα ψυχικόν, ἐγείρεται σῶμα πνευματικόν· Ja. i. 19, πᾶς ἄνθρωπος ταχὺς εἰς τὸ ἀκοῦσαι, βραδὺς εἰς τὸ λαλῆσαι: compare also Mk. xvi. 6, Jo. iv. 22, vi. 63, viii. 41.[1] So also in parallelism of sentences generally; as A. xxv. 12, καίσαρα ἐπικέκλησαι, ἐπὶ καίσαρα πορεύσῃ: compare Eurip. *Iph. Aul.* 464.

c. Especially when a reason (motive) or explanation is appended to a sentence (Krüg. p. 254), or when an application or admonition is deduced from what has preceded:[2] Rev. xxii. 10,[3] μὴ σφραγίσῃς τοὺς λόγους τῆς προφητείας τοῦ βιβλίου τούτου· ὁ καιρὸς ἐγγύς ἐστιν· Jo. iv. 24, viii. 18, xvii. 17, Rom. vi. 9, 1 C. vii. 4, 15, 2 C. xii. 11, Rev. xvi. 6, 15, 1 P. v. 8, 2 P. ii. 16, (Rev. xiv. 5 *v. l.*); H. iii. 12, βλέπετε (compare ver. 7–11) μήποτε ἔσται ἔν τινι ὑμῶν καρδία πονηρὰ ἀπιστίας· 1 C. vi. 18, v. 7, 13, vii. 23, 2 C. xi. 30 (see Meyer),[4] Jo. xii. 35. One case deserves mention as a special variety of asyndeton,—where a saying is followed up by an explanatory clause (without καί) in which the principal word is repeated: Jo. x. 11, ἐγώ εἰμι ὁ ποιμὴν ὁ καλός· ὁ ποιμὴν ὁ καλὸς τὴν ψυχὴν αὐτοῦ τίθησιν ὑπὲρ τῶν προβάτων· xv. 13, 1 C. viii. 2. In such passages we have only to supply in thought a ὅτι (γάρ) or an οὖν (ὥστε), in order to feel how the presence of a conjunction weakens the expression. Compare Lysias, *in Nicomach.* 23, Æsch. *Ctesiph.* 48 (Kritz, *Sallust,* I. 184). It is not uncommon to meet with asyndeton when a writer is developing and working out a thought: see H. xi. 3.

It was formerly an inveterate habit of commentators to supply some particle before a sentence which was appended ἀσυνδέτως, and by this means to bring the sentence into connection with the preceding words; the rhetorical effect produced by the omission of the

---

[1] Stallb. Plat. *Crit.* p. 144, and Plat. *Protag.* p. 52.
[2] Stallb. Plat. *Alcib.* 2. p. 319.
[3] [The most probable reading is ὁ καιρὸς γὰρ ἐγγύς ἐστιν.]
[4] ["Ver. 30 expresses the *result* of verses 23–29, which establish the ὑπὲρ ἐγώ of ver. 23." Meyer *in loc.*—It will be seen that some of the passages quoted in this paragraph are mentioned above as examples of *grammatical* asyndeton. It is not possible to define exactly the boundaries of each kind.]

conjunction was thus entirely overlooked : see, for example, 1 C. iii. 17, vii. 23, Ja. v. 3 (Pott *in loc.*). The same fault was also committed by transcribers of MSS., who frequently introduced connecting particles into the text.

3. The connexion of sentences with one another is most simply effected by means of the copulative particles καί and τε, —negatively by οὐδέ. These particles denote nothing more than mere annexation (§ 53); and hence in the historical style, in accordance with oriental simplicity, they frequently afford the means of passing from one fact to another,—καί both in the Gospels and in the Acts, τε (Madv. 185, Jelf 754. 3) almost exclusively in the Acts. For καί thus used, compare Mt. iv. 23-25, vii. 25, viii. 23-25, ix. 1-4, xiii. 53-58, Mk. i. 13, ii. 1 sq., Jo. ii. 7 sq., 13-16, iii. 22, iv. 27, v. 9, A. ii. 1-4, xii. 7-9, [xiv.] 24-26; for τε, A. xii. 6, 12, 17, xiii. 4, 46, 50,[1] 52, xiv. 11-13, 21, xv. 4, 6, xvi. 23, 34, xvii. 26, xviii. 4, 26, xix. 2 sq., 6, 11, xx. 3, 7, xxv. 2, xxvii. 3, 8, 29, xxviii. 2.[2] In particular, a writer will sometimes first specify the time of an occurrence in an independent sentence, and then subjoin by means of καί the statement of the occurrence itself; see Mk. xv. 25, ἦν ὥρα τρίτη καὶ ἐσταύρωσαν αὐτόν· Jo. xi. 55, ἦν ἐγγὺς τὸ πάσχα καὶ ἀνέβησαν πολλοί· iv. 35, al. (compare § 53.3). This has become a standing usage in Greek writers in cases where the note of time is to be brought into prominence (Madv. 185 b, Jelf 752).

The narration is however still more regularly continued by means of the more strongly marked connective particles δέ and οὖν (see § 53). As the former of these annexes some other thing, something different or new, and the latter indicates a consequence, both particles, loosely applied, are peculiarly adapted to the historical style; and hence the N. T. writers by an interchange of καί, δέ, and οὖν have imparted to their narration a certain variety, which even in the Gospels conceals the Hebrew tinge. Compare Jo. ii. 1 καί twice, 2 δέ, 3 καί, 8 καί, 8 sq. δέ; Jo. iv. 4 δέ, 5 οὖν, 6 δέ and οὖν; iv. 39 δέ, 40 οὖν, 41 καί, 42 τε; A. xii. 1-3 δέ four times, 5 οὖν and δέ, 6 δέ, 7 καί twice

---

[1] [Τε does not occur in this verse. In A. xiii. 52 and xvi. 23 (as often in the Acts) it is doubtful whether we should read τε or δέ.]

[2] Rost's remark (p. 723 sq.) on τε as a connective of sentences in Attic prose hardly receives confirmation from Luke's usage. [Rost's remark (omitted in ed. 7) is to the effect that in Attic prose we find τε . . . τε only when the words connected express ideas which are strongly opposed to each other.]

and δέ, 8 δέ twice and καί, 9 καί twice and δέ, 10 καί twice and δέ, 11 καί, 12 τε, 13 δέ, 14 καί and δέ, 15 δέ three times, 16 δέ twice, 17 δέ, τε, and καί, 18 δέ, 19 δέ and καί, 20 δέ twice, 21 and 22 δέ, 23 δέ and καί, 24 sq. δέ ; A. xxv. 1 οὖν, 2 τε, 4 and 5 οὖν, 6 and 7 δέ; etc.

Other connectives in the historical style—not much more definite in their character, but adopted for the sake of greater variety —are τότε (mainly in Matthew), μετὰ τοῦτο or ταῦτα (mainly in John and Luke), ἐν ἐκείναις ταῖς ἡμέραις, etc.; εἶτα is only found in isolated instances.

The design of the polysyndeton between sentences which are not purely narratory is, to give prominence to them as separate parts of one whole sentence: Jo. x. 3, τούτῳ ὁ θυρωρὸς ἀνοίγει καὶ τὰ πρόβατα τῆς φωνῆς αὐτοῦ ἀκούει καὶ τὰ ἴδια πρόβατα φωνεῖ κατ' ὄνομα καὶ ἐξάγει αὐτά· x. 9, 12. Compare A. xiii. 36, xvii. 28, 1 C. xii. 4 sqq.

4. Of a closer kind is that connexion of sentences which is based on opposition; either generally, where two sentences (like arsis and thesis, as it were) are joined by μέν ... δέ (Madv. 188) or καί ... καί (Madv. 185), negatively by οὔτε ... οὔτε; or where an affirmative sentence stands opposed to a negative, or a negative to an affirmative. Examples of the former are A. xxii. 9, τὸ μὲν φῶς ἐθεάσαντο, τὴν δὲ φωνὴν οὐκ ἤκουσαν· xxiii. 8, xxv. 11, i. 5 (compare § 53. 7), Mk. ix. 13, καὶ Ἠλίας ἐλήλυθεν καὶ ἐποίησαν αὐτῷ ὅσα ἤθελον· Jo. ix. 37 (see § 53. 4). For examples of the latter see Jo. iii. 17, οὐκ ἀπέστειλεν ὁ θεὸς τὸν υἱὸν αὐτοῦ ἵνα κρίνῃ τὸν κόσμον, ἀλλ' ἵνα σωθῇ ὁ κόσμος· Rom. ix. 1, ἀλήθειαν λέγω ἐν Χριστῷ, οὐ ψεύδομαι (compare § 55. 8). To this type—that of opposition or contrast—may also be reduced

a. Sentences of comparison: Mt. xii. 40, ὥσπερ ἦν Ἰωνᾶς ἐν τῇ κοιλίᾳ τοῦ κήτους τρεῖς ἡμέρας καὶ τρεῖς νύκτας, οὕτως ἔσται ὁ υἱὸς τοῦ ἀνθρώπου ἐν τῇ καρδίᾳ τῆς γῆς· Mt. v. 48, ἔσεσθε ὑμεῖς τέλειοι, ὡς ὁ πατὴρ ὑμῶν τέλειός ἐστιν· Jo. iii. 14, καθὼς Μωϋσῆς ὕψωσεν .... οὕτως ὑψωθῆναι δεῖ· L. vi. 31, καθὼς θέλετε, ἵνα ποιῶσιν ὑμῖν οἱ ἄνθρωποι ... καὶ ὑμεῖς ποιεῖτε αὐτοῖς ὁμοίως.

b. Temporal sentences (see § 53. 8): L. i. 23, ὡς ἐπλήσθησαν αἱ ἡμέραι ... ἀπῆλθεν· A. xxvii. 1, Jo. iv. 1, Mt. xvii. 25, ὅτε εἰσῆλθεν εἰς τὴν οἰκίαν ... προέφθασεν· vi. 2, ὅταν οὖν ποιῇς ἐλεημοσύνην, μὴ σαλπίσῃς ἔμπροσθέν σου, al.

c. Even conditional sentences (§ 53. 8): 1 C. ix. 17, εἰ ἑκὼν τοῦτο πράσσω, μισθὸν ἔχω· L. vii. 39, εἰ ἦν προφήτης, ἐγίνωσκεν ἄν· Jo. vii. 17, ἐάν τις θέλῃ τὸ θέλημα αὐτοῦ ποιεῖν, γνώσεται κ.τ.λ. That these sentences really come in here, is shown by the construction (examined elsewhere) in Ja. v. 13, κακοπαθεῖ τις ἐν ὑμῖν, προςευχέσθω, where the conditional sentence takes an independent form, *some one among you is afflicted* (I put the case), *let him pray*; 1 C. vii. 21, δοῦλος ἐκλήθης, μή σοι μελέτω. Compare Ja. ii. 19 sq. (Madv. 194. Rem. 3, Jelf 860. 8). Some supply εἰ in such a case, but improperly: it is however just as inadmissible to take the first clause interrogatively. See above, p. 355; and compare Bernh. p. 385, Dissen, Demosth. *Cor.* p. 284 sq. Similarly in Latin: Terent. *Eunuch.* 2. 2. 21, negat quis, nego; ait, ajo.[1]

5. In the three cases just adduced, *a*, *b*, and *c*,—as also in causal sentences,—an antecedent clause (or *protasis*) and a consequent clause (or *apodosis*) stand contrasted with each other: L. i. 1, v. 4, Mt. iv. 3, v. 13, H. ii. 14, al. In most instances, however, there is no special indication of the commencement of the consequent clause, marked in German by *so;* and hence it has sometimes been a matter of doubt where the apodosis begins (e.g., in Ja. iii. 3 sq., iv. 15, al.). Where οὕτως appears to be used for such a purpose, or where the apodosis is introduced by εἶτα, τότε, or in hypothetical clauses by ἀλλά, δέ,[2] ἄρα (οὖν? see § 63 [3])—as in Mk. xiii. 14, Mt. xii. 28, Jo. vii. 10, xi. 6, xii. 16, 1 C. i. 23, xv. 54, xvi. 2, 2 C. xiii. 4 [*Rec.*], 1 Th. v. 3, al.— the design is to give prominence to the apodosis: οὕτως, in particular, alludes again to the circumstances expressed in the protasis. Only in sentences of comparison (4. *a*) we frequently find οὕτως or καί before the apodosis, answering to the ὡς or ὥςπερ or καθώς of the antecedent clause; see Rom. v. 15, 2 C. xi. 3 [*Rec.*], 1 Th. ii. 7 sq., Mt. xii. 40, Jo. v. 21, xv. 4, 9, xx. 21. (It is after ὥςπερ that οὕτως most regularly occurs.) Where οὕτως follows a conditional clause, it was formerly considered to be purely pleonastic. In Rev. xi. 5, however, οὕτως is *hoc modo* (see the previous sentence), and in 1 Th. iv. 14 it points to the

---

[1] Heindorf, Horat. *Serm.* 1. 1. 45, Kritz, *Sall.* II. 349. [Madv. *Lat. Gr.* 442. *Obs.* 2, Munro on Lucr. 3. 935.]
[2] Jacobs, Æl. *Anim.* p. 27 sq. *Præf.*
[3] [Perhaps § 53. 10. 4.]

identity of the lot of the faithful with that of Christ (ἀπέθανε καὶ ἀνέστη): these examples are not even parallel with those adduced by Matthiæ 610. *extr.*—Still less is οὕτως redundant when it follows participles, as in Jo. iv. 6, A. xx. 11 : see § 65. 9.

In the case of an accumulation of antecedent and consequent clauses, it sometimes occurs that the protasis is repeated after the apodosis, usually in a definite form, so that here we have a doubled apodosis. See Rev. ii. 5, μετανόησον· εἰ δὲ μὴ (μετανοεῖς), ἔρχομαί σοι ταχύ . . ., ἐὰν μὴ μετανοήσῃς; here the length of the sentence gave occasion to the repetition. Mt. v. 18 is probably not an example of this kind: see § 65. 6.

6. The conception of objective sentences, sentences of consequence and purpose, and causal sentences, is one of distinct dependence, and therefore of subordination to a principal sentence. Hence they are appended in the form of dependent sentences, by means of ὅτι, ὡς,—ὥστε, ὡς (not ἵνα, see § 53. 10. 6), also οὖν, ἄρα,—ἵνα, ὅπως,—γάρ, ὅτι, etc. (see § 53); and in some instances the character of grammatical dependence is further indicated by the use of the indirect moods of the verb. Since the causal is akin to the objective sentence, ὅτι (*quod*) may stand at the head of either, signifying both *because* and *that*. There is one case in which εἰ (like *si* in Latin) apparently takes the place of the objective ὅτι, viz., after verbs which express a mental emotion (Madv. 194 c,[1] Jelf 804. 9). See *e.g.* Mk. xv. 44, ἐθαύμασεν εἰ ἤδη τέθνηκεν, *miratus est si jam mortuus fuerit*; 1 Jo. iii. 13, μὴ θαυμάζετε, εἰ μισεῖ ὑμᾶς ὁ κόσμος; compare Fritz. *Mark*, p. 702. Here however ὅτι is used where that which occasions the wonder (grief, etc.) is actually existent ; εἰ where it hovers before the mind of the speaker only as a case supposed, or appears to him uncertain, or at all events is to be represented as uncertain,—' marvel not *if* the world hates you.'[2] A. xxvi. 8 is a similar instance. In the latter case it is sometimes modesty which leads to the choice of this mode of expression; as in our own language we sometimes say, *He asked him whether he would not give* etc. Compare with this A. viii. 22.

The affinity between objective and relative sentences is shown by A. xiv. 27, ἀνήγγελλον, ὅσα ἐποίησεν ὁ θεὸς μετ' αὐτῶν καὶ ὅτι ἤνοιξεν κ.τ.λ.

---

[1] Hoogeveen, *Doctr. Part.* p. 228 sq. (ed. Schütz) ; Jacob on Lucian, *Toxar.* p. 52.

[2] Weber, *Demosth.* p. 535, Matth. 617. 2, Rost p. 628 sq.

7. The character of dependence is still more decidedly exhibited by

a. Relative sentences, where they are appositional—whether they be more or less essential to the integrity of the sentence: Mt. ii. 9, ὁ ἀστήρ, ὃν εἶδον, προῆγεν αὐτούς· Rom. v. 14, Ἀδάμ, ὅς ἐστι τύπος τοῦ μέλλοντος· 1 C. i. 30, Χριστῷ, ὃς ἐγενήθη σοφία ἡμῖν κ.τ.λ., A. i. 2, xv. 10. But the form of the relative sentence is also employed in two other cases:—

(*a*) Where ὅς is continuative, and can be resolved into καὶ οὗτος;[1] examples of this kind are mainly found in narration. A. xiii. 43, ἠκολούθησαν πολλοί ... τῷ Παύλῳ καὶ τῷ Βαρνάβᾳ, οἵτινες προςλαλοῦντες ἔπειθον αὐτούς κ.τ.λ. ; A. xvi. 24, ἔβαλον εἰς φυλακὴν παραγγείλαντες τῷ δεσμοφύλακι ... ὃς παραγγελίαν τοιαύτην κ.τ.λ. ; L. x. 30, A. iii. 3, xiii. 31, xiv. 9, xvi. 14, 16, xvii. 10, xix. 25, xxi. 4, xxii. 4, xxiii. 14, xxviii. 23. (Jelf 834.)

(β) Where the subject or predicate is a relative sentence: A. xiii. 25, ἔρχεται, οὗ οὐκ εἰμὶ ἄξιος τὸ ὑπόδημα λῦσαι· xiii. 48, ἐπίστευσαν, ὅσοι ἦσαν τεταγμένοι εἰς ζωὴν αἰώνιον· xiii. 37, Jo. xi. 3, ὃν φιλεῖς, ἀσθενεῖ· Mt. x. 27, xxiii. 12, Jo. i. 46, iii. 34, xv. 7, 1 Jo. ii. 5, iv. 6, Rom. viii. 25. In this case the relative sentence is frequently placed before the principal, as in Jo. iii. 34, xiii. 7, 1 Jo. iii. 17, A. x. 15, Rom. viii. 25 ; or the principal sentence contains a demonstrative which points back to the relative sentence,—see Mt. v. 19, L. ix. 26, Jo. v. 19, 1 Jo. ii. 5.

Not unfrequently several relative sentences are combined (1 P. iii. 19-22) ; either co-ordinate, A. xiv. 15 sq., i. 2 sq., iii. 2 sq., xxvii. 23, xxiv. 6, 8 (Tisch.) ; or subordinated one to another, A. xiii. 31 (Ἰησοῦς) ὃς ὤφθη τοῖς συναναβᾶσιν αὐτῷ ... οἵτινες νῦν εἰσὶν μάρτυρες αὐτοῦ κ.τ.λ., xxv. 15 sq., xxvi. 7, Rom. i. 2, 5, 6.

b. Indirect interrogative sentences,—which native Greeks characterise by the peculiar form of the interrogative words ὅστις, ὁποῖος, ὁπόσος, etc.: Jo. vi. 64, ᾔδει τίνες εἰσὶν οἱ μὴ πιστεύοντες· Mt. x. 11, ἐξετάσατε τίς ἄξιός ἐστιν· Jo. iii. 8, οὐκ οἶδας πόθεν ἔρχεται καὶ ποῦ ὑπάγει· A. x. 18, ἐπυνθάνοντο εἰ Σίμων ἐνθάδε ξενίζεται· L. xxii. 23, ἤρξαντο συζητεῖν πρὸς ἑαυτοὺς τὸ τίς ἄρα εἴη ἐξ αὐτῶν ὁ τοῦτο μέλλων πράσσειν· A. xxv.

---

[1] [Rost p. 679, Kühner II. 938 (ed. 2). This usage is much more common in Latin (Zumpt 803, Madvig 448): A. Buttmann holds that the frequency of such examples in later Greek is to be ascribed to Latin influence (p. 282 sq.).]

SECT. LX.] CONNEXION OF SENTENCES WITH ONE ANOTHER. 681

20, ἀπορούμενος ἐγώ ... ἔλεγον, εἰ βούλοιτο πορεύεσθαι κ.τ.λ.—
On this compare Schleiermacher, *Herm.* p. 131.

8. So far, the connexion of sentences with one another has depended upon certain conjunctions,—under which head, if we take the word in a wider sense, the relatives may be included. This connexion is also effected by means of inflexional forms, especially the infinitive and the participle, through which the subordinate sentences are grammatically incorporated with a principal sentence, as constituent parts of it. For example:—

a. 1 C. xvi. 3, τούτους πέμψω ἀπενεγκεῖν τὴν χάριν (ἵνα ἀπενέγκωσι), Mk. iv. 3 [*Rec.*], ἐξῆλθεν ὁ σπείρων τοῦ σπεῖραι· A. xxvi. 16, εἰς τοῦτο ὤφθην σοι, προχειρίσασθαί σε· Ph. i. 7, διὰ τὸ ἔχειν με ἐν τῇ καρδίᾳ ὑμᾶς (ὅτι ὑμᾶς ἐν τῇ καρδίᾳ ἔχω), A. xviii. 2, xxvii. 9, xix. 1, ἐγένετο ἐν τῷ τὸν Ἀπολλὼ εἶναι ἐν Κορίνθῳ· xx. 1, μετὰ τὸ παύσασθαι τὸν θόρυβον ... ὁ Παῦλος ἐξῆλθεν. Especially do infinitives with a preposition serve to give compactness and roundness to sentences. The same may be said of the accusative with the infinitive, which usually represents an objective sentence; e.g., H. vi. 11, ἐπιθυμοῦμεν ἕκαστον ὑμῶν τὴν αὐτὴν ἐνδείκνυσθαι σπουδήν· 1 Tim. ii. 8, βούλομαι προσεύχεσθαι τοὺς ἄνδρας κ.τ.λ. (§ 44. 3).

b. 2 C. vii. 1, ταύτας ἔχοντες τὰς ἐπαγγελίας καθαρίσωμεν ἑαυτούς· L. iv. 35, A. xxv. 13 [*Rec.*], κατήντησαν ἀσπασόμενοι τὸν Φῆστον· A. xxv. 1, Φῆστος ἐπιβὰς τῇ ἐπαρχίᾳ ... ἀνέβη· L. iv. 2, ἤγετο ἐν τῇ ἐρήμῳ πειραζόμενος· A. xii. 16, ἐπέμενε κρούων (§ 45. 4). Especially are participles so used in the construction of the genitive absolute, to denote accessory circumstances of place or time (§ 30. Rem., p. 259): e.g., A. xxv. 13, ἡμερῶν διαγενομένων τινῶν Ἀγρίππας καὶ Βερνίκη κατήντησαν· x. 9, ἐκείνων τῇ πόλει ἐγγιζόντων ἀνέβη Πέτρος· L. iv. 40, δύνοντος τοῦ ἡλίου πάντες ... ἤγαγον· ix. 42, ἔτι προσερχομένου αὐτοῦ ἔρρηξεν αὐτὸν τὸ δαιμόνιον· Mk. xiv. 3, καὶ ὄντος αὐτοῦ ἐν Βηθανίᾳ ἐν τῇ οἰκίᾳ Σίμωνος τοῦ λεπροῦ, κατακειμένου αὐτοῦ, ἦλθεν γυνή κ.τ.λ. By degrees this construction became so fully established as an idiom of the language, that it is used even where the subject with which the participle is joined is identical with the subject of the principal sentence: see p. 260. Moreover the same principal sentence frequently contains several participial constructions, either co-ordinate or subordinated to one another, by which means the structure of the sentence becomes more organic. See A. xii. 25, Βαρνάβας καὶ Σαῦλος ὑπέστρεψαν ἐξ Ἱερουσαλήμ, πληρώσαντες τὴν διακονίαν, συμπαραλαβόντες καὶ Ἰωάννην· xvi. 27, ἔξυπνος γενόμενος ὁ δεσμοφύλαξ καὶ ἰδὼν ἀνεῳγμένας τὰς θύρας τῆς φυλακῆς, σπασάμενος μάχαιραν ἤμελλεν ἑαυτὸν ἀναιρεῖν, νομίζων ἐκπεφευγέναι τοὺς δεσμίους· xxiii. 27, τὸν ἄνδρα τοῦτον συλλημφθέντα ὑπὸ τῶν Ἰουδαίων καὶ μέλλοντα ἀναιρεῖσθαι ὑπ' αὐτῶν ἐπιστὰς σὺν τῷ στρατεύματι ἐξειλάμην αὐτόν, μαθών κ.τ.λ.; A. xiv. 19, xviii. 22 sq., xxv. 6 sq., 2 Tim. i. 4, Tit. ii. 12 sq., 1 C. xi. 4, L. vii. 37 sq.

Hence it must in general be acknowledged, not only that these constructions impart greater variety to the style, but also that they unite the sentences more closely with one another, and consequently give to the periods greater roundness. The latter purpose is answered still more effectually when two independent sentences are so interwoven as to form but one,—by *Attraction* (§ 66), for which the relatives in particular possess extensive aptitude (§ 24). Attraction itself however is very varied, and occurs in the N. T. in many forms, from the most simple (L. v. 9, ἐπὶ τῇ ἄγρᾳ τῶν ἰχθύων, ᾗ συνέλαβον· A. iv. 13, ἐπεγίνωσκον αὐτοὺς ὅτι σὺν τῷ Ἰησοῦ ἦσαν) to the complicated, e.g., Rom. iii. 8, τί ἔτι κἀγὼ ὡς ἁμαρτωλὸς κρίνομαι; καὶ μή, καθὼς βλασφημούμεθα καὶ καθώς φασίν τινες ἡμᾶς λέγειν, ὅτι ποιήσωμεν τὰ κακά, ἵνα ἔλθῃ τὰ ἀγαθά;

Rem. A contrast to this fusion of sentences is presented when a writer, instead of contenting himself with the simple infinitive, substitutes for this a complete sentence: Mk. xiv. 21, καλὸν αὐτῷ εἰ οὐκ ἐγεννήθη ὁ ἄνθρωπος ἐκεῖνος· 1 Jo. v. 2, ἐν τούτῳ ἐγνώκαμεν, ὅτι . . . . , ὅταν τὸν θεὸν ἀγαπῶμεν (ii. 3), A. xxvii. 42, τῶν στρατιωτῶν βουλὴ ἐγένετο, ἵνα τοὺς δεσμώτας ἀποκτείνωσιν (contrast ver. 12), Rev. xix. 8. This mode of expression is not always to be ascribed to a love of expansion (characteristic of the later language); it is sometimes adopted in order to give the clause greater prominence, sometimes for the sake of a more flexible construction.

9. By means of these different connectives the style of the N. T. is made to possess an organic texture by no means wanting in variety, though less diversified than the style of Greek writers generally. We even find somewhat lengthy periods thus formed, particularly in Luke (and more especially in the Acts): e.g. L. i. 1-3, A. xii. 13 sq., xv. 24-26, xvii. 24 sq., xx. 9, 20 sq., xxiii. 10, xxvi. 10-14, 16-18, Rom. i. 1-7, 1 P. iii. 18-22, H. ii. 2-4, 2 P. i. 2-7. Yet it must not be concealed that, in cases

where a long period had been planned, the thread of the construction is frequently broken, and either the paragraph ends in some anacoluthon or is left altogether without conclusion (Rom. iii. 8, xii. 6–8, xvi. 25 sq., 27, Mk. vi. 8 sq., G. ii. 4 sq., 2 P. ii. 4–8, 2 Th. ii. 3 sq.,—see § 63), or at all events the construction is commenced anew (2 P. ii. 5 sq., E. v. 27, Jo. viii. 53, Rev. ii. 2, 9).

One means of constructing ramified sentences the N.T. writers have renounced. When words spoken by others are quoted, even when contained in a brief compass, they are not, as a rule, brought into the structure of the sentence in the indirect construction, but are expressed in the direct form; and indeed are not always introduced by ὅτι [1] as an external connective, or by λέγων. See Mt. ix. 18, xxvi. 72, Mk. xi. 32, L. v. 12, Jo. i. 20, xxi. 17, G. i. 23, A. iii. 22, v. 23, al. So also, when a writer has begun by quoting words indirectly, he will frequently pass very quickly into the *oratio directa*: L. v. 14, A. i. 4, xxiii. 22 (see § 63. II. 2). This peculiarity is especially met with after verbs of *asking*, which are followed, not by an indirect statement of the request or intreaty in the form of an infinitive or a clause with ἵνα (§ 44. 8), but by the very words of the speaker: L. xiv. 18, ἐρωτῶ σε, ἔχε με παρῃτημένον· xiv. 19, v. 12, Jo. iv. 31, ix. 2, Ph. iv. 3, A. ii. 40, xvi. 15, xxi. 39, Mt. viii. 31, xviii. 29, 1 C. iv. 16. But what the style thus loses in conciseness, it gains on the other hand in liveliness and clearness. See further Schleiermacher, *Herm.* p. 131.

Rem. It is interesting to notice in parallel sections, especially of the Synoptic Gospels, the variety displayed in the formation and connexion of sentences. In such a comparison Luke always stands

---

[1] [In his interesting dissertations on *Primitive Liturgies*, Dr. Jessop complains, perhaps with reason, that Winer notices too slightly the recitative ὅτι, which is certainly of frequent occurrence in the N. T. (Bruder points out about one hundred examples, but this number should be increased by twenty or more.) In many passages it is difficult to decide whether ὅτι is recitative or whether it introduces an ordinary dependent clause; see *e. g.* the varying judgments of editors in Mt. x. 7, L. vii. 4, Ph. ii. 11. Now and then we have to decide between ὅτι recitative and ὅτι causal, as in Mt. xvi. 7, L. i. 25, Jo. xx. 13 (all these are probably examples of the former), and in some quotations from the O. T., where ὅτι may or may not belong to the words quoted (Mt. iv. 6, Rom. viii. 36, al.). Of course, any construction of the *oratio recta* may thus follow ὅτι: e. g., a direct question (Mk. iv. 21, viii. 4), or an imperative, (2 Th. iii. 10). Not unfrequently we find quotations with and without ὅτι standing side by side (L. xx. 5, Jo. viii. 33,—compare L. iv. 4, 8, 10, 12). The omission of ὅτι (after εὐχαριστῶ) in 1 C. xiv. 18 is remarkable: Greek writers frequently omit this particle after οἶμαι, οἶδα, etc. (Krüg. p. 216, Jelf 798. 1. *a*).]

out as the more practised writer; as indeed he is also more careful than the others in his choice of words,—preferring, for instance, idiomatic expressions, *verba composita* and *decomposita*. But this subject belongs to a treatise on N. T. style.

Section LXI.

POSITION OF WORDS AND CLAUSES,—ESPECIALLY WHEN IRREGULARLY ARRANGED (HYPERBATON).

1. The arrangement of the several words of a sentence is in general determined by the order in which the conceptions are formed, and by the closer relations in which certain parts of the sentence (as groups of words) stand to one another. The latter consideration requires, for instance, that the adjective should, as a rule, be placed in the most immediate contact with its substantive, the adverb with its verb or adjective, the genitive with its governing noun, the preposition with its case, one member of an antithesis with the other. In particular instances, the union of a sentence with what has gone before (H. xi. 1, 1 Tim. vi. 6, Col. ii. 9, Ph. iv. 10), the greater (rhetorical) emphasis which is to fall upon a word, and also in a greater or less degree a desire for euphony and for such grouping as will minister to it, furnish grounds for determining the position of the words: sometimes, moreover, the order of succession in which words should be placed will be fixed by the nature or the conventional estimate of the ideas which they express (e. g., *terra marique*, *Land und Leute*, etc.). Emphasis does not require that the word which receives the stress should be placed *first*: it may even stand last (see *e. g.* Jacob, Luc. *Alex.* p. 74), and indeed may occupy any place in which, according to the constitution of the particular sentence, a word will stand out from the main body with most marked prominence. It is from a wish to effect a connexion with what has preceded that *e. g.* the relative pronoun, even when in an oblique case, commonly begins a sentence.

Hence it is by the laws of the succession of thought and by rhetorical considerations (Herm. Soph. *Trach.* p. 131) that the position of words is determined; and although these allow wide scope for the free action of the mind, and by the cultivated writer will never be felt as fetters, yet in the arrangement of words—for the very reason that logical and rhetorical purposes are so decidedly served by it—there are usually but few peculiarities which have become so habitual to a writer that we can give them a *leading* place among the characteristics of his style.[1]

2. The position of words in the N. T. is in the main subject to the same rules as are followed by the Greek prose writers; for it is only in a very small measure that these rules are national. We may however notice:—

a. That in the didactic writings, of Paul especially, the arrangement of words is freer and more varied than in the historical books,—as indeed in the former rhetorical considerations have more weight. In the (Synoptic) Gospels, on the other hand, the Hebrew type of arrangement prevails.

b. That, especially in narrative, the N. T. writers avoid any great separation of the two main elements of the sentence, subject and verb (predicate); and, in accordance with the Hebrew mode of expression, either draw the verb nearer to the subject, or, if the subject is complex, place the principal subject only before the verb, leaving the rest to follow (§ 58. 6), that the reader's attention may not be kept on the stretch too long. Relative clauses likewise are, whenever it is possible, so placed as to come in after the completion of the principal sentence.

On the whole, the collocation of words in the N. T. is simple and free from all mannerisms, as well as from stiffness or monotony. Gersdorf indeed, in his well-known work,[2] has specified many peculiarities of this kind as characterising the several writers; but a closer scrutiny of his examples will show

(*a*) That he has not paid due regard to the various considerations on which the order and succession of words usually depend in each particular case;

(*b*) That, holding the opinion that it may have become a habit with a writer invariably to place (for instance) the adverb

---

[1] I am not acquainted with any thorough and complete treatment of the arrangement of words in Greek. Kühner, however, deserves thanks for his attempt to claim for this subject, under the name "Topik," its due place in grammar: see his Gramm. II. 622 sqq. [II. 1094–1104: ed. 2]. Madvig also has some remarks on this head in his *Syntax*, § 217 sqq. In Latin, the collocation of words earlier received more special notice, in connexion with the doctrine of euphony, and the subject is well treated in brief by Zumpt, *Gr.* 786 sqq. Compare also Hand, *Lehrb. des lat. Styls* p. 307 sqq., Gernhard, *Commentatt. Gramm.* part 8 (Jen. 1828). On the ancient languages, in general, see H. Weil, *De l'ordre des mots dans les langues anciennes* etc. (Par. 1844). —As to habits acquired by particular authors, Tzschirner, for example, who aimed at a prosaic rhythm, is not to be mistaken in any of his writings. (Jelf 901.) [Many examples, collected from the best authors, are given by Dr. C. Short, *The Order of Words in Attic Greek Prose* (New York, 1870).]

[2] [C. G. Gersdorf, *Beiträge zur Sprach-Characteristik der Schriftsteller des Neuen Testaments* (Leipzig, 1816).]

before (or *after*) the verb, he has proposed, and to some extent has carried out, a plan of critical procedure which cannot but be censured as one-sided. A more rational treatment of this subject would be of great service to textual criticism.

It is not in itself a matter of indifference whether we have τὸ πνεῦμα τοῦ θεοῦ or τὸ πνεῦμα τὸ τοῦ θεοῦ (compare § 20. 1), and without the article πνεῦμα θεοῦ or θεοῦ πνεῦμα. It would be necessary to examine severally all the examples of this phrase which occur in the N. T., according to the special conformation of the style of each passage. To neglect all such considerations in making use of the MSS. (and even of the ancient versions, and of the Fathers—who quote more or less freely), and to force upon a writer some *one* of these collocations whenever he uses the words, is empirical pedantry. If the adjective *usually* follows the noun (φόβος μέγας, ἔργον ἀγαθόν), or the adverb the adjective (χαλεπὸς λίαν, μεγάλη σφόδρα, Strabo 17. 801), the arrangement is a very natural one: if the reverse is adopted, it is either from a wish to give prominence to the meaning of the adjective or adverb—occasioned perhaps in the case of many writers by an antithesis habitually present to their mind (thus καλὰ ἔργα usually in Paul); or else the (antithetical) *nature* of the meaning of the adjective in question may require that it should stand first,—e.g., ἄλλος, εἷς, ἴδιος, etc. Nor can it be thought strange that ὁ ἄνθρωπος οὗτος should occur more frequently than οὗτος ὁ ἄνθρωπος: the latter involves an emphasis on the pronoun (*this* man—no other) which can only exist when the words are spoken δεικτικῶς or with vehemence. The predominance of the latter order in John (Gersdorf p. 444 sq.) is in the first place by no means decided; and, secondly, whenever this arrangement of the words is chosen, the reason may be easily perceived. Ταῦτα πάντα in L. xii. 30 is not identical with πάντα ταῦτα in Mt. vi. 32 (Gersdorf p. 447 sq.). The former signifies *these things all taken together;* the latter, *all these things*. In the first, πάντα is added to define ταῦτα more exactly; in the second, πάντα is indicated demonstratively by means of ταῦτα. Πάντα ταῦτα may indeed be less usual (as perhaps *omnia hæc* is in Latin), but it is the best attested reading in Mt. xxiii. 36,[1] xxiv. 33 sq., L. vii. 18: compare Bengel on Mt. xxiv. 33.—If a narrator, passing from one event to another, and making time the connecting link, says ἐν ἐκείναις ταῖς ἡμέραις, etc., no attentive reader will regard this as an arbitrary departure from the usual order, ἡ πόλις ἐκείνη. And what is the use of such remarks as this: "πάλιν, ἐκεῖθεν, etc., sometimes precede, sometimes follow"?[2]—How, in fine, Gersdorf (p. 335) could so entirely misapprehend the proper position of the adjective in Mt. xiii. 27, xv. 20, as to be even inclined to correct the text,

---

[1] [In this passage and the next the reading is doubtful.]
[2] Even Van Hengel's more exact remark (*Phil.* p. 201) on πάλιν in Paul's Epistles I cannot regard as a canon to be followed unconditionally in criticism or exegesis. As to Ph. ii. 28 I hold to what is said above, p. 435.

I cannot understand. If in Mt. xv. 34 we find πόσους ἄρτους ἔχετε; οἱ δὲ εἶπον· ἑπτὰ καὶ ὀλίγα ἰχθύδια, but in Mk. viii. 7, καὶ εἶχον ἰχθύδια ὀλίγα, in the one passage ὀλίγα is antithetical to ἑπτά, and therefore must stand before its noun; whilst in the other "loaves" and "fishes" stand contrasted,—"of fish also they had a small supply." That Paul writes οἴνῳ ὀλίγῳ in 1 Tim. v. 23, and James in c. iii. 5 ὀλίγον (v. l. ἡλίκον) πῦρ, will indeed surprise no one who studies language with attention.

In Jo. v. 22, τὴν κρίσιν πᾶσαν δέδωκε τῷ υἱῷ, the position of πᾶσαν immediately before δέδωκε, to which it belongs ("he gave it to him not partially, but wholly," 1 C. xii. 12), is very appropriate. Compare also Mt. ix. 35, Rom. iii. 9, xii. 4, A. xvi. 26, xvii. 21, 1 C. x. 1, Xen. *Hell.* 2. 3. 40, Thuc. 7. 60, al. (Jelf 714. *Obs.* 2). Besides the order πᾶσα ἡ πόλις, we also find ὁ πᾶς νόμος G. v. 14, τὸν πάντα χρόνον A. xx. 18, 1 Tim. i. 16 : Thuc. 4. 61, Isocr. *Dem.* p. 1, Herod. 1. 14. 10, Stallb. Plat. *Phileb.* 48 [see above, p. 138]. On such examples as the following, in which a word which involves emphasis is simply placed first, no remark is needed : Jo. vi. 57, viii. 25, ix. 31, xiii. 6, Rom. vii. 23, xiii. 14, 1 C. xii. 22, xiv. 2, xv. 44, L. ix. 20, xii. 30, xvi. 11, H. x. 30, Ja. iii. 3, 1 P. iii. 21, 2 P. i. 21. See however below, no. 3.

The constant adherence to one order in the apostolic benediction χάρις ὑμῖν καὶ εἰρήνη (so also in 1 and 2 Peter) is certainly designed to point out χάρις as the chief and the fuller idea to which εἰρήνη is added as consequent.

The vocative with or without ὦ is sometimes prefixed to the sentence; viz., when it expresses a call (Mk. xiv. 37), or when, as an address, it is intended to awaken attention for what is to follow : see Mt. viii. 2, xv. 28, xviii. 32, xxv. 26, Mk. ix. 19, L. viii. 48, xxiv. 25, Jo. vi. 68, xiii. 6, xxi. 15 sqq., A. i. 11, ii. 29, v. 35, vii. 59, ix. 13, xiii. 10, xxv. 24, Rom. ix. 20, G. iii. 1, 1 Tim. vi. 20. Sometimes it is inserted in the body of the sentence, viz., when attention is assumed to exist on the part of the person addressed, and what follows is simply to be referred to him: see Mt. ix. 22, xvi. 17, xx. 31 [*Rec.*], Jo. xii. 15, A. i. 1, xxvi. 19, 24, 27, G. i. 11, Ph. i. 12, iii. 17, Phil. 20, 2 P. i. 10, Rev. xv. 4. In this case the vocative has its place after one word or after several, according to the degree of closeness in the connexion of these words (Mt. xvi. 17, Jo. xii. 15, Rev. xv. 4, al.) : in some instances, when it is supplementary, it stands at the end of the sentence, see L. v. 8, Jo. xiv. 9, A. xxvi. 7.

3. The grounds of every singular arrangement (transposition) of words which originates in the writer's free preference may be more or less clearly perceived. The following cases should be distinguished :[1]

a. Those in which the strikingly unusual position of the words arises from *rhetorical* causes, and is therefore intentional.

---

[1] [Jelf 904, Don. p. 611, Riddell, Plat. *Apol.* p. 228.]

Thus in 1 P. ii. 7 the apposition (Weber, *Dem.* p. 152) τοῖς πιστεύουσιν is reserved for the close of the sentence, because in this position the conditioning words "as believers," "if we believe," stand out more prominently,—especially as they are thus brought so near the antithetical ἀπειθοῦσι.[1] Compare 1 Jo. v. 13, 16, Jo. xiii. 14, Rom. xi. 13, H. vi. 18 (Stallb. Plat. *Euthyd.* p. 144); also H. vii. 4, ᾧ καὶ δεκάτην ᾿Αβραὰμ ἔδωκεν ἐκ τῶν ἀκροθινίων, ὁ πατριάρχης, *to whom Abraham also gave tithes, the patriarch*; xi. 17, 1 P. iv. 4. Other examples of the kind are H. vi. 19, ἣν ὡς ἄγκυραν ἔχομεν τῆς ψυχῆς ἀσφαλῆ τε καὶ βεβαίαν καὶ εἰςερχομένην κ.τ.λ., x. 34, 1 P. i. 23; 1 C. xiii. 1, ἐὰν ταῖς γλώσσαις τῶν ἀνθρώπων λαλῶ καὶ τῶν ἀγγέλων· A. xxiv. 17, xxvi. 22. The genitive in particular is thus postponed : 1 Th. i. 6, Jo. vii. 38, 1 Tim. iii. 6,[2] al. As to words brought forward in position (see above, no. 2), there is manifestly antithesis in 1 C. x. 11, ταῦτα τύποι συνέβαινον ἐκείνοις, ἐγράφη δὲ πρός κ.τ.λ., L. xvi. 12, xxiii. 31, Jo. ix. 17 [*Rec.*],[3] xxi. 21; also in 2 C. ii. 4, οὐχ ἵνα λυπηθῆτε, ἀλλὰ τὴν ἀγάπην ἵνα γνῶτε· xii. 7, 1 C. ix. 15, A. xix. 4, Rom. xi. 31, Col. iv. 16, G. ii. 10 (Cic. *Div.* 1. 40, *Mil.* 2 *fin.*, Krüg. p. 267); and no less in 1 C. vi. 4, βιωτικὰ μὲν οὖν κριτήρια ἐὰν ἔχητε (examples of ἐάν thus kept back occur frequently in Demosthenes, Klotz p. 484),[4] Rom. xii. 3, ἑκάστῳ ὡς ἐμέρισεν μέτρον πίστεως· 1 C. iii. 5, vii. 17, Jo. xiii. 34 (Cic. *Off.* 2. 21, 72), 2 Th. ii. 7, μόνον ὁ κατέχων ἄρτι ἕως ἐκ μέσου γένηται; lastly in Rom. viii. 18, οὐκ ἄξια τὰ παθήματα τοῦ νῦν καιροῦ πρὸς τὴν μέλλουσαν δόξαν ἀποκαλυφθῆναι· G. iii. 23, H. x. 1, 1 C. xii. 22.

b. In other instances, some closer specification which did not occur to the writer until after he had arranged the sentence is brought in afterwards: A. xxii. 9, τὸ μὲν φῶς ἐθεάσαντο, τὴν δὲ φωνὴν οὐκ ἤκουσαν τοῦ λαλοῦντός μοι· iv. 33, μεγάλῃ δυνάμει ἀπεδίδουν τὸ μαρτύριον οἱ ἀπόστολοι τῆς ἀναστάσεως τοῦ κυρίου Ἰησοῦ· H. xii. 11, Jo. i. 49, iv. 39, vi. 66 [*Rec.*]; xii. 11, 1 C. x. 27, L. xix. 47, 1 P. i. 13, v. 12, 2 P. iii. 2 (A. xix. 27); compare Arrian, *Alex.* 3. 23. 1, τοὺς ὑπολειφθέντας ἐν τῇ διώξει

---

[1] With this compare Demosth. Fals. Leg. 204 c, εἰμὶ τοίνυν ὁ κατηγορῶν ἐξ ἀρχῆς ἐγὼ τούτων, τούτων δ᾿ οὐδεὶς ἐμοῦ.
[2] [See p. 238, Ellicott on G. ii. 6, 9, A. Buttm. p. 387.—In some of the examples in (*b*) the order is probably adopted for emphasis or clearness.]
[3] [Τίς often stands second (*third* in Rom. xiv. 10, Jo. xxi. 21), that an emphatic word may precede. Compare 1 C. xv. 36. (A. Buttm. p. 388 sq.)]
[4] [In 1 C. xv. 2 a sentence precedes τί. Compare Jo. x. 36. (A. Buttm. *l.c.*)]

τῆς στρατιᾶς. Under this head Rev. vii. 17 should probably come. In 2 P. iii. 1, ἐν αἷς διεγείρω ὑμῶν ἐν ὑπομνήσει τὴν εἰλικρινῆ διάνοιαν, the words ἐν ὑπομνήσει are brought into the current of the sentence as a supplementary addition defining διεγείρω more precisely.

c. Words which are to be connected with one another are brought closer together: Rom. ix. 21, ἔχει ἐξουσίαν ὁ κεραμεὺς τοῦ πηλοῦ ἐκ τοῦ αὐτοῦ φυράματος ποιῆσαι κ.τ.λ., 1 P. ii. 16, 1 C. ii. 11.—In E. ii. 3 φύσει belongs to τέκνα, and hence occupies the most suitable place.

d. In some cases the transposition was unavoidable: H. xi. 32, ἐπιλείψει γάρ με διηγούμενον ὁ χρόνος περὶ Γεδεών, Βαράκ τε καὶ Σαμψών κ.τ.λ. As a whole series of names follows, to which a relative clause is to be appended (ver. 33), no other arrangement was possible. See H. vi. 1, 2, 1 C. i. 30.

e. An effort to throw an unemphatic word into the shade may be perceived in H. iv. 11, ἵνα μὴ ἐν τῷ αὐτῷ τις ὑποδείγματι πέσῃ κ.τ.λ.,[1] v. 4, 1 P. ii. 19, A. xxvi. 24. So perhaps in 1 C. v. 1, ὥστε γυναῖκά τινα τοῦ πατρὸς ἔχειν· L. xviii. 18. See Weber, *Dem.* p. 139, 251. In H. ix. 16 also, ὅπου διαθήκη, θάνατον ἀνάγκη φέρεσθαι τοῦ διαθεμένου, the force of the main thought θάνατον ἀνάγκη κ.τ.λ. would have been lessened if the last word had been placed anywhere else. Here and there, in the case of the more practised of the N. T. writers, even the 'aurium judicium,' to which Cicero attaches so much importance, may have exerted an influence, and have produced a more flowing and rhythmical arrangement of words.

On such examples as κακοὺς κακῶς ἀπολέσει, in which similar words or repetitions of the same word are placed together, see § 68. 1. Compare Kühner II. 628 [II. 1103 in ed. 2, Jelf 904. 2].

When the predicate is brought forward in the sentence—as in Jo. i. 1, 49 (compare ver. 47), iv. 19, 24, vi. 60, Rom. xiii. 11, 2 P. i. 10, 14, 19, Ph. iii. 20, ii. 11, 1 Jo. i. 10, Rev. ii. 9—we must estimate each case according to the above principles. It is natural that in those sentences particularly which have the character of exclamations, as in blessings (μακαρισμοί), the predicate should stand at the head; in such a case it has become usual to omit the substantive verb. See Mt. xxi. 9, εὐλογημένος ὁ ἐρχόμενος ἐν ὀνόματι κυρίου· xxiii. 39, L. i. 42, 68, 2 C. i. 3, 1 C. ii. 11 [?], 1 P. i. 3; Mt. v. 3, μακάριοι οἱ πτωχοὶ τῷ πνεύματι· v. 4-11, xxiv. 46. This remark also applies, as a

---

[1] [See Riddell, Plat. *Apol.* p. 230.]

rule, to the doxologies of the O. T. (בָּרוּךְ, מְבֹרָךְ) : Gen. ix. 26, 1 S. xxvi. 25, 2 S. xviii. 28, Ps. cvi. (cv.) 48, al. But it is only by empirical commentators that this arrangement can be regarded as unalterably fixed ; for where the subject expresses the main idea, and especially where it is antithetical to another subject, the predicate both may and will stand after it; compare Ps. lxvii. 20 (LXX). Hence in Rom. ix. 5, if the words ὁ ὢν ἐπὶ πάντων θεὸς εὐλογητός κ.τ.λ. are referred to God, this collocation of the words is perfectly suitable, and indeed necessary : Harless (see his note on E. i. 3) and many others are mistaken here.[1]

On a genitive placed before its governing noun see § 30. 3. Rem. 4 ; a careful writer will avoid such an arrangement where it may give rise to any mistake. Hence in H. vi. 2 βαπτισμῶν διδαχῆς does not stand for διδαχῆς βαπτισμῶν,—the more especially as in the other groups the position of the genitive is regular. In the passages quoted by Tholuck from Thucydides and Plutarch there is no possibility of ambiguity.

4. If the earlier students of the N. T. noticed the arrangement of words in those cases only where certain parts of a sentence were separated from the words to which they logically belong (1 Th. ii. 13, 1 P. ii. 7, Rom. xi. 13, H. ii. 9),—examples of "Trajection," so called,[2]—this limitation in range was less to be censured than the almost entire neglect to inquire into the motives which led to the trajection in each particular case. By such motives (having their existence, it is true, mainly in instinct and feeling) the N. T. writers were always guided. Most rarely are transpositions met with where the nature of the ideas (Quintil. *Instit.* 9. 4. 24) suggested the order of the words (Mt. vii. 7, Jo. vii. 34, Rev. xxi. 6, xxii. 13, Mt. viii. 11, H. xiii. 8), or where the relative position of words which form a group had become settled conventionally, according to the nature or the estimation of the ideas,—in some instances not without regard to ease of pronunciation. Thus we find ἄνδρες καὶ γυναῖκες, A. viii. 3, ix. 2 ; γυναῖκες καὶ παιδία or τέκνα, Mt. xiv. 21, xv. 38, A. xxi. 5 ; ζῶντες καὶ νεκροί, A. x. 42, 2 Tim. iv. 1, 1 P. iv. 5 ; νύκτα καὶ ἡμέραν, A. xx. 31, xxvi. 7 ; νυκτὸς καὶ ἡμέρας, 1 Th. ii. 9, iii. 10 ; σὰρξ καὶ αἷμα, Mt. xvi. 17, G. i. 16, Jo. vi. 54, 56 ; ἐσθίειν (τρώγειν)

---

[1] [On Rom. ix. 5 see Alford and Vaughan *in loc.*; Green, *Cr. Notes*, p. 121 sq. ; Gifford's note in *Speak. Com.* III. 178 sq. ; and the discussion in the *Expositor*, IX. 217, 397, X. 232. Compare Ellicott on E. i. 3.]

[2] On such trajections in Greek authors see Abresch, *Aristænet.* p. 218, Wolf, Demosth. *Lept.* p. 300, Reitz, *Lucian* VII. 448 (Bip.), Krüger, *Dion. Hal.* p. 139, 318, Engelhardt, *Euthyphr.* p. 123 sq.

καὶ πίνειν, Mt. xi. 18, L. vii. 34, xii. 45, 1 C. xi. 22, 29; βρῶσις καὶ πόσις, Rom. xiv. 17, Col. ii. 16; ἔργῳ καὶ λόγῳ, L. xxiv. 19 (Fritz. *Rom*. III. 268); ὁ οὐρανὸς καὶ ἡ γῆ, Mt. v. 18, xi. 25, xxiv. 35, A. iv. 24, al.; ὁ ἥλιος καὶ ἡ σελήνη, L. xxi. 25, Rev. xxi. 23; ἡ γῆ καὶ ἡ θάλασσα, A. iv. 24, xiv. 15, Rev. vii. 1, 3, xiv. 7, al.; *right ... left*, Mt. xx. 21, xxv. 33, Mk. x. 40, L. xxiii. 33, 2 C. vi. 7, Rev. x. 2; δοῦλοι ... ἐλεύθεροι, 1 C. xii. 13, G. iii. 28, E. vi. 8; Ἰουδαῖοι καὶ Ἕλληνες, A. xviii. 4, xix. 10, Rom. iii. 9, 1 C. i. 24 (compare Rom. ii. 9 sq.);—with other examples of the same kind. Deviations from this order occur but sparingly (cases indeed may be conceived in which the reverse arrangement is more in accordance with truth, compare Rom. xiv. 9 [1]): when this reverse arrangement is supported by the preponderant or unanimous testimony of the MSS., it must without hesitation be received. Thus we must read αἷμα καὶ σάρξ in E. vi. 12, H. ii. 14; ἡ θάλασσα καὶ ἡ ξηρά, Mt. xxiii. 15; ἡμέρας καὶ νυκτός, A. ix. 24, L. xviii. 7; λόγῳ καὶ ἔργῳ (Diod. S. *Exc. Vat.* p. 23), Rom. xv. 18; Ἕλλην καὶ Ἰουδαῖος, Col. iii. 11.[2] (In Mt. xiv. 21, xv. 38, the reading of D is παιδία καὶ γυναῖκες: compare Cæsar, *B. Gall.* 2. 28, 4. 14.) The order οἱ πόδες καὶ αἱ χεῖρες seems to predominate in the N. T.: Mt. xxii. 13, Jo. xi. 44, xiii. 9, A. xxi. 11. L. xxiv. 39, 40, are the only examples of the reverse, τὰς χεῖράς μου καὶ τοὺς πόδας. Here perhaps there is a reference to the circumstance that *the hands only* of the crucified were pierced, so that τὰς χεῖρας is the principal member of the clause; indeed John mentions the hands alone. In Rom. xiv. 9, the order νεκροὶ καὶ ζῶντες is determined by the preceding words ἀπέθανεν καὶ ἔζησεν.

The N. T. writers move more freely when they bring together a series of notions. In this case we do not find general and special ideas separately grouped, but the order of the words is regulated by a loose association of ideas, or even by similarity

---

[1] Heusinger, Plut. *Educ.* 2. 5.
[2] [It will be understood that these are not the only examples in which the order given above is departed from. In A. xvii. 12 we find γυναικῶν ... καὶ ἀνδρῶν: in Mt. xv. 38 the order παιδία καὶ γυναῖκες is found in ℵ as well as in D, and is received by Tisch. (ed. 8): of ἡμέρας καὶ νυκτός there are 5 examples in Revelation, against 5 or 6 of νυκτὸς καὶ ἡμέρας in the rest of the N. T. (see Ellicott on 1 Tim. v. 5, Lob. *Paral.* p. 62 sq.). With Rom. xv. 18 may be compared Col. iii. 17 and A. vii. 22 (ἔργῳ καὶ λόγῳ occurs twice only): *earth* stands before *heaven* in L. xii. 56, Rev. xx. 11, al.,—also *sea* before *land* in Rev. x. 5, 8 (but compare ver. 2): in Rev. xiii. 16, xix. 18, δοῦλος follows ἐλεύθερος.]

of sound (Rom. i. 29, 31, Col. iii. 5). On the whole see Lobeck, *Paralip.* p. 62 sqq.

We must be cautious in applying the name *Hysteron proteron* (compare *Odyss.* 12. 134, τὰς μὲν ἄρα θρέψασα τεκοῦσά τε· Thuc. 8. 66 [1]) to such abnormal collocations. It may be observed in passing that Jo. i. 52, ἀγγέλους θεοῦ ἀναβαίνοντας καὶ καταβαίνοντας, has been rightly explained by Lücke;[2] and that we must not suppose the ideas inverted in Jo. vi. 69, πεπιστεύκαμεν καὶ ἐγνώκαμεν (compare x. 38), because in 1 Jo. iv. 16 we find ἐγνώκαμεν καὶ πεπιστεύκαμεν (Jo. xvii. 8).[3] Nor can we admit this figure of speech in other N. T. passages. In 1 Tim. ii. 4 πάντας ἀνθρώπους θέλει σωθῆναι καὶ εἰς ἐπίγνωσιν ἀληθείας ἐλθεῖν, the general ultimate end is first mentioned, and then the immediate end (as a means towards attaining the former,—καί being *and accordingly*). A. xiv. 10 ἥλατο καὶ περιεπάτει is as possible in point of fact as περιπατῶν καὶ ἁλλόμενος, A. iii. 8. In 2 P. i. 9 μυωπάζων is added for the sake of more exact definition. The Hysteron proteron which in A. xvi. 18 Bornemann accepts from D[4] rests on insufficient authority. See further Wilke, *N. T. Rhetorik,* p. 226.

5. f. Sometimes, however, there is a real misplacement of particular words, through some inadvertence, or rather because the ancients, having only intelligent readers in view, were not anxious about minute precision. In particular, the Greek prose writers not unfrequently transpose certain adverbs,[5] to which every reader will assign their true position according to the sense, though the writer may not have arranged them with logical accuracy. It is so with ἀεί in Isocr. *Paneg.* 14, διετέλεσαν κοινὴν τὴν πόλιν παρέχοντες καὶ τοῖς ἀδικουμένοις ἀεὶ τῶν Ἑλλήνων ἐπαμύνουσαν· Xen. *Œc.* 19. 19, Thuc. 2. 43, al.[6] With πολλάκις: see Stallb. Plat. *Rep.* I. 93. With ἔτι in Rom. v. 6, ἔτι Χριστὸς ὄντων ἡμῶν ἀσθενῶν,[7] for ἔτι ὄντων ἡμῶν ἀσθενῶν

---

[1] Nitzsch, *Odyss.* I. 251 sq. [Several of Nitzsch's examples are quoted by Hayman on *Od.* 4. 208: see also Riddell, Plat. *Apol.* p. 237 sq., Jelf 904. 4.]

[2] [As signifying that the angels are not regarded as now *beginning* to descend: the scene displayed to view will be that of *an already existing* intercourse between earth and heaven.]

[3] See Baumg.-Crusius *in loc.* [In Jo. x. 38 read γνῶτε καὶ γινώσκητε.]

[4] [The transposition of διαπονηθεὶς and ἐπιστρέψας.]

[5] Stallb. Plat. *Phæd.* p. 123 (Jelf. 904. *Obs.* 2, Don. p. 611).

[6] See Krüger, *Dion.* p. 252, Schæf. *Demosth.* II. 234.

[7] [This reading is retained by most editors: see Reiche, *Comm. Cr.* p. 34–39. On the reading ἔτι γὰρ . . . ἀσθενῶν ἔτι (אACD, Griesbach, Lachmann, Tregelles) see Vaughan, who takes the first ἔτι as *moreover* (L. xvi. 26, al.). Alford reads εἴγε . . . ἀσθενῶν ἔτι, with B: so also Westcott and Hort (doubtfully), see their *Appendix,* p. 178.]

(compare ver. 8): Plat. *Rep.* 2. 363 d, Achill. *Tat.* 5. 18, and Poppo, *Thuc.* I. i. 300 sqq. Lastly, with ὅμως: 1 Cor. xiv. 7, ὅμως τὰ ἄψυχα φωνὴν διδόντα ... ἐὰν διαστολὴν τοῖς φθόγγοις μὴ δῷ, πῶς γνωσθήσεται τὸ αὐλούμενον κ.τ.λ., instead of, τὰ ἄψυχα, (καίπερ) φωνὴν διδόντα, ὅμως, ἐὰν μή κ.τ.λ.; G. iii. 15, ὅμως ἀνθρώπου κεκυρωμένην διαθήκην οὐδεὶς ἀθετεῖ, instead of, ὅμως οὐδεὶς ἀθετεῖ.[1] Compare Plat. *Phæd.* 91 c, φοβεῖται μὴ ἡ ψυχὴ ὅμως καὶ θειότερον καὶ κάλλιον ὂν τοῦ σώματος προαπολλύηται.[2] (Jelf 697. d.)

In the case of the negative also a trajection is not very uncommon in Greek writers, especially the poets (see Hermann, Eurip. *Hec.* 12). When this takes place, either there is a tacit antithesis, as in Plat. *Crit.* 47 d, πειθόμενοι μὴ τῇ τῶν ἐπαϊόντων δόξῃ· *Legg.* 12. 943 a, Xen. *Mem.* 3. 9. 6 (compare Kühner II. 628,[3] Jelf 904. *Obs.* 3); or the negation, instead of being attached to the negatived word, is prefixed to the whole sentence, as in Plat. *Apol.* 35 d, ἃ μήτε ἡγοῦμαι καλὰ εἶναι μήτε δίκαια· Xen. Eph. 3. 8, ὅτι μὴ τὸ φάρμακον θανάσιμον ἦν·—so also in A. vii. 48, ἀλλ' οὐχ ὁ ὕψιστος ἐν χειροποιήτοις κατοικεῖ. By many commentators it is supposed that there is a misplacement of the negative[4] in Rom. iii. 9, τί οὖν; προεχόμεθα; οὐ πάν-

---

[1] See Bengel, and my note *in loc.*
[2] See Hermann and Lobeck on Soph. *Aj.* 15, Döderlein, Soph. *Œd. C.* p. 396, Pflugk, Eurip. *Andr.* p. 10, and *Hel.* p. 76.—We must not however, with Fritz. *Mark*, p. 19, bring εὐθέως (εὐθύς) under this head. In Mk. ii. 8, v. 30, it belongs to the particle beside which it is placed: in other instances, Mk. i. 10, ix. 15, it stands at the head of the sentence (see above in the text), and may then be easily connected with the principal verb. Πάλιν also is not transposed in 2 C. xii. 21, but is prefixed to the whole sentence,—*lest again when I come God should humble me.* So probably σχεδόν in H. ix. 22 : *and almost* may this rule be laid down, "Everything is purified by blood, etc." Compare Galen, *Protrept.* c. 1, τὰ μὲν ἄλλα ζῶα σχεδὸν ἄτεχνα πάντ' ἐστί· Aristot. *Polit.* 2. 8, Lysias I. 204 (ed. Auger).
[3] What Valckenaer quotes in his *Schol. N. T.*, II. 574, is not all well chosen. On other passages in which even recent scholars have wrongly assumed a trajection of the negative (e. g., Thuc. 1. 5, 3. 57) see Sintenis, Plut. *Themist.* p. 2.
[4] The assertion made by some of these commentators, that Grotius's rendering "not in all respects" is *ungrammatical*, I do not understand. As little however can I comprehend how οὐ πάντως, *omnino non*, can be called a Hebraism. The meaning of לֹא כֹל—the particles standing thus in immediate connexion—is *non omnis;* and whenever οὐ πᾶς is used in the sense of οὐδείς the particles are separated in such a way that the *verb* is negatived by οὐ (§ 26. 1). בְּכֹל אַל, with an ellipsis of the verb (adduced by Koppe *in loc.*), I cannot call to mind as occurring in the O. T.

τως, i. e., *by no means* (πάντως οὔ, 1 C. xvi. 12). The words οὐ πάντως must have this meaning here, whether προεχόμεθα be rendered *have we a pre-eminence?* or *have we an excuse?* That such an explanation is philologically possible, is shown by Theogn. 305 (250 sq.)[1] and Epiphan. *Hær.* 38. 6, and also by the analogy of such expressions as οὐδὲν πάντως Her. 5. 34, 65;[2] but there is no real transposition of the negative. The phrase was rather conceived thus,—*no, absolutely,—no, in no way;* and the distinction between οὐ πάντως as *not altogether* and as *altogether not* would probably be marked by the mode of utterance. Hence there was no occasion for the despair expressed by Van Hengel, who holds that in the text as it stands there is some corruption, the nature of which is not clearly indicated. On the other hand, in 1 C. v. 9 sq., ἔγραψα ὑμῖν ... μὴ συναναμίγνυσθαι πόρνοις, οὐ πάντως τοῖς πόρνοις τοῦ κόσμου τούτου, the meaning of οὐ πάντως is *non omnino* (Sext. Emp. *Math.* 11. 18), and the last words are corrective and explanatory of μὴ συναναμίγνυσθαι πόρνοις: *to hold no intercourse with fornicators, —not generally with the fornicators of this world, for in that case ye must needs sever yourselves from the world* (but, in strictness, only with the unchaste members of the church). So the passage was taken by Luther. H. xi. 3, εἰς τὸ μὴ ἐκ φαινομένων τὰ βλεπόμενα γεγονέναι, has been wrongly referred to this category. Schulz correctly renders the words: *That, therefore, what has been seen has nevertheless not arisen out of things visible;* compare also Bengel *in loc.* The proposition denied is ἐκ φαινομένων τὰ βλεπόμενα γεγονέναι; and to this the negative is pre-

---

[1] Οἱ κακοὶ οὐ πάντως κακοὶ ἐκ γαστρὸς γεγόνασιν,
Ἀλλ' ἄνδρεσσι κακοῖς συνθέμενοι φιλίην.

[2] But οὐ πάνυ (μὴ πάνυ) invariably means *not particularly*. Sometimes it is mild in expression only, and in meaning strong,—on the principle of Litotes; see Weber, *Demosth.* p. 340, Franke, *Demosth.* p. 62. In Rom. *l.c.* the context and the tone of the passage prevent our applying this principle, and rendering οὐ πάντως *not altogether* (either seriously or ironically). [In Rom. iii. 9 the rendering "*by no means*" is accepted by most. A. Buttm. (p. 389), remarking that if the ellipsis were filled up we should have οὐ προιχόμεθα πάντως, refers the phrase to the idiom noticed in § 26. 1: Meyer seems to connect it with the instances in which οὐ reverses the meaning of the word before which it stands (§ 55. 1). This latter principle is frequently applied to οὐ πάνυ: see Don. p. 558, Jelf 738. Obs. 1, Buttm. p. 496, Krüg. p. 304, Hartung II. 87, Liddell and Scott s.v. πάνυ, Meyer on Rom. *l.c.* On the other side see Rost u. Palm s.v. πάνυ, Riddell, Plat. *Apol.* p. 171 sq., who take the same view as Winer ("the universal meaning of οὐ πάνυ is *hardly, scarcely:*" Riddell *l. c.*).]

fixed in perfect accordance with rule.¹ The passage appealed to as containing a transposed negative, 2 Macc. vii. 28, ὅτι οὐκ ἐξ ὄντων ἐποίησεν αὐτὰ ὁ θεός, is uncertain, since this reading is found in the *Cod. Alex.* only: Tischendorf reads ἐξ οὐκ ὄντων. In 2 C. iii. 4 sq., πεποίθησιν ... ἔχομεν, οὐχ ὅτι ἱκανοί ἐσμεν κ.τ.λ., we cannot take οὐχ ὅτι as standing for ὅτι οὐχ (μή). The true rendering is: *This conviction have we ...; not* (having in mind 2 C. i. 24) *that we are able through ourselves, but our ability is from God.* In 2 C. xiii. 7 Paul expresses the purpose of εὐχόμεθα ... μηδέν in the first instance negatively, in the words οὐχ ἵνα ἡμεῖς δόκιμοι φανῶμεν, *not in order that I* (if ye keep yourselves from evil) *may appear approved* (as your teacher). In 1 Jo. iv. 10 it is evident at once that the words οὐχ ὅτι are correctly placed. Nor is there any misplacement of the negative in Rom. iv. 12; the strangeness consists in the repetition of the article before στοιχοῦσιν,—a negligence of style which Fritzsche seeks to hide by a forced interpretation, but which Philippi freely admits. In regard to 1 C. xv. 51, πάντες (μὲν) οὐ κοιμηθησόμεθα, πάντες δὲ ἀλλαγησόμεθα, even after all that has been said by Fritzsche² and Van Hengel, I can but agree with Meyer. Ver. 52 shows that the word ἀλλάττεσθαι is not used in the wider sense (as also applying to those who are raised), but in the narrower, as an antithesis to ἐγείρεσθαι. The only possible translation is: *We all* (the generation which Paul is addressing³) *shall—not sleep—shall however all be changed.* Had Paul supposed that some of the πάντες must die, these would belong to the number of the νεκροί spoken of in ver. 52,

---

¹ [On this passage see Alford. Compare also Riddell, *Plat. Apol.* p. 232.]
² Fritzsche, *De conform. text. Lachm.* p. 38 sq.: Van Hengel, *Cor.* p. 216 sqq.
³ ["Paul himself and all those who will, with him, be living at the time of the παρουσία," is a more exact expression of Meyer's view. But surely this arbitrary restriction of the meaning of πάντες involves as great a difficulty as the supposition that the meaning of ἀλλάττεσθαι varies somewhat in the two verses. Reiche (*Comm. Cr. in loc.*) argues in favour of a transposition of the negative; and De Wette concedes that this is possible, as the emphasis lies on πάντες (compare Num. xxiii. 13). De Wette himself, however, refers the first πάντες as well as the second to ἀλλαγησόμεθα, the words (μὲν) οὐ κοιμηθησόμεθα being quasi-parenthetical, *we all shall—not die—shall however all be changed* (Billroth, Olshausen, Stanley). See further Alford *in loc.*, A. Buttm. p. 121.—The reading of *Rec.* (so far as the position of οὐ is concerned,—μὲν must probably be omitted) is retained by Tischendorf, Reiche, Meyer, De Wette, Stanley, Alford, Tregelles (who places in the margin κοιμηθησόμεθα οὐ, πάντες δέ), Green (*Dev. Crit.* p. 141 sq.): also by Westcott and Hort, see their *Appendix*, p. 118. See also Reiche, *Comm. Cr.* p. 297-317.]

and ἡμεῖς would be an incorrect antithesis. The doubt whether Paul could utter such a prediction as this, cannot induce me to give to ἀλλάττεσθαι in ver. 51 a meaning different from that which it bears in ver. 52. Other objections are answered by Meyer.—That in Rom. xiii. 14 τῆς σαρκὸς πρόνοιαν μὴ ποιεῖσθε εἰς ἐπιθυμίας does not stand for μὴ εἰς ἐπιθυμίας, seems clear in any case: see Fritzsche *in loc.* In 2 C. xii. 20 the translators —as far back as Luther—have taken the liberty of transposing the negative; in the Greek, however, all is in order.

In Rom. xv. 20 οὐχ ὅπου, assumed to stand for ὅπου οὐκ, is said by Bengel "majorem emphasin habere," by Baumg.-Crusius to be a milder and more modest phrase; whereas it is simply the only correct expression,—οὕτως, οὐχ ὅπου . . . ἀλλά κ.τ.λ. In Rom. viii. 12 οὐ τῇ σαρκί of itself calls forth the antithesis ἀλλὰ τῷ πνεύματι. Attention was called by Bengel to the different positions (each of them in accordance with the sense to be expressed) which the negative occupies in Rom. ii. 14, ἔθνη τὰ μὴ νόμον ἔχοντα and νόμον μὴ ἔχοντες; see also Meyer *in loc.*[1]

Several have supposed a *hyperbaton* to exist in 2 Tim. ii. 6, τὸν κοπιῶντα γεωργὸν δεῖ πρῶτον τῶν καρπῶν μεταλαμβάνειν. The apostle seems (from ver. 5) to intend to say, "the husbandman who first labours must enjoy the fruits," i.e., the husbandman must first labour before he enjoys the fruits: in this case πρῶτον belongs to κοπιᾶν, and the sentence should properly have been arranged accordingly. Compare Xen. *Cyr.* 1. 3. 18, ὁ σὸς πρῶτος πατὴρ τεταγμένα ποιεῖ; i.e., ὁ σὸς πατὴρ πρῶτος τετ. ποιεῖ. To evade the *hyperbaton*, Grotius takes πρῶτον as *demum*, which is not admissible. Recent commentators, laying the emphasis on κοπιῶντα thus thrown forward in the sentence, explain the words to mean, "the labouring"—not the idle —"husbandman has the first right to enjoy the fruits": see especially Wiesinger *in loc.* Similar and even more remarkable *hyperbata* are not rare in Greek prose: see Plat. *Rep.* 7. 524 a, Xen. *Cyr.* 2. 1. 5.[2]

A Greek writer will sometimes take one or more words out of a relative sentence, and bring them in before the relative[3] for the sake of emphasis: see above, no. 3. Several commentators have introduced this usage into A. i. 2, punctuating the words thus: τοῖς ἀποστόλοις, διὰ πνεύματος ἁγίου οὓς ἐξελέξατο. This arrangement however has little probability, for it is only the ἐντέλλεσθαι διὰ πνεύματος ἁγίου that could here be of importance to Luke (for the subse-

---

[1] [Bengel: "*non* legem habent . . . *legem* non habent." Meyer: in the former case it is the possession of the *law* that is denied (and the contrast is between *the law* and φύσις): in the latter, the *possession* of the law (the Gentiles are contrasted with the Jews who *have* it).]

[2] Compare Bornem. Xen. *Anab.* p. 21, Franke, *Demosth.* p. 33.

[3] Stallb. Plat. *Rep.* I. 109.

quent contents of the book of Acts) ; whereas the ἐκλέγεσθαι διὰ τοῦ πνεύματος falls within the sphere of the Gospel, and should not be first related here. The general reference to the past contained in οὓς ἐξελέξατο—in which words the apostles are especially indicated—is not without meaning, since it was through this previous choice that they became qualified to receive the commands διὰ τοῦ πνεύματος. See Valcken. *in loc.*—There would be more ground for such an arrangement of words in A. v. 35, προσέχετε ἑαυτοῖς, ἐπὶ τοῖς ἀνθρώποις τί μέλλετε πράσσειν (see Bornem. *in loc.*); though the other punctuation gives a suitable sense,—*take heed to yourselves in regard to these men, what ye are about to do.*

On the other hand it is inconceivable that in A. xxvii. 39 Luke can have written κόλπον τινὰ κατενόουν ἔχοντα αἰγιαλόν for αἰγιαλὸν ἔχοντα κόλπον τινά. The explanation had already been given by Grotius : non frustra hoc additur, sunt enim sinus quidam maris, qui litus non habent, sed præruptis rupibus cinguntur. See also Bengel. Besides, αἰγιαλὸν ἔχοντα must be strictly connected with the relative clause εἰς ὃν κ.τ.λ.,—*which had a shore on which they resolved to land,* i. e., a shore of such a nature that they could be led to this resolve.[1] Equally harsh is the arrangement which some have proposed in Rom. vii. 21, εὑρίσκω ἄρα τὸν νόμον τῷ θέλοντι ἐμοὶ ποιεῖν τὸ καλὸν ὅτι ἐμοὶ τὸ κακὸν παράκειται,—viz., τῷ θέλοντι ἐμοὶ τὸν νόμον ποιεῖν, τὸ καλόν, κ.τ.λ. It has always seemed to me that the words are most simply grouped thus : εὑρίσκω ἄρα τὸν νόμον, τῷ θέλοντι . . . . ὅτι ἐμοὶ τὸ κακὸν παράκειται, *invenio hanc legem* (normam) *volenti mihi honestum facere, ut mihi* etc.[2] See also Philippi *in loc.*

Such expressions as the following are considered by many to be examples of a trajection which has become established, and which even influences the case of the noun (Matth. 380. Rem. 2) : Jo. xii. 1, πρὸ ἓξ ἡμερῶν τοῦ πάσχα, *six days before the passover;* xi. 18, ἦν ἡ Βηθανία ἐγγὺς τῶν Ἱεροσολύμων ὡς ἀπὸ σταδίων δεκαπέντε, *about fifteen stadia from it.* Compare Jo. xxi. 8, Rev. xiv. 20. Were the prepositions in their right place, it is said, the words would run ἓξ ἡμέραις πρὸ τοῦ πάσχα, ὡς σταδίους δεκαπέντε ἀπὸ Ἱεροσολύμων (L. xxiv. 13). It is probable, however, that in Greek they set out from a different view of the matter, and in specifying distance said ἀπὸ σταδίων δεκαπέντε (properly, *lying off from 15 stadia,* i. e., *where the 15 stadia terminate, at the end of the 15 stadia*); just as in Latin, e. g.,

---

[1] [See Smith, *Voyage of St. Paul* p. 136, Alford *in loc.*]
[2] [If we take this as the most natural division of the words, there are two chief interpretations between which we have to choose. (1.) That given in the text, which is, perhaps, most commonly adopted. The weak point is the explanation of τὸν νόμον, which throughout the context denotes the *Mosaic* law. (2.) " I find then with regard to the law, that to me, etc." On this view we have a broken construction ; τὸν νόμον being put "as if the intention had been to complete the sentence thus, *I find then the law powerless to effectuate in me that well-doing which my will approves*" (Vaughan).—Meyer takes νόμον as governed by θέλοντι. Bengel and others give ὅτι the sense of *because.* See Meyer's note ; also *Speak. Comm.* III. 142, 145.]

Liv. 24. 46, Fabius cum *a quingentis fere passibus* castra posuisset.[1] If now it was also necessary to define the position of the speaker, this was expressed by means of a genitive added to the formula. So also in specifications of time. As it was customary to say πρὸ ἐξ ἡμερῶν for *six days ago*,[2] the same formula was retained when it was necessary to give an indication of the point of time in reference to which the calculation was made; hence πρὸ ἐξ ἡμερῶν τοῦ πάσχα (compare *Evang. Apocr.* p. 436 sq.). In whatever way the matter may be regarded, this mode of expression (in relation to both space and time) is sufficiently common in later writers. Compare Ælian, *Anim.* 11. 19, πρὸ πέντε ἡμερῶν τοῦ ἀφανισθῆναι τὴν Ἑλίκην· Xen. Eph. 3. 3, Lucian, *Cronos.* 14, *Geopon.* 12. 31. 2, Achill. Tat. 7. 14 (and Jacobs *in loc.*), Epiphan. *Opp.* II. 248 a, Strabo 10. 483, 15. 715, καταλαβεῖν ἄνδρας πεντεκαίδεκα ἀπὸ σταδίων εἴκοσι τῆς πόλεως· Plutarch, *Philop.* 4, ἦν ἀγρὸς αὐτῷ καλὸς ἀπὸ σταδίων εἴκοσι τῆς πόλεως· Diod. S. 2. 7, *Acta Apocr.* p. 39, 61 ; see Reiske, *Const. Porphyrog.* II. 20 (Bonn ed.), Schæf. *Long.* p. 129. In the LXX Kühnöl has pointed out the following examples : Am. i. 1, πρὸ δύο ἐτῶν τοῦ σεισμοῦ· iv. 7, πρὸ τριῶν μηνῶν τοῦ τρυγητοῦ ; with a singular, ἀπὸ μιᾶς ἡμέρας τῆς Μαρδοχαϊκῆς ἡμέρας 2 Macc. xv. 36 (Joseph. *Antt.* 15. 11. 4, Plut. *Symp.* 8. 1. 1). We also find similar formulas (in a temporal sense) with μετά: Plut. *Coriol.* 11, μεθ' ἡμέρας ὀλίγας τῆς τοῦ πατρὸς τελευτῆς· Malal. 4. p. 88, μετὰ νβ' ἔτη τοῦ τελευτῆσαι τὴν Πασιφάην· Anon. *Chronol.* (prefixed to Malalas in the Bonn ed.) p. 10, μετὰ δύο ἔτη τοῦ κατακλυσμοῦ. See Schæfer *ad Bos, Ellips.* p. 553 sq.

6. Certain particles and enclitic pronouns have their place in a Greek sentence fixed with more or less definiteness, in accordance with the weight which they possess in the sentence. Thus μέν (μενοῦνγε, μέντοι), οὖν, δέ, γάρ, γε, τοίνυν, ἄρα, are not allowed to stand at the commencement of a sentence. (Ἄρα cannot even be the first word in the consequent clause ; see Xen. *Cyr.* 1. 3. 2, 8. 4. 7.) In regard to most of these words the rule is observed by the N. T. writers ;[3] and δέ, γάρ and οὖν occupy sometimes the second, sometimes the third, sometimes even the

---

[1] Ramshorn p. 273 [Zumpt 396, Madvig 234 b. *Obs.*, 270. *Obs.* 4].—An illustration is also afforded by Polyæn. 2. 35, τοὺς πολλοὺς ἐκέλευσεν ἀπὸ βραχέος διαστήματος ἕπεσθαι.

[2] [This mode of expression (with a numeral) belongs to late Greek, and its prevalence is to be attributed more or less to the influence of the Latin : see Liddell and Scott s. v. πρό, A. Buttm. p. 153. Compare πρὸ πολλοῦ, Her. 7. 130 (also 2 Tim. i. 9, Tit. i. 2). In the N. T. see further A. x. 30 (Meyer, Alford), 2 C. xii. 2 : see Grimm, *Clavis* s. vv. ἀπό, πρό, Jelf 905. 3.]

[3] Once only do we find ἔφη inserted in the midst of words directly quoted as spoken (A. xxiii. 35) ; but φησί is so placed in Mt. xiv. 8, A. xxv. 5, 22, xxvi. 25, al. [φασίν, 2 C. x. 10 Lachm.]. The N. T. writers commonly prefix ὁ Παῦλος ἔφη, ὁ δὲ ἔφη, etc., to the words quoted : in Greek authors this is the less usual arrangement (Madvig 219). [On μέν and δέ see Jelf 765 ; on δέ, Ellicott on G. iii. 23.]

SECT. LXI.] POSITION OF WORDS AND CLAUSES. 699

fourth place. The MSS., it is true, do not always agree among themselves. These three particles have the third or fourth place especially when it is proper to avoid separating words which are closely connected:[1] e.g., G. iii. 23, πρὸ τοῦ δὲ ἐλθεῖν· Mk. i. 38, εἰς τοῦτο γὰρ ἐξελήλυθα· L. vi. 23, xv. 17, 2 C. i. 19, ὁ τοῦ θεοῦ γὰρ υἱός· A. xxvii. 14, μετ' οὐ πολὺ δὲ ἔβαλε κ.τ.λ., Jo. viii. 16, καὶ ἐὰν κρίνω δὲ ἐγώ· 1 Jo. ii. 2, οὐ περὶ τῶν ἡμετέρων δὲ μόνον· 1 C. viii. 4, περὶ τῆς βρώσεως οὖν τῶν εἰδωλοθύτων· 2 C. x. 1, ὃς κατὰ πρόσωπον μὲν ταπεινός· Jo. xvi. 22, A. iii. 21. On δέ (Her. 8. 68, Æl. *Anim.* 7. 27, Xen. *Mem.* 2. 1. 16, 5. 4. 13, Diod. S. 11. 11, Thuc. 1. 6, 70, Arrian, *Al.* 2. 2. 2, Xen. *Eq.* 11. 8, Lucian, *Eunuch.* 4, *Dial. Mort.* 5. 1, Sext. Emp. *Math.* 7. 65, Strabo 17. 808)—see Herm. *Orph.* p. 820, Boisson. *Aristænet.* p. 687, Poppo, *Thuc.* I. i. 302, III. i. 71, Stallb. *Phileb,* p. 90, Franke, *Demosth.* p. 208. On γάρ see Schæf. *Melet. Crit.* p. 76, V. Fritzsche, *Quæst. Lucian.* p. 100. On μέν see Herm. *Orph. l.c.,* Bornem. Xenoph. *Conv.* p. 61, Weber, *Demosth.* p. 402. On the other hand, ἄρα (see Herm. Soph. *Antig.* 628) frequently occupies the first place, contrary to Greek usage: e. g., L. xi. 48, Rom. x. 17, 2 C. v. 15, G. ii. 21, v. 11, al. Similarly ἄρα οὖν, Rom. v. 18, vii. 3, 2 Th. ii. 15, E. ii. 19, al. Μενοῦνγε also begins a period in L. xi. 28 [*Rec.*], Rom. ix. 20, x. 18 (see Lob. *Phryn.* p. 342); and τοίνυν in H. xiii. 13.[2] The latter particle very rarely stands first in the better Greek authors; for examples from later writers see Lob. *Phryn. l.c.* In Sextus Empiricus, in particular, they are not uncommon: see *Math.* 1. 11, 14, 25, 140, 152, 155, 217, al. Amongst the Byzantines compare Cinnam. p. 125, 136 (Bonn ed.).[3]

It has been questioned whether the indefinite τὶς can commence a sentence: see Matthiæ, Eurip. *Suppl.* 1187 and *Sprachl.* 487. 6. The instances in which it has the first place may indeed, from the nature of the case, be rare; but approved critics have with good reason assigned it this position in Soph. *Trach.* 865, *Œd. R.* 1471 (compare ver. 1475), Æschyl. *Choeph.* 640 (Herm.). In prose see Plat. *Theæt.* 147 c, Plut. *Tranq.* c. 13. In the N. T., however, there

---

[1] [Lünemann adds: "especially in prepositional combinations." To Winer's list of examples he adds H. i. 13.]
[2] [Τοίνυν stands second in 1 C. ix. 26, L. xx. 25 *Rec.*: first in H. xiii. 13, L. xx. 25 (in the best texts). In Ja. ii. 24 it is probably not genuine.]
[3] Μέντοι however is always placed after some other word which commences the sentence. It is otherwise in later writers: see Boissonade, *Anecd.* II. 27.

are undoubted examples of this kind : Mt. xxvii. 47, L. vi. 2, Jo. xiii. 29, 1 Tim. v. 24, Ph. i. 15. (Jelf 660.)

The particles ἀλλά γε, *yet at all events*, are in earlier writers always separated by some word (be it only a particle) : see Klotz, p. 15 sq. This rule is not observed in L. xxiv. 21, ἀλλά γε σὺν πᾶσι τούτοις τρίτην ταύτην ἡμέραν ἄγει : see Bornemann *in loc.*

The particle μέν is regularly placed after the word to which it belongs in sense[1] (Jelf 765). To this rule also there are some exceptions : A. xxii. 3, ἐγὼ μέν εἰμι ἀνὴρ Ἰουδαῖος, γεγεννημένος ἐν Ταρσῷ τῆς Κιλικίας, ἀνατεθραμμένος δὲ ἐν τῇ πόλει ταύτῃ, instead of, ἐγώ εἰμι ἀνὴρ Ἰουδαῖος γεγεννημένος μέν κ.τ.λ. ; Tit. i. 15, πάντα μὲν καθαρὰ τοῖς καθαροῖς, τοῖς δὲ μεμιασμένοις καὶ ἀπίστοις οὐδὲν καθαρόν, instead of τοῖς μὲν καθαροῖς πάντα καθαρά κ.τ.λ., or πάντα μὲν καθαρά . . . οὐδὲν δὲ καθαρὸν τοῖς μεμιασμένοις ; 1 C. ii. 15. Compare Xen. *Mem.* 2. 1. 6, 3. 9. 8, Æl. *Anim.* 2. 31, Diog. L. 6. 60 : see Herm. Soph. *Œd. R.* 436, Hartung, *Part.* II. 415 sq. In these three passages of the N. T., however, μέν is omitted in good MSS., and recent editors[2] have followed these authorities. But may not the offence which the particle gave to transcribers have been the very cause of the omission ?

The proper position of τε is immediately after a word which stands in parallelism with some other word : A. xiv. 1, Ἰουδαίων τε καὶ Ἑλλήνων πολὺ πλῆθος· ix. 2, xx. 21, xxvi. 3. Not unfrequently, however, it is placed more freely (A. xxvi. 22[3]) ; in particular, it stands immediately after a preposition or article (A. x. 39, ii. 33, xxviii. 23, Jo. ii. 15, al.), in which case it sometimes indicates that this word belongs to the two parallel members, in common,—as in A. xxv. 23, σύν τε χιλιάρχοις καὶ ἀνδράσιν, xiv. 5 [?], x. 39. Compare Plat. *Legg.* 7. 796 d, εἴς τε πολιτείαν καὶ ἰδίους οἴκους· Thuc. 4. 13, and the examples collected by Elmsley, Eurip. *Heracl.* 622 (also Joseph. *Antt.* 17. 6. 2), and by Ellendt, *Lexic. Soph.* II. 796[4] (Jelf 756). In the same way γε is placed after the article or a monosyllabic particle, as Rom. viii. 32, 2 C. v. 3, E. iii. 2 ; compare Xen. *Mem.* 1. 2. 27, 3. 12. 7, 4. 2. 22, Diod. S. 5. 40.[5]

---

[1] If several words are connected together grammatically,—as article and noun, preposition and noun,—μέν may stand immediately after the first : e. g., L. x. 2, ὁ μὲν θερισμός· H. xii. 11, πρὸς μὲν τὸ παρόν· A. i. 1, viii. 4, al. (Demosth. *Lacrit.* 595 a). So also μὲν οὖν : Lysias, *Pecun. Publ.* 3, ἐν μὲν οὖν τῷ πολέμῳ. Compare Bornem. Xen. *Conv.* p. 61. This is true of other conjunctions also ; see above, p. 455. — Even names of one person are sometimes separated by such conjunctions : Jo. xviii. 10, Σίμων οὖν Πέτρος.

[2] [In the last passage authorities are much divided. Westcott and Hort retain μέν.]

[3] Elmsley, Eurip. *Heracl.* 622 : yet compare Schoem. *Isæus* p. 325.

[4] On the whole see Sommer in Jahn's *Archiv*, I. 401 sqq.

[5] See Matthiæ, Eurip. *Iphig. Aul.* 498, Ellendt *l. c.* I. 344. [In L. xi. 8 γε is inserted between a preposition and its case : see Klotz, *Dev.* II. 327 sq., Jelf 735. *Obs.* 2.—Xάριν follows its genitive except in 1 Jo. iii. 12 : Herm. *Vig.* p. 700 sq., Jelf 621. *Obs.* 2.]

Several commentators (e. g., Schott) discover a trajection of καί (*even*) in H. vii. 4, ᾧ καὶ δεκάτην Ἀβραὰμ ἔδωκεν,—as standing for ᾧ δεκάτην καὶ Ἀβραὰμ ἔδωκεν. But here it is on the giving of the tenth that the emphasis rests: Schulz has correctly translated the words.

7. In certain passages a violent displacement of *clauses*[1] has been supposed to exist:—

a. In A. xxiv. 22, ὁ Φῆλιξ, ἀκριβέστερον εἰδὼς τὰ περὶ τῆς ὁδοῦ, εἴπας, ὅταν Λυσίας καταβῇ, διαγνώσομαι κ.τ.λ., Beza, Grotius and others bring εἰδώς κ.τ.λ. into the sentence introduced by εἴπας, and translate: *Felix, quando accuratius . . . . cognovero, inquit, et Lysias huc venerit* etc. Here however the whole is quite in order, as the more recent commentators have perceived.[2]

b. In 2 C. viii. 10, οἵτινες οὐ μόνον τὸ ποιῆσαι ἀλλὰ καὶ τὸ θέλειν προενήρξασθε ἀπὸ πέρυσι, some have supposed that the clauses are inverted (*non velle solum sed facere incepistis*[3]), because in ver. 11 we find ἡ προθυμία τοῦ θέλειν. But there is no ground for such an assumption. The "wishing" strictly denotes only the determination (to collect), and may, if προενήρξασθε is said comparatively—i. e., in comparison with the Christians of Macedonia—stand before the ποιῆσαι, as a more important moment of thought. Not merely in the arrangement, but even in the *purpose*, ye were before the Macedonians: the more becoming is it then to bring the collection to a complete conclusion.[4] It would have been quite possible that the resolve of the Macedonians might have first moved the Corinthians to a like resolve. Meyer's treatment of the words is forced, and he comes at last to Fritzsche's view,[5] which De Wette ably opposes.

---

[1] W. Kahler, *Satura duplex de veris et fictis textus sacri trajectionibus ex Evangeliis et Actis Apostolorum collectis* (Lemgov. 1728); E. Wassenbergh, *De transpositione, saluberrimo in sanandis veterum scriptis remedio* (Franecq. 1786),—reprinted in Seebode's *Miscell. Crit,* I. 141 sqq.

[2] Comp. Bornemann in Rosenmüller, *Repertorium* II. 281 sq.

[3] Grotius, Schott, Stolz, and others. Syriac:

[4] I cannot admit that if this were the meaning we should necessarily have καὶ ἐπιτελέσατε τὸ ποιῆσαι in ver. 11. The θέλειν was, naturally, completed long ago, but it was also of importance to bring the ποιῆσαι to a conclusion.

[5] *Diss. in Cor.* II. 9. [Fritzsche explained τὸ ποιῆσαι of what had been already done in the way of collection, τὸ θέλειν of the purpose to continue in the same course. Meyer now (ed. 2, 3, 4) agrees with De Wette and Winer: so also Wieseler, Alford, Stanley.]

Of recent commentators De Wette was the first to return to the above explanation.[1] I retract my former interpretation of the passage.—On Jo. xi. 15 see above, § 53. 10. 6.

In Mk. xii. 12 a trajection is not to be thought of: after the completion of the first sentence, consisting of two members, the writer assigns the reason of the fact expressed in the former member, and the result is then given in the words καὶ ἀφέντες κ.τ.λ. Mk. xvi. 3 is a similar case. In Ph. i. 16 sq., according to the best evidence, the two clauses should be thus arranged, οἱ μὲν ἐξ ἀγάπης . . . . οἱ δὲ ἐξ ἐριθείας : hence they refer to the members of ver. 15 in the reverse order,—an arrangement which cannot mislead any reader.

Whenever, in the arrangement of particular clauses, the dependent are made to precede the principal—as final clauses (Mt. xvii. 27, A. xxiv. 4, Jo. i. 31, xix. 28, 31, 2 C. xii. 7, Rom. ix. 11, —see Fritzsche, *Rom.* II. 297), or relative (Mk. xi. 23, Jo. iii. 11, Rom. viii. 29, al.), or conditional (1 C. vi. 4, xiv. 9),—the reason for this arrangement is obvious to any attentive reader. Compare Kühner II. 626 (Jelf 903. 2). Under this head should probably come 1 C. xv. 2, τίνι λόγῳ εὐηγγελισάμην ὑμῖν εἰ κατέχετε : see Meyer *in loc.*

Section LXII.

INTERRUPTED STRUCTURE OF SENTENCES: PARENTHESIS.

1. We give the name of "interrupted sentences" to those sentences whose grammatical course is arrested by the intervention of a sentence which is complete in itself :[2] A. xiii. 8, ἀνθίστατο αὐτοῖς Ἐλύμας ὁ μάγος—οὕτως γὰρ μεθερμηνεύεται τὸ ὄνομα αὐτοῦ—ζητῶν διαστρέψαι κ.τ.λ. ; Rom. i. 13, οὐ θέλω ὑμᾶς ἀγνοεῖν ὅτι πολλάκις προεθέμην ἐλθεῖν πρὸς ὑμᾶς—καὶ ἐκωλύθην ἄχρι τοῦ δεῦρο—ἵνα τινὰ καρπὸν σχῶ καὶ ἐν ὑμῖν. This intervening sentence is called a parenthesis ;[3] and it is

---

[1] [Given previously by Cajetan and Estius.—Winer's "former interpretation" is that given in ed. 4, in which θέλων is taken to mean *do willingly* or *readily.*]

[2] The explanation given in Ruddiman's *Institutiones* (II. 396, ed. Stallb.) is not amiss : " parenthesis est sententia sermoni, antequam absolvatur, interjecta." Wilke's definition (*Rhetor.* p. 227) is too wide. (Jelf 798. 2.)

[3] Ch. Wolle, *Comment. de parenthesi sacra* (Lips. 1726) ; J. F. Hirt, *Diss. de parenthesi et generatim et speciatim sacra* (Jen. 1745) ; A. B. Spitzner, *Comment. philol. de parenthesi libris V. et N. T. accommodata* (Lips. 1773) ; J. G. Lindner, 2 *Comment. de parenthesibus Johanneis* (Arnstad. 1765,—a treatise " de parenthe-

customary to present it to the eye as severed from the main sentence, by the use of the familiar marks of parenthesis.[1]

According to the above definition we cannot, in the first place, regard as a parenthesis any accessory sentence which is introduced (even though it be of considerable length), if—either by means of a relative or as a genitive absolute—it stands connected in construction with the principal sentence: Rom. xvi. 4, ix. 1, 1 P. iii. 6, 1 C. v. 4, L. i. 70, ii. 23, E. vi. 2, A. iv. 36. Still less can this name be given to appositional clauses, as Jo. xiv. 22, xv. 26, 1 P. iii. 21, 2 Jo. 1, A. ix. 17, Mk. vii. 2, 1 C. ix. 21; to clauses which are appended to a *completed* sentence to give an illustration, explanation, or reason, as Jo. iv. 6, 8, 10,[2] xi. 2, 51 sq., xiii. 11, xviii. 5, xix. 23, Mk. vii. 3 sq., 26, Mt. i. 22 sq., L. i. 55, A. i. 15, viii. 16, Rom. viii. 36, 1 C. ii. 8, xv. 41, G. ii. 8, E. ii. 8, H. v. 13, viii. 5, vii. 11, Rev. xxi. 25; or, lastly, to clauses which grammatically support any part of the sentence which lies beyond their own limits,[3] e. g., 1 C. xvi. 5, ἐλεύσομαι πρὸς ὑμᾶς, ὅταν Μακεδονίαν διέλθω (Μακεδονίαν γὰρ διέρχομαι), πρὸς ὑμᾶς δὲ τυχὸν παραμενῶ,—where it is clear that Μακεδονίαν and ὑμᾶς, διέρχομαι and παραμενῶ, are mutually related,—G. iv. 24, H. iii. 4, Jo. xxi. 8, Rom. ix. 11, Mk. v. 13, vii. 26.

Parentheses are either brought in ἀσυνδέτως, or are introduced by καί (Fritzsche, *Rom.* I. 35), δέ, or γάρ: Rom. i. 13, vii. 1, E. v. 9, H. vii. 11, Jo. xix. 31, 1 Tim. ii. 7, A. xii. 3, xiii. 8, 1 Jo. i. 2. After a parenthesis the construction either proceeds regularly, or is taken up again (sometimes in a somewhat altered form) by means of the repetition of a word from the principal sentence, with or without a conjunction,—as in 2 C. v. 8, 1 Jo. i. 3. Such a resumption of the construction, however, does not in itself give us a right to regard a series of words as forming a

---

sibus *Paullinis*" is more to be wished for).—Compare further Clerici *Ars Crit.* II. 144 sqq. (Lips.); Baumgarten, *Ausführl. Vortr. über die Hermeneutik*, p. 217 sqq.; Keil, *Lehrb. der Hermen.* p. 58 sq. (for the most part incorrect).

[1] To omit all external indications of a (true) parenthesis would be an inconsistency, if punctuation is to be retained at all. Still, in by far the greatest number of cases commas are sufficient for marking off inserted words. The round brackets seem the most suitable marks of parenthesis.

[2] [Probably this should be iv. 9.—A. i. 15, G. ii. 8, H. vii. 11, are subsequently quoted by Winer as true parentheses.]

[3] [It is hard to see how Jo. xxi. 8, Rom. ix. 11, Mk. v. 13, answer to this description. In the next paragraph Lünemann adds Jo. xvii. 10.]

parenthesis: E. i. 13, ἐν ᾧ καὶ ὑμεῖς ἀκούσαντες τὸν λόγον τῆς ἀληθείας, τὸ εὐαγγέλιον τῆς σωτηρίας ὑμῶν, ἐν ᾧ καὶ πιστεύσαντες ἐσφραγίσθητε κ.τ.λ., ii. 11 sqq., 1 C. viii. 1 (see Meyer [1]), 2 C. v. 6 sqq., Jo. xxi. 21. When the construction which had been commenced is not taken up again grammatically, but the train of thought is continued in a new and independent manner (as in Rom. v. 12 sqq.), we have not a parenthesis, but an anacoluthon (§ 63).

2. The number of parentheses in the N. T. is not small, but it is not as large as the earlier commentators and editors (Knapp included) supposed. Besides the insertion of single words, which is common in both Greek and Latin authors (compare *nudius tertius*),—as 2 C. viii. 3 κατὰ δύναμιν, μαρτυρῶ, καὶ παρὰ δύναμιν αὐθαίρετοι· H. x. 29, πόσῳ, δοκεῖτε, χείρονος ἀξιωθήσεται τιμωρίας· [2] 2 C. x. 10, αἱ μὲν ἐπιστολαί, φησίν, βαρεῖαι (see above, § 58. 9), xi. 21, Rom. iii. 5,—we frequently find in the historical books explanatory statements in regard to place, time, occasion, etc., parenthetically introduced: A. xii. 3, προσέθετο συλλαβεῖν καὶ Πέτρον—ἦσαν δὲ ἡμέραι τῶν ἀζύμων—ὅν κ.τ.λ., i. 15, xiii. 8, L. ix. 28, ἐγένετο μετὰ τοὺς λόγους τούτους, ὡσεὶ ἡμέραι ὀκτώ, καί κ.τ.λ. (compare Isocr. *Phil.* p. 216, Lucian, *Dial. Mar.* 1. 4),[3] A. v. 7, ἐγένετο δέ, ὡς ὡρῶν τριῶν διάστημα, καὶ ἡ γυνή κ.τ.λ., Mt. xv. 32 (compare

---

[1] [Meyer remarks that the words ἡ γνῶσις ... αὐτοῦ, constitute a *logical*, but not a *grammatical* parenthesis. 2 C. v. 6 sqq. has just been quoted: see also § 63. I. 2. b. On Rom. v. 12 sqq. see § 63. I. 1.]

[2] Aristoph. *Acharn.* 12, πῶς τοῦτ᾽ ἔσεισί μου, δοκεῖς, τὴν καρδίαν; Villois. *Anecd.* II. 24, πόσων, οἴεσθε, θυγατέρας ... ἐξέδωκεν;

[3] The Greek construction to which this is compared by Kühnöl and others (the so-called *Schema Pindaricum*,—see Fischer, *Weller* III. 345 sq., Vig. p. 192 sq., Herm. Soph. *Trach.* 517, Boeckh, *Pindar* II. ii. 684 sq., J. B. Brigleb, *Diss. in loc. Luc. ix.* 28: Jen. 1739) lies too remote, being almost confined to poetry (Kühner II. 50 sq., Jelf 386. 1); nor is the application of this idiom recommended by the ἐγένετο, which usually stands absolutely (in no instance do we find ἐγένοντο ἡμέραι ὀκτώ, etc.).—The above explanation of L. ix. 28 must be applied to Mt. xv. 32, ὅτι ἤδη ἡμέραι τρεῖς, προςμένουσί μοι,—as the best MSS. read: Fritzsche, not recognising that such definitions of time are loosely introduced, adopted the reading of D, ἤδη ἡμέραι τρεῖς εἰσὶ καὶ προςμένουσι κ.τ.λ., which is a manifest correction. In his note on Mk. viii. 2, however, he acknowledges the correctness of the usual text: see also his *Sendschreiben über die Verdienste Tholucks*, p. 17. In L. xiii. 16, also, ἣν ἔδησεν ὁ σατανᾶς, ἰδοὺ δέκα καὶ ὀκτὼ ἔτη κ.τ.λ., I have no hesitation in taking the words (with Bengel) in the same way. [Fritzsche *l. c.* decides for the reading ἤδη ἡμέραι τρεῖς in both passages: Winer's words may seem to imply that Fritzsche adopted the received text.]

Lucian, *Dial. Mar.* 1. 4, Schæf. *Demosth.* V. 388), L. xxiii. 51, Jo. iii. 1, ἦν ἄνθρωπος, Νικόδημος ὄνομα αὐτῷ, ἄρχων τῶν Ἰουδαίων· xix. 31 (Diog. L. 8. 42), L. xiii. 24, πολλοί, λέγω ὑμῖν, ζητήσουσιν κ.τ.λ. In several instances a narrator introduces an explanatory clause of this kind in the midst of the direct words of a speaker: Mk. vii. 11, ἐὰν εἴπῃ ἄνθρωπος· κορβᾶν, ὅ ἐστιν δῶρον, ὃ ἐὰν ἐξ ἐμοῦ ὠφεληθῇς· Jo. i. 39, οἱ δὲ εἶπον αὐτῷ· ῥαββί, ὃ λέγεται ἑρμηνευόμενον διδάσκαλε, ποῦ μένεις;[1] A summons or injunction is sometimes inserted in the same way: Mt. xxiv. 15 sq., ὅταν ἴδητε τὸ βδέλυγμα ... ἑστὸς ἐν τόπῳ ἁγίῳ, ὁ ἀναγινώσκων νοείτω, τότε οἱ ἐν τῇ Ἰουδαίᾳ κ.τ.λ.

3. There is no parenthesis in Jo. xi. 30. This verse is appended to ver. 29 that the place to which Mary went may be specified; and now that the departure of Mary is fully related, the narrator passes to those who were with her (ver. 31), who also went out. In Jo. xix. 5 all proceeds regularly, for the change of subjects does not show the necessity of a parenthesis. Nor are the parenthetical marks needed in Mt. xvi. 26 (though Schulz has retained them), for ver. 26 brings into view the preciousness of the ψυχή, in connexion with τὴν δὲ ψυχὴν ζημιωθῇ: the proof contained in ver. 27 relates to ver. 25 inclusively of ver. 26, and no interruption of the structure is to be seen anywhere. Mt. xxi. 4 sq. is an addition by the narrator, who however in ver. 6 continues his narrative in a very simple manner. Jo. vi. 6 is a similar instance.—In Jo. i. 14 it is probable that the clause καὶ ἐθεασάμεθα ... πατρός was not, in the writer's conception, a parenthetical insertion: after completing the complex sentence, he sums up with the words πλήρης χάριτος καὶ ἀληθείας, grammatically independent,—somewhat as in Ph. iii. 19 or Mk. xii. 40.—In L. vii. 29 sq. we have no parenthesis (Lachmann); the two verses contain words of Christ, who is repre-

---

[1] It is a different case when the writer *subjoins* such an explanation to the words of another, and then continues in his own language: Jo. ix. 7, ὕπαγε νίψαι εἰς τὴν κολυμβήθραν τοῦ Σιλωάμ, ὃ ἑρμηνεύεται ἀπεσταλμένος. ἀπῆλθεν οὖν κ.τ.λ.; i. 42, 43, Mt. i. 22 sq., xxi. 4 sq. In no such instance can a parenthesis be thought of. In Mt. ix. 6 we have not so much a parenthesis as a blending of the *oratio directa* and *indirecta*. In H. x. 8 the writer certainly does bring his own words into the midst of a quotation, but it is by means of a relative sentence. [As to Mt. ix. 6 compare what is said below, § 63. II. 2, 66. 1. a.]

sented as speaking both before and afterwards (ver. 31). It is not sufficient to assume a parenthesis in Mk. iii. 17; the structure varies in ver. 16-19,—see § 63. II. 1. Jo. vi. 23 is not in the least parenthetical: it stands connected with ὅτι of ver. 22.

Zeigler's proposal[1] to regard the words καὶ ἦσαν ... γυναικῶν in A. v. 12 sqq. as a parenthesis has very properly found no favour with the editors (Schott excepted). But those also who suspect that there is something spurious in ver. 12-15[2] have come to this conclusion too hastily. The words ὥϛτε κατὰ τὰς πλατείας ἐκφέρειν τοὺς ἀσθενεῖς κ.τ.λ. accord very well with ver. 14: it is from the two circumstances, that the people magnified the apostles, and that the number of the believers increased, that it is easy to understand why the sick were brought out into the streets. Indeed these words accord with ver. 14 much better than with ver. 12. Are we to suppose the πολλὰ σημεῖα καὶ τέρατα (ἐν τῷ λαῷ) merely to have been *previous* occurrences, the effect of which is expressed by ὥϛτε ἐκφέρειν κ.τ.λ.? To assume this would be to sacrifice the perspicuity of the narrative. And what then could these πολλὰ σημεῖα have been but miracles of *healing*? Hence in the words ὥϛτε κατά κ.τ.λ. the writer recurs, in a different connexion, to what he had only indicated summarily in ver. 12, in order that he may recount it more in detail (ver. 15 sq.). For these reasons I am also unable to agree with Lachmann in considering ver. 14 a parenthesis. In A. x. 36, however, τὸν λόγον is probably connected with ver. 37, and the words οὗτος κ.τ.λ.—which, as an independent sentence, express a leading thought, which Peter could not well annex by means of a relative—form a parenthesis: after this interruption the speaker proceeds in ver. 37, *extending* the thought.

4. In the Epistles also we may observe, first of all, certain short parentheses, which contain sometimes a limitation (1 C. vii. 11), sometimes a corroboration (1 Tim. ii. 7, 1 Th. ii. 5), sometimes a proof or a more exact explanation, as in Rom. vii. 1, 2 C. v. 7, vi. 2, x. 4, xii. 2, G. ii. 8, E. ii. 5, v. 9, Ja. iv. 14, 2 Th. i. 10, 1 Jo. i. 2, 1 Tim. iii. 5;—or indeed any thought which forced itself upon the writer (Col. iv. 10, Rom. i. 13). There are however some parentheses of greater length; e. g., H. vii. 20 sq.,

---

[1] In Gabler's *Journ. für theolog. Lit.* I. 155.
[2] Eichhorn, Beck, Kühnöl.

SECT. LXII.] INTERRUPTED STRUCTURE OF SENTENCES. 707

οἱ μὲν γάρ . . . εἰς τὸν αἰῶνα,—for καθ' ὅσον οὐ χωρὶς ὀρκωμοσίας (ver. 20) is manifestly connected with κατὰ τοσοῦτο κρείττονος κ.τ.λ. of ver. 22. So also in Rom. ii. 13–15, since ver. 16, ἐν ἡμέρᾳ ὅτε κρινεῖ κ.τ.λ., is certainly most suitably connected with κριθήσονται in ver. 12 : indeed the word κρινεῖ points back to κριθήσονται. Verses 13–15 constitute a group of thoughts complete in itself, added to ver. 12 for the purpose of explanation. It is the doing of the law that is of moment, and not the hearing (ver. 13) : but heathen who live righteously are doers of the law (ver. 14, 15).[1]—Many however of the lengthy insertions are not parentheses, but digressions; since they merely delay the progress of the thought, and do not interrupt the construction. Thus in 1 C. viii. 1–3, after the grammatically complete sentence περὶ δὲ . . . ἔχομεν, Paul introduces a digression (ἡ γνῶσις . . . ὑπ' αὐτοῦ) on γνῶσις in relation to ἀγάπη, and then returns to ver. 1, beginning afresh with περὶ τῆς βρώσεως οὖν κ.τ.λ. (ver. 4). The case is similar in 1 C. xv. 9, 10, and in 2 C. iii. 14–18 (iv. 1 attaches itself to iii. 12) : also in Rom. xiii. 9 sq.,— in καὶ τοῦτο εἰδότες (ver. 11) Paul returns to μηδενὶ μηδὲν ὀφείλετε, which in thought must be repeated.

But in most of the passages which it has been usual to adduce as parenthetical there is neither parenthesis nor digression. In Tit. i. 1 sqq. κατὰ πίστιν is connected with ἀπόστολος, and the destination of the apostle is completely stated in the words κατὰ πίστιν . . . αἰωνίου; to ζωῆς αἰωνίου is then appended the relative sentence ἣν ἐπηγγ . . . θεοῦ. In Rom. i. 1–7, where Schott in his last edition assumes two parentheses, the whole passage continues with one unbroken thread; only the words expressing the main ideas are enlarged by means of relative clauses (ver. 3 sq., 5, 6). The same may be said of Col. iii. 12–14, where ἀνεχόμενοι (which is in conformity with ἐνδύσασθε) is attached to μακροθυμίαν (perhaps also to πραότητα) as a specification of manner, and is itself supported by καθώς κ.τ.λ. It is only by the clause οὕτω καὶ ὑμεῖς that the structure can be at all inter-

---

[1] [Others carry back still farther the reference of ἐν ἡμέρᾳ (e. g., Alford to ver. 10, Ewald to ver. 5); whilst Lachmann and Meyer include two verses only (14 and 15) in a parenthesis. In former editions Winer had substantially agreed with Bengel, De Wette, al., in connecting ver. 16 with the preceding verse: similarly—though with some difference of interpretation—Fritzsche, Vaughan, and others.]

rupted, the thought expressed by these words being already implied in the καθώς which introduces the preceding clause; but supply χαριζόμενοι, and the construction is regular. In H. xii. 20, 21, we are the less able (with Lachmann) to assume a parenthesis, since in ver. 22 the verb προςεληλύθατε is repeated from ver. 18, and a new sentence therefore commenced,—an affirmative, corresponding to the negative sentence contained in ver. 18–21. In 1 C. i. 8 ὅς relates to Χριστός, ver. 7; and verses 5 and 6 do not form a parenthesis. The two relative sentences in Rom. xvi. 4, which are annexed to each other, and which do not really interrupt the construction, cannot be regarded as a parenthesis. In 1 P. iii. 6 ἀγαθοποιοῦσαι connects itself with ἐγενήθητε, and the words ὡς ... τέκνα are not parenthetical. In E. iii. 5 the clause ὃ ἑτέραις κ.τ.λ. attaches itself to ἐν μυστηρίῳ τοῦ Χριστοῦ (ver. 4); and in 2 P. i. 5 (Schott) the words αὐτὸ τοῦτο δὲ σπουδὴν παρεισενέγκαντες stand on the same level with ὡς πάντα ... δεδωρημένης κ.τ.λ., ver. 4 being a relative sentence explanatory of the words διὰ δόξης καὶ ἀρετῆς. 1 Jo. iv. 17 sqq. and E. i. 21 hardly require remark. In E. ii. 11 οἱ λεγόμενοι ... χειροποιήτου is an apposition to τὰ ἔθνη ἐν σαρκί, and the repetition of ὅτι in ver. 12 cannot make the preceding words a parenthesis. Lastly, we have anacolutha, not parentheses, in Col. iii. 16, 2 P. ii. 4–8 (in the latter instance the anacoluthon is partly occasioned by the sentence in ver. 8,—see § 63. I. 1), and 1 Tim. i. 3 sqq.

In E. iii. 1 sqq. the predicate is not ὁ δέσμιος: in this case, if the meaning were *ego Paulus vinculis detineor*, we could not have the article, and the sense "I am the prisoner of Christ (κατ' ἐξοχήν)" does not commend itself. The simplest procedure is (after Theodoret) to consider the τούτου χάριν of ver. 14 as the resumption of the interrupted thought of ver. 1; especially as the circumstance that Paul has by his imprisonment been taken away from his personal labours might so well give rise to the prayer of ver. 14 sqq.: by this means, also, the τούτου χάριν of ver. 1 receives its natural interpretation. Others, with much less probability, connect iv. 1 with iii. 1, on the ground that ὁ δέσμιος (iv. 1) seems to point back to ἐγὼ ὁ δέσμιος. Compare further Cramer's version of this Epistle, p. 71 sqq., where other conjectures are mentioned and examined; also Harless *in loc.*

Section LXIII.

SENTENCES IN WHICH THE CONSTRUCTION IS BROKEN OFF OR CHANGED: ANACOLUTHON: ORATIO VARIATA.

I. 1. Anacoluthon[1] is said to exist when the construction with which a sentence opens has no grammatical continuation; whether it be that something which intervenes (in particular, a parenthesis[2]) has led the writer entirely away from the construction with which he began, or that, a preferable turn of expression presenting itself,[3] he is induced to give the sentence a different conclusion from that required by the form of its commencement.[4] Hence anacolutha are partly involuntary, partly intentional. In the latter class are included those which rest on a rhetorical basis (Stallb. Plat. *Gorg.* p. 221), or which arise, as Hermann says (*Vig.* p. 895), "a motu animi vel ab arte oratoris vim aliquam captante." It is in writers of great mental vivacity—more taken up with the thought than with the mode of its expression—that we may expect to find anacolutha most frequently: hence they are particularly numerous in the epistolary style of the apostle Paul. The following are examples. A. xv. 22, ἔδοξεν τοῖς ἀποστόλοις .... ἐκλεξαμένους ἄνδρας ἐξ αὐτῶν πέμψαι .... γράψαντες διὰ χειρὸς αὐτῶν. With this compare Lys. *in Eratosth.* 7, ἔδοξεν αὐτοῖς .... ὥσπερ ... πεποιηκότες· Antiphon p. 613 (Reiske), ἔδοξεν αὐτῇ βουλομένῃ βέλτιον εἶναι μετὰ δεῖπνον δοῦναι, ταῖς Κλυταιμνήστρας τῆς τούτου μητρὸς ὑποθήκαις ἅμα διακονοῦσα; conversely, Plat. *Legg.* 3. 686 d, ἀποβλέψας πρὸς τοῦτον τὸν στόλον, οὗ πέρι

---

[1] Herm. *Vig.* p. 894 sqq. (whose illustrations are almost confined to poetical anacolutha), Poppo, *Thuc.* I. i. 360 sqq., Kühner II. 616 sqq. [II. 1091 sqq.: ed. 2], Madv. 216, F. Richter, *De præcipuis Græcæ linguæ anacoluthis* (Mühlh. 1827-28: 2 spec.), De Wannowski, *Syntaxeos anomalæ Græcorum pars* etc. (Lips. 1835), F. W. Engelhardt, *Anacolutha Platonica* (Gedani, 1834 etc.: spec. 1-3): compare Gernhard, Cic. *Offic.* p. 441 sq., Matthiæ, *De anacoluthis apud Ciceronem* in Wolf, *Analect. Lit.* III. 1 sqq. For the N. T. see Fritzsche, *Conjectanea*, spec. 1 p. 33 sq. (Lips. 1825). [See also (Don. p. 609) Jelf 900, Riddell, Plat. *Apol.* p. 223 sqq., and Campbell, Plat. *Theæt.* Appendix A: for the N. T., A. Buttm. p. 378 sqq. (Green p. 234 sq.).]
[2] See Beier, Cic. *Offic.* II. 365.
[3] Weber, *Demosth.* p. 538.
[4] Hence in 1 Jo. i. 1 sqq. there is nothing of the character of an anacoluthon; after the parenthesis of the 2nd verse the writer accurately connects ver. 3 with the beginning of the sentence, repeating—in full accordance with grammatical rule—some of the words of ver. 1.

διαλεγόμεθα, ἔδοξέ μοι πάγκαλος εἶναι (this is very common with ἔδοξε), Plat. *Apol.* 21 c, Xen. *Cyr.* 6, 1. 31, Lucian, *Astrol.* 3, Schwarz, *Solœcism.* p. 86 sq.[1] A. xx. 3, ποιήσας μῆνας τρεῖς, γενομένης αὐτῷ ἐπιβουλῆς .... μέλλοντι ἀνάγεσθαι εἰς τὴν Συρίαν, ἐγένετο γνώμη κ.τ.λ. In Rom. xvi. 25, 27, τῷ δυναμένῳ ... μόνῳ σοφῷ θεῷ διὰ Ἰησοῦ Χριστοῦ, ᾧ ἡ δόξα εἰς τοὺς αἰῶνας, Paul has been led away from the construction he intended by the lengthened statement in regard to God which is contained in ver. 25, 26; and, instead of simply adding ἡ δόξα εἰς τοὺς αἰῶνας, he expresses the substance of the doxology by a relative clause, just as if the dative θεῷ had concluded a sentence. A. xxiv. 5 sq. is a similar case. The participial clause εὑρόντες τὸν ἄνδρα τοῦτον κ.τ.λ. should have been followed by the verb ἐκρατήσαμεν in ver. 6; but Luke, led away by the relative sentence ὃς καί κ.τ.λ., has brought this verb also into the relative construction (ὃν καὶ ἐκρατήσαμεν).

The anacolutha which occur in periods of less extent are more remarkable:[2] e.g., A. xix. 34, ἐπιγνόντες, ὅτι Ἰουδαῖός ἐστι, φωνὴ ἐγένετο μία ἐκ πάντων (instead of ἐφώνησαν ἅπαντες); Mk. ix. 20, ἰδὼν (ὁ παῖς) αὐτόν, τὸ πνεῦμα εὐθὺς ἐσπάραξεν αὐτόν (instead of ὑπὸ τοῦ πνεύματος ἐσπαράχθη). With the latter passage Fritzsche compares *Anthol. Pal.* 11. 488 (?), κἀγὼ δ' αὐτὸν ἰδών, τὸ στόμα μου δέδεται; see also Plat. *Legg.* 6. 769 c. In L. xi. 11, τίνα ἐξ ὑμῶν τὸν πατέρα αἰτήσει ὁ υἱὸς ἄρτον, μὴ λίθον ἐπιδώσει αὐτῷ; the question "he will surely not give?" presupposes such a protasis as, *a father asked by his son for bread*, or *a father of whom his son asks bread* (Mt. vii. 9). A. xxiii. 30 [*Rec.*], μηνυθείσης μοι ἐπιβουλῆς εἰς τὸν ἄνδρα μέλλειν ἔσεσθαι: here the proper continuation of the sentence would be μελλούσης ἔσεσθαι, whereas μέλλειν would be in place if the sentence had opened with some such construction as μηνυσάντων ἐπιβουλήν κ.τ.λ. Compare § 45. 6. The construction is probably altered intentionally in 1 C. xii. 28, οὓς μὲν ἔθετο ὁ θεὸς ἐν τῇ

---

[1] In Latin compare Hirtius, *Bell. Afric.* 25, dum hæc ita fierent, *rex Juba*, cognitis...., *non est visum* etc.; Plin. *Ep.* 10. 34.
[2] One of the most remarkable, perhaps, is that which is quoted by Kypke (II. 104): Hippocr. *Morb. Vulg.* 5. 1, ἐν Ἠλίδι ἡ τοῦ κηπωροῦ γυνὴ πυρετὸς εἶχεν αὐτὴν ξυνεχὴς καὶ φάρμακα πίνουσα οὐδὲν ὠφελεῖτο. Compare also Bar. i. 9, μετὰ τὸ ἀποικίσαι Ναβουχοδονόσορ τὸν Ἰεχονίαν.... καὶ ἤγαγεν αὐτόν κ.τ.λ.; *Act. Apocr.* p. 69.

ἐκκλησίᾳ πρῶτον ἀποστόλους, δεύτερον προφήτας, τρίτον διδασκάλους κ.τ.λ. Paul at first intended to write οὓς μὲν ... ἀποστόλους, οὓς δὲ προφήτας κ.τ.λ., but instead of a mere enumeration prefers an arrangement in order of rank. Hence οὓς μέν is altogether suspended in the sentence; and the abstract nouns which follow (ἔπειτα δυνάμεις κ.τ.λ.) attach themselves to the simple ἔθετο, which alone was still present to the writer's mind. So also in Tit. i. 3: when the apostle adds ἐφανέρωσεν δέ κ.τ.λ., he seizes on a more suitable turn of expression by the introduction of τὸν λόγον αὐτοῦ. Compare further 2 C. vii. 5 (1 C. vii. 26). The parts of the sentence which display the anacoluthon stand farther apart in Jo. vi. 22 sqq., τῇ ἐπαύριον ὁ ὄχλος .... ἰδών,[1] ὅτι ... (ἄλλα δὲ ἦλθε πλοιάρια ...), ὅτε οὖν εἶδεν ὁ ὄχλος κ.τ.λ.: here εἶδεν, in consequence of the words inserted, has gained a more comprehensive object than belonged to ἰδών. In G. ii. 6, ἀπὸ δὲ τῶν δοκούντων εἶναί τι—ὁποῖοί ποτε ἦσαν, οὐδέν μοι διαφέρει—ἐμοὶ γὰρ οἱ δοκοῦντες οὐδὲν προςανέθεντο, the apostle should have continued by means of a passive verb, but was so much disturbed in the construction by the parenthesis ὁποῖοι ... διαφέρει, that he forms a new sentence with γάρ.[2] In G. ii. 4 sq., διὰ δὲ τοὺς παρεισάκτους ψευδαδέλφους .... οἷς οὐδὲ πρὸς ὥραν εἴξαμεν τῇ ὑποταγῇ κ.τ.λ., the parenthesis introduced in ver. 4 has occasioned the anacoluthon. The apostle might either have said, *On account of the false brethren* (in order to please them) ... *we did not permit Titus to be circumcised*, or *To the false brethren we could* (in this respect) *by no means give way*: he has here blended the two constructions.[3] In Rom. ii. 17 sqq., verses 17-20 constitute the

---

[1] [Lachmann, Tregelles, Tischendorf, Alford, Westcott and Hort, read εἶδον for ἰδών. The 23rd verse is said above (§ 62. 3) *not* to be parenthetical.—Similar to this passage (with the reading ἰδών) is Rom. xv. 23 sq., if we omit ἐλεύσομαι πρὸς ὑμᾶς, and inclose ἐλπίζω ... ἐμπλησθῶ within a parenthesis: see Alford.]

[2] In sense, Hermann's explanation (*Progr. de locis Ep. ad Gal.* p. 7) agrees with this. Hermann assumes, however, an aposiopesis after ἀπὸ δὲ τῶν δοκούντων ... τι: against this see Fritzsche, 2. *Progr.* p. 13 (*Opusc. Fritzschiorum* p. 211 sq.). The latter writer regards the words ἀπὸ ... τι (which should, he thinks, form the conclusion of ver. 5) as parallel to διὰ δὲ τοὺς παρεισάκτους ψευδαδίλφους, and translates: *propter irreptitios autem et falsos sodales* (se circumcidi non passus est), *quippe qui ... quibus ... ut ... a viris autem, qui auctoritate valerent* (circumcisionis necessitatem sibi imponi non sivit). Against this see Meyer. I have seen no reason to alter my view of the passage. [Winer's rendering is: Principibus vero (qualescunque demum erant, id nihil ad me, Deus enim externa hominis non curat) principes, inquam, nihil (*novi*) mecum communicarunt. Similarly Ellicott, Lightfoot, al.]

[3] It is in no respect easier to repeat (with Fritzsche, *Progr.* 1. *in Ep. ad*

protasis, and the apodosis begins in ver. 21. As Paul carries through several clauses the thought which he premises as protasis, he loses recollection of the εἰ of ver. 17 ; and when he brings in the apodosis (ver. 21), he passes to another turn of expression by means of οὖν, which particle points to anacoluthon. The case is but little altered if we take οὖν as the conjunction which resumes and gathers up the protasis (Klotz, *Dev.* II. 718 sq.),—as in Greek authors it so frequently commences the apodosis; for still the words ὁ διδάσκων . . . ὁ κηρύσσων κ.τ.λ., whether taken as a question or as an assertion of reproach, alter the natural course of the sentence. After εἰ δέ κ.τ.λ. the most simple apodosis would be: *thou oughtest to prove this knowledge of the law by living thyself according to the law* (compare ver. 23). It is at once evident to every one that the turn which Paul has chosen is more forcible.[1]

In the following passages the anacoluthon is harsher. In 2 P. ii. 4 the protasis εἰ γὰρ ὁ θεὸς ἀγγέλων οὐκ ἐφείσατο κ.τ.λ. has no grammatical apodosis. The apostle intended to say, *so neither* (indeed still less) *will he spare these false teachers;* but as one example of God's punishment after another presents itself to him (ver. 4–8), it is not until ver. 9 that he returns to the thought which should have formed the apodosis, and then with a changed construction and in a more general form. In Rom. v. 12 we might expect the words ὥσπερ δι' ἑνὸς ἀνθρώπου ἡ

Gal. p. 24, *Opusc.* p. 178 sq.) after διὰ δὲ τοὺς παρεισάκτους ψευδαδέλφους the words οὐκ ἠναγκάσθη περιτμηθῆναι (ὁ Τίτος). These words could only be omitted by Paul (unless we would regard him as an unskilled writer) if the subjoined relative clauses had caused him to lose sight of the commencement of the period. This being so, the explanations of the sentence—which in any case is irregular—amount pretty much to the same thing.—There would be nothing extraordinary in the style of such a sentence as this: "But not even did Titus .... allow himself to be forced into undergoing circumcision: on account of the false brethren who had crept in, however, he did not allow himself to be forced (into circumcision)." * [Fritzsche's explanation is adopted by Meyer, Ellicott, Alford, al.: see further Lightfoot *in loc.*, Green, *Cr. Notes* p. 150.]

[1] In a grammatical point of view compare Xen. *Cyr.* 6. 2. 9 sqq., where the commencement, ἐπεὶ δὲ . . . ἦλθον κ.τ.λ., is in § 12 taken up again in the words ὡς οὖν ταῦτα ἤκουσεν ὁ στρατὸς τοῦ Κύρου, to which the apodosis is then attached.

---

* "The Tr. submits his impression, that the most natural interpretation of the passage is to supply περιτμήθη: Titus was not *compelled* to be circumcised, but on account of the false brethren . . . (was circumcised). Paul protested against the alleged necessity of circumcision; but, while refusing to give in τῇ ὑποταγῇ to the measure on doctrinal grounds, he approved it as a matter of Christian expediency."—*Note by the former Translator*, *Prof. Masson.*

ἁμαρτία εἰς τὸν κόσμον εἰσῆλθε to be followed by the apodosis οὕτω δι' ἑνὸς ἀνθρώπου (Χριστοῦ) δικαιοσύνη καὶ διὰ τῆς δικαιοσύνης ἡ ζωή. But by the explanations of εἰσῆλθεν ἡ ἁμαρτία καὶ ὁ θάνατος which verses 12-14 contain, the regular construction is broken off (though in the words ὅς ἐστι τύπος τοῦ μέλλοντος there is an indication of the antithesis); and moreover the apostle remembers that not merely may a simple *parallel* be drawn between Adam and Christ (ὥσπερ ... οὕτως), but that what is derived from Christ surpasses, both in extent and in influence, that which proceeds from Adam: hence the epanorthosis πολλῷ μᾶλλον,—as was perceived by Calvin. The resumption is effected by means of the words ἀλλ' οὐχ ὡς τὸ παράπτωμα κ.τ.λ. (ver. 15), which logically absorb the apodosis, and in εἰ γάρ ... ἀπέθανον the substance of the protasis in ver. 12 is briefly recapitulated: then in ver. 18 Paul sums up the twofold parallel (equality and inequality) in one final result.[1]— 1 Tim. i. 3 sqq. must be judged of in a similar way. Καθὼς παρεκάλεσα is left entirely without any consequent clause: as Paul at once introduces into the protasis the object of the παρακαλεῖν, the apodosis—which should have run thus, οὕτω καὶ νῦν παρακαλῶ, ἵνα παραγγείλῃς κ.τ.λ.—escapes his attention. It is altogether unnatural to consider verses 5-17 parenthetical, as even Bengel does; but it is still more preposterous to take καθώς as a particle of transition, not to be expressed in translation (Heydenreich).

By many commentators, both ancient and modern, Rom. ix. 22 sqq. has been regarded as a very remarkable, and in part a double anacoluthon: see the various opinions in Reiche's *Commentarius Criticus*. But it is probably simpler to attach the καὶ ἵνα of ver. 22 to ἤνεγκεν, and to regard the apodosis as suppressed at the end of ver. 23: *If God, determined to show his wrath ... with all longsuffering endured the vessels of his wrath .... also in order to make known the riches .... : how then? what shall we say to it?* (must not all censure then be silenced?) The enduring of the σκεύη ὀργῆς is not regarded merely as a proof of

---

[1] [So Vaughan, Webster and Wilkinson. Most commentators take a similar view of the *general* construction of this passage. Others would commence the apodosis with καὶ οὕτως in ver. 12 (Green, *Cr. Notes* p. 115), or with καὶ διὰ τῆς ἁμαρτίας: Alford supplies "it was" before ὥσπερ.]

his μακροθυμία, but also as occasioned by the purpose of manifesting the riches of his glory, which he has destined for the σκεύη ἐλέους. The immediate destruction of the σκεύη ὀργῆς (here, the unbelieving Jews) would have been perfectly just. But God endured them with long-suffering (thus softening his justice by kindness); and at once the purpose and the result of this was the clear manifestation (by means of the contrast) of the greatness of his grace towards the σκεύη ἐλέους. The δέ of ver. 22 is not οὖν; and hence it is not probable that this verse is a continuation of the thought expressed in verses 20, 21. That God is entirely free in bestowing his tokens of grace, had been sufficiently declared. The creature cannot rise up against the Creator: that is enough. But, Paul resumes, God is not even altogether as rigorous as he might be, without having reason to apprehend censure from men.[1]

On A. x. 36 see above, § 62. 3: on Rom. xii. 6 sqq. see below, II. 1. In Col. i. 21 there is in any case anacoluthon,—whether we read ἀποκατηλλάγητε, with Lachmann, or retain the received reading ἀποκατήλλαξεν. On 2 P. i. 17 see p. 442; on 1 C. xii. 2, Meyer.[2]

In some other passages in which commentators have supposed the existence of anacoluthon, I can discover nothing of the kind. Rom. vii. 21, εὑρίσκω ἄρα τὸν νόμον τῷ θέλοντι ἐμοὶ ποιεῖν τὸ καλόν, ὅτι ἐμοὶ τὸ κακὸν παράκειται, formerly regarded by Fritzsche[3] as a blending of two constructions, has since been differently explained by him,—in accordance with Knapp's view of the passage: see above, p. 697. Nor is there a mixture of two constructions in H. viii. 9 (Fritz. *Conj.* p. 34). Ἐν ἡμέρᾳ ἐπιλαβομένου μου τῆς χειρὸς αὐτῶν (taken from the LXX) may perhaps be an unusual mode of expression, but is not incorrect; and the Hebrew words (for this is a quotation from Jer. xxxi. 32), בְּיוֹם הֶחֱזִיקִי בְיָדָם, have certainly given occasion, so to speak, to the use of this phrase. The participle is chosen in the place of the infinitive, as in Jer. xxix. 2: compare Bar. ii. 28.—In 1 P. ii. 7 ἀπειθοῦσι δέ stands grammatically connected with the words of the

---

[1] [Lünemann suggests that it is still simpler to take εἰ ... ἤνεγκεν as protasis, and καὶ (scil. ἤνεγκεν) ἵνα in ver. 23 as apodosis: *if God endured ... he endured them also* (or *at the same time*) *in order to* ... Similarly Ewald.]

[2] [In the edition referred to, I believe, Meyer held that Paul proceeds with ὅτι through forgetfulness that he had begun with οἴδατε ὅτι (not οἴδατε merely): see Alford *in loc.* In edition 4 Meyer supplies ἦτε with the participle.]

[3] *Conject.* p. 50. [Fritzsche considered that the two sentences εὑρίσκω ἄρα τὸν νόμον τῷ θέλοντι ἐμοὶ ποιεῖν τὸ καλὸν τὸ κακὸν παρακεῖσθαι (*per id, quod mihi ... malum adjacet*) and εὑρίσκω ἄρα ὅτι ἐμοὶ θέλοντι ... παράκειται are here blended.]

quotation, οὗτος ἐγενήθη κ.τ.λ. As to Rom. i. 26, 27, the variation of reading between ὁμοίως δὲ καί and ὁμοίως τε καί of itself renders it difficult to come to a decision. The former appears to have more external authority on its side,[1] and it has been adopted by Bornemann[2] (as also by Lachmann), and defended as being a formula of frequent occurrence in the N. T.: see Mt. xxvi. 35, xxvii. 41 (Mk. xv. 31), L. v. 10, x. 32, 1 C. vii. 3 sq., Ja. ii. 25 (also Diod. Sic. 17. 111). But in none of these instances does τε precede, and hence they are all inadequate: compare however the passage cited by Fritzsche from Plat. *Symp.* 186 e, ἥ τε οὖν ἰατρική . . . ὡσαύτως δὲ καὶ γυμναστική. This reading of the most important MSS., then, might be justified grammatically; and, as the apostle obviously wishes to give the greater prominence to what was done by the ἄρρενες (he dwells on this in ver. 27, severely denouncing the crime), it would even be very appropriate. The question now is, whether an *anacoluthon* is involved by either or by both of these readings. With the reading ὁμοίως τε καί there is as little anacoluthon as in the Latin "nam *et* feminæ . . . *et* similiter etiam mares:" if however we receive ὁμοίως δὲ καί, the natural sequence is interrupted, just as in "et feminæ . . . similiter vero etiam mares" (Klotz, *Devar.* II. 740).

The apodosis of H. iii. 15 is probably to be sought in ver. 16, τίνες γάρ, *quinam* etc. (Bleek, Tholuck, al.). In 2 C. viii. 3 αὐθαίρετοι connects itself with ἑαυτοὺς ἔδωκαν (ver. 5). In 1 C. v. 11 there is no anacoluthon in τῷ τοιούτῳ μηδὲ συνεσθίειν (so Erasmus); these words take up and strengthen the συναναμίγνυσθαι. In Ja. ii. 2 sqq. the anacoluthon disappears if we take ver. 4 (καὶ οὐ κ.τ.λ.) interrogatively,[3] as is now done by most critics, Lachmann included. In Jo. xiii. 1 there is no anacoluthon in point of grammar: it is to hermeneutics that the removal of the difficulty belongs. 1 C. ix. 15, if ἵνα before τις is spurious (Tischendorf has received it again[4]), is rather an example of aposiopesis than of anacoluthon: see Meyer. Lastly, in E. iii. 18 the participles are probably to be joined with the sentence ἵνα ἐξισχύσητε: see Meyer *in loc.*

2. The illustrations of anacoluthon which have been given thus far are of such a nature that they might well occur in any language. We have now to mention some particular kinds of

---

[1] [Τὶς has the support of the two oldest MSS., B and ℵ, and is retained by Tischendorf, Tregelles, Alford, Westcott and Hort: δέ is preferred by Tisch. (ed. 7), Meyer, A. Buttmann (p. 361), al. In some of the passages quoted below for ὁμοίως δὲ καί the reading is doubtful.]

[2] *Neues theol. Journ.* VI. 145.

[3] [The case is not altered if we omit καί, with Tischendorf and others.]

[4] [The editors are divided, not between τὶς and ἵνα τις, as Winer's words might seem to imply, but between οὐδείς (Tisch. ed. 1, 8, Lachm., Treg., Meyer) and ἵνα τις (Tisch. ed. 2, 7, De W., Reiche). Meyer now takes a different view of the construction (see above, p. 551), considering that the aposiopesis would be too bold for the N. T.]

anacoluthon, which have especially established themselves in Greek usage :—

a. When the construction is continued by means of participles, these frequently appear in an abnormal case, as standing at a distance from the governing verb.[1] E. iv. 2 sq., *παρακαλῶ ὑμᾶς . . . περιπατῆσαι . . . ἀνεχόμενοι ἀλλήλων ἐν ἀγάπῃ, σπουδάζοντες κ.τ.λ.*, as if the exhortation had been in the direct form, *περιπατήσατε*: also E. i. 18, where Meyer raises unnecessary difficulties.[2] Col. iii. 16, *ὁ λόγος τοῦ Χριστοῦ ἐνοικείτω ἐν ὑμῖν πλουσίως, ἐν πάσῃ σοφίᾳ διδάσκοντες καὶ νουθετοῦντες ἑαυτούς κ.τ.λ.*; ii. 2, *ἵνα παρακληθῶσιν αἱ καρδίαι αὐτῶν συμβιβασθέντες ἐν ἀγάπῃ κ.τ.λ.* (as if the *παρακαλεῖσθαι* had been made to relate to the persons themselves), Col. ii. 10;[3] 2 C. ix. 10 sq., *ὁ ἐπιχορηγῶν . . . χορηγήσαι καὶ πληθύναι τὸν σπόρον ὑμῶν . . . ὑμῶν, ἐν παντὶ πλουτιζόμενοι κ.τ.λ.*; ver. 12 sq., *ἡ διακονία (ἐστὶ) περισσεύουσα διὰ πολλῶν εὐχαριστιῶν, διὰ τῆς δοκιμῆς τῆς διακονίας ταύτης δοξάζοντες τὸν θεόν* (as if *ὅτι πολλοὶ εὐχαριστοῦσιν* had preceded); compare Xen. *Cyr.* 1. 4. 26. See also 2 C. i. 7,[4] vii. 5, Ph. i. 29 sq., iii. 10, 2 P. iii. 3, A. xxvi. 3,[5] Jude 16.[6]

Anacolutha of this kind may in part be regarded as *intentional*. The conceptions, thus expressed by the *casus recti* of the participles, stand out with greater prominence; had an oblique case been used, they would be kept back in the body of the sentence (see especially Jude 16), and be represented as only accessory. In most instances, however, the anacoluthon is oc-

---

[1] See Vig. p. 337 sqq., Rost p. 712 sq. [Jelf 707, A. Buttm. p. 298 sq., Green p. 235.]

[2] [In his 3rd and 4th editions Meyer *substantially* agrees with Winer. See Ellicott and Alford *in loc.*; also A. Buttm. p. 94, 317, who prefers to regard the accusatives as governed by *δῴη*.—The peculiarity of this example is, that the "abnormal case" is the *accusative*, not the *nominative*: A. xxvi. 3 is somewhat different, as the personal pronoun is repeated.]

[3] [A mistake : no doubt, for i. 10.]

[4] [That is, if the clause *ἡ ἐλπίς . . . . ὑπὲρ ὑμῶν* immediately precedes *εἰδότες*, as it does in *Rec.*, and also in the reading adopted by Griesbach, Meyer, Tischendorf, Westcott and Hort.—Lachm., De W., Reiche, Alford, and Tregelles bring in this clause before *εἴτε παρακαλούμεθα . . .* : with this reading *εἰδότες* is quite regular.]

[5] [A. Buttmann takes *ὄντα σε* as an accus. absolute (p. 317) : see Jelf 700, Ellic. on E. i. 18. Jelf and Green (*Gr. Notes* p. 102) supply a participle from *ἥγημαι* : see Jelf 895. 1. Meyer and Alford agree with Winer.]

[6] Compare in general Markland, *Lys.* p. 364 (Reiske, Vol. V.), Buttm. Soph. *Philoct.* p. 110, Seidler, Eurip. *Iphig. T.* 1072, Kühner II. 377 sq., Schwarz, *Solœcism.* p. 89 ; also Stallb. Plat. *Apol.* p. 135 sq. and *Sympos.* p. 33.

casioned by forgetfulness: the writer, losing sight of the principal word actually used in the earlier part of the sentence, supposes that he has used some other word of kindred sense. Compare further *Evang. Apocr.* p. 169, 445.

Mk. xii. 40 and Ph. iii. 18 sq. are of a different description: see § 59. 8. b.—In Rom. xiii. 11 καὶ τοῦτο εἰδότες must be joined to ὀφείλετε, ver. 8 [p. 707]; and 1 P. ii. 16 attaches itself (as the ideas themselves suggest) to the imperative ὑποτάγητε in ver. 13.

b. After a participle we often find a transition to the construction with a finite verb: in this case the verb may be accompanied by δέ. Thus: Col. i. 26, πληρῶσαι τὸν λόγον τοῦ θεοῦ, τὸ μυστήριον τὸ ἀποκεκρυμμένον ἀπὸ τῶν αἰώνων ... νυνὶ δὲ ἐφανερώθη· instead of νυνὶ δὲ φανερωθέν (compare Her. 6. 25, Thuc. 1. 67), 1 C. vii. 37, ὃς ἕστηκεν ἐν τῇ καρδίᾳ, μὴ ἔχων ἀνάγκην, ἐξουσίαν δὲ ἔχει (for ἔχων).[1] We must not bring in here 1 C. iv. 14 (as Meyer does), or E. ii. 3, where ἦμεν is parallel to ἀνεστράφημεν. The transition takes place without δέ in E. i. 20, κατὰ τὴν ἐνέργειαν ... ἣν ἐνήργησεν ἐν τῷ Χριστῷ, ἐγείρας αὐτόν ... καὶ ἐκάθισεν·[2] 2 C. vi. 9, Jo. v. 44, Col. i. 6 (Paus. 10. 9. 1). On 2 Jo. 2 see below, II. 1. An effort to attain a simpler structure or to give prominence to the second thought (see especially 2 C. vi. 9, and compare Xen. *Cyr.* 5. 4. 29) is not unfrequently the cause of this anacoluthon.— H. viii. 10 (a quotation from the O. T.) must be explained on the same principle: αὕτη ἡ διαθήκη, ἣν διαθήσομαι τῷ οἴκῳ Ἰσραήλ ... διδοὺς νόμους μου εἰς τὴν διάνοιαν αὐτῶν καὶ ἐπὶ καρδίας αὐτῶν ἐπιγράψω αὐτούς. Some (e. g., Böhme) render the καί before ἐπιγράψω by *etiam;* but this is forced, and anything but favoured by x. 16. Of Jo. i. 32, τεθέαμαι τὸ πνεῦμα καταβαῖνον ... καὶ ἔμεινεν ἐπ' αὐτόν (compare ver. 33, ἐφ' ὃν ἂν ἴδῃς τὸ πνεῦμα καταβαῖνον καὶ μένον ἐπ' αὐτόν), Baumg.-Crusius has already pointed out the right view.[3] In such passages the MSS. sometimes have the participle as a correction of the finite verb; e. g., in E. i. 20, where however καθίσας is received by Lachmann as genuine. A similar kind of anacoluthon is pre-

---

[1] The case noticed by Hermann (Soph. *El.* p. 153) and Buttmann (Demosth. *Mid.* p. 149) is different from this.

[2] [The best texts now have καθίσας here, and in Col. i. 6 omit καί before ἐστίν.]

[3] Compare further Schæf. *Dion. H.* p. 31, *Demosth.* II. 75, V. 437, 573, *Plutarch* IV. 323, Blume, *Lycurg.* p. 147, Matth. 632. 4.

sented by 2 C. v. 6 sqq., θαρροῦντες οὖν πάντοτε ... θαρροῦμεν δὲ καὶ εὐδοκοῦμεν: several clauses having intervened, Paul repeats the θαρροῦντες—which he had intended to construe with εὐδοκοῦμεν—in the form of the finite verb. (Jelf 705, 759.)

c. A sentence which has begun with ὅτι concludes with the (accusative and) infinitive, as if this particle had not been used: A. xxvii. 10, θεωρῶ, ὅτι μετὰ ὕβρεως καὶ πολλῆς ζημίας ... μέλλειν ἔσεσθαι τὸν πλοῦν; compare Plat. *Gorg.* 453 b, ἐγὼ γὰρ εὖ ἴσθ' ὅτι, ὡς ἐμαυτὸν πείθω, εἴπερ ... καὶ ἐμὲ εἶναι τούτων ἕνα· and see above, p. 426. Conversely, in Ælian 12. 39 the construction intended in the words φασὶ Σεμίραμιν is that of the accusative with the infinitive, but μέγα ἐφρόνει follows, as if ὅτι had preceded. Plaut. *Trucul.* 2. 2. 62 is a similar instance. We might compare with this Jo. viii. 54, ὃν ὑμεῖς λέγετε ὅτι θεὸς ὑμῶν ἐστί (where θεὸν ὑμῶν εἶναι might have been said): this however is rather to be regarded as an example of attraction, see below [§ 66. 5]. (Jelf 804. 7.)

d. At the head of a sentence there stands a nominative or an accusative with which the verb of the sentence is not made to agree (*casus pendentes*):[1] 1 Jo. ii. 24, ὑμεῖς, ὃ ἠκούσατε ἀπ' ἀρχῆς, ἐν ὑμῖν μενέτω· and ver. 27, καὶ ὑμεῖς, τὸ χρῖσμα ὃ ἐλάβετε ἀπ' αὐτοῦ ἐν ὑμῖν μένει, *and ye, the anointing which* .... *abides in you.* In either passage, to join ὑμεῖς with the relative clause (as Lachmann does) would be giving to the pronoun, so prominently thrown forward, an undue weight of emphasis. L. xxi. 6, ταῦτα ἃ θεωρεῖτε, ἐλεύσονται ἡμέραι, ἐν αἷς οὐκ ἀφεθήσεται λίθος ἐπὶ λίθῳ κ.τ.λ., *that which ye see* (here), *days will come in which* (it will be overthrown to the very last stone) *not one stone* (of it) *will be left upon another*. So also in Jo. vi. 39, vii. 38, xv. 2, Mt. vii. 24 [*Rec.*], xii. 36, Rev. ii. 26, iii. 12, 21, vi. 8: compare Ex. ix. 7, Xen. *Cyr.* 2. 3. 5, *Œc.* 1. 14, Æl. 7. 1.

2 C. xii. 17, μή τινα ὧν ἀπέσταλκα πρὸς ὑμᾶς, δι' αὐτοῦ ἐπλεονέκτησα ὑμᾶς; instead of, *Have I sent* or *made use of any one of those whom* etc. *in order to rob you?* Rom. viii. 3, τὸ ἀδύνατον τοῦ νόμου, ἐν ᾧ ἠσθένει .... ὁ θεὸς τὸν ἑαυτοῦ υἱὸν πέμψας ... κατέκρινε τὴν ἁμαρτίαν ἐν τῇ σαρκί, *what was impossible to the law .... God, sending his Son, condemned sin in the flesh*: instead of, *that God did, and condemned* etc.

---

[1] Wannowski, *Syntax. Anomal.* p. 54 sq.: see however *H. L.-Z.* 1836, 1. 338. [Jelf 477, Green, *Gr.* p. 233 sq.]

Here however τὸ ἀδύνατον may also be taken as a predicate prefixed to a sentence which is complete in itself, and may be resolved into ὃ γὰρ ἀδύνατόν ἐστι,[1]—as in H. viii. 1, κεφάλαιον ἐπὶ τοῖς λεγομένοις, τοιοῦτον ἔχομεν ἀρχιερέα κ.τ.λ.: see above, § 32. 7, and compare Kühner II. 156.

Several commentators, amongst whom is Olshausen, have supposed that we have an accusative absolute (?) in A. x. 36, τὸν λόγον ὃν ἀπέστειλε τοῖς υἱοῖς Ἰσραήλ κ.τ.λ., *a word which* (or *which word*) *he first delivered to the children of Israel* (viz., the word ἐν παντὶ ἔθνει κ.τ.λ., ver. 35). See however § 62. 3.

An anacoluthon peculiar to the N. T. meets us sometimes, when a writer proceeds, not in his own words, but in those of some passage of the O. T.: e. g., Rom. xv. 3, καὶ γὰρ ὁ Χριστὸς οὐχ ἑαυτῷ ἤρεσεν ἀλλά, καθὼς γέγραπται, οἱ ὀνειδισμοὶ τῶν ὀνειδιζόντων σε ἐπέπεσαν ἐπ' ἐμέ (instead of, " in order to please God, he submitted to the most cruel abuse"); ver. 21, ix. 7: compare 1 C. ii. 9, iii. 21,[2] H. iii. 7. See however below, § 64. 7.

e. Under the head of anacoluthon comes also the use of μέν without any subsequent parallel clause (marked by δέ): see Hermann, *Vig.* p. 841 sq.[3] In this case, either

(*a*) The parallel member may easily be supplied from the clause with μέν, and is in some measure already implied in it. E. g.: H. vi. 16, ἄνθρωποι μὲν γὰρ κατὰ τοῦ μείζονος ὀμνύουσι, *men swear by the greater,* but God can only swear by himself,— compare ver. 13 (Plat. *Protag.* 334 a); here however μέν is doubtful. Col. ii. 23, ἄτινά ἐστι λόγον μὲν ἔχοντα σοφίας ἐν ἐθελοθρησκείᾳ καί κ.τ.λ., *which have indeed an appearance of wisdom,* but are in fact no wisdom at all (Xen. *An.* 1. 2. 1): Rom. x. 1,—where Paul may have designedly avoided expressing

---

[1] [It comes to the same thing if (with Meyer, Fritzsche, De Wette, Alford) we speak of τὸ ἀδύνατον as a nominative in apposition to the sentence (Krüg. p. 246).—It will be observed that in many passages quoted above the form of the word does not show whether the case is nominative or accusative : a comparison of these examples with others, however, leaves little or no doubt that Winer is right in considering the *casus pendens* as a nominative. See A. Buttm. p. 382: contrast Green, *Gr.* p. 233.]

[2] [A mistake,—perhaps for i. 31. 1 C. ii. 9 is noticed more particularly in § 64. 7 : on the different explanations of H. iii. 7 sqq. see Alford's note.]

[3] [Don. p. 577, *New Crat.* p. 281 sq., Jelf 766, Madvig 188; and for the N. T., A. Buttm. p. 365, Grimm, *Clavis* s. v., Ellicott on 1 Th. ii. 18.—Most grammarians agree in this explanation of μέν *solitarium*. See however Rost u. Palm, *Lex.* II. 175, 177, where it is maintained that there are certainly examples in Attic prose in which the single μέν has the same force (= μήν) as in the combinations μέντοι, μενοῦν: see also Bernh. p. 487, Krüger p. 361, and compare 2 C. xi. 4.—When μέν is joined with γάρ, each of the particles retains its proper force : in this and similar combinations, however, μέν *solitarium* is of frequent occurrence,—see Hartung, *Partik.* II. 414.]

the painful antithesis (which appears in ver. 3,—softened however by a commendation): see also 1 C. v. 3. Compare Xen. *Hier.* 1. 7, 7. 4, *Mem.* 3. 12. 1, Plat. *Phæd.* 58 a, Aristoph. *Pax* 13.[1]—Or

(β) The contrasted member is perceptibly subjoined, though with a different turn of expression: Rom. xi. 13 sq., ἐφ' ὅσον μὲν οὖν εἰμὶ ἐγὼ ἐθνῶν ἀπόστολος, τὴν διακονίαν μου δοξάζω, εἴπως παραζηλώσω μου τὴν σάρκα κ.τ.λ. Here the δέ clause is included in εἴπως παραζηλώσω: had Paul continued the sentence regularly, the words would run, *Inasmuch as I am apostle of the gentiles, I glorify my office* (preaching to the gentiles zealously), *but in this I have in view the benefit of the Jews* (I would by this means provoke the Jews to jealousy);—as to my sphere of labour I am apostle of the gentiles, but in purpose I am also apostle of the Jews.—Or

(γ) The construction is altogether broken off, and the parallel clause must be deduced by the reader from the sequel: e.g., A. i. 1, τὸν μὲν πρῶτον λόγον ἐποιησάμην περὶ πάντων ... ἀνελήφθη. Here the writer should have continued thus, *but from this point of time* (that of the Ascension) *I will now carry on the narrative in the second part of my work:* through the mention of the apostles in ver. 3, however, he allows himself to be led to the mention of Christ's appearances after his resurrection, and immediately subjoins to this the sequel of the narration. Rom. vii. 12, ὥστε ὁ μὲν νόμος ἅγιος καὶ ἡ ἐντολὴ ἁγία καὶ δικαία καὶ ἀγαθή, *the law indeed is holy, and the commandment holy* etc.,—but sin, stirred up in the σάρξ, misuses these (in the manner indicated in ver. 8): this thought is pursued by Paul in ver. 13, with a different turn of expression. Compare further Rom. i. 8, iii. 2, 1 C. xi. 18 (in each case πρῶτον μέν,—see below), H. ix. 1, 2 C. xii. 12 (see Rückert *in loc.*), A. iii. 13, xix. 4 (in the last passage μέν is not fully established), xxvi. 4. For examples from Greek writers see Eurip. *Orest.* 8, Xen. *Cyr.* 2. 1. 4, 4. 5. 50, *Mem.* 1. 2. 2, 2. 6. 3, Plat. *Apol.* 21 d, Reisig, Soph. *Œd. Col.* p. 398, Locella, *Xen. Ephes.* p. 225, etc., etc. In L. viii. 5 sqq., Jo. xi. 6, xix. 32, Ja. iii. 17, the correlative particle is not entirely omitted, δέ being simply

---

[1] See Stallb. Plat. *Crit.* p. 105; Held, Plut. *Æm. P.* p. 123.

replaced by ἔπειτα,¹ or by καί : that Greek writers frequently use μέν . . . ἔπειτα, μέν . . . καί (Thuc. 5. 60, 71), μέν . . . τε, as correlatives, is a well-known fact, and in no way strange.² The clause with δέ occasionally stands at some distance, as in 2 C. ix. 1, 3 (Thuc. 2. 74),—probably also 1 C. xi. 18³ (see below); or is not entirely parallel in point of expression (G. iv. 24, 26).

In Rom. i. 8, πρῶτον μὲν εὐχαριστῶ κ.τ.λ., there is certainly an anacoluthon : when the apostle wrote these words he had in view a δεύτερον or an εἶτα, which, however, through the change of structure, does not follow. Wyttenbach's remark (on Plut. *Mor.* I. 47 : ed. Lips.) is here in point : " si solum posuisset πρῶτον, poterat accipi pro *maxime, ante omnia*" (so almost all commentators here) : "nunc quum μέν addidit, videtur voluisse alia subjungere, tum sui oblitus esse." Compare also Isocr. *Areop.* p. 344, Xen. *Mem.* 1. 1. 2, Schæf. *Demosth.* IV. 142, Mätzner, *Antiph.* p. 191.—1 C. xi. 18, πρῶτον μὲν γὰρ συνερχομένων ὑμῶν κ.τ.λ. : the ἔπειτα δέ is probably included in ver. 20 sqq., and Paul really intended to write, *First of all, I hear that in your assemblies there are divisions amongst you,—and then, that at the Lord's Supper disorders occur.* The latter Paul looks at from a different point of view,—not from that of *divisions*. Rom. iii. 2 was correctly explained by Tholuck.⁴

So also in Mt. viii. 21, ἐπίτρεψόν μοι πρῶτον ἀπελθεῖν καὶ θάψαι κ.τ.λ., the word πρῶτον has nothing which corresponds to it. But we should ourselves say, *Let me first of all (first) go away and bury;* and every one at once supplies from the context, *afterwards I will return (and follow thee,* ver. 19, 22).—If in the combination τε . . . καί we find πρῶτον inserted after τε, it means *especially* (Rom. i. 16, ii. 9 sq.) : in 2 C. viii. 5, also, πρῶτον . . . καί does not stand for πρῶτον . . . ἔπειτα,—see Meyer *in loc.*

An anacoluthon similar to that with μέν sometimes occurs with καί, in cases where καί should properly have been repeated (*both . . . and*). Thus in 1 C. vii. 38, ὥστε καὶ ὁ ἐκγαμίζων καλῶς ποιεῖ, ὁ δὲ μὴ ἐκγαμίζων κρεῖσσον ποιεῖ, the sentence is really planned for καὶ ὁ μή . . . . καλῶς ποιεῖ, as its second member : but as Paul is about to write these words, he corrects himself, and uses the comparative adverb ; and now, of course, the adversative particle appears to him more suitable. As however there are weighty authorities against δέ, καί may have been the original reading, changed by transcribers who considered δέ more appropriate.

---

¹ Heind. Plat. *Phæd.* p. 133, Schæf. *Melet.* p. 61.
² Compare Ast, Plat. *Legg.* p. 230, Matthiæ, Eurip. *Orest.* 24, Baiter, *Ind. ad* Isocr. *Paneg.* p. 133, Weber, *Demosth.* p. 257, Mätzner, *Antiph.* p. 209, 257 (Jelf 765).
³ [If connected with xii. 1 (Meyer),—but not as explained below.]
⁴ [Who holds that Paul intended a clause with δέ to follow.]

II. 1. Different from anacoluthon is the *oratio variata*[1] (Matth. 633, Jelf 909. *Obs.* 1). This term is applied where in parallel sentences or members of sentences two different (though synonymous) constructions, each complete in itself, are adopted, so that the period is *heterogeneous* in its structure. In careful writers we meet with the *oratio variata* mainly where a construction, if continued, would have been clumsy or obscure, or not altogether appropriate to the thought;[2] sometimes also a desire for variety has exerted an influence.

We give first some examples of a simple kind. 1 Jo. ii. 2, ἱλασμὸς περὶ τῶν ἁμαρτιῶν ἡμῶν, οὐ περὶ τῶν ἡμετέρων δὲ μόνον, ἀλλὰ καὶ περὶ ὅλου τοῦ κόσμου: here we might either have had περὶ τῶν ὅλου τοῦ κόσμου instead of περὶ ὅλου τοῦ κόσμου, or περὶ ἡμῶν instead of περὶ τῶν ἡμετέρων. Similarly H. ix. 7, A. xx. 34 (1 K. iii. 1, iv. 30, Lucian, *Parasit.* 20). E. v. 33, καὶ ὑμεῖς οἱ καθ' ἕνα ἕκαστος τὴν ἑαυτοῦ γυναῖκα οὕτως ἀγαπάτω ὡς ἑαυτόν, ἡ δὲ γυνὴ ἵνα φοβῆται τὸν ἄνδρα (compare § 43. 5 and Jo. xiii. 29). E. v. 27, ἵνα παραστήσῃ ἑαυτῷ ἔνδοξον τὴν ἐκκλησίαν, μὴ ἔχουσαν σπῖλον ... ἀλλ' ἵνα ᾖ (ἡ ἐκκλησία) ἁγία καὶ ἄμωμος;[3] compare *Act. Apocr.* p. 179. Ph. ii. 22, ὅτι, ὡς πατρὶ τέκνον, σὺν ἐμοὶ ἐδούλευσεν εἰς τὸ εὐαγγέλιον, *that he, as a son his father, so has served* (*me* in my apostolic office— or more fitly) *with me* etc.; Rom. iv. 12 (Æl. *An.* 2. 42), L. ix. 1, i. 73 sq.,[4] 1 P. ii. 7, Rom. i. 12.[5] 1 C. xiv. 1, ζηλοῦτε τὰ πνευματικά, μᾶλλον δὲ ἵνα προφητεύητε, where Paul might have written τὸ προφητεύειν: compare verses 5 and 11, Rev. iii. 18, A. xxii. 17.

In the following examples the divergence is greater. Mk. xii. 38 sq., τῶν θελόντων ἐν στολαῖς περιπατεῖν καὶ ἀσπασμοὺς (ἀσπάζεσθαι) ἐν ταῖς ἀγοραῖς κ.τ.λ. Jo. viii. 53, μὴ σὺ μείζων εἶ τοῦ πατρὸς ἡμῶν Ἀβραάμ, ὅστις ἀπέθανε; καὶ οἱ προφῆται ἀπέθανον: here regularity of construction would require that the question should be continued, καὶ τῶν προφητῶν, οἵτινες ἀπέθανον. 1 C. vii. 13, γυνή, ἥτις ἔχει ἄνδρα ἄπι-

---

[1] Jacob, Luc. *Alex.* p. 22, Jacobs, *Ælian* p. 6, Bremi, *Æschin.* II. 7.
[2] Engelhardt, Plat. *Menex.* p. 254, Beier, Cic. *Offic.* II. 38.
[3] Jo. xi. 52, (ἤμελλεν ἀποθνήσκειν) οὐχ ὑπὲρ τοῦ ἔθνους μόνον, ἀλλ' ἵνα καὶ τὰ τέκνα ... συναγάγῃ εἰς ἕν, does not come under this head. There was here no more convenient mode of expressing the second clause.
[4] In L. i. 55, however, τῷ Ἀβραάμ κ.τ.λ. must be joined [not with ἐλάλησε, but] with μνησθῆναι ἐλέους, mainly on account of εἰς τὸν αἰῶνα.
[5] Compare Matth. 632. 5, Schwarz, *Solœc.* p. 89 sq.

στον καὶ οὗτος συνευδοκεῖ (καὶ συνευδοκοῦντα) οἰκεῖν μετ' αὐτῆς, μὴ ἀφιέτω αὐτόν: see above, p. 186, and compare the similar examples in L. xvii. 31, Jo. xv. 5.—In Rom. xii. 6 sqq., ἔχοντες δὲ χαρίσματα κατὰ τὴν χάριν . . . εἴτε προφητείαν κατὰ τὴν ἀναλογίαν τῆς πίστεως, εἴτε διακονίαν ἐν τῇ διακονίᾳ, εἴτε ὁ διδάσκων ἐν τῇ διδασκαλίᾳ, εἴτε ὁ παρακαλῶν ἐν τῇ παρακλήσει, the construction (accusatives in dependence upon ἔχοντες) is kept up only as far as ἐν τῇ διακονίᾳ, and then begins a new construction, with concrete nouns: Paul might have written instead, εἴτε διδασκαλίαν . . . παράκλησιν κ.τ.λ.—In 2 C. xi. 23 sqq. Paul is enumerating the sufferings which are attendant on the apostolic office, by means of which he has proved himself a servant of Christ, and that in a higher degree. First, he simply appends ἐν κόποις περισσοτέρως κ.τ.λ., each particular brought into relief by an adverb of degree; then follow narrative aorists and perfects (ver. 24 sq.); and, lastly, Paul returns to substantives, interchanging the instrumental dative and the instrumental ἐν (ver. 26, 27). See further Jo. v. 44, Ph. i. 23 sq., 1 Jo. iii. 24. In 2 Jo. 2, διὰ τὴν ἀλήθειαν τὴν μένουσαν ἐν ἡμῖν, καὶ μεθ' ἡμῶν ἔσται εἰς τὸν αἰῶνα, it is obvious that the construction was intentionally changed in the second clause, in order that the thought might be brought out more forcibly than it would have been had this clause fallen into the construction of the first.[1] In Rom. ii. 9 sq., also, Paul first writes ἐπὶ πᾶσαν ψυχήν (speaking of trouble), but afterwards (speaking of the blessings of salvation) substitutes the more appropriate personal dative.—The *oratio variata* is combined with ellipsis in 2 C. viii.

---

[1] We could hardly (with Fritzsche) bring Mk. ii. 23, ἐγίνετο παραπορεύεσθαι αὐτόν . . . διὰ τῶν σπορίμων, καὶ ἤρξαντο οἱ μαθηταί κ.τ.λ., under the head of *variatio structuræ* (taking the last clause to stand for ἄρξασθαι τοὺς μαθητάς), even if we were to apply the standard of cultivated prose: for the narrative style of the Evangelists such a construction (ἄρξασθαι τοὺς μαθητάς) would be too heavy. Besides, the ἐγίνετο stands in no necessary relation to ἄρξασθαι τοὺς μαθητάς (q. d., "it came to pass that, as he . . ., the disciples plucked ears of corn"); but Mark's meaning is, It came to pass that he went through the cornfields *on a Sabbath*, and (then) the disciples plucked etc.—Still less can I find any change of construction that is worth noticing in 1 C. iv. 14, E. ii. 11-13 (or in Ph. i. 13!). No writer is so anxious about uniformity as not to allow himself to say "Not shaming you do I write this, but as my beloved children I admonish you," instead of "I do not . . . shaming . . . but admonishing." In A. xxi. 28, however (Fritz. *Conject.* I. 42 sq.), the words ἔτι τε of themselves show that Luke desires to give prominence to that which follows, and the independent construction of the new sentence accords with this purpose. [In 1 C. iv. 14 Tischendorf and Westcott and Hort read νουθετῶν.]

23, Rom. ii. 8, xi. 22 : also in Mk. vi. 8,¹ παρήγγειλεν αὐτοῖς, ἵνα μηδὲν αἴρωσιν εἰς ὁδόν... ἀλλ᾽ ὑποδεδεμένους σανδάλια (scil. πορεύεσθαι) καὶ μὴ ἐνδύσασθαι (here the better reading is ἐνδύσησθε) δύο χιτῶνας,—see Fritzsche *in loc.*. In Rom. xii. 2, however, we should probably read the infinitive συσχηματίζεσθαι,² not the imperative συσχηματίζεσθε.

Many examples of a similar kind may be collected from Greek authors : e.g., Paus. 1. 19. 5, τοῦ Νίσου λέγεται θυγατέρα ἐρασθῆναι Μίνω καὶ ὡς ἀπέκειρε τὰς τρίχας τοῦ πατρός· 5. 1. 2, 8. 22. 4, Πείσανδρος δὲ αὐτὸν ὁ Καμιρεὺς ἀποκτεῖναι τὰς ὄρνιθας οὐ φησίν, ἀλλὰ ὡς ψόφῳ κροτάλων ἐκδιώξειεν αὐτάς· Thuc. 8. 78, Xen. *Mem.* 2. 7. 8, *Hell.* 2. 3. 19, *An.* 2. 5. 5, Ælian, *Anim.* 10. 13. With Mk. xii. 38 sq., in particular, compare Lysias, *Cæd. Eratosth.* 21. From the LXX may be quoted Gen. xxxi. 33, Jud. xvi. 24, 3 (1) Esd. iv. 48, viii. 22, 80, Neh. x. 30.

In Mk. iii. 14 sqq., to the principal words ἐποίησεν δώδεκα, ἵνα κ.τ.λ. (ver. 14, 15), which are complete in themselves, Mark first attaches an isolated notice καὶ ἐπέθηκεν ὄνομα τῷ Σίμωνι κ.τ.λ. (ver. 16), in regard to the chief apostle, and then subjoins the names of the remaining apostles in direct dependence on ἐποίησεν (ver. 17-19) ; merely introducing in ver. 17 a second notice, similar to the former, by which the flow of the words is no more interrupted than it is in ver. 19 by ὃς καὶ παρέδωκεν κ.τ.λ. All would have been regular if in ver. 16 the evangelist had said Σίμωνα, ᾧ ἐπέθηκεν ὄνομα κ.τ.λ.

Under this head comes also the transition from the relative construction to that with the personal pronoun : 1 C. viii. 6, εἷς θεός... ἐξ οὗ τὰ πάντα καὶ ἡμεῖς εἰς αὐτόν· 2 P. ii. 3, οἷς τὸ κρίμα ἔκπαλαι οὐκ ἀργεῖ καὶ ἡ ἀπώλεια αὐτῶν οὐ νυστάζει; Rev. ii. 18 ; see above, p. 186, Weber, *Demosth.* p. 355 sq. L. x. 8, εἰς ἣν ἂν πόλιν εἰσέρχησθε, καὶ δέχωνται (οἱ πολῖται) ὑμᾶς κ.τ.λ., is substantially of the same kind.

On Rev. vii. 9, εἶδον καὶ ἰδοὺ ὄχλος... ἑστῶτες... περιβεβλημένους (compare xiv. 14), see above, § 59. 11. In both passages there is a blending of two constructions. So also in Rev. xviii. 12 sq., where first of all genitives of apposition are joined to τὸν γόμον, then an accusative (πᾶν ξύλον) comes in, then (καὶ ἵππων

---

¹ [Is not this rather an example of anacoluthon, ὑποδεδεμένους being used as if an infinitive had preceded? See A. Buttm. p. 384, Meyer *in loc.*]
² [The imperative is retained by Tischendorf, Tregelles, Westcott and Hort.]

κ.τ.λ.) genitives again, and lastly another accusative (ψυχὰς ἀνθρώ-πων). In Rev. ii. 17, however, where δώσω governs first the genitive and then the accusative, the distinction between the cases is correctly observed.

2. Deserving of special notice is the transition from the *oratio obliqua* to the *oratio recta*, and *vice versa*:[1] this transition is very common in Greek prose. A. xxiii. 22, ἀπέλυσε τὸν νεανίαν παραγγείλας μηδενὶ ἐκλαλῆσαι, ὅτι ταῦτα ἐνεφάνισας πρός με· xxiii. 23 sq., εἶπεν· ἑτοιμάσατε . . . κτήνη τε παραστῆσαι· L. v. 14, παρήγγειλεν αὐτῷ μηδενὶ εἰπεῖν, ἀλλὰ ἀπελθὼν δεῖξον· Mk. vi. 9. Compare Xen. *Hell.* 2.1.25, *An.* 1. 3. 14, and the passages which Kypke (I. 229 sq.) quotes from Josephus. Mk. xi. 31 sq., ἐὰν εἴπωμεν· ἐξ οὐρανοῦ, ἐρεῖ· διατί οὖν οὐκ ἐπιστεύσατε αὐτῷ ; ἀλλ᾽ εἴπωμεν· ἐξ ἀνθρώπων; ἐφοβοῦντο τὸν λαόν: in the last clause the narrator continues in his own words. With A. i. 4 compare Lysias, *in Diogit.* 12, ἐπειδὴ δὲ συνήλθομεν, ἤρετο αὐτὸν ἡ γυνή, τίνα ποτὲ ψυχὴν ἔχων ἀξιοῖ περὶ τῶν παίδων τοιαύτῃ χρῆσθαι, ἀδελφὸς μὲν ὢν τοῦ πατρός, πατὴρ δ᾽ ἐμός κ.τ.λ. (*Geopon.* 1. 12. 6). See further Jo. xiii. 29, A. xvii. 3. In Mt. ix. 6, however, the clause τότε λέγει τῷ παραλυτικῷ is inserted by the narrator in the midst of the words of Christ (compare Mk. ii. 10, L. v. 24). This is the simplest view of the passage; Meyer's explanation is forced.[2]

We find a transition from singular to plural, and *vice versa*, in Rom. iii. 7 sq., xii. 16 sqq., 20, 1 C. (iv. 2) iv. 6 sq. (Ælian 5. 8), 2 C. xi. 6, Ja. ii. 16, G. iv. 6 sq. (vi. 1).[3] Rom. ii. 15 also, ἐν ταῖς καρδίαις αὐτῶν, συμμαρτυρούσης αὐτῶν τῆς συνειδήσεως, may be brought in here. The change from singular to plural in L. v. 4 is intentional: see Bornemann *in loc.* On a plural in apposition to a singular, as in 1 Jo. v. 16, see § 59. 8.

Words of dissimilar character stand in apposition to each other in Rev. i. 6, ἐποίησεν ἡμᾶς βασιλείαν ἱερεῖς τῷ θεῷ: see § 59. 8. In other constructions besides this Greek writers sometimes place concretes and abstracts side by side; see Bremi on Æschin. *Ctesiph.*

---

[1] D'Orville, *Charit.* p. 89, 347, Heind. *Protag.* p. 510 sq., Jacobs, *Ælian* p. 46, 475, Ast, Plat. *Legg.* p. 160, Held, Plut. *Timol.* p. 451, Bornem. Xen. *Mem.* p. 253, Fritz. *Mark*, p. 212 (Jelf 890).
[2] Mt. xvi. 11, πῶς οὐ νοεῖτε, ὅτι οὐ περὶ ἄρτων εἶπον ὑμῖν· προσέχετε δὲ ἀπὸ τῆς ζύμης τῶν Φαρισαίων κ.τ.λ., is of a different kind : here we have merely a repetition of the direct words of Jesus (ver. 6), as such. Nor is there anything singular in Jo. x. 36. [In Mt. xvi. 11 it seems much simpler to make the question end at ὑμῖν. So the passage now stands in the best texts.]
[3] Schweigh. Arrian, *Epict.* II. 1, 94, 278, Matthiæ, Eurip. *Orest.* 111, Schæf. *Demosth.* IV. 106, Schwarz, *Solœc.* 107.

§ 25, Weber, *Demosth.* p. 260. Compare also Cæsar, *Civ.* 3. 32, erat plena *lictorum* et *imperiorum* provincia.

Section LXIV.

Incomplete Structure: Ellipsis,[1] Aposiopesis.

1. Until a very recent period the ideas generally entertained in regard to ellipsis (and pleonasm) were both inaccurate and fluctuating: hence the uncritical collections of L. Bos[2] and his followers, and of the N. T. philologers in particular (compare Haab p. 276 sqq.). It was from Hermann's acute examination of the subject[3] that these words first received an accurate definition and fixed meaning. Hermann is in the main followed in the present section, in which my immediate aim is simply to determine the various classes of ellipsis, a large number of examples having already been accumulated by Glass and Haab.[4]

I. Ellipsis (excluding aposiopesis, on which below, no. II.) consists in the omission of a word which, though absent itself from the sentence, yet in its idea must necessarily (for completeness of the sentence) be present to the thought.[5] Such omission of words to be supplied by the mind (whether it be occasioned by

---

[1] See K. F. Krumbholz, *De ellipseos in N. T. usu frequenti*, in his *Operarum subsecivarum lib.* 1. No. 11 (Norimb. 1736); F. A. Wolf, *De agnitione ellipseos in interpretatione librorum sacrorum*, Comm. i.-xi. (Lips. 1800-1808,—Comm. i.-vi. are reprinted in Pott's *Sylloge Comment. Theol.* IV. 107 sqq., VII. 52 sqq., VIII. 1 sqq.),—an uncritical collection. Compare further Bauer, *Philol. Thucyd.-Paull.* 162 sqq.; Bloch, *Ueber die Ellipsen in den paul. Briefen*, in his *Theologen* (Odensee, 1791), 1 St. [Jelf 891 sqq., Don. p. 609, Webster, *Synt.* p. 257.]

[2] Lamb. Bos, *Ellipses Græcæ* (Franecq. 1712, Traj. ad Rhen. 1755); *ed.* C. Schoettgen, 1713, 1728; *ed.* J. F. Leisner, Lips. 1749, 1767; *ed.* N. Schwebel, Norimb. 1763; *cum notis* C. B. Michaelis, Hal. 1765; *cum priorum editorum suisque observationibus ed.* G. H. Schæfer, Lips. 1808 (reprinted at Oxford, 1813). Compare Fischer, *Weller* III. i. 119 sqq., III. ii. 29 sqq.

[3] Hermann, *De ellipsi et pleonasmo*, in Wolf and Buttmann's *Museum antiquitatis studiorum*, Vol. I. Fasc. I. p. 97-235, and in Hermann's *Opuscula*, I. 148-244; also, in brief, *ad Vig.* p. 869 sqq.—Ellipsis in Latin is treated by J. W. Schlickeisen, *De formis linguæ Latinæ ellipticis*, 2 Pr. (Mühlhausen, 1830, 1843). An earlier work, by J. G. Lindner (*Ueber die lateinischen Ellipsen*: Frankf. on M. 1780), is of little importance even as a collection of examples.

[4] How much the books of the Bible have had to suffer from commentators in regard to ellipsis is intimated by Hermann (*Opusc.* p. 217), when he calls these books "cereos flecti quorundam artibus."

[5] Hermann, *Opusc.* p. 153: Ellipseos propria est ratio grammatica, quæ posita est in eo, ut oratio, etiamsi aliquid omissum sit, integra esse censeatur, quia id, quod omissum est, necessario tamen intelligi debeat, ut quo non intellecto sententia nulla futura sit.

SECT. LXIV.] INCOMPLETE STRUCTURE. 727

convenience, or by a desire for conciseness)[1] can take place only when the language used contains a clear intimation of what has been suppressed (Hermann, *Opusc.* p. 218),—either by means of the build of the particular sentence, or in consequence of some conventional usage.[2] As there are three constituent parts of the simple sentence, ellipses would range themselves under the three main heads of ellipsis of the subject, of the predicate, and of the copula (Herm. *Vig.* p. 870). Of the predicate, however, a real—i. e., an entire—ellipsis does not and probably cannot occur (Herm. *Vig.* p. 872); for the predicates of a subject are so manifold, that a writer cannot leave this part of the sentence to be supplied by the reader. Hence there remain only two kinds of ellipsis: of these the ellipsis of the subject is from the nature of the case the more limited.

The case in which a word or phrase which is expressed in one clause must be repeated in a subsequent and connected clause (Glass I. 632 sqq.)—either unaltered, or with some change of form required by the construction—cannot be called ellipsis, for here there is no real omission of the word.[3] The following are examples of this case :—

a. 2 C. i. 6, εἴτε θλιβόμεθα, ὑπὲρ τῆς ὑμῶν σωτηρίας, scil. θλιβόμεθα (v. 13, vii. 12); L. xxii. 36, ὁ ἔχων βαλλάντιον, ἀράτω . . . . ὁ μὴ ἔχων, scil. βαλλάντιον (καὶ πήραν), Ja. ii. 10, Jo. iv. 26 ; Jo. xii. 28, δόξασόν σου τὸ ὄνομα . . . . καὶ ἐδόξασα καὶ πάλιν δοξάσω, scil. τὸ ὄνομά μου. Compare further Rom. iii. 27, viii. 4, xi. 6, xiii. 1 (αἱ δὲ οὖσαι, scil. ἐξουσίαι,—this word is supplied by inferior authorities only),[4] Jo. iv. 53, A. xxiii. 34, 1 C. vii. 3 sq., xi. 25

---

[1] The omission of a word may sometimes arise from rhetorical considerations, either entirely, or at all events in part. See below, no. 3.

[2] To neither of these can *e.g.* those commentators appeal, who, in order to escape the archæological difficulty of Jo. xviii. 31, supply *hoc die* (festo) with ἡμῖν οὐκ ἔξεστιν ἀποκτεῖναι οὐδένα.

[3] Hermann, *Vig.* p. 869, *Opusc.* p. 151 sq., Poppo, *Thuc.* I. i. 282.—It must be acknowledged that this mode of expression gives more roundness and compactness to the style: the repetition of the same or similar forms of words would in most cases be very clumsy.

[4] 1 Jo. iii. 20 would come in here according to Lücke's explanation of the passage, which supplies γινώσκομεν (οἴδαμεν) from ver. 19 before the second ὅτι. I confess, however, that to me this explanation seems very harsh. Why may not a transcriber have inadvertently written ὅτι twice? Lachmann indeed rejects the second ὅτι, with A ; but it is just as likely that the particle was left out because it was not understood. Or why may not the repetition of ὅτι be ascribed to the author himself, as in E. ii. 11 sq. (see Fritz. 3. *Progr. ad Gal.* p. 5, or Fritzschiorum *Opusc.* p. 236)? The passage has not yet been sufficiently explained. [In his smaller edition Lachmann rejected the second ὅτι, but restored it in his larger work, reading the *pronoun* ὅ τι in the former clause : Bengel, Ewald, Huther, and others accept the pronoun, which seems certainly

(compare ver. 23), xv. 27, 2 C. xi. 11, Rev. ii. 9. So especially in answers: Jo. xviii. 5, τίνα ζητεῖτε; .... Ἰησοῦν τὸν Ναζωραῖον· xviii. 7, L. xx. 24, τίνος ἔχει εἰκόνα καὶ ἐπιγραφήν; ἀποκριθέντες εἶπον· Καίσαρος· vii. 43, Mt. xxvii. 21; H. v. 4, οὐχ ἑαυτῷ τις λαμβάνει τὴν τιμήν, ἀλλὰ καλούμενος ὑπὸ τοῦ θεοῦ, scil. λαμβάνει τὴν τιμήν (λαμβάνει having, however, the meaning *receives*).

b. Mk. xiv. 29, εἰ πάντες σκανδαλισθήσονται, ἀλλ' οὐκ ἐγώ (σκανδαλισθήσομαι, compare Mt. xxvi. 33); E. v. 24, ὥσπερ ἡ ἐκκλησία ὑποτάσσεται τῷ Χριστῷ, οὕτω .... αἱ γυναῖκες τοῖς ἀνδράσιν (ὑποτασσέσθωσαν); 2 Tim. i. 5, ἥτις ἐνῴκησεν ἐν τῇ μάμμῃ σου .... πέπεισμαι δέ, ὅτι καὶ ἐν σοί (ἐνοικεῖ); Rom. xi. 16, εἰ ἡ ἀπαρχὴ ἁγία, καὶ τὸ φύραμα (ἅγιον); H. v. 5, ὁ Χριστὸς οὐχ ἑαυτὸν ἐδόξασεν ... ἀλλ' ὁ λαλήσας πρὸς αὐτόν (ἐδόξασεν αὐτόν); 1 C. xi. 1, μιμηταί μου γίνεσθε, καθὼς κἀγὼ Χριστοῦ (μιμητής εἰμι); xiv. 27, εἴτε γλώσσῃ τις λαλεῖ, κατὰ δύο ἢ τὸ πλεῖστον τρεῖς (λαλείτωσαν), compare 1 P. iv. 11 ; L. xxiii. 41, ἐν τῷ αὐτῷ κρίματι εἶ· καὶ ἡμεῖς μὲν δικαίως (ἐσμέν, scil. ἐν τῷ κρίματι τούτῳ); 1 C. ix. 12, 25, xi. 16 ; 2 C. iii. 13, καὶ οὐ καθάπερ Μωϋσῆς ἐτίθει κάλυμμα ἐπὶ τὸ πρόσωπον ἑαυτοῦ (τίθεμεν κάλυμμα ἐπὶ τὸ πρόσωπον ἡμῶν).[1] Compare further Mt. xx. 23, xxvi. 5, Jo. xiii. 9, xv. 4, 5, xvii. 22, xviii. 40, Rom. i. 21 [?], ix. 32, xiv. 23, Ph. ii. 5, iii. 4, H. (ii. 13) x. 25, xii. 25, Rev. xix. 10, Mt. xxv. 9. Under this head will also come 1 C. vii. 21, δοῦλος ἐκλήθης, μή σοι μελέτω, if we supply the ellipsis in the simplest way, by understanding τῆς δουλείας (Lob. *Paralip.* p. 314): see Meyer, who has overlooked the fact that I proposed this in my 5th edition.[2] The most remarkable accumulation of such necessary repetitions of words is found in Rom. xii. 6 sq.

c. Nor is there a real ellipsis when it is necessary to supply an affirmative from a preceding negative word,—a case of frequent occurrence in Greek authors (e. g., Thuc. 2. 98. 3, πορευομένῳ αὐτῷ ἀπεγίγνετο μὲν οὐδὲν τοῦ στρατοῦ εἰ μή τι νόσῳ, προςεγίγνετο δέ):[3] 1 C. vii. 19, ἡ περιτομὴ οὐδέν ἐστι, ἀλλὰ τήρησις ἐντολῶν θεοῦ (ἐστί τι or τὰ πάντα ἐστί), iii. 7, 1 C. x. 24, μηδεὶς τὸ ἑαυτοῦ ζητείτω, ἀλλὰ τὸ τοῦ ἑτέρου (scil. ἕκαστος). Of a different kind are E. iv. 29 and 1 C. iii. 1. Conciseness of expression is carried still farther in Mk. xii. 5, καὶ πολλοὺς ἄλλους, τοὺς μὲν δέροντες, τοὺς δὲ ἀποκτείνοντες; from these two participles we must supply a finite verb

---

the most probable reading. In the examples by Winer and Fritzsche for the repetition of ὅτι the particle has the meaning *that*, not *because*.]

[1] This case, in which the verb is construed, not with the principal subject, but with the subject of the subordinate clause, may be regarded as a species of attraction. See Krüger, *Gramm. Untersuch.* III. 72, where many similar examples are adduced, e.g., Xen. *Cyr.* 4. 1. 3, Thuc. 1. 82, 3. 67.

[2] [The notice in ed. 5 (p. 654) has reference to the latter part of the verse only : Winer supplies τῇ δουλείᾳ, from δοῦλος, as object of χρῆσαι (so Bengel, Meyer, De W., Alford, al.). Compare Lightfoot, *Col.* p. 390 sq., *Speak. Comm.* III. 294.]

[3] See Stallbaum, Plat. *Apol.* p. 78, *Sympos.* p. 80, *Euthyd.* p. 158, Mätzner, *Antiph.* p. 176 (Jelf 895. 9). In regard to Latin, compare Bremi, *Nep.* p. 345, Kritz, *Sallust* II. 573.

which will comprehend both verbal notions, such as *ill-treat* (compare Fritzsche *in loc.*). So also in Rom. xiv. 21, καλὸν τὸ μὴ φαγεῖν κρέα μηδὲ πιεῖν οἶνον, μηδὲ ἐν ᾧ ὁ ἀδελφός σου προσκόπτει κ.τ.λ., we should probably supply after the second μηδέ the general word ποιεῖν (Aristot. *Nicom.* 8. 13. 6), or some such word as *taste*. On Ph. ii. 3 see below, no. 2 (Lob. *Paralip.* p. 382). In H. x. 6, 8, ὁλοκαυτώματα καὶ περὶ ἁμαρτίας οὐκ εὐδόκησας, we must from ὁλοκαυτώματα supply the general notion θυσίας to the words περὶ ἁμαρτίας; similarly, in H. x. 38 the general term ἄνθρωπος is to be supplied from δίκαιος (compare Kühner II. 37 [1]). In Rev. vi. 4 the subject of σφάξουσι must be supplied from the clause λαβεῖν τὴν εἰρήνην ἐκ τῆς γῆς, viz., the concrete οἱ κατοικοῦντες ἐπ' αὐτῆς. But here also the suppressed notion is partially present.—(For Latin examples similar to the above see Lindner, *Lat. Ellips.* p. 240 sqq.)

In all these cases the necessity of some supplement is shown by the incompleteness of the sentence, considered grammatically and logically. Not so in Jo. viii. 15, ὑμεῖς κατὰ τὴν σάρκα κρίνετε, ἐγὼ οὐ κρίνω οὐδένα: rather is the second clause so concluded by οὐδένα, that we can perceive no requirement to supply anything,—*Ye judge according to the flesh, but I judge no one* (not merely, *I judge no one according to the flesh*, but absolutely, *I judge no one*). The only justification for supplying κατὰ τὴν σάρκα from the preceding clause would be found in the inappropriateness of the thought which would otherwise be presented: no such inappropriateness, however, am I able to discover, any more than Olshausen and Lücke. As to the meaning, see especially Baumg.-Crusius *in loc.*

After εἰ δὲ μή, εἰ δὲ μή γε (Mt. vi. 1, L. x. 6, xiii. 9, 2 C. xi. 16, al.),[2] and after the formula οὐ μόνον δέ (. . . ἀλλὰ καί), so frequently used by Paul, it is particularly common to have to repeat in thought a preceding word or phrase. For the latter see Rom. v. 3, οὐ μόνον δέ (scil. καυχώμεθα ἐπ' ἐλπίδι τῆς δόξης, ver. 2), ἀλλὰ καὶ καυχώμεθα κ.τ.λ.; Rom. v. 11, καταλλαγέντες σωθησόμεθα . . . οὐ μόνον δέ (καταλλαγέντες σωθησόμεθα), ἀλλὰ καὶ καυχώμενοι· viii. 23, 2 C. viii. 19. In Rom. ix. 10, οὐ μόνον δέ, ἀλλὰ καὶ Ῥεβέκκα κ.τ.λ. something more remote seems to be omitted. It is easiest to fill up the sense thus, from ver. 9 (compare ver. 12): *But not only did Sarah receive a divine promise respecting her son*, but also Rebekah, though she was the mother of two legitimate sons, etc. In Greek writers compare Diog. L. 9. 39, πεντακοσίοις ταλάντοις τιμηθῆναι, μὴ μόνον δέ, ἀλλὰ καὶ χαλκαῖς εἴκοσι. Lucian, *Vit. Auct.* 7, οὐ μόνον, ἀλλὰ καὶ

---

[1] [Jelf 373. 6. On this passage see § 58. 9.]
[2] Compare Plat. *Gorg.* 503 c, *Phæd.* 63 d, Hoogeveen, *Partic. Gr.* I. 345 sq. [The strengthened form εἰ δὲ μή γε, which in the N. T. occurs more frequently than the other, is not unclassical: see Plat. *Rep.* 425 e. Both are found after negative (*otherwise, otherwise indeed*), as well as after affirmative sentences: see Jelf 860. 4, Alford on Mt. vi. 1, Grimm, *Clavis* p. 115, 74.]

ἢν θυρωρεῖν αὐτὸν ἐπιστήσῃς, πολὺ πιστοτέρῳ χρήσῃ τῶν κυνῶν· *Toxar.* 1.[1] An analogous formula in earlier writers is οὐ μόνον γε . . . . ἀλλά: Plat. *Phæd.* 107 b, οὐ μόνον γ', ἔφη ὁ Σωκράτης (scil. ἀπιστίαν σε δεῖ ἔχειν περὶ τῶν εἰρημένων), ἀλλὰ ταῦτά τε εὖ λέγεις κ.τ.λ., *Meno* 71 b, *Legg.* 6. 752 a; see Heindorf and Stallbaum on Plat. *Phæd. l. c.* In 2 C. vii. 7 the clause introduced by οὐ μόνον δέ is actually expressed, by a repetition of preceding words.—The use of κἄν in the sense of *vel certe*[2] is also the result of an omission; e. g., Mk. vi. 56, ἵνα κἂν τοῦ κρασπέδου . . . ἄψωνται (properly, ἵνα ἄψωνται αὐτοῦ, κἂν τοῦ κρασπέδου ἅψωνται), 2 C. xi. 16. The same may be said of εἰ καί in 2 C. vii. 8; compare Bengel *in loc.*[3]

Still less can we give the name of ellipsis to the case in which a word expressed but once must in *the same* principal sentence be supplied a second time (in a different form): A. xvii. 2, κατὰ τὸ εἰωθὸς τῷ Παύλῳ εἰσῆλθε πρὸς αὐτούς (Παῦλος), xiii. 3, ἐπιθέντες τὰς χεῖρας αὐτοῖς ἀπέλυσαν (αὐτούς). In Rom. ii. 28, οὐχ ὁ ἐν τῷ φανερῷ Ἰουδαῖός ἐστιν οὐδὲ ἡ ἐν τῷ φανερῷ περιτομή, the predicative words Ἰουδαῖος and περιτομή must also be supplied with the subjects ὁ ἐν τῷ φανερῷ and ἡ ἐν τῷ φανερῷ. Compare also A. viii. 7.

Rem. It may sometimes happen that some form of a word must be supplied from a *subsequent* clause;[4] compare 1 C. vii. 39. In Rom. v. 16, however, the opinion that παραπτώματος must be supplied with ἐξ ἑνός, from ἐκ τῶν πολλῶν παραπτωμάτων, may now be regarded as obsolete: see Philippi *in loc.* In 2 C. viii. 5 the verb ἔδωκαν in the second clause also belongs to the clause beginning with καὶ οὐ (a very common case), only it must the first time be taken absolutely: *and they did not give as* (in the measure that) *we hoped, but they gave themselves* (personally) etc. But in Mk. xv. 8, ἤρξατο αἰτεῖσθαι καθὼς ἀεὶ ἐποίει αὐτοῖς, it might appear that with the verb αἰτεῖσθαι we must supply ποιεῖν, from ἐποίει. Strictly, however, the words run thus, . . . *to make request in accordance with what he always did for them* (granted to them): from this we may infer the object of the request, but have no right grammatically to supply it.—On E. iv. 26, where it has been proposed to take the μή

---

[1] Kypke, *Obs.* II. 165, Hoogev. *Partic.* II. 956.

[2] Vig. p. 527, Boisson. Philostr. *Epp.* p. 97. [Similarly Meyer, De W., Fritzsche (2. *Diss.* p. 120), A. Buttm. (p. 360), Rost (*Gr.* p. 614), and others. For a different explanation of the process by which κἄν came to mean *if only, even* (κἄν being taken for καὶ ἄν, not καὶ ἐάν), see Rost und Palm, Liddell and Scott, s. v., Jebb on Soph. *Ajax* 1078 or *El.* 1483. See further Green p. 230, Mullach p. 398.—To the N. T. examples of κἄν thus used add A. v. 15.]

[3] [Bengel takes the εἰ καί before πρὸς ὥραν as used elliptically, so as to give the meaning *for a season only—if indeed at all*: "contristavit vos, inquit, epistola, tantummodo ad tempus, vel potius ne ad tempus quidem." Meyer objects (1) that such an ellipsis is found with εἰ καὶ ἄρα, εἴπερ ἄρα, εἰ ἄρα, but never with the simple εἰ καί: (2) that on this view πρὸς ὥραν would naturally precede εἰ καί: (3) that the thought itself would be inappropriate.]

[4] Herm. *Opusc.* p. 151, Jacob, Luc. *Alex.* p. 109, Lindner, *Lat. Ellips.* p. 251 sqq.

of the second clause as belonging to the first also, see above, p. 392.

2. The most common case of actual ellipsis is the omission of the simple copula εἶναι: viz.—

a. In the form ἐστί (more rarely ᾖ),[1]—for this is really implied in the mere juxtaposition of subject and predicate:[2] H. v. 13, πᾶς ὁ μετέχων γάλακτος ἄπειρος (ἐστί) λόγου δικαιοσύνης· ix. 16, x. 4, 18, xi. 19, Mk. xiv. 36, Rom. xi. 16, xiv. 21, 2 C. i. 21, Ph. iv. 3, E. i. 18, iv. 4, v. 17, 2 Th. iii. 2, 1 P. iv. 17. Particularly also in questions, L. iv. 36, A. x. 21, Rom. iii. 1, viii. 27, 31, 2 C. ii. 16, vi. 14, Rev. xiii. 4, H. vi. 8 (compare Kritz, *Sallust*, I. 251); and exclamations, A. xix. 28, 34, μεγάλη ἡ Ἄρτεμις Ἐφεσίων. This omission is however most common in certain established formulas: Ja. i. 12, μακάριος ἀνήρ, ὅς κ.τ.λ. (Mt. v. 3, 5-10, xiii. 16, L. i. 45, Rom. iv. 8, xiv. 22, Rev. xvi. 15, —compare 1 P. iv. 14); δῆλον ὅτι, 1 C. xv. 27,[3] 1 Tim. vi. 7; ἀνάγκη with an infinitive, H. ix. 16, 23, Rom. xiii. 5; πιστὸς ὁ θεός, 1 C. i. 9, x. 13, 2 C. i. 18, or πιστὸς ὁ λόγος, 1 Tim. i. 15, iii. 1, 2 Tim. ii. 11; ὁ κύριος ἐγγύς, Ph. iv. 5; ἄξιος ὁ ἐργάτης τῆς τροφῆς, Mt. x. 10, 1 Tim. v. 18,—compare Rev. v. 2; ἔτι μικρόν, Jo. xiv. 19; μικρὸν ὅσον ὅσον, H. x. 37; εἰ δυνατόν, Mt. xxiv. 24, Rom. xii. 18, G. iv. 15; ὥρα with an infinitive, Rom. xiii. 11 (Plat. *Ap.* p. 42); τί γάρ, Ph. i. 18, Rom. iii. 3; τί οὖν, Rom. iii. 9, vi. 15; τί ἐμοὶ καὶ σοί,[4] Mk. v. 7, i. 24, L. viii. 28, Jo. ii. 4 (Her. 5. 33, Demosth. *Aphob.* 564 b, Arrian, *Epict.* 1. 1. 16, 1. 19. 16); τί τὸ ὄφελος, 1 C. xv. 32, Ja. ii. 14, 16; ᾧ ὄνομα or ὄνομα αὐτῷ, followed by the name, L. ii. 25, Jo. i. 6, iii. 1, al. (Demosth. *Zenoth.* p. 576 b); compare also A. xiii. 11, ii. 29. In the latter examples, as in the former, brevity and conciseness are altogether in place: compare Vig. p. 236.[5]

---

[1] Compare however Stallbaum, Plat. *Rep.* I. 133.
[2] Rost p. 468 sq., Krüg. p. 272 sq.: compare Wannowski, *Syntax. Anom.* p. 210 sq. [See Jelf 376, Don. p. 400 sq., A. Buttm. p. 136 sqq. In a few of the examples quoted here (e. g., H. ix. 16, E. iv. 4) it is the substantive verb that is omitted (see below) not the copula: in some others ἦν rather than ἐστί must be supplied.—H. vi. 8 is not a *question:* probably Winer had intended to mention the frequent omission of εἶναι in *relative* clauses (Don. p. 401, Jelf 376. d), which is illustrated by this passage (H. ii. 10, iv. 13, ix. 2, 4, al.).]
[3] [Unless we supply πάντα ὑποτίτακται (Meyer, and Winer above, 1. a); see Jelf 895. 1. a.—In 1 Tim. l. c. δῆλον is absent from the best texts.]
[4] [So in Mt. xxvii. 19, μηδὲν σοὶ καὶ τῷ δικαίῳ ἐκείνῳ (ἔστω): A. Buttm. p. 138.]
[5] Under this head comes also the formula τί (ἐστιν) ὅτι, Mk. ii. 16 [*Rec.*], A. v. 4 (Bar. iii. 10): see Fritz. *Mark,* p. 60.

The conjunctive ᾖ is to be supplied after ἵνα in (Rom. iv. 16) 2 C. viii. 11, 13.

b. More rarely is the substantive verb omitted in other forms. Εἰμί: 2 C. xi. 6, εἰ δὲ καὶ ἰδιώτης τῷ λόγῳ ἀλλ' οὐ τῇ γνώσει, where λογίζομαι μηδὲν ὑστερηκέναι τῶν ὑπερλίαν ἀποστόλων precedes.[1] Εἰσί: Rom. iv. 14, xi. 16, 1 C. xiii. 8, i. 26 (see Meyer [2]), Rev. xxii. 15, H. ii. 11 (Schæf. *Melet.* p. 43 sq.). Ἐσμέν: Rom. viii. 17, 2 C. x. 7, Ph. iii. 15 (Plin. *Epp.* 6. 16). Εἶ: Rev. xv. 4 (Plat. *Gorg.* 487 d). Ἔστω: Rom. xii. 9, Col. iv. 6, H. xiii. 4, 5 (Fritz. *Rom.* III. 65); also with χάρις τῷ θεῷ, Rom. vi. 17, 2 C. viii. 16, ix. 15 (Xen. *An.* 3. 3. 14). Εἴη in wishes: Rom. i. 7, xv. 33, Jo. xx. 19, 21, 26, Mt. xxi. 9, L. i. 28,[3] Tit. iii. 15. Two different forms of this verb are omitted in close succession in Jo. xiv. 11, ὅτι ἐγὼ ἐν τῷ πατρὶ καὶ ὁ πατὴρ ἐν ἐμοί· xvii. 23. In historical narration the aorist also is left out: e.g., 1 C. xvi. 9[4] (Xen. *An.* 1. 2. 18, *Cyr.* 1. 6. 6, Thuc. 1. 138, al.). On the future see below, p. 734. In the simple language of the N. T. the form to be supplied is always clearly indicated by the context (in Greek authors the determination is often more difficult, see Schæf. *Melet.* p. 43 sq., 114); hitherto, however, commentators have been very lavish in allowing an ellipsis of the substantive verb, and in particular have by this means turned a multitude of participles into finite verbs (compare § 45. 6).[5]

---

[1] The case is simpler in Mk. xii. 26 (from the LXX), ἐγὼ ὁ θεὸς Ἀβραάμ. A. vii. 32: also in 2 C. viii. 23. Compare Soph. *Antig.* 634. [In the passage from which Mk. xii. 26 and A. vii. 32 are taken (Ex. iii. 6) εἰμί is expressed. In 2 C. viii. 23 the form to be supplied is εἰσί.]

[2] [Meyer supplies εἰσί between πολλοί and σοφοί. Compare the *Journal of Philology*, p. 158 sq. (Cambridge, 1868), where it is maintained that the reference is to the *preachers*, and that St. Paul, when he wrote οὐ πολλοὶ σοφοί κ.τ.λ., had ἐξελέχθησαν in his mind as the verb of the sentence.]

[3] [It seems much more probable that ἐστί should be supplied here (Meyer, De W., Bleek, al.).—See Ellicott on E. i. 2.]

[4] [This is an example of the omission of εἰσί.]

[5] [In Green's *Grammar* (p. 180) it is strangely asserted that "the absolute use of the participle as an imperative is a marked feature of the language of the New Testament:" see also his *Critical Notes* p. 36, Wratislaw, *Notes* etc. p. 168, and (less positively) Webster, *Synt.* p. 116. The only passages which I find quoted in illustration of this "Aramaism" (?) are 2 P. i. 20, 1 P. ii. 12, 2 P. iii. 3 (Mk. vi. 9), 1 P. ii. 18, iii. 1, 6 sqq., Rom. xii. 9-19, H. xiii. 5. The first of these passages is surely perfectly regular; the second and third are simple examples of the participial anacoluthon noticed above, § 63. 2 : as to Mk. vi. 9, it is hard to conceive anything more unnatural than the explanation of ὑποδεδεμένους as an "indirect imperative" (Green, *Cr. Notes l. c.*). On 1 P. ii. 18-iii.

The imperative plural ἐστέ,[1] also, is suppressed in such cases as Rom. xii. 9 (1 P. iii. 8), as appears from the whole tone of the sentence; and it is not necessary to explain the participle ἀποστυγοῦντες as an anacoluthon.—In εὐλογητὸς ὁ θεός, etc., Rom. ix. 5, 2 C. i. 3, E. i. 3, we must supply, not ἐστί (Fritz. *Rom.* I. 75), but εἴη or ἔστω (compare 1 P. x. 9,[2] Job i. 21).

We sometimes find the same omission of ἐστί, etc., when this verb is more than the mere copula, and denotes *existence, subsistence* (Rost p. 469, Jelf 376): 1 C. xv. 21, δι' ἀνθρώπου ὁ θάνατος (*exists*), 1 C. xv. 40, Rom. iv. 13.

It will also be sufficient to supply εἶναι or γίνεσθαι in most of those passages in which an oblique case or a preposition appears to require a verb of more special meaning. See 1 C. vi. 13, τὰ βρώματα τῇ κοιλίᾳ καὶ ἡ κοιλία τοῖς βρώμασι· A. x. 15, φωνὴ πάλιν ἐκ δευτέρου πρὸς αὐτόν (ἐγένετο, compare ver. 13), Mt. iii. 17 (in Jo. xii. 28, ἦλθεν φωνή[3]), 1 C. iv. 20, οὐκ ἐν λόγῳ ἡ βασιλεία τοῦ θεοῦ, ἀλλ' ἐν δυνάμει (compare ii. 5), Rom. x. 1, xi. 11, 2 C. iv. 15, viii. 13 (Meyer[4]), 1 P. iii. 12, H. vii. 20. The preposition or the case shows what verbal notion must be supplied in thought: (whose final lot) *leads to burning, is destined for, came to him,*[5] etc. As in the last passage [A. x. 15] ἐγένετο is obviously sufficient, so also in the first two, considering the simplicity of the style, nothing but ἐστί must be supplied. Similarly in 1 C. v. 12, τί γάρ μοι καὶ τοὺς ἔξω κρίνειν; (Arrian, *Epict.* 2. 17. 14, τί μοι νῦν τὴν πρὸς ἀλλήλους μάχην παραφέρειν;

9, see above, p. 442. In H. xiii. 5, Rom. xii. 9 sqq., it must not be forgotten that by the side of the participles stand *adjectives*, with which the imperative of εἶναι is confessedly to be supplied.]

[1] In E. i. 13, also, Meyer would supply ἐστί after ἐν ᾧ: this ἐν ᾧ, however, seems rather to be taken up again, after the clause ἀκούσαντες κ.τ.λ., in the second ἐν ᾧ. Between ἀκούσαντες and πιστεύσαντες there can hardly come εἶναι ἐν Χριστῷ. [Meyer does supply ἐστί, but it is the indicative, not the imperative.]

[2] [This is no doubt a mistake for 1 K. x. 9.—On this question see Ellicott on E. i. 3, Lightfoot on G. i. 5, A. Buttm. p. 137.]

[3] It is always the more simple notion that is omitted; and if a writer here and there introduces a verb of special meaning into a formula which is commonly elliptical, it does not follow that this is the verb by which the ellipsis is to be supplied. Thus Antipater in the *Greek Anthology* says εἴ τί τοι ἐκ βίβλων ἦλθεν ἡμῶν ὄφελος; but we must not on this account supply ἦλθε in the formula τί μοι τὸ ὄφελος (so Palairet p. 415), but only the simple ἐστί. Similarly in Lucian, *Merc. Cond.* 25, we find τί κοινὸν λύρᾳ καὶ ὄνῳ; but it does not follow that in the formula τί ἐμοὶ καὶ σοί; the word κοινόν is to be supplied. See Fritz. *Mark,* p. 33.

[4] [Meyer supplies γίνεται with περίσσευμα.]

[5] [These three renderings relate to H. vi. 8, 1 C. vi. 13, A. x. 15,—as is shown by ed. 5. The omission of H. vi. 8 in the sixth and seventh editions is probably accidental: this passage is misplaced above, p. 731.]

4. 6. 33), and in Jo. xxi. 22, τί πρὸς σέ ;[1] (compare the Latin *hoc nihil ad me, quid hoc ad me ?*). In Jo. xxi. 21 also, οὗτος δὲ τί ; it will be sufficient to supply ἔσται (γενήσεται): the future is suggested by the context. Compare 1 P. iv. 17. Lastly, the formula ἵνα τί (scil. γένηται or γένοιτο) also comes under this head: see Herm. *Vig.* p. 849.

Verbs which express not merely the copula but also the predicate (or a part of it)[2] can be left unexpressed only where they are indicated by the conformation of the sentence (Bar. iv. 1). Compare such well-known phrases as *zwölf einen Thaler* [or our *three a penny*], *manum de tabula, hæc hactenus,* etc. Thus in A. ix. 6 *Rec.*, ὁ κύριος πρὸς αὐτόν, we readily supply εἶπε (ver. 15), to which πρὸς αὐτόν points; as in A. ii. 38, xxv. 22 (Ælian 1. 16 *v.l.*[3]). In Rom. iv. 9, ὁ μακαρισμὸς οὗτος ἐπὶ τὴν περιτομὴν ἢ καὶ ἐπὶ τὴν ἀκροβυστίαν ; the meaning obviously is, *does this . . . refer* etc.; but the word to be supplied is not πίπτει (Theophylact), but rather λέγεται,[4]—compare ver. 6 (λέγειν εἴς τινα, Eurip. *Iphig. T.* 1180). A. xviii. 6, τὸ αἷμα ὑμῶν ἐπὶ τὴν κεφαλὴν ὑμῶν· Mt. xxvii. 25, τὸ αἷμα αὐτοῦ ἐφ' ἡμᾶς (2 S. i. 16, Plat. *Euthyd.* 283 e),—scil. ἐλθέτω, compare Mt. xxiii. 35 (though ἔστω would be sufficient).[5] In Rom. v. 18, ὡς δι' ἑνὸς παραπτώματος εἰς πάντας ἀνθρώπους εἰς κατάκριμα, supply the impersonal ἀπέβη, *res cessit, abiit in* etc.; and with the following words, οὕτω καὶ δι' ἑνὸς δικαιώματος εἰς πάντας ἀνθρώπους εἰς δικαίωσιν ζωῆς, supply ἀποβήσεται (in accordance with ver. 19, —so Fritzsche[6]), or rather a second ἀπέβη (Meyer). 2 C. ix. 7, ἕκαστος καθὼς προῄρηται τῇ καρδίᾳ, μὴ ἐκ λύπης,—scil. δότω,

---

[1] See Hermann, *Opusc.* p. 157 sq., 169, Bos, *Ellips.* p. 598 (Jelf 590. *Obs.*): on the Latin phrase see Kritz, *Sallust* II. 146 [Madvig 479. d. *Obs.* 1].
[2] Hermann, *Opusc.* p. 156 sq. (Jelf 895).
[3] This ellipsis is carried to a great extent in both Greek and Latin : e. g., Charit. 6. 1, ταῦτα μὲν οὖν οἱ ἄνδρες· Val. Flacc. 5. 254, vix ea. Compare also Cic. *N. D.* 2. 4. 11, augures rem ad Senatum, and many examples of a similar kind, especially in the epistolary style: see Cic. *Fam.* 4. 8, 7. 9, *Attic.* 15. 8, 17, 16. 9,—particularly the examples from *ad Atticum*.
[4] Fritzsche *in loc.* [See p. 509, where H. vii. 13 is quoted for λέγειν ἐπί τινα. In Rom. iv. 9 Meyer prefers the simple ἐστί (compare Rom. ii. 2, 9, A. iv. 33).]
[5] When similar imprecations occur in Greek authors,—e. g., ἐς κεφαλήν σοι, Aristoph. *Pax* 1063,—it is customary to supply τραπέσθω, in accordance with Mosch. 4. 123, Phalar. *Ep.* 128. See Bos, *Ellips.* p. 657 sq. (Jelf 891. 4).
[6] [This reference to Fritzsche must be understood as applying to the *tense* only: Fritzsche supplies τὸ κρίμα ἐγένετο and τὸ χάρισμα γενήσεται in the two members of this verse.]

from the whole context. In L. xxii. 26, ὑμεῖς δὲ οὐχ οὕτως, it will be simplest to supply ποιήσετε, from κυριεύουσιν κ.τ.λ.; perhaps however ἔσεσθε would be sufficient.[1] In Ph. ii. 3, μηδὲν κατὰ ἐριθείαν, nothing more is required than the repetition of φρονοῦντες from the preceding verse.[2] In G. ii. 9, δεξιὰς ἔδωκαν ἐμοὶ καὶ Βαρνάβᾳ κοινωνίας, ἵνα ἡμεῖς μὲν εἰς τὰ ἔθνη, αὐτοὶ δὲ εἰς τὴν περιτομήν, as the words relate to preachers of the Gospel, we may easily supply εὐαγγελιζώμεθα, εὐαγγελίζωνται (2 C. x. 16, like κηρύττειν εἴς τινα in 1 Th. ii. 9), and not, with Fritzsche and Meyer [in earlier editions], the less significant πορευθῶμεν, πορευθῶσι, etc. In the proclamation of Rev. vi. 6, χοῖνιξ σίτου δηναρίου καὶ τρεῖς χοίνικες κριθῶν δηναρίου (*A measure of wheat for a denarius!*), the necessary supplement is as readily suggested by the genitive of price (p. 258), as it is in similar notices of sale in our own language. On the formulas of salutation in letters, as Rev. i. 4, Ἰωάννης ταῖς ἑπτὰ ἐκκλησίαις ταῖς ἐν τῇ Ἀσίᾳ· Ph. i. 1, Παῦλος πᾶσιν τοῖς ἁγίοις . . . τοῖς οὖσιν ἐν Φιλίπποις (scil. χαίρειν λέγει), or in A. xxiii. 26, Κλαύδιος Λυσίας τῷ κρατίστῳ ἡγεμόνι Φήλικι χαίρειν (scil. λέγει), A. xv. 23, Ja. i. 1, see Fritzsche, *Rom.* I. 22.

In the proverb 2 P. ii. 22, ἡ λουσαμένη εἰς κύλισμα βορβόρου, the verb is included in εἰς; and we might easily supply ἐπιστρέψασα, in accordance with the preceding words. In proverbs, however, which demand brevity of expression, even verbs of special meaning are omitted (by conventional usage); compare *fortuna fortes*, γλαῦκ᾽ εἰς Ἀθήνας, and see Bernh. p. 351[3] (Jelf 891. 4).

3. The subject can be *entirely* suppressed (Krüg. p. 264) in the following cases only:—

a. Where the subject is at once obvious, because the predicate, either from the nature of the case or through some conventional usage, can be asserted of one (definite) subject only: e. g., βροντᾷ (ὁ Ζεύς), σαλπίζει (ὁ σαλπιγκτής), ἀναγνώσεται (Demosth. *Mid.* 386 b) scil. *scriba*: see above, § 58. 9. From Jewish phraseology we may bring in here the formula of quotation λέγει, H. i. 7; εἴρηκε, H. iv. 4; φησί, H. viii. 5 (μαρτυρεῖ, H. vii. 17 *Rec.*). See above, § 58. 9. On H. xiii. 5 see Bleek.[4]

---

[1] [Or even ἐστί (Meyer, Bornemann): compare Mk. x. 43.]
[2] [So Alford, Ellicott: see however Lightfoot *in loc.* ("do nothing") and on G. v. 13.]
[3] Grotefend, *Ausf. lat. Grammat.* II. 397 sq., Zumpt, *Lat. Grammat.* 759.
[4] [Bleek's opinion may be seen in Alford's note. On Col. i. 19 (quoted below) compare the notes of Ellicott and Lightfoot.]

b. When a saying is quoted the subject of which any reader can at once supply, from his own knowledge or reading: Jo. vi. 31, ἄρτον ἐκ τοῦ οὐρανοῦ ἔδωκεν αὐτοῖς φαγεῖν (scil. ὁ θεός), 2 C. ix. 9 (Ps. cxi. 9), 1 C. xv. 27 (but in ver. 25 Χριστός is the subject), Col. i. 19, Jo. xii. 40, xv. 25, Rom. ix. 18 sq.; see Van Hengel, *Cor.* p. 120 sq. On Jo. vii. 51 see p. 656 : 1 Tim. iii. 16 is noticed below, and Mt. v. 38 in no. 6.[1] (Jelf 373.)

When the 3rd person plural is used impersonally, as in Jo. xx. 2, ἦραν τὸν κύριον ἐκ τοῦ μνημείου (compare § 58. 9), there is no omission ; for this person itself really contains the general subject *people* or *men.* See also L. xii. 20, and Bornemann *in loc.* The same may be said of the genitive absolute, as in L. viii. 20 [*Rec.*], ἀπηγγέλη αὐτῷ λεγόντων, i. e., *men saying, as they said.* Compare 1 K. xii. 9, 1 Chr. xvii. 24, Thuc. 1. 3, Xen. *Cyr.* 3. 3. 54, Diog. L. 6. 32.[2]

In 1 Tim. iii. 16, with the reading ὅς, the subject of the following relative clauses is wanting ; unless we suppose, with some recent commentators, that the apodosis begins at ἐδικαιώθη. This however is not advisable on account of the parallelism : it is more probable that all the members are co-ordinate, and that the apostle took the whole from some hymn (such as were already current in the apostolic church), the more readily suppressing the subject— which was known to all—as he was here only concerned with the predicates, which involved the μυστήριον. (On the simple αὐτός, of a well-known subject, see § 22. 3.) On 1 C. vii. 36 see § 67. 1.

Under (a) come also H. xi. 12, διὸ καὶ ἀφ' ἑνὸς ἐγεννήθησαν,— where one readily supplies *children (descendants),* a notion which is indeed already contained in γεννᾶσθαι (compare Gen. x. 21); and Rom. ix. 11, μήπω γὰρ γεννηθέντων μηδὲ πραξάντων, where moreover the idea τέκνων or υἱῶν is sufficiently indicated in the words Ῥεβέκκα ἐξ ἑνὸς κοίτην ἔχουσα κ.τ.λ. (ver. 10). In L. xvi. 4 the subject is *the debtors :* compare ver. 5.

Where the subject is not left out but must be repeated from the context (this is not the case in H. viii. 4), there may sometimes be room for a difference of opinion : e. g., in Rom. vii. 1, 1 C. xv. 25 (H. ix. 1). The decision in such cases belongs to hermeneutics, not to grammar.[3]

---

[1] Rhetorical considerations have sometimes an influence in such cases, the subject being suppressed through indignation and displeasure. Rom. ix. 19 and 2 P. iii. 4 (Gerhard) may perhaps be examples of this kind.

[2] Döderlein, Soph. *Œdip. Col.* p. 393, Valcken. *Herod.* p. 414, Schæf. *Demosth.* V. 301. [In the best texts, Mt. xvii. 14, 26, L. xii. 36, A. xxi. 10, Rom. ix. 11, and perhaps Rev. xvii. 8, are examples of the genitive absolute with subject omitted (A. Buttm. p. 316). See Jelf 695. *Obs.* 1.]

[3] [In classical Greek we not unfrequently find the indefinite τὶς omitted with the 3rd pers. sing. of a verb (Kühner II. 32). The difficulty of Jo. viii. 44 is relieved if ὅταν λαλῇ be rendered *whenever one speaketh :* ὁ πατὴρ αὐτοῦ will then denote the devil, the father of the liar. Compare Job xxviii. 3, 2 S. xvi. 23 ; also such examples as Mt. xix. 3, 1 Th. iv. 9, Mk. v. 43, where an indefinite subject may be supplied with the dependent infinitive. See Westcott's note.]

4. On the other hand, it frequently happens that only a part of the subject or of the (words joined to the copula[1] to form the) predicate is expressed; the part omitted we must then supply from what is before us, having respect to conventional usage. A. xxi. 16, συνῆλθον καὶ τῶν μαθητῶν, *there also came together* (τινές, *some*) *of the disciples;* so with ἐκ or ἀπό, L. xi. 49, ἐξ αὐτῶν ἀποκτενοῦσι (τινας), xxi. 16, Jo. xvi. 17, xxi. 10, vi. 39, Rev. ii. 10 (v. 9), xi. 9[2] (compare p. 253); Jo. iv. 35, ὅτι ἔτι τετράμηνός ἐστι (χρόνος), Xen. *Hell.* 2. 3. 9; L. xii. 47 sq., ἐκεῖνος ὁ δοῦλος ... δαρήσεται πολλάς ... ὀλίγας (compare 2 C. xi. 24). The notion of *stripes* is contained in δέρειν, and hence one easily supplies πληγάς. This elliptical phrase is of frequent occurrence in Greek authors: e. g., Xen. *An.* 5. 8. 12, τοῦτον ἀνέκραγον ὡς ὀλίγας παίσειεν· Ælian, *Anim.* 10. 21, μαστιγοῦσι πολλαῖς· Aristoph. *Nub.* 971, Schol. *ad* Thuc. 2. 39 (οἱ πλείονας ἐνεγκόντες).[3]

Ellipsis is carried farther in 2 C. viii. 15, ὁ τὸ πολὺ οὐκ ἐπλεόνασε, καὶ ὁ τὸ ὀλίγον οὐκ ἠλαττόνησε (from Ex. xvi. 18, compare ver. 17), where we may supply ἔχων.[4] Many such phrases (consisting of the article with an accusative) are found in later writers—e. g., Lucian, *Catapl.* 4, ὁ τὸ ξύλον· *Bis accus.* 9, ὁ τὴν σύριγγα· *Dial. M.* 10. 4 (Bernh. p. 119)—and hence they are as fully established in usage as the formulas mentioned above. See Bos, *Ellips.* p. 166. Some have awkwardly introduced this idiom into Mt. iv. 15.—In Rom. xiii. 7, ἀπόδοτε πᾶσι τὰς ὀφειλάς, τῷ τὸν φόρον, τὸν φόρον κ.τ.λ., it is simplest to supply ἀποδιδόναι κελεύοντι, i. e. ἀπαιτοῦντι. In 1 C. iv. 6, ἵνα ἐν ἡμῖν μάθητε τὸ μὴ ὑπὲρ ἃ γέγραπται, if φρονεῖν be rejected as spurious, an infinitive is wanting (*per ellipsin,*—not *per aposiopesin,* as Meyer maintains[5]): we need nothing more than the general expression *go beyond*—exalt yourselves above—*what* etc. On the other hand, in 1 C. x. 13, ὑπὲρ ὃ δύνασθε, there is nothing to be

---

[1] See above, no. 2.
[2] Compare Heindorf, Plat. *Gorg.* p. 148, Volc. Fritzsche, *Quæstion. Lucian.* 201.—Some have clumsily introduced this ellipsis into Jo. iii. 25.
[3] Compare Jacobs, *Achill. Tat.* p. 737, Ast, Plat. *Legg.* p. 433, Valcken. *ad Luc. l. c.* (Jelf 436); and on something similar, Bos, *Ellips.* s.v. αἴκισμα. Compare also our own expression " er zählte ihm zwanzig auf" (*he counted him out twenty*).
[4] [Or rather συλλέξας, as Ex. xvi. 17 suggests.]
[5] [Not in his latest edition.]

supplied: the verb is used absolutely, as the Latin *posse* often is. Luther correctly renders the words *above your power*.

In 1 P. ii. 23, παρεδίδου τῷ κρίνοντι δικαίως, several commentators supply κρίσιν, from κρίνοντι. This is not impossible in itself, but παρεδίδου probably has the reflexive sense which is so common:[1] *he committed himself* (his cause) to him who judgeth righteously. There is no ellipsis whatever in Mt. xxiii. 9, πατέρα μὴ καλέσητε ὑμῶν ἐπὶ τῆς γῆς, *on the earth name not* (any one) *your father;* i. e., use not upon earth (that is, amongst and of men) the appellation " our father." Similarly, in 1 Tim. v. 9, χήρα καταλεγέσθω μὴ ἔλαττον ἐτῶν ἑξήκοντα γεγονυῖα κ.τ.λ., the meaning is, *As a widow let one be registered* (enrolled) *who is not under sixty years of age.* The widows entered on the list, however, are (from ver. 16) those who received maintenance from the funds of the church.

5. In particular, we find many substantives regularly omitted in certain definite formulas, or in a special context,— attributives only being expressed, which of themselves suggest the substantives. Compare Bernh. p. 183 sqq. (Don. p. 356 sqq., Jelf 436). The following are examples of words thus omitted:—

Ἡμέρα (Bos s. v.). In the formulas ἡ ἑβδόμη, H. iv. 4 (of the Sabbath); ἕως or μέχρι τῆς σήμερον, Mt. xxvii. 8, 2 C. iii. 15 (2 Chr. xxxv. 25, Malal. 12. 309,—here ἡμέρας is usually expressed in the LXX and the N. T.[2]); ἡ αὔριον, Ja. iv. 14, Mt. vi. 34, A. iv. 3, 5 (3 Macc. v. 38); ἡ ἑξῆς, A. xxi. 1, L. vii. 11;[3] τῇ ἐχομένῃ, L. xiii. 33, A. xx. 15; τῇ ἐπιούσῃ, A. xvi. 11; τῇ ἑτέρᾳ (*postridie*), A. xx. 15; τῇ τρίτῃ, L. xiii. 32 (Xen. *Cyr.* 5. 3. 27, Plut. *Pædag.* 9. 26, τὴν μέσην τέμνειν).[4]

Ὁδός.[5] L. xix. 4, ἐκείνης ἤμελλε διέρχεσθαι· L. v. 19, μὴ εὑρόντες ποίας εἰσενέγκωσιν αὐτόν (Cic. *Att.* 9. 1, qua ituri sint,

---

[1] [Winer's meaning no doubt is, that we often meet with verbs thus used in an apparently reflexive sense (§ 38. 1). As to παραδιδόναι itself the case is not made out very clearly. A. Buttm. (p. 145) allows this meaning to the aorist only (Mk. iv. 29), quoting Is. xlvii. 3; see also Plat. *Phædr.* 250 e, and Heindorf and Thompson *in loc.* In 1 P. i. 23 he would supply τὰ ἑαυτοῦ or κρίσιν; Huther, τὸ λοιδορεῖσθαι κ.τ.λ. (Wiesinger); Alford, "the revilers etc." In Mk. iv. 29, Meyer maintains that the ordinary explanation is not justified by usage, and would render "when the fruit permits,—i. e., is ripe enough :" so also Bleek, Grimm.]

[2] [As to the N. T., ἡμέρας is expressed in Rom. xi. 8, 2 C. iii. 14; and omitted in Mt. xi. 23, xxvii. 8. Mt. xxviii. 15 is doubtful.]

[3] [Here Tregelles and Westcott and Hort read ἐν τῷ ἑξῆς, scil. χρόνῳ : similarly L. viii. 1, ἐν τῷ καθεξῆς. Compare also ἀφ' οὗ, etc.]

[4] In A. xix. 38, ἀγόραιοι ἄγονται (Strab. 13. 629), most supply ἡμέραι; and this is quite appropriate. [Meyer supplies σύνοδοι.]

[5] Fischer *l.c.* p. 259 sq., Lob. *Paralip.* p. 363.

Cic. *Divin.* 1. 54. 123);[1] L. iii. 5, ἔσται τὰ σκολιὰ εἰς εὐθείας κ.τ.λ. (where however ὁδούς follows in the second member). Compare Lucian, *Dial. M.* 10. 13, εὐθεῖαν ἐκείνην προϊόντες· Paus. 8. 23. 2 ; in Latin, compendiariâ ducere (Senec. *Ep.* 119), rectâ ire.[2]

Ὕδωρ (Bos p. 501 sqq.). Mt. x. 42, ὃς ἐὰν ποτίσῃ . . . ποτήριον ψυχροῦ· Ja. iii. 11, Epictet. *Ench.* 29. 2, Arrian, *Epict.* 3. 12. 17, 3. 15. 3, Lucian, *Mors Peregr.* 44 ; as we say *a glass of red* (wine), *a bottle of brown* (beer), *a pint of Bavarian.* So also θερμόν (scil. ὕδωρ), Aristoph. *Nub.* 1040, Arrian, *Epict.* 3. 22. 71, al. In Latin, *frigida*, Plin. *Ep.* 6. 16 ; *calida*, Tac. *Germ.* 22 ; *gelida*, Hor. *Serm.* 2. 7. 91.

Ἱμάτιον (Bos p. 204 sq.). Jo. xx. 12, θεωρεῖ δύο ἀγγέλους ἐν λευκοῖς καθεζομένους, *in white garments;* Mt. xi. 8, Rev. xviii. 12, 16. Compare Ex. xxxiii. 4 in the LXX ; also Arrian, *Epict.* 3. 22. 10, ἐν κοκκίνοις περιπατῶν. See Wetst. I. 381, 958, Bos p. 204.

Γλῶσσα. Rev. ix. 11, ἐν τῇ ἑλληνικῇ.

Αὔρα.[3] A. xxvii. 40, ἐπάραντες τὸν ἀρτέμονα τῇ πνεούσῃ ;

---

[1] The local meaning of the genitive, *that way*—as in German we use the genitive *des Weges* [in the same sense]—is questioned by Bornemann (*Luc.* p. 37, 118), who in L. v. 19 and xix. 4 would read ποίᾳ and ἐκείνῃ. Hermann, however (*Vig.* p. 881), found no difficulty in this local genitive, which indeed has established itself in the pronominal adverbs οὗ, ποῦ. Of this very phrase, however, τῆς (αὐτῆς) ὁδοῦ,—compare Bernh. p. 138—several examples have been adduced, and not from poets merely (Krüger, *Sprachl.* II. 2. p. 9) : compare especially Thuc. 4. 47. 2 and Krüger *in loc.*, Thuc. 4. 33. 3. If we wish to bring the local genitive nearer to the original signification of the case (§ 30. 1), we might perhaps take it as meaning *proceeding from that* (way) ; but it is simpler to connect it with those applications of the genitive which are noticed in § 30. 11. (Jelf 522).

[2] Many adverbial expressions find their explanation in an ellipsis of ὁδός (Buttm. *Ausf. Sprachl.* II. 341) or of χώρα (Bos. p. 561), such as ἰδίᾳ, κατ' ἰδίαν, δημοσίᾳ (A. xvi. 37, al.) : these expressions, however, are used without any consideration of their origin (Bernh. p. 185 sq.). Such an adverbial formula is ἀπὸ μιᾶς, L. xiv. 18, which is not found in Greek writers, though probably it was current in the spoken language. It is equivalent to *with one mind* (ἐκ μιᾶς ψυχῆς, Dion. H. II. 1058), or *with one voice* (*uno ore*, ἐκ μιᾶς φωνῆς, Herod. 1. 4. 21) : Wahl's explanation (*Clav.* p. 45), after Camerarius, is too artificial.—It is possible that in such formulas no substantive at all was originally supplied by the Greeks, and that the feminine (as an abstract form—Ewald, *Hebr. Gr.* 645) was used just as independently as the neuter (see Schæfer on Bos, *Ellips.* p. 43, and a review in *L. Lit. Zeit.* 1825, no. 179): this however Hermann will not admit (*Opusc.* p. 162). [On ἀπὸ μιᾶς Meyer says : "We must understand some notion of manner, which was originally presented under a *local* aspect ; see especially Lob. *Paral.* p. 363." Similarly Jelf I. p. 457.]

[3] Bos p. 49 : compare Lobeck, *Paral.* p. 314.

compare Lucian, *Hermot.* 28 (like τῷ πνέοντι, scil. ἀνέμῳ, Lucian, *Char.* 3).

Χώρα (Bos p. 560 sqq.). Ἐξ ἐναντίας, *ex adverso*, Mk. xv. 39 ; this phrase is then also used in a figurative sense, Tit. ii. 8. The same word is supplied in L. xvii. 24, ἡ ἀστραπὴ ἡ ἀστράπτουσα ἐκ τῆς ὑπ' οὐρανὸν εἰς τὴν ὑπ' οὐρανὸν λάμπει (Job xviii. 4, Pr. viii. 29).

Ἡ ὀρεινή (L. i. 39) became a substantive at an early period, —*the mountain-district;* see Xen. *Cyr.* 1. 3. 3, Ptol. *Geogr.* 5. 17. 3, 6. 9. 4.

Ὥρα (*time*). It is supposed that there is an ellipsis of this word in the formula ἀφ' ἧς, 2 P. iii. 4, L. vii. 45, A. xxiv. 11 ; this phrase, it is true, had already completely assumed the nature of an adverb (compare however Mt. xv. 28). So also in ἐξ αὐτῆς (Mk. vi. 25, A. x. 33, al.), which many even write as one word, ἐξαυτῆς.

Δόμος (or οἶκος). A. ii. 27, 31, εἰς ᾅδου (compare Bos p. 14, Vechner, *Hellenol.* p. 124 sq.) ; but the best MSS. have εἰς ᾅδην.[1]

Γῆ. Mt. xxiii. 15, ἡ ξηρά (opposed to ἡ θάλασσα), *the continent :* see Kypke *in loc.* We should have to supply the same substantive in H. xi. 26, with Lachmann's reading οἱ ἐν Αἰγύπτου θησαυροί : compare Her. 8. 3, Diod. S. 12. 34. But the reading οἱ Αἰγύπτου θησαυροί is better supported.

Χείρ. In ἡ δεξιά, ἡ ἀριστερά, Mt. vi. 3, al. ; δεξιὰν διδόναι, G. ii. 9 (Xen. *An.* 1. 6. 6, 2. 5. 3) ; ἐν δεξιᾷ, ἐπὶ τὴν δεξιάν, E. i. 20, Mt. xxvii. 29 [*Rec.*].

Δραχμή. A. xix. 19, εὗρον ἀργυρίου μυριάδας πέντε ; just as we say, *he is worth a million.* Compare Lucian, *Eun.* 3, 8, Achill. T. 5. 17. So also we find the names of measures suppressed (Ruth iii. 15).

Ὑετός. Ja. v. 7, μακροθυμῶν ἐπ' αὐτῷ (καρπῷ), ἕως λάβῃ πρώϊμον καὶ ὄψιμον.

In all these formulas the ellipsis has established itself through long-continued usage ; and for this reason the meaning is clear, especially in certain contexts, to any one who is acquainted with the *usus loquendi.*[2] Other omissions are of a more special

---

[1] [In ver. 31 Tregelles reads ᾅδου.—In L. ii. 49, ἐν τοῖς τ. π. μ. may mean either "my Father's *house*" (τοῖς οἰκήμασι) or (less probably) "my Father's *business.*"]

[2] Compare in German *er setzte rothen vor, er sass zur rechten, er fuhr mit sechsen*, etc. (*he set down red, he sat on the right, he drove in a coach and six*).

character, belonging to the *usus loquendi* of a particular city or community; e. g., προβατική (πύλη, Neh. iii. 1) Jo. v. 2,[1] —yet see Bos s. v. πύλη. Similar examples are οἱ δώδεκα, οἱ ἑπτά (διάκονοι), A. xxi. 8: compare οἱ τριάκοντα (τύραννοι) in Greek writers.

To this head have been wrongly referred many expressions and formulas in which a neuter adjective or pronoun stands by itself, without any ellipsis (Krüg. p. 4, Jelf 436). To this class belong *e.g.* those adjectives which have long had a substantival character, τὸ ἱερόν (*the temple*), τὸ διοπετές (A. xix. 35), τὸ σηρικόν (Rev. xviii. 12); in biblical language, τὸ ἅγιον, *the holy place* (in the tabernacle and the temple), τὸ ἱλαστήριον, etc. Also τὰ ἴδια *his own* (property), Jo. i. 11; τὰ σά, *what is thine*, L. vi. 30; τὰ κατώτερα τῆς γῆς, E. iv. 9 (where however good MSS. add μέρη): still further τὸ τρίτον τῶν κτισμάτων, Rev. viii. 9, al., and the adverbial expressions ἐν παντί, εἰς κενόν, τὸ λοιπόν (§ 54. 1). In H. xiii. 22, διὰ βραχέων, we must not suppose that λόγων is to be supplied, any more than that in the Latin *paucis* there is an ellipsis of *verbis* or the like; nor must τόπῳ be supplied with ἐν ἑτέρῳ, A. xiii. 35, H. v. 6 (in quotations). In 1 C. xv. 46, also, τὸ πνευματικόν and τὸ ψυχικόν are substantival, and we have no right to understand σῶμα. Lastly, in ἐν τῷ μεταξύ, Jo. iv. 31, there is no ellipsis of χρόνῳ; the phrase is to be referred to τὸ μεταξύ (Lucian, *Dial. D.* 10. 1).

Nor is the genitive of relationship elliptical, Σώπατρος Πύρρου (A. xx. 4), Ἰούδας Ἰακώβου, Ἐμμὸρ τοῦ Συχέμ (§ 30. 3); but the genitive expresses the general idea of *appertaining to*.[2] For examples from the Greeks and Romans see Vechner, *Hellenolog.* p. 122 sq., Jani, *Ars Poet.* p. 187 sq. But even if there were in such cases a real omission of υἱός, ἀδελφός, or the like, it would still be altogether preposterous to supply υἱός with the genitive in G. iii. 20, ὁ δὲ μεσίτης ἑνὸς οὐκ ἔστιν.[3] A word can be left out only when the idea which it expresses is supplied by the context, or may be supposed to be familiar to the reader. But he who writes " the mediator is not of one " has not given even the most remote indication that " son " is the idea he would have the reader supply. The words in themselves simply say, *he appertains not to one*. That however he appertains *as son* (and not—to specify what surely must be regarded as lying nearest—in this very function of *mediator*) the reader would be left to guess!

In like manner, a number of (transitive) verbs, which in combination with a governed noun formed various familiar phrases,

---

[1] As when in Leipsic one speaks of going out "zum Grimmaischen," *by the Grimma (gate)*.
[2] As we ourselves say *Prussia's Blücher*. See Herm. *Opusc.* p. 120, Kühner II. 118 sq. (Jelf 436. b, Don. p. 356, 468).
[3] Kaiser, *De apologet. ev. Joa. consiliis*, II.

have in course of time dropped the noun, being now used by themselves to express the meaning which the combination had conveyed :[1] e. g., διάγειν, *to live* (in an ethical sense), Tit. iii. 3, —properly *to pass,* scil. τὸν βίον (1 Tim. ii. 2). This verb is frequently so used in Greek writers; see Xen. *Cyr.* 1. 2. 2, 8. 3. 50, Diod. S. 1. 8. Similarly, διατρίβειν *to remain* in a place, Jo. iii. 22,—properly, *to spend,* scil. τὸν χρόνον: see Kühnöl *in loc.* In Latin compare *agere, degere* (Vechner, *Hellenol.* p. 126 sq.).—Συμβάλλειν τινί or πρός τινα, A. iv. 15, xvii. 18, *to converse* (confer), *consult with* some one,—originally συμβάλλειν λόγους, *sermonem conferre* (Ceb. 33) : the earlier Greek writers mostly used the middle συμβάλλεσθαι.—Προςέχειν τινί, *give heed to,* scil. τὸν νοῦν; compare the Latin *advertere, attendere.* Similarly, ἐπέχειν, L. xiv. 7, A. iii. 5. Ἐνέχειν also is perhaps to be taken thus[2] in Mk. vi. 19, L. xi. 53. Here however the word is sometimes explained as meaning *to be angry,* —scil. χόλον (Her. 1. 118, 6. 119); but of the omission of this particular accusative no example is to be found.—Ἐπιτιθέναι τινί (τὰς χεῖρας), A. xviii. 10 : compare Xen. *Mem.* 2. 1. 15, *Cyr.* 6. 3. 6.—Συλλαμβάνειν, *concipere, become pregnant,* L. i. 31. —Several verbs thus used absolutely have become technical expressions: e. g., διακονεῖν, Jo. xii. 2, *to wait* (at table); προςφέρειν, H. v. 3, *to offer ;* προςκυνεῖν, *to worship, perform devotions,* Jo. xii. 20, A. viii. 27; λατρεύειν, Ph. iii. 3, L. ii. 37, A. xxvi. 7; καλεῖν, *to invite,* 1 C. x. 27 (Xen. *Cyr.* 2. 2. 23, 8. 4. 1); κρούειν, *to knock* (at a door), Mt. vii. 7, al. ; προβάλλειν, *to shoot forth* (of trees), L. xxi. 30,—a horticultural term. Nautical terms: αἴρειν, *to weigh* (anchor), A. xxvii. 13,—scil. τὰς ἀγκύρας (Bos p. 15, see Thuc. 2. 23), as in Latin *solvere* (Cæs. *Gall.* 4. 23); κατέχειν εἰς, A. xxvii. 40,—see Wahl, s. v.

We must however be careful not to bring in here those

---

[1] [Against supplying any object see Jelf 359 : compare Don. p. 423.]
[2] [Meyer also and A. Buttm. (p. 144) take ἐνέχειν τινί in these two passages as *observe,* watch hostilely : in Mk. vi. 19 *Vulg.* has "insidiabatur ei." On the other side are De W., Bleek, Grimm, al. (There would not however be much more difficulty in tracing ἐνέχειν in the sense of *to be enraged* to the familiar phrase ἐνέχειν χόλον τινί, than in assuming an ellipsis of φωνήν with ῥῆξον in G. iv. 27,—so Winer *in loc.,* De W., A. Buttm. p. 146 : see Ellicott on G. iv. 27.) With προςέχειν and ἐπέχειν, as above (see Ellicott on 1 Tim. i. 4, iv. 16), compare ἐπιβαλών, Mk. xiv. 72 (A. V. : "when he thought thereon ") : see A. Buttm. p. 145, Alford *in loc.*]

verbs which in themselves contain a complete notion, or those which in the particular context are intended to express nothing more than the action which they denote, and are used absolutely. Of this kind are e.g. ἐν γαστρὶ ἔχειν, to be with child ; διορύσσειν, to break through, break in, Mt. vi. 19 ; στρωννύειν ἑαυτῷ, sibi sternere, A. ix. 34, to prepare a bed for oneself ;[1] ἀποστέλλειν to send—personally or by letter, L. vii. 19, A. xix. 31 [2] (Vechner, Hellenol. p. 126); μὴ ἔχειν to be poor, 1 C. xi. 22 (Boisson. Philostr. Epp. p. 128,—compare the Latin habere, Jani, Ars poet. p. 189); ἀγοράζειν καὶ πωλεῖν, Rev. xiii. 17. For verbs used in an abstract sense, see e. g. 1 C. iii. 1, x. 13, H. xii. 25, Col. ii. 21, Ph. ii. 12, Ja. iv. 2 sq. On πάσχειν, in particular, see Wahl, Clav. p. 387 ; compare Weber, Dem. p. 384. In L. ix. 52, ὥστε ἑτοιμάσαι αὐτῷ, the verb should probably be taken thus,—to make preparations for him : the context clearly shows for what purpose, and we have not to supply ξενίαν (from Phil. 22). The same may be said of 1 C. xi. 4, κατὰ κεφαλῆς ἔχων (compare 2 C. v. 12), and of Rev. xxii. 19, ἐάν τις ἀφέλῃ ἀπὸ τῶν λόγων τοῦ βιβλίου,—where to supply τι would betray a total want of linguistic perception. Lastly, δύνασθαι when used absolutely denotes to have power, and does not need a complementary infinitive,—not even in 1 C. x. 13, where δύνασθαι ὑπενεγκεῖν immediately follows : compare Rom. viii. 7, 1 C. iii. 2, 2 C. xiii. 8.—(We also find substantives with the article so used, as dogmatic technical terms,[3] where some would expect a personal genitive (θεοῦ) : e. g., ἡ ὀργή, Rom. iii. 5, v. 9, xii. 19, 1 Th. i. 10, ii. 16, and τὸ θέλημα, Rom. ii. 18.)

The cases are very rare in which an adjective which is used attributively with a substantive can be suppressed. It may very well be conceived that, as the phrase λαλεῖν ἑτέραις (or καιναῖς) γλώσσαις was in frequent use, the adjective might be dropped, and γλώσσαις λαλεῖν itself thus become a technical term.[4] But beyond the range of local and individual usage—as in such examples as libri (i. e., Sibyllini), bishop in partibus (for in partibus infidelium)—we shall not find any omission of this kind ; for so manifold are the epithets which may be attached to a substantive, that it cannot be

---

[1] Compare in German the use of streuen (in winter).
[2] [These two passages are examples of πέμπειν, not of ἀποστέλλειν. Lünemann adds a reference to Mt. xxiii. 34 as containing verbs (ἀποκτενεῖτε, μαστιγώσετε) thus used absolutely (Meyer in loc.) ; but see above, p. 253.]
[3] [Green, Gr. p. 26.]
[4] De Wette, Apostelg. p. 33. [Alford on A. ii. 4, Dict. of Bible, III. 1558.]

left to the reader to conjecture which he should supply. In 2 P. ii. 10, ὀπίσω σαρκὸς πορεύεσθαι must not be supplemented by ἑτέρας, from Jude 7: the phrase is intelligible as it stands. In 1 C. vi. 20, ἠγοράσθητε τιμῆς, there is no ellipsis of μεγάλης. The words simply mean, *ye have been bought for a price;* and the emphasis lies on the verb,—*bought,* not acquired without cost. In Mt. xii. 32, ὃς ἂν εἴπῃ λόγον κατὰ τοῦ υἱοῦ τοῦ ἀνθρώπου, we have not to supply βλάσφημον: *to speak a word against some one* is a phrase complete in itself. In Rev. ii. 6, also, the translation *hoc* (laudabile) *habes* does not presuppose the omission of some similar word in the Greek. More plausible are such examples as A. v. 29, ὁ Πέτρος καὶ οἱ ἀπόστολοι, i. e., οἱ ἄλλοι or οἱ λοιποὶ ἀπόστολοι; but see above, § 58. 7. Rem. In such cases as Mt. xv. 23, οὐκ ἀπεκρίθη αὐτῇ λόγον· L. vii. 7, εἰπὲ λόγῳ, to supply ἕνα (ἑνί), or to supply τινῶν (Jacobs, *Ach. Tat.* p. 440) in Mk. ii. 1, δι᾽ ἡμερῶν, or πολύν in L. xviii. 4, ἐπὶ χρόνον, would be absurd. The *one* is implied in the singular number, as the *some* in the plural. Compare Lucian, *Herm.,* ταλάντου *for a talent; Eun.* 6, ἡμέραν *unum diem* (compare the Latin *ut verbo dicam*); *Alex.* 15, ἡμέρας οἴκοι ἔμεινεν; Xen. Eph. 5. 2, Charit. 5. 9. With L. xviii. 4, in particular, compare the familiar expression χρόνῳ (Schoemann, *Isæus* p. 444).

Rem. Nothing however is more absurd than to assume an ellipsis of adverbs and conjunctions; and yet this assumption has been made in a number of instances, and by N. T. commentators. Of such commentators Hermann says (*Opusc.* p. 204): qui si cogitassent, adverbia conjunctionesque proprietatibus quibusdam et sententiarum inter se consociationibus ac dissociationibus indicandis inservire, quæ nisi disertim verbis expressæ vel propterea intelligi nequeant, quod, si ellipsi locus esset, etiam aliena intelligi possent: numquam adeo absonam opinionem essent amplexi, ut voculas, quarum omissio longe aliter quam adjectio sententias conformat, per ellipsin negligi potuisse crederent. In some cases there lies at the root of this opinion a want of acquaintance with the nature of the moods. Thus it has been held that we should supply ἵνα or ὅπως in θέλεις εἴπωμεν, L. ix. 54, H. viii. 5, al. (against this see Hermann p. 207, and compare § 41. *a.* 4); εἰ or ἐάν in such sentences as 1 C. vii. 21, δοῦλος ἐκλήθης, μή σοι μελέτω (Hermann p. 205, compare § 60. 4); ἄν (Schwarz, *Solœc.* p. 125) in Jo. xv. 22, εἰ μὴ ἦλθον . . . . ἁμαρτίαν οὐκ εἶχον, and similar sentences (Hermann p. 205, see § 42. 2); and frequently μόνον in the formula οὐκ . . . ἀλλά (compare § 55. 8), or in 1 C. ix. 9.[1] It has also been supposed that ἤ is left out after

---

[1] Μὴ τῶν βοῶν μέλει τῷ θεῷ; Paul here is looking only at the spiritual meaning of the law, which he considers from the same point of view as Philo, who says, οὐ γὰρ ὑπὲρ τῶν ἀλόγων ὁ νόμος ἀλλ᾽ ὑπὲρ τῶν νοῦν καὶ λόγον ἐχόντων: see Meyer. The πάντως which follows should of itself have prevented such a weakening of the words. In Rom. iv. 9 there is no need of μόνον before ἢ καί, *an etiam;* and in Rom. iii. 28, where πίστει and χωρὶς ἔργων νόμου are placed in juxtaposition,—as in Paul πίστει and ἔργοις are antitheses which are mutually exclusive—such an addition would be altogether superfluous, and would make the sentence awkward. On Rom. iv. 14 see Fritzsche.

SECT. LXIV.]　　INCOMPLETE STRUCTURE.　　　　　　745

a comparative in Jo. xv. 13, 3 Jo. 4 (Baumg.-Crusius); but in each of these passages the clause with ἵνα is an explanatory adjunct to the demonstrative pronoun, and the genitive of this pronoun is dependent on the comparative. Nor is ἤ to be supplied in such cases as A. iv. 22, ἐτῶν ἦν πλειόνων τεσσαράκοντα· xxiii. 13, 21, xxiv. 11, xxv. 6, Mt. xxvi. 53, although in other places this particle is used. The Greek had accustomed himself thus to condense the phrase; and probably the πλείονες presented itself to his mind not as a comparative (more *than*), but as a defining adjunct,—just as elsewhere the neuter (adverb) πλέον is introduced even *extra constructionem:* see Lob. *Phryn.* p. 410 sq., and compare Matth. 455. Rem. 4. [See above § 35. 1, 37. 5]. Lastly, in 2 P. iii. 4, ἀφ᾽ ἧς οἱ πατέρες ἐκοιμήθησαν, πάντα οὕτως διαμένει ἀπ᾽ ἀρχῆς κτίσεως, some (and still Pott) would supply ὡς before ἀπ᾽ ἀρχῆς κτίσεως: the meaning obtained would certainly be suitable, but how empirical and arbitrary the process! The writer here brings together in one sentence two *termini a quo*, one nearer, the other more remote,—οἱ πατέρες being taken as referring to those fathers (see Semler, especially) who had received the promise of the παρουσία.

We should have a half ellipsis in the case of a particle, if οὐ were used for οὔπω.[1] In Jo. vi. 17,[2] however, after ἤδη in the preceding clause there was at all events no need of οὔπω: *already had darkness come on, and Jesus had not appeared.* In Jo. vii. 8 οὔπω is in reality a mere correction: if οὐκ is the true reading, we cannot remove what I may call the moral difficulty of the passage by substituting for it a philological difficulty.[3] If οὔπω occurs in Mt. xv. 17, it does not follow that in Mk. vii. 18 οὐ stands for οὔπω: in the former passage, however, οὐ is the best attested reading. In Mk. xi. 13 *not* is perfectly sufficient.—Against the admission of another kind of half ellipsis, the use of simple in the place of compound verbs, see my *Progr. de verborum simplicium pro compositis in N. T. usu et caussis* (Leipsic, 1833).

6. Occasionally we meet with a partial ellipsis of both subject and predicate in one sentence. G. v. 13, μόνον μὴ τὴν ἐλευθερίαν εἰς ἀφορμὴν τῇ σαρκί (κατέχητε, τρέψητε,—Œcumenius, ἀποχρήσησθε): the preceding ἐκλήθητε makes the subject clear, as the second person, and the part of the predicate which belongs to the copula (κατέχοντες κ.τ.λ. ἦτε [or rather ἐστέ], Herm. *Vig.* p. 872) is readily supplied from εἰς ἀφορμήν (compare Jacobs, *Philostr.* p. 525). Mt. xxvi. 5 (Mk. xiv. 2), μὴ ἐν τῇ ἑορτῇ, scil. τοῦτο γενέσθω or τοῦτο ποιῶμεν; unless we prefer to

---

[1] Compare especially Withof, *Opusc.* (Ling. 1778), p. 32 sqq.
[2] [Here the best texts have οὔπω. On Jo. vii. 8 see Ellic. *Hist. L.* p. 247, Alford *in loc.*: οὔπω is received by Westcott and Hort.]
[3] See also Boisson. Philostr. *Her.* p. 502, Jacobs, Philostr. *Imagg.* 357, and Ælian, *Anim.* II. 250.

repeat the two verbs κρατήσωμεν καὶ ἀποκτείνωμεν from ver. 4. There is no aposiopesis in these words, or in G. v. 13 (Meyer[1]), any more than when we say, *only not at the feast.* On the partial ellipsis in clauses with μή, see Klotz, *Devar.* II. 669. In 2 C. ix. 6, with τοῦτο δέ we apparently ought to supply λέγω (G. iii. 17, 1 Th. iv. 15) or φημί (1 C. vii. 29, xv. 50),[2] or even λογίζεσθε. (Meyer in his 1st edition connected τοῦτο δέ with the following ὁ σπείρων, but—as he himself has felt—this would be a very rugged construction: his present explanation of τοῦτο δέ, as an accusative absolute, is forced.) So also in the formula οὐχ ὅτι (... ἀλλά), used for the purpose of avoiding misapprehension, "I say" or "I mean" was originally present in thought before ὅτι:[3] Jo. vii. 22,[4] οὐχ ὅτι ἐκ τοῦ Μωϋσέως ἐστίν (ἡ περιτομή), ἀλλ' ἐκ τῶν πατέρων· vi. 46, 2 C. i. 24, iii. 5, Ph. iv. 17, 2 Th. iii. 9. The formula, however, became so fully established in usage, that its origin was no longer thought of; and hence Paul could write, in Ph. iv. 11, οὐχ ὅτι καθ' ὑστέρησιν λέγω.

In parallelism with this οὐχ ὅτι may be placed the οὐχ οἷον ὅτι of Rom. ix. 6, οὐχ οἷον δὲ ὅτι ἐκπέπτωκεν ὁ λόγος τοῦ θεοῦ: i. e., οὐ τοῖον δὲ λέγω, οἷον ὅτι κ.τ.λ. *non tale* (dico) *quale* (hoc est) *excidisse* etc. With this again we may compare the οἷον ὅτι of later writers (Schæf. *Greg. Cor.* p. 105), and—in regard to the circumstantiality of the expression—the combinations noticed by Lobeck (*Phryn.* p. 427), ὡς οἷον, οἷον ὥσπερ. We have before us two other modes of resolving this Pauline formula.

---

[1] [Not in his last edition.]
[2] Bos p. 632 sq., Franke, *Demosth.* p. 83 : compare Herm. *Æschyl.* II. 362.
[3] Schæf. *Bos* p. 775, Herm. *Vig.* p. 804.
[4] [Whether this passage should come in here, or should be compared with Jo. xii. 6, is a disputed point: see Westcott's note.—There is a curious difference between the meanings which this formula has in the N. T. and in classical Greek (Jelf 762. 2, Herm. *Vig.* p. 790, Buttm. *Gr. Gramm.* p. 513 sq. ;—see Xen. *Mem.* 2. 9. 8, Dem. *Timocr.* p. 702, *Aristocr.* p. 671, Thuc. 2. 97, Dio C. p. 285), though the ellipsis must be supplied in (nearly) the same manner in both cases. In classical Greek "*I will* (or *do*) *not say that . . . but*" is used rhetorically, = "*not only . . . but:*" in the N. T., as Winer remarks, "*I do not mean that . . . .*" is used to avoid misconception. A. Buttmann, in comparing the N. T. usage with that of classic writers (*Gr.* p. 372), overlooks such examples as are given above (quoted mainly from Buttmann); and only speaks of the other use of οὐχ ὅτι— in the sense of *although* (Jelf 891. 5. *b*, Don. p. 571, Riddell, Plat. *Apol.* p. 177 sq.,—Plat. *Protag.* p. 336 d, al.).—With ἵνα μὴ λέγωμεν, 2 C. ix. 4 (Phil. 19), compare the Latin *ne dicam:* A. Buttm. p. 241, Krüger p. 194 (Jelf 905. 5. *b*, Madvig, *Lat. Gr.* 440 b).—On μήτι γε, 1 C. vi. 3, *to say nothing of, nedum*, see Liddell and Scott, s. v. μῆτις, Jelf 762, Don. p. 578.]

(a.) By some it is rendered, *but it is not possible that* etc. In this signification οἶον is generally accompanied by τε, but this particle is not in itself essential, and actually is omitted in the passage which Wetstein quotes from Gorgias Leontinus, σοὶ οὐκ ἦν οἶον μόνον μάρτυρας ... εὑρεῖν:[1] perhaps indeed we might read οὐχ οἶόν τε δέ (Ælian 4. 17) in Rom. ix. 6. The usual infinitive construction ἐκπεπτωκέναι τὸν λόγον would here be resolved into a sentence with ὅτι: this is quite in the manner of the later language,—compare in Latin *dico quod*.[2] De Wette's objection[3] falls to the ground if Fritzsche's explanation of λόγος θεοῦ is adopted. (b.) Others, with Fritzsche, take οὐχ οἶον in a sense which it frequently bears in later writers,—that of a negative adverb, *not at all, by no means* (properly, οὐ τοιοῦτόν ἐστιν ὅτι, *the thing is not of such a kind that*): Polyb. 3. 82. 5, 18. 18. 11. In this case, it is true, the finite verb always follows (without ὅτι); but ὅτι here may be pleonastic (as in ὡς ὅτι), or Paul may have taken οὐχ οἶον in the sense of *multum abest (ut), far from its being the case that,* and have construed accordingly. Meyer's analysis of the phrase is in no way preferable.

In Rom. ix. 16, ἄρα οὖν οὐ τοῦ θέλοντος οὐδὲ τοῦ τρέχοντος κ.τ.λ., where it is sufficient to supply ἐστί, the subject of the impersonal sentence (*it depends not then on him that wills, it is not a matter of willing*,—on εἶναί τινος see above, p. 243 sq.) must be obtained from the context, and is *the attainment of the divine mercy* (ver. 15). Similarly in Rom. iv. 16, διὰ τοῦτο ἐκ πίστεως (ἐστί), ἵνα κατὰ χάριν (ᾖ), *therefore from faith* springs that of which I am speaking, viz., ἡ κληρονομία (supplied directly by ver. 14). On Rom. v. 18 see above, no. 2.

In Mt. v. 38, also, ὀφθαλμὸν ἀντὶ ὀφθαλμοῦ καὶ ὀδόντα ἀντὶ ὀδόντος, there are wanting both the subject and a part of the pre-

---

[1] Compare also Kayser, Philostr. *Soph.* p. 348. Examples of the personal οἶός ἐστι, such as those which Meyer quotes from Polybius, have nothing to do with the subject. Compare Weber, *Demosth.* p. 469.

[2] On the relation which the infinitive construction bears to a sentence with ὅτι, see Krüger p. 286.

[3] [Viz., that St. Paul is not speaking of the impossibility that God's word should fail, but of the *fact* that it has not failed. Fritzsche understands by λόγος θεοῦ God's decree to save *a remnant only* of Israel.—The best commentators agree substantially in the explanation of οὐχ οἶον ὅτι. In his analysis Meyer uses the same words as Winer (οὐ τοῖον δὲ λέγω, οἶον ὅτι), but supposes that the formula originated in the fusion of two expressions οὐχ οἶον (as used in later Greek,—see above, and Phryn. p. 372) and οὐχ ὅτι. The same view is taken by A. Buttm. (p. 372): Fritzsche also prefers this explanation to any other, with the exception of that quoted in the text. See A. Buttmann *l. c.*, but especially Fritzsche *in loc.*]

dicate, though an implication of the latter is contained in ἀντί. These words, however, are taken from Ex. xxi. 24, where they are preceded by δώσει.¹ In such familiar sayings as passages of the law, which were present to the mind of all, and had almost become proverbial, even verbs which in other cases could not be left out without ambiguity might very well be suppressed; see above, 3. b.²

7. An entire sentence is sometimes suppressed *per ellipsin* (Hermann, *Opusc.* p. 159, *Vig.* p. 872, Jelf 860. 896).

a. Rom. xi. 21 [*Rec.*], εἰ γὰρ ὁ θεὸς τῶν κατὰ φύσιν κλάδων οὐκ ἐφείσατο, μήπως οὐδὲ σοῦ φείσεται, scil. δέδοικα or ὁρᾶτε,—which however is indicated in μήπως. Mt. xxv. 9 *Rec.*, μήποτε οὐκ ἀρκέσῃ,—for which however the weight of evidence requires us to read μήποτε οὐ μὴ ἀρκέσῃ: with the latter reading, μήποτε must be taken by itself (as expressing refusal), *by no means!* scil. δῶμεν (ver. 8), or γενέσθω τοῦτο;³ compare Rev. xix. 10, xxii. 9, Ex. x. 11.

In L. xvi. 8 it is not so much that φησί or ἔφη is omitted, as that what is further said by him to whom the words ὅτι φρονίμως ἐποίησεν belong is introduced in the direct form. Similarly in L. v. 14. The only cases in which we find ἔφη, etc., left out in Greek prose are when an indication of the person speaking is given by ὁ δέ, οἱ δέ (Ælian 9. 29, *Anim.* 1. 6), and when the setting of the sentence itself shows that it belongs to some particular person (to another speaker),—a very common case in dialogues. Van Hengel (*Annotatt.* p. 8 sqq.) has wrongly applied this ellipsis—ἔφη ὁ θεός—to Mt. xxiii. 34: against this see Fritzsche *in loc.* Bengel's note on 1 C. ix. 24 is incorrect.⁴ In Mt. xvi. 7, however, διελογίζοντο ἐν ἑαυτοῖς λέγοντες· ὅτι ἄρτους οὐκ ἐλάβομεν, it is much more appropriate to supply the simple sentence ταῦτα λέγει before ὅτι, and to render this word *because*, than to take ὅτι as the particle introducing the *oratio recta.* In Jo. v. 6, 7, the words ἄνθρωπον οὐκ ἔχω, ἵνα ... βάλῃ με εἰς τὴν κολυμβήθραν do not seem suitable as a direct answer to the question θέλεις ὑγιὴς γενέσθαι; and we might

---

¹ [It is singular that in Dt. xix. 21 these accusatives occur without any verb (Alford on Mt. *l. c.*): Lev. xxiv. 20 is similar.]
² Akin to this accusative in the citation of a law is that which we find in all languages in orders, demands: e.g., παῖ λοφνίαν. See Bos p. 601.
³ [On these two passages see above, p. 632 sq.]
⁴ ["Non semel reticetur verbum *inquit, inquiunt* ... Itaque hîc quoque sensus est: *ita,* inquiunt, *currite.*"]

therefore suppose a simple *yes truly, certainly*, to be left out. But the sick man does not stop to make this simple affirmation, but at once passes on to speak of the hindrance which up to this time has frustrated his wish. On such passages as Jo. i. 8, οὐκ ἦν ἐκεῖνος τὸ φῶς, ἀλλ᾿ ἵνα μαρτυρήσῃ· ix. 3, see p. 398.

b. A protasis of some length is sometimes left without any consequent clause. Thus with 2 Th. ii. 3 sq., ὅτι ἐὰν μὴ ἔλθῃ ἡ ἀποστασία πρῶτον .... ὅτι ἔστιν θεός, we have to supply (from ver. 1) *the* παρουσία τοῦ κυρίου *does not take place.* The omission is occasioned by the length of the protasis.[1] In particular, we find a protasis with ὥσπερ without any apodosis, Mt. xxv. 14, Rom. v. 12, ix. 22 sqq.:[2] see § 63. 1. (Jelf 860. 3.)[3]

In quotations from the O. T. it sometimes appears as if a whole sentence has been left out; e. g., in 1 C. i. 31, ἵνα, καθὼς γέγραπται, ὁ καυχώμενος ἐν κυρίῳ καυχάσθω. We may supply with ἵνα a γένηται or a πληρωθῇ. The apostle, however, unconcerned about the grammatical sequence, directly annexes to his own words the words of the Scripture, as an integral member of the sentence, just as in Rom. xv. 3 he introduces the words of Christ in the direct form, from Ps. lxix. : compare Rom. xv. 21. In 1 C. ii. 9 sq., however, we must not follow Meyer in regarding ver. 10 as the apodosis corresponding to ἃ ὀφθαλμός κ.τ.λ. : instead of proceeding with τοῦτο ἡμῖν κ.τ.λ., in connexion with ἀλλά, Paul directly subjoins the antithesis to the words of the quotation, and thus leaves ἀλλά without grammatical sequence.[4]

II. *Aposiopesis.* Aposiopesis is the suppression of a sentence or a part of a sentence in consequence of excited feeling (e. g., of anger,[5] sorrow, fear, etc.[6]), the member omitted being

---

[1] Some bring in here Ja. iii. 3,—with what is no doubt the correct reading, εἰ δέ. Here however the apodosis is probably contained in the words καὶ ὅλον τὸ σῶμα : see Wiesinger's careful examination of the passage.

[2] [The protasis here does not commence with ὥσπερ, but with εἰ.]

[3] [It is not uncommon to find a protasis (with εἰ) suppressed in connexion with ἐπεί, which may therefore be rendered *since otherwise* (Rom. iii. 6, H. ix. 26, al.): see Liddell and Scott s. v. II. 3. c (where however the words "protasis" and "apodosis" are accidentally transposed), Vaughan on Rom. xi. 22, A. Buttm. p. 359 (Jelf 860. 2),—also above, p. 354.]

[4] [Similarly De Wette : Meyer now considers ver. 9 as depending upon λαλοῦμεν (as Winer in ed. 5, p. 530).—1 C. ii. 10 (Meyer ed. 1, 2, Alford, Evans) and i. 23 (Meyer, Alford) should have been mentioned above, p. 553, as passages in which δέ has been regarded as introducing the apodosis : compare also 2 P. i. 5.]

[5] Compare Stallbaum, Plat. *Apol.* p. 35. So in the well-known example *quos ego—!* or in our own " warte, ich will dich—!" ("Stay, and I'll—"!). The aposiopesis may appear in the form of a question ; as in Num. xiv. 27, ἕως τίνος τὴν συναγωγὴν τὴν πονηρὰν ταύτην ; Compare A. xxiii. 9 (Lachmann).

[6] Compare Quintilian 9. 2. 54 ; Tiberius and Alexander, *De Figuris*, in Walz,

supplied by the gesture of the speaker (Hermann p. 153). In certain formulas of swearing this figure is of common occurrence, as is noticed above (§ 55. Rem., p. 627). Besides this case, however, we meet with aposiopesis after a conditional sentence in the following passages. L. xix. 42, εἰ ἔγνως καὶ σύ, καίγε ἐν τῇ ἡμέρᾳ σου ταύτῃ, τὰ πρὸς εἰρήνην σου, *if thou also hadst known what is for thy peace!* scil. " how happy would it be (for thee)." L. xxii. 42, πάτερ, εἰ βούλει παρενεγκεῖν[1] τὸ ποτήριον τοῦτο ἀπ' ἐμοῦ· πλὴν κ.τ.λ. In both these examples the apodosis is suppressed through sorrow.—A. xxiii. 9, οὐδὲν κακὸν εὑρίσκομεν ἐν τῷ ἀνθρώπῳ τούτῳ· εἰ δὲ πνεῦμα ἐλάλησεν αὐτῷ ἢ ἄγγελος: *we find no evil in this man; if however a spirit has spoken to him, or an angel*—(said by the Pharisees with gestures expressive of doubt), scil. " the case is a doubtful one," or " we must be on our guard." Others take the words interrogatively (Lachmann): *if however . . . . has spoken?* how then? what should then be done? On the whole see Fritzsche, *Conject.* I. 30 sq. The words μὴ θεομαχῶμεν, which are added in some MSS., are a gloss. Bornemann has tacitly withdrawn his earlier conjecture.[2] Still it may be doubted whether this is really an example of aposiopesis, or whether the sentence is merely broken off by a sudden interruption.—In Jo. vi. 62 the apodosis is suppressed in the triumphant tone of the passage, but it is at once suggested by ver. 61, *how will that amaze you!* In Mk. vii. 11, ὑμεῖς λέγετε· ἐὰν εἴπῃ ἄνθρωπος τῷ πατρὶ ἢ τῇ μητρί· κορβᾶν . . . . ὃ ἐὰν ἐξ ἐμοῦ ὠφεληθῇς· καὶ οὐκέτι ἀφίετε κ.τ.λ., we must supply as apodosis (from ver. 10) *he acts rightly in keeping his vow;* in this case, therefore, ye set him free from the τιμᾶν τὸν πατέρα κ.τ.λ. See Krebs *in loc.*[3] 2 Th. ii. 3 sqq.

Rhetor. Græc. VIII. 536, 450. [Jelf 897, A. Buttm. p. 396, Webster p. 258, Zumpt 758.]

[1] [Lachmann, Tregelles, Westcott and Hort, read παρένεγκε.]

[2] [Winer refers, I believe, to the conjecture that we should read οἱ δὲ πνεῦμα. See Bornem. *Luc.* p. 182.]

[3] Several commentators regard the parallel passage Mt. xv. 5 as also containing an aposiopesis (?): ὃς ἂν εἴπῃ τῷ πατρὶ ἢ τῇ μητρί· δῶρον ὃ ἐὰν ἐξ ἐμοῦ ὠφεληθῇς· καὶ οὐ μὴ τιμήσῃ τὸν πατέρα αὐτοῦ—namely, *he acts rightly* (acts according to the law). Perhaps, however, we should (with Grotius and Bengel) commence the apodosis at καὶ οὐ μή: *he who says to his parents . . . has also* (in such a case) *no need to honour his parents,—he, on doing this, is also* (in this instance) *free from* the command τίμα τὸν πατέρα κ.τ.λ. So taken, the καί would not be pleonastic. [Both in Mk. vii. 12 and in Mt. xv. 5 the καί before οὐ μή is probably spurious. The objection to Winer's explanation of Mt. xv. 5 is, that οὐ μὴ τιμήσει does not

SECT. LXIV.] INCOMPLETE STRUCTURE. 751

is an example of anacoluthon, not of aposiopesis. In Ph. i. 22 an aposiopesis (Rilliet) is not to be thought of.[1]

In Greek writers,[2] as in the N. T., aposiopesis occurs most frequently after conditional clauses (Plat. *Symp.* 220 d). Where there are two parallel conditional clauses, it is very common to find the apodosis belonging to the first suppressed,[3] the speaker hastening on to the second, as the more important: Plat. *Protag.* 325 d, ἐὰν μὲν ἑκὼν πείθηται· εἰ δὲ μή . . . εὐθύνουσιν ἀπειλαῖς καὶ πληγαῖς· *Rep.* 9. 575 d, οὐκοῦν ἐὰν μὲν ἑκόντες ὑπείκωσιν· ἐὰν δὲ μή κ.τ.λ., Thuc. 3. 3. So in L. xiii. 9, κἂν μὲν ποιήσῃ καρπόν· εἰ δὲ μήγε, εἰς τὸ μέλλον ἐκκόψεις αὐτήν; *if it bear fruit, it is well* (it may be left standing), *but if not, cut it down* (though here we might also supply ἄφες αὐτήν from the words preceding).—On the suppression, after εἰ δὲ μή or εἰ δὲ μήγε, of an entire hypothetical clause to be supplied from the previous context, see p. 729.

We might also regard ὅρα μή, Rev. xix. 10, xxii. 9, as an example of aposiopesis; and might compare it with the formulas of deprecation so common in the tragedians, as μὴ ταῦτα (Eurip. *Ion* 1335), μὴ σύ γε, etc. (Jelf 897). Yet see above, p. 729.

In Rom. vii. 24 sq., the words of complaint τίς με ῥύσεται ἐκ τοῦ σώματος τοῦ θανάτου τούτου are followed, through the overmastering pressure of joy, by a brief *Thanks be to God!* This also is a kind of aposiopesis. "Thanks be to God that *he* has already delivered me" would be calm and passionless.

It has been assumed that some idea is suppressed in 2 C. vii. 12, ἄρα εἰ καὶ ἔγραψα ὑμῖν: even Billroth would supply χαλεπόν τι. In this case the word would be left out by Paul designedly, because the subject was still painful to him. But ἔγραψα is complete in itself.

---

mean *he need not,* but either *he will not* (so Fritzsche, who considers this clause part of the protasis), or—according to the usage of the LXX (Green, *Gr.* p. 193 sq.,—see above, p. 636, note⁴)—*he shall not* (Ewald). In Mt. xv. 5 Meyer, De W., Alford, al., suppose an aposiopesis after ὠφιληθῆς, as in Mk. vii. 12: Bleek agrees with Winer. See Green, *Gr.* p. 194, *Crit. Notes* p. 18 sq., 38.]

[1] [Lightfoot assumes an aposiopesis in this verse: see his note,—also Green, *Cr. Notes* p. 161.]

[2] In the O. T. compare Ex. xxxii. 32, Dan. iii. 15, Zech. vi. 15: see Köster, *Erläut. der heil. Schrift,* p. 97.

[3] Poppo, Xen. *Cyr.* p. 256, Stallb. Plat. *Gorg.* p. 197. [Jelf 860. 3, Riddell, Plat. *Apol.* p. 217.]

Section LXV.

Redundant Structure: Pleonasm (Redundance [1]), Diffuseness.

1. Pleonasm[2] is the opposite of ellipsis, as superfluity is the opposite of deficiency. Hence pleonasm would naturally consist in the use of a word the notion of which is not to be included in the conception of the sentence (Hermann, *Opusc.* I. 217, 222). It was believed, indeed, by the older grammarians that certain words—particles especially—might be mere expletives (Hermann *l. c.* p. 226); and Kühnöl[3] even thinks that τὸ ὄρος can be used in the place of ὄρος. As however it is altogether absurd to talk of a pleonasm of the definite article, so also is the existence of expletives in written Greek a pure figment. There is only one form in which pleonasm (which mainly occurs in the predicate of a sentence, Hermann *l.c.* p. 219) can appear,—viz., when there are introduced into a sentence words the notion of which has already been fully expressed *in some other part of the same sentence* (or period), whether by the same word or by one of equivalent meaning. This however cannot take place on any rational principles except in the following cases:—

a. A writer may express the same thing a second time (especially in a lengthy sentence) through inadvertence, or through want of confidence in the attention of the reader: *nonne tibi ad me venienti nonne dixi?* Here it is not really intended that the *nonne* should be presented to the mind more than once. So also in Col. ii. 13, καὶ ὑμᾶς νεκροὺς ὄντας ἐν

---

[1] See Fischer, *Weller* III. i. 269 sqq.; B. Weiske, *Pleonasmi Græci sive commentarius de vocibus, quæ in sermone Græco abundare dicuntur* (Lips. 1807); Poppo, *Thuc.* I. i. 197 sqq. In reference to the N. T., see Glass, *Phil. Sacra* I. 641 sqq. (this writer, however, deals with the O. T. more than with the N. T., and his general treatment of the subject is but poor); Bauer, *Philol. Thuc. Paull.* p. 202 sqq.; Tzschucke, *De sermon. J. Chr.* p. 270 sqq.; Haab p. 324 sqq.; J. H. Maius, *De pleonasmis linguæ Græcæ in N. T.* (Giess. 1728,—10 sheets). The last named writer had intended to write a treatise on pleonasm generally: see his *Observationes in libr. sacr.* I. 52. Another work, by M. Nascou—announced by a *Prodromus* (Havn. 1787)—also failed to appear. [Jelf 899, Don. p. 610, A. Buttm. p. 340 sqq., Webster p. 258 sq.]

[2] Glass *l. c.* writes sensibly on the meaning of the term pleonasm: compare also Flacius, *Clavis scriptorum sacrorum* II. 4, 224, and my first *Progr. de verbis compositis* p. 7 sq. Quintilian (*Instit.* 8. 3. 53) gives a simple, but—if rightly understood—an adequate definition: "pleonasm. vitium, cum supervacuis verbis oratio oneratur."

[3] On Mt. v. 1. Compare Weiske, *Pleon.* p. 34. [See above, § 18. 8.]

SECT. LXV.]   REDUNDANT STRUCTURE.   753

τοῖς παραπτώμασι . . . συνεζωοποίησεν ὑμᾶς σὺν αὐτῷ· Mt.
viii. 1, E. ii. 11 sq., Ph. iv. 15 *v. l.* ;[1] Mk. vii. 25, γυνή, ἧς εἶχεν
τὸ θυγάτριον α ὐ τ ῆ ς πνεῦμα ἀκάθαρτον· Rev. vii. 2 (see § 22. 4):
Demosth. *Euerg.* 688 b, οὗτοι ᾤοντο ἐ μ έ, εἰ πολλά μου λάβοιεν
ἐνέχυρα, ἄσμενον ἀφήσειν με τοὺς μάρτυρας· 1 C. vii. 26, νομίζω
τοῦτο καλὸν ὑπάρχειν . . . ὅτι καλὸν ἀνθρώπῳ· Rev. xii. 9 (?);[2]
2 Tim. iv. 9,[3] σ π ο ύ δ α σ ο ν ἐλθεῖν πρός με τ α χ έ ω ς· 2 C. viii. 24,
τὴν ἔνδειξιν τῆς ἀγάπης . . . ἐνδεικνύμενοι (see however § 32.
2); compare Plat. *Legg.* 12. 966 b, τὴν ἔνδειξιν τῷ λόγῳ ἀδυνατεῖν ἐνδείκνυσθαι (Xen. *Cyr.* 8. 2. 5). Under this head
we may bring Rom. ix. 29 (from the LXX), ὡς Γόμορρα ἂν
ὡμοιώθημεν (in the parallel member, ὡς . . . ἂν ἐγενήθημεν).
Also λογίζεσθαί or ἡγεῖσθαί τινα ὡς, 2 C. x. 2, 2 Th. iii. 15,
Lucian, *Peregr.* 11 (instead of the simple accusative,—compare
הָשַׁב בְּ, Job xix. 11); as in Greek writers we even meet with
νομίζειν ὡς[4] and the like. Of a different kind are L. xx. 2, εἶπον
πρὸς αὐτὸν λέγοντες· Mk. xii. 26, πῶς εἶπεν αὐτῷ ὁ θεὸς
λέγων· A. xxviii. 25, τὸ πνεῦμα ἐλάλησεν . . . λέγον, etc.:
in all these instances the participle is used (as it frequently is
in the LXX) to introduce the direct words of the speaker (compare the well-known ἔφη λέγων, Döderl. *Synon.* IV. 13),—though
certainly these might have been directly appended to the verb
εἶπον, εἶπε. Mt. xxii. 1 and L. xii. 16 differ again from these
examples: still more do L. xiv. 7, xvi. 2, xviii. 2, al.

Another mode of introducing the *oratio recta*—e. g., L. xxii. 61,
ὑπεμνήσθη τοῦ λόγου τοῦ κυρίου ὡς εἶπεν αὐτῷ· A. xi. 16, ἐμνήσθην
τοῦ ῥήματος τοῦ κυρίου, ὡς ἔλεγεν—must be referred to circumstantiality of expression (see below, no. 4), and not be regarded as
pleonasm. We meet with it even in Attic writers, e. g., Xen. *Cyr.*
8. 2. 14, λόγος αὐτοῦ ἀπομνημονεύεται, ὡς λέγοι: see Bornem. *Schol.*
p. 141.

2. b. One of the two synonymous words may in actual
usage have partially lost its meaning,[5] e. g., ἀπ᾽ οὐρανόθεν (*Il.* 8.

---

[1] Vechner, *Hellenol.* p. 177 sq. [Lünemann adds Mt. iv. 16.]
[2] Compare V. Fritzsche, *Quæst. Lucian.* p. 14 sq.
[3] [See however Ellicott *in loc.*]
[4] Yet see Stallb. Plat. *Phileb.* p. 180. [With Rom. ix. 29 compare ὅμοιος ὥσπερ, Æsch. *Agam.* 1311 ; ὅμοιον ὡς, Plat. *Legg.* 628 d (Liddell and Scott s. v., Jelf 594. *Obs.* 5). On 2 C. x. 2, al., see Jelf 703. *Obs.* 2.]
[5] In the department of Accidence the double comparatives μειζότερος, etc., belong to this class; see § 11. 2. In German, compare *mehrere*,—for which purist pedants would both say and write *mehre*. [In English compare *lesser, innermost*, etc.: see Latham, *Eng. Lang.* II. 184, 191, Angus, *Handb.* p. 154, 191.]

48

365), ἔξοχος ἄλλων;[1] or a repetition, which originally was emphatic, may have become weakened in the course of time, as πάλιν αὖθις (Herm. *Vig.* p. 886). So in the N. T. ἀπὸ μακρόθεν, Mt. xxvi. 58, Mk. xv. 40, Rev. xviii. 10 (West. I. 524 sq.); ἀπὸ ἄνωθεν, Mt. xxvii. 51, Mk. xv. 38; ἔπειτα μετὰ τοῦτο, Jo. xi. 7 (εὐθέως παραχρῆμα, A. xiv. 10, in D). Compare ἔπειτα μετὰ ταῦτα, Dem. *Neær.* 530 a; εἶτα μετὰ τοῦτο or ταῦτα, Arist. *Rhet.* 2. 9. 13, Plat. *Lach.* 190 e. For similar examples see Poppo, *Thuc.* III. i. 343, III. ii. 38 :[2] in Latin, compare *deinde postea* (Cic. *Mil.* 24. 65), *post deinde, tum deinde,* etc.[3] Other examples are L. xix. 4, προδραμὼν ἔμπροσθεν (Xen. *Cyr.* 2. 2. 7, 7. 1. 36); iv. 29, ἐκβάλλειν ἔξω; L. xxiv. 50, ἐξάγειν ἔξω[4] (Rev. iii. 12); A. xviii. 21, πάλιν ἀνακάμπτειν (Ceb. 29, compare Kritz, *Sall.* 1. 88); Mk. vii. 36, μᾶλλον περισσότερον (§ 35. 1[5]); L. xxii. 11, ἐρεῖτε τῷ οἰκοδεσπότῃ τῆς οἰκίας;[6] Rev. xviii. 22 (compare *Odyss.* 14. 101, συῶν συβόσια; Her. 5. 64, στρατηγὸν τῆς στρατιῆς; Plat. *Legg.* 2. 671 d, Cedren. I. 343, Theocr. 25. 95); Jo. xii. 13, τὰ βαΐα τῶν φοινίκων (βαΐον of itself signifies *a palm-branch*); A. ii. 30, ὅρκῳ ὤμοσεν ὁ θεός,—compare Ex. xxv. 12.[7]

Under this head also come the following constructions, which have almost assumed the character of established *schemata* :—

a. Particles of comparison are followed by καί, though the "also" is contained in the comparison itself, which asserts that in connexion with a second object *also* some circumstance exists. A. xi. 17, εἰ τὴν ἴσην δωρεὰν ἔδωκεν αὐτοῖς ὁ θεὸς ὡς καὶ ἡμῖν· 1 C. vii. 7, θέλω πάντας ἀνθρώπους εἶναι ὡς καὶ ἐμαυτόν. See above, p. 549.

---

[1] Hermann, Hom. *Hymn. in Cerer.* 362.
[2] From later writers compare ἀπὸ πανταχόθεν, Const. Manass. p. 127; ἀπὸ πρωΐθεν or μηκόθεν, Theophan. Cont. 519, 524; ἐκ δυσμόθεν, Nicet. Annal. 18. p. 359 d; ἐκ παιδόθεν or νηπιόθεν, Malalas 18. p. 429, 5. p. 117; ἕνεκα περί, Cedrenus I. p. 716; περί ... ἕνεκα, Niceph. Cpolit. p. 6, 35; ἀνθ' ὧν ἕνεκα, Theophan. Cont. p. 138; ἀνθ' ὧν ὅτι, Dt. xxviii. 62. On the latter examples see Herm. *Opusc.* p. 220. [We find ἐκ παιδόθεν in Mk. ix. 21.]
[3] Vechner, *Hellenol.* p. 156 sqq.
[4] Lob. Soph. *Ajax* p. 337, Bornem. *Schol.* p. 166 sq.
[5] Compare Herm. *Opusc.* p. 222, Vechner, *Hellenol.* p. 166 sqq.
[6] See Bornemann *in loc.* Οἰκοδομεῖν οἶκον (L. vi. 48) is no more an example of pleonasm than *ædificare domum;* in the *usus loquendi* both verbs very early assumed the (general) meaning *build.* For other examples of the same kind see Lob. *Paral.* p. 501 sq.
[7] See Jacob, *Quæst. Lucian.* p. 10, Bornem. Xen. *Conv.* p. 186, Pflugk, Eurip. *Hec.* p. 18, Lob. *Paralip.* p. 534 sqq.

β. Into a sentence which depends upon a verb of denying, and which forms its complement, a negative is introduced : 1 Jo. ii. 22, ὁ ἀρνούμενος, ὅτι ᾽Ιησοῦς οὐκ ἔστιν ὁ Χριστός· L. xx. 27, ἀντιλέγοντες, ἀνάστασιν μὴ εἶναι (Xen. *Cyr.* 2. 2. 20, *An.* 2. 5. 29, Isocr. *Trapez.* 360, Demosth. *Phorm.* 585, Thuc. 1. 77), H. xii. 19, οἱ ἀκούσαντες παρῃτήσαντο μὴ προςτεθῆναι αὐτοῖς λόγον (Thuc. 5. 63), G. v. 7, τίς ὑμᾶς ἐνέκοψεν τῇ ἀληθείᾳ μὴ πείθεσθαι (Eurip. *Hec.* 860). Compare further L. iv. 42, A. xx. 27, 1 P. iii. 10 (Thuc. 5. 25, 7. 53, Plat. *Phæd.* 117 c, Demosth. *Phænipp.* 654 b); and see Vig. p. 459, 811, Matth. 534. Rem. 5 [1] (Jelf 749, Don. p. 591). We have similar examples in German, in colloquial language, and in Greek also the usage may be explained as arising out of the circumstantiality which belongs to the language of conversation. The negation which the verbs contain gradually became less sensible, and hence it was expressly revived in the dependent sentence (compare Madvig 211). Modern grammarians, indeed, are not disposed to allow that this construction is an example of pleonasm;[2] logically, however, one of the negations is undeniably superfluous.—The dependent negative is sometimes omitted in the N. T., as in classical Greek : e. g., after verbs of *hindering,* L. xxiii. 2, A. viii. 36, Rom. xv. 22. Compare Matth. *l. c.,* Madv. 210. Rem. 1, Klotz, *Devar.* II. 668 (Don. *l. c.,* Jelf 749. *Obs.*).

There is a difference between the above examples and A. x. 15, πάλιν ἐκ δευτέρου (compare Jo. iv. 54), Jo. xxi. 16, πάλιν δεύτερον (Plut. *Philop.* c. 15), G. iv. 9, πάλιν ἄνωθεν (Isocr. *Areopag.* p. 338, πάλιν ἐξ ἀρχῆς), *rursus denuo* (Hand, *Tursell.* II. 279) : in all these instances a more definite word is annexed for the sake of explanation. This difference is still greater in A. v. 23, with the reading τοὺς φύλακας ἔξω ἑστῶτας πρὸ τῶν θυρῶν (Xen. *Cyr.* 7. 1. 23); also L. ii. 36, αὕτη (ἦν) προβεβηκυῖα ἐν ἡμέραις πολλαῖς (compare i. 7, 18),—for this means "she was *far* advanced in years" (Lucian, *Peregr.* 27, πορρωτάτω γήρως προβεβηκώς) ; Rev. ix. 7, τὰ ὁμοιώματα τῶν ἀκρίδων ὅμοια ἵπποις, for ὁμοιώματα means *forms* (compare Ez. x. 22) ; 1 P. iii. 17, εἰ θέλοι τὸ θέλημα τοῦ θεοῦ, *si placuerit voluntati divinæ,*—θέλημα denoting the will in itself, θέλειν its active operation (like " the flood

---

[1] Alberti, *Observ.* p. 470 sq., Thilo, *Act. Thom.* p. 10, Buttm. *Exc.* 2 *in Mid.* p. 142 sqq. [Green p. 189, Webster p. 140, Farrar, *Gr. Synt.* p. 176 sq.]
[2] Hermann, *Opusc.* p. 232, Klotz, *Devar.* II. 668 : " non otiosam esse negationem in ejusmodi locis, sed ita poni infinitivum, ut non res, quæ prohibenda videatur, intelligatur, sed quæ vi ac potestate istius prohibitionis jam non fiat." [See also Ellicott on G. v. 7, Madvig 156. Rem. 4 (Don. p. 591). To the passages cited in the next sentence Lünemann adds 1 Th. ii. 16.]

flows," etc.),—compare Ja. iii. 4 : in Jo. xx. 4, προέδραμεν τάχιον τοῦ Πέτρου signifies *he ran on before, faster than Peter* (added for the sake of more exact definition). In 2 P. iii. 6, if ὑδάτων be supplied with δι' ὧν, yet ὕδατι will not be superfluous : this word would denote the water as an element, whereas ὕδατα (compare Gen. vii. 11) would signify the concrete (separate) masses of water. Compare further Jude 4. On H. vi. 6 see my 3rd *Progr. de verbis compositis*, p. 10.[1] That L. xx. 43, ὑποπόδιον τῶν ποδῶν σου (H. i. 13), *footstool for thy feet*, and Gen. xvii. 13, ὁ οἰκογενὴς τῆς οἰκίας σου (Dt. vii. 13), are not exactly similar to the examples given above, is evident from the appended genitive. Lastly, such passages as Mk. viii. 4, ὧδε ... ἐπ' ἐρημίας· xiii. 29, ἐγγὺς ... ἐπὶ θύραις· 2 Tim. ii. 10, come under the head not of pleonasm (Heinichen, *Eus.* II. 186), but of apposition. So also Mk. xii. 23, ἐν τῇ ἀναστάσει, ὅταν ἀναστῶσι· can hardly be called an example of diffuseness, for the latter clause is an application of the general ἐν τῇ ἀναστάσει to the brothers mentioned in ver. 20 sqq. See Lob. *Paral.* p. 534. Ὀσμὴ εὐωδίας in E. v. 2 (both words derived from ὄζω) might be regarded as a semi-pleonasm, and might perhaps be compared with παίδων ἄπαις (Eurip. *Androm.* 613, Herm. *Opusc.* p. 221). The words however mean *odour of fragrance:* ὀσμή is the scent as inhaled, εὐωδία its property. [Compare § 34. 3. *b.*]

3. c. Lastly, many redundancies of expression are to be explained as arising from a mixture of two constructions (Herm. *Opusc.* p. 224, *Vig.* p. 887): L. ii. 21, ὅτε ἐπλήσθησαν ἡμέραι ὀκτώ ... καὶ ἐκλήθη τὸ ὄνομα (instead of ἐπλήσθησαν δὲ ἡμέραι ... καί, or ὅτε ἐπλήσθησαν ... ἐκλήθη) ; L. vii. 12, ὡς ἤγγισε τῇ πύλῃ τῆς πόλεως, καὶ ἰδοὺ ἐξεκομίζετο τεθνηκώς ; A. x. 17.[2] Rom. ix. 29 also might be brought under this head (see above, p. 753), and even the use of ὅτι before the *oratio recta,* in its original conception (Rost, *Gr.* p. 646, Jelf 802. *Obs.* 8). With greater certainty we may apply this explanation to the pleonastic negative in the formula ἐκτὸς εἰ μή (Devar. I. 74): 1 C. xiv. 5,

---

[1] ["Ceterum πάλιν ἀνακαινίζειν non puto abundanter dictum ... Sed hanc vim habere videtur : *denuo renovare* scil. eos, quorum animi jam olim, cum Christo nomen dedissent, renovati essent, ad bonam mentem revocare." Winer *l. c.*]

[2] [That is, when after a particle of time the apodosis is introduced by καί (or by ו in Hebrew,—see Winer, *Simonis* s. v.), the construction is regarded by Winer as a kind of anacoluthon : see above, p. 546 sq., Herm. *Vig. l. c.,* Krüger p. 352. (For a different explanation of the Greek construction, see Kühner II. 422, Jelf 759. *Obs.* 3 : compare also Ewald, *Lehrb.* p. 826, 832.) It is usual to class together as examples of καί *in apodosi* such passages as L. ii. 21 (which occur frequently in the LXX,—e. g., Ex. xvi. 10, xxxiii. 22, Lev. xiv. 34 sq., xxiii. 10, xxv. 2, Jos. iii. 8, iv. 1, viii. 24, x. 24), and those in which καί follows καὶ ἐγένετο or ἐγένετο δέ (with a note of time, see p. 760) : see De W., Bleek, Alford *ll. cc.,* A. Buttm. p. 276 sq., 362. When the usage of the LXX is considered, it is hard to see how Meyer can be justified in giving to καί the meaning *also* in L. ii. 21, vii. 12, A. i. 10, x. 17 *Rec.*]

μείζων ὁ προφητεύων ἢ ὁ λαλῶν γλώσσαις, ἐκτὸς εἰ μὴ διερμηνεύῃ, *except if he add an interpretation;* 1 C. xv. 2, 1 Tim. v. 19.[1] Here we might have had either ἐκτὸς εἰ διερμηνεύῃ or εἰ μὴ διερμηνεύῃ. Of this and similar formulas (as πλὴν εἰ μή) many examples have been collected by Lobeck (*Phryn.* p. 459): compare also Jacobs, *Achill. Tat.* p. 869, Döderlein, *Œd. Col.* p. 382 sqq. (Jelf 860. *Obs.* 3). On the other hand, when εἰ δὲ μή γε (after a negative clause) appears to have the meaning, *if however this be the case*,[2] *otherwise*—as in Mt. vi. 1, ix. 17, 2 C. xi. 16—the negative may not have been looked upon as pleonastic, as the formula was originally conceived: see Fritzsche, *Matt.* p. 255 (Jelf 860. 6).

4. Most of what has received the name of pleonasm in the N. T. (and elsewhere) should rather be referred to *circumstantiality*, or, more commonly still, to *fulness* of expression.[3] The former is the result of an effort to be very clearly understood; the latter aims at vividness, impressiveness (solemnity), roundness of style. It must not be forgotten that the language of the N. T. consists to a great extent of spoken words, or is formed on the model of the spoken language; and that in oriental phraseology the qualities just mentioned are very highly prized. The distinction between true pleonasm and such expressions as we have now in view is, that in the latter no words or parts of words express conceptions which are not to be included in the general conception of the sentence, though all may not be absolutely required for the logical completeness of the thought. Thus in Mk. i. 17 we have ποιήσω ὑμᾶς γενέσθαι ἁλιεῖς ἀνθρώπων, but in Mt. iv. 19 ποιήσω ὑμᾶς ἁλιεῖς ἀνθρώπων. The opposite of this is not ellipsis but conciseness.

The examples of circumstantiality of expression may be divided into the following classes:—

a. A word which, so far as the thought is concerned, need not be expressed more than once, is sometimes found repeated in

---

[1] We often use similar expressions in our colloquial language: e.g., *alle waren zugegen, ausgenommen du nicht,—ich komme nicht, bevor du nicht gesagt hast.*

[2] [That is: in Mt. vi. 1, *but if ye do* etc.; ix. 17, *but if they do put* etc. Fritzsche's explanation is to the effect that εἰ δὲ μή after a negative clause properly means, *but if ye do not attend to the prohibition, if ye do not abstain from,* etc.]

[3] Herm. *Opusc.* p. 222 sqq., *Vig.* p. 887, Poppo, *Thuc.* I. i. 204 sqq.

a parallel member wherever it would be supplied by the mind :[1] H. ii. 16, οὐ γὰρ ἀγγέλων ἐπιλαμβάνεται, ἀλλὰ σπέρματος Ἀβραὰμ ἐπιλαμβάνεται· Jo. xii. 3, ἤλειψεν τοὺς πόδας τοῦ Ἰησοῦ καὶ ἐξέμαξεν ταῖς θριξὶν αὐτῆς τοὺς πόδας αὐτοῦ· Rev. xiv. 2, ἤκουσα φωνὴν ἐκ τοῦ οὐρανοῦ . . . . καὶ ἡ φωνή, ἣν ἤκουσα· Rev. ix. 21, xvi. 18, 1 C. xii. 12, xv. 54, Ph. ii. 16, iv. 17, Jo. x. 10, Rev. ix. 1 sq., Mk. i. 40, Mt. xviii. 32. In Greek writers compare Xen. *Mem.* 2. 10. 3, Demosth. *Zenoth.* 576 c, Long. 2. 3, Lucian, *Cynic.* 9 (Jacob, Luc. *Alex.* 117, Poppo, *Thuc.* III. ii. 23): in Latin, compare the expressions which Julius Cæsar, in particular, so frequently makes use of, *in ea loca, quibus in locis,—dies, quo die*, etc. By such repetitions the writer ensures that his meaning shall be understood, especially where the words to be connected stand somewhat widely apart. In some cases a repetition is of a rhetorical nature: see no. 5.

b. The instrument by which an action is ordinarily or necessarily performed (e.g., a member of the human body) is expressly mentioned in connexion with the action: A. xv. 23, γράψαντες διὰ χειρὸς αὐτῶν (they were to deliver the letter), A. xi. 30 (2 C. xvii. 13 [2]), xix. 11 ; A. iii. 18, προκατήγγειλε διὰ στόματος πάντων τῶν προφητῶν· xv. 7, L. i. 70, al. From the Greek poets compare Eurip. *Ion* 1187 v. l., χερσὶν ἐκχέων σπονδάς· *Hec.* 526 sq., Theocr. 7. 153, ποσσὶ χορεῦσαι : see Lobeck, *Ajax* p. 222 sq. (Wunder, *Recens.* p. 17 sq.). But in Rom. x. 15 (from the LXX), ὡς ὡραῖοι οἱ πόδες τῶν εὐαγγελιζομένων εἰρήνην, the idea of *arrival* which is implied in πόδες is anything but an idle addition; and in 1 Jo. i. 1, ὃ ἑωράκαμεν τοῖς ὀφθαλμοῖς ἡμῶν (L. ii. 30), the writer has manifestly added the last words for the sake of emphasis,—as when we speak of seeing *with one's own eyes* (Hesiod, *Theog.* 701, Thuc. 2. 11, Aristot. *Mirab.* 160, Heliod. 4. 19 [3]). As to Mk. vi. 2, A. v. 12, it must be recollected that the miracles spoken of were performed by the laying on of hands. Πρὸ προςώπου, however, as used in L. i. 76, προπορεύσῃ πρὸ προςώπου κυρίου· L. ix. 52 (לְפָנָיו), is analogous to the

---

[1] A different view must be taken of many repetitions used by the orators, who when writing, had before their minds the delivery of the oration in the presence of the people : compare Foertsch, *De locis Lysiæ* p. 29. The repetition of the same word, moreover (e. g., Plat. *Charm.* 168 a), is of a different nature.
[2] [This is probably intended for 2 K. xvii. 13.]
[3] See Bremi, *Æsch.* I. 124 ; and compare Jani, *Ars Poet.* p. 220 sq.

examples quoted above. This formula came to be used in the simple sense *before* (in reference to inanimate objects), e. g., A. xiii. 24, πρὸ προςώπου τῆς εἰςόδου αὐτοῦ: compare Num. xix. 4, ἀπέναντι τοῦ προςώπου τῆς σκηνῆς· Ps. xciv. 6,[1] κατὰ προςώπου ἀνέμου.

c. When an action must from the nature of the case be preceded by another action, this latter is nevertheless expressly related,—usually by means of a participle: Mt. xxvi. 51, ἐκτείνας τὴν χεῖρα ἀπέσπασεν τὴν μάχαιραν αὐτοῦ· ii. 8, ὅπως κἀγὼ ἐλθὼν προςκυνήσω αὐτῷ (xiv. 33), Jo. vi. 5, ἐπάρας τοὺς ὀφθαλμοὺς καὶ θεασάμενος· Mt. xiii. 31, ὁμοία κόκκῳ σινάπεως, ὃν λαβὼν ἄνθρωπος ἔσπειρεν· xiii. 33, A. xvi. 3 (Xen. Eph. 3. 4, ὁ δὲ αὐτὸν λαβὼν ἄγει πρὸς τὴν Ἀνθίαν, see Locella p. 141), Jo. vi. 15, γνοὺς ὅτι μέλλουσιν ἔρχεσθαι καὶ ἁρπάζειν αὐτόν· Mt. xix. 21. So also in 1 C. ii. 1, κἀγὼ ἐλθὼν πρὸς ὑμᾶς, ἀδελφοί, ἦλθον οὐ κ.τ.λ., the participle was not required: the examples quoted by Bornemann (on Xen. *Cyr.* 5. 3. 2) are not really similar, as in these several words intervene between the participle and its finite verb. On the other hand, L. i. 31, συλλήψῃ ἐν γαστρὶ καὶ τέξῃ υἱόν, is not a mere redundancy of language; the high importance of the favour destined for her is expressed by the prominence thus given to every particular involved. In L. xxiv. 50, ἐπάρας τὰς χεῖρας αὐτοῦ εὐλόγησεν αὐτούς, the participial clause indicates the symbolical gesture of the person blessing; in E. ii. 17 ἐλθών marks an important moment of thought, to be dwelt upon independently,—as in L. xii. 37.—In Jo. xxi. 13, also, ἔρχεται Ἰησοῦς καὶ λαμβάνει τὸν ἄρτον καὶ δίδωσιν αὐτοῖς, the writer designedly mentions each single act of the wonderful occurrences,—bringing the whole, as it were, before our eyes. In Jo. xi. 48 the words ἐλεύσονται οἱ Ῥωμαῖοι relate to the approach of Roman armies. See further Mt. viii. 3, 7, ix. 18, xxvii. 48, L. vi. 20 (Æl. 12. 22), Jo. xv. 16, Rev. xvi. 1, 2. In A. viii. 35, ἀνοίξας ὁ Φίλιππος τὸ στόμα αὐτοῦ καὶ ἀρξάμενος ἀπὸ τῆς γραφῆς ταύτης εὐηγγελίσατο κ.τ.λ., the clause ἀνοίξας τὸ στόμα is probably used as a (solemn) introduction of an important statement; this is certainly the case in Mt. v. 2 (see Fritzsche *in loc.*).[2]

---

[1] [A mistake: either for Ps. lxxxii. 14 or for Ps. xxxiv. 5.]
[2] Compare generally Fischer, *De vitiis lexicorum*, p. 223 sqq., Pflugk, Eurip. *Hel.* p. 134.

d. A word which is usually regarded as included in another is sometimes expressed by the side of the latter: A. iii. 3, ἠρώτα ἐλεημοσύνην λαβεῖν¹ (compare Virg. Æn. 5. 262, loricam . . . donat *habere* viro). Mk. i. 17, ποιήσω ὑμᾶς γενέσθαι ἁλιεῖς ἀνθρώπων (see above, p. 757): compare Ex. xxiii. 15, Demosth. *Ep.* 3. p. 114 b, ἢ καὶ τοὺς ἀναισθήτους ἀνεκτοὺς ποιεῖν δοκεῖ γίνεσθαι.

e. In the progress of a narration, the Hebraistic καὶ ἐγένετο is prefixed to the detail of the several facts: Mt. vii. 28, καὶ ἐγένετο, ὅτε συνετέλεσεν . . . ἐξεπλήσσοντο,—for which a Greek writer would simply say καὶ ὅτε (or ὅτε δὲ) συνετέλεσεν.² On the other hand, in Jo. xi. 11, ταῦτα εἶπεν, καὶ μετὰ τοῦτο λέγει αὐτοῖς, neither ταῦτα εἶπεν nor μετὰ τοῦτο is superfluous: the latter marks a pause.

Under (c) will come the use of the participle ἀναστάς in such cases as Mt. ix. 9, ἀναστὰς ἠκολούθησεν αὐτῷ· Mk. ii. 14, vii. 24, L. i. 39 (like the Hebrew וַיָּקָם). But though ἀναστάς was not required here, yet in other passages which the commentators bring under the same head this particle is by no means redundant. Thus in Mt. xxvi. 62, ἀναστὰς ὁ ἀρχιερεὺς εἶπεν αὐτῷ, the meaning obviously is, *he stood up* from indignation, *he started up* (from his seat): A. v. 17 is a similar instance. Mk. i. 35, πρωῒ ἔννυχον λίαν ἀναστὰς ἐξῆλθε, *rising in the morning, when it was still very dark.* L. xv. 18, ἀναστὰς

---

¹ See Wetstein *in loc.*, and Boisson. *Eunap.* p. 459.

² This formula is only met with where the principal sentence is preceded by some note of time. The principal verb is sometimes appended by means of καί (on this see Fritzsche, *Matt.* p. 341), as in Mt. ix. 10, L. v. 1, 12, ix. 51; more commonly it follows without any copula (Mt. xi. 1, xiii. 53, xix. 1, xxvi. 1, Mk. iv. 4, L. i. 8, 41, ii. 1, al.). This idiom is used most frequently by Luke, in his Gospel. It was an unhappy thought of Bornemann's (*Schol.* p. 25) that καί in this construction should be rendered *also*.—Ἐγένετο here is really pleonastic, for the note of time might be directly attached to the principal verb. [The construction of καὶ ἐγένετο (ἐγένετο δέ) with the accusative and infinitive (Mk. ii. 23, al.,—A. ix. 37, al.) is noticed above, p. 406 sq.: this construction seems not to occur in the LXX or Apocrypha (compare however 2 Macc. iii. 16). For καὶ ἐγένετο (ἐγένετο δέ) followed by καί and the finite verb, see Gen. xxiv. 30, xxxix. 13 sq., Jos. v. 1, xxiii. 1, 1 Macc. x. 64, 88 (Gen. xxvi. 32, xxvii. 1, xxxix. 19, xli. 8): for the same without καί, Gen. xxii. 1, xxiv. 45, Judith xii. 10, xiii. 12 (Gen. xxiv. 52, xxvii. 34, xl. 1, 20, xli. 1). In Mk. ii. 15 Tischendorf, Meyer, Westcott and Hort read γίνεται with accusative and infinitive: Alford, γίνεται with καί and finite verb. In the LXX ἐγενήθη frequently takes the place of ἐγένετο (e.g., 1 S. iv. 1, xi. 1, Esth. v. 1); also, when the future is spoken of, καὶ ἔσται . . . καί, Ex. xiii. 11 sq., Dt. xi. 29,—or without a second καί, e.g., Lev. xiv. 9, Dt. xxi. 14, Judith xiv. 2 (A. ii. 17, 21, iii. 23, Rom. ix. 26,—all quotations from the O. T.). On the meaning of καί after ἐγένετο δέ etc. (explained by Fritzsche *l.c.* as "nempe"), see above, p. 756, note ⁴. A. x. 25, ἐγένετο τοῦ εἰσελθεῖν, is noticed above, p. 412.—See A. Buttm. p. 276 sq.]

πορεύσομαι πρὸς τὸν πατέρα μου (*I will rise up and go*), *I will forthwith go* etc. There has been a general tendency to set down too many participles to the account of N. T. diffuseness. Here and there there may be doubt in a particular case, but very many of these participles express ideas which would be missed, if left unexpressed: e.g., 1 C. vi. 15, ἄρας οὖν τὰ μέλη τοῦ Χριστοῦ ποιήσω πόρνης μέλη; (see Bengel *in loc.*, Aristoph. *Eq.* 1130, Soph. *Œd. R.* 1270), 1 P. iii. 19, τοῖς ἐν φυλακῇ πνεύμασι πορευθεὶς ἐκήρυξεν. In L. xii. 37, παρελθὼν διακονήσει αὐτοῖς, *he will come to them and serve them*, the sentence—even if judged of by our own feeling—is more graphic and vivid than it would have been without παρελθών. Nor can I regard παρελθών as superfluous in Æl. 2. 30.[1]

With A. iii. 3, quoted above under (d), may also be compared A. xi. 22, ἐξαπέστειλαν Βαρνάβαν διελθεῖν ἕως Ἀντιοχείας (where the ancient versions leave out the infinitive, as unnecessary, though the translators certainly had it in the text before them[2]): these words, however, properly mean, *they sent him away* with the commission *to go, that he should go* etc. Similarly in A. xx. 1, ἐξῆλθεν πορευθῆναι εἰς τὴν Μακεδονίαν, *he departed in order to go to Macedonia*. Compare also Cæsar, *Civ.* 3. 33. But I cannot (with Bornemann) find a mere redundancy in L. xx. 35, οἱ δὲ καταξιωθέντες τοῦ αἰῶνος ἐκείνου τυχεῖν. Here τυχεῖν expresses something which in strictness is not implied in καταξιοῦσθαι, and it is only when this word is added that the phrase becomes complete and clear. Compare Demosth. *Cor.* p. 328 b, κατ' αὐτὸ τοῦτο ἄξιός εἰμι ἐπαίνου τυχεῖν· and Bos, *Exercit.* p. 48 (Bornem. *Schol.* p. 125).

Such sentences as Mk. xi. 5, τί ποιεῖτε λύοντες τὸν πῶλον, and A. xxi. 13, τί ποιεῖτε κλαίοντες καὶ συνθρύπτοντές μου τὴν καρδίαν, have a circumstantial appearance, when compared with the ordinary expressions τί λύετε, τί κλαίετε. But "what do ye, loosing?" properly means *what is your aim in this? quid hoc sibi vult?* Hence ποιεῖν has not here the general meaning "do," which is already contained in every verb of special signification; and we should rather regard τί λύετε[3] as a condensed expression than τί ποιεῖτε λύοντες as diffuse.

5. Fulness of expression—the aim of which is sometimes didactic or rhetorical emphasis (solemnity), sometimes vividness of effect—is met with mainly in the following forms:—

a. The same word is repeated one or more times in parallel members (Xen. *An.* 3. 4. 45). E. ii. 17, εὐηγγελίσατο εἰρήνην

---

[1] Compare in general Schæf. *Soph.* I. 253, 278, II. 314, *Demosth.* IV. 623, Pflugk, Eurip. *Hel.* p. 134, Matth. 558. Rem. 2 (Jelf 698. *Obs.*).
[2] [This word is absent, not from these versions only, but also from the MSS. אAB: it is rejected by the best editors.]
[3] [Winer adds a rendering (*was löset ihr*) which imitates the Greek, as in this construction τί was originally an accusative of the object (§ 21. 3. Rem. 2).]

ὑμῖν τοῖς μακρὰν καὶ εἰρήνην τοῖς ἐγγύς· Jo. vi. 63, τὰ ῥήματα . . . πνεῦμά ἐστιν καὶ ζωή ἐστιν· Col. i. 28, νουθετοῦντες πάντα ἄνθρωπον καὶ διδάσκοντες πάντα ἄνθρωπον· Jo. i. 10, ix. 5, xiv. 26, 27, xv. 19, xix. 10, Mt. xii. 37, Rom. v. 12, xiv. 14, 1 C. i. 24, 27, xiii. 11, 2 C. xi. 26 ; Rom. (iii. 31), viii. 15, οὐκ ἐλάβετε πνεῦμα δουλείας . . . ἀλλὰ ἐλάβετε πνεῦμα υἱοθεσίας (in H. xii. 18, 22, the repetition was necessary for the sake of clearness): 1 C. x. 1 sq., οἱ πατέρες ἡμῶν πάντες ὑπὸ τὴν νεφέλην ἦσαν καὶ πάντες διὰ τῆς θαλάσσης διῆλθον, καὶ πάντες εἰς τὸν Μωϋσῆν ἐβαπτίσαντο, καὶ πάντες . . . . καὶ πάντες κ.τ.λ. (Cæs. *Bell. Gall.* 1. 31), Ph. iii. 2, iv. 8, 2 C. vii. 2 ; 1 C. xiv. 24, Rev. viii. 7, 12 ; 1 C. vi. 11, ἀλλὰ ἀπελούσασθε, ἀλλὰ ἡγιάσθητε, ἀλλὰ ἐδικαιώθητε· i. 20, iv. 8, 1 Tim. v. 10, 2 C. vi. 2, ἰδοὺ νῦν καιρὸς εὐπρόςδεκτος, ἰδοὺ νῦν ἡμέρα σωτηρίας (Arrian, *Epict.* 3. 23. 20), xi. 20, E. vi. 12, 17, v. 10,[1] 1 Jo. i. 1, Rev. xiv. 8, xviii. 2. (The examples of *polysyndeton* may also be brought under this head: Rev. vii. 12, Rom. ii. 17 sq., 1 C. xiii. 2.) Such repetitions frequently occur in urgent address, as Mt. xxv. 11, κύριε, κύριε, ἄνοιξον ἡμῖν· xxiii. 37, L. viii. 24, x. 41, xxii. 31, A. ix. 4 ; and also in demands, Jo. xix. 6 (Krüg. *Dion.* p. 11). In all these examples the writer is unwilling to leave it to the reader to repeat in thought a word which has been once expressed ; that the importance of this word may be properly felt, he prefers himself to express it in every instance in which it comes before the mind. (So especially ἐκ παραλλήλου: Rom. xi. 32, 1 C. xv. 21.)

b. A thought which is to be brought out with great precision is in very many instances (especially in John) expressed both affirmatively and negatively in parallel members (*parallelismus antitheticus*[2]). Jo. i. 20, ὡμολόγησε καὶ οὐκ ἠρνήσατο· E. v. 15, μὴ ὡς ἄσοφοι ἀλλ' ὡς σοφοί· v. 17, Jo. i. 3, iii. 16, x. 5 (xviii. 20), xx. 27, 1 Jo. i. 6, ii. 4, 27, L. i. 20, A. xviii. 9, 1 Tim. ii. 7, Ja. i. 5, 23, 1 P. i. 23, v. 2, H. vii. 21, x. 37 (from the LXX), xii. 8, Rev. ii. 13, iii. 9 (Dt. xxviii. 13, Is. iii. 9,[3] xxxviii. 1, Ez. xviii. 21, Hos. v. 3). For examples in Greek

---

[1] [Inserted by mistake.—I have corrected Mt. xxiii. 27 (below) into 37, from ed. 5.]
[2] Herm. *Opusc.* p. 223 (Jelf 899. 6).
[3] [A mistake.—Some of the passages quoted above are but questionable examples of the usage here noticed.]

writers see Eurip. *El.* 1057, φημὶ κοὐκ ἀπαρνοῦμαι· Æl. *An.* 2. 43, οὐκ ἀρνοῦνται οἱ ἄνθρωποι ἀλλ' ὁμολογοῦσι ; and especially the orators, e. g., Demosth. *Fals. Leg.* p. 200 c, φράσω καὶ οὐκ ἀποκρύψομαι.[1]

c. The following combinations aim at vividness of effect : A. xxvii. 20, περιηρεῖτο ἐλπὶς πᾶσα· Rom. viii. 22, πᾶσα ἡ κτίσις συστενάζει καὶ συνωδίνει· Mt. ix. 35. Compare Diod. S. IV. 51, περινιψάμενος τὸ σῶμα πᾶν· Strabo 11. 500, πολλαῖς συμπληρούμενος πηγαῖς· Lucian, *Paras.* 12, Long. 4. 15; Cic. *Sen.* 18, *con*surrexisse *omnes;* Liv. 33. 29, cum *omnia* terrore et fuga *com*plessent. See my second *Progr. de verbis compositis*, p. 21 sq.

d. The form of address in A. i. 11, ἄνδρες Γαλιλαῖοι· iii. 12, ἄνδρες Ἰσραηλῖται· ii. 14, v. 35, xiii. 16, conveys the same (respectful) emphasis (*men of Israel !*) as the familiar ἄνδρες Ἀθηναῖοι—which itself occurs in A. xvii. 22—or ἄνδρες δικασταί. See § 59. 1.

In 2 C. ii. 16, οἷς μὲν ὀσμὴ θανάτου εἰς θάνατον, οἷς δὲ ὀσμὴ ζωῆς εἰς ζωήν, every word is needed. *A savour of death to death, a savour of life to life*, means a savour of death, which from its very nature can bring nothing but death, etc.

A pleonastic character has often been wrongly ascribed to passages in which synonyms seem brought together for the purpose of expressing one main idea,—a common case in Demosthenes.[2] Paul however —from whose writings these examples are in the main derived—is not in the habit of bringing real synonyms into the same sentence. (Nor has he done so in E. i. 5, 19, ii. 1, iv. 23, 1 C. i. 10, ii. 4, 1 Tim. ii. 1, v. 5 : compare also Ja. iii. 13, Jo. xii. 49, 1 P. i. 4, iv. 9, 1 Jo. i. 1, al.,—and see Fritz. *Rom.* II. 372.) A more careful study of the Greek language in general, and of the diction of the apostles in particular, will preserve us from adopting any such principle,—which *e. g.* would greatly weaken the apostolic salutation χάρις, ἔλεος καὶ εἰρήνη.[3]—In the combinations θυμὸς ὀργῆς Rev. xvi. 19, πέλαγος τῆς

---

[1] See Maius, *Observ. Sacr.* II. 77 sqq., Kypke I. 350 sq., Poppo, *Thucyd.* I. i. 204, Herm. *Med.* p. 361 (ed. Elmsley), and Soph. *Œd. Col.* p. 41, *Philoct.* p. 44, Jacob, *Quæst. Lucian.* p. 19, Weber, *Demosth.* p. 314, Boisson. *Eunap.* p. 164 sqq., Mätzner, *Antiph.* p. 157.

[2] See Schæfer, *Demosth.* I. 209, 320, 756, *Plutarch* IV. 387, V. 106, Weber, *Demosth.* p. 376, Franke, *Demosth.* p. 12, Bremi, *Æschin.* I. 79, Lucian, *Alex.* p. 24 (ed. Jacob), Poppo, *Thuc.* III. i. 619, Schoem. Plut. *Agis* p. 171. Compare Lob. *Paralip.* p. 61 sq.

[3] Schæfer's observation (*Demosth.* I. 320)—"usus (synonymorum) duplex, gravior alter, ut vim concilient orationi, alter levior, ut vel aures expleant vel numeros reddant jucundiores"—has immediate reference to the orators only.

θαλάσσης Mt. xviii. 6, ἐπιφάνεια τῆς παρουσίας 2 Th. ii. 8, σπλάγχνα ἐλέους or οἰκτιρμοῦ L. i. 78, Col. iii. 12, there is nothing pleonastic. The second was long ago correctly rendered by Wetstein *æquor maris:* πέλαγος signifies the expanse (of the sea), and thus is also used of the surface of a river,—see Schwarz, *Commentar.* p. 1067.[1] In L. i. 78, Col. iii. 12, σπλάγχνα is the wider expression, which is more exactly defined by the genitive annexed.

The *parallelismus membrorum,* which appears here and there in the N. T. (see § 68. 3), has nothing to do with pleonasm. On the partition of points of dogma between parallel members, as in Rom. iv. 25, x. 10, see De Wette on the former passage.

6. Pleonasm of entire sentences is a thing inconceivable. Whenever a writer repeats a sentence with but slight variation, his aim is to give very marked prominence to a thought, or to exhibit it under different aspects. 2 C. xii. 7, τῇ ὑπερβολῇ τῶν ἀποκαλύψεων ἵνα μὴ ὑπεραίρωμαι, ἐδόθη μοι σκόλοψ . . . ἵνα με κολαφίζῃ, ἵνα μὴ ὑπεραίρωμαι: the last words are omitted in good MSS.,—but, no doubt, only because they appeared superfluous.[2] Rev. ii. 5, μετανόησον καὶ τὰ πρῶτα ἔργα ποίησον· εἰ δὲ μὴ (μετανοεῖς), ἔρχομαί σοι ταχὺ καὶ κινήσω τὴν λυχνίαν σου ἐκ τοῦ τόπου αὐτῆς, ἐὰν μὴ μετανοήσῃς: compare Plat. *Gorg.* 514 a, ἡμῖν ἐπιχειρητέον ἐστί . . . . θεραπεύειν, ὡς βελτίστους αὐτοὺς τοὺς πολίτας ποιοῦντας· ἄνευ γὰρ δὴ τούτου, ὡς ἐν τοῖς ἔμπροσθεν εὑρίσκομεν, οὐδὲν ὄφελος . . . ἐὰν μὴ καλὴ κἀγαθὴ ἡ διάνοια ᾖ τῶν μελλόντων κ.τ.λ. (Stallb. Plat. *Apol.* p. 23). On 1 C. xiv. 6 see Meyer; and on 1 C. vii. 26 see above, no. 1. On the other hand, in 1 Jo. ii. 27, ὡς τὸ αὐτὸ χρίσμα διδάσκει ὑμᾶς . . . . καί, καθὼς ἐδίδαξεν ὑμᾶς, μενεῖτε ἐν αὐτῷ, the resumptive formula καθὼς ἐδίδαξεν ὑμᾶς is so far from being pleonastic that it could hardly be dispensed with. Similarly in Rev. x. 3, 4.[3]—Of a different kind is Rev. ii. 13, οἶδα ποῦ κατοικεῖς· ὅπου ὁ θρόνος τοῦ σατανᾶ;

---

[1] The investigation of N. T. synonyms (commenced by Bengel, not without success) has been pursued by Tittmann (*De Synonymis N. T. lib.* I.: Lips. 1829): his method is not so much the historical as that of free combination.—Compare also Bornemann's examples and observations in his *Diss. de glossem. N. T.* p. 29 sqq. [This dissertation is prefixed to Bornemann's *Scholia* on Luke.—On N. T. synonyms see especially Trench's work; also Webster, *Synt.* p. 186-237, Green, *Crit. Notes.*]

[2] [On the reading see Westcott and Hort's *Appendix,* p. 120. On 1 C. xiv. 6, vii. 26, quoted below, compare Evans's notes, in *Speak. Comm.* III. 344, 291.]

[3] On such examples as the above see Hermann, Eurip. *Bacch.* 1060, Soph. *Antig.* 691, and *Philoct.* 269, 454; Reisig, *Conject. Aristoph.* p. 314 sq.; Heindorf, Plat. *Phæd.* p. 52 and Cic. *Nat. D.* 1. 16; Schæf. *Demosth.* V. 726; Matth. 636. 2. [§ 60. 5, Jelf 860. 10.

where ὅπου ὁ θρόνος is immediately subjoined in explanation of (as if in answer to) ποῦ κατοικεῖς. So also might Mk. ii. 24 be taken; here however τί is probably *why?* 2 C. vii. 8 and Jo. xiii. 17 do not come in here. In 1 C. i. 22 sq. also, the sentence ἐπειδὴ καὶ Ἰουδαῖοι ... μωρίαν is obviously not a mere repetition of ἐπειδὴ γὰρ ... τὸν θεόν in ver. 21, any more than ἡμεῖς δὲ κηρύσσομεν (ver. 23) is a mere repetition of εὐδόκησεν ὁ θεός κ.τ.λ. (ver. 21). In Rom. vi. 16, οὐκ οἴδατε, ὅτι ᾧ παριστάνετε ἑαυτοὺς δούλους εἰς ὑπακοήν, δοῦλοί ἐστε ᾧ ὑπακούετε, there would be no expression of *idem per idem,* even if δοῦλοι were not immediately followed by the defining clause ἤτοι ἁμαρτίας εἰς θάνατον ἢ ὑπακοῆς εἰς δικαιοσύνην. Nor is there any more reason for regarding the two clauses in Rom. vi. 6, ἵνα καταργηθῇ τὸ σῶμα τῆς ἁμαρτίας, τοῦ μηκέτι δουλεύειν ἡμᾶς τῇ ἁμαρτίᾳ, as identical in meaning: the former clause speaks generally of the καταργηθῆναι of the σῶμα τῆς ἁμαρτίας, the latter expresses concretely the purpose of this καταργηθῆναι. 1 P. ii. 16 has not the remotest connexion with this subject: 2 P. iii. 4 also is of a different kind. On Mt. v. 18 there may be a difference of opinion, according as πάντα in the last clause is taken as referring to the law (so Olshausen, Meyer), or is explained in a general sense, as by Fritzsche,—*donec omnia (quæ mente fingere queas) evenerint.* The latter explanation, however, is less satisfactory.

7. We will now refer to certain cases in which N. T. commentators, both ancient and modern, have assumed the existence of pleonasm, though in reality there is no redundancy of language whatever. First of all, an observation is current even in recent commentaries, supported by misinterpreted parallel passages of Greek authors, to the effect that in the N. T. several verbs—viz., ἄρχεσθαι, δοκεῖν, θέλειν, τολμᾶν, δύνασθαι,—are often pleonastic when joined with an infinitive: Kühnöl, indeed (on L. i. 1), even includes ἐπιχειρεῖν in the number (comp. Weiske, *Pleon.* s. vv.). The whole canon rests on error.

a. In L. i. 1, ἐπειδήπερ πολλοὶ ἐπεχείρησαν ἀνατάξασθαι διήγησιν κ.τ.λ., the verb ἐπιχειρεῖν is no more used without specific meaning,[1] than is the Latin *aggredi* in *aggressus sum scribere.* Luther well renders the words, *Since many have*

---

[1] Though even classical philologers have taken this view,—see Herbst, Xen. *Mem.* p. 38; on the other side see Heind. Plat. *Soph.* p. 450.

ventured etc.; and in all the passages quoted by Kühnöl from Greek authors the verb has this meaning.

b. Similarly, τολμᾶν (Weiske p. 121 sq.) is *to undertake something*, and is always used in reference to important or difficult affairs,—*sustinere, bring oneself to*[1] (Rom. v. 7, 1 C. vi. 1). In Jo. xxi. 12, however, it simply signifies *audere, to venture;* and it is only as to *the reason why* they were afraid to make this inquiry of Jesus that we can be at all in doubt. Markland's observation, *Lysias* p. 159 (ed. Taylor), ought not to have led any commentator astray.

c. As to δοκεῖν compare Fritzsche's note on Mt. iii. 9, and what was said still earlier by J. D. Michaelis in the *Nov. Miscell. Lips.* IV. 45. In 1 C. x. 12, ὁ δοκῶν ἑστάναι obviously means *he who thinks (imagines) he stands;* compare G. vi. 3. In Mk. x. 42, οἱ δοκοῦντες ἄρχειν τῶν ἐθνῶν signifies *those who are accounted, are recognised as, the rulers of the nations.* G. ii. 9, Susann. 5, Joseph. *Antt.* 19. 6. 3, are similar examples: the parallel passage, Mt. xx. 25, has simply οἱ ἄρχοντες. L. xxii. 24, τίς αὐτῶν δοκεῖ εἶναι μείζων, *quis videatur habere* (habiturus esse) *principatum,—who must be judged to have the preeminence* (over the rest): the matter is still future, and hence can only be a subject for probable judgment. 1 C. xi. 16, εἴ τις δοκεῖ φιλόνεικος εἶναι, *if any one thinks he may be contentious;* or, as Meyer,[2] De Wette, *if any one appears to be contentious* (urbanity of expression). L. viii. 18, ὃ δοκεῖ ἔχειν, *what he thinks he possesses.* 1 C. iii. 18, vii. 40, viii. 2, xiv. 37, H. iv. 1 (here Böhme regards δοκεῖ as "elegantius,"—Kühnöl and Bleek[3] take a more correct view), require no remark. Compare generally Bornemann, *Schol.* p. 52 sq.

---

[1] Blume, *Lycurg.* p. 89.

[2] [In his earlier editions: he now renders the words, *thinks of being* etc. (not "thinks that he *may* be"). Lightfoot takes the same view; see his note on Ph. iii. 4.—On this verb see Trench, *Syn.* s. v., Ellicott and Lightfoot on G. ii. 2, 6, Ph. iii. 4.]

[3] [Bleek, Lünemann, Delitzsch, Alford, and others take δοκεῖν here as practically synonymous with φαίνεσθαι,—"appear," in the sense of *being found* or *shown* (to have come short). If this view is correct, this is the only passage in the N. T. in which δοκεῖν is used in an objective sense (see Trench *l. c.*). Kurtz *in loc.* says: "δοκεῖν, *videri, seem,* is used . . . because in such a question as *whether,* and *in what case,* the ὑστερηκέναι already exists as an accomplished, irrevocable fact, human observation cannot go beyond a mere *videtur.*" Another explanation is that the word has reference to the opinion of the judge (of a race, etc.): *lest any one be held* (almost " be adjudged ") *to have come short of it.*]

d. Most of the passages of the Gospels in which ἄρχεσθαι has been alleged to be pleonastic (compare also Valcken. *Selecta* I. 87) are more correctly explained by Fritzsche (*Matt.* p. 539 sq.,—compare p. 766). The true explanation of L. iii. 8 had already been given by Bengel: omnem excusationis etiam conatum præcidit. In particular, it is altogether absurd to regard this verb as pleonastic in L. xii. 45, xxi. 28, 2 C. iii. 1. In Jo. xiii. 5 ἤρξατο indicates the commencement of the action whose termination is related in ver. 12. A. xxvii. 35 is explained by the following verse: by Paul's ἄρχεσθαι ἐσθίειν the others were called upon to do the same. In A. xi. 15 Kühnöl gives the following reason for considering ἄρξασθαι λαλεῖν equivalent to λαλεῖν: ex x. 43 patet, Petrum jam multa de religione christiana disseruisse etc. But ἄρχεσθαι λαλεῖν strictly denotes only the beginning of the discourse, and the use of the phrase here shows that the discourse was not completed: Peter was intending to say more,—see x. 44, ἔτι λαλοῦντος τοῦ Πέτρου. One cannot see on what ground this beginning should be limited to the first six or eight words spoken. Besides, we must not forget that here (A. xi. 15), in a spoken address, ἐν τῷ ἄρξασθαί με λαλεῖν is a more forcible expression,—q. d., "hardly had I said a few words, when etc." In A. xviii. 26, ἤρξατο must be taken in connexion with the following words, ἀκούσαντες δὲ αὐτοῦ κ.τ.λ. On A. ii. 4 see Meyer. As to A. xxiv. 2, the speech of Tertullus, which—to judge from the introduction (ver. 3)—was certainly intended to be of greater length, was probably interrupted (at ver. 9) by the corroboration of the Jews, Paul himself coming in immediately after. Or else we must understand ver. 2 thus: *When he was called, Tertullus began,*—without delay he began his speech.

e. As to θέλειν,[1] Jo. v. 35, see Lücke's careful investigation of the passage. A more plausible example would be 2 Tim. iii. 12, πάντες οἱ θέλοντες εὐσεβῶς ζῆν ἐν Χριστῷ; but these words mean, *all who resolve to live godly,*—all who have this in view. H. xiii. 18 is clear of itself. Jo. vii. 17 has already been correctly explained by Kühnöl. In Jo. vi. 21 the same commentator has rejected Bolten's arbitrary explanation: we must recognise a discrepancy between this passage and Mk. vi.

---

[1] Gataker, *Marc. Anton.* 10. 8.

51.¹ In 1 C. x. 27, καὶ θέλετε πορεύεσθαι means *and ye are minded, resolve, to go* (instead of declining the invitation). On 1 P. iii. 10 see Huther.²

f. In opposition to Kühnöl, who in Mt. ix. 15 takes δύνασθαι as pleonastic, see Fritzsche: Baumg.-Crusius wrongly renders the word *may*. Still less can we suffer the dictum "redundat" to lead us astray in L. xvi. 2, Jo. vii. 7; in the latter passage especially a distinction is obviously intended between δύναται μισεῖν and μισεῖ.

Among substantives, ἔργον in particular, when followed by a genitive, has been regarded as occasionally pleonastic:³ e. g., Rom. ii. 15, ἔργον νόμου, E. iv. 12, 1 Th. i. 3 (see Koppe). Against this see Fritzsche, *Rom.* I. 117. In 1 Th. i. 3, the parallelism of ἔργον τῆς πίστεως with κόπος τῆς ἀγάπης is of itself sufficient to show that ἔργον cannot be pleonastic: see De Wette *in loc.* E. iv. 12 has already been correctly explained by Flatt. Nor are any examples of a pleonasm of ἔργον to be found in Greek writers. In Polyæn. 1. 17, ἔργον τοῦ λογίου certainly signifies the subject of the oracle, the *deed* predicted in the oracle; in Diog. L. *procem.* 1, τὸ τῆς φιλοσοφίας ἔργον means *the occupation of philosophising,* the cultivation of philosophy,—compare soon after ἄρξαι φιλοσοφίας (in Latin, compare Curt. 8. 14. 37, virtutis *opus,* and Petr. *Fragm.* 28. 5, proditionis *opus*),—not exactly the fabric⁴ of philosophy. We cannot put ἔργον and χρῆμα side by side; nor indeed is χρῆμα really pleonastic, when followed by a genitive: see Liddell and Scott s. v. Ὄνομα, which has very frequently been regarded as pleonastic,⁵ is correctly explained by Wahl (compare Van Hengel, *Phil.* p. 160): see also my edition of Simon. *Lex. Hebr.* s. v. שֵׁם. This word, however, deserves greater exactness of treatment at the hands of N. T. lexicographers. (On a periphrastic use of ὄνομα found in Greek poetry, see Matth. 430. k, Jelf 442. e.) In Col. ii. 16, ἐν μέρει ἑορτῆς ἢ νουμηνίας ἢ σαββάτων, there is no more pleonasm than when we say *in respect of* (or *in the matter of*) the fasts, new moons, etc. Lastly, in Rom. vi. 6 the words σῶμα τῆς ἁμαρτίας express a single idea, *the sin-body;*—i.e., the body (of man), on the relation of which to sin no reader of Paul's Epistles can stand in doubt. See above, p. 235.

---

¹ [See above, p. 587. On Jo. vii. 17 see Alford's note.]
² [In his 1st edition, to which Winer refers, Huther understands ζωήν to refer to *eternal* life, and remarks thus on the singular expression θέλων ἀγαπᾶν ζωήν: "the love of life, no less than the possession of it, is conditioned by a certain course of conduct." In ed. 2 he refers ζωή to the *present* life, and follows Bengel's explanation: "qui vult ita vivere ut ipsum non tædeat vitæ."]
³ Boisson. *Nicet.* p. 59.
⁴ [As the phrase is explained by Fritzsche *l. c.*]
⁵ See also Kühnöl, *Joh.* p. 133. [On this word see Grimm, *Clavis* s. v., Cremer, *Bibl.-theol. Wörterb.* s. v.]

8. In the opinion of almost all the earlier commentators we have a kind of half pleonasm in the use of καλεῖσθαι for εἶναι,[1] —a usage which has also been regarded as a Hebraism (נִקְרָא, esse). This opinion was long ago corrected by Bretschneider (*Lex. Man.* p. 209), who says "*sum* videlicet *ex aliorum sententia:*" compare Van Hengel, *Cor.* p. 53 sq., and on נִקְרָא see my Simon. *Lex.* p. 867. In the N. T. καλεῖσθαι never has any other meaning than *to be named* or *called* (Ja. ii. 23, Mt. v. 19, xxi. 13). It is especially used of titles of honour, which indicate the possession of a certain dignity (see Mt. v. 9, L. i. 76, 1 Jo. iii. 1, Rom. ix. 26); and in some instances is even antithetical to "being," as in 1 C. xv. 9 (to have even the name of an apostle), L. xv. 19. As little right have we to fritter down ὀνομάζεσθαι into a bare *esse* in Rom. xv. 20 (1 C. v. 1), E. i. 21, iii. 15, v. 3: sometimes it is even the emphatic word, as is shown by μηδέ in the passage last quoted.[2] Of H. xi. 18, ἐν Ἰσαὰκ κληθήσεταί σοι σπέρμα, several commentators have even given the absurd translation *existet tibi posteritas:* Schulz's rendering also, *thou wilt receive posterity*, is very inaccurate.

We are also told that εὑρίσκεσθαι[3] (together with נִמְצָא in Hebrew) is frequently used for εἶναι. Between these two verbs, however, there is always this distinction, that, whilst εἶναι indicates the quality of a thing in itself, εὑρίσκεσθαι indicates the quality in so far as it is discovered, detected, recognised in the subject. Mt. i. 18, εὑρέθη ἐν γαστρὶ ἔχουσα, *it was found (it appeared) that she was with child* (ἦν ἐν γαστρὶ ἔχουσα might have been said even earlier than this); L. xvii. 18, οὐχ εὑρέθησαν ὑποστρέψαντες δοῦναι δόξαν τῷ θεῷ εἰ μὴ ὁ ἀλλογενὴς οὗτος; *were none found* (q. d., *did none show themselves*) *who returned?* A. viii. 40, Φίλιππος εὑρέθη εἰς Ἄζωτον, *Philip was found* (compare ver. 39, πνεῦμα κυρίου ἥρπασε τὸν Φίλιππον) *in Ashdod*,— properly, *was found removed to Ashdod*, viz., by the πνεῦμα

---

[1] Graev. *Lection. Hesiod.* p. 22; Porson, Eurip. *Hippol.* v. 2; Blomfield, Æsch. *Pers.* p. 128. On the other side see Ellendt, *Lex. Soph.* I. 912.

[2] The passages from Greek writers quoted by Schwarz (*Comment.* p. 719 sq.), as exemplifying the use of καλεῖσθαι or ὀνομάζεσθαι in the place of εἶναι, will be set aside at once by any attentive reader. It is really laughable, however, to find *nominari* taken as used for *esse* in Cic. *Flacc.* 27.

[3] See still Pott on 1 C. iv. 2; and compare the commentators on Plut. *Educ.* 13. 5. Against such a view of נִמְצָא see my *Simonis*, p. 575.

κυρίου that carried him away; Rom. vii. 10, εὑρέθη μοι ἡ ἐντολὴ ἡ εἰς ζωὴν αὕτη εἰς θάνατον, *it was found, it proved* (by experience obtained in his own case, ver. 8-10), *that the commandment for life had become for me a commandment for death;* G.ii.17,εἰ δὲ ... εὑρέθημεν καὶ αὐτοὶ ἁμαρτωλοί, *if however we ... were ourselves discovered* (in the sight of both God and men) *to be sinners;* 1 C. iv. 2, 2 C. v. 3, Ph. iii. 9; Rev. xii. 8, οὐδὲ τόπος εὑρέθη αὐτῶν ἔτι ἐν τῷ οὐρανῷ, *their place was no longer found* (was no longer to be shown) *in heaven,*—just as we say, *all traces of them were destroyed* (compare Rev. xvi. 20, xviii. 21, xx. 11); 1 P. ii. 22, οὐδὲ εὑρέθη δόλος ἐν τῷ στόματι αὐτοῦ, *there was not found in his mouth any deceit,*—no deceit could be detected in his words (Rev. xiv. 5). Ph. ii. 7 was correctly translated by Luther.

The parallels which are quoted from Greek authors by Kypke (I. 2), Palairet (p. 198), Schwarz, and others, prove nothing. In Marc. Anton. 9. 9, τὸ συναγωγὸν ἐν τῷ κρείττονι ἐπιτεινόμενον εὑρίσκετο κ.τ.λ., this verb retains its true meaning, *to be found, met with.* Hierocl. *in carm. Pythag.* p. 88 (ed. Lond.), ἀρχὴ μὲν τῶν ἀρετῶν ἡ φρόνησις εὑρίσκεται, means, *prudentia virtutum principium esse deprehenditur;* i.e., *those who reflect find that* etc. Eurip.*Iph.Taur.*777 (766), ποῦ ποτ' ὄνθ' εὑρήμεθα; *ubi tandem esse deprehendimur (deprehensi sumus)?* 'whither are we found to have wandered ? In Joseph.*Antt.* 17. (not 7.) 5. 8, εὑρίσκεσθαι has reference to the persons to whose view Herod was unwilling that so unwelcome a result should be exposed. Compare further Soph. *Trach.* 410, *Aj.* 1114 (1111), Diod. Sic. 3. 39, 19. 94, Athen. I. 331, Schweigh. Philostr. *Apoll.* 7. 11, Alciphr. 1. 30. In Ignat. *ad Rom.* 3, λέγεσθαι χριστιανόν and εὑρίσκεσθαι χριστιανόν stand contrasted with each other.[1]

9. Amongst particles, ὡς in particular has frequently been considered pleonastic: e.g., in 2 P. i. 3, ὡς πάντα ἡμῖν τῆς θείας δυνάμεως αὐτοῦ ... δεδωρημένης. This particle, however, when joined to a participle in the construction of the genitive absolute, gives to the idea expressed by the verb a subjective character,[2]

---

[1] The same remark applies to the Latin *inveniri* (e. g., Cic. *Lœl.* 12. 42), which Schwarz clumsily explains as equivalent to *esse*. Even in Malalas εὑρίσκεσθαι clearly retains in most instances the meaning *inveniri:* e. g., 14. p. 372. So also in Theophanes : see the index in the Bonn edition.

[2] [Not in the construction of the genitive absolute only, see below : see also Ellicott on 1 Th. ii. 4, A. Buttm. p. 307, Jelf 701, Goodwin, *Syntax* p. 219 sq., Grimm, *Clavis* s. v. Compare also Ellicott on E. v. 22, Lightfoot on Ph. ii. 12.]

the character of a conception or of a purpose. Hence the words just quoted from 2 P. i. 3 must be connected with ver. 5, and rendered, *Being assured (remembering) that the divine power has given us all things, strive* etc.,—ἡγούμενοι, ὅτι ἡ θεία δύναμις . . . δεδώρηται (1 C. iv. 18). Compare Xen. *Cyr.* 3. 3. 4, ὡς εἰρήνης οὔσης, *on the ground that there is peace;* 3. 1. 9, ὡς τἀληθῆ ἐροῦντος, *assured that I speak [will speak] the truth.* Compare also 6. 1. 37, *Mem.* 1. 6. 5, Strabo 9. 401, Xen. Eph. 4. 2, Dion. H. III.1925.[1] Greek writers also join this particle with the accusative absolute: e.g., Xen. *Cyr.* 1. 4. 21, *An.* 7. 1. 40. With the same signification ὡς is prefixed to a dative governed by a verb in A. iii. 12, ἢ ἡμῖν τί ἀτενίζετε ὡς ἰδίᾳ δυνάμει . . . πεποιηκόσιν κ.τ.λ. In Rom. xv. 15, ὡς ἐπαναμιμνήσκων, ὡς means *as* (expressing quality): *as one who reminds you* in conformity with the grace of God.

In Rom. ix. 32, ὅτι οὐκ ἐκ πίστεως, ἀλλ' ὡς ἐξ ἔργων νόμου, ἐκ πίστεως indicates the objective rule or norm, ὡς ἐξ ἔργων one that is merely imagined. 2 C. xiii. 7, Jo. vii. 10, and Phil. 14 must also be brought under the head of comparison. And in Mt. vii. 29, ἦν διδάσκων ὡς ἐξουσίαν ἔχων· Jo. i. 14, δόξαν ὡς μονογενοῦς παρὰ πατρός· the meaning simply is, "*as* one who has authority," "*as* of the only-begotten." Even here the particle does not in itself signify *re vera*, though *as regards the sense* this idea is implied by the comparison,—*altogether as, just as,* i. e., *the true, perfect* glory of the Son of God.[2]

As to ὡς ἐπί, A. xvii. 14, it should be observed that ὡς, when joined with a preposition denoting direction (ἐπί, πρός, εἰς), expresses either the definite intention of following a certain direction, or a mere pretence or feint of doing so (Kühner II. 280, Jelf 626. *Obs.* 1). In this passage Beza, Grotius, and others, take the words in the latter sense, but the former is simpler, and suits the context better. As parallel passages compare Thuc. 5. 3, 6. 61, Xen. *An.* 1. 9. 23, 7. 7. 55, Diod. S. 14. 102, Polyb. 5. 70. 3, Arrian, *Al.* 2. 17. 2, 3. 18. 14: see further Ellendt, *Lex. Soph.* II. 1004. So also when ὡς is immediately followed by ὅτι[3] (q. d., "as that"), ὡς properly indicates that the clause with ὅτι expresses the thought of another, a thought which is merely reported, or even feigned: see *e. g. Argum.* of Isocr. *Busir.* p. 520, κατηγόρουν αὐτοῦ ὡς ὅτι καινὰ δαιμόνια εἰσφέρει. So in 2 Th. ii. 2,

---

[1] See Ast, Plat. *Polit.* p. 320, Lösner, *Obs.* p. 483, Lob. Soph. *Aj.* p. 203, Fritz. *Rom.* II. 360.
[2] [See above, p. 151. In A. xvii. 14, quoted below, the reading ἕως ἐπί is strongly supported, and now stands in the best texts.]
[3] The case is different with ὡς ὅτι in Aristot. *Pol.* 3. 7; here ὡς corresponds to οὕτως which precedes.

εἰς τὸ μὴ σαλευθῆναι ὑμᾶς . . . μήτε διὰ λόγου μήτε δι' ἐπιστολῆς . . . ὡς ὅτι ἐνέστηκεν ἡ ἡμέρα τοῦ κυρίου. In 2 Cor. xi. 21 also this meaning may still be recognised (see Meyer *in loc.*[1]); and in 2 C. v. 19, if we regard the sentence as expressing the content of the διακονία τῆς καταλλαγῆς which has been *committed* to them. Ὡς ὅτι occurs in the same sense in older writers, see Xen. *Hell.* 3. 2. 14, Dion. H. III. 1776;[2] as to the later (Theodoret, *Epp.* p. 1294) see Thilo, *Act. Thom.* p. 10 sq., Lehrs, *De Aristarch.* p. 34. A similar example, but decidedly of a pleonastic character, is ὡς ἵνα in Byzantine Greek, Duc. 8. p. 31, 127, Jo. Canan. p. 467, 470 sq.: still more singular is ἵν' ὅπως, Constant. Man. p. 62, Geo. Acropol. p. 62. (On the formula ὡς οἷον, which is found in earlier writers, see Bast, *Ep. Crit.* p. 43, Herm. *Opusc.* I. 219 sq.)

Οὕτως also has been considered redundant in Jo. iv. 6 (Kühnöl) ὁ Ἰησοῦς κεκοπιακὼς ἐκ τῆς ὁδοιπορίας ἐκαθέζετο οὕτως. This adverb, however, is frequently brought in thus after a participle, the idea of which is by this means taken up again,—*wearied from the journey he sat down thus* (sic ut erat, in consequence of this weariness): Xen. *An.* 4. 5. 29, *Cyr.* 5. 2. 6, 7. 5. 71, *Hellen.* 7. 4. 20, Arrian, *Al.* 5. 27. 13, Ellendt, *Arrian* I. 4 (Jelf 696. *Obs.* 5). On οὕτω at the commencement of the apodosis, see § 60. 5.

10. Palairet (p. 305), following Glass, finds a half pleonasm of a particle in A. xiii. 34, μηκέτι μέλλοντα ὑποστρέφειν εἰς διαφθοράν, maintaining that μηκέτι here stands for the simple μή (for Christ *never* went to corruption). But, as was seen by Bengel, the formula εἰς διαφθορὰν ὑποστρέφειν simply denotes (death and) burial. Æl. 12. 52 proves nothing at all; μηκέτι here means *no longer* (as heretofore), just as οὐκέτι in Jo. xxi. 6. —A similar doctrine has been taught by many in regard to οὐκέτι, but with no more reason. In Rom. vii. 17, νυνὶ δὲ οὐκέτι ἐγὼ κατεργάζομαι αὐτό, ἀλλ' ἡ . . . ἁμαρτία, the meaning is, *But now*, when this has been observed by me (ver. 14 sqq.), *it is no longer I that do the evil;* i.e., I can no longer regard *myself* as the primary cause of it (compare ver. 20).[3] Rom. xi. 6, εἰ δὲ χάριτι, οὐκέτι ἐξ ἔργων, *if by grace, then no longer* (does it come) *from works;* i.e., the latter thought is annulled by the former, and it can now be entertained no longer. Rom. xiv. 13, 15, 2 C. i. 23, G. ii. 20, iii. 18, are plain. In Jo. iv. 42 οὐκέτι

---

[1] [See Alford *in loc.* and Ellicott's note on 2 Th. ii. 2. In 2 C. v. 19, Meyer, De W., Stanley, A. Buttmann (p. 358), Waite (*Speak. Comm.* III. 423) take ὡς ὅτι as *because* or *seeing that:* so Winer in ed. 5 (p. 688).]

[2] Separated from each other—ὡς being in the course of the sentence taken up by ὅτι—these particles are found in early writers: see Schoem. *Isæus* p. 294, Jacobs, *Achill. Tat.* p. 566.

[3] [See Gifford's note *in loc.*, and Lightfoot on G. iii. 18.]

is made clear by the preceding verse, in which διὰ τὸν λόγον αὐτοῦ appears as the antithesis to διὰ τὸν λόγον τῆς γυναικός in ver. 39: a distinction is made between two motives for the πιστεύειν,—one earlier, the other later. On Jo. xv. 15 see Lücke.[1]—Xen. *An.* 1. 10. 12 cannot be quoted in confirmation of such a (pleonastic) use of οὐκέτι; still less Xen. Eph. 1. 13 (μηκέτι). In Paus. 8. 28. 2 recent editors read οὐκ ἔστι, but see Siebelis *in loc.* Compare further Lucian, *Parasit.* 12, Sext. Emp. *Math.* 2. 47, Arrian, *Epict.* 3. 22. 86. In Ælian, *Anim.* 4. 3 also, Jacobs admits that οὐκέτι is used for the simple negative *paullo majore cum vi.*

Section LXVI.

CONDENSATION AND RESOLUTION OF SENTENCES (BREVILOQUENCE, CONSTRUCTIO PRÆGNANS, ATTRACTION, ETC.).

1. The inherent tendency which led the Greek to condense his sentences, and by this means give to them a closer consistence and more roundness, shows itself not in poetry only but also in prose, in various idioms of the language, some of which are not unknown to the N. T. writers. All these idioms agree in this particular, that some intermediate member, not absolutely required for the intelligibility of the sentence, is passed over, and the other members drawn together so as to form one compact whole.[2] This breviloquence is akin to ellipsis and yet different from it; in an elliptical sentence the grammatical structure always points to the omission of some particular word, whilst in an example of breviloquence the *lacuna* is concealed by the structure of the sentence.

To breviloquence belong the following cases:—

a. Between a protasis and the apodosis which follows it there is sometimes no direct link of connexion: Rom. xi. 18, εἰ δὲ κατακαυχᾶσαι, οὐ σὺ τὴν ῥίζαν βαστάζεις, ἀλλὰ ἡ ῥίζα σέ, *but if thou* . . . ., then know or consider that *thou dost not* etc. (1 C. xi. 16). To make the structure complete, we must have ἴσθι

---

[1] [Stier's explanation of the apparent discrepancy between this verse and L. xii. 4, Jo. xv. 20, substantially agrees with Lücke's: see *Words of the Lord Jesus,* VI. 292 (Transl.). See also Westcott's note.]
[2] Compare Matth. 634, Döderlein, *De brachylogia sermonis Græci et Latini* (Erlang. 1831). (Jelf 892 sqq.)

(διανοοῦ), ὅτι οὐ σύ κ.τ.λ.: compare Clem. *ad Cor.* 1. 55. The sentence could not be called elliptical unless it ran thus, εἰ δὲ κατακαυχᾶσαι, ὅτι οὐ σύ κ.τ.λ.; in this case ὅτι would point to a word which had been actually left out, such as *know, reflect*. In the same way, *scito* is often suppressed in Latin between protasis and apodosis: see Cic. *Or.* 2. 12. 51. Compare further 1 Jo. v. 9, εἰ τὴν μαρτυρίαν τῶν ἀνθρώπων λαμβάνομεν, ἡ μαρτυρία τοῦ θεοῦ μείζων ἐστίν, we must remember that *the testimony of God* etc.; or, then we must also receive the testimony of God, which indeed etc.; 1 C. ix. 17.[1] Also Mt. ix. 6, ἵνα δὲ εἰδῆτε, ὅτι ἐξουσίαν ἔχει ὁ υἱὸς τοῦ ἀνθρώπου .... (τότε λέγει τῷ παραλυτικῷ) ἐγερθεὶς ἆρόν σου τὴν κλίνην, where the words introduced by the narrator do not enter into the construction of the sentence: *that ye may know ... stand up and take* etc.,—i.e. the sick man shall immediately stand up at my command, I command the sick man, "Stand up etc." Analogous to this are such examples as Demosth. *Cor.* 329 c, ἵνα τοίνυν εἰδῆτε, ὅτι αὐτός μοι μαρτυρεῖ ... λαβὼν ἀνάγνωθι τὸ ψήφισμα ὅλον: these are of frequent occurrence in the orators, see Kypke and Fritzsche *in loc.* Jo. ix. 36, καὶ τίς ἐστι, κύριε, ἵνα πιστεύσω εἰς αὐτόν; scil. *I wish to know this, in order that* etc. Compare Jo. i. 22.

A breviloquence similar to that in clauses with ἵνα obtains where an event is referred back to predictions of the prophets, by means of ἀλλ' ἵνα, as in Jo. xv. 25, xiii. 18, Mk. xiv. 49; compare 1 C. ii. 9. In these passages, however, the missing member may commonly be supplied before ἵνα from the previous context: see Fritz. *Matt.* Exc. 1, p. 841. [§ 43. 5.]

b. To a general predicate is directly attached a special verb (with its predicate), the verb which would suit the general predicate being passed over. Ph. iii. 13 sq., ἐγὼ ἐμαυτὸν οὐ λογίζομαι κατειληφέναι, ἓν δέ, τὰ μὲν ὀπίσω ἐπιλανθανόμενος, τοῖς δέ ... κατὰ σκοπὸν διώκω κ.τ.λ.; instead of ἓν δὲ ποιῶ, κατὰ σκοπὸν διώκω. Compare Liv. 35. 11: in eos se impetum facturum et nihil prius (facturum), quam flammam tectis injecturum. 2 C. vi. 13, τὴν δὲ αὐτὴν ἀντιμισθίαν ... πλατύνθητε καὶ ὑμεῖς; instead of τὸ δὲ αὐτὸ ὅ ἐστιν ἀντιμισθία κ.τ.λ. See Fritz. *Diss. in* 2. *Cor.* II. 115; on the accusative, however, compare Herm. *Opusc.* I.

---

[1] In Rom. ii. 14 however (Fritzsche) protasis and apodosis hang together without any difficulty. [Fritzsche (I. 117) had maintained that δῆλον ὅτι was suppressed. On 1 C. ix. 17 see Meyer and Alford.]

168 sq.¹ Similarly in Jude 5, ὅτι ὁ κύριος λαὸν ἐκ γῆς Αἰγύπτου σώσας τὸ δεύτερον τοὺς μὴ πιστεύσαντας ἀπώλεσεν. Here the verb connected with τὸ δεύτερον should properly have been οὐκ ἔσωσε (ἀλλά κ.τ.λ.): the Lord, after having saved, *the second time* (when they needed his helping grace) refused them his saving grace and left .... to destruction. Compare further Rom. xi. 23, δυνατός ἐστιν ὁ θεὸς πάλιν ἐγκεντρίσαι αὐτούς. By αὐτοί are meant those that grew on the stock κατὰ φύσιν; and hence cannot be *a second time* grafted on the stock. The strict expression would be: to bring them *a second time* into union with the stock, viz., by being grafted in.

In Col. iii. 25, however, ὁ ἀδικῶν κομιεῖται ὃ ἠδίκησε, if judged by Greek idiom, is hardly an example of brachylogy. This expression, in accordance with the meaning of κομίζεσθαι, resembles our own, *he will reap the wrong he has done:* it is not the wrong itself that he will receive, but the fruits of it, the recompense for it,—the wrong in the form of punishment. Compare E. vi. 8. We have a similar example in Jo. xii. 5, διὰ τί τοῦτο τὸ μύρον οὐκ ἐπράθη ... καὶ ἐδόθη πτωχοῖς, *and* (the proceeds) *given to the poor;*—properly, and (in the form of the money obtained by the sale of it) given to the poor. So also in 1 C. xv. 37.

c. A. i. 1, ὧν ἤρξατο ὁ Ἰησοῦς ποιεῖν τε καὶ διδάσκειν ἄχρι ἧς ἡμέρας κ.τ.λ.: i.e., *what Jesus began to do and to teach,* and continued to do and to teach *until the day* (ver. 22?). Similar to this is L. xxiii. 5, διδάσκων καθ' ὅλης τῆς Ἰουδαίας, ἀρξάμενος ἀπὸ τῆς Γαλιλαίας ἕως ὧδε, *beginning from Galilee and continuing up to this place;* also Mt. xx. 8, Jo. viii. 9, Strabo 12. 541. The construction proposed by Fritzsche for the latter class of passages—διδάσκων ἕως ὧδε, ἀρξάμενος ἀπὸ τῆς Γαλιλαίας² (Lucian, *Somn.* 15)—is too artificial. The assertion of Valckenaer and Kühnöl that in A. i. 1 ἄρχεσθαι is pleonastic, is a mere subterfuge to avoid the difficulty.

2. The following forms of brachylogy are of peculiarly frequent occurrence, and were noticed by earlier grammarians.

d. The so-called *constructio prægnans*, in which a preposition

---

¹ [Hermann, *l. c.* is speaking of the construction πλήττομαι πόδα, and of the accusatives ἀκμήν, ἀρχήν (see above, p. 581).—Meyer would bring this passage under § 63. 2. d, supposing Paul to have changed the construction after writing (the object) τὴν αὐτὴν ἀντιμισθίαν. It is surely simpler to take the accusative as the "quantitative object" (p. 285). Compare De W. *in loc.,* A. Buttm. p. 189 sq.]
² [Similarly Meyer (see his note on Mt. xx. 8): A. Buttm. (p. 374), Bleek and others agree with Winer. On A. i. 1 see Alford.]

is joined to a verb which includes another verb as its consequent. 2 Tim. iv. 18, σώσει εἰς τὴν βασιλείαν, *he will save me into his kingdom*, i. e., *will save me*, removing me *into* etc.; A. xxiii. 24, 1 P. iii. 20 (Her. 7. 230, Xen. *An.* 2. 3. 11, Polyb. 8. 11, Lucian, *Asin.* 56, al.[1]); 2 Tim. ii. 26, ἀνανήψωσιν ἐκ τῆς τοῦ διαβόλου παγίδος· Mt. v. 22, ἔνοχος ἔσται εἰς τὴν γέενναν (§ 31. 5); Rom. viii. 21, ἐλευθερωθήσεται ἀπὸ τῆς δουλείας τῆς φθορᾶς εἰς τὴν ἐλευθερίαν τῆς δόξης κ.τ.λ. (see Fritzsche *in loc.*); A. v. 37, ἀπέστησε λαὸν ἱκανὸν ὀπίσω αὐτοῦ· xx. 30, 2 C. xi. 3, μήπως . . . φθαρῇ τὰ νοήματα ὑμῶν ἀπὸ τῆς ἁπλότητος· A. viii. 40, Φίλιππος εὑρέθη εἰς Ἄζωτον (Rom. vii. 10). See further A. xxiii. 11, L. iv. 38, xviii. 3, G. v. 4, Rom. vii. 2, ix. 3 (xv. 28), xvi. 20, 1 C. xii. 13, xv. 54, 2 C. x. 5, H. ii. 3, x. 22, E. ii. 15, 1 Tim. v. 15, 1 P. iii. 10. According to some H. v. 7 also falls under this head, see Bleek[2] *in loc.* (Ps. xxii. 22 in the Hebrew, Ps. cxvii. 5 in the LXX): a more certain example is Mk. vii. 4.[3] This abbreviated structure is frequently met with in Greek prose:[4] as to Hebrew see Ewald p. 620. Such phrases as κρύπτειν or κλείειν τι ἀπό τινος (1 Jo. iii. 17), μετανοεῖν ἀπὸ τῆς κακίας (A. viii. 22) or ἐκ τῶν ἔργων, etc. (Rev. ix. 20 sq., xvi. 11), ἀποβλέπειν and ἀφορᾶν εἰς (H. xi. 26, xii. 2), παραλαμβάνειν εἰς (Mt. iv. 5), ἀσφαλίζεσθαι τοὺς πόδας εἰς τὸ ξύλον (A. xvi. 24), συγκλείειν τοὺς πάντας εἰς ἀπείθειαν (Rom. xi. 32), arise in like manner out of a pregnancy of expression, which however is hardly felt by us (conceal *from*, shut up *in*). On βαπτίζειν τινὰ εἴς τινα see Fritz. *Rom.* I. 359. On the

---

[1] Compare my *Comment. 5. de verbis compositis*, p. 9. [Winer here notices the frequency with which the *constructio prægnans* occurs in the N. T. in combination with compounds of διά. In 1 P. iii. 20 he takes διά (ὕδατος) as *through*, not as used in an instrumental sense. On G. v. 4 (Rom. vii. 2) see Ellicott.]

[2] [Bleek does not himself take this view of the passage. See Alford's note.]

[3] This passage must be rendered: (coming) *from the market* (Arrian, *Epict.* 3. 19. 5, ἂν μὴ εὕρωμεν φαγεῖν ἐκ βαλανείου), *except they have washed themselves they eat nothing*. The objection to our referring βαπτίσωνται to the *articles of food* (so Kühnöl) does not lie so much in the usage of the language—for βαπτισμός, derived from βαπτίζειν, is evidently applied to *things* in ver. 4,—or in the use of the middle voice (for this might mean *wash for themselves*), as in the circumstance that we should thus introduce a very ordinary thought, and one which would not be looked for in this connexion. To wash articles of food which had been purchased was certainly not a mere precept of Pharisaism, but was a proceeding required by the nature of the case and by the spirit of the Mosaic laws of purification.

[4] Compare Markland, Eurip. *Suppl.* 1205; Stallb. Plat. *Euthyphr.* p. 60; Poppo, *Thuc.* I. i. 292 sq. [Jelf 645 sq., Green p. 209 sq.: for Hebrew, Gesen. p. 224 (Trans.), Ewald, *Lehrb.* p. 700, Kalisch I. 311.]

general subject compare further Fritz. *Mark*, p. 322; also § 50. 4.

e. Zeugma (Synizesis): when two nouns are construed with one verb, though only one of them—the first—directly suits the verb.[1] 1 C. iii. 2, γάλα ὑμᾶς ἐπότισα, οὐ βρῶμα: from ἐπότισα, which suits γάλα only, we must apply the verb *feed* for βρῶμα (compare *Act. Apocr.* p. 60). L. i. 64, ἀνεῴχθη τὸ στόμα αὐτοῦ ... καὶ ἡ γλῶσσα αὐτοῦ: where, properly speaking, ἐλύθη—which is found in some few authorities—must be supplied with γλῶσσα (compare Mk. vii. 35); see Raphel *in loc.*[2] In 1 Tim. iv. 3, κωλυόντων γαμεῖν, ἀπέχεσθαι βρωμάτων, we must supply before the latter infinitive κελευόντων (or, with a scholiast in Matthæi, εἰσηγουμένων) from κωλυόντων, which is equivalent to κελευόντων μή.[3] Another example is 1 C. xiv. 34 [*Rec.*]. Compare Soph. *Œd. R.* 242, Eurip. *Phœn.* 1223, Plat. *Rep.* 2. 374 b (yet see Stallbaum *in loc.*), *Protag.* 327 c, Demosth. *Cor.* § 55 (see Dissen *in loc.*), Arrian, *Al.* 7. 15. 5. So in Greek authors we have sometimes to supply from the first verb a verb of directly opposite meaning, for the second member of the sentence: see Kühner II. 604, Stallb. Plat. *Cratyl.* p. 169 (Jelf 895. 9). Some have introduced this idiom into Ja. i. 9, 10, supplying with ὁ δὲ πλούσιος the verb ταπεινούσθω (or αἰσχυνέσθω):[4] this however is unnecessary, and the thought is finer if καυχάσθω is carried on to the second clause,—see my *Observationes in ep. Jacobi*, p. 6. On 1 C. vii. 19 see above, § 64. 1.[5] (Jelf 895, Don. p. 610.)

f. In comparisons:[6] i. e., with the comparative degree (compare

---

[1] Compare Lobeck, Soph. *Ajax* p. 429 sq.

[2] That ἀνοίγειν γλῶσσαν can be used in plain prose, is not proved by the examples adduced by Segaar *in loc.*—We may remark in passing that the zeugma usually quoted from Her. 4. 106 disappears in Schweighäuser's edition, in which we read ἐσθῆτα δὲ φορέουσι . . . γλῶσσαν δὲ ἰδίην ἔχουσι. As however no MS. has ἔχουσι, later editors have rightly omitted the word.

[3] [See Westcott and Hort's *Appendix*, p. 134.—Lünemann adds 1 Th. ii. 8, with τὰς ἑαυτῶν ψυχάς supplying δοῦναι from the compound verb μεταδοῦναι.]

[4] The passage quoted by Hottinger *in loc.* from Plat. *Rep.* 2. 367 d runs thus in the recent editions, on MS. authority: τοῦτ' οὖν αὐτὸ ἐπαίνεσον δικαιοσύνης, ὃ αὐτὴ δι' αὑτὴν τὸν ἔχοντα ὀνίνησι καὶ ἀδικία βλάπτει [instead of . . . ὀνίνησι· καὶ ἀδικίαν, ὃ βλάπτει.] Hence it is no longer a parallel.

[5] For examples of zeugma in Greek and Latin writers see D'Orville, *Charit.* p. 440 sq.; Wyttenb. Plut. *Moral.* I. 189 sq. (ed. Lips.); Schæf. *Dion.* p. 105; Engelhardt, Plat. *Apol.* p. 221; Bremi, *ad Lys.* exc. 3; Volc. Fritzsche, *Quæst. Lucian.* p. 132; Funkhänel, Demosth. *Androt.* p. 70; Hand, *Lat. Styl* p. 424 sq.

[6] Jacobs, *Anthol. Pal.* III. 63, 494, *Achill. Tat.* p. 747; Fritz. *Mark*, p. 147.

§ 35. 5), and in combinations with adjectives expressing *likeness*, e.g., Rev. xiii. 11, εἶχε κέρατα δύο ὅμοια ἀρνίῳ (properly ἀρνίου κέρασι),[1] as in *Iliad* 17. 51, κόμαι Χαρίτεσσιν ὁμοῖαι· Wisd. ii. 15, vii. 3 ; 2 P. i. 1, τοῖς ἰσότιμον ἡμῖν λαχοῦσι πίστιν (for ἰσότιμον τῇ ἡμῶν πίστει), Jude 7. Compare further Xen. *Cyr.* 5. 1. 3, ὁμοίαν ταῖς δούλαις εἶχε τὴν ἐσθῆτα· 6. 1. 50, ἅρματα ἐκ τοῦ ἱππικοῦ τοῦ ἑαυτοῦ ὅμοια ἐκείνῳ (i.e., τοῖς ἐκείνου), *Iliad* 1. 163, οὐ μέν σοί ποτε ἶσον ἔχω γέρας (i.e., ἶσον τῷ σῷ), Arrian, *Epict.* 1. 14. 11 (Matth. 453, Jelf 781. *d*). This breviloquence in comparison is used by Greek writers with much greater variety of form : see Xen. *Cyr.* 5. 4. 6, 2. 1. 15, *Hier.* 1. 38, Isocr. *Evag.* c. 14, Diod. S. 3. 18, Æl. *Anim.* 4. 21, Dion. H. I. 111.[2] Under this head will also come 1 Jo. iii. 11 sq., αὕτη ἡ ἀγγελία ἣν ἠκούσατε ἀπ' ἀρχῆς, ἵνα ἀγαπῶμεν ἀλλήλους· οὐ καθὼς Κάϊν ἐκ τοῦ πονηροῦ ἦν κ.τ.λ. Here there is, strictly speaking, nothing to be supplied (ὦμεν or ποιῶμεν would not suit οὐ), but the comparison is negligently expressed. The reader easily adjusts the clauses for himself : *that we should love one another,—not as Cain was of the wicked one* . . . will or may it be with us.[3]

We might bring under this head L. xiii. 1, ὧν τὸ αἷμα Πιλᾶτος ἔμιξε μετὰ τῶν θυσιῶν αὐτῶν (for μετὰ τοῦ αἵματος τῶν θυσιῶν?); but this explanation is not necessary, see Meyer.

3. g. It may also be considered a kind of breviloquence when a word which should have formed a sentence of its own is simply appended (or even prefixed) to a sentence, as an apposition: e. g., 2 Tim. ii. 14, Rom. viii. 3, al. (see § 59. 9), and—according to the ordinary reading[4]—Mk. vii. 19, εἰς τὸν ἀφεδρῶνα ἐκπο-

---

[1] Rev. ix. 10 probably should not come in here : the comparison of the tails with scorpions does not seem alien to the style of the poet, and indeed has been pointed out elsewhere : see ver. 19, and compare Züllig *in loc.*

[2] See Wyttenb. Plut. *Mor.* I. 480 sq. ; Schæf. *Apollon. Rhod.* II. 164, *Melet.* p. 57, *Demosth.* III. 463 ; Stallb. Plat. *Protag.* p. 153, *Rep.* I. 134 ; also Heinichen, *Euseb.* II. 154.

[3] Compare Demosth. *Mid.* p. 415 a, οὐ γὰρ ἐκ πολιτικῆς αἰτίας, οὐδ' ὥσπερ Ἀριστοφῶν ἀποδοὺς τοὺς στεφάνους ἔλυσε τὴν προβολήν, *not on account of a political offence, and not as Aristophon quashed the impeachment;* i.e., and not acting in the manner in which Aristophon quashed etc. Against Reiske, who would here insert ὅς in the text, see Spalding *in loc.*

[4] [Καθαρίζων now stands in the best texts. Many regard this word as a loose apposition to ἀφεδρῶνα (§ 59. 8. b) : see Meyer, Green, *Crit. Notes* p. 38, A. Buttm. p. 79. But an ancient and very probable interpretation connects καθαρίζων with λέγει in ver. 18 : *He saith to them,* "*Are ye also* . . . *?*"—*making all meats clean ;* i.e., by this saying pronouncing all meats henceforth clean.]

ρεύεται, καθαρίζον πάντα τὰ βρώματα. Akin to this is the proleptic use of the *adjectiva effectus* (in a kind of apposition), as in Soph. *Œd. Col.* 1202, τῶν σῶν ἀδέρκτων ὀμμάτων τητώμενος, for ὥςτε γενέσθαι ἄδερκτα: this idiom is not confined to the poets and orators,[1] but also occurs in ordinary prose [2] (Don. p. 534, Jelf 439. 2). As N. T. examples might be quoted Mt. xii. 13, (ἡ χεὶρ) ἀπεκατεστάθη ὑγιής·[3] Rom. i. 21, ἐσκοτίσθη ἡ ἀσύνετος αὐτῶν καρδία· 2 C. iv. 4, θεὸς ἐτύφλωσε τὰ νοήματα τῶν ἀπίστων· 1 Th. iii. 13, στηρίξαι τὰς καρδίας ὑμῶν ἀμέμπτους· Ph. iii. 21, μετασχηματίσει τὸ σῶμα . . . ἡμῶν σύμμορφον τῷ σώματι (where after ἡμῶν some MSS. add εἰς τὸ γενέσθαι αὐτό), 1 C. i. 8. But in Rom. i. 21 and 2 C. iv. 4, at all events, this explanation is hardly admissible. In the former passage (as was seen by Flatt) less is implied by ἀσύνετος (which has reference to ἐματαιώθησαν which precedes) than by σκοτίζεσθαι. In 2 C. iv. 4, Paul probably regards the illumination as proceeding from a general faith in Christ; because they did not turn to Christ, but at once rejected him, the illumination did not become theirs.

By the side of the examples first quoted should be placed L. xxiv. 46 sq., ἔδει παθεῖν τὸν Χριστόν . . . καὶ ἀναστῆναι . . . καὶ κηρυχθῆναι ἐπὶ τῷ ὀνόματι αὐτοῦ μετάνοιαν . . . . ἀρξάμενον ἀπὸ Ἱερουσαλήμ. Here, as is often the case with ἐξόν, παρόν (Vig. p. 329, Don. p. 463, Jelf 700. 2), the participle is used absolutely and impersonally,—*a beginning being made (so as to begin)*; compare Her. 3. 91, ἀπὸ δὲ Ποσειδηΐου πόλιος . . . ἀρξάμενον ἀπὸ ταύτης μέχρι Αἰγύπτου . . . πεντήκοντα καὶ τριηκόσια τάλαντα φόρος ἦν.[4]

---

[1] Schæf. *Demosth.* I. 239, V. 641; Erfurdt, Soph. *Antig.* 786; Lob. Soph. *Ajax* p. 278; Heller, Soph. *Œd. Col.* p. 522 sqq.
[2] Ast, Plat. *Legg.* p. 150 sq., Plat. *Polit.* p. 592; Volc. Fritzsche, *Quæst. Lucian.* p. 39, 57; Weber, *Demosth.* p. 497. See in general Meyer, *De epithetis ornantibus,* p. 24; and Ahlemeyer, *Pr. über die dichterische Prolepsis des Adjectivs* (Paderborn, 1827).
[3] Bornem. *Schol.* p. 39; Stallb. Plat. *Protag.* p. 76; Winer, *Simonis* p. 262.
[4] See J. L. Schlosser, *Vindicatio N. T. locorum, quorum integritatem J. Marclandus suspectam reddere non dubitavit* (Hamb. 1732), p. 18 sq. This English critic (ad *Lysiam* p. 653, Vol. VI., Reiske) proposed to read ἀρξαμένων. [Lachmann placed this reading in his margin: Tischendorf, Tregelles, Alford, Westcott and Hort, read ἀρξάμενοι. That Winer regards ἀρξάμενοι as *masculine* (as Bleek supposes, *Syn. Erkl.* II. 516) is not probable, as he refers to the similar use of ἐξόν, etc.: in § 32. 7 his language is less clear. (In Her. 3. 91 Blakesley considers ἀρξάμενον the masculine accusative: but see Krüger *in loc.*, Jelf 700. 2.) With the reading ἀρξάμενοι A. Buttmann (p. 375) would connect the participle with ἔθνη; see Jelf 696. *Obs.* 1, and for the irregularity in case and gender § 59. 8. b, 21. 2: this however would be very harsh. Others assume an anacoluthon, the participle being used as if the personal construction with an active verb had

There is a kind of breviloquence in A. i. 21, ἐν παντὶ χρόνῳ, (ἐν) ᾧ εἰσῆλθε καὶ ἐξῆλθεν ἐφ' ἡμᾶς ὁ κύριος Ἰησοῦς, instead of εἰσῆλθεν ἐφ' ἡμᾶς καὶ ἐξῆλθεν ἀφ' ἡμῶν. Such diffuseness as this, however, would not be tolerated by any Greek writer: compare Eurip. *Phœn.* 536, ἐς οἴκους εἰσῆλθε καὶ ἐξῆλθ' (though here, it is true, the arrangement of the words is simpler), and Valckenaer *in loc.* See also Poppo, *Thuc.* I. i. 289.

Rem. A. x. 39, καὶ ἡμεῖς μάρτυρες πάντων ὧν ἐποίησεν . . ., ὃν καὶ (the reading of the best authorities) ἀνεῖλον κρεμάσαντες ἐπὶ ξύλου, may be an example of brachylogy,—the sense being, *we are witnesses of all that he did, also of the fact that they put him to death.* This explanation however is not necessary. But whatever view may be taken of the passage, καί certainly has here no other meaning than *etiam* (adeo); *tamen* (Kühnöl) would be a precarious rendering in this connexion. It is only when judged of by the idiom of our own language that L. xxiv. 21, τρίτην ταύτην ἡμέραν ἄγει σήμερον (compare 2 C. xii. 14, xiii. 1), can appear an example of brachylogy: in Greek the numeral is simply looked upon as a predicative adjunct. Compare Achill. Tat. 7. 11 (Jac.), τρίτην ταύτην ἡμέραν γέγονεν ἀφανής· Dion. Hal. IV. 2095, τριακοστὸν ἔτος τοῦτο ἀνεχόμεθα κ.τ.λ.; see Bornem. *Luc.* p. 161, and on analogous cases Krüger p. 269 (Don. p. 352, Jelf 453).—Nor must we have recourse to brachylogy in 1 C. i. 12, ἕκαστος ὑμῶν λέγει· ἐγὼ μέν εἰμι Παύλου, ἐγὼ δὲ Ἀπολλώ, ἐγὼ δὲ Κηφᾶ, ἐγὼ δὲ Χριστοῦ. In these four sayings Paul intends to include *all* the declarations of religious partisanship which were current in the church: *every one* uses some one of the following formulas. Compare 1 C. xiv. 26. Lastly, 1 C. vi. 11, ταῦτά τινες ἦτε, rightly understood, has nothing of the nature of brachylogy: see § 58. 3, [§ 59. 7].

4. A Greek, however, possessed the means of binding together still more closely his sentences and parts of sentences, and thus giving roundness and condensation to his language: this means is commonly known as *attraction* (Buttm. *Gr.* § 138. 1). It is only from one point of view that attraction can be regarded as a species of brachylogy. As used by recent grammarians, the name is given to those cases in which two members (especially clauses) which are logically (in sense) connected with each other are also bound together grammatically (formally), by bringing a word (or group of words) which properly belongs to one member alone into grammatical relation to the other, and thus attaching it to both members jointly,—to one logically, to the other grammatically. Thus in " urbem, quam statuo, vestra est," *urbs* properly belongs to *vestra est* (for there are two sentences,—*urbs vestra est* and *quam statuo*), but is *attracted* by the relative clause,

---

preceded. But it is not improbable that the sentence should end at ἔθνη, and that ἀρξάμενοι belongs to ὑμεῖς (Westcott and Hort in margin).]

SECT. LXVI.] CONDENSATION AND RESOLUTION OF SENTENCES. 781

and brought into its construction; so that now it belongs at once to both clauses,—logically to *vestra est*, grammatically to *quam statuo*. See Herm. *Vig.* p. 891 sqq.;[1] but especially G. T. A. Krüger, *Gramm. Untersuch.* 3. Theil. The great variety of form under which attraction occurs in Greek authors is not found in the N. T.: even here, however, we meet with several examples of this figure which were not recognised as such by earlier commentators, and which at all events threw many an obstacle in the way of the interpretation of the N. T.[2]

5. Attraction may generally, so far as it affects the connexion of the sentences, be divided into three principal cases. Either (1) something is attracted from the dependent by the principal sentence; or (2) the principal sentence has given up something to the dependent sentence; or (3) two sentences predicated of the same subject are contracted into one. The first case comprises the following constructions:—

a. 1 C. xvi. 15, οἴδατε τὴν οἰκίαν Στεφανᾶ ὅτι ἐστὶν ἀπαρχὴ τῆς Ἀχαΐας· A. ix. 20, ἐκήρυσσεν τὸν Ἰησοῦν ὅτι οὗτός ἐστιν ὁ υἱὸς τοῦ θεοῦ. This construction occurs very frequently where an objective sentence follows a verb of *perceiving, knowing, showing* or *declaring*: Mk. xi. 32, xii. 34, A. iii. 10, iv. 13, xiii. 32, xv. 36, xvi. 3 [*Rec.*], xxvi. 5, 1 C. iii. 20, xiv. 37, 2 C. xii. 3 sq. 1 Th. ii. 1, 2 Th. ii. 4, Jo. iv. 35, v. 42, vii. 27, viii. 54 (Arrian, *Al.* 7. 15. 7), xi. 31, Rev. xvii. 8 (Gen. i. 4, 1 Macc. xiii. 53, 2 Macc. ii. 1, 1 K. v. 3, xi. 28, al.). Also where an interrogative clause follows: L. iv. 34, οἶδά σε, τίς εἶ· Mk. i. 24;[3] L. xix. 3, ἰδεῖν τὸν Ἰησοῦν, τίς ἐστι·[4] Jo. vii. 27, τοῦτον οἴδαμεν, πόθεν ἐστίν (Kypke *in loc.*); A. xv. 36, ἐπισκεψώμεθα τοὺς ἀδελφούς . . . πῶς ἔχουσι· 2 C. xiii. 5, Jo. xiii. 28 (Achill. Tat. 1. 19, Theophr. *Char.* 21, Philostr. *Ep.* 64). The same anticipation is found with sentences introduced by ἵνα, μή, etc.: Col. iv. 17, βλέπε τὴν διακονίαν, ἵνα αὐτὴν πληροῖς· Rev. iii. 9, ποιήσω αὐτούς, ἵνα ἥξωσι· G. vi. 1, σκοπῶν σεαυτόν, μὴ καὶ σὺ

---

[1] Hermann *l. c.*: Est attractio in eo posita, si quid eo, quod simul ad duas orationis partes refertur, ad quarum alteram non recte refertur, ambas in unam conjungit. Compare Krüger *l.c.*, p. 39 sq. Many make a distinction between assimilation and attraction: compare Hand, *Lat. Styl* p. 376 sqq.
[2] See *e. g.* Bowyer, *Conject.* I. 147.
[3] See Heupel and Fritzsche *in loc.*; Boissonade, Philostr. *Epp.* p. 143.
[4] Compare Schæfer, *Ind. Æsop.* p. 127.—1 C. xv. 2 does not come in here: see § 61. 7.

πειρασθῇς· iv. 11,[1] φοβοῦμαι ὑμᾶς, μήπως εἰκῆ κεκοπίακα εἰς ὑμᾶς. Compare Diod. S. 4. 40, τὸν ἀδελφὸν εὐλαβεῖσθαι, μήποτε ... ἐπίθηται τῇ βασιλείᾳ· Soph. Œd. R. 760, δέδοικ' ἐμαυτόν ... μὴ πόλλ' ἄγαν εἰρημέν' ᾖ μοι· Thuc. 3. 53; Ignat. ad Rom. 1, φοβοῦμαι τὴν ὑμῶν ἀγάπην, μὴ αὐτή με ἀδικήσῃ· Varro, R. R. 3. 10. 6, Cæs. B. Gall. 1. 39 ; compare [G. T. A.] Krüger p. 164 sq. Similarly with a passive verb: 1 C. xv. 12, Χριστὸς κηρύσσεται ὅτι ἐκ νεκρῶν ἐγήγερται.[2] (Jelf 898. 2.)

b. Rom. i. 22, φάσκοντες εἶναι σοφοὶ ἐμωράνθησαν· 2 P. ii. 21, κρεῖττον ἦν αὐτοῖς μὴ ἐπεγνωκέναι ... ἢ ἐπιγνοῦσιν ἐπιστρέψαι κ.τ.λ.: see § 44. 2, Kühner II. 355. This attraction is neglected in A. xv. 22, 25 [Rec.] (Elsner, Obs. I. 428 sq.), xxvi. 20, H. ii. 10, 1 P. iv. 3, L. i. 74. Compare Bremi, Æschin. Fals. Leg. p. 196.

c. A. xvi. 34, ἠγαλλιάσατο πεπιστευκὼς τῷ θεῷ· 1 C. xiv. 18 v.l., εὐχαριστῶ τῷ θεῷ πάντων ὑμῶν μᾶλλον γλώσσαις λαλῶν: see § 45. 4.

d. The simplest kind of attraction—of very frequent occurrence—is that by which the relative, instead of being adapted in case (the accusative) to the verb of the relative sentence, is made to correspond to the verb of the principal sentence, and consequently stands in the case governed by this verb: Jo. ii. 22, ἐπίστευσαν τῷ λόγῳ ᾧ εἶπεν (instead of ὅν). See § 24. 1.

e. Lastly, under this head would come 1 P. iv. 3, ἀρκετὸς ὁ παρεληλυθὼς χρόνος τὸ βούλημα τῶν ἐθνῶν κατειργάσθαι, if we were (with Wahl) to resolve this sentence into ἀρκετόν ἐστιν ἡμῖν, τὸν χρόνον κατειργάσθαι: compare Buttm. § 138. 1, 7 (Don. p. 403, Jelf 677. 1). But this subtlety is not needed.

On the other hand, it cannot be said that attraction is

---

[1] [It is doubtful whether Col. iv. 17, G. vi. 1, iv. 11, should come in here. In Col. iv. 17 and G. iv. 11 the subject of the dependent verb is not identical with the object of the principal verb (see Ellicott and Alford on G. iv. 11): A. xiii. 32 and Jo. xiii. 28 are similar. See however Soph. Œd. R. l. c., and the examples quoted by Krüger, Sprachl. § 61. 6. 6, and Riddell, Plat. Apol. p. 207.—A. xiii. 32, ix. 20, iii. 10 (Col. iv. 17, G. vi. 1), are distinguished from the other examples quoted above by the presence of the pronoun in the dependent clause : compare Krüger l. c.—In 2 Macc. ii. 1 the principal verb is passive.]

[2] See in general J. A. Lehmann, De Grœcæ linguæ transpositione (Danz. 1832), p. 18 sqq.; Schwarz, De solœc. p. 97. We cannot properly assume an "anticipation" in these cases, unless the writer, when he expresses the subject, has in his mind the predication which follows in the dependent sentence, as connected with the subject. On the other hand, especially where parenthetical clauses intervene, e.g., A. xv. 36, ἐπισκεψώμεθα τοὺς ἀδελφούς may have been all that the speaker at first intended to say ; and πῶς ἔχουσιν may have been added merely for the sake of further explanation.—As to Hebrew see Gesen. Lehrg. p. 854.

neglected in Ph. i. 7, δίκαιον ἐμοὶ τοῦτο φρονεῖν being said instead of δίκαιός εἰμι τοῦτο φρονεῖν (Matth. p. 756); for Greek writers also use δίκαιόν ἐστι impersonally with an infinitive, though less inclined to join with it a personal dative than to attach the personal word to the infinitive and place it in the accusative case (Her. 1. 39). The former construction is simpler in conception and more natural.

(2) The secondary clause exerts an attraction on the principal.—The simplest case is that in which the relative pronoun, which properly takes its number and gender from its antecedent in the principal clause,—is made to agree with the noun in the subordinate clause: 1 Tim. iii. 15, ἐν οἴκῳ θεοῦ, ἥτις ἐστὶν ἐκκλησία· Rom. ix. 24, (σκεύη ἐλέους) οὓς καὶ ἐκάλεσεν ἡμᾶς [§ 24. 3]. This attraction is carried farther in the following cases :—

a. 1 C. x. 16, τὸν ἄρτον ὃν κλῶμεν οὐχὶ κοινωνία τοῦ σώματος· Jo. vi. 29, ἵνα πιστεύσητε εἰς ὃν ἀπέστειλεν ἐκεῖνος (see § 24. 2); or Mk. vi. 16, ὃν ἐγὼ ἀπεκεφάλισα Ἰωάννην, οὗτός ἐστιν (see § 24. 2),—compare Mt. vii. 9.

b. 1 Jo. ii. 25, αὕτη ἐστὶν ἡ ἐπαγγελία, ἣν αὐτὸς ἐπηγγείλατο ἡμῖν τὴν ζωὴν τὴν αἰώνιον,—instead of ἡ ζωή, in apposition to ἐπαγγελία (see § 59. 7); Phil. 10 sq.; Rom. iv. 24, ἀλλὰ καὶ δι' ἡμᾶς, οἷς μέλλει λογίζεσθαι τοῖς πιστεύουσιν κ.τ.λ. (Rev. xvii. 8 *v.l.* ?). Luther has taken Ph. iii. 18 in this way. Compare further Fritz. *Mark*, p. 328, Stallb. Plat. *Rep.* I. 216, II. 146, Kühner II. 515 (Jelf 824. II. 4).

c. Mt. x. 25, ἀρκετὸν τῷ μαθητῇ, ἵνα γένηται ὡς ὁ διδάσκαλος αὐτοῦ, καὶ ὁ δοῦλος ὡς ὁ κύριος αὐτοῦ ; instead of καὶ τῷ δούλῳ (ἵνα γένηται) ὡς ὁ κύριος κ.τ.λ.

d. Rom. iii. 8, τί ἔτι κἀγὼ ὡς ἁμαρτωλὸς κρίνομαι ; καὶ μή, καθὼς βλασφημούμεθα καὶ καθώς φασί τινες ἡμᾶς λέγειν, ὅτι ποιήσωμεν τὰ κακά, ἵνα κ.τ.λ. Here the apostle should have made the ποιεῖν κακά κ.τ.λ. dependent upon καὶ μή, but, led away by the parenthesis, joins it to λέγειν in the *oratio recta*. This is not an uncommon case in Greek writers, especially when a relative clause is introduced. See Herm. *Vig.* p. 745, Krüger, *Untersuch.* p. 457 sqq., Dissen, Dem. *Cor.* 177 ; as to Latin, see Beier, Cic. *Off.* I. 50 sq., Grotefend, *Ausf. Gr.* p. 462 sq.[1]

(3) Two successive interrogative sentences, predicated of the

---

[1] [Similar examples are noticed by Jelf (898. 4), but are differently explained. Kühner's remarks (II. 1085 : ed. 2) substantially agree with those in the text.]

same subject, are fused into one: A. xi. 17, ἐγὼ δὲ τίς ἤμην δυνατὸς κωλῦσαι τὸν θεόν; *but who was I? was I powerful enough to hinder?* Compare Cic. *Nat. D.* 1. 27. 78: quid censes, si ratio esset in belluis, non suo quasque generi plurimum tributuras fuisse ? L. xix. 15, τίς τί διεπραγματεύσατο; Mk. xv. 24, τίς τί ἄρῃ;[1] For other examples of interrogative sentences interwoven by attraction, see Kühner II. 588 sq. [II. 1021 sq., ed. 2; Jelf 883.] Interrogative and relative sentences are blended in L. xvi. 2, τί τοῦτο ἀκούω περὶ σοῦ; *quid est quod de te audio?* See Bornemann *in loc.* (Jelf *l.c.*). A. xiv. 15, τί ταῦτα ποιεῖτε; is similar.

L. i. 73 also I regard as a case of attraction: μνησθῆναι διαθήκης ἁγίας αὐτοῦ, ὅρκον (for ὅρκου) ὃν ὤμοσε κ.τ.λ. Others (e. g., Kühnöl) consider that we have here a twofold construction of μνησθῆναι, which is found with an accusative in the LXX (Gen. ix. 16, Ex. xx. 8).[2] 2 P. ii. 12, ἐν οἷς ἀγνοοῦσι βλασφημοῦντες, is probably to be resolved into ἐν τούτοις, ἃ ἀγνοοῦσι, βλασφημοῦντες. A similar construction, βλασφημεῖν εἴς τινα, is frequently met with (§ 32. 1): compare also חָרַף בְּ, 2 S. xxiii. 9; קָלַל בְּ, Is. viii. 21. Perhaps also we may compare μυκτηρίζειν ἔν τινι, 3 (1) Esdr. i. 49; but see 2 Chr. xxxvi. 16. Ἀγνοεῖν ἔν τινι, however, is not without example in later Greek; see Fabric. *Pseudepigr.* II. 717.

6. But attraction is sometimes restricted to a single sentence. The principal case of this kind is that in which two local prepositions are blended into one, so as to give greater terseness to the language (Herm. *Vig.* p. 893, Jelf 647). L. xi. 13, ὁ πατὴρ ὁ ἐξ οὐρανοῦ δώσει πνεῦμα ἅγιον; for ὁ πατὴρ ὁ ἐν οὐρανῷ δώσει ἐξ οὐρανοῦ πνεῦμα ἅγιον. Col. iv. 16, τὴν ἐκ Λαοδικείας (ἐπιστολὴν) ἵνα καὶ ὑμεῖς ἀναγνῶτε: not *the letter written from Laodicea*, but *the letter written to Laodicea* and brought to the Colossians *from* Laodicea.[3] Compare also L. ix. 61 (Mk. v. 26). So also with adverbs of place: L. xvi. 26 [*Rec.*] may be brought under this head (Franke, *Demosth.* p. 13). With the passages first quoted may be reckoned H. xiii. 24, ἀσπάζονται ὑμᾶς οἱ ἀπὸ τῆς Ἰταλίας (i.e., οἱ ἐν τῇ Ἰταλίᾳ ἀπὸ τῆς Ἰταλίας); but the

---

[1] See Herm. Soph. *Ajax* 1164, Eurip. *Ion* 807; Lobeck, Soph. *Ajax* 454 sq.; Ellendt, *Lex. Soph.* II. 824; Weber, *Demosth.* p. 348; and as to Latin, Grotefend, *Ausführliche Grammatik* II. 96, Kritz, *Sallust* I. 211.

[2] This explanation had been given earlier, by an anonymous writer in the *Alt. und Neu.* of 1735, p. 336 sq.

[3] From ignorance of the prevalence of this idiom, some commentators have been induced, in spite of the context, to retain in their translation "the epistle (written by Paul) from Laodicea." [To the examples given in the text Lünemann adds Mt. xxiv. 17, ἆραι τὰ ἐκ τῆς οἰκίας.]

translation "those of Italy"—the Italian Christians (who were with the writer)—is also possible. A critical argument as to the place at which the Epistle was written should never have been founded on these words. 2 C. ix. 2 and Ph. iv. 22 may be understood without assuming an attraction.—This fusion of clauses is very common in Greek writers. Compare Xen. *Cyr.* 7. 2. 5, ἁρπασόμενοι τὰ ἐκ τῶν οἰκιῶν· Thuc. 2. 80, ἀδυνάτων ὄντων ξυμβοηθεῖν τῶν ἀπὸ θαλάσσης Ἀκαρνάνων· Demosth. *Phil.* 3. 46 a, τοὺς ἐκ Σερρίου τείχους ... στρατιώτας ἐξέβαλεν· Paus. 4. 13. 1, ἀπορρίψαι τὰ ἀπὸ τῆς τραπέζης· Demosth. *Timocr.* 483 b, Xen. *An.* 1. 2. 18, Plat. *Apol.* p. 32 b, Thuc. 3. 5, 7. 70, Lucian, *Eunuch.* 12, Theophr. *Char.* 2, Xen. Eph. 1. 10, Isocr. *Ep.* 7. p. 1012 (Judith viii. 17, Sus. 26).[1]

7. Conversely, we sometimes find one sentence resolved grammatically into two, which are connected by καί. Rom. vi. 17, χάρις τῷ θεῷ, ὅτι ἦτε δοῦλοι τῆς ἁμαρτίας, ὑπηκούσατε δέ κ.τ.λ.: for this Paul might have said ὄντες ποτὲ δοῦλοι τῆς ἁμαρτίας ὑπηκούσατε ἐκ καρδίας.[2] L. xxiv. 18, σὺ μόνος παροικεῖς Ἰερουσαλὴμ καὶ οὐκ ἔγνως; for which, in a language which wields the participial construction with such facility, we might have had, with greater correctness, σὺ μόνος παροικῶν Ἰερουσαλὴμ οὐκ ἔγνως; See also Mt. xi. 25, and probably 1 C. iv. 4. See Fritzsche, *Matt.* p. 287, 413, Gesenius on Is. v. 4; and compare what is said by Buttmann (§ 136. 1) on sentences which are connected with each other by μέν and δέ, and by Kühner (II. 415 sq., Jelf 751 sq.) on the subject of *parataxis* generally. In some of these passages, however, this structure may have been adopted for the purpose of fully securing to the first sentence the attention it requires. This purpose shows itself still more clearly in Jo. iii. 19, αὕτη ἐστὶν ἡ κρίσις, ὅτι τὸ φῶς ἐλήλυθεν εἰς τὸν κόσμον καὶ ἠγάπησαν οἱ ἄνθρωποι μᾶλλον τὸ σκότος

---

[1] See Fischer, Plat. *Phæd.* p. 318 sq.; Schæfer, *Demosth.* IV. 119; Hermann, Soph. *Electr.* 135, and Æsch. *Agam.* 516; Ast, Theophr. *Char.* p. 61; Poppo, *Thuc.* I. i. 176 sq., III. ii. 389; Weber, *Demosth.* p. 191, 446.

[2] By others—as at last by Fritzsche also—the stress is laid on the preterite ἦτε, "that ye *were*" (that this state is now past); and the position in which ἦτε stands may be claimed as an argument on this side. So understood, however, Paul's language is somewhat artificial; for, strictly, ἦτε does no more than point to their condition as existing formerly,—does not contemplate it from the standpoint of present time as now at an end ("ye were servants,"—not "ye have been etc."). [Meyer agrees with Fritzsche.—In his note on Mt. xi. 25 Fritzsche had favoured the explanation of Rom. vi. 17 which is given in the text.]

κ.τ.λ.,—see Baumg.-Crusius, and especially Lücke *in loc.*: compare also vi. 50. So also in Jo. vii. 4, οὐδείς τι ἐν κρυπτῷ ποιεῖ καὶ ζητεῖ αὐτὸς ἐν παρρησίᾳ εἶναι, John prefers to express the two inconsistent actions by these parallel sentences (no one does the two things together) instead of writing, οὐδεὶς ... ποιεῖ ζητῶν αὐτός κ.τ.λ. On Mt. xviii. 21 see above, § 45. Rem. 2 [p. 446]. In 1 P. iv. 6, however, the two sentences depending upon ἵνα must be regarded as co-ordinate; only the meaning of κρίνεσθαι in this connexion must be rightly understood.

Parallel to this idiom, but more restricted in its character, would be the figure of speech known as ἓν διὰ δυοῖν (*hendiadys*). This figure consists in the use of two substantives in the place of a single substantive with an adjective or genitive (of quality)—the quality of the object being, for the sake of emphasis, raised to equal grammatical independence with the object itself: e. g., "pateris libamus et auro," i. e., *pateris aureis*. This is essentially an instance of apposition,— *pateris et quidem auro, pateris* h. e. *auro*.[1] Commentators have discovered this figure in the N. T.:[2] many of them indeed (as Heinrichs) have applied it without any limit and in the most foolish way,—e.g., in Mt. iii. 11, A. xiv. 13, Jo. i. 14, iii. 5, H. vi. 10. (Wilke, *Rhet.* p. 149.) But even of the examples which have been more carefully sifted there is not one which is undoubted. Either the nouns combined express two notions which are really distinct (2 Tim. iv. 1, 2 P. i. 16); or the second substantive is added epexegetically (and therefore by way of supplement), as in (Rom. i. 5) A. i. 25, xxiii. 6, E. vi. 18,[3]—compare also 2 C. viii. 4 (καί meaning *and indeed, namely*, p. 545 sq.). Examples of the latter class, though in genus allied to hendiadys, are yet specifically different. To find a hendiadys in the verb, as commentators have done (e. g., in Ph. iv. 18), is altogether absurd.

Section LXVII.

ABNORMAL RELATION OF PARTICULAR WORDS IN THE SENTENCE (HYPALLAGE).

1. A departure from rule may occasionally be observed in regard to the relation sustained by particular words of a sen-

---

[1] See Fritzsche, *Matt.* exc. 4; Teipel in the *Archiv f. d. Stud. d. neuern Sprachen* (Vol. x. Part 1). For a more accurate view of the subject see C. F. Müller in Schneidewin's *Philologus*, VII. 297 sqq.

[2] Glass, *Philol. Sacra* I. 18 sq.

[3] ["The two substantives προσκαρτερήσει καὶ δεήσει, though not merely equivalent to 'precantes sedulo,' still *practically* amount to a 'hendiadys.' According to the regular rule, the substantive which contains the 'accidens' ought to *follow* rather than precede (see Winer, *de Hypallage et Hendiadyi* p. 19), still here προσκαρτερήσει so clearly receives its explanation from καὶ δεήσει, that the expression, though not a strict and grammatical, is yet a virtual, or what might be termed a *contextual* ἓν διὰ δυοῖν: see especially Fritz. *Matth.* p. 857." Ellicott *in loc.*]

tence. Sometimes this irregularity arises from the *constructio ad sensum*, so familiar to the Greeks: here no one who attentively follows the connexion can find the explanation either difficult or doubtful. In other cases the cause is inadvertence on the part of the writer: full of the thoughts with which he is occupied, he loses sight of correctness of expression.

We notice the following cases :—

a. The *constructio ad sensum* (πρὸς τὸ σημαινόμενον or κατὰ σύνεσιν). Of this construction with predicate and attributive examples have been given in § 58; with pronouns, in § 21. (Compare also Rev. iii. 4.)

b. The subject is suppressed, and must be *indirectly* supplied from the previous context. 1 C. vii. 36, γαμείτωσαν, viz., the two young persons who have become acquainted with each other; this is suggested by the mention of the marriageable daughter in the preceding part of the verse. G. i. 23, μόνον ἀκούοντες ἦσαν: from ταῖς ἐκκλησίαις, ver. 22, must be gathered the notion of *members* of the churches. (Compare Cæs. *B. G.* 4. 14.) 1 Tim. ii. 15 would be a similar example, if with ἐὰν μείνωσιν ἐν πίστει the word τέκνα were supplied from the preceding τεκνογονίας. In point of grammar this explanation is admissible,—compare Plat. *Legg.* 10. 886 d, where γενόμενοι stands in relation to θεογονίαν, just as if the expression used had been θεῶν γένεσις:[1] but see above, § 58. 4. In 1 Tim. v. 4 the subject of μανθανέτωσαν is probably χῆραι, deduced from the collective τὶς χήρα (see Huther *in loc.*[2]),—as indeed we often find a plural used in reference to τὶς (Rev. xiv. 11): see Herbst, Xen. *Mem.* p. 50 (Jelf 390). In Rom. xiii. 6, however, λειτουργοὶ θεοῦ εἰσίν refers to οἱ ἄρχοντες, ver. 3.

c. Sometimes we find a sudden change of subject: Jo. xix. 4 sq., ἐξῆλθεν οὖν πάλιν ὁ Πιλᾶτος καὶ λέγει αὐτοῖς· Ἴδε ἄγω ὑμῖν αὐτὸν ἔξω..... ἐξῆλθεν οὖν ὁ Ἰησοῦς ἔξω.... καὶ λέγει αὐτοῖς, viz. *Pilate* (compare xix. 38); L. xix. 4, προδραμὼν.... ἀνέβη ἐπὶ συκομορέαν (Ζακχαῖος), ἵνα ἴδῃ αὐτόν (Ἰησοῦν), ὅτι ἐκείνης ἤμελλε (Ἰησοῦς) διέρχεσθαι. Compare L. xiv. 5, xv. 15, xvii. 2, Mk. ix. 20, A. vi. 6, x. 4, Rom. x. 14 sq., Judith v. 8. On 1 Jo. v. 16 see § 58. 9. This transition from one subject to another is not uncommon in Greek prose. See Her. 6. 30, ὁ δὲ

---

[1] See Zell, Aristot. *Ethic.* p. 209; Poppo, Xen. *Cyr.* p. 29, 160; Küster (Reisig), Xen. *Œcon.* p. 247 sq.
[2] [See Ellicott and Alford on this passage.]

788   ABNORMAL RELATION OF PARTICULAR WORDS   [PART III.

(*Histiæus*) οὔτ' ἂν ἔπαθε κακὸν οὐδέν, δοκέειν ἐμοί, ἀπῆκέ (*Darius*) τ' ἂν αὐτῷ τὴν αἰτίην· Demosth. c. *Phorm.* 587 a, ὃς οὐκ ἔφασκεν οὔτε τὰ χρήματα ἐντεθεῖσθαι τοῦτον (*Phormion*), οὔτε τὸ χρυσίον ἀπειληφέναι (*Lampis*); Plutarch, *Poplic. compar.* 5, . . . προςέλαβεν (*Poplicola*) ὅσα δόντα ἀγαπητὸν ἦν νικῆσαι· καὶ γὰρ τὸν πόλεμον διέλυσε (*Porsena*) κ.τ.λ.; *Vit. Lysandr.* 24, ἄλλο δ' οὐδὲν ἐχρήσατο (*Agesilaus*) αὐτῷ πρὸς τὸν πόλεμον· ἀλλὰ τοῦ χρόνου διελθόντος ἀπέπλευσεν (*Lysander*) εἰς τὴν Σπάρτην κ.τ.λ.; *Ages.* 40, τὴν βασιλείαν Ἀρχίδαμος . . . παρέλαβε, καὶ (scil. αὕτη) διέμεινε τῷ γένει· *Artax.* 15, τοῦ κροτάφου τυχὼν κατέβαλον τὸν ἄνδρα, καὶ τέθνηκεν (οὗτος) κ.τ.λ.; Lysias, *Cæd. Eratosth.* 10, ἵνα τὸν τιτθὺν αὐτῷ (παιδίῳ) διδῷ καὶ μὴ βοᾷ (τὸ παιδίον).[1] As to Hebrew, see Gesen. *Lehrgeb.* p. 803.

d. Words expressing reference are sometimes used with some looseness. As to αὐτός see § 22. 3. Thus in G. ii. 2 αὐτοῖς refers to Ἱεροσόλυμα in ver. 1, the *inhabitants* of the city being meant: A. xvii. 16[2] is similar. In 2 P. iii. 4 αὐτοῦ must be understood of Christ, who, though not expressly named, is indicated in the word παρουσία. In Jo. xv. 6 αὐτά stands in relation to the singular τὸ κλῆμα, which belongs as an apposition to εἴ τις. In a different manner we find αὐτούς in A. iv. 7 used in reference, not to αὐτῶν (ver. 5), but to verses 1 and 2. In A. x. 7 αὐτῷ points, not to Simon (ver. 6), but to Cornelius (ver. 1–5): this is expressly indicated in some MSS., which read τῷ Κορνηλίῳ—an obvious gloss. In A. vii. 24 we have πατάξας τὸν Αἰγύπτιον, though nothing has been previously said about any Egyptian; only in ἀδικούμενον the ἀδικῶν is implied, and that he was an Egyptian is assumed to be known from the connexion of the narrative. Lastly, in 2 Jo. 7 οὗτος points back to πολλοὶ πλάνοι, and comprehends the many in the unity of this person. Conversely, in 1 Jo. iv. 4 αὐτούς has reference to ἀντιχρίστου, ver. 3. Of a simpler kind is the reference of αὐτοῦ in Jo. xx. 7, αὐτόν in Jo. xx. 15; as also that of ἐκεῖνοι to the nearest subject in Jo. vii. 45 (see p. 196). There is also incorrectness when a single form of a pronoun (especially a relative pronoun), must, as regards construction, serve for two cases;

---

[1] Compare Poppo, *Observ. in Thucyd.* p. 189; Schæf. *Demosth.* IV. 214, *Plutarch* IV. 281, 331, V. 86, 295; Stallb. Plat. *Gorg.* p. 215; Mätzner, *Antiph.* p. 145; Schoem. *Isæus* p. 294.

[2] [There seems to be some mistake in this reference.—See further § 22. 3.]

as in 1 C. ii. 9, ἃ ὀφθαλμὸς οὐκ εἶδεν καὶ οὖς οὐκ ἤκουσεν καὶ ἐπὶ καρδίαν ἀνθρώπου οὐκ ἀνέβη (from the LXX). This belongs, in essence, to the subject treated in § 64. 1. Similar examples are of frequent occurrence, both in Greek and also in Latin (Kritz, *Sall.* I. 67, II. 295 sq.).

e. The first of two parallel members is sometimes expressed so generally as to seem to include the second, in cases where from the nature of the case this is impossible. A. xxvii. 22, ἀποβολὴ ψυχῆς οὐδεμία ἔσται ἐξ ὑμῶν πλὴν τοῦ πλοίου, literally means, *there will be no loss of life, except of the ship;* whereas the meaning intended is, *there will be no loss of life, only of the ship will there be loss.* G. i. 19, ἕτερον τῶν ἀποστόλων οὐκ εἶδον, εἰ μὴ Ἰάκωβον τὸν ἀδελφὸν τοῦ κυρίου· would be similar to this, if we were (with Fritzsche, *Matt.* p. 482) to render the words, *alium apostolum non vidi, sed vidi Jacobum* etc.,—εἶδον alone being repeated before Ἰάκωβον: but see my *Comment.*[1] and Meyer *in loc.*[2] We have an approach to such a use of εἰ μή in Rev. xxi. 27, οὐ μὴ εἰσέλθῃ . . . πᾶν κοινὸν καὶ ὁ ποιῶν βδέλυγμα . . . εἰ μὴ οἱ γεγραμμένοι ἐν τῷ βιβλίῳ τῆς ζωῆς, where the γεγραμμένοι are not to be included under πᾶν κοινόν: the meaning is, *Nothing profane shall enter, only those who are inscribed . . . shall enter.* See also Rev. ix. 4. Compare 1 K. iii. 18, οὐκ ἔστιν οὐθεὶς μεθ᾽ ἡμῶν παρὲξ ἀμφοτέρων ἡμῶν ἐν τῷ οἴκῳ.

2. The inadvertence of the writer has disturbed the very structure of the sentence in L. xxiv. 27: ἀρξάμενος ἀπὸ Μωσέως καὶ ἀπὸ πάντων τῶν προφητῶν διηρμήνευεν αὐτοῖς ἐν πάσαις ταῖς γραφαῖς τὰ περὶ αὐτοῦ. Here we can hardly assume that with Moses and the prophets are contrasted any other books of the O. T., which Jesus went on to explain; nor can we suppose, with Kühnöl, that Jesus first quoted the sayings of the prophets, and then proceeded in the second place to interpret them (see Van Hengel, *Annot.* p. 104). The meaning intended by Luke is probably this: *Jesus, beginning from* (with) *Moses, went through all the prophets* (see also Baumg.-Crusius *in loc.*): instead of expressing himself thus, having the ἀπό in his mind when he appended the πάντες προφῆται, he wrote these words in the genitive case. The expedient on which Meyer has lighted[3] is

---

[1] [Winer *l. c.* hesitates between Fritzsche's view and the identification of James the Lord's brother with James son of Alphæus. Meyer, Ellicott, Lightfoot, al., consider that James is here called an apostle.—See p. 566.]

[2] In H. xii. 25, εἰ ἐκεῖνοι οὐκ ἐξέφυγον . . . πολὺ μᾶλλον ἡμεῖς κ.τ.λ., those (Kühnöl and others) who render πολὺ μᾶλλον *multo minus* repeat for the apodosis no more than ἐκφευξόμεθα. The formula retains, however, its usual meaning *multo magis*, and the entire negative notion οὐκ ἐκφευξόμεθα must be repeated with it. Compare Cæsar, *B. G.* 1. 47.

[3] [That (as Alford says) he began with Moses first;—that he began with each of the prophets as he came to them. See Ellicott, *Hist. L.* p. 395 sq.]

but a sorry one. By the side of this passage we may place A. iii. 24, πάντες οἱ προφῆται ἀπὸ Σαμουὴλ καὶ τῶν καθεξῆς ὅσοι ἐλάλησαν καὶ κατήγγειλαν κ.τ.λ. Luke might have written either, *All prophets, Samuel* (as the first) *and those who followed* (in order) *all* etc., or, *All prophets from Samuel onwards, as many of them as* etc. As the words stand there is an unmistakeable tautology. Nor will the punctuation which Casaubon suggested, and which has been adopted by a host of commentators (Valckenaer included), τῶν καθεξῆς ὅσοι ἐλάλησαν, afford any substantial help. We still have *all prophets from Samuel onwards*, and then, as if not included in the first clause, *all who followed Samuel and prophesied.* The expedient which Van Hengel (*Annotat.* p.103) has proposed—to supply ἕως Ἰωάννου (Mt. xi. 13)—is arbitrary, and after all only gives us a thought which is equally unsuitable, *from Samuel and the following prophets onwards ... until John;* whereas we expect to find two extremes of this series mentioned. And even thus Van Hengel merely gains the brachylogy noticed above [p. 775] as used by Luke: ἄρχεσθαι ἀπὸ ... ἕως ...

3. Earlier commentators went farther still in the discovery of such inaccuracies, resulting from negligence on the part of the writer.

a. A mistake in the connexion of attributive and noun, influencing the grammatical form of the attributive, was supposed to have been detected—not only in A. v. 20, τὰ ῥήματα τῆς ζωῆς ταύτης (for ταῦτα), Rom. vii. 24, on which see p. 297 sq., but also[1]—in E. ii. 2, κατὰ τὸν ἄρχοντα τῆς ἐξουσίας τοῦ ἀέρος, τοῦ πνεύματος κ.τ.λ. (for τὸ πνεῦμα), E. iii. 2, 2 C. iii. 7, L. viii.32, xxii. 20; and this species of "hypallage"[2] was supported by examples drawn from ancient authors. In a sentence of some length, comprising relations of various kinds, such a mistake might be possible, especially in the case of the less practised writers: in poetry, indeed, there may be passages which cannot be explained in any natural manner without such an assumption.[3] In prose, however, such examples are probably rare in

---

[1] Bengel on L. xxii. 20 ; Bauer, *Philol. Thucyd.-Paul.* p. 263.
[2] Compare Glass, *Philol. Sacr.* I. 652 sqq.; Jani, *Ars Poet. Lat.* p. 258 sqq. On the other side see Elster, *de Hypallage* (Helmst. 1845).
[3] Compare Lobeck, Soph. *Ajax* p. 73 sq.; Hermann, *Vig.* p. 891, Soph. *Philoct.* p. 202, and Eur. *Hel.* p. 7 ; Krüger, *Grammat. Untersuch.* III. 37 sq. (Jelf 440, Don. p. 387).

the extreme;[1] and in the N. T. there is not one clear instance of the kind.[2] L. viii. 32 is explained at once. On E. iii. 2 see my *Progr. de Hypallage et Hendiadyi in N. T. libris* (Erlang. 1824) p. 15, and Harless *in loc.* In E. ii. 2, where the apostle might most easily have been led aside from the correct construction, πνεῦμα is the spirit which rules in and influences the men of the world, of which spirit Satan is regarded as the lord and master. See Meyer's note: Heinichen (*Euseb.* II. 99) holds fast to hypallage. In 2 C. iii. 7, εἰ ἡ διακονία τοῦ θανάτου ἐν γράμμασιν ἐντετυπωμένη ἐν λίθοις, Paul might have more simply said, in contrast with διακονία τοῦ πνεύματος, ἡ διακονία τοῦ γράμματος ἐντετυπωμένου ἐν λίθοις. Still the existing connexion of the words is not incorrect. Moses' ministration of death was itself ἐν λίθοις ἐντετυπωμένη, in so far as it consisted in bringing to the people, and exercising amongst them, this legislation which threatened and brought death. The letter of the law contained the ministry which Moses had to fulfil. With this passage may grammatically be compared Tac. *Annal.* 14. 16: quod species ipsa carminum docet, non impetu et instinctis nec ore uno *fluens*. In H. ix. 10 ἐπικείμενα is certainly not to be construed with δικαιώμασι, as standing for ἐπικειμένοις; δικαιώμασι is in apposition to ἐπὶ βρώμασιν κ.τ.λ., and ἐπικείμενα is parallel to μὴ δυνάμεναι, the neuter gender being chosen because both δῶρα and θυσίαι are included. With the other reading δικαιώματα, which is well attested, ἐπικείμενα may be referred to this appositional word without any irregularity whatever. A more plausible example is L. xxii. 20, where τὸ ὑπὲρ ὑμῶν ἐκχυνόμενον might be construed with ἐν τῷ αἵματι. Considering the shortness of the sentence, however, it is not likely that Luke can have written ἐκχυνόμενον through inadvertence. It is more probable that he construes ἐκχυνόμενον with ποτήριον, as διδόμενον with σῶμα, meaning by ποτήριον the contents of the cup; and this metonymy will still be easier than the other, τὸ ποτήριον ἡ καινὴ διαθήκη. This irregularity is clearly of a logical, not of a grammatical description; though "to pour out a cup" is a perfectly correct expression. Still, it was not necessary for Schult-

---

[1] Poppo, *Thuc.* I. i. 161; Bornemann, Xen. *Anab.* p. 206; Heinichen, *Euseb.* II. 175.
[2] See F. Woken, *Pietas critica in hypallagas biblicas* (Viteb. 1718).

hess¹ to wax so warm on this point. In H. vi. 1 the hypallage assumed by Palairet and others has already been rejected by Kühnöl. On Jo. i. 14, πλήρης χάριτος κ.τ.λ., see § 62. 3 ; on 2 C. xi. 28, Rev. i. 5, see § 59. 8. That in 2 C. iv. 17 αἰώνιον βάρος δόξης cannot stand for αἰωνίου βάρος δόξης, is sufficiently proved by one single consideration—that the exactness of arrangement at which the apostle manifestly aimed (παραυτίκα . . . αἰώνιον, ἐλαφρόν . . . βάρος, θλῖψις . . . δόξα) would be destroyed by such a change. On 1 C. iv. 3 see Meyer, against Billroth and Rückert. A. xi. 5, εἶδον καταβαῖνον σκεῦός τι, ὡς ὀθόνην μεγάλην, τέσσαρσιν ἀρχαῖς καθιεμένην, is not (through comparison with x. 11, καθιέμενον) to be regarded as an instance of hypallage: the attributives might be joined to σκεῦος as correctly as to ὀθόνη. It is hard to come to a decision upon 2 C. xii. 21, μή . . . πενθήσω πολλοὺς τῶν προημαρτηκότων καὶ μὴ μετανοησάντων κ.τ.λ. The question arises, why not *all* unrepentant sinners ? Can Paul have intended to write τοὺς μὴ μετανοήσαντας ? As however in ver. 21 he mentions a category of sins different from that in ver. 20, we may assume, with Meyer, that the προημαρτηκότες are more exactly defined by means of μὴ μετανοησάντων, as persons who have remained impenitent only in regard to those sins of sensuality which are specified in the words which immediately follow.²

b. Akin to hypallage is *antiptosis*,—a figure which is discovered by some (Kühnöl amongst others) in H. ix. 2, πρόθεσις ἄρτων, these words being taken as standing for ἄρτοι προθέσεως.³ In some such way have been explained Plotin. *Enn.* 2. 1. p. 97 g, πρὸς τὸ βούλημα τοῦ ἀποτελέσματος ὑπάρχειν προσήκει· Thuc. 1. 6, οἱ πρεσβύτεροι τῶν εὐδαιμόνων (see the scholiast),—as standing for πρὸς τὸ τοῦ βουλήματος ἀποτέλεσμα, οἱ εὐδαίμονες τῶν πρεσβυτέρων. In this passage of the N. T., however, we must keep to the simple rendering, *the setting forth of the loaves* (the sacred custom of setting forth

---

¹ *Vom Abendmahl,* p. 155 sq. [See Green p. 236.]
² [Meyer joins the clause ἐπί κ.τ.λ. with πενθήσω, not with μετανοησάντων.— De Wette and others suppose that πενθεῖν here includes the idea of *inflicting punishment,* and by this means explain the use of πολλούς. See Waite's note on this verse, *Speak. Comm.* III. 474.]
³ On this marvellous figure see Hermann, *Vig.* p. 890, Soph. *Electr.* p. 8 ; Blomfield, Æsch. *Agam.* 148, 1360 ; Wyttenb. Plat. *Phæd.* p. 232.

the loaves).¹ Valckenaer would even take ἡ τράπεζα καὶ ἡ πρόθεσις τῶν ἄρτων as standing for ἡ τράπεζα τῶν ἄρτων τῆς προθέσεως. Lastly, some (including Bengel) have taken Rom. ix. 31, διώκων νόμον δικαιοσύνης, as standing for διώκων δικαιοσύνην νόμου : this is preposterous, see Fritzsche *in loc.* On other absurdities of this kind compare Fritzsche's instructive excursus, *Mark*, p. 759 sqq.

Section LXVIII.

REGARD TO SOUND IN THE STRUCTURE OF SENTENCES: PARONOMASIA AND PLAY UPON WORDS (ANNOMINATIO): PARALLELISM: VERSE.

1. The euphony which we usually find in the language of the N. T. (examples of the contrary presenting themselves but rarely, e.g., in 1 C. xii. 2 ²) is not in general the result of any deliberate aim on the part of the writers: it is only in the instance of *paronomasia* and play upon words that we can ascribe much to design.

Paronomasia ³—which consists in the combination of like-sounding words, and which is a favourite figure with oriental writers ⁴—is especially common in Paul's Epistles. In some instances the combination seems to have naturally presented itself; in others, to have been sought by the writer for the purpose of giving a cheerful liveliness to his language, or greater emphasis to the thought. L. xxi. 11, καὶ λιμοὶ καὶ λοιμοὶ ἔσονται.⁵ Hesiod, *Opp.* 226, Plutarch, *Coriol.* c. 13,—see Valcken. *in loc.*; A. xvii. 25, ζωὴν καὶ πνοήν⁶ (compare Varro, *R. R.* 3. 2. 13, utrum propter *oves*, an propter *aves*); H. v. 8, ἔμαθεν ἀφ' ὧν ἔπαθεν⁷ (compare Her. 1. 207), see Wetstein

---

¹ [So Bleek, Lünemann, Kurtz: Tholuck, Delitzsch, and Alford give to πρόθεσις a passive and concrete meaning.]
² Compare Lobeck, Soph. *Ajax* p. 105, *Paralip.* p. 53 sq.
³ See Glass, *Philol. Sacra.* I. 1335–1342; C. B. Michaelis, *De paronomasia sacra* (Hal. 1737); also Lob. *Paralip.* p. 501 sqq. J. F. Böttcher's treatise *De paronomasia finitimisque ei figuris Paulo Apostolo frequentatis* (Lips. 1823) is a valuable and exhaustive monograph.
⁴ See Verschuir, *Dissertat. philol.-exeg.* p. 172 sqq.
⁵ Compare the German *Hunger und Kummer* (*want and woe*).
⁶ Compare our *leben und weben*,—also *Hülle und Fülle*, *Saus und Braus*, *rädern und ädern.* See Baiter, Isocr. *Paneg.* p. 117.
⁷ "Seine *Leiden leiteten* ihn zum Gehorsam."

and Valcken. *in loc.;* Rom. xi. 17, τινὲς τῶν κλάδων ἐξεκλάσθησαν.—Thus in a series of words we find those of similar sound placed together: Rom. i. 29, 31 (πορνείᾳ, πονηρίᾳ), φθόνου, φόνου . . . ἀσυνέτους, ἀσυνθέτους (Wetst. *in loc.*). Elsewhere we find words of similar derivation brought together : 1 C. ii. 13, ἐν διδακτοῖς πνεύματος, πνευματικοῖς πνευματικὰ συγκρίνοντες· 2 C. viii. 22, ἐν πολλοῖς πολλάκις σπουδαῖον· ix. 8, ἐν παντὶ πάντοτε πᾶσαν αὐτάρκειαν· A. xxiv. 3, 2 C. x. 12, αὐτοὶ ἐν ἑαυτοῖς ἑαυτοὺς μετροῦντες· Rom. viii. 23, αὐτοὶ ἐν ἑαυτοῖς στενάζομεν· Ph. i. 4. Xen. *Mem.* 3. 12. 6, δυςκολία καὶ μανία πολλάκις πολλοῖς . . . ἐμπίπτουσιν· 4. 4. 4, πολλῶν πολλάκις ὑπὸ τῶν δικαστῶν ἀφιεμένων· *An.* 2. 4. 10, αὐτοὶ ἐφ' ἑαυτῶν ἐχώρουν· 2. 5. 7, πάντῃ γὰρ πάντα τοῖς θεοῖς ὕποχα καὶ πανταχῇ πάντων ἴσον οἱ θεοὶ κρατοῦσι· Polyb. 6. 18. 6, Athen. 8. 352, Arrian, *Epict.* 3. 23. 22 ; Synes. *Prov.* 2. p. 116 b, πάντα πανταχοῦ πάντων κακῶν ἔμπλεα ἦν.[1]—Mt. xxi. 41, κακοὺς κακῶς ἀπολέσει αὐτούς :[2] Demosth. *Mid.* 413 b, εἶτα θαυμάζεις, εἰ κακὸς κακῶς ἀπολῇ· adv. Zenoth. 575 c, Aristoph. *Plut.* 65, 418, Diog. L. 2. 76, Alciphr. 3. 10 ; compare also Æschyl. *Pers.* 1041, Plaut. *Aulular.* 1. 1. 3 sq.[3] Writers will sometimes use rare or uncommon words or forms of words in order to produce a paronomasia (Gesen. *Lehrg.* p. 858) : e.g., G. v. 7 sq., πείθεσθαι . . . . ἡ πεισμονή (see my *Comment. in loc*).[4]

2. The *play on words* is akin to paronomasia, but differs from it in having respect to the meaning of the words as well as to their similarity in sound ;[5] hence it commonly occurs in anti-

---

[1] See Krüg. Xen. *An.* 1. 9. 2 ; Lob. Soph. *Ajax* p. 138, 380 ; Boisson. *Nicet.* p. 243 ; Beier, Cic. *Off.* I. 128 ; Jahn, *Archiv* II. 402.

[2] *Die Schlimmen wird er schlimm verderben:* [q. d., *he will miserably destroy these miserable men*].

[3] Schæfer, Soph. *Electr.* 742 ; Lobeck, Soph. *Aj.* p. 471, *Paralip.* p. 8, 56 sqq. ; Foertsch, *De locis Lysiæ* p. 44. See also Döderlein, *Progr. de brachylogia* p. 8 sq. In particular, E. A. Diller has collected many such examples of paronomasia in his *Progr. de consensu notionum qualis est in vocibus ejusdem originis diversitate formarum copulatis* (Misen. 1842).

[4] Compare "Die *Bisthümer* sind verwandelt in *Wüstthümer*, die *Abteien* sind nun—*Raubteien*" (Schiller, in *Wallensteins Lager*) ; " *Verbesserungen* nicht *Verböserungen.*" In the *Agenda* of Duke Heinrich of Saxony (1539), it is said in the preface respecting the Popish priest : " Sein Sorge ist nicht *Seelsorge* sondern *Meelsorge.*" [" He cares for the *meal*, not the *weal*, of his people,"—" for their *goods*, not their *good.*"]

[5] E. g., " Träume sind Schäume." [Literally, " dreams are bubbles."—An example in English would be " What is *fame*, but a *name* ?"]

thesis. Mt. xvi. 18, σὺ εἶ Πέτρος, καὶ ἐπὶ ταύτῃ τῇ πέτρᾳ οἰκοδομήσω κ.τ.λ.; Rom. v. 19, ὥσπερ διὰ τῆς παρακοῆς τοῦ ἑνὸς ἀνθρώπου ἁμαρτωλοὶ κατεστάθησαν οἱ πολλοί, οὕτω καὶ διὰ τῆς ὑπακοῆς τοῦ ἑνὸς δίκαιοι κατασταθήσονται· i. 20, τὰ ἀόρατα αὐτοῦ . . . . καθορᾶται· Ph. iii. 2 sq., βλέπετε τὴν κατατομήν, ἡμεῖς γάρ ἐσμεν ἡ περιτομή (Diog. L. 6. 24, τὴν Εὐκλείδου σχολὴν ἔλεγε χολήν, τὴν δὲ Πλάτωνος διατριβὴν κατατριβήν); Ph. iii. 12, 2 C. iv. 8, ἀπορούμενοι, ἀλλ' οὐκ ἐξαπορούμενοι· 2 Th. iii. 11, μηδὲν ἐργαζομένους, ἀλλὰ περιεργαζομένους (compare Seidler, Eurip. *Troad.* p. 11); 2 C. v. 4, ἐφ' ᾧ οὐ θέλομεν ἐκδύσασθαι, ἀλλ' ἐπενδύσασθαι· A. viii. 30, ἆρά γε γινώσκεις, ἃ ἀναγινώσκεις; Jo. ii. 23 sq., πολλοὶ ἐπίστευσαν εἰς τὸ ὄνομα αὐτοῦ . . . αὐτὸς δὲ Ἰησοῦς οὐκ ἐπίστευεν ἑαυτὸν αὐτοῖς· Rom. i. 28, iii. 3, xi. 17,[1] xii. 3, xvi. 2, E. i. 23, iii. 14 sq., 19, G. iv. 17, 1 C. iii. 17, vi. 2, xi. 29, 31, xiv. 10, 2 C. iii. 2, v. 21, x. 3, 1 Tim. i. 8 sq., 2 Tim. iii. 4, iv. 7, 3 Jo. 7 sq., Rev. xxii. 18 sq. In Phil. 20 the allusion made by ὀναίμην to the name of the slave Ὀνήσιμος is of a more covert kind.[2] The remark made above in regard to the employment of unusual words is also applicable here, and is perhaps exemplified in G. v. 12 : compare my *Comment. in loc.*, and also Terent. *Hecyr. prol.* 1, 2, *orator ad vos venio ornatu prologi, sinite exorator sim.*

As may readily be supposed, the works of Greek authors (especially the orators) are not wanting in similar examples of paronomasia and

---

[1] [Quoted above, in no 1. Lünemann adds Mt. vi. 16.]
[2] For a play on words in which the allusion is to *signification only*, see Phil. 11, Ὀνήσιμον τὸν ποτέ σοι ἄχρηστον, νυνὶ δὲ σοὶ καὶ ἐμοὶ εὔχρηστον. Still more latent would be the play upon words in 1 C. i. 23, κηρύσσομεν Χριστὸν ἐσταυρωμένον, Ἰουδαίοις μὲν σκάνδαλον, ἔθνεσι δὲ μωρίαν, αὐτοῖς δὲ τοῖς κλητοῖς . . . σοφίαν, if Paul here had in his mind the words מֻשְׁבָּל (Chaldee), *crux*, and מִבְשׁוּל, σκάνδαλον,—סָכָל, *stultus*, and שֵׂכֶל, *sapientia* (Glass, *Philol.* I. 1339). I am not, however, acquainted with the word מֻשְׁבָּל in Chaldee, and it is only in Æthiopic that we find משקל, *cross*. The whole assertion is a piece of learned trifling.—Equally improbable is Jerome's conjecture in regard to G. i. 6, that in the word μετατίθεσθε the apostle alludes to the oriental etymology of the name Γαλάται (from גלה or גלל) : see my note *in loc.*, and Böttcher *l. c.*, p. 74 sq. In the discourses of Jesus, delivered in the Syro-Chaldaic language, a play on words may in many instances have been lost through translation into Greek : compare Glass *l. c.*, p. 1339. The attempts which modern scholars have made to restore some of these—e.g., in Mt. viii. 21 (Eichhorn, *Einl. ins N. T.* I. 504 sq.), and in Jo. xiii. 1 (μεταβῆ, פֶּסַח, פֶּסַח)—must be pronounced very unfortunate.

play upon words. Examples have been collected by Tesmar, in *Institut. Rhetor.* p. 156 sqq.; Elsner, in *Diss. II. Paulus et Jesaias inter se comparati* (Vratisl. 1821), p. 24; Bremi, *ad Isocr.* exc. 6; Weber, *Demosth.* p. 205. Compare (in addition) the following: Demosth. *Aristocr.* 457 b, ἀνθρώπους οὐδὲ ἐλευθέρους ἀλλ' ὀλέθρους· Plat. *Phæd.* 83 d, ὁμότροπός τε καὶ ὁμότροφος· Æsch. *Ctesiph.* § 78, οὐ τὸν τρόπον ἀλλὰ τὸν τόπον μόνον μετήλλαξεν· Strabo 9. 402, φάσκειν ἐκείνους συνθέσθαι ἡμέρας, νύκτωρ δὲ ἐπιθέσθαι· Antiph. 5. 91, εἰ δέοι ἁμαρτεῖν ἐπί τῳ, ἀδίκως ἀπολῦσαι ὁσιώτερον ἂν εἴη τοῦ μὴ δικαίως ἀπολέσαι· Diod. S. 11. 57, δόξας παραδόξως διασεσῶσθαι· Thuc. 2. 62, μὴ φρονήματι μόνον, ἀλλὰ καὶ καταφρονήματι (Rom. xii. 3): Lys. *in Philon.* 17, Xen. *An.* 5. 8. 21, Plat. *Rep.* p. 580 b, *Lach.* p. 188 b, Diod. Sic. *Exc. Vat.* p. 27. 5, Appian, *Civ.* 5. 132, τῶν νυκτοφυλάκων ἔθος καὶ εἶδος· Diog. L. 5. 17, 6. 4, Ælian, *Anim.* 14. 1.[1] From the Apocrypha and the writings of the Fathers, compare especially Sus. 54, 55, εἰπόν, ὑπὸ τί δένδρον εἶδες αὐτούς... ὑπὸ σχῖνον. Εἶπε δὲ Δανιήλ... σχίσει σε μέσον. 58, 59, εἶπεν· ὑπὸ πρῖνον. Εἶπε δὲ Δανιήλ.... τὴν ῥομφαίαν ἔχων πρίσαι σε μέσον (compare Africani *Ep. ad Orig. de hist. Susan.* p. 220, ed. Wetstein); 3 (1) Esdr. iv. 62, ἄνεσιν καὶ ἄφεσιν· Wisd. i. 10, ὅτι οὖς ζηλώσεως ἀκροᾶται τὰ πάντα καὶ θροῦς γογγυσμῶν οὐκ ἀποκρύπτεται· xiv. 5, θέλεις μὴ ἀργὰ εἶναι τὰ τῆς σοφίας σου ἔργα.[2] *Acta Apocr.* p. 243, ἐξ ἀπειρίας μᾶλλον δὲ ἀπορίας· Macar. *Hom.* 2. 1, τὸ σῶμα οὐχὶ ἓν μέρος ἢ μέλος πάσχει. As to Latin see Jani, *Ars Poet.* p. 423 sq.

3. The *parallelismus membrorum*, well known as the form of Hebrew poetry, also occurs in the N. T., where the style rises to the elevation of rhythm. This parallelism is sometimes the synonymous, as in Mt. x. 26, Jo. i. 17 [?], vi. 35, xiv. 27, Rom. ix. 2, xi. 12, 33, 1 C. xv. 54, 2 Th. ii. 8, H. xi. 17,[3] Ja. iv. 9, 2 P. ii. 3, al.; sometimes the antithetic, as in Rom. ii. 7 sq., Jo. iii. 6, 29 sq., 2 P. iv. 6,[4] 1 Jo. ii. 10 sq., 17, al.,—see especially the hymn in L. i. 46 sqq. (compare § 65. 5).[5] In some instances, points of dogma which might have been expressed in a single sentence are thus divided between parallel members: Rom. iv.

---

[1] See Buttm. Soph. *Philoct.* p. 150, Lob. Soph. *Ajax* p. 138.
[2] Compare Grimm, *Comment. z. B. der Weisheit,* p. 40 (*Einleit.*).
[3] [This verse is taken differently on p. 688.]
[4] [A mistake,—no doubt for 1 P. iv. 6.]
[5] E. G. Rhesa, *De parallelismo sententiarum poet. in libris N. T.* II. (Regiom. 1811); J. J. Snouk Hurgronje, *De parallelismo membrorum in Jesu Christi dictis observando* (Utr. 1836). [See Smith, *Dict. of Bible* s. v. "Poetry," Davidson in Horne's *Introd.* II. 430 sqq., and the authorities quoted by the writers. To these add Davidson, *Introduction to O. T.* II. 271 sqq. (for the O. T.), Forbes on the Ep. to the Romans (Edinburgh, 1868).]

25, x. 10. 1 Tim. iii. 16 also, where with parallelism there is combined complete similarity of clauses, appears to be taken from a hymn of the apostolic church.

4. The verses or parts of verses[1] which are met with in the N. T. either are formal quotations from Greek poets, or appear suddenly in the midst of prose without any announcement whatever. The examples of the latter class may be familiar poetical sentences from unknown poets. More frequently, however, the writer has unconsciously arranged his words in a metrical form: in this manner verses have sometimes found their way even into good prose, though the ancient rhetoricians pronounced them blemishes in composition.[2]

The poetical quotations are confined to the writings of the apostle Paul. They are three in number:[3]—

a. In Tit. i. 12, an entire hexameter, quoted from Epimenides of Crete (ἴδιος αὐτῶν προφήτης,—compare ver. 5):

$$- \smile \; - | \; - \smile \smile | \; - \smile \smile | \; - \smile \smile | \; - \smile \smile | \; - \smile$$
Κρητες ἀει ψευ|σται κακα | θηρια | γαστερες | ἀργαι.

b. In A. xvii. 28, a half hexameter:

$$- \; - | \; - \smile \smile | \; - \smile$$
του γαρ | και γενος | ἐσμεν.

Compare Aratus, *Phænom.* 5, where the verse concludes with ὁ δ᾽ ἤπιος ἀνθρώποισι (δεξιὰ σημαίνει); a spondee occupying the 5th place, as is often the case—especially in Aratus (10, 12, 32, 33).

c. In 1 C. xv. 33, an iambic trimeter acatalectic (senarius):

$$- \; - | \smile \; - | \; - \; - | \; \smile \; - | \smile \; - | \smile \; -$$
φθειρουσιν ἠ|θη χρησθ᾽ | ὁμι|λιαι | κακαι;

spondees occupying the uneven places 1 and 3, as is frequently

---

[1] Loeffler, *De versibus qui in soluta N. T. oratione habentur* (Leipsic, 1718); Kosegarten, *De poetarum effatis Græc. in N. T.*,—also included in his *Dissertatt. Acad.* (ed. Mohnike), p. 135 sqq. [See also the Introduction to Neale's *Hymns of the Eastern Church.*]

[2] Compare Cic. *Orat.* 56. 189 (mis-quoted by Weber, *Demosth.* p. 208); Quintil. *Instit.* 9. 4. 52, 72 sqq.; Fabric. *Biblioth. Latin.* (ed. Ernesti) II. 389; Nolten, *Antibarb.* s. v. "versus ;" Jacob, Luc. *Alex.* p. 52 sq.; Dissen, Demosth. *Cor.* p. 315; Franke, *Demosth.* p. 6; also the *Classical Journal*, no. 45, p. 40 sqq. The treatise by Loeffler (Moeller), *De versu inopinato in prosa* (Leipsic, 1668), I have not seen. The censure passed on verses which appear in the midst of prose is qualified and corrected by Hermann, in his *Opusc.* I. 121 sqq.

[3] J. Hoffmann, *De Paulo apostolo scripturas profanas ter allegante* (Tubing. 1770).

the case¹ (Don. p. 623). This quotation is from the well-known comic poet Menander,—according to H. Stephanus, from his *Thais*.² The best MSS. of the N. T., however, read χρηστά, without elision.

5. The second of the above-mentioned classes³ will comprehend

a. The hexameter verse in Ja. i. 17,—which was recognised by early commentators:

πασα δο|σις ἀγα|θη και | παν δω|ρημα τε|λειον;

the lengthening of σις in the second foot being quite admissible, in the *arsis*. See the commentators *in loc*. Schulthess endeavoured to arrange the rest of the passage in a metrical form, as two verses; but the rhythm would be harsh, and the fact that James makes use of poetical words does not justify us in inferring the existence of actual verses, and putting these together by means of violent alterations and transpositions.

b. On the other hand, we have the true rhythm of a hexameter in H. xii. 13, in the words

και τροχι|ας ὀρ|θας ποι|ησατε | τοις ποσιν | ὑμων.

c. In A. xxiii. 5, also, the words quoted from the LXX may be scanned as an iambic trimeter acatalectic.

ἀρχον|τα του | λαου | σου οὐκ | ἐρεις | κακως;

though certainly the three spondees which occur in the 1st, 3rd, and 4th places would render the verse unpleasing to a Grecian ear.—Lastly, in Jo. iv. 35 the words τετράμηνος . . . ἔρχεται will have the rhythm of a trimeter acatalectic, if we read

---

¹ Hermann, *Doctr. Metr.* p. 74. (On p. 139, "in *impari* sede" is surely a misprint for "in *pari* sede.")

² See Menandri *Fragm.* p. 75 (ed. Meineke), and *Fragm. Comic. Gr.* IV. 132 (ed. Meineke).

³ The search after such verses is so much the more a matter of idle curiosity, as the rhythm of prose is different from that of poetry, and in some instances will not allow these sentences to stand out as verses: Hermann *l. c.* p. 124, Thiersch in the *Münchner gel. Anzeigen*, 1849, vol. 28, no. 118. We have selected such lines only as in themselves express a complete thought. For examples of half—or at all events incomplete—sentences which contain a rhythm, see the *Classical Journal l. c.*, p. 46 sq. On 2 P. ii. 22, also, iambic verses have been forced, by a combination of the two proverbs: see Bengel *in loc.*

SECT. LXVIII.]　　　OF SENTENCES.　　　799

$$\breve{\ }\breve{\ }-|\breve{\ }-|\breve{\ }-|\ \ |\breve{\ }-|\breve{\ }-|\breve{\ }-$$
τετραμη|νος ἐσ|τι χὠ | θερισ|μος ἐρ|χεται.

Here there is an anapæst in the first place (Herm. *Doctr. Metr.*
p. 119 sq., Don. p. 623): on χὠ[1] for καὶ ὁ see Buttm. I. 122.

---

[1] [Surely this should be χὠ: see Buttm. *l. c.*, Don. p. 67, Jelf 13.]

INDEX.

I.—PASSAGES OF THE NEW TESTAMENT EXPLAINED OR ILLUSTRATED.

MATTHEW.

i. 2-16,	.	. 141	vi. 7,	.	. 484	xi. 5,	.	.	326
i. 11 sq.,	.	. 234	vi. 9,	.	. 668	xi. 8,	.	.	739
i. 17,	.	. 137	vi. 12,	.	. 561	xi. 11,	.	.	305
i. 18,	. 260, 570,	769	vi. 19,	.	. 149	xi. 25,	.	.	785
i. 20,	. 488,	500	vi. 25,	.	. 195	xii. 4,	.	.	566
i. 21,	.	. 187	vi. 32,	.	. 560	xii. 7,	.	.	381
i. 22,	.	. 576	vi. 34,	.	257, 649	xii. 9,	.	.	183
ii. 2,	.	. 558	vii. 4,	.	. 356	xii. 13,	.	663,	779
ii. 3,	.	. 137	vii. 6,	.	. 630	xii. 14,	.	.	360
ii. 4,	. 88,	333	vii. 8,	.	. 333	xii. 15,	.	.	183
ii. 6,	.	. 141	vii. 9,	.	211, 643	xii. 21,	.	.	261
ii. 13,	.	. 334	vii. 12,	.	423, 570	xii. 23,	.	.	642
ii. 20,	.	. 219	vii. 14,	.	208, 562	xii. 24,	.	.	157
ii. 22,	.	. 257	vii. 16,	.	349, 465	xii. 26,	.	.	217
iii. 5,	.	. 546	vii. 21,	.	. 214	xii. 30,	.	.	606
iii. 7,	.	. 509	vii. 24,	.	349, 718	xii. 32,	.	626,	744
iii. 10,	.	. 333	vii. 29,	.	. 771	xii. 36,	.	.	718
iii. 11,	.	. 333	viii. 1,	.	. 275	xii. 41,	.	472,	495
iii. 12,	.	. 185	viii. 4,	.	182, 183	xii. 42,	.	.	150
iii. 14,	.	. 336	viii. 8,	.	. 423	xii. 50,	.	139,	187
iii. 16,	. 183,	189	viii. 11,	.	. 220	xiii. 3,	.	.	132
iii. 17,	. 347,	733	viii. 19,	.	. 145	xiii. 14,	265,	445,	584
iv. 1,	.	. 132	viii. 21,	.	. 721	xiii. 15,	.	.	630
iv. 3,	.	. 421	viii. 28,	.	. 276	xiii. 18,	.	.	231
iv. 4,	. 350, 486,	490	viii. 32,	.	. 391	xiii. 23,	.	.	578
iv. 15,	. 234,	289	viii. 34,	.	. 137	xiii. 25,	.	.	413
iv. 16,	.	. 309	ix. 6,	705, 725,	774	xiii. 28,	.	.	356
iv. 23,	. 181,	233	ix. 8,	.	. 219	xiii. 30,	.	.	282
v. 3,	.	. 689	ix. 13,	.	. 621	xiii. 34,	.	.	336
v. 9,	.	. 769	ix. 17,	.	. 757	xiii. 52,	.	.	265
v. 18,	. 216,	765	ix. 34,	.	. 486	xiv. 3,	.	.	515
v. 19,	.	. 308	ix. 35,	.	181, 233	xiv. 6,	.	.	276
v. 20,	.	. 307	x. 1,	.	. 231	xiv. 7,	.	.	471
v. 21,	.	. 275	x. 5,	.	. 234	xiv. 22,	.	.	372
v. 22,	. 138, 267,	776	x. 11,	.	. 385	xiv. 24,	.	.	591
v. 25,	. 371,	630	x. 16,	.	. 515	xiv. 25,	.	.	468
v. 28,	.	. 255	x. 19,	.	. 210	xiv. 31,	.	.	252
v. 34,	.	. 486	x. 25,	.	423, 783	xiv. 36,	.	.	384
v. 35,	.	. 495	x. 26,	.	. 375	xv. 4,	.	427,	585
v. 38,	.	. 747	x. 28,	100, 149,	280	xv. 5,	158,	636,	750
v. 45,	. 557,	572	x. 29,	.	. 216	xv. 16,	.	.	582
v. 46,	. 332	sq.	x. 32,	.	283, 570	xv. 23,	.	216,	744
vi. 1,	. 32,	757	x. 33,	.	. 386	xv. 32,	.	210,	704
vi. 5,	.	. 586	x. 42,	.	. 739	xvi. 6,	.	.	280
			xi. 1,	.	. 181	xvi. 7,	.	.	748

Winer Grammar.   51

xvi. 11,	.	.	. 725	xxiv. 2,	. . . 604	xxvii. 66,	.	. . 472
xvi. 13,	.	.	. 664	xxiv. 6,	. . . 628	xxviii. 17,	.	. . 130
xvi. 14,	.	.	. 654	xxiv. 9,	. . . 438	xxviii. 19,	.	. . 240
xvi. 20,	.	.	. 421	xxiv. 12,	. . . 137			
xvi. 26,	.	. 164, 705	xxiv. 22,	. . . 214	MARK.		
xvii. 11,	.	.	. 332	xxiv. 26,	. . . 219			
xvii. 12,	.	.	. 273	xxiv. 27,	. . . 220	i. 1,	.	. . 233
xvii. 14,	.	.	. 736	xxiv. 32,	. . . 111	i. 4,	.	. 235, 440
xvii. 16,	.	.	. 102	xxiv. 38,	. . . 204	i. 9,	.	517 sq.
xvii. 18,	.	.	. 178	xxiv. 40,	. . . 333	i. 10,	.	. . 693
xvii. 20,	.	.	. 309	xxiv. 43,	. . . 212	i. 16,	.	. . 520
xvii. 25,	.	.	. 463	xxiv. 45,	. . . 659	i. 17,	.	. . 760
xvii. 26,	.	.	. 736	xxiv. 47,	. . . 490	i. 22,	.	. . 653
xviii. 1,	.	. 305, 556	xxiv. 50,	. . . 525	i. 35,	.	. . 760
xviii. 3,	.	.	. 589	xxv. 1,	. . . 24	i. 39,	.	517 sq.
xviii. 5,	.	.	. 490	xxv. 6,	. . . 259	i. 44,	.	. 182, 183
xviii. 6,	.	. 424, 764	xxv. 9,	. . 632, 748	ii. 1,	.	476, 516, 518
xviii. 7,	.	.	. 465	xxv. 14,	. 578, 749	ii. 8,	.	. . 693
xviii. 8,	.	.	. 302	xxv. 21,	. . . 509	ii. 10,	.	. . 725
xviii. 19,	.	.	. 369	xxv. 24,	. . . 198	ii. 15,	.	. . 760
xviii. 21,	.	.	. 446	xxv. 27,	. . . 352	ii. 16,	160, 208, 572, 731
xviii. 22,	.	.	. 314	xxv. 34,	. . . 236	ii. 18,	.	. 181, 438
xviii. 24,	.	.	. 146	xxv. 40,	. . . 509	ii. 23,	.	320, 406, 723
xviii. 25,	.	.	. 607	xxvi. 2,	. . . 331	ii. 24,	.	. . 765
xviii. 27,	.	.	. 255	xxvi. 5,	. . . 745	ii. 26,	.	. . 469
xix. 2,	.	.	. 183	xxvi. 9,	. . . 352	iii. 2,	.	. . 374
xix. 5,	.	. 328, 539	xxvi. 17,	. . . 356	iii. 6,	.	. . 374
xix. 8,	.	.	. 505	xxvi. 18,	. . . 88	iii. 11,	.	. . 388
xix. 12,	.	.	. 152	xxvi. 23,	. . . 515	iii. 14 sqq.,	.	. 724
xix. 13,	.	.	. 359	xxvi. 24,	. 352, 473	iii. 16,	.	. . 344
xix. 22,	.	.	. 438	xxvi. 26,	. . . 144	iii. 16 sqq.,	.	. 706
xx. 1,	.	.	. 267	xxvi. 26 sq.,	. . . 131	iii. 20,	.	. . 614
xx. 2,	.	.	. 461	xxvi. 28,	. . . 428	iii. 21,	.	. 346, 458
xx. 8,	.	.	. 775	xxvi. 33,	. . . 366	iii. 28,	.	. . 176
xx. 15,	.	.	. 639	xxvi. 35,	. . . 636	iv. 1,	.	. . 504
xx. 18,	.	.	. 263	xxvi. 38,	. . . 194	iv. 12,	.	. 577, 630
xx. 20,	.	.	. 213	xxvi. 44,	. . . 527	iv. 19,	.	. . 240
xx. 23,	.	. 566, 728	xxvi. 45,	. . . 391	iv. 29,	.	. 360, 738
xxi. 2,	.	.	. 194	xxvi. 50,	207 sq.	iv. 38,	.	. . 187
xxi. 3,	.	.	. 567	xxvi. 53,	. . . 300	iv. 39,	.	. . 395
xxi. 5,	.	.	. 194	xxvi. 54,	. . . 356	v. 2,	.	. . 276
xxi. 7,	.	. 179, 219	xxvi. 59,	. 361, 546	v. 3,	.	. . 615
xxi. 19, 145, 468 sq., 629	xxvi. 61,	. . . 476	v. 5,	.	. . 438
xxi. 20,	.	.	. 345	xxvi. 62,	. . . 760	v. 11,	.	. . 438
xxi. 23,	.	.	. 276	xxvi. 63,	477 sq.	v. 23,	.	. . 396
xxi. 41,	. 180, 386, 794	xxvi. 66,	. . . 253	v. 25,	.	. . 230
xxi. 42,	298, 457, 482	xxvi. 67,	. . . 130	v. 26,	.	. 458, 784
xxii. 5,	.	.	. 191	xxvii. 1,	. . . 400	v. 30,	.	. . 693
xxii. 25,	.	.	. 596	xxvii. 5,	. 481, 516	v. 36,	.	. . 436
xxii. 36,	.	.	. 308	xxvii. 7,	265, 461	v. 43,	.	. . 360
xxiii. 5,	.	.	. 567	xxvii. 15,	. . . 500	vi. 3,	.	. . 142
xxiii. 9,	.	.	. 738	xxvii. 19,	. . . 731	vi. 7,	.	. . 312
xxiii. 15,	.	.	. 740	xxvii. 22,	. . . 179	vi. 8,	.	. . 724
xxiii. 25,	.	.	. 251	xxvii. 23,	. . . 559	vi. 8 sq.,	.	. 397
xxiii. 30,	.	.	. 380	xxvii. 25,	. . . 734	vi. 9,	.	. 725, 732
xxiii. 31,	.	.	. 265	xxvii. 33,	. . . 207	vi. 16,	.	. . 205
xxiii. 32,	.	. 391, 545	xxvii. 37,	. . . 344	vi. 19,	.	. . 742
xxiii. 33,	.	.	. 356	xxvii. 40,	169, 444	vi. 20,	.	. . 437
xxiii. 34,	.	.	. 748	xxvii. 44,	219, 285	vi. 25,	.	. . 423
xxiii. 35,	.	.	. 578	xxvii. 49,	. . . 356	vi. 36,	.	. . 210
xxiii. 37,	.	.	. 288	xxvii. 54,	. . . 338	vi. 37,	.	. . 190

NEW TESTAMENT. 803

						LUKE.	
i. 39 sq.,	286, 312, 581	xii. 12,	.	545, 702			
i. 45,	. . . 372	xii. 14,	. .	. 595	i. 1,	. .	344, 765
i. 52,	. . . 489	xii. 18,	. .	. 209	i. 4,	. .	. 206
i. 56,	. . . 384	xii. 19,	. .	. 361	i. 6,	. .	. 158
ii. 4,	. 401, 776	xii. 23,	. .	. 756	i. 9,	. .	. 443
ii. 11,	. . . 750	xii. 24,	. .	. 201	i. 17,	. .	. 182
ii. 15,	. . . 142	xii. 26,	.	470, 753	i. 20,	. 204,	438, 610
ii. 19,	668, 669, 778	xii. 28,	. .	. 222	i. 21,	. .	. 292
ii. 26,	. . . 118	xii. 32,	. .	. 528	i. 22,	. .	. 187
ii. 36,	. . . 300	xii. 33,	. .	. 158	i. 24,	. .	. 107
iii. 2,	. . . 704	xii. 38,	.	280, 587	i. 25,	. .	. 525
iii. 3,	. . . 106	xii. 38 sq.,	.	. 722	i. 27,	. .	. 86
iii. 4,	. . . 468	xii. 38 sqq.,	228, 668, 705		i. 28,	. .	. 732
iii. 6,	. . . 359	xiii. 3, 16,	.	. 516	i. 31,	. .	. 759
iii. 8,	. . . 664	xiii. 9,	. .	. 517	i. 32,	. .	. 151
iii. 11,	. . . 429	xiii. 10,	. .	. 267	i. 36,	. .	. 80
iii. 12,	. . . 627	xiii. 14,	. .	. 661	i. 37,	214, 216,	350, 492
iii. 15,	. . . 280	xiii. 19,	. .	. 184	i. 39,	. .	. 740
iii. 19,	. . . 267	xiii. 20,	. .	. 382	i. 42,	. .	. 308
iii. 22,	. . . 186	xiii. 25,	. .	. 437	i. 43,	. .	424 sq.
iii. 26,	. . . 614	xiii. 28,	. .	. 111	i. 51,	. .	. 346
iii. 27,	. . . 234	xiii. 34,	. .	. 578	i. 55,	. .	. 722
iii. 35,	. 189, 385	xiv. 1,	. .	. 374	i. 57,	. .	. 408
x. 6,	. . . 374	xiv. 2,	.	630, 632	i. 58,	. .	. 471
x. 8,	. . . 566	xiv. 3,	121, 235, 477, 537		i. 59,	. .	336, 511
x. 11,	. 208, 572	xiv. 4,	. .	. 438	i. 62,	. .	. 386
x. 12,	. . . 577	xiv. 5,	. .	. 313	i. 64,	. .	. 777
x. 15,	. . . 693	xiv. 6,	. .	. 273	i. 68,	. .	. 589
x. 17,	. . . 348	xiv. 8,	. .	. 586	i. 70,	. .	165, 703
x. 20,	. . . 710	xiv. 10,	. .	. 360	i. 72,	. .	. 471
x. 23,	. . . 135	xiv. 12,	. .	. 356	i. 73,	. .	205, 784
x. 28,	. 208, 572	xiv. 13,	. .	. 235	i. 73 sq.,	.	410, 722
x. 30,	. 360, 423	xiv. 36,	. .	. 211	i. 74,	. .	. 402
x. 34,	. . . 305	xiv. 40,	. .	. 374	i. 76,	. .	. 769
x. 37,	. . . 138	xiv. 43,	. .	. 457	i. 78,	. .	. 764
x. 42,	. . . 304	xiv. 47,	. .	. 145	i. 79,	. .	. 110
x. 43,	. . . 302	xiv. 49,	. .	. 398	ii. 1,	. .	318, 401
x. 45,	. . . 302	xiv. 53,	. .	. 269	ii. 2,	. .	. 306
x. 47,	. . . 402	xiv. 54,	. .	. 438	ii. 4,	. .	210, 456
i. 2,	. . . 429	xiv. 58,	. .	. 476	ii. 8,	. .	. 282
i. 7,	. . . 539	xiv. 68,	. .	. 615	ii. 12,	. .	. 434
i. 10,	. . . 517	xiv. 70,	. .	. 337	ii. 13,	. .	. 80
i. 13,	. . . 359	xiv. 72,	. .	. 742	ii. 21,	. 408,	546, 756
i. 20,	. . . 317	xv. 1,	.	159, 321	ii. 22,	. .	. 183
i. 21,	. 280, 590	xv. 3,	. .	. 254	ii. 23,	. .	. 152
i. 30,	. . . 472	xv. 4,	. .	. 254	ii. 26,	. .	371, 388
i. 32,	. . . 438	xv. 8,	. .	. 730	ii. 28,	. .	. 187
i. 37,	. . . 423	xv. 16,	. .	206 sq.	ii. 31,	. .	. 218
i. 38,	. . . 282	xv. 20,	. .	. 361	ii. 34,	. .	229, 496
i. 42,	. . . 766	xv. 21,	. .	. 150	ii. 35,	. .	. 389
ii. 5,	. . . 761	xv. 25,	. .	. 543	ii. 36,	. .	. 755
ii. 13,	. 376, 556	xv. 36,	. .	. 356	ii. 41,	. .	. 269
ii. 14,	. . . 628	xv. 39,	. .	. 740	ii. 45,	. .	. 429
ii. 18,	. . . 374	xv. 44,	.	339, 679	ii. 49,	. .	. 740
ii. 19,	. . . 389	xvi. 2,	. .	. 431	iii. 1,	. .	. 173
ii. 21,	. . . 345	xvi. 3,	.	454, 702	iii. 5,	. .	. 739
ii. 22,	. . . 232	xvi. 5,	. .	. 434	iii. 8,	. .	. 767
ii. 25,	. . . 388	xvi. 7,	.	546, 654	iii. 15,	. .	. 374
ii. 32,	. . . 725	xvi. 8,	. .	. 566	iii. 20,	. .	. 490
iii. 5,	. . . 728	xvi. 9,	. .	. 311	iii. 23,	. .	. 439
iii. 11,	. . . 298	xvi. 14,	. .	. 557	iii. 23-38,	.	. 141

iv. 6,	.	.	.	338	ix. 46,	.	.	.	305	xiii. 9,	.	.	369, 751
iv. 10,	.	.	.	410	ix. 49,	.	.	.	490	xiii. 16,	.	.	. 704
iv. 14,	.	.	.	477	ix. 51,	.	.	.	187	xiii. 34,	.	.	. 189
iv. 15,	.	181, 187, 443	ix. 52,	.	.	400, 743	xiii. 35,	.	.	. 372
iv. 16,	.	.	.	264	ix. 54,	.	.	.	356	xiv. 7,	.	.	335, 742
iv. 18,	.	.	339, 561	ix. 61,	.	.	.	784	xiv. 8 sq.,	.	.	631
iv. 20,	.	.	.	131	ix. 62,	.	.	.	267	xiv. 10,	.	87, 361, 574
iv. 22,	.	.	.	297	x. 1,	.	.	592, 665	xiv. 18,	.	345, 526, 739
iv. 23,	.	.	.	518	x. 4,	.	.	.	619	xiv. 23,	.	.	. 158
iv. 26 sq.,	.	.	566	x. 7,	.	.	.	458	xv. 6,	.	.	. 321
iv. 29,	.	.	.	400	x. 8,	.	.	.	724	xv. 7,	.	.	. 302
iv. 35,	.	57, 433, 607	x. 9,	.	.	.	508	xv. 16,	.	.	. 248
iv. 42,	.	.	.	409	x. 13,	.	.	.	648	xv. 18,	.	.	. 760
v. 4,	.	.	.	725	x. 18,	.	.	.	336	xv. 29,	.	.	. 156
v. 5,	.	.	.	491	x. 19,	.	.	.	342	xvi. 2,	.	.	. 784
v. 14,	.	182, 183, 725	x. 20,	.	.	484, 621	xvi. 3,	.	.	. 436
v. 16,	.	.	187, 515	x. 21,	.	.	.	262	xvi. 4,	.	.	. 736
v. 17,	.	.	.	183	x. 23 sq.,	.	.	191	xvi. 8,	.	254, 297, 748
v. 19,	.	.	259, 738	x. 29,	.	.	.	163	xvi. 9,	.	.	. 321
v. 24,	.	.	.	725	x. 36,	.	.	.	163	xvi. 18,	.	.	. 152
v. 25,	.	.	.	508	x. 37,	.	.	321, 471	xvi. 20,	.	.	. 85
v. 32,	.	.	.	339	x. 42,	.	.	.	308	xvi. 23,	.	.	. 220
vi. 1,	.	.	.	124	xi. 3,	.	.	120 sq.	xvi. 24,	.	.	. 252
vi. 11,	.	.	.	386	xi. 4,	.	.	.	138	xvii. 1,	.	.	. 412
vi. 12,	.	.	.	231	xi. 5,	.	.	349, 357	xvii. 2,	.	.	302, 424
vi. 16,	.	.	.	238	xi. 7,	.	.	516, 518	xvii. 6,	.	.	. 383
vi. 18,	.	.	.	464	xi. 8,	.	.	250, 554	xvii. 7,	.	.	. 87
vi. 34,	.	.	.	369	xi. 11,	.	.	643, 710	xvii. 8,	.	109, 210, 371
vi. 35,	.	.	.	151	xi. 12,	.	.	.	369	xvii. 15,	.	.	. 471
vi. 42,	.	.	.	356	xi. 13,	.	.	.	784	xvii. 18,	.	.	. 769
vi. 48,	.	.	588, 754	xi. 14,	.	.	.	186	xvii. 24,	.	.	. 740
vii. 4,	.	.	.	386	xi. 18,	.	.	.	557	xvii. 25,	.	.	. 464
vii. 5,	.	.	.	187	xi. 22,	.	.	.	32	xvii. 27,	.	.	. 204
vii. 8,	.	.	.	438	xi. 28,	.	.	.	556	xvii. 31,	.	.	. 723
vii. 11,	.	.	.	738	xi. 29,	.	.	.	236	xviii. 1,	.	.	. 414
vii. 12,	.	264, 546, 756	xi. 33,	.	.	.	298	xviii. 3,	.	.	. 776
vii. 22,	.	.	.	326	xi. 35,	.	.	374, 631	xviii. 4,	.	.	554, 744
vii. 29 sq.,	.	.	705	xi. 49,	.	.	494, 737	xviii. 6,	.	.	. 297
vii. 30,	.	.	.	267	xi. 53,	.	.	.	742	xviii. 7,	.	.	321, 620
vii. 33,	.	.	.	607	xii. 1,	.	.	.	482	xviii. 9,	.	.	. 136
vii. 44,	.	.	.	137	xii. 4,	.	.	100, 201	xviii. 12,	.	.	. 342
vii. 47,	.	.	571 sq.	xii. 6,	.	.	.	216	xviii. 14,	.	.	. 302
viii. 1,	.	.	.	738	xii. 8,	.	.	283, 570	xviii. 15,	.	.	. 135
viii. 14,	.	.	.	462	xii. 12,	.	.	.	166	xviii. 21,	.	.	. 317
viii. 17,	.	.	375, 386	xii. 20,	.	228, 320, 656	xviii. 31,	.	.	. 265
viii. 18,	.	.	.	766	xii. 26,	.	600, 614 sq.	xviii. 34,	.	.	. 183
viii. 20,	.	.	.	736	xii. 30,	.	.	193, 686	xix. 2,	.	.	. 200
viii. 29,	.	.	.	273	xii. 36,	.	.	.	736	xix. 4,	259, 738, 754, 787
viii. 34,	.	.	.	517	xii. 37,	.	.	.	761	xix. 7,	.	.	. 492
viii. 43,	.	.	.	267	xii. 44,	.	.	.	490	xix. 11,	.	.	. 588
viii. 46,	.	.	.	435	xii. 46,	.	.	.	525	xix. 15,	.	189, 360, 784
viii. 47,	.	.	.	208	xii. 47,	.	283, 607, 737	xix. 23,	.	.	378 sq.
ix. 1,	.	.	.	722	xii. 48,	204, 283, 656, 737	xix. 29,	.	.	. 226
ix. 3,	.	.	397 sq.	xii. 49,	.	.	.	562	xix. 37,	.	.	493, 661
ix. 9,	.	.	.	190	xii. 51,	.	.	.	552	xix. 40,	.	107, 348, 369
ix. 13,	.	145, 368, 649	xii. 53,	.	.	.	489	xix. 42,	.	.	. 750
ix. 14,	.	.	.	286	xii. 54,	.	.	144, 332	xix. 43,	.	.	. 544
ix. 19,	.	.	.	131	xii. 58,	.	.	568, 630	xix. 48,	.	.	107, 374
ix. 22,	.	.	.	464	xiii. 1,	.	.	.	778	xx. 2,	.	.	. 753
ix. 28,	.	.	648, 704	xiii. 2,	.	.	338, 503	xx. 10,	.	.	. 361
ix. 45,	.	.	.	574	xiii. 4,	.	.	.	481	xx. 11 sq.,	.	.	588

NEW TESTAMENT.   805

xx. 19,	. . 505	JOHN.		v. 6 sq.,	. . 748
xx. 20,	160, 253, 400	i. 1,	. . 151, 504	v. 13,	. . 112
xx. 26,	. . 253	i. 6,	. . 440, 457	v. 18,	. . 336
xx. 27,	. 668, 755	i. 8,	. . . 398	v. 22,	. . 687
xx. 35,	. . 761	t. 9,	. . . 439	v. 24,	. . 341
xx. 36,	. 614 sq.	i. 13,	. . . 220	v. 29,	. . 235
xx. 42,	. . 139	i. 14,	151, 705, 771	v. 32,	. . 136
xx. 43,	. . 756	i. 15,	. . 306, 342	v. 36,	166, 307
xx. 46,	. . 587	i. 16,	. . 456, 545	v. 37 sq.,	613 sq.
xxi. 6,	. . 718	i. 18,	. 429, 517 sq.	v. 44,	190,416,583,717,723
xxi. 11,	. . 793	i. 19,	. . . 547	v. 45,	. 136, 341
xxi. 19,	. . 342	i. 22,	. . . 774	vi. 1,	. . 239
xxi. 21,	. . 183	i. 25,	. . . 616	vi. 3,	. 131 sq.
xxi. 24,	. . 438	i. 27,	. . . 423	vi. 7,	. . 423
xxi. 25,	. 149, 150	i. 30,	. . 190, 306	vi. 9,	. . 145
xxi. 30,	. . 742	i. 32,	. . 150, 717	vi. 10,	. 288, 571
xxi. 37,	227, 517 sq.	i. 34,	. . . 341	vi. 17,	. . 745
xxii. 2,	. . 374	i. 42,	. . . 583	vi. 19,	. . 468
xxii. 9,	. . 356	i. 51,	. . . 201	vi. 21,	469, 586 sq.
xxii. 11,	. . 754	i. 52,	. . . 692	vi. 22,	. . 343
xxii. 15,	. . 584	ii. 6,	. 496 sq., 502	vi. 22 sqq.,	. . 711
xxii. 19,	. . 191	ii. 9,	. . . 248	vi. 23,	. . 706
xxii. 20,	. . 791	ii. 17,	. . . 231	vi. 27,	. 622, 670
xxii. 23,	. 374, 556	ii. 18,	. . . 557	vi. 29,	. . 425
xxii. 24,	. 305, 766	ii. 19,	. . . 482	vi. 31,	. . 736
xxii. 26,	. . 735	ii. 20,	. . . 273	vi. 33,	. . 431
xxii. 30,	. . 361	ii. 21,	. . . 666	vi. 35,	. . 635
xxii. 41,	. . 288	ii. 25,	. . 143, 426	vi. 36,	. . 548
xxii. 42,	. . 750	iii. 10,	. . . 143	vi. 39,	. . 718
xxii. 49,	. . 348	iii. 13,	. . . 429	vi. 40,	. . 425
xxii. 53,	. . 193	iii. 15,	. . . 267	vi. 45,	. . 236
xxii. 61,	. . 753	iii. 16,	. . 215, 377	vi. 46,	. . 746
xxiii. 5,	. 477, 775	iii. 18,	. . 594, 602	vi. 50,	. . 431
xxiii. 8,	. . 459	iii. 19,	. . . 785	vi. 55,	. . 584
xxiii. 12,	. 440, 586	iii. 22,	. . . 742	vi. 57,	. . 498
xxiii. 15,	. . 274	iii. 26,	. . . 265	vi. 62,	. . 750
xxiii. 19,	. 209, 439	iii. 29,	. . . 584	vi. 64,	. . 596
xxiii. 31,	. . 356	iii. 34,	. . . 527	vii. 3,	. . 361
xxiii. 32,	. . 665	iii. 36,	. . . 332	vii. 4,	. . 786
xxiii. 44,	. . 543	iv. 1,	. . . 180	vii. 8,	. . 745
xxiii. 45,	. . 163	iv. 5,	. . . 494	vii. 10,	. . 771
xxiii. 48,	. . 509	iv. 6,	459, 489, 772	vii. 15,	. . 607
xxiii. 51,	. 182, 438	iv. 11,	. . . 619	vii. 16,	. . 621
xxiii. 53,	. . 626	iv. 14,	. . . 496	vii. 21 sq.,	. . 68
xxiv. 1,	. . 259	iv. 15,	. . . 363	vii. 22,	. . 746
xxiv. 13,	. . 438	iv. 18,	. . . 582	vii. 23,	. . 574
xxiv. 15,	. 139, 187	iv. 23,	263, 523, 528, 662	vii. 31,	. . 641
xxiv. 16,	. . 409	iv. 29,	. . . 642	vii. 34,	. . 61
xxiv. 18,	. . 785	iv. 31,	. . . 741	vii. 35,	. 234, 375
xxiv. 21,	488, 554, 655,	iv. 33,	. . . 642	vii. 36,	. . 61
	700, 780	iv. 34,	. . 423, 425	vii. 38,	. 109, 718
xxiv. 25,	. . 407	iv. 35,	676, 737, 781, 798	vii. 40,	. . 253
xxiv. 27,	. . 789	iv. 37,	. . . 142	vii. 45,	. . 196
xxiv. 29,	. . 150	iv. 42,	. . . 772	vii. 49,	. . 611
xxiv. 32,	. . 438	iv. 44,	. . 560, 569	vii. 51,	. 334, 656
xxiv. 35,	. . 275	iv. 48,	. . . 637	vii. 52,	. 333, 391
xxiv. 36,	. . 187	iv. 52,	. . . 288	viii. 4,	. . 84
xxiv. 39 sq.,	. 691	v. 1,	. . . 155	viii. 9,	. . 775
xxiv. 46 sq.,	. 290, 779	v. 2,	. 335, 489, 741	viii. 12,	. . 636
xxiv. 47,	. 267, 490	v. 4,	. . . 515	viii. 15,	. . 729
xxiv. 50,	. . 759	v. 5,	. . 288, 321	viii. 20,	. . 481

806 INDEX.

viii. 21,	. 484 sq.	xii. 23, . . 426, 576	xvii. 25, . . . 548
viii. 25,	546, 581 sq.	xii. 26, . . . 332	xvii. 26, . . . 282
viii. 29,	. . 346	xii. 40, . . 575, 630	xviii. 3, . . . 132
viii. 36,	. . 369	xii. 44, . . 622 sq.	xviii. 11, . 184, 642
viii. 37,	. 515 sq.	xii. 47, . . 180, 249	xviii. 12, . . 344
viii. 38,	. . 570	xiii. 1, . . 426, 715	xviii. 28, . . 360
viii. 39,	. 382 sq.	xiii. 2, . . 315, 360	xviii. 31, . . 727
viii. 44, 142, 173, 181, 586, 736		xiii. 4, . . . 220	xviii. 37, . . 643
		xiii. 5, . . . 767	xviii. 39, . . 426
viii. 53,	. 210, 722	xiii. 6, . . . 332	xix. 6, . . . 160
viii. 54,	. . 718	xiii. 10, . . . 638	xix. 11, . . . 383
viii. 55,	. . 243	xiii. 12, . . . 339	xix. 14, . . . 236
viii. 56,	. . 426	xiii. 13, . . . 227	xix. 23, . . . 220
viii. 58,	. . 334	xiii. 18, . . . 398	xix. 25, . . 164, 238
viii. 59,	. . 588	xiii. 24, . . . 387	xix. 28, . . 575, 702
ix. 2,	. . 574	xiii. 27, . 304, 332, 391	xix. 31, . . . 645
ix. 3,	. . 398	xiii. 28, . . 781 sq.	xix. 35, . . . 428
ix. 5,	. . 180	xiii. 29, . . . 722	xix. 37, . . . 197
ix. 7,	. 517, 705	xiii. 31, . . . 346	xx. 2, . . 522, 736
ix. 17,	. . 557	xiii. 34, . . 583, 658	xx. 4, . . . 756
ix. 21,	. . 189	xiv. 3, . . . 332	xx. 7, . . . 788
ix. 22,	. . 423	xiv. 7, . . . 342	xx. 12, . . . 739
ix. 25,	. . 429	xiv. 11, . . . 732	xx. 15, . . . 183
ix. 30,	. 230, 559	xiv. 16, . . . 665	xx. 19, . . . 198
ix. 33,	. . 382	xiv. 19, . . . 731	xx. 23, . . . 340
ix. 36,	. . 774	xiv. 23, . . . 320	xx. 28, . . . 228
ix. 37,	. . 342	xiv. 28, . . 381, 383	xx. 29, . . . 340
x. 4,	. . 646	xiv. 30 sq., . . 69	xxi. 1, . . . 468
x. 7,	. . 234	xv. 2, . . 67, 718	xxi. 4, . . . 508
x. 11,	. . 132	xv. 3, . . . 497	xxi. 8, . . . 697
x. 18,	. . 463	xv. 4, . . . 395	xxi, 12, . . . 766
x. 27,	. . 646	xv. 5, . . 625, 723	xxi. 13, . . . 759
x. 29,	. . 151	xv. 6, . 177, 345, 788	xxi. 16, . . . 755
x. 32,	. . 332	xv. 8, . 347, 423, 425	xxi. 18, . . . 321
x. 36,	. . 688	xv. 11, . . . 172	xxi. 21, . . . 734
x. 37,	. . 600	xv. 13, . . 425, 745	xxi. 22, . . 370, 734
xi. 1,	. . 512	xv. 16, . . . 363	xxi. 23, . . . 332
xi. 2,	. . 431	xv. 18, . . 306, 339	xxi. 25, . . 419, 605
xi. 4,	. . 479	xv. 20, . . . 365	
xi. 13,	. . 666	xv. 22, . . . 382	Acts.
xi. 15,	. 574, 702	xv. 24, . . . 548	i. 1,] . . 720, 775
xi. 18,	. . 697	xv. 25, . . . 398	i. 2, . . 204, 696
xi. 19,	. . 506	xv. 27, . . . 334	i. 3, . . 235, 259
xi. 30,	. . 705	xvi. 2, . . . 426	i. 4, . . . 725
xi. 33,	. . 269	xvi. 7, . . . 424	i. 5, . . . 201
xi. 37,	. . 423	xvi. 8, . . . 524	i. 7, . . 244, 550
xi. 44,	. . 348	xvi. 9, . . . 557	i. 8, . . . 156
xi. 47,	. . 354	xvi. 11, . . . 342	i. 10, . 218, 546, 756
xi. 48,	. . 759	xvi. 14 sq., . . 333	i. 11, . . . 763
xi. 49,	. . 213	xvi. 17, . . 88, 253	i. 12, . . . 227
xi. 50,	. . 424	xvi. 24, . . . 575	i. 13, . . 160, 238
xi. 52,	. . 722	xvi. 27, . . . 187	i. 14, . . . 654
xi. 55,	. . 676	xvi. 30, . . 426, 484	i. 18, . . . 108
xi. 56,	. . 637	xvi. 32, . . 426, 648	i. 21, . . 508, 780
xii. 1,	. . 697	xvii. 2, . 181, 231, 361	i. 22, . . 204, 775
xii. 3,	121 sq., 251, 659	xvii. 3, . . 363, 425	i. 24, . . . 430
xii. 5,	. . 775	xvii. 4, . . 345 sq.	i. 25, . . . 786
xii. 7,	. . 342	xvii. 10, . . 341, 486	i. 26, . . . 540
xii. 9,	. . 166	xvii. 18, . . . 346	ii. 1, . . . 412
xii. 13,	. 264, 754	xvii. 22, . . . 342	ii. 3, . . . 648
xii. 16,	. . 491	xvii. 24, . . . 332	ii. 12, . . . 379

NEW TESTAMENT. 807

ii. 25,	. . 108, 495	vii. 7,	. . . 385	xi. 17,	. . 199, 553, 784
ii. 26,	. . . 528	vii. 10,	. . . 173	xi. 19,	. . 465, 489
ii. 27,	. . . 740	vii. 14,	. . . 488	xi. 22,	. . . 761
ii. 28,	. . . 470	vii. 16,	. . 112, 237	xi. 28,	. . . 661
ii. 29,	. . . 731	vii. 19,	. . . 410	xii. 3,	. . . 588
ii. 30,	. . . 570	vii. 20,	. . 265, 310	xii. 11,	. . . 189
ii. 31,	. . . 740	vii. 22,	. . . 284	xii. 14,	. . . 57
ii. 33,	. 268, 297, 666	vii. 24,	. . 323, 788	xii. 19,	. . 517 sq.
ii. 36,	. . . 137	vii. 26,	. . . 336	xii. 21,	. . . 178
ii. 38,	. . 490, 734	vii. 29,	. . . 484	xiii. 2,	. 328, 524 sq.
ii. 39,	. . 517 sq.	vii. 34,	. . . 445	xiii. 9,	. . . 133
ii. 43,	. . 194, 473	vii. 36,	. . . 149	xiii. 10,	. . 396, 641
ii. 45,	. . . 384	vii. 38,	. . . 147	xiii. 11,	. . . 610
ii. 47,	. . . 136	vii. 40,	. . 226, 375	xiii. 13,	. . . 506
iii. 1,	. . . 509	vii. 42,	. . 315, 589	xiii. 17,	. . . 472
iii. 2,	. . . 444	vii. 42 sq.,	. . . 642	xiii. 19,	. . . 547
iii. 3,	. . . 760	vii. 45,	. . 111, 218	xiii. 20,	. . . 273
iii. 5,	. . . 742	vii. 48,	. . . 693	xiii. 25,	. . . 211
iii. 10,	. . 781 sq.	vii. 53,	. . 286, 496	xiii. 26,	. . . 298
iii. 12,	. 410, 763, 771	viii. 2,	. . . 321	xiii. 27,	. . . 569
iii. 13,	185, 186, 196, 720	viii. 5,	. . . 181	xiii. 32,	166, 284, 781 sq.
iii. 16,	. . . 491	viii. 9,	. . . 213	xiii. 34,	. . . 772
iii. 17,	. . . 501	viii. 11,	. . . 273	xiii. 35,	. . . 741
iii. 19,	. . 389, 578	viii. 16,	. . . 440	xiii. 39,	. . . 524
iii. 23,	. . . 194	viii. 22,	. . 376, 556	xiii. 40,	. . . 219
iii. 24 sq.,	. . . 789	viii. 26,	. . 147, 195	xiii. 45,	. . . 446
iii. 26,	. . 168, 413	viii. 31,	. . 369, 379	xiii. 48,	. . . 328
iv. 2,	. . . 486	viii. 35,	. . . 759	xiii. 49,	. . . 472
iv. 5,	. . 183, 517	viii. 40,	516, 518, 769	xiv. 1,	. . . 500
iv. 7,	. . 212, 788	ix. 1,	. . . 255	xiv. 9,	. . . 407
iv. 11,	. . . 195	ix. 2,	. . . 133	xiv. 10,	. . 99, 692
iv. 12,	. 273, 569, 619	ix. 4,	. . . 436	xiv. 12,	. . . 187
iv. 13,	. . . 337	ix. 6,	. . 210, 734	xiv. 15,	. . . 784
iv. 15,	. . . 742	ix. 9,	. . . 610	xiv. 16,	. . . 274
iv. 17,	. . 490, 584	ix. 11,	. . . 569	xiv. 17,	. . . 195
iv. 20,	. . . 624	ix. 20,	. . 781 sq.	xiv. 18,	. . . 409
iv. 21,	. . . 374	ix. 21,	. . . 359	xiv. 26,	. . . 592
iv. 22,	. . 666, 745	ix. 31,	. . . 477	xiv. 27,	. . . 471
iv. 29,	. . . 48	ix. 35,	. . . 343	xv. 1,	. . . 270
iv. 35,	. . . 384	ix. 37,	. . . 222	xv. 4,	. . . 471
v. 4,	266, 621, 623, 731	ix. 42,	. . . 477	xv. 7,	. . . 283
v. 7,	. . . 704	x. 3,	. . . 288	xv. 10,	. . . 400
v. 12 sqq.,	. . . 706	x. 7,	. . 181, 788	xv. 12,	. . . 222
v. 15,	. . . 730	x. 10,	. . 182, 184	xv. 16,	. . . 588
v. 17,	. . . 760	x. 14,	. . . 214	xv. 17,	. . . 389
v. 19,	. . . 475	x. 15,	. . 733, 755	xv. 22,	. . 319, 709
v. 20,	. . . 297	x. 17,	464, 546, 756	xv. 23,	. 160, 397, 735
v. 23,	. . 469, 755	x. 22,	. . . 406	xv. 24,	. . . 405
v. 26,	. . 359, 634	x. 25,	. . . 412	xv. 27,	. . . 429
v. 28,	. . 490, 584	x. 28,	. . . 563	xv. 36,	. . . 177
v. 29,	. 651, 654, 744	x. 30,	. . . 698	xv. 38,	. . . 465
v. 31,	. . . 268	x. 32,	. . . 172	xvi. 9,	. . 275, 475
v. 32,	. . . 239	x. 36,	205, 706, 719	xvi. 11,	. . . 79
v. 35,	. . 489, 697	x. 37,	. . . 477	xvi. 16,	. . . 322
v. 36,	. . 213, 327	x. 39,	. . . 780	xvi. 22,	. . . 337
v. 38 sq.,	. . . 369	x. 41,	. . . 174	xvi. 27,	. . . 420
v. 40,	. . . 490	x. 45,	. . . 527	xvi. 33,	. . 246, 465
v. 42,	. . . 434	x. 47,	. . . 409	xvi. 34,	. . . 435
vi. 9,	. . . 160	xi. 5,	. . . 792	xvi. 37,	. . . 559
vii. 4,	. . . 517	xi. 15,	. . . 767	xvi. 40,	. . . 494
vii. 5,	. . . 344	xi. 16,	. . . 753	xvii. 2,	. . 264, 465

808 INDEX.

xvii. 3,	. . 725	xxii. 3,	. 237, 428, 700	xxvi. 26,	. 626 sq.
xvii. 4,	. . 328	xxii. 5,	. . . 592	xxvi. 29,	. . 379
xvii. 10,	. . 475	xxii. 6,	. . . 276	xxvi. 31,	. . 334
xvii. 11,	. . 374	xxii. 17,	. 276, 406, 722	xxvi. 32,	. . 383
xvii. 14,	. . 771	xxii. 18,	. . . 172	xxvii. 1,	. . 410
xvii. 18,	. 379, 742	xxii. 21,	. . . 494	xxvii. 2,	. . 280
xvii. 20,	. . 212	xxii. 22,	. . . 352	xxvii. 10,	. 426, 718
xvii. 21,	. . 305	xxii. 24,	. . . 208	xxvii. 12,	. 375, 499
xvii. 22,	. . 305	xxii. 25,	. . . 261	xxvii. 13,	. 304, 742
xvii. 25,	. . 793	xxii. 30,	. . 457, 496	xxvii. 14,	. 183, 477
xvii. 27,	374 sq., 556	xxiii. 1,	. . . 328	xxvii. 20,	. 149, 763
xvii. 28,	129, 193, 499,	xxiii. 5,	. . . 798	xxvii. 21,	. . 352
	569, 797	xxiii. 6,	. . 546, 786	xxvii. 22,	. . 789
xvii. 29,	. . 617	xxiii. 8,	. . . 618	xxvii. 28,	. . 315
xvii. 31,	. . 486	xxiii. 9,	. . 749, 750	xxvii. 33,	. . 437
xviii. 6,	. 220, 734	xxiii. 13,	. . . 320	xxvii. 34,	. . 467
xviii. 10,	. . 742	xxiii. 14,	. . . 584	xxvii. 35,	. . 767
xviii. 15,	. . 193	xxiii. 15,	. . . 407	xxvii. 38,	. . 131
xviii. 17,	. . 257	xxiii. 21,	. . . 241	xxvii. 39,	. 367, 697
xviii. 21,	. . 517	xxiii. 22,	. . . 725	xxvii. 40,	74, 739, 742
xix. 3,	. . 496	xxiii. 23,	. 212, 393	xxvii. 42,	. 423, 630
xix. 4,	. . 720	xxiii. 23 sq.,	. . 725	xxviii. 3,	322, 461, 465
xix. 14,	. . 212	xxiii. 26,	. . . 735	xxviii. 20,	. . 287
xix. 19,	. . 740	xxiii. 27,	. . . 168	xxviii. 23,	. . 150
xix. 22,	. 315, 517 sq.	xxiii. 30,	. . . 710	xxviii. 25,	. . 753
xix. 26,	. . 624	xxiii. 31,	. . . 475	xxviii. 26,	. . 58
xix. 27,	. 229, 245, 548	xxiii. 34,	. 212, 456	xxviii. 27,	630 sq.
xix. 29,	. . 443	xxiv. 2,	. . . 767		
xix. 34,	. . 710	xxiv. 3,	. . . 52	ROMANS.	
xix. 35,	. 294, 741	xxiv. 5 sq.,	. 442, 710	i. 1,	. . 155
xix. 38,	. . 738	xxiv. 8,	. . . 254	i. 1 sqq.,	. . 707
xx. 2,	. . 181	xxiv. 10,	. 435, 459	i. 3,	. . 233
xx. 3,	. . 710	xxiv. 11,	. . . 204	i. 4,	. 235, 297, 460
xx. 4,	. . 173	xxiv. 12 sq.,	. . 616	i. 5,	. 232, 474
xx. 9,	465, 468 sq., 537	xxiv. 14,	. . . 275	i. 6,	. . 243
xx. 13,	. . 328	xxiv. 17,	. 267, 475	i. 7,	. . 294
xx. 14,	. 517 sq.	xxiv. 18,	. . . 176	i. 8,	473, 720 sq.
xx. 16,	. . 367	xxiv. 19,	. . . 352	i. 9,	. . 563
xx. 18,	. . 204	xxiv. 21,	. . . 203	i. 10,	. 374, 470
xx. 24,	. 233, 401	xxiv. 22,	. . . 701	i. 12,	. . 722
xx. 27,	. . 409	xxiv. 25,	. . . 580	i. 13,	. . 549
xx. 29,	. . 494	xxv. 4,	. . . 518	i. 15,	. 289, 294
xx. 34,	. . 722	xxv. 7,	. . . 659	i. 16,	. 310, 721
xx. 35,	. . 301	xxv. 10,	. . . 304	i. 17,	. 170, 232
xxi. 2,	. . 429	xxv. 11,	254, 317, 334	i. 19,	. . 295
xxi. 3,	326, 439, 592	xxv. 12,	. . . 675	i. 20,	. . 295
xxi. 4,	. . 405	xxv. 15,	. . . 161	i. 21,	. . 779
xxi. 8,	. 168, 741	xxv. 16,	. 371 sq.	i. 23,	. 258, 485
xxi. 10,	. . 736	xxv. 18,	. . . 466	i. 24,	330, 410, 519
xxi. 13,	. 516, 518, 761	xxv. 22,	. 353, 734	i. 25,	. . 504
xxi. 16,	205, 253, 268,	xxv. 27,	. . . 402	i. 26,	. . 297
	386, 737	xxvi. 3,	193, 290, 499, 716	i. 26 sq.,	. . 715
xxi. 21,	. . 405	xxvi. 4,	. . . 720	i. 28,	. 603, 610
xxi. 24,	. . 361	xxvi. 8,	. . . 679	i. 30,	. . 61
xxi. 25,	. . 159	xxvi. 10,	. . . 548	i. 32,	. . 432
xxi. 26,	. . 343	xxvi. 14,	. . . 436	ii. 1,	. 169, 484, 668
xxi. 28,	. 548, 723	xxvi. 16,	. 178, 329	ii. 3,	. . 200
xxi. 31,	. . 269	xxvi. 18,	. . . 174	ii. 5,	234, 501, 519
xxi. 33,	. . 375	xxvi. 22,	174, 436, 570	ii. 7,	. . 233
xxi. 38,	. . 641	xxvi. 23,	. . . 120	ii. 8,	. 527, 724
xxii. 1,	. . 249	xxvi. 24,	. . . 134	ii. 9,	. . 194

NEW TESTAMENT.

ii. 9 sq.,	721, 723	vi. 3,	. . . 639	ix. 15,	. . . 108
ii. 12,	. . 432	vi. 4,	. 170 sq., 296	ix. 16,	. . . 747
ii. 13 sqq.,	. . 707	vi. 5,	. . . 552	ix. 18,	. . . 736
ii. 14,	174, 388, 696, 774	vi. 6,	235, 409, 765, 768	ix. 19,	. 342, 736
ii. 15,	. . 725	vi. 10,	209, 263, 285, 532	ix. 20,	. . . 584
ii. 17 sqq.,	. 711 sq.	vi. 11,	. . 263, 486	ix. 21,	. . . 689
ii 18,	. . 743	vi. 12,	. . 148, 658	ix. 22 sqq.,	. 713, 749
ii. 21 sq.,	. . 405	vi. 13,	. . . 394	ix. 24,	. . . 662
ii. 26,	. 181 sq.	vi. 14,	. . 349, 397	ix. 26,	. . . 769
ii. 27,	168, 432, 475	vi. 16,	. . 549, 765	ix. 29,	. . . 753
ii. 28,	. 568, 730	vi. 17,	205, 327, 732, 785	ix. 30,	. 174, 553
iii. 2,	. 720 sq.	vi. 20,	. . . 263	ix. 31,	. . . 793
iii. 4,	. 318, 389	vi. 21,	. 177, 197, 277	ix. 32,	. . . 771
iii. 5,	. 641 sq.	vi. 22,	. . . 519	ix. 33,	. . . 542
iii. 6,	348, 743, 749	vii. 2,	. 235, 339, 776	x. 1,	. 479, 719, 733
iii. 7,	. 546, 579	vii. 3,	. . . 408	x. 2,	. 231, 502
iii. 8,	. . 783	vii. 4,	. . 263, 476	x. 3,	. . . 232
iii. 9,	330, 693 sq.	vii. 5,	. . . 414	x. 10,	. . . 495
iii. 11,	. . 136	vii. 6,	. . 198, 296	x. 14,	197, 249, 348, 356
iii. 19,	. 137, 576	vii. 7,	. . 383, 561	x. 15,	. 356, 758
iii. 20,	. 214, 350	vii. 10,	. . . 770	x. 18,	. 183, 642
iii. 21,	. . 232	vii. 12,	. . . 720	x. 19,	141, 491, 597, 662
iii. 22,	232, 521, 553	vii. 13,	. . . 435	x. 20,	. 274, 588 sq.
iii. 23,	. . 443	vii. 14,	. . . 507	x. 21,	. 23, 505
iii. 24,	. . 272	vii. 17,	. . 579, 772	xi. 2,	. . . 481
iii. 25,	. 119, 171, 189, 318, 497	vii. 21,	185, 670, 697, 714	xi. 4,	. . . 223
		vii. 22,	. . . 540	xi. 6,	. 354, 772
iii. 27,	. . . 212	vii. 24,	. 235, 298, 358	xi. 7,	. . . 250
iii. 28,	. . 744	vii. 24 sq.,	. . 751	xi. 8,	. . . 117
iii. 30,	350, 453, 512	viii. 1,	. . . 168	xi. 11,	. 574, 733
iv. 2,	. . 384	viii. 2,	. . . 171	xi. 13,	. . . 509
iv. 3,	. . 567	viii. 3,	. 290, 484, 670, 718, 778	xi. 13 sq.,	. . . 720
iv. 4,	. . 36			xi. 14,	. . . 374
iv. 9,	509, 734, 744	viii. 6,	. . 560, 568	xi. 17,	. . . 488
iv. 11,	. 475, 666	viii. 8,	. . . 566	xi. 18,	. . . 773
iv. 12,	274, 695, 722	viii. 11,	. . . 498	xi. 20,	. 270, 394
iv. 13,	232, 260, 568	viii. 12,	. . 410, 696	xi. 21,	241, 595, 632, 748
iv. 16,	. . 747	viii. 15,	. . . 483	xi. 23,	. . . 776
iv. 17,	. 204, 206	viii. 18,	. . 267, 505	xi. 27,	. . . 241
iv. 19,	. . 610	viii. 20,	. . . 498	xi. 30,	. . . 270
iv. 20,	270, 327, 430	viii. 21,	. . 666, 776	xi. 31,	. 191, 575, 688
v. 2,	. . 170	viii. 22,	. . . 763	xi. 32,	. . . 496
v. 3,	. . 729	viii. 23,	145, 233, 667, 729	xi. 33,	. 238, 652
v. 5,	133, 232, 516	viii. 24,	271, 355, 545	xi. 36,	. 134, 521
v. 6,	. 692, 568	viii. 25,	. . . 527	xii. 1,	66, 477, 669
v. 7,	145, 349, 568	viii. 26,	. . . 120	xii. 2,	. . . 724
v. 8,	. . 172	viii. 27,	. . . 499	xii. 5,	. . . 137
v. 9,	. . 743	viii. 29,	. . . 243	xii. 6 sqq.,	. 723, 728
v. 11,	. 441, 729	viii. 30,	. . 346 sq.	xii. 9,	. . . 733
v. 12,	180, 491, 494, 712 sq., 749	viii. 32,	. . . 555	xii. 9 sqq.,	. . . 732
		viii. 35,	. . . 232	xii. 12,	. . . 271
v. 12 sqq.,	. . 713	viii. 36,	. . . 235	xii. 15,	. 397 sq.
v. 14,	. . 492	ix. 1,	. . . 487	xii. 16,	. . . 275
v. 15,	. . 137	ix. 3,	. . 353, 776	xii. 18,	. . . 289
v. 16,	. . 730	ix. 4,	. . . 221	xii. 19,	. . . 743
v. 18,	. 235, 734	ix. 5,	166, 289, 690, 733	xii. 20,	. . . 394
v. 19,	. . 137	ix. 6,	. . 746 sq.	xiii. 1,	. 194, 454
v. 20,	. . 561	ix. 7,	. . . 719	xiii. 2,	. . . 265
v. 20 sq.,	. . 575	ix. 8,	. . . 137	xiii. 7,	. . . 737
v. 21,	. . 520	ix. 10,	. . . 729	xiii. 8,	. . . 629
vi. 2,	. 263, 349	ix. 11,	. 241, 608, 736	xiii. 9 sq.,	. . . 707

810 INDEX.

xiii. 11,	243, 717	ii. 5,	733	vii. 1,	198
xiii. 14,	696	ii. 6,	273	vii. 2,	192, 497
xiv. 1,	496	ii. 7,	172	vii. 3,	132
xiv. 2,	130, 405	ii. 9,	398, 719, 788	vii. 5,	380, 527
xiv. 4,	263	ii. 9 sq.,	749	vii. 7,	354, 567, 584, 754
xiv. 8,	369	ii. 10,	749	vii. 10,	622
xiv. 9,	691	ii. 11,	689	vii. 11,	328
xiv. 11,	262, 563, 572	ii. 12,	241	vii. 13,	186, 722
xiv. 14,	189, 487, 566	ii. 13,	242	vii. 14,	354, 486, 556
xiv. 20,	475	ii. 15,	700	vii. 15,	390, 519
xiv. 21,	597, 729	iii. 1,	122, 728	vii. 17,	566
xiv. 23,	341	iii. 2,	619, 777	vii. 18,	211
xv. 1,	597	iii. 5,	546, 570	vii. 19,	728
xv. 3,	719, 749	iii. 7,	728	vii. 20,	525
xv. 4,	191, 236	iii. 10,	376	vii. 21,	555, 678, 728, 744
xv. 5,	231, 501	iii. 11,	504	vii. 24,	493
xv. 8,	479	iii. 13,	332	vii. 26,	403, 570
xv. 9,	405, 417	iii. 14,	60	vii. 28,	265, 346, 354, 366
xv. 13,	231	iii. 17,	206	vii. 29,	132, 575
xv. 15,	304, 347, 771	iii. 19,	443	vii. 31,	262
xv. 16,	279, 486, 666	iv. 2,	424	vii. 35,	264, 445, 582
xv. 17,	289	iv. 3,	229, 424	vii. 36,	787
xv. 20,	696	iv. 4,	484, 560, 785	vii. 37,	241, 717
xv. 21,	719, 749	iv. 5,	134	vii. 38,	304, 721
xv. 23 sq.,	711	iv. 6,	217, 362 sq., 478, 483, 737	viii. 1 sqq.,	707
xv. 25,	429			viii. 3,	329
xv. 27,	560	iv. 7,	554, 567	viii. 6,	186, 522, 724
xv. 28,	472	iv. 8,	377	viii. 7,	231, 270, 584
xv. 30,	477	iv. 9,	149, 158 sq.	viii. 9,	566
xvi. 2,	198	iv. 11,	114	viii. 11,	491, 559
xvi. 4,	708	iv. 14,	156, 430, 717	ix. 2,	265, 554, 602
xvi. 5,	496	iv. 15,	552	ix. 5,	321, 401, 657
xvi. 10,	238	iv. 18,	771	ix. 7,	271
xvi. 12,	487	iv. 20,	733	ix. 9,	559, 744
xvi. 19,	560	iv. 21,	356	ix. 10,	491, 559
xvi. 20,	776	v. 1,	210, 689	ix. 11,	368
xvi. 25,	273	v. 2,	576	ix. 12,	231
xvi. 25 sqq.,	710	v. 3,	568, 720	ix. 15,	202, 361, 424, 483, 551, 715
xvi. 26,	232, 494	v. 5,	575		
xvi. 27,	134	v. 7,	48, 354	ix. 17,	774
		v. 8,	666	ix. 18,	172, 361
1 Corinthians.		v. 9,	132, 347	ix. 19,	429
i. 2,	294, 330	v. 9 sq.,	694	ix. 20,	347
i. 6,	231	v. 10,	161, 354, 602	ix. 22,	213
i. 8,	196, 519, 708	v. 11,	347, 715	ix. 24,	748
i. 9,	473	v. 12,	733	ix. 26,	609
i. 10,	477	vi. 1,	318	x. 2,	319
i. 11,	238	vi. 2,	482	x. 3,	166
i. 12,	780	vi. 3,	155, 746	x. 4,	336, 659
i. 21,	476	vi. 4,	556	x. 9,	179
i. 22,	765	vi. 5,	218	x. 11,	567
i. 23,	168, 678, 749, 795	vi. 7,	318, 556, 579	x. 12,	766
i. 25,	307	vi. 9 sq.,	613	x. 13,	408, 737, 743
i. 26,	732	vi. 10,	626	x. 16,	204, 237
i. 27,	237	vi. 11,	202, 319, 645, 664, 780	x. 17,	137, 251, 461
i. 28,	161, 608			x. 19,	61
i. 29,	214	vi. 13,	733	x. 21,	237
i. 30,	464	vi. 15,	761	x. 22,	355
i. 31,	749	vi. 16,	656	x. 24,	728
ii. 1,	231, 430	vi. 19,	218	x. 27,	768
ii. 2,	597	vi. 20,	744	x. 30,	198, 271

NEW TESTAMENT.

x. 33, . . . 607	xv. 24, . . 360, 387	iii. 11, . 474, 512, 527
xi. 2, . . 285, 567	xv. 25, . . . 656	iii. 13, . . . 728
xi. 4, 138, 433, 477, 743	xv. 27, . 387, 731, 736	iii. 14, . . . 669
xi. 5, . . 222, 271	xv. 29, . 219, 349, 478	iii. 14 sqq., . . 707
xi. 6, . . 391, 600	xv. 31, . . 191, 649	iii. 18, . . 287, 318
xi. 12, . . . 476	xv. 33, . . 43, 797	iv. 2, . . . 103
xi. 15, . . 339, 455	xv. 34, . . . 392	iv. 3, . . 273, 554
xi. 16, . . 766, 774	xv. 35, . . . 333	iv. 4, . . . 779
xi. 18, . 515, 720, 721	xv. 36, . . . 228	iv. 7, . . . 576
xi. 20, . . . 403	xv. 37, . . . 775	iv. 10, . . . 236
xi. 22, . . . 743	xv. 42, . . . 656	iv. 13, . . . 441
xi. 23, . . 337, 464	xv. 46, . . . 741	iv. 15, . . . 733
xi. 24, . . . 191	xv. 49, . . . 345	iv. 16, . . 552, 581
xi. 26, . . . 568	xv. 51 sq., . . 695	iv. 17, . . . 792
xi. 27, . 161, 253, 550	xv. 52, 109, 482, 544, 655	iv. 18, . . 260, 608
xi. 28, . . . 566	xv. 54, . . . 776	v. 1, . 333, 366, 666
xi. 30, . . . 334	xv. 57, . . . 428	v. 2, . . 184, 444
xi. 31, . . . 381	xvi. 1, . . . 467	v. 4, . . 133, 491
xii. 2, . . 384, 714	xvi. 2, . . . 500	v. 5, . . . 666
xii. 3, . . . 486	xvi. 3, . . 219, 476	v. 6, . . . 442
xii. 8, . . . 501	xvi. 5, . . . 703	v. 6 sqq., . . 717
xii. 8 sq., . . . 522	xvi. 6, . . . 446	v. 7, . . . 474
xii. 15, . 461, 504, 625	xvi. 9, . . . 545	v. 8, . . . 553
xii. 22, . . . 301	xvi. 12, . . . 467	v. 11, . . . 417
xii. 28, . . . 710	xvi. 17, . . . 191	v. 12, . . 442, 743
xii. 31, . . . 584	xvi. 21, . . . 664	v. 14, . . . 232
xiii. 3, . 89, 284, 361	xvi. 22, . . 601, 602	v. 19, . 181, 438, 772
xiii. 6, . . 263, 540		v. 20, . . 328, 480
xiii. 12, . 191, 329, 476	2 CORINTHIANS.	v. 21, . . 232, 608
xiii. 13, . . . 303	i. 3, . . . 733	vi. 1, . . . 417
xiv. 1, . . 567, 722	i. 4, . . . 203	vi. 3, . . . 608
xiv. 4, . . . 152	i. 5, . . . 236	vi. 4, . . . 225
xiv. 5, . 368, 722, 756	i. 7, . . . 716	vi. 13, . . 665, 774
xiv. 7, . . 433, 693	i. 9, . . 340, 575	vi. 14, . . . 276
xiv. 9, . . . 438	i. 10, . . . 341	vi. 17, . . . 183
xiv. 11, . 273, 483, 722	i. 12, . . . 309	vii. 5, . 442, 711, 716
xiv. 13, . . . 575	i. 15, . . . 270	vii. 7, . . 169, 304
xiv. 15, . . . 349	i. 17, . . . 576	vii. 8, . . . 730
xiv. 18, . . 434, 683	i. 18, . . 557, 563	vii. 9, . 501, 576, 622
xiv. 19, . . . 302	i. 24, . . 263, 746	vii. 11, . . . 271
xiv. 20, . . . 270	ii. 1, . . . 265	vii. 12, . . 347, 751
xiv. 22, . . . 229	ii. 2, . . 460, 547	vii. 13, . . 464, 490
xiv. 33, . . . 244	ii. 3, . 198, 347, 352	vii. 14, . . . 469
xiv. 34, . . . 777	ii. 4, . . 459, 474	viii. 2, . . 477, 528
xiv. 36, . . . 494	ii. 5, . . . 623	viii. 3, . . . 715
xiv. 38, . . . 390	ii. 6, . . . 649	viii. 5, . . 721, 730
xv. 2, 211, 332, 688, 757	ii. 7, . . . 406	viii. 6, . . . 414
xv. 3, . . . 513	ii. 9, . . . 347	viii. 7, . 241, 396, 565
xv. 4, . . . 339	ii. 10, . . . 327	viii. 8, . . . 476
xv. 6, . . . 313	ii. 12, . . 495, 567	viii. 9, . . . 196
xv. 8, . . 60, 131	ii. 13, 181, 265, 340, 413	viii. 10, . . . 701
xv. 9, . . . 769	ii. 14, . . . 24	viii. 11, . . . 461
xv. 10, . . . 621	ii. 16, . . . 763	viii. 12, . . . 385
xv. 12, . . . 782	ii. 17, . . . 136	viii. 13, . . 527, 733
xv. 13, . . . 601	iii. 3, . . . 122	viii. 15, . . . 737
xv. 13 sq., . . 567	iii. 4 sq., . . . 695	viii. 16, . . . 732
xv. 15, . 231, 477, 556	iii. 5, . . . 746	viii. 17, . . . 304
xv. 16, . . . 365	iii. 6, . . 238, 546	viii. 18, . . . 347
xv. 18, . . . 487	iii. 7, . 428, 790, 791	viii. 19, . . 488, 729
xv. 21, . . . 733	iii. 8, . . . 349	viii. 20, . . . 441
xv. 22, . . . 486	iii. 9, . . . 569	viii. 23, . . 723 sq.

812 INDEX.

viii. 24,	.	.	753	GALATIANS.		iv. 27,	. 301, 609, 742
ix. 2,	.	.	241	i. 1,	. . 474, 521	iv. 28,	. . . 501
ix. 4,	.	.	746	i. 4,	. . 166, 659	v. 1,	. . . 263
ix. 6,	.	489,	746	i. 5,	. . . 134	v. 4,	. . . 776
ix. 7,	.	.	734	i. 6,	. . . 795	v. 6,	. . . 319
ix. 9,	.	.	588	i. 7,	. . 136, 566	v. 7,	. . . 755
ix. 10 sq.,	.	.	716	i. 8,	. . 649, 650	v. 7 sq., .	. . 794
ix. 11,	.	.	264	i. 8 sq.,	. . . 369	v. 10,	. . . 292
ix. 12,	.	.	264	i. 12,	464, 614, 618	v. 12,	. . 319, 377
ix. 12 sq.,	.	.	716	i. 13,	. . 336, 584	v. 13,	. . . 745
ix. 13,	. 170, 232,	476	i. 15,	. . . 459	v. 16,	. . . 636
ix. 14,	.	.	271	i. 16,	. . . 273	v. 26,	. . . 629
ix. 15,	.	.	732	i. 18,	. . . 313	vi. 1,	. . 781 sq.
x. 1,	.	.	477	i. 19,	. . 566, 789	vi. 3,	. . . 766
x. 2,	325, 404, 406,	553	i. 20,	. . . 563	vi. 10,	. . 355, 561
x. 4,	. 265,	310	i. 23,	. . 444, 787	vi. 11,	. . 347 sq.
x. 5,	.	.	232	i. 24,	. . . 484	vi. 12,	. . . 270
x. 7,	.	.	465	ii. 1,	. . . 475	vi. 14,	. . . 153
x. 9,	. 380,	390	ii. 2,	553, 633, 788	vi. 16,	. . . 546
x. 10,	.	.	655	ii. 4,	. . . 361	vi. 17,	. 190, 259
x. 12,	.	.	273	ii. 4 sq.,	. . . 711		
x. 13,	203, 400, 495,	665	ii. 5,	. . . 296	EPHESIANS.	
x. 14,	. 430, 494,	595	ii. 6,	558, 579, 711	i. 3,	. . . 733
xi. 1,	. 377,	551	ii. 7,	. . . 339	i. 5,	. . . 502
xi. 2,	. 231, 323,	670	ii. 8,	. . . 495	i. 6,	. . . 203
xi. 3,	.	.	776	ii. 9,	. . 735, 766	i. 7,	. . . 486
xi. 4,	. 136,	383	ii. 10,	. . 178, 185	i. 8,	. . 138, 204
xi. 6,	.	.	552	ii. 11,	. . . 431	i. 9,	. . . 189
xi. 7,	.	638 sq.	ii. 13,	. . 271, 377	i. 10,	. . . 495
xi. 9,	.	.	168	ii. 14,	48, 296, 505	i. 11,	. . . 328
xi. 10,	.	.	563	ii. 15 sq.,	. . . 655	i. 12,	. . . 167
xi. 12,	. 357,	547	ii. 16,	232, 350, 566	i. 13,	260, 271, 704, 733
xi. 16,	. 730,	757	ii. 17,	. . 640, 770	i. 14,	. . 206 sq.
xi. 17,	.	.	501	ii. 19,	. . . 263	i. 15,	. . 169, 193
xi. 18,	.	.	145	ii. 20,	. . 209, 285	i. 16,	. . . 470
xi. 20,	.	.	320	iii. 1,	101, 168, 185, 279	i. 17,	. . 189, 363
xi. 21,	. 502,	772	iii. 4,	. . . 561	i. 18,	. . . 716
xi. 23,	. 526,	584	iii. 7,	. . . 527	i. 20,	. . 273, 717
xi. 23 sqq.,	.	.	723	iii. 9,	. . . 488	i. 23,	207, 323, 325, 669
xi. 24,	. 503,	737	iii. 10,	. . . 461	ii. 2,	. 298, 501, 790
xi. 26,	.	.	234	iii. 11,	. . . 170	ii. 3,	. 220, 238, 270,
xi. 28,	. 264,	668	iii. 14,	. . . 297		689, 717
xi. 29,	.	.	191	iii. 15,	. . . 693	ii. 4,	. . 282, 553
xi. 30,	.	.	675	iii. 16,	206 sq., 469, 656	ii. 5,	. . . 148
xii. 1,	.	.	569	iii. 17,	. . . 494	ii. 6,	. . 295, 347
xii. 2,	. 200, 520,	698	iii. 18,	. . . 579	ii. 7,	. . 172, 319
xii. 6,	.	.	568	iii. 19,	. . . 474	ii. 8,	. . 148, 272
xii. 7,	. 276,	764	iii. 20,	. . 144, 741	ii. 10,	. . 185, 193
xii. 8,	.	.	479	iii. 21,	. . 174, 381	ii. 11,	. 166, 169, 708
xii. 9,	. 300, 339,	354	iii. 22,	. . . 232	ii. 11 sq.,	. . 753
xii. 11,	.	.	352	iii. 23,	. . . 494	ii. 11 sqq.,	. . 704
xii. 12,	. 132,	720	iv. 7,	. . 473 sq.	ii. 12,	. . . 221
xii. 13,	.	.	502	iv. 8,	. . . 610	ii. 14,	. . . 666
xii. 15,	.	.	194	iv. 9,	. . 329, 755	ii. 15,	. . 170, 275
xii. 17,	.	.	718	iv. 11,	. . 632, 782	ii. 16,	. . . 519
xii. 20,	. 274,	696	iv. 13,	. . . 499	ii. 17,	. . . 759
xii. 20 sq.,	.	.	632	iv. 15,	. . . 382	ii. 21,	138, 169, 186, 430
xii. 21,	. 491, 693,	792	iv. 17,	. . . 362	iii. 1,	. . . 236
xiii. 1,	.	.	314	iv. 19,	. . . 176	iii. 1 sqq.,	. . 708
xiii. 4,	. 484, 552,	555	iv. 20,	. . . 353	iii. 4,	. . . 170
xiii. 7,	. 576,	695	iv. 25,	. . 136, 223	iii. 5,	. . . 273

NEW TESTAMENT. 813

iii. 6,	.	. 400, 486	vi. 16 sq.,	.	. 666	iii. 21,	. .	. 779
iii. 8,	.	. . 81	vi. 18,	.	. 546, 786	iv. 3,	. .	. 210
iii. 10,	.	161, 295, 575	vi. 19,	.	. . 363	iv. 5,	. .	. 275
iii. 11,	.	. . 320	vi. 20,	.	. . 482	iv. 7,	. .	. 232
iii. 12,	.	. 172, 232	vi. 22,	.	. . 200	iv. 10,	. .	106, 399
iii. 13,	170, 206 sq., 210					iv. 11,	. .	501, 746
iii. 15,	.	. . 137	PHILIPPIANS.			iv. 15,	. .	. 250
iii. 16,	.	363, 496, 520	i. 1,	.	. . 735	iv. 16,	. .	286, 515
iii. 18,	.	159, 180, 715	i. 3,	.	. . 489	iv. 18,	. .	297, 458
iii. 19,	.	232, 272, 435	i. 6,	.	. . 285	iv. 19, 21,	.	. 172
iii. 20,	.	. . 526	i. 7,	.	. 414, 783	iv. 22,	. .	. 785
iii. 21,	.	. . 134	i. 8,		236 sq., 563			
iv. 1,		169, 203, 485	i. 9,	.	. . 518	COLOSSIANS.		
iv. 2 sq.,	.	. . 716	i. 11,	.	. 174, 287	i. 3 sq.,	. .	. 433
iv. 3,	.	. . 483	i. 12,	.	. . 304	i. 4,	. .	. 169
iv. 4,	.	. . 519	i. 14,	.	. . 171	i. 6,	171, 204, 319, 717	
iv. 6,	.	. . 521	i. 16 sq.,	.	. 460, 702	i. 8,	. .	. 169
iv. 8,	.	. 282, 656	i. 17 (16),	.	. . 229	i. 9,	. .	. 172
iv. 9,	.	136, 666, 741	i. 18,	.	. . 196	i. 10,	. .	. 716
iv. 11,	.	. . 130	i. 19,	.	. 159, 161	i. 12,	. .	. 170
iv. 13,	.	. . 238	i. 22,	.	374, 547, 751	i. 13,	. .	. 297
iv. 14,	.	. . 575	i. 23,	.	. 300, 413	i. 15,	. .	. 153
iv. 15,	.	. . 496	i. 23 sq.,	.	. . 723	i. 16,	. 144, 340, 521	
iv. 16,	.	. . 483	i. 26,	.	. 170, 584	i. 17,	. .	. 187
iv. 18,	.	. 233, 660	i. 27,	.	. . 265	i. 19,	. .	. 736
iv. 21,	.	. 249, 488	i. 28,	.	. . 206	i. 20,	. 222, 266, 495	
iv. 22,	.	404 sq., 430	i. 29 sq.,	.	. . 716	i. 21,	. 270, 553, 714	
iv. 23,	.	270, 330, 405	ii. 1,	.	. . 661	i. 22,	. .	. 235
iv. 24,	.	. . 501	ii. 3,	.	. . 735	i. 23,	. .	. 596
iv. 26,	.	391, 392, 620	ii. 4,	.	. . 624	i. 24,	. .	170, 236
iv. 27,	.	. . 616	ii. 6,	.	221, 406	i. 26,	. .	. 717
iv. 28,	.	. . 444	ii. 7,	.	. . 430	i. 27,	. .	. 207
iv. 29,	.	216, 454, 728	ii. 9,	.	. . 175	ii. 1,	. .	. 568
iv. 30,	.	. . 494	ii. 10,	.	. 238, 487	ii. 2,	. .	. 716
v. 2,	.	. . 756	ii. 11,	.	. . 361	ii. 5,	552, 554, 588 sq.	
v. 3 sq.,	.	. 338, 610	ii. 12,	.	. . 597	ii. 7,	. .	. 271
v. 5, 159, 163, 209, 215, 446			ii. 13,	.	. . 479	ii. 8,	. 136, 501, 631	
v. 9,	.	. . 230	ii. 15,	.	. . 591	ii. 13,	. .	. 430
v. 12,	.	. 177, 182	ii. 18,	.	. . 285	ii. 14,	. .	. 275
v. 13,	.	. . 323	ii. 20,	.	. . 209	ii. 15,	. .	. 323
v. 14,	.	. 110, 392	ii. 22,	.	. 525, 722	ii. 16,	. .	. 768
v. 15,	.	. 376, 595	ii. 23,	.	. . 48	ii. 17,	. .	. 667
v. 19,	.	. . 265	ii. 27,	.	. . 508	ii. 18, 233, 291, 310, 586,		
v. 21,	.	. . 441	ii. 28,	.	. . 304			603
v. 23,	.	. . 665	ii. 30,	.	. . 115	ii. 19, 159, 177, 281, 309,		
v. 24,	.	. . 565	iii. 2,	.	. . 280			609
v. 26,	.	. 153, 172	iii. 3,	.	262, 271, 609	ii. 20,	. .	316, 326
v. 27,	.	. . 722	iii. 5,	.	. . 270	ii. 22,	. .	. 158
v. 31,	.	328, 456, 539	iii. 6,	.	. . 174	ii. 23,	. .	209, 719
v. 32,	.	. 190, 553	iii. 7,	.	. 342 sq.	iii. 5,	145, 207, 210, 393,	
v. 33,	.	. 396, 722	iii. 8,	.	. . 552			666
vi. 2,	.	. . 488	iii. 9,		172, 174, 232, 487	iii. 6,	. .	. 332
vi. 3,	.	. . 361	iii. 10,	.	. 409, 716	iii. 8,	. .	. 133
vi. 4,	.	236 sq., 485	iii. 11,	.	. . 374	iii. 12,	. .	. 764
vi. 5,	.	. . 172	iii. 12,		345, 374, 491 sq.	iii. 12 sqq.,	.	. 707
vi. 8,	.	. . 775	iii. 13 sq.,	.	. . 774	iii. 14,	. .	207, 490
vi. 11,	.	. . 236	iii. 14,	.	. . 169	iii. 15,	. .	232, 546
vi. 12,	.	. 299, 524	iii. 16,	.	. 397 sq.	iii. 16,	. .	. 716
vi. 13,	.	. . 236	iii. 18,	.	. . 665	iii. 18,	. .	. 338
vi. 14,	.	. . 666	iii. 18 sq.,		228, 668, 705	iii. 24,	. .	463, 666
vi. 16,	.	. 168, 490	iii. 20,	.	. 177, 568	iii. 25,	. .	. 775

814   INDEX.

iv. 3,	. . . 649	
iv. 6,	. 398, 400	
iv. 12,	. . . 138	
iv. 15,	. . 128, 181	
iv. 16,	. 133, 423, 784	
iv. 17,	. . 781 sq.	

1 Thessalonians.

i. 1,	. . . 170
i. 2,	. . . 470
i. 3,	. . 233, 768
i. 7,	. . . 218
i. 9,	. . . 181
i. 10,	. . 444, 743
ii. 3,	. . . 618
ii. 6,	. . . 512
ii. 7,	. . . 385
ii. 8,	. . 125, 777
ii. 10,	. . . 584
ii. 12,	. . . 414
ii. 13,	. . . 323
ii. 16,	. 172, 567, 743
ii. 17,	. . . 305
ii. 20,	. . 558 sq.
iii. 3,	. . 229, 413
iii. 5,	. . . 633
iii. 6,	. . . 464
iii. 8,	. . 369, 579
iii. 9,	. . . 283
iii. 13,	. . 519, 779
iv. 2,	. . . 474
iv. 3,	. . 401 sq.
iv. 6,	. 61, 143, 403
iv. 7,	. . . 519
iv. 8,	. . . 623
iv. 9,	. . 414, 426
iv. 13,	. . . 335
iv. 14,	. . . 678
iv. 15,	. . 483, 636
iv. 16,	169, 310, 482, 487
v. 1,	. . . 426
v. 2,	. . . 174
v. 4,	. . 573, 575
v. 10,	. . . 368
v. 11,	. . . 217
v. 12,	. . . 483
v. 15,	. . . 360
v. 22,	. . . 149

2 Thessalonians.

i. 1,	. . . 170
i. 4,	. . . 204
i. 4 sq.,	. . . 669
i. 6,	. . . 562
i. 7,	. . . 297
i. 8,	. . . 596
i. 9,	. . . 465
i. 10,	. . 326, 486
i. 12,	. . 162 sq.
ii. 1,	. . . 479
ii. 2,	. . 619, 771

ii. 3,	. 132, 298, 299
ii. 3 sq.,	. . . 749
ii. 6,	. . . 579
ii. 7,	. . . 688
ii. 10,	. . . 236
ii. 11,	. . . 296
ii. 12,	. . . 157
ii. 13,	. 232, 260, 519
iii. 3,	. . . 110
iii. 4,	. . . 292
iii. 5,	. . . 232
iii. 7,	. . . 557
iii. 8,	. . 442, 619
iii. 9,	. . . 746
iii. 12,	. . . 477
iii. 14,	. . . 147

1 Timothy.

i. 2,	. . . 171
i. 3,	. . . 404
i. 3 sqq.,	. . . 713
i. 4,	. . 174 sq.
i. 6,	. . . 245
i. 7,	. . . 211
i. 9,	. . . 265
i. 12,	. . . 437
i. 18,	. . . 484
ii. 1,	. . . 321
ii. 2,	. . . 81
ii. 4,	. . . 692
ii. 6,	. . . 669
ii. 8,	. . . 80
ii. 9,	. . . 80
ii. 10,	. . . 197
ii. 12,	. . . 152
ii. 15,	. . 648, 787
iii. 2,	. . . 146
iii. 5,	. . . 567
iii. 12,	. . . 146
iii. 13,	. . . 175
iii. 14,	. . . 304
iii. 15,	. . 206 sq.
iii. 16,	326, 736, 796 sq.
iv. 1,	. . . 233
iv. 3,	. . . 777
iv. 8,	. . . 175
iv. 13,	. . . 370
iv. 14,	. . . 471
v. 4,	. . . 787
v. 5,	. . . 162
v. 9,	. . . 738
v. 11,	. . . 388
v. 13,	. . 436, 603
v. 19,	. . 469, 757
v. 23,	. . . 624
vi. 3,	. . . 64
vi. 4,	. . . 506
vi. 5,	. . 126, 287
vi. 8,	. . . 89
vi. 12,	. . . 392
vi. 13,	. . . 469

vi. 17,	170, 240, 296, 341
vi. 20,	. . . 317

2 Timothy.

i. 1,	. . . 502
i. 3,	. . 465, 561
i. 8,	. . . 236
i. 9,	. . . 698
i. 12,	. . . 546
i. 13,	. . . 174
i. 16,	. . . 86
i. 18,	. . 304, 458
ii. 2,	. . . 473
ii. 6,	. . . 696
ii. 10,	. . . 175
ii. 11,	. . . 179
ii. 14,	. 602, 669, 778
ii. 25,	. . 374, 631
iii. 1,	. . . 154
iii. 8,	. . . 288
iii. 12,	. . . 767
iii. 16,	. . . 120
iv. 2,	. . . 653
iv. 8,	. . . 341
iv. 9,	. . . 753
iv. 18,	. . . 776

Titus.

i. 1,	. . . 502
i. 1 sqq.,	. . . 707
i. 2,	. . . 698
i. 3,	. . 670, 711
i. 5,	. . . 322
i. 6,	. . . 146
i. 11,	. . . 603
i. 12,	. 80, 192, 797
i. 15,	. 108, 651, 700
ii. 2,	. . . 405
ii. 4,	. . . 363
ii. 7,	. . . 322
ii. 8,	. . 527, 740
ii. 13,	. . 162 sq.
iii. 3,	. . . 742
iii. 5,	. 174, 487, 502
iii. 7,	. . . 196

Philemon.

1,	. . . 236
5,	. . . 511
6,	. . 519, 578
9,	. . . 236
10,	. . . 205
11,	. . . 795
13,	. . 236, 479
14,	. . . 771
19,	. . 347, 746
20,	. . 172, 795

Hebrews.

i. 2,	. . . 219
i. 3,	. . 233, 297

NEW TESTAMENT. 815

i. 6,	. . .	387
i. 7,	. . .	505
i. 8,	. . .	227
i. 9,	. .	346, 504
i. 11,	. . .	333
i. 13,	. . .	756
ii. 3,	. .	474, 776
ii. 7,	. . .	503
ii. 8,	. . .	560
ii. 9,	.	497, 578, 670
ii. 10,	. .	402, 431
ii. 11,	. . .	458
ii. 14,	. . .	339
ii. 16,	. . .	334
ii. 17,	. .	284, 289
ii. 18,	. .	198, 484
iii. 3,	. .	237, 300
iii. 5,	. . .	428
iii. 6,	. . .	196
iii. 7,	. . .	719
iii. 8,	. . .	500
iii. 11,	. .	578, 627
iii. 12,	.	242, 413, 632
iii. 13,	. . .	236
iii. 15,	. .	628, 715
iii. 16,	.	60, 551, 641
iii. 19,	. . .	546
iv. 1,	. . .	766
iv. 2,	. .	275, 326
iv. 3,	.	332, 578, 627
iv. 4,	. . .	656
iv. 8,	. .	183, 380
iv. 11,	. . .	483
iv. 13,	. .	183, 506
iv. 15,	. . .	112
iv. 16,	. . .	496
v. 1,	. . .	289
v. 2,	. . .	287
v. 4,	. . .	728
v. 5,	. . .	400
v. 6,	. . .	741
v. 7,	.	189, 540, 776
v. 8,	. .	206, 793
v. 11,	. . .	143
v. 12,	.	426, 440, 497
vi. 1,	. .	234, 666
vi. 2,	.	233, 240, 690
vi. 5,	. . .	248
vi. 6,	.	265, 432, 756
vi. 7,	. .	174, 546
vi. 8,	. . .	441
vi. 13,	. . .	478
vi. 14,	.	445, 553, 627
vi. 16,	. .	478, 719
vi. 17,	. . .	484
vi. 18,	. . .	482
vii. 2,	. . .	441
vii. 4,	. .	688, 701
vii. 6,	. .	341, 610
vii. 9,	341, 399, 473, 563
vii. 11,	. .	327, 605
vii. 12,	. . .	568
vii. 17,	. . .	656
vii. 20,	. . .	733
vii. 20 sq.,	.	706 sq.
vii. 21,	. . .	471
vii. 24,	. . .	134
vii. 26,	. . .	546
vii. 27,	. . .	192
viii. 1,	. .	670, 719
viii. 3,	. . .	386
viii. 5,	. . .	356
viii. 6,	. .	110, 327
viii. 8,	.	183, 261, 544
viii. 9,	. . .	714
viii. 10,	.	229, 536, 717
viii. 11,	. .	217, 636
ix. 1,	.	166, 542, 720
ix. 2,	.	175, 296, 792
ix. 3,	. .	221, 308
ix. 4,	. . .	481
ix. 5,	. . .	403
ix. 6,	. . .	334
ix. 7,	. . .	722
ix. 8,	. . .	234
ix. 9,	.	207, 500, 608
ix. 10,	. . .	791
ix. 11,	. . .	237
ix. 12,	.	105, 431, 475
ix. 15,	. .	231, 489
ix. 16,	. . .	689
ix. 17,	. .	491, 602
ix. 19,	. . .	241
ix. 22,	. . .	693
ix. 23,	. .	219, 221
ix. 26,	.	354, 489, 749
x. 2,	. . .	379
x. 5 sq.,	. . .	346
x. 6,	. . .	729
x. 8,	.	442, 705, 729
x. 10,	.	172, 483, 486
x. 14,	. . .	339
x. 16,	. .	442, 717
x. 20,	. . .	663
x. 22,	. .	88, 776
x. 24,	. . .	231
x. 27,	. . .	212
x. 28,	. . .	489
x. 33,	. . .	178
x. 34,	. .	194, 659
x. 35,	. . .	210
x. 37,	. .	309, 731
x. 38,	.	170, 656, 729
x. 39,	. . .	244
xi. 1,	. . .	68
xi. 2,	.	326, 484, 513
xi. 3,	.	414, 694
xi. 7,	. . .	502
xi. 11,	.	187, 504
xi. 12,	.	202, 432, 736
xi. 13,	. . .	502
xi. 15,	.	257, 381 sq., 383
xi. 17, 336, 340, 546, 688,		796
xi. 18,	. .	505, 769
xi. 26,	. .	480, 740
xi. 28,	.	114, 183, 340
xi. 29,	. . .	510
xi. 32,	. .	349, 689
xi. 35,	443, 459, 576, 609
xi. 39,	. .	476, 513
xi. 40,	. . .	323
xii. 1,	. . .	527
xii. 2,	. . .	456
xii. 3,	. . .	23
xii. 7,	. . .	495
xii. 10,	. . .	509
xii. 11,	. .	244, 666
xii. 13,	. . .	798
xii. 15,	.	246, 316, 632
xii. 17,	. . .	183
xii. 18,	. .	271, 431
xii. 19,	. . .	755
xii. 20 sqq.,	. .	708
xii. 25,	. . .	789
xii. 27,	. . .	576
xiii. 2,	. . .	585
xiii. 4,	. . .	732
xiii. 5,	. .	637, 732
xiii. 9,	. . .	487
xiii. 10,	. .	248, 459
xiii. 13,	. .	236, 430
xiii. 15,	. . .	262
xiii. 18,	. . .	649
xiii. 19,	. . .	304
xiii. 20,	. . .	172
xiii. 22,	. . .	741
xiii. 23,	. .	304, 435
xiii. 24,	. . .	784

JAMES.

i. 1,	.	397 sq., 735
i. 2,	. . .	138
i. 7,	. . .	559
i. 7 sq.,	. . .	670
i. 9 sq.,	. . .	777
i. 11,	.	346, 347, 590
i. 12,	. . .	666
i. 13,	.	120, 242, 464
i. 15,	. . .	107
i. 17,		62, 236, 438, 798
i. 18,	. . .	212
i. 24,	. .	340, 347
i. 25,	. .	175, 297
i. 27,	. . .	246
ii. 1,	. . .	232
ii. 2 sqq.,	. . .	715
ii. 4,	.	231, 233, 547
ii. 5,	. .	236, 265
ii. 6,	. . .	217
ii. 8,	. . .	554
ii. 9,	. . .	443
ii. 10,	.	253, 350, 386

ii. 11,	.	.	. 601	ii. 12,	. . 484, 732	ii. 12,	. .	198, 784
ii. 13,	.	.	. 124	ii. 14,	. . . 474	ii. 14,	. .	108, 242
ii. 14,	.	.	. 134	ii. 16,	. . 689, 717	ii. 16,	. .	. 118
ii. 15,	.	.	440, 566	ii. 17,	. . . 394	ii. 18,	. .	430, 664
ii. 18,	.	.	. 349	ii. 18,	. . . 732	ii. 19,	. .	. 275
ii. 22,	.	.	. 540	ii. 19,	. . . 650	ii. 20,	. .	. 199
ii. 23,	.	.	. 567	ii. 22,	. . . 770	ii. 21,	. .	352, 605
ii. 26,	.	.	. 144	ii. 23,	. . . 738	ii. 22,	. 135 sq., 443,
iii. 3,	.	.	. 749	ii. 24,	. . 185, 263			735, 798
iii. 4,	.	.	. 756	iii. 1,	. 89, 361, 442,	iii. 1,	. .	177, 689
iii. 6,	.	.	. 62		602, 732	iii. 3,	. .	716, 732
iii. 7,	.	.	. 275	iii. 3,	. . . 666	iii. 4,	. 183, 334, 736,
iii. 8,	.	668, 672	iii. 4,	. . . 483			745, 788
iii. 11,	.	.	. 739	iii. 6,	. 281, 578, 708	iii. 5,	272, 441, 522, 586
iii. 12,	.	.	. 619	iii. 6 sqq.,	. . 732	iii. 9,	. .	. 246
iii. 13,	.	.	172, 211	iii. 8,	. . 288, 733	iii. 10,	. .	156, 646
iii. 14,	.	590, 620, 642	iii. 10,	. . 409, 768	iii. 11,	. .	. 430
iii. 15,	.	.	. 439	iii. 12,	. . . 733	iii. 12,	. .	196, 498
iii. 18,	.	.	. 275	iii. 14,	. 182, 281, 367	iii. 13,	. .	. 658
iv. 2,	.	.	. 589	iii. 17,	. . 367, 755	iii. 14,	. .	. 274
iv. 2 sq.,	.	.	. 321	iii. 18,	. . . 513	iii. 17,	. .	. 271
iv. 4,	.	.	. 223	iii. 19,	. . . 761			
iv. 5,	.	.	. 529	iii. 20,	. 194, 537, 776		1 John.	
iv. 10,	.	.	. 327	iii. 21,	237, 239, 242, 663	i. 1,	. .	. 758
iv. 13,	.	.	145, 201	iv. 1,	. . 328, 513	i. 1 sqq.,	. .	. 709
iv. 14,	.	135 sq., 175	iv. 2,	. . . 101	i. 9,	. .	. 577
iv. 15,	.	.	357, 547	iv. 3,	. . 400, 782	ii. 2,	. .	. 722
v. 2,	.	.	. 342	iv. 6,	. 351, 501, 786	ii. 5,	. .	. 232
v. 3,	.	.	154, 265	iv. 7,	. . . 495	ii. 7 sq., .	.	. 658
v. 4,	.	.	. 464	iv. 8,	. . . 134	ii. 8,	. .	. 335
v. 5,	.	.	195, 519	iv. 11,	. . 134, 196	ii. 12,	. .	. 183
v. 6,	.	.	. 132	iv. 12,	. . . 262	ii. 13,	. .	. 348
v. 7,	.	.	. 740	iv. 14,	. . 136, 165	ii. 15,	. .	. 232
v. 11,	.	.	. 309	iv. 19,	. . 57, 151	ii. 19,	. .	. 398
v. 13,	.	211, 355, 678	v. 2,	. . . 481	ii. 21,	. .	215, 347
v. 14,	.	.	. 508	v. 6,	. . . 327	ii. 22,	. .	. 755
v. 17,	.	.	. 584	v. 7,	. . 441 sq.	ii. 24,	. .	. 718
				v. 8,	. . 154, 173	ii. 25,	. .	. 665
	1 Peter.		v. 9,	. . . 270	ii. 26,	. .	. 347
i. 1,	.	.	. 141	v. 10,	. . . 167	ii. 27,	346, 426, 718, 764
i. 2,	.	171, 234, 297	v. 12,	. . . 347	ii. 28,	. .	. 280
i. 3,	.	.	. 502			iii. 1,	. .	575, 769
i. 5,	.	.	154, 486		2 Peter.	iii. 5,	. .	. 334
i. 7,	.	.	174, 295	i. 1,	162 sq., 250, 778	iii. 8,	. .	. 334
i. 8,	.	.	. 609	i. 3,	. 328, 476, 770	iii. 11,	. .	. 425
i. 9,	.	.	. 429	i. 4,	. . . 196	iii. 11 sq.,	. .	. 778
i. 10,	.	.	. 242	i. 5,	. 178, 708, 749	iii. 13,	. .	. 679
i. 11,	.	.	. 242	i. 9,	233, 569, 603, 692	iii. 17,	. .	. 232
i. 12,	.	.	. 621	i. 17,	. . 442, 462	iii. 18,	. .	. 629
i. 14,	.	.	. 443	i. 19,	. . . 305	iii. 19 sq.,	. .	. 727
i. 15,	.	.	138, 501	i. 20,	. 244 sq., 732	iii. 23,	. .	. 425
i. 18,	.	166, 659, 662	ii. 1,	. . . 441	iii. 24,	. .	200, 723
i. 22,	.	.	232, 486	ii. 3,	186, 272, 279, 482,	iv. 2,	. .	. 435
i. 24,	.	.	346 sq.		584, 724	iv. 4,	. .	. 788
i. 25,	.	.	. 267	ii. 4,	. . 429, 712	iv. 9,	. .	273, 519
ii. 3,	.	.	. 562	ii. 5,	. . 312, 432	iv. 17,	. .	172, 425
ii. 6,	.	.	. 316	ii. 6,	. . . 263	iv. 20,	. .	. 342
ii. 7,	.	688, 714, 722	ii. 7,	. . . 461	v. 6,	. .	. 475
ii. 8,	.	.	. 546	ii. 9,	. . . 429	v. 9,	. .	. 774
ii. 10,	.	.	. 431	ii. 10,	. . 297, 744	v. 10,	. .	. 594
ii. 11,	.	.	179, 442	ii. 11,	. . 305, 493	v. 13,	. .	. 348

NEW TESTAMENT.

v. 15, . . . 369
v. 16, . 595, 656, 665
v. 20, 166, 195, 202, 363, 524

2 John.

2, . . . 512, 723
4, ... 660
6, ... 183
7, 168, 175, 177, 435, 606, 788
12, ... 347

3 John.

2, ... 467
4, . 81, 201, 425, 745
6, ... 152
7, ... 463
10, ... 619
12, ... 326

Jude.

1, . . . 265, 524
4, ... 162
5, ... 775
7, . . . 288, 778
11, . . . 236, 258
14, . . . 265, 346
15, . . . 203, 279
16, ... 716
21, . . . 172, 496

Revelation.

i. 4, 79, 141, 227, 735
i. 5, . 246, 668, 672
i. 5 sq., . . . 672
i. 6, ... 725
i. 10, ... 230
i. 19, ... 646
i. 20, ... 290
ii. 5, . 194, 679, 764
ii. 13, . 525, 593, 764
ii. 14, ... 284
ii. 16, . . 194, 268
ii. 17, . . 247, 725
ii. 20, . . 97, 671
ii. 26, ... 718
iii. 2, ... 646
iii. 3, ... 288
iii. 9, 361, 423, 660, 781
iii. 10, ... 297
iii. 12, . 637, 672, 718
iii. 15, . . 377 sq.
iii. 19, ... 590
iii. 20, ... 547
iii. 21, ... 718
iv. 1, ... 672
iv. 3, ... 80
iv. 4, ... 671
iv. 7, ... 134

iv. 8, . 497, 660, 673
iv. 9, . . 350, 388
iv. 11, ... 134
v. 3, ... 616
v. 4, ... 616
v. 6, ... 673
v. 7, ... 340
v. 9, ... 487
v. 11 sq., . . . 671
v. 12, . . 158, 672
v. 13, . . 134, 436
vi. 4, . . 361, 729
vi. 6, ... 735
vi. 8, . . 135, 718
vi. 11, . . 218, 361
vi. 14, ... 459
vii. 2, . . 149, 429
vii. 9, . . 671, 724
vii. 11, ... 93
vii. 14, ... 340
vii. 17, ... 689
viii. 1, ... 389
viii. 3, ... 361
viii. 4, ... 270
viii. 5, ... 340
viii. 9, ... 672
viii. 11, ... 135
viii. 12, ... 575
viii. 13, . . 145, 461
ix. 4, . . 214, 602
ix. 7, ... 755
ix. 10, ... 778
ix. 11, . . 227, 739
ix. 12, . . 223, 648
ix. 14, . . 671, 672
ix. 18, . . 4 0, 465
ix. 20, . . 575, 616
ix. 21, ... 616
x. 7, . . 346, 547
x. 9, ... 398
x. 11, ... 491
xi. 4, ... 672
xi. 5, . . 368, 678
xi. 9, ... 253
xi. 11, ... 515
xi. 14, ... 223
xi. 15, ... 660
xii. 6, ... 184
xii. 7, ... 411
xii. 8, . . 616, 770
xii. 9, ... 753
xii. 11, ... 498
xii. 14, . . 184, 221
xii. 17, ... 491
xiii. 1, ... 510
xiii. 3, . . 297, 327
xiii. 10, ... 161
xiii. 11, ... 778
xiii. 12, . . 185, 361
xiii. 13, ... 577

xiii. 16, . . . 361
xiii. 17, . . . 673
xiv. 1, . . . 673
xiv. 4, . . . 384
xiv. 6, . . . 109
xiv. 7, . . . 672
xiv. 9, . . . 510
xiv. 10, . . 107, 547
xiv. 12, . . 232, 672
xiv. 13, 361, 398 sq., 487, 576
xiv. 14, . . 671, 724
xiv. 19, . . 661, 672
xiv. 20, ... 697
xv. 2, . 310, 444, 460
xvi. 3, . . . 672
xvi. 7, . . . 259
xvi. 9, . . . 281
xvi. 19, . . . 763
xvi. 21, . . . 461
xvii. 2, . . . 186
xvii. 3, . . 251, 287
xvii. 4, . . . 287
xvii. 8, 259 sq., 327, 736, 781, 783
xvii. 9, . . . 185
xvii. 12, . . . 646
xvii. 16, . . . 177
xviii. 11, . . . 491
xviii. 12, 204, 739, 741
xviii. 12 sq., . . 724
xviii. 14, . . . 194
xviii. 17, . . . 279
xviii. 24, . . . 221
xix. 5, . . . 262
xix. 6, . . . 672
xix. 10, . . 748, 751
xix. 12, . . . 672
xix. 13, . . . 135
xix. 16, . . 308 sq.
xx. 2, . . . 671 sq.
xx. 3, . . . 673
xx. 4, . . . 132
xx. 5, . . . 372
xxi. 4, . . . 626
xxi. 8, . . . 431
xxi. 9, . . . 165
xxi. 11, . . . 310
xxi. 10 sq., . . 672
xxi. 13, . . . 150
xxi. 16, . . 244, 509
xxi. 17, . 244, 290, 669
xxi. 25, . . . 636
xxi. 27, . . 214, 566, 789
xxii. 3, . . . 216
xxii. 9, . . 748, 751
xxii. 11, . . . 391
xxii. 14, . . . 360
xxii. 16, . . . 491
xxii. 19, . . . 743

Winer Grammar.

II.—PASSAGES OF THE OLD TESTAMENT[1] AND APOCRYPHA EXPLAINED OR ILLUSTRATED.

GENESIS.

iv. 13,	300
iv. 24,	314
vi. 4,	389
x. 9,	310
x. 21,	736
[xi. 7,	578]
[xiv. 13,	143]
xv. 1,	672
[xv. 12,	412]
xvii. 13,	756
xxii. 17,	627
xxii. 20,	672
xxiii. 3 sq.,	223
xxiv. 3,	185
xxiv. 7,	204
xxiv. 37,	185
xxvi. 10,	39
xxvii. 30,	389
xxx. 42,	389
xxxi. 16,	205
xxxiii. 17,	334
xxxviii. 9,	388
xxxviii. 13,	672
xxxviii. 26,	302
xxxix. 16,	334
xl. 8,	136
xli. 8,	136
xliii. 3 sq.,	368
xliv. 4,	260
xlv. 16,	672
xlviii. 2,	672

EXODUS.

i. 12,	309
i. 16,	363, 388
iv. 21,	260
v. 14,	672
viii. 14,	581
viii. 21,	71, 369
ix. 21,	603
x. 11,	748
xiv. 4,	484
xiv. 18,	260
xv. 16,	387
xvi. 3,	377
xvi. 7,	170
xvii. 3,	256
xvii. 11,	388 sq.
xxv. 40,	356
xxxii. 32,	97, 751

[xxxii. 32,	230]
xxxii. 33,	177
xxxiii. 4,	739
xxxiii. 8,	389
xxxiv. 23,	314
xxxiv. 34,	389
xxxvi. 1,	185
xl. 36,	389

LEVITICUS.

i. 14,	369
xv. 16,	185
xvi. 32,	185
xix. 18,	188
xxi. 17,	211
xxi. 20,	185
xxii. 4,	185
xxiii. 15,	204
xxiv. 20,	748

NUMBERS.

ix. 10,	41
xi. 9,	389
xii. 6,	302
xiv. 2,	377
xiv. 27,	749
xix. 22,	205
xx. 3,	377
xx. 19,	248
xxiii. 13,	695
xxxiii. 38 sq.,	338

DEUTERONOMY.

v. 27,	385
vii. 13,	756
viii. 3,	350
ix. 11,	476
x. 22,	488
xi. 30,	289
xvi. 16,	314
xix. 21,	748
xxii. 7,	361
xxii. 27,	136
xxviii. 62,	754
xxix. 18,	211
xxxi. 6,	637
xxxi. 8,	637

JOSHUA.

v. 15,	510
x. 17,	672

xxii. 26,	411
xxiii. 13,	411

JUDGES.

ii. 14,	291
ii. 21,	411
v. 3,	191
vi. 3,	389
vi. 10,	185
vi. 18,	191
ix. 37,	411
x. 18,	385
xi. 24,	385
xi. 27,	191
xi. 34,	265
xii. 6,	411
xiii. 23,	384
xvi. 2,	672
xvi. 24,	724
xvii. 8,	320
xix. 30,	39
xxi. 3,	411
xxi. 7,	411

RUTH.

i. 12,	411
ii. 2,	185
ii. 10,	408
iii. 3,	411
iii. 15,	740

1 SAMUEL.

[ii. 3,	589]
[iii. 7,	267]
vii. 2 sq.,	137
ix. 9,	227
ix. 12,	646
xi. 2,	39
xii. 23,	411
xiv. 39,	136
xv. 12,	672
xvi. 9,	283
xvii. 34,	389
[xvii. 34,	143]
xviii. 22,	291
xxv. 20,	71

2 SAMUEL.

i. 16,	734
vi. 20,	562
xv. 4,	358
xix. 43,	314

[1] [When the figures are inclosed in brackets, the reference is to the Hebrew text; otherwise, to the Greek.]

OLD TESTAMENT AND APOCRYPHA. 819

1 Kings.
ii. 2, . . . 191
iii. 1, . . . 722
iii. 11, . . . 411
iii. 18, . . . 789
viii. 16, . . . 283
viii. 37, . . . 572
viii. 48, . . . 289
xii. 9, . . . 736
xii. 10, . . . 672
xiii. 16, . . . 411
xvi. 19, . . . 410
xvi. 31, . . . 411
xx. 23, . . . 627

2 Kings.
vi. 10, . . . 314
xvii. 29, . . . 41

1 Chronicles.
ix. 27, . . . 41
xvii. 6, . . . 208
xvii. 24, . . . 736
xxi. 24, . . . 487
xxviii. 4, . . . 283
xxviii. 20, . . . 637

2 Chronicles.
vi. 38, . . . 289
[xvii. 9, . . . 284]
xxxv. 10, . . . 86

Ezra.
[ix. 14, . . . 297]

Nehemiah.
iv. 16, . . . 137
v. 18, . . . 488
ix. 7, . . . 283
xiii. 14, . . . 39
xiii. 25, . . . 627

Esther.
i. 5, . . . 516

Job.
xiv. 13, . . . 377
xviii. 4, . . . 740
[xix. 3, . . . 589]
xxii. 3, . . . 369

Psalms.
iv. 5, . . . 391
[xviii. 5, . . . 32]
xxii. 1, . . . 280
[xxii. 22, . . . 776]
xxiv. 8, . . . 327
xxxix. 6, . . . 211
xl. 3, . . . 24

l. 6, . . . 574
lxii. 2, . . . 256
lxvii. 20, . . . 690
lxxxix. 2, . . . 334
xciv. 11, . . . 578
[xcv. 11, . . . 578]
ci. 3, . . . 384
cxi. 1, . . . 291
cxvii. 5, . . . 776
cxvii. 23, . . 39, 298
cxviii. 33, . . . 327
cxviii. 50, . . 24, 39
cxviii. 159, . . . 563
cxix. 7, . . . 389
[cxix. 164, . . . 314]
cxxxvii. 7, . . . 23
cxlvi. 10, . . . 291

Proverbs.
viii. 28, . . . 740
[xviii. 14, . . . 661]

Canticles.
ii. 7, . . . 627
iii. 5, . . . 627
vii. 6, . . . 562

Isaiah.
i. 9, . . . 86
vi. 4, . . . 204
ix. 1, . . . 289
xxvi. 20, . . . 309
xxix. 10, . . . 117
xxxvi. 12, . . . 574
xlv. 23, . . . 627
xlvii. 3, . . . 738

Jeremiah.
i. 5, . . . 334
ii. 36, . . . 208
x. 24, . . . 392
xi. 5, . . . 410
xxiii. 20, . . . 387
[xli. 7, . . . 517]
xlix. 4, . . . 385

Lamentations.
i. 20, . . . 563

Ezekiel.
xvii. 19, . . . 627
xxi. 11, . . . 497
xxxiii. 27, . . . 627
xxxiv. 8, . . . 627
xxxv. 6, . . . 627
xliv. 9, . . . 216

Daniel.
iii. 15, . . . 751

v. 5, . . . 24
vii. 25, . . . 221
xi. 2, . . . 282

Hosea.
ii. 8, . . . 223

Joel.
ii. 21, . . . 411

Amos.
i. 1, . . . 698
iv. 7, . . . 698

Jonah.
i. 3, . . . 182
iii. 3, . . . 310
iii. 4, . . . 411

Zephaniah.
i. 4, . . . 223

Zechariah.
vi. 15, . . . 751

3 (1) Esdras.[1]
i. 31, . . . 170
i. 49, . . . 784
iv. 48, . . . 724
iv. 54, . . . 185
v. 67, . . . 411
vi. 31, . . . 427
viii. 22, . . . 724

Tobit.
iii. 6, . . . 302
iv. 15, . . . 265
v. 14, . . . 41
vii. 11, . . . 389

Judith.
ii. 3, . . . 177
iv. 2, . . . 309
ix. 2, . . . 185
ix. 14, . . . 408
x. 7, . . . 671
xiii. 20, . . . 411

Wisdom.
ii. 14, . . . 229
ii. 15, . . . 778
vii. 3, . . . 778
ix. 6, . . . 229
xi. 15, . . . 134
xv. 12, . . . 655
xvi. 17, . . . 290
xvi. 20, . . . 23
xvii. 2, . . . 236
xviii. 3, . . . 242
xix. 12, . . . 192

[1] [1 Esdras in editions of the LXX; 3 Esdras in the Vulgate and the English Apocrypha.]

820   INDEX.

ECCLESIASTICUS.		iii. 10,	.	.	.	731	v. 39,	.	.	.	408
vi. 34,	. . . 211	iii. 36,	.	.	.	505	vi. 27,	.	.	.	411
xi. 21,	. . . 292						vi. 59,	.	.	.	411
xxii. 26,	. . . 368	SUSANNA.					xiii. 52,	.	.	.	458
xxiii. 14,	. . . 562	5,	.	.	.	766					
xliv. 18,	. . . 423	27,	.	.	.	214	2 MACCABEES.				
		33,	.	.	.	458	ii. 1,	.	.	.	782
BARUCH.		54 sqq.,	.	.	.	796	v. 10,	.	.	.	617
i. 9,	. . . 710	61,	.	.	.	223	vi. 1,	.	.	.	270
i. 19,	. . . 204						vii. 28,	.	.	.	695
ii. 12,	. . . 229	1 MACCABEES.					xi. 22,	.	.	.	316
ii. 28,	. . . 714						xv. 30,	.	.	.	698
ii. 29,	. . . 627	ii. 58,	.	.	.	231					

III.—INDEX OF SUBJECTS.

Abbreviated forms of proper names, 26, 127 sq.; of other nouns, 24 sq., 117.
Abnormal relation of words in a sentence, 786-793.
Abstract nouns, forms of, 115-118; use of the article with, 147-155, 138; plural of, 220; supplied from concrete, 181; combined with concrete, 665 sq., 725 sq.
Accentuation, 55-63; words distinguished by, 55 sq., 58, 60 sqq.; changes in later Greek, 56 sq.; of certain personal names, 58 sqq.; of indeclinable names, 59; of elided words, 43.
Accumulation of prepositions, 521 sq.
Accusative case, 277-290; with transitive verbs, 277-280; of place, 280; of cognate noun, 281-283, 203; double, 284 sq., 285 sq.; of neuter adjectives and pronouns, 285, 250; quantitative, 285, 775; with passive verbs, 286 sq., 326; of the remoter object, 287; of time and space, 287 sq.; of exact definition, 288; adverbial, 288 sq., 581 sq.; absolute, 226, 290, 716, 718 sq.; after prepositions, 494-509; after verbs compounded with prepositions, 530-540; in apposition to a sentence, 290, 669; with infinitive, 402, 404 sq., 406 sq., 414 sq.; after ὅτι, 426, 718; is ἐν used as a periphrasis for the? 283; (sing.) of 3d decl. with appended ν, 76 sq.
Active voice, 314-316; apparently used in a reflexive, 315, 738,—or a passive sense, 316; with ἑαυτόν, 316, 321 sq.; sometimes used for the middle voice, 320-322, 24, 35.
Adjectives: of two and three terminations, 25, 80; declension of, 80, 71-77; comparison of, 81, 300-310; double comparatives, 81, 753; derived from verbs, 119,—from adjectives, 120 sqq.,—from substantives, 122 sq.; compound, 123 sqq.; as attributives, 163-166, 174 sq., 657-663; used as substantives, 135, 217 sq., 293-295, 299, 649 sq.,—neuter, so used, 119, 294 sq., 299, 649 sq., 741; accus. of, used adverbially, 288; neuter, used as adverbs, 314, 580; is the femin. used for the neuter? 298, 39; expressing an effect, proleptic use of, 663, 779; joined to substantives with the article, 163-166,—to anarthrous nouns, 174 sq.,—to the vocative case, 229,—to two or more substantives, 661 sq.; connected by καί, 659; differing from their substantive in number, gender, or case, 660 sq., 672 sq., 705, 790-792; predicative, 134, 647 sqq., 662 sq.; in apposition, relating to a sentence, 669 sq.; in the place of adverbs, 582-584; ellipsis of, 743 sq.; periphrases for, 298 sq., 526-529; followed by the genitive, 242 sq.; position of, 163-166, 657-659, 686 sq.
Adverbs, 447 sq., 578-643, 123; use of, by the N. T. writers, 579; derived from adjectives, 579 sq.; with the article, 135; joined to nouns, 582, 584; whether used for adjectives, 584; periphrases for, 526-529; replaced by adjectives, 582-584,—by participles or the dative case, 445 sq., 584 sq.,—by finite verbs, 585-590; demonstrative, included in relative, 198; governing a case, 590 sq.;

combinations of, 591,—with prepositions, 525 sq.; prepositions used as, 526; of place, interchanged, 591-593, —used of persons, 593; apposition joined to, 664; irregular position of, 692 sqq.; no real ellipsis of, 744 sq.; in *ι* or *υ*, 47; comparison of, 81; compound, 127.

Adversative sentences, 551-555, 677-679.

Æolic forms, 37, 77, 90, 100, 104.

Affirmative word supplied from negative, 728, 777.

Alexandrian dialect of Greek, 20-22, etc., 90; its peculiar orthography, 53 sqq. See *Septuagint*.

Anacoluthon: particular kinds of, 716-722; various examples of, 709-722, 209, 397, 442, 554, 561, 578, 670-673, 704, 708; punctuation, 67.

Annominatio, 794 sqq.

Antiptosis, 792 sq.

Aorist tense, 343-348; when used for the pluperfect, 343 sq.; never stands for the perfect, 344 sq.,—or the future, 345 sq.,—or the present, 347; iterative or gnomic aorist, 346 sq.; epistolary aorist, 347 sq.; not used de conatu in the N. T., 348; has the aor. middle a passive sense? 319 sq.; aor. passive in middle sense, 327 sq.; proper translation of, 345; aor. indic. with ἄν, 380 sq.,—without ἄν in apodosis, 382 sq.; 2 aor. with ending α, 86 sq., 103; 1 aor. with Æolic opt., 90; 1 aor. in the place of 2 aor., 38, 99, 101 sqq., 106 sqq. See also *Imperative*, etc.

Apocalypse, peculiarities in the language and style of the, 41, 150, 263, 350, 451, 485, 577, 670 sqq.

Apocryphal writings, general style of the, 22.

Apodosis, introduced by καί, 357, 546 sq., 678, 756,—by δέ, 553, 678, 749, —by ἀλλά, 552, 678,—by οὖν, 712, —by οὕτως, 548 sq., 678 sq.; commencement of, not marked, 678; suppressed, 578, 627, 712 sq., 749; doubled, 679; link between protasis and apodosis wanting, 773 sq.; forms of, in conditional sentences, 364-367, 378-384; peculiar use of the perfect and the aorist in, 341 sq., 345 sq.

Aposiopesis, 749-751, 551, 627, 715.

Apostrophe in the N. T., 42 sq.

Apposition, 663-673, 657; different kinds of, 663 sq.; construction of words in, 665-669; irregularities, 670-673, 668, 705; genitive of, 666-668; to a genit. included in a possessive pron., 664; to an adverb, 664; to a sentence, 290, 668 sqq.; preposition not repeated with a noun in, 524; a clause in apposition attracted into a relative clause, 665, 783; article with words in, 172 sq.; position of words in, 669 sq. (687 sq.)

Aquila, 39.

Aramaic language, 30 sq., 187, 224, 544; Aramaisms, 30 sq., 217, 439 (732).

Article, definite, 129-175; as a demonstr. pron., 129 sqq. (comp. 133); with nouns, 131-136; designating a class, 132, 217; is it used for the relative? 133; peculiar uses of, 134 sq., 136, 743; in the place of a pers. pron., 135; in appellations, 135; with adjectives, adverbs, sentences, etc., 135; neuter article with masc. or fem. nouns, 136, 223; with demonstr. pron., 137,—τᾶς, 137 sq.,—τοιοῦτος, etc., 138 sq.; with proper names, 137, 139-141; in the predicate, (136), 141 sq.; never indefinite, 143; cases in which it may either be inserted or omitted, 143, 147-163; frequently omitted after a prepos., 139, 149, 151, 157,—in superscriptions, 140, 155,—before quasi-proper names and abstract nouns, 147-155,—before nouns which are followed by a defining genitive, 153, 155 sq., 175,—in enumerations, 149, 175,—with ordinal numerals, 154, 156,—by the law of correlation, 175; the use of the art. sometimes a characteristic of style, 146 sq.; variation of MSS. in regard to, 146 sq.; repetition of, with nouns connected by conjunctions, 157-162; with attributives, 163-175; with nouns in apposition, 172 sq.; sometimes found with the attributive of an anarthrous substantive, 174 sq.; questions in regard to the art. which are not fully settled, 175; works upon, 129; position, 147.

Article, indefinite, never expressed by ὁ, ἡ, τό, 143; indicated by τὶς, and sometimes by εἷς, 145 sq.

Assimilation of consonants, neglected, 54; in Latin, 55.

Asyndeton, 653, 659, 673-676.

Attic forms, 22 sq., 37, 88 sq.

Attraction, 682, 780-785; of relative pronoun or adverb, 197, 202 sqq., 206, 782; of antecedent, 204 sqq., 783; of an apposition into a relative clause, 665, 783; of the subject of a dependent sentence, 781 sq.; of prepositions, 454, 493, 784 sq.; with infinitives, 402, 404, 782.

Attributives, 657-673; article with, 163-175; ellipsis of, 743 sq.
Augment: temporal for syllabic, 82, 102; syllabic for temporal, 82 sq.; superfluous, 82, 111; neglected, 83-86, 108; irregular, 84 sq.; double, 84 sq.; in verbs beginning with ἐυ, 83,—with ρ, 88; position of, in compound verbs, 83-85, 97.

Bengel (J. A.), 8, 310.
Beth essentiæ, 40, 230.
Blending of two constructions, 426, 546, 566, 670-673, 714, 724 sq., 747, 756 sq.
Brachylogy. See *Breviloquence*.
Breathings, interchanged, 48 sq.; over ρρ, 53; aspirate over initial ρ, 53.
Breviloquence, 773-785; in comparisons, 307, 777 sq.; in questions, 783 sq.; in use of ἄρχεσθαι, 775, 790; miscellaneous exx. of, 460, 472, 514 sqq., 557, 665.
Byzantine writers, notices of their language and style, *passim*; in general, 17, 22, 27 sq.; forms of words, 70, 71, 72, 76, 81, 84, 87, 90 sq., 93 sq., 99, 108, 113, 119, 123 sq., 127, 128, 390, 423; words and phrases, 19, 23, 327; syntax, 38, 133, 139, 191, 224, 286, 295, 299, 312, 335, 361 sq., 368, 389, 396, 400, 407, 411, 422, 439 sq., 446, 455, 464, 506, 520, 577, 592, 647, 699, 754, 770, 772.

Cardinal numeral, used for ordinal, 311; numeral *one* expressed by the singular number, 311; repeated, in the place of a distributive, 40, 312; in the place of a numeral adverb, 314.
Cases, in general, 224 sqq.; not really interchanged, 225; used absolutely, 225 sq. (see *Genitive*, etc.); relation between prepositions and, 449 sq., 451 sq.; not interchanged, with prepositions, 455, 458, 476, 492 sq., 508, 511; their meaning lost in late Greek, 38; nominative and vocative, 225-230; genitive, 230-260; dative, 260-277; accusative, 277-290.
Causal conjunctions, originally objective or temporal, 541, 561, 679; causal sentences, 555, 557-561, 679.
Chaldee, 221, 224, 656, 795.
Chiasm (the figure), 511, 658.
Christian element in N. T. Greek, 36, 451.
Cilicisms, 28, 88.
Circumstantiality of expression, 33, 753, 757-761.

Cognate substantive, accus. of, 281-283, 203.
Collective nouns, construction of, 647 (181); collective use of the singular, 218 (177).
Comma, improper use of, 65 sq.; where necessary, 66 sq. (628); a half-comma desirable, 67.
Comparative degree, 300-307; strengthened by μᾶλλον, 300 sq.; followed by prepositions, 301, 303, 502 sqq., —by ἤ, 300; whether used for the superlative, 303, 305 sq.,—or the positive, 301, 303 sqq.; correlative comparatives, 306; peculiarities in the form of, 81; of adverbs, 81.
Comparison, sentences of, 548 sq., 677; pleonasm in, 549, 753 sq.; breviloquence in, 307, 777 sq.
Compound verbs, 125-127; construction of, 529-540; used for simple, and *vice versa*, 25, 745.
Concessive sentences, 551, 554 sq. (432 sq.)
Concrete nouns, supplied from abstract, 181, 787; combined with abstract, 665 sq., 725 sq.
Conditional sentences, 678; forms of protasis, 363-370, 380-384; of apodosis, 364-367, 378-384. See *Protasis, Apodosis*.
Conjunctions, 447 sq., 541-579; limited use of, in N. T. Greek, 33, 448, 579; various classes of, 541; copulative, 541-548; correlative, 547 sq.; comparative, 548 sq.; disjunctive, 549-551; adversative, 551-554; concessive, 551, 554 sq.; temporal, 555, 370 sq., 387, 561; consecutive, 377, 400, 555-557, 563, 578; causal, 555, 557-561; conditional, 555, 561 sq., 363 sq.; final, 563, 358, 627; objective, 563; repetition of, 652 sq.; position of, 455, 547, 557, 698-701; never really interchanged, 543, 545, 549 sq., 563-578; no real ellipsis of, 744 sq.; omission of—see *Asyndeton*.
Conjunctive mood, 351; in independent sentences, 355-357; in dependent sentences, 358-390; with ἄν, 364-367, 385 sq., 389; with particles of design, 358-363; after εἰ, ἐάν, 364-369; after particles of time, 371 sq., 387 sq.; in indirect questions, 373 sq.; in relative sentences, 385 sq.; with ἵνα, for an imperative, 396; with μή, 628-634; with οὐ μή, 634-637; aorist and present of, 351, 385, 387; future of, 89, 95.
Consecutive sentences, 377, 400, 679.
Consequent clause. See *Apodosis*.

SUBJECTS. 823

Consonants, unusual combinations of, 49, 54 sq.
Constructio ad sensum, 787 ; in regard to gender, 176 sq., 648, 660 sq.,— number, 177, 181, 645-648, 660 ; in the Apocalypse, 670-673.
Constructio prægnans, 776 sq., 454, 465, 495, 514 sqq.
Constructions, blending of two. See *Blending*.
Contracted verbs, 91 sq. ; contracted forms of proper names, 26, 127 sq., —of other nouns, 24 sq., 117.
Contraction, 51; neglected, 51, 72, 74 sq.
Co-ordination instead of subordination, 33, 446 sq., 543, 676.
Copula suppressed, 654, 689, 731-734.
Crasis, 51.

Dative case, 260-277 ; with verbs and adjectives, expressing the remoter object, 261-264 ; with εἶναι, γίνεσθαι, 264 ; with ὁ αὐτός, 186 ; joined to substantives, 264 sq. ; of reference, 261, 265, 270 ; of opinion or judgment, 264 sq., 310 ; dativus commodi, incommodi, 265 ; dat. ethicus, 194 ; of the sphere, rule, cause, etc., 270 ; of the mode, instrument, 271, 283, 289, 427, 584 sq. ; of time and place, 273 sq. ; with passive verbs, 274 sq. ; absolute, 226, 275 ; double, 276 ; is it used for the local εἰς or πρός ? 268 sq. ; with verbs of coming, 269 ; prepositions akin to, 266-268, 272 ; differs from διά with the genitive, 272 ; after prepositions, 480-493 ; after verbs compounded with ἀνά, ἀντί, ἐν, ἐπί, παρά, περί, πρός, σύν (ὑπό), 530-540 ; of infinitive, 412 sq.
Dawes's Canon, 636 sq.
Declensions of nouns, unusual forms in, 69-80.
Defective verbs, 98-112.
Demonstrative pronouns, 195-202 ; joined to nouns with the article, 137 ; as predicates, 137 ; used adverbially in the neuter, 178 ; included in the relative, 197, 206 ; repetition of, 198 sqq. ; introduced (for emphasis) before verbs, 199,—before ὅτι, ἵνα, etc., a predicative infinitive, a participial clause, etc., 200 sq. ; sometimes used with some looseness of reference, 195 sq., 788 ; in -δε, 202.
Deponents, 323-325.
Derivation, by terminations, 113-123 ; by composition, 123-127.
Derivative verbs, 113-115, 125 sqq. ; substantives, 115-119, 123 sq. ; adjectives, 120-125.

Diæresis, 47, 49.
Dialects of Greek, in general, 20 ; Alexandrian dialect, 20-22, 53 sqq., 90 (see *Septuagint*), Macedonian, 20 (23), 113 ; Hellenistic, 20 sqq., 28 sq., and *passim* ; ἡ κοινή, 20 ; writers of ἡ κοινή, 22 ; dialects mingled in later Greek, 20 sq.
Diffuseness, 757-764.
Digressions, 707.
Diminutives in later Greek, 25 sq., 119.
Distributive numerals, how expressed in the N. T., 19, 40, 312, 496 sq., 500 ; compare 41.
Doric forms, 22, 37 (52), 95, 96 sq., 128.
Doxologies, 689 sq.
Dual, not found in the N. T., 221 ; rare in later Greek, 27, 38.
Dynamic dative, 271 ; dyn. middle, 318 sq.

Elision, rare in the N. T., 42 sq.
Ellipsis, 726-749 ; ellipsis, improperly so called, 727-730 ; ellipsis of εἶναι or γίνεσθαι, 437, 440, 584, 731-734 ; of other verbs, 734 sq. ; of substantives, with attributives, 294, 738-741,— after ἐν, εἰς, 480, 740 ; of object, with transitive verbs, 741 sq. ; of attributive adjective, 743 sq. ; (partial) of both subject and predicate, 745-748 ; in commands, 748 ; of the subject, 735-738 (787) ; of sentences, 748 sq. ; ellipsis of adverbs or conjunctions impossible, 744 sq. ; additional examples of, 396, 398, 480, 632, 723 sq. ; of δεῖν with infinitives (?), 405.
Empirical philology, characteristics of, 7 sq.
Enallage of gender or number, in pronouns, 176 sq.,—in nouns, 217 sqq. ; of case, 225, 455 ; of number, in the verb, 645-649 ; of gender, in the predicate, 648 sqq. ; of tense, 330 sq. ; of prepositions, 450, 453 sqq., 514-521.
Enclitic pronouns, 62 sq. ; position of, 699 sq.
Euphony, 793.

Feminine gender, in adverbial formulas, 739 ; does it ever stand for the neuter? 39, 223, 298.
Final ς (in οὕτως, etc.), 43 sqq. ; final ν (ν ἐφελκυστικόν), 43 sqq.
Final sentences. See *Purpose*.
Foreign names, declension of, 77 sqq.
Formulas of citation, 656, 735 ; of asseveration, 445 sq., 563, 627.
Fritzsche (K. F. A.), 10.
Fulness of expression, 757, 761-764.

Future tense, 348-350; expressing what *may* or *must* take place, 348 sq.; used of a possible case, 349 sq., 356; never stands for the optative mood, 350,— or for a past tense, 350; sometimes borders on the present tense, 350; used for the imperative, 396 sq.; future indic. after μή, 630 sq.,—after οὐ μή, 634-636; affinity between the future and the conjunctive mood, 349, 356 sq., 361, 374, 385, 630-632, 635 sq.; with ἄν, 372, 388; futurum exactum, 385, 387, 417; future middle in a passive sense, 319; 3d future, 348; Attic future, 88 sq.; future conjunctive, 89, 95; active form of future in the place of the middle form, 98, etc.; (periphrases for, 41).

Gataker, 14.
Gender of nouns, 222 sq.; sometimes changed in later Greek, 26, 38, 73, 76. See *Constructio ad sensum*.
General notion supplied from special, 728 sq., 774 sq.
Genitive case, 230-260; attributive, appended with repeated article, 163 sq.; of quality, 40, 231, 297; partitive, 231, 247 sq., 250-253,—after adverbs, 253; of the object, 231-233; of the subject, 232 sq., 236 sq.; expressing remote relations of dependence, 234-237; expressing relations of place or time (attributively), 234; topographical, 234; of content, 235; of material, 297; of apposition, 237, 242, 666-668; of kindred, 164, 237 sq., 741; of relation, 242 sq., 252; of separation, 245-247; of price and exchange, 258; of place and time, 204, 258 sq., 739; genitive absolute, 226, 259,—used irregularly, 259 sq., 681 sq.,—used impersonally, 736; after adjectives and participles, 242 sq.; after εἶναι, γίνεσθαι, 243-245; after verbs of giving, tasting, etc., 247 sq.,—of participating in, 250,—of perception, 249,—of fulness and want, 251,—of touching, laying hold of, etc., 252 sq.,—of accusing, etc., 254 sq.,—of feeling, desiring, caring for, remembering, etc., 255 sqq.,—of ruling, 252, 257; after verbs containing a notion of comparison, 252; after comparatives, 300, 303, 307; after prepositions, 455-480; after verbs compounded with ἀπό, ἐκ, κατά, πρό, ὑπέρ, 530-540; several genitives, dependent on one another, 238; genitive placed before, 239, 690,—or separated from, its governing noun, 233; two genitives depending on one noun, 239; periphrases for, 240-242; representing the subject of a sentence, 253, 737; genitive of the infinitive, 407-412, 420; distinction between the genit. and accus. after certain verbs, 247, 250, 252, 255-257; general remarks on the case, 260.
Gentile nouns, 118 sq.
Georgi (C. S.), 6, 15, 17.
Gersdorf, 4, 173, 685-687.
Græcisms in Latin, 34.
Grammar of N. T. Greek: its object and treatment, 1-4; its history, 4-19; works upon, 10 sq.
Greek, later, *passim;* works illustrative of, 3; its general character, 20; lexical peculiarities, 22-27, 28 sq.; grammatical peculiarities, 27, 37 sq. —Peculiarities of the popular spoken language: in general, 20-22 (55); in words and phrases, 22-27, 229; forms of words, 76, 95, 127; syntax, 170, 179, 352, 403, 407, 424, 438, 450, 592.
Greek, modern, 76, 77, 88, 90, 91, 97, 98, 106, 115, 230, 313,—30; peculiarities of syntax, 38, 179, 187, 188, 190, 192, 210, 212, 221, 224, 246, 251, 266, 287, 301, 312, 316, 345, 352, 356, 362, 382, 389, 390, 422, 423, 424, 464, 471, 520, 558, 562, 599, 606, 614, 641, 645.

Haab, 6.
Hebraisms, various opinions respecting, 13 sq.; perfect (pure) and imperfect, 32, 40; lexical, 18 sq., 28-36, 23 (194); grammatical, 40; Hebraisms in connexion with pronouns, 176, 184 sq., 216 sq. (297 sq.); with numerals, 216, 311, 312; positive for superlative adjective, 308 sq.; future for imperative, 396 sq.; finite verb with adverbial force, 587-590; imitations of the Hebrew infinitive absolute, 39 sq., 427, 445 sq., 584 sq.; Hebraistic use of prepositions, 229, 257, 268, 280, 285 sq., 662, 291, 293, 450 sq., 470 sq., 485, 487 sq.; ὁδόν, *towards*, 289; υἱός (τέκνον) in periphrases, 298 sq.; οὐ . . . πᾶς, 214 sq.; εἰ in formulas of swearing, 627; καὶ ἐγένετο, ἐγένετο δέ, 406 sq., 756, 760; θέλειν τι, 587; καλὸν ἤ, 302; ἀστεῖος τῷ Θεῷ, 310; εἶναι (γίνεσθαι) εἴς τι, 229; εἰς with predicate, 285 sq., 662; ἡμέρα καὶ ἡμέρᾳ, 581. (See further 230, 514 sq., 329, 331, 391, 297 sq., 309 sq.) General influence of Hebrew on the Greek of the N.

SUBJECTS. 825

T., 28, 32 sq., 224, 448, 450 sq., 543, 685, 759.
Hebraists, 12-15.
Hebrew language, general characteristics of the, 9, 16, 28, 32 sq.; Hebrew words and phrases noticed, 33, 34, 117; Hebrew constructions noticed, 145, 214, 216, 217, 229 sq., 267, 283, 289, 291, 297 sq., 310, 331, 334, 341, 358, 391, 396, 412, 445 sq., 451 sq., 471, 472, 485, 514 sq., 517, 564, 571, 573 sqq., 578, 587, 589, 594, 627, 652, 656, 661, 689 sq., 693, 756, 760, 769, 776.
Hebrews, peculiarities in the language and style of the Ep. to the, 35, 151, 414, 441, 446, 541, 557.
Hellenistic Greek, 19 sqq., 28 sq.
Hendiadys, 786.
Heteroclites, 70, 72-79.
Historic present, 334.
Hypallage, 297 sq., 786-792.
Hyperbaton, 687-702.
Hypodiastole, 50.
Hypothetical sentences. See *Conditional*.

Illative or consecutive sentences, 377, 400, 679.
Imperative mood, 390-399; in a permissive sense, 390 sq.; two imperatives connected by καί, how resolved, 391-393; not used for the future, 393; aorist and present of, 351, 393-395, 628 sq.; perfect of, 395 sq.; substitutes for, 396-398; with μή, 628 sq.; 3d plural, form of, 91.
Imperfect indicative, 335-338; is it used for other tenses? 336-338; combined with the aor., 337; peculiar use of the, 352 sqq.; with ἄν, 353, 380, 381 sq.; without ἄν, in the apodosis, 382 sq.; variation of MSS. between aor. and imperfect, 337.
Impersonal verbs, 655 sq., 735 sq.; impersonal use of participles, 779, 736.
Inclination of the accent, 62 sq.
Indeclinable nouns, 70, 78 sq. (226 sq.); accentuation, 59.
Indefinite pronoun τὶς, 212 sq.; position of, 213, 689, 699 sq.
Indicative mood, 351, 352-390; apparently used for the conjunctive, 354 sq.; after particles of design, 360-363, 673 (386); in conditional sentences, 364-370, 378-384; in temporal sentences, 370 sqq., 388 sq.; in indirect questions, 373-376; in relative sentences, 384-386; in illative sentences, 377; with ὄφελον, 377; after μή, 630-634.

Indirect quotation, rare in the N. T., 33, 376, 683.
Infinitive absolute (Hebrew), how translated, 39 sq., 427, 445 sq., 584 sq.
Infinitive mood, 399-427, 681; epexegetic, 399-401, 410 sq.; expressing purpose or consequence, 399 sq., 408 sqq.; after ὥστε, 377, 400; as the subject of a sentence, 401-403; accus. with, 402, 404 sq., 406 sq., 414 sq.; nominative and other cases with, 402, 404, 415, 782; as object, 403-407; expressing what *ought to be*, 405 sq.; for imperative, 397 sq., 399, 644; with the article, 402, 406-415; present and aorist of, 415-419; future, 416, 419-421; perfect, 417, 420; active, for passive, 426; replaced by finite verb with εἰ, ἐάν, 403, 682,—with ὅταν, 682,—with ἵνα, 403 sq., 420-426, 682,—with ὅτι, 404, 407, 747; after ἐστί, 403; after ἐγένετο, 406 sq.; with ἄν, 390; with a negative, 604 sq.; after πρίν, 415; after ὅτι, 426, 718; genitive of, 407-412, 420; dative, 412 sq.; after prepositions, 40, 413-415, 420; replaced by the participle, 434-437, 782.
Interjections, 447, 579.
Interrogative particles, 638-643.
Interrogative pronouns, direct and indirect, 176, 210, 680; can they take the place of relative pronouns (or *vice versa*)? 210 sq., 207 sq.; used adverbially in the neuter, 178.
Interrogative sentences, direct and indirect, 638-643, 680 sq.; indirect, construction of, 373-376, 386 sq., 680 sq.; negative, 641-643; two fused into one, 783 sq.; blended with relative, 784.
Interrupted sentences, 702-708.
Ionic forms, 23, 37, 45 sq., 71, 73 sq., 75, 102 sq., 106, 109 sq., 363.
Iota subscript, 51 sq.
Irregular verbs, 98-112.
Itacism, 138, 53.

James (St.), peculiarities in the language and style of, 674, 798.
John (St.), peculiarities in the language and style of, 11, 35, 79, 146, 149 sq., 151, 166, 199, 200, 229, 235, 263, 266, 332, 425 sq., 451, 554, 576 sq., 673, 676 sq., 762.
Josephus, language and style of, 21, 34, 59, 79, 352.

Latin language: its influence on the syntax of N. T. Greek, 41, 229, 340, 422, 460, 680, 698; Latin words in

the N. T. and in later Greek, 27, 128, 29 (119); notices of Latin constructions, 16, 178, 201, 210 sq., 293, 306, 373, 407, 421, 424, 452, 454, 459, 504, 583, 597, 625, 645, 667 sq., 741, 743, 758; orthography of Latin words, 55; Græcisms in Latin, 34.
Lexicology and lexicography, 1.
Libri Pseudepigraphi, style of, 22.
Luke (St.), peculiarities in the language and style of, 31, 35, 79, 135, 146, 149 sq., 151, 226 sq., 266, 320, 372, 408, 412, 422, 428, 446, 477, 518, 541, 543, 556 sq., 561, 639, 641, 676 sq., 680, 683, 685, 760, 763, 767, 789 sq.

Mark (St.), peculiarities in the language and style of, 79, 146, 149 sq., 151, 181, 208, 263, 266, 543, 676, 685.
Masculine gender, is it used for the feminine? 222 sq.
Matthew (St.), peculiarities in the language and style of, 35, 79, 146, 149 sq., 151, 263, 266, 422, 543, 576, 674, 676 sq., 685.
Metaplasmus, 72 sq., 76.
Middle voice, 316-325; meaning of, 316-318; joined with pers. pronouns, 179, 318, 322; tenses of, with passive meaning, 319 sq.; used for the active, 322 sq.; active used in its place, 320-322 (98, etc.).
Moods, used with less strictness in later Greek, 38. See *Indicative*, etc.

Negative particles, 593-638; joined to particular words in a sentence, 597 sqq., 601 sq., 605 sq., 609, 641; with participles, 606-611; expressing a continued negation, 611-619; followed by καί (τι), 619 sq.; combinations of, 624-627, 634-638; trajection of, 693-696; pleonasm of, 755-757; affirmative word supplied from negative, 728, 777; is the absolute negation used for the relative? 620-624.
Neuter gender, used of persons, 222; is it used for the feminine? 222; neuter plural with singular verb, 645-647; neuter adjective, for an abstract noun, 294. See *Gender* and *Constructio ad sensum*.
Neuter verbs. See *Verbs, intransitive*.
Nominative case, 226-230; nomin. tituli, 226 sq.; used absolutely, 226, 290 (672), 718 sq.; for the vocative, 227 sq.; periphrases for, 229 sq.; with an infinitive, 404, 415, 782; in exclamations, 228, 668, 672; of participle, irregularly used, 716, 779;
in apposition to a sentence, 669, 719.
Nouns, unusual inflexions of, in 1st decl., 69 sqq.; 2d decl., 72 sq.; 3d decl., 73-77. See *Substantives*.
Number of nouns, 217-222.
Numerals, 311-314; cardinal, 23, 311, 313; ordinal, 311 sq.; proportional, 311; distributive, 312, 496 sq., 500; qualified by που, ὡς, ὡσεί, 578 sq.,— by τίς, 212; numeral adverbs, 314; accentuation of numerals in -ιτης, 56.

Object expressed by ἐκ with the genitive, 253; common to two verbs, 654; ellipsis of, 742.
Objective sentence (with ὅτι, ὡς), 563, 679; negative in an, 605; akin to the relative sentence, 679 sq.
Opposition, 551-555, 677-679.
Optative mood, 351; in independent sentences, 357 sq., 379; replaced by a question, 39, 41, 358; with ἄν, 353, 379, 386 sq.; in final sentences, 358 sqq., 363; after εἰ, 364, 367 sq.; after πρίν, 372; in oratio obliqua, 376, 372; in indirect questions, 374 sq., 386 sq.; rare in later Greek, 28, 38, 352, 360; replaced by the conjunctive, 359 sq., 372; aorist and present, 351.
Oratio obliqua, 372, 376; passing into, or intermingled with, the oratio recta, 376, 683, 705, 725; comparatively rare in the N. T., 33, 376, 683.
Oratio variata, 722-726, 525, 672.
Ordinal numerals, a peculiar use of, 312; cardinal, instead of, 311.
Oriental names, declension of, 77 sq.
Orthography, principles of, 42-55; of particular words, 45-49; Alexandrian, 53 sqq.

Palestine, language of, in the time of our Lord, 20 sq., 30.
Parallel members inexactly expressed, 789; parallel passages, abuse of, 330, 431, 454, 520, 550, 571.
Parallelismus antitheticus, 762 sq.; par. membrorum, 764, 796.
Parenthesis, 702-708; consisting of single words, 704; followed by γάρ, 558,—by δέ, 553; introduced by καί, δέ, γάρ, 703; in the historical books, 704-706; in the epistles, 706-708, 289; marks of, 69, 703.
Paronomasia, 793 sq., 796.
Participle, 427-447, 681 sq.; as attributives, with and without the art., 167-169, 657-663; with the article, 135

sq., 138, 167-169, 444 sq.,—as predicate, 136, 440, 645; governing a genitive, 242 sq. (445); with the case of its verb, 427, 444; future, rare in the N. T., 428; present, 427, 431,—is it used for other tenses? 428 sqq., 444,—with article, as a timeless substantive, 444 sq.; aorist, 428, 430,—not used for other tenses, 431 sq.; perfect, 428, 430 sq.; resolution of, by subordinate sentences, 168, 432 sq.; with καίτοι, καίπερ, 432 sq.; two or more partic. unconnected by conjunctions, 433; in the place of an infinitive, 434-437, 782; not used for a finite verb, 440-443, 732 sq.; whether it expresses the principal notion, 320, 443 sq., 585-587; with εἶναι, 30, 437-440; replaced by a finite verb, 446, 544; with negatives, 606-611; used absolutely, 446, 779 (669), —in the genitive, 259 sq., 681 sq., 736; with ὡς, 770 sq.; in combination with some part of its own verb, 445 sq., 584 sq.; transition from, to a finite verb, 717 sq.; in an abnormal case, 716 sq.; in apposition, in the place of a sentence, 669, 778 sq.

Particles, various classes of, 447 sq.; sparingly used in the N. T., 448, 579; no real ellipsis of, 744 sq.; position of, 698-701; written separately or joined, 49, 526.

Partitive formulas, 130, 216 sq.; with first member suppressed, 130 sq.

Pasor, 4 sq.

Passive voice, 326-330; of verbs which govern the dative or genitive, 287, 326 sq.; tenses of, in middle sense, 327 sq.; not used like the Hebrew Hophal, 329; accompanied by a dative, 274,—by prepositions, 461-464; with an accus., 286 sq., 326.

Paul (St.), peculiarities in the language and style of, 21, 28, 31, 35, 146, 150 sq., 154, 162, 169 sq., 193, 200, 209, 232, 235, 238, 263, 320, 323, 362, 408, 414, 430, 446, 451, 501, 521, 556 sq., 562, 640, 685, 709, 729, 746, 763, 793, 797.

Peculiarities in the diction of N. T. writers, general remarks on, 4, 30, 41, 240, 684 sq. See *Matthew*, *Mark*, etc.

Perfect tense, 338-343; combined with the aorist, 339 sq.; used in an aoristic sense, 340; is it used for other tenses? 340-342; with present meaning, (341), 342; passive, in a middle sense, 328; —not used for the perfect active, 328; with ἄν, 369. See also *Imperative*, etc.

Personal pronouns, 176, 178-191; used with great frequency in the N. T., 176, 178 sq., 184; sometimes omitted where they might have been expected, 179; replaced by nouns, 180 sq.; used with some looseness of reference, 181-184, 788; redundancy of, in relative sentences, 184 sq.; repeated, with a different reference, 186; nomin. of, when expressed, 190 sq.; position of, 193; periphrases for, 193, 241; dativus ethicus (?), 194; enclitic forms of, 62 sq. (193).

Peter (St.), peculiarities in the language and style of, 11, 35, 146, 150 sq., 154.

Pfochen, 13.

Philo, 21, 34.

Play upon words, 794-796.

Pleonasm, 752-773; of negatives, 755, 756 sq.; of sentences, impossible, 764; alleged pleonasm of certain verbs (ἄρχεσθαι, etc.), 765-770,—substantives (ἔργον, etc.), 768,—particles, 770-773.

Pluperfect tense, with the meaning of the imperfect, 341 sq.; passive, in a middle sense, 328; expressed by means of the aorist, 343 sq.; with ἄν, 381, 379; indic., 3d plural, 93; without augment, 85 sq.

Plural number, apparently used for the singular, 201, 218-221, 649; in a dual sense, 221; implying 'some,' 744; of abstract nouns, 220; plur. majestatis, 221, 649; neuter, with singular verb, 645-647; transition from, to singular (and *vice versa*), 725, 649.

Polysyndeton, 652 sq., 677, 762.

Position of words in a sentence, 684-702; of adjectives used attributively and predicatively, 163-166, 657-659, 686 sq.; of the genitive of pers. pronouns, 193 sq.; of demonstr. pron., 202, 686 sq.; of relative clauses, 209, 685, 696 sq., 702; of τις, 212, 688,— τίς, 213, 689, 699 sq.; of the predicate, 689 sq.; of the genitive, 193, 238 sq., 690; of the vocative, 687; of prepositions, 455; of adverbs, 692 sq.; of negatives, 693-696; of conjunctions, etc., 455, 547, 557, 698-701; of emphatic words generally, 684, 686 sq.; of words in apposition, 669 sq. (687 sq.); conventional arrangement of certain substantives, 690 sq.; dependent clauses placed before princi-

INDEX.

pal, 702 ; regard to sound in the arrangement of words, 689, 794. See also *Trajection*.

Positive degree, with μᾶλλον or ἤ, instead of a comparative, 301 sq. ; followed by παρά, ὑπέρ, 301, 503 sq. ; is it used for the superlative ? 308.

Possessive pronouns, sometimes used objectively, 191 ; replaced by ἴδιος, 191 sq. ; periphrases for, 193, 499 ; with apposition in the genitive, 664.

Predicate, construction of, 644-656, 660, 662 sq., 285 sq. ; enlargement of, 657, etc. ; ellipsis of, 734-738 ; partial ellipsis of both subject and predicate, 745-748 ; article in, 136, 141 sq. ; placed first, 689 sq.

Prepositions, in general, 447-455 ; compound, 127 ; governing the genitive, 455, etc.,—the dative, 480, etc.,—the accus., 494, etc. ; originally adverbs, 447 ; used adverbially, 312 sq., 526 ; joined with adverbs, 525 sq. ; their relation to cases, 449 sq., 451 sq. ; used when the simple case would have sufficed, 32, 40, 224, 245-249, 251, 253, 258, 266, 272, 280, 450 ; forming periphrases for adjectives and adverbs, 526-529 ; interchange of, 450, 453 sqq., 512-521 ; the same relation expressed by various prepositions in different languages, 452 sq., 459, 468, 487, 528 ; attraction of, 454, 493, 784 sq. ; repetition of, 522-525 ; not repeated with the relative, 197 sq., 524 sq. ; with different cases in the same sentence, 510 sq. ; different prepositions in the same sentence, 511 sq.,—or joined to one noun, 521 sq. ; after comparatives, 301, 303, 502 sqq. ; after intransitive verbs, 277-280, 291-293 (529, etc.) ; of rest, joined to verbs of motion, 492 sq., 514-516 (compare 591-593) ; of motion, joined to verbs of rest, 503, 514, 516-518 (comp. 592); construction of verbs compounded with, 529-540 ; apparent transposition of, 697 sq. (127) ; position of, 455 ; quasi-prepositions, 590 sq. (155 sq., 218, 758 sq.) ; prepositional clauses as attributives, 163, 166, 169-172, 174, 527 sq.

Present tense, 331-335 ; combined with the aorist, 333 sq. ; includes a preterite, 334 ; in the sense of a perfect, 343 ; is it used for other tenses ? 331-335 ; historic, 334 ; with ἄν, 384, 369, 388 ; in the dependent moods—see *Imperative*, etc.

Preterite, prophetic, 341.

Prolepsis, 341 sq., 345 sq., 347, 663, 779.

Pronouns, in general, 176-178 ; personal, 178-191 ; possessive, 191-193 ; demonstrative, 195-202 ; relative, 202-210 ; interrogative, 210-212 ; indefinite, 212 sq. ; expressed in a Hebraistic manner, 214-217 ; construed ad sensum, 176 sq., 181 sq., 787 sq. ; are they used with prospective reference ? 178 ; neuter of, used adverbially, 178, 285, 250,—or as a substantive, 741.

Proper names, in ἅς, ας, 69 sq., 127 sq. ; with other endings, 77 sq. ; indeclinable, 70, 78 sq., 226 sq. ; in contracted forms, 26, 127 sq. ; with and without the article, 137, 139-141 ; accentuation of certain, 58 sq.

Protasis of conditional sentences, 363-370, 380-384, 678 ; not expressed, 353, 378 sq., 749 ; replaced by a principal sentence, 211, 355, 678,— by an imperative, 391 sqq. ; negatives in, 598-602 ; aposiopesis after, 627, 750 sq.

Proverbial expressions, 443, 735, 747 sq.

Prozeugma of the demonstrative pronoun, 202.

Punctuation, 63-69 (628).

Purists, 12-19.

Purpose, adverbial sentences of, 679, 358-363, 389 ; expressed by the infinitive, 399 sq., 408 sqq.,—by the participle, 428,—by a relative sentence, 386.

Questions, of doubt or uncertainty, 348 sq., 356 sq. ; used to express a wish, 39, 41, 358 ; direct, 638-643 ; indirect, 373-376, 386 sq., 638-640 ; negative, for the imperative, 396 ; breviloquence in, 783 sq.

Quotations joined by καί, 542 ; sentences abruptly concluded by, 719, 749 ; poetical, 797 ; how introduced, 656, 735.

Rabbinisms, 30, 34 (36).
Rational philology, 8-10.
Reciprocal formulas, 217.
Redundance. See *Pleonasm*.
Reduplication, in verbs beginning with ρ, 88 ; instead of augment, 86.
Reflexive pronouns, 187-189 ; 3d person used for 1st and 2d, 187 sq. ; replaced by pers. pronouns, 188 sq., —by ἴδιος, 191 sq.
Relative pronouns, 202-210 ; in the place of demonstrative, 130, 209 ;

SUBJECTS. 829

including demonstrative, 197 sq., 206; construed ad sensum, 176 sq.; adverbial use of the neuter, 178, 209; are they used for direct interrogatives? 207 sq.; combined with interrog. pron., 211; after verbs of knowing, etc., 208; repeated, 209; attraction of, 197, 202 sqq., 206, 782; taking their gender or number from a following noun, 206 sq., 783; their antecedent, sometimes remote, 196; continuative force of, 680; prepos. not repeated with, 197 sq., 524 sq.; with $γε$, 555,—or other particles, 578 sq.

Relative sentences, 680; expressing purpose, 386; construction of, 384-386; replaced by principal sentences, 186, 711, 724,—by participles, 167 sq., 432; redundancy of pronouns in, 184 sq.; position of, 209, 685, 696 sq., 702.

Rhetoric of the N. T., 1 sq.; rhetorical usages, 308 sq., 622-624, 674 sq., 684 sq., 687 sq., 709, 736.

Rosetta inscription, 22.

Schema $κατ' ἐξοχήν$, 654; $ἀπὸ κοινοῦ$, 252, 262, 265, 518; Pindaricum, 648 sq., 704.

Schwarz (J. C.), 8, 15.

Sentence (the) and its elements, 644-656, 64 sq.; one logical, resolved into two grammatical, 446, 785 sq.; with the article, 135; simple, how enlarged, 657-673; apposition to, 290, 668 sqq.; sentences connected by particles and relatives, 676-681, —by inflexional forms, 681 sq.; opposed sentences, 677-679; ellipsis of sentences, 748 sq.; repetition of sentences, 764 sq.; trajection of sentences, 701 sq.

Septuagint version,[1] its language and style, *passim;* general remarks, 20, 21, 28-30, 32-34, 36, 39-41; relation between the language of the LXX and that of the N. T., 21, 31, 32, 36, 40, 41; peculiarities in words and forms, 24, 32, 141, 327,—46, 47, 48, 53, 54, 71, 73, 77, 78, 79, 86, 88, 89, 90, 91, 97, 313, 390; in syntax, 39-41, 137, 156, 167, 177, 179, 185, 186, 189, 191, 203, 204, 211, 215, 216, 217, 221, 223, 229, 248, 255, 256, 257, 258, 286, 289, 291, 292, 293, 298, 300, 301, 302, 309, 310, 311, 313, 314, 317, 334, 341, 360, 368, 369, 378, 384, 385, 389, 390, 409, 410, 411, 422, 427, 431, 439, 445, 471, 520, 562, 572, 585, 587, 588, 591, 592, 626, 627, 628, 634, 636, 637, 639, 648, 667, 671, 672, 690, 698, 714, 724, 738, 751, 753, 756, 759, 760.

Sharp's (Granville) 'first rule,' 162 sq.

Singular number, apparently used for the plural, 212; in a collective sense, 132, 177, 217 sq.; transition from, to the plural, 725; used distributively, 218.

Subject of a sentence, 644; with the article, 141; expressed by a genitive, with or without a prepos., 253, 737; not expressed, 654-656, 735-738, 787, 190; partial ellipsis of both subject and predicate, 745-748; complex, construction of, 650-654, 685,—prominence given to one member, 651 sq.; enlargement of, 657-673; change of, 787 sq.; attraction of the subject of a dependent sentence, 781 sq.

Substantives, declension of, 69-80; derived from verbs, 115-117,—from adjectives, 117 sq.,—from substantives, 118 sq.; compound, 123-127; article with, 131-163, 172 sq.; in the place of pronouns, 180 sq.,—of adjectives, 295-297; substantives which are commonly used in the plural, 219 sqq.; cognate, accus. of, 281-283, 203; repeated, with adverbial force, 581.

Superlative, periphrases for, 308 310; strengthened by $πάντων$, 310.

Synizesis, 777.

Synonyms combined, 753-755, 763 sq.

Syriac version (Peshito), references to the, 217, 227, 247, 298, 312, 521, 625.

Technical terms belonging to the N. T., 36; formed by ellipsis with verbs, 742,—by substantives with the article, 743.

Temporal adverbs, used in an argumentative sense, 579.

Temporal sentences, 370-373, 387-389, 677 sq.; expressed by participles, 168, 432,—by infinitives (with prepos.), 413 sq.,—by principal sentences, 543 sq., 676, 704.

Tenses of the Greek verb, 330 sq.; in no case really interchanged, *ib.;* the present, 331-335; the imperfect, 335-338; the perfect, 338-343; the aorist, 343-348; the future, 348-350; combination of different tenses, 350;

---

[1] [Under this head are included the Apocryphal books of the Old Testament.]

tenses of the dependent moods, 350 sq.; peculiar forms in, 82, etc.
Thiersch (H. W. J.), 32.
Thomas Magister, 22.
Time as expressed by prepositions, 452, 475,—by the cases, 258 sq., 273 sq., 288; notices of, introduced parenthetically, 704.
Tittmann, 449.
Trajection (or transposition) of words, 687-698 (201, 240); of clauses, 701 sq. (559 sq.).
Transition from the participle to the finite verb, 717 sq.; from the relative to the demonstrative construction, 186, 724 (711); from the oratio obliqua to the or. recta, and *vice versa*, 376, 683, 725; from singular to plural, and *vice versa*, 725, 649.

Verbals in τος, 120.
Verbs, derivative, 113-115; compound, 125 sqq.; double compounds, 126 sq.; compound, used for simple (and *vice versa*), 25, 529 sq., 745; inflexion of, 82-112; verbs in ω used for verbs in μι, 25 (93-98, 100, 106 sq., 108); intransitive verbs, made transitive, 24, 314, 329,—with accusative (*accus. rei*), 285,—accompanied by ὑπό, παρά, 462,—connected by prepositions with the dependent noun, 291-293; partially intransitive, 315 sq.; transitive, used intransitively, 315 (742 sq.); compounded with prepositions, construction of, 529-540; used impersonally, 655 sq., 735 sq.; finite, with adverbial force, 585-590; of commanding, asking, etc., 410 sq., 414 (416), 421 sq.; ellipsis of, 731-735.
Verses (hexameter, etc.) occurring in the N. T., 797.
Versions, as critical authorities, 133, 571, 664.
Vocative case, not a part of the sentence, 66; with and without ὦ, 228 sq.; accompanied by an adjective in the nomin., 229, 668; position, 687.
Voices of the verb, 314-330.
Vorst, 14, 30.

Wahl, 451.
Wish, expressed by a question, 39, 41, 358; by the optative, 357 sq., 378; by ὄφελον, 377; by εἰ? 562.
Words (and phrases) supplied in connected clauses, 727-730; arrangement of—see *Position, Trajection.*
Wyss (Caspar), 4 sq.

Zeugma, 777.

IV.—INDEX OF GREEK WORDS AND FORMS.

α intensive, 125.
α privative, 124.
α changed into ε, 46, 73 sq., 90, 107; -άω for -έω, 25, 104; α, ας, etc., for ον, ες, etc., in the 2 aorist, 86 sq.
-α, -ᾶ, as a genitive termination, 69.
-α, genit. -ης, after vowels and ρ, 71; genit. -ας, after δ and θ, 70 sq.
ἀγαθοεργέω, 26 sq.
ἀγαθοποιέω, 26.
ἀγαθός, comparison of, 81; ἀγ. πρός τι, 454.
ἀγαθουργέω, 26.
ἀγαθωσύνη, 26.
ἀγαλλιάω, ἀγαλλίασις, 25, 26.

ἀγαπάω, not used adverbially, 590.
ἀγάπη τοῦ Θεοῦ (Χριστοῦ), 232.
Ἅγαρ, τό, 223.
ἀγγέλλω (and compounds), 98.
ἄγγελοι, οἱ ἄγγελοι, 155.
ἄγε with plural subject, 649.
ἀγενεαλόγητος, 26 sq.
ἅγια (τά), 220 sq.; ἅγια ἁγίων, 221, 308.
ἁγιότης, 26.
ἀγνοέω, construction,[1] 198, 784.
ἁγνότης, 26.
ἄγνυμι (κατάγνυμι), 82.
ἀγορά without article, 150.
ἀγόραιοι, ἀγοραῖοι, 61.
ἀγριέλαιος, 26.

---

[1] [This will be understood to mean 'notices of construction.' It does not necessarily imply that the pages specified contain a *complete* register of the constructions of the word.]

ἀγρός without article, 150 sq.
ἄγω (and compounds), 99 ; used intransitively, 315 ; ἄγω τινί, 268 sq.; ἄγει used impersonally, 655.
ἀδελφός omitted, 238.
ἀδικέω, meaning, 334.
ἁδρότης, accent, 60.
ἀετός, 22.
ἄζυμα, 220.
-άζω, verbs in, 26, 114.
'Ἀθῆναι, plural, 220.
ἀθροίζω, 25.
ἀθῶος, ἀθῷος, 53 ; construction, 246.
Αἴγυπτος anarthrous, 139.
αἷμα, cædes, 31 ; αἵματα, 220 sq.; αἷμα ἐκχέειν, 34.
αἱματεκχυσία, 26 sq., 116, 123.
αἰνέω with dative, 673.
-αίνω, verbs in, 114 ; 1 aor. of verbs in -αίνω, -αίρω, 89.
αἱρέω (and compounds), 86, 99.
αἴρω, 1 aorist, etc., 52 ; used absolutely, 742.
αἰσχύνομαι with infin. and partic., 435 sq.
αἰτέω, construction, 284 ; αἰτοῦμαι, 321.
αἴτημα, 25.
αἰτίωμα, 116.
αἰφνίδιος used adverbially, 583.
αἰχμαλωτίζω, -τεύω, 26, 113 sq.
αἰῶνες, 219 sq.
αἰώνιος, α, ον, 80.
ἀκαίρως, 579 sq.
ἀκατάκριτος, 296.
ἀκατάπαστος, 108.
ἀκμήν, 288, 581 sq.
ἀκολουθέω ὀπίσω τ., 293.
ἀκούω, construction, 249, 259, 434, 436 ; audisse, 343, ἀκούσω, 99.
ἀκροβυστία, ἀκρόβυστος, 123 sq.
ἀκρογωνιαῖος, 123, 296.
ἀλάβαστρος (-τρον), 73.
ἀλάλητος, 24, 120.
ἀλεκτοροφωνία, 26.
ἀλέκτωρ, 24.
'Ἀλεξανδροινός (-ῖνος), 60.
ἀλήθω, 22.
ἁλιεῖς (ἁλεεῖς), 49.
ἀλλά: how it differs from δέ, 551 sq. ; can it stand for other conj.? 565 sq. ; various uses of, 551-554 ; commencing the apodosis, 552,
678 ; ἀλλά γε, 554, 700 ; ἀλλὰ μὲν οὖν, 552 ; ἀλλ' ἵνα, 398, 774 ; ἀλλ' ἤ, 552.
ἀλλάσσω, constr., 258, 485.
ἀλλ' ἤ, 552.
ἅλλομαι, 99.
ἄλλος omitted (?), 654, 744 ; apparently pleonastic, 664 sq.
ἀλλοτριοεπίσκοπος, 26, 123 sq.
ἅμα as a prepos., 590.
ἁμαρτάνω, 99 sq. ; construction, 293.
ἀμετανόητος, 124.
ἀμήν, 579.
'Ἀμπλίας, 128.
ἀμύνομαι, 323.
ἀμφί, not found in the N. T., 466.
ἀμφιέννυμι, ἀμφιάζω, -έζω, 100.
-αν for -ασι in 3 plur. perf. act., 90.
-ᾶν not -ᾷν, as termination of infin., 52.
ἄν with the indic., conj., and optat. moods, 364, 366 sq., 369, 370-372, 378-390 ; omitted, 353 sq. 382-385, 419, 744 ; in relative sentences, 384-386 ; in indirect questions, 386 sq. ; without a verb, 380 ; ἄν for ἐάν, 364, 380 ; ἐάν for ἄν, 390.
ἀνά with accus., 496 sq. ; expressing distribution, 312, 496 sq.
ἀνά, construction of verbs compounded with, 532 sq.[1]
ἀνάβα, 94.
ἀνάγκη, 31 ; omission of ἐστί with, 731.
ἀνάθεμα, 24, 34.
ἀναθεματίζω, 34.
ἀνακάμπτω intransitive, 315.
ἀνάκειμαι, 23.
ἀνακλίνομαι, 23.
ἀναλύω intransitive, 315.
ἀναμιμνήσκομαι, constr., 256.
ἀναξίως, 579 sq.
ἀναπαήσομαι, 108.
ἀνάπειρος, 49.
ἀναπίπτω, 22 ; ἀνάπεσαι, 87.
ἀναστάς, pleonastic (?), 760 sq.
ἀναστατόω, 113.
ἀνατέλλω intransitive, 315.
ἀνατίθημι, act. and midd., 317.
ἀνατολαί, plur., 220 ; without art., 150.
ἀναφαίνομαι, construction, 326.
ἀνέλεος, 124.
ἀνεξερεύνητος, 124.

---

[1] [As a rule, the contents of § 52 are referred to here in this general manner, and not in connexion with the particular verbs.]

ἀνεξιχνίαστος, 124.
ἀνεπαίσχυντος, 296.
ἄνευ with genit., 591.
ἀνέχομαι, augment, 85; future, 100; construction, 204, 253.
ἀνῆκεν, 338.
ἀνήρ without art., 152; with personal nouns, 657, 763.
ἀνθρωπάρεσκος, 26. 124.
ἀνθρώπινον λέγω, 28.
ἄνθρωπος joined to personal nouns, 657; κατ' ἄνθρωπον, 501.
ἀνοίγω, augment, 85; inflexions, 85, 100; ἀ. τὸ στόμα, τοὺς ὀφθαλμούς, 34, 759.
ἀνόμως, 579 sq.
ἀνορθώθη, 86.
-ανος, termination of patronymics, etc., 119.
ἀνταποκρίνομαι, 26.
ἀντέχομαι, construction, 253.
ἀντί with genit., 258, 455 sq.; with infin., 414; ἀνθ' ὧν, 202, 456.
ἀντί, construction of verbs compounded with, 533.
ἄντικρυς, ἀντικρύ, 45; with genitive, 591.
ἀντιλέγω, 23.
ἀντίλυτρον, 26.
'Αντίπας, 128.
ἀντιπέρα, accent, 60; with genit., 591.
ἄντλημα, 116.
ἀνώγαιον (ἀνάγαιον), 46.
ἀνώτερος, 81.
ἄξιος ἵνα, 421.
ἀπαντάω, 100.
ἀπάντησις, 25; εἰς ἀπάντησιν, 31.
ἀπαράβατος, 26.
ἀπαρτισμός, 25.
ἀπειλέω, ἀπειλοῦμαι, 321.
ἀπείραστος, 120, 242 sq.
ἀπεκατέστη, ἀπεκατεστάθη, 84.
ἀπεκδύομαι, 323.
ἀπελπίζω, 25.
ἀπέναντι, 591.
ἀπερισπάστως, 579.
ἀπέχω, 343.
ἀπό, 456 sq., 462-466; how it differs from ἐκ, 456 sq.,—from παρά, when used with passives, 463 sq.; interchanged with ὑπό, 464; replacing the simple genitive, 241 (?), 246-249, 251, 463, 737; in periphrases for adverbs, 526; with the infin., 413; attraction with ἀπό, 784; transposed (?), 697 sq.; ἀφ' οὗ,

204, 370, 387, 738; ἀφ' ἧς ἡμέρας, 204; ἀπὸ μικροῦ ἕως μεγάλου, 18 sq.; ἀπὸ τότε, ἀπὸ πέρυσι, 525 sq.; ἀπὸ μακρόθεν, 753 sq.
ἀπό, construction of verbs compounded with, 531 sq.
ἀποδεκτός, accent, 60.
ἀποθνήσκω with dative, 263.
ἀποκεφαλίζω, 26.
ἀποκρίνομαι, 19, 317; ἀπεκρίθην, 23, 327.
ἀπόκρυφος used adverbially, 583.
ἀποκτείνω, ἀποκτέννω, 23, 100.
ἀποκυέω, ἀποκυόω, 107 sq.
ἀπόλλυμι, ἀπολλύω, 108; future, 100; οἱ ἀπολλύμενοι, 430.
'Απολλώς, 127.
ἀπορρίπτω intrans., 315.
ἀποστασία, 25.
ἀποτάσσομαι, 23.
ἀποτόμως, 579 sq.
ἀπροσωπολήπτως, 126.
ἄπταιστος, 120.
ἀπώσατο, 111.
ἄρα, meaning, 555 sq.; occupying the first place, 698 sq.; ἄρα οὖν, 556; ἄρα γε, 556; εἰ ἄρα, 556.
ἆρα, meaning, 640; ἆρά γε, 556, 640.
ἄραφος, 53.
ἀργός, ἡ, όν, 25, 80.
ἀργύρια, 220.
ἀρεσκεία, ἀρέσκεια, 57.
ἀρέσκω, construction, 293.
-άριον, diminutives in, 119; common in later Greek, 25.
ἀριστερά without art., 152; plural, 220.
ἀρκέομαι, construction, 292.
ἁρμόζομαι, 323.
ἀρνέομαι, 25, 324.
ἀροτριάω, 25.
ἁρπάζω, 101.
ἄρσην, 23, 49.
'Αρτεμᾶς, 127.
ἀρτέμων, declension, 74.
ἄρτον φαγεῖν, 34; ἀ. κλᾶν, 36.
ἀρχή without art., 154; (τὴν) ἀρχήν used adverbially, 288, 581 sq.
ἄρχομαι, peculiar use of, 789 sq.; breviloquence with, 775; is it ever pleonastic? 767; ἀρξάμενον used absolutely, 779.
-αρχος, -άρχης, substantives in, 70 sq.
-ᾶς, -ας, proper names in, 26, 69 sq., 128.
ἀσεβέω, construction, 279.
ἀστοχέω, construction, 245.

GREEK WORDS AND FORMS.   833

ἀσφαλῆν, 76 sq.
ἀτενίζω, 25, 124.
ἄτερ with genit., 591.
αὐθεντέω, 24.
αὐξάνω intrans., 315; αὔξω, 101.
αὔρα omitted, 739 sq.
αὐτοκατάκριτος, 296.
αὐτόματος used adverbially, 583.
αὐτός, used with some looseness of reference, 181-184, 788; referring to a noun which follows (?), 178; redundant, 179, 184 (652),—in connexion with participles, 184, 276,—in relative sentences, 184 sq.; repeated, 186; καὶ αὐτός in the place of a relative, 186, 724; is the nomin. of αὐτός the unemphatic *he* ? 186 sq.; αὐτός used of Christ, 182 sq., 187; αὐτός and ἐκεῖνος in one sentence, 196; αὐτοῦ placed before its governing noun, 193; ὁ αὐτός, αὐτός ὁ, 139; ὁ αὐτός with a dative, 186; τὸ αὐτό with intransitive verbs, 285; τὰ αὐτά, ταὐτά, 51; αὐτὸ τοῦτο used adverbially, 178.
αὐτοῦ, αὑτοῦ, 188 sq.
ἀφεδρών, 118.
ἀφέθησαν, 97.
ἀφεῖς, 97.
ἀφελῶ, 99.
ἀφέωνται, 96 sq.
ἀφίδω, 48.
ἀφίημι, 96 sq.; ἄφες (ἄφετε) with conjunctive, 356; ἀφ. ὀφειλήματα, 31, 34.
ἀχειροποίητος, 296.
ἀχρεόω, 49.
ἄχρι, ἄχρις, 44 sq.; with genit., 591; ἄ. οὗ, ἄ. οὗ ἄν, 204, 370 sq., 387 sq.; ἄχρι ἧς ἡμέρας, 204, 370.

Βάαλ, ἡ, 223.
βαθμός, 23.
βαίνω (and comp.), 94.
βαΐον, 754.
βαλλάντιον, 46.
βάλλω (and comp.) intrans., 315.
βαπτίζομαι, 776.
βάπτισμα, 26 sq., 36, 115.
βάπτω with genit., 252.
βαρέω (βαρύνω), 25, 101.
βασιλεύω, constr., 24, 257, 314.
βασίλισσα, 25.
βασκαίνω, 1 aor. of, 89, 101; construction, 279.
βάτος, gender, 73.

Winer Grammar.

βέβαιος, α, ον, 80.
Βηθαβαρᾶ, 70.
Βηθσαϊδά, 70.
βιβλαρίδιον, 25, 119.
βιῶσαι, 101.
βλαστάνω, 101; intrans., 315.
βλασφημέω, construction, 278, 784.
βλέπω ἀπό τ., 40, 280; βλ. εἴς τ., 293; βλέπε μή, 631 sq.
βορρᾶς, genit., 69; without art., 150.
βούλομαι followed by the conjunctive, 356; ἐβουλόμην without ἄν, 353.
βουνός, 23.
βραδύνω with genit., 246.
βραδυτής, accent, 60.
βρέχω, 24.
βρώσιμος, 296.

γαμέω, 101, 107 (585).
γαμίσκω, 114 sq.
γάμοι, 220.
γάρ, etymology and meaning, 558-561; in questions, 559; can it stand for other conj.? 568 sqq.; introducing a parenthesis, 558, 703; after a parenth., 558; position, 455, 698-700; ἦ γάρ, 302; καὶ γάρ, 560 sq.; τί γάρ, 559, 731; τε γάρ, 561.
γε, 547, 554, 556, 561, 640, 729, 746; position, 455, 698, 700.
γελάω, 102.
γέμω (γεμίζω), construction, 251, 287.
γένει, τῷ γένει, 148.
γενέσια, 24; plural, 220.
γέννημα, 23, 26; γένημα, 49.
γεύομαι, figur. used, 34; constr., 248.
γῆ omitted, 480, 740; without art., 149 (137).
γήρει, 73 sq.
γίνομαι, 102; γέγονα, 340; with genitive, 243 sqq.; with dative, 264; with a participle, 440; omitted, 733 sq., 745 sq., 748; γίν. εἴς τι, 229; καὶ ἐγένετο, ἐγέν. δέ (γίνεται, ἐγενήθη), with finite verb, 756, 760, —with infin., 406 sq., 760; ἐγέν. τοῦ with infin., 411 sq.
γινώσκω, meanings of, 18, 329 sq.; forms, 89, 102; γνοῖ, 102, 360; passive, 329; with a participle, 435.
γλῶσσα, *nation*, 34; omitted, 739; is the phrase γλώσσαις λαλεῖν elliptical? 743.
γλωσσόκομον, γλωσσοκομεῖον, 24, 117.
γνωστός, 295.

53

834 INDEX.

γογγύζω, 23.
Γολγοθᾶ, 70.
Γόμορρα, 70.
γράφω with dative, 265; in aorist, 347 sq.
γρηγορέω, 27, 115.
γυμνητεύω (γυμνι-), 26, 114.
γυνή without art., 152; omitted, 237.

δαίμων, δαιμόνιον, 23.
δανείζομαι, 318.
Δαυίδ (-είδ), Δαβίδ, 47.
δέ, 551-554, 676 sq.; how it differs from ἀλλά, 551 sq.; can it stand for other conj.? 566 sq., 570 sq.; in the apodosis, 553, 678, 749 (199); introducing a parenth., 703; after a parenth., 553; position, 455, 698 sq.; elided before ἄν, 42; ὁ δέ, 130 sq.; οὐ (μή) ... δέ, 551 (620 sqq.); καί ... δέ, δὲ καί, 553.
-δε, demonstratives in, 202.
δεῖ, construction, 402; ἔδει without ἄν, 352-354, 383; ellipsis of δεῖν (?), 405.
δειγματίζω, 25, 113.
δείκνυμι, 108.
δεκαδύο, 23.
δεκαπέντε, 313.
δεκατόω, 25, 113.
δεξιά, without art., 152; plural, 220; ἐκ δεξιᾶς, δεξιῶν, 459.
δεξιολάβος, 126.
δέομαι, construction, 247, 414, 422; ἐδέετο, 51; ἐδεεῖτο, 102.
δέρω πολλάς, 283, 286 sq.
δεσμή, δέσμη, 60.
δεσμός, plural of, 72.
δεσμοφύλαξ, 124.
δευτεραῖος used adverbially, 583.
δεύτερον adverbial, 314.
δευτερόπρωτος, 124.
δή, 578 (394).
δῆλον ὅτι, 731.
Δημᾶς, 128.
δημοσίᾳ, 53, 739.
δήποτε, δήπου, 578.
διά with genit., 452, 472-477; can it denote the *causa principalis?* 473 sq.; sometimes akin to the dative, 272 ; διὰ 'I. Χριστοῦ, 473 ; in periphrases for adj. or adverbs, 474, 526 sq.; with the accus., 497-499; with the infin., 414.
διά, construction of verbs compounded with, 537.

διαβεβαιόομαι, 317.
διάβολος without art., 154 sq.
διάγω used absolutely, 742.
διαθῆκαι, 221.
διακονέω, augment, 85; used absolutely, 742.
Δίαν, 76 sq.
διαπαρα-, compounds with, 126 sq.
διαπαρατριβή, 126 sq.
διαπονέομαι, 23.
διασκορπίζω, 26, 113.
διατρίβω used absolutely, 742.
διαφέρω, construction, 245, 252.
διδάσκω τινί, 279; ἔν τινι, 284.
δίδωμι (and comp.), inflexions, 89, 93, 94, 95, 102; δῴη, δώῃ, 94, 363; δώσῃ, 89, 95; διδοῖ, δοῖ, 95, 360; διδ. ἔν τ., 515.
διερμήνευε, 86.
διίστημι intrans. in 1 aor., 315.
δικαιοκρισία, 26, 123.
δικαιοσύνη, *alms* (?), 32, 33; δικ. Θεοῦ, 232.
διό, διόπερ, 557.
διοπετές (τό), 294, 741.
διότι, 557.
διπλότερος, 81.
διψάω, meaning and constr., 17, 256; διψᾶν, διψῆν, 52, 92.
διώκω, 31; future, 102.
δοκέω never really pleonastic, 766; οἱ δοκοῦντες, 444, 766.
δόμος omitted, 740.
δόξα, *brightness, splendour*, 33; ἡ δόξα, 134.
δραχμή omitted, 740.
δύναμαι, augment, 82; δύνῃ, 90; never pleonastic, 768; ἠδυνάμην without ἄν, 352; used absolutely, 743.
δυνάμεις, *miracles*, 33.
δύο, declension, 74; δύο δύο, 40, 312; δύο with plural noun, 221.
δυσεντέριον, 73.
δυσμαί, 220; without art., 150.
δύω, δύνω, διδύσκω (and compounds), 102.
δωδεκάφυλος, 124.
δῴη, 94, 363.
δῶμα, 24.
δώσῃ, 89, 95.

ε for α, 46, 73 sq., 90, 107; -έω for -άω, 104; ε and αι interchanged in MSS., 87; ε and η interchanged, 53, 637.
ἔα, 579.

GREEK WORDS AND FORMS. 835

ἐάν, εἰ, 363 sq., 368 sqq.; ἐάν with indic., 369, 388 sq., 357; with conj., 363 sq., 366 sq., 368; ἐάν with a finite verb replacing an infin., 403; no real ellipsis of ἐάν, 744; ἐὰν μή in oaths, 627; ἐὰν μή not used for ἀλλά, 566; ἐάν for ἄν, 390; ἄν for ἐάν, 364, 380.
ἐάνπερ, 562.
ἑαυτοῦ for 1 and 2 pers., 187 sq.; ἑαυτοῦ, ἑαυτόν, with the middle, 322 sq.,—or with the active voice, 28, 321 sq.; αὑτοῦ, 188 sq.; ἑαυτῶν for ἀλλήλων, 188; ἀφ' ἑαυτῶν, ἐφ' ἑαυτοῦ, 465; καθ' ἑαυτόν, 500.
ἐάω: οὐκ ἐάω, 597, 599.
ἐγάμησα, 101.
ἐγγύς with genit. and dative, 243, 591; ἐγγὺς εἶναι, 584.
ἐγείρω intrans., 315 sq.; ἐγείρομαι, 316.
ἐγενήθην, 102.
ἐγκαίνια, 220.
ἐγκαινίζω, 34.
ἐγκακέω, 26.
ἐγκαλέω, construction, 254.
ἐγκρατεύομαι, 26.
ἐγώ, when expressed, 190; μοί dativus ethicus (?), 194; μοῦ standing before the governing noun, 193; πρός με, 62 sq.; καθ' ἡμᾶς, 193, 499.
ἔδει a true imperf. indic., 353 sq.
ἐδολιοῦσαν, 91.
ἐδώκαμεν, 102.
ἐθελοθρησκεία, 124.
ἐθέλω, θέλω, 102, 586. See θέλω.
ἐθνικῶς, 580.
ἐθύθη, 48.
-εί or -ί, adverbial ending, 47.
-ει as termination of 2 sing. indic. passive, 89 sq.
εἰ, meaning, 365 sq., 638; with indic., 364-366, 369 sq., 380-384, 374-376; with conj., 368, 374; with optative, 367; εἰ, ἐάν, 363 sq., 368 sqq.; εἰ with a finite verb replacing an infin., 403, 682; εἰ μή, εἰ οὐ, 598-602; no real ellipsis of εἰ, 678, 744; εἰ in oaths, 40, 627; εἰ as indirect interrogative, 638,—its construction, 373 sq., 375 sq.; εἰ in direct interrogation, 638 sqq.; εἰ for ὅτι, 679, 562, 600; for ἐπεί, 562, 600; εἰ ἄρα, 556, 375 sq.; εἰ καί, καὶ εἰ, 554 sq.; εἰ δὲ μή, εἰ δὲ μή γε, used elliptically, 729 sq., 757.

-εια or -ια as termination of subst., 49, 118.
εἴγε, 561 sq.
εἰδέα, 53.
(εἴδω) εἶδον, inflexions, 102 sq., 86, 88; ἴδε, ἰδέ, 55 sq.; followed by a participle, 434; ἰδεῖν θάνατον, 17 sq.; ἔφιδε, ἐφείδεν, ἀφίδω, 48.
εἰδωλεῖον, 118.
εἰδωλόθυτον, 27, 124
εἰδωλολατρεία, 27.
εἰδωλολάτρης, 124.
εἴδωλον, 120.
εἰκῆ, εἰκῇ, 52.
εἴκοσι (-ιν), 45.
εἰλικρίνεια, εἰλικρινής, 124.
εἰλίσσω, 23.
εἰ μή in oaths, 627; not used for ἀλλά, 566, 789; εἰ μή τι ἄν, 380; ἐκτὸς εἰ μή, 757, 368; οὐ (οὐδείς) ... εἰ μή, 638.
εἰ μήν (ἦ μήν), 553, 627.
εἰμί, 95 sq.; εἰμί, εἶμι, 61; ἐστί, ἔστι, 61; the substantive verb, 584, 656; ἦν as an aorist, 381; ὤν a past partic., 428 sq.; with a partic., 437-440, 30,—negatived by μή, 606; omitted, 437, 440 sq., 731-735, 745 sqq.; ἔστι, it is possible, 403; εἶναί τινος, 243 sq.,—τινι, 264,—εἴς τι, 229,— ἔκ τινος, 461; καὶ ἔσται ... καί, 760.
εἶμι (and comp.), 105, 93, 331; εἶμι, εἰμί, 61.
εἵνεκεν. See ἕνεκα.
-εινός, adj. in, 123.
εἴπερ, 561 sq.
εἶπον, inflexions, 103 sq.; εἰπόν, 23, 58, 103; ἐρρήθην, ἐρρέθην, 103 sq.; εἴρηκε (εἶπε) in citations, 656, 735; ellipsis of εἶπε, 734; εἰπεῖν ἵνα, 422; ὡς ἔπος εἰπεῖν, 399, 563.
εἴπως, 374, 376, 562.
εἴρω, ἐρῶ. See εἶπον.
-εις, plural termination (for -εας), 74.
εἰς with accus., 494-496; in periphrases, 285 sq., 527, 662; does it form a periphrasis for the nomin.? 229; can εἰς be used for ἐν? 514, 516-521,—or as a nota dativi? 266 sq.,—or accusativi? 285 sq., 662; εἰς with the infin., 413 sq., 420.
εἰς, constr. of verbs compounded with, 535.
εἷς for τις, 145 sq. (30); εἷς τις, 146, 213; εἷς and ὁ εἷς, 144; εἷς for πρῶτος, 33, 311; εἷς ... καὶ εἷς (and

similar expressions), 216 sq.; εἷς τὸν ἕνα, 217; εἷς ... οὐ, 216; οὐδὲ εἷς, 216; εἷς καθ᾽ εἷς, etc., 312.
-εισαν for -εσαν, in pluperf., 93, 103.
εἰσέρχεσθαι εἰς τὸν κόσμον, 18.
εἴτε, 549, 638 (368).
εἶτεν, 23.
ἐκ, 458-461, 453, 456 sq.; how it differs from ἀπό, 456 sq.; not used for ἐν, 461; replacing the simple genit., 241 (?), 246, 248 sq., 251, 253, 258, 458, 737; in periphrases for adverbs, 527 sq.; attraction with ἐκ, 784 sq.; ἔκπαλαι, 25, 525.
ἐκ, constr. of verbs compounded with, 533 sq.
ἕκαστος with the art., 138 sq.; with plural predicate, 648.
ἐκγαμίζω, 127.
ἐκεῖ for ἐκεῖσε, and *vice versa*, 591 sqq.
ἐκεῖνος referring to the nearest subject, 196, 788; taking up the subject or predicate, 199, 206; position, 199, 202, 686; joined to a noun with the art., 137; apparently used for οὗτος, 196; occurring in the same sentence with αὐτός, 196.
ἐκέρδησα, 107.
ἐκκακέω, 26.
ἐκκλησία without art., 152.
ἐκλέγομαι ἔν τινι, 283.
ἐκμυκτηρίζω, 26.
ἐκούσιον (κατὰ), 580.
ἔκραξα, 107.
ἔκρυβον, 107.
ἐκτένεια, 26.
ἐκτενῶς, 26, 579 sq.
ἐκτός with genit., 591; ἐκτὸς εἰ μή, 368, 757.
ἐκχέω, ἐκχύνω (-χύννω), 25, 104; fut. ἐκχεῶ, 91 sq., 104; ἐκχέετε, 51.
ἑκών used adverbially, 583.
ἐλαιών, 118, 226 sq.
ἐλάκησα, 108.
ἐλάττων, 49; without ἤ, 300 (745).
ἐλαχιστότερος, 81, 753.
ἐλεάω, 104.
ἐλεεινός, 123.
ἔλεος, 76.
ἐλεύσομαι, 104 sq.
ἑλκόω, augment, 85.
ἑλκύω, 57, 104.
ἑλληνίζω, 29, 116 sq.
ἑλληνιστής, 116.
ἐλλογάω, 104.

ἐλπίζω with dative, 261; other constructions, 292, 404, 416 sq.
ἐλπίς: ἐφ᾽ ἐλπίδι, etc., 48.
ἐμός sometimes used objectively, 191.
ἐμπιπλῶν, 94.
ἐμπνέω with genit., 255.
ἐμπορεύομαι, constr., 279.
ἔμπροσθεν with genit., 591.
ἐν with dative, 480-488; apparently with genit., 480 (with accus., 455); with infin., 413; with dative of time or place, 274; differs from διά with genit., 486; in periphrases for adj. or adverbs, 528; apparently used for εἰς, 514-516, 518-521; can ἐν represent the dative? 272 sq.,— or the accus.? 283,—or the nomin. (*Beth essentiæ*)? 230, 644; ἐν ᾧ, 482, 484, 370; ἐν Χριστῷ (ἐν Κυρίῳ), 484, 486 sq.,—used attributively, 169 sq.; ἐν ὀνόματι, 487.
ἐν, constr. of verbs compounded with, 534 sq.
ἔναντι with genit., 591.
ἐναντίον, 268, 293; with genit., 591.
ἔνατος, ἔννατος, 46.
ἐνδείκνυμαι, 318.
ἐνδύομαι figur., 31.
ἐνέγκας, 110 sq.
ἔνεδρον, 73.
ἕνεκα, ἕνεκεν, εἵνεκεν, 45 sq.; with genit., 591; with infin., 414; οὗ εἵνεκεν, 561.
ἐνενήκοντα, 46.
ἐνεός, ἐννεός, 48.
ἐνέπαιξα, 108.
ἐνεργέω, ἐνεργοῦμαι, 323.
ἐνέχω used absolutely, 742.
ἐνθάδε, 592.
ἔνι, 96.
ἐνισχύω intrans., 315.
ἔνοχος with genit., 253; with dative, 264, 267; with εἰς, 267, 776.
ἐντός with genit., 591.
ἐντρέπομαί τινα, 277.
ἐνώπιον, 268, 293, 591; ἐν. τοῦ Θεοῦ, 34.
ἐνωτίζομαι, 34.
ἐξάπινα, 25.
ἐξεκρέμετο, 107.
ἐξένευσε, 112.
ἔξεστι, construction, 402; ἐξόν ἐστι, 25.
ἐξομολογέομαί τινι and ἔν τινι, 31, 33, 262.
ἐξορκίζω, 127.
ἐξ οὗ, *whence*, 177.

GREEK WORDS AND FORMS.

ἐξουδενέω, -όω, ἐξουθενέω, -όω, 26, 113.
ἐξυπνίζω, 25.
ἔξω with genit., 591.
ἔξωθεν, 592; with genit., 591.
ἐξῶσεν, 111.
ἔοικα, 342.
ἐπαγγέλλομαι with aor. infin., 417.
ἐπαινέσω, 104.
ἔπαιξα, 108.
ἐπαισχύνθη, 86.
ἐπάν, 387.
ἐπάνω with genit., 591; without influence on case, 313.
Ἐπαφρᾶς, 128.
ἐπεί, 541, 561; with indic. present, 354; introducing a question, 603; with a suppressed protasis, 354, 749; ἐπεὶ μή, 602; ἐπεὶ ἄρα, 556.
ἐπειδή, 541, 561.
ἐπειδήπερ, 561.
ἐπείπερ, 561.
ἔπειτα μετὰ τοῦτο, 754.
ἐπέκεινα, accent, 59; with genit., 591.
ἐπενδύτης, 26, 117.
ἐπερωτάω, 25; ἐπ. ἐν, 39.
ἐπέχω used absolutely, 742.
ἐπί with genit., 468-470, 465; with dative, 488-492, 452 sq.; with accus., 507-509; in periphrases for adverbs, 528; with different cases in one sentence, 510; ἐφ' ᾧ, 491 sq.; ἐφ' οἷς, 197 sq., 202; ἐπὶ τρίς, 525.
ἐπί, constr. of verbs compounded with, 535 sq.
ἐπιβάλλω used absolutely, 742.
ἐπιγαμβρεύω, 27.
ἐπιδιορθόομαι, 322 sq.
ἐπιθυμέω, construction, 255 sq.
ἐπικαλέομαι, 330.
ἐπιλαμβάνομαι, constr., 252 sq.
ἐπιλανθάνομαι, constr., 256.
ἐπιλησμονή, 116.
ἐπιμένω, construction, 537; with a participle, 434.
ἐπιορκέω, future, 104.
ἐπιούσιος, 120 sq.
ἐπιποθέω, construction, 256.
ἐπιπόθητος, 296.
ἐπίσταμαι with participle, 435.
ἐπιστέλλω, 23.
ἐπιστολαί, 219.
ἐπιστρέφομαι, ἐπιστροφή, 27.
ἐπιτίθημί τινι, used absolutely, 742.
ἐπιτυγχάνω, construction, 249 sq.
ἐπιφᾶναι, 110.

ἐπιφαύσει, 110.
ἐπιχειρέω, alleged pleonasm of, 765.
ἐραυνάω, 49.
ἐργάζομαί τι, 279; augment, 85.
ἔργον not pleonastic, 768.
ἐρεύγομαι, 23.
ἔρημος, ον, 80; accent, 59.
ἐριθεία, 116; accent, 57.
ἔρις, plural, 75.
Ἑρμᾶς, 128.
ἐρρήθην, ἐρρέθην, 103 sq.
ἔρχομαι (and comp.), 104 sq., 86; present in future sense, 331 sq.; ὁ ἐρχόμενος, 428.
ἐρωτάω, 23, 25, 31, 33; construction, 284, 414, 422.
ἐρωτέω, 104.
-ες for -ας in 2 sing. perf., 90.
ἐσήμανα, 89, 109 sq.
ἔσθησις, 23.
ἐσθίω (ἔφαγον), construction, 248 sq.; φάγομαι, φάγεσαι, 110.
ἔσθω, 24, 105.
ἐσσόομαι (ἡττάομαι), 49, 106.
ἑστάναι, 93.
ἔσχατος predicative, 164; used adverbially, 583.
ἐσχάτως, 579 sq.; ἐσχ. ἔχειν, 27, 580.
ἔσω, εἴσω, 60; meaning, 592; with genit., 591; ἐσώτερος, 81.
ἔσωθεν, 592.
ἕτερος apparently pleonastic, 665; ἐν ἑτέρῳ, 741.
-ετης, accent. of numeral adj. in, 56.
ἔτι, 579; with comparatives, 300 sq.; trajection of, 692.
ἑτοιμάζω used absolutely, 743.
ἕτοιμος, ον, 80; accent, 59; with aor. infin., 417.
ἑτοίμως, 579 sq.
ευ-, augment of verbs beginning with, 83.
εὐαγγελίζω, active voice, 25; augment, 83; construction, 267, 279, 284, 287, 326.
εὐαγγέλιον τοῦ Χριστοῦ, 233; εὐ. κατὰ Ματθαῖον, 501.
εὐαρέστως, 579 sq.
εὖ γε, 554.
εὐδοκέω, 26; derivation, 125; augment, 83; εὐδ. ἔν τινι, 39, 291; other constructions, 266, 279.
εὔθετος, construction, 267.
εὐθύμως, 579 sq.
εὐθύς figur., 34; εὐθύς (εὐθέως), position of, 693.

εὐλογέω, 83; augment, 83; εὐλογημένος (εὐλογητός), position of, 689 sq.,—ellipsis of εἴη (ἔστω) with, 733.
εὐπερίστατος, 124.
εὐπροςωπέω, 114.
εὑρίσκω (and comp.), 87, 89, 105; augment, 83; εὑρίσκειν χάριν (ἔλεος), 18, 35; εὑρίσκομαι with dative of agent, 274 sq.; is εὑρίσκομαι used for εἰμί? 769 sq.
εὐσχήμων, 23.
εὐχαριστέω, 20, 23; augment, 83; with accus., 279; with participle, 434 sq.
εὔχομαι, augment, 83; construction, 266; ηὐχόμην without ἄν, 353.
-εύω, verbs in, 114 sq.
εὐώνυμα without art., 152; plural, 220.
ἐφάπαξ, 525.
ἔφη. See φημί.
ἔφθασα, 111.
ἐφίδε, 48.
ἐχθές (χθές), 25, 48.
ἔχω (and compounds), inflexions, 88, 100; intransitive, 315; ἔχομαί τινος, 253; ἔχειν and μὴ ἔχειν used absol., 743; ellipsis of ἔχων, 737.
-έω, derivative verbs in, 114 sq.; verbs in -έω which retain ε in the future, 92; -έω for άω, 104.
ἐωνησάμην, 82, 112.
-έως for -έος in genit. of adj., 75.
ἕως with genit., 590 sq.; with infin., 414; ἕως οὗ (ὅτου), 370, 591; constr. of the conj. ἕως (ἕ. οὗ, ἕ. ὅτου), with and without ἄν, 370 sqq., 387 sq.; ἕως πότε, etc., 591; ἕως ἐπί τ., 771.

ζάω, 105 sq.; ζῆν without ι subscript, 52; transitive in the LXX, 24.
ζβεννύω, 49.
ζηλεύω, 114.
ζῆλος, neuter, 76
ζημιόομαι, 17.
Ζηνᾶς, 128.
ζητέω with infin., 403; ζητ. ψυχήν, 34 (18).
ζῷον, ζῶον, 53.

ἤ disjunctive, 549-551; not used for καί, 549 sq.; repeated 652; ἤ ... ἤ καί, 549; in questions, 638 sq.
ἤ comparative, 549; after comparatives, 300; after adj. in the positive, 301 sq.; no real ellipsis of, 744 sq.

(300); θέλω ἤ, 301 sq.; λυσιτελεῖ ἤ, 302; ἤ γάρ, 302.
ἦ μήν (εἰ μήν), 553, 627.
ἤδη (ἤδη ποτέ), 579.
ἥκω, inflexions, 106; meaning, 343.
ἡλίκος, 210.
ἥλιος without art., 148 sq.
ἡμάρτησα, 99 sq.
ἤμεθα, 95 sq.
ἡμεῖς and ὑμεῖς interchanged, 330.
ἤμελλε, 82.
ἡμέρα omitted, 738; ἄχρι (and ἀφ᾽) ἧς ἡμέρας, 204; ἡμέρᾳ καὶ ἡμέρᾳ, 581; δἰ ἡμερῶν, 476.
ἤμην, 95 sq.
ἡμίση (ἡμίσεια), ἡμίσους, 73, 75.
ἡμίωρον, 125.
ἡνίκα (ἤν. ἄν), 370 sq., 387, 389
ἦξα, 106.
ἤπερ, 303, 549.
ἤρεμος, 81.
-ήριον, subst. in, 119.
ἠρχόμην, 105.
ἦς for ἦσθα, 96.
ἤτοι, 549.
ἡττάομαι, 106.
ἤτω, 95.
ἤφιε, 97.
ἦχος, 76.

θάλασσα without art., 150.
θάλλω, 106.
θανατηφόρος, 126.
θάνατος, 30; without art., 152; θάνατον ἰδεῖν (θεωρεῖν), 17 sq.
θαυμάζω, inflexions, 327; constr., 292; θαυμ. εἰ, 562, 679, 600.
θεατρίζω, 25, 113.
θέλημα, meaning, 755 sq.; τὸ θέλ., 743.
θέλω (ἐθέλω), 102, 586; is it used with adverbial force? 586 sq.; is it ever pleonastic? 767 sq.; θέλω ἤ, malo, 301 sq.; οὐ θέλω, nolo, 597; θ. ποιῆσαι, 356; θ. ἵνα, 420, 422 sq.; θέλω ἔν τινι, 291 sq.; θέλω τί, 587.
θεόπνευστος, 120.
Θεός without art., 151; Θεέ, 72; ἀστεῖος (δυνατός) τῷ Θεῷ, 310, 265.
θεοστυγής, 24; accent, 61 sq.
Θευδᾶς, 128.
θθ for τθ, 49.
θλῖψις, θλίψις, 56.
θνήσκω, 106.
θρῆσκος, θρησκός, 57.
θριαμβεύω τινά, 24, 314.

GREEK WORDS AND FORMS. 839

Θυάτειρα, 70.
θυγάτηρ omitted, 237.
θύρα without art., 152; θύραι, 220.
θυρεός, 24.
-θω, verbs in, 114.

ι subscript, in certain words and classes of words, 51-53.
ι and ει interchanged, 49, 53; -ια or -εια as ending of nouns, 49, 118.
ί or εί as adverbial ending, 47.
-ια, subst. in, 116, 118 sq., 126.
ἰδέ, ἴδε, 55 sq.; ἴδε, ἰδού, 229, 319, 563; ἴδε combined with a plural verb, 649; εἶδον καὶ ἰδού with accus. and nomin., 671, 724.
ἴδιος for a possess. pron., 191 sq.; joined to a pers. pron., 192; ἰδίᾳ, 53, 739.
ἱέρισσα, 25.
Ἰεριχώ, declension, 79.
ἱερουργέω as a transit. verb, 279.
Ἰερουσαλήμ, Ἰεροσόλυμα, 79; with and without art., 140; plural form, 220.
-ίζω, verbs in, 27, 113; contracted future, 88 sq.
ἵημι (and comp.), inflexions, 96 sq.
Ἰησοῦς, declension, 77.
ἱκεσία, 24.
ἱλάσκομαι, 106; with accus., 284 sq.
ἱλαστήριον, 119, 741.
ἵλεως, 22.
ἱμάτιον omitted, 739; plural, 220.
ἵνα, 563; construction, 358-363, 673; with optat., 363; forming a periphrasis for the imperative, 396,—for the infin., 28, 403, 420-426, 682,—in St. John, 425 sq.; ἐκβατικῶς, 572-577; for ὥςτε, 577; for ὅτι (?), 577; no real ellipsis of, 356, 744; ἵνα τί, 212, 734; ἀλλ' ἵνα, 398, 774; ἵνα πληρωθῇ, 576 sq.; ἵνα μὴ λέγω, 746.
-ινος, -ινός, adj. in, 122 sq.; common in later Greek, 26.
-ιον, subst. in, 119.
Ἰούδα, accent, 59; art. with, 141.
ἰουδαΐζω, 114.
ἰσάγγελος, 124.
ἴσος, ἶσος, 60; ἴσα adverbial, 221.
ἱστάνω, 106, 94.
ἱστάω, 93 sq.
ἵστημι (and comp.), inflexions, 84, 93-95, 106; meaning, 315 sq., 342.
Ἰωάννης, Ἰωάνης, 49; declension, 77.
Ἰωσῆς, 77.

καθά, 548.
καθαιρέομαι, construction, 245.
καθάπερ, 548.
καθάπτω, 322.
καθέζομαι, 106.
καθεῖς, καθ' εἷς, 312.
καθερίζω, 46.
καθεύδω, augment, 83.
καθῆκεν, 352, 338.
κάθημαι (κάθη, κάθου), 98.
καθό, 385 sq., 548.
καθότι, 548, 555; κ. ἄν with indic., 384.
κάθου, 98.
καθώς, 27, 548, 555, 561.
καθώςπερ, 548.
καί, 541-548, 676; connecting numerals, 313; in questions, 545; as an adversative (?), 545; not used for ἤ, 549 sq.; epexegetic, 545 sq., 786; joining the special to the general, 544, 546, 653 sq.; does καί mean *especially*? 546; commencing the apodosis, 357, 546 sq., 756; in comparisons, 548 sq., 754; trajection of (?), 701; crasis with καί, 51; καί ... καί, 547 sq. (the 2d καί omitted, 721); τε ... καί, 547 sq.; τε καί, 548; καί ... δέ, 553; καίγε, 547; καὶ γάρ, 560 sq.; εἰ καί, καὶ εἰ, 554 sq.; οὐ ... ἀλλὰ καί, 624.
καινότερος, 305.
καίπερ with participle, 432 sq.
καιρός without art., 154; καιροί for dual, 221.
καίτοι, 432 sq., 554.
καίτοιγε, 554.
καίω (and comp.), 89, 106.
κακός, comparison, 81.
καλέω, *invite*, 742; is καλεῖσθαι used for εἶναι? 769.
καλὸν ἤ, 302; κ. ἦν, 352, 383.
καλοποιέω, 26 sq.
καμμύω, 25, 51.
κἄν, 380, 730.
κασαδοκέω, 125.
καρδία not used for a pers. pron., 195.
καρδιογνώστης, 124.
καρπὸς ὀσφύος (κοιλίας), χειλέων, 34.
κατά with genit., 477 sq.; with accus., 499-502, 453; in periphrases for adj. or adverbs, 528 sq.,—for the genit. (?), 241; with accus. of pers. pron. for a possessive pron., 193, 499; expressing distribution, 312,

500; sometimes akin to the dative, 272.
κατά, constr. of verbs compounded with, 537.
κατάβα, 94.
καταβραβεύω, 28.
καταγινώσκω, construction, 254.
κατακαήσομαι, 106.
κατακαυχάομαι, constr., 254; κατακαυχᾶσαι, 90.
κατακρίνω θανάτῳ, 263 sq.
καταλαμβάνω, 317, 321.
καταλείπω, aorist, 106.
κατάλυμα, 26, 116.
καταλύω intrans., 315.
καταμαρτυρέω, construction, 254.
καταναρκάω, 28.
κατάνυξις, 117.
καταποντίζω, 25.
καταράομαι, construction, 278.
καταστολή, 24.
καταχράομαι, construction, 262.
κατεαγῶ (κατεάξω, κατέαξαν), 82.
κατείδωλος, 296.
κατέναντι with genit., 591.
κατενώπιον with genit., 591.
κατέχω εἰς, 743.
κατηγορέω, construction, 254.
κατήγωρ, 117.
κάτω, 592; κατώτερος, 81.
καυχάομαι, construction, 279, 292 sq.; καυχᾶσαι, 90.
κεκέρασμαι, 107.
κέκτημαι, 342.
κελεύω, construction, 337, 417, 422.
κενῶς, 579.
κεράννυμι, 107.
κέρατα, 75.
κερδαίνω, 89, 107.
κεφαλαιόω, 113.
κεφαλίς, 23.
κῆρυξ, κήρυξ, 56.
κηρύσσω εἴς τ., 267; κηρύξαι, -ῠ-, 57.
κλαίω, constr., 278; future, 107.
κλάω (τὸν) ἄρτον, 36.
κλείς, declension, 75.
Κλεόπας, 128.
κλέψω, 107.
κληρονομέω, construction, 250.
κλίβανος, 22.
κλίνω (ἐκκλίνω) intrans., 315.
κοιλία: ἐκ κοιλίας, καρπὸς κ., 34.
κοιμάομαι, 17, 334 sq., 342.
κοινός, 19.
κοινόω, 112.
κοινωνέω, construction, 250 sq.

κοινωνός, construction, 250.
Κολοσσαί, Κολασσαί, 47.
κόλποι, 220.
κομίζομαι, 775; future, 89.
κόπτομαί τινα, 278.
κοράσιον, 24.
κόσμιος, ον, 80.
κόσμος, 27; without art., 153; ὁ κόσμος, 133.
κράβαττος, 26, 46.
κράζω, 107; fut., 107, 348; κέκραγα, 342; κρᾶζον, 57.
κρατέω, construction, 252, 409.
κρέας, 75.
κρείττων, 49, 81; κρεῖττον ἦν, 352.
κρέμαμαι, 107.
κρίμα, κρῖμα, 56 sq.
κρούω used absol., 742.
κρυπτή, 298.
κρύπτω, 25; inflexions, 107; construction, 246, 284.
κτάομαι, 342.
κτίσις, creature, 33; without art., 153.
κτιστής, κτίστης, 57 sq.
κύπτω, quantity of υ, 57.
κυριακός, 296.
κύριος and ὁ κύριος, 154.
κύω, κυέω, 107.

λαγχάνω, construction, 250, 401.
λάθρα, λάθρᾳ, 52.
λαῖλαψ, λαίλαψ, 56; gender, 22.
λαλέω with participle, 436.
λαλιά, 24.
λαμβάνω, fut. λήμψομαι, 53 sq.; λαβέ, 395,—accent, 55 sq.; is λαβών pleonastic? 759; λαμβ. τὴν ἐπαγγελίαν, 297.
λαμπάς, 24.
λανθάνω with participle, 585.
λάσκω, 108.
λεγεών, λεγιών, 49.
λέγω, construction, 266; implying command, 405; ellipsis of, 746; λέγει in citations, 656, 735; λέγων pleonastic, 753; λέγων, λέγοντες, used absolutely, 672; λέγ. περί, 452.
λείπω, 106.
ληνός, gender, 661.
λιβανωτός, 73.
λιθοβολέω, 26, 126.
λιμός femin., 73, 22, 661.
λογία, 26.
λογίζομαι, 324 sq.; λογ. εἴς τι, 229, 286.

GREEK WORDS AND FORMS. 841

λοιβή, 24.
λοιπός, τοῦ λοιποῦ, τὸ λοιπόν, 580 ; apparent ellipsis of, 654, 744.
Λουκᾶς, 128.
Λύδδα, 70.
λυσιτελεῖ ᾗ, 302.
Λύστρα, 70.
λυτρόω, active and middle, 318.
λυχνία, 25.
λύω figur., 34.

-μα, substantives in, 26, 115 sq.; their meaning, 116 ; common in later Greek, 26, 115.
μαθητεύω transitive, 24, 314.
μακάριος, 689.
μακρόθεν, 580 ; ἀπὸ μ., 753 sq.
μᾶλλον omitted, 301 sq.; with the comparative, 300, 754 ; with the positive, 301, 306 sq.; not joined with the superlative, 300.
μάμμη, 26.
μανθάνω with infin. and partic., 436 sq.
μαρτυρέομαι, construction, 326.
μασάομαι, 49.
μάταιος, ον, 80.
μαχαίρης, μαχαίρῃ, 71.
μεγαλύνω, 31.
μεγαλωσύνη, 27, 118.
μέθυσος, 24.
μεθύω (μεθύσκομαι), constr., 251, 272.
μειζότερος, 28, 81, 753.
μέλει, construction, 257.
μελίσσιος, 25.
μέλλω with infin., 419 sq.; with augment, 82.
μεμιαμμένος, 108.
μέν, position of, 698-700, 455; μέν... δέ, 130, 551, 553 sq., 677 ; μέν not followed by δέ, 553 sq., 719-721 ; μὲν γάρ, 719 ; μὲν οὖν, 552, 556.
μενοῦνγε, 556 ; at the beginning of a sentence, 699.
μέντοι, 551, 554 ; its position, 699.
μεριμνάω, construction, 257, 261.
μεσημβρία without art., 150.
μεσιτεύω, 26.
μεσονύκτιον, 24.
μέσος predicative, 163 sq.; μέσον without art., 153,—with genit., 591.
μετά with genit., 470-472 ; akin to the dative, 268, 272 ; with verbs of following, 293 ; πολεμεῖν μετά τ., 471, 506 ; with accus., 502 sq.; with an infin., 414.

μετά, constr. of verbs compounded with, 287, 538.
μεταμορφόω, construction, 287, 538.
μεταξύ with genit., 591 ; τὸ μετ., 741.
μετέχω, construction, 250 sq.
μετοικεσία, 24.
μέχρι, μέχρις, 44 sq.; with genit., 591 ; μ. οὗ, 370 sq.
μή : how it differs from οὐ, 593, etc.; used for οὐ, 610 sq.; with the optat., 597 sq.,—the imper., 598, 628 sq., —the infin., 604 sq.; μή with partic. and adjectives, 606-611 ; pleonastic use of μή, 409, 755 ; μή after relatives, 603 sq.; in conditional and final sentences, 598 ; in prohibitions, 598, 628 sq.; in questions, direct, 641-643,—and indirect, 374 ; μὴ οὐ, 642 ; οὐ μή, 634-637, 642, 750 sq.; trajection of μή, 693-696 ; μή after verbs of fearing, 631-634 ; μή, final, 630-634 ; μή ... μηδέ, 612 ; μή ... ἀλλά (δέ), 620-624 ; μή ... ἀλλὰ καί, 624 ; μή ... πᾶς for μηδείς, 214 sq.
μηδέ: distinctive use of μηδέ and μήτε, 611-619 ; how μηδέ differs from καὶ μή, 619 ; μή ... μηδέ, 612 ; μηδέ ... μηδέ, 614 ; μηδέ ... μήτε, 617 sq.
μηθείς, 48.
μηκέτι not used for μή, 772 sq.
μήν, 541, 553.
μήποτε, 374, 579, 603, 630 sqq., 748.
μήπου, 579.
μήπως, 562, 630-634, 748 ; with aor. indic., 633 sq.; with two different moods, 633 sq.
μήτε : distinctive use of μηδέ and μήτε, 611-619 ; apparently used for μηδέ, 614 sq.; μήτε ... μήτε, 612-617 ; μήτε ... καί (τε), 619 sq.; μηδέ ... μήτε, 617 sq.
μήτηρ without art. 151 sq.; omitted, 237.
μήτι (εἰ μήτι), 641 ; μήτιγε, 746.
μητρολῴας, 49.
μιαίνω, 108, 651.
μίγμα, μῖγμα, 56 sq.
μιμνήσκομαι, constr., 256, 784.
μισθαποδοσία, 25.
μισθόομαι, 318.
μισθωτός, 58.
μνημονεύω, construction, 256 sq.
μνηστεύομαι, redupl., 86.
μοιχαλίς, 25, 223.
-μονή, subst. in, 116.
μόνος predicative, 164 ; alleged ellipsis

of μόνον, 620-624, 744; οὐ μόνον ... ἀλλά, 624; οὐ μόνον δέ (ellipt.), 729 sq.
μονόφθαλμος, 25.
-μος, subst. in, 115.
μοσχοποιέω, 27.
μύριοι, μυρίοι, 60.
μωμάομαι, 324.
μῶρος, 59 sq.
Μωϋσῆς (Μωυσῆς), Μωσῆς, 47; declension, 77 sq.

ν ἐφελκυστικόν, 43 sqq.; ν not changed before γ, μ, etc., 53 sqq.; ν and νν in certain words, 46, 49, 53; ν added to accus. sing. of 3 decl., 53, 76 sq.
ναί, 579.
Νεάπολις, declension, 79.
νεκρός, gender, 223; νεκροί without art., 153; ἀνάστασις νεκρῶν, 235.
νή, 579.
νῆστις, declension, 75.
νηφάλιος (νηφαλέος), 49.
νικάω ἔκ τ., 460; ὁ νικῶν, 444.
νικέω, 104.
νῖκος, 25.
νίπτω, 108.
νοΐ, νοός, 72.
νομοθετέω, construction, 327.
νόμος without art., 152 sq.
νοσσός (νεοσσός), etc., 25, 49.
νότος without art., 150.
νουθεσία, 25.
Νυμφᾶς (Νύμφα), 127 sq.
νύμφη, daughter-in-law, 33.
νῦν, νυνί, 579; νυνί, 24.
νυχθήμερον, 26.
νῶτος, νῶτον, 73.

ξενίζομαί τινι, 262.
ξενοδοχεύς, 26.
ξηρά, 18.
ξύλον, 23.
ξυράω, 25.

ο or ω in certain words, 46, 48, 49.
ὁ μέν, ὁ δέ (and similar expressions), 130; ὁ δέ without ὁ μέν, 130 sq.; τό before sentences, adverbs, etc., 135, 644,—before masc., or femin. nouns, 136, 223; τό (τοῦ, τῷ) before the infin., 402 sq., 406-415, 420.
ὅδε, 201 sq.
ὁδός figur., 34; omitted, 738 sq.;

ὁδῷ without prepos., 274; ὁδόν, towards, 289; ὁδὸν ποιεῖν, 320.
δύνασαι, 90.
ὅθεν, 557.
οἶδα (ᾔδειν), 342, 381, 435 (93).
οἰκήματα omitted, 740.
οἰκοδεσπότης, 26.
οἰκοδομέω (and comp.), augment, 83 sq.; used figur., 31, 36; οἰκ. ἔν τινι, 39; οἰκοδ. οἶκον, 754.
οἰκοδομή, 25, 36.
οἶκος omitted, 480, 740.
οἰκουργός, 125.
οἰκτείρω, future, 108.
οἰκτιρμοί, 220.
-οῖν for -οῦν in infin. active, 92, 52.
οἷος, 210; οἷος δηποτοῦν, 578.
ὀλίγος predicative, 164.
ὀλοθρεύω, ὀλεθρεύω, 114.
ὁλοκαύτωμα, 34.
ὁλόκληρος, 26.
ὅλος predicative, 164.
Ὀλυμπᾶς, 128.
ὀμείρομαι, 125 sq.
ὀμνύω, ὄμνυμι, 25, 108; construction, 278 sq., 282 sq., 417, 486, 495.
ὁμοιάζω, 26.
ὅμοιος, ον, 80; accent, 59 sq.; with genit., 243; with dative, 262.
ὁμοίωμα, form, 755.
ὁμολογέω with a partic., 435; ὁμ. ἔν τινι, 40, 283; ὁμ. τινί, 262.
ὅμως, 433, 551, 554; trajection of, 693.
ὀνάριον, 25.
ὀνειδίζω, construction, 278.
ὀνειδισμός, 25.
ὄνομα, various constructions, 227; is it ever pleonastic? 768; ἐπὶ τῷ ὀνόματι, 490; ἐν ὀνόματι, 487.
ὀνομάζομαι not equivalent to εἰμί, 769.
ὄπισθεν with genit., 591.
ὀπίσω with genit., 591; πορεύεσθαι ὀπ. τινός, 31; ἀκολουθεῖν ὀπ. τ., 293.
ὁποῖος, 210.
ὁπότε, 370, 389, 640.
ὅπου, 561, 593, 640; for ὅποι, 592; ὅπου ἄν with indic., 384.
ὀπτασία, 25.
ὅπως, 563, 640; construction, 358-361, 425; is it used for ὥστε? 578, 576; ὅπως ἄν, 389; ὅρα ὅπως, 425; ὅ. πληρωθῇ, 576 sq.; omitted (?), 356, 744.
ὁράω (and comp.), forms, 86, 89, 108; ἑώρακα, 342; ὀφθῆναί τινι, 275; ὅρα

GREEK WORDS AND FORMS.

ποιήσεις, 356; ὅρα μή, 628, 630-632, 751; ὅρα ὅπως, 425.
ὀργή (ἡ), 743.
ὀρεινή (ἡ), 740.
ὀρέων, 74.
ὀρθοποδέω, 27, 126.
ὀρθοτομέω, 27, 125.
ὀρθοῖζω, 26, 34, 113.
ὀσκωμοσία, 25, 124.
ὁροθεσία, 26.
ὅς, ὅςτις, 209 sq.; ὅς referring to a remote antecedent, 196; used for the interrog., 207 sq.; attraction, 202-204, 780 sqq.; ὅς with conj. and with fut. indic., expressing purpose, 375, 386; ὅς ἄν with conj. and indic., 384-386; ὅς = καὶ οὗτος, 680; replaced by καί and a demonstr. pron., 186, 724; ὅ prefixed to sentences, 209 (285); ὅς μέν... ὅς δέ (and similar expressions), 130; ὅς γε, 555; ὅς δή, ὅς δήποτε, 578; ἐξ οὗ, whence, 177; ἕως οὗ, etc.,—see ἕως, ἀπό, ἄχρι, μέχρι, ἕνεκα; ἐν ᾧ, 370, 482, 484; ἐφ᾽ ᾧ, 491 sq.; ἐφ᾽ οἷς, 197 sq., 202; ἀνθ᾽ ὧν, 202, 456.
ὁσάκις ἄν, 387.
-οσαν, 3 plur. of historical tenses, 91.
ὅσιος, ον, 80.
ὅσος, 210; ὅσοι ἄν with indic., 384; ὅσον ὅσον, 309.
ὀστέα, ὀστέων, 72.
ὅστις, ὅς τις, 50 sq.; ὅστις, ὅς, 202, 209 sq.; in an indirect question, 210; with conj. or fut. indic., expressing purpose, 375, 386; is ὅ,τι used for τί in a direct qu.? 208 sq., 572; ὅστις ἄν, 384-386, 603; ἕως ὅτου, 75, 370 sq.
-οσύνη, substantives in, 118.
ὅταν, constructions, 363, 387-389; ὅταν with a finite verb instead of an infinitive, 682.
ὅτε with indic., 370 sq.; with conj., 372 sq.
ὅ,τι, ὅ τι, 50 sq.
ὅτι, 541, 557, 563, 679, 756; is it used for other conj.? 571 sq.; interchanged with ὅτε in MSS., 572; with infin., 426 sq., 718; introducing the oratio recta, 756, 683; ὅτι with finite verb replacing an infin., 404, 407, 436, 747; omitted, 683; repeated, 708, 727 sq.; ὅτι οὐ, μή, 602, 605 (594); οὐχ ὅτι, οὐχ οἷον ὅτι, 746 sq.; δῆλον ὅτι, 731; τί ὅτι, 731; ὡς ὅτι, 771 sq.

ὅτου (ἕως ὅ.), 75.
οὐ: distinctive use of οὐ and μή, 593-611; οὐ in conditional sentences, 598-602; with partic. and adj., 606-611; with the infin., 605; with subst., 597 sq.; after relatives, 603 sq.; with the fut. in prohibitions, 396 sq., 629; οὐ with single words in final clauses, etc., 600, 602, 605, 608; οὐ reversing the meaning of verbs, etc., 597, 599 sq., 605, 608-611; οὐ for μή in antitheses, 601, 602, 606; in questions, 641-643, 396; pleonastic, 755; trajection of οὐ, 693-696; οὐ μή, 634-637, 642, 750 sq.; μὴ οὐ, 642; εἰ οὐ, 599-602; οὐ... ἀλλά (δέ), 620-624; οὐ... ἀλλὰ καί, οὐ μόνον... ἀλλά, 624; οὐ or οὐδείς... εἰ μή (πλήν, ἤ), 638; οὐ... οὐδέ, 612; οὐ... οὔτε, 615 sq.; οὐκ ἄοσ, 641; οὐχ ὅτι, οὐχ οἷον ὅτι, 746 sq.; οὐ μόνον δέ (elliptical), 729 sq.; οὐ... πᾶς for οὐδείς, 31, 214 sq.; οὐ πάντως, πάντως οὐ, 693 sq.; οὐ πάνυ, 694; οὐ... ποτέ, 216; οὐ for οὔπω (?), 745; οὔ, οὐχί, 598; (οὐκ ἕστηκεν, οὐχ ἰδού, 48).
οὗ, 561, 592.
οὐά (οὐά), 60, 579.
οὐαί (ἡ), 223.
οὐδέ: distinctive use of οὐδέ and οὔτε, 611-619; how it differs from καὶ οὐ, 619; οὐδέ, not even, 611, 617 sq., 626; οὐδὲ εἷς, 216; οὐ... οὐδέ, 612; οὐδέ... οὐδέ, 614; οὐδέ... οὔτε, 617 sqq.; οὐδέ... δέ, 620.
οὐδείς ἐστιν ὅς, 375; with οὐ, 604.
οὐδείς, 48.
οὐκέτι, 579; not used for οὐ, 772 sq.
οὔκουν, οὐκοῦν, 555, 643.
οὖν, 555-557, 676; is it used for other conj.? 570 sq.; in 3d or 4th place, 698 sq.; in apodosis, 712; ἄρα οὖν, 557; τί οὖν, 731; μὲν οὖν, 552, 556.
οὐράνιος, ον, 80.
οὐρανόθεν, 580; ἀπ᾽ οὐρ., 753.
οὐρανός without art., 144, 149 sq.; οὐρανοί, 220.
οὔτε: distinctive use of οὔτε and οὐδέ, 611-619; οὔτε apparently used for οὐδέ, 615; οὔτε... οὔτε, 612-617, 677; οὔτε... καί (τε), 619 sq.; οὔτε... καὶ οὐ, 613 sq.; οὔτε... οὐδέ, 616 sq.

ούτος referring to a remote subject, 195 sq. ; taking up the subject or predicate, 199, 206 ; repeated, 198 sqq. ; joined to a noun which has the art., 137 ; position, 199, 202, 686 ; before ὅτι, ἵνα, etc., 200 ; τοῦτο adverbial, 178 ; τοῦτο μέν ... τοῦτο δέ, 178 ; τοῦτ' ἔστιν epexeg., 665 ; ταῦτα πάντα, πάντα ταῦτα, 686 ; ταῦτα referring to a single object, 201 sq.; καὶ ταῦτα, 202, 432 ; ἐν τούτῳ, 484 ; ἐν ταύτῃ, 39 ; μετὰ ταῦτα, 201.
οὕτως, 548 sq., 678 sq. ; οὕτως, οὕτω, 43 sq.; is it used for οὗτος ? 584 ; οὕτως εἶναι, 584 ; commencing the apodosis, 678 sq.; pleonastic (?), 678 sq., 772.
οὐχί, 598.
ὀφείλημα, sin, 31, 33 sq.; ὀφ. ἀφιέναι, 31, 34.
ὀφείλω, imperfect without ἄν, 352.
ὄφελον with indic., 377.
ὀφθαλμοδουλεία, 124.
ὀψάριον, 23.
ὀψέ with genit., 591.
ὄψησθε, 89, 108.
ὄψιμος, 25.
ὀψώνιον, 23 ; plural, 220.
-όω, verbs in, 26, 113.

παθητός, 120.
παιδάριον, 25.
παιδεύω, 23.
παιδιόθεν, 27, 580 ; ἐκ π., 754.
παίζω, 108.
πάλιν, position, 693 ; pleonastic, 754 sqq.
παμπληθεί, 124.
πανδοχεύς, 26.
πανοικί, 27 ; form, 47.
πανταχῆ, -χῇ, 53.
πάντη, πάντῃ, 52.
πάντοτε, 27.
πάντως οὐ, οὐ πάντως, 693 sq.
πάνυ : οὐ (μὴ) πάνυ, 694.
παρά with genit., 457 ; different from ἀπό, 456 sq., 463 sq.; after passive verbs, 457 ; with dative, 492 sq.; with accus., 503 sq.; in comparisons, 301, 503 sq.
παρά, construction of verbs compounded with, 538.
παραβάτης, 27.
παραβολεύομαι, 115.
παραδιατριβή, 127.

παραδίδωμι intrans., 315, 738 ; παρ. εἴς τ., 268 ; παραδίδοσθαι, 36.
παραινέω with accus., 279.
παρακαλέω, 23 ; construction, 422 ; with aor. infin., 417.
παρακαταθήκη, 127.
παραπλήσιον with a dative, 590.
παρασκευή, derivation, 116 ; π. τοῦ πάσχα, 236.
παραφρονία, 25, 118.
παρείσακτος, 296.
παρεκτός with genit., 591.
παρεμβολή, 23.
παρέχω, παρέχομαι, 322.
Παρμενᾶς, 128.
παρρησία, 24.
πᾶς with art., 137 sq.; with abstract nouns, 138 ; with participles, 138 ; position of, 138, 686 sq. ; πᾶς ... οὐ (μή) for οὐδείς (μηδείς), 31, 214 sq. (694); τὰ πάντα, 133, 144 ; πάντα ταῦτα and ταῦτα πάντα, 686 ; πάντα with intrans. verbs, 285 ; πάντων with superl., 222, 310, —with compar., 303.
πάσχα indeclinable, 79.
πάσχω, 36.
Πάταρα, plural, 220.
πατήρ without art., 151; omitted, 237.
πατριάρχης, 27, 70.
πατρολῴας, 49.
πατροπαράδοτος, 124.
παύω (καταπαύω), constructions, 245, 409 ; with a partic., 434.
παχύνω figur., 18.
πεζός used adverbially, 583 ; πεζῇ, 53.
πειθός, 119.
πεινάω, 52, 92 ; with accus., 256.
πειράζω, 112.
πεισμονή, 116, 794.
πέλαγος τῆς θαλάσσης, 763 sq.
πέμπω in a past tense, 347.
πενθέω, 792.
πεντηκοστή, 27.
πεπειραμένος, 112.
πέποιθα, construction, 268, 292.
πεποίθησις, 26.
πέρ, 561.
πέραν with genit., 591, 31.
πέρατα τῆς γῆς, 31.
περί with genit., 466 sq.; different from ὑπέρ, 466, 478 sq., 513,—from ἀμφί, 466 ; with accus., 506 ; in periphrases, 240 sq., 506.
περί, constr. of verbs compounded with, 538.

GREEK WORDS AND FORMS. 845

περιάγω, περιάγομαι, 322 sq.
περιέχει, 316.
περίκειμαι, construction, 287.
περιούσιος, 120 sq.
περιπατέω, *live*, 34 ; with a dative, 274.
περισπάομαι, 23.
περισσοτέρως, 81, 304 sq.
πετάομαι, 25, 109.
πέτομαι, 109.
τηχῶν, 75.
πιάζω, 22.
πιέζω, 109.
πίεσαι, 109.
Πιλᾶτος, accent, 59.
πίνω, 109, 112.
πίπτω (and comp.), 86 sq.; ἔπεσα, 86 sq.; *irritum esse*, 18.
πιστεύω εἰς, ἐπί τινα, 267, 292 ; πιστεύεσθαι, construction, 287, 326.
πιστικός, 121 sq.
πίστις with objective genit., 232; with prepos., 267 (171).
-πλασίων, 311.
πλατύνω τὴν καρδίαν, 31.
πλείων, πλέων, 81 ; without ἤ, 300.
πλέω with accusative, 280.
πληγή omitted, 737.
πλήθει, τῷ πλ., 148.
πλημμύρης, 71.
πλήν, 552, 591, 638.
πληροφορία, 26.
πληρόω, constr., 251, 272, 287.
πλησίον as a prepos., 590 ; ὁ πλ., 63, 25.
πλησμονή, 116.
πλοός, 72.
πλούσιος, construction, 251.
πλοῦτος neuter, 76.
πνεῦμα ἅγιον without the art., 151.
πνευματικός, 296.
ποία, 22.
ποιέω (καλῶς, εὖ) τινί, 278; π. τοῦ with infin., 410 sq.; π. ἵνα, 423 ; ποιεῖν, ποιεῖσθαι, 320 sq.; ποιεῖν ἔλεος (χάριν) μετά τινος, 34, 471.
ποιμαίνω, *rule*, 17.
ποίμνιον, ποιμνίον, 60.
ποῖος for τίς, 212.
πολεμέω μετά τ., 471, 506.
πόλις, ellipsis of, 79.
πολιτεύομαι, 325, 328.
πολυμερῶς, 580.
πολυποίκιλος, 124.
πολύς joined to a subst. with an adj., 659 sq.; πολλοί and οἱ π., 136 sq.;

πολύ with compar., 301 ; πολλά adverbial, 580.
πολυτρόπως, 580.
πορεύομαι with dative, 270, 274.
ποταμοφόρητος, 124.
ποταπός, 25.
ποτέ, 579. See μήποτε.
πότε for ὁπότε, 640.
πότερος, 211 ; πότερον ... ἤ, 638.
ποτήριον, *lot*, 18, 33 ; ποτ. πίνειν (fig.), 18 ; ποτ. ἐκχυνόμενον, 791.
που, 578 sq.
ποῦ for ὅπου, 640 ; for ποῖ, 592 sq.
ποῦς, πούς, 56.
πρᾶος (πρᾷος), 52.
πραΰς, πραΰτης (πρᾷος, πραότης), 48.
πρέπει (πρέπον ἐστί), construction, 402.
πρηνής, 23.
πρίν, πρὶν ἤ, 371 sq., 415, 417.
πρό with genit., 466 ; transposed (?) in temporal phrases, 697 sq.; with the infin., 414.
πρό, construction of verbs compounded with, 538 sq.
προβάλλω used absol., 742.
προβλέπω, -ομαι, 323.
πρόθεσις ἄρτων, 296 sq., 792 sq.
πρόϊμος, 49.
προκόπτω, 315.
προορώμην, 86.
πρός with genit., 467 sq. ; with dative, 493 ; with accus., 453, 504 sqq. ; πρός με, σε, 62 sq. ; in periphrases, 529 ; with the infin., 414 ; akin to the simple dative, 266 sq.
πρός, construction of verbs compounded with, 539 sq.
προςέχω τινί, 742.
προσήλυτος, 25, 27, 120.
προςκυνέω, construction, 263.
προςτίθημι with adverbial force, 40, 587 sq.
προςφάγιον, 26.
προςφάτως, 580.
προςφέρω used absol., 742.
προςωπολημπτέω, 34, 126.
προςωπολήπτης, 126.
προςωπολημψία, 126.
πρόςωπον without art., 152 ; πρ. λαμβάνειν, 31, 34 ; πρ. στηρίζειν, 34 ; κατὰ πρόςωπον, 499, 218 ; πρὸ προςώπου, 156, 218, 758 sq.
προφητεύω, augment, 84.
πρύμνα, 22.
πρωΐ, 52.

πρώρα (πρώ-, πρῷ-), 53, 60; πρώρης, 71.
πρῶτος, πρῶτον, 583; πρῶτον, 721; πρ.
   μου, 306; πρῶτος for πρότερος, 306;
   εἷς for πρῶτος, 33, 311.
πτύον, 25.
πτῶμα, 23.
πύλη omitted, 741; πύλαι, 220.
πύρινος, 296.
πω, 579.
πως. See εἴπως, μήπως.
πῶς for ὅπως, 640.

ρ not doubled after a prepos. or the
   augment, 53, 88; ῥ (ῤῥ) or ρ (ρρ),
   53.
ῥάκκος, 49.
ῥαντίζω, 25; ῥεραντισμένος (ῥερ.), 88.
ῥαφίς, 26.
ῥέω, 109.
ῥῆμα, 18, 216; without art., 153.
ῥήσσω (ῥήγνυμι), 23; used absol., 742.
ῥητῶς, 580.
ῥίπτω: ῥῖψαν, ῥίψαν, 57; ῥεριμμένοι
   (ῥερ-, ἐρ-), 88.
ρρ, ρσ, 49.
ῥύμη, 23 sq.
ῥυπαρεύομαι, 114.

σ, ς, 45.
ς in οὕτως, etc., 43 sqq.
σάββατον, declension, 72 sq.; σάββατα,
   221.
σαλπίζω, 109.
σάρδιον, 73.
σαρκικός, σάρκινος, 122 sq.
σὰρξ καὶ αἷμα, 19; πᾶσα σάρξ, 34;
   κατὰ σάρκα, 169, 500 sq.
σαρόω, 25, 113.
Σατανᾶς, Σατᾶν, 78; with art., 155.
σεβάζομαι, 23.
σελήνη and ἡ σελ., 148 sq.
σημαίνω, 109 sq.
σητόβρωτος, 124.
-σθωσαν, 3 plur. imper., 91.
σίκερα, indeclin., 79.
Σίλας, 128.
σιρικόν, 49.
-σις, subst. in, 115 sq.
σιτομέτριον, 26.
σῖτος, plural, 73.
σκανδαλίζω, 34.
σκάνδαλον, figur., 33.
σκέπτομαι, 110.
σκηνοπηγία, 27, 126.
σκληροκαρδία, 27, 123.
σκληροτράχηλος, 27, 123

σκληρύνω, 114.
σκόλοψ, 276.
σκορπίζω, 23, 113.
σκότος, ὁ, 22, 76.
-σκω, verbs in, 114.
Σολομών, form and declension, 78.
Σπανία, 26.
σπάω, σπάομαι, 321.
σπείρης, 71.
σπεκουλάτωρ, declension, 74.
σπέρμα, offspring, 17, 31.
σπεύδω intransitive, 315.
σπῖλος, 26, 57.
σπλάγχνα, 18, 764.
σπλαγχνίζομαι, 31, 34, 113; construction, 255, 277, 292.
σπουδάζω, 110.
σσ, ττ, 48.
στάδιον, plural, 73.
στάμνος, 24.
στέγω, 22.
στήκω, 25, 27, 106; construction, 263.
στηρίζω, 110.
στιβάς (στοιβάς), 49.
Στοϊκός (-ω-), 49.
στόμα, edge, 18, 31.
στρέφω (ἀνα-, ἐπι-) intrans., 315; is
   it used with adverbial force? 588
   sq.
στρηνιάω, 22, 26.
στῦλος, στύλος, 57.
σύ, when expressed, 190 sq.; σοῦ, position of, 193; σοί dat. ethicus (?),
   194; πρός σε, 62 sq.; καθ' ὑμᾶς,
   193.
συγγενῆν, 76 sq.
συγγενίς, femin. of συγγενής, 80.
συγκρίνω, 23.
συγκυρία, 25.
συκομορέα (-μω-), 49.
συλλαμβάνω used absolutely, 742.
συμβάλλω τινί, 742.
συμμαθητής, 26.
συμφέρει ἵνα, 424.
σύν with dative, 488; different from
   μετά, 488.
σύν, construction of verbs compounded
   with, 269, 540; adj. compounded
   with σύν governing the genit., 243;
   subst. compounded with σύν common
   in later Greek, 26.
συνειδυίης, 71.
-σύνη, subst. in, 118.
συνιοῦσι, 97.
συνίστημι, 23.
συντρίβω (ῑ or ῐ), 57.

ΣυροΦοινίκισσα, ΣυροΦοίνισσα, 118
σύρτις, σύρτις, 60.
σΦυρίς (σπ-), 49.
σχολή, 24.
σώζω εἴς τι, 776; οἱ σωζόμενοι, 430.
Σώπατρος, 128.

ταμεῖον, 25, 117.
ταπεινοΦροσύνη, 27, 123.
ταπεινόΦρων, 123, 296.
ταρταρόω, 25.
ταῦτα. See οὗτος.
τάχιον, 81; not used as a positive, 304.
τε, 542, 676; different from καί, 542; τε...τε, 547; τε...καί, 547 sq.; τε καί, 548; τε...δέ, 548, 715; position, 455, 700; τε γάρ, 561.
τεκνίον, 60.
τέκνον in periphrases, 298 sq.
τελείως, 580.
τέρας, 75.
τεσσαρεςκαιδέκατος, 311.
τέσσερ-ες, -α, -άκοντα, 46.
τέτευχε, 110.
τηλικοῦτος, 210.
-της, subst. in, 116 sqq.
τίθημι, 93; θέσθαι ἐν τῇ καρδίᾳ, 24.
τίς not used for εἴ τις, 211, 678, 744; with subst. and adj., 212 sq.; may either precede or follow its subst., 213; may have the first place, 699 sq.; in reference to a plural, 787; as antithesis of οὐδέν, 213; τί with emphasis, 213; τί, accus. with intrans. verbs, 285; του, τῳ, 60 sq., 213; εἴς τις, 146, 213; εἴς for τίς, 29, 145 sq.; ellipsis of, 736.
τίς in indirect qu. and for the relative, 210 sq.; for πότερος, 211; τίς ἐστιν ὅς with the indic., 375,—with οὐ, 604; for ποῖος, 212; position, 212, 688; τί, why? 178; τί for ὡς, 562; ἵνα τί, 212, 734; τί ὅτι, 731; τί ἐμοὶ καὶ σοί, 731, 733; τί γάρ, τί οὖν, 559, 731.
τό. See ὁ.
τοι, 541. See μέντοι, etc.
τοιγαροῦν, 557.
τοίνυν, 555, 557, 699.
τοιοῦτος, 210; with the art., 138.
τολμάω not pleonastic, 766.
-τος, verbals in, 120.
τοσοῦτος, 210; τοσούτῳ... ὅσῳ, 306.
τουτέστι, 49, 665.
τοῦτο. See οὗτος.

τρίτον, 314.
τρόπος, accus. used adverbially, 288.
τροΦοΦορέω, 125.
τρόχος, τροχός, 62.
Τρωάς, 53.
ττ, σσ, 48.
τυγχάνω, 110; construction, 249 sq.
τυχόν, 446.
-τωσαν, 3 plur. imperative, 91.

ὕαλος, 22.
ὑβρίζω with accus., 277.
ὑγιή, 74.
ὕδωρ omitted, 739.
ὑετός omitted, 740.
υἱός in periphrases, 34, 298 sq.; omitted, 297, 741.
ὑμέτερος used objectively, 191.
-υνω, verbs in, 114.
ὑπάρχω with partic., 440.
ὑπέρ with genit., 478-480; how it differs from περί, 466, 478 sq., 513; with accus., 502; in comparisons, 301; ὑπερλίαν, 525; as an adverb, 526.
ὑπέρ, constr. of verbs compounded with, 540.
ὑπεράνω with genit., 591.
ὑπερέκεινα, 580; with genit., 591; accent, 59.
ὑπερεκπερισσοῦ with genit., 591.
ὑπερῷον, 119.
ὑπό with genit., 456 sq., 461 sq.; interchanged with ἀπό, 463 sq.; with accus., 507.
ὑπό, constr. of verbs compounded with, 540.
ὑποκάτω with genit., 591.
ὑποπόδιον, 27.
ὑπωπιάζω, 46.
ὑστερέω, construction, 245 sq., 251 sq., 280.
ὕψιστος without art., 151.
-υω for -υμι, 25, 108.

Φ for π, 48 sq.
Φάγομαι, Φάγεσαι, 110.
Φάγος, Φαγός, 58, 120.
Φαίνω, 110; construction, 293.
Φαύσκω, 110.
Φείδομαι, constr., 39, 257.
Φειδομένως, 123.
Φειδός, 120.
Φέρω, 110 sq.
Φεύγω, construction, 280, 409.
Φημί, ellipsis of, 746; Φησί (Φασί),

655 sq., 735 ; position of φησί, ἔφη, 698 ; ἔφη omitted, 748.
φθάνω, 23 ; inflexions, 111 ; construction, 586.
φιάλη, 22.
Φίλιπποι, plural, 220.
φοβέομαι, construction, 279 sq. ; φοβ. μή, 631.
φόβηθρον, 119.
Φοῖνιξ, φοίνιξ, 56.
φορτίον, 26.
φρυάσσω, 25.
φυλακτήριον, 27, 119.
φυλάσσω, 31, 317 ; construction, 279 sq.
φυσιόομαι, 25.
φύω, inflexions, 111 ; intransitive, 23, 316.
φωνή, 203 ; ellipsis of, 739.

χαίρω, 111 ; construction, 263, 291 ; χαίρειν, 397 sq., 735.
χαρίζομαι, 325, 327 ; future, 111.
χάριν with genit., 591, 700.
χάριτα, 75.
χαριτόω, 113.
χεῖλος, shore, 18, 31 ; language, 34 ; χειλέων, 74.
χείρ omitted, 740.
Χερουβίμ, 79.
χέω (χύνω), 104 (51) ; χεῶ future, 91 sq., 104.
χολάω, 25.
χορτάζω, 18, 23.
χράομαι, construction, 262.
χρεοφειλέτης, 48.
χρή, construction, 402.
χρήζω, construction, 250.
χρηματίζω, 23 ; χρηματίζομαι, 326.
χρηστότης, 22.
χρίσμα, χρῖσμα, 56 sq.
Χριστός and ὁ Χρ., 146 ; is Χριστός used to intensify the meaning of a subst. ? 310 ; ἐν Χριστῷ, 169 sq., 484, 486 sq. ; διὰ Χριστοῦ, 473.
χρόνος omitted, 738.
χρύσεος, declension, 72

χρυσοδακτύλιος, 27.
-χυσία, subst. in, 116.
χώ, 799.
χώρα omitted, 740.
χωρίς as a prepos., 590 sq.

ψεύδομαι, construction, 266.
ψεῦσμα, 25.
ψιθυριστής, 25.
ψιχίον, 25, 119.
ψυχή omitted, 739 ; is it a periphrasis for a pers. pron. ? 194 sq.
ψῦχος, ψύχος, 56 sq.
ψωμίζω, 23 ; with accus., 284.

-ω, accus. ending, 72.
-ω, verbs in, for verbs in μι, 25 (93-98, 100, 106 sq., 108).
ὦ with the vocative, 228 sq.
ὧδε, 592.
ὠδίν, 75 ; ὠδῖνες, 82.
ὠθέω, 82 sq., 111.
-ωλός, adj. in, 120.
ἄν for a past partic., 428 sq.
ὠνέομαι, 82, 112.
ᾠόν, 53.
ὥρα without art., 154 ; omitted, 740.
ὠρώμην, 108.
-ως, genit. -ω, in proper names, 72.
ὡς, 370, 548 sq., 555, 561, 563, 578, 662 ; with infin., 380, 390, 400 sq. ; with participles, 770 sq. ; with the predicate, 286, 753 ; ὡς ἄν, 384 sq., 387, 389 ; omitted (?), 745 ; pleonastic (?), 770-772, 753 ; with numerals, 578 sq. ; ὡς ἔπος εἰπεῖν, 399, 563 ; ὡς ὅτι, 771 sq. ; ὡς ἐπί, 771 ; ὡς καί, 549 ; for οὕτως (?), 578.
ὠσάμην, 83, 111.
ὡσεί with numerals, 578 sq.
ὥσπερ, 548, 678 ; protasis with ὥσπερ without apodosis, 749.
ὥστε with infin., 377, 400 ; with finite verb, 377 ; ὥ. (οὐ and) μή, 602.
ὠτάριον, 25.
ὠτίον, 26.
ὠφέλιμος πρός τι, 267.

www.ingramcontent.com/pod-product-compliance
Lightning Source LLC
Chambersburg PA
CBHW052106010526
44111CB00036B/1483